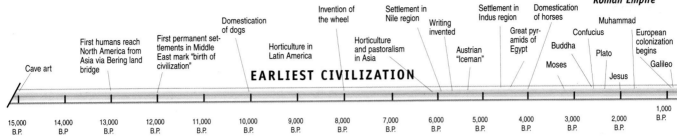

W9-BSM-060

Earliest horticultural and pastoral societies

Rise of agriculture and bureaucracy

European Middle Ages

Roman Empire

Invention of the wheel

Settlement in Nile region

Writing invented

Settlement in Indus region

Domestication of horses

Muhammad

Domestication of dogs

Horticulture in Latin America

Horticulture and pastoralism in Asia

Austrian "Iceman"

Great pyramids of Egypt

Confucius

Buddha

Plato

European colonization begins

First humans reach North America from Asia via Bering land bridge

First permanent settlements in Middle East mark "birth of civilization"

Moses

Jesus

Galileo

Cave art

EARLIEST CIVILIZATION

| 15,000 B.P. | 14,000 B.P | 13,000 B.P. | 12,000 B.P. | 11,000 B.P. | 10,000 B.P. | 9,000 B.P. | 8,000 B.P. | 7,000 B.P. | 6,000 B.P. | 5,000 B.P. | 4,000 B.P. | 3,000 B.P. | 2,000 B.P. | 1,000 B.P. |

"Baby bust"

Civil Rights Movement

Women's movement intensifies

U.S. life expectancy 77 years

1974 Punk begins

1997 Backstreet Boys lead revival of pop

1960 Rise of folk era and Motown

1961 Surfing music is born

1981 MTV debuts

1999 Eminem merges musical styles

1969 Woodstock

1979 SugarHill Gang popularizes rap

1977 Disco peaks

1991 Nirvana takes grunge mainstream

1964 British music invasion (The Beatles)

1970 First Earth Day

1987 Rhode Island enacts statewide recycling law

2000 60% of U.S. women in labor force

1965 Foreign-born Japanese eligible for citizenship

1968 First interracial kiss on TV (*Star Trek*)

1998 President Clinton impeached

2004 Massachusetts is first state to legalize same-sex marriage

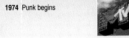
1955 First McDonald's restaurant

1964 LBJ declares war on poverty

1968 Dr. Martin Luther King Jr. assassinated

1975 First women's shelter

1980 Women earn majority of college degrees

1981 First AIDS cases reported

1984 *The Cosby Show* symbolizes upward mobility of many African American families

1997 Nelson Mandela becomes first black president of South Africa

1999 Euro introduced

2005 Hurricane Katrina draws attention to depth of poverty in U.S.

1954 *Brown v. Board of Education*

1961 European colonization of Africa ends

1969 Stonewall riot begins gay rights movement

1977 First gay TV character

1988 Last U.S. Playboy Club closes

Sept. 11, 2001 Terrorist attacks

1954 "Under God" added to Pledge of Allegiance

1973 *Roe v. Wade*

1978 Microsoft antitrust trial begins

1994 Rwanda genocide begins

2001 War on Terrorism

Revolutions in USSR and Eastern Europe 1989–1990

Persian Gulf War 1991

Iraq War 2003–

Vietnam War 1963–1975

1975

2000

1955 Cable TV invented

1960 Birth control pill invented

1965 Compact disc invented

1981 Space shuttle

1990 Human Genome Project

2002 Birth control patch invented

1977 First computerized arcade game

1969 First human on moon

1975 Microsoft founded

1990s Expansion of the Internet

2001 Apple introduces the iPod

1952 DNA discovered

1957 Sputnik launched

1978 World's first test-tube baby

2000 First hybrid cars sold in U.S.

1961 Laser invented

1973 First cell phone call

1982 Modern Internet opens

1952 First frozen "TV dinners" appear in supermarkets

1971 E-mail invented

1983 Laptop computers hit the market

1996 First cloned mammal: Dolly the sheep

1968 First heart transplant

Postindustrial era

Information Revolution

| 3 billion | 4 billion | 5 billion | 6 billion |

292.2 million

1959 Goffman debuts "dramaturgical analysis"

1981 Bernard nurtures gender studies

Piaget probes how we learn

WANT TO GET A BETTER GRADE?
Use these helpful tools!

"MAKING THE GRADE" CHAPTER REVIEW

The end-of-chapter review material will help you make the best use of your textbook as a study tool and be more successful in your course. A two-page visual summary helps you focus on important concepts. A full page of sample test questions (all written by John Macionis) allows you to test your knowledge.

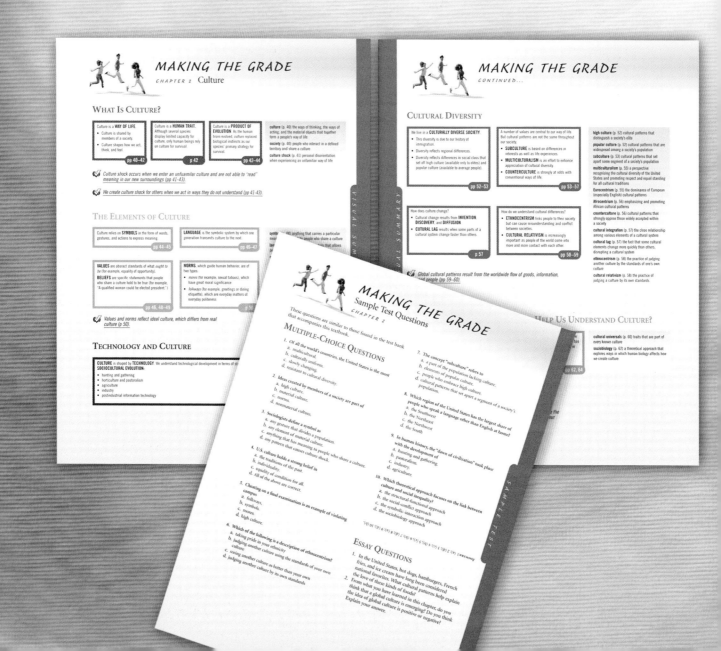

"APPLYING THEORY" TABLES

"Applying Theory" tables summarize at a glance how the various theoretical approaches view the topic at hand.

APPLYING THEORY

Social Stratification

	Structural-Functional Approach	Social-Conflict Approach	Symbolic-Interaction Approach
What is the level of analysis?	Macro-level	Macro-level	Micro-level
What is social stratification?	Stratification is a system of unequal rewards that benefits society as a whole.	Stratification is a division of a society's resources that benefits some and harms others.	Stratification is a factor that guides people's interaction in everyday life.
What is the reason for our social position?	Social position reflects personal talents and abilities in a competitive economy.	Social position reflects the way society divides resources.	The products we consume all say something about social position.
Are unequal rewards fair?	Yes. Unequal rewards boost economic production by encouraging people to work harder and try new ideas. Linking greater rewards to more important work is widely accepted.	No. Unequal rewards only serve to divide society, creating "haves" and "have-nots." There is widespread opposition to social inequality.	Maybe. People may or may not define inequality as fair. People may view their social position as a measure of self-worth, justifying inequality in terms of personal differences.

" ✓ YOUR LEARNING" FEATURE

All theoretical discussions are followed by "Critical Review" sections. At the end of the section, a new feature—"Check Your Learning"—challenges you to focus on the main ideas of the discussion.

> **CRITICAL REVIEW** A micro-level analysis of social stratification helps us see patterns of social inequality in our everyday lives. At the same time, the limitation of this approach is that it has little to say about how and why broad patterns of social inequality exist, which was the focus of the structural-functional and social-conflict approaches. The Applying Theory table summarizes the contributions of the three theoretical approaches to social stratification.
>
> ✓ **YOUR LEARNING** Point to several ways in which social stratification shapes the way people of different social positions behave in the course of a typical day.

"SUMMING UP" TABLES

"Summing Up" tables recap the key points of text discussions.

SUMMING UP

Three Research Orientations in Sociology

	Scientific	Interpretive	Critical
What is reality?	Society is an orderly system. There is an objective reality "out there."	Society is ongoing interaction. People construct reality as they attach meanings to their behavior.	Society is patterns of inequality. Reality is that some categories of people dominate others.
How do we conduct research?	Researcher gathers empirical, ideally quantitative, data. Researcher tries to be a neutral observer.	Researcher develops a qualitative account of the subjective sense people make of their world. Researcher is a participant.	Research is a strategy to bring about desired social change. Researcher is an activist.
Corresponding theoretical approach	Structural-functional approach	Symbolic-interaction approach	Social-conflict approach

This book is offered to teachers of sociology in the hope that it will help our students understand their place in today's society and in tomorrow's world.

John J. Macionis

NINTH EDITION

SOCIETY
the basics

JOHN J. MACIONIS

Kenyon College

PEARSON

Prentice
Hall

Upper Saddle River, New Jersey 07458

Library of Congress Cataloging-in-Publication Data

Macionis, John J.
   Society : the basics / John J. Macionis. — 9th ed.
     p. cm.
   Includes bibliographical references and index.
   ISBN 0-13-228490-1 (alk. paper)
    1. Sociology. I. Title.

HM586.M1657 2007
301—dc22

2006043688

Editorial Director: *Leah Jewell*
Publisher: *Nancy Roberts*
Editor in Chief of Development: *Rochelle Diogenes*
Development Editor: *Karen Trost*
VP, Director of Production and Manufacturing: *Barbara Kittle*
Production Editor: *Barbara Reilly*
Copyeditors: *Bruce Emmer, Amy Macionis*
Proofreader: *Beatrice Marcks*
Editorial Assistant: *Lee Peterson*
Prepress and Manufacturing Manager: *Nick Sklitsis*
Prepress and Manufacturing Buyer: *Brian Mackey*
Director of Marketing: *Brandy Dawson*
Executive Marketing Manager: *Marissa Feliberty*

Marketing Assistant: *Irene Fraga*
Creative Design Director: *Leslie Osher*
Senior Art Director: *Anne B. Nieglos*
Interior and Cover Designer: *Ilze Lemesis*
Line Art Illustrations: *Mirella Signoretto*
Director, Image Resource Center: *Melinda Patelli*
Manager, Rights and Permissions: *Zina Arabia*
Manager, Visual Research: *Beth Brenzel*
Image Permissions Coordinator: *Debra Hewitson*
Photo Researcher: *Teri Stratford*
Manager, Cover Visual Research and Permissions: *Karen Sanatar*
Director, Media and Assessment: *Shannon Gattens*
Senior Media Editor: *Deborah O'Connell*
Cover Photo: *Frederic Cirou/AGE Fotostock America, Inc.*

This book was set in 10/12 Minion by Pine Tree Composition, Inc., and was printed and bound by
RR Donnelley & Sons Company. The cover was printed by Phoenix Color Corp.

Pearson Education LTD.
Pearson Education Singapore, Pte. Ltd
Pearson Education, Canada, Ltd
Pearson Education—Japan
Pearson Education Australia PTY, Limited

Pearson Education North Asia Ltd
Pearson Educación de Mexico, S.A. de C.V.
Pearson Education Malaysia, Pte. Ltd
Pearson Education, Upper Saddle River, New Jersey

10 9 8 7 6 5 4
ISBN 0-13-228490-1

BRIEF CONTENTS

CONTENTS

CHAPTER 1

Sociology: Perspective, Theory, and Method   *1*

CHAPTER 2

Culture   *39*

CHAPTER 3

Socialization: From Infancy to Old Age *69*

CHAPTER 4

Social Interaction in Everyday Life *95*

CHAPTER 5

Groups and Organizations *119*

CHAPTER 6

Sexuality and Society *145*

CHAPTER 9

Global Stratification   *243*

CHAPTER 10

Gender Stratification   *271*

CHAPTER **13**

Family and Religion *371*

CHAPTER 14

Education, Health, and Medicine *409*

CHAPTER 15

Population, Urbanization, and Environment *449*

CHAPTER *16*

Social Change: Modern and Postmodern Societies 481

BOXES

THINKING GLOBALLY

THINKING ABOUT DIVERSITY: RACE, CLASS, AND GENDER

SEEING SOCIOLOGY IN EVERYDAY LIFE

The New York Times IN THE Times

MAPS

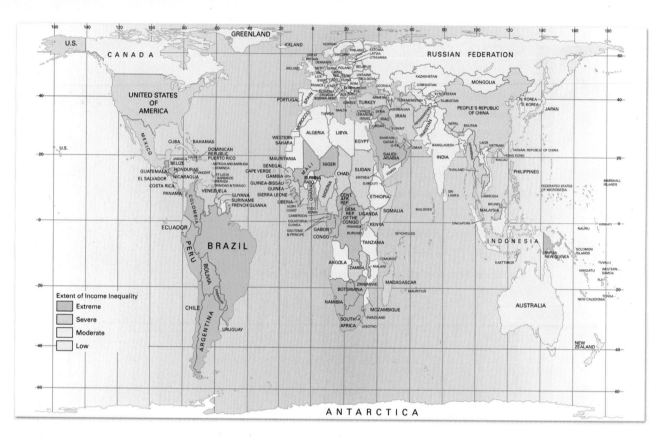

GLOBAL MAPS

WINDOW ON THE WORLD

NATIONAL MAPS

SEEING OURSELVES

PREFACE

An Invitation to Students, a Welcome to Instructors

I did not start out to become a sociologist. Guided by teachers and counselors who pointed to my good grades in mathematics and physics, I applied to and entered engineering school. The first year went well enough. Early in my sophomore year, however, I realized that I had lost my interest in engineering. To be honest, my school was also losing its interest in me, and my engineering career came to a crashing halt soon after I posted a grade point average of 1.3 for the fall semester.

The personal crisis that followed caused me to take a hard look at other fields of study, and the following spring, I enrolled in my first sociology class. This one course would truly change my life. From the very beginning, sociology helped me make sense of the world, and just as important, sociology was *fun*. Thirty-five years later, I can still say the same thing.

The importance of one person's story lies in the fact that countless people have been turned on to sociology in much the same way. Thousands of students have discovered the excitement of sociology in an introductory class, and many have gone on to make it their life's work.

To students: I invite you to open this book, to enjoy it, and to find a new and very useful way of looking at the world. To my colleagues teaching sociology: I stand with you in knowing the deep satisfaction that comes from making a difference in the lives of our students. There is surely no greater reward for our work and, in my case, no better reason for striving for ever-better revisions of *Society: The Basics*, which, along with the longer, hardcover version, *Sociology*, stands out as the discipline's most popular text.

The new ninth edition of *Society: The Basics* is exciting, covers it all, and—as students' e-mail messages testify—is plain fun to read. This major revision raises sociology's most popular text to a still higher standard of excellence and is an unparalleled resource to help today's students learn about our diverse and changing world.

Students using this book can log on to a full-featured Web site at http://www.prenhall.com/macionis. From the main page, simply click on the cover of *Society: The Basics, Ninth Edition,* to find chapter overviews and learning objectives, suggested essay questions and paper topics, multiple-choice and true-false questions that the server will grade, and chapter-relevant Web destinations with learning questions.

Instructors and students will benefit from our other technology innovation. MySocLab™—a "one-stop shop" for teaching and learning materials—will transform both the classroom and the learning experience. Pulling together the many resources available with this textbook, MySocLab has the power to make instructors more effective and students more engaged.

Textbook, Web site, and MySocLab—a multimedia package that is the foundation for sound learning in this new information age. I invite you to examine these important pieces of the learning process!

Organization of This Text

Society: The Basics presents sociology's basic ideas, research, and insights in sixteen logically organized chapters. Chapter 1 ("Sociology: Perspective, Theory, and Method") explains how the discipline's distinctive point of view illuminates the world in a new and exciting way. In addition, the first chapter introduces major theoretical approaches and explains the methods sociologists use to test and refine their knowledge.

The next six chapters examine sociology's core concepts. Chapter 2 ("Culture") explores the fascinating diversity of human living that marks our world. Chapter 3 ("Socialization: From Infancy to Old Age") investigates how people everywhere develop their humanity as they learn to participate in society. While highlighting the importance of the early years to the socialization process, this chapter describes important changes that occur over the entire life course, including old age. Chapter 4 ("Social Interaction in Everyday Life") takes a micro-level look at how people construct the daily realities that we often take for granted. Chapter 5 ("Groups and Organizations") focuses on social groups, within which we have many of our most meaningful experiences. It also highlights the expansion of formal organizations and points up some of the problems of living in a bureaucratic age. Chapter 6 ("Sexuality and Society") explains the social foundation of human sexuality. Based on recent research, this chapter surveys sexual patterns in the United States and also explores variations in sexual practices through history and around the world today. Chapter 7 ("Deviance") analyzes how the routine operation of society promotes deviance as well as conformity.

The next four chapters survey social inequality and provide more coverage of this important topic than any other brief text. Chapter 8 ("Social Stratification") introduces basic concepts that describe social hierarchy throughout history and around the world today. The chapter then highlights dimensions of social difference in the United States. Chapter 9 ("Global Stratification") extends this text's commitment to global education by analyzing the social ranking of entire nations. Why, in other words, do people in some societies have abundant wealth while in others people struggle every day just to survive? *Society: The Basics* also provides full-chapter coverage of two additional dimensions of social difference. Chapter 10 ("Gender Stratification") describes how gender is a central element of social stratification in the United States, as it is worldwide. Chapter 11 ("Race and Ethnicity") explores racial and ethnic diversity in the United States, explaining how societies use physical and cultural traits to construct and rank categories of people in a hierarchy.

Next are three chapters that survey all the major social institutions. Chapter 12 ("Economics and Politics") examines the political economy of U.S. society in global context. Beginning with a historical look at how the Industrial Revolution transformed the Western world, this chapter contrasts capitalist and socialist economic models and investigates how economic systems are linked to a society's distribution of wealth and power. It also contains coverage of the military, issues of war and peace, and an expanded discussion of terrorism.

Chapter 13 ("Family and Religion") spotlights two institutions central to the symbolic organization of social life. The chapter begins by focusing on the variety of families in the United States, making frequent comparisons to kinship systems in other parts of the world. The basic elements of religious life are presented next, along with an overview of recent religious trends.

Chapter 14 ("Education, Health, and Medicine") examines two institutions with special importance in the modern world. The chapter looks first at the historical expansion of schooling, noting many ways in which the scope and substance of education in any society are linked to other social institutions. Next, we look at the vital social issue of health, including the emergence of medicine as a central institution during the past century and a half.

The final two chapters of the text focus on dimensions of social change. Chapter 15 ("Population, Urbanization, and Environment") is a synthesis that begins by spotlighting the growth of population in the world. Then, our attention turns to the rise of cities in the United States and to the urban explosion now taking place in poor nations of the world. Finally, the chapter explains how the state of the natural environment reflects social organization. Chapter 16 ("Social Change: Modern and Postmodern Societies") concludes the text with summaries of major theories of social change, a look at how people forge social movements to encourage or resist change, and analysis of the various benefits and liabilities of modern social patterns as well as the emergence of a "postmodern" way of life.

Continuity: Established Features of *Society: The Basics*

Society: The Basics is no ordinary textbook: In sociology, it represents *the* standard of excellence, which explains why this book is selected by far more faculty than any other. The extraordinary strength of *Society: The Basics* results from a combination of the following features.

The best writing style. Most important, this text offers a writing style widely praised by students and faculty alike as elegant and inviting. *Society: The Basics* is an enjoyable text that encourages students to read—even beyond their assignments. No one says it better than the students themselves, whose recent e-mail includes testimonials such as these:

> I am currently a student at Columbus State, and my sociology professor is utilizing your book, *Society: The Basics,* in his lectures. I just wanted to let you know that I have thoroughly enjoyed reading your book. I have read several sociology books, . . . I love the fact that you intertwine sociological concepts with real-life situations. It is fascinating to view different cultures through the eyes of a sociologist, and it is amazing how much can be learned. . . . Between your book and my professor, sociology has become a passion for me. Keep up the good work, and please, write another book!

> Mr. Macionis, It meant the whole world to me that you personally wrote back. I don't know exactly how to tell you how much your work and love have put passion in my heart that I never knew was there. I have been completely overwhelmed by the power of your words and educational standards. Thank you once again for doing what you do and being who you are.

> I just want to tell you this is the best text I have ever used.

> I want to thank you for providing us with such a comprehensive, easy-to-read, and engaging book. . . . In fact, my instructor thought it was so interesting and well done, she read the book from cover to cover. Your work has been a great service to us all. My sociology book is the only textbook that I currently own that I actually enjoy reading. Thank you!

> My sociology class used your book and it was by far the best textbook I have ever used. I actually liked to read it for pleasure as well as to study. I just want to say it was great.

> I am taking a Sociology 101 class using your text, a book that I have told my professor is the best textbook that I have ever seen, bar none. I've told her as well that I will be more than happy to take more sociology classes as long as there is a Macionis text to go with them.

> I am fascinated by the contents of this textbook. In contrast to texts in my other classes, I actually enjoy the reading. Thank you for such a thought-provoking, well-written textbook.

I am a student of nursing in Arizona. Once I began reading *Society: The Basics*, I was enthralled. Your sociological acumen causes you to write in a way that conveys (perfectly) your excitement about the subject to us, the students. I wish you could be my instructor. Thank you for your work!

Dude, your book *rocks!*

Instructors, too, offer praise for this text:

I began using your intro text my first semester of teaching seventeen years ago, and I continue to use your intro text today. I am thrilled with the style, the content, the updated nature of the examples used, and the impressive photo layouts. I have enjoyed it for years and look forward to continued success with your new editions. The author has definitely written this textbook with the student in mind. Other texts talk over the student, yet *Society: The Basics* has always been excellent reading for all levels of student ability. I have had hundreds of students who would not have done as well in my introductory course had I not used this textbook. Macionis does a terrific job of explaining difficult topics in a down-to-earth manner.

I have been adopting this text for my introductory classes for many years, and my students consistently find it to be both rewarding and entertaining. And over the years, these teaching assignments have run the gamut—both day and evening classes, both traditional and adult learners, both community colleges and universities. I have been loyal to this text because I can find no better teaching tool and because students say they could not meet high academic standards and expectations without it.

A focus on careers. *Society: The Basics* is written to help students see the relevance of sociology to their future careers. Chapter 1 explains how the introductory course gives students a "sociology advantage" in the world of work. All the chapters that follow apply the perspective and findings of sociology to various careers. These discussions are marked by the **Sociology @ Work** icon.

A global perspective. *Society: The Basics* has taken a leading role in expanding the horizons of our discipline beyond the United States. It was the first brief text to mainstream global content, the first to introduce global maps, and the first to offer comprehensive coverage of global topics such as stratification and the natural environment. It is no wonder that *Sociology* and *Society: The Basics* have been adapted and translated into half a dozen languages for use around the world. Each chapter explores the world's social diversity and explains why social trends in the United States—from musical tastes to the price of wheat to the growing disparity of income—are influenced by what happens elsewhere. Just as important, students will learn ways in which social patterns and policies in the United States affect poor nations around the world.

A celebration of social diversity. *Society: The Basics* invites students from all social backgrounds to discover a fresh and exciting way to see themselves within the larger social world. Readers will discover in this text the diversity of U.S. society—people of African, Asian, European, and Latino ancestry, as well as women and men of various class positions and at all points in the life course. Just as important, without ignoring the problems that marginalized people face, this text does not treat minorities as social problems but notes their achievements. A decade ago, the American Sociological Association's journal *Teaching Sociology* recognized Macionis's *Sociology* (the hardcover companion to this text) as the best of all the leading texts in terms of integrating racial and ethnic material throughout (Stone, 1996).

Emphasis on critical thinking. Critical-thinking skills include the ability to challenge common assumptions by formulating questions, to identify and weigh appropriate evidence, and to reach reasoned conclusions. This text not only teaches but also encourages students to learn on their own.

Engaging and instructive chapter openings. One of the most popular features of earlier editions of *Society: The Basics* has been the engaging vignettes that begin each chapter. These openings—for instance, using the tragic sinking of the *Titanic* to illustrate the life-and-death consequences of social inequality, describing a sociology class in a community college classroom to illustrate the increasing social diversity of the United States, or recounting how a fire in a Bangladesh sweatshop that manufactures clothing for sale in the United States left dozens of low-paid workers dead—spark the interest of readers as they introduce important themes. While keeping the best chapter-opening vignettes from earlier editions, this revision offers six that are new.

Inclusive focus on women and men. Beyond devoting two full chapters to the important concepts of sex and gender, *Society: The Basics* mainstreams gender into *every* chapter, showing how the topic at hand affects women and men differently and explaining how gender operates as a basic part of social organization.

Theoretical clarity and balance. This text makes theory easy. The discipline's major theoretical approaches are introduced in Chapter 1 and are carried through later chapters. The text highlights the social-conflict, structural-functional, and symbolic-interaction approaches and also introduces social-exchange analysis, ethnomethodology, cultural ecology, and sociobiology.

Recent research and the latest data. *Society: The Basics, Ninth Edition,* blends classic sociological statements with the latest research as reported in the leading publications in the field. While some texts ignore new work in sociology journals, *Society: The Basics* reflects recent research in a dozen of the discipline's top publications. More than 1,000 research citations support this revision, most published in the past ten years. Using the latest sources ensures that the text's content and statistical data are the most recent available. All statistical data are the latest available—in many cases, for 2005.

Learning aids. This text has many features to help students learn. In each chapter, **Key Concepts** are identified by boldfaced type, and following each appears *a precise, italicized definition.* Key concepts and their definitions appear at the end of each chapter, and a complete **Glossary** is found at the end of the book. At the end of each chapter, you will find **Applying Sociology in Everyday Life,** three learning activities that are easy for introductory students to do and that make sociology come alive. Each chapter also includes our new feature, **Making the Grade,** which makes it easy for students to review content and assess their learning. More about Making the Grade is found in the discussion of features new to this edition.

Outstanding images: Photography and fine art. *Society: The Basics, Ninth Edition,* offers the finest and most extensive program of photography and artwork available in any comparable book. For each new edition, I search extensively to obtain the finest images of the human condition and present them with insightful captions, often in the form of thought-provoking questions. Both photographs and artwork present people of various social backgrounds and historical periods. For example, alongside art by Europeans such as Pieter Brueghel the Elder and U.S. artists including George Tooker, this edition has paintings by celebrated African American artists Henry Ossawa Tanner and Jonathan Green, outstanding Latino artist Carmen Lomas Garza, and renowned folk artist Anna Bell Lee Washington.

Thought-provoking theme boxes. Although boxed material is common to introductory texts, *Society: The Basics, Ninth Edition,* provides a wealth of uncommonly good boxes, many new to this edition. Each chapter typically contains three or four boxes—for a total of fifty-four—and the boxes fall into five types that amplify central themes of the text. All the boxes are followed by three "What Do You Think?" questions that help readers generate critical thought and stimulate spirited class discussion.

Applying Sociology boxes show readers how to apply the perspective, theory, and methods of sociology to learn more about issues, including crime, disabilities, and social inequality. **Seeing Sociology in Everyday Life** boxes focus on familiar experiences, such as encountering stereotypes, computer technology, or the campus culture of "hooking up," and explain how sociological thinking provides deeper understanding. **Thinking About Diversity: Race, Class, and Gender** boxes focus on multicultural issues and present the voices of women and people of color. **Thinking Critically** boxes teach students to ask sociological questions about their surroundings and help them evaluate important, controversial issues. **Thinking Globally** boxes encourage readers to think about their own way of life by examining the fascinating social diversity that characterizes our world.

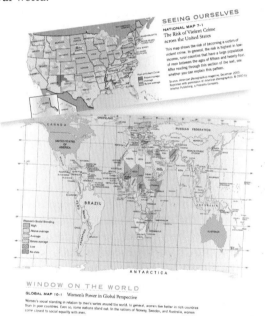

An unparalleled program of thirty-nine global and national maps. Another popular feature of *Society: The Basics* is the program of global and national maps. **Window on the World** global maps—twenty in all—are true sociological maps offering a comparative look at income inequality, favored languages, the extent of prostitution, permitted marriage forms, the degree of political freedom, the incidence of HIV/AIDS infection, and a host of other issues. The global maps use the non-Eurocentric projection devised by cartographer Arno Peters that accurately portrays the relative size of all the continents.

Seeing Ourselves national maps—nineteen in all—help illuminate the social diversity of the United States. Most of these maps offer a close-up look at all 3,141 U.S. counties, highlighting suicide rates, teen pregnancy, risk of violent crime, poverty, racially mixed people, most widespread religious affiliation, and, as measures of recent trends, obesity across the country or where the jobs will be by the end of the decade. Each national map includes an explanatory caption that poses a question to stimulate students' thinking about social forces. A complete listing of the Seeing Ourselves national maps as well as the Window on the World global maps follows the table of contents.

An annotated instructor's edition. This is the only brief text available in an instructor's edition with a full program of helpful annotations—written by the author—on every page. These annotations provide additional data, notable quotations, comments about maps, and pop culture observations.

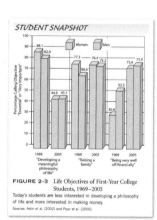

Applying Theory tables. Sociological theory is important, but it can be challenging to students. All theoretical sections are followed by a **Critical Review** discussion that highlights the approach's strengths and limitations. In addition, **Applying Theory** tables provide quick and easy summaries of the key insights of each theoretical approach.

Snapshot figures. Among the popular features of *Society: The Basics* are the **Global Snapshots,** colorful graphs that compare social patterns in the United States with those in other nations; **Diversity Snapshots,** figures that illustrate differences by race, ethnicity, class, or gender; and **Student Snapshots,** figures that document trends in the behaviors and opinions of college students based on the surveys conducted by the Higher Education Research Institute at the University of California at Los Angeles.

FIGURE 2-3 Life Objectives of First-Year College Students, 1969–2005
Today's students are less interested in developing a philosophy of life and more interested in making money.
Sources: Astin et al. (2002) and Pryor et al. (2005).

Innovation: Changes in the Ninth Edition

Each new edition of *Society: The Basics* and *Sociology* has broken new ground, one reason that more than 5 million students have learned from these sociological best-sellers. In fact, one reason this book has always been the best-seller is that it never stands still. A revision raises high expectations, but after two years of planning and hard work, we are pleased to offer a major revision that sets a new standard of excellence for brief texts. Here is an overview of the innovations that define *Society: The Basics, Ninth Edition.*

Student friendly: A fresh design. As instructors understand, today's students are visually oriented—in a world of rapid-fire images, they respond to what they see. Just as important, the photographs that they find in newspapers, on television, and online are more sociological than ever. As a result, this new edition of *Society: The Basics* offers more and better images, and the text has a fresh design that is clean, attractive, and sure to boost student interest.

Society: The Basics encourages students to use images to learn. Bold, vibrant, and colorful photos pull students into the chapter material and become teaching opportunities, not just elements that add visual appeal. Students will be inspired by the visuals and educated by the context.

Student friendly: A fresh feel. A fresh look also calls for a fresh feel to the text. The goal of this new edition can be stated in the form of a promise: Every student in every class will be able to immediately understand the material on every page of the text. This promise does not mean that I have left out any of the content you expect. What it does mean is that I have prepared this revision with the greatest care and with an eye toward making language and arguments as clear as they can be.

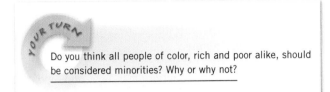

YOUR TURN

Do you think all people of color, rich and poor alike, should be considered minorities? Why or why not?

Student friendly: Interactive "Your Turn" questions. To make this edition of *Society: The Basics* more engaging and interactive, I have placed "Your Turn" questions at five or six points in every chapter. "Your Turn" questions ask readers to apply the ideas being discussed to a new issue or to link the ideas to their own lives.

people favor Weber's multidimensional hierarchy, others think, in light of this trend, that Marx's view of the rich versus the poor is closer to the truth.

✔ YOUR LEARNING According to Weber, which of the three dimensions of social inequality would you expect to be the most important in United States? Why?

Student friendly: "Check Your Learning." After each theoretical discussion, a quick "Check Your Learning" question helps students assess how well they understand the material.

Student friendly: "Applying Sociology in Everyday Life." The value of sociology depends on students' ability to apply what they learn to their own lives. This revision illustrates the discipline's concepts in familiar ways that encourage students to see sociology in their everyday lives. In addition, a new feature—"Applying Sociology in Everyday Life"—is found at the end of each chapter. This feature offers students three easy-to-do activities that will connect important sociological ideas to their everyday lives.

Student friendly: A greater focus on careers. Most students who enroll in a sociology course expect to find something useful for their future careers. They will. *Society: The Basics, Ninth Edition*, has even more discussion of how sociology can help students in their future careers. Chapter 1

But sociology is not just for people who want to be sociologists. People who work in criminal justice—including jobs in police departments, probation offices, and correction facilities—gain the "sociology advantage" by learning what categories of people are most at risk of becoming criminals as well as victims, how effective various policing policies and programs are at preventing crime, and why people turn to crime in the first place. Similarly, people who work in health care—including doctors, nurses, and technicians—also gain a "sociology advantage" by learning about patterns of health and illness within the population, as well as how factors such as race, gender, and social class affect human health.

explains how this text can give students a "sociology advantage" in their careers. In later chapters, look for the **Sociology @ Work** icon to learn how to make marketing efforts more multicultural (Chapter 2, "Culture"), why physicians should understand the social dynamics of an office visit or a medical examination (Chapter 4, "Social Interaction in Everyday Life"), and what sociology teaches us about the criminal justice system (Chapter 7, "Deviance") and the medical establishment (Chapter 14, "Education, Health, and Medicine").

Student friendly: "In the *Times*" readings. What better way to bring sociology to life than to provide students with brief, well-written news articles that apply sociology to today's world! In this edition, each and every chapter includes an article about some dimension of U.S. society that recently appeared in *The New York Times*. These articles present important and current issues that are sure to engage student readers:

Chapter 1 ("Sociology: Perspective, Theory, and Method") *"For Illegal Immigrants, a Harsh Lesson"*

Chapter 2 ("Culture") *"Cast from Their Ancestral Home, Creoles Worry about Culture's Future"*

Chapter 3 ("Socialization: From Infancy to Old Age") *"Adultescent"*

Chapter 4 ("Social Interaction in Everyday Life") *"Seriously, the Joke Is Dead"*

Chapter 5 ("Groups and Organizations") *"The Beast That Feeds on Boxes: Bureaucracy"*

Chapter 6 ("Sexuality and Society") *"Children, Media, and Sex: A Big Book of Blank Pages"*

Chapter 7 ("Deviance") *"Despite Drop in Crime, an Increase in Inmates"*

Chapter 8 ("Social Stratification") *"Surge in Homeless Families Sets Off Debate on Cause"*

Chapter 9 ("Global Stratification") *"Shantytown Dwellers in South Africa Protest Sluggish Pace of Change"*

Chapter 10 ("Gender Stratification") *"Men Are Becoming the Ad Target of the Gender Sneer"*

Chapter 11 ("Race and Ethnicity") *"Around the World in Five Boroughs"*

Chapter 12 ("Economics and Politics") *"Rewards of a 90-Hour Week: Poverty and Dirty Laundry"*

Chapter 13 ("Family and Religion") *"Crisis of Indian Children Intensifies as Families Fail"*

Chapter 14 ("Education, Health, and Medicine") *"The College Dropout Boom"*

Chapter 15 ("Population, Urbanization, and Environment") *"Dump Trash, Add Scavengers, Mix and Get a Big Mess"*

Chapter 16 ("Social Change: Modern and Postmodern Societies") *"Modernity Tips Balance in a Remote Corner of Kashmir"*

Student friendly: Expanded and improved timeline. An easy way to help students put their lives in historical perspective is the timeline, an exclusive feature found inside the front cover of *Society: The Basics, Ninth Edition*. This revision features an expanded and updated timeline incorporating more material about popular culture and social diversity, as well as a number of color images.

Both students and faculty benefit from the following innovations:

Student friendly: "Making the Grade." A major innovation in this edition is an entirely new approach to end-of-chapter material. "Making the Grade" is intended to assist students in what matters most—doing well in the course. This material includes a **Visual Summary,** which is a graphic review of the main points of the chapter as well as all the key concepts. The Visual Summary is useful to students for study and to instructors as lecture notes. In addition, there is a **Practice Test,** including both multiple-choice questions (with answers provided) and suggested essay questions. These questions are very similar to those found in the Test Item File that is provided to instructors using this text. I have written all the testing material accompanying *Society: The Basics* myself.

More on the mass media and popular culture. Because of the importance of the mass media and popular culture to our everyday lives, this edition of *Society: The Basics* includes new and expanded discussions of these topics

throughout the text. In addition, there are now many more photographs dealing with films, television, and other sources of popular culture.

Updated features. This revision has new and updated sociological maps, six new opening vignettes, and new and updated boxes.

The latest statistical data. Instructors count on this text to include the very latest statistical data. The *Ninth Edition* comes through again, making use of the latest data from various government agencies and private organizations. I have worked with Amy Marsh Macionis to ensure that the newest statistics are used throughout the text—in most cases for 2004, 2005, or even 2006. In addition, instructors will find dozens of new research citations as well as many familiar current events that raise the interest of students.

Keeping up with the field. As surprising as it may seem, some textbooks do not reflect new work in the field, making few references to sociology's journals and taking little notice of new books. In preparing this revision, I have reviewed new publications—including the *American Journal of Sociology, American Sociological Review, Rural Sociology, Social Forces, Sociological Focus, Sociological Forum, Society, The Public Interest, Social Problems, Population Bulletin, Teaching Sociology, Contemporary Sociology,* and *Social Science Quarterly*—as well as popular press publications that keep us abreast of current trends and events. Of course, material selected for inclusion in an introductory textbook must be both interesting and relevant to the lives of students.

New topics. *Society: The Basics, Ninth Edition* is completely updated with new and expanded discussions in every chapter. Here is a partial listing, by chapter.

- **Chapter 1, "Sociology: Perspective, Theory, and Method"**
  To show the power of society on individual behavior, Chapter 1 presents the most recent data on birth rates around the world and suicide rates here in the United States; new "Your Turn" features help students apply Durkheim's theory of suicide, to imagine their lives had they been born elsewhere, and to engage in other learning exercises; there is more on C. Wright Mills and the "sociological imagination," including a Seeing Sociology in Everyday Life box; students will find a new and expanded discussion applying sociology to their careers and their own personal growth; the chapter now includes the idea of "debunking"; a new Applying Sociology box shares insights gained by Barbara Ehrenreich during the research for her book *Nickel and Dimed;* a new "In the *Times*" article suggests that societal forces play a powerful role in college attendance; there are new sections providing more dis-

cussion of the feminist approach and the race-conflict approach, including a Thinking About Diversity box on the important contributions to sociology made by W. E. B. Du Bois; discussion of experiments in sociology has been expanded; and "Making the Grade," the new end-of-chapter feature, helps students assess their learning and review important material.

- **Chapter 2, "Culture"** A new journal entry describes cultural patterns high in the Andes Mountains of Peru; new discussions include the topics of emerging values and value clusters, by which cultural values work together; a new section highlights the range of distinct cultures in the United States and the world and points out that the number of different cultures is declining; an expanded and updated Applying Sociology box deals with the new symbols linked to the use of instant messaging; a new discussion of values in global perspective contrasts dominant cultural values in high-income and low-income nations; a new "In the *Times*" article takes a look at the challenges faced by Creoles in Louisiana trying to preserve their culture after being displaced by Hurricane Katrina; and the chapter contains an update on the number of states enacting laws making English the official language.

- **Chapter 3, "Socialization: From Infancy to Old Age"** A new journal entry highlights the power of the mass media to change cultural patterns; a new "In the *Times*" explores the complexity of defining "adulthood"; the chapter includes updates on income, wealth, and poverty among older people in the United States; there is a new, short discussion of Nancy Chodorow's theory of gender development; finally, a new national map shows where multiracial people are most and least common.

- **Chapter 4, "Social Interaction in Everyday Life"** A new Applying Sociology box shows how the concept "master status" can be applied to people with physical disabilities; numerous "Your Turn" questions invite student reaction to the material; and a new "In the *Times*" article suggests that declining tolerance for put-down humor in today's society may explain the "death" of traditional joke-telling.

- **Chapter 5, "Groups and Organizations"** A series of new "Your Turn" features helps students apply concepts to their own lives; a critical discussion of Stanley Milgram's claim about "six degrees of separation" has been added; a new "In the *Times*" article delves into how difficult it is to cut back on inefficient government bureaucracy; and there are new examples of organizational inefficiency based on the government's response to the disastrous hurricane season of 2005.

- **Chapter 6, "Sexuality and Society"** A new chapter opening describes controversy surrounding changing patterns of sexual behavior in Iraq; a new "In the *Times*" article suggests that, despite concerns that sexual content may be harmful to young people, we have yet to learn very much about this issue; a new section traces patterns of sexuality over the life course; there is an update on the legal status of gay marriage and civil unions; the latest statistics on the incidence of rape

in the United States are provided; a number of sections have been rewritten to improve clarity and present the most current examples; and discussion of the social-conflict analysis of sexuality has been expanded.

- **Chapter 7, "Deviance"** A new chapter opening uses the jailing of Martha Stewart to raise questions about common stereotypes about criminals; as in all chapters, many examples have been revised to increase their relevance to students; readers will find a report assessing new research on the role of genetics in criminal behavior; the discussion of structural-functional theory is now illustrated using the classic research of Kai Erikson; the 2006 lobbying scandals in Congress have been added to the discussion; there are updates on white-collar crime, corporate crime, hate crimes, and all the latest crime statistics from the FBI; and a new "In the *Times*" article explores the dramatic increase in the prison population in the United States despite a drop in the crime rate.

- **Chapter 8, "Social Stratification"** This chapter has been reorganized to provide a clearer and better flow; it updates trends in inequality found in China and other countries; it contains the latest available details on social inequality in the United States, including statistics on the unequal distribution of both income and wealth and current poverty data; there is a new micro-level discussion of social stratification and social interaction; a discussion of how family patterns affect income and wealth has been added; and a new "In the *Times*" article looks at homelessness in small communities, explaining that the problem is getting bigger.

- **Chapter 9, "Global Stratification"** A new Global Map shows the latest classification of high-, middle-, and low-income nations around the world; the chapter now includes reports on recent changes in the economic ranking of India and China; discussion of theoretical approaches to global inequality has been updated and expanded; there is a new discussion of the North American Free Trade Agreement (NAFTA) and the effects of the increasing globalization of the economy on people in low-income nations as well as people here in the United States; finally, a new "In the *Times*" article takes a look at the problem of poverty in the shantytowns of Durban, South Africa.

- **Chapter 10, "Gender Stratification"** Discussion of the Musuo, a small apparently matriarchal society, has been added to this chapter; the chapter contains updates from the United Nations on the nations that have the greatest and the least gender equality; a new discussion of body image and eating disorders has been included; statistics on women in the labor force and on women's and men's incomes have been updated; discussion of the "glass ceiling" has been expanded; there is an updated list of women's "firsts" in U.S. politics; one of the many new "Your Turn" features asks students if they think the United States should enact a law requiring at least 25 percent of candidates for elected office be women; a new Applying Theory table calls attention to the key differences between various types of feminism; and a new "In the *Times*" article investigates recent television advertising that has portrayed men in unfairly negative terms.

- **Chapter 11, "Race and Ethnicity"** A new chapter-opening story describing a classroom discussion of race and ethnicity demonstrates that social diversity does not always involve simple "black and white" categories; discussion of the social construction of race has been expanded; the definition of the concept "minority" has been modified to include the issue of power; a new "In the *Times*" article describes the remarkable and changing ethnic diversity of New York City's neighborhoods; there are updated statistics on the population size and social standing of the various racial and ethnic categories of the U.S. population; the chapter has a new section on Arab Americans, highlighting their social diversity as well as their concerns about becoming targets of hate crimes and government surveillance; and a new national map shows the distribution of the Arab American population in the United States.

- **Chapter 12, "Economics and Politics"** The chapter contains statistical updates on all economic indicators and employment patterns; discussion of the recent gains made by socialism in South America has been added; information on underemployment and forced reductions in employee pensions and other benefits has been expanded; new statistics on social diversity in the U.S. workplace are given; an update from Freedom House presents the extent of political democracy in countries around the world in 2005, as well as new statistics on political lobbying and campaign spending in the 2004 presidential election; there is a new discussion of the social class background of U.S. military personnel; finally, there is an update on the global spread of nuclear weapons.

- **Chapter 13, "Family and Religion"** A new chapter-opening story describes the decision of one Latina living in the United States to have fewer children in order to make a better life for her family; feminist theory is given a higher profile in the social-conflict analysis of family life; numerous "Your Turn" features invite students to apply important ideas to their own lives; a new "In the *Times*" article describes the crisis facing families on the Lummi Indian reservation in Washington; there are updates on income and other family patterns for various racial and ethnic categories of U.S. families; the latest statistics on family violence are included; there is the latest information on countries now permitting same-sex marriage, as well as lawful gay marriage in Massachusetts; discussion of religion has been expanded to include new age spirituality, the latest information on patterns of religious affiliation and belief, and a new journal entry about visiting the Inca ceremonial center of Machu Picchu; and a new Thinking Critically box addresses the current controversy over intelligent design, explaining how science and religion provide different understandings of the world.

- **Chapter 14, "Education, Health, and Medicine"** A new chapter-opening vignette features a woman in her thirties who describes the career importance of returning to college; there is a new journal entry about schooling in the highlands

of Peru; included are the latest statistics on schooling in the United States, along with data on how schooling boosts income; there is a new theoretical discussion applying the symbolic-interaction approach to schooling; a new national map shows differences in teacher salaries across the United States; a new Thinking About Diversity box describes how unequal funding affects the everyday lives of students in various schools; there is a new discussion of how schools reduce but do not eliminate differences in social capital based on students' home environments; a new "In the *Times*" article shows how class position plays into the decision by young people to drop out of college; information on grade inflation has been updated; an expansive discussion of obesity has been added, including a new national map showing rates of obesity across the United States; and there are also updated statistics regarding the health of the U.S. population, as well as the latest data on the prevalence of sexually transmitted diseases.

- **Chapter 15, "Population, Urbanization, and Environment"** A new chapter opener describes the incentives offered by a number of rural communities in the Great Plains that are trying to reverse population loss and attract new residents; all the demographic statistics, including global population, fertility, mortality, and infant mortality rates, have been updated; a new "In the *Times*" article describes the lives of trash-pickers living and working in the Shanghai dump; and there are various updates on the state of the global environment.

- **Chapter 16, "Social Change: Modern and Postmodern Societies"** The chapter has a new section on claims making; there is new coverage of disasters, describing major types of disasters and the social effects of this type of unexpected change; a new Applying Sociology box describes how the social consequences of disasters continue for years—even generations—after the event; there are updated statistics on ways in which life in the United States has improved and ways in which it has not; one of the many "Your Turn" questions asks students to assess Alvin Toffler's idea of "future shock" by explaining whether they think life is changing too fast or not fast enough; and finally, a new "In the *Times*" article describes the patterns of change coming to a traditional village in Kashmir.

A Word about Language

This text's commitment to describing the social diversity of the United States and the world carries with it the responsibility to use language thoughtfully. In most cases, this text uses the terms "African American" and "person of color" rather than the word "black." Similarly, the text uses the terms "Latino" and "Hispanic" to refer to people of Spanish descent. Most tables and figures refer to "Hispanics" because this is the term the Census Bureau uses when collecting statistical data about our population.

Students should realize, however, that many individuals do not describe themselves using these terms. Although the word "Hispanic" is commonly used in the eastern part of the United States and "Latino" and the feminine form "Latina" are widely heard in the West, across the United States people of Spanish descent identify with a particular ancestral nation, whether it be Argentina, Mexico, some other Latin American country, or Spain or Portugal in Europe.

The same holds for Asian Americans. Although this term is a useful shorthand in sociological analysis, most people of Asian descent think of themselves in terms of a specific country of origin (say, Japan, the Philippines, Taiwan, or Vietnam).

In this text, the term "Native American" refers to all the inhabitants of the Americas (including Alaska and the Hawaiian Islands) whose ancestors lived here prior to the arrival of Europeans. Here again, however, most people in this broad category identify with their historical society (for example, Cherokee, Hopi, Seneca, or Zuni). The term "American Indian" refers to only those Native Americans who live in the continental United States, not including Native peoples living in Alaska or Hawaii.

On a global level, this text avoids the word "American"—which literally designates two continents—to refer to just the United States. For example, referring to this country, the term "the U.S. economy" is more correct than "the American economy." This convention may seem a small point, but it implies the significant recognition that we in this country represent only one society (albeit a very important one) in the Americas.

A Word about Web Sites

Because of the increasing importance of the Internet, each chapter of this new edition of *Society: The Basics* contains numerous Internet icons identifying useful Web sites. The goal is to provide sites that are current, informative, and above all, relevant to the topic at hand.

Please keep in mind that Web sites change all the time. Although my publisher and I make every effort to ensure that the sites listed meet our high standards, readers may find that sites have changed and some may have gone away entirely.

Second, sites have been selected to provide different points of view on various issues. The listing of a site does not imply that the publisher or I agree with everything—or even anything—on the site. For this reason, we urge students to examine all sites with a critical eye.

Supplements

Society: The Basics, Ninth Edition, is the heart of an unprecedented multimedia learning package that includes a wide range of proven instructional aids as well as several new ones. As the author of the text, I maintain a keen interest in all the supplements to ensure their quality and integration with the text. The supplements for this revision have been thoroughly updated, improved, and expanded.

FOR THE INSTRUCTOR

Annotated Instructor's Edition (0-13-228497-9). The AIE is a complete student text with author's annotations on every page. These annotations—which have been thoroughly revised for this edition—have won praise from instructors for enriching class presentations. Margin notes include summaries of research findings, statistics from the United States or other nations, insightful quotations, information highlighting patterns of social diversity in the United States, and high-quality survey data from the National Opinion Research Center (NORC) General Social Survey and the World Values Survey data from the Inter-University Consortium for Political and Social Research (ICPSR).

Instructor's Manual (0-13-228494-4). Formerly called the *Data File,* this is the instructor's manual that is of interest even to those who have never used one before. Providing far more than detailed chapter outlines and discussion questions, it contains statistical profiles of the United States and other nations, summaries of important developments, recent articles from *Teaching Sociology* that are relevant to the classroom, and supplemental lecture material for every chapter of the text.

Test Item File (0-13-228498-7). I have written this key supplement to reflect all the material in the textbook—in terms of both content and language. The file contains over 2,000 items—at least 100 per chapter—in multiple-choice, true-false, and essay formats, plus new questions based on the supplemental items that allow educators to assess a student's use of these important tools.

TestGEN-EQ (0-13-228499-5). This computerized software allows instructors to create their own personalized exams, to edit any or all of the existing test questions, and to add new questions. Other special features of this program include random generation of test questions, creation of alternative versions of the same test, scrambling question sequence, and test preview before printing.

Faculty Resources on CD (0-13-228504-5). Pulling together all of the media assets available to instructors, this interactive CD allows instructors to insert media—video, PowerPoint, graphs, charts, maps—into their interactive classroom presentations. In addition, electronic versions of the Instructor's Manual, Test Item File, teaching annotations, and Personal Response System questions are located on this valuable resource.

Prentice Hall Film and Video Guide: *Introductory Sociology,* Seventh Edition (0-13-154744-5). Newly updated by Peter Remender of the University of Wisconsin–Oshkosh, this guide links important concepts in the text directly to compelling, student-focused feature films and documentaries. Each film is summarized, and critical-thinking questions allow the instructor to highlight the relevance of each film or video to concepts in sociology.

ABCNEWS *ABC News*/Prentice Hall Video Library for Sociology (0-13-189132-4). Few educators will dispute that video is the most dynamic supplement one can use to enhance a class. Prentice Hall and *ABC News* are working together to bring to you the best and most comprehensive video material available in the college market. Through its wide variety of award-winning programs—*Nightline, This Week, World News Tonight,* and *20/20*—*ABC News* offers a resource for feature and documentary-style videos related to the chapters in *Society: The Basics, Ninth Edition.* An excellent instructor's guide carefully and completely integrates the videos into lectures. The guide has a synopsis of each video, showing its relation to the chapter, and discussion questions to help students focus on how concepts and theories apply to real-life situations. The videos are available in both DVD and VHS formats.

Presentation PowerPoints™ for *Society: The Basics, Ninth Edition.* These PowerPoint slides combine graphics and text in a colorful format to help instructors convey sociological principles in a new and exciting way. Each chapter of the textbook has fifteen to twenty-five slides that communicate the key concepts of that chapter. For easy access, they are available on the Instructor Resource CD-ROM or in the instructor portion of MySocLab for *Society: The Basics, Ninth Edition.*

MEDIA SUPPLEMENTS

mysoclab MySocLab™ is an engaging student and faculty learning system for introductory sociology courses. It allows students to test their mastery of the concepts in the book by providing chapter-by-chapter diagnostic tests. Results from the diagnostic tests build a customized study plan, and students are provided rich supplementary content to help them learn any concepts they have not yet mastered.

MySocLab allows instructors to track the progress of both individual students and the class as a whole. Based on the diagnostic results of the class, instructors receive a suggested customized lesson plan. The customized lesson plan provides opportunity for a compelling classroom experience based on actual student performance.

MySocLab is available as a premium Web site with no course management features or requirements, or it can be accessed through either BlackBoard™ or WebCT™ course management platforms.

Additionally, MySocLab offers the major faculty and student resources for *Society: The Basics, Ninth Edition,* in one convenient location.

Companion Website™. In tandem with the text, students and professors can now take full advantage of the Internet to enrich their study of sociology. Features of the site include chapter objectives, study questions, and links to interesting material and information from other sites on the Web that will reinforce and enhance the content of each chapter. The Companion Website is available to both students and instructors: Go to http://www.prenhall.com/macionis, and click on the cover of *Society: The Basics, Ninth Edition.*

Research Navigator™. Research Navigator can help students complete research assignments efficiently and confidently by providing three exclusive databases of high-quality scholarly and popular articles accessed by easy-to-use search engines.

- **EBSCO's ContentSelect™ Academic Journal Database,** organized by subject, contains fifty to one hundred of the leading academic journals for sociology. Instructors and students can search the online journals by keyword, topic, or multiple topics. Articles include abstract and citation information and can be cut, pasted, e-mailed, or saved for later use.
- ***The New York Times* Search-by-Subject™ Archive** provides articles specific to sociology and is searchable by keyword or multiple keywords. Instructors and students can view full-text articles from the world's leading journalists writing for *The New York Times.*
- **Link Library** offers editorially selected "Best of the Web" sites for sociology. Link Libraries are continually scanned and kept up-to-date, providing the most relevant and most accurate links for research assignments.

Students and instructors can gain access to Research Navigator by using the access code found in the front of the brief *Prentice Hall Guide to Research Navigator*™. The access code for Research Navigator is included with every guide and can be packaged for no extra charge with *Society: The Basics, Ninth Edition*. Please contact your Prentice Hall representative for more information.

Telecourse. The Macionis texts *Sociology* and *Society: The Basics* have been selected for use in the new telecourse "The Way We Live," available on DVD from INTELECOM. To find out more about this truly outstanding course, go to http://www.intellecom.org and, under the Alphabetical Listing of Courses, click on "The Way We Live"; or call (800) 576-2988.

FOR THE STUDENT

Study Guide (0-13-228493-6). This complete guide helps students review and reflect on the material presented in *Society: The Basics, Ninth Edition*. Each of the sixteen chapters in the Study Guide provides an overview of the corresponding chapter in the student text, summarizes its major topics and concepts, offers applied exercises, and features end-of-chapter tests with answers.

VangoNotes. These chapter reviews from *Society: The Basics, Ninth Edition*, in downloadable MP3 format allow students to study on the go. Students can listen to the following selections for each chapter of the textbook:

- **Big Ideas:** The "need to know" for each chapter
- **Practice Test:** A gut check for the Big Ideas—tells students if they need to keep studying
- **Key Terms:** Audio "flashcards" to help students review key concepts and terms
- **Rapid Review:** A quick drill session to be used right before the test

VangoNotes are *flexible;* students can download all the material directly to an MP3 player or only the chapters they need. The notes can be used in the car, at the gym, or while walking to class.

VangoNotes can be accessed at VangoNotes.com. To purchase the complete set of VangoNotes, use ISBN 0-13-228498-2. To purchase individual chapters, use ISBN 0-13-224992-8.

***Time* Special Edition (0-13-154734-8).** Showing how the popular media write with a sociological eye, this special edition of *Time* magazine, updated for 2006, pulls together the best articles of the past two years dealing with sociological topics. Contact your local Prentice Hall sales representative for more information.

Sociological Classics: A Prentice Hall Pocket Reader (0-13-191806-0). Compiled by the sociologist David Kauzlarich, this edited volume features fourteen selections from classical sociological theorists. Contact your local Prentice Hall sales representative for more information.

"10 Ways to Fight Hate" brochure (0-13-028146-8). Produced by the Southern Poverty Law Center, the leading hate crime and crime watch organization in the United States, this free supplement walks students through ten steps that they can take on their own campus or in their own neighborhood to fight hate every day.

In Appreciation

The usual practice of crediting a book to a single author hides the efforts of dozens of women and men that have resulted in *Society: The Basics, Ninth Edition*. I would like to express my thanks to the Prentice Hall editorial team, including Yolanda de Rooy, division president; Leah Jewell, editorial director; and Nancy Roberts, publisher, for their steady enthusiasm and for pursuing both innovation and excellence.

Day-to-day work on the book is shared by the author and the production team. Barbara Reilly, production editor at Prentice Hall, is a key member of the team who is responsible for the attractive page layout of the book; indeed, if anyone "sweats the details" more than I do, it is Barbara! Amy Marsh Macionis, my "in house" editor, checks virtually everything, untangling awkward phrases and catching errors and inconsistencies in all the statistical data. Amy is a most talented editor who is relentless in her pursuit of quality. My debt to her is great indeed.

I also have a large debt to the members of the Prentice Hall sales staff, the men and women who have given this text such remarkable support over the years. Thanks, especially, to Brandy Dawson and Marissa Feliberty, who carry out our marketing campaign.

Thanks, too, to Ilze Lemesis for providing the interior design of the book, which was coordinated in-house by creative design director Leslie Osher and art director Anne Nieglos. Developmental and copy editing of the manuscript was skillfully done by Karen Trost, Bruce Emmer, and Amy Marsh Macionis.

It goes without saying that every colleague knows more about a number of topics covered in this book than the author does. For that reason, I am grateful to the hundreds of faculty and the many students who have written to me to offer comments and suggestions. More formally, I am grateful to the following people who have reviewed some or all of this manuscript:

Kimberly A. Alexander, Lock Haven University
Shawn Bingham, University of South Florida
Elizabeth Bodien, Northampton Community College
Karen Bourg, Nashville State Community College
Cris Braesch, Hennepin Technical College
Yang Cai, Caldwell College
Allison Cotton, Prairie View A & M University
Sophia DeMasi, Montgomery County Community College
Lilli M. Downes, Polk Community College
Stacie Carolyn Golin, Sussex County Community College
Ada Haynes, Tennessee Tech University
Shirley A. Jackson, Southern Connecticut State University
Robert M. Khoury, St. John's University
Denise S. Malloy, University of Memphis
Kathleen Mentink, Chippewa Valley Technical College
Fatima Rodriguez, Reedley College
Vaso Thomas, Bronx Community College
Linda Vang, California State University and Fresno City College
David Wachtel, Bluegrass Community and Technical College

I also wish to thank the following colleagues for sharing their wisdom in ways that have improved this book:

Doug Adams (Ohio State University), Francis O. Adeola (University of New Orleans), Arfa Aflatooni (Linn-Benton Community College), Kip Armstrong (Bloomsburg University), Rose Arnault (Fort Hays State University), Scott Beck (Eastern Tennessee State University), Lois Benjamin (Hampton University), Philip Berg (University of Wisconsin—La Crosse), Janet Carlisle Bogdan (LeMoyne College), Alessandro Bonanno (Sam Houston State University), Charlotte Brauchle (Southwest Texas Junior College and Saint Mary's University), Bill Brindle (Monroe Community College), John R. Brouillette (Colorado State University), Cathryn Brubaker (Georgia Perimeter College), Brent Bruton (Iowa State University), Richard Bucher (Baltimore City Community College), Karen Campbell (Vanderbilt University), Cecilia Cantrell (Georgia State University), Harold Conway (Blinn College), Gerry Cox (Fort Hays State University), Lovberta Cross (Southwest Tennessee Community College), James A. Davis (Harvard University), Sumati Devadutt (Monroe Community College), Mary Donaghy (Arkansas State University), Keith Doubt (Northeast Missouri State University), William Dowell (Heartland Community College), Denny Dubbs (Harrisburg Area Community College), Travis Eaton (Northeast Louisiana State University), Helen Rose Fuchs Ebaugh (University of Houston), John Ehle (Northern Virginia Community College), Roger Eich (Hawkeye Community College), Tracy Elliott (Collin County Community College), Kevin Everett (Radford University), Heather Fitz Gibbon (College of Wooster), Kevin Fitzpatrick (University of Alabama—Birmingham), Dona Fletcher (Sinclair Community College), Charles Frazier (University of Florida), Karen Lynch Frederick (Saint Anselm College), Patricia Gagné (University of Kentucky—Louisville), Pam Gaiter (Collin County Community College), Jarvis Gamble (Owen's Technical College), Patricia L. Gibbs (Foothill College), Steven Goldberg (City College, City University of New York), Charlotte Gotwald (York College of Pennsylvania), Norma B. Gray (Bishop State Community College), Rhoda Greenstone (DeVry Institute), Jeffrey Hahn (Mount Union College), Harry Hale (Northeast Louisiana State University), Dean Haledjian (Northern Virginia Community College), Dick Haltin (Jefferson Community College), Marvin Hannah (Milwaukee Area Technical College), Charles Harper (Creighton University), Michael Hart (Broward Community College), Adonna Helmig (Pittsburgh State University), Gary Hodge (Collin County Community College), Elizabeth A. Hoisington (Heartland Community College), Sara Horsfall (Stephen F. Austin State University), Peter Hruschka (Ohio Northern University), Glenna Huls (Camden County College), Jeanne Humble (Lexington Community College), James Hunter (Indiana University–Purdue University at Indianapolis), Richard Hutchinson (Weber State University), Cynthia Imanaka (Seattle Central Community College), Miles Jackson (Clark College), Patricia Johnson (Houston Community College), Ed Kain (Southwestern University), Audra Kallimanis (Mount Olive College), Paul Kamolnick (Eastern Tennessee State University), Irwin Kantor (Middlesex County College), Jessica Kelley-Moore (Purdue University), Douglas B. Kennard (Mount Vernon Nazarene University), Thomas Korllos (Kent State University), Rita Krasnow (Virginia Western Community College), Donald Kraybill (Elizabethtown College), Michael Lacy (Colorado State University), Michael Levine (Kenyon College), George Lowe (Texas Tech University), Don Luidens (Hope College), Larry Lyon (Baylor University), Li-Chen Ma (Lamar University), Karen E. B. McCue (University of New Mexico—Albuquerque), Ronald McGriff (College of the Sequoias), Meredith McGuire (Trinity College), Lisa McMinn (Wheaton College), Setma Maddox (Texas Wesleyan University), Errol Magidson (Richard J. Daley College), Kooros Mahmoudi (Northern Arizona University), Jean-Louis Marchand (Chesapeake College), Allan Mazur (Syracuse University), Jack Melhorn (Emporia State University), Ken Miller (Drake University), Richard Miller (Navarro College), Joe Morolla (Virginia Commonwealth University), Peter B. Morrill (Bronx Community College), Craig Nauman (Madison Area Technical

College), Dina B. Neal (Vernon College), Therese Nemec (Fox Valley Technical College), Joong-Hwan Oh (Hunter College, City University of New York), Toby Parcel (Ohio State University), Fernando Parra (California State Polytechnic University), Anne Peterson (Columbus State Community College), Marvin Pippert (Roanoke College), Lauren Pivnik (Monroe Community College), Nevel Razak (Fort Hays State College), Jim Rebstock (Broward Community College), George Reim (Cheltenham High School), Virginia Reynolds (Indiana University of Pennsylvania), Laurel Richardson (Ohio State University), Keith Roberts (Hanover College), Ellen Rosengarten (Sinclair Community College), Michael Ryan (Dodge City Community College), Marvin Scott (Butler University), Ray Scupin (Lindenwood College), Steve Severin (Kellogg Community College), Harry Sherer (Irvine Valley College), Walt Shirley (Sinclair Community College), Anson Shupe (Indiana University–Purdue University at Fort Wayne), Ree Simpkins (Missouri Southern State University), Glen Sims (Glendale Community College), Paula Snyder (Columbus Community Col-

lege), Thomas Soltis (Westmoreland Community College), Nancy Sonleitner (University of Oklahoma), Larry Stern (Collin County Community College), Randy Ston (Oakland Community College), Verta Taylor (University of California–Santa Barbara), Vickie H. Taylor (Danville Community College), Mark J. Thomas (Madison Area Technical College), Len Tompos (Lorain County Community College), Christopher Vanderpool (Michigan State University), Phyllis Watts (Tiffin University), Murray Webster (University of North Carolina—Charlotte), Debbie White (Collin County Community College), Marilyn Wilmeth (Iowa University), Stuart Wright (Lamar University), William Yoels (University of Alabama—Birmingham), Dan Yutze (Taylor University), Wayne Zapatek (Tarrant County Community College), Assata Zerai (Syracuse University), and Frank Zulke (Harold Washington College).

Finally, I would like to dedicate this edition of the book to all the students who, after opening this book, accept my invitation to learn about sociology, to enjoy it, and to make it part of their daily lives.

College), Dina B. Neal (Vernon College), Therese Nemec (Fox Valley Technical College), Joong-Hwan Oh (Hunter College, City University of New York), Toby Parcel (Ohio State University), Fernando Parra (California State Polytechnic University), Anne Peterson (Columbus State Community College), Marvin Pippert (Roanoke College), Lauren Pivnik (Monroe Community College), Nevel Razak (Fort Hays State College), Jim Rebstock (Broward Community College), George Reim (Cheltenham High School), Virginia Reynolds (Indiana University of Pennsylvania), Laurel Richardson (Ohio State University), Keith Roberts (Hanover College), Ellen Rosengarten (Sinclair Community College), Michael Ryan (Dodge City Community College), Marvin Scott (Butler University), Ray Scupin (Lindenwood College), Steve Severin (Kellogg Community College), Harry Sherer (Irvine Valley College), Walt Shirley (Sinclair Community College), Anson Shupe (Indiana University–Purdue University at Fort Wayne), Ree Simpkins (Missouri Southern State University), Glen Sims (Glendale Community College), Paula Snyder (Columbus Community College), Thomas Soltis (Westmoreland Community College), Nancy Sonleitner (University of Oklahoma), Larry Stern (Collin County Community College), Randy Ston (Oakland Community College), Verta Taylor (University of California–Santa Barbara), Vickie H. Taylor (Danville Community College), Mark J. Thomas (Madison Area Technical College), Len Tompos (Lorain County Community College), Christopher Vanderpool (Michigan State University), Phyllis Watts (Tiffin University), Murray Webster (University of North Carolina—Charlotte), Debbie White (Collin County Community College), Marilyn Wilmeth (Iowa University), Stuart Wright (Lamar University), William Yoels (University of Alabama—Birmingham), Dan Yutze (Taylor University), Wayne Zapatek (Tarrant County Community College), Assata Zerai (Syracuse University), and Frank Zulke (Harold Washington College).

The sociological perspective shows us
that the society around us influences how we act
and even what we think and feel. Learning to see
the world sociologically is useful in many ways—
and it is also fun!

CHAPTER 1

Sociology: Perspective, Theory, and Method

WHAT makes the sociological perspective a new and exciting way of seeing the world?

WHY is sociology an important tool for your future career?

HOW do sociologists conduct research to learn about the social world?

I f you were to ask 100 people in the United States, "Why do couples marry?" it is a safe bet that at least 90 would reply, "People marry because they fall in love." Most of us find it hard to imagine a marriage being happy without love; for the same reason, when people fall in love, we expect them to think about marriage.

But is the decision about whom to marry really just a matter of personal feelings? There is plenty of evidence that if love is the key to marriage, Cupid's arrow is carefully aimed by the society around us.

In short, society has a number of "rules" about whom we should and should not marry. In all states but Massachusetts, the law rules out half the population, banning people from marrying someone of the same sex even if the couple is deeply in love. But there are other rules as well. Sociologists have found that people, especially when they are young, are very likely to marry someone close in age, and people of all ages typically marry someone of the same race, of a similar social class background, of much the same level of education, and with the same degree of physical attractiveness (Chapter 13, "Family and Religion," gives details). People end up making choices about whom to marry, but society certainly narrows the field (Gardyn, 2002; Zipp, 2002).

When it comes to love and most other dimensions of our lives, the decisions we make do not simply result from what philosophers call "free will." The essential wisdom we gain from sociology is that our social world guides our actions and life choices in much the same way that the seasons influence our choice of clothing.

The author's Web site is a great resource for new sociologists: http://www. TheSociologyPage.com (or www.macionis.com).

The Sociological Perspective

Sociology is *the systematic study of human society*. At the heart of this discipline is a distinctive point of view called the *sociological perspective*.

SEEING THE GENERAL IN THE PARTICULAR

Years ago, Peter Berger (1963) described the **sociological perspective** as *seeing the general in the particular*. By this he meant that sociology helps us see *general* patterns in the behavior of *particular* people. Although every individual is unique, society shapes the lives of people in various *categories* (such as children and adults, women and men, the rich and the poor) very differently. We begin to think sociologically by realizing how the general categories into which we fall shape our particular life experiences.

This text explores the power of society to guide our actions, thoughts, and feelings. We may think of marriage as the simple product of personal feelings. Yet the sociological perspective shows us that patterns involving our sex, age, race, and social class guide our selection of a partner. It might be more accurate to think of love as a feeling we have for others who match up with what society teaches us to want in a mate.

SEEING THE STRANGE IN THE FAMILIAR

At first, many people find that using the sociological perspective amounts to *seeing the strange in the familiar*. Consider how you would react if someone were to say to you, "You fit all the right categories; you would make a wonderful husband. Let's get married!" Looking at life sociologically requires giving up the *familiar* idea that we live our lives only in terms of what we decide in favor of the initially *strange* notion that society shapes these decisions, as it does all our experiences.

WINDOW ON THE WORLD

GLOBAL MAP 1-1 Women's Childbearing in Global Perspective

Is childbearing simply a matter of personal choice? A look around the world shows that it is not. In general, women living in poor countries have many more children than women in rich nations. Can you point to some of the reasons for this global disparity? In simple terms, such differences mean that if you had been born into another society (whether you are female or male), your life might be quite different from what it is now.

Sources: Data from Hamilton et al. (2005) and United Nations (2006). Map projection from *Peters Atlas of the World* (1990).

For individualistic North Americans, learning to see how society affects us may take a bit of practice. Consider the decision by women to bear children. Like the selection of a mate, the choice of how many children to have would seem to be a personal one. Yet there are social patterns here as well. As shown in Global Map 1–1, the average woman in the United States has about two children during her lifetime. In India, however, the "choice" is about three; in Cambodia, about four; in Ethiopia, about five; in Yemen, about six; and in Niger, about seven.

For a look at how society has shaped celebrity names, click on the "Play 'The Name Game'" link at http://www. TheSociologyPage.com

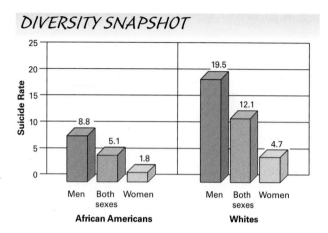

DIVERSITY SNAPSHOT

FIGURE 1–1   Rate of Death by Suicide, by Race and Sex, for the United States

Suicide rates are higher for white people than for black people and higher for men than for women. Rates indicate the number of deaths by suicide for every 100,000 people in each category for 2003.

Source: Hoyert et al. (2006).

What accounts for these striking differences? As later chapters explain, women in poor countries have less schooling and fewer economic opportunities, are more likely to remain in the home, and are less likely to use contraception. Clearly, society has much to do with the decisions women and men make about childbearing.

SEEING PERSONAL CHOICE IN SOCIAL CONTEXT

What could be a more lonely personal act than taking your own life? Emile Durkheim (1858–1917), one of sociology's pioneers, showed that social forces are at work even in such an intensely personal action as suicide, providing strong evidence of how social forces affect individual behavior.

Examining official records in and around his native France, Durkheim (1966, orig. 1897) found that some categories of people were more likely than others to take their own lives. He found that men, Protestants, wealthy people, and the unmarried each had much higher suicide rates than women, Catholics and Jews, the poor, and married people. Durkheim explained these differences in terms of *social integration*: Categories of people with strong social ties had low suicide rates, and more individualistic people had high suicide rates.

In the male-dominated societies Durkheim studied, men had much more freedom than women. But despite its advantages, freedom also contributes to social isolation and a higher suicide rate. Likewise, self-reliant Protestants were

more likely to commit suicide than more tradition-bound Catholics and Jews, whose rituals encourage stronger social ties. The wealthy have much more freedom than the poor but, once again, at the cost of a higher suicide rate.

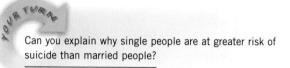

Can you explain why single people are at greater risk of suicide than married people?

A century later, Durkheim's analysis still holds true. Figure 1–1 shows suicide rates for four categories of the U.S. population. In 2003, there were 12.1 recorded suicides for every 100,000 white people, which is more than twice the rate for African Americans (5.1). For both races, suicide was more common among men than among women. White men (19.5) are more than four times as likely as white women (4.7) to take their own lives. Among African Americans, the rate for men (8.8) was almost five times that for women (1.8). Applying Durkheim's logic, the higher suicide rate among white people and men reflects their greater wealth and freedom, just as the lower rate among women and people of color reflects their limited social choices. Just as Durkheim did a century ago, we can see general sociological patterns in the actions of particular individuals.

SEEING SOCIOLOGICALLY: MARGINALITY AND CRISIS

Anyone can learn to see the world using the sociological perspective. But two situations help people see clearly how society shapes individual lives: living on the margins of society and living through a social crisis.

From time to time, everyone feels like an "outsider." For some categories of people, however, being an *outsider*—not part of the dominant group—is an everyday experience. The greater people's social marginality, the better able they are to use the sociological perspective.

For example, no African American grows up in the United States without understanding the importance of race in shaping people's lives. Rap lyrics by groups such as Three 6 Mafia, who say that they "Done seen people killed, done seen people deal, done seen people live in poverty with no meals," show that some people of color—especially African Americans living in the inner city—feel like their hopes and dreams are crushed by society. But white people, as the dominant majority, think less often about race and the privileges it provides, believing that race affects only people of color and not themselves as well. People at the margins of social life, including women, gay people, people with disabilities, and the very old, are aware of social patterns that others rarely think about. To become better at using the sociological perspective, we must step back from our familiar routines and look at our lives with a new curiosity.

Periods of change or crisis make everyone feel a little off balance, encouraging us to use the sociological perspective. The sociologist C. Wright Mills (1959) illustrated this idea using the Great Depression of the 1930s. As the unemployment rate soared to 25 percent, people without jobs could not help but see general social forces at work in their particular lives. Rather than saying, "Something is wrong with me; I can't find a job," they took a sociological approach and realized, "The economy has collapsed; there are no jobs to be found!" Mills believed that using what he called the "sociological imagination" in this way helps people understand their society and how it affects their own lives. The Seeing Sociology in Everyday Life box on page 6 takes a closer look.

People with the greatest privileges tend to see individuals as responsible for their own lives. Categories of people who are at the margins of society, by contrast, are quick to see how race, class, and gender can create disadvantages. The music of Three 6 Mafia and other popular hip-hop groups expresses the frustration felt by many African Americans living in our country's inner cities.

The Importance of a Global Perspective

As new information technology draws even the farthest reaches of the planet closer together, many academic disciplines are taking a **global perspective,** *the study of the larger world and our society's place in it.* What is the importance of a global perspective for sociology?

First, global awareness is a logical extension of the sociological perspective. Sociology shows us that our place in society profoundly affects our life experiences. It stands to reason, then, that the position of our society in the larger world system affects everyone in the United States.

The world's 192 nations can be divided into three broad categories according to their level of economic development (see Global Map 9–1 on page 247). **High-income countries** are *the nations with the highest overall standards of living.* The roughly fifty nations in this category include the United States and Canada, Argentina, the nations of Western Europe, South Africa, Israel, Saudi Arabia, Japan, and Australia. Taken together, these nations generate most of the world's goods and services, and the people who live in them own most of the planet's wealth. Economically speaking, people in these countries are very well off, not because they are smarter or work harder than anyone else but because they were lucky enough to be born in a rich region of the world.

A second category is **middle-income countries,** *nations with a standard of living about average for the world as a*

whole. People living in any of these eighty nations—many of the countries of Eastern Europe, some of Africa, and almost all of Latin America and Asia—are as likely to live in rural villages as in cities and to walk or ride tractors, scooters, bicycles, or animals as to drive automobiles. On average, they receive six to eight years of schooling. Most middle-income countries also have considerable social inequality within their own borders, meaning that some people are extremely rich (members of the business elite in nations across North Africa, for example) but many more lack safe housing and adequate nutrition (people living in the shanty settlements that surround Mexico City or Lima, Peru).

The remaining sixty or so nations of the world are **low-income countries,** *nations with a low standard of living in which most people are poor.* Most of the poorest countries in the world are in Africa, and a few are in Asia. Here again, a few people are very rich, but the majority struggle to get by with poor housing, unsafe water, too little food, and, perhaps most serious of all, little chance to improve their lives.

Chapter 9 ("Global Stratification") explains the causes and consequences of global wealth and poverty. But every chapter of this text makes comparisons between the United States and other nations for four reasons:

The Sociological Imagination: Turning Personal Problems into Public Issues

The power of the sociological perspective lies not just in making sense of our individual lives but in transforming society. As C. Wright Mills saw it, society, not people's personal failings, is the main cause of poverty and other social problems. The sociological imagination brings people together to create change by transforming personal *problems* into public *issues*. In this excerpt,* Mills (1959:3–5) explains the need for a sociological imagination:

> When society becomes industrialized, a peasant becomes a worker; a feudal lord is liquidated or becomes a businessman. When classes rise or fall, a man is employed or unemployed; when the rate of investment goes up or down,

a man takes new heart or goes broke. When wars happen, an insurance salesman becomes a rocket

To find out more about C. Wright Mills, visit the Gallery of Sociologists at http://www.TheSociologyPage.com

launcher; a store clerk, a radar man; a wife lives alone; a child grows up without a father. Neither the life of an individual nor the history of a society can be understood without understanding both.

> Yet men do not usually define the troubles they endure in terms of historical change. . . . The well-being they enjoy, they do not usually impute to the big ups and downs of the society in which they live. Seldom aware of the intricate connection between the patterns of their own lives and the course of world history, ordinary men do not usually know what this connection means for the kind of men they are

becoming and for the kinds of history-making in which they might take part. They do not possess the quality of mind essential to grasp the interplay of men and society, of biography and history, of self and world. . . .

> What they need . . . is a quality of mind that will help them to [see] what is going on in the world and . . . what may be happening within themselves. It is this quality . . . [that] may be called the sociological imagination.

WHAT DO YOU THINK?

1. As Mills sees it, how are personal troubles different from public issues?

2. Living in the United States, why do we typically blame ourselves for the problems we face?

3. By using the sociological imagination, how do we gain the power to change the world?

*In this excerpt, Mills uses "man" and male pronouns to apply to all people. Note that even an outspoken critic of society reflected the conventional writing practices of his time as far as gender was concerned.

1. **Where we live shapes the lives we lead.** As we saw in Global Map 1–1 on page 3, women living in rich and poor nations have very different lives, as suggested by the number of children they have. To understand ourselves and appreciate how others live, we must understand something about how societies differ, which is one good reason to pay attention to the global maps found throughout this text.

2. **Societies throughout the world are increasingly interconnected.** Historically, people in the United States took only passing note of the countries beyond our own borders. In recent decades, however, the United States and the rest of the world have become linked as never before. Electronic technology now transmits pictures, sounds, and written documents around the globe in seconds.

One effect of new technology, as later chapters will explain, is that people all over the world now share many tastes in food, clothing, and music. Rich countries such as the United States influence other nations, whose people are ever more likely to gobble up our Big Macs and Whoppers, dance to the latest hip-hop music, and speak the English language.

But the larger world also has an impact on us. We all know the contributions of famous immigrants such as Arnold Schwarzenegger (who came to the United States from Austria) and Gloria Estefan (who came from Cuba). More than 1 million immigrants enter the United States each year, bringing their skills and talents along with their fashions and foods, greatly increasing the racial and cultural diversity of this country.

A global perspective helps us to see the power of society over the individual. Here are six photos of children from nations around the world—Bolivia, Ethiopia, Thailand, Botswana, South Korea, and El Salvador. In what ways would the lives of children in the United States be different had they been born in one of these nations?

Trade across national boundaries has also created a global economy. Large corporations make and market goods worldwide. Stock traders in New York pay close attention to the financial markets in Tokyo and Hong Kong even as wheat farmers in Iowa watch the price of grain in the former Soviet republic of Georgia. Because most new U.S. jobs involve international trade, greater global understanding has never been more important.

3. **Many social problems that we face in the United States are far more serious elsewhere.** Poverty is a serious problem in this country, but as Chapter 9 ("Global Stratification") explains, poverty in Latin America, Africa, and Asia is both more common and more serious. In the same way, although women have lower social standing than men in the United States, gender inequality is much greater in the world's poor countries.

4. **Thinking globally helps us learn more about ourselves.** We cannot walk the streets of a distant city without thinking about what it means to live in the United States. Comparing life in various settings often leads to unexpected lessons. For instance, in Chapter 9, we visit a squatter settlement in Madras, India. There, despite a desperate lack of basic material goods, people thrive in the love and support of family members. Why, then, are so many poor people in the United States angry and alone? Are material things—so central to our definition of a "rich" life—the best way to measure human well-being?

In sum, in an increasingly interconnected world, we can understand ourselves only to the extent that we understand others. Sociology is an invitation to learn a new way of looking at the world around us. Is this invitation worth accepting? What are the benefits of applying the sociological perspective?

and school busing to laws regulating divorce. For example, in her study of how divorce affects people's income, the sociologist Lenore Weitzman (1985, 1996) discovered that women who leave marriages typically experience a dramatic loss of income. Recognizing this fact, many states passed laws that have increased women's claims to marital property and enforced fathers' obligations to provide support for women raising their children.

SOCIOLOGY AND PERSONAL GROWTH

By applying the sociological perspective, we are likely to become more active and aware and to think more critically in our everyday lives. Using sociology benefits us in four ways:

1. **The sociological perspective helps us assess the truth of "common sense."** We all take many things for granted, but that does not make them true. One good example is the idea that we are free individuals who are personally responsible for our lives. If we think we decide our fate, we may be quick to praise successful people as superior and consider others with fewer achievements personally deficient. A sociological approach, by contrast, encourages *debunking* common sense—it encourages us to ask whether common beliefs are really true and, to the extent that they are not, why they are so widely held. The Applying Sociology box gives an example of how the sociological perspective debunks some common-sense ideas we have about people who do low-wage work.

2. **The sociological perspective helps us see the opportunities and constraints in our everyday lives.** Sociological thinking leads us to see that in the game of life, we have a say in how to play our cards, but it is society that deals us the hand. The more we understand the game, the better players we will be. Sociology helps us learn more about the world around us so that we can more effectively pursue our goals.

    For instance, do you think going to college is just a matter of personal choice? "In the *Times*" on pages 10–11 suggests that societal forces play a powerful role in shaping college attendance.

To view maps showing patterns of interest to sociologists, go to http://www.nationalatlas.gov

3. **The sociological perspective empowers us to be active participants in our society.** The better we understand how society operates, the more effective citizens we become. As C. Wright Mills explained in the box on page 6, it is the sociological perspective

One important reason to gain a global understanding is that, living in a high-income nation, we scarcely can appreciate the suffering that goes on in much of the world. This family, living in the African nation of Zambia, has none of the security most of us take for granted. In poor nations, children have only a fifty-fifty chance of surviving to adulthood.

YOUR TURN

How would your life be different if you had been born into a poor family in an Asian farming village? What might you be doing right now instead of reading this textbook?

Applying the Sociological Perspective

Applying the sociological perspective is useful in many ways. First, sociology is at work guiding many of the laws and policies that shape our lives. Second, on an individual level, making use of the sociological perspective leads to important personal growth and expanded awareness. Third, studying sociology is excellent preparation for the world of work.

SOCIOLOGY AND PUBLIC POLICY

Sociologists have helped shape public policy—the laws and regulations that guide how people in communities live and work—in countless ways, from racial desegregation

APPLYING SOCIOLOGY

Nickel and Dimed: On (Not) Getting By in America

All of us know people who work at low-wage jobs as waitresses at diners, clerks at drive-throughs, or sales associates at discount stores such as Wal-Mart. We see such people just about every day. Many of us actually *are* such people. In the United States, "common sense" tells us that the jobs people have and the amount of money they make reflect their personal abilities as well as their willingness to work hard.

Barbara Ehrenreich (2001) had her doubts. To find out what the world of low-wage work is really like, the successful journalist and author decided to leave her comfortable middle-class life to live and work in the world of low-wage jobs. She began in Key West, Florida, taking a job as a waitress for $2.43 an hour plus tips. Right away, she found out she had to work much harder than she ever imagined. By the end of a shift, she was exhausted, but after sharing tips with the kitchen staff, she averaged less than $6.00 an hour. This was barely above the national minimum wage and provided just enough income to pay the rent on her tiny apartment, buy food, and cover other basic expenses. She had to hope that

she didn't get sick, because the job did not provide health insurance and she couldn't afford to pay for a visit to a doctor's office.

After working for more than a year at a number of other low-wage jobs, including cleaning motels in Maine and working on the floor of a Wal-Mart in Minnesota, she had rejected quite a bit of "common sense." First, she now knew that tens of millions of people with low-wage jobs work very hard every day. If you don't think so, Ehrenreich says, take on one of these jobs for yourself. Second, these jobs require not only hard work (imagine completely cleaning three motel rooms every hour all day long) but also special skills and real intelligence (try waiting on ten tables in a restaurant at the same time and keeping everybody happy). She found that the people she worked with were, on average, just as smart, clever, and funny as others she knew who wrote books for a living or taught at a college.

Why, then, do we think of low-wage workers as lazy or as having less ability? It surprised Ehrenreich to learn that many low-wage workers felt this

way about themselves. In a society that teaches us to believe that personal ability is everything, we learn to size people up by their job. Ehrenreich discovered that many low-wage workers, subject to constant supervision, random drug tests, and other rigid rules that usually come with such jobs, end up feeling unworthy, even to the point of not trying for anything better. Such beliefs, she concludes, help support a society of extreme inequality in which some people live better because of the low wages paid to the rest.

WHAT DO YOU THINK?

1. Have you ever held a low-wage job? If so, would you say you worked hard? What was your pay? Were there any benefits?

2. Ehrenreich claims that most well-off people in the United States are dependent on low-wage workers. What does she mean by this?

3. Do most people with jobs at Wendy's or Wal-Mart have a real chance to enroll in college and to work toward a different career? Why or why not?

---

that turns a private problem (such as being out of work) into a public issue (a lack of good jobs). As we come to see how society affects us, we may decide to support society as it is, or we may set out with others to change it.

4. **The sociological perspective helps us live in a diverse world.** North Americans represent just 5 percent of the world's population, and as the remaining chapters of this book explain, much of the other 95 percent live very differently than we do. Still, like people everywhere, we tend to view our own way of life as "right," "natural," and "better." The sociological perspective

prompts us to think critically about the strengths and weaknesses of all ways of life, including our own.

CAREERS: THE "SOCIOLOGY ADVANTAGE"

Most students at colleges and universities today are very interested in getting a good job. A background in sociology is excellent preparation for the working world. Of course, completing a bachelor's degree in sociology is the right choice for people who decide they would like to go on to graduate work and eventually become a professor or researcher in this field. Throughout the United States, tens of thousands of men and women teach sociology in univer-

Times

The New York Times

June 19, 2005

For Illegal Immigrants, a Harsh Lesson

By SUSAN DONALDSON JAMES

TRENTON—Esteban Navarro's disappearance broke a lot of hearts at Trenton Central High School, where the dropout rate among Hispanic students is triple the state average.

Two years ago, Mr. Navarro, a quiet and gifted student, was headed for top honors. His teachers said he was a star soccer player who received a perfect score on the advanced-placement calculus exam and was named class valedictorian. By senior year, the long-haired teenager was being courted by Princeton, where he took advanced math classes.

But by spring 2003, when he was a senior, Mr. Navarro's plans to attend college unraveled. As the son of illegal immigrants, Mr. Navarro, who was born in Costa Rica, had no Social Security number. Had he been a citizen, his parents' meager income as a cook and a

house cleaner might have qualified him for financial aid, but federal law barred him from receiving assistance.

Afraid to risk flouting federal law, Princeton and other leading universities could not process Mr. Navarro's applications, . . . And at graduation, as the principal called on him to deliver the valedictory speech, Mr. Navarro had already dropped out—his dream of becoming a mathematician dashed in a tangle of immigration laws.

Now 21, Mr. Navarro, who had attended school in the United States since the first grade, works in a pizza shop outside Philadelphia.

Nor is the plight of Mr. Navarro an isolated case. Currently, about 60,000 high school students who have spent nearly their entire lives in the United States are considered illegal immigrants. . . . And because 56 percent of them are from low-income families, the cost of college is out of reach.

One solution is embodied in the In-State Tuition Act, first introduced in the New Jersey Legislature in 2003, which would allow illegal immigrants like Mr. Navarro to attend public colleges at in-state tuition rates. . . .

To qualify for in-state status, according to the legislation, students would have to prove that they had attended a New Jersey high school for at least four years and planned to apply for citizenship. . . .

The issue is particularly pressing in New Jersey, which has the fifth-largest immigrant population in the nation. Some migration studies say that as many as 500,000 residents are illegal immigrants, although the real numbers are hard to determine. . . . They often shuttle among low-wage jobs as cooks, construction workers and janitors. Their children tend to attend low-performing schools and drop out early to help their families scratch out a living. . . .

---

sities, colleges, and high schools. But just as many professional sociologists work as researchers for government agencies or private foundations and businesses, gathering important information

In a short video, the author offers a personal response to the question, "Why would someone want to be a sociologist?" See the Video Gallery at http://www.TheSociologyPage.com

on how people live, what they think, and how they spend their money. In today's cost-conscious world, agencies and companies want to be sure that the products, programs, and policies they create get the job done at the lowest cost. Sociologists, especially those with advanced research skills, are in high demand for this type of evaluation research (Deutscher, 1999).

In addition, a smaller but increasing number of people work as clinical sociologists. These women and men work, much as clinical psychologists do, with the goal of improv-

ing the lives of troubled clients. A basic difference is that sociologists focus on difficulties not in the personality but in the individual's web of social relationships.

But sociology is not just for people who want to be sociologists. People who work in criminal justice—including jobs in police departments, probation offices, and correction facilities—gain the "sociology advantage" by learning what categories of people are most at risk of becoming criminals as well as victims, how effective various policing policies and programs are at preventing crime, and

why people turn to crime in the first place. Similarly, people who work in health care—including doctors, nurses, and technicians—also gain a "sociology advantage" by learning about patterns of health and illness within the population, as well as how factors such as race, gender, and social class affect human health.

Based on New Jersey Census figures, there may be as many as 100,000 illegal immigrants in the public schools. But in 2003, . . . only about 1,200 had actually considered applying to college. . . .

So far, federal and state laws have sent immigrants mixed signals. In 1982, the United States Supreme Court ruled that public school students in kindergarten through 12th grade could not be denied an education because of their immigration status. A decade later, the national Immigration Reform and Control Act of 1996 largely cut social benefits to illegal immigrant families, including access to federal financial aid. The law also included a provision prohibiting in-state tuition rates for illegal immigrants.

After 2001, California and Texas were the first states to counter that act with laws to treat illegal immigrant students as residents if they had been educated almost exclusively in the United States.

Those two states were followed by Utah, Illinois, Oklahoma, New York and Washington.

But many New Jersey legislators are hesitant to act. . . .

Immigration papers arrived in April for the Navarro family. But they were too late for Esteban, who gave up his dream to go to college two years ago and cut off all contact with high school friends and teachers.

"It hurts me a lot," said his brother, Julio, who recently graduated from high school and plans to attend Middlebury College, where he was awarded a scholarship. . . . "I see a lot of kids get the door shut in their face. You don't hear many success stories. It keeps me up a lot of nights, wondering why."

WHAT DO YOU THINK?

1. How does the fact that Esteban Navarro was unable to attend college show that our achievements and failures involve not just our personal efforts but the operation of society?

2. In what other ways are the lives and destinies of people like Esteban affected by their undocumented status in the United States? Point to specific facts in the article that support your answer.

3. Are laws that deny people certain rights because they are not legal immigrants just or unjust? Explain your opinion.

Adapted from the original article by Susan Donaldson James published in *The New York Times* on June 19, 2005. Copyright © 2005 by The New York Times Company. Reprinted with permission.

The American Sociological Association (2002) reports that sociology is also excellent preparation for jobs in dozens of fields, including advertising, banking, business, education, government, journalism, law, public relations, and social work. In almost any type of work, success depends on understanding how various categories of people differ in beliefs, family patterns, and other ways of life. Unless you have a job that never involves dealing with people, you should consider the workplace benefits of taking courses in sociology.

YOUR TURN

Write down five jobs that appeal to you, then identify ways in which sociological thinking would increase your chances for success in each one.

The Origins of Sociology

Like the "choices" made by individuals, major historical events rarely just "happen." Sociology was born as the result of powerful social forces.

SOCIAL CHANGE AND SOCIOLOGY

Striking changes in Europe during the eighteenth and nineteenth centuries made people think more about society and their place in it, spurring the development of sociology. Three significant changes that transformed society were the rise of a factory-based economy, the explosive growth of cities, and new ideas about democracy and political rights.

Industrial Technology

During the Middle Ages, most people in Europe plowed fields near their homes or engaged in small-scale *manufact-*

Here we see Galileo, one of the great pioneers of the scientific revolution, defending himself before church officials, who were greatly threatened by his claims that science could explain the operation of the universe. Just as Galileo challenged the common sense of his day, pioneering sociologists such as Auguste Comte later argued that society is neither rigidly fixed by God's will nor set by human nature. On the contrary, Comte claimed, society is a system we can study scientifically, and based on what we learn, we can act intentionally to improve our lives.

North Wind Picture Archives

uring (a word derived from Latin words meaning "to make by hand"). By the end of the eighteenth century, inventors were using new sources of energy—the power of moving water and then steam—to operate large machines in mills and factories. As a result, instead of laboring at home or in tightly knit groups, workers became part of a large and anonymous labor force under the control of strangers who owned the factories. This change in the system of production took people away from their homes, weakening the traditions that had guided community life for centuries.

The Growth of Cities

Across Europe, landowners took part in what historians call the "enclosure movement"—they fenced off more and more farmland to create grazing areas for sheep, the source of wool for the thriving textile mills. Without land, countless tenant farmers had little choice but to head for the cities in search of work in the new factories.

As cities grew larger, these urban migrants faced many social problems, including pollution, crime, and homelessness. Moving through streets crowded with strangers, they faced a new, impersonal world.

Political Change

Economic development and the growth of cities also brought new ways of thinking. In the writings of Thomas Hobbes (1588–1679), John Locke (1632–1704), and Adam Smith (1723–1790), we find a shift from a focus on people's moral duties to God and king to the pursuit of self-interest.

In the new political climate, philosophers spoke of *individual liberty* and *individual rights*. Echoing the thoughts of Locke, our own Declaration of Independence clearly states that each citizen has "certain unalienable rights," including "life, liberty, and the pursuit of happiness."

The French Revolution, which began in 1789, was an even greater break with political and social tradition. As the French social analyst Alexis de Tocqueville (1805–1859) declared, the change in society in the wake of the French Revolution amounted to "nothing short of the regeneration of the whole human race" (1955:13, orig. 1856). As the new industrial economy, enormous cities, and fresh political ideas combined to draw attention to society, the new discipline known as sociology developed in France, Germany, and England, the countries experiencing the greatest changes.

SCIENCE AND SOCIOLOGY

Throughout history, the nature of society has fascinated people, including the brilliant philosophers K'ung Fu-tzu, or Confucius (551–479 B.C.E.), in China and Plato (427–347 B.C.E.) and Aristotle (384–322 B.C.E.) in Greece.[1] Later, the Roman emperor Marcus Aurelius (121–180), the medieval thinkers Saint Thomas Aquinas (c. 1225–1274) and Chris-

---

[1]The abbreviation B.C.E. means "before the common era." We use this throughout the text instead of the traditional B.C. ("before Christ") to reflect the religious diversity of our society. Similarly, in place of the traditional A.D. (*anno Domini,* or "in the year of our Lord"), we use the abbreviation C.E. ("common era").

SEEING OURSELVES

NATIONAL MAP 1-1
Suicide Rates across the United States

This map shows which states have high, average, and low suicide rates. Look for patterns. By and large, high suicide rates occur where people live far apart from one another. More densely populated states have low suicide rates. Do these data support or contradict Durkheim's theory of suicide? Why?

Source: Hoyert et al. (2006).

Number of Suicides per 100,000 People

- Above average: 14.1 or more
- Average: 10.0 to 14.0
- Below average: 9.9 or fewer

tine de Pizan (c. 1363–1431), and the great English playwright William Shakespeare (1564–1616) wrote about the workings of society.

Yet these thinkers were more interested in imagining the ideal society than they were in studying society as it really was. It was the French social thinker Auguste Comte (1798–1857) who coined the term *sociology* in 1838 to describe this new way of thinking. This makes sociology among the youngest of the academic disciplines—far newer than history, physics, or economics, for example.

Comte (1975, orig. 1851–54) saw sociology as the product of three stages of historical development. During

 For a biographical sketch of Comte, visit the Gallery of Sociologists at http://www. TheSociologyPage.com

the earliest *theological stage*, from the beginning of human history up to the end of the European Middle Ages about 1350 C.E., people took the religious view that society expressed God's will.

With the dawn of the Renaissance in the fifteenth century, the theological stage gave way to a *metaphysical stage* in which people saw society as a natural rather than supernatural phenomenon. The English philosopher Thomas Hobbes, for example, suggested that society reflected not the perfection of God as much as the failings of a selfish human nature.

What Comte called the *scientific stage* began with the work of early scientists such as the Polish astronomer Nicolaus Copernicus (1473–1543), the Italian astronomer and physicist Galileo Galilei (1564–1642), and the English physicist and mathematician Isaac Newton (1642–1727). Comte's contribution came in applying the scientific approach, originally used to analyze the physical world, to the study of society.

Comte's approach is called **positivism,** *a way of understanding based on science.* As a positivist, Comte believed that society operates according to certain laws, just as the physical world operates according to gravity and other laws of nature.

At the beginning of the twentieth century, sociology took hold as an academic discipline in the United States, strongly influenced by Comte's ideas. Today, most sociologists still consider science a crucial part of sociology. But we now realize that human behavior is far more complex than the movement of planets. We are creatures of imagination and spontaneity, so human behavior can never be explained by any rigid "laws of society." In addition, early sociologists such as Karl Marx (1818–1883) were deeply troubled by the striking inequality of the new industrial society. They wanted the new discipline of sociology not just to understand society but also to bring about change toward social justice.

Sociological Theory

The desire to translate observations into understanding brings us to the important part of sociology known as *theory.* A **theory** is *a statement of how and why specific facts are related.* The job of sociological theory is to explain social behavior in the real world. For example, recall Durkheim's theory that categories of people with low social integration (men, Protestants, the wealthy, and the unmarried) are at higher risk of suicide.

Sociologists conduct research to test and refine their theories. National Map 1–1 shows the suicide rates for each of the fifty states and gives you a chance to do some theorizing of your own.

The structural-functional approach highlights how social patterns help society operate. It suggests that we consider how college functions as a "marriage market," bringing together young people who have the chance to link up with others who share their life interests. The social-conflict approach offers a different insight. It suggests that college is a common experience mainly for young people from privileged families, preparing them for successful careers and helping them to meet and marry others of similar background; in this way, colleges help extend the class structure into a new generation.

In building theory, sociologists face two basic questions: What issues should we study? And how should we connect the facts? In answering these questions, sociologists look to one or more theoretical approaches or "road maps." Think of a **theoretical approach** as *a basic image of society that guides thinking and research*. Sociologists make use of three theoretical approaches: the *structural-functional approach,* the *social-conflict approach,* and the *symbolic-interaction approach*.

The Structural-Functional Approach

The **structural-functional approach** is *a framework for building theory that sees society as a complex system whose parts work together to promote solidarity and stability*. As its name suggests, this approach points to **social structure,** *any relatively stable pattern of social behavior*. Social structure

gives our lives shape in families, the workplace, or the college classroom. This approach also looks for each structure's **social functions,** *the consequences of a social pattern for the operation of society as a whole*. All social patterns, from a simple handshake to complex religious rituals, function to keep society going, at least in its present form.

The structural-functional approach owes much to Auguste Comte, who pointed out the need to keep society unified when many traditions were breaking down. Emile Durkheim, who helped establish sociology in French univer-

 Find biographical sketches of Durkheim and Spencer in the Gallery of Sociologists at http://www.TheSociologyPage.com

sities, also based his work on this approach. A third structural-functional pioneer was the English sociologist Herbert Spencer (1820–1903). Spencer compared society to the human body: Just as the structural parts of the human body—the skeleton, muscles, and internal organs—function together to help the entire organism survive, social structures work together to preserve society. The structural-functional approach, then, leads sociologists to identify various structures of society and investigate their functions.

The U.S. sociologist Robert K. Merton (1910–2003) expanded our understanding of social function by pointing out that any social structure probably has many functions, some more obvious than others. He distinguished between **manifest functions,** *the recognized and intended consequences of any social pattern*, and **latent functions,** *the unrecognized and unintended consequences of any social pattern*. For example, the obvious function of this country's system of higher education is to give young people the information and skills they will need to perform jobs after graduation. Perhaps just as important, although less often acknowledged, is college's function as a "marriage broker," bringing together young people of similar social backgrounds. Another latent function of higher education is to limit unemployment by keeping millions of people out of the labor market, where many of them might not easily find jobs.

But Merton also recognized that the effects of social structure are not all good and certainly not good for everybody. Thus a **social dysfunction** is *any social pattern that may disrupt the operation of society*. People often disagree on what is helpful and what is harmful for society as a whole. In addition, what is functional for one category of people (say, a plan to provide high profits for factory owners) may well be dysfunctional for another category of people (by providing low wages for factory workers).

CRITICAL REVIEW The main idea of the structural-functional approach is its vision of society as stable and orderly. The main goal of sociologists who use this approach, then, is to figure out "what makes society tick."

We can use the sociological perspective to look at sociology itself. All of the most widely recognized pioneers of the discipline were men. This is because, in the nineteenth century, it was all but unheard of for women to be college professors, and few women took a central role in public life. But Harriet Martineau in England, Jane Addams in the United States, and others made contributions to sociology that we now recognize as important and lasting.

In the mid-1900s, most sociologists favored the structural-functional approach. In recent decades, however, its influence has declined. By focusing attention on social stability and unity, critics point out, structural-functionalism ignores inequalities of social class, race, ethnicity, and gender, which cause tension and conflict. In general, its focus on stability at the expense of conflict makes this approach somewhat conservative. As a critical response, sociologists developed the social-conflict approach.

✔ YOUR LEARNING How do manifest functions differ from latent functions? Give an example of a manifest function and a latent function of automobiles in the United States.

THE SOCIAL-CONFLICT APPROACH

The **social-conflict approach** is *a framework for building theory that sees society as an arena of inequality that generates conflict and change.* Unlike the structural-functional emphasis on solidarity, this approach highlights how factors such as class, race, ethnicity, gender, and age are linked to inequality in terms of money, power, education, and social prestige. A conflict analysis rejects the idea that social structure promotes the operation of society as a whole, focusing instead on how any social pattern benefits some people while hurting others.

Sociologists use the social-conflict approach to look at ongoing conflict between dominant and disadvantaged categories of people—the rich in relation to the poor, white people in relation to people of color, or men in relation to women. Typically, people on top try to protect their privileges while the disadvantaged try to gain more for themselves.

A conflict analysis of our educational system shows how schooling reproduces class inequality from one generation to the next. For example, secondary schools assign students to either college preparatory or vocational training programs. From a structural-functional point of view, such "tracking" benefits everyone by providing schooling that fits students' abilities. But conflict analysis argues that tracking often has less to do with talent than with social background, meaning that well-to-do students are placed in higher tracks while poor children end up in lower tracks.

In this way, young people from privileged families get the best schooling, which leads them to college and later to high-income careers. The children of poor families, by contrast, are not prepared for college and, like their parents before them, typically get stuck in low-paying jobs. In both cases, the social standing of one generation is passed on to the next, with schools justifying the practice in terms of individual merit (Bowles & Gintis, 1976; Oakes, 1982, 1985).

Many sociologists who use social-conflict analysis try not just to understand society but also to reduce inequality. Karl Marx championed the cause of workers in what he saw as their battle against factory owners. In a well-known statement (inscribed on his monument in London's Highgate Cemetery), Marx declared, "The philosophers have only interpreted the world, in various ways; the point, however, is to change it."

FEMINISM AND THE GENDER-CONFLICT APPROACH

One important type of conflict analysis is the **gender-conflict approach,** *a point of view that focuses on inequality and conflict between women and men.* The gender-conflict

An Important Pioneer: Du Bois on Race

One of sociology's pioneers in the United States, William Edward Burghardt Du Bois saw sociology as the key to solving society's problems, especially racial inequality.

Du Bois spoke out against racial separation and was a founding member of the National Association for the Advancement of Colored People (NAACP). He helped his colleagues in sociology—and people everywhere—see the deep racial divisions in the United States. White people can simply be "Americans," Du Bois pointed out; African Americans, however, have a "double consciousness," reflecting their status as citizens who are never able to escape identification based on the color of their skin.

In his sociological classic *The Philadelphia Negro: A Social Study* (1899), Du Bois explored Philadelphia's African American community, identifying both the strengths and the weaknesses of people wrestling with overwhelming social problems on a day-to-day basis. He challenged the belief—widespread at that time—that blacks were inferior to whites, and he blamed white prejudice for the problems African Americans faced. He also criticized successful people of color for being so eager to win white acceptance that they gave up all ties with

the black community, which needed their help.

Du Bois described race as the major problem facing the United States in the twentieth century. Early in his career, he was hopeful about overcoming racial divisions. By the end of his life, however, he had grown bitter, believing that little had changed. At the age of ninety-three, Du Bois left the United States for Ghana, where he died two years later.

WHAT DO YOU THINK?

1. If he were alive today, do you think that Du Bois would still consider race a major problem in the twenty-first century? Why or why not?

2. How much do you think African Americans today experience "double consciousness"?

3. How can sociology help us understand and reduce racial conflict?

Sources: Based in part on Baltzell (1967) and Du Bois (1967, orig. 1899).

---

approach is closely linked to **feminism,** *the advocacy of social equality for women and men.*

The importance of the gender-conflict approach lies in making us aware of the many ways in which our society places men in positions of power over women, in the home (where men are usually considered the "head of the household"), in the workplace (where men earn more income and hold most positions of power), and in the mass media (how many hip-hop stars are women?).

Another contribution of the gender-conflict approach is making us aware of the importance of women to the development of sociology. Harriet Martineau (1802–1876) is regarded as the first woman sociologist. Martineau, who was born to a wealthy English family, first made her mark in 1853 by translating the writings of Auguste Comte from French into English. She later documented the evils of slavery and argued for laws to protect factory workers, defending work-

ers' right to unionize. She was particularly concerned about the position of women in society and fought for changes in education policy so that women could look forward to more in life than marriage and raising children.

In the United States, Jane Addams (1860–1935) was a sociological pioneer whose contributions began in 1899 when she helped found Hull House, a Chicago settlement house that provided assistance to immigrant families. Although widely published (Addams wrote eleven books and hundreds of articles), Addams chose the life of a public activist over that of a university sociologist, speaking out on issues involving inequality, immigration, and the pursuit of peace. After years of controversy due to her pacifism during World War I, she was awarded the Nobel Peace Prize in 1931.

All chapters of this book consider the importance of gender and gender inequality. For an in-depth look at feminism and the social standing of women and men, see Chapter 10 ("Gender Stratification").

THE RACE-CONFLICT APPROACH

Another important type of social-conflict analysis is the **race-conflict approach,** *a point of view that focuses on inequality and conflict between people of different racial and ethnic categories.* Just as men have power over women, white people have numerous social advantages over people of color, including, on average, higher incomes, more schooling, better health, and longer life expectancy.

The race-conflict approach also points out the contributions to the development of sociology made by people of color. Ida Wells Barnett (1862–1931) was born to slave parents but rose to become a teacher and then a journalist and newspaper publisher. She campaigned tirelessly for racial equality and, especially, to put an end to the lynching of black people. She wrote and lectured about racial inequality throughout her life (Lengerman & Niebrugge-Brantley, 1998).

An important contribution to understanding race in the United States was made by William Edward Burghardt Du Bois (1868–1963). Born to a poor Massachusetts family, Du Bois enrolled at Fisk University in Nashville, Tennessee, and then at Harvard University, where he earned the first doctorate awarded by that university to a person of color. Like most people who follow the social-conflict approach (whether focusing on class, gender, or race), Du Bois believed that scholars should try not simply to learn about society's problems but also to solve them. He therefore studied the black community, spoke out against racial inequality, and participated in the founding of the National Association for the Advancement of Colored People (NAACP). The Thinking About Diversity box takes a closer look at the ideas of W. E. B. Du Bois.

> **CRITICAL REVIEW** The various social-conflict approaches have gained a large following in recent decades, but like other approaches, they have met with criticism. Because any conflict analysis focuses on inequality, it largely ignores how shared values and interdependence can unify members of a society. In addition, say critics, to the extent that it pursues political goals, a social-conflict approach cannot claim scientific objectivity. Supporters of social-conflict analysis respond that *all* theoretical approaches have political consequences.
>
> A final criticism of both the structural-functional and social-conflict approaches is that they paint society in broad strokes—in terms of "family," "social class," "race," and so on. A third theoretical

The basic insight of the symbolic-interaction approach is that people create the reality they experience as they interact. In other words, as these three students engage one another in conversation, they are literally deciding "what's going on?"

approach views society less in general terms and more as the specific, everyday experiences of individual people.

✓ **YOUR LEARNING** Why do sociologists characterize the social-conflict approach as "activist"? What is it trying to achieve?

THE SYMBOLIC-INTERACTION APPROACH

The structural-functional and social-conflict approaches share a **macro-level orientation,** meaning *a broad focus on social structures that shape society as a whole.* Macro-level sociology takes in the big picture, rather like observing a city from a helicopter and seeing how highways help people move from place to place or how housing differs from rich to poor neighborhoods. Sociology also uses a **micro-level orientation,** *a close-up focus on social interaction in specific situations.* Exploring city life in this way occurs at street level, where you might watch how children invent games on a school playground or observe how pedestrians respond to homeless people they pass on the street. The **symbolic-interaction approach,** then, is *a framework for building theory that sees society as the product of the everyday interactions of individuals.*

How does "society" result from the ongoing experiences of tens of millions of people? One answer, detailed in Chapter 4 ("Social Interaction in Everyday Life"), is that society is nothing more than the reality people construct for themselves as they interact with one another. That is, human beings are creatures who live in a world of symbols, attaching meaning to virtually everything from the words on this page to a wink of an eye. "Reality," therefore, is

APPLYING THEORY

Major Theoretical Approaches

	Structural-Functional Approach	Social-Conflict Approach	Symbolic-Interaction Approach
What is the level of analysis?	Macro-level	Macro-level	Micro-level
What image of society does the approach have?	Society is a system of interrelated parts that is relatively stable. Each part works to keep society operating in an orderly way. Members generally agree about what is morally right and morally wrong.	Society is a system of social inequalities based on class (Marx), gender (feminism and gender-conflict approach), and race (race-conflict approach). Society operates to benefit some categories of people and to harm others. Social inequality causes conflict that leads to social change.	Society is an ongoing process. People interact in countless settings using symbolic communications. The reality people experience is variable and changing.
What core questions does the approach ask?	How is society held together? What are the major parts of society? How are these parts linked? What does each part do to help society work?	How does society divide a population according to class, gender, race, and age? How do advantaged people protect their privileges? How do disadvantaged people challenge the system seeking change?	How do people experience society? How do people shape the reality they experience? How do behavior and meaning change from person to person and from one situation to another?

simply how we define our surroundings, our duties toward others, and even our own identities.

The symbolic-interaction approach has roots in the thinking of Max Weber (1864–1920), a German sociologist who emphasized understanding a particular setting from the point of view of the people in it. Since Weber's time, sociologists have taken micro-level sociology in a number of directions. Chapter 3 ("Socialization: From Infancy to Old Age") discusses the ideas of George Herbert Mead (1863–1931), who explored how our personalities develop as a result of social experience. Chapter 4 ("Social Interaction in Everyday Life") presents the work of Erving Goffman (1922–1982), whose *dramaturgical analysis* describes how we resemble actors on a stage as we play out our various roles. Other contemporary sociologists, including George Homans and Peter Blau, have developed *social-exchange analysis,* the idea that interaction is guided by what each person stands to gain and lose from others. In the ritual of courtship, for example, people seek mates who can offer them at least as much—in terms of physical attractiveness, intelligence, and social background—as they offer in return.

CRITICAL REVIEW Without denying the existence of macro-level social structures such as the family and social class, the symbolic-interaction approach reminds us that

society basically amounts to *people interacting*. That is, micro-level sociology shows us how individuals construct and experience society. However, by emphasizing what is unique in each social scene, this approach risks overlooking the widespread influence of culture, as well as factors such as class, gender, and race.

✅ **YOUR LEARNING** How does a micro-level analysis differ from a macro-level analysis?

The Applying Theory table summarizes the features of the structural-functional, social-conflict, and symbolic-interaction approaches. As you read the chapters in this book, keep in mind that each is helpful in answering particular types of questions. As the Applying Sociology box on pages 20–21 shows, the fullest understanding of society comes from using all three approaches.

Three Ways to Do Sociology

All sociologists want to learn about the social world. But just as they may prefer one theoretical approach to another, they may prefer one research orientation. The following sections describe three ways to do sociological research: scientific, interpretive, and critical sociology.

SCIENTIFIC SOCIOLOGY

Probably the most popular way to do sociological research is based on **science,** *a logical system that bases knowledge on direct, systematic observation.* **Scientific sociology,** then, is *the study of society based on systematic observation of social behavior.* Scientific sociology is sometimes called *empirical sociology* because it is based on **empirical evidence,** which is *information we can verify with our senses.*

A scientific orientation often challenges what we accept as "common sense." Here are three examples of widely held beliefs that are not supported by scientific evidence:

1. **"Differences in the behavior of females and males reflect 'human nature.'"** Wrong. Much of what we call human nature is constructed by the society in which we live. We know this because researchers have found that definitions of "feminine" and "masculine" change over time and vary from one society to another (see Chapter 10, "Gender Stratification").

2. **"The United States is a middle-class society in which most people are more or less equal."** Not true. As Chapter 8 ("Social Stratification") explains, the richest 5 percent of U.S. families control more than half of the country's wealth, while almost half of all families have scarcely any wealth at all.

3. **"People marry because they are in love."** Not exactly. In our own society, as already explained, many social rules guide the selection of mates. Around the world, as Chapter 13 ("Family and Religion") explains, research indicates that marriages in most societies are arranged by parents and have little to do with love.

These examples confirm the old saying that "it's not what we *don't* know that gets us into trouble as much as the things we *do* know that just aren't so." Scientific sociology is a useful way to assess many kinds of information.

Concepts, Variables, and Measurement

A basic element of science is the **concept,** *a mental construct that represents some part of the world in a simplified form.* Sociologists use concepts to label aspects of social life, including "the family" and "the economy," and to categorize people in terms of their "gender" or "social class."

A **variable** is *a concept whose value changes from case to case.* The familiar variable "height," for example, has a value that varies from person to person. The concept "social class" can describe people's social standing using the values "upper-class," "middle-class," "working-class," or "lower-class."

The use of variables depends on **measurement,** *a procedure for determining the value of a variable in a specific case.* Some variables are easy to measure, as when a nurse checks our height at a medical office. But measuring sociological variables can be far more difficult. For example, how would you measure a person's social class? You might start by looking at clothing, listening to how people speak, or noting where they live. Or trying to be more precise, you might ask about income, occupation, and education. Because there are many ways to measure a complex variable like social class, researchers must make decisions about how to *operationalize* a variable, stating exactly what they are measuring.

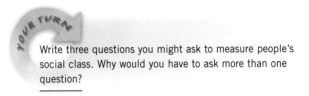

Write three questions you might ask to measure people's social class. Why would you have to ask more than one question?

Statistics

Sociologists also face the problem of dealing with large numbers of people. For example, how do you report income for thousands or even millions of individuals? Listing streams of numbers would carry little meaning and tell us nothing about the people as a whole. To solve this problem, sociologists use *descriptive statistics* to state what is "average" for a large population. The most commonly used descriptive statistics are the *mean* (the arithmetic average of all measures, obtained by adding them up and dividing by the number of cases), the *median* (the score at the halfway point in an ascending series of numbers), and the *mode* (the score that occurs most often).

Reliability and Validity

Good measurement must be reliable and valid. **Reliability** is *consistency in measurement.* For measurement to be reliable, in other words, the process must yield the same results when repeated. However, even measurement that yields consistent results may not be valid. **Validity** is *actually measuring exactly what you intend to measure.* Valid measurement means more than hitting the same spot somewhere on a target again and again; it means hitting the exact target, the bull's-eye.

Say you want to know just how religious the students at your college are. You might ask students how often they attend religious services. But is going to a church, temple, or mosque really the same thing as being religious? Maybe not, because people take part in religious rituals for many reasons, some of them having little to do with religion; in addition, some strong believers avoid organized religion altogether. Thus even when a measure yields consistent

Sports: Playing the Theory Game

Who doesn't enjoy sports? Children and teens may play as many as two or three organized sports. For adults who don't participate themselves, weekend television is filled with sporting events, and whole sections of our newspapers are devoted to teams and players and scores. What can we learn by applying sociology's three theoretical approaches to this familiar element of life in the United States?

Structural-Functional Approach

According to the structural-functional approach, the manifest functions of sports include recreation, getting in shape, and letting off steam in a relatively harmless way. Sports have important latent functions as well, from building social relationships to creating countless jobs. Perhaps the most important latent function of sports is to encourage competition, which is central to our society's way of life.

Of course, sports also have dysfunctional consequences. For example, colleges and universities that try to field winning teams sometimes recruit students for their athletic skill rather than their academic ability. This practice not only lowers a school's academic standards but also shortchanges athletes, who spend little time doing the academic work that will prepare them for future careers (Upthegrove, Roscigno, & Charles, 1999).

Social-Conflict Approach

A social-conflict analysis points out how sports are linked to social inequal-

ity. Some sports—tennis, swimming, golf, skiing—are expensive, so participation is largely limited to the well-to-do. Football, baseball, and basketball, however, are accessible to people at almost all income levels. Thus the games people play are not simply a

INTERNET To read the 2005 Racial and Gender Report Cards for U.S. sports, go to http://www.bus.ucf.edu/sport/cgi-bin/site/sitew.cgi?page=/ides/index.htx

matter of choice but also a reflection of their social standing.

Throughout history, men have dominated the world of sports. The first modern Olympic Games, held in 1896, excluded women from competition. In the United States through most of the twentieth century, Little League teams barred girls from the playing field based on the traditional ideas that girls lack the strength and the stamina to play sports and that they risk losing their femininity if they do. Both the Olympics and the Little League are now

open to females as well as males, but even today, women still take a back seat to men, particularly in sports with the greatest earnings and social prestige.

Although our society long excluded people of color from professional sports, opportunities have expanded in recent decades. In 1947, Jackie Robinson crossed the "color line" to become the first African American player in Major League Baseball. More than fifty years later, professional baseball retired the legendary Robinson's number 42 on *all* teams. In 2005, African Americans (12 percent of the U.S. population) accounted for 9 percent of Major League Baseball players, 66 percent of National Football League (NFL) players, and 73 percent of National Basketball Association (NBA) players (Lapchick, 2006).

One reason for the increasing share of African Americans in professional sports is the fact that athletic performance—in terms of batting average or number of points scored per game—can be precisely measured and is not influenced by racial prejudice. It is also true that some people of color make a particular effort to excel in athletics, where they see more opportunity than in other careers (S. Steele, 1990; Edwards, 2000; Harrison, 2000). In recent years, in fact, African American athletes have earned higher salaries, on average, than white players.

But racial discrimination still exists in professional sports. For one thing, race is linked to

The film *Fever Pitch* suggests the importance of sports—in this case, passion for the Boston Red Sox—to our way of life in the United States.

the positions athletes play on the field, a pattern called "stacking." The figure shows the results of a study of race in football. Notice that white players dominate the offense and also play the central positions on both sides of the line. More broadly, African Americans have a large share of players only in five major sports: basketball, football, baseball, boxing, and track. And across all professional sports, the vast majority of managers, head coaches, and team owners are still white (Lapchick, 2006).

Who benefits most from professional sports? Although some players get sky-high salaries and millions of fans love following their teams, the vast profits sports generate are controlled by a small number of people—predominantly, white men. In sum, sports in the United States are bound up with inequalities based on gender, race, and wealth.

Symbolic-Interaction Approach
At the micro-level, a sporting event is a complex, face-to-face interaction. In part, play is guided by the players' assigned positions and the rules of the game. But players are also spontaneous and unpredictable. Following the symbolic-interaction approach, we see sports less as a system and more as an ongoing process.

From this point of view, too, we would also expect each player to understand the game a little differently. Some players enjoy stiff competition; for others, love of the game may be greater than the need to win. In

addition, the behavior of any single player is likely to change over time. A rookie in professional baseball, for example, may feel self-conscious during the first few games in the big leagues but go on to develop a comfortable sense of fitting in with

the team. Coming to feel at home on the field was slow and painful for Jackie Robinson, who knew that many white players and millions of white fans resented his presence. In time, however, his outstanding ability and his confident, cooperative manner won him the respect of the entire nation.

The three theoretical approaches provide different insights into sports, and none is entirely correct. Applied to any issue, each approach provides part of a complex picture. To fully appreciate the power of the sociological perspective, you should become familiar with all three.

WHAT DO YOU THINK?
1. Describe how a macro-level approach to sports differs from a micro-level approach. Which theoretical approaches are macro-level, and which one is micro-level?
2. Make up three questions about sports, one that reflects the focus of each of the three theoretical approaches.
3. How might you apply the three approaches to other social patterns, such as the workplace or family life?

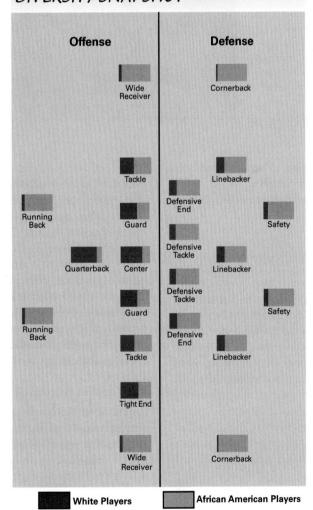

DIVERSITY SNAPSHOT

Race and Sport: "Stacking" in Professional Football

Does race play a part in professional sports? Looking at the various positions in professional football, we see that white players are more likely to play the central and offensive positions. What do you make of this pattern?

Source: Lapchick (2006).

When two factors appear to go together, we speak of correlation. But recognizing a correlation is not the same as knowing which one causes the other. For example, we know that many homeless people abuse alcohol. But is alcohol abuse the cause of homelessness? Or does being homeless encourage people to use a drug to soften their suffering? Can both be true?

results (meaning that it is reliable), it can still miss the intended target (and therefore lack validity). Good sociological research depends on careful measurement, which is always a challenge to researchers.

Correlation and Cause

The real payoff in scientific research is determining how variables are related. **Correlation** means *a relationship in which two (or more) variables change together.* But sociologists want to know not just how variables change but which variable changes the other. The scientific ideal is to determine **cause and effect,** which means *a relationship in which change in one variable causes change in another.* As we noted earlier, Emile Durkheim found that the degree of social integration (the cause) affected the suicide rate (the effect) among categories of people. Scientists refer to the cause as the *independent variable* and the effect as the *dependent variable.* Understanding cause and effect is valuable because it allows researchers to *predict* how one pattern of behavior will produce another.

Just because two variables change together does not necessarily mean that they have a cause-and-effect relationship. For instance, the marriage rate in the United States falls to its lowest point in January, the month when the national death rate is highest. Does this mean that people drop dead because they don't marry or that they don't marry because they die? Of course not. More likely, it is the cold and often stormy weather across much of the country in January (perhaps combined with the postholiday blues) that is responsible for both the low marriage rate and the high death rate.

When two variables change together but neither one causes the other, sociologists describe the relationship as a *spurious,* or false, correlation. A spurious correlation between two variables usually results from some third factor. For example, delinquency rates are high where young people live in crowded housing, but this is not because crowded housing causes youngsters to "turn bad." Both crowded housing and delinquency result from a third factor: poverty. To be sure of a real cause-and-effect relationship, we must show that (1) variables are correlated, (2) the independent (causal) variable occurs before the dependent variable, and (3) there is no evidence that a third variable has been overlooked, causing a spurious correlation.

The Ideal of Objectivity

A guiding principle of scientific study is *objectivity,* or personal neutrality, in conducting research. The ideal of objective research is to allow the facts to speak for themselves and not be influenced by the personal values and biases of the researcher. In reality, of course, achieving total neutrality is impossible for anyone. But carefully observing the rules of scientific research will maximize objectivity.

The German sociologist Max Weber noted that people usually choose *value-relevant* research topics—topics they care about. But, he cautioned, once their work is under way, researchers should try to be *value-free.* That is, we must be dedicated to finding truth as it *is* rather than as we think it *should be.* For Weber, this difference sets science apart from politics. Researchers (unlike politicians) must stay openminded and be willing to accept whatever results come from their work, whether they personally agree with them or not.

Weber's argument still carries much weight in sociology, although most researchers realize that we can never be completely value-free or even aware of all our biases (Demerath, 1996). Keep in mind, however, that sociologists are not "average" people: Most are highly educated white men and women who are more politically liberal than the population as a whole. Sociologists need to remember that they, too, are influenced by their social backgrounds.

YOUR TURN

Why do you think many doctors, teachers, and police officers avoid working professionally with their own children?

INTERPRETIVE SOCIOLOGY

Not all sociologists agree that the scientific orientation is the best way to study human society. Unlike planets or other elements of the natural world, humans do not simply move about; we engage in *meaningful* action. A second type of research is **interpretive sociology,** *the study of society that focuses on the meanings people attach to their social world.* Max Weber, the pioneer of this framework, argued that the proper focus of sociology is *interpretation,* or understanding the meanings people create in their everyday lives.

The Importance of Meaning

Interpretive sociology differs from scientific, or empirical, sociology in three ways. First, scientific sociology focuses on action, on what people do; interpretive sociology, by contrast, focuses on the meanings people attach to their actions. Second, scientific sociology sees an objective reality "out there," but interpretive sociology sees reality constructed by people themselves in the course of their everyday lives. Third, scientific sociology tends to favor *quantitative* data—numerical measurements of social behavior—and interpretive sociology favors *qualitative* data, researchers' perceptions of how people understand their surroundings. In sum, the scientific orientation is well suited for research in a laboratory, where investigators stand back and take careful measurements. The interpretive orientation is better suited for research in a natural setting, where investigators interact with people, learning how they make sense of their everyday lives.

Weber's Concept of *Verstehen*

Max Weber claimed that the key to interpretive sociology lies in *Verstehen,* the German word for "understanding." It is the interpretive sociologist's job not just to observe *what* people do but also to share in their world of meaning, coming to appreciate *why* they act as they do. Subjective thoughts and feelings, which scientists tend to dismiss because they are difficult to measure, are the focus of the interpretive sociologist's attention.

CRITICAL SOCIOLOGY

Like the interpretive orientation, critical sociology developed in reaction to the limitations of scientific sociology. In this case, however, the problem involves the central principle of scientific research: objectivity. Scientific sociology holds that reality is "out there," and the researcher's job is to study and document this reality. But Karl Marx, who founded the critical orientation, rejected the idea that society exists as a "natural" system with a fixed order. To assume this, he claimed, is the same as saying that society cannot be changed. Scientific sociology, in his view, ends up supporting the status quo. **Critical sociology,** by contrast, is *the study of society that focuses on the need for social change.*

The Importance of Change

Rather than asking the scientific question "How does society work?" critical sociologists ask moral and political questions, especially, "Should society exist in its present form?" Their answer, typically, is that it should not. One recent account of this orientation, echoing Marx, claims that the point of sociology is "not just to research the social world but to change it in the direction of democracy and social justice" (Feagin & Hernán, 2001:1). In making value judgments about how society should be changed, critical sociology rejects Weber's goal that sociology be value-free and emphasizes instead that sociologists should be activists in pursuit of greater social equality.

Sociologists using the critical orientation seek to change not only society but also the character of research itself. They often identify personally with their research subjects and encourage them to help decide what to study and how to do the work. Often researchers and subjects use their findings to provide a voice for less powerful people and advance the political goal of a more equal society (Hess, 1999; Feagin & Hernán, 2001; Perrucci, 2001).

Sociology as Politics

Scientific sociologists object to taking sides in this way, claiming that critical sociology (whether feminist, Marxist, or of some other critical orientation) becomes political, lacks objectivity, and cannot correct for its own biases. Critical sociologists respond that *all* research is political in that either it calls for change or it does not; sociologists thus have no choice about their work being political, but they can choose *which* positions to support.

SUMMING UP

Three Research Orientations in Sociology

	Scientific	Interpretive	Critical
What is reality?	Society is an orderly system. There is an objective reality "out there."	Society is ongoing interaction. People construct reality as they attach meanings to their behavior.	Society is patterns of inequality. Reality is that some categories of people dominate others.
How do we conduct research?	Researcher gathers empirical, ideally quantitative, data. Researcher tries to be a neutral observer.	Researcher develops a qualitative account of the subjective sense people make of their world. Researcher is a participant.	Research is a strategy to bring about desired social change. Researcher is an activist.
Corresponding theoretical approach	Structural-functional approach	Symbolic-interaction approach	Social-conflict approach

Critical sociology is an activist approach that ties knowledge to action and seeks not just to understand the world but also to improve it. Generally speaking, scientific sociology tends to appeal to researchers with nonpolitical or more conservative political views; critical sociology appeals to those whose politics ranges from liberal to radical left.

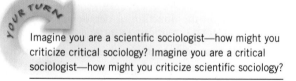

Imagine you are a scientific sociologist—how might you criticize critical sociology? Imagine you are a critical sociologist—how might you criticize scientific sociology?

METHODS AND THEORY

Is there a link between research orientations and sociological theory? There is no precise connection, but each of the three ways to do sociology—scientific, interpretive, and critical—does stand closer to one of the theoretical approaches presented earlier in this chapter. The scientific orientation is linked to the structural-functional approach (because both are concerned with understanding society as it is), the interpretive orientation to the symbolic-interaction approach (because both focus on the meanings people attach to their social world), and the critical orientation to the social-conflict approach (because both seek to reduce social inequality). The Summing Up table provides a quick review of the differences among the three ways to do sociology. Many sociologists favor one orientation over another; however, because each provides useful insights, it is a good idea to become familiar with all three.

Gender and Research

In recent years, sociologists have become aware that research is affected by **gender,** *the personal traits and social positions that members of a society attach to being female or male.* Gender can affect sociological research in five ways (Eichler, 1988; Giovannini, 1992):

1. **Androcentricity.** *Androcentricity* (literally, "focus on the male") means approaching an issue from a male perspective. Sometimes researchers act as if only men's activities are important, ignoring what women do. For years, sociologists studying occupations focused on the paid labor of men and overlooked the housework and child care traditionally performed by women. Research that tries to explain human behavior cannot ignore half of humanity.

    The parallel concept of *gynocentricity*—seeing the world from a female perspective—is a problem too. However, in our male-dominated society, this problem arises less often.

2. **Overgeneralizing.** This problem occurs when sociologists gather data only from men but then use that information to draw conclusions about all people. For example, a researcher might speak to a handful of male public officials and then form conclusions about an entire community.

3. **Gender blindness.** Failing to consider gender at all is called *gender blindness.* The lives of men and women differ in many ways. A study of growing old in the United States might suffer from gender blindness if it overlooked the fact that most elderly men live with spouses but elderly women generally live alone.

4. **Double standards.** Researchers must be careful not to judge men and women by different standards. For example, a family researcher who labels a couple "man and wife" may define the man as the "head of the household" and treat him as important while assuming that the woman simply engages in family "support work."

5. **Interference.** Another way gender can distort a study is if a subject reacts to the sex of the researcher, interfering with the research operation. While studying a small community in Sicily, for instance, Maureen Giovannini (1992) found that many men treated her as a *woman* rather than as a *researcher*. Some thought it inappropriate for a single woman to speak privately with a man. Others denied Giovannini access to places they considered off-limits to women.

There is nothing wrong with focusing research on people of one sex or the other. But all sociologists, as well as people who read their work, should be mindful of how gender can affect an investigation.

Think of three research topics in U.S. society that might be affected by the gender of the researcher. In each case, explain why.

Research Ethics

Like all other scientific investigators, sociologists must be aware that their work can harm as well as help subjects and communities. For this reason, the American Sociological Association—the major professional organization of sociologists in North America—has established formal guidelines for conducting research (1997).

Sociologists must try to be skillful and fair-minded in their work. They must disclose all research findings without omitting significant data. They should make their results available to other sociologists who may want to conduct a similar study.

Go to the American Sociological Association Web site at http://www.asanet.org, click on "Ethics," and read the profession's Code of Ethics.

Sociologists must also make sure that subjects taking part in a research project are not harmed, and they must stop work right away if they suspect that any subject is at risk of harm. Researchers are also required to protect the privacy of individuals involved in a research project, even if they come under pressure from authorities, such as the police or the courts, to release confidential information. Researchers must also get the *informed consent* of participants, which means that the subjects fully understand their responsibilities and the risks that the research involves and agree to take part before the work begins.

Another guideline concerns funding. Sociologists must include in their published reports all sources of financial support. They must avoid taking money from a source if there is any question about a conflict of interest. For example, researchers must never accept funding from any organization that seeks to influence the research results for its own purposes.

The federal government also plays a part in research ethics. Every college and university that seeks federal funding for research involving human subjects must have an *institutional review board* (IRB) that reviews grant applications and ensures that research will not violate ethical standards.

Finally, there are global dimensions to research ethics. Before beginning work in another country, an investigator must become familiar enough with that society to understand what people *there* are likely to regard as a violation of privacy or a source of personal danger. In a diverse society such as our own, the same rule applies to studying people whose cultural background differs from your own. The Thinking About Diversity box on page 26 offers tips on the sensitivity outsiders should apply when studying Hispanic communities.

Research Methods

A **research method** is *a systematic plan for doing research.* Four widely used methods of sociological investigation are experiments, surveys, participant observation, and the use of existing sources. None is better or worse than any other. Rather, just as a carpenter selects a particular tool for a particular job, researchers choose a method according to whom they want to study and what they want to learn.

TESTING A HYPOTHESIS: THE EXPERIMENT

The **experiment** is *a research method for investigating cause and effect under highly controlled conditions.* Experiments test a specific *hypothesis,* a statement of how two (or more) variables are related. A hypothesis is really an educated guess about how variables are linked, usually as an *if-then* statement: *If* one thing were to happen, *then* something else will result.

An experimenter gathers the evidence needed to reject or not to reject the hypothesis in four steps: (1) State which variable is the *independent variable* (the "cause" of the change) and which is the *dependent variable* (the "effect," the thing that is changed). (2) Measure the initial value of

Studying the Lives of Hispanics

Because our society is socially diverse, sociologists often find themselves studying people who differ from themselves. Learning, in advance, the ways of life of any category of people can ease the research process and ensure that no hard feelings are caused along the way.

Gerardo Marín and Barbara Van Oss Marín (1991) have identified five areas of concern when conducting research with Hispanic people:

1. **Be careful with terms.** The Maríns point out that "Hispanic" is a label of convenience used by the U.S. Census Bureau. Few people of Spanish descent think of themselves as "Hispanic"; most identify with a particular country, such as Cuba, Argentina, or Spain.

2. **Be culturally aware.** By and large, the U.S. population is individualistic and competitive. Many Hispanics, by contrast, place more value on cooperation and community. An outsider may judge the behavior of a Hispanic subject as conformist or overly trusting when in fact the person is simply trying to be helpful. Researchers should also realize that Hispanic respondents might agree with a particular statement merely out of politeness.

3. **Anticipate family dynamics.** Hispanic cultures have strong family loyalties. Asking subjects to reveal

information about another family member may make them uncomfortable or even angry. The Maríns add that a researcher's request to speak privately with a Hispanic woman in the home may provoke suspicion or outright disapproval from her husband or father.

4. **Take your time.** Spanish cultures, the Maríns explain, tend to place the quality of relationships above simply getting a job done. A non-Hispanic researcher who tries to hurry an interview with a Hispanic family out of a desire not to delay the family's dinner may be considered rude for not proceeding at a more sociable and relaxed pace.

5. **Think about personal space.** The Maríns point out that people of Spanish descent typically maintain

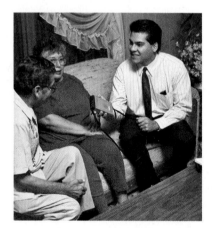

closer physical contact than many non-Hispanics. Therefore, researchers who seat themselves across the room from their subjects may come across as standoffish. Conversely, researchers may also wrongly label Hispanics "pushy" when they move in closer than a non-Hispanic researcher may find comfortable.

Of course, Hispanics differ among themselves just as people in any category do, and these generalizations apply to some more than to others. But investigators should be aware of cultural dynamics when carrying out any research, especially in the United States, where hundreds of distinctive categories of people make up our multicultural society.

WHAT DO YOU THINK?

1. Give a specific example of harm that might occur to a study if researchers are not sensitive to the culture of their subjects.

2. What do researchers need to do to avoid the kinds of problems noted in this box?

3. Discuss the research process with classmates from various cultural backgrounds. In what ways are the concerns raised by people of different cultural backgrounds similar? In what ways do they differ?

the dependent variable. (3) Expose the dependent variable to the independent variable (the "cause" or "treatment"). (4) Measure the dependent variable again to see what change, if any, took place. If the expected change took place, the experiment supports the hypothesis; if not, the hypothesis must be modified.

Successful experiments depend on careful control of all factors that might affect what the experiment is trying to measure. Control is easiest in a research laboratory. But experiments in an everyday location—"in the field," as sociologists say—have the advantage of letting researchers observe subjects in their natural settings.

Illustration of an Experiment: The "Stanford County Prison"

Prisons can be violent settings, but is this due simply to the "bad" people who end up there? Or as Philip Zimbardo suspected, does prison itself somehow cause violent behavior? To answer this question, Zimbardo devised a fascinating experiment, which he called the "Stanford County Prison" (Zimbardo, 1972; Haney, Banks, & Zimbardo, 1973).

Zimbardo thought that once inside a prison, even emotionally healthy people are likely to engage in violence. So Zimbardo treated the *prison setting* as the independent variable capable of causing *violence,* the dependent variable.

To test this hypothesis, Zimbardo and his research team first constructed a realistic-looking "prison" in the basement of the psychology building on the campus of Stanford University. Then they placed an ad in a local newspaper, offering to pay young men to help with a two-week research project. To each of the seventy who responded they administered a series of physical and psychological tests and then selected the healthiest twenty-four.

The next step was to assign randomly half the men to be "prisoners" and half to be "guards." The plan called for the guards and prisoners to spend the next two weeks in the mock prison. The prisoners began their part of the experiment when real police officers "arrested" them at their homes. After searching and handcuffing the men, the police drove them to the local police station, where they were fingerprinted. Then police transported their captives to the Stanford prison, where the guards locked them up. Zimbardo started his video camera rolling and watched to see what would happen next.

The experiment turned into more than anyone had bargained for. Both guards and prisoners soon became embittered and hostile toward one another. Guards humiliated the prisoners by giving them jobs such as cleaning toilets with their bare hands. The prisoners resisted and insulted the guards. Within four days, the researchers had removed five prisoners who displayed "extreme emotional depression, crying, rage and acute anxiety" (Hanley, Banks, & Zimbardo, 1973:81). Before the end of the first week, the situation had become so bad that the researchers had to end the experiment.

The events that unfolded at the "Stanford County Prison" supported Zimbardo's hypothesis that prison violence is rooted in the social character of jails themselves, not in the personalities of individual guards and prisoners. This finding raises questions about our society's prisons, suggesting the need for basic reform. Zimbardo's experiment also shows the potential of research to threaten the physical and mental well-being of subjects. Such dangers are not always as obvious as they were in this case. Therefore, researchers must consider carefully the potential harm to subjects at all stages of their work and close down any study, as Zimbardo did, if subjects may suffer harm of any kind.

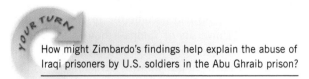

How might Zimbardo's findings help explain the abuse of Iraqi prisoners by U.S. soldiers in the Abu Ghraib prison?

ASKING QUESTIONS: SURVEY RESEARCH

A **survey** is *a research method in which subjects respond to a series of statements or questions in a questionnaire or an interview.* The most widely used of all research methods, the survey is well suited to studying what cannot be observed directly, such as political attitudes or religious beliefs.

A survey targets some *population,* such as unmarried mothers or adults living in rural counties in Wisconsin. Sometimes every adult in the country is the survey population, as in polls taken during national political campaigns.

 To better understand the use of polls in political campaigns, go to http://faculty.vassar.edu/lowry/polls.html

Of course, contacting a vast number of people is all but impossible, so researchers usually study a *sample,* a much smaller number of subjects selected to represent the entire population. Surveys using samples of only 1,500 people commonly give accurate estimates of public opinion for the entire country.

Beyond selecting subjects, the survey must have a specific plan for asking questions and recording answers. The most common way to do this is to give subjects a *questionnaire* with a series of written statements or questions. Often the researcher lets subjects choose possible responses to each item, as on a multiple-choice test. Sometimes, though, a researcher may want subjects to respond freely, to permit all opinions to be expressed. Of course, this free-form approach means that the researcher later has to make sense out of what can be a bewildering array of answers.

In an *interview,* a researcher personally asks subjects a series of questions, thereby solving one problem common to the questionnaire method: the failure of some subjects to return the questionnaire to the researcher. A further difference is that interviews give participants freedom to respond as they wish. Researchers often ask follow-up questions to clarify an answer or to probe a bit more deeply. In doing this, however, a researcher must avoid influencing the subject even in subtle ways, such as by raising an eyebrow as the subject offers an answer.

Illustration of Survey Research: Studying the African American Elite

Do highly successful African Americans escape the sting of racism? The sociologist Lois Benjamin—herself a successful college professor who had become the first black faculty member at the University of Tampa—thought the answer was no. To investigate the effects of racism on talented African American men and women, Benjamin set out to conduct survey research.

Benjamin chose to interview subjects rather than distribute a questionnaire because, first, she wanted to enter into a conversation with her subjects, to ask follow-up questions, and to be able to pursue topics that might come up in conversation. A second reason Benjamin favored interviews over questionnaires is that racism is a sensitive topic. A supportive researcher can make it easier for subjects to answer painful questions more freely.

Because conducting interviews takes a great deal of time, Benjamin had to limit the number of people in her study. She settled for 100 men and women. Even this small number kept Benjamin busy for more than two years of scheduling, traveling, and meeting with respondents. She spent another two years transcribing the tapes of her interviews, sorting out what the hours of talk told her about racism, and writing up her results.

Benjamin began by interviewing people she knew and asking them to suggest others. This strategy is called *snowball sampling* because the number of individuals included grows rapidly over time. Snowball sampling is appealing because it is an easy way to do research: We begin with familiar people, who provide introductions to their friends and colleagues. The drawback, however, is that snowball sampling rarely produces a sample that is representative of the larger population. Benjamin's sample probably contained many like-minded individuals, and it was certainly biased toward people willing to talk openly about race. She understood these problems and tried to include in her sample people of both sexes, different ages, and representing different regions of the country. The Thinking Critically box presents a statistical profile of Benjamin's respondents and some tips on how to read tables.

Benjamin based all her interviews on a series of questions and allowed her subjects to answer however they wished. As usually happens, the interviews took place in a wide range of settings. She met subjects in offices (hers or theirs), in hotel rooms, and in cars. In each case, Benjamin tape-recorded the conversation, which lasted from two-and-one-half to three hours, so that she would not be distracted by taking notes.

As research ethics demand, Benjamin offered complete anonymity to participants. Even so, many—including nota-bles such as Vernon E. Jordan Jr., the former president of the National Urban League, and Yvonne Walker-Taylor, the first woman president of Wilberforce University—were accustomed to being in the public eye and permitted Benjamin to use their names.

What surprised Benjamin most about her research was how eagerly many subjects responded to her request for an interview. These normally busy men and women appeared to go out of their way to contribute to her project. Furthermore, once the interviews were under way, many of her subjects became very emotional. Benjamin reports that at some point in the conversation, about 40 of her 100 subjects cried. For them, apparently, the research provided an opportunity to release feelings and share experiences they had never revealed before. How did Benjamin respond to such sentiments? She reports that she cried along with her respondents.

Of the research orientations described earlier in this chapter, you will see that Benjamin's research fits best under interpretive sociology (she wanted to find out what race meant to her subjects) and critical sociology (she undertook the study partly to show that racial prejudice still exists). Many of her subjects reported fearing that race might someday undermine their success, and others spoke of a race-based "glass ceiling" preventing them from reaching the highest positions in U.S. society. Summarizing her findings, Benjamin concluded that despite the improving social standing of African Americans, black people in the United States still suffer the sting of racial hostility.

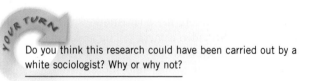

Do you think this research could have been carried out by a white sociologist? Why or why not?

In the Field: Participant Observation

Participant observation is *a research method in which investigators systematically observe people while joining them in their routine activities.* This method lets researchers study everyday social life in any natural setting, from nightclubs to a religious seminary. Cultural anthropologists use participant observation to study other societies, calling this method *fieldwork.*

At the beginning of a field study, most researchers do not have a specific hypothesis in mind. In fact, they may not yet realize what the important questions will turn out to be. This makes most participant observation *exploratory* and *descriptive,* falling within interpretive sociology and producing mostly qualitative, rather than quantitative, data. Compared with experiments and surveys, participant observation has few hard-and-fast rules. But this flexibility

THINKING CRITICALLY

Reading Tables: An Important Skill

A table provides a lot of information in a small amount of space, so learning to read tables can increase your reading efficiency. When you spot a table, look first at the title to see what information it contains. The title of the table presented here provides a profile of the 100 subjects participating in Lois Benjamin's research. Across the top of the table, you will see eight variables that define these men and women. Reading down each column, note the categories within each variable; the percentages in each column add up to 100.

Starting at the top left, we see that Benjamin's sample was mostly men (63 percent, versus 37 percent women). In terms of age, most of the respondents (68 percent) were in the middle stage of life, and most grew up in a predominantly black community in the South or in the North or Midwest region of the United States.

These individuals are indeed a professional elite. Notice that half have earned either a doctorate (32 percent) or a medical or law degree (17 percent). Given their extensive education (and Benjamin's own position as a professor), we should not be surprised that the largest share (35 percent) work in academic institutions. In terms of income, these are wealthy individuals, with most (64 percent) earning more than $50,000 annually about 1990 (a

salary that only 31 percent of full-time workers make even today).

Finally, we see that these 100 individuals are generally left-of-center in their political views. In part, this reflects their extensive schooling (which encourages progressive thinking) and the tendency of academics to fall on the liberal side of the political spectrum.

WHAT DO YOU THINK?

1. Statistical data, such as those in this table, are an efficient way to convey lots of information. Can you explain why?

2. Looking at the table, can you determine how long it took most people to become part of this elite? Explain.

3. Do you see any ways in which this African American elite might differ from a comparable white elite? What are they?

THE TALENTED 100: LOIS BENJAMIN'S AFRICAN AMERICAN ELITE

Sex	Age	Childhood Racial Setting	Childhood Region	Highest Educational Degree	Job Sector	Annual Income (about 1990)	Political Orientation
Male 63%	35 or younger 6%	Mostly black 71%	West 6%	Doctorate 32%	College or university 35%	More than $50,000 64%	Radical left 13%
Female 37%	36 to 54 68%	Mostly white 15%	North or Midwest 32%	Medical or law 17%	Private, for-profit 17%	$35,000 to $50,000 18%	Liberal 38%
	55 or older 26%	Racially mixed 14%	South 38%	Master's 27%	Private, nonprofit 9%	$20,000 to $34,999 12%	Moderate 28%
			Northeast 12%	Bachelor's 13%	Government 22%	Less than $20,000 6%	Conservative 5%
			Other 12%	Less 11%	Self-employed 14%		Depends on issue 14%
					Retired 3%		Unknown 2%
100%	100%	100%	100%	100%	100%	100%	100%

Source: Adapted from Lois Benjamin, *The Black Elite: Facing the Color Line in the Twilight of the Twentieth Century* (Chicago: Nelson-Hall, 1991), p. 276.

Sociologists can carry out research in almost any setting. Tammy Anderson of the University of Delaware visited many night spots in order to understand how and why young people participate in "raves."

Tammy L. Anderson, Ph.D.

allows investigators to explore the unfamiliar and adapt to the unexpected.

Participant observers try to gain entry into a setting without disturbing the routine behavior of others. Their role is twofold: To gain an insider's viewpoint, they must become participants in the setting, "hanging out" for months or even years, trying to act, think, and even feel the same way as the people they are observing; at the same time, they must remain observers, standing back from the action and applying the sociological perspective to social patterns that others take for granted.

Because the personal impressions of a single researcher play such a central role, critics claim that participant observation falls short of scientific standards. Yet its personal approach is also a strength: Where a high-profile team of sociologists administering a formal survey might disrupt a setting, a sensitive participant-observer often can gain profound insight into people's behavior.

Illustration of Participant Observation: *Street Corner Society*

Did you ever wonder what everyday life was like in an unfamiliar neighborhood? In the late 1930s, a young graduate student at Harvard University named William Foote Whyte

(1914–2000) set out to study social life in a rather rundown section of Boston. His curiosity ultimately led him to carry out four years of participant observation in this neighborhood, which he called "Cornerville."

At the time, Cornerville was home to first- and second-generation Italian immigrants. Most were poor, and many Bostonians considered Cornerville a place to avoid, a slum inhabited by criminals. Wanting to learn the truth, Whyte set out to discover for himself exactly what life was like inside this community. His celebrated book, *Street Corner Society* (1981, orig. 1943), describes Cornerville as a community with its own code of values, complex social patterns, and particular social conflicts.

To start, Whyte considered a range of research methods. He could have taken questionnaires to one of Cornerville's community centers and asked local people to fill them out. Or he could have invited members of the community to come to his Harvard office for interviews. But it is easy to see that such formal strategies would have gained little cooperation from the local people and produced few insights. Whyte decided, therefore, to ease into Cornerville life and slowly build a personal understanding of this rather mysterious place.

Soon enough, Whyte discovered the challenges of even getting started in field research. As an upper-middle-class WASP graduate student from Harvard, he stood out on the streets of Cornerville. Even a friendly overture from such an outsider could seem pushy and rude. Early on, Whyte dropped in at a local bar, hoping to buy a woman a drink and encourage her to talk about Cornerville. Looking around the room, he could find no woman alone. He thought he might have an opportunity when he saw a man sit down with two women. He walked over and asked, "Pardon me. Would you mind if I joined you?" Instantly, he realized his mistake:

> There was a moment of silence while the man stared at me. Then he offered to throw me down the stairs. I assured him that this would not be necessary, and demonstrated as much by walking right out of there without any assistance. (1981:289)

As this incident suggests, gaining entry to a community is the vital—and sometimes hazardous—first step in field research. "Breaking in" requires patience, ingenuity, and a little luck. Whyte's big break came in the form of a young man named "Doc," whom he met in a local social service agency. Whyte complained to Doc about how hard it was to make friends in Cornerville. Doc responded by taking Whyte under his wing and introducing him to others in the community. With Doc's help, Whyte soon became a neighborhood regular.

Whyte's friendship with Doc illustrates the importance of a *key informant* in field research. Such people not only introduce a researcher to a community but often remain a source of information and help. But using a key informant also has its risks. Because any person has a particular circle of friends, a key informant's guidance is certain to "spin" the study in one way or another. Moreover, in the eyes of others, the reputation of the key informant, for better or worse, usually rubs off on the investigator. So although a key informant is helpful early on, a participant-observer must seek a broader range of contacts.

Having entered the Cornerville world, Whyte quickly learned another lesson: A field researcher needs to know when to speak and when to shut up. One evening, he joined a group discussing neighborhood gambling. Wanting to get the facts straight, Whyte asked innocently, "I suppose the cops were all paid off?"

> The gambler's jaw dropped. He glared at me. Then he denied vehemently that any policeman had been paid off and immediately switched the conversation to another subject. For the rest of that evening I felt very uncomfortable.

The next day, Doc offered some sound advice:

> "Go easy on that 'who,' 'what,' 'why,' 'when,' 'where' stuff, Bill. You ask those questions and people will clam up on you. If people accept you, you can just hang around, and you'll learn the answers in the long run without even having to ask the questions." (1981:303)

In the months and years that followed, Whyte became familiar with everyday life in Cornerville and even married a local woman with whom he would spend the rest of his life. In the process, he learned that the common stereotypes were wrong. In Cornerville, most people worked hard, many were quite successful, and some even boasted of sending children to college. Even today, Whyte's book makes for fascinating reading about the deeds, dreams, and disappointments of immigrants and their children living in one ethnic community, and it contains the rich detail that can only come from years of participant observation.

Give an example of a topic for sociological research that would be best studied using (a) an experiment, (b) a survey, and (c) participant observation.

USING AVAILABLE DATA: EXISTING SOURCES

Not all research requires that investigators collect new data. Sometimes sociologists make use of existing sources, data collected by others.

The data most widely used by researchers are gathered by government agencies such as the U.S. Census Bureau. Data about other nations in the world are found in various publications of the United Nations and the World Bank.

For statistical data about the U.S., your own state, and your own county, go to http://quickfacts.census.gov/qfd/

Using available information—whether government statistics or data collected by other sociologists—saves time and money. This method has special appeal to sociologists with low budgets. For anyone, however, government data are usually more extensive and more accurate than what researchers could obtain on their own.

But using available data has problems of its own. Data may not be available in the exact form that is needed. For example, you may be able to find the average salaries paid to professors at your school but not separate figures for the amounts paid to women and men. Further, there are always questions about how accurate the existing data are. In his nineteenth-century study of suicide, described earlier, Emile Durkheim used official records. But Durkheim had no way to know if a death classified as a suicide was really an accident or vice versa.

Illustration of the Use of Existing Sources: A Tale of Two Cities

Why might one city have been home to many famous people and another's history shows hardly any famous people at all? To those of us living in the present, historical data offer a key to unlocking secrets of the past. The award-winning study *Puritan Boston and Quaker Philadelphia*, by E. Digby Baltzell (1979), shows how a researcher can use available data to do historical research.

The story begins with Baltzell making a chance visit to Bowdoin College in Maine. As he walked into the college library, he saw on the wall three portraits—of the celebrated author Nathaniel Hawthorne, the famous poet Henry Wadsworth Longfellow, and Franklin Pierce, the fourteenth president of the United States. He soon learned that all three men were members of the same class at Bowdoin, graduating in 1825. How could it be, Baltzell wondered, that this small college had graduated more famous people in a single year than his own, much bigger University of Pennsylvania had graduated in its entire history? To answer this question, Baltzell was soon paging through historical documents to see whether the New England states had indeed produced more famous people than his native Pennsylvania.

What were Baltzell's data? He turned to the *Dictionary of American Biography,* twenty volumes profiling more than 13,000 outstanding men and women in fields such as politics, law, and the arts. The dictionary told Baltzell who was

SUMMING UP

Four Research Methods

	Experiment	Survey	Participant Observation	Existing Sources
Application	For explanatory research that specifies relationships between variables Generates quantitative data	For gathering information about issues that cannot be directly observed, such as attitudes and values Useful for descriptive and explanatory research Generates quantitative or qualitative data	For exploratory and descriptive study of people in a "natural" setting Generates qualitative data	For exploratory, descriptive, or explanatory research whenever suitable data are available
Advantages	Provides the greatest opportunity to specify cause-and-effect relationships Replication of research is relatively easy	Sampling, using questionnaires, allows surveys of large populations Interviews provide in-depth responses	Allows study of "natural" behavior Usually inexpensive	Saves time and expense of data collection Makes historical research possible
Limitations	Laboratory settings have an artificial quality Unless the research environment is carefully controlled, results may be biased	Questionnaires must be carefully prepared and may yield a low return rate Interviews are expensive and time-consuming	Time-consuming Replication of research is difficult Researcher must balance roles of participant and observer	Researcher has no control over possible biases in data Data may only partially fit current research needs

great, and he realized that the longer the biography, the more important the person is thought to be.

By the time Baltzell had identified the seventy-five individuals with the longest biographies, he saw a striking pattern. Massachusetts had the most by far, with twenty-one of the seventy-five top achievers. The New England states, combined, claimed thirty-one entries. By contrast, Pennsylvania could boast of only two, and all the states in the Middle Atlantic region had just twelve. Looking more closely, Baltzell discovered that most of New England's great achievers had grown up in and around the city of Boston. Again, in stark contrast, almost no one of comparable standing came from his own Philadelphia, a city with many more people than Boston.

What could explain this remarkable pattern? Baltzell drew inspiration from the German sociologist Max Weber (1958, orig. 1904–5), who argued that a region's record of achievement was influenced by its major religious beliefs (see Chapter 13, "Family and Religion"). In the religious differences between Boston and Philadelphia, Baltzell found the answer to his puzzle. Boston was a Puritan settlement, founded by people who highly valued the pursuit of excellence and public achievement. Philadelphia, by contrast, was settled by Quakers, who believed in equality and avoided public notice.

Both the Puritans and the Quakers had fled religious persecution in England, but the two religious traditions produced quite different cultural patterns. Convinced of humanity's innate sinfulness, Boston Puritans built a rigid society in which family, church, and school regulated people's behavior. They celebrated hard work as a means of glorifying God and viewed public success as a reassuring sign of God's blessing. In short, Puritanism fostered a disciplined life in which people both sought and respected achievement.

Philadelphia's Quakers, by contrast, built their way of life on the belief that all human beings are basically good. They saw little need for strong social institutions to "save" people from sinfulness. They believed in equality, so that even those who became rich considered themselves no better than anyone else. Thus rich and poor alike lived modestly and discouraged one another from standing out by seeking fame or running for public office.

In Baltzell's sociological imagination, Boston and Philadelphia took the form of two social "test tubes": Puritanism was poured into one, Quakerism into the other. Centuries later, we can see that different "chemical reactions" occurred in each case. The two belief systems apparently led to different attitudes toward personal achievement, which in turn shaped the history of each

Is Sociology Nothing More than Stereotypes?

"Protestants are the ones who kill themselves!"

"People in the United States? They're rich, they love to marry, and they love to divorce!"

"Everybody knows that you have to be black to play professional basketball!"

Everyone—including sociologists—loves to generalize. Seeing social patterns in everyday life is nothing more than making generalizations about people. But beginning students of sociology may wonder how sociological generalizations differ from simple stereotypes.

Each of the three statements in quotation marks is an example of a **stereotype,** *an exaggerated description applied to every person in some category.* First, rather than describing specific individuals or averages, each statement describes every person in some category in exactly the same extreme way; second, each leaves out relevant facts and distorts reality (even though many stereotypes do contain an element of truth); third, a stereotype is often motivated by bias and can sound more like a put-down than a fair-minded observation.

Good sociology makes generalizations, but they must meet three conditions. First, sociologists do not carelessly apply any generalization to everyone. Second, sociologists make sure that a generalization squares with all available facts. Third, sociologists make generalizations fair-mindedly, in the interest of getting at the truth.

Earlier in this chapter, we noted that the suicide rate among Protestants is higher than the rate among Catholics or Jews. However, the statement "Protestants are the ones who kill themselves" is not a fair generalization because most Protestants do no such thing. It would be just as wrong to jump to the conclusion that a particular friend, because he is a Protestant male, is about to end his own life. (Imagine refusing to lend money to a roommate, who happens to be a Baptist, explaining, "Well, given your risk of suicide, I might never get paid back!")

Second, sociologists shape their generalizations to available facts. A more factual version of the second statement is that by world standards, the U.S. population, on average, has a very high standard of living. It is also true that our marriage rate is one of the highest in the world. And although few people take pleasure in divorcing, our divorce rate is also among the world's highest.

Third, sociologists try to be fair-minded, and they have a passion for truth. The last of the statements, about African Americans and basketball, is not good sociology for two reasons. First, it is simply not true, and second, it seems motivated by racial bias rather than truth-seeking.

Good sociology, then, stands apart from harmful stereotyping. But a sociology course is an excellent setting for talking about common stereotypes. The classroom encourages discussion and offers the factual information you need to decide whether a particular belief is a valid sociological generalization or just a stereotype.

A sociology classroom is a great place to get at the truth behind common stereotypes.

WHAT DO YOU THINK?

1. Can you think of a common stereotype of sociologists? What is it? After reading this chapter, do you still think it is valid? How would you know?

2. Do you think taking a sociology course challenges people's stereotypes? Why or why not?

3. Can you think of a stereotype of your own that might be challenged by sociological research?

region. Today, we can see that Boston's Kennedys (despite being Catholic) are only one of that city's many families that exemplify the Puritan pursuit of recognition and leadership. By contrast, there has never been even one family with such stature in the entire history of Philadelphia.

Baltzell's study uses scientific logic, but it also illustrates the interpretive approach by showing how people understood their world. His research reminds us that sociological investigation often involves mixing research orientations to fit a particular problem. The Summing Up table provides a quick review of the four major methods of sociological investigation.

Why is the use of existing sources especially important in doing historical research? What other questions might you wish to answer using existing sources?

Putting It All Together: Ten Steps in Sociological Research

The following ten questions will guide you through a research project in sociology:

1. **What is your topic?** Being curious and using the sociological perspective can generate ideas for social research at any time and in any place. Pick a topic you find important to study.

2. **What have others already learned?** You are probably not the first person with an interest in some issue. Visit the library and search the Internet to see what theories and methods other researchers have applied to your topic. In reviewing the existing research, note problems that have come up to avoid repeating past mistakes.

3. **What, exactly, are your questions?** Are you seeking to explore an unfamiliar setting? To describe some category of people? To investigate cause and effect between variables? Clearly state the goals of your research and operationalize all variables.

4. **What will you need to carry out research?** How much time and money are available to you? What special equipment or skills does the research require? Can you do all the work yourself?

5. **Are there ethical concerns?** Might the research harm anyone? How can you minimize the chances for injury? Will you promise your subjects anonymity? If so, how will you ensure that anonymity will be maintained?

6. **What method will you use?** Consider all major research strategies and combinations of methods. The most suitable method will depend on the kinds of questions you are asking and the resources available to you.

7. **How will you record the data?** The research method you use guides your data collection. Be sure to record information accurately and in a way that will make sense to you later on (it may be months before you write up the results of your work). Watch out for any personal bias that may creep into your work.

8. **What do the data tell you?** Determine what the data say about your initial questions. If your study involves a specific hypothesis, you should be able to confirm, reject, or modify it on the basis of your findings. Keep in mind that there will be several ways to interpret your results, depending on the theoretical approach you apply, and you should consider them all.

9. **What are your conclusions?** Prepare a final report explaining what you have learned. Also, evaluate your own work. What problems arose during the research process? What questions were left unanswered?

10. **How can you share what you have learned?** Consider making a presentation to a class or maybe even to a meeting of professional sociologists. The important point is to share what you have learned with others and to let them respond to your work.

The Seeing Sociology in Everyday Life box on page 33 discusses the use of the sociological perspective and reviews many of the ideas presented in this chapter. This box will help you apply what you have learned to the question of how sociological generalizations differ from the common stereotypes we hear every day.

APPLYING SOCIOLOGY IN EVERYDAY LIFE

1. Explore your local area, and draw a sociological map of the community. Include the types of buildings (for example, "big, single-family homes," "rundown business district," "new office buildings," "student apartments") found in various places, and guess at the categories of people who live or work there. What patterns do you see?

2. Figure 13–2 on page 385 shows the U.S. divorce rate over the past century. Using the sociological perspective, and with an eye to the timeline inside the front cover of this book, try to identify societal factors that caused the divorce rate to rise or fall.

3. Say you were going to observe several teachers to grade their teaching skills. How would you operationalize the concept "good teaching"? What, exactly, would you look for? Do you think students are the best judges of good and bad teaching? Why or why not?

MAKING THE GRADE

WHAT IS THE SOCIOLOGICAL PERSPECTIVE?

The **SOCIOLOGICAL PERSPECTIVE** reveals the power of society to shape individual lives.

- C. Wright Mills called this point of view the "sociological imagination," which transforms personal troubles into public issues.
- Being an outsider or experiencing social crisis can encourage the sociological perspective.

pp 2–6

APPLYING the sociological perspective has many benefits:

- helping us understand the barriers and opportunities in our lives
- giving us an advantage in our careers
- guiding public policy

pp 8–11

 Global awareness is an important part of the sociological perspective because our society's place in the world affects us all (pp 5–8).

ORIGINS OF SOCIOLOGY

RAPID SOCIAL CHANGE helped trigger the development of sociology:

- rise of an industrial economy
- explosive growth of cities
- new political ideas

pp 11–12

AUGUSTE COMTE named sociology in 1838.

- Early philosophers tried to describe the ideal society, but Comte wanted to understand society as it really is.
- Karl Marx and many later sociologists used sociology to try to make society better.

pp 12–13

 The countries that experienced the most rapid social change were those in which sociology developed first (p 12).

THEORY: LINKING FACTS TO CREATE MEANING

┌──── **macro-level** ────┐

The **STRUCTURAL-FUNCTIONAL APPROACH** explores how social structures work together to help society operate.

- Auguste Comte, Emile Durkheim, and Herbert Spencer helped develop the structural-functional approach.

pp 14–15

The **SOCIAL-CONFLICT APPROACH** shows how inequality creates conflict and causes change.

- Two important types of conflict analysis are the *gender-conflict approach*, linked to *feminism*, and the *race-conflict approach*.
- Karl Marx helped develop the social-conflict approach.

pp 15–17

micro-level

The **SYMBOLIC-INTERACTION APPROACH** studies how people, in everyday interaction, construct reality.

- Max Weber and George Herbert Mead helped develop the symbolic-interaction approach.

pp 17–18

⊞ See the Applying Theory table on page 18.

 To get the full benefit of the sociological perspective, apply all three approaches.

---

sociology (p. 2) the systematic study of human society

sociological perspective (p. 2) the special point of view of sociology that sees general patterns of society in the lives of particular people

global perspective (p. 5) the study of the larger world and our society's place in it

high-income countries (p. 5) the nations with the highest overall standards of living

middle-income countries (p. 5) nations with a standard of living about average for the world as a whole

low-income countries (p. 5) nations with a low standard of living in which most people are poor

positivism (p. 13) a way of understanding based on science

theory (p. 13) a statement of how and why specific facts are related

theoretical approach (p. 14) a basic image of society that guides thinking and research

structural-functional approach (p. 14) a framework for building theory that sees society as a complex system whose parts work together to promote solidarity and stability

social structure (p. 14) any relatively stable pattern of social behavior

social functions (p. 14) the consequences of a social pattern for the operation of society as a whole

manifest functions (p. 14) the recognized and intended consequences of any social pattern

latent functions (p. 14) the unrecognized and unintended consequences of any social pattern

social dysfunction (p. 14) any social pattern that may disrupt the operation of society

social-conflict approach (p. 15) a framework for building theory that sees society as an arena of inequality that generates conflict and change

gender-conflict approach (p. 15) a point of view that focuses on inequality and conflict between women and men

feminism (p. 16) the advocacy of social equality for women and men

race-conflict approach (p. 17) a point of view that focuses on inequality and conflict between people of different racial and ethnic categories

macro-level orientation (p. 17) a broad focus on social structures that shape society as a whole

micro-level orientation (p. 17) a close-up focus on social interaction in specific situations

symbolic-interaction approach (p. 17) a framework for building theory that sees society as the product of the everyday interactions of individuals

VISUAL SUMMARY

MAKING THE GRADE

CONTINUED...

VISUAL SUMMARY

RESEARCH: DOING SOCIOLOGY

SCIENTIFIC SOCIOLOGY uses the logic of science to understand how variables are related.
- tries to establish cause and effect
- demands that researchers try to be objective

pp 19, 22–23

INTERPRETIVE SOCIOLOGY focuses on the meanings that people attach to behavior.
- People construct reality in their everyday lives.
- Weber's *Verstehen* is learning how people understand their world.

p 23

CRITICAL SOCIOLOGY uses research to bring about social change.
- focuses on inequality
- rejects the principle of objectivity, claiming that all research is political

pp 23–24

 See the Summing Up table on page 24.

 Gender, involving both researcher and subjects, can affect all research (pp 24–25).

 All researchers must follow professional ethical guidelines for conducting research (p 25).

science (p. 19) a logical system that bases knowledge on direct, systematic observation

scientific sociology (p. 19) the study of society based on systematic observation of social behavior

empirical evidence (p. 19) information we can verify with our senses

concept (p. 19) a mental construct that represents some part of the world in a simplified form

variable (p. 19) a concept whose value changes from case to case

measurement (p. 19) a procedure for determining the value of a variable in a specific case

reliability (p. 19) consistency in measurement

validity (p. 19) actually measuring exactly what you intend to measure

correlation (p. 22) a relationship in which two (or more) variables change together

cause and effect (p. 22) a relationship in which change in one variable (the independent variable) causes change in another (the dependent variable)

interpretive sociology (p. 23) the study of society that focuses on the meanings people attach to their social world

critical sociology (p. 23) the study of society that focuses on the need for social change

gender (p. 24) the personal traits and social positions that members of a society attach to being female or male

METHODS: STRATEGIES FOR DOING RESEARCH

The **EXPERIMENT** allows researchers to study cause and effect between two or more variables in a controlled setting.
- example of an experiment: Zimbardo's "Stanford County Prison"

pp 25–27

SURVEY research uses questionnaires or interviews to gather subjects' responses to a series of questions.
- example of a survey: Benjamin's "Talented 100"

pp 27–29

Through **PARTICIPANT OBSERVATION**, researchers join with people in a social setting for an extended period of time.
- example of participant observation: Whyte's *Street Corner Society*

pp 28, 30–31

Researchers take data collected by others from **EXISTING SOURCES** to save time and money.
- example of using existing sources: Baltzell's *Puritan Boston and Quaker Philadelphia*

pp 31–34

research method (p. 25) a systematic plan for doing research

experiment (p. 25) a research method for investigating cause and effect under highly controlled conditions

survey (p. 27) a research method in which subjects respond to a series of statements or questions in a questionnaire or an interview

participant observation (p. 28) a research method in which investigators systematically observe people while joining them in their routine activities

stereotype (p. 33) an exaggerated description applied to every person in some category

 See the Summing Up table on page 32.

 Which method the researcher uses depends on the question being asked.

Researchers combine these methods depending on the specific goals of their study.

36

MAKING THE GRADE
Sample Test Questions
CHAPTER 1

These questions are similar to those found in the test bank that accompanies this textbook.

MULTIPLE-CHOICE QUESTIONS

1. **What does the sociological perspective show us about whom any individual chooses to marry?**
   a. There is no explaining personal feelings like love.
   b. People's actions reflect human free will.
   c. The operation of society guides many of our personal choices.
   d. In the case of love, opposites attract.

2. **The personal value of studying sociology includes**
   a. seeing the opportunities and constraints in our lives.
   b. the fact that it is good preparation for a number of careers.
   c. being more active participants in society.
   d. All of the above are correct.

3. **The discipline of sociology first developed in**
   a. countries experiencing rapid social change.
   b. countries with strong traditions.
   c. countries with a history of warfare.
   d. the world's poorest countries.

4. **Which early sociologist coined the term *sociology* in 1838?**
   a. Karl Marx
   b. Auguste Comte
   c. Adam Smith
   d. Herbert Spencer

5. **Sociology's social-conflict approach draws attention to**
   a. how structure contributes to the overall operation of society.
   b. how people construct meaning through interaction.
   c. patterns of social inequality.
   d. the stable aspects of society.

6. ***Empirical evidence* refers to**
   a. quantitative rather than qualitative data.
   b. what people consider "common sense."
   c. information we can verify with our senses.
   d. patterns found in every known society.

7. **When trying to measure people's "social class," you would have to keep in mind that**
   a. your measurement can never be both reliable and valid.
   b. there are several different ways to operationalize this variable.
   c. there is no way to measure "social class."
   d. in the United States, everyone agrees on what "social class" means.

8. **Interpretive sociology is a research orientation that**
   a. focuses on people's actions.
   b. sees an objective reality "out there."
   c. seeks to increase social justice.
   d. focuses on the meanings people attach to behavior.

9. **In participant observation, the problem of "breaking in" to a setting is often solved with the help of a**
   a. key informant.
   b. research assistant.
   c. bigger budget.
   d. All of the above are correct.

10. **The critical sociology research orientation is linked most closely to which theoretical approach?**
    a. structural-functional approach
    b. social-conflict approach
    c. symbolic-interaction approach
    d. None of the above is correct.

ANSWERS: 1 (c); 2 (d); 3 (a); 4 (b); 5 (c); 6 (c); 7 (b); 8 (d); 9 (a); 10 (b).

ESSAY QUESTIONS

1. Explain why using the sociological perspective can make us seem less in control of our lives. In what ways does it actually give us greater power over our lives?
2. Guided by the discipline's three major theoretical approaches, come up with sociological questions about (a) television, (b) war, and (c) colleges and universities.
3. Compare and contrast scientific sociology, interpretive sociology, and critical sociology. Why might a sociologist prefer one to another? Why is it important for a student of sociology to understand all three?

The way we dress, the places we go, and the work that we do are all part of a way of life we call culture. This woman in Peru weaves fabrics that she sells in the local marketplace.

CHAPTER **2**

Culture

WHAT is culture?

WHY is it so important
to understand people's
cultural differences?

HOW does culture
support social
inequality?

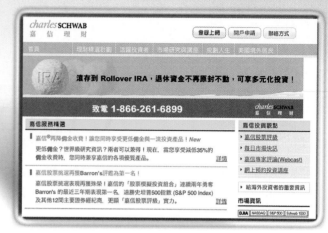

Back in 1990, executives of Charles Schwab & Co., a large investment brokerage corporation, gathered in a conference room at the company's headquarters in San Francisco to discuss ways they could expand their business. One idea was that the company would profit by giving greater attention to the increasing racial and ethnic diversity of the United States. In particular, they pointed to Census Bureau data showing the rising number of Asian Americans, not just in San Francisco but throughout the country. The data showed (then as now) not only that Asian Americans are much more numerous, but they are also, on average, doing pretty well, with more than one-third of households earning more than $75,000 a year (in today's dollars).

This meeting led Schwab to launch a diversity initiative, assigning three executives to work just on building awareness of the company among Asian Americans. In the years since then, the scope of the program grew and Schwab employed as many as 300 people speaking Chinese, Japanese, Korean, Vietnamese, or another Asian language. Knowing these languages is important because research shows that most Asian Americans and others who come to the United States prefer to communicate in their first language. In addition, the company has launched Web sites using Chinese and other Asian languages. Finally, the company has opened branch offices in many predominantly Asian American neighborhoods in cities on the East and West Coasts.

Has this diversity initiative been successful? Schwab has gained a much larger share of investments made by Asian Americans. Because Asian Americans spend more than $300 billion a year, any company

 would be smart to follow the lead Schwab has taken. Other racial and ethnic categories that represent even larger markets in the United States are Hispanic Americans (who spend $580 billion each year) and African Americans ($600 billion) (Fattah, 2002; Karrfalt, 2003).

Businesses like Schwab are taking note of the fact that the United States is the most *multicultural* of all the world's nations. This cultural diversity reflects our long history of receiving immigrants from all over the world. The ways of life found around the world differ, not only in terms of languages and forms of dress, but also in preferred foods, musical tastes, family patterns, and beliefs about right and wrong. Some of the world's people have many children, while others have few; some honor the elderly, while others seem to glorify youth. Some societies are peaceful and others warlike, and they embrace a thousand different religious beliefs and ideas about what is polite and rude, beautiful and ugly, pleasant and repulsive. This amazing human capacity for so many different ways of life is a matter of human culture.

What Is Culture?

Culture is *the ways of thinking, the ways of acting, and the material objects that together form a people's way of life.* When studying culture, sociologists consider both thoughts and things. *Nonmaterial culture* includes ideas created by members of a society, ranging from art to Zen; *material culture* refers to physical things, ranging from armchairs to zippers.

The terms "culture" and "society" obviously go hand in hand, but their precise meanings differ. Culture is a shared way of life or social heritage; **society** refers to *people who interact in a defined territory and share a culture.* Neither society nor culture could exist without the other.

Human beings around the globe create diverse ways of life. Such differences begin with outward appearance: Contrast the women shown here from Brazil, Kenya, New Guinea, and South Yemen, and the men from Taiwan (Republic of China), India, Canada, and New Guinea. Less obvious, but of even greater importance, are internal differences, since culture also shapes our goals in life, our sense of justice, and even our innermost personal feelings.

Culture not only shapes what we do but also what we think and how we feel—elements of what we commonly but wrongly describe as "human nature." The warlike Yanomamö of the Brazilian rain forest think aggression is natural, but halfway around the world, the Semai of Malaysia live quite peacefully. The cultures of the United States and Japan both stress achievement and hard work, but members of our society value individualism more than the Japanese, who value collective harmony.

Given the extent of cultural differences in the world and people's tendency to view their own way of life as "natural," it is no wonder that we often feel **culture shock,** *personal disorientation when experiencing an unfamiliar way of life.* People can experience culture shock right here in the United States when, say, African Americans explore an Iranian neighborhood in Los Angeles, college students venture into the Amish countryside in Ohio, or New Yorkers travel through small towns in the Deep South. But culture shock

All societies contain cultural differences that can provoke a mild case of culture shock. This woman traveling on a French bus looks with disapproval at another woman wearing the Muslim hijab head covering. France recently debated banning such clothing.

is most intense when we travel abroad. The Thinking Globally box tells the story of a U.S. researcher making his first visit to the home of the Yąnomamö people living in the Amazon region of South America.

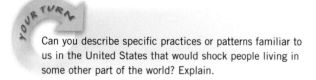

Can you describe specific practices or patterns familiar to us in the United States that would shock people living in some other part of the world? Explain.

January 2, high in the Andes Mountains of Peru. In the rural highlands, people are poor and depend on one another. The culture is built on cooperation among fami-

lies and neighbors who have lived nearby for many generations. Today, we spend an hour watching a new house being built. A young couple invited their families and neighbors, who arrived about 6:30 in the morning, and right away they began building. By midafternoon, most of the work had been done, and the couple then provided a large meal, drinks, and music that continued for the rest of the day.

No way of life is "natural" to humanity, even though most people around the world view their own behavior that way. The cooperation that comes naturally in small communities high in the Andes Mountains of Peru is very different from the competitive lifestyle that is natural to so many people living in, say, Chicago or New York. Such variations come from the fact that we are creatures of culture who join together to create our own way of life. Every other animal, from ants to zebras, behaves very much the same all around the world because their behavior is determined by instincts, biological programming over which the species has no control. A few animals—notably chimpanzees and related primates—have some capacity for culture, as researchers have learned by observing them using tools and teaching simple skills to their offspring. But the creative power of humans is far greater than that of any other form of life. In short, only humans rely on culture rather than instinct to ensure their survival (M. Harris, 1987). To understand how human culture came to be, we need to look back at the history of our species.

CULTURE AND HUMAN INTELLIGENCE

Scientists tell us that our planet is 4.5 billion years old (see the timeline inside the front cover of this text). Life appeared about 1 billion years later. Fast-forward another 2 to 3 billion years, and we find dinosaurs ruling Earth. It was when these giant creatures disappeared—some 65 million years ago—that our history took a crucial turn with the appearance of the animals we call primates.

The importance of primates is that they have the largest brains relative to body size of all living creatures. About 12 million years ago, primates began to evolve along two different lines, setting apart humans from the great apes, our closest relatives. Some 3 million years ago, our distant human ancestors climbed down from the trees of Central Africa to move around in the tall grasses. There, walking upright, they learned the advantages of hunting in groups and made use of fire, tools, and weapons; built simple shelters; and fashioned basic clothing. These Stone Age achievements mark the point at which our ancestors embarked on a distinct evolutionary course, making culture their

Confronting the Yąnomamö: The Experience of Culture Shock

A small aluminum motorboat chugged steadily along the muddy Orinoco River, deep within South America's vast tropical rain forest. The anthropologist Napoleon Chagnon was nearing the end of a three-day journey to the home territory of the Yąnomamö, one of the most technologically simple societies on Earth.

Some 12,000 Yąnomamö live in villages scattered along the border of Venezuela and Brazil. Their way of life could hardly be more different from our own. The Yąnomamö wear little clothing and live without electricity, cars, or other conveniences most people in the United States take for granted. They use bows and arrows for hunting and warfare, as they have for centuries. Many of the Yąnomamö have had little contact with the outside world, so Chagnon would be as strange to them as they would be to him.

By 2:00 in the afternoon, Chagnon had almost reached his destination. The hot sun and humid air were becoming unbearable. Chagnon's clothes were soaked with sweat, and his face and hands were swollen from the bites of gnats swarming around him. But he scarcely noticed, so focused was he on the fact that in just a few moments, he would be face to face with people unlike any he had ever known.

Chagnon's heart pounded as the boat slid onto the riverbank. He and his guide climbed from the boat and walked toward the Yąnomamö village, stooping as they pushed their way through the dense undergrowth. Chagnon describes what happened next:

> I looked up and gasped when I saw a dozen burly, naked, sweaty, hideous men staring at us down the shafts of their drawn arrows! Immense wads of green tobacco were stuck between their lower teeth and lips, making them look even more hideous, and strands of dark green slime dripped or hung from their nostrils—strands so long that they clung to their [chests] or drizzled down their chins.
> My next discovery was that there were a dozen or so vicious, underfed dogs snapping at my legs, circling me as if I were to be their next meal. I just stood there holding my notebook, helpless and pathetic. Then the stench of the decaying vegetation and filth hit me and I almost got sick. I was horrified. What kind of welcome was this for the person who came here to live with you and learn your way of life, to become friends with you? (1992:11–12)

Fortunately for Chagnon, the Yąnomamö villagers recognized his guide and lowered their weapons. Reassured that he would survive the afternoon, Chagnon still was shaken by his inability to make any sense of these people. And this was to be his home for a year and a half! He wondered why he had given up physics to study human culture in the first place.

WHAT DO YOU THINK?

1. As they came to know Chagnon, might the Yąnomamö, too, have experienced culture shock? Why?

2. Can you think of an experience you had that is similar to the one described here?

3. Can studying sociology help reduce the experience of culture shock? How?

primary strategy for survival. By about 250,000 years ago, our species, *Homo sapiens*—derived from the Latin meaning "thinking person"—had emerged. Humans continued to evolve so that by about 40,000 years ago, people who looked more or less like us roamed the planet. With larger brains, these "modern" *Homo sapiens* developed culture rapidly, as the wide range of tools and cave art from this period suggests.

People throughout the world communicate not just with spoken words but also with bodily gestures. Because gestures vary from culture to culture, they can occasionally be the cause for misunderstandings. For instance, the commonplace "thumbs up" gesture we use to express "Good job!" can get a person from the United States into trouble in Australia, where people take it to mean "Up yours!"

By 12,000 years ago, the founding of permanent settlements and the creation of specialized occupations in the Middle East (in what is today Iraq and Egypt) marked "the birth of civilization." At this point, the biological forces we call instincts had disappeared, replaced by a more efficient survival scheme: *fashioning the natural environment to our purposes.* Ever since, humans have made and remade their world in countless ways, resulting in today's fascinating cultural diversity.

HOW MANY CULTURES?

In the United States, how many cultures are there? One indicator of culture is language; the Census Bureau lists more than 200 languages spoken in this country, most of which were brought by immigrants from nations around the world.

Globally, experts document almost 7,000 languages, suggesting the existence of as many distinct cultures. Yet the number of languages spoken around the world is declining, and roughly half now are spoken by fewer than 10,000 people. Experts expect that the coming decades may see the disappearance of hundreds of these languages, including Gullah, Pennsylvania German, and Pawnee (all spoken in the United States), Han (spoken in northwestern Canada),

Oro in the Amazon region (Brazil), Sardinian (spoken on the European island of Sardinia), Aramaic (the language of Jesus of Nazareth in the Middle East), Nu Shu (a language spoken in southern China that is the only one known to be used only by women), and Wakka Wakka and several other Aboriginal tongues spoken in Australia. Why the decline? Likely reasons for the trend include high-technology communication, increasing international migration, and an expanding global economy, all of which are reducing global cultural diversity (UNESCO, 2001; Barovick, 2002; Hayden, 2003).

To learn more about how anthropologists study other cultures, go to http://www.aaanet.org

The Elements of Culture

Although cultures vary greatly, they all have common elements, including symbols, language, values, and norms. We begin our discussion with the one that is the basis for all the others: symbols.

SYMBOLS

Like all creatures, human beings sense the surrounding world, but unlike others, we also give the world *meaning.* Humans transform the elements of the world into *symbols.* A **symbol** is *anything that carries a particular meaning recognized by people who share a culture.* A word, a whistle, a wall of graffiti, a flashing red light, a raised fist—all serve as symbols. The human capacity to create and manipulate symbols is almost limitless—think of the variety of meanings associated with the simple act of winking an eye, which can convey such messages as interest, understanding, or insult.

Societies create new symbols all the time. The Applying Sociology box describes some of the symbols that have developed along with our increasing use of computers for communication.

We are so dependent on our culture's symbols that we often take them for granted. We become keenly aware of the importance of a symbol, however, when it is used in an unconventional way, as when someone burns a U.S. flag during a political demonstration. Entering an unfamiliar culture also reminds us of the power of symbols; culture shock is really the inability to "read" meaning in unfamiliar surroundings. Not understanding the symbols of a culture leaves a person feeling lost and isolated, unsure of how to act, and sometimes frightened.

Culture shock is a two-way process. On one hand, the traveler *experiences* culture shock when meeting people whose way of life is different. For example, North Americans

APPLYING SOCIOLOGY

New Symbols in the World of Instant Messaging

Soc was Gr8!

    What happened?

I was :´-D

    Y?

The prof looks like =(_8^(1)

    Maybe his wife looks like
    >@@@@8^)

GMTA

    See you B4 class. B4N

BCNU

The world of symbols changes all the time. One reason that people create new symbols is that we develop new ways to communicate. Today, more than 50 million people in the United States (most of them young, and many of them students) communicate using an instant messaging (IM) program. All you need to have is a computer and a connection to the Internet.

The exchange above starts with one roommate telling the other how much she enjoyed her new sociology class. If you can't read all the symbols in the message, check the following list of IM symbols. (To appreciate the "emoticon" faces, rotate the page 90° to the right.)

:´-D I am laughing so hard I'm crying.

:-(I am sad.

:-() I am shocked.

:-) I am smiling.

:-)8 I am smiling and wearing a bow tie.

:-O Wow!

:-|| I am angry with you!

:-P I'm sticking my tongue out at you!

%-} I think I've had too much to drink.

:-x My lips are sealed!

-:(Somebody cut my hair into a mohawk!

@}————>——— Here's a rose for you!

=(_8^(1) Homer Simpson

>@@@@8^) Marge Simpson

AFAIK As far as I know

AWHFY Are we having fun yet?

B4 Before

B4N 'Bye for now

BBL Be back later

BCNU Be seeing you

CU See you!

GAL Get a life!

GMTA Great minds think alike.

Gr8 Great

HAGN Have a good night.

H&K Hugs and kisses

IMBL It must be love.

J4F Just for fun

KC Keep cool.

L8r Later

LTNC Long time no see

MYOB Mind your own business.

PCM Please call me.

QPSA? ¿Que pasa?

U You

UR You are

Wan2 Want to

X! Typical woman!

Y! Typical man!

Y Why

2bctd To be continued

2g4u Too good for you

2L8 Too late

WHAT DO YOU THINK?

1. What does the fact that we create new symbols all the time suggest about culture?

2. Do you think using symbols such as the ones described here is a good way to communicate? Does it lead to confusion or misunderstanding? Why or why not?

3. What other kinds of symbols can you think of that are new to your generation?

Sources: J. Rubin (2003) and Berteau (2005).

who consider dogs beloved household pets might be put off by the Masai of eastern Africa, who ignore dogs and never feed them. The same travelers might be horrified to find that in parts of Indonesia and in the northern regions of the People's Republic of China, people roast dogs for dinner.

On the other hand, a traveler can *inflict* culture shock on others by acting in ways that offend them. The North American who asks for a cheeseburger in an Indian restau-

rant offends Hindus, who consider cows sacred and never to be eaten. Global travel provides endless opportunities for misunderstanding.

Symbolic meanings also vary within a single society. In the debate about flying the Confederate flag over the South Carolina state house a few years ago, some people saw the flag as a symbol of regional pride, while others saw it as a symbol of racial oppression.

إقرأ **Arabic**	**Read** English	독서 **Korean**
կարդա **Armenian**	διαβαζω Greek	بخوانيد **Persian**
(Cambodian script) **Cambodian**	אקרא׃ **Hebrew**	читать **Russian**
閱讀 **Chinese**	पढ़ना Hindi	¡Ven a leer! Spanish

FIGURE 2–1 Human Languages: A Variety of Symbols

Here the single English word "Read" is written in twelve of the hundreds of languages humans use to communicate with one another.

LANGUAGE

The heart of a symbolic system is **language,** *a system of symbols that allows people to communicate with one another.* Humans have created many alphabets to express the hundreds of languages we speak. Several examples are shown in Figure 2–1. Even rules for writing differ: Most people in Western societies write from left to right, people in northern Africa and western Asia write from right to left, and people in eastern Asia write from top to bottom. Global Map 2–1 shows where in the world we find the three most widely spoken languages, English, Chinese, and Spanish.

Language not only allows communication but is the key to **cultural transmission,** *the process by which one generation passes culture to the next.* Just as our bodies contain the genes of our ancestors, our cultural heritage contains countless symbols created by those who came before us. Language is the key that unlocks centuries of accumulated wisdom.

YOUR TURN

List three cultural elements that were passed to you by earlier generations. List three different elements that emerged in your own generation; do you think these will last to be passed to your children and grandchildren?

Language skills may link us to the past, but they also spark the human imagination to connect symbols in new ways, creating an almost limitless range of future possibilities. Language sets apart human beings as the only creatures

Can animals use language? To learn more, go to http://www.newscientist.com/article. ns?id=dn3218

who are self-conscious, aware of our limitations and our ultimate mortality, yet are able to dream and hope for a future better than the present.

Does Language Shape Reality?

Does someone who speaks Cherokee, an American Indian language, experience the world differently from North Americans who think in Spanish or English? Edward Sapir and Benjamin Whorf claimed that the answer is yes, because each language has its own distinct symbols that serve as the building blocks of reality (Sapir, 1929, 1949; Whorf, 1956, orig. 1941). Further, they noted that each symbolic system has words or expressions not found in any other symbolic system. Finally, all languages connect symbols with distinctive emotions, so, as multilingual people know, a single idea may "feel" different if spoken in Spanish rather than in English or Chinese.

Formally, the **Sapir-Whorf thesis** holds that *people see and understand the world through the cultural lens of language.* In the decades since Sapir and Whorf published their work, however, scholars have taken issue with this proposition. Current thinking is that although we do fashion reality out of our symbols, evidence does not support the notion that language *determines* reality in the way Sapir and Whorf claimed. For example, we know that children understand the idea of "family" long before they learn that word; similarly, adults can imagine new ideas or things before devising a name for them (Kay & Kempton, 1984; Pinker, 1994).

VALUES AND BELIEFS

What accounts for the popularity of movie characters such as James Bond, Neo, Erin Brockovich, Lara Croft, and Rocky? Each is ruggedly individualistic, going it alone and relying on personal skill and savvy to challenge "the system." In admiring such characters, we are supporting certain **values,** *culturally defined standards that people use to decide what is desirable, good, and beautiful and that serve as broad guidelines for social living.* Values are standards that people who share a culture use to make choices about how to live.

Values are broad principles that underlie **beliefs,** *specific statements that people hold to be true.* In other words, values are abstract standards of goodness, and beliefs are particular matters that people accept as true or false. For example, because most U.S. adults share the value of providing equal opportunity for all, they believe that a qualified woman could serve as president of the United States (NORC, 2005).

WINDOW ON THE WORLD

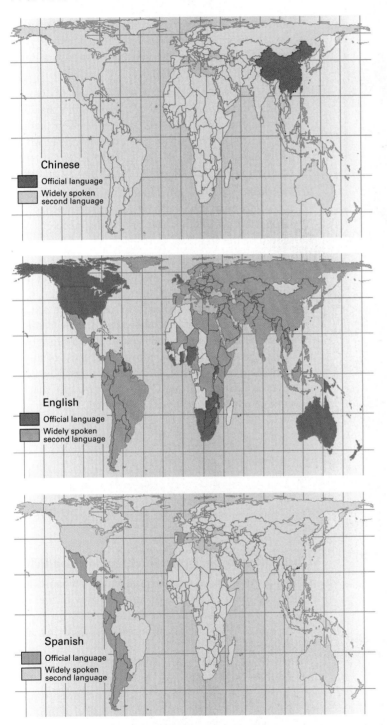

Chinese
- Official language
- Widely spoken second language

English
- Official language
- Widely spoken second language

Spanish
- Official language
- Widely spoken second language

GLOBAL MAP 2-1

Language in Global Perspective

Chinese (including Mandarin, Cantonese, and dozens of other dialects) is the native tongue of one-fifth of the world's people, almost all of whom live in Asia. Although all Chinese people read and write with the same characters, they use several dozen dialects. The "official" dialect, taught in schools throughout the People's Republic of China and the Republic of Taiwan, is Mandarin (the dialect of Beijing, China's historical capital city). Cantonese, the language of Canton, is the second most common Chinese dialect; it differs in sound from Mandarin roughly the way French differs from Spanish.

English is the native tongue or official language in several world regions (spoken by one-tenth of humanity) and has become the preferred second language in most of the world.

The largest concentration of Spanish speakers is in Latin America and, of course, Spain. Spanish is also the second most widely spoken language in the United States.

Source: *Peters Atlas of the World* (1990); updated by the author.

What does the popularity of the television show *The Apprentice* tell you about the values at the heart of U.S. culture?

Key Values of U.S. Culture

The sociologist Robin Williams Jr. (1970) identified ten values as central to our way of life:

1. **Equal opportunity.** People in the United States believe in not *equality of condition* but *equality of opportunity.* This means that society should provide everyone with the chance to get ahead according to individual talents and efforts.

2. **Individual achievement and personal success.** Our way of life encourages competition so that each person's rewards should reflect personal merit. A successful person is given the respect due a "winner."

3. **Material comfort.** Success in the United States generally means making money and enjoying what it will buy. Although people sometimes remark that "money won't buy happiness," most of us pursue wealth all the same.

4. **Activity and work.** Our heroes, from television's Buffy the Vampire Slayer to golf champion Tiger Woods, are "doers" who get the job done. Our culture values *action* over *reflection* and taking control of events over passively accepting fate.

5. **Practicality and efficiency.** We value the practical over the theoretical, "doing" over "dreaming." "Major in something that will help you get a job!" parents say to their college-age children.

6. **Progress.** We are an optimistic people who, despite waves of nostalgia, believe that the present is better than the past. We celebrate progress, viewing the "very latest" as the "very best."

7. **Science.** We expect scientists to solve problems and to improve our lives. We believe that we are rational people, which probably explains our cultural tendency (especially among men) to devalue emotion and intuition as sources of knowledge.

8. **Democracy and free enterprise.** Members of our society recognize numerous individual rights that governments should not take away. We believe that a just political system is based on free elections in which adults select government leaders and on an economy that responds to the choices of individual consumers.

9. **Freedom.** We favor individual initiative over collective conformity. While we know that everyone has responsibilities to others, we believe that people should be free to pursue personal goals.

10. **Racism and group superiority.** Despite strong ideas about individualism and freedom, most people in the United States still judge others according to gender, race, ethnicity, and social class. In general, U.S. culture values males over females, whites over people of color, people with northwestern European backgrounds over those whose ancestors came from other parts of the world, and rich over poor. Although we describe ourselves as a nation of equals, there is little doubt that some of us are "more equal" than others.

Can you see how cultural values can shape the way people see the world? For example, how does our cultural emphasis on individual achievement blind us to the power of society to give some people great advantages over others?

Values: Often in Harmony, Sometimes in Conflict

In many ways, cultural values go together. Williams's list includes examples of *value clusters* in our way of life. For instance, we value activity and work because we expect effort to lead to achievement and success and result in material comfort.

Sometimes, however, one core cultural value contradicts another. Take the first and last items on Williams's list, for example: People may believe in equality of opportunity, yet they may also look down on others because of their sex or race. Value conflict causes strain and often leads to awkward balancing acts in our beliefs. Sometimes we decide that one value is more important than another by, for example, supporting equal opportunity while opposing the

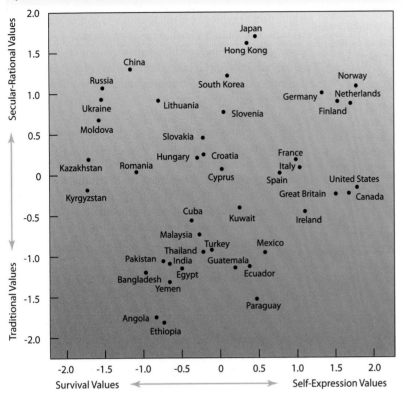

FIGURE 2–2 Cultural Values of Selected Countries

Higher-income countries are secular-rational and favor self-expression. The cultures of lower-income countries are more traditional and concerned with economic survival.

Source: *Modernization, Cultural Change and Democracy* by Ronald Inglehart and Christian Welzel, New York: Cambridge University Press, 2005.

acceptance of homosexual people in the U.S. military. In these cases, we simply learn to live with the contradictions.

Emerging Values

Like all elements of culture, values change over time. People in the United States have always valued hard work. In recent decades, however, we have placed increasing importance on leisure—having time off from work to do things such as reading, travel, or community service that provide enjoyment and satisfaction. Similarly, although the importance of material comfort remains strong, more people are seeking personal growth through meditation and other spiritual activity.

YOUR TURN

Would you say that physical fitness is an emerging cultural value? Why or why not?

Values: A Global Perspective

Values vary from culture to culture around the world. In general, the values that are important in higher-income countries differ somewhat from those in lower-income countries.

People in lower-income nations develop cultures that value survival. This means that people place a great deal of importance on physical safety and economic security. They worry about having enough to eat and a safe place to sleep at night. In addition, lower-income nations tend to be traditional, with values that celebrate the past and emphasize the importance of family and religious beliefs. These nations, in which men have most of the power, typically discourage or forbid practices such as divorce and abortion.

People in higher-income countries develop cultures that value individualism and self-expression. These countries are rich enough that most of the people take survival for granted, focusing their attention instead on which "lifestyle" they prefer and how to achieve the greatest personal happiness. In addition, these cultures tend to be secular-rational, placing less emphasis on family ties and religious beliefs and more on people thinking for themselves and being tolerant of others who differ from them. In higher-income nations, women have social standing more equal to men, and there is widespread support for practices such as divorce and abortion (World Values Survey, 2004). Figure 2–2 shows how selected countries of the world compare in terms of cultural values.

NORMS

Most people in the United States are eager to gossip about "who's hot" and "who's not." Members of American Indian societies, however, typically condemn such behavior as rude and divisive. Both patterns illustrate the operation of **norms,** *rules and expectations by which a society guides the behavior of its members.* In everyday life, people respond to each other with *sanctions,* rewards or punishments that encourage conformity to cultural norms.

William Graham Sumner (1959, orig. 1906), an early U.S. sociologist, coined the term **mores** (pronounced "more rays") to refer to *norms that are widely observed and have great moral significance.* Mores, or *taboos,* include our society's insistence that adults not engage in sexual relations with children.

People pay less attention to **folkways,** *norms for routine or casual interaction.* Examples include ideas about appropriate greetings and proper dress. A man who does not wear a tie to a formal dinner party may raise an eyebrow for violating folkways or "etiquette." If he were to arrive at the dinner party wearing *only* a tie, however, he would violate cultural mores and invite a more serious response.

YOUR TURN

Give two examples of campus folkways and two examples of campus mores. What are the likely consequences of violating each type of norm?

As we learn cultural norms, we gain the capacity to evaluate our own behavior. Doing wrong (say, downloading a term paper from the Internet) can cause both *shame*—the painful sense that others disapprove of our actions—and also *guilt*—a negative judgment we make of ourselves. Only cultural creatures can experience shame and guilt. This is what the writer Mark Twain had in mind when he remarked that people "are the only animals that blush—or need to."

IDEAL AND REAL CULTURE

Values and norms do not describe actual behavior so much as they suggest how we *should* behave. We must remember that *ideal culture* always differs from the *real culture* that actually occurs in everyday life. For example, most women and men agree on the importance of sexual faithfulness in marriage. Even so, in one study, 25 percent of married men and 10 percent of married women reported having been sexually unfaithful to their spouses at some point in the marriage (Laumann et al., 1994). But a culture's moral standards are important all the same, calling to mind the old saying, "Do as I say, not as I do."

Technology and Culture

In addition to symbolic elements such as values and norms, every culture includes a wide range of physical human creations called *artifacts.* The Chinese eat with chopsticks rather than knives and forks, the Japanese place mats rather than rugs on the floor, and many men and women in India prefer flowing robes to the close-fitting clothing common in the United States. The material culture of a people can seem as strange to outsiders as their language, values, and norms.

A society's artifacts partly reflect underlying cultural values. The warlike Yąnomamö carefully craft their weapons and prize the poison tips on their arrows. By contrast, our society's embrace of individuality and independence goes a long way to explain our high regard for the automobile: We own more than 230 million motor vehicles—more than one for every licensed driver—and even in an age of high gasoline prices, many of these are the large sport utility vehicles that we might expect rugged, individualistic people to choose.

In addition to expressing values, material culture also reflects a society's level of **technology,** *knowledge that people use to make a way of life in their surroundings.* The more complex a society's technology, the easier it is for members of that society to shape the world for themselves.

Gerhard Lenski (Nolan & Lenski, 2004) argues that a society's level of technology is crucial in determining what cultural ideas and artifacts emerge or are even possible. Thus, he sees *sociocultural evolution*—the historical changes in culture brought about by new technology—in terms of four major levels of development: hunting and gathering, horticulture and pastoralism, agriculture, and industry.

HUNTING AND GATHERING

The oldest and most basic way of living is **hunting and gathering,** *the use of simple tools to hunt animals and gather vegetation for food.* From the time of our earliest human ancestors 3 million years ago until about 1800, most people in the world lived as hunters and gatherers. Today, however, this technology supports only a few societies, including the Kaska Indians of northwestern Canada, the Pygmies of Central Africa, the Bushmen of southwestern Africa, the Aborigines of Australia, and the Semai of Malaysia. Typically, hunters and gatherers spend most of their time searching for game and edible plants. Their societies are small, generally with several dozen people living in a nomadic, familylike group, moving on as they use up an area's vegetation or follow migratory animals.

Everyone helps search for food, with the very young and the very old doing what they can. Women usually gather vegetation—the primary food source for these peoples—while men do most of the hunting. Despite their different roles, the two sexes are regarded as having about the same social importance (Leacock, 1978).

Hunters and gatherers do not have formal leaders. They may look to one person as a *shaman,* or priest, but this position does not excuse the person from the daily work of finding food. Overall, hunting and gathering is a simple and egalitarian way of life.

Limited technology leaves hunters and gatherers vulnerable to the forces of nature. Storms and droughts can easily destroy their food supply, and they have few effective ways to respond to accidents or disease. Many children die in childhood, and only half live to the age of twenty.

As people with powerful technology steadily close in on them, hunting and gathering societies are vanishing. Fortunately, studying their way of life has produced valuable information about our sociocultural history and our fundamental ties to the natural environment.

HORTICULTURE AND PASTORALISM

Horticulture, *the use of hand tools to raise crops,* appeared around 10,000 years ago. The hoe and the digging stick (used to punch holes in the ground for planting seeds) first turned up in fertile regions of the Middle East and Southeast Asia, and by 6,000 years ago, these tools were in use from Western Europe to China. Central and South Americans also learned to cultivate plants, but rocky soil and mountainous land forced members of many societies to continue to hunt and gather even as they adopted this new technology (Fisher, 1979; Chagnon, 1992).

In especially dry regions, societies turned not to raising crops but to **pastoralism,** *the domestication of animals.* Throughout the Americas, Africa, the Middle East, and Asia, many societies combine horticulture and pastoralism.

Growing plants and raising animals allows societies to feed hundreds of members. Pastoral peoples remain nomadic, but horticulturalists make permanent settlements. In a horticultural society, a material surplus means that not everyone has to produce food; some people are free to make crafts, become traders, or serve as full-time priests. Compared with hunters and gatherers, pastoral and horticultural societies are more unequal, with some families operating as a ruling elite.

Because hunters and gatherers have little control over nature, they generally believe that the world is inhabited by spirits. As they gain the power to raise plants and animals, however, people come to believe in one God as the creator of the world. The pastoral roots of Judaism and Christianity are evident in the term "pastor" and the common view of God as a "shepherd" who stands watch over all.

What would it be like to live in a society with simple technology? That's the premise of the television show *Survivor.* What advantages do societies with simple technology afford their members? What disadvantages do you see?

AGRICULTURE

Five thousand years ago, technological advances led to **agriculture,** *large-scale cultivation using plows harnessed to animals or machines.* Agrarian technology first appeared in the Middle East and gradually spread throughout the world. The invention of the animal-drawn plow, the wheel, writing, numbers, and new metals changed societies so much that historians call this era the "dawn of civilization."

By turning the soil, plows allow land to be farmed for centuries, so agrarian people can live in permanent settlements. With large food surpluses that can be transported by animal-powered wagons, populations grow into the millions. As members of agrarian societies become more and more specialized in their work, money is used as a form of common exchange, replacing the earlier system of barter. Although the development of agrarian technology expands human choices and fuels urban growth, it also makes social life more individualistic and impersonal.

Agriculture also brings about a dramatic increase in social inequality. Most people live as serfs or slaves, but a few elites are freed from labor to cultivate a "refined" way of life based on the study of philosophy, art, and literature. At all levels, men gain pronounced power over women.

People with only simple technology live much the same the world over, with minor differences caused by regional variations in climate. But, Lenski explains, agrarian technology gives people enough control over the world that cultural diversity dramatically increases.

INDUSTRY

Industrialization occurred as societies replaced the muscles of animals and humans with new forms of power. Formally, **industry** is *the production of goods using advanced sources of energy to drive large machinery.* The introduction of steam power, starting in England about 1775, greatly boosted productivity and transformed culture in the process.

Agrarian people work in or near the home, but most people in industrial societies work in large factories under the supervision of strangers. In this way, industrialization pushes aside traditional cultural values that guided family-centered agrarian life for centuries.

Industry also made the world seem smaller. In the nineteenth century, railroads and steamships carried people across land and sea faster and farther than ever before. In the twentieth century, this process continued with the invention of the automobile, the airplane, radio, television, and computers.

Industrial technology also raises living standards and extends the human life span. Schooling becomes the rule because industrial jobs demand more and more skills. In addition, industrial societies reduce economic inequality and steadily extend political rights.

It is easy to see industrial societies as "more advanced" than those relying on simpler technology. After all, industry raises living standards and stretches life expectancy to the seventies and beyond—about twice that of the Yąnomamö. But as industry intensifies individualism and expands personal freedom, it weakens human community. Also, industry has led people to abuse the natural environment, which threatens us all. And although advanced technology gives us labor-saving machines and miraculous forms of medical treatment, it also contributes to unhealthy levels of stress and has created weapons capable of destroying in a flash everything that our species has achieved.

POSTINDUSTRIAL INFORMATION TECHNOLOGY

Going beyond the four categories discussed by Lenski, we see that many industrial societies, including the United States, have now entered a postindustrial era in which more and more economic production makes use of *new information technology.* Production in industrial societies centers on factories that make *things,* but postindustrial production centers on computers and other electronic devices that create, process, store, and apply *ideas and information.*

The emergence of an information economy changes the skills that define a way of life. No longer are mechanical abilities the only key to success. People find that they must learn to work with symbols by speaking, writing, computing, and creating images and sounds. One result of this change is that our society now has the capacity to create symbolic culture on an unprecedented scale. The Seeing Sociology in Everyday Life box takes a closer look.

Cultural Diversity

In the United States, we are aware of our cultural diversity when we hear several different languages being spoken while riding a subway in New York, Washington, D.C., or Los Angeles. Compared to a country such as Japan, whose historical isolation makes it the most *monocultural* of all high-income nations, centuries of heavy immigration have made the United States the most *multicultural* of all high-income countries.

Between 1820 (when the government began keeping track of immigration) and 2006, about 75 million people came to our shores. A century ago, almost all immigrants hailed from Europe; today, the majority of newcomers arrive from Latin America and Asia. To understand the reality of life in the United States, we must move beyond shared cultural patterns to consider cultural diversity.

HIGH CULTURE AND POPULAR CULTURE

Cultural diversity can involve social class. In fact, in everyday talk, we usually use the term "culture" to mean art forms such as classical literature, music, dance, and painting. We describe people who attend the opera or the theater as "cultured," thinking that they appreciate the "finer things in life."

We speak less kindly of ordinary people, assuming that everyday culture is somehow less worthy. So we are tempted to judge the music of Haydn as "more cultured" than hip-hop, couscous as better than cornbread, and polo as more polished than Ping-Pong.

These differences arise because many cultural patterns are readily accessible to only some members of a society. Sociologists use the term **high culture** to refer to *cultural patterns that distinguish a society's elite* and **popular culture** to describe *cultural patterns that are widespread among a society's population.*

Virtual Culture: Is It Good for Us?

January 16, Orlando, Florida. Walt Disney World is a delight for the kids but a little disturbing for the sociologist. It is ready-made culture: Streets, stores, and events re-create a storybook-perfect small town, populated by Disney characters. Here, life is carefully controlled to ensure a good time, with the ultimate purpose of relieving us of whatever cash we have.

The Information Revolution is now generating symbols—words, sounds, and images—faster than ever before and rapidly spreading them across the nation and around the world. What does this new information technology mean for our way of life?

For our ancestors, culture was a way of life passed down from generation to generation. It was a heritage—a society's collective memory—that was authentically our own because it was created in people's everyday lives. But in our emerging cybersociety, more and more cultural symbols are new, intentionally *created* by a small cultural elite of composers, writers, filmmakers, and others who work in the expanding information economy.

Consider the changing character of cultural heroes, people who serve as role models and represent cultural ideals. A century ago, our heroes were real men and women who made a difference in the life of our nation: George Washington, Abigail Adams, Betsy Ross, Davy Crockett, Daniel Boone, Abraham Lincoln, Harriet Tubman. Today, by contrast, children consume

Culture used to be a way of life passed across many generations. Today, large corporations and the mass media create culture to entertain—and to make money.

virtual culture, images that spring from the minds of contemporary culture makers and that reach them through the television, movie, or computer screen. Today's "heroes" are Lara Croft, Aragorn, Anakin Skywalker, Rug Rats, Scooby Doo, Batman, Barbie, a continuous flow of Disney characters, and the ever-smiling Ronald McDonald. Some of these cultural icons embody values that shape our way of life. But few of them have any historical reality, and almost all have been created for a single purpose: to make money.

WHAT DO YOU THINK?

1. Over the course of the twenty-first century, do you think virtual culture will become more or less important? Explain your answer.

2. Does virtual culture weaken or strengthen our cultural traditions? Is that good or bad?

3. What image of this country do U.S. movies and television shows give to people abroad?

Source: I thank Roland Johnson for the basic idea for this box.

Common sense may suggest that high culture is superior to popular culture, but sociologists are uneasy with such judgments, for two reasons. First, neither elites nor ordinary people share all the same tastes and interests; people in both categories differ in numerous ways. Second, do we praise high culture because it is really better than popular culture or simply because its supporters have more money, power, and prestige? For example, there is no difference between a violin and a fiddle; however, we name the instrument one way when it is used to produce a type of music typically enjoyed by a person of higher position and

the other way when it produces music appreciated by people with lower social standing.

SUBCULTURE

The term **subculture** refers to *cultural patterns that set apart some segment of a society's population.* People who ride "chopper" motorcycles, traditional Korean Americans, New England "Yankees," Ohio State football fans, the southern California "beach crowd," and wilderness campers all display subcultural patterns. "In the *Times*" on pages 54–55 takes a look at the challenges faced by Creoles in Louisiana

October 11, 2005

Cast from Their Ancestral Home, Creoles Worry about Culture's Future

By SUSAN SAULNY

Natchitoches Parish, La.—It is peaceful here on the Cane River, beyond the fluffy tops of high cotton and towering magnolia trees, but it is not home. For the New Orleans Creoles living in exodus here and elsewhere around Louisiana, their city was far more than home—it was homeland, the capital of an ethnic nation unique in this country....

The Creoles, the population of mixed-race families who trace their roots to the city's French and Spanish colonial era,...have been more distinctly connected to a place—New Orleans—than perhaps any other American ethnic group but their rural Louisiana neighbors, the Cajuns. But unlike the Cajuns, who settled in Louisiana after being expelled from Canada by the British, the Creoles lived in the birthplace of their culture.

And now, after the recent storms and the blows they dealt to Creole communities around New Orleans, scattering them to states from coast to coast, many Creoles fear that without a geographical base, their already fragile culture and their very identity could be lost....

Many Creoles trace their roots to immigrants and slaves from the former French and Spanish colonies in the Caribbean, particularly Cuba and what is now Haiti. Historians say it was New Orleans's position as a crossroads and port town that allowed for the easy mingling of races and nationalities that in turn gave birth, in the eighteenth century, to a part-European, part-Afro-Caribbean society that grew to an estimated 20,000 people in Louisiana by the mid-1800's. The Creole culture that developed over generations—known for a distinctive cuisine, language and music—contributed to New Orleans's

singular identity and helped define Louisiana to the world. Before Hurricane Katrina, experts estimated that 10 to 20 percent of black people in New Orleans—30,000 to 60,000 people—considered themselves Creole by way of ancestry, but even more lived lives influenced by the culture because of their proximity to it.

And now most are gone.

With their geographic underpinnings swept away, many New Orleanians of Creole descent are trying to figure out how best to preserve a community separated from both its birthplace and home base....

Last month, the evacuation scattered people haphazardly, not even giving them a chance to say goodbye or tell one another where they were going. Families that had lived within blocks of each other for generations ended up in different states....

---

trying to preserve their culture after being displaced by Hurricane Katrina.

List five subcultures that are part of your life. Which are the most important?

It is easy but often inaccurate to put people in subcultural categories because almost everyone participates in many subcultures without having much commitment to any one of them. In some cases, ethnicity and religion set people apart from one another, with tragic results. Consider the former nation of Yugoslavia in southeastern Europe. The 1990s civil war there was fueled by extreme cultural diversity. This *one* small country with a population about equal to the Los Angeles metropolitan area made use of *two* alphabets, embraced *three* major religions, spoke *four* major

languages, was home to *five* major nationalities, was divided into *six* separate republics, and absorbed the cultural influences of *seven* surrounding countries. The cultural conflict that plunged this nation into civil war shows that subcultures are a source not only of pleasing variety but also of tension and even violence.

Many people view the United States as a melting pot where many nationalities blend into a single "American" culture (Gardyn, 2002). But given so much cultural diversity, how accurate is the melting pot image? For one thing, subcultures involve not just *difference* but *hierarchy*. Too often what we view as dominant or "mainstream" culture are the patterns favored by powerful segments of the population, and we view the lives of disadvantaged people as "subculture." But are the cultural patterns of rich skiers in Aspen, Colorado, any less a subculture than the cultural patterns of skateboarders in Los Angeles? Some sociologists therefore prefer to level the playing field of society by emphasizing multiculturalism.

The Creoles in New Orleans were an economically diverse group. Some lived in simple but historic houses in the Tremé area near the French Quarter, while others were concentrated in Gentilly and in more modern, upscale neighborhoods in New Orleans East. Large swaths of the last two areas were damaged beyond repair in the flood and are likely to be condemned....

Many Creoles think their recent trials will make them only stronger.

"Katrina was not a death knell for Creole culture, quite the opposite," Janet Ravare Colson, the assistant director of the Creole Heritage Center at Northwestern State University in Natchitoches, said. "I think it was an awakening. People want to know about their heritage now more than ever."...

Some Creoles predict that the area around Natchitoches (pronounced NACK-ih-tish), which already had a siz-able, generations-old Creole community, will become the new center of the culture....

It is not clear, however, what will happen to New Orleans without its Creoles.

"Much of what made New Orleans unique was the Creole influence," said Mary Gehman, an assistant professor of English at Delgado Community College in New Orleans and the author of several works on Creole history. "With the razing of large areas of condemned buildings and replacing them with modern housing with faux touches, the displacement of neighborhoods, the emphasis on a Las Vegas-style entertainment destination in the new New Orleans, I fear little will survive of the original spirit of the place."

Adapted from the original article by Susan Saulny published in *The New York Times* on October 11, 2005. Copyright © 2005 by The New York Times Company. Reprinted with permission.

WHAT DO YOU THINK?

1. How does having a place to call home help people maintain strong cultural traditions?

2. This article suggests that people lose more than their homes and property when a natural disaster like Hurricane Katrina strikes. Explain why this is true.

3. What cultural patterns are part of your ethnic background? How have they been tied to your living in a specific place?

MULTICULTURALISM

Multiculturalism is *a perspective recognizing the cultural diversity of the United States and promoting respect and equal standing for all cultural traditions.* Multiculturalism represents a sharp change from the past, when U.S. society downplayed cultural diversity, defining itself in terms of its European and especially English immigrants. Today there is spirited debate about whether we should continue to focus on historical traditions or highlight contemporary diversity.

E pluribus unum, the Latin phrase that appears on each U.S. coin, means "out of many, one." This motto symbolizes not only our national political union but also the idea that the varied experiences of immigrants from around the world come together to form a new way of life.

But from the outset, the many cultures did not melt together as much as harden into a hierarchy. At the top were the English, who formed a majority and established English as the nation's dominant language. Further down, people of other backgrounds were advised to model themselves after "their betters" so that the "melting" was really a process of Anglicization—adoption of English ways. As multiculturalists see it, early in its history, U.S. society set up the English way of life as an ideal that everyone else should imitate and by which everyone should be judged.

Since then, historians have reported events from the point of view of the English and others of European ancestry, paying little attention to the perspectives and accomplishments of Native Americans and people of African and Asian descent. Multiculturalists criticize this as **Eurocentrism,** *the dominance of European (especially English) cultural patterns.* Molefi Kete Asante, a supporter of multiculturalism, argues that like "the fifteenth-century Europeans who could not cease believing that the Earth was the center of the universe, many ... find it difficult to cease viewing European culture as the center of the social universe" (1988:7).

One controversial issue involves language. Some people believe that English should be the official language of the

Of more than 268 million people age five or older in the United States, the Census Bureau reports that 52 million (19 percent) speak a language other than English at home. Of these, 62 percent speak Spanish and 15 percent use an Asian language (the Census Bureau lists 29 languages, each of which is favored by more than 100,000 people). The map shows that non–English speakers are concentrated in certain regions of the country. Which ones? What do you think accounts for this pattern?

Source: U.S. Census Bureau (2003, 2006).

Percentage of Population That Speaks a Language Other than English at Home

- 60.0% or more
- 35.0% to 59.9%
- 17.9% to 34.9%
- 4.6% to 17.8%
- 0.4 % to 4.5%

U.S. average = 19.4%

United States; by 2006, legislatures in twenty-seven states had enacted laws making it the official language. But some 52 million U.S. adults—nearly one in six—speak a language other than English at home. Spanish is the second most commonly spoken language in the United States, and several hundred other tongues are heard across the country, including Italian, German, French, Filipino, Japanese, Korean, Vietnamese, Russian, and a host of Native American languages. National Map 2–1 shows where in the United States large numbers of people speak a language other than English at home.

Supporters of multiculturalism say it is a way of coming to terms with our country's increasing social diversity. With the Asian and Hispanic populations increasing rapidly, some analysts predict that today's children will live to see people of African, Asian, and Hispanic ancestry become the *majority* of this country's population.

Supporters also claim that multiculturalism is a good way to strengthen the academic achievement of African American children. To counter Eurocentrism, some multicultural educators are calling for **Afrocentrism,** *emphasizing and promoting African cultural patterns,* which they see as a strategy for correcting centuries of ignoring the cultural achievements of African societies and African Americans.

Although multiculturalism has found favor in recent years, it has drawn criticism as well. Opponents say it encourages divisiveness rather than unity because it urges people to identify with only their own category rather than with the nation as a whole. In addition, critics say, multiculturalism actually harms minorities themselves. Multicultural policies (from African American studies departments to all-black dorms) seem to support the same racial separa-

tion that our nation has struggled so long to overcome. Furthermore, in the early grades, an Afrocentric curriculum may deny children important knowledge and skills by forcing them to study only certain topics from a single point of view.

Finally, the global war on terror has drawn the issue of multiculturalism into the world spotlight. In 2005, British Prime Minister Tony Blair responded to a terrorist attack in London, stating, "It is important that the terrorists realize [that] our determination to defend our values and our way of life is greater than their determination to . . . impose their extremism on the world." He went on to warn that the British government would expel Muslim clerics who encouraged hatred and terrorism (Barone, 2005). In a world of cultural difference and conflict, we all have much to learn about tolerance and peacemaking.

COUNTERCULTURE

Cultural diversity also includes outright rejection of conventional ideas or behavior. **Counterculture** refers to *cultural patterns that strongly oppose those widely accepted within a society.*

During the 1960s, for example, a youth-oriented counterculture rejected mainstream culture as too competitive, self-centered, and materialistic. Instead, hippies and other counterculturalists favored a collective and cooperative lifestyle in which "being" was more important than "doing" and the capacity for personal growth—or "expanded consciousness"—was prized over material possessions like fancy homes and cars. Such differences led some people to "drop out" of the larger society.

Countercultures are still flourishing. At the extreme, small militaristic communities (made up of people born and bred in this country) or bands of religious militants (from other countries) exist in the United States, some of them engaging in violence intended to threaten our way of life.

CULTURAL CHANGE

Perhaps the most basic human truth is that "all things shall pass." Even the dinosaurs, which thrived on this planet for 160 million years (see the timeline), remain today only as fossils. Will humanity survive for millions of years to come? All we can say with certainty is that given our reliance on culture, the human record will show continuous change.

Figure 2–3 shows changes in student attitudes between 1969 (the height of the 1960s counterculture) and 2005. Some attitudes have changed only slightly: Today, as a generation ago, most men and women look forward to raising a family. But today's students are much less concerned than those of the 1960s with developing a philosophy of life and are much more interested in making money.

Change in one dimension of a cultural system usually sparks changes in others. For example, today's college women are much more interested in making money because women are much more likely to be in the labor force than their mothers or grandmothers were. Working for income may not change their interest in having a family, but it does increase their age at first marriage and the divorce rate. Such connections illustrate the principle of **cultural integration,** *the close relationships among various elements of a cultural system.*

Some parts of a cultural system change faster than others. William Ogburn (1964) observed that technology moves quickly, generating new elements of material culture (such as test-tube babies) faster than nonmaterial culture (such as ideas about parenthood) can keep up with them. Ogburn called this inconsistency **cultural lag,** *the fact that some cultural elements change more quickly than others, disrupting a cultural system.* In a world in which a woman can give birth to a child by using another woman's egg, which has been fertilized in a laboratory with the sperm of a total stranger, how are we to apply traditional ideas about motherhood and fatherhood?

Cultural changes are set in motion in three ways. The first is *invention,* the process of creating new cultural elements, such as the telephone (1876), the airplane (1903), and the computer (late 1940s), each of which changed our way of life. The process of invention goes on all the time, as indicated by the thousands of applications submitted annually to the U.S. Patent Office. The timeline inside the front cover of this book shows other inventions that have helped change our way of life.

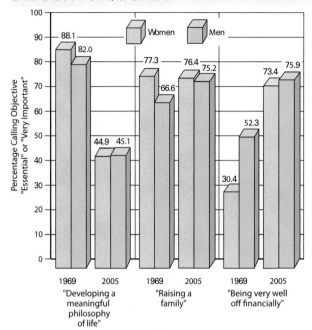

STUDENT SNAPSHOT

FIGURE 2-3 Life Objectives of First-Year College Students, 1969–2005

Today's students are less interested in developing a philosophy of life and more interested in making money.

Sources: Astin et al. (2002) and Pryor et al. (2005).

Discovery, a second cause of change, involves recognizing and better understanding something already in existence, from a distant star to the foods of another culture to women's athletic ability. Many discoveries result from painstaking scientific research, and others happen by a stroke of luck, as in 1898 when Marie Curie unintentionally left a rock on a piece of photographic paper, noticed that emissions from the rock had exposed the paper, and thus discovered radium.

The third cause of cultural change is *diffusion,* the spread of objects or ideas from one society to another. Because new information technology sends information around the globe in seconds, cultural diffusion has never been greater than it is today.

Our own way of life has contributed many significant cultural elements to the world, ranging from computers to jazz music. Of course, diffusion works the other way, too, so that much of what we assume is "American" actually comes from elsewhere. Most of the clothing we wear and the furniture we use, as well as the watch we carry and the money we spend all had their origins in other cultures (Linton, 1937a).

In the world's low-income countries, most children must work to provide their families with needed income. This seven-year-old boy in eastern Ilam, Nepal, works long hours in a tea field. Is it ethnocentric for people living in high-income nations to condemn the practice of child labor because we think youngsters belong in school? Why or why not?

ETHNOCENTRISM AND CULTURAL RELATIVISM

December 10, a small village in Morocco. Watching many of our fellow travelers browsing through a tiny ceramics factory, we have little doubt that North Americans are among the world's greatest shoppers. We delight in surveying hand-woven carpets in China or India, inspecting finely crafted metals in Turkey, or collecting the beautifully colored porcelain tiles we find here in Morocco. Of course, all these items are wonderful bargains. But one major reason for the low prices is unsettling to people living in rich countries: Many products from the world's low- and middle-income countries are produced by children—some as young as five or six—who work long days for pennies per hour.

We think of childhood as a time of innocence and freedom from adult burdens such as work. In poor countries throughout the world, however, families depend on income earned by their children. So what people in one society

think of as right and natural, people elsewhere find puzzling or even immoral. Perhaps the Chinese philosopher Confucius had it right when he noted that "all people are the same; it's only their habits that are different."

Just about every imaginable idea or behavior is commonplace somewhere in the world, and this cultural variation causes travelers both excitement and distress. The Australians flip light switches down to turn them on, but North Americans flip them up. The Japanese give names to city blocks; North Americans name city streets. Egyptians stand very close to others in conversation; North Americans are used to maintaining several feet of "personal space." Bathrooms lack toilet paper in much of rural Morocco, causing considerable discomfort for North Americans, who recoil at the thought of using the left hand for bathroom hygiene, as the locals do.

Given that a particular culture is the basis for every person's reality, it is no wonder that people everywhere exhibit **ethnocentrism,** *the practice of judging another culture by the standards of one's own culture.* Some degree of ethnocentrism is necessary for people to be emotionally attached to their way of life. But ethnocentrism also generates misunderstanding and sometimes conflict.

Even our language is culturally biased. Centuries ago, people in North America or Europe referred to China as the "Far East." But this term, unknown to the Chinese, is an ethnocentric expression for a region that is far east *of us.* The Chinese name for their country translates as "Central Kingdom," suggesting that they, like us, see their society as the center of the world. The map in Figure 2–4 challenges our ethnocentrism by presenting a "down under" view of the Western Hemisphere.

The alternative to ethnocentrism is **cultural relativism,** *the practice of judging a culture by its own standards.* Cultural relativism can be difficult for travelers to adopt: It requires not only openness to unfamiliar values and norms but also the ability to put aside cultural standards we have known all our lives. Even so, as people of the world increasingly come into contact with one another, the importance of understanding other cultures becomes ever greater.

As noted in the opening to this chapter, businesses in the United States are learning the value of marketing to a culturally diverse population. Similarly, businesses now know that success in the global economy depends on awareness of cultural patterns around the world. IBM, for example, now provides technical support for its products using Web sites in twenty-two languages (Fonda, 2001).

This trend is a change from the past, when many companies used marketing strategies that lacked sensitivity to cultural diversity. The translation of Coors's phrase "Turn It Loose" startled Spanish-speaking customers by proclaiming that the beer would cause diarrhea. Braniff Airlines translated its slogan "Fly in Leather" into Spanish so carelessly that it read "Fly Naked"; similarly, Eastern Airlines's slogan "We Earn Our Wings Every Day" became "We Fly Daily to Heaven," discouraging timid air travelers. Even the poultry magnate Frank Perdue fell victim to poor marketing when his pitch "It Takes a Tough Man to Make a Tender Chicken" was transformed into the Spanish phrase "A Sexually Excited Man Will Make a Chicken Affectionate" (Helin, 1992).

But cultural relativism introduces problems of its own. If almost any behavior is the norm *somewhere* in the world, does that mean everything is equally right? Does the fact that some Indian and Moroccan families benefit from their children working long hours justify child labor?

Because we are all members of a single human species, surely there must be some universal standards of proper conduct. But what are they? And in trying to develop them, how can we avoid imposing our own standards on others? There are no simple answers to these questions. But when

 In two brief videos, the author considers issues of cultural relativism at http://www.TheSociologyPage.com

confronting an unfamiliar cultural practice, it is best to resist making judgments before grasping what "they" think of the issue. Remember also to think about your own way of life as others might see it. After all, what we gain most from studying others is better insight into ourselves.

A Global Culture?

Today more than ever, we can observe many of the same cultural patterns the world over. Walking the streets of Seoul, South Korea; Kuala Lumpur, Malaysia; Chennai, India; Cairo, Egypt; or Casablanca, Morocco, we see jeans, hear familiar music, and read ads for many of the same products we use at home. Recall, too, from Global Map 2–1 that English is firmly established as the preferred second language in most parts of the world. Are we witnessing the birth of a single global culture?

Societies around the world now have more contact with one another than ever before, thanks to the flow of goods, information, and people:

1. **Global economy: The flow of goods.** International commerce is at an all-time high. The global economy has spread many consumer goods (from cars and TV shows to music and fashion) throughout the world.

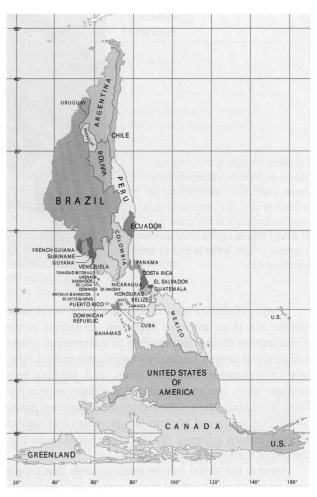

FIGURE 2-4 The View from "Down Under"

North America should be "up" and South America "down," or so we think. But because we live on a globe, "up" and "down" have no meaning at all. The reason this map of the Western Hemisphere looks wrong to us is not that it is geographically inaccurate; it simply violates our ethnocentric assumption that the United States should be "above" the rest of the Americas.

2. **Global communication: The flow of information.** The Internet and satellite-assisted communication enable people to experience events taking place thousands of miles away, often as they happen.

3. **Global migration: The flow of people.** Knowledge about the rest of the world motivates people to move where they imagine life will be better, and modern transportation technology, especially air travel, makes moving about faster than ever before. As a result, in most nations, significant numbers of current residents were born elsewhere (including some 34 million people in the United States—12 percent of the population).

Using an evolutionary perspective, sociobiologists explain that different reproductive strategies give rise to a double standard: Men treat women as sexual objects more than women treat men that way. While this may be so, many sociologists counter that behavior—such as that shown in Ruth Orkin's photograph, *American Girl in Italy*—is more correctly understood as resulting from a culture of male domination.

Copyright 1952, 1980 Ruth Orkin.

Yet by stressing the divisiveness of culture, this approach understates ways in which cultural patterns integrate members of a society. Thus we should consider both social-conflict and structural-functional insights for a fuller understanding of culture.

✔ **YOUR LEARNING** How does a social-conflict analysis of college fraternities and sororities differ from a structural-functional analysis?

EVOLUTION AND CULTURE: SOCIOBIOLOGY

We know that culture is a human creation, but does human biology influence how this process unfolds? A third theoretical approach, standing with one leg in biology and the other in sociology, is **sociobiology**, *a theoretical approach that explores ways in which human biology affects how we create culture.*

Sociobiology rests on the theory of evolution proposed by Charles Darwin in his book *On the Origin of Species* (1859). Darwin asserted that living organisms change over long periods of time as a result of *natural selection,* a matter of four simple principles. First, all living things live to reproduce themselves. Second, the blueprint for reproduction is in the genes, the basic units of life that carry traits of one generation into the next. Third, some random variation in genes allows each species to "try out" new life patterns in a particular environment. This variation enables some organisms to survive better than others and to pass on their advantageous genes to their offspring. Fourth and finally, over thousands of generations, the genes that promote reproduction survive and become dominant. In this way, as

biologists say, a species *adapts* to its environment, and dominant traits emerge as the "nature" of the organism.

Sociobiologists claim that the large number of cultural universals reflects the fact that all humans are members of a single biological species. It is our common biology that underlies, for example, the apparently universal "double standard." As the sex researcher Alfred Kinsey put it, "Among all people everywhere in the world, the male is more likely than the female to desire sex with a variety of partners" (quoted in Barash, 1981:49). But why?

We all know that a child results from joining a woman's egg with a man's sperm. But the biological significance of a single sperm is very different from that of a single egg. For healthy men, sperm is a "renewable resource" produced by the testes throughout most of the life course. A man releases hundreds of millions of sperm in a single ejaculation—technically, enough to fertilize every woman in North America (Barash, 1981:47). A newborn girl's ovaries, however, contain her entire lifetime supply of follicles, or immature eggs. A woman releases a single egg cell from the ovaries each month. So although men are biologically capable of fathering thousands of offspring, a woman is able to bear a relatively small number of children.

Given this biological difference, men reproduce their genes most efficiently by engaging in sex readily and often. But women look at reproduction differently. Each of a woman's pregnancies demands that she carry the child, give birth, and provide care for some time afterward. Efficient reproduction on the part of the woman therefore depends on selecting a man whose qualities (beginning with the likelihood that he will simply stay around) will contribute to her child's survival and, later, successful reproduction.

This trend is a change from the past, when many companies used marketing strategies that lacked sensitivity to cultural diversity. The translation of Coors's phrase "Turn It Loose" startled Spanish-speaking customers by proclaiming that the beer would cause diarrhea. Braniff Airlines translated its slogan "Fly in Leather" into Spanish so carelessly that it read "Fly Naked"; similarly, Eastern Airlines's slogan "We Earn Our Wings Every Day" became "We Fly Daily to Heaven," discouraging timid air travelers. Even the poultry magnate Frank Perdue fell victim to poor marketing when his pitch "It Takes a Tough Man to Make a Tender Chicken" was transformed into the Spanish phrase "A Sexually Excited Man Will Make a Chicken Affectionate" (Helin, 1992).

But cultural relativism introduces problems of its own. If almost any behavior is the norm *somewhere* in the world, does that mean everything is equally right? Does the fact that some Indian and Moroccan families benefit from their children working long hours justify child labor?

Because we are all members of a single human species, surely there must be some universal standards of proper conduct. But what are they? And in trying to develop them, how can we avoid imposing our own standards on others? There are no simple answers to these questions. But when

 In two brief videos, the author considers issues of cultural relativism at http://www.TheSociologyPage.com

confronting an unfamiliar cultural practice, it is best to resist making judgments before grasping what "they" think of the issue. Remember also to think about your own way of life as others might see it. After all, what we gain most from studying others is better insight into ourselves.

A GLOBAL CULTURE?

Today more than ever, we can observe many of the same cultural patterns the world over. Walking the streets of Seoul, South Korea; Kuala Lumpur, Malaysia; Chennai, India; Cairo, Egypt; or Casablanca, Morocco, we see jeans, hear familiar music, and read ads for many of the same products we use at home. Recall, too, from Global Map 2–1 that English is firmly established as the preferred second language in most parts of the world. Are we witnessing the birth of a single global culture?

Societies around the world now have more contact with one another than ever before, thanks to the flow of goods, information, and people:

1. **Global economy: The flow of goods.** International commerce is at an all-time high. The global economy has spread many consumer goods (from cars and TV shows to music and fashion) throughout the world.

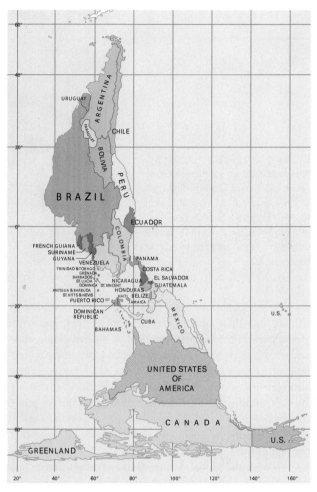

FIGURE 2–4   The View from "Down Under"

North America should be "up" and South America "down," or so we think. But because we live on a globe, "up" and "down" have no meaning at all. The reason this map of the Western Hemisphere looks wrong to us is not that it is geographically inaccurate; it simply violates our ethnocentric assumption that the United States should be "above" the rest of the Americas.

2. **Global communication: The flow of information.** The Internet and satellite-assisted communication enable people to experience events taking place thousands of miles away, often as they happen.

3. **Global migration: The flow of people.** Knowledge about the rest of the world motivates people to move where they imagine life will be better, and modern transportation technology, especially air travel, makes moving about faster than ever before. As a result, in most nations, significant numbers of current residents were born elsewhere (including some 34 million people in the United States—12 percent of the population).

Following the structural-functional approach, what do you make of the Amish practice of "barn raising," by which everyone in a community joins together to raise a family's new barn in a day? Why is such a ritual almost unknown in rural areas outside of Amish communities?

These global links make the cultures of the world more similar. But there are three important limitations to the global culture thesis. First, the flow of information, goods, and people is uneven. Generally speaking, urban areas (centers of commerce, communication, and people) have stronger ties to one another, and rural villages remain isolated. In addition, the greater economic and military power of North America and Western Europe means that nations in these regions influence the rest of the world more than the rest of the world influences them.

Second, the global culture thesis assumes that people everywhere are able to afford the new goods and services. As Chapter 9 ("Global Stratification") explains, desperate poverty in much of the world deprives people of even the basic necessities of a safe and secure life.

Third, although many cultural elements have spread throughout the world, people everywhere do not attach the same meanings to them. Do children in Tokyo draw the same lessons from reading the Harry Potter books as children in New York or London? Similarly, we enjoy foods from around the world while knowing little about the lives of the people who created them. In short, people everywhere look at the world through their own cultural lenses.

Theoretical Analysis of Culture

Sociologists investigate how culture helps us make sense of ourselves and the surrounding world. Here we will examine several macro-level theoretical approaches to understanding culture. A micro-level approach to the personal experience of culture, which emphasizes how individuals not only conform to cultural patterns but create new patterns in their everyday lives, is the focus of Chapter 4 ("Social Interaction in Everyday Life").

THE FUNCTIONS OF CULTURE: STRUCTURAL-FUNCTIONAL ANALYSIS

The structural-functional approach explains culture as a complex strategy for meeting human needs. Drawing from the philosophical doctrine of *idealism,* this approach considers values to be the core of a culture (Parsons, 1966; R. M. Williams, 1970). In other words, cultural values direct our lives, give meaning to what we do, and bind people together. Countless other cultural traits have various functions that support the operation of society.

Structural-functional analysis helps us understand unfamiliar ways of life. Consider the Amish farmer in Ohio plowing hundreds of acres with a team of horses. His methods may violate the U.S. cultural value of efficiency, but from the Amish point of view, hard work functions to develop the discipline necessary for a devoutly religious way of life. Long days of working together not only make the Amish self-sufficient but also strengthen family ties and unify local communities.

Of course, Amish practices have dysfunctions as well. The hard work and strict religious discipline are too demanding for some, who end up leaving the community. Also, strong religious beliefs sometimes prevent compromise, and as a result, slight differences in religious practices have caused the Amish to divide into different communities (Kraybill, 1989; Kraybill & Olshan, 1994).

If cultures are strategies for meeting human needs, we would expect to find many common patterns around the world. **Cultural universals** are *traits that are part of every*

APPLYING THEORY

Culture

	Structural-Functional Approach	Social-Conflict Approach	Sociobiology Approach
What is the level of analysis?	Macro-level	Macro-level	Macro-level
What is culture?	Culture is a system of behavior by which members of societies cooperate to meet their needs.	Culture is a system that benefits some people and disadvantages others.	Culture is a system of behavior that is partly shaped by human biology.
What is the foundation of culture?	Cultural patterns are rooted in a society's core values and beliefs.	Cultural patterns are rooted in a society's system of economic production.	Cultural patterns are rooted in humanity's biological evolution.
What core questions does the approach ask?	How does a cultural pattern help society operate? What cultural patterns are found in all societies?	How does a cultural pattern benefit some people and harm others? How does a cultural pattern support social inequality?	How does a cultural pattern help a species adapt to its environment?

known culture. Comparing hundreds of cultures, George Murdock (1945) identified dozens of cultural universals. One common element is the family, which functions everywhere to control sexual reproduction and to oversee the care of children. Funeral rites, too, are found everywhere because all human communities cope with the reality of death. Jokes are another cultural universal, serving as a safe means of releasing social tensions.

CRITICAL REVIEW The strength of structural-functional analysis lies in showing how culture operates to meet human needs. Yet by emphasizing a society's dominant cultural patterns, this approach largely ignores cultural diversity. Also, because this approach emphasizes cultural stability, it downplays the importance of change. In short, cultural systems are neither as stable nor a matter of as much agreement as structural-functional analysis leads us to believe. The Applying Theory table summarizes this theoretical approach's main lessons about culture.

✔ YOUR LEARNING In the United States, what are some of the functions of sports, July Fourth celebrations, and county fairs?

INEQUALITY AND CULTURE: SOCIAL-CONFLICT ANALYSIS

The social-conflict approach draws attention to the link between culture and inequality. From this point of view, any cultural trait benefits some members of society at the expense of others.

Why do certain values dominate a society in the first place? Many conflict theorists, especially Marxists, argue that culture is shaped by a society's system of economic production. Social-conflict theory, then, is rooted in the philosophical doctrine of *materialism,* which holds that a society's system of material production (such as our own capitalist economy) has a powerful effect on the rest of a culture. This materialist approach contrasts with the idealistic leanings of structural-functionalism.

Social-conflict analysis ties our cultural values of competitiveness and material success to our country's capitalist economy, which serves the interests of the nation's wealthy elite. The culture of capitalism teaches us that rich and powerful people work harder or longer than others and therefore deserve their wealth and privileges; it also encourages us to view capitalism as "natural," discouraging us from trying to reduce economic inequality.

Eventually, however, the strains of inequality erupt into movements for social change. Two examples are the civil rights movement and the women's movement. Both sought greater equality, and both encountered opposition from defenders of the status quo.

CRITICAL REVIEW The social-conflict approach suggests that cultural systems do not address human needs equally, allowing some people to dominate others. This inequality in turn generates pressure toward change.

Using an evolutionary perspective, sociobiologists explain that different reproductive strategies give rise to a double standard: Men treat women as sexual objects more than women treat men that way. While this may be so, many sociologists counter that behavior—such as that shown in Ruth Orkin's photograph, *American Girl in Italy*—is more correctly understood as resulting from a culture of male domination.

Copyright 1952, 1980 Ruth Orkin.

Yet by stressing the divisiveness of culture, this approach understates ways in which cultural patterns integrate members of a society. Thus we should consider both social-conflict and structural-functional insights for a fuller understanding of culture.

✓ YOUR LEARNING How does a social-conflict analysis of college fraternities and sororities differ from a structural-functional analysis?

EVOLUTION AND CULTURE: SOCIOBIOLOGY

We know that culture is a human creation, but does human biology influence how this process unfolds? A third theoretical approach, standing with one leg in biology and the other in sociology, is **sociobiology**, *a theoretical approach that explores ways in which human biology affects how we create culture.*

Sociobiology rests on the theory of evolution proposed by Charles Darwin in his book *On the Origin of Species* (1859). Darwin asserted that living organisms change over long periods of time as a result of *natural selection,* a matter of four simple principles. First, all living things live to reproduce themselves. Second, the blueprint for reproduction is in the genes, the basic units of life that carry traits of one generation into the next. Third, some random variation in genes allows each species to "try out" new life patterns in a particular environment. This variation enables some organisms to survive better than others and to pass on their advantageous genes to their offspring. Fourth and finally, over thousands of generations, the genes that promote reproduction survive and become dominant. In this way, as

biologists say, a species *adapts* to its environment, and dominant traits emerge as the "nature" of the organism.

Sociobiologists claim that the large number of cultural universals reflects the fact that all humans are members of a single biological species. It is our common biology that underlies, for example, the apparently universal "double standard." As the sex researcher Alfred Kinsey put it, "Among all people everywhere in the world, the male is more likely than the female to desire sex with a variety of partners" (quoted in Barash, 1981:49). But why?

We all know that a child results from joining a woman's egg with a man's sperm. But the biological significance of a single sperm is very different from that of a single egg. For healthy men, sperm is a "renewable resource" produced by the testes throughout most of the life course. A man releases hundreds of millions of sperm in a single ejaculation—technically, enough to fertilize every woman in North America (Barash, 1981:47). A newborn girl's ovaries, however, contain her entire lifetime supply of follicles, or immature eggs. A woman releases a single egg cell from the ovaries each month. So although men are biologically capable of fathering thousands of offspring, a woman is able to bear a relatively small number of children.

Given this biological difference, men reproduce their genes most efficiently by engaging in sex readily and often. But women look at reproduction differently. Each of a woman's pregnancies demands that she carry the child, give birth, and provide care for some time afterward. Efficient reproduction on the part of the woman therefore depends on selecting a man whose qualities (beginning with the likelihood that he will simply stay around) will contribute to her child's survival and, later, successful reproduction.

The United States and Canada: Are They Culturally Different?

The United States and Canada are two of the largest high-income nations in the world, and they share a common border of about 4,000 miles. But do the United States and Canada share the same culture?

One important point to make right away is that both nations are *multicultural*. Not only do both countries have hundreds of Native American societies, but immigration has brought people from all over the world to both the United States and Canada. In both countries, most early immigrants came from Europe, but in recent years, most immigrants have come from nations in Asia and Latin America. The Canadian city of Vancouver, for example, has a Chinese community about the same size as the Latino community in Los Angeles.

Canada differs from the United States in one important respect—historically, Canada has had *two* dominant cultures: French (about 25 percent of the population) and British (roughly 40 percent). People of French ancestry are a large majority in the province of Quebec (where French is the official language) and a large minority in New Brunswick (which is officially bilingual).

Are the dominant values of Canada much the same as those we have described for the United States? Seymour Martin Lipset (1985) finds that they differ to some degree. The United States declared its independence from Great Britain in 1776; Canada did not formally separate from Great Britain until 1982. For this reason, Lipset concludes, the dominant culture of Canada lies between the culture of the United States and that of Great Britain.

The culture of the United States is more individualistic, and Canada's is more collective. In the United States, individualism is seen in the historical importance of the cowboy, a self-sufficient loner, and even outlaws such as Jesse James and Billy the Kid are regarded as heroes because they challenged authority. In Canada, it is the Mountie—Canada's well-known police officer on horseback—who is looked on with great respect.

Politically, people in the United States tend to think that individuals ought to do things for themselves. In Canada, much as in Great Britain, there is a strong sense that government should look after the interests of everyone. This is one reason that Canada has a much broader social welfare system (including universal health care) than the United States (the only high-income nation without such a program). It also helps explain the fact that about half of all U.S. households own one or more guns and why the idea that individuals are entitled to own a gun, although controversial, is widespread. In Canada, by contrast, few households have guns, and government greatly restricts gun ownership, as in Great Britain.

WHAT DO YOU THINK?

1. Why do you think some Canadians feel that their way of life is overshadowed by that of the United States?

2. Ask your friends to name the capital city of Canada. Are you surprised by how few know the answer? Why or why not?

3. Why do many people in the United States not know very much about either Canada or Mexico, countries with which we share long borders?

Who members of a society celebrate as heroic is a good indication of people's cultural values. In the United States, outlaws such as Jesse James (and, later, Bonnie and Clyde) were regarded as heroes because they represented the strength of the individual standing up against authority. In Canada, by contrast, people have always looked up to the Mountie, who symbolizes society's authority over the individual.

The double standard certainly involves more than biology and is tangled up with the historical domination of women by men. But sociobiology suggests that this cultural pattern, like many others, has an underlying "bio-logic." Simply put, the double standard exists around the world because women and men everywhere tend toward distinctive reproductive strategies.

CRITICAL REVIEW Sociobiology provides intriguing insights into the biological roots of some cultural patterns. But this approach remains controversial for two reasons.

First, some critics fear that sociobiology may revive the biological arguments of a century ago that claimed the superiority of one race or sex. But defenders counter that sociobiology rejects the past pseudoscience of racial and gender superiority. In fact, they say, sociobiology unites all humanity because all people share a single evolutionary history. Sociobiology does assert that men and women differ biologically in some ways that culture cannot easily overcome. But far from claiming that males are somehow more important than females, sociobiology emphasizes that both sexes are vital to human survival.

Second, sociobiologists have little evidence to support their theories. Research to date suggests that biological forces do not *determine* human behavior in any rigid sense. Rather, humans *learn* behavior within a culture. The contribution of sociobiology, then, lies in explaining why some cultural patterns are more common and seem easier to learn than others (Barash, 1981).

✔ **YOUR LEARNING** Explain the role of human biology in making some cultural patterns, such as sibling rivalry, widespread.

Because any analysis of culture requires a broad focus on the workings of society, the three approaches discussed in this chapter are macro-level in scope. The symbolic-interaction approach, with its micro-level focus on people's behavior in specific situations, will be explored in Chapter 4.

Culture and Human Freedom

This entire chapter leads us to ask an important question: To what extent are human beings, as cultural creatures, free? Does culture bind us to each other and to the past? Or does it enhance our capacity for individual thought and independent choice?

As symbolic creatures, humans cannot live without culture. But the capacity for culture does have some drawbacks. We may be the only animals who name ourselves, but living in a symbolic world means that we are also the only creatures who experience alienation. In addition, culture is largely a matter of habit, which limits our choices and drives us to repeat troubling patterns, such as racial prejudice and sex discrimination, in each new generation.

Our society's emphasis on competitive achievement urges us toward excellence, yet this same pattern also isolates us from one another. Material things comfort us in some ways but divert us from the security and satisfaction that come from close relationships and spiritual strength.

For better and worse, human beings are cultural creatures, just as ants and bees are prisoners of their biology. But there is a crucial difference. Biological instincts create a ready-made world; culture forces us to choose as we make and remake a world for ourselves. No better evidence of this freedom exists than the cultural diversity of our own society and the even greater human diversity around the world.

Learning about this cultural diversity is one goal shared by sociologists. The Thinking Globally box on page 63 offers some contrasts between the cultures of the United States and Canada. Wherever we may live, the better we understand the workings of the surrounding culture, the better prepared we will be to use the freedom it offers us.

◖ APPLYING SOCIOLOGY IN EVERYDAY LIFE

1. New words are created all the time. What was going on in the United States that helps explain the creation of the following new words (Herzog, 2004): *sweatshop* (1892); *motel* (1925); *supermarket* (1933); *teenager* (1938); *workaholic* (1971); *couch potato* (1976); and *soccer mom* (1996)?

2. Find someone on campus who has lived in another country, and ask how the culture of that society differs from the way of life here. Look for ways in which the other person sees U.S. culture differently from people who have lived here all their lives.

3. Watch an animated Disney film such as *Finding Nemo, The Lion King, The Little Mermaid, Aladdin,* or *Pocahontas.* One reason for the popularity of these films is that they all share cultural themes. Using the list of key values of U.S. culture on page 48 as a guide, what makes the film you selected especially "American"?

MAKING THE GRADE

CHAPTER 2 Culture

WHAT IS CULTURE?

| Culture is a **WAY OF LIFE**.
• Culture is shared by members of a society.
• Culture shapes how we act, think, and feel.

pp 40–42 | Culture is a **HUMAN TRAIT**. Although several species display limited capacity for culture, only human beings rely on culture for survival.

p 42 | Culture is a **PRODUCT OF EVOLUTION**. As the human brain evolved, culture replaced biological instincts as our species' primary strategy for survival.

pp 42–44 |

culture (p. 40) the ways of thinking, the ways of acting, and the material objects that together form a people's way of life

society (p. 40) people who interact in a defined territory and share a culture

culture shock (p. 41) personal disorientation when experiencing an unfamiliar way of life

 Culture shock occurs when we enter an unfamiliar culture and are not able to "read" meaning in our new surroundings (pp 41-43).

 We create culture shock for others when we act in ways they do not understand (pp 41-43).

THE ELEMENTS OF CULTURE

| Culture relies on **SYMBOLS** in the form of words, gestures, and actions to express meaning.

pp 44–45 | **LANGUAGE** is the symbolic system by which one generation transmits culture to the next.

pp 46–47 |

symbol (p. 44) anything that carries a particular meaning recognized by people who share a culture

language (p. 46) a system of symbols that allows people to communicate with one another

cultural transmission (p. 46) the process by which one generation passes culture to the next

Sapir-Whorf thesis (p. 46) the idea that people see and understand the world through the cultural lens of language

| **VALUES** are abstract standards of what *ought to be* (for example, equality of opportunity).
BELIEFS are specific statements that people who share a culture hold to be true (for example, "A qualified woman could be elected president.")

pp 46, 48–49 | **NORMS**, which guide human behavior, are of two types:
• *mores* (for example, sexual taboos), which have great moral significance
• *folkways* (for example, greetings or dining etiquette), which are matters of everyday politeness

p 50 |

values (p. 46) culturally defined standards that people use to decide what is desirable, good, and beautiful and that serve as broad guidelines for social living

beliefs (p. 46) specific statements that people hold to be true

norms (p. 50) rules and expectations by which a society guides the behavior of its members

mores (p. 50) norms that are widely observed and have great moral significance

folkways (p. 50) norms for routine or casual interaction

 Values and norms reflect ideal culture, which differs from real culture (p 50).

TECHNOLOGY AND CULTURE

| **CULTURE** is shaped by **TECHNOLOGY**. We understand technological development in terms of stages of **SOCIOCULTURAL EVOLUTION**:
• hunting and gathering
• horticulture and pastoralism
• agriculture
• industry
• postindustrial information technology

pp 50–52 |

technology (p. 50) knowledge that people use to make a way of life in their surroundings

hunting and gathering (p. 50) the use of simple tools to hunt animals and gather vegetation for food

horticulture (p. 51) the use of hand tools to raise crops

pastoralism (p. 51) the domestication of animals

agriculture (p. 51) large-scale cultivation using plows harnessed to animals or machines

industry (p. 52) the production of goods using advanced sources of energy to drive large machinery

MAKING THE GRADE

CONTINUED...

V I S U A L   S U M M A R Y

CULTURAL DIVERSITY

We live in a **CULTURALLY DIVERSE SOCIETY**.

- This diversity is due to our history of immigration.
- Diversity reflects regional differences.
- Diversity reflects differences in social class that set off high culture (available only to elites) and popular culture (available to average people).

pp 52–53

A number of values are central to our way of life. But cultural patterns are not the same throughout our society.

- **SUBCULTURE** is based on differences in interests as well as life experiences.
- **MULTICULTURALISM** is an effort to enhance appreciation of cultural diversity.
- **COUNTERCULTURE** is strongly at odds with conventional ways of life.

pp 53–57

How does culture change?

- Cultural change results from **INVENTION**, **DISCOVERY**, and **DIFFUSION**.
- **CULTURAL LAG** results when some parts of a cultural system change faster than others.

p 57

How do we understand cultural differences?

- **ETHNOCENTRISM** links people to their society but can cause misunderstanding and conflict between societies.
- **CULTURAL RELATIVISM** is increasingly important as people of the world come into more and more contact with each other.

pp 58–59

 Global cultural patterns result from the worldwide flow of goods, information, and people (pp 59–60).

high culture (p. 52) cultural patterns that distinguish a society's elite

popular culture (p. 52) cultural patterns that are widespread among a society's population

subculture (p. 53) cultural patterns that set apart some segment of a society's population

multiculturalism (p. 55) a perspective recognizing the cultural diversity of the United States and promoting respect and equal standing for all cultural traditions

Eurocentrism (p. 55) the dominance of European (especially English) cultural patterns

Afrocentrism (p. 56) emphasizing and promoting African cultural patterns

counterculture (p. 56) cultural patterns that strongly oppose those widely accepted within a society

cultural integration (p. 57) the close relationships among various elements of a cultural system

cultural lag (p. 57) the fact that some cultural elements change more quickly than others, disrupting a cultural system

ethnocentrism (p. 58) the practice of judging another culture by the standards of one's own culture

cultural relativism (p. 58) the practice of judging a culture by its own standards

THEORETICAL ANALYSIS OF CULTURE

The **STRUCTURAL-FUNCTIONAL APPROACH** views culture as a relatively stable system built on core values. All cultural patterns play some part in the ongoing operation of society.

pp 60–61

The **SOCIAL-CONFLICT APPROACH** sees culture as a dynamic arena of inequality and conflict. Cultural patterns benefit some categories of people more than others.

pp 61–62

SOCIOBIOLOGY explores how the long history of evolution has shaped patterns of culture in today's world.

pp 62, 64

cultural universals (p. 60) traits that are part of every known culture

sociobiology (p. 62) a theoretical approach that explores ways in which human biology affects how we create culture

See the Applying Theory table on page 61.

Culture can limit the choices we make. Yet as cultural creatures, we have the capacity to shape and reshape our world to meet our needs and pursue our dreams (p 64).

MAKING THE GRADE
Sample Test Questions
CHAPTER 2

These questions are similar to those found in the test bank that accompanies this textbook.

MULTIPLE-CHOICE QUESTIONS

1. Of all the world's countries, the United States is the most
   a. multicultural.
   b. culturally uniform.
   c. slowly changing.
   d. resistant to cultural diversity.

2. Ideas created by members of a society are part of
   a. high culture.
   b. material culture.
   c. norms.
   d. nonmaterial culture.

3. Sociologists define a symbol as
   a. any gesture that divides a population.
   b. any element of material culture.
   c. anything that has meaning to people who share a culture.
   d. any pattern that causes culture shock.

4. U.S. culture holds a strong belief in
   a. the traditions of the past.
   b. individuality.
   c. equality of condition for all.
   d. All of the above are correct.

5. Cheating on a final examination is an example of violating campus
   a. folkways.
   b. symbols.
   c. mores.
   d. high culture.

6. Which of the following is a description of ethnocentrism?
   a. taking pride in your ethnicity
   b. judging another culture using the standards of your own culture
   c. seeing another culture as better than your own
   d. judging another culture by its own standards

7. The concept "subculture" refers to
   a. a part of the population lacking culture.
   b. elements of popular culture.
   c. people who embrace high culture.
   d. cultural patterns that set apart a segment of a society's population.

8. Which region of the United States has the largest share of people who speak a language other than English at home?
   a. the Southwest
   b. the Northeast
   c. the Northwest
   d. the South

9. In human history, the "dawn of civilization" took place with the development of
   a. hunting and gathering.
   b. pastoralism.
   c. industry.
   d. agriculture.

10. Which theoretical approach focuses on the link between culture and social inequality?
    a. the structural-functional approach
    b. the social-conflict approach
    c. the symbolic-interaction approach
    d. the sociobiology approach

ANSWERS: 1 (a); 2 (d); 3 (c); 4 (b); 5 (c); 6 (b); 7 (d); 8 (a); 9 (d); 10 (b).

ESSAY QUESTIONS

1. In the United States, hot dogs, hamburgers, French fries, and ice cream have long been considered national favorites. What cultural patterns help explain the love of these kinds of foods?

2. From what you have learned in this chapter, do you think that a global culture is emerging? Do you think the idea of global culture is positive or negative? Explain your answer.

Socialization is the process by which older members of a society teach their way of life to the young. In a traditional region of South Africa, this father teaches his four-year-old son to hunt with a bow and arrow.

CHAPTER 3

Socialization: From Infancy to Old Age

WHY is social experience the key to human personality?

WHAT familiar social settings have special importance to how we live and grow?

HOW do our experiences change over the life course?

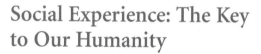

On a cold winter day in 1938, a social worker walked quickly to the door of a rural Pennsylvania farmhouse. Investigating a case of possible child abuse, the social worker entered the house and soon discovered a five-year-old girl hidden in a second-floor storage room. The child, whose name was Anna, was wedged into an old chair with her arms tied above her head so that she couldn't move. She was wearing filthy clothes, and her arms and legs were as thin as matchsticks (K. Davis, 1940).

Anna's situation can only be described as tragic. She was born in 1932 to an unmarried and mentally impaired woman of twenty-six who lived with her strict father. Angry about his daughter's "illegitimate" motherhood, the grandfather did not even want the child in his house, so for the first six months of her life, Anna was passed among various welfare agencies. But her mother could not afford to pay for her care, and Anna returned to the hostile home of her grandfather.

To lessen the grandfather's anger, Anna's mother kept the child in the storage room and gave her just enough milk to keep her alive. There she stayed—day after day, month after month, with almost no human contact—for five long years.

Learning about the discovery of Anna, sociologist Kingsley Davis immediately went to see the child. He found her with local officials at a county home. Davis was stunned by the emaciated girl, who could not laugh, speak, or even smile. Anna was completely unresponsive, as if alone in an empty world.

Social Experience: The Key to Our Humanity

Socialization is so basic to human development that we sometimes overlook its importance. But in this terrible case of an isolated child, we can see what humans would be like without social contact. Although physically alive, Anna hardly seems human. We can see that without social experience, a child is not able to act or communicate in a meaningful way and seems to be as much an object as a person.

Sociologists use the term **socialization** to refer to *the lifelong social experience by which people develop their human potential and learn culture.* Unlike other living species, whose behavior is biologically set, humans need social experience to learn their culture and to survive. Social experience is also the basis of **personality,** *a person's fairly consistent patterns of acting, thinking, and feeling.* We build a personality by internalizing—taking in—our surroundings. But without social experience, as Anna's case shows, personality hardly develops at all.

HUMAN DEVELOPMENT: NATURE AND NURTURE

Anna's case makes clear the fact that humans depend on others to provide the care needed not only for physical growth but also for personality to develop. A century ago, however, people mistakenly believed that humans were born with instincts that determined their personality and behavior.

The Biological Sciences: The Role of Nature

Charles Darwin's groundbreaking study of evolution, described in Chapter 2 ("Culture"), led people to think that human behavior was instinctive, simply our "nature." Such ideas led to claims that the U.S. economic system reflects "instinctive human competitiveness," that some people are "born criminals," or that women are "naturally" emotional and men are "naturally" more rational (Witkin-Lanoil, 1984).

People trying to understand cultural diversity also misunderstood Darwin's thinking. Centuries of world exploration had taught Western Europeans that people around the world behaved quite differently from society to society. But Europeans linked these differences to biology rather than culture. It was an easy, although incorrect and very damaging, step to claim that members of technologically simple societies were biologically less evolved and therefore "less human." This ethnocentric view helped justify colonialism: Why not take advantage of others if they seem not to be human in the same way that you are?

The Social Sciences: The Role of Nurture

In the twentieth century, biological explanations of human behavior came under fire. The psychologist John B. Watson (1878–1958) developed a theory called *behaviorism,* which held that behavior is not instinctive but learned. Thus people everywhere are equally human, differing only in their cultural patterns. In short, Watson rooted human behavior not in nature but in *nurture.*

Today, social scientists are cautious about describing *any* human behavior as instinctive. This does not mean that biology plays no part in human behavior. Human life, after all, depends on the functioning of the body. We also know that children often share biological traits (such as height and hair color) with their parents and that heredity plays a part in intelligence, musical and artistic talent, and personality (such as how you deal with frustration). However, whether you develop your inherited potential depends on how you are raised. For example, unless children use their brains early in life, the brain does not fully develop (Goldsmith, 1983; Begley, 1995).

Without denying the importance of nature, then, nurture matters more in shaping human behavior. More precisely, *nurture is our nature.*

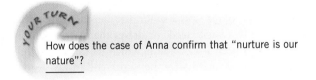

How does the case of Anna confirm that "nurture is our nature"?

SOCIAL ISOLATION

As the story of Anna shows, cutting people off from the social world is very harmful. For ethical reasons, researchers can never place human beings in total isolation to study what happens. But in the past, they have studied the effects of social isolation on nonhuman primates.

Research with Monkeys

In a classic study, the psychologists Harry and Margaret Harlow (1962) placed rhesus monkeys—whose behavior is

in some ways surprisingly similar to human behavior—in various conditions of social isolation. They found that complete isolation (with adequate nutrition) for even six months seriously disturbed the monkeys' development. When returned to their group, these monkeys were passive, anxious, and fearful.

The Harlows then placed infant rhesus monkeys in cages with an artificial "mother" made of wire mesh with a wooden head and the nipple of a feeding tube where the breast would be. These monkeys also survived but were unable to interact with others when placed in a group.

But monkeys in a third category, isolated with an artificial "mother" covered with soft terry cloth, did better. Each of these monkeys would cling to the "mother" closely. Because these monkeys showed less developmental damage than the earlier groups, the Harlows concluded that the monkeys benefited from this closeness. The experiment confirmed how important it is that adults cradle infants affectionately.

Finally, the Harlows discovered that infant monkeys could recover from as much as three months of isolation. But after about six months, isolation caused irreversible emotional and behavioral damage.

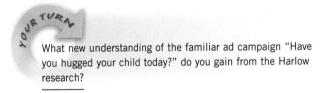

What new understanding of the familiar ad campaign "Have you hugged your child today?" do you gain from the Harlow research?

Studies of Isolated Children

The rest of Anna's story squares with the Harlows' findings. After her discovery, Anna received extensive social contact and soon showed improvement. When Kingsley Davis (1940) revisited her after ten days, he found her more alert and even smiling (perhaps for the first time in her life!). Over the next year, Anna made slow but steady progress, showing more interest in other people and gradually learning to walk. After a year and a half, she could feed herself and play with toys.

But as the Harlows might have predicted, Anna's five years of social isolation had caused permanent damage. At age eight, her mental development was still less than that of a two-year-old. Not until she was almost ten did she begin to use words. Because Anna's mother was mentally retarded, perhaps Anna was similarly challenged. The riddle was never solved, however, because Anna died at age ten of a blood disorder, possibly related to the years of abuse she suffered (K. Davis, 1940, 1947).

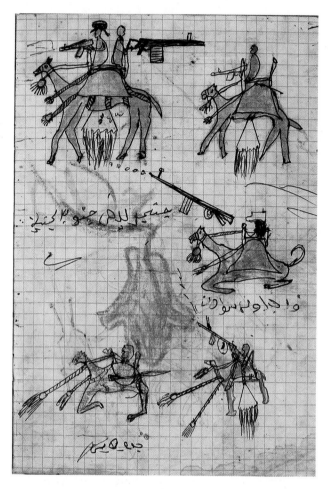

The personalities we develop depend largely on the environment in which we live. When a child's world is shredded by violence, the damage can be profound and lasting. This drawing was made by thirteen-year-old Rahid in the Darfur region of Sudan, where armed militia have killed more than 150,000 people since 2003. What are the likely effects of such experiences on a young person's self-confidence and capacity to form trusting ties with others?

Courtesy of Dr. Annie Sparrow, Human Rights Watch

A more recent case of childhood isolation involves a California girl abused by her parents (Curtiss, 1977; Rymer, 1994). From the time she was two, Genie was tied to a potty chair in a dark garage. In 1970, when she was rescued at age thirteen, Genie weighed only fifty-nine pounds and had the mental development of a one-year-old. With intensive treatment, she became physically healthy, but her language ability remains that of a young child.

Learn more about the life of Genie at http://www.pbs.org/wgbh/nova/transcripts/2112gchild.html

Today, Genie lives in a home for developmentally disabled adults.

CRITICAL REVIEW All evidence points to the crucial role of social experience in forming personality. Human beings can sometimes recover from abuse and short-term isolation. But there is a point—exactly when is unclear from the small number of cases studied—at which isolation in infancy causes permanent developmental damage.

 YOUR LEARNING What do studies of isolated children teach us about the importance of social experience?

Understanding Socialization

Socialization is a complex, lifelong process. The following sections highlight the work of six researchers who made lasting contributions to our understanding of human development.

SIGMUND FREUD'S ELEMENTS OF PERSONALITY

Sigmund Freud (1856–1939) lived in Vienna at a time when most Europeans considered human behavior biologically fixed. Trained as a physician, Freud turned to the study of personality and eventually developed the celebrated theory of psychoanalysis.

Visit the Sigmund Freud Museum of Vienna, Austria, at http://www.freud-museum.at/

Basic Human Needs

Freud claimed that biology plays a major part in human development, although not in terms of specific instincts, as is the case in other species. Rather, he theorized that humans have two basic needs or drives that are present at birth. First is a need for bonding, which he called the "life instinct," or *eros* (named after the Greek god of love). Second, we share an aggressive drive he called the "death instinct," or *thanatos* (the Greek word for "death"). These opposing forces, operating at an unconscious level, generate deep inner tension.

Freud's Model of Personality

Freud combined basic human drives and the influence of society into a model of personality with three parts: id, ego, and superego. The **id** (Latin for "it") represents *the human being's basic drives,* which are unconscious and demand immediate satisfaction. Rooted in biology, the id is present at birth, making a newborn a bundle of demands for attention, touching, and food. But society opposes the self-centered id, which is why one of the first words a child usually learns is "no."

To avoid frustration, a child must learn to approach the world realistically. This is done through the **ego** (Latin for "I"), which is *a person's conscious efforts to balance innate pleasure-seeking drives with the demands of society.* The ego arises as we gain awareness of our distinct existence and face the fact that we cannot have everything we want.

In the human personality, **superego** (Latin for "above or beyond the ego") is *the cultural values and norms internalized by an individual.* The superego operates as our conscience, telling us *why* we cannot have everything we want. The superego begins to form as a child becomes aware of parental demands and matures as the child comes to understand that everyone's behavior should take account of cultural norms.

Personality Development

To the id-centered child, the world is a jumble of physical sensations that bring either pleasure or pain. As the superego develops, however, the child learns the moral concepts of right and wrong. Initially, in other words, children can feel good only in a physical way (as when being held and cuddled), but after three or four years, they feel good or bad according to how they judge their behavior against cultural norms (doing "the right thing").

The id and the superego remain in conflict, but in a well-adjusted person, the ego manages these opposing forces. If conflicts are not resolved during childhood, they may surface as personality disorders later on.

Culture, in the form of superego, *represses* selfish demands, forcing people to look beyond their own desires. Often the competing demands of self and society result in a compromise Freud called *sublimation,* which changes selfish drives into socially acceptable behavior. For example, marriage makes the satisfaction of sexual urges socially acceptable, and competitive sports are an outlet for aggression.

CRITICAL REVIEW In Freud's time, few people were ready to accept sex as a basic drive. More recent critics have charged that Freud's work presents humans in male terms and devalues women (Donovan & Littenberg, 1982). Freud's theories are also difficult to test scientifically. But Freud influenced everyone who later studied human personality. Of special importance to sociology are his ideas that we internalize social norms and that childhood experiences have a lasting impact on our personalities.

YOUR LEARNING What are the three elements in Freud's model of personality? What does each mean?

JEAN PIAGET'S THEORY OF COGNITIVE DEVELOPMENT

The Swiss psychologist Jean Piaget (1896–1980) studied human *cognition:* how people think and understand. As Piaget watched his own three children grow, he wondered not only what they knew but how they made sense of the world; he went on to identify four stages of cognitive development.

 To learn more about Piaget and his work, visit http://www.piaget.org

The Sensorimotor Stage

Stage one is the **sensorimotor stage,** *the level of human development at which individuals experience the world only through their senses.* For about the first two years of life, infants know the world only by touching, tasting, smelling, looking, and listening. "Knowing" to very young children amounts to what their senses tell them.

The Preoperational Stage

About age two, children enter the **preoperational stage,** *the level of human development at which individuals first use language and other symbols.* Now children begin to think about the world using their imagination. But "pre-op" children between about two and six attach meanings only to specific experiences and objects. They can identify a toy as their "favorite" but cannot describe what *types* of toys they like.

Lacking abstract concepts, a child cannot judge size, weight, or volume. In one of his best-known experiments, Piaget placed two identical glasses containing equal amounts of water on a table. He asked several five- and six-year-olds whether the amount in each was the same. They nodded that it was. The children then watched Piaget take one of the glasses and pour its contents into a taller, narrower glass, raising the level of the water. He asked again whether each glass held the same amount. The typical five- or six-year-old now insisted that the taller glass held more water. By about age seven, children are able to think more abstractly and realize that the amount of water stays the same.

The Concrete Operational Stage

Next comes the **concrete operational stage,** *the level of human development at which individuals first see causal connections in their surroundings.* Between the ages of seven and eleven, children focus on how and why things happen. In addition, they attach more than one symbol to an event or object. If, for example, you say to a child of five, "Today is Wednesday," she might respond, "No, it's my birthday!"

indicating that she can use just one symbol at a time. But an older child at the concrete operational stage would be able to respond, "Yes, and today is also my birthday."

The Formal Operational Stage

The last step in Piaget's model is the **formal operational stage,** *the level of human development at which individuals think abstractly and critically.* At about age twelve, young people begin to reason in the abstract rather than think only of concrete situations. For example, if you ask a child of seven, "What would you like to be when you grow up?" you will get a concrete response such as "a teacher." But most teenagers can consider the question more abstractly and might respond, "I would like a job that helps others." As they gain the capacity for abstract thought, young people also learn to understand metaphors. Hearing the phrase "A penny for your thoughts" might lead a child to ask for a coin, but a teenager will recognize a gentle invitation to intimacy.

YOUR TURN

Using Piaget's concepts, can you explain why young children will reach for a nickel rather than a dime?

CRITICAL REVIEW Freud saw human beings passively torn by opposing forces of biology and culture. Piaget saw the mind as active and creative. He saw the ability to engage the world unfolding in stages as the result of both biological maturation and social experience.

But do people in all societies pass through all four of Piaget's stages? Living in a traditional society that changes slowly probably limits the capacity for abstract and critical thought. Even in the United States, perhaps 30 percent of people never reach the formal operational stage (Kohlberg & Gilligan, 1971).

✓ **YOUR LEARNING** What are Piaget's four stages of cognitive development? What does his research teach us about human development?

LAWRENCE KOHLBERG'S THEORY OF MORAL DEVELOPMENT

Lawrence Kohlberg (1981) built on Piaget's work to study *moral reasoning,* how people come to judge situations as right or wrong. Here again, development occurs in stages.

Young children who experience the world in terms of pain and pleasure (Piaget's sensorimotor stage) are at the *preconventional* level of moral development. At first, "rightness" amounts to "what feels good to me."

The *conventional* level, Kohlberg's second stage, appears by the teens (corresponding to Piaget's final, formal operational stage). At this point, young people lose some of their selfishness as they learn to define right and wrong in terms of what pleases parents and conforms to cultural norms.

In Kohlberg's final stage of moral development, the *postconventional* level, people move beyond their society's norms to consider abstract ethical principles. As they think about ideas such as liberty, freedom, or justice, they may argue that what is lawful still may not be right.

CRITICAL REVIEW Like the work of Piaget, Kohlberg's model explains moral development in terms of distinct stages. But whether this model applies to people in all societies remains unclear. Further, many people in the United States apparently never reach the postconventional level of moral reasoning, although why is still an open question.

Another problem with Kohlberg's research is that all his subjects were boys. He committed a common research error, described in Chapter 1 ("Sociology: Perspective, Theory, and Method"), by generalizing the results of male subjects to all people. This problem led a colleague, Carol Gilligan, to investigate how gender affects moral reasoning.

✓ **YOUR LEARNING** What are Kohlberg's three stages of moral development? What do they teach us about human development?

CAROL GILLIGAN'S THEORY OF GENDER AND MORAL DEVELOPMENT

Carol Gilligan (1982) set out to compare the moral development of girls and boys and concluded that the two sexes use different standards of rightness. Boys, she claims, have a *justice perspective,* relying on formal rules to define right and wrong. Girls, by contrast, have a *care and responsibility perspective,* judging a situation with an eye toward personal relationships and loyalties. For example, as boys see it, stealing is wrong because it breaks the law. Girls are more likely to wonder why someone would steal and to be sympathetic toward someone who steals, say, to feed a hungry child.

Kohlberg treats rule-based male reasoning as morally superior to the person-based female perspective. Gilligan notes that impersonal rules have long governed men's lives in the workplace, but personal relationships are more relevant to women's lives as mothers and caregivers. Why, then, Gilligan asks, should we set up male standards as the norms by which to judge everyone?

Childhood is a time to learn principles of right and wrong. According to Carol Gilligan, however, boys and girls define what is "right" in different ways. After reading about Gilligan's theory, can you suggest what these two might be arguing about?

CRITICAL REVIEW Gilligan's work sharpens our understanding of both human development and gender issues in research. Yet the question remains, does nature or nurture account for the differences between females and males? In Gilligan's view, cultural conditioning is at work, a view that finds support in other research. For example, Nancy Chodorow (1994) claims that children grow up in homes in which, typically, mothers do much more nurturing than fathers. As girls learn to identify with mothers, they become more concerned with care and responsibility to others. By contrast, boys become more like fathers, who are often away from the home, and they may develop more detached personalities and a greater concern for abstract rules. Perhaps the moral reasoning of females and males will become more similar as more women organize their lives around the workplace.

✔ **YOUR LEARNING** According to Gilligan, how do boys and girls differ in their approach to right and wrong?

GEORGE HERBERT MEAD'S THEORY OF THE SOCIAL SELF

George Herbert Mead (1863–1931) developed a theory of *social behaviorism* to explain how social experience develops an individual's personality (1962, orig. 1934).

The Self

Mead's central concept is the **self,** *the part of an individual's personality composed of self-awareness and self-image.*

Mead's genius lay in seeing the self as the product of social experience.

First, said Mead, *the self develops only with social experience.* The self is not part of the body and does not exist at birth. Mead rejected the idea that personality is guided by biological drives (as Freud asserted) or even biological maturation (as Piaget claimed). For Mead, self develops only as the individual interacts with others. Without interaction, as we see from cases of isolated children, the body grows, but no self emerges.

Second, Mead explained, *social experience is the exchange of symbols.* Only people use words, a wave of the hand, or a smile to create meaning. We can train a dog using reward and punishment, but the dog attaches no meaning to its actions. By contrast, human beings find meaning in action by imagining people's underlying intentions. In short, a dog responds to *what you do,* but a human responds to *what you have in mind* as you do it. You can train a dog to go to the hallway and bring back an umbrella. But without understanding intention, if the dog cannot find the umbrella, it is incapable of the *human* response: to look for a raincoat instead.

Third, Mead continues, *understanding intention requires imagining a situation from the other's point of view.* Using symbols, we imagine ourselves in another person's shoes and see ourselves as that person does. This capacity lets us anticipate how others will respond to us even before we act. A simple toss of a ball, for example, requires stepping outside yourself to imagine how the other person will catch your throw. All symbolic interaction, then, involves seeing ourselves as others see us, a process Mead called *taking the role of the other.*

The Looking-Glass Self

In effect, others are a mirror (which people used to call a "looking glass") in which we see ourselves. What we think of ourselves, then, depends on how we think others see us. For example, if we think others see us as clever, we will think of ourselves in the same way. But if we feel they think of us as clumsy, then that is how we will see ourselves. Charles Horton Cooley (1864–1929) used the phrase **looking-glass self** to mean *a self-image based on how we think others see us.*

The I and the Me

Mead's fourth point is that *by taking the role of another, we become self-aware.* Another way of saying this is that the self has two parts. One part of the self operates as subject, being active and spontaneous. Mead called the subjective side of the self the "I" (the subjective form of the personal pronoun). The other part of the self

 Mead is featured in the Gallery of Sociologists at http://www.TheSociologyPage.com

works as an object, the way we imagine others see us. Mead called the objective side of the self the "me" (the objective form of the personal pronoun). All social experience has both components: We initiate action (the I-phase, or subjective side, of the self), and we evaluate the action based on how others respond to us (the me-phase, or objective side, of the self).

Development of the Self

According to Mead, the key to developing the self is learning to take the role of the other. With limited social experience, infants can do this only through *imitation.* They mimic the behavior of other people without understanding the underlying intention, and so at this point, they have no self.

As children learn to use language and other symbols, the self emerges in the form of *play.* Play involves assuming roles modeled on **significant others,** *people, such as parents, who have special importance for socialization.* Playing "mommy" or "daddy" begins to teach children to imagine the world from a parent's point of view.

Gradually, children learn to take the roles of several others at once. This skill lets them move from simple play (say, playing catch) involving one other person to complex *games* (such as baseball) involving many others. By about age seven, most children have the social experience needed to engage in team sports.

Have you ever seen young children put on their parents' shoes, literally putting themselves "in the shoes" of another person? How does this help children learn to "take the role of the other"?

Figure 3–1 charts the progression from imitation to play to games. But there is a final stage in the development of the self. A game involves dealing with a limited number of other people in just one situation. Everyday life demands that we see ourselves in terms of cultural norms as *any* member of our society might. Mead used the term **generalized other** to refer to *widespread cultural norms and values we use as a reference in evaluating ourselves.*

As life goes on, the self continues to change along with our social experiences. But no matter how much the world shapes us, we always remain creative beings able to act back toward the world. Thus, Mead concluded, we play a key role in our own socialization.

CRITICAL REVIEW Mead's work explores the essence of social experience itself. In the symbolic interaction of human beings, he believed he had found the root of both self and society.

Mead's view is completely social, allowing no biological element at all. This is a problem for followers of Freud (who said our drives are rooted in the body) and Piaget (whose stages of development are tied to biological maturity).

Be careful not to confuse Mead's concepts of the I and the me with Freud's id and superego. For Freud, the id originates in our biology, but Mead rejected any biological element of self (although he never clearly spelled out the origin of the I). In addition, the id and the superego are locked in continual combat, but the I and the me work cooperatively together (Meltzer, 1978).

YOUR LEARNING Identify one important similarity between the theories of Mead and Piaget. What is one important difference?

ERIK H. ERIKSON'S EIGHT STAGES OF DEVELOPMENT

Although some analysts (including Freud) point to childhood as the crucial time when personality takes shape, Erik H. Erikson (1902–1994) took a broader view of socialization. He explained that we face challenges throughout the life course (1963, orig. 1950).

Stage 1: Infancy—the challenge of trust (versus mistrust). Between birth and about eighteen months,

The self is able simultaneously to take the role of:	*no one* (no ability to take the role of the other)	*one* other in *one* situation	*many* others in *one* situation	*many* others in *many* situations
when:	engaging in imitation	engaging in play	engaging in games	recognizing the generalized other

FIGURE 3–1 Building on Social Experience

George Herbert Mead described the development of the self as a process of gaining social experience. That is, the self develops as we expand our capacity to take the role of the other.

infants face the first of life's challenges: to gain a sense of trust that their world is a safe place. Family members play a key role in how any infant meets this challenge.

Stage 2: Toddlerhood—the challenge of autonomy (versus doubt and shame). The next challenge, up to age three, is to learn skills to cope with the world in a confident way. Failure to gain self-control leads children to doubt their abilities.

Stage 3: Preschool—the challenge of initiative (versus guilt). Four- and five-year-olds must learn to engage their surroundings—including people outside the family—or experience guilt at having failed to meet the expectations of parents and others.

Stage 4: Preadolescence—the challenge of industriousness (versus inferiority). Between ages six and thirteen, children enter school, make friends, and strike out on their own more and more. They either feel proud of their accomplishments or fear that they do not measure up.

Stage 5: Adolescence—the challenge of gaining identity (versus confusion). During the teen years, young people struggle to establish their own identity. In part, teens identify with others, but they also want to be unique. Almost all teens experience some confusion as they struggle to establish an identity.

Stage 6: Young adulthood—the challenge of intimacy (versus isolation). The challenge for young adults is to form and keep intimate relationships with others. Making close friends (and especially, falling in love) involves balancing the need to bond with the need to have a separate identity.

Stage 7: Middle adulthood—the challenge of making a difference (versus self-absorption). The challenge of middle age is to contribute to the lives of others in the family, at work, and in the larger world. Failing at this, people become self-centered, caught up in their own limited concerns.

Stage 8: Old age—the challenge of integrity (versus despair). Near the end of their lives, people hope to look back on what they have accomplished with a sense of integrity and satisfaction. For those who have been self-absorbed, old age brings only a sense of despair over missed opportunities.

CRITICAL REVIEW Erikson's theory views personality formation as a lifelong process, with success at one stage (say, an infant gaining trust) preparing us to meet the next challenge. However, not everyone faces these challenges in the exact order presented by Erikson. Nor is it clear that failure to meet a challenge at one stage of life means that a person is doomed to fail in life's later stages. A broader question, raised earlier in our discussion of Piaget's ideas, is whether people in other cultures and at other times in history would define a successful life in Erikson's terms.

In sum, Erikson's model points out how several factors, including the family and school, shape our personalities. In the next section, we take a closer look at these important agents of socialization.

✔ **YOUR LEARNING** In what ways does Erikson take a broader view of socialization than other thinkers presented in this chapter?

Agents of Socialization

Every social experience we have affects us in at least a small way. However, several familiar settings have special importance to the socialization process. Among them are the family, the school, the peer group, and the mass media.

THE FAMILY

The family affects socialization in many ways. For most people, the family may be the most important socializing agent of all.

Sociological research indicates that wealthy parents tend to encourage creativity in their children while poor parents tend to foster conformity. Although this general difference may be valid, parents at all class levels can and do provide loving support and guidance by simply involving themselves in their children's lives. Henry Ossawa Tanner's painting *The Banjo Lesson* stands as a lasting testament to this process.

Henry Ossawa Tanner, *The Banjo Lesson*, 1893. Oil on canvas. Hampton University Museum, Hampton, Virginia.

Nurture in Early Childhood

Responsibility for the care of infants, who are totally dependent on others, typically falls on parents and other family members. For several years—at least until children begin school—the family has the job of teaching children skills, values, and beliefs. Overall, research suggests, nothing is more likely to produce a happy, well-adjusted child than a loving family (Gibbs, 2001).

Not all family learning results from intentional teaching by parents. Children also learn from the type of environment adults create. Whether children learn to see themselves as strong or weak, smart or stupid, loved or sim-

ply tolerated—and as Erik Erikson suggests, whether they see the world as trustworthy or dangerous—depends largely on the quality of the surroundings provided by parents and other caregivers.

Race and Class

The family also gives children a social identity. In part, social identity involves race. Racial identity is complex because, as Chapter 11 ("Race and Ethnicity") explains, societies define race in various ways. In addition, in the 2000 U.S. census, more than 7 million people (about 2.5 percent) said they consider themselves to be in two or more racial categories. This number is rising, and 5 percent of all births in the United States are now recorded as interracial. National Map 3–1 shows where people who describe themselves as racially mixed live.

Social class position, like race, plays a large part in shaping a child's personality. Whether born into families of high or low social position, children gradually come to realize that their family's social standing affects how others see them and, in time, how they come to see themselves.

In addition, research shows that the class position of parents affects not just how much money parents have to spend on their children but also what parents expect of them (Ellison, Bartowski, & Segal, 1996). When people in the United States were asked to pick from a list of traits they thought most desirable in a child, those with lower-class standing favored obedience and conformity. Well-to-do people, by contrast, chose good judgment and creativity (NORC, 2005).

Why the difference? Melvin Kohn (1977) explains that people of lower social standing usually have only limited education and hold jobs that involve performing routine tasks under close supervision. Expecting that their children will grow up to take similar positions, they encourage obedience and may even use physical punishment such as spanking to get it. Because well-off parents generally have had more schooling, they usually have jobs that demand imagination and creativity, so they try to inspire the same qualities in their children. Consciously or not, all parents act in ways that encourage their children to follow in their footsteps.

Wealthier parents typically provide their children with an extensive program of leisure activities, including sports, vacation travel, and music lessons. These enrichment activities—far less available to children growing up in low-income families—represent important *cultural capital* that advances children's learning and creates a sense of confidence that they will be successful throughout their lives (Lareau, 2002).

SEEING OURSELVES

NATIONAL MAP 3–1
Racially Mixed People
across the United States

This map shows the distribution of people who described themselves as racially mixed in the 2000 census. How do you think growing up in an area with a high level of racially mixed people (such as Los Angeles or New York) would be different from growing up in an area with few such people (for example, the Plains States in the middle of the country)?

Source: U.S. Census Bureau (2001).

Number of People
Indicating Two or
More Races

- 50,000 to 469,800
- 10,000 to 49,999
- 5,000 to 9,999
- 1,000 to 4,999
- 100 to 999
- 0 to 99

THE SCHOOL

Schooling enlarges children's social world to include people with backgrounds different from their own. It is only as they encounter people who differ from themselves that children come to understand the importance of factors such as race and social class position. As they do, they are likely to cluster together in play groups made up of their own class, race, and gender.

Gender

Schools join with families in socializing children into gender roles. Studies show that at school, boys engage in more physical activities and spend more time outdoors, and girls are more likely to help teachers with various housekeeping chores. Boys also engage in more aggressive behavior in the classroom, where girls are typically quieter and better behaved (Lever, 1978; R. Best, 1983; Jordan & Cowan, 1995). Gender differences continue right through to college as women tend toward majoring in the arts or humanities and men lean toward economics, the physical sciences, and computing.

YOUR TURN

In what specific ways is life on your campus different for women and men?

What Children Learn

Schooling teaches children a wide range of knowledge and skills. Schools also informally teach many other things, which together might be called the *hidden curriculum.* Activities such as spelling bees, for example, teach children not only how to spell but also how society divides the population into "winners" and "losers." Sports help students develop their strength and skills and also teach children important lessons in cooperation and competition.

For most children, school is also their first experience with bureaucracy. The school day is based on impersonal rules and a strict time schedule. Not surprisingly, these are also the traits of the large organizations that will employ them later in life.

THE PEER GROUP

By the time they enter school, children have also discovered the **peer group,** *a social group whose members have interests, social position, and age in common.* Unlike the family and the school, the peer group allows children to escape the direct supervision of adults. Among their peers, children learn how to form relationships on their own. Peer groups also offer the chance to discuss interests that adults may not share (such as clothes and popular music) or permit (such as drugs and sex).

It is not surprising, then, that parents express concern about who their children's friends are. In a rapidly changing society, peer groups have great influence, and the attitudes of young and old may be different enough to form a "generation gap." The importance of peer groups typically peaks during adolescence, when young people begin to break away from their families and think of themselves as adults.

Even during adolescence, however, parental influence on children remains strong. Peers may affect short-term

GLOBAL SNAPSHOT

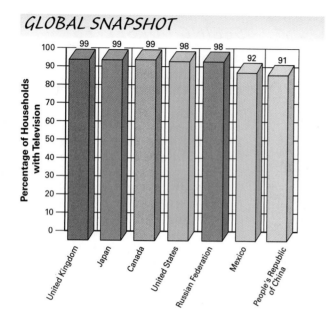

FIGURE 3-2 Television Ownership in Global Perspective

Television is popular in high- and middle-income countries, where almost every household owns as least one TV set.

Sources: U.S. Census Bureau (2005) and International Telecommunication Union (2006).

interests such as music or television shows, but parents have greater influence on long-term goals such as going to college (Davies & Kandel, 1981).

Finally, any neighborhood or school is made up of many peer groups. As Chapter 5 ("Groups and Organizations") explains, individuals tend to view their own group in positive terms and put down other groups. In addition, people are influenced by peer groups they would like to join, a process sociologists call **anticipatory socialization,** *learning that helps a person achieve a desired position.* In school, for example, young people may copy the clothing styles and speech of a group they hope will accept them. Later in life, a young lawyer who hopes to move up may conform to the attitudes and behavior of the firm's partners in order to be accepted.

THE MASS MEDIA

August 30, Isle of Coll, off the west coast of Scotland. The last time we visited this remote island, there was no electricity and most people spoke the ancient Gaelic language. Now that a power cable comes from the mainland, homes have lights and appliances and—television!

Almost with the flip of a switch, this tiny place has been thrust into the modern world. It is no surprise that traditions are fast disappearing and a rising share of the population is now mainlanders who come out to their vacation homes. And nearly everyone speaks English.

The **mass media** are *the means for delivering impersonal communications to a vast audience.* The term *media* comes from the Latin word for "middle," suggesting that the media connect people. *Mass* media resulted as communications technology (first newspapers and then radio, television, films, and the Internet) spread information on a mass scale. The mass media are important not only because they are so powerful but also because their influence is likely to differ from that of the family, the local school, and the peer group. In short, the mass media introduce people to ideas and images that are new and different.

In the United States, television was introduced in the 1930s and quickly became the dominant medium. Today, 98 percent of U.S. households have at least one television

 An online chapter on the mass media is available at http://www.prenticehall.ca/macionis/massmedia.html

(by comparison, just 96 percent have telephones). Two of three households also have cable television.

As Figure 3–2 indicates, the United States has one of the highest rates of television ownership in the world. In this country, it is people with lower incomes who spend the most time watching TV.

The Extent of Television Viewing

Just how "glued to the tube" are we? National surveys show that the average household has at least one set turned on for more than eight hours each day and that people spend half their free time watching television. A study by the Kaiser Family Foundation found that youngsters between the ages of two and eighteen average 5½ hours a day "consuming media," including almost three hours of television and the rest watching video movies and playing video games (MacPherson, 1999; Cornell, 2000; Nielsen Media Research, 2005).

Years before children learn to read, television watching is a part of their daily routine. As they grow, children spend as many hours in front of a television as they do in school or interacting with their parents. This continues to be so despite research that suggests that television makes children more passive and less likely to use their imagination (American Psychological Association, 1993; Fellman, 1995).

Television and Politics

The comedian Fred Allen once quipped that we call television a "medium" because it is "rarely well done." For a vari-

Concern with violence and the mass media extends to the world of video games, especially those popular with young boys. Among the most controversial games, which include high levels of violence, is *Grand Theft Auto*. Do you think the current rating codes are sufficient to guide parents and children who buy video games, or would you support greater restrictions on game content?

ety of reasons, television (as well as other mass media) provokes plenty of criticism. Some liberal critics argue that for most of television's history, racial and ethnic minorities have been invisible or have been included only in stereotypical roles (such as African Americans playing butlers, Asian Americans playing gardeners, or Hispanics playing new immigrants). In recent years, however, minorities have moved closer to center stage on television. There are now far more Hispanic actors on primetime television than there were a generation ago, and they play a far wider range of characters (Lichter & Amundson, 1997; Fetto, 2003b).

On the other side of the fence, conservative critics charge that the television and film industries are dominated by a liberal "cultural elite." In recent years, they claim, "politically correct" media have advanced liberal causes including feminism and gay rights (Rothman, Powers, & Rothman, 1993; B. Goldberg, 2002). But not everyone agrees, and some counter that the popularity of the Fox Network, home to Sean Hannity, Bill O'Reilly, Brit Hume, and other conservative commentators, suggests that television programming reflects political "spin" from both sides of the political spectrum.

Television and Violence

A final issue concerns violence and the mass media. In 1996, the American Medical Association (AMA) issued the startling statement that violence in television and films had reached such a high level that it posed a hazard to our health. More recently, a study found a strong link between aggressive behavior and the amount of time elementary school children spend watching television and using video games (Robinson et al., 2001). The public is concerned about this issue: Three-fourths of U.S. adults have either walked out of a movie or turned off television because of too much violence. Almost two-thirds of television programs contain violence, and in most scenes, violent characters show no remorse and are not punished (B. J. Wilson, 1998).

In 1997, the television industry adopted a rating system for programs. But we are left to wonder whether watching sexual or violent programming harms people as much as critics say. More important, why do the mass media contain so much sex and violence in the first place?

Television and other mass media have enriched our lives with entertaining and educational programming. The media also increase our exposure to other cultures and provoke discussion of current issues. At the same time, the power of the media—especially television—to shape how we think remains controversial.

Other spheres of life beyond family, school, peer group, and the media also play a part in social learning. For most people in the United States, these include religious organizations, the workplace, the military, and social clubs. In the end, socialization is not a simple learning process but a complex balancing act as we absorb information from a variety of sources. In the process of sorting and weighing all the information we receive, we form our own distinctive personalities.

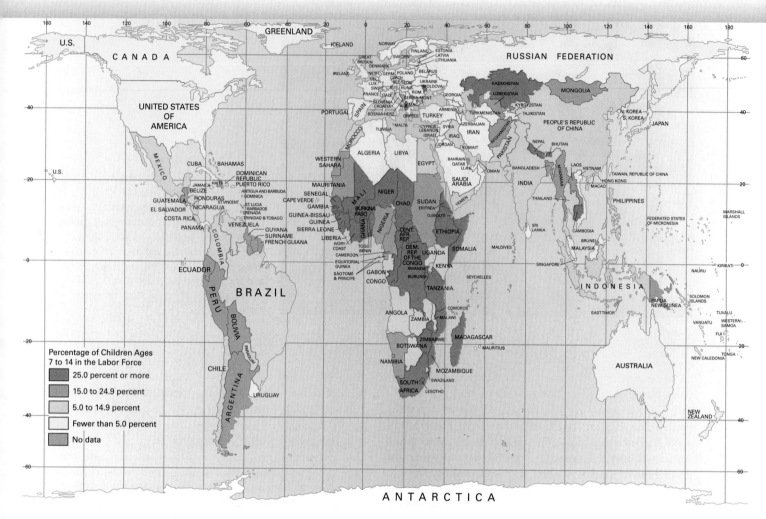

WINDOW ON THE WORLD

GLOBAL MAP 3-1 Child Labor in Global Perspective

Industrialization extends childhood and discourages children from work and other activities considered suitable only for adults. This is why child labor is uncommon in the United States and other high-income countries. In less economically developed nations of the world, however, children are a vital economic asset, and they typically begin working as soon as they are able. How would childhood in, say, the African nations of Chad or Sudan differ from that in the United States or Canada?

Sources: World Bank (2005, 2006) and author estimates; map projection from *Peters Atlas of the World* (1990).

Socialization and the Life Course

Although childhood has special importance in the socialization process, learning continues throughout our lives. An overview of the life course reveals how society organizes human experience according to age—childhood, adolescence, adulthood, and old age.

CHILDHOOD

A few years ago, the Nike corporation, maker of popular athletic shoes, came under fire. The company's shoes are made in Taiwan and Indonesia, in many cases by young children who spend their days working in factories

instead of going to school. In fact, some 250 million of the world's children work, half of them full time, earning about 50 cents an hour (Human Rights Watch, 2006). Global Map 3–1 shows that child labor is most common in the nations of Africa and Asia.

Criticism of Nike springs from the fact that most North Americans think of *childhood*—roughly the first twelve years of life—as a carefree time of learning and play. In fact, as the historian Philippe Ariès (1965) explains, the whole idea of "childhood" is fairly new. In the Middle Ages, children of four or five were treated like adults and expected to take care of themselves.

We defend our idea of childhood because youngsters are biologically immature. But a look back in time and around the world shows that the concept of childhood is grounded not in biology but in culture (LaRossa & Reitzes, 2001). In rich countries today, not everyone has to work, so childhood is extended to allow time for young people to learn the skills they will need in a high-technology workplace.

 Human Rights Watch reports on child soldiers around the world at http:// www.hrw.org/campaigns/crp/ index.htm

In 2005, a thirteen-year-old soccer player named Freddy Adu was offered a $1 million contract by Nike. In what ways do you think our society might be encouraging children to grow up too fast?

ADOLESCENCE

At the same time that industrializing societies came to regard childhood as a distinct stage of life, adolescence emerged as a buffer between childhood and adulthood. We generally link *adolescence,* or the teenage years, with emotional and social turmoil as young people develop their own identities. Again, we are tempted to say that teenage turbulence comes from the biological changes of puberty. But it really comes from cultural inconsistency. For example, the mass media glorify sex and schools hand out condoms, even as parents urge restraint. Consider, too, that an eighteen-year-old may face the adult duty of going to war but lacks the adult right to drink a beer. In short, adolescence is a time of social contradictions, when people are no longer children but not yet adults.

Like all stages of life, adolescence varies according to social background. Most young people from working-class families move right from high school to the adult world of work and parenting. Such men and women typically are considered adults by the time they reach age twenty. How-

In recent decades, some people have become concerned that U.S. society is shortening childhood, pushing children to grow up faster and faster. Do films such as *Thirteen,* which show young girls dressing and behaving as if they were much older, encourage a "hurried childhood"? Do you see this as a problem or not?

ever, wealthier teens have the resources to attend college and perhaps graduate school, thereby stretching adolescence to the late twenties and even the thirties (T. W. Smith, 2003).

Many of our soldiers in Iraq are still teenagers. Why should we not be surprised to learn that most of these young men and women performing adult jobs are from small-town, working-class families?

ADULTHOOD

If stages of the life course were based on biological changes, it would be easy to define *adulthood.* However, as "In the

Times

December 26, 2004

Adultescent

By JOHN TIERNEY

Adultescent came of age in 2004, but only as a word. The adult it describes is too busy playing Halo 2 on his Xbox or watching SpongeBob at his parents' house to think about growing up. The editors of the *Webster's New World College Dictionary* chose *adultescent* as word of the year; they said there were enough examples to constitute a "Peter Pandemic."

Since 1970, the median age for Americans to marry has risen four years, to 25 for women and 27 for men. Meanwhile, the proportion of people in their early 30s who have never married has tripled.

There are four million Americans between 25 and 34 still living with their parents, not always happily, as the apartments.com Web site discovered last year

when it offered $10,000 for the best essay from an adultescent desperate for money to get his or her own place. The winner was a 25-year-old woman who told of sharing a room with her 17-year-old brother.

But being unencumbered by rent—or mortgages or children—can leave lots of disposable income, which is why marketers have happily focused on adultescents since at least 1996. That was the year an article in the magazine *Precision Marketing* referred to the "adultescent marketplace," the earliest citation discovered by Paul McFedries, the author of the wordspy.com Web site.

Other variations would later appear—*adultolescents, adulescents, kidults* and *rejuveniles*—but nothing else quite captured the person with teenage tastes and an adult credit card. Someone free to do nothing, like the characters on *Seinfeld*,

or party all night, like the ones in *Sex in the City*. Someone with a connoisseur's passion for plasma televisions, Kelly bags, Harry Potter movies and low-riding Gap jeans. Someone with a ritual call at birthday parties: "30 is the new 20," "40 is the new 30," etc.

One common explanation for the rise in adultescence is the cost of housing and education, which has made it harder for young people (especially in places like New York [City]) to afford homes and children. Another explanation is that young adults now enjoy some pleasures of marriage without the consequences.

But if you ask adultescents why they haven't grown up, they may give you a simple answer: Because they don't have to.

Times" explains, deciding when someone is an adult turns out to be more complicated than it may seem.

Regardless of exactly when it begins, adulthood is the time of life when most accomplishments take place, including pursuing a career and raising a family. Personalities are largely formed by then, although dramatic change in a person's environment—such as unemployment, divorce, or serious illness—can cause significant change to the self.

During early adulthood—until about age forty—young adults learn to manage day-to-day affairs for themselves, often juggling conflicting priorities: parents, partner, children, schooling, and work. Women are especially likely to try to "do it all" because our culture gives them major responsibility for child rearing and household chores even if they have demanding jobs outside the home.

In middle adulthood—roughly between ages forty and sixty—people sense that their life circumstances are pretty

well set. They also become more aware of the fragility of health, which the young typically take for granted. Women who have devoted many years to raising a family can find middle adulthood emotionally trying. Children grow up and require less attention, and husbands become absorbed in their careers, leaving some women with spaces in their lives that are difficult to fill. Many women who divorce during middle adulthood also face serious financial problems (Weitzman, 1985, 1996). For all these reasons, an increasing number of women in middle adulthood return to school and seek new careers.

For everyone, growing older means facing physical decline, a prospect our culture makes especially painful for women. Because good looks are considered more important for women, the appearance of wrinkles and graying hair can be traumatic. Men have their own particular difficulties as they grow older. Some must admit that they are never going

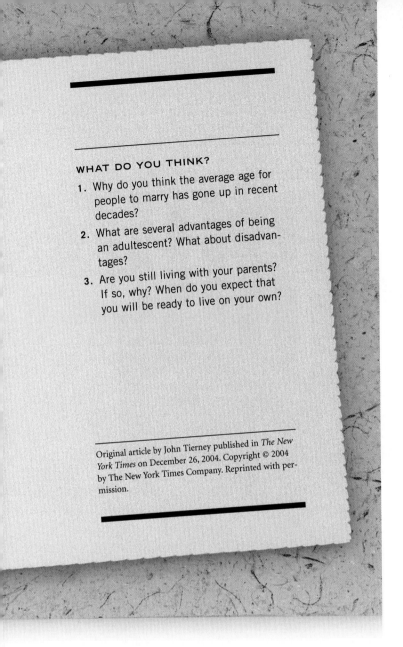

to reach earlier career goals. Others realize that the price of career success has been neglect of family or personal health.

Based on national survey data, the sociologist Tom Smith (2003) identified five factors that people consider important in deciding when a young person becomes an "adult": finishing school, no longer living with parents, having the ability to support a family, marrying, and becoming a parent. How many of these conditions do you meet? In what order do you expect to reach the remaining ones?

Old Age

Old age—the later years of adulthood and the final stage of life—begins around the mid-sixties. With people living longer, the elderly population is growing nearly as fast as the U.S. population as a whole. As Figure 3–3 on page 86 shows, about one in eight people is over age sixty-five, and the elderly now outnumber teenagers. By 2030, the number of seniors will double to 71 million, and almost half the country's people will be over forty (U.S. Census Bureau, 2004, 2006).

We can only begin to imagine the full consequences of the "graying of the United States." As more and more people retire from the labor force, the share of nonworking adults—already ten times greater than in 1900—will go up, increasing demand for health care and other social products and services. But perhaps most important, elderly people will be more visible in everyday life. As the twenty-first century goes on, the young and the old will interact more and more.

The aging of the U.S. population is the focus of **gerontology** (*geron* in Greek means "old person"), *the study of aging and the elderly.* Gerontologists study both the physical and the social dimensions of growing old.

Aging and Biology

For most of our population, gray hair, wrinkles, and declining energy begin in middle age. After about age fifty, bones become more brittle, injuries take longer to heal, and the risks of chronic illnesses (such as arthritis and diabetes) and life-threatening conditions (such as heart disease and cancer) rise steadily. Sensory abilities—taste, sight, touch, smell, and especially hearing—become less sharp with age (Treas, 1995; Metz & Miner, 1998).

Even so, most older people are neither disabled nor discouraged by their physical condition. Only one in five seniors reports trouble walking, and fewer than one in twenty needs care in a hospital or nursing home. Overall, although 26 percent of people over age sixty-five characterize their health as "fair" or "poor," 74 percent consider their overall condition "good" to "excellent." On average, the health of U.S. seniors is steadily improving (Lethbridge-Çejku, Rose, & Vickerie, 2006).

Aging and Culture

Culture shapes how we understand growing old. In low-income countries, old age gives people great influence and respect because elders control the most land and have wisdom gained over the course of a lifetime. For these reasons, a preindustrial society usually takes the form of a **gerontocracy,** *a form of social organization in which the elderly have the most wealth, power, and prestige.*

Industrialization lessens the social standing of the elderly, giving more wealth, power, and prestige to younger

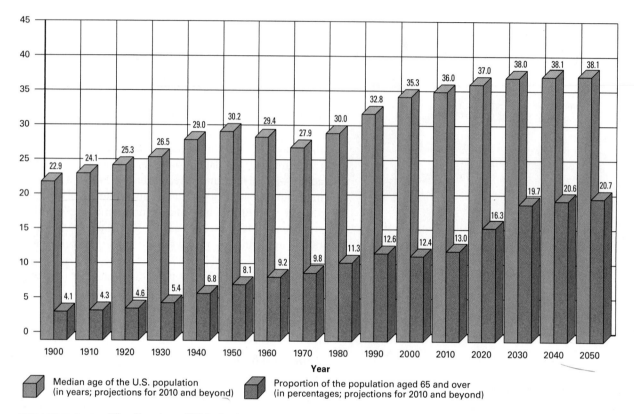

Median age of the U.S. population
(in years; projections for 2010 and beyond)

Proportion of the population aged 65 and over
(in percentages; projections for 2010 and beyond)

FIGURE 3–3 The Graying of U.S. Society

The proportion of the U.S. population over the age of sixty-five tripled during the last century. The median age of the U.S. population has now passed thirty-five years and will continue to rise.

Source: U.S. Census Bureau (2004, 2006).

people. This trend seems to be continuing: The average age of today's corporate executives is fifty-five, compared to fifty-nine in 1980 (Herring, 2005). In an industrial society, older people typically live apart from their grown children, and rapid social change makes much of what seniors know obsolete, at least from the point of view of younger people. A problem common to industrial societies, then, is **ageism,** *prejudice and discrimination against older people.*

November 1, approaching Kandy, Sri Lanka. Our little van struggles up the steep mountain incline. Breaks in the lush vegetation offer spectacular views that interrupt our conversation about growing old. "Then there are no old-age homes in your country?" I ask. "In Colombo and other cities, I am sure," our driver responds, "but not many. We are not like you Americans." "And how is that?" I ask, stiffening a bit. His eyes remain fixed on the road: "We would not leave our fathers and mothers to live alone."

Not surprisingly, growing old in the United States is challenging. When we're young, becoming older means taking on new roles and responsibilities. In old age, the opposite happens as people leave behind roles that have given them identity, pleasure, and prestige. When people retire from familiar work routines, some find restful recreation or new activities, but others lose their self-worth and suffer outright boredom.

Aging and Income

Reaching old age means living with less income. But today, the U.S. elderly population is doing better than ever. In 1960, some 35 percent of the elderly were poor; in 2005, this figure fell to 10.1 percent—less than the poverty rate of 12.6 percent for the population as a whole (U.S. Census Bureau, 2006). A generation ago, old age carried the highest risk of poverty; today, that is true of childhood.

Why the change? An increasing share of older couples have had double incomes, which helps people save more. In

The reality of growing old is as much a matter of culture as it is of biology. In the United States, being elderly often means being inactive; yet in many other countries of the world, elders often continue many familiar and productive routines.

addition, better health allows older people to continue to work for income. Government programs have become more generous, so that almost half of all government spending now goes to programs that assist the elderly even as spending on children has remained more or less flat. Despite these gains, many seniors have lost some of the pension income they were counting on, and more of today's workers are not receiving pension benefits at all.

Since 1980, on average, seniors have posted a 35 percent increase in income (in constant dollars), which is double the increase for people under thirty-five (U.S. Census Bureau, 2006). Today's average senior has a net worth of $160,000. A reasonable question, then, is whether we should continue to favor the oldest members of our society and risk slighting the youngest, who now suffer most from poverty.

YOUR TURN

Would you favor replacing the common "senior discounts" found at many local businesses with discounts for low-income people? What about single parents with children? Explain your view.

DEATH AND DYING

Throughout most of human history, low living standards and limited medical technology meant that death, caused most often by disease or accident, could come at any stage of life. Today, however, 84 percent of people in the United States die after age fifty-five (Hoyert et al., 2006).

After observing many dying people, the psychologist Elisabeth Kübler-Ross (1969) described death as an orderly transition involving five distinct stages. Typically, a person first reacts to the prospect of dying with *denial*, perhaps to be expected in a culture that doesn't like to talk about death. The second phase is *anger* as the person facing death sees it as a gross injustice. Third, anger gives way to *negotiation* as the person imagines it might be possible to avoid death by striking a bargain with God. The fourth stage, *resignation*, is often accompanied by psychological depression. Finally, a complete adjustment to death requires *acceptance*. At this point, no longer paralyzed by fear and anxiety, the person whose life is ending sets out to make the most of whatever time remains.

As older people become a larger share of the U.S. population, we can expect our culture to become more comfortable with the idea of death. In recent years, for example, people in the United States and in other high-income nations have been discussing death more openly, and the trend is toward viewing dying as preferable to prolonged suffering. More married couples are taking steps to prepare for death with legal and financial planning; this openness may help ease the pain of the surviving spouse, a consideration for women who, more often than not, outlive their husbands.

THINKING ABOUT DIVERSITY: RACE, CLASS, AND GENDER

The Development of Self among High School Students

Adolescence is a time when people ask questions like "Who am I?" and "What do I want to become?" In the end, we all have to answer these questions for ourselves. But race and ethnicity are likely to have an effect on what our answers turn out to be.

Grace Kao (2000) investigated the identity and goals of students enrolled in Johnstown High School, a large (3,000-student) school in a Chicago suburb. Johnstown High is considered a good school, with above-average test scores. It is also racially and ethnically diverse: 47 percent of the students are white, 43 percent are African American, 7 percent are Hispanic, and 3 percent are of Asian descent.

Kao interviewed sixty-three Johnstown students—female and male—both individually and in small groups with others of the same race and ethnicity. Talking with them, she learned how important racial and ethnic stereotypes are in young people's developing sense of self.

What are these stereotypes? White students are seen as hardworking and studious and concerned about getting high grades. African American students are thought to study less, either because they are not as smart or because they just don't try as hard. In any case, students see African Americans as at high risk of failure in school. Because the stereotype says that Hispanics are headed for manual occupations—as gardeners or laborers—they are seen as not caring very much about doing well in school. Finally, Asian American students are seen as hardworking high achievers, either because they are smarter or because they focus on academics rather than, say, sports.

From her interviews, Kao learned that most students think these stereotypes are true and take them personally. They expect people, including themselves, to perform in school more or less the way the stereotype predicts. In addition, young people—whether white, black, Hispanic, or Asian—mostly hang out with others like themselves, which gives them little chance to find out that their attitudes are wrong.

Students of all racial and ethnic categories say they *want* to do well in school. But not getting to know those who differ from themselves means that they measure success *only in relation to their own category.* To African American students, in other words, "success" means doing as well as other black students and not flunking out. To Hispanics, "success" means avoiding manual labor and ending up with any job in an office. Whites and Asians define "success" as earning high grades and living up to the high-achievement stereotype. For all these young people, then, "self" develops through the lens of how U.S. society defines race and ethnicity.

WHAT DO YOU THINK?

1. Were you aware of racial and ethnic stereotypes, similar to those described here, in your high school? What about your college? Explain.

2. Do you think gender stereotypes affect the performance of women and men in school as much as racial and ethnic stereotypes? Explain.

3. What can be done to reduce the damaging effects of racial and ethnic stereotypes?

THE LIFE COURSE: PATTERNS AND VARIATIONS

This brief examination of the life course points to two major conclusions. First, although each stage of life reflects the biological process of aging, the life course is largely a social construction. For this reason, people in different societies may experience a stage of life quite differently or not at all. Second, in any society, the stages of the life course present certain problems and transitions that involve learning something new and, in many cases, unlearning familiar routines.

Societies organize the life course according to age, but other forces such as class, race, ethnicity, and gender also shape people's lives. Thus the general patterns described in this chapter apply somewhat differently to various categories of people. The Thinking About Diversity box provides an example of how race and ethnicity can shape the academic performance of high school students.

People's life experiences also vary depending on when, in the history of a society, they are born. A **cohort** is *a category of people with something in common, usually their age.* Because members of a particular age cohort generally are influenced by the same economic and cultural trends, they tend to develop similar attitudes and values. Women and men born in the late 1940s and 1950s grew up during a period of economic expansion that gave them a sense of optimism. Today's college students, who have grown up in an age of economic uncertainty, are less confident about the future.

What major events or trends have shaped the personalities of people your age?

Resocialization: Total Institutions

A final type of socialization, experienced by more than 2 million people in the United States at any one time, involves being confined—often against their will—in prisons or mental hospitals. This is the special world of the **total institution,** *a setting in which people are isolated from the rest of society and manipulated by an administrative staff.*

According to Erving Goffman (1961), total institutions have three important characteristics. First, staff members supervise all aspects of daily life, including where residents (often called "inmates") eat, sleep, and work. Second, life in a total institution is controlled and standardized, with the same food, uniforms, and activities for everyone. Third, formal rules dictate when, where, and how inmates perform their daily routines.

The purpose of such rigid routines is **resocialization,** *radically changing an inmate's personality by carefully controlling the environment.* Prisons and mental hospitals physically isolate inmates behind fences, barred windows, and locked doors and control their access to the telephone, computers, mail, and visitors. The institution becomes their entire world, making it easier for the staff to bring about personality change—or at least obedience—in the inmate.

Resocialization is a two-part process. First, the staff breaks down a new inmate's existing identity. For example, an inmate must surrender personal possessions, including clothing and grooming articles used to maintain a distinctive appearance. Instead, the staff provides standard-issue clothes so that everyone looks alike. The staff subjects new inmates to "mortifications of self," which can include searches, medical examinations, head shaving, fingerprinting, and assignment of a serial number. Once inside the walls, individuals also give up their privacy as guards routinely inspect their living quarters.

In the second part of the resocialization process, the staff tries to build a new self in the inmate through a system of rewards and punishments. Having a book to read, watching television, or making a telephone call may seem like minor pleasures to the outsider, but in the rigid environment of the total institution, the opportunity to gain such

Prisons are one example of a total institution in which inmates dress alike and carry out daily routines under the direct supervision and control of the institutional staff. What do we expect prison to do to young people convicted of crimes? How well do you think prisons do what people expect them to?

simple privileges as these can be a powerful motivation to conform. The length of confinement typically depends on how well the inmate cooperates with the staff.

Total institutions affect people in different ways. Some inmates may end up "rehabilitated" or "recovered," but others may change little, and still others may become hostile or bitter. Over a long period of time, living in a rigidly controlled environment can leave some *institutionalized,* without the capacity for independent living.

But what about the rest of us? Does socialization crush our individuality or empower us to reach our creative potential? The Applying Sociology box on page 90 takes a closer look at this vital question.

Are We Free within Society?

This chapter stresses one key theme: Society shapes how we think, feel, and act. If this is so, then in what sense are we free? To answer this important question, consider the Muppets, puppet stars of television and film. Watching the antics of Kermit the Frog, Miss Piggy, and the rest of the troupe, we almost believe they are real rather than objects controlled from backstage. As the sociological perspective points out, human beings are like puppets in that we, too, respond to backstage forces. Society gives us a culture and shapes our lives according to class, race, and gender. If this is so, can we really claim to be free?

Sociologists answer this question with many voices. The politically liberal response is that individuals are *not* free of society—in fact, as social creatures, we never could be. But if we are condemned to live in a society with power over us, it is important to do what we can to make our world as just as possible, by working to lessen class differences and other barriers to opportunity for minorities, including women. Conservatives answer that we *are* free because society can never dictate our dreams. Our history as a nation, right from the revolutionary act that led to

its founding, is one story after another of individuals pursuing personal goals despite great odds.

Both attitudes are found in George Herbert Mead's analysis of socialization. Mead recognized that society makes demands on us, sometimes limiting our options. But he also reminded us that human beings are spontaneous

Are we free within society? No and yes. Society does affect our actions, thoughts, and feelings. But we also have the ability to act back on the world around us.

and creative, capable of acting on society and bringing about change. Mead noted the power of society while still affirming the human capacity to evaluate, criticize, and ultimately choose and change.

In the end, we may seem like puppets, but only on the surface. A crucial difference is that we can stop, look up at the "strings" that make us move, and even yank on them defiantly (Berger, 1963:176). If our pull is strong enough, we may accomplish more than we might think. As Margaret Mead once remarked, "Do not make the mistake of thinking that concerned people cannot change the world; it's the only thing that ever has."

WHAT DO YOU THINK?

1. Do you think our society gives more freedom to males than to females? Why or why not?

2. Are people living in modern, high-income countries more free than those living in traditional, low-income nations? Explain your answer.

3. Has learning about socialization increased or decreased your feeling of freedom? Why?

APPLYING SOCIOLOGY IN EVERYDAY LIFE

1. Get together with several members of your sociology class, and gather data by asking classmates and friends to name traits they consider elements of "human nature." Then compare notes and discuss the extent to which these traits come from nature or nurture.

2. Here is an easy and effective way to better understand George Herbert Mead's claim that the self is composed of two parts, the "I" and the "me." Place your left hand, palm down, on a desk or table; then run your right hand softly over the back of your left hand. Focus on how your left hand feels using the

sensations provided through the fingertips of your right hand. In this exercise, the right hand (the one that is active) represents the I. The left hand (the one being examined) is the me. Of course, as Mead would quickly add, both hands are part of a single self.

3. Watch several hours of primetime programming on network or cable television. Keep track of all the violence you see and calculate the average number of violent scenes per hour. On the basis of observing a small and unrepresentative sample of programs, what are your conclusions?

MAKING THE GRADE

WHAT IS SOCIALIZATION?

Socialization is a **LIFELONG PROCESS**.

- Socialization develops our humanity as well as our particular personalities.
- The importance of socialization is seen in the fact that extended periods of social isolation result in permanent damage (cases of Anna and Genie).

pp 70–72

Socialization is a matter of **NURTURE** rather than **NATURE**.

- A century ago, most people thought human behavior resulted from biological instinct.
- For us as human beings, it is our nature to nurture.

pp 70–71

socialization (p. 70) the lifelong social experience by which people develop their human potential and learn culture

personality (p. 70) a person's fairly consistent patterns of acting, thinking, and feeling

IMPORTANT CONTRIBUTIONS TO OUR UNDERSTANDING OF SOCIALIZATION

SIGMUND FREUD'S model of the human personality has three parts:

- *id:* innate, pleasure-seeking human drives
- *superego:* the demands of society in the form of internalized values and norms
- *ego:* our efforts to balance innate, pleasure-seeking drives and the demands of society

pp 72–73

LAWRENCE KOHLBERG applied Piaget's approach to stages of moral development:

- We first judge rightness in *preconventional* terms, according to our individual needs.
- Next, *conventional* moral reasoning takes account of parental attitudes and cultural norms.
- Finally, *postconventional* reasoning allows us to criticize society itself.

p 74

To **GEORGE HERBERT MEAD,**

- the self is part of our personality and includes self-awareness and self-image;
- the self develops only as a result of social experience;
- social experience involves the exchange of symbols;
- social interaction depends on understanding the intention of another, which requires taking the role of the other;
- human action is partly spontaneous (the I) and partly in response to others (the me);
- we gain social experience through imitation, play, games, and understanding the *generalized other.*

pp 75–76

JEAN PIAGET believed that human development involves both biological maturation and gaining social experience. He identified four stages of cognitive development:

- First, the *sensorimotor stage* involves knowing the world only through the senses.
- Next, the *preoperational stage* involves starting to use language and other symbols.
- Next, the *concrete operational stage* allows individuals to understand causal connections.
- Finally, the *formal operational stage* involves abstract and critical thought.

pp 73–74

CAROL GILLIGAN found that gender plays an important part in moral development, with males relying more on abstract standards of rightness and females relying more on the effects of actions on relationships.

pp 74–75

CHARLES HORTON COOLEY used the term *looking-glass self* to explain that we see ourselves as we imagine others see us.

p 76

ERIK H. ERIKSON identified challenges that individuals face at each stage of life from infancy to old age.

pp 76–77

id (p. 72) Freud's term for the human being's basic drives

ego (p. 73) Freud's term for a person's conscious efforts to balance innate pleasure-seeking drives with the demands of society

superego (p. 73) Freud's term for the cultural values and norms internalized by an individual

sensorimotor stage (p. 73) Piaget's term for the level of human development at which individuals experience the world only through their senses

preoperational stage (p. 73) Piaget's term for the level of human development at which individuals first use language and other symbols

concrete operational stage (p. 73) Piaget's term for the level of human development at which individuals first see causal connections in their surroundings

formal operational stage (p. 74) Piaget's term for the level of human development at which individuals think abstractly and critically

self (p. 75) George Herbert Mead's term for the part of an individual's personality composed of self-awareness and self-image

looking-glass self (p. 76) Charles Horton Cooley's term for a self-image based on how we think others see us

significant others (p. 76) people, such as parents, who have special importance for socialization

generalized other (p. 76) Mead's term for widespread cultural norms and values we use as a reference in evaluating ourselves

MAKING THE GRADE

CONTINUED...

AGENTS OF SOCIALIZATION

The **FAMILY** is usually the first setting of socialization.

- Family has the greatest impact on attitudes and behavior.
- A family's social position, including race and social class, shapes a child's personality.
- Ideas about gender are learned first in the family.

pp 77–78

SCHOOLS give most children their first experience with bureaucracy and impersonal evaluation.

- Schools teach knowledge and skills needed for later life.
- Schools expose children to greater social diversity.
- Schools reinforce ideas about gender.

p 79

The **PEER GROUP** helps shape attitudes and behavior.

- The peer group takes on great importance during adolescence.
- The peer group frees young people from adult supervision.

pp 79–80

The **MASS MEDIA** have a huge impact on socialization in modern, high-income societies.

- The average U.S. child spends as much time watching television and videos as attending school and interacting with parents.
- The mass media often reinforce stereotypes about gender and race.
- The mass media expose people to a great deal of violence.

pp 80–81

peer group (p. 79) a social group whose members have interests, social position, and age in common

anticipatory socialization (p. 80) learning that helps a person achieve a desired position

mass media (p. 80) the means for delivering impersonal communications to a vast audience

SOCIALIZATION AND THE LIFE COURSE

The concept of **CHILDHOOD** is grounded not in biology but in culture. In high-income countries, childhood is extended.

pp 82–83

The emotional and social turmoil of **ADOLESCENCE** results from cultural inconsistency in defining people who are not children but not yet adults. Adolescence varies by social class position.

p 83

ADULTHOOD is the stage of life when most accomplishments take place. Although personality is now formed, it continues to change with new life experiences.

pp 83–85

OLD AGE is defined differently from culture to culture.

- In high-income countries, old age is a time of disengagement and loss of social importance.
- The "graying of the United States" means that our country's average age is going up.

pp 85–87

gerontology (p. 85) the study of aging and the elderly

gerontocracy (p. 85) a form of social organization in which the elderly have the most wealth, power, and prestige

ageism (p. 86) prejudice and discrimination against older people

cohort (p. 88) a category of people with something in common, usually their age

✓ *Every stage of life is socially constructed in ways that vary from society to society.*

TOTAL INSTITUTIONS

TOTAL INSTITUTIONS include prisons, mental hospitals, and monasteries.

- Staff members supervise all aspects of life.
- Life is standardized with all inmates following set rules and routines.

p 89

RESOCIALIZATION is a two-part process:

- breaking down inmates' existing identity
- building a new self through a system of rewards and punishments

p 89

total institution (p. 89) a setting in which people are isolated from the rest of society and manipulated by an administrative staff

resocialization (p. 89) radically changing an inmate's personality by carefully controlling the environment

VISUAL SUMMARY

These questions are similar to those found in the test bank that accompanies this textbook.

MULTIPLE-CHOICE QUESTIONS

1. Kingsley Davis's study of Anna, the girl isolated for five years, shows that
   a. humans have all the same instincts found in other animal species.
   b. without social experience, a child never develops personality.
   c. personality is present in all humans at birth.
   d. many human instincts disappear in the first few years of life.

2. Most sociologists take the position that
   a. humans have instincts that direct behavior.
   b. biological instincts develop in humans at puberty.
   c. it is human nature to nurture.
   d. All of the above are correct.

3. Lawrence Kohlberg explored socialization by studying
   a. cognition.
   b. the importance of gender in socialization.
   c. the development of biological instincts.
   d. moral reasoning.

4. Carol Gilligan added to Kohlberg's findings by showing that
   a. girls and boys typically use different standards in deciding what is right and wrong.
   b. girls are more interested in right and wrong than boys are.
   c. boys are more interested in right and wrong than girls are.
   d. today's children are far less interested in right and wrong than their parents are.

5. The "self," said George Herbert Mead, is
   a. the part of the human personality made up of self-awareness and self-image.
   b. the presence of culture within the individual.
   c. basic drives that are self-centered.
   d. present in infants from birth.

6. Why is the family so important to the socialization process?
   a. Family members provide necessary care for infants and children.
   b. Families give children social identity in terms of class, ethnicity, and religion.
   c. Parents greatly affect a child's self-concept.
   d. All of the above are correct.

7. Compared to higher-income parents, lower-income parents are more likely to emphasize which of the following?
   a. independence
   b. creativity
   c. obedience
   d. imagination

8. In global perspective, which statement about childhood is correct?
   a. In every society, the first ten years of life are a time of play and learning.
   b. Rich societies extend childhood much longer than poor societies do.
   c. Poor societies extend childhood much longer than rich societies do.
   d. Childhood is defined by being biologically immature.

9. Modern, high-income societies typically define people in old age as
   a. the wisest of all.
   b. the most up-to-date on current fashion and trends.
   c. less socially important than younger adults.
   d. All of the above are correct.

10. According to Erving Goffman, the purpose of a total institution is
    a. to reward someone for achievement in the outside world.
    b. to give a person more choices about how to live.
    c. to encourage lifelong learning in a supervised context.
    d. to radically change a person's personality or behavior.

ANSWERS: 1 (b); 2 (c); 3 (d); 4 (a); 5 (a); 6 (d); 7 (c); 8 (b); 9 (c); 10 (d).

ESSAY QUESTIONS

1. State the two sides of the "nature-nurture" debate. In what sense are human nature and nurture not opposed to each other?

2. We have all seen very young children place their hands in front of their faces and exclaim, "You can't see me!" They assume that if they cannot see you, you cannot see them. What does this behavior suggest about a young child's ability to "take the role of the other"? Should a parent expect a young child to "see things from *my* point of view"? Explain.

Sociology points to the many rules that guide behavior in everyday situations. The more we learn about the rules of social interaction, the better we can play the game.

CHAPTER *4*

Social Interaction in Everyday Life

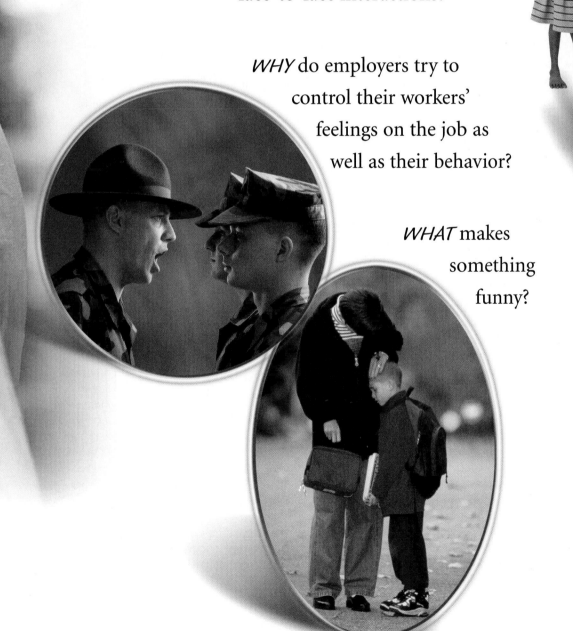

HOW do we create reality in our face-to-face interactions?

WHY do employers try to control their workers' feelings on the job as well as their behavior?

WHAT makes something funny?

Harold and Sybil are late for their visit to another couple's home in an unfamiliar area near Fort Lauderdale, Florida. For the last twenty minutes, they have traveled in circles, searching in vain for Coconut Palm Road. Harold, gripping the wheel ever more tightly, is muttering under his breath. Sybil, sitting next to him, looks straight ahead, afraid to say a word.

Harold and Sybil are lost in more ways than one: They are unable to understand why they are growing angry at their situation and at each other. Like most men, Harold cannot stand getting lost, and the longer he drives around, the more incompetent he feels. Sybil cannot understand why Harold does not pull into a gas station and ask someone where Coconut Palm Road is. If she were driving, she thinks to herself, they would already have arrived and would now be comfortably settled in with their friends.

Why don't men like to ask for directions? Because men value their independence, they are uncomfortable asking for help (and they are also reluctant to accept it). To ask someone for assistance is the same as saying, "You know something I don't." If it takes Harold a few more minutes to find Coconut Palm Road on his own—and keep his self-respect in the process—he thinks that's the way to go.

Women are more in tune with others and strive for connectedness. From Sybil's point of view, asking for help is right because sharing information builds social bonds and gets the job done. Asking for directions seems as natural to her as searching on his own is to Harold. Obviously, getting lost is sure to create conflict as long as neither one understands the other's point of view.

Such everyday social patterns are the focus of this chapter. The central concept is **social interaction,** *the process by which people act and react in relation to others.* We begin by presenting the rules and building blocks of common experience and then explore the almost magical way in which face-to-face interaction creates the reality in which we live.

Social Structure: A Guide to Everyday Living

 October 21, Ho Chi Minh City, Vietnam. This morning we leave the ship and make our way along the docks toward the center of Ho Chi Minh City, known to an earlier generation as Saigon. Government security officers wave us through the heavy iron gates. Pressed against the fence are dozens of men who operate cyclos (bicycles with small carriages attached to the front), the Vietnamese version of taxicabs. We wave them off but spend the next twenty minutes shaking our heads at several persistent drivers who pedal alongside, pleading for our business. The pressure is uncomfortable. We decide to cross the street but realize suddenly that there are no stop signs or signal lights—and the street is an unbroken stream of bicycles, cyclos, motorbikes, and small trucks. The locals don't bat an eye; they just walk at a steady pace across the street, parting waves of vehicles that immediately close in again behind them. Walk right into traffic? With our small children on our backs? Yup, we did it; that's the way it works in Vietnam.

 For a short video ("Sociology and Cultural Relativity") on the difficulty of traveling to unfamiliar places, go to http://www.TheSociology Page.com

Members of every society rely on social structure to make sense out of daily situations. As our family's introduction to the streets of Vietnam suggests, the world can be disorienting, even frightening, when society's rules are unclear. We turn now to other building blocks of everyday life.

Status

In every society, people build their lives using the idea of **status,** *a social position that a person holds.* In everyday use, the word "status" generally refers to "prestige," as when a college president is said to have more "status" than a newly hired assistant professor. But sociologically speaking, both "president" and "professor" are statuses, or positions, within the collegiate organization.

Status is part of our social identity and defines our relationships to others. As Georg Simmel (1950:307, orig. 1902), one of the founders of sociology, once pointed out, before we can deal with anyone, we need to know who the person is.

Each of us holds many statuses at once. The term **status set** refers to *all the statuses a person holds at a given time.* A teenage girl may be a daughter to her parents, a sister to her brother, a student at her school, and a goalie on her hockey team.

Status sets change over the life course. A child grows up to become a parent, a student graduates to become a lawyer, and a single person marries to become a husband or a wife, sometimes becoming single again as a result of death or divorce. Joining an organization or finding a job enlarges our status set; retirement or withdrawing from activities makes it smaller. Over a lifetime, people gain and lose dozens of statuses.

ASCRIBED AND ACHIEVED STATUS

Sociologists classify statuses in terms of how people attain them. An **ascribed status** is *a social position a person receives at birth or takes on involuntarily later in life.* Examples of ascribed statuses are being a daughter, a Cuban, a teenager, or a widower. Ascribed statuses are matters about which we have little or no choice.

By contrast, an **achieved status** refers to *a social position a person takes on voluntarily that reflects personal ability and effort.* Achieved statuses in the United States include honors student, Olympic athlete, software writer, and thief.

In the real world, of course, most statuses involve a combination of ascription and achievement. That is, people's ascribed statuses influence the statuses they achieve. People who achieve the status of lawyer, for example, are likely to share the ascribed benefit of being born into relatively well-off families. By the same token, many less desirable statuses, such as criminal, drug addict, or unemployed worker, are more easily achieved by people born into poverty.

In any rigidly ranked setting, no interaction can proceed until people assess each other's social standing. Thus, military personnel wear insignia, clear symbols of their level of authority. Don't we size up one another in much the same way in routine interactions, noting a person's rough age, quality of clothing, and manner for clues about social position?

Make a list of ten important statuses in your life. Indicate whether each one is ascribed or achieved. Is this difficult to do? Explain your answer.

MASTER STATUS

Some statuses matter more than others. A **master status** is *a status that has special importance for social identity, often shaping a person's entire life.* For most people, a job is a master status because it reveals a great deal about social background, education, and income. In a few cases, a person's name is a master status; being in the "Bush" or "Kennedy" family attracts attention and creates opportunities.

A master status can be negative as well as positive. Consider serious illness. Sometimes people, even lifelong friends, avoid cancer patients or people with acquired immune deficiency syndrome (AIDS) because of their illnesses. As another example, the fact that all societies limit opportunities for women makes gender a master status.

Sometimes a physical disability can serve as a master status to the point that we dehumanize people by seeing them only in terms of their disability. The Applying Sociology box on page 98 shows how.

APPLYING SOCIOLOGY

Physical Disability as Master Status

Physical disability works in much the same way as class, gender, or race in defining people in the eyes of others. In the following interviews, two women explain how a physical disability can become a master status—a trait that overshadows everything else about them. The first voice is of twenty-nine-year-old Donna Finch, who lives with her husband and son in Muskogee, Oklahoma, and holds a master's degree in social work. She is also blind.

Most people don't expect handicapped people to grow up; they are always supposed to be children. . . . You aren't supposed to date; you aren't supposed to have a job; somehow you're just supposed to disappear. I'm not saying this is true of anyone else, but in my own case I think I was more intellectu-

ally mature than most children, and more emotionally immature. I'd say that not until the last four or five years have I felt really whole.

Rose Helman is an elderly woman who has retired and lives near New York City. She suffers from spinal meningitis and is also blind.

You ask me if people are really different today than in the '20s and '30s. Not too much. They are still fearful of the handicapped. I don't know if fearful is the right word, but uncomfortable at least. But I can understand it somewhat; it happened to me. I once asked a man to tell me which staircase to use to get from the subway out to the street. He started giving me directions that were confusing, and

I said, "Do you mind taking me?" He said, "Not at all." He grabbed me on the side with my dog on it, so I asked him to take my other arm. And he said, "I'm sorry, I have no other arm." And I said, "That's all right, I'll hold onto the jacket." It felt funny hanging onto the sleeve without the arm in it.

WHAT DO YOU THINK?

1. Have you ever had a disease or disability that became a master status? If so, how did others react?

2. How might such a master status affect someone's personality?

3. Can being very fat or very thin serve as a master status? Why or why not?

Source: Based on Orlansky & Heward (1981).

Role

A second important social structure is **role,** *behavior expected of someone who holds a particular status.* A person *holds* a status and *performs* a role (Linton, 1937b). For example, holding the status of student leads you to perform the role of attending classes and completing assignments.

Both statuses and roles vary by culture. In the United States, the status "uncle" refers to a brother of either mother or father; in Vietnam, however, the word for "uncle" is different when referring to the mother's or father's side of the family, and the two men have different responsibilities. In every society, actual role performance varies according to a person's unique personality, and some societies permit more individual expression than others.

Because we hold many statuses at once—a status set—everyday life is a mix of many roles. Robert Merton (1968) introduced the term **role set** to identify *a number of roles attached to a single status.*

Figure 4–1 shows four statuses of one person, each status linked to a different role set. First, as a professor, this

woman interacts with students (the teacher role) and other academics (the colleague role). Second, as a researcher, she gathers and analyzes data (the fieldwork role) that she uses in her publications (the author role). Third, the same woman holds the status of "wife," with a marital role (such as confidante and sexual partner) toward her partner, with whom she shares a domestic role toward the household. Fourth, she holds the status of "mother," with routine responsibilities for her children (the maternal role) as well as involvement in their school and other organizations (the civic role).

A global perspective shows us that the roles people use to define their lives differ from society to society. In low-income countries, people spend fewer years as students, and family roles are typically very important to social identity. In high-income nations, people spend more years as students, and family roles may or may not be very important to social identity. Another dimension of difference involves housework. As Global Map 4–1 on page 100 shows, especially in poor nations of the world, housework is an important role that falls heavily on women.

Role Conflict and Role Strain

People in modern, high-income countries juggle many responsibilities demanded by their various statuses and roles. As most mothers can testify, being a parent and working outside the home both involve physically and emotionally draining roles. Sociologists thus recognize **role conflict** as *conflict among the roles connected to two or more statuses.*

Even roles linked to a single status can make competing demands on us. **Role strain** is *tension among the roles connected to a single status.* A college professor may enjoy being friendly with students. At the same time, however, the professor must maintain the personal distance needed to evaluate students fairly. In short, performing the roles of even a single status can be something of a balancing act.

One strategy for minimizing role conflict is separating parts of our lives so that we perform roles for one status at one time and place and we carry out roles for another status in a completely different setting. A familiar example of this is deciding to "leave the job at work" before heading home to the family.

YOUR TURN

Give one example of role conflict and one example of role strain in your own life.

Role Exit

After she left the life of a Catholic nun to become a university sociologist, Helen Rose Fuchs Ebaugh (1988) began to study her own experience of *role exit,* the process by which people disengage from important social roles. In studying a range of "exes," including ex-nuns, ex-doctors, ex-husbands, and ex-alcoholics, Ebaugh saw a pattern in the process of becoming an "ex."

According to Ebaugh, the process begins as people come to doubt their ability to continue in a certain role. As they imagine alternative roles, they ultimately reach a tipping point when they decide to pursue a new life. Even at this point, however, a past role can continue to influence their lives. "Exes" carry with them a self-image shaped by an earlier role, which can interfere with building a new sense of self. For example, an ex-nun may hesitate to wear stylish clothing and makeup.

"Exes" must also rebuild relationships with people who knew them in their earlier life. Learning new social skills is another challenge. For example, Ebaugh reports, ex-nuns who enter the dating scene after decades in the church are often surprised to learn that today's sexual norms are very different from those they knew when they were teenagers.

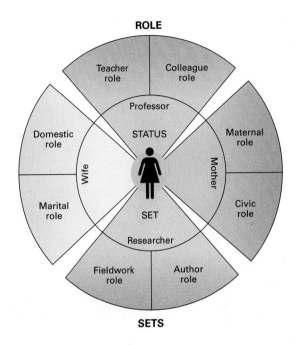

FIGURE 4–1 Status Set and Role Sets

A status set includes all the statuses a person holds at a given time. The status set defines "who we are" in society. The many roles linked to each status define "what we do."

The Social Construction of Reality

In 1917, the Italian playwright Luigi Pirandello wrote a play titled *The Pleasure of Honesty,* about a character named Angelo Baldovino, a brilliant man with a checkered past. Baldovino enters the fashionable home of the Renni family and introduces himself in a peculiar way:

> Inevitably we construct ourselves. Let me explain. I enter this house and immediately I become what I have to become, what I can become: I construct myself. That is, I present myself to you in a form suitable to the relationship I wish to achieve with you. And, of course, you do the same with me. (1962:157–58)

Baldovino suggests that although behavior is guided by status and role, we have considerable ability to shape what happens from moment to moment. In other words, "reality" is not as fixed as we may think.

The **social construction of reality** is *the process by which people creatively shape reality through social interaction.* This idea is the foundation of the symbolic-interaction approach, described in Chapter 1 ("Sociology: Perspective, Theory, and Method"). As Baldovino's remark suggests,

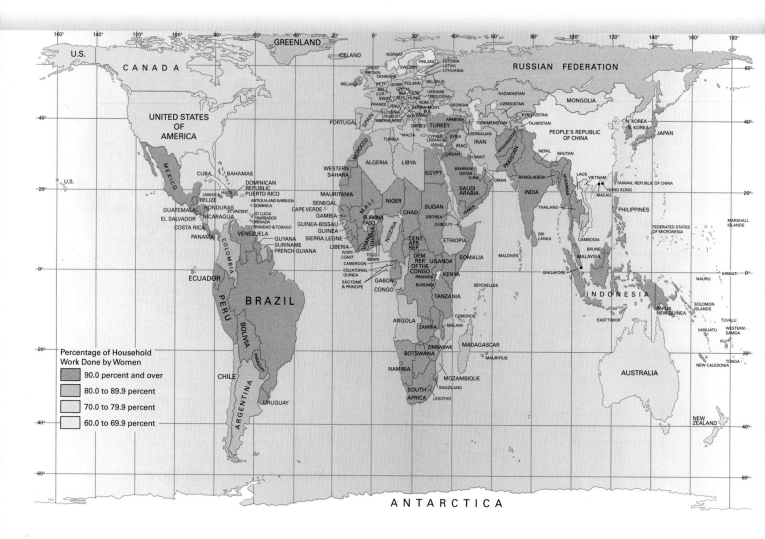

WINDOW ON THE WORLD

GLOBAL MAP 4–1   Housework in Global Perspective

Throughout the world, housework is a major part of women's routines and identities. This is especially true in poor nations of Latin America, Africa, and Asia, where the social position of women is far below that of men. But our society also defines housework and child care as "feminine" activities, even though women and men have the same legal rights and most women work outside the home.

Source: *Peters Atlas of the World* (1990); updated by the author.

Percentage of Household Work Done by Women

- 90.0 percent and over
- 80.0 to 89.9 percent
- 70.0 to 79.9 percent
- 60.0 to 69.9 percent

---

quite a bit of "reality" remains unclear in everyone's minds, especially in unfamiliar situations. So we present ourselves in terms that suit the setting and our purposes, and as others do the same, reality takes shape.

Social interaction, then, is a complex negotiation that builds reality. Most everyday situations involve at least some agreement about what's going on, but participants' percep-

tions of events are based on their different interests and intentions.

"STREET SMARTS"

What people commonly call "street smarts" is actually a form of constructing reality. In his autobiography, *Down These*

Mean Streets, Piri Thomas recalls moving to a new apartment in Spanish Harlem. Returning home one evening, young Piri found himself cut off by Waneko, the leader of the local street gang, who was flanked by a dozen others.

"Whatta ya say, Mr. Johnny Gringo," drawled Waneko.

Think man, I told myself, *think your way out of a stomping. Make it good.* "I hear you 104th Street coolies are supposed to have heart," I said. "I don't know this for sure. You know there's a lot of streets where a whole 'click' is made out of punks who can't fight one guy unless they all jump him for the stomp." I hoped this would push Waneko into giving me a fair one. His expression didn't change.

"Maybe we don't look at it that way."

Crazy, man, I cheer inwardly, *the cabron is falling into my setup.* . . . "I wasn't talking to you," I said. "Where I come from, the pres is president 'cause he got heart when it comes to dealing."

Waneko was starting to look uneasy. He had bit on my worm and felt like a sucker fish. His boys were now light on me. They were no longer so much interested in stomping me as seeing the outcome between Waneko and me. "Yeah," was his reply. . . .

I knew I'd won. Sure, I'd have to fight; but one guy, not ten or fifteen. If I lost, I might still get stomped, and if I won I might get stomped. I took care of this with my next sentence. "I don't know you or your boys," I said, "but they look cool to me. They don't feature as punks."

I had left him out purposely when I said "they." Now his boys were in a separate class. I had cut him off. He would have to fight me on his own, to prove his heart to himself, to his boys, and most important, to his turf. He got away from the stoop and asked, "Fair one, Gringo?" (1967:56–57)

This situation reveals the drama—sometimes subtle, sometimes savage—by which human beings creatively build everyday reality. Of course, not everyone enters a situation with equal power. Should a police officer have come upon the fight that took place between Piri and Waneko, both young men might have ended up in jail.

THE THOMAS THEOREM

By using his wits and boxing with Waneko until they both tired, Piri Thomas won acceptance by the gang. What took place that evening in Spanish Harlem is an example of the **Thomas theorem,** named after W. I. Thomas (1966:301, orig. 1931): *Situations that are defined as real are real in their consequences.*

Applied to social interaction, the Thomas theorem means that although reality is "soft" as it is being shaped, it can become "hard" in its effects. In the case just described, local gang members saw Piri Thomas act in a worthy way, so in their eyes, he *became* worthy.

Flirting is an everyday experience in reality construction. Each person offers information to the other and hints at romantic interest. Yet the interaction proceeds with a tentative and often humorous air so that either individual can withdraw at any time without further obligation.

ETHNOMETHODOLOGY

Most of the time, we take social reality for granted. To become more aware of the social world we help create, Harold Garfinkel (1967) came up with **ethnomethodology,** *the study of the way people make sense of their everyday surroundings.* This approach begins by pointing out that everyday behavior rests on a number of assumptions. When you ask someone the simple question "How are you?" you could be referring to how someone is doing physically, mentally, spiritually, or even financially. The person, however, assumes that you are asking a polite question and are really not interested in the details.

One good way to investigate the assumptions we make about everyday reality is to purposely break the rules. For example, the next time someone asks, "How're you doing?" offer details from your last physical examination or explain all the good and bad things that have happened since you woke up that morning and see how the person reacts.

By seeing what happens, we get a better idea of the "rules" of everyday social interaction. The person will most likely become confused or irritated by your unexpected

People build reality from their surrounding culture. Yet, because cultural systems are marked by diversity and even outright conflict, reality construction always involves tensions and choices. Turkey is a nation with a mostly Muslim population, but it is also a country that has embraced Western culture. Here, women confront starkly different definitions of what is "feminine."
Staton R. Winter, *The New York Times*.

behavior—a reaction that helps us see not only what the rules are but how important they are to everyday reality.

Members of every culture have rules about how close people should stand while talking. To test this assumption, during a conversation slowly move closer and closer to the other person and see what happens.

REALITY BUILDING: CLASS AND CULTURE

People do not build everyday experience out of thin air. In part, how we act or what we see in our surroundings depends on our interests. Gazing at the sky on a starry night, for example, lovers discover romance, and scientists see hydrogen atoms fusing into helium. Social background also affects what we see, which is why the residents of Spanish Harlem experience a different world than people living on Manhattan's pricey Upper East Side.

In global perspective, reality construction varies even more. Consider these everyday situations: People waiting for a bus in London typically "queue up" in a straight line; people in New York City are rarely so orderly. The law in Saudi Arabia forbids women to drive cars, a ban unthinkable in the United States. In this country, a "short walk" means a few blocks or a few minutes; in the Andes Mountains of Peru, this same phrase means a few miles.

The point is that people build reality from the surrounding culture. Chapter 2 ("Culture") explains how

people the world over find different meanings in specific gestures, so inexperienced travelers can find themselves building an unexpected and unwelcome reality. Similarly, in a study of popular culture, JoEllen Shively (1992) screened films set in the American West to men of European descent and to Native American men. The men in both categories claimed to enjoy the films but for different reasons. White men interpreted the films as praising rugged people striking out for the frontier and conquering the forces of nature. Native American men saw in the same films a celebration of land and nature. Given their different cultures, it is as if people in the two categories saw two different films.

Films also have an effect on the reality we all experience. The 2004 film *Ray,* for example, about the life of the musician Ray Charles, who overcame the challenge of blindness, is one of a series of recent films that have changed people's awareness of disabilities.

Dramaturgical Analysis: The "Presentation of Self"

Erving Goffman (1922–1982) was another sociologist who analyzed social interaction, explaining how people live their lives much like actors performing on a stage. If we imagine ourselves as directors observing what goes on in the theater of everyday life, we are doing what Goffman called **dramaturgical analysis,** *the study of social interaction in terms of theatrical performance.*

Dramaturgical analysis offers a fresh look at the concepts of status and role. A status is like a part in a play, and a role is a script, supplying dialogue and action for the characters. Goffman described each person's performance as the **presentation of self,** *a person's efforts to create specific impressions in the minds of others.* This process, sometimes called *impression management,* begins with the idea of personal performance (Goffman, 1959, 1967).

PERFORMANCES

As we present ourselves in everyday situations, we reveal information to others both consciously and unconsciously. Our performances include the way we dress (costume), the objects we carry (props), and our tone of voice and the way we carry ourselves (demeanor). In addition, we vary our performances according to where we are (the set). We may joke loudly in a restaurant, for example, but lower our voices when entering a church. People design settings, such as homes or offices, to bring about desired reactions in others.

An Application: The Doctor's Office

Consider how a physician uses an office to convey particular information to an audience of patients. The fact that medical doctors enjoy high prestige and power in the United States is clear upon entering one of their offices.

First, the doctor is nowhere to be seen. Instead, in what Goffman describes as the "front region" of the setting, the patient encounters a receptionist, or gatekeeper, who decides whether and when the patient can meet the doctor. A simple survey of the doctor's waiting room, with patients (often impatiently) waiting to gain entry to the inner sanctum, leaves little doubt that the doctor and the staff are in charge.

The "back region" is composed of the examination rooms as well as the doctor's private office. Once inside the office, the patient can see a wide range of props, such as medical books and framed degrees, that give the impression that the doctor has the specialized knowledge necessary to call the shots. The doctor usually is seated behind a desk—the larger and grander the desk, the greater the statement of power—and the patient is given only a chair.

The doctor's appearance and manner offer still more information. The usual white lab coat (costume) may have the practical function of keeping clothes from becoming dirty, but its social function is to let others know at a glance the physician's status. A stethoscope around the neck and a black medical bag in hand (more props) have the same purpose. The doctor uses highly technical language that is often mystifying to the patient, again emphasizing that the doctor

is in charge. Finally, patients use the title "doctor," but they, in turn, are often addressed only by their first names, which further shows the doctor's dominant position. The overall message of a doctor's performance is clear: "I will help you, but you must allow me to take charge."

Try doing a similar analysis of the offices of several faculty members on your campus. What differences do you notice? How can you explain the patterns?

NONVERBAL COMMUNICATION

The novelist William Sansom describes the performance of a character named Mr. Preedy, an English vacationer on a beach in Spain:

> He took care to avoid catching anyone's eye. First, he had to make it clear to those potential companions of his holiday that they were of no concern to him whatsoever. He stared through them, round them, over them—eyes lost in space. The beach might have been empty. If by chance a ball was thrown his way, he looked surprised; then let a smile of amusement light his face (Kindly Preedy), looked around dazed to see that there were people on the beach, tossed it back with a smile to himself and not a smile *at* the people. . . .

[He] then gathered together his beach-wrap and bag into a neat sand-resistant pile (Methodical and Sensible Preedy), rose slowly to stretch his huge frame (Big-Cat Preedy), and tossed aside his sandals (Carefree Preedy, after all). (1956:230–31)

Without saying a single word, Mr. Preedy offers a great deal of information about himself to anyone watching him. This is the process of **nonverbal communication,** *communication using body movements, gestures, and facial expressions rather than speech.*

Many parts of the body can be used to generate *body language,* that is, to convey information to others. Facial expressions are the most significant form of body language. Smiling, for example, shows pleasure, although we distinguish among the deliberate smile of Kindly Preedy on the beach, a spontaneous smile of joy at seeing a friend, a pained smile of embarrassment, and the full, unrestrained smile of self-satisfaction we often associate with winning some important contest.

Eye contact is another crucial element of nonverbal communication. Generally, we use eye contact to invite social interaction. Someone across the room "catches our eye," sparking a conversation. Avoiding another's eyes, by contrast, discourages communication. Hands also speak for us. Common hand gestures within our culture convey, among other things, an insult, a request for a ride, an invitation for someone to join us, or a demand that others stop in their tracks. Gestures also add meaning to spoken words. For example, pointing in a threatening way gives greater emphasis to a word of warning, shrugging the shoulders adds an air of indifference to the phrase "I don't know," and rapidly waving the arms lends urgency to the single word "Hurry!"

Body Language and Deception

As any actor knows, it is very difficult to pull off a perfect performance in front of others. In everyday performances, unintended body language can contradict our planned meaning: A teenage boy explains why he is getting home so late, for example, but his mother doubts his words because he avoids looking her in the eye; the movie star on a television talk show claims that her recent flop at the box office is "no big deal," but the nervous swing of her leg suggests otherwise. Because nonverbal communication is hard to control, it provides clues to deception, in much the same way that changes in breathing, pulse rate, perspiration, and blood pressure recorded on a lie detector suggest that a person is lying.

Look at the two faces in the Seeing Sociology in Everyday Life box. Can you tell which one is the honest smile and which one is phony? Recognizing dishonest performances is difficult, because no one bodily gesture tells us for sure that someone is lying. But because any performance involves so many forms of body language, few people can keep up a lie without some slip-up, raising the suspicions of a careful observer. Therefore, the key to detecting lies is to view the whole performance with an eye for inconsistencies.

GENDER AND PERFORMANCES

Because women are socialized to respond to others, they tend to be more sensitive than men to nonverbal communication. In fact, gender is a central element in personal performances.

Demeanor

Demeanor—the way we act and carry ourselves—is a clue to social power. Simply put, powerful people enjoy more personal freedom in how they act. Off-color remarks, swearing, or putting your feet on the desk may be acceptable for the boss but rarely for employees. Similarly, powerful people can interrupt others, but less powerful people are expected to show respect through silence (Smith-Lovin & Brody, 1989; Henley, Hamilton, & Thorne, 1992; C. Johnson, 1994).

Because women generally occupy positions of less power, demeanor is a gender issue as well. As Chapter 10 ("Gender Stratification") explains, 43 percent of all working women in the United States hold secretarial or service jobs under the control of supervisors who are usually men. Women, then, learn to craft their personal performances more carefully than men and defer to men more often in everyday interaction.

Use of Space

How much space does a personal performance require? Power plays a key role here; the more power you have, the more space you use. Men typically command more space than women, whether pacing back and forth before an audience or casually sitting on a bench. Why? Our culture has traditionally measured femininity by how *little* space women occupy—the standard of "daintiness"—and masculinity by how *much* territory a man controls—the standard of "turf" (Henley, Hamilton, & Thorne, 1992).

For both sexes, **personal space** is *the surrounding area over which a person makes some claim to privacy.* In the United States, people generally stay several feet apart when speaking; throughout the Middle East, by contrast, people stand much closer. But just about everywhere, men (with their greater social power) often intrude into women's personal space. If a woman moves into a man's personal space, however, he is likely to take it as a sign of sexual interest.

Spotting Lies: What Are the Clues?

Deception is common in today's world. There may be no way to rid the world of dishonesty, but researchers have learned a great deal about how to tell when someone is lying. According to Paul Ekman, a specialist in analyzing social interaction, clues to deception can be found in four elements of a performance: words, voice, body language, and facial expressions.

1. **Words.** People who are good liars mentally go over their lines, but they may say something that is inconsistent, thereby suggesting deception. In addition, a simple slip of the tongue—something the person did not mean to say in quite that way—can occur in even a carefully prepared performance. Any such "leak" might indicate that the person is hiding something.

2. **Voice.** Tone and patterns of speech contain clues to deception because they are hard to control. Especially when hiding a powerful emotion, a person cannot easily prevent the voice from trembling or breaking. Speed provides another clue; an individ-

ual may speak more quickly than normal, suggesting anger, or more slowly, indicating sadness.

3. **Body language.** A "leak" conveyed through body language, which is also difficult to control, may tip off an observer to deception. Subtle body movements, sudden swallowing, or rapid breathing may show that the person is nervous. Powerful emotions that flash through a performance and change body language—what Ekman calls a "hot spot"—are good clues to deception.

4. **Facial expressions.** Because there are forty-three different muscles in the face, facial expressions are more difficult to control than other

body language. Look at the two faces in the photos. Can you tell which is the lying face? It's the one on the left. A real smile is usually accompanied by a relaxed expression and lots of "laugh lines" around the eyes; a phony smile seems forced and unnatural, with fewer wrinkles around the mouth and eyes.

We all try to fake emotions—some of us more successfully than others.

 For more on detecting deception, visit http://www.sciencenews.org/articles/20040731/bob8.asp

But the more powerful the emotion, the more difficult it is to deceive others.

WHAT DO YOU THINK?

1. Why can parents usually tell if their children are not being entirely truthful?

2. How might a police officer stopping a motorist make use of Ekman's research?

3. Are there "good liars" and "bad liars"? Explain.

Sources: Based on Ekman (1985), F. Golden (1999), and R. L. Kaufman (2002).

Staring, Smiling, and Touching

Eye contact encourages interaction. In conversations, women hold eye contact more than men. But men have their own brand of eye contact: staring. When men stare at women, they are claiming social dominance and defining women as sexual objects.

Although it often shows pleasure, smiling can also be a sign of trying to please someone or of submission. In a male-dominated world, it is not surprising that women smile more than men (Henley, Hamilton, & Thorne, 1992).

Finally, mutual touching suggests intimacy and caring. Apart from close relationships, however, touching is generally something men do to women (but rarely, in our culture, to other men). A male doctor touches the shoulder of his female nurse as they examine a report, a young man touches the back of his woman friend as he guides her across the street, or a male instructor touches the arms of young women as he teaches them to ski. In such examples, the intent of the touching may be harmless and may bring little response, but it amounts to a subtle ritual by which men claim dominance over women.

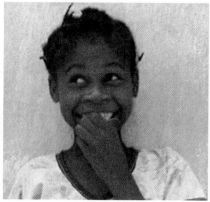

Hand gestures vary widely from one culture to another. Yet people everywhere chuckle, grin, or smirk to indicate that they don't take another person's performance seriously. Therefore, the world over, people who cannot restrain their mirth tactfully cover their faces.

YOUR TURN

Watch female-male couples holding hands. Which person has the hand to the front and which has the hand to the rear? Can you see a pattern and offer an explanation?

IDEALIZATION

People behave the way they do for many, often complex reasons. Even so, Goffman suggests, we construct performances to *idealize* our intentions. That is, we try to convince others (and perhaps ourselves) that our actions reflect ideal cultural standards rather than selfish motives.

Idealization is easily illustrated by returning to the world of doctors and patients. In a hospital, doctors engage in a performance known as "making rounds." Upon entering a patient's room, the doctor often stops at the foot of the bed and silently examines the patient's chart. Afterward, doctor and patient talk briefly. In ideal terms, this routine represents a personal visit to check on a patient's condition.

In reality, the picture is not so perfect. A doctor may see dozens of patients a day and remember little about many of them. Reading the chart is a chance to recall the patient's name and medical problems, but revealing the impersonality of the patient's care would undermine the cultural ideal of the doctor as deeply concerned about the welfare of others.

Doctors, college professors, and other professionals typically idealize their motives for entering their chosen careers. They describe their work as "making a contribution to science," "serving the community," or even "answering a call from God." Rarely do people admit the more common, less honorable motives: the income, power, prestige, and leisure time that these occupations provide.

We all use idealization to some degree. When was the last time you smiled and made polite remarks to someone you did not like? Such little lies ease our way through social interactions. Even when we suspect that others are putting on an act, we are unlikely to challenge their performance, for reasons that we shall examine next.

EMBARRASSMENT AND TACT

The famous speaker keeps mispronouncing the dean's name; the visiting ambassador rises from the table to speak, unaware of the napkin that still hangs from his neck; the president becomes ill at a state dinner. As carefully as people may craft their performances, slip-ups of all kinds happen. The result is *embarrassment,* or discomfort after a spoiled performance. Goffman describes embarrassment as "losing face."

Embarrassment is an ever-present danger because idealized performances typically contain some deception. In addition, most performances involve juggling so many elements that one thoughtless moment can shatter the intended impression.

A curious fact is that an audience often overlooks flaws in a performance, allowing the actor to avoid embarrassment. If we do point out a misstep ("Excuse me, but do you know your fly is open?"), we do it quietly and only to help someone avoid even greater loss of face. In Hans Christian Andersen's classic fable "The Emperor's New Clothes," the child who blurts out the truth, that the emperor is parading about naked, is scolded for being rude.

Often members of an audience actually help the performer recover from a flawed performance. *Tact* is helping someone "save face." After hearing a supposed expert make an embarrassingly inaccurate remark, for example, we

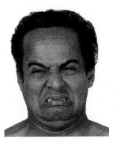

To most people in the United States, these expressions convey anger, fear, disgust, happiness, surprise, and sadness. But do people elsewhere in the world define them in the same way? Research suggests that all human beings experience the same basic emotions and display them to others in the same basic ways. But culture plays a part by specifying the situations that trigger one emotion or another.

might ignore the comment, as if it had never been spoken. Or with mild laughter we could treat what was said as a joke. Or we could simply respond, "I'm sure you didn't mean that," hearing the statement but not allowing it to destroy the actor's performance. With these options in mind, it is easier to understand Abraham Lincoln's comment, "Tact is the ability to describe others the way they see themselves."

Why is tact so common? Embarrassment creates discomfort not only for the actor but also for everyone else. Just as the entire audience feels uneasy when an actor forgets a line, people who observe the awkward behavior of others are reminded of how fragile their own performances often are. Socially constructed reality thus functions like a dam holding back a sea of chaos. Should one person's performance spring a leak, others tactfully help make repairs. After all, everyone lends a hand in building reality, and no one wants it to be suddenly swept away.

In sum, Goffman's research shows that although behavior is spontaneous in some respects, it is more patterned than we like to think. Almost 400 years ago, William Shakespeare captured this idea in lines that still ring true:

All the world's a stage,
And all the men and women merely players:
They have their exits and their entrances;
And one man in his time plays many parts.
(*As You Like It*, act 2, scene 7)

Using Goffman's approach, explain the importance of performances, nonverbal communication, idealization, and tact using, as much as you can, examples from your own life.

Interaction in Everyday Life: Three Applications

The final sections of this chapter illustrate the major elements of social interaction by focusing on three important dimensions of everyday life: emotions, language, and humor.

Is it possible to build a machine capable of human interaction? Check out http://www.ai.mit.edu/projects/humanoid-robotics-group/

EMOTIONS: THE SOCIAL CONSTRUCTION OF FEELING

Emotions, more commonly called *feelings,* are an important dimension of everyday life. Indeed, what we *do* often matters less than how we *feel* about it. Emotions seem very personal because they are "inside." Even so, just as society guides our behavior, it guides our emotional life.

The Biological Side of Emotions

Studying people all over the world, Paul Ekman (1980a, 1980b) reported that people everywhere express six basic emotions: happiness, sadness, anger, fear, disgust, and surprise. In addition, Ekman found that all people use much the same facial expressions to show these emotions. Indeed, he argues, some emotional responses seem to be "wired" into human beings, that is, biologically programmed in our facial features, muscles, and central nervous system.

Why? Over centuries of evolution, emotions developed in the human species because they serve a social purpose: supporting group life. Emotions are powerful forces that allow us to overcome our individualism and build connections with others. Thus the capacity for emotion arose in our ancestors along with the capacity for culture (Turner, 2000).

Many of us think emotions are simply part of our biological makeup. While there is a biological foundation to human emotion, sociologists have demonstrated that what triggers an emotion—as well as when, where, and to whom the emotion is displayed—is shaped by culture. For example, many jobs not only regulate a worker's behavior, but also expect workers to display a particular emotion, as in the case of the always-smiling airline flight attendant. Can you think of other jobs that regulate emotions in this way?

The Cultural Side of Emotions

But culture does play an important role in guiding human emotions. First, Ekman explains, culture defines *what triggers* an emotion. Whether people define the departure of an old friend as joyous (causing happiness), insulting (arousing anger), a loss (creating sadness), or a mystical event (causing surprise and awe) has a lot to do with the culture. Second, culture provides rules for the *display* of emotions. For example, most people in the United States express emotions more freely with family members than with others in the workplace. Similarly, we expect children to express emotions to parents, although parents tend to hide their emotions from their children. Third, culture guides how we *value* emotions. Some societies encourage the expression of emotion, while others expect members to control their feelings and maintain a "stiff upper lip." Gender also plays a part; traditionally at least, many cultures expect women to show emotions while condemning emotional expression by men as a sign of weakness. In some cultures, of course, this pattern is less pronounced or even reversed.

Emotions on the Job

In the United States, most people are freer to express their feelings at home than on the job. This is because, as Arlie Russell Hochschild (1979, 1983) explains, the typical company does indeed try to control not only the behavior but also the emotions of its employees. Take the case of an airline flight attendant who offers passengers a pillow, a drink, and a smile. Although this smile might convey real pleasure at serving the customer, Hochschild's study of flight attendants points to a different conclusion: The smile is an emotional script demanded by the airline as the right way to perform the workplace role. Therefore, we see that the "presentation of self" described by Erving Goffman can involve not just surface acting but also the "deep acting" of emotions.

SOCIOLOGY ⨁ WORK

With these patterns in mind, it is easy to see that we socially construct our emotions as part of our everyday reality, a process sociologists call *emotion management*. The Thinking Critically box relates the very different emotions displayed by women who decide to have an abortion, depending on their personal view of terminating a pregnancy.

LANGUAGE: THE SOCIAL CONSTRUCTION OF GENDER

As Chapter 2 ("Culture") explains, language is the thread that weaves members of a society in the symbolic web we call culture. Language conveys not only a surface message but also deeper levels of meaning. One important level involves gender. Language defines men and women differently in terms of both power and value (Henley, Hamilton, & Thorne, 1992; Thorne, Kramarae, & Henley, 1983).

Language and Power

A young man proudly rides his new motorcycle up his friend's driveway and asks, "Isn't she a beauty?" On the surface, the question has little to do with gender. Yet why does he use the pronoun *she* rather than *he* or *it* to refer to his prized possession?

The answer is that language helps men establish control over their surroundings. That is, a man attaches a female pronoun to a motorcycle (or car, boat, or other object) because doing so reflects *ownership*. Perhaps this is also why, in the United States and elsewhere, traditionally a woman who marries takes the last name of her husband. Because today's women in the United States value their independence, many (about 15 percent) now keep their own name or combine the two family names.

Language and Value

Typically, the English language treats as masculine whatever has greater value, force, or significance. For instance, the

Managing Feelings: Women's Abortion Experiences

Few issues today generate as much emotion as abortion. In a study of women's abortion experiences, the sociologist Jennifer Keys (2002) discovered emotional scripts or "feeling rules" that guide how women feel about ending a pregnancy.

Keys explains that different emotional scripts arise from the political controversy surrounding abortion. The antiabortion movement defines abortion as a personal tragedy, the "killing of an unborn child." Given this definition, women who end a pregnancy through abortion are doing something very wrong and can expect to feel grief, guilt, and regret. So intense are these feelings, according to supporters of this position, that such women often suffer from "postabortion syndrome."

Those who take the pro-choice position have an opposing view of abortion. From this point of view, the woman's problem is the *unwanted pregnancy;* abortion is an acceptable medical solution. Therefore, the emotion to be expected in a woman who ends a pregnancy is not guilt but relief.

In her research, Keys conducted in-depth interviews with forty women who had recently had abortions and found that all of them used such scripts to "frame" their situation in an antiabortion or pro-choice manner. In part, this construction of reality reflects the woman's own attitude about abortion. In addition, however, women's partners

and friends typically encouraged specific feelings about the event. Ivy, one young woman in the study, had a close friend who was also pregnant. "Congratulations!" she exclaimed when she learned of Ivy's condition. "We're going to be having babies together!" Such a statement established one "feeling rule": having a baby is *good,* which sent the message to Ivy that her planned abortion should trigger guilt. Working in the other direction, Jo's partner was horrified at the news that she was pregnant. Doubting his own ability to be a father, he blurted out, "I would rather put a gun to my head than have this baby!" His panic not only defined having the child as a mistake but alarmed Jo as well. Clearly, her partner's reaction made the decision to end the pregnancy a matter of relief from a terrible problem.

Medical personnel also play a part in the process of reality construction by using specific terms. Nurses and doctors who talk about "the baby" encourage the antiabortion framing of abortion and provoke grief and guilt. On the other hand, those who use language such as "pregnancy tissue," "fetus," or "the contents of the uterus" encourage the pro-choice framing of abortion as a simple medical procedure leading to relief. Olivia began using the phrase "products of conception," which she picked up from her doctor. Denise spoke of her procedure as "taking the

extra cells out of my body." She explained, "Yeah, I did feel some guilt when I thought that this was the beginning of life, but my body is full of life—you have lots of cells in you."

After the procedure, most women reported actively trying to manage their feelings. Explained Ivy, "I never used the word 'baby.' I kept saying to myself that it was not formed yet. There was nothing there yet. I kept that in my mind." On the other hand, Keys found that all of the women in her study who had undergone abortions but nevertheless leaned toward the antiabortion position did use the term "baby." When interviewed, Gina explained, "I do think of it as a baby. The truth is that I ended my baby's life and I should not have done that. Thinking that makes me feel guilty. But—considering what I did—maybe I *should* feel guilty." Believing that what she had done was wrong, in other words, Gina actively called out the feeling of guilt—in part, Keys concluded, to punish herself.

WHAT DO YOU THINK?

1. In your own words, what are "emotional scripts" or "feeling rules"?

2. Can you apply the idea of "scripting feelings" to the experience of getting married?

3. In light of this discussion, to what extent is it correct to say that our feelings are not as personal as we might have thought?

adjective "virtuous," meaning "morally worthy" or "excellent," is derived from the Latin word *vir,* meaning "man." On the other hand, the adjective "hysterical," meaning "uncontrollable emotion," comes from the Greek word *hyster,* meaning "uterus."

In many familiar ways, language also confers a different value on the two sexes. Traditional masculine terms

such as "king" or "lord" have a positive meaning, while comparable terms, such as "queen," "madam," or "dame," can have negative meanings. Similarly, the use of the suffixes "-ess" and "-ette" to indicate femininity usually devalues the words to which they are added. For example, a "major" has higher standing than a "majorette," as does a "host" in relation to a "hostess" or a "master" to a "mis-

SOCIAL INTERACTION IN EVERYDAY LIFE   CHAPTER 4   **109**

Gender and Language: "You Just Don't Understand!"

In the story that opened this chapter, Harold and Sybil faced a situation that rings all too true to many people: When they are lost, men grumble to themselves and perhaps blame their partners but avoid asking for directions. For their part, women can't understand why men refuse help when they need it.

Deborah Tannen (1990) explains that men typically define most everyday encounters as competitive. Therefore, getting lost is bad enough without asking for help, which lets someone else get "one up." By contrast, because women traditionally have had a subordinate position, they find it easy to ask for help. Sometimes, Tannen points out, women ask for assistance even when they don't need it.

A similar gender-linked pattern involves what women consider "trying to be helpful" and men call "nagging." Consider the following exchange (adapted from Adler, 1990):

SYBIL: What's wrong, honey?
HAROLD: Nothing.
SYBIL: Something is bothering you. I can tell.
HAROLD: I told you nothing is bothering me. Leave me alone.
SYBIL: But I can see that something is wrong.
HAROLD: OK. Just why do you think something is bothering me?
SYBIL: Well, for one thing, you're bleeding all over your shirt.
HAROLD: (*now irritated*) Yeah, well, it doesn't bother me.
SYBIL: (*losing her temper*) WELL, IT SURE IS BOTHERING ME!
HAROLD: Fine. I'll go change my shirt.

The problem couples face in communicating is that what one partner *intends* by a comment is not always what the other *hears* in the words. To Sybil, her opening question is an effort at cooperative problem solving. She can see that something is wrong with Harold (who has cut himself while doing yard work), and she wants to help him. But Harold interprets her pointing out his problem as belittling

him and tries to close off the discussion. Sybil, confident that Harold would be more positive toward her if he just understood that she only wants to be helpful, repeats her question. This sets in motion a vicious circle in which Harold, thinking his wife is trying to make him feel incapable of looking after himself, responds by digging in his heels. This, in turn, makes his wife all the more sure that she needs to do something. And around it goes until somebody gets really angry.

In the end, Harold agrees to change his shirt but still refuses to discuss the original problem. Defining his wife's concern as "nagging," Harold just wants Sybil to leave him alone. For her part, Sybil fails to understand her husband's view of the situation and walks away convinced that he is a stubborn grouch.

WHAT DO YOU THINK?

1. Based on this box, how would you describe the basic difference between the way men and women talk?

2. What are the reasons for any gender differences in language?

3. Do you think that understanding Tannen's conclusions would help female-male couples communicate better? Why or why not?

tress." Thus language both mirrors social attitudes and helps perpetuate them.

List words that describe a very sexually active female. Are they positive or negative in meaning? Repeat the same exercise for a male. What differences do you notice?

Given the importance of gender to social interaction in everyday life, perhaps we should not be surprised that women and men sometimes have trouble communicating with each other. In the Thinking About Diversity box, Harold and Sybil, whose misadventures finding their friends' home were described in the opening to this chapter, return to illustrate how the two sexes often seem to be speaking different languages.

Reality Play: The Social Construction of Humor

Humor plays an important part in everyday life. Everyone laughs at a joke, but few people think about what makes something funny. We can apply many of the ideas developed in this chapter to explain how, by using humor, we "play with reality" (Macionis, 1987).

The Foundation of Humor

Humor is produced by the social construction of reality; specifically, it arises as people create and contrast two different realities. Generally, one reality is *conventional,* that is, what people in a specific situation expect. The other reality is *unconventional,* an unexpected violation of cultural patterns. In short, humor arises from the contradictions, ambiguities, and double meanings found in differing definitions of the same situation.

There are countless ways to mix realities and thereby generate humor. Contrasting realities emerge from statements that contradict themselves, such as "Nostalgia is not what it used to be"; statements that repeat themselves, such as Yogi Berra's line "It's *déjà vu* all over again"; or statements that mix up words, such as Oscar Wilde's line, "Work is the curse of the drinking class." Even switching around syllables does the trick, as in the case of the country song "I'd Rather Have a Bottle in Front of Me than a Frontal Lobotomy."

Of course, a joke can be built the other way around, so that the comic leads the audience to expect an unconventional answer and then delivers a very ordinary one. When a reporter asked the famous criminal Willy Sutton why he robbed banks, for example, he replied dryly, "Because that's where the money is." Regardless of how a joke is constructed, the greater the opposition or difference between the two definitions of reality, the greater the humor.

When telling jokes, the comedian uses various strategies to strengthen this opposition and make the joke funnier. One common technique is to present the first, conventional remark in conversation with another actor and then turn toward the audience or the camera to deliver the second, unexpected line. In a Marx Brothers movie, Groucho remarks, "Outside of a dog, a book is a man's best friend." Then, raising his voice and turning to the camera, he adds, "And *inside* of a dog, it's too dark to read!" Such "changing channels" emphasizes the difference between the conventional and unconventional realities. Following the same logic, many stand-up comedians also "reset" the audience to conventional expectations by adding "But seriously, folks, . . ." between jokes. Monty Python comedian John Cleese did this with his trademark line, "And now for something completely different."

Because humor involves challenging established conventions, most U.S. comedians—including Dave Chappelle—have been social "outsiders," members of racial and ethnic minorities.

Comedians pay careful attention to their performances—the precise words they use and the timing of their delivery. A joke is well told if the comic times the lines to create the sharpest possible opposition between the realities; in a careless performance, the joke falls flat. Because the key to humor lies in the collision of realities, we can see why the climax of a joke is termed the "*punch* line."

The Dynamics of Humor: "Getting It"

After someone told you a joke, did you ever have to say, "I don't get it"? To "get" humor, members of an audience must understand the two realities involved well enough to appreciate their difference. A comedian may make getting the joke harder by leaving out some important information. In other words, the audience must pay attention to the stated elements of the joke and fill in the missing pieces on their own. As a simple example, consider the comment of movie producer Hal Roach upon reaching his hundredth birthday: "If I had known I would live to be one hundred, I would

May 22, 2005

Seriously, the Joke Is Dead

By WARREN ST. JOHN

In case you missed its obituary, the joke died recently after a long illness. . . . Its passing was barely noticed, drowned out, perhaps, by the din of ironic one-liners, snark and detached bons mots that pass for humor these days. . . .

It's a matter of faith among professional comics that jokes—the kind that involve a narrative setup, some ridiculous details and a punch line—have been displaced by observational humor and one-liners. . . .

The joke hung on for a while, lurking in backwaters of male camaraderie like bachelor parties and trading floors and in monthly installments of Playboy's "Party Jokes" page. Then jokes practically vanished. To tell a joke at the office or a party these days is to pronounce oneself a cornball, an attention hog, and of course to risk offending someone, a high social crime. . . .

Among comics, the most cited culprit in the death of the joke is so-called "political correctness" or, at least, a heightened sensitivity to offending people. . . .

Older comics tend to put the blame on the failings of younger generations. Robert Orben, 78, a former speechwriter for President Gerald R. Ford and the author of several manuals for comedians, said he believed a combination of shortened attention spans and lack of backbone among today's youth made them ill-suited for joke telling. . . .

While humor has always been around . . . the joke has gone in and out of fashion. In modern times its heyday was probably the 1950's, but the joke's demise began soon after, a result of several seismic cultural shifts. The first of those . . . was the threat of nuclear annihilation. . . .

Around the same time, said John Morreall, a religion professor and humor scholar at the College of William and Mary, the roles of men and women began to change. . . .

Telling old-style jokes, he said, was a masculine pursuit because it allowed men to communicate with one another without actually revealing anything about themselves. Historically women's humor was based on personal experience, and conveyed a sense of the teller's likes and dislikes, foibles and capacity for self-deprecation. . . .

Over time men let down their guard, and comics like Lenny Bruce, George

---

have taken better care of myself!" Here, getting the joke depends on realizing the unstated fact that Roach must have taken pretty good care of himself because he did make it to one hundred. Or take one of W. C. Fields's lines: "Some weasel took the cork out of my lunch!" "What a lunch!" we think to ourselves to "finish" the joke.

Here is an even more complex joke: What do you get if you cross an insomniac, a dyslexic, and an agnostic? Answer: A person who stays up all night wondering if there is a dog. To get this one, you must know that insomnia is an inability to sleep, that dyslexia causes a person to reverse letters in words, and that an agnostic doubts the existence of God.

Why would an audience be required to make this kind of effort to understand a joke? Our enjoyment of a joke is increased by the pleasure of figuring out all the pieces needed to "get it." In addition, "getting" the joke makes you an "insider" compared to those who don't "get it." We have all experienced the frustration of *not* getting a joke: fear of being judged stupid, coupled with a sense of being excluded from a pleasure shared by others. Sometimes someone may tactfully explain a joke so the other person doesn't feel left out. But as the old saying goes, if a joke has to be explained, it won't be very funny.

The Topics of Humor

All over the world, people smile and laugh, making humor a universal element of human culture. But because the world's people live in different cultures, humor rarely travels well.

 October 1, Kobe, Japan. Can you share a joke with people who live halfway around the world? At dinner, I ask two Japanese college women to tell me a joke. "You know 'crayon'?" Asako asks. I nod. "How do you ask for a crayon in Japanese?" I respond that I have no idea. She laughs out loud as she says what sounds like "crayon crayon." Her companion Mayumi laughs, too. My wife and I sit awkwardly, straight-faced. Asako relieves some of our embarrassment by explaining that the Japanese word for "give me" is <u>kureyo,</u> which sounds like "crayon." I force a smile.

Carlin and later Jerry Seinfeld, embraced the personal, observational style.

"A very common quip was, 'Women can't tell jokes,'" Mr. Morreall said. " . . . Their humor is observational humor about the people around that they care about." . . .

"Women's-style humor was ahead of the curve," he said. "In the last 30 years all humor has caught up with women's humor."

The mingling of the sexes in the workplace and in social situations wasn't particularly good for the joke either, as jokes that played well in the locker room didn't translate to the conference room or the co-ed dinner party. . . . In any event, . . . in a social situation wit plays better than old-style joke telling. Witty remarks push the conversation along and enliven it, encouraging others to contribute.

Jokes, on the other hand, cause conversation to screech to a halt and require everyone to focus on the joke teller, which can be awkward. . . .

The torrent of e-mail jokes in the late 1990's and joke Web sites made every joke available at once. . . . Forwarding a joke by e-mail takes hardly any effort at all. So everyone did it, until it wasn't funny anymore. . . .

One paradox about the death of the joke: It may result in more laughs. Joke tellers, after all, are limited by the number of jokes they can memorize, while observational wits never run out of material. And . . . the threshold for getting a laugh is lower for them than for joke tellers, who always battle high expectations.

"Jon Stewart just has to twist his eye brows a little bit, and people laugh," [Mr. Morreall] said. "It's a much easier medium." . . .

WHAT DO YOU THINK?

1. What factors does the article suggest explain the decline of traditional joke-telling?

2. In what ways have the changing relationships between men and women affected humor?

3. What types of humor are common in your everyday life?

Adapted from the original article by Warren St. John published in *The New York Times* on May 22, 2005. Copyright © 2005 by The New York Times Company. Reprinted with permission.

What is humorous to the Japanese, then, may be lost on the Chinese, Iraqis, or people in the United States. Even the social diversity of this country means that people will find humor in different situations. New Englanders, southerners, and westerners have their own brands of humor, as do Latinos and Anglos, fifteen- and fifty-year-olds, Wall Street bankers and rodeo riders.

But for everyone, topics that lend themselves to double meanings or controversy generate humor. For example, in the United States, the first jokes many of us learned as children concerned bodily functions kids are not supposed to talk about. The mere mention of "unmentionable acts" or certain parts of the body can dissolve young faces in laughter.

Are there jokes that can break through the cultural barrier? Yes, but they must touch on universal human experiences such as, say, turning on a friend:

I think of a number of jokes, but none seems likely to work. Understanding jokes about the United States is difficult for people who know little about our culture. Is there something more universal? Inspiration: "Two men are walking in the woods and come upon a huge bear. One guy leans over and tightens up the laces on his running shoes. 'Jake,' says the other, 'what are you doing? You can't outrun that bear!' 'I don't have to outrun the bear,' responds Jake. 'I just have to outrun you!'" Smiles all around.

The controversy found in humor often walks a fine line between what is funny and what is "sick." During the Middle Ages, people used the word "humors" (derived from the Latin *humidus*, meaning "moist") to mean a balance of bodily fluids that regulated a person's health. Researchers today document the power of humor to reduce stress and improve health, confirming the old saying, "Laughter is the best medicine" (Haig, 1988; Bakalar, 2005). At the extreme, however, people who always take conventional reality lightly risk being defined as deviant or even mentally ill (a common stereotype shows insane people laughing uncontrollably, and for a long time mental hospitals were known as "funny farms").

Then, too, every social group considers certain topics too sensitive for humorous treatment. If you joke about such things, you risk criticism for telling a "sick" joke (and being labeled "sick" yourself). People's religious beliefs, tragic accidents, or appalling crimes are some of the subjects of "sick" jokes or no jokes at all. Even years later, there have been no jokes about the victims of the September 11, 2001, terrorist attacks.

Here is a joke about sociologists: How many sociologists does it take to change a light bulb? Answer: None. There is nothing wrong with the light bulb; it's *the system* that needs to be changed! What makes this joke funny? What sort of people are likely to get it? What kind of people probably won't? Why?

The Functions of Humor

Humor is found everywhere because it works as a safety valve for potentially disruptive sentiments. Put another way, humor provides an acceptable way to discuss a sensitive topic without appearing to be serious or offensive. Having said something controversial, people often use humor to defuse the situation by simply stating, "I didn't mean anything by what I said—it was just a joke!"

People also use humor to relieve tension in uncomfortable situations. One study of medical examinations found that most patients try to joke with doctors to ease their own nervousness (P. S. Baker et al., 1997).

Humor and Conflict

Humor holds the potential to liberate those who laugh, but it can also be used to put down others. Men who tell jokes about women, for example, typically are voicing hostility toward them (Powell & Paton, 1988; Benokraitis & Feagin, 1995). Similarly, jokes about gay people reveal tensions about sexual orientation. Real conflict can be masked by humor when people choose not to bring the conflict out into the open (Primeggia & Varacalli, 1990).

"Put-down" jokes make one category of people feel good at the expense of another. After collecting and analyz-ing jokes from many societies, Christie Davies (1990) confirmed that ethnic conflict is a driving force behind humor in most of the world. The typical ethnic joke makes fun of some disadvantaged category of people, at the same time making the joke teller feel superior. Given the Anglo-Saxon traditions of U.S. society, Poles and other ethnic and racial minorities have long been the butt of jokes, as have New-foundlanders in eastern Canada, Scots in England, Irish in Scotland, Sikhs in India, Turks in Germany, Hausas in Nigeria, Tasmanians in Australia, and Kurds in Iraq. The fact that there is less tolerance today for such "put-down" humor may be one reason for the decline of traditional joke-telling, as "In the *Times*" on pages 112–13 explains.

Of course, disadvantaged people also make fun of the powerful, although usually with some care. Women in the United States joke about men, just as African Americans find humor in white people's ways and poor people poke fun at the rich. Throughout the world, people target their leaders with humor, and officials in some countries take such jokes seriously enough to arrest those who do not show proper respect (Speier, 1998).

In 2006, many in the Islamic world were enraged when European newspapers published cartoons depicting the prophet Muhammad. How does one person's humor become another's sacrilege?

In sum, humor is much more important than we may think. It is a means of mental escape from a conventional world that is not entirely to our liking (Flaherty, 1984, 1990; Yoels & Clair, 1995). This fact helps explain why so many of our nation's comedians come from the ranks of historically marginalized peoples, including Jews and African Americans. As long as we maintain a sense of humor, we assert our freedom and are never prisoners of reality. By putting a smile on our faces, we change ourselves and the world just a little—ideally, for the better.

APPLYING SOCIOLOGY IN EVERYDAY LIFE

1. Sketch out your own status set and role set. Identify any statuses and also any sources of role conflict and role strain.
2. During the next twenty-four hours, every time people ask "How are you?" stop and actually give a full and truthful answer. What happens when you respond to a polite question in an honest way? Listen to how people respond, and also watch their body language. What can you conclude?
3. Stroll around downtown or at a local mall. Pay attention to how many women and men you find at various locations. From your observations, are there stores that are "gendered" so that there are "female spaces" and "male spaces"? How and why are spaces "gendered"?

MAKING THE GRADE

CHAPTER 4 Social Interaction in Everyday Life

WHAT IS SOCIAL STRUCTURE?

SOCIAL STRUCTURE refers to social patterns that guide our behavior in everyday life.

p 96

The building blocks of social structure are
- **STATUS**—a social position that is part of our social identity and that defines our relationships to others
- **ROLE**—the action expected of a person who holds a particular status

pp 97–98

 A person holds a status and performs a role.

ASCRIBED STATUSES are involuntary.
ACHIEVED STATUSES are earned.
A **MASTER STATUS** has special importance for a person's identity.

pp 97–98

ROLE CONFLICT results from tension among roles linked to two or more statuses.

ROLE STRAIN results from tension among roles linked to a single status.

p 99

 A person's status set changes over the life course (p 97).

social interaction (p. 96) the process by which people act and react in relation to others

status (p. 97) a social position that a person holds

status set (p. 97) all the statuses a person holds at a given time

ascribed status (p. 97) a social position a person receives at birth or takes on involuntarily later in life

achieved status (p. 97) a social position a person takes on voluntarily that reflects personal ability and effort

master status (p. 97) a status that has special importance for social identity, often shaping a person's entire life

role (p. 98) behavior expected of someone who holds a particular status

role set (p. 98) a number of roles attached to a single status

role conflict (p. 99) conflict among the roles connected to two or more statuses

role strain (p. 99) tension among the roles connected to a single status

THE SOCIAL CONSTRUCTION OF REALITY

Through **SOCIAL INTERACTION**, we construct the reality we experience.

pp 99–100

The **THOMAS THEOREM** says that the reality people construct in their interaction has real consequences for the future.

p 101

Both **CULTURE** and **SOCIAL CLASS** shape the reality people construct.

p 102

ETHNOMETHODOLOGY is a strategy to reveal the assumptions people have about their social world.

pp 101–2

social construction of reality (p. 99) the process by which people creatively shape reality through social interaction

Thomas theorem (p. 101) W. I. Thomas's statement that situations defined as real are real in their consequences

ethnomethodology (p. 101) Harold Garfinkel's term for the study of the way people make sense of their everyday surroundings

 Through the social construction of reality, people creatively shape their social world (pp 99-101).

VISUAL SUMMARY

115

We carry out much of our daily lives as members of groups and organizations. As members of a church choir, these children learn the importance not only of music but of working together as members of a group.

MAKING THE GRADE

CHAPTER 4 Social Interaction in Everyday Life

WHAT IS SOCIAL STRUCTURE?

> **SOCIAL STRUCTURE** refers to social patterns that guide our behavior in everyday life.
>
> **p 96**

> The building blocks of social structure are
> - **STATUS**—a social position that is part of our social identity and that defines our relationships to others
> - **ROLE**—the action expected of a person who holds a particular status
>
> **pp 97–98**

 A person holds *a status* and performs *a role.*

> **ASCRIBED STATUSES** are involuntary.
> **ACHIEVED STATUSES** are earned.
> A **MASTER STATUS** has special importance for a person's identity.
>
> **pp 97–98**

> **ROLE CONFLICT** results from tension among roles linked to two or more statuses.
>
> **ROLE STRAIN** results from tension among roles linked to a single status.
>
> **p 99**

 A person's status set changes over the life course (p 97).

social interaction (p. 96) the process by which people act and react in relation to others

status (p. 97) a social position that a person holds

status set (p. 97) all the statuses a person holds at a given time

ascribed status (p. 97) a social position a person receives at birth or takes on involuntarily later in life

achieved status (p. 97) a social position a person takes on voluntarily that reflects personal ability and effort

master status (p. 97) a status that has special importance for social identity, often shaping a person's entire life

role (p. 98) behavior expected of someone who holds a particular status

role set (p. 98) a number of roles attached to a single status

role conflict (p. 99) conflict among the roles connected to two or more statuses

role strain (p. 99) tension among the roles connected to a single status

THE SOCIAL CONSTRUCTION OF REALITY

> Through **SOCIAL INTERACTION,** we construct the reality we experience.
>
> **pp 99–100**

> The **THOMAS THEOREM** says that the reality people construct in their interaction has real consequences for the future.
>
> **p 101**

> Both **CULTURE** and **SOCIAL CLASS** shape the reality people construct.
>
> **p 102**

> **ETHNOMETHODOLOGY** is a strategy to reveal the assumptions people have about their social world.
>
> **pp 101–2**

social construction of reality (p. 99) the process by which people creatively shape reality through social interaction

Thomas theorem (p. 101) W. I. Thomas's statement that situations defined as real are real in their consequences

ethnomethodology (p. 101) Harold Garfinkel's term for the study of the way people make sense of their everyday surroundings

 Through the social construction of reality, people creatively shape their social world (pp 99-101).

115

DRAMATURGICAL ANALYSIS: THE "PRESENTATION OF SELF"

DRAMATURGICAL ANALYSIS explores social interaction in terms of theatrical performance: A status operates as a part in a play and a role is a script.

PERFORMANCES are the way we present ourselves to others.
- Performances are both conscious (intentional action) and unconscious (nonverbal communication).
- Performances include costume (the way we dress), props (objects we carry), and demeanor (tone of voice and the way we carry ourselves).

pp 102–4

---

dramaturgical analysis (p. 102) Erving Goffman's term for the study of social interaction in terms of theatrical performance

presentation of self (p. 103) Erving Goffman's term for a person's efforts to create specific impressions in the minds of others

nonverbal communication (p. 104) communication using body movements, gestures, and facial expressions rather than speech

personal space (p. 104) the surrounding area over which a person makes some claim to privacy

---

GENDER affects performances because men typically have greater social power than women. Gender differences involve *demeanor, use of space,* and *staring, smiling, and touching.*

pp 104–6

DEMEANOR—With greater social power, men have more freedom in how they act.

p 104

USE OF SPACE—Men typically command more space than women.

p 104

STARING and **TOUCHING** are generally done by men to women.

SMILING, as a way to please another, is more commonly done by women.

p 105

IDEALIZATION of performances means we try to convince others that our actions reflect ideal culture rather than selfish motives.

p 106

EMBARRASSMENT is the "loss of face" in a performance. People use **TACT** to help others "save face."

pp 106–7

INTERACTION IN EVERYDAY LIFE: THREE APPLICATIONS

EMOTIONS: The Social Construction of **FEELING**

The same basic emotions are biologically programmed into all human beings, but culture guides what triggers emotions, how people display emotions, and how people value emotions. In everyday life, the presentation of self involves managing emotions as well as behavior.

pp 107–9

LANGUAGE: The Social Construction of **GENDER**

Gender is an important element of everyday interaction. Language defines women and men as different types of people, reflecting the fact that society attaches greater power and value to what is viewed as masculine.

pp 108–10

REALITY PLAY: The Social Construction of **HUMOR**

Humor results from the difference between conventional and unconventional definitions of a situation. Because humor is a part of culture, people around the world find different situations funny.

pp 111–14

MAKING THE GRADE
Sample Test Questions
CHAPTER 4

These questions are similar to those found in the test bank that accompanies this textbook.

MULTIPLE-CHOICE QUESTIONS

1. **Which term defines who and what we are in relation to others?**
   a. role
   b. status
   c. role set
   d. master status

2. **In U.S. society, which of the following might be a master status?**
   a. occupation
   b. physical or mental disability
   c. race or color
   d. All of the above are correct.

3. *Role set* refers to
   a. a number of roles found in any one society.
   b. a number of roles attached to a single status.
   c. a number of roles that are more or less the same.
   d. a number of roles within any one organization.

4. **Frank excels at football at his college, but he doesn't have enough time to study as much as he wants to. This problem is an example of**
   a. role set.
   b. role strain.
   c. role conflict.
   d. role exit.

5. **The Thomas theorem states that**
   a. our statuses and roles are the key to our personality.
   b. most people rise to their level of incompetence.
   c. people know the world only through their language.
   d. situations defined as real are real in their consequences.

6. **Which of the following is the correct meaning of "presentation of self"?**
   a. efforts to create impressions in the minds of others
   b. acting out a master status
   c. thinking back over the process of role exit
   d. trying to take attention away from others

7. **Paul Ekman points to what is an important clue to deception by another person?**
   a. smiling
   b. using tact
   c. inconsistencies in a presentation
   d. All of the above are correct.

8. **In terms of dramaturgical analysis, tact is understood as**
   a. helping someone take on a new role.
   b. helping another person "save face."
   c. making it hard for someone to perform a role.
   d. negotiating a situation to get your own way.

9. **In her study of human emotion, Arlie Hochschild explains that companies typically**
   a. try to regulate the emotions of workers.
   b. want workers to be unemotional.
   c. encourage people to express their true emotions.
   d. profit from making customers more emotional.

10. **People are likely to "get" a joke when they**
    a. know something about more than one culture.
    b. have a different social background than the joke teller.
    c. understand the two different realities being presented.
    d. know why someone wants to tell the joke.

ANSWERS: 1 (b); 2 (d); 3 (b); 4 (c); 5 (d); 6 (a); 7 (c); 8 (b); 9 (a); 10 (c).

ESSAY QUESTIONS

1. Explain Erving Goffman's claim that we engage in a "presentation of self." What are the elements of this presentation? Apply this approach to an analysis of a professor teaching a class.
2. In what ways are human emotions rooted in our biology? In what ways are emotions guided by culture?

We carry out much of our daily lives as members of groups and organizations. As members of a church choir, these children learn the importance not only of music but of working together as members of a group.

CHAPTER 5

Groups and Organizations

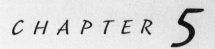

HOW do groups affect how we behave?

WHY can "who you know" be as important as "what you know"?

In *WHAT* ways have large business organizations changed in recent decades?

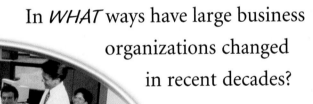

Back in 1948, people in Pasadena, California, paid little attention to the opening of a new restaurant by brothers Maurice and Richard McDonald. Yet this one small business would not only transform the restaurant industry but also introduce a new organizational model copied by countless businesses of all kinds.

The McDonald brothers' basic concept, which was soon called "fast food," was to serve meals quickly and cheaply to large numbers of people. The brothers trained employees to do highly specialized jobs: One person grilled hamburgers while others "dressed" them, made French fries, whipped up milkshakes, and handed the food to the customers in assembly-line fashion.

As the years went by, the McDonald brothers prospered, and they opened several more restaurants, including one in San Bernardino. It was there, in 1954, that Ray Kroc, a traveling blender and mixer salesman, paid them a visit.

Kroc was fascinated by the efficiency of the brothers' system and saw the potential for a whole chain of fast-food restaurants. The three launched the plan as partners. Soon Kroc bought out the McDonalds (who returned to running their original restaurant) and went on to become one of the greatest success stories of all time. Today, McDonald's has become one of the mostly widely known brand names in the world, with more than 30,000 restaurants that serve 50 million people daily throughout the United States and in 118 other countries.

 For a history of McDonald's, go to http://www.wemweb.com/chr66a/sbr66_museum/sbr66_museum.html

The success of McDonald's points to more than just the popularity of hamburgers and French fries. The organizational principles that guide this company are coming to dominate social life in the United States and elsewhere.

We begin this chapter by looking at *social groups,* the clusters of people with whom we interact in our daily lives. As you will learn, the scope of group life expanded greatly during the twentieth century. From a world of families, local neighborhoods, and small businesses, our society now relies on the operation of huge corporations and other bureaucracies that sociologists describe as *formal organizations.* Understanding this expansion of social life and appreciating what it means for us as individuals are the main objectives of this chapter.

Social Groups

Almost everyone wants a sense of belonging, which is the essence of group life. A **social group** is *two or more people who identify and interact with one another.* Human beings come together as couples, families, circles of friends, churches, clubs, businesses, neighborhoods, and large organizations. Whatever the form, groups contain people with shared experiences, loyalties, and interests. While keeping their individuality, members of social groups also think of themselves as a special "we."

Not every collection of individuals forms a group. People with a status in common, such as women, African Americans, homeowners, soldiers, millionaires, college graduates, and Roman Catholics, are not a group but a *category.* Though they know that others hold the same status, most are strangers to one another. Similarly, students sitting in a large lecture hall interact to a very limited extent. Such a loosely formed collection of people is a *crowd* rather than a group.

However, the right circumstances can quickly turn a crowd into a group. Events from power failures to terrorist attacks can make people bond quickly with strangers.

PRIMARY AND SECONDARY GROUPS

People often greet one another with a smile and the simple phrase "Hi! How are you?" The response is usually "Fine, thanks. How about you?" This answer is often more scripted than truthful. Explaining how you are *really* doing might make people feel so awkward that they would beat a hasty retreat.

Social groups fall into one of two types, based on their members' degree of genuine personal concern for one another. According to Charles Horton Cooley (1864–1929), a **primary group** is *a small social group whose members share personal and lasting relationships.* Joined by *primary relationships,* people spend a great deal of time together, engage

To learn more about Cooley, visit the Gallery of Sociologists at http://www.TheSociologyPage.com

in a wide range of activities, and feel that they know one another pretty well. In short, they show real concern for one another. The family is every society's most important primary group.

Cooley called personal and tightly integrated groups "primary" because they are among the first groups we experience in life. In addition, family and friends have primary importance in the socialization process, shaping our attitudes, behavior, and social identity.

Members of primary groups help one another in many ways, but they generally think of their group as an end in itself rather than as a means to other ends. In other words, we tend to think that family and friendship link people who "belong together." Members of a primary group also tend to view each other as unique and irreplaceable. Especially in the family, we are bound to others by emotion and loyalty. Brothers and sisters may not always get along, but they always remain "family."

In contrast to the primary group, the **secondary group** is *a large and impersonal social group whose members pursue a specific goal or activity.* In most respects, secondary groups have characteristics opposite to those of primary groups. *Secondary relationships* involve weak emotional ties and little personal knowledge of one another. Many secondary groups exist for only a short time, beginning and ending without particular significance. Students in a college course, who may or may not see one another after the semester ends, are one example of a secondary group.

Secondary groups include many more people than primary groups. For example, dozens or even hundreds of people may work in the same company, yet most of them pay only passing attention to one another. Sometimes the passage of time transforms a group from secondary to primary, as with co-workers who share an office for many years and develop closer relationships. But generally, members of a

As human beings, we live our lives as members of groups. Such groups may be large or small, temporary or long-lasting, and can be based on kinship, cultural heritage, or some shared interest.

secondary group do not think of themselves as "we." Secondary ties need not be hostile or cold, of course. Interactions among students, co-workers, and business associates are often quite pleasant even if they are impersonal.

Unlike members of primary groups, who display a *personal orientation,* people in secondary groups have a *goal orientation.* Primary group members define each other according to *who* they are in terms of family ties or personal qualities, but people in secondary groups look to one another for *what* they are, that is, what they can do for each other. In secondary groups, we tend to "keep score," aware of what we give others and what we receive in return. This goal orientation means that secondary group members usually remain formal and polite. It is in a secondary relationship, therefore, that we ask the question "How are you?" without expecting (or even wanting) a truthful answer.

The Summing Up table on page 122 reviews the characteristics of primary and secondary groups. Keep in mind that these traits define two types of groups in ideal terms; most real groups contain elements of both. For example, a

Become a member of a virtual group at http://groups.yahoo.com

women's group on a university campus may be quite large (and therefore secondary), but its members may identify strongly with one another and provide lots of mutual support (making it seem primary).

SUMMING UP

Primary Groups and Secondary Groups

	Primary Group ⟷	Secondary Group
Quality of relationships	Personal orientation	Goal orientation
Duration of relationships	Usually long-term	Variable; often short-term
Breadth of relationships	Broad; usually involving many activities	Narrow; usually involving few activities
Perception of relationships	As ends in themselves	As means to an end
Examples	Families, circles of friends	Co-workers, political organizations

Many people think that small towns and rural areas emphasize primary relationships and that large cities are characterized by secondary ties. This generalization is partly true, but some urban neighborhoods—especially those populated by people of a single ethnic or religious category—can be very tightly knit.

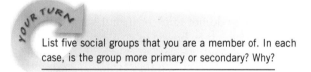

List five social groups that you are a member of. In each case, is the group more primary or secondary? Why?

GROUP LEADERSHIP

How do groups operate? One important element of group dynamics is leadership. Although a small circle of friends may have no leader at all, most large secondary groups place leaders in a formal chain of command.

Two Leadership Roles

Groups typically benefit from two kinds of leadership. **Instrumental leadership** refers to *group leadership that focuses on the completion of tasks.* Members look to instrumental leaders to make plans, give orders, and get things done. **Expressive leadership,** by contrast, is *group leadership that focuses on the group's well-being.* Expressive leaders take less of an interest in achieving goals and focus on promoting the well-being of members and minimizing tension and conflict among members.

Because they concentrate on performance, instrumental leaders usually have formal, secondary relationships with other members. These leaders give orders and reward or punish people according to how much they contribute to the group's efforts. Expressive leaders build more personal, primary ties. They offer sympathy to members going through tough times, keep the group united, and lighten serious moments with humor. Typically, successful instrumental leaders enjoy more *respect* from members and expressive leaders generally receive more personal *affection.*

Three Leadership Styles

Sociologists also describe leadership in terms of its decision-making style. *Authoritarian leadership* focuses on instrumental concerns, takes personal charge of decision making, and demands that group members obey orders. Although this leadership style may win little affection from the group, a fast-acting authoritarian leader is appreciated in a crisis.

Democratic leadership is more expressive, making a point of including everyone in the decision-making process. Although less successful in a crisis situation, where there is little time for discussion, democratic leaders generally draw on the ideas of all members to develop creative solutions to problems.

Laissez-faire leadership allows the group to function more or less on its own (*laissez-faire* in French means "leave it alone"). This style typically is the least effective in promoting group goals (White & Lippitt, 1953; Ridgeway, 1983).

GROUP CONFORMITY

Groups influence the behavior of their members, often promoting conformity. "Fitting in" provides a secure feeling of belonging, but at the extreme, group pressure can be unpleasant and even dangerous. Interestingly, as experiments by Solomon Asch and Stanley Milgram showed, even strangers can encourage group conformity.

Asch's Research

Solomon Asch (1952) recruited students for what he told them was a study of visual perception. Before the experiment began, he explained to all but one member of a small group that their real purpose was to put pressure on the remaining person. Placing six to eight students around a table, Asch showed them a "standard" line, as drawn on Card 1 in Figure 5–1, and asked them to match it to one of the three lines on Card 2.

Anyone with normal vision can see that the line marked "A" on Card 2 is the correct choice. Initially, as planned, everyone made the matches correctly. But then Asch's secret accomplices began answering incorrectly, leaving the naive subject (seated at the table so as to answer next to last) bewildered and uncomfortable.

What happened? Asch found that one-third of all subjects chose to conform by answering incorrectly. Apparently, many of us are willing to compromise our own judgment to avoid the discomfort of being different, even from people we do not know.

Milgram's Research

Stanley Milgram, a former student of Solomon Asch's, conducted conformity experiments of his own. In Milgram's controversial study (1963, 1965; A. G. Miller, 1986), a researcher explained to male recruits that they would be taking part in a study of how punishment affects learning. One by one, he assigned them to the role of teacher and placed another person—actually an accomplice of Milgram's—in a connecting room to pose as a learner.

The teacher watched as the learner sat down in what looked like an electric chair. The researcher applied electrode paste to one of the learner's wrists, explaining that this would "prevent blisters and burns." The researcher then attached an electrode to the wrist and secured the leather straps, explaining that they would "prevent excessive movement while the learner was being shocked." Although the shocks would be painful, the researcher reassured the teacher, they would cause "no permanent tissue damage."

The researcher then led the teacher back into the adjoining room, pointing out that the "electric chair" was connected to a "shock generator," actually a phony but realistic-looking piece of equipment with a label that read "Shock Generator, Type ZLB, Dyson Instrument Company, Waltham, Mass." On the front was a dial that supposedly regulated electric current from 15 volts (labeled "Slight Shock") to 300 volts ("Intense Shock") to 450 volts ("Danger: Severe Shock").

Seated in front of the "shock generator," the teacher was told to read aloud pairs of words. Then the teacher was to repeat the first word of each pair and wait for the learner

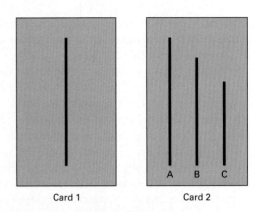

FIGURE 5-1 Cards Used in Asch's Experiment in Group Conformity

In Asch's experiment, subjects were asked to match the line on Card 1 to one of the lines on Card 2. Most subjects agreed with the wrong answers given by others in their group.
Source: Asch (1952).

to recall the second word. Whenever the learner failed to answer correctly, the teacher was told to apply an electric shock.

The researcher directed the teacher to begin at the lowest level (15 volts) and to increase the shock by 15 volts every time the learner made a mistake. And so the teacher did. At 75, 90, and 105 volts, the teacher heard moans from the learner; at 120 volts, shouts of pain; by 270 volts, screams; at 315 volts, pounding on the wall; after that, dead silence. None of the forty subjects assigned to the role of teacher during the initial research even questioned the procedure before reaching 300 volts, and twenty-six of the subjects—almost two-thirds—went all the way to 450 volts. Even Milgram was surprised at how readily people obeyed authority figures.

YOUR TURN

Thinking back to Chapter 1 ("Sociology: Perspective, Theory, and Method"), do you think that sociologists today would consider Milgram's research ethical? Why or why not?

Milgram (1964) then modified his research to see whether ordinary people—not authority figures—could pressure people to administer electrical shocks, in the same way that Asch's groups had pressured individuals to match lines incorrectly.

This time, Milgram formed a group of three teachers, two of whom were his accomplices. Each of the teachers was to suggest a shock level when the learner made an error; the rule was that the group would then administer the *lowest* of the three suggested levels. This arrangement gave the naive subject the power to deliver a lesser shock regardless of what the others said.

The accomplices suggested increasing the shock level with each error, putting pressure on the subject to do the same. The subjects in these groups applied voltages three to four times higher than those applied by subjects acting alone. Thus Milgram's research suggests that people are likely to follow the directions not only of legitimate authority figures but also of groups of ordinary individuals, even when it means harming another person.

Janis's "Groupthink"

Experts also cave in to group pressure, says Irving L. Janis (1972, 1989). Janis argues that a number of U.S. foreign policy blunders, including the failure to foresee the Japanese attack on Pearl Harbor during World War II and our ill-fated involvement in the Vietnam War, resulted from group conformity among our highest-ranking political leaders.

Common sense tells us that group discussion improves decision making. Janis counters that group members often seek agreement that closes off other points of view. Janis called this process **groupthink,** *the tendency of group members to conform, resulting in a narrow view of some issue.*

A classic example of groupthink resulted in the disastrous 1961 invasion of the Bay of Pigs in Cuba. Looking back, Arthur Schlesinger Jr., an adviser to President Kennedy, confessed feeling guilty "for having kept so quiet during those crucial discussions in the Cabinet Room," adding that the group discouraged anyone from challenging what, in hindsight, Schlesinger considered "nonsense" (quoted in Janis, 1972:30, 40). Groupthink may also have been a factor in 2003, when U.S. leaders were led to believe that Iraq had stockpiles of weapons of mass destruction.

REFERENCE GROUPS

How do we assess our own attitudes and behavior? Frequently, we use a **reference group,** *a social group that serves as a point of reference in making evaluations and decisions.*

A young man who imagines his family's response to a woman he is dating is using his family as a reference group. A supervisor who tries to predict her employees' reaction to a new vacation policy is using them in the same way. As these examples suggest, reference groups can be primary or secondary. In either case, our need to conform shows how others' attitudes affect us.

We also use groups we do *not* belong to for reference. Being well prepared for a job interview means showing up

dressed the way people in that company dress for work. Conforming to groups we do not belong to is a strategy to win acceptance and illustrates the process of *anticipatory socialization,* described in Chapter 3 ("Socialization: From Infancy to Old Age").

Stouffer's Research

Samuel A. Stouffer and his colleagues (1949) conducted a classic study of reference groups during World War II. Researchers asked soldiers to rate their own, or any competent soldier's, chances of promotion in their army unit. You might guess that soldiers serving in outfits with high promotion rates would be optimistic about advancement. Yet Stouffer's research pointed to the opposite conclusion: Soldiers in army units with low promotion rates were actually more positive about their chances to move ahead.

The key to understanding Stouffer's results lies in the groups against which soldiers measured themselves. Those assigned to units with lower promotion rates looked around them and saw people making no more headway than they were. Although they had not been promoted, neither had many others, so they did not feel deprived. However, soldiers in units with higher promotion rates could think of many people who had been promoted sooner or more often than they had. With such people in mind, even soldiers who had been promoted themselves were likely to feel short-changed.

The point is that we do not make judgments about ourselves in isolation, nor do we compare ourselves with just anyone. Regardless of our situation in *absolute* terms, we form a subjective sense of our well-being by looking at ourselves *relative* to specific reference groups (Merton, 1968; Mirowsky, 1987).

IN-GROUPS AND OUT-GROUPS

Each of us favors some groups over others, whether because of political outlook, social prestige, or just manner of dress. On some college campuses, for example, left-leaning student activists may look down on fraternity members, whom they view as conservative; fraternity members, in turn, may snub the computer "nerds" who work too hard. People in just about every social setting make similar positive and negative evaluations of members of other groups.

Such judgments illustrate another key element of group dynamics: the opposition of in-groups and out-groups. An **in-group** is *a social group toward which a member feels respect and loyalty.* An **out-group,** by contrast, is *a social group toward which a person feels a sense of competition or opposition.* In-groups and out-groups are based on the idea that "we" have valued traits that "they" lack.

Tensions between groups sharpen the groups' boundaries and give people a clearer social identity. However, members of in-groups generally hold overly positive views of themselves and unfairly negative views of various out-groups.

Power also plays a part in intergroup relations. A powerful in-group can define others as a lower-status out-group. Historically, in countless U.S. cities and towns, many white people viewed people of color as an out-group and subordinated them socially, politically, and economically. Internalizing these negative attitudes, minorities often struggled to overcome negative self-images. In this way, in-groups and out-groups foster loyalty but also generate conflict (Tajfel, 1982; Bobo & Hutchings, 1996).

In terms of in-groups and out-groups, explain what happens when people who may not like each other discover they have a common enemy.

GROUP SIZE

The next time you go to a party, try to arrive first. If you do, you will be in a position to observe some fascinating group dynamics. Until about six people enter the room, every person who arrives usually shares a single conversation. As more people arrive, the group soon divides into two or more clusters, and it divides again and again as the party grows. Group size plays a crucial role in how group members interact.

To understand why, note the mathematical number of relationships possible among two to seven people. As shown in Figure 5–2, two people form a single relationship; adding a third person results in three relationships; a fourth person yields six. Increasing the number of people further boosts the number of relationships much more rapidly because every new individual can interact with everyone already there. Thus by the time seven people join one conversation, twenty-one "channels" connect them. With so many open channels, at this point the group usually divides.

The Dyad

The German sociologist Georg Simmel (1858–1918) explored the dynamics in the smallest social groups. Simmel (1950, orig. 1902) used the term **dyad** (Greek for "pair") to designate *a social group with two members*. Simmel explained that social interaction in a dyad typically is more intense than in larger groups because neither member shares the other's attention with anyone else. In the United States, love affairs, marriages, and the closest friendships are dyadic.

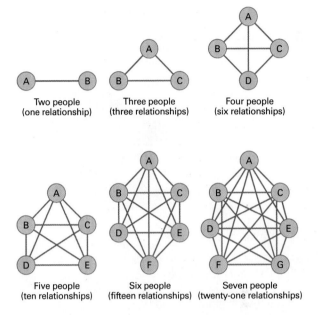

FIGURE 5–2 Group Size and Relationships

As the number of people in a group increases, the number of relationships that link them increases much faster. By the time six or seven people share a conversation, the group usually divides into two. Why are relationships in smaller groups typically more intense?

Source: Created by the author.

But like a stool with only two legs, dyads are unstable. Both members of a dyad must work to keep the relationship going; if either withdraws, the group collapses. Because stable marriages are important to society, the marital dyad is supported with legal, economic, and often religious ties.

The Triad

Simmel also studied the **triad,** *a social group with three members*, which contains three relationships, each uniting two of the three people. A triad is more stable than a dyad because one member can act as a mediator if relations between the other two become strained. Such group dynamics help explain why members of a dyad (say, a married couple) often seek out a third person (such as a counselor) to sort out tensions between them.

On the other hand, two of the three can pair up to press their views on the third, or two may intensify their relationship, leaving the other feeling left out. For example, when two of the three members of a triad develop a romantic interest in each other, they will come to understand the meaning of the old saying, "Two's company, three's a crowd."

The triad, illustrated by Jonathan Green's painting *Friends,* includes three people. A triad is more stable than a dyad because conflict between any two persons can be mediated by the third member. Even so, should the relationship between any two become more intense in a positive sense, those two are likely to exclude the third.

Jonathan Green, *Friends,* 1992. Oil on masonite, 14 in. × 11 in. © Jonathan Green, Naples, Florida. Collection of Patric McCoy.

As groups grow beyond three people, they become more stable and capable of withstanding the loss of one or more members. At the same time, increases in group size reduce the intense interaction possible in only the smallest groups. This is why larger groups are based less on personal attachments and more on formal rules and regulations.

Social Diversity: Race, Class, and Gender

Race, ethnicity, class, and gender each play a part in group dynamics. Peter Blau (1977; Blau, Blum, & Schwartz, 1982; South & Messner, 1986) points out three ways in which social diversity influences intergroup contact:

1. **Large groups turn inward.** Blau explains that the larger a group is, the more likely its members are to concentrate relationships among themselves. Say a college is trying to enhance social diversity by increasing the number of international students. These students may add a dimension of difference, but as their numbers rise, they become more likely to form their own social group. Thus efforts to promote social diversity may have the unintended effect of promoting separatism.

2. **Heterogeneous groups turn outward.** The more socially diverse a group is, the more likely its members are to interact with outsiders. Campus groups that recruit people of both sexes and various social backgrounds typically have more intergroup contact than those with members of one social category.

3. **Physical boundaries create social boundaries.** To the extent that a social group is physically segregated from others (by having its own dorm or dining area, for example), its members are less likely to interact with other people.

Networks

A **network** is *a web of weak social ties.* Think of a network as a "fuzzy" group containing people who come into occasional contact but lack a sense of boundaries and belonging. If you think of a group as a "circle of friends," think of a network as a "social web" expanding outward, often reaching great distances and including large numbers of people.

Some networks come close to being groups, as in the case of college friends who stay in touch years after graduation by e-mail and telephone. More commonly, however, a network includes people we *know of* or who *know of us* but with whom we interact rarely, if at all. As one woman known as a community organizer puts it, "I get calls at home, [and] someone says, 'Are you Roseann Navarro? Somebody told me to call you. I have this problem. . . .'" (Kaminer, 1984:94).

Network ties often give us the sense that we live in a "small world." In a classic experiment, Stanley Milgram (1967; Watts, 1999) gave letters to subjects in Kansas and Nebraska intended for specific people in Boston who were unknown to the original subjects. No addresses were given, and the subjects in the study were told to send the letters to others they knew personally who might know the target people. Milgram found that the target people received the letters with, on average, six people passing them on. This result led Milgram to claim that everyone is connected to everyone else by "six degrees of separation." Later research, however, has cast doubt on Milgram's claim. Examining Milgram's original data, Judith Kleinfeld noted that most of Milgram's letters (240 out of 300) never arrived at all (Wildavsky, 2002). Most of those that did reach their destination had been given to people who were wealthy, a fact that led Kleinfeld to conclude that rich people are far better connected across the country than ordinary men and women.

Network ties may be weak, but they can be a powerful resource. For immigrants trying to become established in a new community, businesspeople seeking to expand their operations, or new college graduates looking for a job, *whom* you know often is just as important as *what* you know (Hagan, 1998; Petersen, Saporta, & Seidel, 2000).

Networks are based on people's colleges, clubs, neighborhoods, political parties, and personal interests. Obviously, some networks are made up of people with more wealth, power, and prestige than others; that explains the importance of being "well connected." The networks of more privileged categories of people—such as the members of a country club—are a valuable form of "social capital," which is more likely to lead people in these categories to higher-paying jobs (Green, Tigges, & Diaz, 1999; Lin, Cook, & Burt, 2001).

To learn more about new Internet-based social networks, visit http://www.friendster.com

Some people also have denser networks than others; that is, they are connected to more people. Typically, the largest social networks include people who are young, well-educated, and living in large cities (Fernandez & Weinberg, 1997; Podolny & Baron, 1997).

Gender also shapes networks. Although the networks of men and women are typically of the same size, women include more relatives (and more women) in their networks, and men include more co-workers (and more men). Women's ties, therefore, may not be quite as powerful as typical "old boy" networks. But research suggests that as gender equality increases in the United States, the networks of men and women are becoming more alike (Reskin & McBrier, 2000; Torres & Huffman, 2002).

Finally, new information technology has generated a global network of unprecedented size in the form of the Internet. But the Internet has not yet linked the entire world. Global Map 5–1 on page 128 shows that Internet use is high in rich countries and far less common in poor nations.

Formal Organizations

As noted earlier, a century ago, most people lived in small groups of family, friends, and neighbors. Today, our lives revolve more and more around **formal organizations,** *large secondary groups organized to achieve their goals efficiently.* Formal organizations such as corporations and government agencies differ from small primary groups in their impersonality and their formally planned atmosphere.

Today's world has so many large organizations that we identify them just by initials: IRS, IBM, FBI, CIA, CNN, WB, WWF, and so on. How many more examples can you think of?
_____

When you think about it, organizing 300 million members of U.S. society is truly remarkable, whether it involves paving roads, collecting taxes, schooling children, or delivering the mail. To carry out most of these tasks, we rely on large formal organizations.

TYPES OF FORMAL ORGANIZATIONS

Amitai Etzioni (1975) identified three types of formal organizations, distinguished by the reasons people participate in them: utilitarian organizations, normative organizations, and coercive organizations.

Utilitarian Organizations

Just about everyone who works for income belongs to a *utilitarian organization,* one that pays people for their efforts. Becoming part of a utilitarian organization—a business, government agency, or school system, for example—usually is a matter of individual choice, although most people must join one or another such organization to make a living.

Normative Organizations

People join *normative organizations* not for income but to pursue some goal they think is morally worthwhile. Sometimes called *voluntary associations,* these include community service groups (such as Amnesty International, the PTA, the League of Women Voters, and the Red Cross), political parties, and religious organizations. In global perspective, people in the United States and in other high-income countries are the most likely to join voluntary associations. A recent study found that 83 percent of first-year college students in the United States said they had participated in some organized volunteer activity within the past year (Curtis, Baer, & Grabb, 2001; Schofer & Fourcade-Gourinchas, 2001; Pryor et al., 2005).

Coercive Organizations

Coercive organizations have involuntary memberships. People are forced to join these organizations as a form of punishment (prisons) or treatment (some psychiatric hospitals). Coercive organizations have special physical features, such as locked doors and barred windows, and are

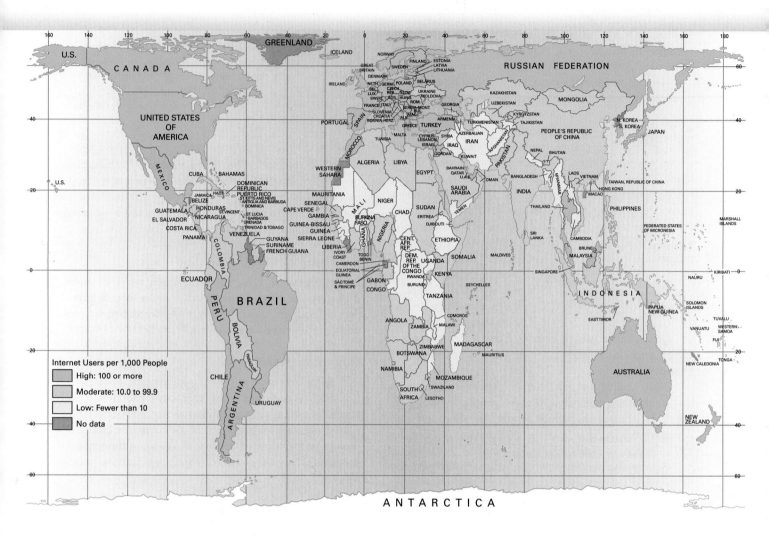

WINDOW ON THE WORLD

GLOBAL MAP 5–1   Internet Users in Global Perspective

This map shows how the Information Revolution has affected countries around the world. In most high-income nations, at least one-third of the population uses the Internet. By contrast, only a small share of people in low-income nations does so. What effect does this have on people's access to information? What does this mean for the future in terms of global inequality?

Sources: United Nations Development Programme (2005) and International Telecommunication Union (2006).

---

supervised by security personnel. They isolate people (whom they label "inmates" or "patients") for a period of time in order to radically change their attitudes and behavior. Recall from Chapter 3 ("Socialization: From Infancy to Old Age") the power of a total institution to change a person's sense of self.

It is possible for a single formal organization to fall into *all* of these categories from the point of view of different individuals. For example, a mental hospital serves as a coercive organization for a patient, a utilitarian organization for a psychiatrist, and a normative organization for a hospital volunteer.

Origins of Formal Organizations

Formal organizations date back thousands of years. Elites who controlled early empires relied on government officials to collect taxes, undertake military campaigns, and build monumental structures from the Great Wall of China to the pyramids of Egypt.

However, early organizations had two limitations. First, they lacked the technology to travel over large distances, to communicate quickly, and to gather and store information. Second, the preindustrial societies they were trying to rule had traditional cultures. **Tradition,** according to the German sociologist Max Weber, consists of *values and beliefs passed from generation to generation.* Tradition makes a society conservative, Weber explained, because it limits an organization's efficiency and ability to change.

By contrast, Weber described the modern worldview as **rationality,** *a way of thinking that emphasizes deliberate, matter-of-fact calculation of the most efficient way to accomplish a particular task.* A rational worldview pays little attention to the past and is open to any changes that might get the job done better or more quickly.

The rise of the "organizational society" rests on what Weber called the **rationalization of society,** *the historical change from tradition to rationality as the main mode of human thought.* Modern society, he claimed, becomes "disenchanted" as sentimental ties give way to a rational focus on science, complex technology, and the organizational structure called bureaucracy.

Characteristics of Bureaucracy

Bureaucracy is *an organizational model rationally designed to perform tasks efficiently.* Bureaucratic officials regularly create and revise policy to increase efficiency. To appreciate the power and scope of bureaucratic organization, consider that any one of more than 300 million phones in the United States can connect you within seconds to any other phone in a home, business, automobile, or even a hiker's backpack on a remote trail in the Rocky Mountains. Such instant communication is beyond the imagination of people who lived in the ancient world.

Our telephone system depends on technology such as electricity, fiber optics, and computers. But the system could not exist without the organizational capacity to keep track of every telephone call—recording which phone called which other phone, when, and for how long—and presenting all this information to more than 100 million telephone users in the form of a monthly bill.

What specific traits promote organizational efficiency? Max Weber (1978, orig. 1921) identified six key elements of the ideal bureaucratic organization:

1. **Specialization.** Our ancestors spent most of their time looking for food and finding shelter. Bureaucracy, by contrast, assigns individuals highly specialized jobs.

2. **Hierarchy of offices.** Bureaucracies arrange workers in a vertical ranking. Each person is thus supervised by "higher-ups" in the organization while in turn supervising others in lower positions. Usually, with few people at the top and many at the bottom, bureaucratic organizations take the form of a pyramid.

3. **Rules and regulations.** Rationally enacted rules and regulations guide a bureaucracy's operation. Ideally, a bureaucracy seeks to operate in a completely predictable fashion.

4. **Technical competence.** Bureaucratic officials have the technical competence to carry out their duties. Bureaucracies typically hire new members according to set standards and then monitor their performance. Such impersonal evaluation contrasts with the ancient custom of favoring relatives, whatever their talents, over strangers.

5. **Impersonality.** Bureaucracy puts rules ahead of personal whim so that both clients and workers are all treated in the same way. From this impersonal approach comes the commonplace image of the "faceless bureaucrat."

6. **Formal, written communications.** It is often said that the heart of bureaucracy is not people but paperwork. Rather than casual, face-to-face talk, bureaucracy depends on formal, written memos and reports, which accumulate in vast files.

YOUR TURN

To what degree is your college or university a bureaucracy? Explain.

Bureaucratic organization promotes efficiency by carefully hiring workers and limiting the unpredictable effects of personal taste and opinion. The Summing Up table on page 130 reviews the differences between small social groups and large formal organizations.

Organizational Environment

All organizations exist in the larger world. How well any organization performs depends not only on its own goals and policies but also on the **organizational environment,**

SUMMING UP

Small Groups and Formal Organizations

	Small Groups	Formal Organizations
Activities	Much the same for all members	Distinct and highly specialized
Hierarchy	Often informal or nonexistent	Clearly defined, corresponding to offices
Norms	General norms, informally applied	Clearly defined rules and regulations
Membership criteria	Variable; often based on personal affection or kinship	Technical competence to carry out assigned tasks
Relationships	Variable and typically primary	Typically secondary, with selective primary ties
Communications	Casual and face to face	Mostly formal and in writing
Focus	Person-oriented	Task-oriented

factors outside an organization that affect its operation. These factors include technology, economic and political trends, current events, the available workforce, and other organizations.

Modern organizations are shaped by *technology,* including copiers, telephones, and computer equipment. Computers give employees access to more information and people than ever before. At the same time, computer technology allows managers to closely monitor the activities of workers (Markoff, 1991).

Economic and political trends affect organizations. All organizations are helped or hurt by periodic economic growth or recession. Most industries also face competition from abroad as well as changes in law—such as new environmental standards—at home.

Current events can have significant effects even on organizations that are far away. The economic slowdown and rise in energy prices following the hurricanes that devastated the Gulf states in 2005 affected both government and business organizations.

Population patterns also affect organizations. The average age, typical level of education, social diversity, and size of a local community determine the available workforce and sometimes the market for an organization's products or services.

Other organizations also contribute to the organizational environment. To be competitive, a hospital must be responsive to the insurance industry and to organizations representing doctors, nurses, and other health care workers. It must also be aware of the medical equipment and health care procedures available at nearby facilities, as well as competitors' prices.

THE INFORMAL SIDE OF BUREAUCRACY

Weber's ideal bureaucracy deliberately regulates every activity. In real-life organizations, however, human beings are creative (and stubborn) enough to resist bureaucratic regulation. Informality may amount to cutting corners on the job at times, but it can also provide the flexibility necessary for an organization to adapt to change.

In part, informality comes from the varying personalities of organizational leaders. Studies of U.S. corporations show that the qualities and quirks of individuals—including personal charisma and interpersonal skills—can have a great effect on organizational success or failure (Halberstam, 1986; Baron, Hannan, & Burton, 1999).

Authoritarian, democratic, and laissez-faire types of leadership (described earlier in this chapter) reflect individual personality as much as any organizational plan. Then, too, in the "real world" of organizations, leaders sometimes seek to benefit personally through abuse of organizational power. Examples include scandals involving corporate executives and members of Congress. More commonly, leaders take credit for the efforts of those who work for them. For example, the responsibilities—and authority—of many secretaries are far greater than their official job titles and salaries suggest.

Communication offers another example of organizational informality. Memos and other written documents are the formal way to spread information through the organization. Typically, however, people create informal networks, or "grapevines," that spread information quickly, if not always accurately. Grapevines, using word of mouth and e-mail, are particularly important to rank-and-file workers

George Tooker's painting *Government Bureau* is a powerful statement about the human costs of bureaucracy. The artist paints members of the public in a drab sameness—reduced from human beings to mere "cases" to be disposed of as quickly as possible. Set apart from others by their positions, officials are "faceless bureaucrats" concerned more with numbers than with providing genuine assistance (notice that the artist places the fingers of the officials on calculators).

George Tooker, *Government Bureau*, 1956. Egg tempera on gesso panel, 19⅝ × 29⅝ inches. The Metropolitan Museum of Art, George A. Hearn Fund, 1956 (56.78). Photograph © 1984 The Metropolitan Museum of Art.

because higher-ups often try to keep important information from them.

The spread of e-mail has "flattened" organizations somewhat, allowing even the lowest-ranking employee to bypass immediate superiors to communicate directly with the organization's leader or all fellow employees at once. Some organizations consider such "open channel" communication unwelcome and limit the use of e-mail. Leaders may also seek to protect themselves from a flood of messages each day. Microsoft Corporation (whose leader, Bill Gates, has an "unlisted" address, which helps him limit his e-mail to hundreds of messages each day) has developed screens that filter out all messages except those from approved people (Gwynne & Dickerson, 1997).

Using new information technology together with age-old human ingenuity, members of formal organizations often find ways to personalize their work and surroundings. Such efforts suggest that we should take a closer look at some of the problems of bureaucracy.

PROBLEMS OF BUREAUCRACY

We rely on bureaucracy to manage everyday life efficiently, but many people are uneasy about large organizations. Bureaucracy can dehumanize and manipulate us, and some say it poses a threat to political democracy.

Bureaucratic Alienation

Max Weber held up bureaucracy as a model of productivity. Yet Weber was keenly aware of bureaucracy's potential to *dehumanize* the people it is supposed to serve. The impersonality that fosters efficiency also keeps officials and clients

from responding to each other's unique personal needs. Typically, officials treat each client impersonally as a standard "case."

Formal organizations create *alienation*, according to Weber, by reducing the human being to "a small cog in a ceaselessly moving mechanism" (1978:988, orig. 1921). Although formal organizations are designed to benefit humanity, Weber feared that people might well end up serving formal organizations.

Bureaucratic Inefficiency and Ritualism

On Labor Day 2005, as people in New Orleans and other coastal areas were battling to survive in the wake of Hurricane Katrina, 600 firefighters from around the country assembled in a hotel meeting room in Atlanta awaiting deployment. Officials of the Federal Emergency Management Agency (FEMA) explained to the crowd that they were first going to be given a lecture on "equal opportunity, sexual harassment, and customer service." Then, the official continued, they would each be given a stack of FEMA pamphlets with the agency's phone number to distribute to people in the devastated areas. A firefighter stood up and shouted, "This is ridiculous. Our fire departments and mayors sent us down here to save lives, and you've got us doing *this*?" The FEMA official thundered back, "You are now employees of FEMA, and you will follow orders and do what you are told" ("Places Where the System Broke Down," 2005:39).

Criticism of the government response to the hurricane disaster of 2005 was widespread and pointed to the problem of bureaucratic *inefficiency*, the failure of a formal organiza-

April 10, 2005

The Beast That Feeds on Boxes: Bureaucracy

By SCOTT SHANE

In the long and dispiriting history of American intelligence failure, from Pearl Harbor to the 2001 attacks to Iraqi weapons, one chronic culprit is that "giant power wielded by pygmies," as Balzac put it: bureaucracy. . . .

"I've been studying bureaucracy for 40 years," said James Q. Wilson, a professor of public policy at Pepperdine University, "and I can't remember a single commission that proposed cutting back."

Little surprise, then, that after two independent commissions and multiple Congressional committees studied the shortcomings of the 15 intelligence agencies, they proposed more bureaucracy.

This . . . worries Richard A. Posner, a federal appeals court judge and the author of a coming book on intelligence reform. "Every time you add a layer of bureaucracy, you delay the movement of information up the chain to the policy maker," Judge Posner said. "And you dilute the information, because at each step some details are taken out.". . .

Through Republican and Democratic administrations, in response to any kind of crisis or failure, in every field from education to national security, and often in the face of stark evidence that it will be counterproductive, the federal government has grown layers, said Dr. [Paul C.] Light, a professor of public service at New York University and senior fellow at the Brookings Institution.

The layering can scramble communication and accountability, he said, and it lies at the heart of many government failures. In the Columbia disaster, NASA engineers' worries never reached top officials. Commanders in Iraq have said that word of abuses at Abu Ghraib did not reach them.

One of the first great students of bureaucracy, the early-20th-century German sociologist Max Weber, saw a lot to like in this form of organization, particularly as a replacement for clan-based or patronage systems. . . . But Weber may not have imagined the scale of bureaucracy at the top of a 21st-century superpower, or its relentless growth.

In 1960, according to Dr. Light's study of federal phone directories, there were 17 different executive titles in the 15 cabinet departments he tracks. By 2004, that had ballooned to 64 titles, as new positions were wedged between existing jobs, creating such choice appellations as "chief of staff to the associate deputy assistant secretary" and "principal deputy deputy assistant secretary" (the repetition is not a typo). . . .

Sometimes growth is a matter of prestige. . . . Sometimes pay freezes lead to the manufacture of new titles to allow bosses to give deserving subordinates raises.

---

tion to carry out the work it exists to perform. People sometimes describe inefficiency by saying that an organization has too much "red tape," meaning that important work does not get done. The term "red tape" is derived from the ribbon used by slow-working eighteenth-century English administrators to wrap official parcels and records (Shipley, 1985). To Robert Merton (1968), red tape amounts to a new twist on the familiar concept of group conformity. He coined the term **bureaucratic ritualism** to describe *a focus on rules and regulations to the point of interfering with an organization's goals*. In short, rules and regulations should be a means to an end, not an end in themselves that takes the focus away from the organization's stated goals.

Do you think FEMA or other large government bureaucracies are necessarily inefficient, or do they just suffer from poor leadership? Explain your answer.

After the terrorist attacks of September 11, 2001, the U.S. Postal Service continued to help deliver mail addressed to Osama bin Laden to a post office in Afghanistan, despite the objections of the FBI. It took an act of Congress to change the policy (Bedard, 2002). "In the *Times*" explains how difficult it is to cut back on inefficient government bureaucracy.

Bureaucratic Inertia

If bureaucrats sometimes have little reason to work very hard, they have every reason to protect their jobs. Thus officials typically work to keep their organization going even when its goal has been realized. As Max Weber put it, "Once fully established, bureaucracy is among the social structures which are hardest to destroy" (1978:987, orig. 1921).

Bureaucratic inertia refers to *the tendency of bureaucratic organizations to perpetuate themselves*. Formal organizations tend to take on a life of their own beyond their

But the real driver for layering is the effort to reform, Dr. Light said, as leaders frustrated by failing bureaucracies add layers to impose discipline on those below. The response to the 9/11 attacks is a clear example. The government first created the Department of Homeland Security, building a florid new superstructure above 22 agencies employing 180,000 people. . . . Atop the layers of the Central Intelligence Agency and its 14 siblings, Congress followed the advice of the 9/11 commission and decided to place a new director of national intelligence, assisted by a staff of more than 500. . . .

Then the presidential commission on Iraqi weapons intelligence weighed in . . . with a list of proposed additions: the CIA's directorate of operations would be swallowed up by a new human intelligence directorate; the FBI's security operations would be consolidated into a National Security Service; "mission managers" under a deputy director of national intelligence for integrated intelligence strategies would coordinate reporting on a single target. And so on, for 74 recommendations.

Each comes with a common-sense rationale. But nearly all would add bulk to the bureaucracy, potentially tangling lines of authority and communication for intelligence, with its dependence on speed and precision. . . .

The hazards of the bureaucratic imperative were not lost on the latest intelligence commission, led by Laurence H. Silberman, a senior federal judge, and Charles S. Robb, the former Virginia senator and governor. . . .

The report frets repeatedly about the danger of bureaucracy and says specifically, "We have tried to eschew the 'boxology' that often dominates discussions of government reform."

But in the end, the commission could not stop itself. On its organizational chart for Mr. Negroponte's operation, there are 34 boxes.

WHAT DO YOU THINK?

1. Max Weber saw many strengths of bureaucracy. But based on this article, what is an important weakness of this type of organization?

2. The article describes the problem of inefficiency in expanding government bureaucracy. To what extent do you think the same problem exists in other types of bureaucracy, such as big business?

3. If people recognize that increasing size causes problems, why do we keep making bureaucratic organizations bigger and more complex?

Adapted from the original article by Scott Shane published in *The New York Times* on April 10, 2005. Copyright © 2005 by The New York Times Company. Reprinted with permission.

---

formal objectives. For example, the U.S. Department of Agriculture still has offices in nearly every county in all fifty states, even though only about one county in ten has any working farms. Usually, an organization manages to stay in business by redefining its goals; for example, the Agriculture Department now performs a broad range of work not directly related to farming, including nutritional and environmental research.

Oligarchy

Early in the twentieth century, Robert Michels (1876–1936) pointed out the link between bureaucracy and political **oligarchy,** *the rule of the many by the few* (1949, orig. 1911). According to what Michels called "the iron law of oligarchy," the pyramid shape of bureaucracy places a few leaders in charge of the resources of the entire organization.

Max Weber believed that a strict hierarchy of responsibility resulted in high organizational efficiency. But Michels countered that hierarchy also weakens democracy because officials can and often do use their access to information, resources, and the media to promote their own personal interests.

Furthermore, bureaucracy helps distance officials from the public, as in the case of the corporate president or public official who is "unavailable for comment" to the local press or the national president who claims "executive privilege" when withholding documents from Congress. Oligarchy, then, thrives in the hierarchical structure of bureaucracy and reduces the accountability of leaders to the people (Tolson, 1995).

Political competition, term limits, a system of checks and balances, and the law prevent the U.S. government from becoming an out-and-out oligarchy. Even so, in U.S. political races, candidates who have the visibility, power, and money that come with already being in office enjoy a significant advantage. In the 2004 congressional elections, only one of every ten congressional officeholders running for reelection was defeated.

The Evolution of Formal Organizations

The problems of bureaucracy—especially the alienation it produces and its tendency toward oligarchy—stem from two organizational traits mentioned earlier: hierarchy and rigidity. To Weber, bureaucracy is a top-down system: Rules and regulations made at the top guide every part of people's work down the chain of command. A century ago in the United States, Weber's ideas took hold in an organizational model called *scientific management*. We take a look at this model and then examine three challenges over the course of the twentieth century that gradually led to a new model: the *flexible organization*.

SCIENTIFIC MANAGEMENT

Frederick Winslow Taylor (1911) had a simple message: Most businesses in the United States were sadly inefficient. Managers had little idea of how to increase their business's output, and workers relied on the same tired skills of earlier generations. To increase efficiency, Taylor explained, business should apply the principles of science. **Scientific management,** then, is *the application of scientific principles to the operation of a business or other large organization.*

Scientific management involves three steps. First, managers carefully observe the job performed by each worker, identifying all the operations involved and measuring the time needed for each. Second, managers analyze their data, trying to discover ways for workers to perform each job more efficiently. For example, managers might decide to give workers different tools or to reposition various work operations within the factory. Third, management provides guidance and incentives for workers to do their jobs more efficiently. If a factory worker moves 20 tons of pig iron in one day, for example, management would show the worker how to do the job more efficiently and then provide higher wages as the worker's productivity rises. Taylor concluded that if scientific principles were applied in this way, companies would become more profitable, workers would earn higher wages, and consumers would pay lower prices.

A century ago, the auto pioneer Henry Ford put it this way: "Save ten steps a day for each of 12,000 employees, and you will have saved fifty miles of wasted motion and misspent energy" (Allen & Hyman, 1999:209). In the early 1900s, the Ford Motor Company and many other businesses followed Taylor's lead and made improvements in efficiency.

The principles of scientific management suggested that decision-making power in the workplace should rest with the owners and executives, who paid little attention to the ideas of their workers. As the decades passed, formal organizations faced important challenges involving race and gender, rising competition from abroad, and the changing nature of work itself. We now take a brief look at each of these challenges.

THE FIRST CHALLENGE: RACE AND GENDER

In the 1960s, critics claimed that big businesses and other organizations engaged in unfair hiring practices. Rather than hiring on the basis of competence as Weber had proposed, they routinely excluded women and other minorities, especially from positions of power. Hiring on the basis of competence is partly a matter of fairness; it is also a matter of enlarging an organization's talent pool to promote efficiency.

Patterns of Privilege and Exclusion

In the early twenty-first century, as shown in Figure 5–3, non-Hispanic white men in the United States—34 percent of the working-age population—still held 56 percent of management jobs. Non-Hispanic white women also made up 34 percent of the population, but they held just 29 percent of managerial positions (U.S. Equal Employment Opportunity Commission, 2005). The members of other minorities lagged further behind.

Rosabeth Moss Kanter (1977; Kanter & Stein, 1979) points out that excluding women and minorities from the workplace ignores the talents of more than half the population. Furthermore, underrepresented people in an organization often feel like members of a socially isolated out-group: uncomfortably visible, taken less seriously, and given fewer chances for promotion.

Opening up an organization so that change and advancement happen more often, Kanter claims, improves everyone's on-the-job performance by motivating employees to become "fast-trackers" who work harder and are more committed to the company. By contrast, an organization with many dead-end jobs turns workers into less productive "zombies" who are never asked for their opinion on anything. An open organization also encourages leaders to seek out the ideas of all employees, which usually improves decision making.

The "Female Advantage"

Some organizational researchers argue that women bring special management skills that strengthen an organization. According to Deborah Tannen (1994), women have a greater "information focus" and more readily ask questions in order to understand an issue. Men, by contrast, have an "image focus" that makes them wonder how asking questions in a particular situation will affect their reputation.

In another study of women executives, Sally Helgesen (1990) found three other gender-linked patterns. First, women place greater value on communication skills and share information more than men do. Second, women are more flexible leaders who typically give their employees greater freedom. Third, compared to men, women tend to emphasize the interconnectedness of all organizational operations. She coined the term *female advantage* for these patterns, which help companies striving to be more flexible and democratic.

In sum, one challenge to conventional bureaucracy is to become more open and flexible in order to take advantage of the experience, ideas, and creativity of everybody, regardless of race or gender. The result goes right to the bottom line: greater profits.

The Second Challenge: The Japanese Work Organization

In 1980, the corporate world in the United States was shaken to discover that the most popular automobile model sold in this country was not a Chevrolet, Ford, or Plymouth but the Honda Accord, made in Japan. As late as the 1950s, the label "Made in Japan" was generally found on products that were cheap and poorly made. But times had changed. The success of the Japanese auto industry (and shortly afterward, companies making electronics, cameras, and many other products) soon had analysts buzzing about the "Japanese organization." How else could so small a country challenge the world's economic powerhouse?

Japanese organizations reflect that nation's strong collective spirit. In contrast to the U.S. emphasis on rugged individualism, the Japanese value cooperation. In effect, formal organizations in Japan are more like large primary groups. A generation ago, William Ouchi (1981) highlighted differences between formal organizations in Japan and in the United States. First, Japanese companies hired new workers in groups, giving everyone the same salary and responsibilities. Second, many Japanese companies hired workers for life, fostering a strong sense of loyalty. Third, with the idea that employees would spend their entire careers there, many Japanese organizations trained workers in all phases of operations. Fourth, although Japanese corporate leaders took ultimate responsibility for their organizations' performance, they involved workers in "quality circles" to discuss decisions that affected them. Fifth, Japanese companies played a large role in the lives of workers, providing home mortgages, sponsoring recreational activities, and scheduling social events. Together, such policies encourage much more loyalty among members of Japanese organizations than is typically the case in their U.S. counterparts.

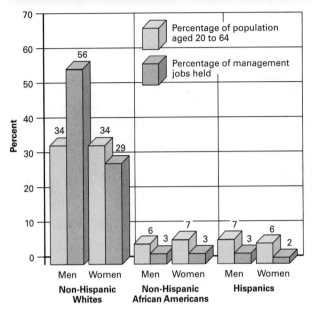

FIGURE 5-3   U.S. Managers in Private Industry by Race, Sex, and Ethnicity, 2003

White men are more likely than their population size suggests to be managers in private industry. The opposite is true for white women and other minorities. What factors do you think may account for this pattern?

Sources: U.S. Census Bureau (2006) and U.S. Equal Employment Opportunity Commission (2005).

For decades, people around the world marveled at the economic "miracle" of Japanese organizations. But the praise was premature. Around 1990, the Japanese economy entered a downward trend that is only now showing signs of ending. As a result of this downturn, most Japanese companies no longer offer workers jobs for life or many of the other benefits noted by Ouchi.

The Third Challenge: The Changing Nature of Work

Beyond rising global competition and the need to provide equal opportunity for all, pressure to modify conventional work organizations is also coming from changes in the nature of work itself. Over the past few decades, the economy of the United States has moved from industrial to postindustrial production. In other words, rather than working in factories using heavy machinery to make *things*, more people today are using computers and other electronic technology to create or process *information*. A

The best of today's information age jobs—including working at the popular search-engine Web site Google—allow people lots of personal freedom as long as they produce good ideas. At the same time, many other jobs—such as working the counter at McDonald's—involve the same routines and strict supervision found in factories a century ago.

postindustrial society, then, is characterized by information-based organizations.

Frederick Taylor developed his concept of scientific management at a time when most jobs involved tasks that, though often backbreaking, were routine. Workers shoveled coal, poured liquid iron into molds, welded body panels to automobiles on an assembly line, or shot hot rivets into steel girders to build skyscrapers. In addition, a large part of the U.S. labor force in Taylor's day was made up of immigrants, most of whom had little schooling and many of whom knew little English. The routine nature of industrial jobs, coupled with the limited skills of the labor force, led Taylor to treat work as a series of fixed tasks set down by management and followed by employees.

Many of today's information age jobs are very different: The work of designers, artists, consultants, writers, editors, composers, programmers, business owners, and others now demands creativity and imagination. What does this mean for formal organizations? Here are several ways in which today's organizations differ from those of a century ago:

1. **Creative freedom.** As one Hewlett-Packard executive put it, "From their first day of work here, people are given important responsibilities and are encouraged to grow" (Brooks, 2000:128). Today's organizations treat employees with information age skills as a vital resource. Executives can set production goals but cannot dictate how to accomplish tasks involving imagination and discovery. This gives highly skilled workers *creative freedom,* which means they are subject to less

day-to-day supervision as long as they generate good results in the long run.

2. **Competitive work teams.** Many organizations allow several groups of employees to work on a problem and offer the greatest rewards to the group that comes up with the best solution. Competitive work teams—a strategy first used by Japanese organizations—draw out the creative contributions of everyone and at the same time reduce the alienation often found in conventional organizations (Maddox, 1994; Yeatts, 1994).

3. **A flatter organization.** By spreading responsibility for creative problem solving throughout the workforce, organizations take on a flatter shape. That is, the pyramid shape of conventional bureaucracy is replaced by an organizational form with fewer levels in the chain of command, as shown in Figure 5–4.

4. **Greater flexibility.** The typical industrial age organization was a rigid structure guided from the top. Such organizations may accomplish a good deal of work, but they are not especially creative or able to respond quickly to changes in their larger environment. The ideal model in the information age is a *more open, flexible* organization, one that both generates new ideas and adapts quickly to the rapidly changing global marketplace.

What does this all mean for organizations? As David Brooks puts it, "The machine is no longer held up as the standard that healthy organizations should emulate. Now,

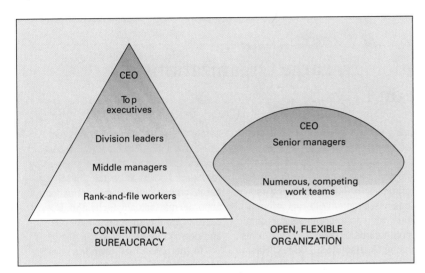

FIGURE 5-4 Two Organizational Models

The conventional model of bureaucratic organizations has a pyramid shape, with a clear chain of command. Orders flow from the top down, and reports of performance flow from the bottom up. Such organizations have extensive rules and regulations, and their workers have highly specialized jobs. More open and flexible organizations have a flatter shape, more like a football. With fewer levels in the hierarchy, responsibility for generating ideas and making decisions is shared throughout the organization. Many workers do their jobs in teams and have a broad knowledge of the entire organization's operation.

Source: Created by the author.

it's the ecosystem" (2000:128). Today's "smart" companies seek out intelligent, creative people (America Online's main building is called "Creative Center One") and nurture the growth of their talents.

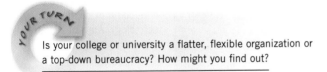

Is your college or university a flatter, flexible organization or a top-down bureaucracy? How might you find out?

Keep in mind, however, that many of today's jobs do not involve creative work at all. In reality, the postindustrial economy has created two very different types of work: highly skilled creative work and low-skilled service work. Work in the fast-food industry, for example, is routine and highly supervised and thus has much more in common  with factory work of a century ago than with the creative teamwork typical of today's information organizations. Therefore, at the same time that some organizations have taken on a flatter, more flexible form, others continue to use a rigid chain of command.

THE "McDONALDIZATION" OF SOCIETY[1]

As noted in the opening to this chapter, McDonald's has enjoyed enormous success, now operating more than 30,000 restaurants in the United States and around the world. Japan has more than 2,400 Golden Arches, and the world's largest McDonald's is found in China's capital, Beijing.

McDonald's is far more than a restaurant chain; it is a symbol of U.S. culture. Not only do people around the world associate McDonald's with the United States, but here at home, one poll found that 98 percent of schoolchildren could identify Ronald McDonald, making him as well known as Santa Claus.

Even more important, the organizational principles that underlie McDonald's are coming to dominate our entire society. Our culture is becoming "McDonaldized," an awkward way of saying that many aspects of life are modeled on the famous restaurant chain. Parents buy toys at worldwide chain stores such as Toys 'R' Us; we drive in to Jiffy Lube for a ten-minute oil change; face-to-face communication is being replaced more and more with voice mail, e-mail, and instant messaging; television presents news in the form of ten-second sound bites; college admissions officers size up students they have never met by glancing at their GPAs and SAT scores; and professors assign ghostwritten textbooks[2] and evaluate students by giving tests mass-produced for them by publishing companies. The list goes on and on.

McDonaldization: Three Principles

What do all these developments have in common? According to George Ritzer (1993), the McDonaldization of society involves three basic organizational principles:

---

[1]The term "McDonaldization" was coined by Jim Hightower (1975); much of this discussion is based on the work of George Ritzer (1993, 1998, 2000) and Eric Schlosser (2002).

[2]A number of popular sociology textbooks were not written by the person whose name appears on the cover. This book is not one of them. The test bank was also written by the author.

Computer Technology, Large Organizations, and the Assault on Privacy

Late for a meeting with a new client, Sarah drives her car through a yellow light as it turns red at a main intersection. A computer linked to a pair of cameras notes the violation and takes one picture of her license plate and another of her sitting in the driver's seat. In the mail seven days later, she receives a summons to appear in court.

Joe calls a toll-free number to check the pollen count. As he listens to a recorded message, caller ID identifies Joe, records the call, and pulls up his profile from a public records database. The computer adds to the profile the fact that Joe suffers from allergies. Several weeks later, tens of thousands of profiles are sold to a drug company, which sends Joe and others a free sample of its new allergy medication.

Julio looks through his mail and finds a letter from a Washington, D.C., data services company informing him that he is one of about 145,000 people whose name, address, and Social Security number have recently been sold to criminals in California posing as businesspeople. With this information, he is told, criminals can obtain credit cards or take out loans in his name (A. Hamilton, 2001; O'Harrow, 2005).

These are all cases showing that today's organizations—which know more about us than ever before and more than most of us realize—pose a growing threat to personal privacy. Large organizations are necessary for today's society to operate. In some cases, organizations using information about us may actually be helpful. But cases of identity theft are on the rise, and personal privacy is on the decline.

In the past, small-town life gave people little privacy. But at least if people knew something about you, you were just as likely to know something about them. Today, unknown people "out there" access information about each of us all the time.

In part, the loss of privacy is a result of more and more complex computer technology. Are you aware that every time you send an e-mail or visit a Web site, you leave a record in one or more computers? Most of these records can be seen by people you don't know, as well as by employers and public officials.

Another part of today's loss of privacy reflects the increasing number and size

Count how many surveillance cameras you see as you go through a typical day. Does the presence of these cameras make you feel more secure? Or do you feel that they intrude into your privacy?

1. **Efficiency.** Ray Kroc, the marketing genius behind the expansion of McDonald's, set out to serve a hamburger, French fries, and a milkshake to a customer in fifty seconds. Today, one of the company's most popular items is the Egg McMuffin, an entire breakfast in a single sandwich. In the restaurant, customers pick up their meals at a counter, dispose of their own trash, and stack their own trays as they walk out the door or, better still, drive away from the pickup window taking whatever mess they make with them. Such efficiency is now central to our way of life. We tend to think that anything done quickly is, for that reason alone, good.

2. **Uniformity.** The first McDonald's operating manual declared the weight of a regular raw hamburger to be 1.6 ounces, its size to be 3.875 inches across, and its fat content to be 19 percent. A slice of cheese weighs exactly half an ounce, and French fries are cut precisely 9/32 of an inch thick.

   Think about how many objects around the home, the workplace, and the campus are designed and mass-produced uniformly according to a standard plan. Not just our environment but our life experiences—from traveling the nation's interstate highways to sitting at home viewing national TV shows—are more standardized than ever before.

of formal organizations. As explained in this chapter, large organizations tend to treat people impersonally, and they have a huge appetite for information. Mix large organizations with ever more complex computer technology, and it is no wonder that most people in the United States are concerned about who knows what about them and what is being done with this information.

For decades, the level of personal privacy in the United States has been declining. Early in the twentieth century, when state agencies began issuing driver's licenses, they created a file for every licensed driver. Today, a touch of a button sends this information to other organizations, including the police. Similarly, the Internal Revenue Service, the Social Security Administration, and government agencies that benefit veterans, students, the unemployed, and the poor all collect mountains of personal information.

Business organizations do much the same thing, although, as the examples show, people may not be aware that their choices and activities end up in corporate databases. Most people today use credit—the U.S. population now holds more than 1 billion credit cards, an average of five per adult—but the companies that do "credit checks" collect information about us and distribute it to almost anyone who asks, including criminals planning to steal our identity.

 See who's walking on Fifth Avenue in New York City right now at this Web site: http://www.riotmanhattan.com/riotmanhattan/webcam.html

Then there are the small cameras that are found not only at traffic intersections but also in stores, public buildings, and parking garages and across college campuses. The number of surveillance cameras that monitor our movements is rapidly increasing with each passing year. So-called "security cameras" may increase public safety in some ways—say, by discouraging a mugger or even a terrorist—but only at the cost of the little privacy we have left.

After the September 11, 2001, terrorist attacks, the federal government took steps (including passage of the USA PATRIOT Act) to strengthen national security. Today, government officials more closely monitor not just who enters the country but also the everyday activities of more and more people who are already here. Steps taken to improve national security make it harder to protect personal privacy.

Some legal protections remain. All the states have enacted laws giving citizens the right to examine some records about themselves kept by employers, banks, and credit bureaus. The U.S. Privacy Act of 1974 also limits the exchange of personal information among government agencies and permits citizens to examine and correct most government files. In response to rising levels of identity theft, Congress is likely to pass more laws to regulate the sale of credit information. But so many organizations (both public and private) now have information about us—experts estimate that 90 percent of U.S. households are profiled in databases somewhere—that current laws simply do not address the extent of the privacy problem.

WHAT DO YOU THINK?

1. If it comes to a choice, do you think most people consider national security or personal privacy to be more important? Can we have both security and privacy? Explain your position.

2. Internet search engines such as Yahoo! (http://www.yahoo.com) have "people search" programs that let you locate almost anyone. Do you think such programs pose a threat to personal privacy?

3. Have you checked your credit history lately? Do you know how to reduce the chances of someone stealing your identity? If not, one place to start is http://www.fightidentitytheft.com

Sources: R. Wright (1998), "Online Privacy" (2000), Rosen (2000), A. Hamilton (2001), Heymann (2002), and O'Harrow (2005).

Almost anywhere in the world, a person can walk into a McDonald's restaurant and buy the same sandwiches, drinks, and desserts prepared in the same way.[3]

---

[3]As McDonald's has "gone global," a few products have been added or changed according to local tastes. For example, in Uruguay, customers enjoy the McHuevo (a hamburger with a poached egg on top); Norwegians can buy McLaks (grilled salmon sandwiches); the Dutch favor the Groenteburger (vegetable burger); in Thailand, McDonald's serves Samurai pork burgers; the Japanese can purchase Chicken Tatsuta Sandwich (chicken seasoned with soy and ginger); Filipinos eat McSpaghetti (spaghetti with tomato sauce and bits of hot dog); and in India, where Hindus eat no beef, McDonald's sells a vegetarian Maharaja Mac (B. Sullivan, 1995).

Uniformity results from a highly rational system that specifies every action and leaves nothing to chance.

3. **Control.** The most unreliable element in the McDonald's system is human beings. After all, people have good and bad days, and they sometimes let their minds wander or decide to do something a different way. To minimize the unpredictable human element, McDonald's has automated its equipment to cook food at a fixed temperature for a set length of time. Even the cash register at McDonald's is keyed to pictures of the items so that ringing up a customer's order is as simple as possible.

Similarly, automatic teller machines are replacing banks, highly automated bakeries produce bread while people stand back and watch, and chickens and eggs (or is it eggs and chickens?) emerge from automated hatcheries. In supermarkets, laser scanners at self-checkouts are phasing out human checkers. Most of our shopping now occurs in malls, where everything from temperature and humidity to the kinds of stores and products sold are subject to continuous control and supervision (Ide & Cordell, 1994).

Can Rationality Be Irrational?

There is no doubt about the popularity or efficiency of McDonald's. But there is another side to the story.

Max Weber was alarmed at the increasing rationalization of the world, fearing that formal organizations would cage our imaginations and crush the human spirit. As he saw it, rational systems were efficient but dehumanizing. McDonaldization bears him out. Each of the principles we have just discussed limits human creativity, choice, and freedom. Echoing Weber, Ritzer states that "the ultimate irrationality of McDonaldization is that people could lose control over the system and it would come to control us" (1993:145). Perhaps even McDonald's understands this—the company has now expanded into more upscale, less McDonaldized restaurants such as Chipotle's and Pret-à-Manger that offer food that is more sophisticated, fresh, and healthful (Philadelphia, 2002).

The Future of Organizations: Opposing Trends

Early in the twentieth century, ever-larger organizations arose in the United States, most taking on the bureaucratic form described by Max Weber. In many respects, these organizations were like armies led by powerful generals who issued orders to their captains and lieutenants. Ordinary soldiers, working in the factories, did what they were told.

With the emergence of the postindustrial economy after 1950, as well as rising competition from abroad, many organizations evolved toward the flatter, more flexible model that encourages communication and creativity. Such "intelligent organizations" (Pinchot & Pinchot, 1993; Brooks, 2000) have become more productive than ever. Just as important, for highly skilled people who enjoy creative freedom, these organizations create less of the alienation that so worried Max Weber.

But this is only half the story. Although the postindustrial economy created many highly skilled jobs, it created even more routine service jobs, such as those offered by McDonald's. Fast-food companies now represent the largest pool of low-wage labor, aside from migrant workers, in the United States (Schlosser, 2002). Work of this kind, which Ritzer calls "McJobs," offers few of the benefits that today's highly skilled workers enjoy. On the contrary, the automated routines that define work in the fast-food industry, telemarketing, and similar fields are not very different from those that Frederick Taylor described a century ago.

Moreover, the organizational flexibility that gives better-off workers more freedom carries, for rank-and-file employees, the ever-present threat of "downsizing" (Sennett, 1998). Organizations facing global competition are eager to attract creative employees, but they are just as eager to cut costs by eliminating as many routine jobs as possible. The net result is that some people are better off than ever while others worry about holding their jobs and struggle to make ends meet—a trend that Chapter 8 ("Social Stratification") explores in detail.

U.S. organizations remain the envy of the world for their productive efficiency. Indeed, there are few places on Earth where the mail arrives as quickly and dependably as it does in this country. But we should remember that the future is far brighter for some than for others. In addition, as the Seeing Sociology in Everyday Life box on pages 138–39 explains, formal organizations pose a mounting threat to our privacy, something to keep in mind as we envision our organizational future.

✎ APPLYING SOCIOLOGY IN EVERYDAY LIFE

1. The next time you are eating at a fast-food restaurant, watch to see how not just employees but also customers are expected to behave in certain ways. For example, many fast-food restaurants expect customers to line up to order, get their own drinks, find their own table, and clean up their own mess. What other norms are at work?
2. Visit a large public building with an elevator. Observe groups of people as they approach the elevator, and enter the elevator with them. Watch their behavior: What happens to the conversations? Where do people fix their eyes? Can you explain these patterns?
3. Using campus publications and your school's Web page (and some assistance from an instructor), try to draw an organizational pyramid for your college or university. Show the key offices and how they supervise and report to one another.

MAKING THE GRADE

WHAT ARE SOCIAL GROUPS?

SOCIAL GROUPS are two or more people who identify and interact with one another.

p 120

A **PRIMARY GROUP** is small, personal, and lasting (examples include family and close friends).

pp 121–22

A **SECONDARY GROUP** is large, impersonal and goal-oriented, and often of shorter duration (examples include a college class or a corporation).

pp 121–22

⊞ See the Summing Up table on page 122.

Elements of Group Dynamics

GROUP LEADERSHIP

- *Instrumental leadership* focuses on completing tasks.
- *Expressive leadership* focuses on a group's well-being.
- *Authoritarian leadership* is a "take charge" style that demands obedience; *democratic leadership* includes everyone in decision making; *laissez-faire leadership* lets the group function mostly on its own.

p 122

GROUP CONFORMITY

- The Asch, Milgram, and Janis research shows that group members often seek agreement and may pressure one another toward conformity.
- Individuals use *reference groups*—including both *in-groups* and *out-groups*—to form attitudes and make evaluations.

p 122–24

GROUP SIZE and DIVERSITY

- Georg Simmel described the *dyad* as intense but unstable; the *triad*, he said, is more stable but can dissolve into a dyad by excluding one member.
- Peter Blau claimed larger groups turn inward, socially diverse groups turn outward, and physically segregated groups turn inward.

p 125–26

SOCIAL NETWORKS are relational webs that link people with little common identity and limited interaction. Being "well connected" in networks is a valuable type of social capital.

p 126–27

WHAT ARE FORMAL ORGANIZATIONS?

FORMAL ORGANIZATIONS are large secondary groups organized to achieve their goals efficiently.

p 127

UTILITARIAN ORGANIZATIONS pay people for their efforts (examples include a business or government agency).

p 127

NORMATIVE ORGANIZATIONS have goals people consider worthwhile (examples include voluntary associations such as the PTA).

p 127

COERCIVE ORGANIZATIONS are organizations people are forced to join (examples include prisons and mental hospitals).

p 127–28

social group (p.120) two or more people who identify and interact with one another

primary group (p. 121) a small social group whose members share personal and lasting relationships

secondary group (p.121) a large and impersonal social group whose members pursue a specific goal or activity

instrumental leadership (p. 122) group leadership that focuses on the completion of tasks

expressive leadership (p. 122) group leadership that focuses on the group's well-being

groupthink (p. 124) the tendency of group members to conform, resulting in a narrow view of some issue

reference group (p. 124) a social group that serves as a point of reference in making evaluations and decisions

in-group (p. 124) a social group toward which a member feels respect and loyalty

out-group (p. 124) a social group toward which a person feels a sense of competition or opposition

dyad (p. 125) a social group with two members

triad (p. 125) a social group with three members

network (p. 126) a web of weak social ties

formal organization (p. 127) a large secondary group organized to achieve its goals efficiently

tradition (p. 129) values and beliefs passed from generation to generation

rationality (p. 129) a way of thinking that emphasizes deliberate, matter-of-fact calculation of the most efficient way to accomplish a particular task

rationalization of society (p. 129) Weber's term for the historical change from tradition to rationality as the main mode of human thought

MAKING THE GRADE

CONTINUED...

WHAT ARE FORMAL ORGANIZATIONS? *CONTINUED*

All formal organizations operate in an **ORGANIZATIONAL ENVIRONMENT** which is influenced by
- technology
- political and economic trends
- current events
- population patterns
- other organizations

pp 129–30

See the Summing Up table on page 130.

bureaucracy (p. 129) an organizational model rationally designed to perform tasks efficiently

organizational environment (p. 129) factors outside an organization that affect its operation

bureaucratic ritualism (p. 132) a focus on rules and regulations to the point of interfering with an organization's goals

bureaucratic inertia (p. 132) the tendency of bureaucratic organizations to perpetuate themselves

oligarchy (p. 133) the rule of the many by the few

scientific management (p. 134) Frederick Taylor's term for the application of scientific principles to the operation of a business or other large organization

Modern Formal Organizations: Bureaucracy

BUREAUCRACY, which Max Weber saw as the dominant type of organization in modern societies, is based on
- specialization
- hierarchy of offices
- rules and regulations
- technical competence
- impersonality
- formal, written communication

pp 129, 130–31

PROBLEMS OF BUREAUCRACY include
- bureaucratic alienation
- bureaucratic inefficiency and ritualism
- bureaucratic inertia
- oligarchy

pp 131–33

The Evolution of Formal Organizations

CONVENTIONAL BUREAUCRACY

In the early 1900s, Frederick Taylor's **SCIENTIFIC MANAGEMENT** applied scientific principles to increase productivity.

p 134

MORE OPEN, FLEXIBLE ORGANIZATIONS

In the 1960s, Rosabeth Moss Kanter proposed that opening up organizations for all employees, especially women and other minorities, increased organizational efficiency.

pp 134–35

In the 1980s, global competition drew attention to the Japanese work organization's collective orientation.

p 135

THE CHANGING NATURE OF WORK

Recently, the rise of a postindustrial economy has created two very different types of work:
- highly skilled and creative work (examples include designers, consultants, programmers, and executives)
- low-skilled service work associated with the "McDonaldization" of society, based on efficiency, uniformity, and control (examples include jobs in fast-food restaurants and telemarketing)

pp 135–40

These questions are similar to those found in the test bank that accompanies this textbook.

MULTIPLE-CHOICE QUESTIONS

1. What term did Charles Cooley give to a small social group whose members share personal and lasting relationships?
   a. expressive group
   b. in-group
   c. primary group
   d. secondary group

2. Which type of group leadership is concerned with getting the job done?
   a. laissez-faire leadership
   b. secondary group leadership
   c. expressive leadership
   d. instrumental leadership

3. The research done by Solomon Asch, in which subjects were asked to pick lines of the same length, showed that
   a. groups encourage their members to conform.
   b. most people are stubborn and refuse to change their minds.
   c. groups often generate conflict.
   d. group members rarely agree on everything.

4. What concept refers to a social group that someone uses as a point of reference in making an evaluation or decision?
   a. out-group
   b. reference group
   c. in-group
   d. primary group

5. A network is correctly thought of as
   a. the most close-knit social group.
   b. a category of people with something in common.
   c. a social group in which most people know one another.
   d. a web of weak social ties.

6. From the point of view of a nurse, a hospital is a
   a. normative organization.
   b. coercive organization.
   c. utilitarian organization.
   d. All of the above are correct.

7. Bureaucracy is a type of social organization characterized by which of the following?
   a. specialized jobs
   b. offices arranged in a hierarchy
   c. lots of rules and regulations
   d. All of the above are correct.

8. According to Robert Michels, bureaucracy always means
   a. inefficiency.
   b. oligarchy.
   c. alienation.
   d. specialization.

9. Rosabeth Moss Kanter claims that large business organizations
   a. need to "open up" opportunity to encourage workers to perform well.
   b. must have clear and stable rules to survive in a changing world.
   c. do well or badly depending on how talented the leader is.
   d. suffer if they do not adopt the latest technology.

10. The "McDonaldization of society" means that
    a. organizations can provide food for people more efficiently than families can.
    b. impersonal organizations concerned with efficiency, uniformity, and control are more and more common.
    c. it is possible for organizations to both do their job and meet human needs.
    d. society today is one vast social network.

ANSWERS: 1 (c); 2 (d); 3 (a); 4 (b); 5 (d); 6 (c); 7 (d); 8 (b); 9 (a); 10 (b).

ESSAY QUESTIONS

1. How do primary groups differ from secondary groups? Give examples of each in your own life.
2. According to Max Weber, what are the six traits that define bureaucracy? What is the advantage of this organizational form? What are several problems that often go along with it?

If you think sex is simply a matter of biology, think again. Sexuality is constructed by society and is an important part of our everyday lives.

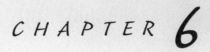

CHAPTER 6

Sexuality and Society

WHAT was the sexual revolution, and how did it change U.S. society?

WHY do societies try to control people's sexual behavior?

HOW does sexuality play a part in social inequality?

D ust swirls from the street as the crowded bus pulls to the curb in downtown Baghdad, and twenty-five-year-old Ali is the first one out the door. He hurries for several blocks past vendors and open stores and then turns down a narrow alley. Halfway along the dark passageway, he walks through a small, open door. This is Abu Abdullah's, a popular brothel in Iraq's capital city. Ali has come to buy sex.

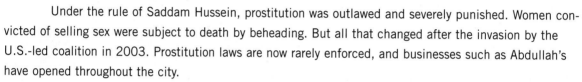

Ali lives in a small village 40 miles west of the city. He is not married. "I don't have enough money to get married," he explains, "so I come here." Abdullah's charges him $1.50 for fifteen minutes alone with a woman.

Under the rule of Saddam Hussein, prostitution was outlawed and severely punished. Women convicted of selling sex were subject to death by beheading. But all that changed after the invasion by the U.S.-led coalition in 2003. Prostitution laws are now rarely enforced, and businesses such as Abdullah's have opened throughout the city.

Asked about the changes since the fall of Saddam Hussein, Ali shrugs his shoulders, smiles, and says "Now we have freedom." But not everyone agrees that such freedom is a good thing. Many Iraqis believe that the spread of prostitution, as well as the opening of "adult cinemas" and the easy availability of pornography over the Internet, is weakening their society. Some blame the United States for causing what they see as moral decline (Caryl, 2003).

The debate about the proper place for sex in Iraqi society will go on for years to come. Much the same discussion is also taking place in the United States, where people disagree about a number of issues, including the pros and cons of prostitution and pornography and how much sex in movies and on television is too much.

This chapter examines the importance of sex to society and presents what researchers have learned about patterns of sexual behavior. As you will see, sexual attitudes are quite diverse around the world, and here in the United States, beliefs about sex have changed dramatically over the past century. Today, we continue to debate a number of social issues involving sexuality, including gay rights, teen pregnancy, prostitution, and date rape.

Understanding Sexuality

How much of your day does *not* involve thoughts that have something to do with sexuality? If you are like most people, the answer is "not very much," because sexuality is not just about having sex. Sexuality is a theme found almost every-where—on campus, in the workplace, and especially in the mass media. The sex industry, including pornography and prostitution, is a multibillion-dollar business. Sexuality is an important part of how we think about ourselves as well as how others evaluate us. In truth, there are few areas of social life in which sexuality does not play some part.

Even so, U.S. culture has long treated sex as taboo; even today, many people avoid talking about it. As a result, although sex can produce much pleasure, it also causes confusion, anxiety, and sometimes outright fear. Even scientists long considered sex off limits as a topic of research. It was not until the middle of the twentieth century that researchers turned their attention to this vital dimension of social life. Since then, as this chapter explains, we have discovered a great deal about human sexuality.

SEX: A BIOLOGICAL ISSUE

Sex refers to *the biological distinction between females and males*. From a biological point of view, sex is the way humans reproduce. A female ovum and a male sperm, each

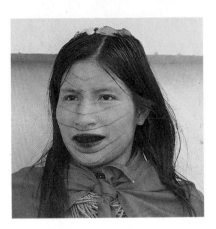

We claim that beauty is in the eye of the beholder, which suggests the importance of culture in setting standards of attractiveness. All of the people pictured here—from Morocco, South Africa, Nigeria, Myanmar, Japan, and Ecuador—are beautiful to members of their own society. At the same time, sociobiologists point out that, in every society on Earth, people are attracted to youthfulness. The reason is that, as sociobiologists see it, attractiveness underlies our choices about reproduction, which is most readily accomplished in early adulthood.

containing twenty-three chromosomes (biological codes that guide physical development), combine to form a fertilized embryo. To one of these pairs of chromosomes, which determines the child's sex, the mother contributes an X chromosome and the father contributes either an X or a Y. A second X from the father produces a female (XX) embryo; a Y from the father produces a male (XY) embryo. A child's sex is determined biologically at the moment of conception.

The sex of an embryo guides its development. If the embryo is male, testicular tissue forms and starts to produce testosterone, a hormone that triggers the development of male genitals (sex organs). If little testosterone is present, the embryo develops female genitals.

Look at the six photos above. Do you think that what people in any society consider beautiful is more a matter of biology or culture? Explain your answer.

SEX AND THE BODY

Some differences in the body set males and females apart. Right from birth, the two sexes have different **primary sex characteristics,** namely, *the genitals, organs used for reproduction.* At puberty, as people reach sexual maturity, additional sex differentiation takes place. At this point, people

The film *Transamerica* was the first widely seen Hollywood production about transsexuality. This story of a man who wishes to become a woman (played by Felicity Huffman) demonstrates that such a transformation involves much more than surgery. Imagine for a moment all the "complications" you would have to deal with if you were planning to change your sex.

develop **secondary sex characteristics,** *bodily development, apart from the genitals, that distinguishes biologically mature females and males.* Sexually mature females have wider hips for giving birth, milk-producing breasts for nurturing infants, and soft, fatty tissue that provides a reserve supply of nutrition during pregnancy and breast feeding. Sexually mature males typically develop more muscle in the upper body, more extensive body hair, and deeper voices. Of course, these are general differences; some males are smaller and have less body hair and higher voices than some females.

Keep in mind that sex is not the same thing as gender. *Gender* is an element of culture and refers to the personal traits and patterns of behavior (including responsibilities, opportunities, and privileges) that a culture attaches to being female or male. Chapter 10 ("Gender Stratification") explains that gender is an important dimension of social inequality.

Intersexual People

Sex is not always as clear-cut as just described. The term **intersexual people** refers to *people whose bodies (including genitals) have both female and male characteristics.* An older term for intersexual people is *hermaphrodite* (a word derived from Hermaphroditus, the child of the mythological Greek gods Hermes and Aphrodite, who embodied both sexes). A true hermaphrodite has both a female ovary and a male testis.

However, our culture demands that sex be clear-cut, a fact evident in the requirement that parents record the sex of their child at birth as either female or male. In the United States, some people respond to intersexual people with confusion or even disgust. But attitudes in other cultures are quite different: The Pokot of eastern Africa, for example, pay little attention to what they consider a simple biological error, and the Navajo look on intersexual people with awe, seeing in them the full potential of both the female and the male (Geertz, 1975).

Transsexuals

Transsexuals are *people who feel they are one sex even though biologically they are the other.* Tens of thousands of people have experienced the feeling of being trapped in a body of the wrong sex and a desire to be the other sex. Most become *transgendered,* meaning that they begin to disregard conventional ideas about how females and males should look and behave. Many go one step further and undergo *gender reassignment,* surgical alteration of their genitals, usually accompanied by hormone treatments. This medical process is complex and takes months or even years, but it helps many people gain a sense of becoming on the outside who they feel they are on the inside (Gagné, Tewksbury, & McGaughey, 1997).

In 2001, San Francisco became the first city with a health plan for city employees that includes paying the cost of gender reassignment surgery (which can cost more than $50,000). Would you support enacting similar policies in other places? Why or why not?

Sex: A Cultural Issue

Sexuality has a biological foundation. But like all other elements of human behavior, sexuality is also very much a cultural issue. Biology may explain some animals' mating rituals, but humans have no similar biological program. Although there is a biological "sex drive" in the sense that people find sex pleasurable and may seek to engage in sexual activity, our biology does not dictate any specific ways of being sexual any more than our desire to eat dictates any particular foods or table manners.

NATIONAL MAP 6–1

First-Cousin Marriage Laws
across the United States

There is no single view on first-cousin marriages
in the United States: Twenty-four states forbid
such unions, twenty allow them, and six allow
them with restrictions.* In general, states that
permit first-cousin marriages are found in New
England, the Southeast, and the Southwest.

First-Cousin Marriage
☐ Allowed
☐ Allowed
  with Restrictions
■ Not Allowed

* Of the six states that allow first-cousin marriages with restrictions, five states permit them only when couples are past childbearing age.

Source: "State Laws regarding Marriages" (2006).

Cultural Variation

Almost every sexual practice shows considerable variation
from one society to another. In his pioneering study of sexuality in the United States, Alfred Kinsey and his colleagues
(1948) found that most couples reported having intercourse
in a single position: face to face, with the woman on the bottom and the man on top. Halfway around the world, in the
South Seas, most couples *never* have sex in this way. In fact,
when the people of the South Seas learned of this practice
from Western missionaries, they poked fun at it as the
strange "missionary position."

Even the simple practice of displaying affection varies
from society to society. Most people in the United States
kiss in public, but the Chinese kiss only in private. The
French kiss publicly, often twice (once on each cheek), and
Belgians kiss three times (starting on either cheek). The
Maoris of New Zealand rub noses, and most people in Nigeria don't kiss at all.

Modesty, too, is culturally variable. If a woman stepping into a bath is disturbed, what body parts does she
cover? Helen Colton (1983) reports that an Islamic woman
covers her face, a Laotian woman covers her breasts, a
Samoan woman covers her navel, a Sumatran woman covers her knees, and a European woman covers her breasts
with one hand and her genital area with the other.

Around the world, some societies restrict sexuality, and
others are more permissive. In China, for example, societal
norms so closely regulate sexuality that few people have sexual intercourse before they marry. In the United States, at
least in recent decades, intercourse before marriage has
become the norm, and some people choose to have sex even
without strong commitment.

THE INCEST TABOO

When it comes to sex, do all societies agree on anything?
The answer is yes. One cultural universal—an element
found in every society the world over—is the **incest taboo,**
a norm forbidding sexual relations or marriage between certain relatives. In the United States, the law, reflecting cultural mores, prohibits close relatives (including brothers
and sisters, parents and children) from having sex or marrying. But in another example of cultural variation, exactly
which family members are included in our society's incest
taboo varies from state to state. National Map 6–1 shows
that twenty-four states outlaw marriage between first
cousins; twenty-six states do not.

Some societies (such as the North American Navajo)
apply incest taboos only to the mother and others on her
side of the family. There are also societies on record (including ancient Peru and Egypt) that have approved brother-sister marriages among the nobility to keep power within a
single family (Murdock, 1965, orig. 1949).

Why does some form of incest taboo exist everywhere?
Part of the reason is biology: Reproduction between close
relatives of any species increases the odds of producing offspring with mental or physical problems. But why, of all
living species, do only humans observe an incest taboo?
This fact suggests that controlling sexuality between close
relatives is a necessary element of *social* organization. For
one thing, the incest taboo limits sexual competition in
families by restricting sex to spouses (ruling out, for example, sex between parent and child). Second, because family
ties define people's rights and obligations toward one
another, reproduction between close relatives would hopelessly confuse kinship; if a mother and son had a daughter,

Times
The New York Times

January 31, 2006

Children, Media and Sex: A Big Book of Blank Pages

By JANE E. BRODY

In last summer's prize-winning R-rated film *Me and You and Everyone We Know*, a barely pubescent boy is seduced into oral sex by two girls perhaps a year older, and his 6-year-old brother logs on to a pornographic chat room and solicits a grown woman with instant messages about "poop."

Is this what . . . teenage children are watching? If so, what message are they getting about sexual mores, and what effect will it have on their behavior?

The journal *Pediatrics* addressed the topic last July in a supplemental report, "Impact of the Media on Adolescent Sexual Attitudes and Behaviors." It is an important and, sad to say, much neglected subject. . . . "Although a great deal is known about the effects of mass media on other adolescent behaviors, such as eating, smoking and drinking, we know basically nothing about the effects of mass media on adolescent sexual behaviors," the report's principal investigator, S. Liliana Escobar-Chaves of the [University of Texas] Center for Health Promotion and Prevention Research, concluded.

But to hazard a guess based on clear evidence that media representations influence teenage eating, smoking and drinking habits, adolescents are almost certainly affected—negatively—by sexual references and images from television, in movies and video games, in music, in magazines and on Web sites. . . .

Despite the advent of V-chips, movie ratings and televised warnings of appropriateness for young people, American teenagers have no trouble getting access to graphic sexual presentations. And no one restricts what they hear in popular songs. The effect of abstinence-only education pales by comparison with the many graphic messages that portray sexual activity—especially unprotected sex outside of marriage—to be a part of our culture as normal and acceptable as eating a Big Mac or drinking a Coke. . . .

Television is the best-studied medium, and the average teenager watches it for more than three hours a day. Two-thirds of youngsters 8 to 18 have TVs in their bedrooms, and two-thirds live in homes with cable TV, providing unsupervised access to sex talk and scenes.

The sexual content of TV is pervasive and increasing. A Kaiser Family Foundation study found that "the shows most watched by adolescents in 2001–2002 had 'unusually high' amounts of sexual content compared with TV as a whole: 83 percent of programs popular with teens had sexual content, and 20 percent contained explicit or implicit intercourse." . . .

The foundation study found that "characters involved in sexual behavior in TV programs rarely experience any

would the child consider the male a father or a brother? Third, by requiring people to marry outside their immediate families, the incest taboo integrates the larger society as people look beyond their close kin when seeking to form new families.

The incest taboo has long been a sexual norm in the United States and throughout the world. But in this country, many other sexual norms have changed over time. In the twentieth century, as the next section explains, our society experienced both a sexual revolution and a sexual counterrevolution.

Sexual Attitudes in the United States

What do people in the United States think about sex? Our culture's attitudes toward sexuality have always been something of a contradiction. Most European immigrants arrived with rigid ideas about "correct" sexuality, typically limiting sex to reproduction within marriage. The early Puritan settlers of New England demanded strict conformity in attitudes and behavior, and they imposed severe punishment for any sexual misconduct, even if it took place in the privacy of the home. Efforts to regulate sexuality continued well into the twentieth century: As late as the 1960s, for example, some states legally banned the sale of condoms in stores. Until 2003, when the Supreme Court struck them down, thirteen states had laws banning sexual acts between partners of the same sex; "fornication" laws, which are still on the books in eleven states, can be used to punish heterosexual intercourse among unmarried couples.

But this is just one side of the story. As Chapter 2 ("Culture") explained, because U.S. culture is individualistic, many believe in giving people freedom to do pretty much as they wish, as long as they cause no direct harm to others. The idea that what people do in the privacy of their own homes is *their* business makes sex a matter of individual freedom and personal choice.

negative consequences." . . .

Furthermore, only 3 percent of sex scenes observed involved protection against disease and unwanted pregnancy.

What little is known about the effects of television sex on teenage attitudes and behavior comes primarily from a national telephone survey conducted twice, in 2001 and again in 2002. . . .

The research indicated that adolescents who watched shows with sexual content tended to overestimate the frequency of certain sexual behaviors and to have more permissive attitudes toward premarital sex.

As for movies, two studies that analyzed the content of top movie videos rented by young people revealed a large amount of sexual content, mostly sex among unmarried partners.

The effects of such viewing have been minimally studied. In a 2001 study of sexually active black girls ages 14 to 18, those who were exposed to X-rated movies were more likely to have multiple sexual partners, to have sex more often, to test positively for chlamydia and to be less likely to use contraception.

The music videos aimed at teenagers are rife with sexuality or eroticism, much of it explicit, the report noted. But the effects of this exposure have yet to be studied. Likewise, nothing of a scientific nature is known about the effects of magazines, advertising or video or computer games on adolescents' attitudes and behavior toward sex.

As for the Internet, one national survey of 10- to 17-year-olds found that one in five had "inadvertently encountered explicit sexual content, and one in five had been exposed to an unwanted sexual solicitation while online."

The report called for better studies to assess the effects of sexuality in the mass media on adolescent beliefs and behavior, especially studies that measure over time how the cumulative effects of sexual content in different media affect teenage sexuality.

Adapted from the original article by Jane E. Brody published in *The New York Times* on January 31, 2006. Copyright © 2006 by The New York Times Company. Reprinted with permission.

WHAT DO YOU THINK?

1. What might account for the fact that there has been so little study of how the mass media may affect young people's sexual behavior?

2. Do you agree with the article's claim that the mass media present sexual activity to young people as being "as normal as drinking a Coke"? Why or why not?

3. Would you support regulating the presentation of sexual activity in the mass media? Why or why not?

When it comes to sexuality, is the United States restrictive or permissive? The answer is both. On one hand, many people in the United States still view sexual conduct as an important sign of personal morality. On the other hand, sex is more and more a part of the mass media—one recent report concluded that the number of scenes in television shows with sexual content had doubled in the last ten years (Kunkel et al., 2005). "In the *Times*" suggests that, despite concerns that sexual content in the mass media may be harmful to young people, we have yet to learn very much about this issue. Within this complex framework, we turn now to changes in sexual attitudes and behavior over the course of the past century.

YOUR TURN

On balance, do you think the mass media encourage young people to engage in sexual activity? Explain.

THE SEXUAL REVOLUTION

Over the past century, the United States witnessed profound changes in sexual attitudes and practices. The first indications of this change came in the 1920s as millions of people migrated from farms and small towns to rapidly growing cities. There, living apart from their families and meeting new people in the workplace, young men and women enjoyed considerable sexual freedom, one reason the decade became known as the "Roaring Twenties."

In the 1930s and 1940s, the Great Depression and World War II slowed the rate of change. But in the postwar period, after 1945, Alfred Kinsey set the stage for what later came to be known as the *sexual revolution*. In 1948, Kinsey and his colleagues published their first study of sexuality in the United States, and it raised eyebrows everywhere. The national uproar resulted mostly from the fact that scientists were actually studying sex, a topic many people were uneasy talking about even in the privacy of their homes.

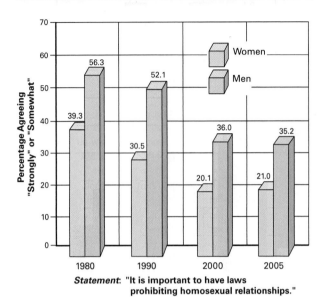

Statement: "It is important to have laws prohibiting homosexual relationships."

FIGURE 6-4 Opposition to Homosexual Relationships: Attitudes of First-Year College Students, 1980–2005

The historical trend among college students is toward greater tolerance of homosexual relationships, a view held by a large majority.

Sources: Astin et al. (2002) and Pryor et al. (2005).

we see a similar trend. In 1980, about half of college students supported laws prohibiting homosexual relationships; by 2005, as Figure 6–4 shows, less than one-third felt the same way (Astin et al., 2002; Pryor et al., 2005).

In large measure, this change was brought about by the gay rights movement, which arose in the middle of the twentieth century. Up to that time, most people in this country did not discuss homosexuality, and it was common for companies (including the federal government and the armed forces) to fire anyone who was accused of being gay. Mental health professionals also took a hard line, describing homosexuals as "sick" and sometimes placing them in mental hospitals, where it was hoped they might be "cured." It is no surprise that most lesbians and gay men remained "in the closet," closely guarding the secret of their sexual orientation. But the gay rights movement gained strength during the 1960s. One early milestone for the movement occurred in 1973 when the American Psychiatric Association declared that homosexuality was not an illness but simply "a form of sexual behavior."

The gay rights movement also began using the term **homophobia** to describe *discomfort over close personal in-*teraction with people thought to be gay, lesbian, or bisexual (Weinberg, 1973). The concept of homophobia, "fear of sameness," turns the tables on society: Instead of asking "What's wrong with gay people?" the question becomes "What's wrong with people who can't accept a different sexual orientation?"

In 2004, a number of cities and towns began to allow gay couples to marry, although these unions were later invalidated. But gay marriage is now legal in the state of Massachusetts, and civil unions (marriage by another name) are legal in Vermont and Connecticut. At the same time, seventeen states have enacted laws that forbid gay marriage and prohibit recognizing such marriages performed elsewhere.

What changes in laws regarding gay marriage do you expect over the next ten years? Why?

Sexual Issues and Controversies

Sexuality lies at the heart of a number of controversies in the United States today. Here we take a look at four key issues: teen pregnancy, pornography, prostitution, and sexual violence.

TEEN PREGNANCY

Because of the risk of pregnancy, engaging in sexual activities—especially intercourse—demands a high level of responsibility. Teenagers may be biologically mature enough to conceive, but many are not emotionally secure enough to appreciate the consequences of their actions. Surveys show that there are nearly 1 million U.S. teen pregnancies in the United States each year, most of them unplanned. This country's rate of births to teens is higher than that of all other high-income countries and is twice the rate in Canada (Darroch et al., 2001).

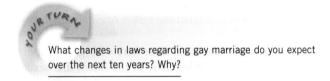

Visit the Web site of the National Campaign to Prevent Teen Pregnancy at http://www.teenpregnancy.org

For young women of all racial and ethnic categories, weak families and low income sharply increase the likelihood of becoming sexually active and having an unplanned child. To make matters worse, having unplanned children raises the risk that young women (as well as young fathers-to-be) will not finish school and will live in poverty (Alan Guttmacher Institute, 2002).

Did the sexual revolution raise the rate of teenage pregnancy? Perhaps surprisingly, the answer is no. The rate of

negative consequences." . . .

Furthermore, only 3 percent of sex scenes observed involved protection against disease and unwanted pregnancy.

What little is known about the effects of television sex on teenage attitudes and behavior comes primarily from a national telephone survey conducted twice, in 2001 and again in 2002. . . .

The research indicated that adolescents who watched shows with sexual content tended to overestimate the frequency of certain sexual behaviors and to have more permissive attitudes toward premarital sex.

As for movies, two studies that analyzed the content of top movie videos rented by young people revealed a large amount of sexual content, mostly sex among unmarried partners.

The effects of such viewing have been minimally studied. In a 2001 study of sexually active black girls ages 14 to 18, those who were exposed to X-rated movies were more likely to have multiple sexual partners, to have sex more often, to test positively for chlamydia and to be less likely to use contraception.

The music videos aimed at teenagers are rife with sexuality or eroticism, much of it explicit, the report noted. But the effects of this exposure have yet to be studied. Likewise, nothing of a scientific nature is known about the effects of magazines, advertising or video or computer games on adolescents' attitudes and behavior toward sex.

As for the Internet, one national survey of 10- to 17-year-olds found that one in five had "inadvertently encountered explicit sexual content, and one in five had been exposed to an unwanted sexual solicitation while online."

The report called for better studies to assess the effects of sexuality in the mass media on adolescent beliefs and behavior, especially studies that measure over time how the cumulative effects of sexual content in different media affect teenage sexuality.

WHAT DO YOU THINK?

1. What might account for the fact that there has been so little study of how the mass media may affect young people's sexual behavior?

2. Do you agree with the article's claim that the mass media present sexual activity to young people as being "as normal as drinking a Coke"? Why or why not?

3. Would you support regulating the presentation of sexual activity in the mass media? Why or why not?

When it comes to sexuality, is the United States restrictive or permissive? The answer is both. On one hand, many people in the United States still view sexual conduct as an important sign of personal morality. On the other hand, sex is more and more a part of the mass media—one recent report concluded that the number of scenes in television shows with sexual content had doubled in the last ten years (Kunkel et al., 2005). "In the *Times*" suggests that, despite concerns that sexual content in the mass media may be harmful to young people, we have yet to learn very much about this issue. Within this complex framework, we turn now to changes in sexual attitudes and behavior over the course of the past century.

On balance, do you think the mass media encourage young people to engage in sexual activity? Explain.

THE SEXUAL REVOLUTION

Over the past century, the United States witnessed profound changes in sexual attitudes and practices. The first indications of this change came in the 1920s as millions of people migrated from farms and small towns to rapidly growing cities. There, living apart from their families and meeting new people in the workplace, young men and women enjoyed considerable sexual freedom, one reason the decade became known as the "Roaring Twenties."

In the 1930s and 1940s, the Great Depression and World War II slowed the rate of change. But in the postwar period, after 1945, Alfred Kinsey set the stage for what later came to be known as the *sexual revolution*. In 1948, Kinsey and his colleagues published their first study of sexuality in the United States, and it raised eyebrows everywhere. The national uproar resulted mostly from the fact that scientists were actually studying sex, a topic many people were uneasy talking about even in the privacy of their homes.

Over the course of the last century, social attitudes in the United States have become more accepting of human sexuality. What do you see as some of the benefits of this greater openness? What are some of the negative consequences?

Kinsey also had some interesting things to say. His two books (Kinsey, Pomeroy, & Martin, 1948; Kinsey et al., 1953) became best-sellers because they revealed that people in the United States, on average, were far less conventional in sexual matters than most had thought. These books encouraged a new openness toward sexuality, which helped set the sexual revolution in motion.

In the late 1960s, the sexual revolution truly came of age. Youth culture dominated public life, and expressions such as "if it feels good, do it" and "sex, drugs, and rock 'n' roll" summed up the new, freer attitude toward sex. The baby boom generation, born between 1946 and 1964, became the first cohort in U.S. history to grow up with the idea that sex was part of people's lives, whether they were married or not.

Technology also played a part in the sexual revolution. The birth control pill, introduced in 1960, not only prevented pregnancy but also made sex more convenient. Unlike a condom or a diaphragm, which has to be applied at the time of intercourse, the pill could be taken anytime during the day. Now women as well as men could engage in sex without any special preparation.

Because women were historically subject to greater sexual regulation than men, the sexual revolution had special significance for them. Society's traditional "double standard" allows (and even encourages) men to be sexually active but expects women to be virgins until marriage and faithful to their husbands afterward. The survey data in Figure 6–1 show the narrowing of the double standard as a result of the sexual revolution. Among people born between 1933 and 1942 (that is, people who are in their sixties and seventies today), 56 percent of men but just 16 percent of women report having had two or more sexual partners by age twenty. Compare this wide gap with the pattern among those born between 1953 and 1962 (people now in their forties and fifties), who came of age after the sexual revolution. In this category, 62 percent of men and 48 percent of women say they had two or more sexual partners by age twenty (Laumann et al., 1994:198). The sexual revolution increased sexual activity overall, but it changed women's behavior more than men's.

Greater openness about sexuality develops as societies become richer and the opportunities for women increase. With these facts in mind, look for a pattern in the global use of birth control shown in Global Map 6–1 on page 154.

THE SEXUAL COUNTERREVOLUTION

The sexual revolution made sex a topic of everyday discussion and sexual activity more a matter of individual choice. However, by 1980, the climate of sexual freedom that had marked the late 1960s and 1970s was criticized by some as evidence of our country's moral decline, and the *sexual counterrevolution* began.

Politically speaking, the sexual counterrevolution was a conservative call for a return to "family values" and a change from sexual freedom back toward what critics saw as the sexual responsibility valued by earlier generations. Critics of the sexual revolution objected not just to the idea of "free love" but to trends such as cohabitation (living together without being married) and unmarried couples having children.

Looking back, the sexual counterrevolution did not greatly change the idea that people should decide for themselves when and with whom to have a sexual relationship. But whether for moral reasons or concerns about sexually transmitted diseases (STDs), more people began choosing to limit their number of sexual partners or not to have sex at all.

Is the sexual revolution over? It is true that people are making more careful decisions about sexuality. But as the rest of this chapter explains, the ongoing sexual revolution is evident in the fact that there is now greater acceptance of premarital sex as well as increasing tolerance for various sexual orientations.

PREMARITAL SEX

In light of the sexual revolution and the sexual counterrevolution, how much has sexual behavior in the United States really changed? One interesting trend involves premarital sex—sexual intercourse before marriage—among young people.

Consider first what U.S. adults *say* about premarital intercourse. Table 6–1 shows that about 35 percent characterize sexual relations before marriage as "always wrong" or "almost always wrong." Another 17 percent consider premarital sex "wrong only sometimes," and about 45 percent say premarital sex is "not wrong at all." Public opinion is more accepting of premarital sex today than a generation ago, but our society clearly remains divided on this issue.

Now let's look at what young people *do*. For women, there has been marked change over time. The Kinsey studies reported that for people born in the early 1900s, about 50 percent of men but just 6 percent of women had premarital sexual intercourse before age nineteen. Studies of baby boomers, born after World War II, show a slight increase in premarital sex among men but a large increase—to about one-third—among women. The most recent studies, targeting men and women born in the 1970s, show that 76 percent of men and 66 percent of women had premarital sexual intercourse by their senior year in high school (Laumann et al., 1994:323–24). Although a significant minority of young people choose abstinence, or not having sexual intercourse, premarital sex is widely accepted among young people today.

Finally, keep in mind that young people can be sexually active without having intercourse. In recent years, the share of young people engaging in oral sex has increased. In many cases, oral sex is chosen rather than intercourse because it does not involve the risk of pregnancy and because some people see it as less than "going all the way." At the same time, however, oral sex can transmit diseases. A recent government study found that only 20 percent of today's teens

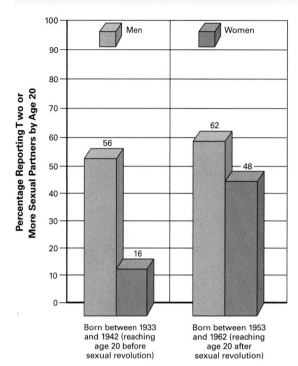

DIVERSITY SNAPSHOT

FIGURE 6-1 The Sexual Revolution:
Closing the Double Standard

A larger share of men than women report having had two or more sexual partners by age twenty. But the sexual revolution greatly reduced this gender difference.

Source: Laumann et al. (1994:198).

TABLE 6-1

How We View Premarital and Extramarital Sex

Survey Question: "There's been a lot of discussion about the way morals and attitudes about sex are changing in this country. If a man and a woman have sexual relations before marriage, do you think it is always wrong, almost always wrong, wrong only sometimes, or not wrong at all? What about a married person having sexual relations with someone other than the marriage partner?"

	Premarital Sex	Extramarital Sex
"Always wrong"	26.3%	79.9%
"Almost always wrong"	8.8	11.9
"Wrong only sometimes"	17.3	4.9
"Not wrong at all"	45.1	2.1
"Don't know"/No answer	2.5	1.2

Source: *General Social Surveys, 1972–2004: Cumulative Codebook* (Chicago: National Opinion Research Center, 2005), p. 291.

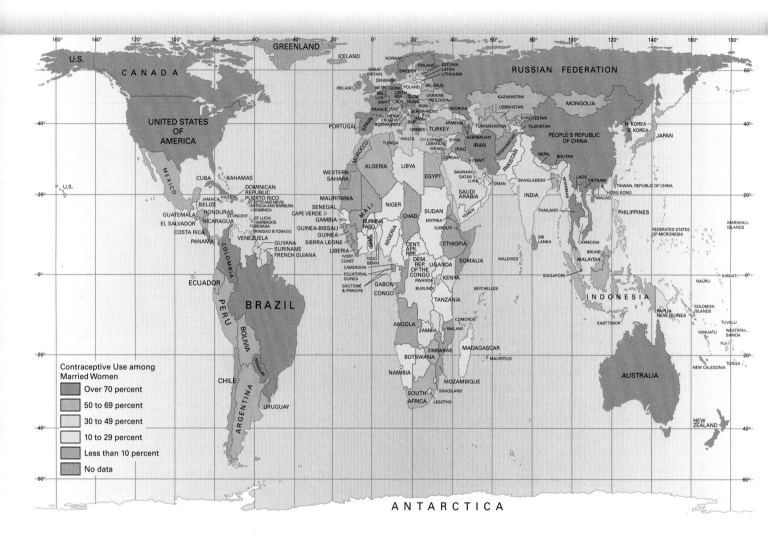

WINDOW ON THE WORLD

GLOBAL MAP 6-1 Contraceptive Use in Global Perspective

The map shows the percentage of married women using modern contraception methods, including barrier methods, contraceptive pill, implants, injectables, intrauterine contraceptive devices (IUDs), and sterilization. In general, in what way do high-income nations differ from low-income nations? Can you explain this difference?

Source: Data from United Nations Development Programme (2005).

have sexual intercourse before reaching the age of fifteen, but half had at least one sexual experience involving oral sex (National Center for Health Statistics, 2005).

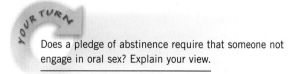

Does a pledge of abstinence require that someone not engage in oral sex? Explain your view.

SEX BETWEEN ADULTS

Judging from the mass media, people in the United States are very active sexually. But do popular images reflect reality? The Laumann study (1994), the largest study of sexuality since Kinsey's groundbreaking research, found that frequency of sexual activity varies widely in the U.S. population. One-third of adults report having sex with a partner a few times a year or not at all, another one-third have sex once or several times a month, and the remaining one-third have sex with a partner two or more times a week. In short, no single stereotype accurately describes sexual activity in the United States.

Despite the widespread image of "swinging singles" promoted on television shows such as *Sex and the City*, it is married people who have sex with partners the most. In addition, married people report the highest level of satisfaction—both physical and emotional—with their partners (Laumann et al., 1994).

EXTRAMARITAL SEX

What about married people having sex outside of marriage? This practice, commonly called "adultery" (sociologists prefer the more neutral term *extramarital sex*), is widely condemned. Table 6–1 shows that more than 90 percent of U.S. adults consider a married person having sex with someone other than the marital partner to be "always wrong" or "almost always wrong." The norm of sexual fidelity within marriage has been and remains a strong element of U.S. culture.

But actual behavior falls short of the cultural ideal. The Laumann study reports that about 25 percent of married men and 10 percent of married women have had at least one extramarital sexual experience. Or stating this the other way around, 75 percent of men and 90 percent of women have remained sexually faithful to their partners (Laumann et al., 1994:214; NORC, 2005:1702).

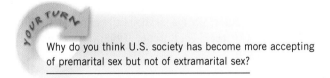

Why do you think U.S. society has become more accepting of premarital sex but not of extramarital sex?

SEX OVER THE LIFE COURSE

Patterns of sexual activity change with age. In the United States, most young men become sexually active by the time they reach sixteen and women by the age of seventeen. By the time they reach their mid-twenties, more than 90 percent of both women and men reported being sexually active with a partner at least once during the past year.

The picture begins to change by about age fifty, after which advancing age is linked to a decline in the share of people who are sexually active. By age sixty, about 15 percent of men and 40 percent of women say they have not been sexually active in the past year. By age seventy, half of women claim not to be sexually active; by age eighty, half of men say the same (Laumann et al., 1994). Contrary to pop-

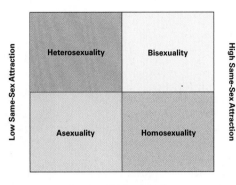

DIVERSITY SNAPSHOT

FIGURE 6-2 Four Sexual Orientations

A person's level of same-sex attraction and opposite-sex attraction are two distinct dimensions that combine in various ways to produce four major sexual orientations.

Source: Adapted from Storms (1980).

ular stereotypes, these data show that sexual activity is a normal part of life for most older adults.

Sexual Orientation

In recent decades, public opinion about sexual orientation has shown a remarkable change. **Sexual orientation** is *a person's romantic and emotional attraction to another person.* The norm in all human societies is **heterosexuality** (*hetero* is a Greek word meaning "the other of two"), meaning *sexual attraction to someone of the other sex.* Yet in every society, a significant share of people experience **homosexuality** (*homo* is the Greek word for "the same"), *sexual attraction to someone of the same sex.* Keep in mind that people do not necessarily fall into just one of these categories; they may have varying degrees of attraction to both sexes.

The idea that sexual orientation is often not clear-cut points to the existence of a third category: **bisexuality,** *sexual attraction to people of both sexes.* Some bisexual people are attracted equally to males and females; many others are attracted more strongly to one sex than the other. Finally, **asexuality** is *no sexual attraction to people of either sex.* Figure 6–2 places each of these sexual orientations in relation to the others.

It is important to remember that sexual *attraction* is not the same thing as sexual *behavior.* Many people have experienced some attraction to someone of the same sex,

The recent film *Brokeback Mountain*, the story of two young men who have a close, lifelong relationship, was widely characterized as a "gay cowboy movie." However, in the film both young men have relationships with women as well as with each other, so it is probably more correct to say that it is a "bisexual movie." Do you think people have more trouble understanding—and accepting—bisexuality than homosexuality? Why or why not?

but far fewer ever actually engage in same-sex behavior. This is in large part because our culture discourages such actions.

In the United States and around the world, heterosexuality is the norm because, biologically speaking, heterosexual relations permit human reproduction. Even so, most societies tolerate homosexuality. Among the ancient Greeks, upper-class men considered homosexuality the highest form of relationship, partly because they looked down on women as intellectually inferior. As men saw it, heterosexuality was necessary only so they could have children, and "real" men preferred homosexual relations (Kluckhohn, 1948; Ford & Beach, 1951; Greenberg, 1988).

For a summary of recent research on sexual orientation, go to http://www.davidmyers.org/Brix?pageID=62

WHAT GIVES US A SEXUAL ORIENTATION?

The question of how people come to have a particular sexual orientation is strongly debated. The arguments cluster into two general positions: sexual orientation as a product of society and sexual orientation as a product of biology.

Sexual Orientation: A Product of Society

This approach argues that people in any society attach meanings to sexual activity, and these meanings differ from place to place and over time. As Michel Foucault (1990, orig. 1978) points out, for example, there was no distinct category of people called "homosexuals" until a century ago, when scientists and eventually the public as a whole began defining people that way. Throughout history, many people no doubt had what we would call "homosexual experiences." But neither they nor others saw in this behavior the basis for any special identity.

Anthropological studies show that patterns of homosexuality differ greatly from one society to another. In Siberia, for example, the Chukchee Eskimo perform a ritual during which one man dresses like a woman and does a woman's work. The Sambia, who dwell in the Eastern Highlands of New Guinea, have a ritual in which young boys perform oral sex on older men in the belief that eating semen will make them more masculine. The existence of such diverse patterns in societies around the world seems to indicate that for human beings, sexual expression is socially constructed (Murray & Roscoe, 1998; Blackwood & Wieringa, 1999).

Sexual Orientation: A Product of Biology

A growing body of research suggests that sexual orientation is innate, or rooted in human biology in much the same way that people are born right-handed or left-handed. Arguing this position, Simon LeVay (1993) links sexual orientation to the structure of a person's brain. LeVay studied the brains of both homosexual and heterosexual men and found a small but important difference in the size of the hypothalamus, a part of the brain that regulates hormones. Such an anatomical difference, he claims, plays a part in shaping sexual orientation.

The American Psychological Association posts answers to commonly asked questions about sexual orientation at http://www.apa.org/topics/orientation.html

Genetics may also influence sexual orientation. One study of forty-four pairs of brothers, all homosexual, found that thirty-three pairs had a distinctive genetic pattern involving the X chromosome. Moreover, the gay brothers had an unusually high number of gay male relatives—but only on their mother's side. Such evidence leads some researchers to think there may be a "gay gene" located on the X chromosome (Hamer & Copeland, 1994).

CRITICAL REVIEW Mounting evidence supports the conclusion that sexual orientation is rooted in biology, although the best guess at present is that both nature and nurture play a part. Remember that sexual orientation is not a matter of neat categories. Most people who think of themselves as homosexual have had one or more heterosexual experiences, just as many people who think of themselves as heterosexual have had one or more homosexual experiences. Explaining sexual orientation, then, is not easy.

There is also a political issue here with great importance for gay men and lesbians. To the extent that sexual orientation is based in biology, homosexuals have no more choice about their sexual orientation than they do about their skin color. If this is so, shouldn't gay men and lesbians expect the same legal protection from discrimination as African Americans?

YOUR LEARNING What evidence supports the position that sexual behavior is constructed by society? What evidence suports the position that sexual orientation is rooted in biology?

HOW MANY GAY PEOPLE ARE THERE?

What share of our population is gay? This is a hard question to answer because, as noted earlier, sexual orientation is not a matter of neat categories. In addition, people are not always willing to discuss their sexuality with strangers or even family members. Sex researcher Alfred Kinsey estimated that about 4 percent of males and 2 percent of females have an exclusively same-sex orientation, although he pointed out that most people experience same-sex attraction at some point in their lives.

Some social scientists put the gay share of the population at 10 percent. But the Laumann survey shows that how homosexuality is defined makes a big difference in the results (Laumann et al., 1994). As Figure 6–3 shows, around 9 percent of men and 4 percent of women between the ages of eighteen and fifty-nine reported engaging in homosexual activity *at some time* in their lives. The second set of numbers in the bar graph shows that fewer men and even fewer women had a homosexual experience during childhood but not after puberty. And 2.8 percent of men and 1.4 percent

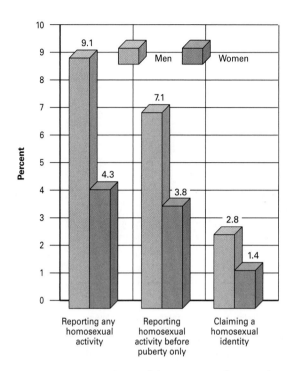

FIGURE 6-3 Share of the U.S. Population That Is Homosexual

The percentage of people who are classified as having a homosexual orientation depends on how this concept is operationalized. Research suggests that 2.8 percent of adult men and 1.4 percent of adult women claim a homosexual identity.

Source: Adapted from Laumann et al. (1994).

of women defined themselves as "partly" or "entirely" homosexual.

In the Laumann survey, less than 1 percent of U.S. adults described themselves as bisexual. But bisexual experiences appear to be fairly common (at least for a time) among younger people, especially on college and university campuses (Laumann et al., 1994; Leland, 1995). Many bisexuals do not think of themselves as either gay or straight, and their behavior reflects elements of both gay and straight living.

THE GAY RIGHTS MOVEMENT

The public's attitude toward homosexuality has been moving toward greater acceptance. Back in 1973, about three-fourths of U.S. adults claimed that homosexual relations were "always wrong" or "almost always wrong." Although that percentage changed little in the 1970s and 1980s, by 2004 it had dropped to 60 percent (NORC, 2005:292). Among college students, who are generally more tolerant of homosexual relationships than the population as a whole,

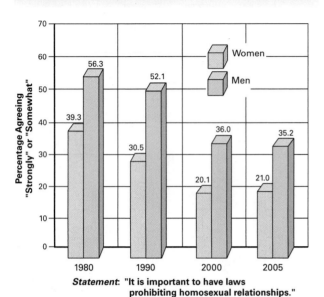

Statement: "It is important to have laws prohibiting homosexual relationships."

FIGURE 6–4 Opposition to Homosexual Relationships: Attitudes of First-Year College Students, 1980–2005

The historical trend among college students is toward greater tolerance of homosexual relationships, a view held by a large majority.
Sources: Astin et al. (2002) and Pryor et al. (2005).

teraction with people thought to be gay, lesbian, or bisexual (Weinberg, 1973). The concept of homophobia, "fear of sameness," turns the tables on society: Instead of asking "What's wrong with gay people?" the question becomes "What's wrong with people who can't accept a different sexual orientation?"

In 2004, a number of cities and towns began to allow gay couples to marry, although these unions were later invalidated. But gay marriage is now legal in the state of Massachusetts, and civil unions (marriage by another name) are legal in Vermont and Connecticut. At the same time, seventeen states have enacted laws that forbid gay marriage and prohibit recognizing such marriages performed elsewhere.

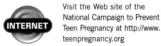

What changes in laws regarding gay marriage do you expect over the next ten years? Why?

Sexual Issues and Controversies

Sexuality lies at the heart of a number of controversies in the United States today. Here we take a look at four key issues: teen pregnancy, pornography, prostitution, and sexual violence.

TEEN PREGNANCY

Because of the risk of pregnancy, engaging in sexual activities—especially intercourse—demands a high level of responsibility. Teenagers may be biologically mature enough to conceive, but many are not emotionally secure enough to appreciate the consequences of their actions. Surveys show that there are nearly 1 million U.S. teen pregnancies in the United States each year, most of them unplanned. This country's rate of births to teens is higher than that of all other high-income countries and is twice the rate in Canada (Darroch et al., 2001).

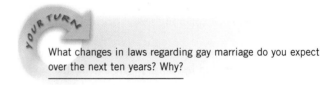

Visit the Web site of the National Campaign to Prevent Teen Pregnancy at http://www.teenpregnancy.org

For young women of all racial and ethnic categories, weak families and low income sharply increase the likelihood of becoming sexually active and having an unplanned child. To make matters worse, having unplanned children raises the risk that young women (as well as young fathers-to-be) will not finish school and will live in poverty (Alan Guttmacher Institute, 2002).

we see a similar trend. In 1980, about half of college students supported laws prohibiting homosexual relationships; by 2005, as Figure 6–4 shows, less than one-third felt the same way (Astin et al., 2002; Pryor et al., 2005).

In large measure, this change was brought about by the gay rights movement, which arose in the middle of the twentieth century. Up to that time, most people in this country did not discuss homosexuality, and it was common for companies (including the federal government and the armed forces) to fire anyone who was accused of being gay. Mental health professionals also took a hard line, describing homosexuals as "sick" and sometimes placing them in mental hospitals, where it was hoped they might be "cured." It is no surprise that most lesbians and gay men remained "in the closet," closely guarding the secret of their sexual orientation. But the gay rights movement gained strength during the 1960s. One early milestone for the movement occurred in 1973 when the American Psychiatric Association declared that homosexuality was not an illness but simply "a form of sexual behavior."

The gay rights movement also began using the term **homophobia** to describe *discomfort over close personal in-*

Did the sexual revolution raise the rate of teenage pregnancy? Perhaps surprisingly, the answer is no. The rate of

NATIONAL MAP 6–2
Teenage Pregnancy Rates
across the United States

The map shows pregnancy rates for 2000 for women aged fifteen to nineteen. In what regions of the country are rates high? Where are they low? What explanation can you offer for these patterns?

Source: Alan Guttmacher Institute (2004).

Pregnancies per 1,000 Women Aged 15 to 19
■ Above average
▨ Average
□ Below average

pregnancy among teens in 1950 was higher than it is today, partly because people back then married at a younger age. Because abortion was against the law, many pregnancies led to quick marriages. As a result, there were many pregnant teenagers, but almost 90 percent were married. Today, by contrast, the number of pregnant teens has fallen, but about 80 percent of these women are unmarried. In a slight majority (57 percent) of such cases, these women keep their babies; in the remainder, they have abortions (29 percent) or miscarriages (14 percent) (Alan Guttmacher Institute, 2004). National Map 6–2 shows pregnancy rates for women between the ages of fifteen and nineteen throughout the United States.

PORNOGRAPHY

Pornography is *sexually explicit material intended to cause sexual arousal.* But what is and is not pornographic has long been a matter of debate. Recognizing that different people view portrayals of sexuality differently, the U.S. Supreme Court gives local communities the power to decide for themselves what type of material violates "community standards" of decency and lacks "redeeming social value."

Definitions aside, pornography is very popular in the United States: X-rated videos, telephone "sex lines," sexually explicit movies and magazines, and thousands of Internet Web sites make up a thriving industry that takes in more than $10 billion each year. The vast majority of consumers of pornography are men.

Traditionally, people have criticized pornography on *moral* grounds. National surveys confirm the concern of 60 percent of U.S. adults that "sexual materials lead to a break-down of morals" (NORC, 2005:293). Today, however,

pornography is also seen as a *political* issue because most of it degrades women, portraying them as the sexual playthings of men.

Some critics also claim that pornography is a cause of violence against women. Although it is difficult to prove a scientific cause-and-effect relationship between what people view and how they act, the public shares a concern about pornography and violence, with almost half of adults holding the opinion that pornography encourages people to commit rape (NORC, 2005:293).

Although people everywhere object to sexual material they find offensive, many also value the principle of free speech and the protection of artistic expression. Nevertheless, pressure to restrict pornography is building from an unlikely coalition of conservatives (who oppose pornography on moral grounds) and liberals (who condemn it for political reasons).

PROSTITUTION

Prostitution is *the selling of sexual services.* Often called the "world's oldest profession," prostitution has existed throughout recorded history. In the United States today, about one in seven adult men reports having paid for sex at some time (NORC, 2005:1701). Because most people think that sex should be an expression of intimacy between two people, they find the idea of sex for money disturbing. As a result, prostitution is against the law everywhere in the United States except for parts of rural Nevada.

Around the world, prostitution is greatest in poor countries where patriarchy is strong and traditional cultural norms limit women's ability to earn a living. Global Map 6–2 on page 160 shows where prostitution is most widespread.

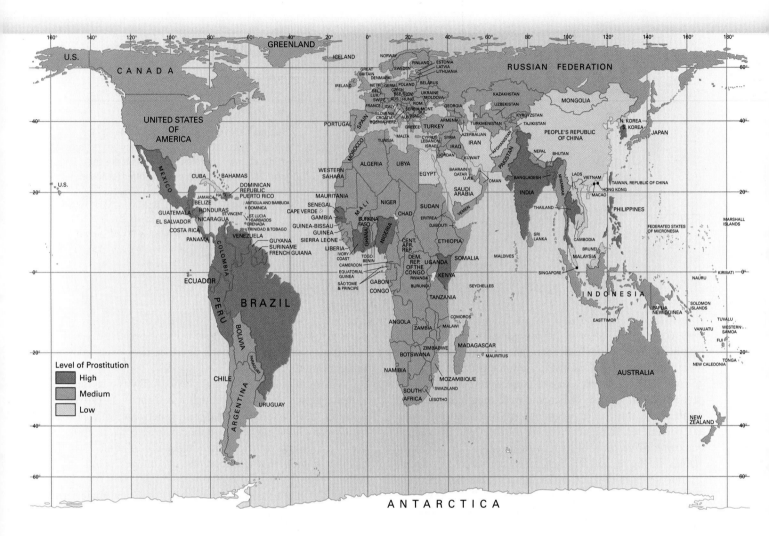

WINDOW ON THE WORLD

GLOBAL MAP 6–2   Prostitution in Global Perspective

Generally speaking, prostitution is widespread in societies where women have low standing. Officially, at least, the People's Republic of China boasts of gender equality, including the elimination of "vice" such as prostitution, which oppresses women. By contrast, in much of Latin America, where patriarchy is strong, prostitution is common. In many Islamic societies, patriarchy is also strong, but religion is a counterbalance, so prostitution is limited. Western, high-income nations have a moderate amount of prostitution.

Sources: *Peters Atlas of the World* (1990) and Mackay (2000).

Types of Prostitution

Most prostitutes (many prefer the morally neutral term "sex workers") are women, but they fall into different categories. *Call girls* are elite prostitutes, typically young, attractive, and well-educated women who arrange their own "dates" with clients by telephone. The classified pages of any large city newspaper contain numerous ads for "escort services," by which women and men offer both companionship and sex for a fee.

Brothels like this one are found in rural counties of Nevada. Some people claim that legalizing prostitution permits the government to protect the health and safety of "sex workers," who have the opportunity to earn a good income. Others claim that selling sex is degrading to women as well as men, and that women's economic opportunity should not depend on selling themselves in this way. Where do you stand on the issue of legalized prostitution? Why?

In the middle are prostitutes employed in "massage parlors" or brothels under the control of managers. These sex workers have less choice about their clients, receive less money for their services, and get to keep no more than half of what they make.

At the bottom of the sex worker hierarchy are *streetwalkers,* women and men who "work the streets" of large cities. Typically, female streetwalkers are under the control of male pimps who take most of their earnings. Some are addicted to drugs and sell sex to buy the drugs they need. All streetwalkers are at high risk of becoming the victims of violence (Davidson, 1998; Estes, 2001).

Most prostitutes offer heterosexual services. However, gay prostitutes also trade sex for money. Researchers report that many gay prostitutes end up selling sex after having suffered rejection by family and friends because of their sexual orientation (Weisberg, 1985; Boyer, 1989; Kruks, 1991).

A Victimless Crime?

Prostitution is against the law almost everywhere in the United States, but many people consider it a victimless crime (defined in Chapter 7, "Deviance," as a crime in which no one claims to be a victim). Consequently, instead of enforcing prostitution laws consistently, police stage only occasional crackdowns. This policy reflects a desire to control prostitution while recognizing that it is impossible to eliminate it totally.

Many people take a "live and let live" attitude about prostitution and say that adults ought to be free to do as they please as long as no one is forced to do anything. But is prostitution really victimless? The sex trade subjects many women to abuse and outright violence and also plays a part in spreading sexually transmitted diseases, including AIDS.

In addition, many poor women—especially in low-income nations—become trapped in a life of selling sex. Thailand, in Southeast Asia, has 2 million prostitutes, representing about 10 percent of all women in the labor force. Many of these women begin working before they are teenagers, are often subjected to physical abuse, and run a high risk of contracting HIV (Wonders & Michalowski, 2001).

In the past, the focus of law enforcement has been on the women who earn money as sex workers. But prostitution would not exist without demand on the part of men. For this reason, police officers are now more likely to target "Johns" when they attempt to buy sex.

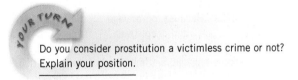

Do you consider prostitution a victimless crime or not? Explain your position.

SEXUAL VIOLENCE: RAPE AND DATE RAPE

Ideally, sexual activity occurs within a loving relationship between consenting adults. In reality, however, sex can sometimes be twisted by hatred and violence. Here we consider two types of sexual violence: rape and date rape.

Rape

Although some people think rape is motivated only by a desire for sex, it is actually an expression of power, a violent act that uses sex to hurt, humiliate, or control another person. According to the Federal Bureau of Investigation, about 95,000 women report being raped to the police each year.

SEEING SOCIOLOGY IN EVERYDAY LIFE

When Sex Is Only Sex: The Campus Culture of "Hooking Up"

Have you ever been in a sexual situation and not been sure of the right thing to do? Most colleges and universities highlight two important rules. First, sexual activity must take place only when both participants have given clear statements of consent. The consent principle is what makes "having sex" different from date rape. Second, no one should knowingly expose a partner to a sexually transmitted disease, especially when the partner is unaware of the danger.

These rules are very important, but they say little about the larger issue of what sex *means*. For example, when is it "right" to have a sexual relationship? How well do you have to know the other person? If you do have sex, are you obligated to see the person again?

Two generations ago, there were informal rules for campus sex. Dating was part of the courtship process. That is, "going out" was a way in which women and men evaluated each other as possible marriage partners while they sharpened their own sense of what they wanted in a mate. Because, on average, marriage took place when people were in their early twenties, many college students became engaged and married while they were still in school. In this cultural climate, sex became part of a

relationship along with commitment—a serious interest in the other person as a possible marriage partner.

Today, the sexual culture of the campus is very different. Partly because people now marry much later, the culture of courtship has declined dramatically. About three-fourths of women in a recent national survey point to a new campus pattern, the culture of "hooking up." What exactly is "hooking up"? Most describe it in words like these: "When a girl and a guy get together for a physical encounter—anything from kissing to having sex—and don't necessarily expect anything further."

Student responses to the survey suggest that "hookups" have three characteristics. First, most couples who hook up know little about each other. Second, a typical hookup involves people who have been drinking alcohol, usually at a campus party. Third, most women are critical of the culture of hooking up and express little satisfaction with these encounters. Certainly, some women (and men) who hook up simply walk away, happy to have enjoyed a sexual experience free of further obligation. But given the powerful emotions that sex can unleash, hooking up often leaves someone wondering

what to expect next. "Will you call me tomorrow?" "Will I see you again?"

The survey asked women who had experienced a recent hookup to report how they felt about the experience a day later. A majority of respondents said they felt "awkward," about half felt "disappointed" and "confused," and one in four felt "exploited." Clearly, for many people, sex is more than a physical encounter. Further, because today's campus is very sensitive to charges of sexual exploitation, there is a need for clearer standards of fair play.

WHAT DO YOU THINK?

1. How extensive is hooking up on your campus? Are you aware of differences in these encounteres between heterosexuals and homosexuals?

2. What do you see as the advantages of sex without commitment? What are the disadvantages of this kind of relationship? Are men and women likely to answer these questions differently? Explain.

3. Do you think college students need more guidance about sexual issues? If so, who should provide this guidance?

Source: Based in part on Marquardt & Glenn (2001).

The actual number of rapes is likely several times higher (Federal Bureau of Investigation, 2005).

The official government definition of rape is "the carnal knowledge of a female forcibly and against her will." Thus official rape statistics include only victims who are women. But men, too, are raped—in perhaps 10 percent of all cases. Most men who rape men are not homosexual; they are heterosexuals who are motivated by a desire not for sex but to dominate another person.

Date Rape

A common myth is that rape involves strangers. In reality, however, only about one-third of all rapes fit this pattern. Three of every four rapes involve people who know each other—more often than not, pretty well—and these crimes usually take place in familiar surroundings, such as the home or a college campus. The term "date rape" or "acquaintance rape" refers to forcible sexual violence

162 CHAPTER 6 SEXUALITY AND SOCIETY

Experts agree that one factor that contributes to the problem of sexual violence on the college campus is the widespread use of alcoholic beverages. What policies are in force on your campus to discourage the kind of drinking that leads to one person imposing sex on another?

against women by men they know (Laumann et al., 1994; U.S. Bureau of Justice Statistics, 2006).

A second myth, often linked specifically to date rape, is the idea that a woman who has been raped must have done something to encourage the man and make him think she wanted to have sex. Perhaps the victim agreed to go out with the offender. Maybe she even invited him to her room. But of course, such actions no more justify rape than they would any other kind of physical assault.

Although rape is a physical attack, it also leaves emotional and psychological scars. Beyond the brutality of being physically violated, rape by an acquaintance also affects a victim's ability to trust others. Psychological scars are especially serious among the half of rape victims who are under eighteen; one-third of these young victims are attacked by their own fathers or stepfathers (Greenfield, 1996).

How common is date rape? One recent study found that about 20 percent of a sample of high school girls in the United States reported being victims of sexual or physical violence inflicted by the boys they were dating (Dickinson, 2001).

Nowhere has the issue of date rape been more widely discussed than on college campuses, where the danger of date rape is high. The collegiate environment promotes easy friendships and encourages trust. At the same time, many young students have much to learn about relationships and about themselves. As the Seeing Sociology in Everyday Life box explains, although college life encourages communication, it provides few social norms to help guide young people's sexual experiences. To counter the problem, many

A government report on the sexual victimization of college women is available at http://www.ojp.usdoj.gov/bjs/abstract/svcw.htm

schools now actively address myths about rape. In addition, greater attention is now focused on the use of alcohol, which increases the likelihood of sexual violence.

Theoretical Analysis of Sexuality

Applying sociology's various theoretical approaches gives us a better understanding of human sexuality. The following sections discuss the three major approaches. The Applying Theory table on page 164 highlights the key insights of each approach.

STRUCTURAL-FUNCTIONAL ANALYSIS

The structural-functional approach explains the contribution of any social pattern to the overall operation of society. Because sexuality can have such important consequences, society regulates this type of behavior.

The Need to Regulate Sexuality

From a biological point of view, sex allows our species to reproduce. But culture and social institutions regulate *with whom* and *when* people reproduce. For example, most societies condemn married people who have sex with someone other than a spouse. To allow the forces of sexual passion to go unchecked would threaten family life, especially the raising of children.

The fact that the incest taboo exists everywhere shows clearly that no society permits a completely free choice of sexual partners. Reproduction resulting from sex between family members other than married partners would break down the kinship system and hopelessly confuse human relationships.

APPLYING THEORY

Sexuality

	Structural-Functional Approach	Symbolic-Interaction Approach	Social-Conflict Approach
What is the level of analysis?	Macro-level	Micro-level	Macro-level
What is the importance of sexuality for society?	Society depends on sexuality for reproduction. Society uses the incest taboo and other norms to control sexuality in order to maintain social order.	Sexual practices vary among the many cultures of the world. Some societies allow individuals more freedom than others in matters of sexual behavior.	Sexuality is linked to social inequality. U.S. society regulates women's sexuality more than men's; this is part of the larger pattern of men dominating women.
Has sexuality changed over time? How?	Yes. As advances in birth control technology separate sex from reproduction, societies relax some controls on sexuality.	Yes. The meanings people attach to virginity and other sexual matters are all socially constructed and subject to change.	Yes and no. Some sexual standards have relaxed, but society still defines women in sexual terms, just as homosexual people are harmed by society's heterosexual bias.

Historically, the social control of sexuality was strong, mostly because sex often led to childbirth. We see these controls at work in the old-fashioned distinction between "legitimate" reproduction (within marriage) and "illegitimate" reproduction (outside marriage). But once a society develops the technology to control births, its sexual norms become more permissive. This occurred in the United States, where over the course of the twentieth century, sex moved beyond its basic reproductive function and became mainly a form of intimacy and even recreation (Giddens, 1992).

Latent Functions: The Case of Prostitution

It is easy to see that prostitution is harmful because it spreads disease and exploits women. But does it have latent functions that help explain why prostitution is so widespread? According to Kingsley Davis (1971), prostitution is one way to meet the sexual needs of a large number of people who do not have ready access to sex, including soldiers, travelers, and people who are not physically attractive enough or are too poor to attract a marriage partner (such as Ali in the opening to this chapter). Some people favor prostitution because they want sex without the "trouble" of a relationship. As one analyst put it, "Men don't pay for sex; they pay so they can leave" (Miracle, Miracle, & Baumeister, 2003:421).

CRITICAL REVIEW The structural-functional approach helps us appreciate the important role sexuality plays in the organization of society. The incest taboo and

other cultural norms suggest that society has always paid attention to who has sex with whom and, especially, who reproduces with whom.

Functional analysis sometimes ignores gender; when Kingsley Davis wrote of the benefits of prostitution for society, he was really talking about the benefits to *men*. In addition, the fact that sexual patterns change over time, just as they differ around the world, is ignored by this perspective. To appreciate the varied and changeable nature of sexuality, we now turn to the symbolic-interaction approach.

YOUR LEARNING Why do modern societies give people more choice about matters involving sexuality?

SYMBOLIC-INTERACTION ANALYSIS

The symbolic-interaction approach highlights how as people interact, they construct everyday reality. As explained in Chapter 4 ("Social Interaction in Everyday Life"), different people construct different realities, so the views of one group or society may well differ from those of another. In the same way, our understanding of sexuality can and does change over time.

The Social Construction of Sexuality

Almost all social patterns involving sexuality saw a lot of change over the course of the twentieth century. One good illustration is the changing importance of virginity. A century ago, our society's norm—for women, at least—was virginity until marriage. This norm was strong because there was no effective means of birth control, and virginity was the only assurance a man had that his bride-to-be was not carrying another man's child.

Today, because we have gone a long way toward separating sex from reproduction, the virginity norm has weakened considerably. In the United States, among people born between 1963 and 1974, just 16.3 percent of men and 20.1 percent of women report being virgins at first marriage (Laumann et al., 1994:503).

Another example of our society's construction of sexuality involves young people's awareness of sex. A century ago, childhood was a time of innocence in sexual matters. In recent decades, however, thinking has changed. Although few people encourage sexual activity between children, most people believe that children should be educated about sex so that they can make intelligent choices about their behavior as they grow older.

Global Comparisons

Around the world, different societies attach different meanings to sexuality. For example, Ruth Benedict (1938), an anthropologist who spent years learning the ways of life of the Melanesian people of southeastern New Guinea, reported that adults paid little attention when young children engaged in sexual experimentation with one another. Parents in Melanesia shrugged off such activity because before puberty, sex cannot lead to reproduction. Is it likely that most parents in the United States would respond the same way?

Sexual practices also vary from culture to culture. Circumcision of infant boys (the practice of removing all or part of the foreskin of the penis) is common in the United States but rare in most other parts of the world. A practice sometimes referred to as female circumcision (removal of the clitoris) is rare in the United States but common in parts of Africa and the Middle East (Crosette, 1995; Huffman, 2000). (For more about this practice, more accurately called "female genital mutilation," see the Thinking About Diversity box on page 286).

CRITICAL REVIEW The strength of the symbolic-interaction approach lies in revealing the socially constructed character of familiar social patterns. Understanding that people "construct" sexuality, we can better appreciate the variety of sexual attitudes and practices found over the course of history and around the world.

One limitation of this approach is that not all sexual practices are so variable. Men everywhere have always

The control of women's sexuality is a common theme in human history. During the Middle Ages, Europeans devised the "chastity belt"—a metal device locked about a woman's groin that prevented sexual intercourse (and probably interfered with other bodily functions as well). While such devices are all but unknown today, the social control of sexuality continues. Can you point to examples?

been more likely to see women in sexual terms than the other way around. Because this pattern is widespread, some broader social structure must be at work, as we shall see in the following section on the social-conflict approach.

✓ YOUR LEARNING What evidence can you provide showing that human sexuality is socially constructed?

SOCIAL-CONFLICT ANALYSIS

As you have seen in earlier chapters, the social-conflict approach highlights dimensions of inequality. This approach shows how sexuality both reflects patterns of social inequality and helps perpetuate them.

Sexuality: Reflecting Social Inequality

Recall our discussion of prostitution, a practice outlawed almost everywhere in our society. Enforcement of prostitution laws is uneven at best, especially when it comes to who is and is not likely to be arrested. Although two people are

The Abortion Controversy

A black van pulls up to a storefront in a busy section of the city. Two women get out of the front seat and look up and down the street. After a moment, one nods to the other, and they open the rear door to let a third young woman out of the van. Standing to the right and left of the woman, the two quickly escort her inside the building.

This scene might describe two federal marshals taking a convict to a police station, but it is actually an account of two clinic workers helping a woman who has decided to have an abortion. Why must they be so cautious? Anyone who has read the papers in recent years knows about the angry confrontations at abortion clinics across North America. Some opponents have even targeted and killed doctors who carry out abortions, some 1.3 million of which are performed in the United States each year. It is one of the most hotly debated issues of our day.

Abortion has not always been so controversial. In colonial times, mid-wives and other healers performed abortions with little community opposition and with full approval of the law. But controversy arose around 1850, when early medical doctors wanted to eliminate the competition they faced from midwives and other traditional health providers, whose income came largely from ending pregnancies. By 1900, medical doctors succeeded in getting every state to pass a law banning abortion.

Such laws greatly reduced the number of abortions. Those that did occur were performed "underground," as secretly as possible. Many women who wanted abortions—especially those who were poor—had little choice but to seek help from unlicensed "back alley" abortionists, sometimes with tragic results due to unsanitary conditions and the use of medically dangerous techniques.

By the 1960s, opposition to laws prohibiting abortions was rising. In 1973, the U.S. Supreme Court rendered a landmark decision (in the cases of *Roe* v. *Wade* and *Doe* v. *Bolton*), striking down all state laws banning abortion. In effect, this action established a woman's legal access to abortion nationwide.

Even so, the abortion controversy continues. On one side of the issue are people who describe themselves as "pro-choice," supporting a woman's right to choose abortion. On the other side are those who call themselves "pro-life," opposing abortion as morally wrong; these people would like to see the Supreme Court reverse its 1973 decision.

How strong is the support for each side of the abortion controversy? A recent national survey asked the question, "Should it be possible for a pregnant woman to obtain a legal abortion if the woman wants it for any reason?" In response, 38.5 percent said yes (placing them in the pro-choice camp), and 56.5 percent said no (expressing the pro-life position); the remaining 5 percent offered no opinion (NORC, 2005:282).

involved, the record shows that police are far more likely to arrest (less powerful) female prostitutes than (more powerful) male clients. Of all women engaged in prostitution, it is streetwalkers—women with the least income and most likely to be minorities—who face the highest risk of arrest (COYOTE Los Angeles, 2006). We might also wonder whether so many women would be involved in prostitution in the first place if they had economic opportunities equal to those of men.

More generally, which categories of people in U.S. society are most likely to be defined and treated as sexual objects? The answer, once again, is those with less power: women compared to men, and people of color compared to whites. In this way, sexuality, a natural part of human life, is used by society to define some people as less worthy.

Sexuality: Creating Social Inequality

Social-conflict theorists, especially feminists, point to sexuality as the root of inequality between women and men. Defining women in sexual terms devalues them from full human beings to objects of men's interest and attention. Is it any wonder that the word "pornography" comes from the Greek word *porne*, meaning "a man's sexual slave"?

If men define women in sexual terms, it is easy to see pornography—almost all of which is consumed by males—as a power issue. Because pornography typically shows women focused on pleasing men, it supports the idea that men have power over women.

Some radical critics doubt that this element of power can ever be removed from heterosexual relations (A. Dworkin, 1987). Most social-conflict theorists do not reject

A closer look shows that particular circumstances make a big difference in how people see this issue. The figure shows that most U.S. adults favor legal abortion if a pregnancy seriously threatens a woman's health, if the woman became pregnant as a result of rape, or if the fetus is very likely to have a serious defect. The bottom line is that about 38 percent support access to abortion under *any* circumstances, but nearly 83 percent support access to abortion under *some* circumstances.

Many of those who take the pro-life position feel strongly that abortion is nothing other than the killing of unborn children, some 42 million since *Roe* v. *Wade* was decided in 1973. To them, people never have the right to end innocent life in this way. But pro-choice people are no less committed to their position, that women must have control over their own bodies. If pregnancy decides the course of women's lives, women will never be able to compete with men on equal terms, whether it is on campus or in the workplace. Therefore, access to legal, safe abortion is a necessary condition to full participation in society.

WHAT DO YOU THINK?

1. The more conservative, pro-life people see abortion as a moral issue, and more liberal, pro-choice people see abortion as a power issue. Compare these positions to how conservatives and liberals view the issue of pornography.

2. Surveys show that men and women have almost the same opinions about abortion. Does this surprise you? Why or why not?

3. Why do you think the abortion controversy is often so bitter? Do you think our nation can find a middle ground on this issue?

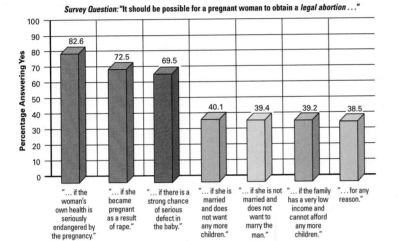

Survey Question: "It should be possible for a pregnant woman to obtain a *legal abortion*..."

When Should the Law Allow a Woman to Choose Abortion?

The extent of public support for legal abortion depends on exactly how the issue is presented. Source: NORC (2005).

heterosexuality, but they do agree that sexuality can and does degrade women. Our culture often describes sexuality in terms of sport (men "scoring" with women) and violence ("slamming," "banging," and "hitting on," for example, are verbs used for both fighting and sex).

Queer Theory

Social-conflict theory has taken aim not only at the domination of women by men but also at heterosexuals dominating homosexuals. In recent years, as many lesbians and gay men have sought public acceptance, a gay voice has risen in sociology. The term **queer theory** refers to *a body of research findings that challenges the heterosexual bias in U.S. society.*

The Queer Resources Directory looks at a wide range of issues from a queer theory perspective: http://www.qrd.org/qrd/

Queer theory begins with the claim that our society is characterized by **heterosexism,** *a view that labels anyone who is not heterosexual as "queer."* Our heterosexual culture victimizes a wide range of people, including gay men, lesbians, bisexuals, transsexuals, and even asexual people. Furthermore, although most people agree that bias against women (sexism) and people of color (racism) is wrong, heterosexism is widely tolerated and sometimes well within the law. For example, U.S. military forces cannot legally discharge a female soldier for "acting like a woman" because that would be a clear case of gender discrimination. But the military forces can discharge her for homosexuality if she is a sexually active lesbian.

Heterosexism is also part of everyday culture (Kitzinger, 2005). When we describe something as "sexy," for example, don't we really mean attractive to *heterosexuals?*

From a social-conflict point of view, sexuality is not so much a "natural" part of our humanity as it is a socially constructed pattern of behavior. Sexuality plays an important part in social inequality: By defining women in sexual terms, men devalue them as objects. Would you consider the behavior shown here to be "natural" or socially directed? Why?

Can you think of three social patterns (like the one just mentioned) that are examples of heterosexism?

CRITICAL REVIEW The social-conflict approach shows how sexuality is both a cause and an effect of inequality. In particular, it helps us understand men's power over women and heterosexual people's domination of homosexual people.

At the same time, this approach overlooks the fact that many people do not see sexuality as a power issue. On the contrary, many couples enjoy a vital sexual relationship that deepens their commitment to one another. In addition, the social-conflict approach pays little attention to steps our society has made toward reducing inequality. Today's men are less likely to describe women as sex objects than they were a few decades ago. One of the most important issues in the workplace today is ensuring that all employees remain free from sexual harassment. Rising public concern (see Chapter 10, "Gender Stratification") has reduced sex abuse in the workplace. There is also ample evidence that the gay rights movement has won greater opportunities and social acceptance for gay people.

YOUR LEARNING How does sexuality play a part in creating social inequality?

This chapter closes with a look at what is perhaps the most divisive sexuality-related issue of all: **abortion,** *the deliberate termination of a pregnancy.* There seems to be no middle ground in the debate over this controversial issue. The Thinking Critically box on pages 166–67 helps explain why.

APPLYING SOCIOLOGY IN EVERYDAY LIFE

1. The most complete study of sexual patterns in the United States to date is *The Social Organization of Sexuality: Sexual Practices in the United States* by Edward Laumann and colleagues (1994). Get a copy from your campus or community library, and read a chapter or two. Did what you read surprise you? Why or why not?

2. Contact your school's student services office, and ask for information about the extent of sexual violence on your campus. Do people typically report such crimes? What policies and procedures does your school have to respond to sexual violence?

3. Use the campus library and Internet sources to learn more about the experiences of women and men involved in prostitution. As you learn more, decide whether you think prostitution should be considered a "victimless crime."

MAKING THE GRADE

CHAPTER 6 Sexuality

WHAT IS SEXUALITY?

SEX is biological, referring to bodily differences between females and males.

p 146

GENDER is cultural, referring to behavior, power, and privileges a society attaches to being female or male.

p 148

Sexuality is a **BIOLOGICAL ISSUE**.

- Sex is determined at conception as a male sperm joins a female ovum.
- Males and females have different genitals (*primary sex characteristics*) and bodily development (*secondary sex characteristics*).
- *Intersexual people* (*hermaphrodites*) have some combination of male and female genitalia.
- *Transsexual people* feel they are one sex although biologically they are the other.

pp 146–48

Sexuality is a **CULTURAL ISSUE**.

- For humans, sex is a matter of cultural meaning and personal choice rather than biological programming.
- Sexual practices vary considerably from one society to another (examples include kissing, ideas about modesty, and standards of beauty).
- The *incest taboo* exists in all societies because regulating sexuality, especially reproduction, is a necessary element of social organization. Specific taboos vary from one society to another.

pp 148–50

sex (p. 146) the biological distinction between females and males

primary sex characteristics (p. 147) the genitals, organs used for reproduction

secondary sex characteristics (p. 148) bodily development, apart from the genitals, that distinguishes biologically mature females and males

intersexual people (p. 148) people whose bodies (including genitals) have both female and male characteristics

transsexuals (p. 148) people who feel they are one sex even though biologically they are the other

incest taboo (p. 149) a norm forbidding sexual relations or marriage between certain relatives

✓ *Sexuality is a theme found throughout most areas of social life in the United States (p 146).*

SEXUAL ATTITUDES IN THE UNITED STATES

The **SEXUAL REVOLUTION**, which peaked in the 1960s and 1970s, drew sexuality out into the open. Baby boomers were the first generation to grow up with the idea that sex was a normal part of social life.

pp 151–52

The **SEXUAL COUNTERREVOLUTION**, which was evident by 1980, aimed criticism at "permissiveness" and urged a return to more traditional "family values."

pp 152–53

Beginning with the work of Alfred Kinsey, researchers have studied sexual behavior in the United States and reached many interesting conclusions:

- Premarital sexual intercourse became more common during the twentieth century.
- About three-fourths of young men and two-thirds of young women have intercourse by their senior year in high school.
- Among all U.S. adults, sexual activity varies: One-third report having sex with a partner a few times a year or not at all; another one-third have sex once to several times a month; the remaining one-third have sex two or more times a week.
- Extramarital sex is widely condemned, and just 25 percent of married men and 10 percent of married women report being sexually unfaithful to their spouses at some time.

p 153–55

MAKING THE GRADE
CONTINUED...

SEXUAL ORIENTATION

SEXUAL ORIENTATION is a person's romantic or emotional attraction to another person. Four sexual orientations are
- heterosexuality
- homosexuality
- bisexuality
- asexuality

pp 155–56

Most research supports the claim that sexual orientation is rooted in biology in much the same way as being right-handed or left-handed.

pp 156–57

Sexual orientation is not a matter of neat categories because many people who think of themselves as heterosexual have homosexual experiences; the reverse is also true.

p 155

- The share of the U.S. population that is homosexual depends on how you define "homosexuality."
- About 9% of adult men and 4% of adult women report engaging in some homosexual activity; 2.8% of men and 1.4% of women consider themselves homosexual.

p 157

The gay rights movement helped change public attitudes toward greater acceptance of homosexuality. Still, just over half of U.S. adults say homosexuality is wrong.

pp 157–58

sexual orientation (p. 155) a person's romantic and emotional attraction to another person

heterosexuality (p. 155) sexual attraction to someone of the other sex

homosexuality (p. 155) sexual attraction to someone of the same sex

bisexuality (p. 155) sexual attraction to people of both sexes

asexuality (p. 155) no sexual attraction to people of either sex

homophobia (p. 158) discomfort over close personal interaction with people thought to be gay, lesbian, or bisexual

SEXUAL ISSUES AND CONTROVERSIES

TEEN PREGNANCY Almost 1 million U.S. teenagers become pregnant each year. The rate of teenage pregnancy has dropped since 1950, when many teens married and had children. Today, most pregnant teens are not married and are at high risk of dropping out of school and being poor.

pp 158–59

PORNOGRAPHY The law allows local communities to set standards of decency. Conservatives condemn pornography on moral grounds; liberals view pornography as a power issue, condemning it as demeaning to women.

p 159

PROSTITUTION The selling of sexual services is illegal almost everywhere in the United States. Many people view prostitution as a victimless crime, but it victimizes women and spreads sexually transmitted diseases.

pp 159–61

SEXUAL VIOLENCE Some 95,000 rapes are reported each year in the United States, but the actual number is probably several times higher. Rapes are violent crimes in which victims and offenders typically know one another.

pp 161–63

ABORTION Laws banned abortion in all states by 1900. Opposition to these laws rose during the 1960s, and in 1973, the U.S. Supreme Court declared these laws unconstitutional. Today, some 1.3 million abortions are performed each year. People who describe themselves as "pro-choice" support a woman's right to choose abortion; people who call themselves "pro-life" oppose abortion on moral grounds.

pp 166–67

pornography (p. 159) sexually explicit material intended to cause sexual arousal

prostitution (p. 159) the selling of sexual services

abortion (p. 168) the deliberate termination of a pregnancy

THEORETICAL ANALYSIS OF SEXUALITY

The **STRUCTURAL-FUNCTIONAL APPROACH** highlights society's need to regulate sexual activity and especially reproduction. One universal norm is the incest taboo, which keeps family relations clear.

pp 163–64

The **SOCIAL-CONFLICT APPROACH** links sexuality to social inequality. *Feminist theory* claims that men dominate women by devaluing them to the level of sexual objects. *Queer theory* claims our society has a heterosexual bias, defining anything different as "queer."

pp 165–68

The **SYMBOLIC-INTERACTION APPROACH** emphasizes the various meanings people attach to sexuality. The social construction of sexuality can be seen in sexual differences between societies and in changing sexual patterns over time.

pp 164–65

queer theory (p. 167) a body of research findings that challenges the heterosexual bias in U.S. society

heterosexism (p. 167) a view that labels anyone who is not heterosexual as "queer"

See the Applying Theory table on page 164.

These questions are similar to those found in the test bank that accompanies this textbook.

MULTIPLE-CHOICE QUESTIONS

1. **What is the term for humans who have some combination of female and male genitalia?**
   a. asexual people
   b. bisexual people
   c. transsexual people
   d. intersexual people

2. **A global perspective on human sexuality shows us that**
   a. although sex involves our biology, it is also a cultural trait that varies from place to place.
   b. people everywhere in the world have the same sexual practices.
   c. people in all societies are uncomfortable talking about sex.
   d. All of the above are correct.

3. **Why is the incest taboo found in every society?**
   a. It limits sexual competition between members of families.
   b. It helps define people's rights and obligations toward one another.
   c. It helps connect members of a family to others in the larger society.
   d. All of the above are correct.

4. **The sexual revolution came of age during the**
   a. 1890s.
   b. 1920s.
   c. 1960s.
   d. 1980s.

5. **Survey data show that the largest share of U.S. adults reject which of the following?**
   a. extramarital sex
   b. homosexuality
   c. premarital sex
   d. sex simply for pleasure

6. **According to the Laumann study of sexuality in the United States,**
   a. only one-third of the adult population is sexually active.
   b. there is great diversity in levels of sexual activity, so no one stereotype is correct.
   c. single people have more sex than married people.
   d. most married men admit to cheating on their wives at some point in their marriage.

7. **What is the concept meaning "sexual attraction to people of both sexes"?**
   a. heterosexuality
   b. homosexuality
   c. bisexuality
   d. asexuality

8. **Compared to 1950, the U.S. rate of teenage pregnancy today is**
   a. higher.
   b. the same, but more teens become pregnant by choice.
   c. the same, but more pregnant teens are married.
   d. lower.

9. **By what age do half of young people in the United States today become sexually active?**
   a. when they marry
   b. by the middle of college
   c. by the end of high school
   d. by age thirteen

10. **If we look back in history, we see that once a society develops birth control technology,**
    a. social control of sexuality becomes more strict.
    b. the birth rate actually goes up.
    c. attitudes about sexuality become more permissive.
    d. people no longer care about incest.

Answers: 1 (d); 2 (a); 3 (d); 4 (c); 5 (a); 6 (b); 7 (c); 8 (d); 9 (c); 10 (c).

ESSAY QUESTIONS

1. What was the "sexual revolution"? What changed? Can you point to reasons for the change?

2. Of the issues discussed in this chapter (prostitution, teen pregnancy, pornography, sexual violence, and abortion), which do you think is the most important for U.S. society today? Why?

We are all familiar with the experience of "being different." Deviance—or standing out from what is normal—is closely linked to the operation of society.

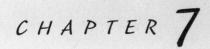

CHAPTER 7

Deviance

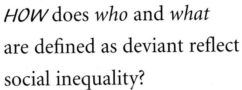

WHY does every society have deviance?

HOW does *who* and *what* are defined as deviant reflect social inequality?

WHAT effect has punishment had in reducing crime in the United States?

The black SUV rolled through the gates of the federal women's prison in Alderson, West Virginia, threading its way among the sea of news reporters, many of whom leaned toward the vehicle to catch a glimpse of the famous woman sitting in back. Martha Stewart had just been released from jail. Stewart was sent to prison in 2004 after being convicted of lying about an improper stock deal. After five months behind bars, she was eager to get home. Soon after leaving the prison, the woman who made a fortune explaining how to live well boarded a private jet that whisked her to her 153-acre ranch in Katonah, New York. Within three days, she reported to her probation officer, who placed an electronic monitor on her ankle and explained that she would have to spend the next five months at home under house arrest.

The day after her release, Wes Smith, a postal carrier in Katonah, smiled at reporters as he delivered mail to Stewart's home. "She's served her time. She's probably a changed person. Maybe she learned her lesson" (Fitzgerald, 2005).

This chapter explores the issue of crime and criminals, showing that individuals accused of wrongdoing do not always fit the common stereotype of the "street" criminal. More broadly, it also tackles the larger question of why societies develop standards of right and wrong in the first place. As we shall see, law is simply one part of a complex system of social control: Society teaches us all to conform, at least most of the time, to countless rules. We begin our investigation by defining several basic concepts.

What Is Deviance?

Deviance is *the recognized violation of cultural norms.* Norms guide virtually all human activities, so the concept of deviance is quite broad. One category of deviance is **crime,** *the violation of a society's formally enacted criminal law.* Even criminal deviance spans a wide range, from minor traffic violations to sexual assault to murder.

Most familiar examples of nonconformity are negative instances of rule breaking, such as stealing from a campus bookstore, assaulting a fellow student, or driving while intoxicated. But we also define especially righteous people—students who speak up too much in class or people who are overly enthusiastic about new computer technology—as deviant, even if we give them a measure of respect. What all deviant actions or attitudes, whether negative or positive, have in common is some element of *difference* that causes us to think of another person as an "outsider" (H. S. Becker, 1966).

Not all deviance involves action or even choice. The very *existence* of some categories of people can be troublesome to others. To the young, elderly people may seem hopelessly "out of it," and to some whites, the mere presence of people of color may cause discomfort. Able-bodied people often view people with disabilities as an out-group, just as rich people may shun the poor for falling short of their standards.

SOCIAL CONTROL

All of us are subject to **social control,** *attempts by society to regulate people's thoughts and behavior.* Often this process is informal, as when parents praise or scold their children or when friends make fun of a classmate's choice of music. Cases of serious deviance, however, may bring action by the **criminal justice system,** *a formal response by police, courts, and prison officials to alleged violations of the law.*

How a society defines deviance, *who* is branded as deviant, and *what* people decide to do about deviance are all issues of social organization. Only gradually, however, have people recognized that deviance is much more than a matter of individual choice, as the chapter now explains.

INTERNET Learn more about juvenile delinquency at http://www.ojjdp.ncjrs.org/

THE BIOLOGICAL CONTEXT

Chapter 3 ("Socialization: From Infancy to Old Age") explained that a century ago, most people understood—or more correctly, misunderstood—human behavior to be the result of biological instincts. Early interest in criminality thus focused on biological causes. In 1876, Cesare Lombroso (1835–1909), an Italian physician who worked in prisons, theorized that criminals stand out physically, with low foreheads, prominent jaws and cheekbones, protruding ears, hairiness, and unusually long arms. All in all, Lombroso claimed that criminals look like our apelike ancestors.

Had Lombroso looked more carefully, he would have found the physical features he linked to criminality throughout the entire population. We now know that no physical traits distinguish criminals from noncriminals.

In the middle of the twentieth century, William Sheldon took a different approach, suggesting that body structure might predict criminality (Sheldon, Hartl, & McDermott, 1949). He cross-checked hundreds of young men for body type and criminal history and concluded that delinquency was most common among boys with muscular, athletic builds. Sheldon Glueck and Eleanor Glueck (1950) confirmed that conclusion but cautioned that a powerful build does not necessarily *cause* or even *predict* criminality. Parents, they suggested, tend to be more distant from powerfully built sons, who in turn grow up to show less sensitivity toward others. In a self-fulfilling prophecy, people who expect muscular boys to be bullies may act in ways that bring about the aggressive behavior they expect.

Today, genetics research seeks possible links between biology and crime. In 2003, scientists at the University of Wisconsin reported results of a twenty-five-year study of crime among 400 boys. The researchers collected DNA samples from each boy and noted any trouble they had had with the law. The researchers concluded that genetic factors (especially defective genes that, say, make too much of an enzyme) together with environmental factors (especially abuse early in life) were strong predictors of adult crime and violence. They noted, too, that these factors together were a better predictor of crime than either one alone (Lemonick, 2003; Pinker, 2003).

CRITICAL REVIEW Biological theories offer a limited explanation of crime. The best guess at present is that biological traits in combination with environmental factors explain some serious crime. Most of the actions we define as deviant are carried out by people who are physically quite normal.

In addition, because a biological approach looks at the individual, it offers no insight into how some kinds of behaviors come to be defined as deviant in the first place.

Deviance is difference that makes a difference. Deviance emerges in everyday life as we encounter people whose appearance or behavior differs from what we consider "normal" or "right." Playing his music on the streets of New York City, the Naked Cowboy is "different" in a way that provides pleasure to many people passing by.

Therefore, although there is much to learn about how human biology may affect behavior, research currently puts far greater emphasis on social influences.

PERSONALITY FACTORS

Like biological theories, psychological explanations of deviance focus on individual abnormality. Some personality traits are inherited, but most psychologists think personality is shaped primarily by social experience. Deviance, then, is viewed as the result of "unsuccessful" socialization.

Classic research by Walter Reckless and Simon Dinitz (1967) illustrates the psychological approach. Reckless and Dinitz began by asking teachers to categorize twelve-year-old male students as either likely or unlikely to get into trouble with the law. They then interviewed both the boys and their mothers to assess each boy's self-concept and how he related to others. Analyzing their results, the researchers found that the "good boys" displayed a strong conscience (what Freud called superego), could handle frustration, and identified with cultural norms and values. The "bad boys," by contrast, had a weaker conscience, displayed little tolerance for frustration, and felt out of step with conventional culture.

As we might expect, the "good boys" went on to have fewer run-ins with the police than the "bad boys." Because all the boys lived in areas where delinquency was widespread, the investigators attributed staying out of trouble to a personality that controlled deviant impulses. Based on this conclusion, Reckless and Dinitz called their analysis *containment theory*.

CRITICAL REVIEW Psychologists have shown that personality patterns have some connection to deviance. Some serious criminals are psychopaths who do not feel guilt or shame, have no fear of punishment, and have little sympathy for the people they harm (Herpertz & Sass, 2000). However, as noted in the case of biological factors, most serious crimes are committed by people whose psychological profiles are normal.

Both biological and psychological research views deviance as a trait of individuals. The reason these approaches have limited value in explaining deviance is that wrongdoing has more to do with the organization of society. We now turn to a sociological approach, which explores where ideas of right and wrong come from, why people define some rule breakers but not others as deviant, and what role power plays in this process.

YOUR LEARNING Why does biological or psychological analysis not explain deviance very well?

THE SOCIAL FOUNDATIONS OF DEVIANCE

Although we tend to view deviance as the free choice or personal failings of individuals, all behavior—deviance as well as conformity—is shaped by society. Three social foundations of deviance identified here will be detailed later in this chapter:

1. **Deviance varies according to cultural norms.** No thought or action is inherently deviant; it becomes deviant only in relation to particular norms. State law permits prostitution in rural areas of Nevada, although the practice is outlawed in the rest of the United States. Eleven states have gambling casinos; twenty-eight have casinos on Indian reservations. In all other states, casino gambling is illegal.

   Further, most cities and towns have at least one unique law. For example, Mobile, Alabama, outlaws the wearing of stiletto-heeled shoes; in Juneau, Alaska, it is illegal to bring a flamingo into a barbershop;

South Padre Island, Texas, bans the wearing of neckties; Mount Prospect, Illinois, has a law against keeping pigeons or bees; Topeka, Kansas, bans snowball fights; Hoover, South Dakota, does not allow fishing with a kerosene lantern; and Beverly Hills, California, regulates the number of tennis balls allowed on the court at one time (Sanders & Horn, 1998; R. Steele, 2000).

   Around the world, deviance is even more diverse. Albania outlaws any public display of religious faith, such as "crossing" oneself; Cuba and Vietnam can prosecute citizens for meeting with foreigners; Malaysia does not allow tight-fitting jeans for women; police in Iran can arrest a woman simply for wearing makeup; and Saudi Arabia bans the sale of red roses on Valentine's Day.

2. **People become deviant as others define them that way.** Everyone violates cultural norms at one time or another. For example, have you ever walked around talking to yourself or "borrowed" a pen from your workplace? Whether such behavior defines us as mentally ill or criminal depends on how others perceive, define, and respond to it.

3. **Both norms and the way people define rule-breaking involve social power.** The law, claimed Karl Marx, is the means by which powerful people protect their interests. A homeless person who stands on a street corner speaking out against the government risks arrest for disturbing the peace; a mayoral candidate during an election campaign does exactly the same thing and gets police protection. In short, norms and how we apply them reflect social inequality.

The Functions of Deviance: Structural-Functional Analysis

The key insight of the structural-functional approach is that deviance is a necessary element of social organization. This point was made a century ago by Emile Durkheim.

DURKHEIM'S BASIC INSIGHT

In his pioneering study of deviance, Emile Durkheim (1964a, orig. 1893; 1964b, orig. 1895) made the surprising statement that there is nothing abnormal about deviance. In fact, it performs four essential functions:

1. **Deviance affirms cultural values and norms.** As moral creatures, people must prefer some attitudes and behaviors to others. But any definition of virtue rests on an opposing idea of vice: There can be no

good without evil and no justice without crime. Deviance is needed to define and support morality.

2. **Responding to deviance clarifies moral boundaries.** By defining some individuals as deviant, people draw a boundary between right and wrong. For example, a college marks the line between academic honesty and deviance by disciplining students who cheat on exams.

3. **Responding to deviance brings people together.** People typically react to serious deviance with shared outrage. In doing so, Durkheim explained, they reaffirm the moral ties that bind them. For example, after the September 11, 2001, terrorist attacks, people across the United States were joined by a common desire to protect the country and bring those responsible to justice.

4. **Deviance encourages social change.** Deviant people push a society's moral boundaries; their lives suggest alternatives to the status quo and encourage change. Today's deviance, declared Durkheim, can become tomorrow's morality (1964b:71, orig. 1895). For example, rock 'n' roll, condemned as immoral in the 1950s, became a mainstream, multibillion-dollar industry just a few years later; in recent decades, hip-hop music has followed the same path.

Keeping in mind Durkheim's claim that society creates deviance to mark moral boundaries, why do we often define people only in terms of their deviance by calling someone an "addict" or a "thief"?

An Illustration: The Puritans of Massachusetts Bay

Kai Erikson's (2005b, orig. 1966) classic study of the Puritans of Massachusetts Bay brings Durkheim's theory to life. Erikson shows that even the Puritans, a disciplined and highly religious group, created deviance to clarify their moral boundaries. In fact, Durkheim might well have had the Puritans in mind when he wrote:

> Imagine a society of saints, a perfect cloister of exemplary individuals. Crimes, properly so called, will there be unknown; but faults which appear [insignificant] to the layman will create there the same scandal that the ordinary offense does in ordinary consciousness. . . . For the same reason, the perfect and upright man judges his smallest failings with a severity that the majority reserve for acts more truly in the nature of an offense. (1964b:68–69)

Deviance is thus not a matter of a few "bad apples" but a necessary condition of "good" social living.

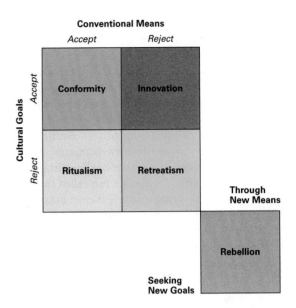

FIGURE 7–1 Merton's Strain Theory of Deviance

Combining a person's view of cultural goals and the conventional means to obtain them allowed Robert Merton to identify various types of deviants.

Source: Merton (1968).

Deviance may be found in every society, but the *kind* of deviance people generate depends on the moral issues they seek to clarify. The Puritans, for example, experienced a number of "crime waves," including the well-known outbreak of witchcraft in 1692. With each response, the Puritans answered questions about the range of proper beliefs by celebrating some of their members and condemning others as deviant.

Erikson discovered that although the offenses changed, the proportion of people the Puritans defined as deviant remained steady over time. This stability, he concluded, confirms Durkheim's claim that society creates deviants to mark its changing moral boundaries. In other words, by constantly defining a small number of people as deviant, the Puritans maintained the moral shape of their society.

MERTON'S STRAIN THEORY

Some deviance may be necessary for a society to function, but Robert Merton (1938, 1968) argued that too much deviance results from particular social arrangements. Specifically, the extent and kind of deviance depend on whether a society provides the *means* (such as schooling and job opportunities) to achieve cultural *goals* (such as financial success). Merton's strain theory of deviance is illustrated in Figure 7–1.

Conformity lies in pursuing cultural goals through approved means. For most of us, a "success" is someone who gains wealth and prestige through talent, schooling, and hard work. But not everyone who wants conventional success has the opportunity to attain it. For example, people living in poverty may see little hope of becoming successful if they play by the rules. According to Merton, the strain between our culture's emphasis on wealth and the lack of opportunities to get rich may encourage some people, especially the poor, to engage in stealing, drug dealing, and other forms of street crime. Merton called this type of deviance *innovation*—using unconventional means (street crime) rather than conventional means (hard work at a "straight" job) to achieve a culturally approved goal (wealth) (see Figure 7–1).

The inability to reach a cultural goal may also prompt another type of deviance that Merton calls *ritualism*. For example, many people may believe they cannot achieve the cultural goal of becoming rich; therefore, they rigidly stick to the rules (the conventional means) in order to at least feel respectable.

A third response to the inability to succeed is *retreatism*: rejecting both cultural goals and means so that one in effect "drops out." Some alcoholics, drug addicts, and street people are retreatists. The deviance of retreatists lies in their unconventional lifestyles and, perhaps more seriously, in what seems to be their willingness to live this way.

The fourth response to failure is *rebellion*. Like retreatists, rebels such as radical "survivalists" reject both the cultural definition of success and the conventional means of achieving it but go one step further by forming a counterculture supporting alternatives to the existing social order.

DEVIANT SUBCULTURES

Richard Cloward and Lloyd Ohlin (1966) extended Merton's theory, proposing that crime results not simply from limited legitimate (legal) opportunity but also from readily accessible illegitimate (illegal) opportunity. In short, deviance or conformity depends on the *relative opportunity structure* that frames a person's life.

The life of Al Capone, a notorious gangster, illustrates Cloward and Ohlin's theory. As a son of poor immigrants, Capone faced barriers of poverty and ethnic prejudice, which lowered his odds of achieving success in conventional terms. Yet as a young man during the Prohibition era (when alcoholic beverages were banned in the United States, from 1920 to 1933), Capone found in his neighborhood people who could teach him how to sell alcohol illegally—a source of illegitimate opportunity. Where the structure of opportunity favors criminal activity, Cloward and Ohlin predict the development of *criminal subcultures,* such as street gangs.

But what happens when people are unable to find *any* opportunities, legal or illegal? Then deviance may take one of two forms: *conflict subcultures* (armed street gangs), in which violence is ignited by frustration and a desire for respect, or *retreatist subcultures,* in which deviants drop out and abuse alcohol or other drugs.

Albert Cohen (1971, orig. 1955) suggests that criminality is most common among lower-class youths because they have the least opportunity to achieve conventional success. Neglected by society, they seek self-respect by creating a deviant subculture that defines as worthy the traits these youths do have. Being feared on the street may win few points with society as a whole, but it may satisfy a youth's desire to "be somebody" in a local neighborhood.

Walter Miller (1970, orig. 1958) adds that deviant subcultures are characterized by (1) *trouble,* arising from frequent conflict with teachers and police; (2) *toughness,* the value placed on physical size, strength, and agility, especially among males; (3) *smartness,* the ability to succeed on the streets, to outsmart or "con" others; (4) *a need for excitement,* the search for thrills, risk, or danger; (5) *a belief in fate,* a sense that people lack control over their own lives; and (6) *a desire for freedom,* often expressed as anger toward authority figures.

Finally, Elijah Anderson (1994, 2002) explains that in poor urban neighborhoods, most people manage to conform to conventional ("decent") values. Yet faced daily with neighborhood crime and violence, indifference or even hostility from police, and sometimes even neglect from their own parents, some young men decide to live by the "street code." To show that he can survive on the street, a young man displays "nerve," a willingness to stand up to any threat. Following this street code, the young man believes that even a violent death is better than being "dissed" (disrespected) by others. Some manage to escape the dangers, but the risk of ending up in jail—or worse—is very high for these young men, who have been pushed to the margins of our society.

CRITICAL REVIEW Durkheim made an important contribution by pointing out the functions of deviance. However, there is evidence that a community does not always come together in reaction to crime; sometimes fear of crime drives people to withdraw from public life (Liska & Warner, 1991; Warr & Ellison, 2000).

Merton's strain theory also has been criticized for explaining some kinds of deviance (stealing, for example) better than others (crimes of passion or mental illness).

Young people cut off from legitimate opportunity often form subcultures that many people view as deviant. Gang subcultures, including tattoos on the fingers, are one way young people gain the sense of belonging and respect denied to them by the larger culture.

Furthermore, not everyone seeks success in conventional terms of wealth, as strain theory suggests.

The general argument of Cloward and Ohlin, Cohen, and Miller—that deviance reflects the opportunity structure of society—has been confirmed by later research (Allan & Steffensmeier, 1989; Uggen, 1999). However, these theories fall short by assuming that everyone shares the same cultural standards for judging right and wrong. If we define crime as including not just burglary and auto theft but the type of illegal stock deals that sent Martha Stewart to prison, then more high-income people will be counted among criminals. There is evidence that people of all social backgrounds have become more casual about breaking the rules, as the Seeing Sociology in Everyday Life box on page 180 explains.

Finally, all structural-functional theories suggest that everyone who breaks the rules will be labeled deviant. However, becoming deviant is actually a highly complex process, as the next section explains.

✔ YOUR LEARNING Why do you think many of the theories just discussed seem to say that crime is more common among people with lower social standing?

Labeling Deviance: Symbolic-Interaction Analysis

The symbolic-interaction approach explains how people come to see deviance in everyday situations. From this point of view, definitions of deviance and conformity are surprisingly flexible.

LABELING THEORY

The central contribution of symbolic-interaction analysis is **labeling theory,** *the idea that deviance and conformity result not so much from what people do as from how others respond to those actions.* Labeling theory stresses the relativity of deviance, meaning that people may define the same behavior in any number of ways.

Consider these situations: A college student takes a sweater off the back of a roommate's chair, a married woman at a convention in a distant city has sex with an old boyfriend, and a mayor gives a big city contract to a major campaign contributor. We might define the first situation as carelessness, borrowing, or theft. The consequences of the second situation depend largely on whether the woman's behavior becomes known back home. In the third situation, is the mayor choosing the best contractor or paying off a political debt? The social construction of reality is a highly variable process of detection, definition, and response.

Primary and Secondary Deviance

Edwin Lemert (1951, 1972) observed that some norm violations—say, skipping school or underage drinking—provoke slight reaction from others and have little effect on a person's self-concept. Lemert calls such passing episodes *primary deviance.*

But what happens if people take notice of someone's deviance and make something of it? For example, if people begin to describe a young man as an "alcohol abuser" and exclude him from their friendship network, he may become bitter, drink even more, and seek the company of those who approve of his behavior. The response to primary deviance can set in motion *secondary deviance,* by which a person

Deviant Subculture: Has It Become OK to Break the Rules?

It's been a couple of bad years for the idea of playing by the rules. First we learn that the executives of not just one but many U.S. corporations are guilty of fraud and outright stealing on a scale that most of us cannot even imagine. Then Martha Stewart, the country's lifestyle guru, is sent to jail for trading stocks illegally and lying about it. Then the Catholic church, which we hold up as a model of moral behavior, has become embroiled in a scandal of its own. In this case, hundreds of priests are said to have sexually abused parishioners (most of them teens and children) over many decades while church officials busied themselves covering up the crimes. By the beginning of 2005, more than 300 priests in the United States had been removed from their duties pending investigations of abuse. Finally, in 2006, a number of members of Congress—the people we elected as our leaders— were found to have accepted money in illegal influence peddling by lobbyists.

There are plenty of ideas about what is causing this widespread wrongdoing. Some suggest that the pressure to win in the highly competitive business and political world—by whatever means necessary—can be overwhelming. As one analyst put it, "You can get away with your embezzlements and your lies, but you can never get away with *failing*."

Such thinking helps explain the wrongdoing among many CEOs in the corporate world or taking illegal money by some members of Congress, but it offers little insight into the problem of abusive priests. In some ways at least, wrongdoing seems to have become a way of life for just about everybody. For example, the Internal Revenue Service reports that U.S. taxpayers cheat on their taxes, failing to pay an estimated $200 billion each year (an average of about $1,600 per tax-

payer). The music industry claims that it has lost a vast amount of money due to illegal piracy of recordings, a practice especially common among young people. Perhaps most disturbing of all, surveys of high school and college students show that at least half say that they cheated on a test at least once during the past year.

Emile Durkheim viewed society as a moral system, built on a set of rules about what people should and should not do. Years earlier, another French thinker named Blaise Pascal made the opposite claim that "cheating is the foundation of society." Today, which of the two statements is closer to the truth?

Do you consider cheating in school to be wrong? Would you turn in someone you saw cheat? Why or why not?

WHAT DO YOU THINK?

1. In your opinion, how widespread is wrongdoing in U.S. society today?

2. Do you think the people who break the rules usually think that their actions are wrong? Why or why not?

3. What do you think are the reasons for the apparent increase in dishonesty?

Sources: Based on "Our Cheating Hearts" (2002) and Bono (2006).

---

begins to take on a deviant identity and repeatedly breaks the rules.

Can you see how the development of secondary deviance is one application of the Thomas theorem (see Chapter 4, "Social Interaction in Everyday Life"), which states that situations people define as real become real in their consequences?

Stigma

Secondary deviance marks the start of what Erving Goffman (1963) called a *deviant career*. As people develop a stronger commitment to deviant behavior, they typically acquire a **stigma**, *a powerfully negative label that greatly changes a person's self-concept and social identity.*

A stigma operates as a master status (see Chapter 4), overpowering other dimensions of identity so that a person is discredited in the minds of others and consequently becomes socially isolated. Sometimes an entire community stigmatizes a person through what Harold Garfinkel (1956) calls a *degradation ceremony.* A criminal prosecution is one example, operating much like a high school graduation ceremony in reverse: A person stands before the community to be labeled in a negative rather than a positive way.

Retrospective and Projective Labeling

Once people stigmatize a person, they may engage in *retrospective labeling,* a reinterpretation of the person's past in light of some present deviance (Scheff, 1984). For example, after discovering that a priest has sexually molested a child, others rethink his past, perhaps musing, "He always did want to be around young children." Retrospective labeling, which distorts a person's biography by being highly selective, typically deepens a deviant identity.

Similarly, people may engage in *projective labeling* of a stigmatized person, using a deviant identity to predict the person's future actions. Regarding the priest, people might say, "He's going to keep at it until he's caught." The more people in someone's social world think such things and act accordingly, the greater the chance that they will come true.

Labeling Difference as Deviance

Is a homeless man who refuses to allow police to take him to a city shelter on a cold night simply trying to live independently, or is he "crazy"? People have a tendency to treat behavior that irritates or threatens them not simply as "difference" but as deviance or even mental illness.

The psychiatrist Thomas Szasz (1961, 1970, 2003, 2004) claims that people are too quick to apply the label of mental illness to conditions that simply amount to a difference we don't like. The only way to avoid this troubling practice, Szasz concludes, is to stop using the idea of mental illness entirely. The world is full of people whose differences in thought or action may irritate us, but such differences are not grounds for defining someone as mentally ill. Such labeling, Szasz says, simply enforces conformity to the standards of people powerful enough to impose their will on others.

Most mental health professionals reject the idea that mental illness does not exist. But they agree that it is important to think carefully about how we define "difference." First, people who are mentally ill are no more to blame for their condition than people who suffer from cancer or some other physical problem. Therefore, having a mental or physical illness is no grounds for being labeled "deviant." Second, people (especially those without the knowledge to diagnose mental illness) should avoid applying such labels just to make people conform to our own standards of behavior.

THE MEDICALIZATION OF DEVIANCE

Labeling theory, particularly the ideas of Szasz and Goffman, helps explain an important shift in the way our society understands deviance. Over the past fifty years, the growing influence of psychiatry and medicine has led to the **medicalization of deviance,** *the transformation of moral and legal deviance into a medical condition.*

Medicalization amounts to swapping one set of labels for another. In moral terms, we judge people or their behavior as "bad" or "good." However, the scientific objectivity of medicine passes no moral judgment, instead using clinical diagnoses such as "sick" or "well."

To illustrate, until the mid-twentieth century, most people viewed alcoholics as morally weak people easily tempted by the pleasure of drink. Gradually, however, medical specialists redefined alcoholism so that most people now consider it a disease, making people "sick" rather than "bad." In the same way, obesity, drug addiction, child abuse, sexual promiscuity, and other behaviors that used to be strictly moral matters are widely defined today as illnesses for which people need help rather than punishment.

When you see a student who is extremely overweight, do you tend to think the person is "sick"? What about a student who has not showered for a week? Explain your view.
———

The Difference Labels Make

Whether we define deviance as a moral or a medical issue has three consequences. First, it affects *who responds* to deviance. An offense against common morality typically brings a reaction from members of the community or the police. A medical label, however, places the situation under the control of clinical specialists, including counselors, psychiatrists, and physicians.

A second issue is *how people respond.* A moral approach defines deviants as offenders subject to punishment. Medically, however, they are patients who need treatment. Punishment is designed to fit the crime, but treatment programs are tailored to the patient and may involve virtually any therapy that a specialist thinks might prevent future illness.

Third, and most important, the two labels differ on the issue of *the personal competence of the deviant person.* From a moral standpoint, whether we are right or wrong, at least we are responsible for our own behavior. Once we are defined as sick, however, we are seen as unable to control (or, if "mentally ill," even to understand) our actions. People who are labeled incompetent are subject to treatment, often against their will. For this reason alone, defining deviance in medical terms should be done with extreme caution.

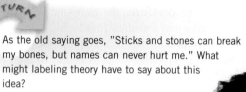

As the old saying goes, "Sticks and stones can break my bones, but names can never hurt me." What might labeling theory have to say about this idea?

SUTHERLAND'S DIFFERENTIAL ASSOCIATION THEORY

Learning any social pattern, whether conventional or deviant, is a process that takes place in groups. According to Edwin Sutherland (1940), a person's tendency toward conformity or deviance depends on the amount of contact with others who encourage or reject conventional behavior. This is Sutherland's theory of *differential association*.

A number of studies confirm the idea that young people are more likely to engage in delinquency if they believe that members of their peer group encourage such activity (Akers et al., 1979; Miller & Matthews, 2001). One recent investigation focused on sexual activity among eighth-grade students. Two strong predictors of such behavior in young girls were having a boyfriend who encouraged sexual relations and having girlfriends they believed would approve of such activity. Similarly, boys were encouraged to become sexually active by friends who rewarded them with high status in the peer group (Little & Rankin, 2001).

HIRSCHI'S CONTROL THEORY

The sociologist Travis Hirschi (1969; Gottfredson & Hirschi, 1995) developed *control theory,* which states that social control depends on people's anticipating the consequences of their behavior. Hirschi assumes that everyone finds at least some deviance tempting. But the thought of a ruined career keeps most people from breaking the rules; for some, just imagining the reactions of family and friends is enough. On the other hand, people who think that they have little to lose from deviance are likely to become rule breakers.

Specifically, Hirschi links conformity to four different types of social control:

1. **Attachment.** Strong social attachments encourage conformity. Weak family, peer, and school relationships leave people freer to engage in deviance.

All social groups teach their members skills and attitudes that encourage certain behavior. In recent years, discussion on college campuses has focused on the dangers of binge drinking that result in about 300 deaths each year in the United States. How much of a problem is binge drinking on your campus?

2. **Opportunity.** The greater a person's access to legitimate opportunity, the greater the advantages of conformity. By contrast, someone with little confidence in future success is more likely to drift toward deviance.

3. **Involvement.** Extensive involvement in legitimate activities—such as holding a job, going to school, or playing sports—inhibits deviance (Langbein & Bess, 2002). By contrast, people who simply "hang out" waiting for something to happen have the time and energy to engage in deviant activity.

4. **Belief.** Strong beliefs in conventional morality and respect for authority figures restrain tendencies toward deviance. By contrast, people with a weak conscience (and who are left unsupervised) are more open to temptation (Stack, Wasserman, & Kern, 2004).

Hirschi's analysis combines a number of earlier ideas about the causes of deviant behavior. Note that a person's relative social privilege as well as family and community environment are likely to affect the risk of deviant behavior (Hope, Grasmick, & Pointon, 2003).

CRITICAL REVIEW The various symbolic-interaction theories all see deviance as a process. Labeling theory links deviance not to *action* but to the *reaction* of others. Thus some people are defined as deviant but others who think or behave in the same way are not. The concepts of secondary deviance, deviant career, and stigma show how being labeled deviant can become a lasting self-concept.

Yet labeling theory has several limitations. First, because it takes a highly relative view of deviance, labeling theory ignores the fact that some kinds of behavior—such as murder—are condemned just about everywhere. Therefore, labeling theory is most usefully applied to less serious issues, such as sexual promiscuity or mental illness. Second, research on the consequences of deviant labeling does not clearly show whether deviant labeling produces further deviance or discourages it (Smith & Gartin, 1989; Sherman & Smith, 1992). Third, not everyone resists being labeled as deviant; some people actively seek it (Vold & Bernard, 1986). For example, people engage in civil disobedience and willingly subject themselves to arrest in order to call attention to social injustice.

Sociologists consider Sutherland's differential association theory and Hirschi's control theory important contributions to our understanding of deviance. But why do society's norms and laws define certain kinds of activities as deviant in the first place? This important question is addressed by social-conflict analysis, the focus of the next section.

✔ YOUR LEARNING   Clearly define secondary deviance, deviant career, and stigma.

Deviance and Inequality: Social-Conflict Analysis

The social-conflict approach links deviance to social inequality. That is, *who* or *what* is labeled "deviant" depends on which categories of people hold power in a society.

DEVIANCE AND POWER

Alexander Liazos (1972) points out that the people we tend to define as deviants—the ones we dismiss as "nuts" and "sluts"—are typically those who share the trait of powerlessness. Bag ladies, not corporate polluters, and unemployed men on street corners, not international arms dealers, carry the stigma of deviance.

Social-conflict theory explains this pattern in three ways. First, all norms and especially the laws of any society generally reflect the interests of the rich and powerful. People who threaten the wealthy, either by taking their property or by advocating a more egalitarian society, are labeled "common thieves" or "political radicals." Karl Marx, a major architect of the social-conflict approach, argued that the law

and all social institutions support the interests of the rich. Or as Richard Quinney puts it, "Capitalist justice is by the capitalist class, for the capitalist class, and against the working class" (1977:3).

Second, even if their behavior is called into question, the powerful have the resources to resist deviant labels. The majority of the corporate executives involved in recent scandals have yet to be arrested; only a few have gone to jail.

Third, the widespread belief that norms and laws are natural and good masks their political character. For this reason, although we may condemn the unequal application of the law, most of us give little thought to whether the laws themselves are really fair or not.

DEVIANCE AND CAPITALISM

In the Marxist tradition, Steven Spitzer (1980) argues that deviant labels are applied to people who interfere with the operation of capitalism. First, because capitalism is based on private control of property, people who threaten the property of others—especially the poor who steal from the rich—are prime candidates for being labeled deviant. Conversely, the rich who take advantage of the poor are less likely to be labeled deviant. For example, landlords who charge poor tenants high rents and evict those who cannot pay are not considered criminals; they are simply "doing business."

Second, because capitalism depends on productive labor, people who cannot or will not work risk being labeled deviant. Many members of our society think people who are out of work, even through no fault of their own, are somehow deviant.

Third, capitalism depends on respect for authority figures, causing people who resist authority to be labeled deviant. Examples are children who skip school or talk back to parents or teachers and adults who do not cooperate with employers or police.

Fourth, anyone who directly challenges the capitalist status quo is likely to be defined as deviant. Such has been the case with labor organizers, radical environmentalists, and antiwar activists.

On the other side of the coin, society positively labels whatever supports the operation of capitalism. For example, winning athletes enjoy celebrity status because they make money and express the values of individual achievement and competition, both vital to capitalism. Also, Spitzer notes, we condemn using drugs of escape (marijuana, psychedelics, heroin, and crack) as deviant but promote drugs (such as alcohol and caffeine) that encourage adjustment to the status quo.

The capitalist system also tries to control people who don't fit into the system. The elderly, people with mental or physical disabilities, and Robert Merton's "retreatists" (peo-

After the collapse of the Enron corporation, CEO Kenneth Lay was convicted of fraud and conspiracy. At the time of his death in 2006, Lay was facing decades of jail time. Along with other corporate executives convicted of crimes, Lay came to symbolize the scandals and corruption that have rocked the corporate world in recent years.

ple addicted to alcohol or other drugs) represent a "costly yet relatively harmless burden" to society. Such people, claims Spitzer, are subject to control by social welfare agencies. But people who openly challenge the capitalist system, including the inner-city "underclass" and revolutionaries—Merton's "innovators" and "rebels"—are controlled by the criminal justice system and, if necessary, military forces such as the National Guard.

Note that both the social welfare and criminal justice systems blame individuals, not the system, for social problems. Welfare recipients are considered unworthy freeloaders, poor people who rage at their plight are labeled rioters, anyone who actively challenges the government is branded a radical or a communist, and those who attempt to gain illegally what they will never get legally are rounded up as common criminals.

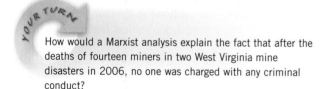

How would a Marxist analysis explain the fact that after the deaths of fourteen miners in two West Virginia mine disasters in 2006, no one was charged with any criminal conduct?

WHITE-COLLAR CRIME

In a sign of things to come, a Wall Street stockbroker named Michael Milken made headlines back in 1987 when he was jailed for business fraud. Milken attracted attention because not since the days of Al Capone had anyone made so much money in one year: $550 million—about $1.5 million a day (Swartz, 1989).

Milken engaged in **white-collar crime,** defined by Edwin Sutherland in 1940 as *crime committed by people of high social position in the course of their occupations.* White-collar crime does not involve violence and rarely brings police with guns drawn to the scene. Rather, white-collar criminals use their powerful offices to illegally enrich themselves or others, often causing significant public harm in the process. For this reason, sociologists sometimes call white-collar offenses "crime in the suites" as opposed to "crime in the streets."

The most common white-collar crimes are bank embezzlement, business fraud, bribery, and antitrust violations. Sutherland (1940) explains that such white-collar offenses typically end up in a civil hearing rather than a criminal courtroom. *Civil law* regulates business dealings between private parties; *criminal law* defines a person's moral responsibilities to society. In practice, someone who loses a civil case pays for damage or injury but is not labeled a criminal. Furthermore, corporate officials are protected by the fact that most charges of white-collar crime target the organization rather than individuals.

In the rare cases that white-collar criminals are charged and convicted, they usually escape punishment. A government study found that those convicted of fraud and punished with a fine ended up paying less than 10 percent of what they owed; most managed to hide or transfer their assets to avoid paying up. Among white-collar criminals convicted of embezzlement, only about half ever served a day in jail. One accounting found that just 53 percent of the embezzlers convicted in the U.S. federal courts served prison sentences; the rest were put on probation or issued a fine (Willing, 2005; U.S. Bureau of Justice Statistics, 2006).

APPLYING THEORY

Deviance

	Structural-Functional Approach	Symbolic-Interaction Approach	Social-Conflict Approach
What is the level of analysis?	Macro-level	Micro-level	Macro-level
What is deviance? What part does it play in society?	Deviance is a basic part of social organization. By defining deviance, society sets its moral boundaries.	Deviance is part of socially constructed reality that emerges in interaction. Deviance comes into being as individuals label something as deviant.	Deviance results from social inequality. Norms, including laws, reflect the interests of powerful members of society.
What is important about deviance?	Deviance is universal: All societies contain deviance.	Deviance is variable: Any act or person may or may not be labeled as deviant.	Deviance is political: People with little power are at high risk of becoming deviant.

CORPORATE CRIME

Sometimes whole companies, not just individuals, break the law. **Corporate crime** consists of *the illegal actions of a corporation or people acting on its behalf.*

Corporate crime ranges from knowingly selling faulty or dangerous products to deliberately polluting the environment (Derber, 2004). The collapse of Enron, Global Crossing, and other corporations in recent years has cost tens of thousands of people their jobs and their pensions. Even more seriously, twenty-four people died in underground coal mines in 2005, and hundreds more died from "black lung" disease resulting from years of inhaling coal dust. The death toll for all job-related hazards in the United States probably exceeds 50,000 each year (Carroll, 1999; J. Jones, 1999; U.S. Census Bureau, 2005).

ORGANIZED CRIME

Organized crime is *a business supplying illegal goods or services.* Sometimes crime organizations force people to do business with them, as when a gang extorts money from shopkeepers for "protection." In most cases, however, organized crime involves selling illegal goods and services—including sex, drugs, or gambling—to willing buyers.

Organized crime has flourished in the United States for more than a century. The scope of its operations expanded among immigrants who found that this society was not willing to share its opportunities with them. Thus some ambitious minorities (such as Al Capone, mentioned earlier) made their own success, especially during Prohibition, when the government banned the production and sale of alcohol.

The Italian Mafia is a well-known example of organized crime. But other criminal organizations involve African Americans, Chinese, Colombians, Cubans, Haitians, and Russians, as well as others of almost every racial and ethnic category. Organized crime today involves a wide range of activities, from selling illegal drugs to prostitution to credit card fraud and selling false identification papers to illegal immigrants (Valdez, 1997).

CRITICAL REVIEW According to social-conflict theory, a capitalist society's inequality in wealth and power shapes its laws and how they are applied. The criminal justice and social welfare systems thus act as political agents, controlling categories of people who are a threat to the capitalist system.

Like other approaches to deviance, social-conflict theory has its critics. First, this approach suggests that laws and other cultural norms are created directly by the rich and powerful. At the very least, this is an oversimplification because the law also protects workers, consumers, and the environment, sometimes opposing the interests of corporations and the rich.

Second, social-conflict analysis argues that criminality springs up only to the extent that a society treats its members unequally. However, as Durkheim noted, deviance exists in all societies, whatever the economic system.

The sociological explanations for crime and other types of deviance that we have discussed are summarized in the Applying Theory table.

✔ YOUR LEARNING Define white-collar crime, corporate crime, and organized crime.

Deviance, Race, and Gender

What people consider deviant reflects the relative power and privilege of different categories of people. The following sections offer two examples: how racial and ethnic hostility motivates hate crimes and how gender is linked to deviance.

HATE CRIMES

The term **hate crime** refers to *a criminal act against a person or a person's property by an offender motivated by racial or other bias.* A hate crime may express hostility toward someone based on race, religion, ancestry, sexual orientation, or physical disability. The federal government recorded about 7,600 hate crimes in 2004.

In 1998, people across the country were stunned by the brutal killing of Matthew Shepard, a gay student at the University of Wyoming, by two men filled with hatred toward homosexuals. The National Gay and Lesbian Task Force reports that one in five lesbians and gay men has been physically assaulted and more than 90 percent have been verbally abused because of sexual orientation (cited in Berrill, 1992:19–20). People who contend with multiple stigmas, such as gay men of color, are especially likely to be victims. Yet it can happen to anyone: A recent study found that about 25 percent of the hate crimes based on race targeted white people (Jenness & Grattet, 2001).

By 2006, forty-seven states and the federal government had enacted legislation that raises penalties for crimes motivated by hatred. Supporters are gratified, but opponents charge that such laws, which increase the penalty for a crime based on the attitudes of the offender, amount to punishing "politically incorrect" thoughts. The Thinking About Diversity box takes a closer look at the issue of hate crime laws.

THE FEMINIST PERSPECTIVE: DEVIANCE AND GENDER

Virtually every society in the world tries to control the behavior of women more than men. Historically, our own society has centered women's lives around the home. In the United States even today, women's opportunities in the workplace, in politics, in athletics, and in the military are more limited than men's. Elsewhere in the world, the constraints on women are greater still. In Saudi Arabia, women cannot vote or legally operate motor vehicles; in Iran, women who expose their hair or wear makeup in public can be whipped; and not long ago, a Nigerian court convicted a divorced woman of bearing a child out of wedlock and sentenced her to death by stoning; her life was later spared out of concern for her child (Eboh, 2002).

Gender also figures into the theories about deviance noted earlier. For example, Robert Merton's strain theory defines cultural goals in terms of financial success. Traditionally at least, this goal has had more to do with the lives of men, because women have been socialized to define success in terms of relationships, particularly marriage and motherhood (Leonard, 1982). A more woman-focused theory might recognize the "strain" that results from the cultural ideal of equality clashing with the reality of gender-based inequality.

According to labeling theory, gender influences how we define deviance because people commonly use different standards to judge the behavior of females and males. Further, because society puts men in positions of power over women, men often escape direct responsibility for actions that victimize women. In the past, at least, men who sexually harassed or assaulted women were labeled only mildly deviant and sometimes escaped punishment entirely.

By contrast, women who are victimized may have to convince others—even members of a jury—that they are not to blame for their own sexual harassment or assault. Research confirms an important truth: Whether people define a situation as deviant—and, if they do, who the deviant is—depends on the sex of both the audience and the actors (King & Clayson, 1988).

Finally, despite its focus on inequality, much social-conflict analysis does not address the issue of gender. If economic disadvantage is a primary cause of crime, as conflict theory suggests, why do women (whose economic position is much worse than men's) commit far *fewer* crimes than men?

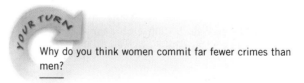

Why do you think women commit far fewer crimes than men?

Crime

Crime is the violation of criminal laws enacted by a locality, state, or the federal government. All crimes are composed of two distinct elements: the *act* itself (or in some cases, a failure to do what the law requires) and *criminal intent* (in legal terminology, *mens rea,* or "guilty mind"). Intent is a matter of degree, ranging from willful conduct to negligence. Someone who is negligent does not set out deliberately to hurt anyone but acts (or fails to act) in such a way that results in harm. Prosecutors weigh the degree of intent in determining whether, for example, to charge someone with

Hate Crime Laws: Do They Punish Actions or Attitudes?

On a cool October evening, Todd Mitchell, an African American teenager, was standing with some friends in front of their apartment complex in Kenosha, Wisconsin. They had just seen the film *Mississippi Burning* and were fuming over a scene that showed a white man beating a young black boy as he knelt in prayer.

"Do you feel hyped up to move on some white people?" asked Mitchell. Minutes later, they saw a young white boy walking toward them on the other side of the street. Mitchell commanded, "There goes a white boy. Go get him!" The group swarmed around the youngster, beating him bloody and leaving him on the ground in a coma. The attackers took the boy's tennis shoes as a trophy.

Police soon arrested the boys and charged them with the beating. Todd Mitchell went to trial as the ringleader, where the jury found him guilty of aggravated battery *motivated by racial hatred*. Instead of the usual two-year prison sentence, Mitchell went to jail for four years.

As this case illustrates, hate crime laws punish a crime more severely if the offender is motivated by bias against some category of people. Supporters make three arguments in favor of hate crime legislation. First, the offender's intentions are always important in weighing criminal responsibility, so considering hatred as an intention is nothing new. Second, a crime motivated by racial or other bias inflames the public more than a crime carried out, say, for money. Third, victims of hate crimes typically suffer more serious injuries than victims of crimes with other motives.

Critics counter that while some hate crime cases involve hard-core racism, most are impulsive acts by young people. Even more important, critics maintain, hate crime laws are a threat to First Amendment guarantees

 Read one critic's ideas about hate crime laws at http://www.andrewsullivan.com/politics.php

of free speech. Hate crime laws allow courts to sentence offenders not just for actions but also for their attitudes. As the Harvard University law professor Alan Dershowitz cautions, "As much as I hate bigotry, I fear much more the Court attempting to control the minds of citizens." In short, according to critics, hate crime laws open the door to punishing beliefs rather than behavior.

In 1993, the U.S. Supreme Court upheld the sentence handed down to Todd Mitchell. In a unanimous decision, the justices reaffirmed that the government should not punish an individual's beliefs. But, they reasoned, a belief is no longer protected when it becomes the motive for a crime.

WHAT DO YOU THINK?

1. Do you think crimes motivated by hate are more harmful than those motivated by, say, greed? Why or why not?

2. Do you think minorities such as African Americans should be subject to the same hate crime laws as white people? Why or why not?

3. On balance, do you favor or oppose hate crime laws? Why?

Sources: Terry (1993) and A. Sullivan (2002).

---

first-degree murder, second-degree murder, or negligent manslaughter. Alternatively, they may consider a killing justifiable, as in self-defense.

TYPES OF CRIME

In the United States, the Federal Bureau of Investigation (FBI) gathers information on criminal offenses and regularly reports the results in a publication called *Crime in the United States*. Two major types of crime make up the FBI "crime index."

Crimes against the person, also referred to as *violent crimes,* are *crimes that direct violence or the threat of violence against others.* Violent crimes include murder and manslaughter (legally defined as "the willful killing of one human being by another"), aggravated assault ("an unlawful attack by one person on another for the purpose of inflicting severe or aggravated bodily injury"), forcible rape ("the carnal knowledge of a female forcibly and against her will"), and robbery ("taking or

 Find a report on the violent victimization of college students at http://www.ojp.usdoj.gov/bjs/pub/pdf/vvcs02.pdf

SEEING OURSELVES

NATIONAL MAP 7–1
The Risk of Violent Crime across
the United States

This map shows the risk of becoming the victim
of a violent crime. In general, the risk is highest
in low-income, rural counties that have a large
population of men between the ages of fifteen
and twenty-four. After reading through this section of the text, can you explain this pattern?

Source: *American Demographics* magazine, December 2000
issue. Copyright © 2004 by Crain Communications, Inc.

attempting to take anything of value from the care, custody, or control of a person or persons, by force or threat of force or violence and/or putting the victim in fear"). National Map 7–1 shows the risk of violent crime for all the counties in the United States.

Crimes against property, also referred to as *property crimes,* are *crimes that involve theft of property belonging to others.* Property crimes include burglary ("the unlawful entry of a structure to commit a [serious crime] or a theft"), larceny-theft ("the unlawful taking, carrying, leading, or riding away of property from the possession of another"), motor vehicle theft ("the theft or attempted theft of a motor vehicle"), and arson ("any willful or malicious burning or attempt to burn the personal property of another").

A third category of offenses, not included in major crime indexes, is **victimless crimes,** *violations of law in which there are no obvious victims.* Also called *crimes without complaint,* they include illegal drug use, prostitution, and gambling. The term "victimless crime" is misleading, however. How victimless is a crime when young drug users embark on a life of crime to support their drug habit? What about a pregnant woman who, by smoking crack, permanently harms her baby? Or a gambler who loses the money needed to support himself and his family? Perhaps it is more correct to say that people who commit such crimes are both offenders and victims.

Because public views of victimless crime vary greatly, laws differ from place to place. Although gambling and prostitution are legal in only limited areas, both activities are common across the country.

Do you think that a student who downloads music in violation of the law is guilty of theft? Why or why not?

CRIMINAL STATISTICS

Statistics gathered by the FBI show crime rates rising from 1960 to 1990 and then declining through 2004. Even so, police still count nearly 12 million serious crimes each year. Figure 7–2 shows the trends for various serious crimes over the past four decades.

Always read crime statistics with caution, however, because they include only crimes known to the police. Almost all murders are reported, but other assaults—especially between people who know one another—often are not. Police records include an even smaller proportion of property crimes, especially when the losses are small.

Researchers check official crime statistics by conducting *victimization surveys,* in which they ask a representative sample of people about their experiences with crime. According to such surveys, the overall crime rate is about three times higher than official reports indicate (Russell, 1995b).

THE STREET CRIMINAL: A PROFILE

Using government crime reports, we can draw a general description of the categories of people most likely to be arrested for violent and property crimes.

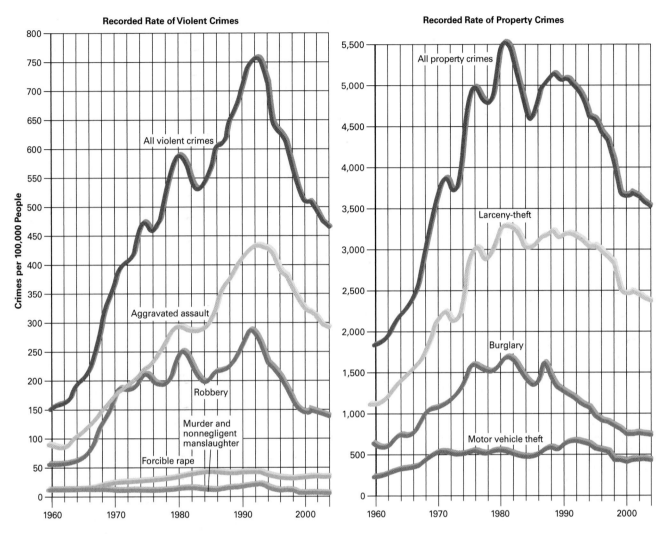

FIGURE 7-2 Crime Rates in the United States, 1960–2004

The graphs represent crime rates for various violent crimes and property crimes during recent decades.
Since about 1990, the trend has been toward lower crime rates.

Source: Federal Bureau of Investigation (2005).

Age

Official crime rates rise sharply during adolescence, peak in the late teens, and fall as people get older. People between the ages of fifteen and twenty-four represent just 14 percent of the U.S. population, but in 2004, they accounted for 39.2 percent of all arrests for violent crimes and 45.6 percent of arrests for property crimes.

Gender

Although each sex makes up roughly half the population, police collared males in 68.1 percent of all property crime arrests in 2004; the other 31.9 percent of arrests involved women. In other words, men are arrested more than twice as often as women for property crimes. In the case of violent crimes, the difference is even greater, with 82.1 percent of arrests involving males and just 17.9 percent females (almost a five-to-one ratio).

It may be that law enforcement officials are reluctant to define women as criminals. In global perspective, the greatest gender difference in crime rates occurs in societies that most severely limit the opportunities of women. In the United States, the difference in arrest rates for women and men has been narrowing, which probably indicates increasing gender equality in our society. Between 1995 and 2004,

"You look like this sketch of someone who's thinking about committing a crime."

there was a 9.2 percent *increase* in arrests of women and an 8.9 percent *drop* in arrests of men (Federal Bureau of Investigation, 2005).

Social Class

The FBI does not assess the social class of arrested persons, so no statistical data of the kind given for age and gender are available. But research has long indicated that street crime is more widespread among people of lower social position (Thornberry & Farnsworth, 1982; Wolfgang, Thornberry, & Figlio, 1987).

Yet the connection between class and crime is more complicated than it appears on the surface. For one thing, many people look upon the poor as less worthy than the rich, whose wealth and power confer "respectability" (Tittle, Villemez, & Smith, 1978; Elias, 1986). And although crime—especially violent crime—is a serious problem in the poorest inner-city communities of the United States, most of these crimes are committed by a few hard-core offenders. The majority of people in inner-city neighborhoods have no criminal record at all (Wolfgang, Figlio, & Sellin, 1972; Elliott & Ageton, 1980; Harries, 1990).

The connection between social standing and criminality also depends on the type of crime. If we expand our definition of crime beyond street offenses to include white-collar crime, the "common criminal" suddenly looks much more affluent and may live in a $100 million home.

Race and Ethnicity

Both race and ethnicity are strongly linked to crime rates, although the reasons are many and complex. Official statistics indicate that 70.8 percent of arrests for index crimes in 2004 involved white people. However, arrests of African Americans are higher in proportion to their share of the general population. African Americans represent 12.3 percent of the population of the United States but 28.2 percent of the arrests for property crimes (versus 69.3 percent for whites) and 36.9 percent of arrests for violent crimes (versus 60.9 percent for whites) (Federal Bureau of Investigation, 2005).

There are several reasons for the disproportionate number of arrests among African Americans. First, in the United States, race is closely linked to social standing, which, as we have already explained, affects the likelihood of engaging in street crimes. Many poor people living in the midst of wealth come to see society as unjust and therefore are more likely to turn to crime to get their share (Blau & Blau, 1982; E. Anderson, 1994; Martinez, 1996).

Second, black and white family patterns differ: Almost three-fourths of non-Hispanic black children (compared with one-fourth of non-Hispanic white children) are born to single mothers. There are two risks associated with single parenting: Children get less supervision and experience a greater risk of poverty. With one-third of African American children growing up in poor families (compared with one in seven white children), no one should be surprised at proportionately higher crime rates for African Americans (Courtwright, 1996; Jacobs & Helms, 1996; U.S. Census Bureau, 2006).

Third, prejudice prompts white police to arrest black people more readily and leads citizens to report African Americans more willingly, so people of color are overly criminalized (Chiricos, McEntire, & Gertz, 2001; Quillian & Pager, 2001; Demuth & Steffensmeier, 2004).

Fourth, remember that the official crime index does not include arrests for offenses ranging from drunk driving to white-collar violations. This omission contributes to the view of the typical criminal as a person of color. If we broaden our definition of crime to include drunk driving, business fraud, embezzlement, stock swindles, and cheating on income tax returns, the proportion of white criminals rises dramatically.

The recent film *Crash* shows how much ideas about race and class color our thinking about crime in the United States. For example, looking at this scene, what do you assume is going on? If the three men were white, would your assumption be the same? What if they were wearing button-down shirts and khakis? Why?

Keep in mind, too, that categories of people with high arrest rates are also at higher risk of being victims of crime. In the United States, for example, African Americans are almost six times as likely to die as a result of homicide as white people (Rogers et al., 2001; Hoyert et al., 2006).

Finally, some categories of the population have unusually low rates of arrest. People of Asian descent, who account for about 4 percent of the population, figure in only 1.1 percent of all arrests. As Chapter 11 ("Race and Ethnicity") explains, Asian Americans enjoy higher than average educational achievement and income. Also, Asian American culture emphasizes family solidarity and discipline, both of which keep criminality down.

CRIME IN GLOBAL PERSPECTIVE

By world standards, the U.S. crime rate is high. Although recent crime trends are downward, there were 16,137 murders in the United States in 2004, which amounts to one every half hour around the clock. In large cities such as New York, rarely does a day pass without someone being killed.

The rate of violent crime (but not property crime) in the United States is several times higher than in Europe. The contrast is even greater between our country and the nations of Asia, including India and Japan, where violent and property crime rates are among the lowest in the world.

Elliott Currie (1985) suggests that crime arises from our culture's emphasis on individual economic success, often at the expense of strong families and neighborhoods. The United States also has extraordinary cultural diversity, a result of centuries of immigration. In addition, economic inequality is higher in this country than in most other high-income nations. Our society's relatively weak social fabric, combined with considerable frustration among the poor, generates widespread criminal behavior.

Another factor contributing to violence in the United States is extensive private ownership of guns. About 70 percent of murder victims in the United States die from shootings. Since the early 1990s, in Texas and several other southern states, shooting deaths have exceeded automobile-related fatalities. The U.S. rate of handgun deaths is about seven times higher than in Canada, a country that strictly limits handgun ownership.

 Read a report on violent victimization and race at http://www.ojp.usdoj.gov/bjs/pub/pdf/vvr98.pdf

Surveys show that about 36 percent of U.S. households have at least one gun. Put differently, there are more guns than adults in this country, and one-third of these weapons are handguns that figure in violent crime. In large part, gun ownership reflects people's fear of crime, yet easy availability of guns in this country makes crime more deadly (NORC, 2005).

But as critics of gun control point out, waiting periods and background checks at retail gun stores do not keep guns out of the hands of criminals, who almost always obtain guns illegally (J. D. Wright, 1995). And gun control is not a magic bullet in the war on crime. Elliot Currie (1985) notes that the number of Californians killed each year by knives alone exceeds the number of Canadians killed by weapons of all kinds. However, most experts think that stricter gun control laws would lower the level of deadly violence.

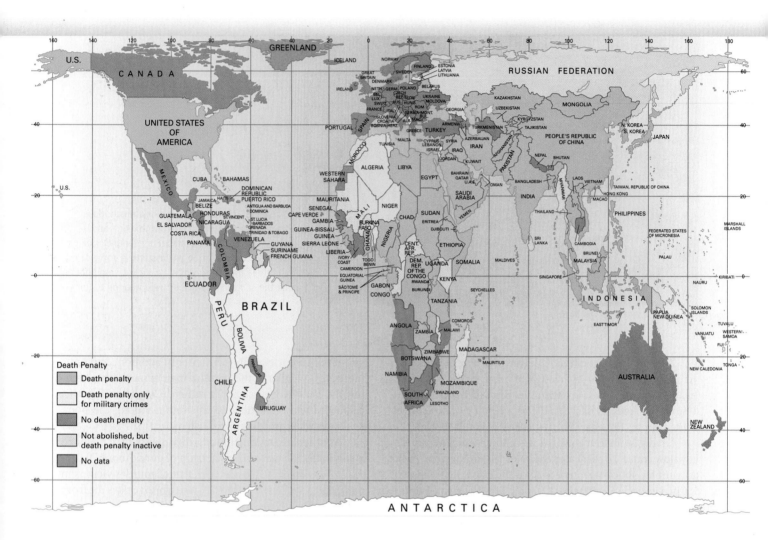

WINDOW ON THE WORLD

GLOBAL MAP 7–1   Capital Punishment in Global Perspective

The map identifies seventy-three countries and territories in which the law allows the death penalty for ordinary crimes; in eleven more, the death penalty is reserved for exceptional crimes under military law or during times of war. The death penalty does not exist in eighty-six countries and territories; in twenty-six more, although the death penalty remains in law, no execution has taken place in more than ten years. Compare rich and poor nations: What general pattern do you see? In what way are the United States and Japan exceptions to this pattern?

Source: Amnesty International (2006a).

 December 24–25, traveling through Peru. In Lima, Peru's capital city, the concern with crime is obvious. Almost every house is fortified with gates, barbed wire, or broken glass embedded in cement at the top of a wall.

Private security forces are everywhere in the rich areas along the coast, where we find the embassies, expensive hotels, and the international airport.

Later on, the picture is very different as we pass through small villages high in the Andes to the east. The *same families have lived in these communities for generations, and people know one another. No gates or fences here. And we've seen only one police car all afternoon.*

Crime rates are high in some of the largest cities of the world, such as Manila, Philippines, and São Paulo, Brazil, which have rapid population growth and millions of desperately poor people. Outside of big cities, however, the traditional character of low-income societies and their strong family structure allow local communities to control crime informally.

Some types of crime have always been multinational, such as terrorism, espionage, and arms dealing (Martin & Romano, 1992). But today, the globalization we are experiencing on many fronts also extends to crime. A recent case in point is the illegal drug trade. In part, the problem of illegal drugs in the United States is a *demand* issue. That is, the demand for cocaine and other drugs in this country is high, and many young people are willing to risk arrest or even violent death for a chance to make money in the drug trade. But the *supply* side of the issue is just as important. In the South American nation of Colombia, at least 20 percent of the people depend on cocaine production for their livelihood. Not only is cocaine Colombia's most profitable export, but it outsells all other exports—including coffee—combined. Clearly, then, drug dealing and many other crimes are closely related to social conditions both in this country and elsewhere.

Different countries have different strategies for dealing with crime. The use of capital punishment is one example. According to Amnesty International (2006b), four nations (China, Iran, Vietnam, and the United States) account for 97 percent of the world's executions carried out by governments. Global Map 7–1 shows which countries currently use capital punishment. The global trend is toward abolishing the death penalty: Since 1985, more than fifty nations have ended this practice.

The U.S. Criminal Justice System

The criminal justice system is a society's formal response to crime. We shall briefly examine the key elements of the U.S.

 criminal justice system: police, courts, and the punishment of convicted offenders. First, however, we must understand an important principle that underlies the entire system, the idea of due process.

DUE PROCESS

Due process is a simple but very important idea: The criminal justice system must operate within the bounds of law.

Police must be allowed discretion if they are to handle effectively the many different situations they face every day. At the same time, it is important that the police treat people fairly. Here we see a police officer deciding whether or not to charge a young woman with driving while intoxicated. What factors do you think enter into this decision?

This principle is grounded in the first ten amendments to the U.S. Constitution—known as the Bill of Rights—

 To read the Bill of Rights, go to http://www.archives.gov/ national_archives_experience/ charters/bill_of_rights.html

adopted by Congress in 1791. The Constitution offers various protections to any person charged with a crime. Among these are the right to counsel, the right to refuse to testify against oneself, and the right to confront all accusers, as well as freedom from being tried twice for the same crime and freedom from being "deprived of life, liberty, or property without due process of law." Furthermore, the Constitution gives all people the right to a speedy and public trial, with a jury if desired, and freedom from excessive bail as well as from cruel and unusual punishment.

To increase the power of punishment to deter crime, capital punishment was long carried out in public. Here is a photograph from the last public execution in the United States, with twenty-two-year-old Rainey Bethea standing on the scaffold moments from death in Owensboro, Kentucky, on August 16, 1937. Children as well as adults were in the crowd. Now that the mass media report the story of executions across the country, states carry out capital punishment behind closed doors.

In general terms, the concept of due process means that anyone charged with a crime must receive (1) fair notice of the proceedings, (2) a hearing on the charges conducted according to law and with the ability to present a defense, and (3) a judge or jury that weighs evidence impartially (Inciardi, 2000).

Due process limits the power of government, with an eye toward this nation's cultural support of individual rights and freedoms. Deciding exactly how far government can go makes up much of the work of the judicial system, especially the U.S. Supreme Court.

POLICE

The police generally serve as the point of contact between a population and the criminal justice system. In principle, the police maintain public order by enforcing the law. Of course, there is only so much that 675,734 full-time police officers across the United States can do to monitor the activities of 300 million people. As a result, the police use a great deal of personal judgment in deciding which situations warrant their attention and whether these situations should or should not involve making an arrest.

How do police officers carry out their duties? In a study of police behavior in five cities, Douglas Smith and Christy Visher (1981; Smith, 1987) concluded that because they must act swiftly, police quickly size up situations in terms of six factors. First, the more serious they think the situation is, the more likely they are to make an arrest. Second, police take account of the victim's wishes in deciding whether or not to make an arrest. Third, the odds of arrest go up the more uncooperative a suspect is. Fourth, police are more likely to take into custody someone they have arrested before, presumably because this suggests guilt. Fifth, the presence of bystanders increases the chances of arrest. According to Smith and Visher, the presence of observers prompts police to take stronger control of a situation, if only to move the encounter from the street (the suspect's turf) to the police department (where law officers have the advantage). Sixth, all else being equal, police are more likely to arrest people of color than to arrest whites, perceiving people of African or Latino descent as either more dangerous or more likely to be guilty.

COURTS

After arrest, a court determines a suspect's guilt or innocence. In principle, U.S. courts rely on an adversarial process involving attorneys—one representing the defendant and another the state—in the presence of a judge who monitors legal procedures.

In practice, however, about 90 percent of criminal cases are resolved before court appearance through **plea bargaining,** *a legal negotiation in which a prosecutor reduces a charge in exchange for a defendant's guilty plea.* For example, the state may offer a defendant charged with burglary a lesser charge, perhaps possession of burglary tools, in exchange for a guilty plea.

same families have lived in these communities for generations, and people know one another. No gates or fences here. And we've seen only one police car all afternoon.

Crime rates are high in some of the largest cities of the world, such as Manila, Philippines, and São Paulo, Brazil, which have rapid population growth and millions of desperately poor people. Outside of big cities, however, the traditional character of low-income societies and their strong family structure allow local communities to control crime informally.

Some types of crime have always been multinational, such as terrorism, espionage, and arms dealing (Martin & Romano, 1992). But today, the globalization we are experiencing on many fronts also extends to crime. A recent case in point is the illegal drug trade. In part, the problem of illegal drugs in the United States is a *demand* issue. That is, the demand for cocaine and other drugs in this country is high, and many young people are willing to risk arrest or even violent death for a chance to make money in the drug trade. But the *supply* side of the issue is just as important. In the South American nation of Colombia, at least 20 percent of the people depend on cocaine production for their livelihood. Not only is cocaine Colombia's most profitable export, but it outsells all other exports—including coffee—combined. Clearly, then, drug dealing and many other crimes are closely related to social conditions both in this country and elsewhere.

Different countries have different strategies for dealing with crime. The use of capital punishment is one example. According to Amnesty International (2006b), four nations (China, Iran, Vietnam, and the United States) account for 97 percent of the world's executions carried out by governments. Global Map 7–1 shows which countries currently use capital punishment. The global trend is toward abolishing the death penalty: Since 1985, more than fifty nations have ended this practice.

The U.S. Criminal Justice System

The criminal justice system is a society's formal response to crime. We shall briefly examine the key elements of the U.S.  criminal justice system: police, courts, and the punishment of convicted offenders. First, however, we must understand an important principle that underlies the entire system, the idea of due process.

DUE PROCESS

Due process is a simple but very important idea: The criminal justice system must operate within the bounds of law.

Police must be allowed discretion if they are to handle effectively the many different situations they face every day. At the same time, it is important that the police treat people fairly. Here we see a police officer deciding whether or not to charge a young woman with driving while intoxicated. What factors do you think enter into this decision?

This principle is grounded in the first ten amendments to the U.S. Constitution—known as the Bill of Rights—adopted by Congress in 1791. The Constitution offers various protections to any person charged with a crime. Among these are the right to counsel, the right to refuse to testify against oneself, and the right to confront all accusers, as well as freedom from being tried twice for the same crime and freedom from being "deprived of life, liberty, or property without due process of law." Furthermore, the Constitution gives all people the right to a speedy and public trial, with a jury if desired, and freedom from excessive bail as well as from cruel and unusual punishment.

 To read the Bill of Rights, go to http://www.archives.gov/ national_archives_experience/ charters/bill_of_rights.html

To increase the power of punishment to deter crime, capital punishment was long carried out in public. Here is a photograph from the last public execution in the United States, with twenty-two-year-old Rainey Bethea standing on the scaffold moments from death in Owensboro, Kentucky, on August 16, 1937. Children as well as adults were in the crowd. Now that the mass media report the story of executions across the country, states carry out capital punishment behind closed doors.

In general terms, the concept of due process means that anyone charged with a crime must receive (1) fair notice of the proceedings, (2) a hearing on the charges conducted according to law and with the ability to present a defense, and (3) a judge or jury that weighs evidence impartially (Inciardi, 2000).

Due process limits the power of government, with an eye toward this nation's cultural support of individual rights and freedoms. Deciding exactly how far government can go makes up much of the work of the judicial system, especially the U.S. Supreme Court.

POLICE

The police generally serve as the point of contact between a population and the criminal justice system. In principle, the police maintain public order by enforcing the law. Of course, there is only so much that 675,734 full-time police officers across the United States can do to monitor the activities of 300 million people. As a result, the police use a great deal of personal judgment in deciding which situations warrant their attention and whether these situations should or should not involve making an arrest.

How do police officers carry out their duties? In a study of police behavior in five cities, Douglas Smith and Christy Visher (1981; Smith, 1987) concluded that because they must act swiftly, police quickly size up situations in terms of six factors. First, the more serious they think the situation is, the more likely they are to make an arrest. Second, police

take account of the victim's wishes in deciding whether or not to make an arrest. Third, the odds of arrest go up the more uncooperative a suspect is. Fourth, police are more likely to take into custody someone they have arrested before, presumably because this suggests guilt. Fifth, the presence of bystanders increases the chances of arrest. According to Smith and Visher, the presence of observers prompts police to take stronger control of a situation, if only to move the encounter from the street (the suspect's turf) to the police department (where law officers have the advantage). Sixth, all else being equal, police are more likely to arrest people of color than to arrest whites, perceiving people of African or Latino descent as either more dangerous or more likely to be guilty.

COURTS

After arrest, a court determines a suspect's guilt or innocence. In principle, U.S. courts rely on an adversarial process involving attorneys—one representing the defendant and another the state—in the presence of a judge who monitors legal procedures.

In practice, however, about 90 percent of criminal cases are resolved before court appearance through **plea bargaining,** *a legal negotiation in which a prosecutor reduces a charge in exchange for a defendant's guilty plea.* For example, the state may offer a defendant charged with burglary a lesser charge, perhaps possession of burglary tools, in exchange for a guilty plea.

SUMMING UP

Four Justifications for Punishment

Retribution	The oldest justification for punishment.
	Punishment is society's revenge for a moral wrong.
	In principle, punishment should be equal in severity to the crime itself.
Deterrence	An early modern approach.
	Crime is considered social disruption which society acts to control.
	People are viewed as rational and self-interested; deterrence works because the pain of punishment outweighs the pleasure of crime.
Rehabilitation	A modern strategy linked to the development of social sciences.
	Crime and other deviance are viewed as the result of social problems (such as poverty) or personal problems (such as mental illness).
	Social conditions are improved; treatment is tailored to the offender's condition.
Societal protection	A modern approach easier to carry out than rehabilitation.
	If society is unable or unwilling to rehabilitate offenders or reform social conditions, people are protected by the imprisonment or execution of the offender.

Plea bargaining is widespread because it spares the system the time and expense of trials. A trial is usually unnecessary if there is little disagreement as to the facts of the case. Moreover, because the number of cases entering the system has doubled over the past decade, prosecutors cannot possibly bring every case to trial even if they wanted to. By quickly resolving most of their work, then, the courts can devote their resources to the most important cases.

But plea bargaining pressures defendants (who are presumed innocent) to plead guilty. A person can exercise the right to a trial, but only at the risk of receiving a more severe sentence if found guilty. Furthermore, low-income defendants must often rely on a public defender—typically an overworked and underpaid attorney who may devote little time to even the most serious cases (Novak, 1999). Plea bargaining may be efficient, but it undercuts the adversarial process and the rights of defendants.

PUNISHMENT

When a young man is shot dead on the street after leaving a restaurant, some people may wonder why it happened, but almost everyone believes that someone should have to "pay" for the crime. Indeed, sometimes the desire to punish is so great that in the end justice may not be done.

Such cases force us to ask why a society should punish its wrongdoers. Scholars answer with four basic reasons which are described in the following sections and summarized in the Summing Up table: retribution, deterrence, rehabilitation, and societal protection.

Retribution

The oldest justification for punishment is to satisfy a society's need for **retribution,** *an act of moral vengeance by which society makes the offender suffer as much as the suffering caused by the crime.* Retribution rests on the view that society exists in a moral balance. When criminality upsets this balance, punishment in equal measure restores the moral order, as suggested by the biblical saying, "An eye for an eye."

In the Middle Ages, most people viewed crime as sin—an offense against God as well as society—that required a harsh response. Although critics point out that retribution does little to reform the offender, many people today still consider vengeance reason enough for punishment.

Deterrence

A second justification for punishment is **deterrence,** *the attempt to discourage criminality through the use of punishment.* Deterrence is based on the eighteenth-century Enlightenment idea that as calculating and rational creatures, humans will not break the law if they think that the pain of punishment will outweigh the pleasure of crime.

Deterrence emerged as a reform measure in response to harsh punishments based on retribution. Why put someone to death for stealing if theft can be discouraged by a prison sentence? As the concept of deterrence gained acceptance in industrial societies, execution and physical mutilation of criminals were replaced by milder forms of punishment such as imprisonment.

DEVIANCE   CHAPTER 7   **195**

November 8, 2004

Despite Drop in Crime, an Increase in Inmates

By FOX BUTTERFIELD

The number of inmates in state and federal prisons rose 2.1 percent last year, even as violent crime and property crime fell, according to a study by the Justice Department released yesterday.

The continuing increase in the prison population, despite a drop or leveling off in the crime rate in the past few years, is a result of laws passed in the 1990s that led to more prison sentences and longer terms, said Allen J. Beck, chief of corrections statistics for the department's Bureau of Justice Statistics and an author of the report.

At the end of 2003, there were 1,470,045 men and women in state and federal prisons in the United States, the report found. In addition, counting those inmates in city and county jails and incarcerated juvenile offenders, the total number of Americans behind bars was 2,212,475 on Dec. 31 last year, the report said.

The report estimated that 44 percent of state and federal prisoners in 2003 were black, compared with 35 percent who were white, 19 percent who were Hispanic and 2 percent who were of other races. The numbers have changed little in the last decade.

Statistically, the number of women in prison is growing fast, rising 3.6 percent in 2003. But at a total of 101,179, they are just 6.9 percent of the prison population.

Alfred Blumstein, a criminologist at Carnegie Mellon University, said one of the most striking findings in the report was that almost 10 percent of all American black men ages 25 to 29 were in prison.

Such a high proportion of young black men behind bars not only has a strong impact on black families, Professor Blumstein said, but "in many ways is self-defeating." The criminal justice system is built on deterrence, with being sent to prison supposedly a stigma, he said. "But it's tough to convey a sense of stigma when so many of your friends and neighbors are similarly stigmatized."

In seeking to explain the paradox of a falling crime rate but a rising prison population, Mr. Beck pointed out that FBI statistics showed that from 1994 to 2003 there was a 16 percent drop in arrests for violent crime, including a 36 percent decrease in arrests for murder and a 25 percent decrease in arrests for robbery.

But the tough new sentencing laws led to a growth in inmates being sent to

---

Punishment may deter crime in two ways. *Specific deterrence* convinces an individual offender that crime does not pay. Through *general deterrence,* punishing one person serves as an example to others.

Rehabilitation

The third justification for punishment, **rehabilitation,** is *a program for reforming the offender to prevent later offenses.* Rehabilitation arose along with the social sciences in the nineteenth century. Since then, sociologists have claimed that crime and other deviance spring from a social environment marked by poverty or lack of parental supervision. Logically, then, if offenders learn to be deviant, they can also learn to obey the rules; the key is controlling the environment. *Reformatories* or *houses of correction* provided a controlled setting where people could learn proper behavior (recall the description of total institutions in Chapter 3, "Socialization: From Infancy to Old Age").

Like deterrence, rehabilitation motivates the offender to conform. But rehabilitation emphasizes constructive improvement, whereas deterrence and retribution simply make the offender suffer. In addition, retribution demands that the punishment fit the crime, but rehabilitation tailors treatment to each offender. Thus identical crimes would prompt similar acts of retribution but different rehabilitation programs.

Societal Protection

A final justification for punishment is **societal protection,** *rendering an offender incapable of further offenses temporarily through imprisonment or permanently by execution.* Like deterrence, societal protection is a rational approach to punishment intended to protect society from crime.

Currently, 2.1 million people are imprisoned in the United States. As "In the *Times*" explains, the crime rate has gone down in recent years, but the number of offenders

prison, from 522,000 in 1995 to 615,400 in 2002, the report said.

Similarly, the report found that the average time served by prison inmates rose from 23 months in 1995 to 30 months in 2001.

Among the new measures were mandatory minimum sentencing laws, which required inmates to serve a specified proportion of their time behind bars; truth-in-sentencing laws, which required an inmate to actually serve the time he was sentenced to; and a variety of three-strikes laws increasing the penalties for repeat offenders.

In the three states with the biggest prison systems, California, Texas and Florida, the number of newly admitted inmates grew last year, but the number of those released either fell or remained stable, Mr. Beck said.

Several states with small prison systems had particularly large increases in new inmates, led by North Dakota, up 11.4 percent, and Minnesota, up 10.3 percent.

New York had a 2.8 percent decrease in new inmates, reflecting the continued sharp fall in crime in New York City, Mr. Beck said.

Overall, Mr. Beck said, the prison population is aging. Traditionally the great majority of inmates are men in their 20s and early 30s, but middle-aged inmates, those 40 to 54, account for about half of the increase in the prison population since 1995, he said.

This is a result both of the aging of the general American population and of the longer sentences, Mr. Beck said.

But the number of elderly inmates is still small, despite longer sentences and more life sentences. Those inmates 65 and older were still only 1 percent of the prison population in 2003.

WHAT DO YOU THINK?

1. Why do you think about 10 percent of young African American men are in prison?

2. Do you favor longer sentences as a way to discourage crime? Why or why not?

3. Why do you think the share of prisoners who are women is increasing?

Adapted from the original article by Fox Butterfield published in *The New York Times* on November 8, 2004. Copyright © 2004 by The New York Times Company, Reprinted with permission.

---

locked up across the country has gone up fourfold since 1980. This rise in the prison population reflects both tougher public attitudes toward crime and punishing offenders and an increasing number of arrests for drug-related crimes. As a result, the United States now imprisons a larger share of its population than any other country in the world (U.S. Bureau of Justice Statistics, 2004; Sentencing Project, 2005).

YOUR TURN

Which of the four reasons for punishment do you think is most important? Why? Do you think most others would agree with you? Explain.

CRITICAL REVIEW The reasons societies punish are many and complex. Accurately assessing the actual consequences of punishment is no simple task.

The value of retribution lies in Durkheim's claim that punishing the deviant person increases society's moral awareness. For this reason, punishment was traditionally a public event. Although the last public execution in the United States took place in Kentucky nearly seventy years ago, today's mass media ensure public awareness of executions carried out inside prison walls (Kittrie, 1971).

Does punishment deter crime? Despite our extensive use of punishment, our society has a high rate of **criminal recidivism,** *later offenses by people previously convicted of crimes.* About three-fourths of state prisoners have been jailed before, and about half will be back within a few years after release (Petersilia, 1997; DeFina & Arvanites, 2002). Such facts raise doubt about how much punishment deters crime. In addition, only about one-third of all crimes are known to police; of these, only about one in five results in an arrest. Most crimes, therefore, go unpunished, so that the old saying "Crime doesn't pay" rings hollow.

Violent Crime Is Down—but Why?

During the 1980s, crime rates shot upward. Just about everyone lived in fear of violent crime, and in many larger cities, the numbers of people killed and wounded made whole neighborhoods appear to be war zones. There seemed to be no solution to the problem.

In the 1990s, something good and unexpected happened: Serious crime rates began to fall until by 2000, they were at levels not seen in more than a generation. Why? Researchers point to several reasons:

1. **A reduction in the youth population.** We have already noted that young people (particularly males) are responsible for much violent crime. Between 1990 and 2000, the share of the pop-

ulation aged fifteen to twenty-four dropped by about 5 percent (perhaps as one unexpected result of the legalization of abortion in 1973).

One reason that crime has gone down is that there are more than 2 million people incarcerated in this country. This has caused severe overcrowding of facilities such as this Maricopa County, Arizona, prison.

2. **Changes in policing.** Much of the drop in crime (like the earlier rise in crime) has taken place in large cities. New York City, where the number of murders fell from 2,245 in 1990 to just 570 in 2004, has adopted a policy of *community policing,* which means that police are concerned not just with making arrests but in preventing crime before it happens. Officers get to know the areas they patrol and frequently stop young men for jaywalking or other minor infractions so they can check them for concealed weapons (the word is out that you can be arrested for carrying a gun). In addition, there are more police at work in large cities. For example, Los Angeles added more than 2,000 police in the 1990s, and it, too, saw its violent

General deterrence is even more difficult to investigate scientifically because we have no way of knowing how people might act if they were unaware of punishments handed down to others. Opponents of capital punishment point to research suggesting that the death penalty has limited value as a general deterrent and note that the United States is the only Western, high-income nation that routinely executes serious offenders. Half of the 3,314 people currently on death row are in just five states: California, Texas, Florida, Pennsylvania, and Ohio.

It is also true that death sentences have been pronounced against innocent people. Between 1973 and 2003, almost 100 people were released from death row after new evidence established their innocence, which means that innocent people may have been put to death. Before leaving office in January 2003, Illinois Governor George Ryan claimed his state's judicial system was flawed and com-

muted the sentences of all 167 of the state's death row inmates to life in prison (S. Levine, 2003).

Despite the growing controversy over the use of the death penalty, a majority of adults in the United States (64 percent) say they support capital punishment for people convicted of murder (NORC, 2005:156). Among first-year college students, about two-thirds express support for the death penalty (Pryor et al., 2005).

Prisons provide short-term societal protection by keeping offenders off the streets, but they do little to reshape attitudes or behavior in the long term (Carlson, 1976; R. A. Wright, 1994). Perhaps rehabilitation is an unrealistic expectation because according to Sutherland's theory of differential association, locking up criminals together for years probably strengthens criminal attitudes and skills. Imprisonment also breaks whatever social ties inmates may have in the outside world, which, following Hirschi's

crime rate fall during that period.

3. **More prisoners.** Between 1985 and 2005, the number of inmates in jails and prisons in the United States soared from 750,000 to more than 2.1 million. The main reason for this increase is tough new laws that demand prison time for many crimes, especially drug offenses. As one analyst put it, "When you lock up an extra million people, it's got to have some effect on the crime rate" (Franklin Zimring, quoted in Witkin, 1998:31).

4. **A better economy.** The U.S. economy boomed during the 1990s. With unemployment down, more people were working, reducing the likelihood that some would turn to crime out of economic desperation. The logic here is simple: More jobs, fewer crimes. By the same token, the economic downturn of the early 2000s slowed the downward crime trend.

5. **The declining drug trade.** Many analysts think that the most important factor in reducing rates of violent crime is the decline of crack cocaine. Crack came on the scene around 1985, and violence spread as young people—especially in the inner cities and increasingly armed with guns—became part of a booming drug trade. Facing few legitimate job opportunities, more people turned to selling illegal drugs, and a generation of young people became caught up in a wave of violence.

By the early 1990s, however, the popularity of crack had begun to fall as people saw the damage the drug was causing to entire communities. This realization, coupled with steady economic improvement and stiffer sentences for drug offenses, helped bring about the turnaround in violent crime.

The current picture looks better relative to what it was a decade ago. The crime problem, says one

researcher, "looks better, but only because the early 1990s were so bad. So let's not fool ourselves into thinking everything is resolved. It's not."

WHAT DO YOU THINK?

1. Do you support the policy of community policing? Why or why not?

2. What do you see as the pros and cons of building more prisons as an anticrime policy?

3. Of all the factors mentioned here, which do you think is the most important in crime control? Which is least important? Why?

Sources: Based on Fagan, Zimring, & Kim (1998), Witkin (1998), Winship & Berrien (1999), Donahue & Levitt (2000), and R. Rosenfeld (2002).

---

control theory, makes inmates likely to commit more crimes upon release.

✓ **YOUR LEARNING** What are society's four justifications for punishment? Does sending offenders to prison accomplish each of them? How?

COMMUNITY-BASED CORRECTIONS

Prisons keep convicted criminals off the streets. But the evidence suggests that locking people up does little to rehabilitate most offenders. Further, prisons are expensive, costing our society at least $25,000 per year to support each inmate, in addition to the initial costs of building the prison facilities.

One recent alternative to the traditional prison that has been adopted by many cities and states across the country is

community-based corrections, *correctional programs operating within society at large rather than behind prison walls.* Community-based corrections have three main advantages: They reduce costs, reduce overcrowding in prisons, and allow for supervision of convicts while eliminating the hardships of prison life and the stigma that accompanies going to jail. In general, the idea of community-based corrections is not so much to punish as to reform; such programs are therefore usually offered to individuals who have committed less serious offenses and who appear to be good prospects for avoiding future criminal violations (Inciardi, 2000).

Probation

One form of community-based corrections is *probation,* a policy of permitting a convicted offender to remain in the community under conditions imposed by a court, including regular supervision. Courts may require that a probationer receive counseling, attend a drug treatment program, hold a job, avoid associating with "known criminals," or anything else deemed appropriate. Typically, a probationer must check in with an officer of the court (the probation officer) on a regular schedule to make sure the guidelines are being followed. Should the probationer fail to live up to the conditions set by the court or commit a new offense, the court may revoke probation and send the offender back to jail.

Shock Probation

A related strategy is *shock probation,* a policy by which a judge orders a convicted offender to prison for a short time and then suspends the remainder of the sentence in favor of probation. Shock probation is thus a mix of prison and probation that is used to impress on the offender the seriousness of the situation while still withholding full-scale imprisonment. In some cases, shock probation takes place in a special "boot camp" facility where offenders might spend one to three months in a military-style setting intended to teach discipline and respect for authority (Cole & Smith, 2002).

Parole

Parole is a policy of releasing inmates from prison to serve the remainder of their sentences in the local community under the supervision of a parole officer. Although some sentences specifically deny the possibility of parole, most inmates become eligible for parole after serving a certain portion of their sentence. At this time, a parole board evaluates the risks and benefits of an inmate's early release from prison. If parole is granted, the parole board monitors the offender's conduct until the sentence is completed. Should the offender not comply with the conditions of parole or be arrested for another crime, the board can revoke parole, returning the offender to prison to complete the sentence.

CRITICAL REVIEW Evaluations of community-based corrections are mixed. There is little question that probation and parole programs are much less expensive than conventional imprisonment; they also free up room in prisons for people who commit more serious crimes. Yet research suggests that although probation and shock probation do seem to work for some people, they do not significantly reduce criminal recidivism. Similarly, parole is useful to prison officials as a means to encourage good behavior among inmates who hope for early release. Yet levels of crime among individuals who have been released on parole are high. Indeed, recidivism among parolees is so high that a number of states have ended their parole programs entirely (Inciardi, 2000).

Such evaluations help us see that the criminal justice system, by itself, cannot eliminate crime. As the Applying Sociology box on pages 198–99 explains, while police, courts, and prisons do affect crime rates, crime and other deviance are not just the acts of "bad people" but reflect the operation of society itself.

YOUR LEARNING Identify and define three types of community-based corrections.

APPLYING SOCIOLOGY IN EVERYDAY LIFE

1. Identity theft is a new type of crime that victimizes as many as 10 million people each year in the United States. Research this crime, and explain how this offense differs from property crime that takes place "on the street." (Consider differences in the crime, the offenders, and the victims.)
2. Rent a wheelchair (check with a local pharmacy or medical supply store), and use it as much as possible for a day or two. Not only will you gain a firsthand understanding of the physical barriers to getting around, but you will discover that people respond to you in many new ways.
3. Watch an episode of the real-action police show *Cops.* Based on this program, how would you describe the people who commit crimes?

MAKING THE GRADE

CHAPTER 7 Deviance

WHAT IS DEVIANCE?

 Deviance refers to norm violations ranging from minor infractions, such as bad manners, to major infractions, such as serious violence (p 174).

Theories of Deviance

BIOLOGICAL THEORIES
- focus on individual abnormality
- explain human behavior as the result of biological instincts

Lombroso claimed criminals have ape-like physical traits; later research links criminal behavior to certain body types and genetics.

p 175

PSYCHOLOGICAL THEORIES
- focus on individual abnormality
- see deviance as the result of "unsuccessful socialization"

Reckless and Dinitz's *containment theory* links delinquency to weak conscience.

pp 175–76

deviance (p. 174) the recognized violation of cultural norms

crime (p. 174) the violation of a society's formally enacted criminal law

social control (p. 174) attempts by society to regulate people's thoughts and behavior

criminal justice system (p. 174) a formal response by police, courts, and prison officials to alleged violations of the law

 Biological and psychological theories provide a limited understanding of crime and other deviance because most violations are carried out by people who are normal (p 176).

SOCIOLOGICAL THEORIES view all behavior—deviance as well as conformity—as products of society. Sociologists point out that
- what is deviant varies from place to place according to cultural norms
- behavior and individuals become deviant as others define them that way
- what and who a society defines as deviant reflect who has and who does not have social power

p 176

THEORETICAL ANALYSIS OF DEVIANCE

The Functions of Deviance: Structural-Functional Analysis

Durkheim claimed deviance is a normal element of society that
- affirms cultural norms and values
- clarifies moral boundaries
- brings people together
- encourages social change

pp 176–77

Merton's *strain theory* explains deviance in terms of a society's cultural goals and the means available to achieve them.

Deviant subcultures are discussed by Cloward and Ohlin, Cohen, Miller, and Anderson.

pp 177–79

labeling theory (p. 179) the idea that deviance and conformity result not so much from what people do as from how others respond to those actions

stigma (p. 180) a powerfully negative label that greatly changes a person's self-concept and social identity

medicalization of deviance (p. 181) the transformation of moral and legal deviance into a medical condition

white-collar crime (p. 184) crime committed by people of high social position in the course of their occupations

corporate crime (p. 185) the illegal actions of a corporation or people acting on its behalf

organized crime (p. 185) a business supplying illegal goods or services

hate crime (p. 186) a criminal act against a person or a person's property by an offender motivated by racial or other bias

Labeling Theory: Symbolic-Interaction Analysis

Labeling theory claims that deviance depends less on what someone does than on how others react to that behavior. If people respond to primary deviance by stigmatizing a person, secondary deviance and a deviant career may result.

pp 179–81

The *medicalization of deviance* is the transformation of moral and legal deviance into a medical condition. In practice, this means a change in labels, replacing "good" and "bad" with "sick" and "well."

pp 181–82

Sutherland's *differential association theory* links deviance to how much others encourage or discourage such behavior.

p 182

Hirschi's *control theory* states that imagining the possible consequences of deviance often discourages such behavior. People who are well integrated into society are less likely to engage in deviant behavior.

p 182

 See the Applying Theory table on page 185.

MAKING THE GRADE

CONTINUED...

THEORETICAL ANALYSIS OF DEVIANCE *CONTINUED*

Deviance and Inequality: Social-Conflict Analysis

Based on Karl Marx's ideas, social-conflict theory holds that laws and other norms operate to protect the interests of powerful members of any society.

- White-collar offenses are committed by people of high social position as part of their jobs. Sutherland claimed such offenses are rarely prosecuted and are most likely to end up in civil rather than criminal court.
- Corporate crime refers to illegal actions by a corporation or people acting on its behalf. Although corporate crimes cause considerable public harm, most cases of corporate crime go unpunished.
- Organized crime has a long history in the United States, especially among categories of people with few legitimate opportunities.

pp 183–85

Deviance, Race, and Gender

- What people consider deviant reflects the relative power and privilege of different categories of people.
- *Hate crimes* are crimes motivated by racial or other bias; they target people with disadvantages based on race, gender, or sexual orientation.
- In the United States and elsewhere, societies control the behavior of women more closely than that of men.

p 186

WHAT IS CRIME?

CRIME is the violation of criminal laws enacted by local, state, or federal governments. There are two major categories of serious crime:
- crimes against the person (violent crime), including murder, aggravated assault, forcible rape, and robbery,
- crimes against property (property crime), including burglary, larceny/theft, auto theft, and arson.

pp 186–88

crimes against the person (p. 187) (violent crimes) crimes that direct violence or the threat of violence against others

crimes against property (p. 188) (property crimes) crimes that involve theft of property belonging to others

victimless crimes (p. 188) violations of law in which there are no obvious victims

PATTERNS OF CRIME IN THE UNITED STATES

- Official statistics show that arrest rates peak in late adolescence and drop steadily with advancing age.
- About 70% of people arrested for property crimes and 82% of people arrested for violent crimes are male.
- *Street crime* is more common among people of lower social position. Including white-collar and corporate crime makes class differences in criminality smaller.
- More whites than African Americans are arrested for street crimes. However, African Americans are arrested more often than whites in relation to their population size. Asian Americans have a lower-than-average rate of arrest.
- By world standards, the U.S. crime rate is high.

pp 188–91

THE U.S. CRIMINAL JUSTICE SYSTEM

Police

The police maintain public order by enforcing the law.
- Police use personal discretion in deciding whether and how to handle a situation.
- Research suggests that police are more likely to make an arrest if the offense is serious, if bystanders are present, or if the suspect is African American or Latino.

p 194

Courts

Courts rely on an adversarial process in which attorneys—one representing the defendant and one representing the state—present their cases in the presence of a judge who monitors legal procedures.
- In practice, U.S. courts resolve most cases through plea bargaining. Though efficient, this method puts less powerful people at a disadvantage.

pp 194–95

Punishment

There are four justifications for punishment:
- retribution
- deterrence
- rehabilitation
- societal protection

pp 195–97

Community-based corrections include probation and parole. These programs lower the cost of supervising people convicted of crimes and reduce prison overcrowding but have not been shown to reduce recidivism.

pp 199–200

plea bargaining (p. 194) a legal negotiation in which a prosecutor reduces a charge in exchange for a defendant's guilty plea

retribution (p. 195) an act of moral vengeance by which society makes the offender suffer as much as the suffering caused by the crime

deterrence (p. 195) the attempt to discourage criminality through the use of punishment

rehabilitation (p. 196) a program for reforming the offender to prevent later offenses

societal protection (p. 196) rendering an offender incapable of further offenses temporarily through imprisonment or permanently by execution

criminal recidivism (p. 197) later offenses by people previously convicted of crimes

community-based corrections (p. 199) correctional programs operating within society at large rather than behind prison walls

See the Summing Up table on page 195.

MAKING THE GRADE
Sample Test Questions
CHAPTER 7

These questions are similar to those found in the test bank that accompanies this textbook.

MULTIPLE-CHOICE QUESTIONS

1. Crime is a special type of deviance that
   a. refers just to violations of law.
   b. involves punishment.
   c. refers to any violation of a society's norms.
   d. always involves a particular person as the offender.

2. Emile Durkheim explains that deviance is
   a. defined by the rich and used against the poor.
   b. harmful not just to victims but to society as a whole.
   c. often at odds with public morality.
   d. found in every society.

3. Using Robert Merton's strain theory, a person selling illegal drugs for a living would fall into which of the following categories?
   a. conformist
   b. innovator
   c. retreatist
   d. ritualist

4. Labeling theory states that deviance
   a. is a normal part of social life.
   b. always changes people's social identity.
   c. arises not from what people do as much as how others respond.
   d. All of the above are correct.

5. When Jake's friends began calling him a "dope-head," he left the group and spent more time smoking marijuana. He also began hanging out with others who used drugs, and by the end of the term, he had dropped out of college. Edwin Lemert would call this situation an example of
   a. primary deviance.
   b. developing secondary deviance.
   c. the formation of a deviant subculture.
   d. the beginning of retreatism.

6. A social-conflict approach claims that who a society calls deviant depends on
   a. who does and does not have power.
   b. a society's moral values.
   c. how often the behavior occurs.
   d. how harmful the behavior is.

7. Stealing a laptop computer from the study lounge in a college dorm is an example of which of the following criminal offenses?
   a. burglary
   b. motor vehicle theft
   c. robbery
   d. larceny-theft

8. The FBI's criminal statistics used in this chapter reflect
   a. all crimes that occur.
   b. offenses known to the police.
   c. offenses that result in an arrest.
   d. offenses that result in a criminal conviction.

9. About 61 percent of the people arrested for violent crime in the United States are
   a. white.
   b. African American.
   c. Hispanic.
   d. Asian.

10. Which of the following is the oldest justification for punishing an offender?
    a. deterrence
    b. societal protection
    c. retribution
    d. rehabilitation

ANSWERS: 1 (a); 2 (d); 3 (b); 4 (c); 5 (b); 6 (a); 7 (d); 8 (b); 9 (a); 10 (c).

ESSAY QUESTIONS

1. How does a sociological view of deviance differ from the commonsense notion that bad people do bad things?

2. Marc Mauer (1999) found that one in three black men between the ages of twenty and twenty-nine is in jail, on probation, or on parole. What factors, noted in this chapter, help explain this pattern?

All societies rank people so that some have more money, power, and prestige than others. What the differences are and how great they are vary from place to place and over time.

CHAPTER *8*

Social Stratification

WHAT is social stratification?

WHY does social inequality exist?

HOW do social classes in the United States differ from one another?

On April 10, 1912, the ocean liner *Titanic* slipped away from the docks of Southampton, England, on its first voyage across the North Atlantic to New York. A proud symbol of the new industrial age, the towering ship carried 2,300 men, women, and children, some of them enjoying more luxury than most travelers today could imagine. Poor passengers crowded the lower decks, journeying to what they hoped would be a better life in the United States.

Two days out, the crew received reports of icebergs in the area but paid little notice. Then, near midnight, as the ship steamed swiftly westward, a stunned lookout reported a massive shape rising out of the dark ocean directly ahead. Moments later, the *Titanic* collided with a huge iceberg, as tall as the ship itself, that split open its side as if the grand vessel were a giant tin can.

Seawater flooded into the ship's lower levels, pulling the ship down by the bow. Within twenty-five minutes of impact, people were rushing for the lifeboats. By 2:00 A.M., the bow was completely submerged, and the stern rose high above the water. Clinging to the deck, quietly observed by those in lifeboats, hundreds of helpless passengers and crew solemnly passed their final minutes before the ship disappeared into the frigid Atlantic (W. Lord, 1976).

The tragic loss of more than 1,600 lives made news around the world. Looking back on this terrible event with a sociological eye, we see that some categories of passengers had much better odds of survival than others. A reflection of that era's traditional ideas about gender, women and children boarded the lifeboats first, with the result that 80 percent of those who died were men. Class was also a factor in who survived and who did not. More than 60 percent of the passengers traveling on first-class tickets were saved because they were on the upper decks, where warnings were sounded first and lifeboats were accessible. Only 36 percent of the second-class passengers survived, and of the third-class passengers on the lower decks, only 24 percent escaped drowning. On board the *Titanic,* class meant more than the quality of accommodations—it was a matter of life or death.

The fate of the passengers on the *Titanic* dramatically illustrates how social inequality affects the way people live and sometimes whether they live at all. This chapter explores the important concept of social stratification and examines social inequality in the United States.

What Is Social Stratification?

Every society is marked by inequality, with some people having more money, schooling, health, and power than others. **Social stratification,** defined as *a system by which a society ranks categories of people in a hierarchy*, is based on four basic principles:

1. **Social stratification is a trait of society, not simply a reflection of individual differences.** Many of us think of social standing in terms of personal talent and effort, exaggerating the extent to which we control our own fate. Did a higher percentage of the first-class passengers on the *Titanic* survive because they were better swimmers than second- and third-class passengers? Hardly. They did better because of their privileged position on the ship. Similarly, children born into wealthy families are more likely than children born into poverty to enjoy good health, do well in school, succeed in a career, and live a long life. Neither the rich nor the poor are responsible for creating

The personal experience of poverty is clear in this photograph of a homeless couple spending the night in a low-cost rooming house. The main sociological insight is that, although we feel the effects of social stratification personally, our social standing is largely the result of the way society (or a world of societies) structures opportunity and reward. To the core of our being, we are all products of social stratification.

social stratification, yet this system shapes the lives of us all.

2. **Social stratification carries over from generation to generation.** We have only to look at how parents pass their social position on to their children to see that stratification is a trait of societies rather than individuals.

    Some individuals, especially in industrial societies, do experience **social mobility,** *a change in position within the social hierarchy.* Social mobility may be upward or downward. We celebrate the achievements of rare individuals such as Britney Spears and Michael Jordan, both of whom rose from modest beginnings to fame and fortune. Some people move downward in the social hierarchy because of business setbacks, unemployment, or illness. More often people move *horizontally;* that is, they switch one job for another at about the same social level. The social standing of most people remains much the same over their lifetime.

3. **Social stratification is universal but variable.** Social stratification is found everywhere. Yet *what* is unequal and *how* unequal it is vary from one society to another. In some societies, inequality is mostly a matter of prestige; in others, wealth or power is the key

element of difference. In addition, some societies contain more inequality than others.

4. **Social stratification involves not just inequality but beliefs as well.** Any system of inequality not only gives some people more than others but also defines these arrangements as fair. Like the *what* of social inequality, the explanation of *why* people should be unequal differs from society to society.

Caste and Class Systems

Sociologists distinguish between *closed systems,* which allow little change in social position, and *open systems,* which permit much more social mobility. The caste system is an example of a closed system, and the class system is more open.

THE CASTE SYSTEM

A **caste system** is *social stratification based on ascription, or birth.* A pure caste system is closed because birth alone determines a person's entire future, with little or no social mobility based on individual effort. People live out their lives in the rigid categories into which they were born, without the possibility for change for the better or worse.

An Illustration: India

Many of the world's societies, most of them agrarian, are caste systems. In India, for example, much of the population still lives in traditional villages, where the caste system persists. The Indian system identifies four major castes (or *varna,* a Sanskrit word that means "color"): Brahmin, Kshatriya, Vaishya, and Sudra. On the local level, however, each of these is composed of hundreds of subcaste groups (*jati*).

From birth, caste position determines the direction of a person's life. First, with the exception of farming, which is open to everyone, families in each caste perform one type of work, as priests, soldiers, barbers, leather workers, sweepers, and so on.

Second, a caste system demands that people marry others of the same ranking. If people were to have "mixed" marriages with members of other castes, what rank would their children hold? Sociologists call this pattern of marrying within a social category *endogamous* marriage (*endo-* stems from the Greek word meaning "within"). According to tradition, Indian parents select their children's marriage partners, often before the children reach their teens.

Third, caste guides everyday life by keeping people in the company of "their own kind." Norms reinforce this practice by teaching, for instance, that a "purer" person of a higher caste position is "polluted" by contact with someone of lower standing.

Fourth, caste systems rest on powerful cultural beliefs. Indian culture is built on the Hindu tradition that doing the caste's life work and accepting an arranged marriage are moral duties.

YOUR TURN

Are there elements of caste in U.S. society? To what extent do parents pass on their social position to children? What about the idea that there are "women's jobs" and "men's jobs"?

Caste and Agrarian Life

Caste systems are typical of agrarian societies because agriculture demands a lifelong routine of hard work. By teaching a sense of moral duty, a caste system ensures that people are disciplined for a lifetime of work and are willing to perform the same jobs as their parents. Thus the caste system has hung on in rural India more than sixty years after being formally outlawed. People living in the industrial cities of India have many more choices about work and marriage partners than people in rural areas.

Another country dominated by caste is South Africa, although the racial system of *apartheid* is now in decline. The Thinking Globally box takes a closer look.

THE CLASS SYSTEM

Because a modern economy must put people to work in many occupations other than farming, it depends on developing people's talents in many diverse fields. This process of schooling and specialization gives rise to a **class system,** *social stratification based on both birth and individual achievement.*

Class systems are more open than caste systems, so people who gain schooling and skills may experience social mobility. As a result, class distinctions become blurred, and even blood relatives may have different social standings. Categorizing people according to their color, sex, or social background comes to be seen as wrong in modern societies as all people gain political rights and, in principle, equal standing before the law. In addition, work is no longer fixed at birth but involves some personal choice. Greater individuality also translates into more freedom in selecting a marital partner.

Meritocracy

The concept of **meritocracy** refers to *social stratification based on personal merit.* Because industrial societies need to develop a broad range of abilities (beyond farming), stratification is based not just on the accident of birth but also on *merit* (from a Latin word meaning "earned"), which includes a person's knowledge, abilities, and effort. A rough measure of merit is a person's job and how well it is done. To increase meritocracy, industrial societies expand equality of opportunity and teach people to expect unequal rewards based on individual performance.

In a pure meritocracy, which has never existed, social position would depend entirely on a person's ability and effort. Such a system would have ongoing social mobility, blurring social categories as individuals continuously move up or down in the system, depending on their latest performance.

Caste societies define merit in terms of loyalty to the system—that is, dutifully performing whatever job comes with a person's birth. Caste systems waste human potential, but they are very orderly. A need for order is the reason that industrial societies keep some elements of caste—such as letting wealth pass from generation to generation—rather than becoming complete meritocracies. A pure meritocracy would weaken families and other social groupings. After all, economic performance is not everything: Would we want to evaluate our family members solely on how successful they are in their jobs outside of the home? Probably not. Class systems in industrial societies move toward meritocracy to

Race as Caste: A Report from South Africa

At the southern tip of the African continent lies South Africa, a country about the size of Alaska with a population of about 47 million. For 300 years, the native Africans who lived there were ruled by white people, first by Dutch traders and farmers in the mid-seventeenth century and then by the British, who colonized the area in the nineteenth century. By the early 1900s, the British had taken over the entire country, naming it the Union of South Africa.

In 1961, the nation declared its independence from Britain, calling itself the Republic of South Africa, but freedom for the black majority was still decades away. To ensure their control over the black population, whites enforced a policy of *apartheid,* or racial separation. Apartheid, written into law in 1948, denied blacks citizenship, ownership of land, and any voice in the government. As a lower caste, blacks received little schooling and performed menial, low-paying jobs. White families of modest wealth had at least one black household servant.

The white minority claimed that apartheid protected their cultural traditions from people they believed to be inferior. When blacks resisted apartheid, whites used brutal military repression to maintain their power.

Even so, steady resistance—especially from younger blacks, who demanded a political voice and economic opportunity—gradually forced change. Criticism from other industrial nations added to the pressure. By the mid-1980s, the tide began to turn as the South African government granted limited rights to people of mixed race and Asian ancestry. This was followed by the rights for all people to form labor unions, to enter various occupations once limited to whites, and to own property. Officials also repealed laws that separated the races in public places.

The pace of change increased in 1990 with the release from prison of Nelson Mandela, who led the fight against apartheid. In 1994, the first national election open to all races made Mandela president, ending centuries of white minority rule.

Despite this dramatic political change, social position in South Africa is still based on race. About one-third of black South Africans have no work, and the majority remain dirt poor. The worst off are the 7 million known as *ukuhleleleka,* which means "marginal people" in the Xhosa language. Soweto-by-the-Sea may sound like the name of a summer getaway, but it is home to thousands of people crammed into ramshackle huts made from packing cases, corrugated metal, cardboard, and other discarded materials. There is little electricity for lights or refrigeration. Without plumbing, people must use buckets to haul sewerage; women line up to take a turn at a single water tap that serves more than 1,000 people. Jobs are hard to come by, and those who do find work are lucky to earn $250 a month.

South Africa's current president, Thabo Mbeki, elected in 1999, leads a nation that is still crippled by its history of racial caste. Tourism is on the upswing and holds the promise of an economic boom in years to come, but the country can shed its past only by providing real opportunity to all its people.

WHAT DO YOU THINK?

1. How has race been a form of caste in South Africa?

2. Although apartheid is no longer law, why does racial inequality continue to shape South African society?

3. Does race operate as an element of caste in the United States? Explain your answer.

Sources: Fredrickson (1981), Wren (1991), Hawthorne (1999), and Mabry & Masland (1999).

Jamie Foxx is among the "celebrities" who stand out in today's popular culture. What we "celebrate" in Foxx is not only his acting ability but the fact that he was born to a family with a very modest income, rising on the basis of his talents to superstardom. In explaining any person's social standing, how much importance should we attribute to birth and how much to individual talent and effort?

promote productivity and efficiency but keep caste elements, such as family, to maintain order and social unity.

Status Consistency

Status consistency is *the degree of consistency in a person's social standing across various dimensions of social inequality.* A caste system has little social mobility and high status consistency, so the typical person has the same relative standing with regard to wealth, power, and prestige. However, the greater mobility of class systems produces less status consistency. In the United States, most college professors with advanced degrees enjoy high social prestige but earn only modest incomes. Low status consistency means that *classes* are much harder to define than *castes*.

CASTE AND CLASS: THE UNITED KINGDOM

The mix of meritocracy and caste in class systems is well illustrated by the United Kingdom (Great Britain—composed of England, Wales, and Scotland—and Northern Ireland), an industrial nation with a long agrarian history.

The Estate System

In the Middle Ages, England had a castelike system of three *estates*. The *first estate* was the clergy, who were thought to speak with the authority of God. Some clergy were local priests, who lived simple lives. But the highest church officials lived in palaces and presided over an organization that owned much land (which was the major source of wealth); they also had a great deal of power to shape the political events of the day.

The *second estate* was a hereditary nobility, making up perhaps 5 percent of the population. The royal family—the king and queen at the top of the power structure—as well as lesser nobles (including those titled as dukes, earls, and barons) together owned most of the nation's land. Most of these men and women had no occupation at all; they thought that engaging in a trade or any other work for income was beneath them. Well tended by servants, nobles used their leisure time to develop skills in horseback riding and warfare and to cultivate refined tastes in art, music, and literature.

To prevent vast landholdings from being divided by heirs when the nobles died, the law of *primogeniture* (from Latin, meaning "firstborn") stated that all landholdings passed to the oldest son or other male relation. Younger sons had to find other means of support. Some became leaders in the church, where they would live as well as they were used to. Others became military officers or judges or took up professions considered honorable for gentlemen. In an age when no woman could inherit her father's property and few women had the chance to earn a living on their own, a noble daughter depended for her security on marrying well.

Below the nobility and the clergy, the vast majority of men and women formed the *third estate,* or commoners. Most commoners were serfs who worked the land owned by nobles or the church. Unlike members of the first and second estates, most commoners had little schooling and were illiterate.

As the Industrial Revolution expanded England's economy with the growth of factories, some commoners living in cities made enough money to challenge the nobility. More emphasis on meritocracy, the growing importance of money, and the expansion of schooling and legal rights eventually blurred social rankings and gave rise to a class system.

Perhaps it is a sign of the times that these days, traditional titles are put up for sale by British nobles who need money. In 1996, for example, Earl Spencer—the brother of Princess Diana—sold his title, Lord of Wimbledon, to raise the $300,000 he needed to redo the plumbing in one of his large homes (McKee, 1996).

The United Kingdom Today

The United Kingdom has a class system, but caste elements of the past are still evident today. A small number of British families still holds considerable inherited wealth and enjoys the highest prestige, schooling at excellent universities, and political influence. A traditional monarch, Queen Elizabeth II, is the United Kingdom's head of state, and Parliament's House of Lords is composed of "peers," about half of whom are of noble birth. However, control of government has passed to the House of Commons, where the prime minister and other ministers typically reach their positions by achievement—winning an election—rather than by birth.

 London's *Sunday Times* publishes a list of the richest people in Great Britain and other countries. Find the "Rich List" at http://www.sunday-times.co.uk/richlist/

Further down in the class hierarchy, roughly one-fourth of the British people fall into the middle class. Some earn comfortable incomes from professions and businesses and are likely to have investments in the form of stocks and bonds. Below the middle class, perhaps half of all Britons consider themselves "working-class," earning modest incomes through manual labor. The remaining one-fourth of the British people make up the lower class, the poor who lack steady work or who work full time but are paid too little to live comfortably. Most lower-class Britons live in the nation's northern and western regions, which have been plagued by closings of mines and factories.

Today's British class system has a mix of caste elements and meritocracy, producing a highly stratified society with some opportunity to move upward or downward. One result of the historical estate system is that social mobility occurs less often in the United Kingdom than in the United States (Kerckhoff, Campbell, & Winfield-Laird, 1985). This more rigid system of inequality in the United Kingdom is reflected in the importance attached to accent. Distinctive patterns of speech develop when people are set off from one another over many generations. In the United States, accent is a clue to where a person lives or grew up (we can easily identify a midwestern "twang" or a southern "drawl"). In the United Kingdom, however, accent is a mark of social class (upper-class people speak the "King's English," but most people speak like "commoners"). So different are these two accents that the British seem to be, as the saying goes, "a single people divided by a common language."

Have you ever heard distinctive accents in the speech of poor people in rural areas or the inner cities of the United States? What do such accents suggest about people's social history?

CLASSLESS SOCIETIES? THE FORMER SOVIET UNION

Nowhere in the world do we find a society without some degree of social inequality. Yet some nations have claimed to be classless.

The Russian Revolution

The Union of Soviet Socialist Republics (USSR), which rivaled the United States as a military superpower in the mid- to late twentieth century, was born out of a revolution in Russia in 1917. The Russian Revolution ended the feudal estate system ruled by a hereditary nobility and transferred most farms, factories, and other productive property from private ownership to state control. Following the lead of Karl Marx, who believed that private ownership of property was the basis for social classes, Soviet leaders boasted of becoming a classless society.

Critics, however, pointed out that based on their jobs, the Soviet people were actually stratified into four unequal categories. At the top were high government officials, or *apparatchiks*. Next came the Soviet intelligentsia, including lower government officials, college professors, scientists, physicians, and engineers. Below them were manual workers and, at the lowest level, the rural peasantry.

In reality, the Soviet Union was not really classless at all. But putting factories, farms, colleges, and hospitals under state control did create more economic equality (although with sharp differences in power) than in capitalist societies such as the United States.

The Modern Russian Federation

In 1985, Mikhail Gorbachev came to power with a new economic program known as *perestroika*, meaning "restructuring." Gorbachev saw that although the Soviet system had reduced economic inequality, living standards lagged far behind those of other industrial nations. Gorbachev tried to generate economic growth by reducing the inefficient centralized control of the economy.

Gorbachev's economic reforms turned into one of the most dramatic social movements in history. People throughout Eastern Europe blamed their poverty and lack of basic freedoms on the repressive ruling class of Communist party officials. Beginning in 1989, people throughout Eastern Europe toppled their socialist governments, and in 1991, the Soviet Union itself collapsed, with its largest republic remaking itself as the Russian Federation.

The Soviet Union's story shows that social inequality involves more than economic resources. Soviet society may not have had the extremes of wealth and poverty found in the United Kingdom and the United States. But an elite class

In recent decades, the government of China has permitted a market economy to operate in limited areas of the country. The result has been increased production and the emergence of a new business class with a lifestyle similar to that of wealthy people in the United States.

existed all the same, based on political power rather than wealth.

What about social mobility in so-called classless societies? In the twentieth century, there was as much upward social mobility in the Soviet Union as in the United Kingdom or the United States. Rapidly expanding industry and government drew many poor rural peasants into factories and offices. This trend illustrates what sociologists call **structural social mobility,** *a shift in the social position of large numbers of people due more to changes in society than to individual efforts.*

 November 24, Odessa, Ukraine. The first snow of our voyage flies over the decks as our ship docks at Odessa, the former Soviet Union's southern port on the Black Sea. Not far from the dock, we gaze up at the Potemkin Steps, the steep stairway up to the city, where the first

shots of the Russian Revolution rang out. It has been six years since our last visit; and much has changed; indeed, the Soviet Union itself has collapsed. Has life improved? For some people, certainly. There are now chic boutiques in which well-dressed shoppers buy fine wines, designer clothes, and imported perfumes. Outside, shiny new Volvos, Mercedes, and even a few Cadillacs stand out against the small Ladas from the "old days." But for most people, life seems much worse. Flea markets line the curbs as families sell their home furnishings. When meat sells for $4 a pound and the average person earns about $30 a month, people become desperate. Even the city has to save money by turning off street lights after 8:00 P.M. The spirits of most people seem as dim as Odessa's streets.

During the 1990s, structural social mobility in the Russian Federation turned downward. One indicator is that the average life span for men dropped by eight years and for women by two years. Many factors are involved, including Russia's poor health care system, but the Russian people clearly have suffered in the turbulent period of economic change that began in 1991 (Bohlen, 1998; Gerber & Hout, 1998).

In the long run, closing inefficient state industries may improve the Russian Federation's economic performance. But in the short run, most citizens face hard times as living standards fall. As businesses have returned to private ownership, the gulf between rich and poor has grown. Today, some Russians praise the recent changes while others hang on, patiently hoping for better times.

CHINA: EMERGING SOCIAL CLASSES

Sweeping political and economic change has affected not just the Russian Federation but also the People's Republic of China. After the Communist revolution in 1949, the state took control of all farms, factories, and other productive property. Communist party leader Mao Zedong declared all work to be equally important, so officially, social classes no longer existed.

The new program greatly reduced economic inequality. But as in the Soviet Union, social differences remained. The country was ruled by a political elite with enormous power and considerable privilege; below them were managers of large factories and skilled professionals; next came industrial workers; at the bottom were rural peasants, who were not even allowed to leave their villages to migrate to cities.

Further economic change came in 1978, when Mao died and Deng Xiaoping became China's leader. The state gradually loosened its hold on the economy, allowing a new class of business owners to emerge. Communist party leaders remain in control of the country, and some have prospered as they have joined the ranks of the small but wealthy elite who control new, privately run industries. China's economy has experienced rapid growth, and the nation has now moved into the middle-income category. By and large, this new prosperity has been concentrated in coastal areas where living standards have soared far above those in China's rural interior.

In China, a new class system is emerging with a mix of the old political hierarchy and a new business hierarchy. Economic inequality in China has increased and, as Figure 8–1 shows, it is almost as great as in the United States. As China becomes a global economic power, new patterns of inequality will emerge, reminding us that social stratification is highly dynamic.

IDEOLOGY: THE POWER BEHIND STRATIFICATION

How do societies persist without sharing their resources more equally? The British estate system lasted for centuries, and for 2,000 years people in India accepted the idea that they should be privileged or poor based on the accident of birth.

A major reason that social hierarchies endure is **ideology,** *cultural beliefs that justify particular social arrangements, including patterns of inequality.* A belief—for example, the idea that the rich are smart and the poor are lazy—is ideological to the extent that it supports inequality by defining it as fair.

Plato and Marx on Ideology

According to the ancient Greek philosopher Plato (427–347 B.C.E.), every culture considers some type of inequality fair. Although Karl Marx understood this, he was far more critical of inequality than Plato. Marx criticized capitalist societies for defending wealth and power in the hands of a few as a "law of the marketplace." Capitalist law, he continued, defines the right to own property, which encourages money to remain within the same families from one generation to the next. In short, Marx concluded, culture and institutions combine to support a society's elite, which is why established hierarchies last a long time.

Historical Patterns of Ideology

Ideology changes along with a society's economy and technology. Because agrarian societies depend on most people's performing a lifetime of labor, they develop caste systems that make doing the duties of a person's social position or "station" a moral responsibility. With the rise of industrial capitalism, an ideology of meritocracy arises, defining wealth and power as prizes to be won by those who perform

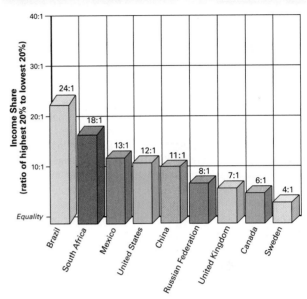

FIGURE 8-1 Economic Inequality in Selected Countries

Many low- and middle-income countries have greater economic inequality than the United States. But this country has more economic inequality than most high-income nations.

These data are the most recent available, representing income share for various years between 1999 and 2004.

Sources: U.S. Census Bureau (2005) and World Bank (2006).

the best. This change means that the poor—often the targets of charity under feudalism—are looked down on under industrial capitalism as personally undeserving. This harsh view is linked to the work of Herbert Spencer, as explained in the Thinking Critically box on page 214.

History shows how difficult it is to change social stratification. However, challenges to the status quo always arise. Traditional ideas about "a woman's place," for example, have given way to economic opportunity for women in societies today. The continuing progress toward racial equality in South Africa is another case of widespread rejection of the ideology of apartheid.

The Functions of Social Stratification

Why does social stratification exist at all? According to the structural-functional approach, social stratification plays a vital part in the operation of society. This argument was

Is Getting Rich "the Survival of the Fittest"?

"The survival of the fittest"—we have all heard these words used to describe society as a competitive jungle. The phrase was coined by one of sociology's pioneers, Herbert Spencer (1820–1903), whose ideas about social inequality are still widespread today.

Spencer, who lived in England, eagerly followed the work of the natural scientist Charles Darwin (1809–1882). Darwin's theory of biological evolution held that a species changes physically over many generations as it adapts to the natural environment. Spencer distorted Darwin's theory, applying it to the operation of society: Society became the "jungle," with the "fittest" people rising to wealth and the "failures" sinking into miserable poverty.

It is no surprise that Spencer's views were popular among the rising U.S. industrialists of the day. John D. Rockefeller (1839–1937), who made a vast fortune building the oil industry, recited Spencer's "social gospel" to young children in Sunday school. As Rockefeller saw it, the growth of giant corporations—and the astounding wealth of their owners—was merely the result of the survival of the fittest, a basic fact of nature. Neither Spencer nor Rockefeller had much sympathy for the poor, seeing poverty as evidence of individuals' failing to measure up in a competitive world. Spencer opposed social welfare programs because he thought they penalized society's "best" people (through taxes) and rewarded its "worst" members (through welfare benefits).

Today, sociologists point out that society is far from a meritocracy, as Spencer claimed. And it is not the case that companies or individuals who generate lots of money necessarily benefit society. Yet Spencer's view that people get what they deserve in life remains part of our individualistic culture.

WHAT DO YOU THINK?

1. What did Herbert Spencer mean when he said that society encourages "the survival of the fittest"?

2. Why are Spencer's ideas still popular in the United States today?

3. Is how much you earn a good measure of your importance to society? Why or why not?

presented many years ago by Kingsley Davis and Wilbert Moore (1945).

THE DAVIS-MOORE THESIS

The **Davis-Moore thesis** states that *social stratification has beneficial consequences for the operation of a society.* How else, ask Davis and Moore, can we explain the fact that some form of social stratification has been found in every society?

Davis and Moore note that modern societies have hundreds of occupational positions of varying importance. Certain jobs—say, washing windows or answering a telephone—are fairly easy and can be performed by almost anyone. Other jobs—such as designing a new generation of computers or transplanting human organs—are very difficult and demand the scarce talents of people with extensive (and expensive) training.

Therefore, Davis and Moore explain, the greater the functional importance of a position, the more rewards a society attaches to it. This strategy promotes productivity and efficiency because rewarding important work with income, prestige, power, or leisure encourages people to do these things and to work better, longer, and harder. In short, unequal rewards (which is what social stratification is) benefit society as a whole.

Davis and Moore claim that any society could be egalitarian, but only to the extent that people are willing to let *anyone* perform *any* job. Equality also demands that someone who performs a job poorly be rewarded just as much as someone who performs the job well. Such a system clearly offers little incentive for people to try their best. The overall effect of equality, therefore, is to reduce a society's productive efficiency.

The Davis-Moore thesis suggests the reason for some form of stratification; it does not state precisely what rewards a society should give to any occupational position or how unequal rewards should be. It merely points out that positions a society considers crucial must offer enough rewards to draw talented people away from less important work.

Following Davis and Moore's thinking, why do professors give grades from A to F? What would happen if they gave every student the same grade? Explain.

CRITICAL REVIEW Although the Davis-Moore thesis is an important contribution to understanding social stratification, it has provoked criticism. Melvin Tumin (1953) wondered, first of all, how we assess the importance of a particular occupation. Perhaps the high rewards our society gives to physicians result partly from deliberate efforts by medical schools to limit the supply of physicians and thereby increase the demand for their services.

Furthermore, do rewards actually reflect the contribution someone makes to society? With income approaching $300 million per year, Oprah Winfrey earns more in one day than the U.S. president earns all year. Would anyone argue that hosting a talk show is more important than leading a country? And what about members of the U.S. military in Iraq? Facing the risks of combat, they earn only about $12,000 a year. Then there are many cases like that of Larry Ellison, the chief executive officer of Oracle, who even as the value of his company slid downward still earned $700 million, an amount it would take a typical U.S. soldier some 60,000 years to earn (M. Benjamin, 2002; Broder, 2002; Dunn, 2003). Do corporate executives deserve such megasalaries for their "contributions to society"?

Second, Tumin claimed that Davis and Moore ignore how the caste elements of social stratification can *prevent* the development of individual talent. Born to privilege, rich children have opportunities to develop their abilities, which is something many gifted poor children never have.

Third, living in a society that places so much importance on money, we tend to overestimate the importance of high-paying work; how do stockbrokers or people who trade international currencies really contribute to society? For the same reason, it is difficult for us to see the importance of work

Do corporate CEOs deserve their high salaries? The AFL-CIO offers a critical view at its Web site, where it tracks CEO salaries: http://www.aflcio.org/corporateamerica/paywatch

not oriented toward making money, such as parenting, creative writing, playing in a symphony, or just being a good friend to someone in need (Packard, 2002).

Finally, by suggesting that social stratification benefits all of society, the Davis-Moore thesis ignores how social inequality promotes conflict and can even provoke revolution. This criticism leads to the social-conflict approach, which provides a very different explanation for social inequality.

YOUR LEARNING State the Davis-Moore thesis in your own words. What are Tumin's criticisms of this thesis?

Stratification and Conflict

Social-conflict analysis argues that rather than benefiting society as a whole, stratification provides some people with advantages over others. This analysis draws heavily on the ideas of Karl Marx, with contributions from Max Weber.

KARL MARX: CLASS CONFLICT

As Marx saw it, the Industrial Revolution promised humanity a society free from want. Yet during Marx's lifetime, the capitalist economy had done little to improve the lives of most people. Marx set out to explain a glaring contradiction: how, in a society so rich, so many could be so poor.

In Marx's view, social stratification is rooted in people's relationship to the means of production. People either own productive property (such as factories and businesses) or sell their labor to others. In feudal Europe, the nobility and the church owned the productive land; the peasants toiled as farmers. Under industrial capitalism, the nobility was replaced by **capitalists** (sometimes called the *bourgeoisie*, a French word meaning "town dwellers"), *people who own and operate factories and other businesses in pursuit of profits.* Peasants became the **proletarians,** *working people who sell their labor for wages.* Capitalists and proletarians have opposing interests and are separated by a vast gulf of wealth and power, making class conflict inevitable.

Marx lived during the nineteenth century, a time when a small number of industrialists in the United States were amassing great fortunes. Andrew Carnegie, J. P. Morgan, and John Jacob Astor (one of the few rich passengers to drown on the *Titanic*) lived in fabulous mansions that were filled with priceless works of art and staffed by dozens of servants. Even by today's standards, their incomes were staggering. For example, Carnegie earned more than $20 million in 1900 (more than $100 million in today's dollars), when the average worker earned roughly $500 a year (Baltzell, 1964; Pessen, 1990).

In time, Marx believed, the working majority would overthrow the capitalists once and for all. Capitalism would bring about its own downfall, Marx reasoned, because it makes workers poorer and poorer and gives them little control over what they make or how they make it. Under capitalism, work produces only **alienation,** *the experience of isolation and misery resulting from powerlessness.*

To replace capitalism, Marx imagined a *socialist* system that would meet the needs of all rather than just the needs of the elite few: "The proletarians have nothing to lose but their

SOCIAL STRATIFICATION **CHAPTER 8** **215**

chains. They have a world to win" (Marx & Engels, 1972:362, orig. 1848).

CRITICAL REVIEW   Marx has had enormous influence on sociological thinking. But his revolutionary ideas, calling for the overthrow of capitalist society, also make his work highly controversial.

One of the strongest criticisms of the Marxist approach is that it ignores a central idea of the Davis-Moore thesis: that a system of unequal rewards is needed to place people in the right jobs and to motivate people to work hard. Marx separated reward from performance; his egalitarian ideal was based on the principle "from each according to ability, to each according to need" (Marx & Engels, 1972:388, orig. 1848). However, failure to reward individual performance may be precisely what caused the low productivity of the former Soviet Union and other socialist economies around the world. Defenders respond to such criticism by asking why we assume that humanity is inherently selfish rather than social; individual rewards are not the only way to motivate people to perform their social roles (M. S. Clark, 1991; Fiske, 1991).

A second problem is that the revolutionary change Marx predicted has failed to happen, at least in advanced capitalist societies. The next section explains why.

✅ **YOUR LEARNING**   How does Marx's view of social stratification differ from the Davis-Moore thesis?

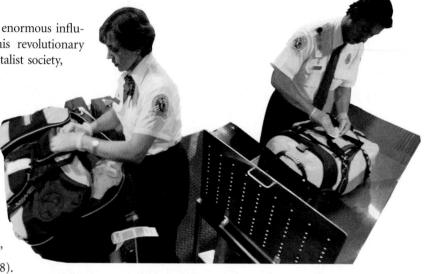

Most workers in the United States today have service jobs; instead of farming or working in a factory, they work with other people. Some analysts say that the spread of service work has made many people feel that they are "getting ahead" and reduced class conflict in U.S. society; others claim that many service jobs actually provide lower pay, fewer benefits, and less job security than many factory jobs of the past. Which argument do you think is more correct? Why?

WHY NO MARXIST REVOLUTION?

Despite Marx's prediction, capitalism is still thriving. Why have industrial workers not overthrown capitalism? Ralf Dahrendorf (1959) suggested four reasons:

1. **Fragmentation of the capitalist class.** Today, tens of millions of stockholders, rather than single families, own most large companies. Day-to-day corporate operations are in the hands of a large class of managers, who may or may not be major stockholders. With stock so widely held—about 50 percent of U.S. households own at least some stocks—more and more people have a direct stake in the capitalist system.

2. **A higher standard of living.** As Chapter 12 ("Economics and Politics") explains, a century ago, most U.S. workers were in factories or on farms in **blue-collar occupations,** *lower-prestige jobs that involve*

mostly manual labor. Today, most workers are in **white-collar occupations,** *higher-prestige jobs that involve mostly mental activity.* These jobs are in sales, management, and other service fields. Most of today's white-collar workers do not think of themselves as an "industrial proletariat." Just as important, the average income in the United States rose almost tenfold over the course of the twentieth century, even allowing for inflation, and the number of hours in the workweek decreased. Most workers today are far better off than workers were a century ago, an example of structural social mobility. One result of this rising standard of living is that more people support the status quo.

3. **More worker organizations.** Workers today have the right to form labor unions that make demands of management, backed by threats of work slowdowns and strikes. As a result, labor disputes are settled without threatening the capitalist system.

4. **Greater legal protections.** Over the past century, new laws made the workplace safer, and unemployment insurance, disability protection, and Social Security now provide workers with greater financial security.

A Counterpoint

These developments suggest that our society has smoothed many of capitalism's rough edges. Yet many observers claim that Marx's analysis of capitalism is still largely valid (Domhoff, 1983; Stephens, 1986; Boswell & Dixon, 1993; Hout, Brooks, & Manza, 1993). First, wealth remains highly concentrated, with 40 percent of all privately owned property in the hands of 1 percent of the U.S. population (Keister, 2000). Second, many of today's white-collar jobs offer no more income, security, or satisfaction than factory work did a century ago. Third, many benefits enjoyed by today's workers came about through the class conflict Marx described; workers still struggle to hold on to what they have; and in recent years, many workers have actually lost pensions and other benefits. Fourth, although workers have gained legal protections, ordinary people still face disadvantages that the law cannot overcome. Therefore, social-conflict theorists conclude, the absence of a socialist revolution in the United States does not mean Marx was wrong about capitalism.

YOUR TURN

Using what you have learned about social inequality in the United States so far, how correct do you think Marx was about the role of capitalism? Explain your answer.

MAX WEBER: CLASS, STATUS, AND POWER

Max Weber agreed with Karl Marx that social stratification causes social conflict, but he viewed Marx's two-class model as simplistic. Instead, he viewed social stratification as involving three distinct dimensions of inequality.

The first dimension, economic inequality—the issue so important to Marx—Weber called *class* position. Weber did not think of classes as well-defined categories but as a continuum ranging from high to low. Weber's second dimension is *status,* or social prestige, and the third is *power*.

The Socioeconomic Status Hierarchy

Marx viewed prestige and power as simple reflections of economic position and did not treat them as distinct dimensions of inequality. But Weber noted that status consistency in modern societies often is quite low: A local government official might exercise great power yet have little wealth or social prestige.

Weber, then, characterizes stratification in industrial societies as a multidimensional ranking rather than a hierarchy of clearly defined classes. In line with Weber's think-

ing, sociologists use the term **socioeconomic status (SES)** to refer to *a composite ranking based on various dimensions of social inequality*.

Inequality in History

Weber observed that each of his three dimensions of social inequality stands out at a different time in the history of human societies. Status or social prestige is the main dimension of difference in agrarian societies, taking the form of honor. Members of these societies gain prestige by conforming to cultural norms that apply to their particular rank.

Industrialization and the development of capitalism level traditional rankings based on birth but generate striking financial inequality. Thus in an industrial society, the crucial difference between people is the economic dimension of class.

Over time, industrial societies witness the growth of a bureaucratic state. Bigger government and the spread of all types of other organizations make power more important in the stratification system. Especially in socialist societies, where government regulates many aspects of life, high-ranking officials become the new ruling elite.

This historical analysis points to a final difference between Weber and Marx. Marx thought societies could eliminate social stratification by abolishing private ownership of productive property. Weber doubted that overthrowing capitalism would significantly lessen social stratification. It might lessen economic differences, he reasoned, but socialism would increase inequality by expanding government and concentrating power in the hands of a political elite. Popular uprisings against socialist bureaucracies in Eastern Europe and the former Soviet Union support Weber's position.

CRITICAL REVIEW Weber's multidimensional view of social stratification influenced sociologists enormously and made the concept of socioeconomic status hierarchy popular. But critics (particularly those who favor Marx's ideas) argue that although social class boundaries may have blurred, industrial and postindustrial nations still show striking patterns of social inequality.

As will be explained shortly, economic inequality has increased recently in the United States. Although some people favor Weber's multidimensional hierarchy, others think, in light of this trend, that Marx's view of the rich versus the poor is closer to the truth.

✔ **YOUR LEARNING** According to Weber, which of the three dimensions of social inequality would you expect to be the most important in United States? Why?

When Class Gets Personal: Picking (with) Your Friends

The sound of banjo music drifted across the field late one summer afternoon. I lay down my brush, climbed over the fence I had been painting, and walked toward the sound of the music to see what was going on. That's how I met my neighbor Max, a retired factory worker who lived just up the road. Max was a pretty good "picker," and within an hour, I was back on his porch with my guitar. I called Howard, a friend who teaches at the college, and he showed up a little while later, six-string in hand. The three of us jammed for a couple of hours, smiling all the while.

The next morning, I was mowing the grass in front of the house when Max came walking down the road. I turned off the lawnmower as he came down the driveway. "Hi, Max," I said. "Thanks for having us over last night. I really had fun."

"Don't mention it," Max responded. Then he shook his head a little and added, "Ya know, I was thinkin' after you guys left. I mean, it was really somethin' how you guys looked like you were having a great time. With somebody like *me!*"

"Well, yeah," I replied, not sure what he meant. "You sure played better than we did."

Max looked down at the ground, embarrassed by the compliment. Then he added, "What I mean is that you guys were having a good time with somebody like *me*. You're both professors, right? *Doctors,* even . . ."

WHAT DO YOU THINK?

1. Why did Max assume that two college teachers would not enjoy spending time with him?

2. How does his reaction suggest that people take social position personally?

3. Can you think of a similar experience you have had with someone of a different social position?

Stratification and Interaction

Because social stratification has to do with the way an entire society is organized, sociologists (Marx and Weber included) typically treat it as a macro-level issue. But a micro-level analysis of social stratification is also important because people's social standing affects their everyday interaction.

In most communities, people interact primarily with others of about the same social standing. To some extent, this is because people tend to live with others like themselves. As we observe people during the course of our everyday activities, such as walking in a downtown shopping area, we see that couples or groups tend to be made up of individuals whose appearance and shopping habits are similar. People with very different social standing commonly keep their distance from one another. Well-dressed people walking down the street on their way to an expensive restaurant, for example, might move across the sidewalk or even cross the street to avoid getting close to others they think are homeless people. The Applying Sociology box gives another example of how differences in social class position can affect interaction.

Finally, just about everyone realizes that the way we dress, the car we drive (or the bus we ride), and even the food and drink we order at the campus snack bar say something about our budget and personal tastes. Sociologists use the term **conspicuous consumption** to refer to *buying and using products with an eye to the "statement" they make about social position.* Ignoring the water fountain in favor of pay-

APPLYING THEORY

Social Stratification

	Structural-Functional Approach	Social-Conflict Approach	Symbolic-Interaction Approach
What is the level of analysis?	Macro-level	Macro-level	Micro-level
What is social stratification?	Stratification is a system of unequal rewards that benefits society as a whole.	Stratification is a division of a society's resources that benefits some and harms others.	Stratification is a factor that guides people's interaction in everyday life.
What is the reason for our social position?	Social position reflects personal talents and abilities in a competitive economy.	Social position reflects the way society divides resources.	The products we consume all say something about social position.
Are unequal rewards fair?	Yes. Unequal rewards boost economic production by encouraging people to work harder and try new ideas. Linking greater rewards to more important work is widely accepted.	No. Unequal rewards only serve to divide society, creating "haves" and "have-nots." There is widespread opposition to social inequality.	Maybe. People may or may not define inequality as fair. People may view their social position as a measure of self-worth, justifying inequality in terms of personal differences.

ing for bottled water tells people that you have extra money to spend. And no one needs a $100,000 automobile to get around, of course, but being seen in such a vehicle says "I have arrived" in more ways than one.

CRITICAL REVIEW A micro-level analysis of social stratification helps us see patterns of social inequality in our everyday lives. At the same time, the limitation of this approach is that it has little to say about how and why broad patterns of social inequality exist, which was the focus of the structural-functional and social-conflict approaches. The Applying Theory table summarizes the contributions of the three theoretical approaches to social stratification.

✓ YOUR LEARNING Point to several ways in which social stratification shapes the way people of different social positions behave in the course of a typical day.

Stratification and Technology: A Global Perspective

We can weave together a number of observations made in this chapter by considering the relationship between a society's technology and its type of social stratification. This analysis draws on Gerhard Lenski's model of sociocultural evolution discussed in Chapter 2 ("Culture").

HUNTING AND GATHERING SOCIETIES

With simple technology, hunters and gatherers produce only what is necessary for day-to-day living. Some people may produce more than others, but the group's survival depends on all sharing what they have. Thus no categories of people are better off than others.

HORTICULTURAL, PASTORAL, AND AGRARIAN SOCIETIES

As technological advances create a surplus, social inequality increases. In horticultural and pastoral societies, a small elite controls most of the surplus. Larger-scale agriculture is more productive still, and striking inequality—as great as at any time in history—places the nobility in an almost god-like position over the masses.

INDUSTRIAL SOCIETIES

Industrialization pushes inequality downward. Prompted by the need to develop people's talents, meritocracy takes hold and weakens the power of traditional elites. Industrial productivity also raises the living standards of the historically poor majority. Specialized work demands schooling for all, sharply reducing illiteracy. A literate population demands a greater voice in political decision making, reducing social inequality and lessening men's domination of women.

Over time, even wealth becomes somewhat less concentrated (contradicting Marx's prediction). In the 1920s,

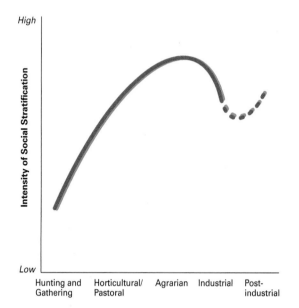

FIGURE 8-2 Social Stratification and Technological Development: The Kuznets Curve

The Kuznets curve shows that greater technological sophistication generally is accompanied by more pronounced social stratification. The trend reverses itself as industrial societies relax rigid, castelike distinctions in favor of greater opportunity and equality under the law. Political rights are more widely extended, and there is even some leveling of economic differences. However, the emergence of postindustrial society has brought an upturn in economic inequality, as indicated by the broken line added by the author.

Source: Created by the author, based on Kuznets (1955) and Lenski (1966).

the richest 1 percent of U.S. families owned about 40 percent of all wealth, a figure that fell to 30 percent by the 1980s (Williamson & Lindert, 1980; Beeghley, 1989; U.S. House of Representatives, 1991). Such trends help explain why Marxist revolutions occurred in *agrarian* societies, such as Russia (1917), Cuba (1959), and Nicaragua (1979), where social inequality is most pronounced, rather than in *industrial* societies as Marx predicted. However, wealth inequality turned upward again after 1990 and is once again about the same as it was in the 1920s (Keister, 2000).

THE KUZNETS CURVE

In human history, then, technological advances first increase but then moderate the intensity of social stratification. Greater inequality is functional for agrarian societies, but industrial societies benefit from a less unequal system. This historical trend, recognized by the Nobel Prize–winning economist Simon Kuznets (1955, 1966), is illustrated by the Kuznets curve, shown in Figure 8–2.

Social inequality around the world generally confirms the Kuznets curve. Global Map 8–1 shows that high-income nations that have passed through the industrial era (including the United States, Canada, and the nations of Western Europe) have somewhat less income inequality than nations in which a larger share of the labor force remains in farming (as is common in Latin America and Africa). Income inequality reflects not just technological development but also a society's political and economic priorities. Of all high-income nations, the United States has the greatest income inequality.

And what of the future? Figure 8–2 extends the trend described by Kuznets to the postindustrial era (the broken line), reflecting increasing social inequality. The fact that U.S. society is now experiencing greater economic inequality suggests that the long-term trend may differ from the one Kuznets observed half a century ago.

Inequality in the United States

The United States differs from most European nations in never having had a titled nobility. With the significant exception of our racial history, we have never known a caste system that rigidly ranks categories of people.

Even so, U.S. society is highly stratified. Not only do the rich have most of the money, but they also receive the most schooling, enjoy the best health, and consume the most goods and services. Such privilege contrasts sharply with the poverty of millions of women and men who worry about paying next month's rent or a doctor's bill when a child becomes ill. Many people think of the United States as a middle-class society, but is this really the case?

INCOME, WEALTH, AND POWER

One important dimension of economic inequality is **income,** *earnings from work or investments.* The Census Bureau reports that the median U.S. family income in 2005 was $56,194. The left side of Figure 8–3 on page 222 shows the distribution of income among all U.S. families.[1] The richest 20 percent of families (earning at least $103,000 annually, with a mean of about $176,000) received 48.1 percent of all income, and the bottom 20 percent (earning less than $26,000, with a mean of about $14,700) received only 4.0 percent.

---

[1]The Census Bureau reports both mean and median incomes for families ("two or more persons related by blood, marriage, or adoption") and households ("two or more persons sharing a living unit"). In 2005, mean family income was $73,304, higher than median family income ($56,194) because high-income families pull up the mean but not the median. For households, these figures are somewhat lower—a mean of $63,344 and a median of $46,326—because families average 3.1 people and households average 2.6.

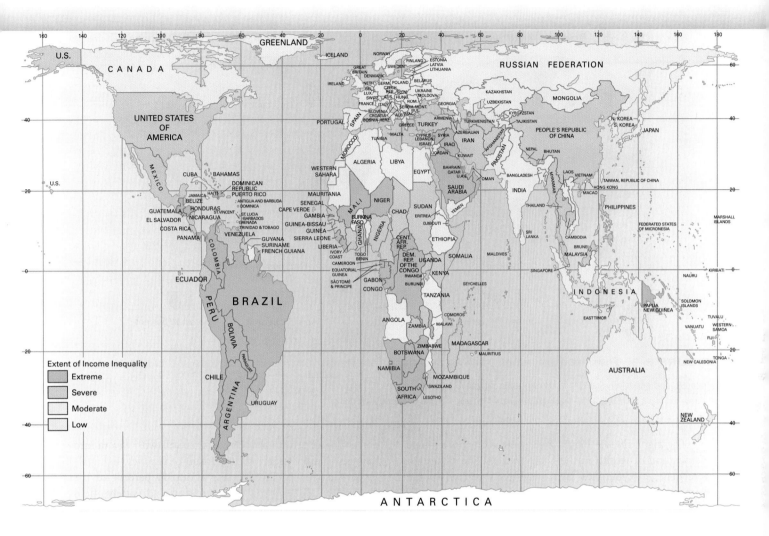

WINDOW ON THE WORLD

GLOBAL MAP 8-1 Income Inequality in Global Perspective

Societies throughout the world differ in the rigidity and extent of their social stratification and their overall standard of living. This map highlights income inequality. Generally speaking, the United States stands out among high-income nations, such as Great Britain, Sweden, Japan, and Australia, as having greater income inequality. The less economically developed countries of Latin America and Africa, including Colombia, Brazil, and the Central African Republic, as well as much of the Arab world, exhibit the most pronounced inequality of income. Is this pattern consistent with the Kuznets curve?

Source: Based on Gini coefficients obtained from World Bank (2006).

Table 8–1 on page 222 takes a closer look at income distribution. In 2005, the highest-paid 5 percent of U.S. families earned at least $185,000 (averaging almost $309,000), or 21.1 percent of all income, more than the total earnings of the lowest-paid 40 percent. At the very top of the pyramid, the richest 0.5 percent earned at least $1.75 million. In short, while a small number of people earn very high incomes, the majority make do with far less.

Income is only one part of a person's or family's **wealth,** *the total value of money and other assets, minus outstanding debts.* Wealth—including stocks, bonds, and real estate—is distributed even more unequally than income.

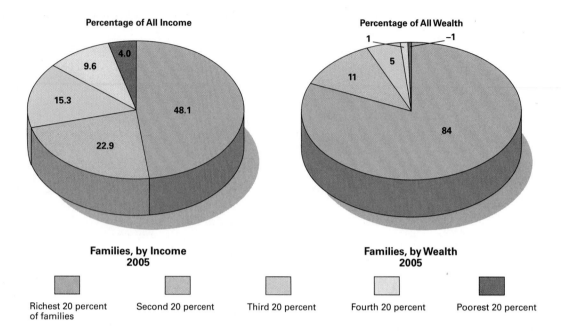

Percentage of All Income

4.0

9.6

15.3

48.1

22.9

Families, by Income
2005

Percentage of All Wealth

1   −1

5

11

84

Families, by Wealth
2005

Richest 20 percent of families   Second 20 percent   Third 20 percent   Fourth 20 percent   Poorest 20 percent

FIGURE 8–3   Distribution of Income and Wealth in the United States

Income, and especially wealth, is divided unequally in U.S. society.

Sources: Income data from U.S. Census Bureau (2006); wealth data based on Keister (2000) and Wolff (2004).

The right side of Figure 8–3 shows the approximate distribution of wealth in the United States. The richest 20 percent of U.S. families own roughly 84 percent of the country's entire wealth. High up in this privileged category are the top 5 percent of families, the "very rich," who own 60

TABLE 8-1

U.S. Family Income, 2005

Highest-paid . . .	Annually Earns at Least . . .
0.5%	$1,750,000
1	400,000
5	185,000
10	125,000
20	103,000
30	80,000
40	68,000
50	58,000
60	45,000
70	34,000
80	26,000
90	10,500

Source: U.S. Census Bureau (2006) and author calculations.

percent of all private property. Richer still, with wealth into the tens of millions, are the 1 percent of families that qualify as "super-rich" and possess about 40 percent of the nation's privately held resources (Keister, 2000; Keister & Moller, 2000; Wolff, 2004). At the top of the wealth pyramid, the ten richest U.S. families have a combined net worth of more than $232 billion (Miller & Serafin, 2006). This amount equals the total property of 3.1 million average families, including enough people to fill the cities of Chicago, Illinois; Chattanooga, Tennessee; and Clearwater, Florida.

See the *Federal Reserve Bulletin* for an analysis of changes in U.S. family wealth and income: http://www.federalreserve. gov/pubs/bulletin/2006/ financesurvey.pdf

The wealth of the average U.S. family is currently about $93,100 (Bucks, Kennickel, & Moore, 2006). Family wealth reflects the total value of homes, cars, investments, insurance policies, retirement pensions, furniture, clothing, and all other personal property, minus a home mortgage and other debts. The wealth of average people is not only less than that of the rich but also different in kind. Most people's wealth centers on a home and a car—property that generates no income—but the greater wealth of the rich is mostly in the form of stocks and other income-producing investments.

When financial assets are balanced against debits, the lowest-ranking 40 percent of families have virtually no wealth at all. The negative percentage shown in Figure 8–3 for the poorest 20 percent means that these families actually live in debt.

In the United States, wealth is an important source of power. The small proportion of families that controls most of the wealth also has the ability to shape the agenda of the entire society. As explained in Chapter 12 ("Economics and Politics"), some sociologists argue that such concentrated wealth weakens democracy because the political system serves the interests of the super-rich.

People of all social classes have the same right to vote. But can you think of ways in which the rich have more power to shape U.S. society than the rest of us?

SCHOOLING

Industrial societies have expanded opportunities for schooling, but some people still receive much more than others. Table 8–2 shows the schooling for women and men aged twenty-five and over in the United States. In 2004, although 85 percent had completed high school, only about 28 percent were college graduates.

Schooling affects both occupation and income because most (but not all) of the better-paying, white-collar jobs listed in Table 8–3 on page 224 require a college degree or other advanced study. Most blue-collar jobs, which bring lower income and less prestige, require less schooling.

OCCUPATIONAL PRESTIGE

In addition to generating income, work is also an important source of prestige. We commonly evaluate each other according to the kind of work we do, giving greater respect to those who do what we consider important work and less to others with more modest jobs.

Sociologists measure the relative social prestige of various occupations (NORC, 2005). Table 8–3 on page 224 shows that people give high prestige to occupations, such as

medicine, law, and engineering, that require extensive training and generate high income. By contrast, less prestigious work—as a waitress or janitor, for example—not only pays less but requires less ability and schooling. Occupational prestige rankings are much the same in all high-income nations (Lin & Xie, 1988).

In any society, high-prestige occupations go to privileged categories of people. In Table 8–3, for example, the highest-ranking occupations are dominated by men. We have to go thirteen jobs down the list to find "registered nurse," a career chosen mostly by women. Similarly, many

TABLE 8-2
Schooling of U.S. Adults, 2004 (aged 25 and over)

	Women	Men
Not a high school graduate	**14.6%**	**15.2%**
8 years or less	6.1	6.5
9–11 years	8.5	8.7
High school graduate	**85.4**	**84.8**
High school only	32.8	31.1
1–3 years of college	26.5	24.3
College graduate or more	26.1	29.4

Source: U.S. Census Bureau (2005).

of the lowest-prestige jobs are commonly performed by people of color.

In Table 8–3, identify jobs that have traditionally been performed by new immigrants. What pattern do you discover?

ANCESTRY, RACE, AND GENDER

A class system rewards individual talent and effort. But nothing affects social standing as much as birth into a particular family, which has a strong bearing on future schooling, occupation, and income. Research suggests that more than one-third of our country's richest people—those with hundreds of millions of dollars in wealth—derived their fortunes mostly from inheritance (Miller & Newcomb, 2005). Inherited poverty shapes the future of tens of millions of others.

Also closely linked to social position in the United States is race. White people have a higher overall occupational standing than African Americans and also receive more schooling. The median African American family income was $35,464 in 2005, just 56 percent of the $63,156 earned by non-Hispanic white families. This difference in income makes a real difference in people's lives. For example, non-Hispanic white families are more likely to own their homes (76 percent do) than black families (48 percent) (U.S. Census Bureau, 2006).

Some of the racial difference in income results from the larger proportion of single-parent families among African Americans. Comparing only families that include a married couple, African American families earned 80 percent as much as non-Hispanic white families.

TABLE 8-3
The Relative Social Prestige of Selected Occupations in the United States

White-Collar Occupations	Prestige Score	Blue-Collar Occupations	White-Collar Occupations	Prestige Score	Blue-Collar Occupations
Physician	86		Funeral director	49	
Lawyer	75		Real estate agent	49	
College/university professor	74		Bookkeeper	47	
Architect	73			47	Machinist
Chemist	73			47	Mail carrier
Physicist/astronomer	73		Musician/composer	47	
Aerospace engineer	72			46	Secretary
Dentist	72		Photographer	45	
Member of the clergy	69		Bank teller	43	
Psychologist	69			42	Tailor
Pharmacist	68			42	Welder
Optometrist	67			40	Farmer
Registered nurse	66			40	Telephone operator
Secondary school teacher	66			39	Carpenter
Accountant	65			36	Bricklayer/stonemason
Athlete	65			36	Child care worker
Electrical engineer	64		File clerk	36	
Elementary school teacher	64			36	Hairdresser
Economist	63			35	Baker
Veterinarian	62			34	Bulldozer operator
Airplane pilot	61			31	Auto body repairer
Computer programmer	61		Retail apparel salesperson	30	
Sociologist	61			30	Truck driver
Editor/reporter	60		Cashier	29	
	60	Police officer		28	Elevator operator
Actor	58			28	Garbage collector
Radio/TV announcer	55			28	Taxi driver
Librarian	54			28	Waiter/waitress
	53	Aircraft mechanic		27	Bellhop
	53	Firefighter		25	Bartender
Dental hygienist	52			23	Farm laborer
Painter/sculptor	52			23	Household laborer
Social worker	52			22	Door-to-door salesperson
	51	Electrician		22	Janitor
Computer operator	50			09	Shoe shiner

Source: Adapted from *General Social Surveys, 1972–2004: Cumulative Codebook* (Chicago: National Opinion Research Center, 2005), pp. 2031–49.

Over time, this income difference builds into a huge wealth gap (Altonji, Doraszelski, & Segal, 2000). A survey of families by the government's Federal Reserve found that median wealth for minority families, including African Americans, Hispanics, and Asian Americans ($27,100), is just 19 percent of the median ($142,700) for non-Hispanic white families (Bucks, Kennickell, & Moore, 2006).

Social ranking involves ethnicity as well. Historically, people of English ancestry have enjoyed the most wealth and wielded the greatest power in U.S. society. The Latino population—the largest U.S. racial or ethnic minority—has long been disadvantaged. In 2005, the median income among Hispanic families was $37,867, which is 60 percent of the median income for non-Hispanic white families. A

People often distinguish between the "new rich" and those with "old money." Men and women who suddenly begin to earn high incomes tend to spend their money on status symbols because they enjoy the new thrill of high-roller living and they want others to know of their success. Those who grow up surrounded by wealth, on the other hand, are used to a privileged way of life and are more quiet about it. Thus, the conspicuous consumption of the lower-upper class (left) can differ dramatically from the more private pursuits and understatement of the upper-upper class (right).

detailed examination of how race and ethnicity affect social standing is presented in Chapter 11 ("Race and Ethnicity").

Of course, both men and women are found in families at every social level. Yet on average, women have less income, wealth, and occupational prestige than men. Among single-parent families, those headed by a woman are almost three times more likely to be poor than those headed by a man. Chapter 10 ("Gender Stratification") examines the link between gender and social stratification.

Social Classes in the United States

As noted earlier, rankings in a caste system are rigid and obvious to all. Defining the social categories in a more fluid class system, however, is not so easy. Followers of Karl Marx see two major social classes: capitalists and proletarians. Other sociologists find as many as six classes (Warner & Lunt, 1941) or even seven (Coleman & Rainwater, 1978). Still others side with Max Weber, believing that people form not clear-cut classes but a multidimensional status hierarchy.

Defining classes in the United States is difficult because of the relatively low level of status consistency. Especially toward the middle of the hierarchy, people's social position on one dimension may not be the same as their standing on another. For example, a government official may have the power to administer a multimillion-dollar budget yet earn only a modest personal income. Similarly, many members of

the clergy enjoy ample prestige but only moderate power and low pay. Or consider a lucky day trader in the stock market who wins no special respect but makes a lot of money.

Finally, the social mobility characteristic of class systems—again, most pronounced near the middle—means that social position may change during a person's lifetime, further blurring class boundaries. With these issues in mind, we can examine four general rankings: the upper class, the middle class, the working class, and the lower class.

THE UPPER CLASS

Families in the upper class—the top 5 percent of the U.S. population—earn at least $185,000, and some earn ten times that much or more. As a general rule, the more a family's income comes from inherited wealth in the form of stocks and bonds, real estate, and other investments, the stronger a family's claim to being upper-class.

In 2006, *Forbes* magazine profiled the richest 400 people in the United States who were worth at least $1 billion (and as much as $53 billion) (Miller & Serafin, 2006). These people form the core of the upper class or Karl Marx's "capitalists"—the owners of the means of production and thus of most of the nation's private wealth. Many of these people spend much of their time managing their own wealth. Many upper-class people with smaller fortunes are business owners, top executives in large corporations, or senior government officials. Historically, the upper class has been composed of white Anglo-Saxon Protestants, but this is less true today (Pyle & Koch, 2001).

Upper-Uppers

The *upper-upper class,* sometimes called "blue bloods" or simply "society," includes less than 1 percent of the U.S. population (Baltzell, 1995). Membership is almost always the result of birth, as suggested by the old remark that the easiest way to become an upper-upper is to be born one. Most of these families possess enormous wealth that is primarily inherited. For this reason, members of the upper-upper class are said to have "old money."

Set apart by their wealth, upper-uppers live in exclusive neighborhoods such as Beacon Hill in Boston, the Rittenhouse Square section of Philadelphia, the Gold Coast of Chicago, and Nob Hill in San Francisco. Their children typically attend private schools with others of similar background and complete their formal education at high-prestige colleges and universities. In the historical pattern of European aristocrats, they study liberal arts rather than vocational skills. Women of the upper-upper class often do volunteer work for charitable organizations. Such activities serve a dual purpose: They help the larger community, and they build networks that broaden this elite's power (Ostrander, 1980, 1984).

Lower-Uppers

Most upper-class people actually fall into the *lower-upper class.* The queen of England is in the upper-upper class based not on her fortune (which is "only" $700 million) but on her family tree. J. K. Rowling, author of the Harry Potter books, is easily worth almost twice as much—more than $1 billion—but this woman (who was once on welfare) is a member of the lower-upper class. The major difference is that members of the lower-upper class are the "working rich" who get their money mostly by earning it rather than inheritance. These "new rich" families—who make up 3 or 4 percent of the U.S. population—generally live in expensive neighborhoods, own vacation homes near the water or in the mountains, and send their children to private schools and good colleges. Yet most do not gain entry into the clubs and associations of "old money" families.

When we think about the "American dream," we imagine rising to which part of the upper class? Explain.

THE MIDDLE CLASS

Made up of 40 to 45 percent of the U.S. population, the large middle class has a tremendous influence on our cul-

ture. Television and movies usually show middle-class people, and most commercial advertising is directed at these average consumers. The middle class contains far more ethnic and racial diversity than the upper class.

Upper-Middles

People in the top half of this category are called the *upper-middle class,* based on their above-average income in the range of $100,000 to $185,000 a year. Such income allows upper-middle-class families to live in a comfortable house in a fairly expensive area, own several automobiles, and build investments. Two-thirds of upper-middle-class children graduate from college, and postgraduate degrees are common. Many go on to high-prestige occupations as physicians, engineers, lawyers, accountants, and business executives. Lacking the power of the richest people to influence national or international events, upper-middles often play an important role in local political affairs.

Average-Middles

The rest of the middle class falls close to the center of the U.S. class structure. *Average-middles* typically work in less prestigious white-collar occupations as bank tellers, middle managers, or sales clerks or in highly skilled blue-collar jobs such as electrical work and carpentry. Family income falls between $45,000 and $100,000 a year, which is roughly the national average.[2]

Middle-class people generally build up a small amount of wealth over the course of their working lives, mostly in the form of a house and a retirement account. Most average-middle-class men and women are likely to be high school graduates, but the odds are just fifty-fifty that they will complete a college degree, usually at a less expensive, state-supported school.

THE WORKING CLASS

About one-third of the population falls within the working class (sometimes called the *lower-middle class*). In Marxist terms, the working class forms the core of the industrial proletariat. The blue-collar jobs held by members of the working class yield a family income of between $25,000 and $45,000 a year, somewhat below the national average. Working-class families have little or no wealth and are vulnerable to financial problems caused by unemployment or illness.

Many working-class jobs provide little personal satisfaction—requiring discipline but rarely imagination—and subject workers to continual supervision. These jobs also

---

[2]In some parts of the United States where the cost of living is very high (say, San Francisco), a family might need $150,000 or more in annual income to reach the middle class.

offer fewer benefits, such as medical insurance and pension plans. About half of working-class families own their homes, usually in lower-cost neighborhoods. College becomes a reality for only about one-third of working-class children.

THE LOWER CLASS

The remaining 20 percent of the population make up the lower class. Low income makes their lives insecure and difficult. In 2005, the federal government classified 37 million people (12.6 percent of the population) as poor. Millions more—called the "working poor"—are slightly better off, holding low-prestige jobs that provide little satisfaction and minimal income. Barely half manage to complete high school, and only one in four ever reaches college.

Society segregates the lower class, especially when the poor are racial or ethnic minorities. About 40 percent of lower-class families own their own home, typically in the least desirable neighborhoods. Although poor neighborhoods are found in inner cities, lower-class families also live in rural areas, especially across the South.

YOUR TURN

If you wanted to assess someone's social class position and could ask only one question, what would it be? Explain your decision.

"So long, Bill. This is my club. You can't come in."

The Difference Class Makes

Max Weber claimed that social stratification affects people's *life chances,* which means it shapes our lives in just about every way imaginable. We will briefly examine some of the ways social standing is linked to our health, values, politics, and family life.

HEALTH

Health is closely related to social standing. Children born into poor families are three times more likely to die from disease, neglect, accidents, or violence during their first year of life than children born into privileged families. Among adults, people with above-average incomes are twice as likely as low-income people to describe their health as excellent. In addition, on average, richer people live seven years longer because they eat more nutritious food, live in safer and less stressful environments, and receive better medical care (Lethbridge-Çejku, Rose, & Vickerie, 2006).

VALUES AND ATTITUDES

Some values and attitudes vary from class to class. The "old rich" have an unusually strong sense of family history because their position is based on wealth passed down from generation to generation. Secure in their birthright privileges, upper-uppers also favor understated manners and tastes; many "new rich" people engage in conspicuous consumption, using homes, cars, and even airplanes as status symbols to make a statement about their social position.

Affluent people with greater education and financial security are also more tolerant of controversial behavior such as homosexuality. Working-class people, who grow up in an atmosphere of greater supervision and discipline and are less likely to attend college, tend to be less tolerant (Lareau, 2002; NORC, 2005).

POLITICS

Do political attitudes follow class lines? The answer is yes, but the pattern is complex. A desire to protect wealth prompts well-off people to take a more conservative approach to *economic* issues, favoring, for example, lower taxes. But on *social* matters such as abortion and gay rights, highly educated, more affluent people are more liberal. People of lower social standing, by contrast, tend to be economic liberals, favoring government social programs that

The mass media are full of suggestions that upward social mobility is within reach of everyone. Recent television shows, including *The Bachelor*, *The Bachelorette*, and *How to Marry a Millionaire* (shown at right), spread the message that getting rich is as easy as saying "I do." How realistic is this claim?

support the poor, but typically have more conservative values on social issues (NORC, 2005).

A clearer pattern emerges when it comes to political involvement. Higher-income people, who are better served by the system, are more likely to vote and to join political organizations than people with low incomes. In presidential elections, three-fourths of adults with family incomes of $75,000 vote, compared to about half of adults with family incomes of $35,000 (Samuelson, 2003).

FAMILY AND GENDER

Social class also shapes family life. Generally, lower-class families are somewhat larger than middle-class families because of earlier marriage and less use of birth control. Another family pattern is that working-class parents encourage children to conform to conventional norms and respect authority figures. Parents of higher social standing pass on a different "cultural capital" to their children, teaching them to express their individuality and imagination more freely (Kohn, 1977; McLeod, 1995; Lareau, 2002).

The more money a family has, the better parents can develop their children's talents and abilities. An affluent family earning $108,700 a year will spend $279,450 raising a child born in 2005 to the age of eighteen. Middle-class people, with an average income of $57,400 a year, will spend $190,980, and a lower-class family earning less than $43,200 will spend $139,110 (Lino, 2006). Privilege leads to privilege as family life reproduces the class structure in each generation.

Class also shapes our world of relationships. In a classic study of married life, Elizabeth Bott (1971, orig. 1957) found that most working-class couples divide their responsibilities

according to gender roles; middle-class couples, by contrast, are more egalitarian, sharing more activities and expressing greater intimacy. More recently, Karen Walker (1995) discovered that working-class friendships typically serve as sources of material assistance; middle-class friendships are likely to involve shared interests and leisure pursuits.

Social Mobility

Ours is a dynamic society marked by quite a bit of social movement. Earning a college degree, landing a higher-paying job, or marrying someone who has a good income contributes to *upward social mobility;* dropping out of school, losing a job, or becoming divorced (especially for women) may result in *downward social mobility.*

Over the long term, though, social mobility is not so much a matter of individual changes as changes in society itself. In the first half of the twentieth century, for example, industrialization expanded the U.S. economy, pushing up living standards. Even people who were not good swimmers rode the rising tide of prosperity. More recently, the closing of U.S. factories has brought downward structural social mobility, dealing economic setbacks to many people.

Sociologists distinguish between shorter- and longer-term changes in social position. **Intragenerational social mobility** is *a change in social position occurring during a person's lifetime* (*intra* is Latin for "within"). **Intergenerational social mobility,** *upward or downward social mobility of children in relation to their parents,* is important because it reveals long-term changes in society that affect everyone (*inter* means "between").

MYTH VERSUS REALITY

In few societies do people think about "getting ahead" as much as in the United States. Moving up, after all, is the American dream. But is there as much social mobility in our country as we like to think?

Studies of intergenerational mobility (most of which have focused only on men) show that almost 40 percent of the sons of blue-collar workers take white-collar jobs and about 30 percent of sons born into white-collar families end up doing blue-collar work. *Horizontal social mobility*—changing jobs at the same class level—is even more common; overall, about 80 percent of sons showed some type of social mobility in relation to their fathers (Blau & Duncan, 1967; Featherman & Hauser, 1978; Hout, 1998).

Research points to four general conclusions about social mobility in the United States:

1. **Social mobility over the course of the past century has been fairly high.** A high level of mobility is what we would expect in an industrial class system.

2. **The long-term trend in social mobility has been upward.** Industrialization, which greatly expanded the U.S. economy, and the growth of white-collar work over the course of the twentieth century have raised living standards.

3. **Within a single generation, social mobility is usually small.** Most young families increase their income over time as they gain education and skills. A typical family headed by a thirty-year-old earned about $53,000 in 2005; a typical family headed by a fifty-year-old earned $73,000 (U.S. Census Bureau, 2006). Yet only a few people move from "rags to riches" (the way J. K. Rowling did) or lose a lot of money (a number of hip-hop stars who made it big had little money left a few years later). Most social mobility involves small movement within one class level rather than large movement between classes.

4. **Social mobility since the 1970s has been uneven.** Real income (adjusted for inflation) rose during the twentieth century until the 1970s. Between 1975 and 1985, gains were far smaller. During the 1980s, real income changed little for many people, rising slowly after 1993 and falling again after 2000. But general trends do not show the experiences of different categories of people, as the next section explains.

MOBILITY BY INCOME LEVEL

Figure 8–4 shows how U.S. families at different income levels made out between 1980 and 2005. Well-to-do families (the highest 20 percent, but not all the same families over

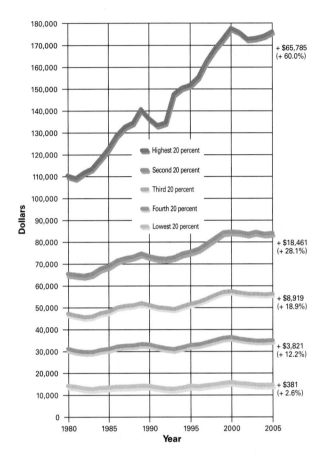

FIGURE 8–4   Mean Annual Income, U.S. Families, 1980–2005 (in 2005 dollars, adjusted for inflation)

The gap between high-income and low-income families is wider today than it was in 1980.

Source: U.S. Census: Bureau (2006).

the entire period) saw their incomes jump 60 percent, from an average $110,507 in 1980 to $176,292 in 2005. People in the middle of the population also had gains, but more modest ones. The lowest-income 20 percent saw only a 2.6 percent increase in earnings.

For families at the top of the income scale (the highest 5 percent), recent decades have brought a windfall. These families, with average income of more than $150,000 in 1980, were making $308,636 in 2005—almost twice as much (U.S. Census Bureau, 2006).

MOBILITY: RACE, ETHNICITY, AND GENDER

White people in the United States have always been in a more privileged position than people of African or Hispanic

As CEOs Get Richer, the Great Mansions Return

I grew up in Elkins Park, Pennsylvania, an older suburban community just north of Philadelphia. Elkins Park was and still is a mostly middle-class community, although like most of suburbia, some neighborhoods boast bigger houses than others.

What made Elkins Park special was that scattered over the area were a handful of great mansions, built a century ago by early Philadelphia industrialists. At that time, all there was to the town was these great "estates," along with fields and meadows. By about 1940, however, most of this land had been split off into lots for the homes of newer middle-class suburbanites. The great mansions suddenly seemed out of place, with heirs disagreeing over who should live there and how to pay the rising property taxes. As a result, many of the great mansions were sold, the buildings taken down, and the land subdivided.

In the 1960s, when I was a teenager, a short bike ride could take me past the Breyer estate (built by the founder of the ice-cream company, now the township police building), the Curtis estate (built by a magazine publisher and transformed into a community park), and the Wanamaker estate (built by the founder of a large Philadelphia department store, now gone entirely). Probably the grandest of them all was the Wiedner estate, modeled after a French chateau, complete with door knobs and window pulls covered in gold; it now stands empty.

In their day, these structures were not just home to a family and many servants; they were also monuments to a time when the rich were, well, *really* rich. By contrast, the community that emerged on the grounds once owned by these rich families is middle-class, with homes built on smaller lots.

But did the so-called Gilded Age of great wealth disappear forever? Hardly. By the 1980s, a new wave of great mansions was being built in the United States. Take the architect Thierry Despont, who designs huge houses for the super-rich. One of Despont's "smaller" homes might be 20,000 square feet (about ten times the size of the average U.S. house), and they go all the way up to 60,000 square feet (as big as any of the Elkins Park mansions built a century ago and almost the size of the White House). These megahomes have kitchens as large as college classrooms, exercise rooms, indoor swimming pools, and even indoor tennis courts (Krugman, 2002).

Megahouses are being built by newly rich chief executive officers (CEOs) of large corporations. Although CEOs have always made more money than most people, recent years have seen executive compensation soar. Between 1970 and 2005, the average U.S. family saw only a modest increase in income (about 20 percent after inflation is taken into account). According to *Fortune* magazine, during the same period, the average compensation for the 100 highest-paid CEOs skyrocketed from $1.3 million (about 40 times the earnings of an average worker at that time) to $37.5 million (roughly a 2,800 percent increase and equal to 1,000 times the salary of today's average worker). Some CEOs, of course, earn far more: In the year before Enron collapsed, for example, Kenneth Lay earned about $150 million. Assuming that Lay worked forty hours a week for fifty weeks that year, that amounts to $75,000 *per hour* (Krugman, 2002).

Some analysts argue that in today's competitive global economy, many CEOs are true "superstars" who build profits and deserve what they earn. Others take a less generous view, suggesting that CEOs have stacked their corporate boards of directors with friends whose "payback" includes approving enormous paychecks and bonuses. In any case, executive pay has become a national scandal. In light of the harm that this pay scandal has done to the corporate world (not to mention cases of outright fraud and theft such as those that are bringing executives like Kenneth Lay to trial), it appears that we have been living in an era of uncontrolled greed.

WHAT DO YOU THINK?

1. Do you consider increasing economic inequality a problem? Why or why not?

2. How many times more than an average worker should a CEO earn? Explain your answer.

3. Does very high CEO pay help or hurt stockholders? What about the general public? Why?

descent. Through the economic expansion of the 1980s and 1990s, more African Americans entered the ranks of the wealthy. But overall, the real income of African Americans has changed little in three decades. African American family income as a percentage of white family income was the same in 2005 as it was in 1970 (60 percent). Compared with white families, Latino families lost ground between 1975 (when their average income was 67 percent of that of white families) and 2005 (when it had slipped to 64 percent) (Pomer, 1986; U.S. Census Bureau, 2006).

Feminists point out that historically, women have had less chance for upward mobility than men because most working women hold clerical jobs (such as secretary) and service positions (such as food server) that offer few opportunities for advancement.

Over time, however, the earnings gap between women and men has been narrowing. Women working full time in 1980 earned 60 percent as much as men working full time; by 2005, women were earning 77 percent as much (U.S. Census Bureau, 2006).

MOBILITY AND MARRIAGE

Research points to the conclusion that marriage has an important effect on social standing. In a study of women and men in their forties, Jay Zagorsky (2006) found that people who marry and stay married accumulate about twice as much wealth as people who remain single or who divorce. Reasons for this difference include the fact that couples who live together typically enjoy double incomes and also pay only half the bills they would have if they were single and living in separate households.

It is also likely that compared to single people, married men and women work harder in their jobs and save more money. Why? Primarily because they are working not just for themselves but to support others who are counting on them (Popenoe, 2006).

Just as marriage pushes social standing upward, divorce usually makes social position go down. Couples who divorce take on the costs of supporting two households, which leaves them with less money for savings or other investment. After divorce, women are hurt more than men because it is typically the man who earns more. Many women who divorce not only lose most of their income but may also lose benefits, including health care and insurance coverage (Weitzman, 1996).

THE AMERICAN DREAM: STILL A REALITY?

The expectation of upward social mobility is deeply rooted in U.S. culture. Through much of our history, the economy has grown steadily, raising living standards. Today, at least for some people, the American dream is alive and well. In 2005, fully 22 percent of U.S. families earned $100,000 or more, compared with just 3 percent back in 1967 (in dollars controlled for inflation). There are now at least 5 million millionaires in the United States, four times the number a decade ago (Rank & Hirschl, 2001; U.S. Census Bureau, 2006).

Yet not all indicators are so positive. Note these disturbing trends:

1. **For many workers, earnings have stalled.** The annual income of a fifty-year-old man working full time climbed by 49 percent between 1958 and 1974 (from $25,671 to $38,190 in constant 2001 dollars). Between 1974 and 2004, however, this worker's income rose only half as quickly, even as the number of hours worked increased and the cost of necessities such as housing, education, and medical care went way up (Russell, 1995a; U.S. Census Bureau, 2006).

2. **More jobs offer little income.** The expanding global economy has moved many industrial jobs overseas, reducing the availability of high-paying factory work here in the United States. At the same time, the expansion of our service economy means more of today's jobs—in fast-food restaurants or large discount stores—offer relatively low wages.

3. **Young people are remaining at home.** For the first time in history, half of young people aged eighteen to twenty-four, unable to support a household, are still living with their parents. Since 1975, the average age at marriage has moved upward four years (to 25.3 years for women and 27.1 years for men).

Over the past generation, more people have become rich, and the rich have become richer; as the Applying Sociology box explains, the highest-paid corporate executives have enjoyed a runaway rise in their earnings. But at the same time, the increasing share of low-paying jobs has brought downward mobility for millions of families, feeding the fear that the chance to enjoy a middle-class lifestyle is slipping away. As Figure 8–5 on page 232 shows, although median family income doubled between 1950 and 1973, it has grown by only 22 percent since then (U.S. Census Bureau, 2005).

THE GLOBAL ECONOMY AND THE U.S. CLASS STRUCTURE

Underlying the shifts in U.S. class structure is global economic change. Much of the industrial production that gave U.S. workers high-paying jobs a generation ago has moved overseas. With less industry at home, the United States now serves as a vast consumer market for industrial goods such

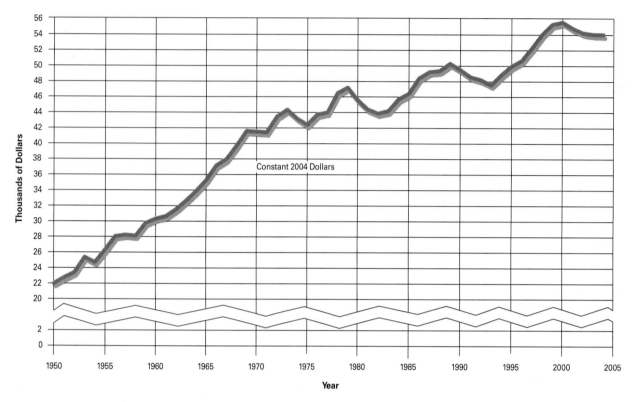

FIGURE 8-5 Median Annual Income, U.S. Families, 1950–2005

Average family income in the United States grew rapidly between 1950 and 1970. Since then, however, the increase has been smaller.

Source: U.S. Census Bureau (2006).

as cars, stereos, cameras, and computers made in China, Japan, South Korea, and elsewhere.

High-paying jobs in manufacturing, held by 26 percent of U.S. workers in 1960, support only 11 percent of workers today. In their place, the economy offers service work, which pays far less. Traditionally high-paying corporations such as USX (formerly United States Steel) now employ fewer people than the expanding McDonald's chain, and fast-food clerks make only a fraction of what steelworkers earn.

The global reorganization of work has not been bad news for everyone. The global economy is driving upward social mobility for educated people who specialize in law, finance, marketing, and computer technology. Global economic expansion also helped push up the stock market (even with the post-2000 declines) almost eightfold between 1980 and 2006, reaping profits for families with money to invest.

But the same trend has hurt many average workers, who have lost their factory jobs and now perform low-wage service work. In addition, many companies (General Motors and Ford are recent examples) have downsized—cutting the ranks of their workforce—to stay competitive in world markets. As a result, although more than 50 percent of all married-couple families contain two or more workers—more than twice the share in 1950—many families are working harder simply to hold on to what they have (A. L. Nelson, 1998; Sennett, 1998; U.S. Census Bureau, 2006).

Poverty in the United States

Social stratification creates both "haves" and "have-nots." All systems of social inequality create poverty, or at least **relative poverty,** *the deprivation of some people in relation to those who have more.* A more serious but preventable problem is **absolute poverty,** *a deprivation of resources that is life-threatening.*

As Chapter 9 ("Global Stratification") explains, almost 1 billion human beings around the world—one person in six—are at risk of absolute poverty. Even in the affluent United States, families go hungry, live in inadequate housing, and suffer poor health because of serious poverty.

THE EXTENT OF POVERTY

In 2005, the government classified 37 million men, women, and children—12.6 percent of the U.S. population—as

African American artist Henry Ossawa Tanner captured the humility and humanity of impoverished people in his painting *The Thankful Poor*. This insight is important in a society that tends to define poor people as morally unworthy and deserving of their bitter plight.

Henry Ossawa Tanner (1859–1937), *The Thankful Poor*. Private collection. Art Resource, N.Y.

poor. This count of relative poverty refers to families with income below an official poverty line, which, for a family of four, was set that year at $19,971. The poverty line is about three times what the government estimates a family will spend for food. But the income of the average poor family was just 60 percent of this amount. This means that the typical poor family had to get by on less than $12,000 in 2005 (U.S. Census Bureau, 2006).

Who Are the Poor?

Although no single description fits all poor people, poverty is greater among certain categories of our population. Where these categories overlap, the problem is especially serious.

Age

A generation ago, the elderly were at greatest risk for poverty. But thanks to better retirement programs offered today by private employers and government, the poverty rate for people over age sixty-five fell from 30 percent in 1967 to 10.1 percent—well below the national average—in 2005. Looking at it from another angle, about 10 percent (3.6 million) of the poor are elderly.

Today, the burden of poverty falls most heavily on children. In 2005, 17.6 percent of people under age eighteen (12.9 million children) were poor. Put another way, 35 percent of the U.S. poor are children.

Race and Ethnicity

Two-thirds of all poor people are white; 25 percent are African American. But in relation to their overall numbers, African Americans are about three times as likely as non-Hispanic whites to be poor. In 2005, some 24.9 percent of African Americans (9.2 million people) lived in poverty, compared with 21.8 percent of Hispanics (9.4 million), 11.1 percent of Asians and Pacific Islanders (1.4 million), and 8.3 percent of non-Hispanic whites (16.2 million). The poverty gap between whites and minorities has changed little since 1975.

People of color have especially high rates of child poverty. Among African American children, 34.5 percent are poor; the comparable figures are 28.3 percent among Hispanic children and 10.0 percent among non-Hispanic white children (U.S. Census Bureau, 2006).

Gender and Family Patterns

Of all poor people age eighteen or older, 61 percent are women and 39 percent are men. This difference reflects the fact that women who head households are at high risk of poverty. Of all poor families, 53 percent are headed by women with no husband present, and just 9 percent are headed by single men.

The United States has experienced the **feminization of poverty**, *the trend of women making up an increasing proportion of the poor*. In 1960, only 25 percent of all poor households were headed by women; the majority of poor families had both wives and husbands in the home. By 2005, however, the proportion of poor families headed by single women had more than doubled to 53 percent.

The feminization of poverty is one result of a larger trend: the rapidly increasing number of households at all class levels headed by single women. When this trend is

SEEING OURSELVES

NATIONAL MAP 8-1
Poverty across the United States

This map shows that the poorest counties in the United States—where the poverty rate is more than twice the national average—are in Appalachia, spread across the Deep South, along the border with Mexico, near the Four Corners region of the Southwest, and in the Dakotas. Can you suggest some reasons for this pattern?

Source: U.S. Census Bureau (2005).

Percentage of
Population below
the Poverty Level

23.5% to 36.2%
17.6% to 23.4%
12.5% to 17.5%
9.8% to 12.4%
2.2% to 9.7%

U.S. average: 12.5%

coupled with the fact that households headed by women are at high risk of poverty, it is easy to see why women and their children now make up a larger share of the U.S. poor.

Urban and Rural Poverty

The greatest concentration of poverty is found in central cities, where the 2005 poverty rate stood at 17.0 percent. The poverty rate in suburbs is 9.3 percent. Thus the poverty rate for urban areas as a whole is 12.2 percent, lower than the 14.5 percent found in rural areas. National Map 8–1 shows that most of the counties with the highest poverty rate in the United States are rural.

EXPLAINING POVERTY

That the richest nation on Earth contains tens of millions of poor people raises serious questions. It is true, as some analysts remind us, that most poor people in the United States are far better off than the poor in other countries: For example, 41 percent of U.S. poor families own their home, 70 percent own a car, and only a few percent report often going without food (Rector, 1998; Gallagher, 1999). But there is little doubt that poverty harms the overall well-being of millions of people in this country.

Why is there poverty in the first place? Here we present two opposing explanations that lead to a lively and important political debate.

One View: Blame the Poor

One view holds that *the poor are primarily responsible for their own poverty.* Throughout the nation's history, people have placed a high value on self-reliance, convinced that social standing is mostly a matter of individual talent and effort. According to this view, society offers plenty of opportunities to anyone able and willing to take advantage of them, and the poor are people who cannot or will not work due to a lack of skills, schooling, or motivation.

In his study of Latin American cities, the anthropologist Oscar Lewis (1961) concluded that the poor become trapped in a *culture of poverty,* a lower-class subculture that can destroy people's ambition to improve their lives. Socialized in poor families, children become resigned to their situation, producing a self-perpetuating cycle of poverty.

In 1996, hoping to free people from what some saw as a culture of poverty in the United States, Congress changed the welfare system, which had provided a federal guarantee of financial assistance to poor people since 1935. The federal government continues to send money to the states to distribute to needy people, but benefits now carry strict limits—in most cases, no more than two years at a stretch and a total of five years altogether if a person moves in and out of the welfare system. The stated purpose of this reform was to force people to be self-supporting and move them away from dependency on government.

 A report on food scarcity in the United States is found at http://www.ers.usda.gov/Publications/err11

Another View: Blame Society

A different position, argued by the sociologist William Julius Wilson (1996a, 1996b; Mouw, 2000), holds that *society is primarily responsible for poverty.* Wilson points to the loss of jobs in our inner cities as the primary cause of poverty, claiming that there is simply not enough work to support families. Wilson sees any apparent lack of trying on the part of the poor as a *result* of little opportunity rather

THINKING CRITICALLY

The Welfare Dilemma

In 1996, Congress ended federal public assistance, which guaranteed some income to all poor people. New state-run programs were enacted that require people who receive aid to get training or find work—or have their benefits cut off.

What, exactly, is welfare? The term "welfare" refers to an assortment of policies and programs designed to improve the well-being of some low-income people. Until the welfare reform of 1996, most people used the term to refer to just one part of the overall system: Aid to Families with Dependent Children (AFDC), a program of monthly financial support to parents (mostly single women) to care for themselves and their children. In 1996, about 5 million households received AFDC for some part of the year.

Conservatives opposed AFDC, claiming that rather than reducing child poverty, AFDC made the problem worse, in two ways. First, they claim that this form of welfare weakened families, because for years after the program began, public assistance regulations provided benefits to poor mothers only if no husband lived in the home. As conservatives see it, AFDC operated as an economic incentive to women to have children outside of marriage, and they blame it for the rapid rise in out-of-wedlock births among poor people. To conservatives, marriage is one key to reducing poverty: Fewer than one in ten married-couple families are poor, and more than nine out of ten AFDC families were headed by an unmarried woman.

Second, conservatives believe that welfare encouraged poor people to become dependent on government handouts, the main reason that eight out of ten poor heads of households did not have full-time jobs. Furthermore, only 5 percent of single mothers receiving AFDC worked full time, compared with more than half of nonpoor single

mothers. Conservatives say that welfare strayed far from its original purpose of short-term help to nonworking women with children (say, after divorce or death of a husband) and became a way of life. Once trapped in dependency, poor women are likely to raise children who will themselves be poor as adults.

Liberals have a different view. Why, they ask, do so many people object to the government's giving money to poor mothers and their children when most "welfare" actually goes to richer people? The AFDC budget was about $25 billion annually—no small sum, to be sure—but just half of the $50 billion in home mortgage deductions that homeowners pocket each year. And it pales in comparison to the $300 billion in annual Social Security benefits Uncle Sam provides to senior citizens, most of whom are not poor. And what about "corporate welfare" to big companies? Their tax write-offs and other benefits run into hundreds of billions of dollars per year.

Liberals add that the stereotype of do-nothing "welfare queens" masks the fact that most poor families who turn to public assistance are truly needy. The typical AFDC household received barely $400 per month, hardly enough to attract people to a life of welfare dependency. In constant dollars, in fact, AFDC payments actually declined over the years. Liberals therefore fault public assistance as a "Band-Aid approach" to the serious social problems of too few jobs and too much income inequality in the United States.

As for the charge that public assistance undermines families, liberals agree that the proportion of single-parent families has risen, but they do not regard AFDC as the reason. Rather, they see single parenting as a broad cultural trend found at all class levels in many countries.

Surveys show that people in the United States, more than people in other high-income nations, tend to see poverty as a mark of laziness and personal failure. It should not be surprising, then, that Congress replaced the federal AFDC program with state-run programs called Temporary Assistance for Needy Families (TANF). States set their own qualification requirements and benefits, but they must limit benefits to two consecutive years, with a lifetime limit of five years.

By 2005, TANF had moved more than half of single parents on welfare into jobs or job training. In addition, the rate of out-of-wedlock birth has fallen. Supporters of welfare reform see the new program as a success. But critics point out that many of the people who are now working earn so little pay that they are hardly better off than before, and half of these workers have no health insurance. In other words, welfare reform has greatly reduced the number of people receiving welfare, but it has done little to reduce poverty. In addition, say the critics, many of these working women now spend less time with their children. For these reasons, the welfare debate goes on.

WHAT DO YOU THINK?

1. How does our cultural emphasis on self-reliance help explain the controversy surrounding public assistance? Why do people not criticize benefits (such as home mortgage deductions) for people who are better off?

2. Do you approve of the benefit time limits built into the TANF program? Why or why not?

3. Why have the welfare reforms done little to reduce poverty?

Sources: Corcoran et al. (2000), U.S. Department of Health and Human Services (2000), Rogers-Dillon (2001), Lichter & Crowley (2002), and Lichter & Jayakody (2002).

June 29, 2004

Surge in Homeless Families Sets Off Debate on Cause

By LESLIE KAUFMAN

ST. CLOUD, Minn—In small cities like this one and big ones like Kansas City, Mo., and New York, families are knocking on the doors of homeless shelters in growing numbers. Inside a faded yellow-brick Victorian on a block near downtown here, dozens of families know of the increase firsthand.

Behind the front door, the 11 rooms of the Landon House Shelter are packed with homeless parents and their children, often exceeding the 48-bed capacity and requiring the staff to roll out cots. . . .

"We are always full," said Darlene Johnson, executive director of the shelter. "Pretty much bursting out of the seams." . . .

This wind-swept Plains city of 60,000 about 60 miles northwest of Minneapolis has seen the number of families requesting shelter climb by 45 percent in the last decade, to an average of 124 families a night. The number of homeless families in Minnesota tripled to 1,341 a night in 2003 from 434 in 1991, when the state first started conducting surveys every three years, and most of the last increase came in rural areas like this one.

And Minnesota is not alone. . . . The Urban Institute, a research group in Washington that surveyed homeless assistance providers in 1996, . . . found that at least 1.4 million children and 2 million adults were homeless, but that number has surely grown as cities like Columbus, Ohio; Philadelphia; St. Louis; and New York have all reported surges at their homeless shelters for the last two or three years. . . .

Family homelessness first emerged as a national problem in the mid 1980s. After a public outcry over the wretched conditions endured by many such families living in crumbling converted hotels, President Ronald Reagan in 1987 signed the McKinney Act, which gave states money to build emergency shelters and help such families. In the years since, billions in federal dollars have financed an explosion in the number of such shelters. In 2003 alone, the federal government spent $1.3 billion on more than 3,700 local programs that run shelters. . . .

Some liberals have expressed concern that these shelters have done little more than hide a shameful epidemic from public view, while conservatives have argued that they have become an expensive magnet for poor families who are unhappy with their living situations and are seeking government help. Yet almost everyone agrees that the number of families knocking on their doors continues to swell. . . .

Many academics and advocates for the homeless cite a widening gulf between income and rents. Real pay for

than as a *cause* of poverty. From Wilson's point of view, Lewis's analysis amounts to blaming the victims for their own suffering (W. Ryan, 1976). To combat poverty and reduce the need for welfare, Wilson argues, the government should fund jobs and provide affordable child care for low-income mothers and fathers.

CRITICAL REVIEW The U.S. public is evenly divided over whether government or people themselves should take responsibility for reducing poverty (NORC, 2005). Government statistics show that 52 percent of the heads of poor families did not work at all during 2005, and an additional 30 percent worked only part time (U.S. Census Bureau, 2006). Such facts seem to support the "blame the poor" position because a major cause of poverty is *not holding a job.*

But the *reasons* that people do not work are more in step with the "blame society" position. Middle-class women may be able to combine working and child rearing, but this is much harder for poor women who cannot afford child care, and few employers provide child care programs. As William Julius Wilson explains, many people are jobless not because they are avoiding work but because there are not enough jobs to go around. In short, the most effective way to reduce poverty is to ensure a greater supply of jobs as well as child care for parents who work (W. J. Wilson, 1996a; Pease & Martin, 1997; Duncan, 1999; Bainbridge, Meyers, & Waldfogel, 2003).

✅ **YOUR LEARNING** Explain the view that the poor should take responsibility for poverty and the view that society is responsible for poverty. Which is closer to your own view?

THE WORKING POOR

Not all poor people are jobless, and the *working poor* command the sympathy and support of people on both sides of the poverty debate. In 2005, some 18 percent of heads of poor families (1.4 million women and men) worked at least fifty weeks of the year and yet could not escape poverty.

the bottom 10 percent of wage earners rose less than 1 percent in adjusted dollars from 1979 to 2003. . . . Welfare payments buy less than half of what they did in 1970, and millions of families no longer receive them at all.

By contrast, housing costs have nearly tripled since 1979, . . . [and] city governments have been steadily eliminating public housing. . . .

If tight rental markets tell part of the story, they are clearly not the whole story. Since the 1980s, a significant body of research has developed to show that the heads of homeless families, like their single, street-sleeping male counterparts, are often drug addicts or mentally impaired or both.

The families are also disproportionately African American and usually headed by unwed mothers or women fleeing domestic violence. . . .

Critics of the shelter system argue that it may be abetting personal dysfunction. The shelter system constructed with federal dollars after the McKinney Act was a vast improvement over the shoddy hotels of the 1980s. Many programs, particularly in New York, place families in the shelter at the top of the list for government subsidized rental apartments, an incentive that New York is considering dropping.

Such a system actually encourages families to enter the shelter system, argues Howard Husock, who teaches at the John F. Kennedy School of Government at Harvard University, particularly those who are doubled up with relatives or living in otherwise uncomfortable situations because of personal choices, including unwed motherhood. . . .

[Philip F.] Mangano, the Bush administration's homelessness chief, said . . . the emergency shelter system that Washington had built might have been a misuse of money.

"If we had an opportunity to go back, we might have created a different response on homeless[ness], one that focused more on investing in housing," he said. "We spent billions of dollars and have had 20 years of shuffling homeless people from one side of town to the other, from one homeless program to another. It is a disgrace."

WHAT DO YOU THINK?

1. Why is homelessness rarely discussed by our political leaders in Congress?

2. What are some of the reasons for homelessness given in the article? Which is most important? Why?

3. What changes in our national policy toward homelessness would you support? Why?

Adapted from the original article by Leslie Kaufman published in *The New York Times* on June 29, 2004. Copyright © 2004 by The New York Times Company. Reprinted with permission.

Another 30 percent of these heads of families (2.3 million people) remained poor despite part-time employment. Put differently, 3.4 percent of heads of families work full-time and earn so little that they remain poor (U.S. Census Bureau, 2006). A key cause of working poverty is the fact that a full-time worker earning $6 per hour—above the 2006 minimum wage of $5.15 per hour—cannot lift an urban family of four above the poverty line.

 For a profile of the working poor, visit http://www.bls.gov/cps/cpswp2003.pdf

Individual ability and personal initiative do play a part in shaping social position. However, the weight of sociological evidence points toward society, not individual character traits, as the primary source of poverty, because entire *categories* of people—female heads of families, people of color, people in inner-city neighborhoods isolated from the larger society—face special barriers and limited opportunities.

The Thinking Critically box on page 235 takes a closer look at the current welfare debate. Understanding this important social issue can help us decide how our society should respond to the problem of poverty, as well as the problem of homelessness discussed next.

HOMELESSNESS

We have no exact count of homeless people. Fanning out across the United States on the night of March 27, 2000, Census Bureau officials counted 170,706 people at emergency and homeless shelters. But experts estimate that a full count of the homeless would probably reach 500,000 on any given night, rising to perhaps three times that number—1.5 million people—at some time during the course of a year. In addition, recent evidence suggests that the number of homeless people in the United States is going up (U.S. Census Bureau, 2000; Wickham, 2000; Marks, 2001). "In the *Times*" provides a closer look at the problem of homelessness.

The familiar stereotypes of homeless people—men sleeping in doorways and women carrying everything they own in shopping bags—have been replaced by the "new homeless": people thrown out of work because of factory closings, people forced out of apartments by rent increases, and others who cannot meet mortgage or rent payments because of low wages or no work at all. Today, no stereotype paints a complete picture of the homeless.

The majority of homeless people report that they do not work, but one study found that 44 percent said they worked at least part time (U.S. Department of Housing and Urban Development, 1999). Working or not, all homeless people have one thing in common: poverty. For that reason, the explanations of poverty just presented also apply to homelessness. Some people blame the *personal traits* of the homeless. One-third of homeless people are substance abusers, and one-fourth are mentally ill. More broadly, a fraction of 1 percent of our population, for one reason or another, seems unable to cope with our complex and highly competitive society (Bassuk, 1984; Whitman, 1989).

A report by the U.S. Conference of Mayors on homelessness is found at http://usmayors.org/uscm/hunger survey/2004/onlinereport/HungerAndHomelessness Report2004.pdf

Others see homelessness resulting from *societal factors,* including low wages and a lack of low-income housing (Kozol, 1988; Schutt, 1989; Bohannan, 1991). Supporters of this position point out that one-third of the homeless consist of entire families, and children are the fastest-growing category of the homeless.

U.S. society has been more generous with the "worthy" poor (such as elderly people) than with the "unworthy" poor (such as able-bodied people who, we assume, should take care of themselves). Why do you think we have not done more to reduce poverty among children, who surely fall into the "worthy" category?

No one disputes that a large proportion of homeless people are personally impaired to some degree, but cause and effect are difficult to untangle. Even so, it is clear that structural changes in the U.S. economy, reduced aid to low-income people, and a real estate market that puts housing out of reach of the poorest members of U.S. society all contribute to homelessness.

CLASS, WELFARE, POLITICS, AND VALUES

We have reviewed many facts about social inequality. In the end, however, our opinions about wealth and poverty depend not just on facts but also on our politics and values. As we might expect, the idea that social standing reflects personal merit is popular among well-off people; the opposing idea, that society should spread wealth more equally, finds favor among those who are less well off (NORC, 2005).

In the United States, our cultural emphasis on individual responsibility encourages us to see successful people as personally worthy and to view poor people as personally lacking. Such attitudes go a long way toward explaining why our society spends much more than other high-income nations on education (to promote opportunity) but much less on public assistance programs (which directly support the poor).

Most members of our society are willing to accept a high level of income inequality, and many hold a harsh view of the poor. To the extent that we define poor people as undeserving, we look on public assistance programs as at best a waste of money and at worst a threat to personal initiative.

Finally, the drama of social stratification extends far beyond the borders of the United States. The most striking social inequality is found not by looking inside one country but by comparing living standards in various parts of the world. In Chapter 9, we broaden our focus by investigating global stratification.

APPLYING SOCIOLOGY IN EVERYDAY LIFE

1. Identify three ways in which social stratification is evident in the everyday lives of students on your campus. In each case, explain exactly what is unequal and what difference it makes. Do you think individual talent or family background is more important in creating these social differences?

2. Sit down with parents, grandparents, or other relatives, and assess the social position of your family over the last three generations. Has social mobility taken place? How much? Why?

3. During an evening of television viewing, assess the social class of the characters you see on various shows. In each case, explain why you assign someone a specific social class position. What patterns do you find?

4. Governor Arnold Schwarzenegger of California recently said, "In this country, it doesn't make any difference where you were born. It doesn't make any difference who your parents were. It doesn't make any difference if, like me, you couldn't even speak English until you were in your 20s. America gave me opportunities, and my immigrant dreams came true. I want other people to get the same chances I did, the same opportunities. And I believe they can." Ask a number of people who came to the United States from another country the extent to which they agree or disagree with this statement.

MAKING THE GRADE

CHAPTER 8 Social Stratification

WHAT IS SOCIAL STRATIFICATION?

SOCIAL STRATIFICATION is a system by which a society ranks categories of people in a hierarchy, so that some people have more money, power, and prestige than others.

Social stratification
• is a trait of society, not simply a reflection of individual differences
• carries over from one generation to the next
• is supported by a system of cultural beliefs that define certain kinds of inequality as just
• takes two general forms: caste systems and class systems

pp 206–7

CASTE SYSTEMS
• are based on birth (ascription)
• permit little or no social mobility
• are common in traditional, agrarian societies

pp 207–8

CLASS SYSTEMS
• are based on both birth (ascription) and meritocracy (individual achievement)
• permit some social mobility
• are common in modern, industrial and postindustrial societies

pp 208–10

social stratification (p. 206) a system by which a society ranks categories of people in a hierarchy

social mobility (p. 207) a change in position within the social hierarchy

caste system (p. 207) social stratification based on ascription, or birth

class system (p. 208) social stratification based on both birth and individual achievement

meritocracy (p. 208) social stratification based on personal merit

status consistency (p. 210) the degree of consistency in a person's social standing across various dimensions of social inequality

structural social mobility (p. 212) a shift in the social position of large numbers of people due more to changes in society than to individual efforts

ideology (p. 213) cultural beliefs that justify particular social arrangements, including patterns of inequality

VISUAL SUMMARY

THEORETICAL ANALYSIS OF SOCIAL STRATIFICATION

The **STRUCTURAL-FUNCTIONAL APPROACH** points to ways social stratification helps society to operate.

• The *Davis-Moore thesis* states that social stratification is universal because of its functional consequences.

• In caste systems, people are rewarded for performing the duties of their position at birth.

• In class systems, unequal rewards attract the ablest people to the most important jobs and encourage effort.

pp 213–15

The **SOCIAL-CONFLICT APPROACH** claims that stratification divides societies in classes, benefiting some categories of people at the expense of others and causing social conflict.

• Karl Marx claimed that capitalism places economic production under the ownership of captalists, who exploit the proletariat who sell their labor for wages.

• Max Weber identified three distinct dimensions of social stratification: economic class, social status or prestige, and power. Conflict exists between people at various positions on a multidimensional hierarchy of socioeconomic status (SES).

pp 215–17

Davis-Moore thesis (p. 214) the assertion that social stratification exists in every society because it has beneficial consequences for the operation of society

capitalists (p. 215) people who own and operate factories and other businesses in pursuit of profits

proletarians (p. 215) working people who sell their labor for wages

alienation (p. 215) the experience of isolation and misery resulting from powerlessness

blue-collar occupations (p. 216) lower-prestige jobs that involve mostly manual labor

white-collar occupations (p. 216) higher-prestige jobs that involve mostly mental activity

socioeconomic status (SES) (p. 217) a composite ranking based on various dimensions of social inequality

conspicuous consumption (p. 218) buying and using products with an eye to the "statement" they make about social position

The **SYMBOLIC-INTERACTION APPROACH**, a micro-level analysis, explains out that we size up people by looking for clues to their social standing. *Conspicuous consumption* refers to buying and displaying products that make a "statement" about social class systems. Most people tend to socialize with others whose social standing is similar to their own.

pp 218–19

See the Applying Theory table on page 219.

SOCIAL STRATIFICATION AND TECHNOLOGY: A GLOBAL PERSPECTIVE

Hunting and Gathering → Horticultural and Pastoral → Agrarian —————— Industrial —————— Postindustrial

• Gerhard Lenski explains that advancing technology initially increases social stratification, which is most intense in agrarian societies.

pp 219–20

• Industrialization reverses the trend, reducing social stratification.

pp 219–20

• In postindustrial societies, social stratification again increases.

p 220

See the Kuznets Curve (Figure 8-2 on page 220).

MAKING THE GRADE

CONTINUED...

INEQUALITY IN THE UNITED STATES

SOCIAL STRATIFICATION involves many dimensions:

- *Income*—Earnings from work and investments are unequal, with the richest 20% of families earning twelve times as much as the poorest 20% of families.
- *Wealth*—The total value of all assets minus debts, wealth is distributed more unequally than income, with the richest 20% of families holding 84% of all wealth.
- *Power*—Income and wealth are important sources of power.
- *Prestige*—Work generates not only income but prestige. White-collar jobs generally offer more income and prestige than blue-collar jobs. Many lower-prestige jobs are performed by women and people of color.
- *Family ancestry*, *race and ethnicity*, and *gender* all affect social standing.

pp 220–25

income (p. 220) earnings from work or investments

wealth (p. 221) the total value of money and other assets, minus outstanding debts

SOCIAL CLASSES IN THE UNITED STATES

$185,000
$185,000

$45,000
$45,000

$25,000
$25,000

UPPER CLASS—5% of the population. Most members of the *upper-upper class*, or "old rich," inherited their wealth; the *lower-upper class*, or "new rich," work at high-paying jobs.

MIDDLE CLASS—40 to 45% of the population. People in the *upper-middle class* have significant wealth; *average-middles* have less prestige, do white-collar work, and most attend college.

WORKING CLASS—one-third of the population. People in the *lower middle class* do blue-collar work; only about one-third of children attend college.

LOWER CLASS—20% of the population. Most people in the lower class lack financial security due to low income; many live below the poverty line; half do not complete high school.

pp 225–27

intragenerational social mobility (p. 228) a change in social position occurring during a person's lifetime

intergenerational social mobility (p. 228) upward or downward social mobility of children in relation to their parents

- People with higher social standing generally have better health, hold certain values and political attitudes, and pass on advantages in the form of "cultural capital" to their children.
- Social mobility is common in the United States, as it is in other high-income countries, but typically only small changes occur from one generation to the next.
- Due to the expansion of the global economy, the richest families now earn more than ever; families near the bottom of the class system have seen only small increases.

pp 227–32

POVERTY IN THE UNITED STATES

POVERTY PROFILE

- The government classifies 37 million people, 12.6% of the population, as poor.
- About 35% of the poor are children under age 18.
- Two-thirds of the poor are white, but in relation to their population, African Americans and Hispanics are more likely to be poor.
- The "feminization of poverty" means that more poor families are headed by women.
- About 48% of the heads of poor families are among the "working poor" who work at least part-time but do not earn enough to lift a family of four above the poverty line.
- An estimated 1.5 million people are homeless at some time during the course of a year.

pp 232–38

EXPLANATIONS OF POVERTY

- Blame individuals: The *culture of poverty* thesis states that poverty is caused by shortcomings in the poor themselves (Oscar Lewis).
- Blame society: Poverty is caused by society's unequal disbribution of wealth and lack of good jobs (William Julius Wilson).

pp 234–36

relative poverty (p. 232) the deprivation of some people in relation to those who have more

absolute poverty (p. 232) a deprivation of resources that is life-threatening

feminization of poverty (p. 233) the trend of women making up an increasing proportion of the poor

These questions are similar to those found in the test bank that accompanies this textbook.

MULTIPLE-CHOICE QUESTIONS

1. *Social stratification* **refers to**
   a. job specialization.
   b. ranking categories of people in a hierarchy.
   c. the fact that some people work harder than others.
   d. inequality of personal talent and individual effort.

2. **A caste system is social stratification**
   a. based on individual achievement.
   b. based on meritocracy.
   c. based on birth.
   d. in which categories of people are unequal.

3. **Sonja has two advanced degrees, an average salary, and is working at a low-prestige job. Which concept best describes her situation?**
   a. low status consistency
   b. horizontal social mobility
   c. upward social mobility
   d. high status consistency

4. **According to the Davis-Moore thesis,**
   a. equality is functional for society.
   b. the more inequality a society has, the more productive it is.
   c. more important jobs must offer enough rewards to draw talent from less important work.
   d. societies with more meritocracy are less productive than those with caste systems.

5. **Karl Marx claimed that society "reproduces the class structure." By this, he meant that**
   a. society benefits from inequality.
   b. class differences are passed on from one generation to another.
   c. class differences are the same everywhere.
   d. a society without classes is impossible.

6. **Max Weber claimed that social stratification is based on**
   a. economic class.
   b. social status or prestige.
   c. power.
   d. All of the above are correct.

7. **The wealthiest 20 percent of people in the United States own about how much of the country's privately owned wealth?**
   a. 34 percent
   b. 54 percent
   c. 84 percent
   d. 94 percent

8. **About what share of U.S. adults over the age of twenty-five are college graduates?**
   a. 10 percent
   b. 28 percent
   c. 40 percent
   d. 68 percent

9. **Which of the following is another term for the "working class"?**
   a. upper-middle class
   b. average-middle class
   c. lower class
   d. lower-middle class

10. **Which quintile (20 percent) of the U.S. population has seen the greatest change in income over the last generation?**
    a. the top quintile
    b. the middle quintile
    c. the lowest quintile
    d. All quintiles have seen the same change.

11. **Change in social position during a person's own lifetime is called**
    a. intergenerational social mobility.
    b. intragenerational social mobility.
    c. structural social mobility.
    d. horizontal social mobility.

12. **Which age category of the U.S. population has the highest poverty rate?**
    a. children
    b. middle-aged people
    c. young people in their twenties
    d. seniors over age sixty-five

ANSWERS: 1 (b); 2 (c); 3 (a); 4 (c); 5 (b); 6 (d); 7 (c); 8 (b); 9 (d); 10 (a); 11 (b); 12 (a).

ESSAY QUESTIONS

1. Explain why social stratification is a creation of society, not just a reflection of individual differences.

2. How do caste and class systems differ? How are they the same? Why does industrialization introduce a measure of meritocracy into social stratification?

3. What is the extent of poverty in the United States? Who are the poor in terms of age, race and ethnicity, and gender?

Around the world, social inequality is dramatic, with some people in some countries earning far more than people living elsewhere. Low wage levels is one reason many corporations that once produced their products in the United States now operate factories in China and other countries.

CHAPTER 9

Global Stratification

WHAT share of the world's people live in absolute poverty?

WHY are some of the world's countries so rich and others so poor?

Are rich nations making global poverty better or worse? *HOW?*

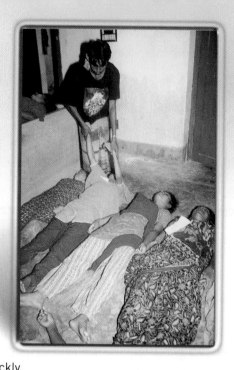

More than 1,000 workers were busily sewing together polo shirts on the fourth floor of the garment factory in Narsingdi, a small town about thirty miles northeast of Bangladesh's capital city of Dhaka. The thumping of hundreds of sewing machines produced a steady roar throughout the long working day.

But in an instant everything changed when an electric gun used to shoot spot remover onto stained fabric gave off a spark, which ignited the flammable liquid. Suddenly, a work table burst into flames. People rushed to smother the fire with shirts, but there was no stopping the blaze: In a room filled with combustible materials, the flames spread quickly.

The workers scrambled toward the narrow staircase that led to the street. At the bottom, however, the human wave pouring down the steep steps collided with a folding metal gate, stretched across the doorway and locked to keep workers from leaving during working hours. Panicked, the people turned, only to be pushed back by the hundreds behind them. In a single terrifying minute of screaming voices, thrusting legs, and pounding hearts, dozens were crushed and trampled. By the time the gates were opened and the fire put out, fifty-two garment workers lay dead.

Garment factories like this one are big business in Bangladesh, where clothing accounts for 75 percent of the country's total economic exports. Half of these garments end up in stores throughout the United States. The reason so much of the clothing we buy is made in poor countries like Bangladesh is simple economics—Bangladeshi garment workers labor for close to twelve hours a day, typically seven days a week, and yet earn only $400 to $500 a year, which is just a few percent of what a garment worker makes in the United States.

Tanveer Chowdhury manages this garment factory owned by his family. He complained bitterly to reporters about the tragedy. "This fire has cost me $586,373, and that does not include $70,000 for machinery and $20,000 for furniture. I made commitments to meet deadlines, and I still have the deadlines. I am now paying for air freight at $10 a dozen when I should be shipping by sea at 87 cents a dozen."

There was one other cost Chowdhury did not mention. To compensate families for the loss of their loved ones in the fire, the factory eventually agreed to pay $1,952 per person. In Bangladesh, life—like labor—is cheap (based on Bearak, 2001).

Garment workers in Bangladesh are part of the roughly 1 billion of the world's people who work hard every day and yet remain poor. As this chapter explains, although poverty is a reality in the United States and other nations, the greatest social inequality is not *within* nations but *between* them (Goesling, 2001). We can understand the full dimensions of poverty only by exploring **global stratification,** *patterns of social inequality in the world as a whole.*

 Visit the United Students against Sweatshops Web site at http://www.students againstsweatshops.org

Global Stratification: An Overview

Chapter 8 ("Social Stratification") described inequality in the United States. In global perspective, however, social stratification is far greater. Figure 9–1 divides the world's total income by fifths of the population. Recall from Chapter 8 that the richest 20 percent of the U.S. population earns about 48 percent of the national income (see Figure

8–3 on page 222). The richest 20 percent of the global population, however, receives about 80 percent of world income. At the other extreme, the poorest 20 percent of the U.S. population earns 4 percent of our national income; the poorest fifth of the world's people, by contrast, struggles to survive on just 1 percent of global income.

Because some countries are so much richer than others, even people in the United States with income below the government's poverty line live far better than the majority of people on the planet. The average person in a rich nation such as the United States is extremely well off by world standards. At the top of the pyramid, the world's richest person (Bill Gates in the United States, who was worth about $53 billion in 2006) has more wealth than the world's forty-five poorest *countries* (United Nations Development Programme, 2005; Miller & Serafin, 2006).

A WORD ABOUT TERMINOLOGY

Classifying the 192 nations on Earth into categories ignores many striking differences. These nations have rich and varied histories, speak different languages, and take pride in their distinctive cultures. However, various models have been developed that classify countries in order to study global stratification.

One such model, developed after World War II, labeled the rich, industrial countries the "First World"; the less industrialized, socialist countries the "Second World"; and the nonindustrialized, poor countries the "Third World." But the "three worlds" model is less useful today. For one thing, it grew out of Cold War politics, when the capitalist West (the First World) faced off against the socialist East (the Second World) while other nations (the Third World) remained more or less on the sidelines. But the sweeping changes in Eastern Europe and the collapse of the former Soviet Union means that a distinctive Second World no longer exists.

A second problem is that the "three worlds" model lumped together more than 100 countries as the Third World. In reality, some better-off nations of the Third World (such as Chile in South America) have thirteen times the per-person productivity seen in the poorest countries of the world (such as Ethiopia in East Africa).

These facts call for a modestly revised system of classification. The fifty-five **high-income countries** are defined as *the richest nations with the highest overall standards of living.* The world's seventy-five **middle-income countries** are not as rich; they are *nations with a standard of living about average for the world as a whole.* The remaining sixty-two **low-income countries** are *nations with a low standard of living in which most people are poor.*

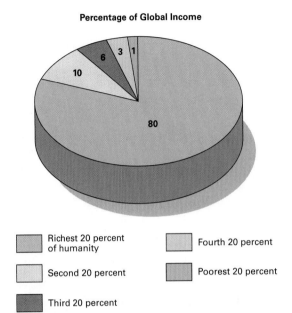

Percentage of Global Income

Legend:
- Richest 20 percent of humanity
- Second 20 percent
- Third 20 percent
- Fourth 20 percent
- Poorest 20 percent

FIGURE 9-1 Distribution of World Income

Global income is very unequal, with the richest 20 percent of the world's people earning eighty times as much as the poorest 20 percent.

Sources: Calculated by the author based on United Nations Development Programme (2000) and World Bank (2001).

This model has two advantages over the "three worlds" system. First, it focuses on economic development rather than whether societies are capitalist or socialist. Second, it gives a better picture of the relative economic development of various countries because it does not lump together all lower-income nations into a single "Third World."

When ranking countries, keep in mind that there is social stratification within every nation. In Bangladesh, for example, members of the Chowdhury family, who own the garment factory described in the chapter-opening story, earn as much as $1 million per year, which is several thousand times more than one of their workers earns. The full extent of global inequality is even greater, because the wealthiest people in rich countries such as the United States live worlds apart from the poorest people in low-income countries such as Bangladesh, Haiti, and Sudan.

HIGH-INCOME COUNTRIES

In nations where the Industrial Revolution first took place more than two centuries ago, productivity increased more than 100-fold. To understand the power of industrial and computer technology, consider that the Netherlands, one small European nation, is more productive than the whole

Japan represents the world's high-income countries, in which industrial technology and economic expansion have produced material prosperity. The presence of market forces is evident in this view of downtown Tokyo (above, left). The Russian Federation represents the middle-income countries of the world. Industrial development and economic performance were sluggish under socialism; as a result, Moscow residents had to wait in long lines for their daily needs (above, right). The hope is that the introduction of a market system will raise living standards, although in the short run, Russian citizens must adjust to increasing economic inequality. Bangladesh (left) represents the world's low-income countries. As the photograph suggests, these nations have limited economic development and rapidly increasing populations. The result is widespread poverty.

continent of Africa south of the Sahara, and tiny South Korea outproduces all of India.

Global Map 9–1 shows that the high-income nations of the world include the United States and Canada, Argentina and Chile, the nations of Western Europe, Israel, Saudi Arabia, South Africa, Singapore, Hong Kong (now part of the People's Republic of China), Japan, South Korea, Australia, and New Zealand.

These countries cover roughly 25 percent of Earth's land area, including parts of five continents, and lie mostly in the Northern Hemisphere. In 2006, the population of these nations was about 1.1 billion, or about 18 percent of the world's people. About three-fourths of the people in high-income countries live in or near cities.

Significant cultural differences exist among high-income countries; for example, the nations of Europe recognize more than thirty official languages. But these societies have something in common: They all produce enough economic goods to enable their people to lead comfortable material lives. Per capita annual income (that is,

average income per person in a year) ranges from about $10,000 annually (in Lithuania and South Africa) to more than $37,000 annually (in the United States and Norway). In fact, people in high-income countries enjoy 79 percent of the world's total income.

Production in rich nations is capital-intensive; that is, it is based on factories, big machinery, and advanced technology. Most of the largest corporations that design and market computers, as well as most computer users, are located in high-income countries. High-income countries also control the world's financial markets, so daily events on the stock exchanges of New York, London, and Tokyo affect people throughout the world.

MIDDLE-INCOME COUNTRIES

Middle-income countries have per capita annual incomes ranging from $2,500 to $10,000, roughly the median for the world's nations. Two-thirds of the people in middle-income countries live in cities, and industrial jobs are common. The

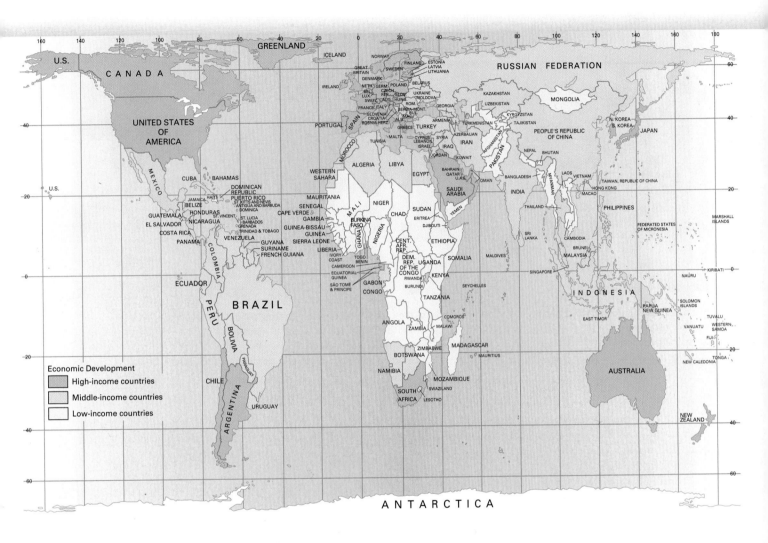

WINDOW ON THE WORLD

GLOBAL MAP 9–1 Economic Development in Global Perspective

In high-income countries—including the United States, Canada, Chile, Argentina, the nations of Western Europe, South Africa, Israel, Saudi Arabia, Australia, and Japan—a highly productive economy provides people, on average, with material plenty. Middle-income countries—including most of Latin America and Asia—are less economically productive, with a standard of living about average for the world as a whole but far below that of the United States. These nations also have a significant share of poor people who are barely able to feed and house themselves. In the low-income countries of the world, poverty is severe and widespread. Although small numbers of elites live very well in the poorest nations, most people struggle to survive on a small fraction of the income common in the United States.

Note: Data for this map are provided by the United Nations. Each country's economic productivity is measured in terms of its gross domestic product (GDP), which is the total value of all the goods and services produced by a country's economy within its borders in a given year. Dividing each country's GDP by the country's population gives us the per capita (per-person) GDP and allows us to compare the economic performance of countries of different population sizes. High-income countries have a per capita GDP of more than $10,000. Many are far richer than this, however; the figure for the United States exceeds $37,000. Middle-income countries have a per capita GDP ranging from $2,500 to $10,000. Low-income countries have a per capita GDP of less than $2,500. Figures used here reflect the United Nations "purchasing power parities" system, which is an estimate of what people can buy using their income in the local economy.

Source: Based on data from United Nations Development Programme (2005); map projection from *Peters Atlas of the World* (1990).

When Hurricane Katrina flooded the city of New Orleans, most of the population evacuated, leaving behind those who were too old, too sick, or too poor to make their way to safety. This disaster revealed the depth of hidden poverty that exists in the United States. More than a year later, the crowds had returned and the tourist center of the city was back in business *(left)*; at the same time, rebuilding had scarcely begun in many of the city's poorest neighborhoods *(right)*.

remaining one-third of the people live in rural areas, where most are poor and lack access to schools, medical care, adequate housing, and even safe drinking water.

Looking at Global Map 9–1, we see that about eighty of the world's nations fall in the middle-income category. At the high end are Mexico (Latin America), Botswana (Africa), and Malaysia (Asia), where annual income is about $9,000. At the low end are Ecuador (Latin America), Egypt (Africa), and Indonesia (Asia), with roughly $3,000 annually in per capita income.

One cluster of middle-income countries consists of what used to be known as the Second World: the former Soviet Union and Eastern Europe. These countries had mostly socialist economies until popular revolts between 1989 and 1991 swept their governments aside. Since then, these nations have begun to introduce free-market systems, but so far the results have been uneven. Some (including Poland) have improving economies, but living standards in others (including Russia) have fallen.

Other middle-income nations include Peru and Brazil in South America and Namibia and Botswana in Africa. Recently, both India and the People's Republic of China entered the middle-income category, which now includes most of Asia.

Taken together, middle-income countries span roughly 55 percent of the world's land area and are home to about 4.5 billion people, or about 70 percent of humanity. Some countries (such as Russia) are far less crowded than others (such as El Salvador), but compared to high-income countries, these societies are densely populated.

Why do you think most people from high-income countries who travel to middle- or low-income nations do so as tourists, but most who travel from low- or middle-income nations to high-income countries do so as immigrants?

LOW-INCOME COUNTRIES

Low-income countries, where most people are very poor, are mostly agrarian societies with some industry. Most of these roughly sixty nations, identified in Global Map 9–1, are found in Central and East Africa and Asia. Low-income countries cover 20 percent of the planet's land area and are home to 12 percent of its people. Population density is generally high, although it is greater in Asian countries (such as Bangladesh and Pakistan) than in Central African nations (such as Chad and the Democratic Republic of the Congo).

In poor countries, one-third of the people live in cities; most inhabit villages and farms as their ancestors have done for centuries. In fact, half the world's people are farmers, most of whom follow cultural traditions. With limited industrial technology, they cannot be very productive—one reason that many endure severe poverty. Hunger, disease, and unsafe housing shape the lives of the world's poorest people.

People living in rich nations such as the United States find it hard to grasp the extent of human poverty in much of the world. From time to time, televised pictures of famine in very poor countries such as Ethiopia and Bangladesh give us shocking glimpses into the poverty that makes every day a life-and-death struggle for many in low-income nations. Behind these images lie cultural, historical, and economic forces that we shall explore in the remainder of this chapter.

Global Wealth and Poverty

October 14, Manila, the Philippines. What caught my eye was how clean she was—a girl no more than seven or eight years old, wearing a freshly washed dress and with her hair carefully combed. She followed us with her eyes: Camera-toting Americans stand out in this, one of the poorest neighborhoods in the entire world.

Fed by methane from the decomposing garbage, the fires never go out on Smokey Mountain, the vast garbage dump on the north side of Manila. Smoke covers the hills of refuse like a thick fog. But Smokey Mountain is more than a dump; it is a neighborhood that is home to thousands of people. It is hard to imagine a setting more hostile to human life. Amid the smoke and the squalor, men and women do what they can to survive. They pick plastic bags from the garbage and wash them in the river, and they collect cardboard boxes or anything else they can sell. What chance do their children have, coming from families that earn a few hundred dollars a year, with hardly any opportunity for schooling, year after year, breathing this foul air? Against this backdrop of human tragedy, one lovely little girl has put on a fresh dress and gone out to play.

Now our taxi driver threads his way through heavy traffic as we head for the other side of Manila. The change is amazing: The smoke and smell of the dump give way to neighborhoods that could be in Miami or Los Angeles. A cluster of yachts floats on the bay in the distance. No more rutted streets; now we glide quietly along wide boulevards lined with trees and filled with expensive Japanese cars. We pass shopping plazas, upscale hotels, and high-rise office buildings. Every block or so we see the gated entrance to an exclusive residential enclave with security guards standing watch. Here, in air-conditioned homes, the rich of Manila live—and many of the poor work.

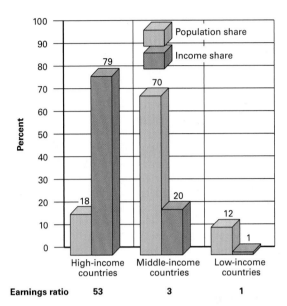

FIGURE 9-2 The Relative Share of Income and Population by Level of Economic Development

For every dollar earned by people in low-income countries, people in high-income countries earn $53.

Sources: Calculated by the author based on United Nations Development Programme (2000) and World Bank (2001).

Low-income nations are home to some rich and many poor people. The fact that most people live with incomes of a few hundred dollars a year means the burden of poverty is far greater than among the poor of the United States. This does not mean that poverty here at home is a minor problem. In so rich a country, too little food, substandard housing, and no medical care for tens of millions of people, one-third of them children, amount to a national tragedy. The Thinking About Diversity box on page 250 profiles the striking poverty that exists along the southwestern border of the United States. Yet poverty in poor countries is both more severe and more widespread than in the United States.

THE SEVERITY OF POVERTY

Poverty in poor countries is more severe than it is in rich countries. A key reason that quality of life differs so much around the world is that economic productivity is lowest in precisely the regions where population growth is highest. Figure 9–2 shows the proportion of global population and global income for countries at each level of economic development. High-income countries are by far the most advantaged, with 79 percent of global income supporting just 18 percent of humanity. In middle-income nations, 70 percent

Las Colonias: "America's Third World"

"We wanted to have something for ourselves," explains Olga Ruiz, who has lived in the border community of College Park, Texas, for eleven years. There is no college in College Park, nor does this dusty stretch of rural land have sewer lines or even running water. Yet this town is one of some 1,800 settlements that have sprouted up in southern Texas along the 1,200-mile border with Mexico that runs from El Paso down to Brownsville. Together, they are home to perhaps 750,000 people, a number expected to pass 1 million by 2010.

Many people speak of *las colonias* (Spanish for "the colonies") as "America's Third World" because these desperately poor communities look much like their counterparts in Mexico or many other middle- or low-income nations. But almost all of the people living in the *colonias* are Latino, 85 percent of them are legal residents, and more than half are U.S. citizens.

Anastacia Ledsema, now seventy-two years old, moved to a *colonia* called Sparks more than forty years ago. Born in Mexico, Ledsema married a Texas man, and together they paid $200 for a quarter-acre lot in a new border community. For months, they

camped out on their land. Step by step, however, they invested their labor and their money to build a modest house. Not until 1995 did their small community get running water—a service promised by developers years before. After the water line came, things changed more than they expected. "When we got water," recalls Ledsema, "that's when so many people came in." The population of Sparks quickly doubled to about 3,000, overwhelming the water supply so that sometimes the faucet does not run at all.

The residents of all the *colonias* know that they are poor. Indeed, the Census Bureau recently declared one border community to be the poorest in

the entire United States. Concerned over the lack of basic services in so many of these communities, Texas officials have banned any new settlements. But most of the people who move here—even those who start off sleeping in their cars or trucks—see these communities as the first step on the path to the American dream. Oscar Solis, a neighborhood leader in Panorama Village, with a population of about 150, is proud to show visitors around the small but growing town. "All of this work we have done ourselves," he says with a smile, "to make our dream come true."

WHAT DO YOU THINK?

1. Are you surprised that such poverty exists in a rich country like the United States? Why or why not?

2. Why do you think such communities get little attention from the U.S. mass media?

3. To what extent do you think the people living in these communities will have their "dreams come true"? Explain your answer.

Source: Based on Schaffer (2002).

of the world's people earn 20 percent of global income. This leaves 12 percent of the planet's population with just 1 percent of global income. For every dollar received by an individual in a low-income country, someone in a high-income nation takes home $53.

Table 9–1 shows the extent of wealth and well-being in specific countries around the world. The first column of figures gives the gross domestic product (GDP) for a number

of high-, middle-, and low-income countries.[1] The United States, a large industrial nation, had a 2003 GDP of more than $10 trillion; Japan's GDP that same year was about $4 trillion. A comparison of GDP figures shows that the

---

[1]Gross domestic product (GDP) is the value of all the goods and services produced by a country's economy within its borders in a given year.

world's richest nations are thousands of times more productive than the poorest countries.

The second column of figures in Table 9–1 divides GDP by the entire population size to give an estimate of what people can buy using their income in the local economy. The per capita GDP for the richest high-income countries, including the United States, Sweden, and Canada, is very high, exceeding $26,000. For middle-income countries, such as Mexico and the Russian Federation, the figures are in the $9,000 range. In the world's low-income countries, per capita GDP is just a few hundred dollars. In the Central African Republic or in Ethiopia, a typical person labors all year to make what the average worker in the United States earns in a week.

The last column of Table 9–1 is a measure of quality of life in the various nations. This index, calculated by the United Nations, combines income, education (extent of adult literacy and average years of schooling), and longevity (how long people typically live). Index values are decimals that fall between extremes of one (highest) and zero (lowest). By this calculation, Norwegians enjoy the highest quality of life (.963), with residents of the United States close behind (.944). At the other extreme, people in the African nation of Niger have the lowest quality of life (.281).

Relative versus Absolute Poverty

The distinction between relative and absolute poverty, made in Chapter 8 ("Social Stratification"), has an important application to global inequality. People living in rich countries generally focus on *relative poverty*, meaning that some people lack resources that are taken for granted by others. By definition, relative poverty exists in every society, rich or poor.

 Find a report by the World Bank on strategies to reduce global poverty at http://www1.worldbank.org/publications/pdfs/14978frontmat.pdf

More important in global perspective, however, is *absolute poverty*, a lack of resources that is life-threatening. Human beings in absolute poverty lack the nutrition necessary for health and long-term survival. To be sure, some absolute poverty exists in the United States. But such immediately life-threatening poverty strikes only a small proportion of the U.S. population; in low-income countries, by contrast, one-third or more of the people are in desperate need.

Because absolute poverty is deadly, one global indicator of this problem is the median age at death. Global Map 9–2 on page 252 identifies the age by which half of all people born in a nation die. In rich countries, most people die after the age of seventy-five, but in poor countries, half of all deaths occur among children under the age of ten.

TABLE 9-1

Wealth and Well-Being in Global Perspective, 2003

Country	Gross Domestic Product (US$ billions)	GDP per Capita (PPP US$)*	Quality of Life Index
High-Income			
Norway	221	37,670	.963
Australia	522	29,632	.955
Sweden	302	26,750	.949
Canada	857	30,677	.949
United States	10,949	37,562	.944
Japan	4,301	27,967	.943
United Kingdom	1,795	27,147	.939
France	1,758	27,677	.938
South Korea	605	17,971	.901
Middle-Income			
Eastern Europe			
Russian Federation	433	9,230	.795
Romania	57	7,277	.792
Belarus	18	6,052	.786
Ukraine	50	5,491	.766
Latin America			
Mexico	626	9,168	.814
Brazil	492	7,790	.792
Venezuela	85	4,919	.772
Asia			
Malaysia	104	9,512	.796
Thailand	143	7,595	.778
People's Republic of China	1,417	5,003	.755
Middle East			
Iran	137	6,995	.736
Syria	22	3,576	.721
Africa			
Algeria	67	6,107	.722
Botswana	8	8,714	.565
Low-Income			
Latin America			
Haiti	3	1,742	.475
Asia			
Cambodia	4	2,078	.571
Pakistan	82	2,097	.527
Bangladesh	52	1,770	.520
Africa			
Guinea	4	2,097	.466
Ethiopia	7	711	.367
Central African Republic	1	1,089	.355
Niger	3	835	.281

*These data are the United Nations' purchasing power parity (PPP) calculations, which avoid currency rate distortion by showing the local purchasing power of each domestic currency.

Source: United Nations Development Programme, *Human Development Report, 2005* (New York: United Nations Development Programme, 2005).

WINDOW ON THE WORLD

GLOBAL MAP 9-2   Median Age at Death in Global Perspective

This map identifies the age below which half of all deaths occur in any year. In the high-income countries of the world, including the United States, it is mostly the elderly who face death, that is, people aged seventy-five or older. In middle-income countries, including most of Latin America, most people die years or even decades earlier. In low-income countries, especially in Africa and parts of Asia, it is children who die, half of them never reaching their tenth birthday.

Source: World Bank (1993), with updates by the author; map projection from *Peters Atlas of the World* (1990).

THE EXTENT OF POVERTY

Poverty in poor countries is more widespread than it is in rich nations such as the United States. Chapter 8 noted that the U.S. government officially classifies almost 13 percent of the population as poor. In low-income countries, however, most people live no better than the poor in the United States, and many are far worse off. As Global Map 9–2 shows, the high death rates among children in Africa indicate that absolute poverty is greatest there, where half the population is malnourished. In the world as a whole, at any given time, 15 percent of the people—about 1 billion—suffer from chronic hunger, which leaves them less able to work and puts them at high risk of disease (United

Tens of millions of children fend for themselves every day on the streets of Latin America, where many fall victim to disease, drug abuse, and outright violence. What do you think must be done to put an end to scenes like this one in San Salvador, the capital city of El Salvador?

Nations Development Programme, 2001; Chen & Ravallion, 2004).

The typical adult in a rich nation such as the United States consumes about 3,500 calories a day, which is actually too much and leads to obesity and related health problems. The typical adult in a low-income country not only does more physical labor but consumes just 2,000 calories a day. The result is undernourishment: too little food or not enough of the right kinds of food.

In the ten minutes it takes to read through this section of the chapter, about 300 people in the world who are sick and weakened from hunger will die. This amounts to about 40,000 people a day, or 15 million people each year. Clearly, easing world hunger is one of the most serious challenges facing humanity today.

POVERTY AND CHILDREN

Death comes early in poor societies, where families lack adequate food, safe drinking water, secure housing, and access to medical care. Organizations fighting child poverty estimate that at least 100 million city children in poor countries beg, steal, sell sex, or work for drug gangs to provide income for their families. Such a life almost always means dropping out of school and puts children at high risk of disease and violence. Many girls, with little or no access to medical assistance, become pregnant, a case of children who cannot support themselves having children of their own.

Analysts estimate that another 100 million of the world's children leave their families altogether, sleeping and living on the streets as best they can or perhaps trying to migrate to the United States. Roughly half of all street children are found in Latin American cities such as Mexico City and Rio de Janeiro, where half of all children grow up in poverty. Many people in the United States know these cities as exotic travel destinations, but they are also home to thousands of children living in makeshift huts, under bridges, or in alleyways (United Nations Development Programme, 2000; Collymore, 2002).

 Read more about the lives of street children at http://www.hrw.org/children/street.htm

 YOUR TURN

How do you think the experience of childhood as a stage of the life course differs in high- and low-income countries?

POVERTY AND WOMEN

In rich societies, the work women do typically is undervalued, underpaid, or overlooked entirely. In poor societies, women face even greater disadvantages. Most of the people who work in sweatshops like the one described in the opening to this chapter are women.

To make matters worse, tradition keeps women out of many jobs in low-income nations; in Bangladesh, women work in garment factories because that nation's conservative Muslim religious norms bar them from most other paid work and limit their opportunities for advanced schooling (Bearak, 2001). At the same time, traditional norms give women primary responsibility for child rearing and maintaining the household. The United Nations estimates that in poor countries, men own 90 percent of the land, a far greater gender disparity in wealth than is found in high-income nations. It is no surprise, then, that about 70 per-

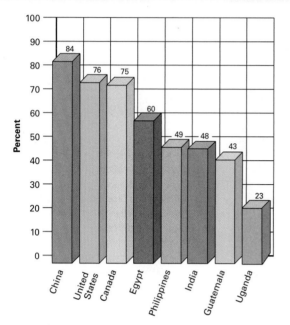

FIGURE 9–3 Use of Contraception by Married Women of Childbearing Age

In the United States, most women of childbearing age use contraception. In many low-income countries, however, most women do not have the opportunity to make this choice.

Source: United Nations Development Programme (2005).

cent of the world's 1 billion people living near absolute poverty are women (Hymowitz, 1995).

Finally, most women in poor countries receive little or no reproductive health care. Limited access to birth control keeps women at home with their children, keeps the birth rate high, and limits the economic production of the country. Figure 9–3 shows that only about one-fourth of women in poor countries such as Uganda use contraceptives for birth control, compared with the United States, where three-fourths of women use contraceptives.

SLAVERY

Poor societies have many problems in addition to hunger, including illiteracy, warfare, and even slavery. The British Empire banned slavery in 1833, followed by the United States in 1865. But according to Anti-Slavery International (ASI), as many as 200 million men, women, and children (about 3 percent of humanity) live today in conditions that amount to slavery.

ASI describes four types of slavery. First is *chattel slavery,* in which one person owns another. The number of chattel slaves is difficult to estimate because this practice is against the law almost everywhere. But the buying and selling of slaves still takes place in many countries in Asia, the Middle East, and especially Africa. The Thinking Globally box describes the reality of one slave's life in the African nation of Mauritania.

A second, more common form of bondage is *child slavery,* in which desperately poor families let their children take to the streets to do what they can to survive. Perhaps 100 million children—many in poor countries of Latin America—fall into this category.

Third, *debt bondage* is the practice by which employers hold workers captive by paying them too little to meet their debts. In this case, workers receive a wage, but it is too small to cover the food and housing provided by the employer; for practical purposes, they are enslaved. Many sweatshop workers in low-income nations fall into this category.

Fourth, *servile forms of marriage* may also amount to slavery. In India, Thailand, and some African nations, families marry off women against their will. Many end up as slaves to their husband's family; some are forced into prostitution.

Finally, one additional form of slavery is *human trafficking,* the movement of men, women, and children from one place to another for the purpose of performing forced labor. For example, women or men are brought to a new country on the promise of a job and then forced to become prostitutes or farm laborers, or "parents" adopt children from another country and then force them to work in sweatshops. Such activity is big business: Next to trading in guns and drugs, trading in people brings the greatest profits to organized crime around the world (Orhant, 2002).

In 1948, the United Nations issued the Universal Declaration of Human Rights, which states, "No one shall be held in slavery or servitude; slavery and the slave trade shall be prohibited in all their forms." Unfortunately, nearly six decades later, this social evil still exists.

 Read the UN's Universal Declaration of Human Rights at http://www.un.org/rights/50/decla.htm

EXPLANATIONS OF GLOBAL POVERTY

What accounts for severe and widespread poverty in much of the world? The rest of this chapter provides answers to this question using the following facts about poor societies:

1. **Technology.** About one-quarter of people in low-income countries farm the land using human muscles or animal power. With such limited energy sources, agricultural production is modest.

"God Made Me to Be a Slave"

Fatma Mint Mamadou is a young woman living in North Africa's Islamic Republic of Mauritania. Asked her age, she pauses, smiles, and shakes her head. She has no idea when she was born. Nor can she read or write. What she knows is tending camels, herding sheep, hauling bags of water, sweeping, and serving tea to her owners. This young woman is one of perhaps 90,000 slaves in Mauritania.

In the central region of this nation, having very dark skin almost always means being a slave to an Arab owner. Fatma accepts her situation; she has known nothing else. She explains in a matter-of-fact voice that she is a slave, like her mother before her and her grandmother before that. "Just as God created a camel to be a camel," she shrugs, "he created me to be a slave."

Fatma, her mother, and her brothers and sisters live together in a squatter settlement on the edge of Nouakchott, Mauritania's capital city. Their home is a nine-by-twelve-foot hut they built from

wood scraps and other building materials taken from construction sites. The roof is nothing more than a piece of cloth; there is no plumbing or furniture. The nearest water comes from a well a mile down the road.

In this region, slavery began more than 500 years ago, about the time Columbus sailed west toward the Americas. As Arab and Berber tribes moved across the African continent spreading Islam, they raided local villages and made slaves of the people, a practice that was continued for dozens of gener-

ations. In 1905, the French colonial rulers of Mauritania banned slavery. After the nation gained independence in 1961, the new government reaffirmed the ban. But such proclamations have done little to change strong traditions. Indeed, people like Fatma have no idea what freedom means.

The next question is more personal: "Are you and other girls ever raped?" Again, Fatma hesitates. With no hint of emotion, she responds, "Of course, in the night the men come to breed us. Is that what you mean by rape?"

WHAT DO YOU THINK?

1. How does tradition play a part in keeping people in slavery?

2. What might explain the fact that the world still tolerates slavery?

3. Explain the connection between slavery and poverty.

Source: Based on Burkett (1997).

2. **Population growth.** As Chapter 15 ("Population, Urbanization, and Environment") explains, the poorest countries have the world's highest birth rates. Despite the death toll from poverty, the populations of poor countries in Africa double every twenty-five years. In these countries, half the people are teenagers or younger. With such a large share of the population just entering the childbearing years, the wave of population growth will continue to roll into the future. In recent years, for example, the population of Chad has swelled by 2.8 percent annually, so that even with economic development, living standards have fallen.

3. **Cultural patterns.** Poor societies are usually traditional. People who hold to long-established ways of

life resist change—even change that promises a richer material life. The Seeing Sociology in Everyday Life box on page 256 explains why traditional people in India respond to their poverty differently than poor people in the United States.

4. **Social stratification.** Low-income nations distribute their wealth very unequally. Chapter 8 ("Social Stratification") explained that social inequality is greater in agrarian societies than in industrial societies. In Brazil, for example, half of all farmland is owned by just 1 percent of the people (Bergamo & Camarotti, 1996).

5. **Gender inequality.** Extreme gender inequality in poor societies keeps women from holding jobs, which typically means they have many children. An expand-

"Happy Poverty" in India: Making Sense of a Strange Idea

Although India has become a middle-income nation, its per capita GDP is only $2,892, less than one-tenth that in the United States. For this reason, India is home to one-fourth of the world's hungry people.

But most North Americans do not easily understand the reality of poverty in India. Many of the country's 1.1 billion people live in conditions far worse than those our society labels "poor." A traveler's first experience of Indian life can be shocking. Chennai (formerly known as Madras), for example, one of India's largest cities with 7 million inhabitants, seems chaotic to the outsider, with streets choked by motorbikes, trucks, carts pulled by oxen, and waves of people. Along the roadway, vendors sit on burlap cloths selling fruits, vegetables, and cooked food while people a few yards away work, talk, bathe, and sleep.

Although some people live well, Chennai is dotted by more than 1,000 shanty settlements, home to half a million people from rural villages who have come in search of a better life. Shantytowns are clusters of huts built with branches, leaves, and pieces of discarded cardboard and tin. These dwellings offer little privacy and lack refrigeration,

running water, and bathrooms. A visitor from the United States may feel uneasy in such an area, knowing that the poorest sections of our own inner cities seethe with frustration and sometimes explode with violence.

But India's people understand poverty differently than we do. No restless young men hang out at the corner, no drug dealers work the streets, and there is little danger of violence. In the United States, poverty often means anger and isolation; in India, even shantytowns are organized around strong families—children, parents, and often grandparents—who offer a smile of welcome to a stranger.

For traditional people in India, life is shaped by *dharma,* the Hindu concept of duty and destiny that teaches people to accept their fate, whatever it may be. Mother Teresa, who worked among the poorest of India's people, goes to the heart of the cultural differences: "Americans have angry poverty," she explains. "In India, there is worse poverty, but it is a happy poverty."

Perhaps we should not describe anyone who clings to the edge of survival as happy. But poverty in India is eased by the strength and support of families and communities, a sense that life has a purpose, and a worldview that encourages each person to accept whatever life offers. As a result, a visitor may come away from a first encounter with Indian poverty rather confused: "How can people be so poor and yet seem content, active, and *joyful?*"

WHAT DO YOU THINK?

1. What did Mother Teresa mean when she said that in India there is "happy poverty"?

2. How might an experience like this change the way you think of being "rich"?

3. Do you know of any poor people in the United States who have attitudes toward poverty similar to these people in India? What would make people seem to accept their poverty?

---

ing population, in turn, slows economic development. Many analysts conclude that raising living standards in much of the world depends on improving the social standing of women.

6. **Global power relationships.** A final cause of global poverty lies in the relationships between the nations of the world. Historically, wealth flowed from poor

societies to rich nations through **colonialism,** *the process by which some nations enrich themselves through political and economic control of other nations.* The countries of Western Europe colonized much of Latin America beginning roughly 500 years ago. Such global exploitation allowed some nations to develop economically at the expense of others.

In rich nations such as the United States, most parents expect their children to enjoy years of childhood, largely free from the responsibilities of adult life. This is not the case in poor nations across Latin America, Africa, and Asia. Poor families depend on whatever income their children can earn, and many children as young as six or seven work full days weaving or performing other kinds of manual labor. Child labor lies behind the low prices of many products imported for sale in this country.

Although 130 former colonies gained their independence during the twentieth century, exploitation continues through **neocolonialism** (*neo* is the Greek word for "new"), *a new form of global power relationships that involves not direct political control but economic exploitation by multinational corporations*. A **multinational corporation** is *a large business that operates in many countries*. Corporate leaders can impose their will on countries in which they do business to create favorable economic conditions, just as colonizers did in the past (Bonanno, Constance, & Lorenz, 2000).

Global Stratification: Theoretical Analysis

There are two major explanations for the unequal distribution of the world's wealth and power: *modernization theory* and *dependency theory*. Each theory suggests a different solution to the suffering of hungry people in much of the world.

Modernization Theory

Modernization theory is *a model of economic and social development that explains global inequality in terms of technological and cultural differences between nations*. Modernization theory, which follows the structural-functional approach, emerged in the 1950s, a time when U.S. society was fascinated with new developments in technology. To showcase the power of protective technology and also to counter the growing influence of the Soviet Union and socialism in much of the world, U.S. policymakers drafted a foreign policy that supported capitalism and free markets. This general policy has been with us ever since (Rostow, 1960, 1978; Bauer 1981; Berger 1986; Firebaugh, 1996; Firebaugh & Sandu, 1998).

Historical Perspective

Until a few centuries ago, the entire world was poor. Because poverty has been the norm throughout human history, modernization theory proposes that it is *affluence* that demands an explanation.

Affluence came within reach of a growing share of people in Western Europe during the late Middle Ages as world exploration and trade expanded. Soon the Industrial Revolution was under way, transforming first Western Europe and then North America. Industrial technology, together with the spirit of capitalism, created new wealth as never before. At first, this new wealth benefited only a few. But industrial technology was so productive that gradually the living standards of even the poorest people began to improve. Absolute poverty, which had plagued humanity throughout history, was finally in decline.

During the twentieth century, the standard of living in high-income countries, where the Industrial Revolution began, jumped at least fourfold. Many nations in Asia and Latin America have industrialized, and they, too, have

Modernization theory claims that corporations that build factories in low-income nations help people by providing them with jobs and higher wages than they had before; dependency theory views these factories as "sweatshops" that exploit workers. Following the dependency theory approach, these students are staging a protest at Gap and Nike stores in Boston.

become richer. But with limited industrial technology, low-income countries have changed much less.

The Importance of Culture

Why didn't the Industrial Revolution sweep away poverty the world over? Modernization theory points out that not every society wants to adopt new technology. Doing so takes a cultural environment that emphasizes the benefits of material wealth and new ideas.

Modernization theory identifies *tradition* as the greatest barrier to economic development. A reverence for the past may discourage people from adopting new technologies that would raise their living standards. Even today, many people—from the Amish in North America to traditional Islamic people in the Middle East to the Semai of Malaysia—oppose new technology because they see it as a threat to their family relationships, customs, and religious beliefs.

Max Weber (1958, orig. 1904–05) found that at the end of the Middle Ages, Western Europe's cultural environment favored change. As Chapter 13 ("Family and Religion") explains, the Protestant Reformation reshaped traditional Catholic beliefs to generate a progress-oriented way of life. Wealth—looked on with suspicion by the Catholic church—became a sign of personal virtue, and the growing importance of individualism steadily replaced the traditional emphasis on family and community. These new cultural patterns nurtured the Industrial Revolution.

Rostow's Stages of Modernization

Modernization theory holds that the door to affluence is open to all. Indeed, as technological advances spread around the world, all societies should gradually industrialize. According to Walt W. Rostow (1960, 1978), modernization occurs in four stages:

1. **Traditional stage.** Socialized to honor the past, people in traditional societies cannot easily imagine that life can or should be any different. They therefore build their lives around families and local communities, following well-worn paths that allow little individual freedom or change. Life is often spiritually rich but lacking in material goods.

   A century ago, much of the world was in this initial stage of economic development. Nations such as Bangladesh, Niger, and Somalia are still at the traditional stage and remain poor.

2. **Take-off stage.** As a society shakes off the grip of tradition, people start to use their talents and imagination, sparking economic growth. A market emerges as people produce goods not just for their own use but to trade with others for profit. Greater individualism, a willingness to take risks, and a desire for material goods also take hold, often at the expense of family ties and time-honored norms and values.

   Great Britain reached take-off by about 1800, the United States by 1820. Thailand, a middle-income country in eastern Asia, is now in this stage. Such development is typically speeded by progressive influences from rich nations, including foreign aid, the availability of advanced technology and investment capital, and opportunities for schooling abroad.

3. **Drive to technological maturity.** As this stage begins, "growth" is a widely accepted idea that fuels a society's pursuit of higher living standards. A diversified economy drives a population eager to enjoy the benefits of industrial technology. At the same time, people begin to realize (and sometimes regret) that industrialization is weakening traditional family and local community life. Great Britain entered this stage by about 1840, the United States by 1860. Today, Mexico, the U.S. territory of Puerto Rico, and South Korea are among the nations driving to technological maturity.

   Absolute poverty is greatly reduced in nations in this stage of development. Cities swell with people who have left rural villages in search of economic opportunity; job specialization makes relationships  less personal, and growing individualism generates social movements demanding greater political rights. Societies approaching technological maturity also provide basic schooling to all their people and advanced training for some. The newly educated consider tradition "backward," opening the door to further change. In addition, the social position of women steadily approaches that of men.

4. **High mass consumption.** Economic development driven by industrial technology raises living standards as mass production stimulates mass consumption. Simply put, people soon learn to "need" the expanding selection of goods that their society produces. The United States, Japan, and other rich nations entered this stage of development by 1900. Approaching this level of economic prosperity today are two former British colonies in eastern Asia: Hong Kong (now part of the People's Republic of China) and Singapore (independent since 1965).

The Role of Rich Nations

Modernization theory claims that high-income countries play four important roles in global economic development:

1. **Controlling population.** Because population growth is greatest in the poorest societies, rising population can overtake economic advances. Rich nations can help limit population growth by exporting birth control technology and promoting its use. Once economic development is under way, birth rates should decline, as they have in industrialized nations, because children are no longer an economic asset.

2. **Increasing food production.** Rich nations can export high-tech farming methods to poor nations to help raise agricultural yields. Such techniques, collectively referred to as the "Green Revolution," include new hybrid seeds, modern irrigation methods, chemical fertilizers, and pesticides for insect control.

3. **Introducing industrial technology.** Rich nations can encourage economic growth in poor societies by introducing machinery and information technology, which raise productivity. Industrialization also shifts the labor force from farming to skilled industrial and service jobs.

4. **Providing foreign aid.** Investment capital from rich nations can boost the prospects of poor societies striving to reach Rostow's take-off stage. Foreign aid can help raise agricultural productivity by enabling poor countries to purchase more fertilizer and build irrigation projects. In addition, financial and technical assistance to build power plants and factories improves industrial output.

CRITICAL REVIEW Modernization theory has many influential supporters among social scientists (Parsons, 1966; W. E. Moore, 1977, 1979; Berger, 1986; Firebaugh, 1996; Firebaugh & Sandu, 1998). For decades, it has shaped the foreign policy of the United States and other rich nations. Supporters point to rapid economic development in Asia—especially in South Korea, Taiwan, Singapore, and Hong Kong—as proof that the affluence created in Western Europe and North America is within the reach of all countries.

But modernization theory faces criticism from socialist countries (and left-leaning analysts in the West) as little more than a defense of capitalism. Its most serious flaw, according to critics, is that modernization simply has not occurred in many poor countries. The United Nations reported that living standards in a number of nations, including Haiti and Nicaragua in Latin America and Sudan, Ghana, and Rwanda in Africa, are actually lower today than they were in 1960 (United Nations Development Programme, 1996).

A second criticism of modernization theory is that it fails to recognize that rich nations, which benefit from the status quo, often block the path to development for poor countries. Centuries ago, rich countries industrialized

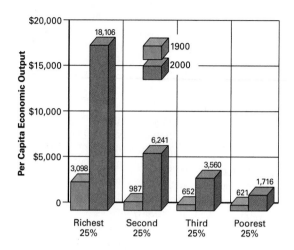

FIGURE 9-5 The World's Increasing Economic Inequality

The gap between the richest and poorest people in the world is twice as big as it was a century ago.

Source: International Monetary Fund (2000).

extreme poverty has become worse. In 1980, sub-Saharan Africa accounted for 11 percent of $1-per-day poverty; by 2001, this share had risen to 29 percent (Sala-i-Martin, 2002; Chen & Ravallion, 2004; Dunphy, 2006).

These trends in economic performance have caused both modernization and dependency theorists to revise their views. Governments have played a large role in the economic growth that has occurred in Asia and elsewhere; this fact challenges modernization theory and its free-market approach to development. On the other hand, since the upheavals in the former Soviet Union and Eastern Europe,

a global reevaluation of socialism has been taking place. Because socialist nations have a record of poor economic performance and political repression, many low-income nations are unwilling to follow the advice of dependency theory and place economic development entirely under government control.

Although the world's future is uncertain, we have learned a great deal about global stratification. One major insight, offered by modernization theory, is that poverty is partly a *problem of technology*. A higher standard of living for a growing world population depends on raising agricultural and industrial productivity. A second insight, derived from dependency theory, is that global inequality is also a *political issue*. Even with higher productivity, the human community must address crucial questions concerning the distribution of resources, both within societies and around the globe.

Although economic development raises living standards, it also places greater strains on the natural environment. As nations such as India and China—with a combined population of 2.4 billion—become more affluent, their people will consume more energy and other natural resources (China has recently passed Japan to become the second largest consumer of oil, behind the United States, which is one reason that oil prices have been rising). Richer nations also produce more solid waste and other forms of pollution.

Finally, the vast gulf that separates the world's richest and poorest people puts everyone at greater risk of war and terrorism as the poorest people challenge the social arrangements that threaten their existence (Lindauer & Weerapana, 2002). In the long run, we can achieve peace on this planet only by ensuring that all people enjoy a significant measure of dignity and security.

APPLYING SOCIOLOGY IN EVERYDAY LIFE

1. Page through several issues of any current news-magazine or travel magazine, and notice any stories or advertising mentioning low-income countries (selling, say, coffee from Colombia or exotic vacations to India). What picture of life in low-income countries does the advertising present? In light of what you have learned in this chapter, how accurate does this image seem to you?
2. Millions of students from abroad study on U.S. campuses. Find a woman and a man on your campus who were raised in a low-income country. After

explaining that you have been studying global stratification, ask if they are willing to share what life is like back home. If they are, ask about stratification as well as their social position in their home country.
3. Pick five of the global maps in this text (the full list is found on page xvi), and identify social traits of high-income countries and those of low-income countries. Try to use both modernization theory and dependency theory to build theoretical explanations of the patterns you find.

country in eastern Asia, is now in this stage. Such development is typically speeded by progressive influences from rich nations, including foreign aid, the availability of advanced technology and investment capital, and opportunities for schooling abroad.

3. **Drive to technological maturity.** As this stage begins, "growth" is a widely accepted idea that fuels a society's pursuit of higher living standards. A diversified economy drives a population eager to enjoy the benefits of industrial technology. At the same time, people begin to realize (and sometimes regret) that industrialization is weakening traditional family and local community life. Great Britain entered this stage by about 1840, the United States by 1860. Today, Mexico, the U.S. territory of Puerto Rico, and South Korea are among the nations driving to technological maturity.

Absolute poverty is greatly reduced in nations in this stage of development. Cities swell with people who have left rural villages in search of economic opportunity; job specialization makes relationships less personal, and growing individualism generates social movements demanding greater political rights. Societies approaching technological maturity also provide basic schooling to all their people and advanced training for some. The newly educated consider tradition "backward," opening the door to further change. In addition, the social position of women steadily approaches that of men.

SOCIOLOGY @ WORK

4. **High mass consumption.** Economic development driven by industrial technology raises living standards as mass production stimulates mass consumption. Simply put, people soon learn to "need" the expanding selection of goods that their society produces. The United States, Japan, and other rich nations entered this stage of development by 1900. Approaching this level of economic prosperity today are two former British colonies in eastern Asia: Hong Kong (now part of the People's Republic of China) and Singapore (independent since 1965).

The Role of Rich Nations

Modernization theory claims that high-income countries play four important roles in global economic development:

1. **Controlling population.** Because population growth is greatest in the poorest societies, rising population can overtake economic advances. Rich nations can help limit population growth by exporting birth control technology and promoting its use. Once economic development is under way, birth rates should decline, as they have in industrialized nations, because children are no longer an economic asset.

2. **Increasing food production.** Rich nations can export high-tech farming methods to poor nations to help raise agricultural yields. Such techniques, collectively referred to as the "Green Revolution," include new hybrid seeds, modern irrigation methods, chemical fertilizers, and pesticides for insect control.

3. **Introducing industrial technology.** Rich nations can encourage economic growth in poor societies by introducing machinery and information technology, which raise productivity. Industrialization also shifts the labor force from farming to skilled industrial and service jobs.

4. **Providing foreign aid.** Investment capital from rich nations can boost the prospects of poor societies striving to reach Rostow's take-off stage. Foreign aid can help raise agricultural productivity by enabling poor countries to purchase more fertilizer and build irrigation projects. In addition, financial and technical assistance to build power plants and factories improves industrial output.

CRITICAL REVIEW Modernization theory has many influential supporters among social scientists (Parsons, 1966; W. E. Moore, 1977, 1979; Berger, 1986; Firebaugh, 1996; Firebaugh & Sandu, 1998). For decades, it has shaped the foreign policy of the United States and other rich nations. Supporters point to rapid economic development in Asia—especially in South Korea, Taiwan, Singapore, and Hong Kong—as proof that the affluence created in Western Europe and North America is within the reach of all countries.

But modernization theory faces criticism from socialist countries (and left-leaning analysts in the West) as little more than a defense of capitalism. Its most serious flaw, according to critics, is that modernization simply has not occurred in many poor countries. The United Nations reported that living standards in a number of nations, including Haiti and Nicaragua in Latin America and Sudan, Ghana, and Rwanda in Africa, are actually lower today than they were in 1960 (United Nations Development Programme, 1996).

A second criticism of modernization theory is that it fails to recognize that rich nations, which benefit from the status quo, often block the path to development for poor countries. Centuries ago, rich countries industrialized

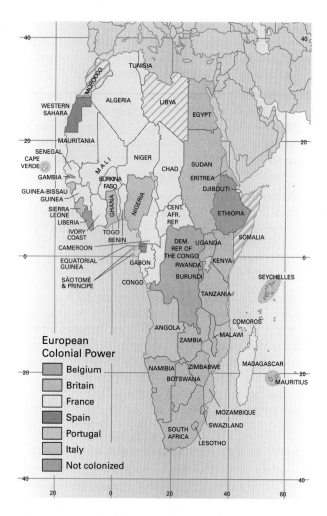

FIGURE 9–4 Africa's Colonial History

For more than a century, most of Africa was colonized by European nations, with France dominating in the northwest region of the continent and Great Britain dominating in the east and south.

European
Colonial Power

- Belgium
- Britain
- France
- Spain
- Portugal
- Italy
- Not colonized

from a position of global strength. Can we expect poor countries today to do so from a position of global weakness?

Third, modernization theory treats rich and poor societies as separate worlds, ignoring the fact that the global economy affects all nations. Many countries in Latin America and Asia are still struggling from the effects of their colonization, which boosted the fortunes of Europe.

Fourth, modernization theory holds up the world's most developed countries as the standard for judging the rest of humanity, revealing an ethnocentric bias. We need to remember that our Western idea of "progress" has

caused us to rush headlong into a competitive, materialistic way of life, which uses up the world's scarce resources and damages the natural environment.

Fifth and finally, modernization theory suggests that the causes of global poverty lie almost entirely within the poor societies themselves. Critics see this analysis as little more than blaming the victims for their own problems. Instead, they argue, an analysis of global inequality should focus just as much on the behavior of rich nations as it does on the behavior of poor ones and also on the global economic system.

Concerns such as these reflect a second major approach to understanding global inequality, dependency theory.

✓ **YOUR LEARNING** State the important ideas of modernization theory. Point to several of its strengths and weaknesses.

DEPENDENCY THEORY

Dependency theory is *a model of economic and social development that explains global inequality in terms of the historical exploitation of poor nations by rich ones.* This analysis, which follows the social-conflict approach, puts primary responsibility for global poverty on rich nations, which for centuries have systematically impoverished low-income countries and made them dependent on the rich ones. This destructive process continues today.

Historical Perspective

Everyone agrees that before the Industrial Revolution, there was little affluence in the world. However, dependency theory asserts that people living in poor countries were actually better off economically in the past than their descendants are now. André Gunder Frank (1975), a noted supporter of this theory, argues that the colonial process that helped develop rich nations also *underdeveloped* poor societies.

Dependency theory is based on the idea that the economic positions of the rich and poor nations of the world are linked and cannot be understood apart from one another. Poor nations are not simply lagging behind rich ones on the "path of progress"; rather, the prosperity of the most developed countries came largely at the expense of less developed ones. In short, some nations became rich only because others became poor. Both are the result of the global economic system that began to develop five centuries ago.

The Importance of Colonialism

Late in the fifteenth century, Europeans began surveying the Americas to the west, Africa to the south, and Asia to the

Although the world continues to grow richer, billions of people are being left behind. The shantytown of Cité Soleil ("City of the Sun") near Port-au-Prince, the capital of Haiti, is built around an open sewer. What would you estimate life expectancy to be in such a place?

east in order to establish colonies. They were so successful that a century ago, Great Britain controlled about one-fourth of the world's land, boasting that "the sun never sets on the British Empire." The United States, itself originally a patchwork of small British colonies on the eastern seaboard of North America, soon pushed across the continent, purchased Alaska, and gained control of Haiti, Puerto Rico, Guam, the Philippines, the Hawaiian Islands, and Guantanamo Bay in Cuba.

Meanwhile, Europeans and Africans engaged in a brutal form of human exploitation—the slave trade—from about 1500 until 1850. Even as the world was rejecting slavery, Europeans took control of Africa itself, as Figure 9–4 shows. European powers dominated most of the continent until the early 1960s.

Formal colonialism has almost disappeared from the world. However, according to dependency theory, political liberation has not meant economic independence. Far from it: The economic relationship between poor and rich nations continues the colonial pattern of domination. This *neocolonialism* is the heart of the capitalist world economy.

Wallerstein's Capitalist World Economy

Immanuel Wallerstein (1974, 1979, 1983, 1984) explains global stratification using a model of the "capitalist world economy." Wallerstein's term "world economy" suggests that the prosperity or poverty of any country results from the operation of the global economic system. The global economy began to take shape with the beginning of colonization more than 500 years ago when Europeans began gathering

wealth from the rest of the world. Because the global economy is based in high-income countries, it is capitalist in character.[2]

Wallerstein calls the rich nations the *core* of the world economy. Colonialism enriched this core by funneling raw materials from around the world to Western Europe, where they fueled the Industrial Revolution. Today, multinational corporations operate profitably worldwide, bringing wealth to North America, Western Europe, Australia, and Japan.

Low-income countries are the *periphery* of the global economy. Drawn into the global economy by colonial exploitation, poor nations continue to support rich ones by providing low-cost labor and a vast market for industrial products. The remaining countries are the *semiperiphery* of the world economy. They include middle-income countries like Mexico and Brazil that have closer ties to the global economic core.

According to Wallerstein, the world economy benefits rich societies (by generating profits) and harms the rest of the world (by causing poverty). The world economy thus makes poor nations dependent on rich ones. This dependency involves three factors:

1. **Narrow, export-oriented economies.** Poor nations produce only a few crops for export to rich countries. Examples include coffee and fruits from Latin American nations, oil from Nigeria, hardwoods from

---

[2]This section also draws on Frank (1980, 1981), Delacroix & Ragin (1981), Bergesen (1983), Dixon & Boswell (1996), and Kentor (1998).

the Philippines, and palm oil from Malaysia. Today's multinational corporations buy raw materials cheaply in poor societies and transport them to core nations, where factories process them for profitable sale. Thus poor nations develop few industries of their own.

2. **Lack of industrial capacity.** Without an industrial base, poor societies depend on selling their inexpensive raw materials to the rich nations and try to buy from the rich nations the few expensive manufactured goods they can afford. In a classic example of this dependency, British colonialists encouraged the people of India to raise cotton but prevented them from weaving their own cloth. Instead, the British shipped Indian cotton to English textile mills in Birmingham and Manchester, manufactured the cloth, and shipped finished goods back to India, where the very people who harvested the cotton bought the garments.

   Dependency theorists claim that the Green Revolution—widely praised by modernization theorists—works the same way. Poor countries sell cheap raw materials to rich nations and then try to buy expensive fertilizers, pesticides, and machinery in return. Typically, rich countries profit from this exchange more than poor nations.

3. **Foreign debt.** Unequal trade patterns have plunged poor countries into debt. Collectively, the poor nations of the world owe rich countries $2.8 trillion; hundreds of billions of dollars are owed to the United States alone. Such staggering debt paralyzes a country, causing high unemployment and rampant inflation (World Bank, 2006).

The Role of Rich Nations

Modernization theory and dependency theory assign rich nations very different roles. Modernization theory holds that rich societies *produce wealth* through capital investment and new technology. Dependency theory views global inequality in terms of how countries *distribute wealth*, arguing that rich nations have *overdeveloped* themselves as they have *underdeveloped* the rest of the world.

Dependency theorists dismiss the idea that programs developed by rich countries to control population and boost agricultural and industrial output raise living standards in poor countries. Instead, they claim, such programs actually benefit rich nations and the ruling elites, not the poor majority, in low-income countries (Kentor, 2001).

The hunger activists Frances Moore Lappé and Joseph Collins (1986) maintain that the capitalist culture of the United States encourages people to think of poverty as somehow inevitable. Following this line of reasoning, poverty results from "natural" processes, including having too many children, and from natural disasters such as droughts. But according to dependency theory, global poverty is far from inevitable; it results from deliberate policies. Lappé and Collins point out that the world already produces enough food to allow every person on the planet to become quite fat. In fact, most of Africa actually exports food, even though many people in African nations go hungry.

According to Lappé and Collins, the contradiction of poverty amid plenty stems from the rich-nation policy of producing food for profit, not people. That is, corporations in rich nations work with elites in poor countries to grow and export profitable crops such as coffee, which means using land that could otherwise produce basics such as beans and corn for local families. Governments of poor countries support the practice of growing for export because they need food profits to help pay off their huge foreign debt. According to Lappé and Collins, the capitalist corporate structure of the global economy is at the core of this vicious cycle.

CRITICAL REVIEW The main idea of dependency theory is that no nation becomes rich or poor in isolation because a single global economy shapes the future of all nations. Pointing to Latin America and other poor regions of the world, dependency theorists claim that development simply cannot proceed under the constraints now imposed by rich countries. Rather, they call for radical reform of the entire world economy so that it operates in the interests of the majority of people.

Critics charge that dependency theory wrongly treats wealth as if no one gets richer without someone else getting poorer. Corporations, small business owners, and farmers can and do create new wealth through their drive and imaginative use of new technology. After all, they point out, the entire world's wealth has increased sixfold since 1950.

Second, dependency theory is wrong in blaming rich nations for global poverty, because many of the world's poorest countries (such as Ethiopia) have had little contact with rich nations. On the contrary, a long history of trade with rich countries has dramatically improved the economies of nations including Sri Lanka, Singapore, and Hong Kong (all former British colonies), as well as South Korea and Japan. In short, say the critics, most evidence shows that foreign investment by rich nations encourages economic growth, as modernization theory claims, not economic decline, as dependency theory says (E. F. Vogel, 1991; Firebaugh, 1992).

APPLYING THEORY

Global Poverty

	Modernization Theory	Dependency Theory
Which theoretical approach is applied?	Structural-functional approach	Social-conflict approach
How did global poverty come about?	The whole world was poor until some countries developed industrial technology, which allowed mass production and created affluence.	Colonialism moved wealth from some countries to others, making some nations poor as it made other nations rich.
What are the main causes of global poverty today?	Traditional culture and a lack of productive technology.	Neocolonialism—the operation of multi-national corporations in the global, capitalist economy.
Are rich countries part of the problem or part of the solution?	Rich countries are part of the solution, contributing new technology, advanced schooling, and foreign aid.	Rich countries are part of the problem, making poor countries economically dependent and in debt.

Third, critics call dependency theory simplistic for pointing the finger at a single factor—the capitalist market system—as the cause of global inequality (Worsley, 1990). Dependency theory views poor societies as passive victims and ignores factors inside these countries that contribute to their economic problems. Sociologists have long recognized the vital role of culture in shaping people's willingness to accept or resist change. Under the rule of the ultratraditional Muslim Taliban, for example, Afghanistan became economically isolated, and its living standards sank to among the lowest in the world. Is it reasonable to blame capitalist societies for that country's stagnation?

Nor can rich societies be held responsible for the reckless behavior of foreign leaders whose corruption and militaristic campaigns impoverish their countries. Examples include the regimes of Ferdinand Marcos in the Philippines, François Duvalier in Haiti, Manuel Noriega in Panama, Mobutu Sese Seko in Zaire (today's Democratic Republic of the Congo), and Saddam Hussein in Iraq. Some leaders even use food supplies as a weapon in internal political struggles, leaving the people starving, as in the African nations of Ethiopia, Sudan, and Somalia. Likewise, many countries throughout the world have done little to improve the status of women or control population growth.

Fourth, critics say dependency theory is wrong to claim that global trade always makes rich nations richer and poor nations poorer. For example, in 2005, the United States had a trade deficit of $716 billion, meaning that this nation imports that much more goods than it sells abroad. Our country's single greatest debt was to China, whose profitable trade has now pushed that country into the ranks of the world's middle-income nations (Crutsinger, 2005).

Fifth, critics fault dependency theory for offering only vague solutions to global poverty. Most dependency theorists urge poor nations to end all contact with rich countries, and some call for nationalizing foreign-owned industries. In other words, dependency theory is really an argument against the market system and for some sort of world socialism. In light of the difficulties socialist countries (even better-off socialist countries such as Russia) have had in meeting the needs of their own people, critics ask, should we really expect such a system to rescue the entire world from poverty?

The Applying Theory table summarizes the main arguments of modernization theory and dependency theory.

✓ YOUR LEARNING State the main ideas of dependency theory. Point to several of its strengths and weaknesses.

Global Stratification: Looking Ahead

Among the most important trends of recent decades is the expansion of the global economy. In the United States, rising production and sales abroad have brought huge profits to many corporations and their stockholders, especially to those who already have substantial wealth. At the same time, the global economy has moved manufacturing jobs abroad, closing factories in this country and hurting many

Times

The New York Times

December 25, 2005

Shantytown Dwellers in South Africa Protest Sluggish Pace of Change

By MICHAEL WINES

Johannesburg—Sending what some call an ominous signal to this nation's leaders, South Africa's sprawling shanty-towns have begun to erupt, sometimes violently, in protest over the government's inability to deliver the better life that the end of apartheid seemed to herald a dozen years ago.

At a hillside shantytown in Durban called Foreman Road, riot police officers fired rubber bullets in mid-November to disperse 2,000 residents marching to the municipal mayor's office downtown. Two protesters were injured; 45 were arrested. The rest burned an effigy of the city's mayor, Obed Mlaba. . . .

Since 1994, South Africa's government has built and largely given away 1.8 million basic houses, usually 16 feet by 20 feet, often to former shantytown dwellers. More than 10 million have gained access to clean water, and count-

less others have been connected to electrical lines or basic sanitation facilities.

Yet at the same time, researchers say, rising poverty has caused 2 million to lose their homes and 10 million more to have their water or power cut off because of unpaid bills. And the number of shanty dwellers has grown by as much as 50 percent, to 12.5 million people—more than one in four South Africans, many living in a level of squalor that would render most observers from the developed world speechless.

For South African blacks, the current plight is uncomfortably close to the one they endured under apartheid. Black shantytowns first rose under white rule, the result of policies inended to keep nonwhites impoverished and powerless. During apartheid, from the 1940s to the 1980s, officials uprooted and moved millions of blacks, consigning many to transit camps that became permanent shantytowns, sending others to black

townships that quickly attracted masses of squatters. . . .

In Durban, the city is erecting some 16,000 starter houses a year, but the shanty population, now about 750,000, continues to grow by more than 10 percent annually.

The city's 180,000 shanties, crammed into every conceivable open space, are a remarkable sight. Both free-standing and sharing common walls, they spill down hillsides between middle-class subdivisions, perch beside freeway exits and crowd next to foul landfills. They are built of scrap wood and metal and corrugated panels and plastic tarpaulin roofs weighed down with concrete chunks. . . . The 1,000 or so hillside shanties at Foreman Road are typical. A standpipe at the top provides water, carried by bucket to each shack for bathing and dishwashing. At the bottom . . . are four hand-dug, scrap-wood privies—each one, on this day, inexplicably pad-

average workers. The net result: economic polarization in the United States.

People who support the global economy claim that the expansion of trade results in benefits for all countries involved. For this reason, they endorse policies such as the North American Free Trade Agreement (NAFTA). Critics of expanding globalization make other claims: Manufacturing jobs are being lost in the United States, and more manufacturing now takes place abroad, where workers are paid little and few laws protect their safety in the workplace. In addition, other critics of expanding globalization point to the ever-greater stress that the world's economy places on the natural environment.

But perhaps the greatest concern is the vast economic inequality that separates the world's nations. "In the *Times*" takes a look at the problem of poverty in the shantytowns of Durban, South Africa. The concentration of wealth in high-

income countries, coupled with grinding poverty in low-income nations, may well be the biggest problem facing humanity in the twenty-first century.

Both modernization theory and dependency theory offer some understanding of this urgent problem. In evaluating these theories, we must consider empirical evidence. Over the course of the twentieth century, living standards rose significantly in most countries of the world. Even the economic output of the poorest 25 percent of the world's people almost tripled during those 100 years. However, the economic output of the other 75 percent of the world's people increased about sixfold. By this measure, although all people are better off in *absolute* terms, there was almost twice as much *relative* economic inequality in the world in 2000 as there was in 1900. As Figure 9–5 on page 266 shows, the poorest of the world's people are being left behind.

locked shut. Residents say they seldom trek down to the privies, relieving themselves instead in plastic bags and buckets that can be periodically emptied or thrown away.

The one-room shacks provide the rudest sort of shelter. A bed typically takes up half the space; a table holds cookware; clothes go in a small chest. There is no electricity, and so no television; entertainment comes from battery-powered radios. Residents use kerosene stoves and candles for cooking and heat, with predictable results. A year ago, a wind-whipped fire destroyed 288 shacks here. A fire at a Cape Town shantytown early this month left 4,000 people homeless.

The residents say Mayor Mlaba promised during his last election campaign to erect new homes on the slum site and on vacant land opposite their hillside. Instead, however, the city proposed to move the slum residents to rural land far off Durban's outskirts—

and far from the gardening, housecleaning and other menial jobs they have found during Foreman Road's 16-odd years of existence.

Lacking cars, taxi fare or even bicycles to commute to work, the residents marched in protest on Nov. 14, defying the city's refusal to issue a permit. . . .

In a shack roughly 7 feet by 8 feet, a third of the way down Foreman Road's ravine, Zamile Msane, 32, lives with her 58-year-old mother and three children, ages 12, 15 and 17. Ms. Msane has no job. A sister gives her family secondhand clothes, and neighbors donate cornmeal for food. In seven years, she has fled three wildfires, in 1998, 2000 and 2004, losing everything each time.

Yet Ms. Msane, who came here from the Eastern Cape eight years ago, said she would not return to the farm where she once lived, because there was nothing to eat.

Ms. Msane said she joined the Nov. 14 march for one reason.

"Better conditions," she said. "It's not good here, because these are not proper houses. There's mud outside. We're always living in fear of fires. Winter is too cold; summer is too warm. Life is so difficult."

WHAT DO YOU THINK?

1. Would you say that the people living in the Foreman Road shantytown are suffering from relative poverty or absolute poverty? Why?

2. What factors that you have read about in this chapter help explain the poverty described here?

3. Do you think conditions are likely to improve for blacks in South Africa in the years ahead? Point to facts in the article in support of your position.

Adapted from the original article by Michael Wines published in *The New York Times* on December 25, 2005. Copyright © 2005 by The New York Times Company. Reprinted with permission.

Most of this economic polarization took place between 1900 and 1970. Since 1970, the degree of economic inequality worldwide has declined. In addition, the numbers of the world's poorest people—those living on less than $1 per day—have fallen from about 1.5 billion in 1980 to about 1 billion in 2001 (Schultz, 1998; Firebaugh, 1999, 2000; Sala-i-Martin, 2002; Chen & Ravallion, 2004).

The greatest reduction in poverty has taken place in Asia, a region generally regarded as an economic success story. Back in 1980, fully 85 percent of global $1-per-day poverty was in Asia; by 2001, that figure had fallen to 64 percent. Since then, two Asian countries—India and China—have joined the ranks of the middle-income nations (Sala-i-Martin, 2002; Chen & Ravallion, 2004; United Nations Development Programme, 2004).

Latin America represents a mixed case. During the 1970s, this world region enjoyed significant economic growth; during the 1980s and 1990s, however, there was little overall improvement. The share of global $1-per-day poverty was about the same in 2001 (4 percent) as it was in 1970 (Sala-i-Martin, 2002; Chen & Ravallion, 2004).

An increasingly popular idea is "fair trade," paying people in poor nations a fair price for their products. Would you pay more for a cup of coffee made using beans for which a farmer in a low-income country was paid a higher price? Why or why not?

In Africa, about half of the nations are showing economic growth greater than in the past. In many countries, however, especially those south of the Sahara, the extent of

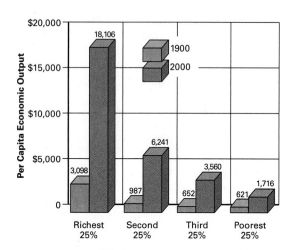

FIGURE 9–5 The World's Increasing Economic Inequality

The gap between the richest and poorest people in the world is twice as big as it was a century ago.

Source: International Monetary Fund (2000).

extreme poverty has become worse. In 1980, sub-Saharan Africa accounted for 11 percent of $1-per-day poverty; by 2001, this share had risen to 29 percent (Sala-i-Martin, 2002; Chen & Ravallion, 2004; Dunphy, 2006).

These trends in economic performance have caused both modernization and dependency theorists to revise their views. Governments have played a large role in the economic growth that has occurred in Asia and elsewhere; this fact challenges modernization theory and its free-market approach to development. On the other hand, since the upheavals in the former Soviet Union and Eastern Europe,

a global reevaluation of socialism has been taking place. Because socialist nations have a record of poor economic performance and political repression, many low-income nations are unwilling to follow the advice of dependency theory and place economic development entirely under government control.

Although the world's future is uncertain, we have learned a great deal about global stratification. One major insight, offered by modernization theory, is that poverty is partly a *problem of technology.* A higher standard of living for a growing world population depends on raising agricultural and industrial productivity. A second insight, derived from dependency theory, is that global inequality is also a *political issue.* Even with higher productivity, the human community must address crucial questions concerning the distribution of resources, both within societies and around the globe.

Although economic development raises living standards, it also places greater strains on the natural environment. As nations such as India and China—with a combined population of 2.4 billion—become more affluent, their people will consume more energy and other natural resources (China has recently passed Japan to become the second largest consumer of oil, behind the United States, which is one reason that oil prices have been rising). Richer nations also produce more solid waste and other forms of pollution.

Finally, the vast gulf that separates the world's richest and poorest people puts everyone at greater risk of war and terrorism as the poorest people challenge the social arrangements that threaten their existence (Lindauer & Weerapana, 2002). In the long run, we can achieve peace on this planet only by ensuring that all people enjoy a significant measure of dignity and security.

⚬ APPLYING SOCIOLOGY IN EVERYDAY LIFE

1. Page through several issues of any current newsmagazine or travel magazine, and notice any stories or advertising mentioning low-income countries (selling, say, coffee from Colombia or exotic vacations to India). What picture of life in low-income countries does the advertising present? In light of what you have learned in this chapter, how accurate does this image seem to you?
2. Millions of students from abroad study on U.S. campuses. Find a woman and a man on your campus who were raised in a low-income country. After

explaining that you have been studying global stratification, ask if they are willing to share what life is like back home. If they are, ask about stratification as well as their social position in their home country.
3. Pick five of the global maps in this text (the full list is found on page xvi), and identify social traits of high-income countries and those of low-income countries. Try to use both modernization theory and dependency theory to build theoretical explanations of the patterns you find.

MAKING THE GRADE

CHAPTER 9 Global Stratification

GLOBAL STRATIFICATION: AN OVERVIEW

HIGH-INCOME COUNTRIES

- contain 18% of the world's people
- generate 79% of global income
- have a high standard of living based on advanced technology
- produce enough economic goods to enable their people to lead comfortable lives
- include about 50 nations, among them the United States, Canada, Argentina, Chile, the nations of Western Europe, Israel, Saudi Arabia, South Africa, Japan, South Korea, and Australia

pp 245–46

MIDDLE-INCOME COUNTRIES

- contain 70% of the world's people
- generate 20% of global income
- have a standard of living about average for the world as a whole
- include about 80 nations, among them Russia, the nations of Eastern Europe, Mexico, Peru, Brazil, Botswana, Namibia, Egypt, Indonesia, India, and the People's Republic of China

pp 246–48

LOW-INCOME COUNTRIES

- contain 12% of the world's people
- generate 1% of global income
- have a low standard of living due to limited industrial technology
- include about 60 nations, generally in Central and East Africa and Asia, among them Chad, the Democratic Republic of the Congo, Ethiopia, Bangladesh, and Pakistan

pp 248–49

See Global Map 9–1 on page 247.

 Although poverty is a reality in the United States and other nations, the greatest social inequality is not within nations but between them.

global stratification (p. 244) patterns of social inequality in the world as a whole

high-income countries (p. 245) the richest nations with the highest overall standards of living

middle-income countries (p. 245) nations with a standard of living about average for the world as a whole

low-income countries (p. 245) nations with a low standard of living in which most people are poor

VISUAL SUMMARY

GLOBAL WEALTH AND POVERTY

All societies contain **RELATIVE POVERTY**, but low-income nations face widespread **ABSOLUTE POVERTY** that is life-threatening.

- Worldwide, about 1 billion people are at risk due to poor nutrition.
- About 15 million people, most of them children, die each year from diseases caused by poverty.
- Throughout the world, women are more likely than men to be poor. Gender bias is strongest in poor societies.
- As many as 200 million men, women, and children (about 3% of humanity) live in conditions that can be described as slavery.

pp 251–54

FACTORS CAUSING POVERTY

- Lack of technology limits production.
- High birth rates produce rapid population increase.
- Traditional cultural patterns make people resist change.
- Extreme social inequality distributes wealth very unequally.
- Extreme gender inequality limits the opportunities of women.
- Colonialism allowed some nations to exploit other nations; neocolonialism continues today.

pp 254–57

colonialism (p. 256) the process by which some nations enrich themselves through political and economic control of other nations

neocolonialism (p. 257) a new form of global power relationships that involves not direct political control but economic exploitation by multinational corporations

multinational corporation (p. 257) a large business that operates in many countries

267

MAKING THE GRADE

CONTINUED...

GLOBAL STRATIFICATION: THEORETICAL ANALYSIS

VISUAL SUMMARY

MODERNIZATION THEORY maintains that nations achieve affluence by developing advanced technology. This process depends on a culture that encourages innovation and change toward higher living standards.

W.W. Rostow identified four stages of development:

- *Traditional stage*—People's lives are built around families and local communities. (Example: Bangladesh)

- *Take-off stage*—A market emerges as people produce goods not just for their own use but to trade with others for profit. (Example: Thailand)

- *Drive to technological maturity*—The ideas of economic growth and higher living standards gain widespread support; schooling is widely available; the social standing of women improves. (Example: Mexico)

- *High mass consumption*—Advanced technology fuels mass production and mass consumption as people now "need" countless goods. (Example: the United States)

pp 257–59

Modernization theory claims

- Rich nations can help poor nations by providing technology to control population size, increase food production, and expand industrial and information economy output, and by providing foreign aid to pay for new economic development.

- Rapid economic development in Asia shows that affluence is within reach of other nations of the world.

p 259

Critics claim

- Rich nations do little to help poor countries and benefit from the status quo. Low living standards in much of Africa and South America result from the policies of rich nations.

- Because rich nations, including the United States, control the global economy, many poor nations struggle to support their people and cannot follow the path to development taken by rich countries centuries ago.

pp 259–60

DEPENDENCY THEORY maintains that global wealth and poverty were created by the colonial process beginning 500 years ago that developed rich nations and underdeveloped poor nations. This capitalist process continues today in the form of neocolonialism—economic exploitation of poor nations by multinational corporations.

Immanuel Wallerstein's model of the capitalist world economy identified three categories of nations:

- *Core*—the world's high-income countries, which are home to multinational corporations

- *Semiperiphery*—the world's middle-income countries, with ties to core nations

- *Periphery*—the world's low-income countries, which provide low-cost labor and a vast market for industrial products

pp 260–61

Dependency theory claims

- Three key factors—export-oriented economies, a lack of industrial capacity, and foreign debt—make poor countries dependent on rich nations and prevent their economic development.

- Radical reform of the entire world economy is needed so that it operates in the interests of the majority of people.

pp 261–62

Critics claim

- Dependency theory overlooks the sixfold increase in global wealth since 1950 and the fact that the world's poorest countries have had weak, not strong, ties to rich countries.

- Rich nations are not responsible for cultural patterns or political corruption that block economic development in many poor nations

pp 262–63

modernization theory (p. 257) a model of economic and social development that explains global inequality in terms of technological and cultural differences between nations

dependency theory (p. 260) a model of economic and social development that explains global inequality in terms of the historical exploitation of poor nations by rich ones

See the Applying Theory table on page 263.

MAKING THE GRADE
Sample Test Questions
CHAPTER 9

These questions are similar to those found in the test bank that accompanies this textbook.

MULTIPLE-CHOICE QUESTIONS

1. In global perspective, the richest 20 percent of all people earn about what percent of the entire world's income?
   a. 20
   b. 40
   c. 60
   d. 80

2. The United States, Canada, and Japan are all considered to be
   a. high-income countries.
   b. middle-income countries.
   c. low-income countries.
   d. Each of these three countries falls into a different category.

3. Low-income nations
   a. are evenly spread in all world regions.
   b. are found mostly in Africa and Asia.
   c. are all in Latin America.
   d. contain a majority of the world's people.

4. China and India are now
   a. the world's poorest countries.
   b. among the world's low-income nations.
   c. among the world's middle-income nations.
   d. among the world's high-income nations.

5. Which of the following is the range of annual personal income for people living in middle-income nations?
   a. $250 to $1,000
   b. $1,000 to $2,500
   c. $2,500 to $10,000
   d. $10,000 to $25,000

6. How does poverty in poor nations compare to poverty in the United States?
   a. In poor nations, poverty is more likely to involve men.
   b. In most poor nations, the problem of poverty has been all but solved.
   c. In poor nations, most people do not consider poverty a problem.
   d. In poor nations, there is far more absolute poverty.

7. *Neocolonialism* refers to the process by which
   a. rich countries gain new colonies to replace older ones.
   b. multinational corporations dominate the economy of a poor country.
   c. rich countries grant independence to their former colonies.
   d. large corporations do business in many countries at once.

8. Which of the following statements is the basis of modernization theory?
   a. The main cause of poverty in the world is low productivity due to simple technology and traditional culture.
   b. Poor nations can never become rich if they remain part of the global capitalist economy.
   c. The main cause of poverty in the world is the operation of multinational corporations.
   d. Most poor nations were richer in the past than they are today.

9. According to Walt Rostow, which is the final stage of economic development?
   a. drive to technological maturity
   b. traditional
   c. high mass consumption
   d. take-off

10. Dependency theory differs from modernization theory by saying that
    a. poor nations are responsible for their own poverty.
    b. capitalism is the best way to produce economic development.
    c. economic development is not a good idea for poor countries.
    d. global stratification results from the exploitation of poor countries by rich countries.

ANSWERS: 1 (d); 2 (a); 3 (b); 4 (c); 5 (c); 6 (d); 7 (b); 8 (a); 9 (c); 10 (d).

ESSAY QUESTIONS

1. What are the differences between relative and absolute poverty? Describe global social stratification using both concepts.

2. Why do many analysts claim that economic development in low-income countries depends on raising the social standing of women?

Gender is more than differences in the ways society expects women and men to behave. It is also a matter of social stratification placing men in positions of power over women.

CHAPTER 10

Gender Stratification

HOW is gender a creation
of society?

WHAT differences does gender
make in people's lives?

WHY is gender an important
dimension of social
stratification?

At first we traveled quite alone . . . but before we had gone many miles, we came on other wagonloads of women, bound in the same direction. As we reached different cross-roads, we saw wagons coming from every part of the country and, long before we reached Seneca Falls, we were a procession.

So wrote Charlotte Woodward in her journal as she made her way in a horse-drawn wagon along the rutted dirt roads leading to Seneca Falls, a small town in upstate New York. The year was 1848, a time when slavery was legal in much of the United States and the social standing of all women, regardless of color, was far below that of men. Back then, in much of the country, women could not own property, keep their own wages if they were married, draft a will, file lawsuits in a court (including lawsuits seeking custody of their own children), or attend college, and husbands were widely viewed as having unquestioned authority over their wives and children.

Some 300 women gathered at Wesleyan Chapel in Seneca Falls to challenge this second-class citizenship. They listened as their leader, Elizabeth Cady Stanton, called for expanding women's rights and opportunities, including the right to vote. Stanton pointed to the fact that the Declaration of Independence stated that "all men are created equal," claiming that in fact "all men and women are created equal." At that time, most people considered the idea of gender equality absurd and outrageous. Even many of those attending the conference were shocked by the idea: Stanton's husband, Henry, rode out of town in protest (Gurnett, 1998).

Much has changed since the Seneca Falls convention, and many of Stanton's "outrageous" proposals are now accepted as matters of basic fairness. But as this chapter explains, women and men still lead different lives in the United States and elsewhere in the world: In most respects, men are still in charge. This chapter explores the importance of gender and explains how, like class position, gender is a major dimension of social stratification.

Gender and Inequality

Chapter 6 ("Sexuality and Society") explained that biological differences divide the human population into categories of female and male. **Gender** refers to *the personal traits and social positions that members of a society attach to being female or male.* Gender, then, is a dimension of social organization, shaping how we interact with others and even how we think about ourselves. More important, gender also involves *hierarchy,* placing men and women in different positions in terms of power, wealth, and other resources.

This is why sociologists speak of **gender stratification,** *the unequal distribution of wealth, power, and privilege between men and women.* In short, gender affects the opportunities and constraints we face throughout our lives.

MALE-FEMALE DIFFERENCES

Many people think there is something "natural" about gender distinctions because biology does make one sex different from the other. But we must be careful not to think of social differences in biological terms. In 1848, for example, women were denied the vote because many people assumed that women did not have enough intelligence or interest in politics. Such attitudes had nothing to do with biology; they reflected the *cultural patterns* of that time and place.

Another example is athletic performance. In 1925, most people—both women and men—believed that the best women runners could never compete with men in a marathon. Today, as Figure 10–1 shows, the gender gap has greatly narrowed, and the best women runners routinely post better times than the fastest men of decades past. Here again, most of the differences between men and women turn out to be socially created.

Do you think female and male athletes should compete on different teams or on the same teams? Why? Do you think men and women see this issue differently?

There are some differences in physical ability between the sexes. On average, males are 10 percent taller than women, 20 percent heavier, and 30 percent stronger, especially in the upper body (Ehrenreich, 1999). On the other hand, women outperform men in the ultimate game of life itself: Life expectancy for men is 75.2 years, and women can expect to live 80.4 years (Miniño, Heron, & Smith, 2006).

In adolescence, males do a bit better in mathematics, and females show stronger verbal skills, a difference that reflects both biology and socialization (Lengermann & Wallace, 1985; Tavris & Wade, 2001). However, research does not point to any overall differences in intelligence between males and females.

Biologically, then, men and women differ in limited ways, with neither one naturally superior. But culture can define the two sexes differently, as the global study of gender described in the next section shows.

GENDER IN GLOBAL PERSPECTIVE

The best way to see how gender is based in culture is by comparing one society to another. Three important studies highlight just how different "masculine" and "feminine" can be.

The Israeli Kibbutz

In Israel, collective Jewish settlements are called *kibbutzim.* The *kibbutz* (the singular form of the word) is an important setting for gender research because gender equality is one of its stated goals; men and women share in both work and decision making.

In kibbutzim, both sexes share most everyday jobs. Both men and women take care of children, cook and clean, repair buildings, and make everyday decisions for the group. Girls and boys are raised in the same way, and from the first weeks of life, children live together in dormitories. Women and men in the kibbutzim have achieved remarkable (although not complete) social equality, evidence that culture defines what is feminine and what is masculine.

Margaret Mead's Research

The anthropologist Margaret Mead carried out groundbreaking research on gender. If gender is based in the bio-

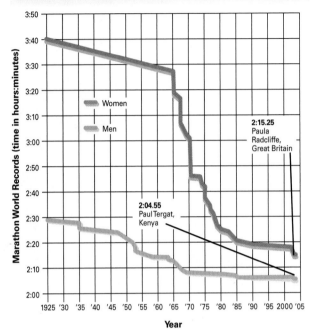

DIVERSITY SNAPSHOT

FIGURE 10-1 Men's and Women's Athletic Performance

Do men naturally outperform women in athletic competition? The answer is not obvious. Early in the twentieth century, men outpaced women by more than an hour in marathon races. But as opportunities for women in athletics have increased, women have been closing the performance gap. Only ten minutes separate the current world marathon records for women and for men (both set in 2003).

Sources: *Christian Science Monitor,* © 1995 Christian Science Monitor and Marathonguide.com (2006). Adapted with permission of the *Christian Science Monitor.*

logical differences between men and women, she reasoned, people everywhere should define "feminine" and "masculine" in the same way; if gender is cultural, these concepts should vary.

Mead studied three societies in New Guinea (1963, orig. 1935). In the mountainous home of the Arapesh, Mead observed men and women with remarkably similar attitudes and behavior. Both sexes, she reported, were cooperative and sensitive to others—in short, what our culture would label "feminine."

Moving south, Mead studied the Mundugumor, whose headhunting and cannibalism stood in striking contrast to the gentle ways of the Arapesh. In this culture, both sexes were typically selfish and aggressive, traits we define as "masculine."

In every society, people assume certain jobs, patterns of behavior, and ways of dressing are "naturally" feminine while others are just as obviously masculine. But in global perspective, we see remarkable variety in such social definitions. These men, Wodaabe pastoral nomads who live in the African nation of Niger, are proud to engage in a display of beauty most people in our society would consider feminine.

Finally, traveling west to the Tchambuli, Mead discovered a culture that, like our own, defined females and males differently. But, Mead reported, the Tchambuli *reversed* many of our ideas of gender: Females were dominant and rational and males were submissive, emotional, and nurturing toward children. Based on her observations, Mead concluded that culture is the key to gender distinctions because what one society defines as masculine another may see as feminine.

Some critics view Mead's findings as "too neat," as if she saw in these societies just the patterns she was looking for. Deborah Gewertz (1981) challenged what she called Mead's "reversal hypothesis," pointing out that Tchambuli males are really the more aggressive sex. Gewertz explains that Mead visited the Tchambuli (who actually call themselves the Chambri) during the 1930s, after they had lost much of their property in tribal wars, and observed men rebuilding their homes, a temporary role for Chambri men.

George Murdock's Research

In a broader study of more than 200 preindustrial societies, George Murdock (1937) found some global agreement on which tasks are feminine and which masculine. Hunting and warfare, Murdock observed, generally fall to men, and home-centered tasks such as cooking and child care tend to be women's work. With their simple technology, preindustrial societies apparently assign roles reflecting men's and women's physical characteristics. With their greater size and strength, men hunt game and protect the group; because women bear children, they do most work in the home.

Beyond this general pattern, Murdock found much variety. Consider agriculture: Women did the farming in about the same number of societies as men; in most societies, the two sexes divided this work. When it came to many other tasks, from building shelters to tattooing the body, Murdock found that preindustrial societies were as likely to turn to one sex as the other.

CRITICAL REVIEW Global comparisons show that overall, societies do not consistently define tasks as feminine or masculine. With industrialization, the importance of muscle power declines, further reducing gender differences (Nolan & Lenski, 2004). In sum, gender is too variable to be a simple expression of biology; what it means to be female and male is mostly a creation of society.

☑ **YOUR LEARNING** By comparing many cultures, what do we learn about the origin of gender differences?

PATRIARCHY AND SEXISM

Conceptions of gender vary, and there is evidence of societies in which women have greater power than men. One example is the Musuo, a very small society in China's Yunnan province, in which women control most property, select their sexual partners, and make most decisions about everyday life. The Musuo appear to be a case of **matriarchy** ("rule of mothers"), *a form of social organization in which females dominate males*, which has only rarely been documented in human history.

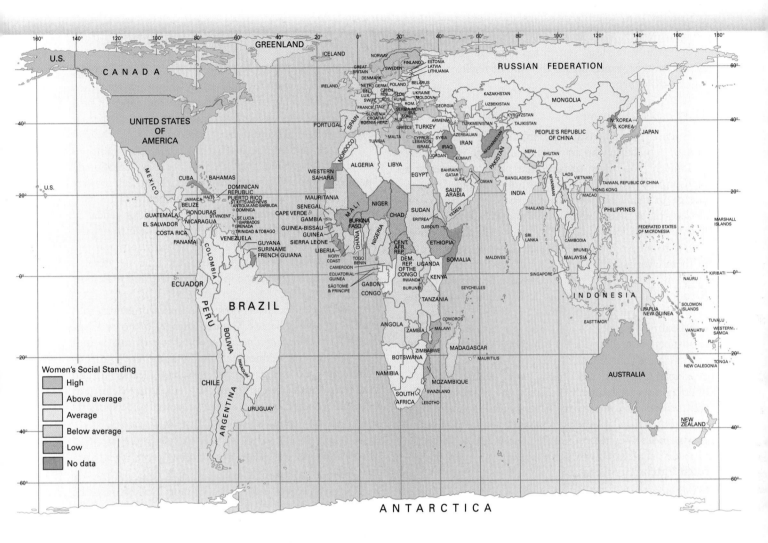

GLOBAL MAP 10–1 Women's Power in Global Perspective

Women's social standing in relation to men's varies around the world. In general, women live better in rich countries than in poor countries. Even so, some nations stand out: In the nations of Norway, Australia, and Iceland, women come closest to social equality with men.

Source: Data from Seager (2003).

The pattern found almost everywhere in the world is **patriarchy** ("rule of fathers"), *a form of social organization in which males dominate females.* Global Map 10–1 shows the great variation in the relative power and privilege of women that exists from country to country. According to the United Nations' gender development index, Norway, Australia, and Iceland give women the highest social standing; by contrast, women in the African nations of Niger,

Burkina Faso, Mali, Sierra Leone, and Chad have the lowest social standing compared with men. Of the world's nations, the United States was ranked eighth in terms of gender equality (United Nations Development Programme, 2005).

The justification for patriarchy is **sexism,** *the belief that one sex is innately superior to the other.* Sexism is not just a matter of individual attitudes; it is built into the institutions of our society. *Institutional sexism* is found throughout the economy, with women highly concentrated in low-paying jobs. Similarly, the legal system has long excused violence against women, especially on the part of boyfriends, husbands, and fathers.

The Costs of Sexism

Sexism limits the talents and the ambitions of the half of the human population who are women. Although men benefit in some respects from sexism, their privilege comes at a high price. Masculinity in our culture encourages men to engage in many high-risk behaviors: using tobacco and alcohol, playing dangerous sports, and even driving recklessly. As Marilyn French (1985) argues, patriarchy drives men to relentlessly seek control, not only of women but also of themselves and their world. Thus masculinity is linked not only to accidents but also to suicide, violence, and stress-related diseases. The *Type A personality*—marked by chronic impatience, driving ambition, competitiveness, and free-floating hostility—is one cause of heart disease and an almost perfect match with the behavior our culture considers masculine (Ehrenreich, 1983).

Finally, as men seek control over others, they lose opportunities for intimacy and trust. As one analyst put it, competition is supposed to "separate the men from the boys." In practice, however, it separates men from men and everyone else (Raphael, 1988).

Must Patriarchy Go On?

In preindustrial societies, women have little control over pregnancy and childbirth, which limits the scope of their lives. In those same societies, men's greater height and physical strength are valued resources. But industrialization, including birth control technology, gives people choices about how to live. In societies like our own, biological differences offer little justification for patriarchy.

But males are dominant in the United States and just about everywhere else. Does this mean that patriarchy is inevitable? Some researchers claim that biological factors such as differences in hormones and slight differences in brain structure "wire" the sexes with different motivations and behaviors—especially aggressiveness in males—making patriarchy difficult or perhaps even impossible to change (S. Goldberg, 1974; Rossi, 1985; Popenoe, 1993b; Udry, 2000). However, most sociologists believe that gender is socially constructed and *can* be changed. Just because the world has long been overwhelmingly patriarchal does not mean that we must stay prisoners of the past.

To understand why patriarchy continues today, we next examine how gender is rooted and reproduced in society, a process that begins in childhood and continues throughout our lives.

Gender and Socialization

From birth until death, gender shapes human feelings, thoughts, and actions. Children quickly learn that their society defines females and males as different kinds of people; by about age three, they begin to apply gender standards to each other and to themselves.

In the past, many people in the United States traditionally described women using terms such as "emotional," "passive," and "cooperative." By contrast, men were described as "rational," "active," and "competitive." It is curious that we were taught for so long to think of gender in terms of one sex being opposite to the other, especially because women and men have so much in common and also because research suggests that most people develop personalities that are some mix of feminine and masculine traits (Bem, 1993).

Just as gender affects how we think of ourselves, so it teaches us how to behave. **Gender roles** (also known as **sex roles**) are *attitudes and activities that a society links to each sex*. A culture that defines males as ambitious and competitive encourages them to seek out positions of leadership and play team sports. To the extent that females are defined as deferential and emotional, they are expected to be supportive helpers and quick to show their feelings.

GENDER AND THE FAMILY

The first question people usually ask about a newborn—"Is it a boy or a girl?"—has great importance because the answer involves not just sex but the likely direction of a child's life. In fact, gender is at work even before a child is born, because especially in lower-income nations, parents hope their firstborn will be a boy rather than a girl.

Soon after birth, family members welcome infants into the "pink world" of girls or the "blue world" of boys (Bernard, 1981). People even send gender messages in the way they handle infants. One researcher at an English university presented an infant dressed as either a boy or a girl to a number of women; her subjects handled the "female" child tenderly, with frequent hugs and caresses, while treating the "male" child more aggressively, often lifting him up high in the air or bouncing him on the knee (Bonner, 1984; Tavris & Wade, 2001). The lesson is clear: The female world revolves around cooperation and emotion, and the male world puts a premium on independence and action.

YOUR TURN

Did you grow up in a home in which females and males had different jobs and responsibilities? How did this affect your view of gender?

A common theme in books and films is an upper-class man "rescuing" a struggling lower-class woman. In the movie *Maid in Manhattan,* a rich and powerful man (played by Ralph Fiennes) staying at an upscale New York hotel meets an attractive young woman (played by Jennifer Lopez), whom he believes to be a hotel guest. The two share a romantic night together, but they soon face the reality that their lives are worlds apart. How is gender inequality evident in this story? Would the same story be as believable if the couple's social positions were reversed?

Gender and the Peer Group

About the time they enter school, children move outside the family, making friends with others of the same age. Considerable research points to the fact that young children tend to form single-sex play groups (Martin & Fabes, 2001).

Peer groups teach additional lessons about gender. After spending a year watching children at play, Janet Lever (1978) concluded that boys favor team sports with complex rules and clear objectives such as scoring runs or touchdowns. Such games nearly always involve winners and losers, reinforcing masculine traits of aggression and control.

Girls, too, play team sports. But, Lever explains, girls also play hopscotch or jump rope or simply talk, sing, or dance. These activities have few rules, and rarely is "victory" the ultimate goal. Instead of teaching girls to be competitive, Lever says, female peer groups encourage interpersonal skills of communication and cooperation, presumably the basis for girls' future roles as wives and mothers.

The games we play offer important lessons for our later lives. Lever's observations recall Carol Gilligan's gender-based theory of moral reasoning, which was introduced in Chapter 3 ("Socialization: From Infancy to Old Age"). According to Gilligan (1982), boys reason according to abstract principles. For them, "rightness" amounts to "playing by the rules." By contrast, girls consider morality a matter of responsibility to others.

Gender and Schooling

Gender shapes our interests and beliefs about our own abilities, guiding areas of study and, eventually, career choices (Correll, 2001). In high school, more girls than boys learn secretarial skills and take vocational classes such as cosmetology and food services. Classes in woodworking and auto mechanics attract mostly young men.

Women have now become a majority (57 percent) of the students on college campuses across the United States. As their numbers have increased, women have become well represented in many fields of study that once excluded them, including mathematics, chemistry, and biology. But men still predominate in many fields, including engineering, physics, and philosophy, and women cluster in the fine arts (including music, dance, and drama) as well as the social sciences (including anthropology and sociology). Newer areas of study are also gender-typed: More men than women take computer science, and more women than men enroll in courses in gender studies.

What is your declared or likely major? What share of students in this major are female and what share are male? Can you explain this pattern?

Gender and the Mass Media

Since television first captured the public imagination in the 1950s, white males have held center stage; racial and ethnic minorities were all but absent from television until the early 1970s. Even when both sexes appeared on camera, men generally played the brilliant detectives, fearless explorers, and skilled surgeons. Women played the less capable characters, often unnecessary except for the sexual interest they added to the story.

The Beauty Myth

The Duchess of Windsor once remarked, "A woman cannot be too rich or too thin." The first half of her observation might apply to men as well, but certainly not the second. After all, the vast majority of ads placed by the $30-billion-a-year U.S. cosmetics industry and the $50-billion diet industry target women.

According to Naomi Wolf (1990), certain cultural patterns create a "beauty myth" that is damaging to women. The beauty myth arises, first, because society teaches women to measure their worth in terms of physical appearance. Yet the standards of beauty embodied by the *Playboy* centerfold or the 100-pound New York fashion model are out of reach for most women.

The way society teaches women to prize relationships with men, whom they presumably attract with their beauty, also supports the beauty myth. Striving for beauty not only drives women to be extremely disciplined but also forces them to be highly attentive and responsive to men. In short, beauty-minded women try to please men and avoid challenging male power.

Belief in the beauty myth is one reason so many young women are focused on body image, particularly being as thin as possible, often to the point of endangering their health. During the past several decades, the share of young women who develop an eating disorder such as anorexia nervosa (dieting to the point of starvation) or bulimia (binge eating followed by vomiting) has risen dramatically.

The beauty myth affects males as well: Men are told repeatedly that they should want to possess beautiful women. Such ideas about beauty reduce women to objects and motivate men to think of women as if they were dolls rather than human beings.

There can be little doubt that the idea of beauty is important in everyday life. According to Wolf, the question is whether beauty is about how we look or how we act.

WHAT DO YOU THINK?

1. Is there a "money myth" that states that people's income is a reflection of their worth? Does it apply more to one sex than to the other?

2. Can you see a connection between the beauty myth and the rise of eating disorders among young women in the United States?

3. Among people with physical disabilities, do you think women or men face more serious issues of "looking different"?

Historically, advertisements have shown women in the home, cheerfully using cleaning products, serving food, trying out appliances, and modeling clothes. Men predominate in ads for cars, travel, banking services, industrial companies, and alcoholic beverages. The authoritative voiceover—the off-screen voice that describes a product in television and radio advertising—is almost always male (D. M. Davis, 1993).

A careful study of gender in advertising reveals that men usually appear taller than women, implying male supe-

riority. Women, by contrast, are more frequently presented lying down (on sofas and beds) or, like children, seated on the floor. Men's facial expressions and behavior give off an air of competence and imply dominance; women often appear childlike, submissive, and sexual. Men focus on the products being advertised, and women often focus on the men (Goffman, 1979; Cortese, 1999).

Finally, advertising perpetuates what Naomi Wolf (1990) calls the "beauty myth." The Applying Sociology box takes a closer look at how this myth affects women.

Gender and Social Stratification

Gender involves more than how people think and act. It is also about social hierarchy. The reality of gender stratification can be seen, first, in the world of work.

WORKING WOMEN AND MEN

Back in 1900, just one-fifth of women were in the U.S. labor force.  Today, this figure has tripled, to 59 percent, and 71 percent of these working women work full time. The once common view that earning income is a man's role no longer holds true.

Factors that have changed the U.S. labor force include the decline of farming, the growth of cities, shrinking family size, and a rising divorce rate. The United States, along with most other nations of the world, now considers women working for income the rule rather than the exception. A report on women in the labor force can be found at http://www.bls.gov/cps/wlf-databook2005.htm

Women make up almost half the U.S. paid labor force, and more than half of all married couples depend on two incomes.

In the past, many younger women in the labor force were childless. But today, 59 percent of married women with children under age six are in the labor force, as are 76 percent of married women with children between six and seventeen years of age. For widowed, divorced, or separated women with children, the comparable figures are 74 percent of women with younger children and 83 percent of women with older children (U.S. Census Bureau, 2005).

Gender and Occupations

Although women are closing the gap with men as far as working for income is concerned, the work done by the two sexes remains very different. The U.S. Department of Labor (2006) reports a high concentration of women in two types of jobs. Administrative support work draws 22 percent of working women, most of whom are secretaries or other office workers. These are called "pink-collar jobs" because 75 percent are filled by women. Another 20 percent of employed women perform service work. Most of these jobs are in the food service industries, child care, and health care.

Table 10–1 shows the ten occupations with the highest concentrations of women. These jobs tend to be at the low end of the pay scale, with limited opportunities for advancement and with men as supervisors (U.S. Department of Labor, 2006).

Men dominate most other job categories, including the building trades, where 99 percent of brickmasons, stonema-

TABLE 10-1

Jobs with the Highest Concentrations of Women, 2005

Occupation	Number of Women Employed	Percentage in Occupation Who Are Women
1. Preschool or kindergarten teacher	719,000	97.7%
2. Secretary or administrative assistant	3,499,000	97.3
3. Dental hygienist	132,000	97.1
4. Dental assistant	259,000	96.1
5. Dietitian or nutritionist	68,000	95.3
6. Word processor or typist	295,000	95.0
7. Child care worker	1,329,000	94.8
8. Licensed practical or licensed vocational nurse	510,000	93.4
9. Occupational therapist	85,000	92.9
10. Receptionist or information clerk	1,376,000	92.4

Source: U.S. Department of Labor (2006).

sons, and heavy-equipment mechanics are men. Likewise, men make up 86 percent of police officers and engineers, 70 percent of lawyers, 68 percent of physicians and surgeons, and 63 percent of corporate managers. According to a recent survey, the top earners in *Fortune* 500 companies include 2,105 men (94 percent of the total) and 145 women (6 percent). Find reports on all aspects of women in business at http://www.catalystwomen.org/bookstore/freematerials.shtml

Just 17 of the 1,000 largest corporations in the United States have a woman as their chief executive officer (Catalyst, 2006; U.S. Department of Labor, 2006).

Gender stratification in everyday life is easy to see: Female nurses assist male doctors, female secretaries serve male executives, and female flight attendants are under the command of male airline pilots. In any field, the greater a job's income and prestige, the more likely it is to be held by a man. For example, women represent 98 percent of kindergarten teachers, 82 percent of elementary and middle school teachers, 57 percent of secondary school educators, 39 percent of professors in colleges and universities, and 18 percent of college and university presidents (*Chronicle of Higher Education*, 2006; U.S. Department of Labor, 2006).

How are women kept out of certain jobs? By defining some kinds of work as "masculine," society defines women as unsuitable workers. In a study of coal mining in southern

West Virginia, Suzanne Tallichet (2000) found that most men considered it "unnatural" for women to work in the mines. Consequently, women who did so were defined as "unnatural" and subject to labeling as "sexually loose" or as lesbians. Such labeling made these women outcasts, presented a challenge to holding the job, and made advancement all but impossible.

In the corporate world, too, the higher in the company we look, the fewer women we find. You hardly ever hear anyone say that women don't belong at the top levels of a company. But many people seem to feel this way, which can prevent women from being promoted. Sociologists describe this barrier as a *glass ceiling* that is not easy to see but blocks women's careers all the same (Benokraitis & Feagin, 1995).

One challenge to male domination in the workplace comes from women who are entrepreneurs. Women now own more than 9 million small businesses, twice the number in 1990 and more than one-third of the total. Although the large majority of these businesses are one-person operations, women-owned businesses employ one-fourth of the entire labor force. Women have shown that they can make opportunities for themselves apart from large, male-dominated companies (U.S. Small Business Administration, 2001b).

Gender, Income, and Wealth

In 2005, the median earnings for women working full time were $31,858, and men working full time earned $41,386. This means that for every dollar earned by men, women earned about 77 cents. These earnings differences are greatest among older workers because older working women typically have less education and seniority than older working men. Earnings differences are smaller among younger workers because younger men and women tend to have similar schooling and work experience.

Among full-time workers of all ages, 33 percent of women earned less than $25,000 in 2005, compared with 22

 The *Monthly Labor Review* reports on the gender earnings gap at http://www.bls.gov/opub/mlr/2003/03/art2full.pdf

percent of comparable men. At the upper end of the income scale, men were almost two and one-half times more likely than women (19.3 percent versus 8.3 percent) to earn more than $75,000 (U.S. Census Bureau, 2006).

The main reason women earn less is the *type* of work they do: largely clerical and service jobs. In effect, jobs and gender interact. People still think of less important jobs as "women's work," just as people devalue work simply because it is performed by women (England, Hermsen, & Cotter, 2000; Cohen & Huffman, 2003).

In recent decades, supporters of gender equality have proposed a policy of "comparable worth," paying people not according to the historical double standard but according to the value of what they do. Several nations, including Great Britain and Australia, have adopted comparable worth policies, but these policies have found limited acceptance in the United States. As a result, women in this country lose as much as $1 billion in income annually.

A second cause of gender-based income inequality has to do with society's view of the family. Both men and women have children, of course, but our culture gives more of the responsibility of parenting to women. Pregnancy and raising small children keep many younger women out of the labor force at a time when their male peers are making significant career advancements. When women workers return to the labor force, they have less job experience and seniority than their male counterparts (Stier, 1996; Waldfogel, 1997).

In addition, women who choose to have children may be unable or unwilling to take on fast-paced jobs that tie up their evenings and weekends. To avoid role strain, they may take jobs that offer shorter commuting distances, more flexible hours, and employer-provided child care services.

 Women pursuing both a career and a family are torn between their dual responsibilities in ways that men are not. Consider this: At age forty, 90 percent of men but only 35 percent of women in executive positions have at least one child (F. N. Schwartz, 1989). This pattern is also found on the campus, where one recent study concluded that young female professors with at least one child were at least 20 percent less likely to have tenure than comparable men in the same field (Shea, 2002).

Consider the statements "He fathered the child" and "She mothered the child." What does each actually mean people did? How do you think gender shapes the meaning of parenting?

The two factors noted so far—type of work and family responsibilities—account for about two-thirds of the earnings difference between women and men. A third factor—discrimination against women—accounts for most of the remainder (Fuller & Schoenberger, 1991). Because discrimination is illegal, it is practiced in subtle ways. Women on their way up the corporate ladder often run into the glass ceiling described earlier; company officials may deny its existence, but it effectively prevents many women from rising above middle management.

For all these reasons, women earn less than men in all major occupational categories. Even so, many people think that women own most of the country's wealth, perhaps because they typically outlive men. Government statistics tell a different story: Fifty-five percent of people with $1 million or more in assets are men, although widows are highly represented in this elite club (Johnson & Raub, 2006). Just 11 percent of the people identified in 2005 by *Forbes* magazine as the richest people in the United States are women (Miller & Serafin, 2006).

HOUSEWORK: WOMEN'S "SECOND SHIFT"

In the United States, housework has always presented a cultural contradiction: We claim that it is essential for family life, but people get little reward for doing it (Bernard, 1981). Here, as around the world, taking care of the home and children has been considered

 What's a homemaker mom really worth? To see, visit http://www.salary.com

"women's work" (see Global Map 4–1 on page 100). As women have entered the labor force, the amount of housework women do has gone down, but the *share* done by women has stayed the same. Figure 10–2 shows that overall, women average 16.5 hours of housework per week, compared with 9.2 hours for men. As the figure shows, women in all categories do significantly more housework than men (Stapinski, 1998).

Men do support the idea of women entering the paid labor force, and most count on the money women earn. But many men resist taking on an equal share of household duties (Heath & Bourne, 1995; Harpster & Monk-Turner, 1998; Stratton, 2001).

GENDER AND EDUCATION

In the past, our society considered schooling more necessary for men, who worked outside the home. But times have changed. By 1980, women earned a majority of all associate and bachelor's degrees; in 2005, their share was 60 percent (National Center for Education Statistics, 2006).

College doors have opened to women, and differences in men's and women's majors are becoming smaller. In 1970, for example, women earned just 17 percent of bachelor's degrees in the natural sciences, computer science, and engineering; by 2004, the proportion had doubled to 34 percent.

In 1992, for the first time, women earned a majority of postgraduate degrees, which are often a springboard to high-prestige jobs. In all areas of study in 2004, women earned 59 percent of all master's degrees and 48 percent of all doctorates (including 60 percent of all Ph.D. degrees in sociology).

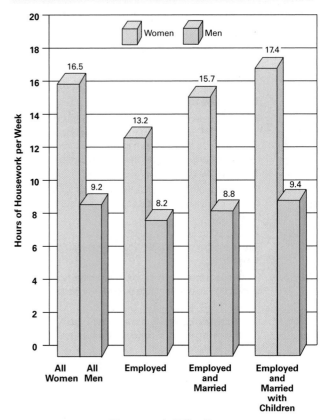

FIGURE 10-2 Housework: Who Does How Much?

Regardless of employment or family status, women do more housework than men. What effect do you think the added burden of housework has on women's ability to advance in the workplace?

Source: Adapted from Stapinski (1998).

Women have also broken into many graduate fields that used to be almost all male. For example, in 1970, only a few hundred women received a

 A report on trends in equal education for girls and women can be found at http://nces.ed.gov/pubs2005/equity/

master's of business administration (M.B.A.) degree, compared to more than 58,000 in 2004 (42 percent of all such degrees) (National Center for Education Statistics, 2006).

Despite this progress, men still predominate in some professional fields. In 2004, men received 51 percent of law degrees (LL.B. and J.D.), 54 percent of medical degrees (M.D.), and 58 percent of dental degrees (D.D.S. and D.M.D.) (National Center for Education Statistics, 2006). Our society still defines high-paying professions (and the drive and competitiveness needed to succeed in them) as masculine. But the

TABLE 10–2

Significant "Firsts" for Women in U.S. Politics

1869	Law allows women to vote in Wyoming territory.
1872	First woman to run for the presidency (Victoria Woodhull) represents the Equal Rights party.
1917	First woman elected to the House of Representatives (Jeannette Rankin of Montana).
1924	First women elected state governors (Nellie Taylor Ross of Wyoming and Miriam "Ma" Ferguson of Texas); both followed their husbands into office. First woman to have her name placed in nomination for the vice-presidency at the convention of a major political party (Lena Jones Springs, a Democrat).
1931	First woman to serve in the Senate (Hattie Caraway of Arkansas); completed the term of her husband upon his death and won reelection in 1932.
1932	First woman appointed to the presidential cabinet (Frances Perkins, secretary of labor in the cabinet of President Franklin D. Roosevelt).
1964	First woman to have her name placed in nomination for the presidency at the convention of a major political party (Margaret Chase Smith, a Republican).
1972	First African American woman to have her name placed in nomination for the presidency at the convention of a major political party (Shirley Chisholm, a Democrat).
1981	First woman appointed to the U.S. Supreme Court (Sandra Day O'Connor).
1984	First woman to be successfully nominated for the vice-presidency (Geraldine Ferraro, a Democrat).
1988	First woman chief executive to be elected to a consecutive third term (Madeleine Kunin, governor of Vermont).
1992	Political "Year of the Woman" yields record number of women in the Senate (six) and the House (forty-eight), as well as (1) first African American woman to win election to U.S. Senate (Carol Moseley-Braun of Illinois), (2) first state (California) to be served by two women senators (Barbara Boxer and Dianne Feinstein), and (3) first woman of Puerto Rican descent elected to the House (Nydia Velazquez of New York).
1996	First woman appointed secretary of state (Madeleine Albright).
2000	First First Lady to win elected political office (Hillary Rodham Clinton, senator from New York).
2001	First woman to serve as national security adviser (Condoleezza Rice); first Asian American woman to serve in a presidential cabinet (Elaine Chao).
2002	Record number of women in the Senate (fourteen).
2005	First African American woman appointed secretary of state (Condoleezza Rice); record number of women in the House (sixty-seven).

Source: Compiled by the author.

share of women in all these professions is steadily rising. For example, the American Bar Association (2006) reported that law school enrollments across the United States were about evenly split between women and men.

GENDER AND POLITICS

A century ago, almost no women held elected office in the United States. In fact, women were legally barred from voting in national elections until the passage of the Nineteenth Amendment to the Constitution in 1920. However, a few women were candidates for political office even before they could vote. The Equal Rights party supported Victoria Woodhull for the U.S. presidency in 1872; perhaps it was a sign of the times that she spent election day in a New York City jail. Table 10–2 identifies milestones in women's gradual movement into political life.

Today, thousands of women serve as mayors of cities and towns across the United States, and tens of thousands more hold responsible administrative jobs in the federal

 For the latest on women in national politics, visit http://www.cawp.rutgers.edu

government. At the state level, 23 percent of state legislators in 2006 were women (up from just 6 percent in 1970). National Map 10–1 shows where in the United States women have made the greatest political gains.

Change is coming more slowly at the highest levels of power, although a majority of U.S. adults claim they would support a qualified woman for any office, including the presidency. In addition, people in both major political parties are talking about women as likely candidates for the 2008 election. In 2006, 8 of the 50 state governors were women (16 percent), and in Congress, women held 67 of the 435 seats in the House of Representatives (15 percent) and 14 of the 100 seats in the Senate (14 percent) (Center for American Women and Politics, 2006).

Women make up half of Earth's population, but they hold just 17 percent of seats in the world's 185 parliaments. Although this represents a rise from 3 percent fifty years ago, only in fourteen countries, among them Sweden and Norway, do women represent more than one-third of the members of parliament (Inter-Parliamentary Union, 2006).

Sweden, Norway, and Denmark have laws that require at least 25 percent of candidates for elected office to be women. Do you think the United States should enact such a law? Why or why not?

Although women make up half of U.S. adults,
just 23 percent of the seats in state legislatures
are held by women. Look at the state-by-state
variation in the map. In which regions of the
country have women gained the greatest political
power? What do you think accounts for this
pattern?

Source: Center for American Women and Politics (2006).

Share of State
Legislative Seats
Held by Women

High: 30.0% and
over

Above average:
25.0% to 29.9%

Average:
20.0% to 24.9%

Below average:
15.0% to 19.9%

Low: 14.9% and
under

U.S. average: 22.8%

GENDER AND THE MILITARY

Since colonial times, women have served in the U.S. armed
forces. Yet in 1940, at the outset of World War II, just 2 percent of armed forces personnel were women. By the time of
the war in Iraq, women represented almost 15 percent of all
deployed U.S. troops as well as people serving in all capaci-
ties in the armed forces.

Clearly, women make up a growing share of the military in the United States, and almost all military assignments are now open to women. But some people object to
opening doors in this way, claiming that women lack the
physical strength of men. Others reply that military women
are better educated and score higher on intelligence tests
than military men. But the heart of the issue is our society's
deeply held view of women as *nurturers*—people who give
life and help others—which clashes with the image of
women trained to kill.

One reason that women are more integrated into
today's military is that high technology blurs the distinction
between combat and noncombat personnel. A combat pilot
can fire missiles at a target miles away; by contrast, non-
fighting medical evacuation teams must travel directly into
the line of fire (Segal & Hansen, 1992; Wilcox, 1992;
Kaminer, 1997).

ARE WOMEN A MINORITY?

A **minority** is *any category of people distinguished by physical or cultural difference that a society sets apart and subordinates.* Given the clear economic disadvantage of being a
woman in our society, it seems reasonable to say that

women are a minority in the United States even though they
outnumber men.[1]

Even so, most white women do not think of themselves
in this way (Hacker, 1951; Lengermann & Wallace, 1985).
This is partly because, unlike racial minorities (including
African Americans) and ethnic minorities (say, Hispanics),
white women are well represented at all levels of the class
structure, including the very top.

Bear in mind, however, that at every class level, women
typically have less income, wealth, education, and power
than men. Patriarchy makes women depend on men—first
their fathers and later their husbands—for their social
standing (Bernard, 1981).

MINORITY WOMEN: INTERSECTION THEORY

If women are defined as a minority, what about minority
women? Are they doubly handicapped? This question lies at
the heart of **intersection theory,** *the interplay of race, class,
and gender, often resulting in multiple dimensions of disadvantage.* Research shows that disadvantages linked to race
and gender often combine to produce especially low social
standing (Ovadia, 2001).

Income data illustrate the truth of this approach. Looking first at race and ethnicity, the median income in 2005
for African American women working full time was

---

[1]We use the term "minority" instead of "minority group" because, as
explained in Chapter 5 ("Groups and Organizations"), women make up a
category, not a group. People in a category share a status or identity but
generally do not know one another or interact.

The basic insight of intersection theory is that various dimensions of social stratification—including race and gender—can add up to great disadvantages for some categories of people. Just as African Americans earn less than whites, women earn less than men. Thus, African American women confront a "double disadvantage," earning just 63 cents for every dollar earned by non-Hispanic white men. How would you explain the fact that some categories of people are much more likely to end up in low-paying jobs like this one?

$30,363, which is 85 percent as much as the $35,797 earned by non-Hispanic white women; Hispanic women earned $25,022—just 70 percent as much as their white counterparts. Looking at gender, African American women earned 89 percent as much as African American men, and Hispanic women earned 93 percent as much as Hispanic men.

Combining these disadvantages, African American women earned 63 percent as much as non-Hispanic white men, and Hispanic women earned 52 percent as much (U.S. Census Bureau, 2006). These differences reflect minority women's lower positions in the occupational and educational hierarchies. These data confirm that although gender has a powerful effect on our lives, it does not operate alone. Class position, race and ethnicity, gender, and sexual orientation form a multilayered system that provides disadvantages for some and privileges for others (Saint Jean & Feagin, 1998).

VIOLENCE AGAINST WOMEN

In the nineteenth century, men claimed the right to rule their households, even to the point of using physical discipline against their wives, and a great deal of "manly" violence is still directed against women. A government report estimates that 387,000 aggravated assaults against women occur annually. To this number can be added 177,000 rapes or sexual assaults and perhaps 1.4 million simple assaults (U.S. Bureau of Justice Statistics, 2006).

 Here is a United Nations report on violence against women and girls around the world: http://www.unicef-icdc.org/publications/pdf/digest6e.pdf

Gender violence is also an issue on college and university campuses. A report from the U.S. Department of Justice (2000) states that in 2000, 1.7 percent of female college students were victims of rape, and another 1.1 percent were victims of attempted rape. In 90 percent of all campus cases, the victim knew the offender, and most of the assaults took place in the woman's living quarters.

Off campus as well, most gender-linked violence occurs where men and women interact most: in the home. Richard Gelles (cited in Roesch, 1984) argues that with the exception of the police and the military, the family is the most violent organization in the United States, and women suffer most of the injuries (Gelles & Cornell, 1990; Smolowe, 1994).

Violence toward women also occurs in casual relationships. As noted in Chapter 7 ("Deviance"), most rapes involve men known, and often trusted, by their victims. Dianne Herman (2001) argues that the extent of sexual abuse shows that the tendency toward sexual violence is built into our way of life. All forms of violence against women—from the catcalls that intimidate women on city streets to a pinch in a crowded subway to physical assaults that occur at home—express what she calls a "rape culture" of men trying to dominate women. Feminists explain that sexual violence is fundamentally about *power*, not sex, and therefore should be understood as a dimension of gender stratification.

In global perspective, violence against women is built into other cultures in many different ways. One case in point is the practice of female genital mutilation, a painful and often dangerous surgical procedure performed in more than forty countries and known to occur in the United States, as shown in Global Map 10–2. The Thinking About Diversity box on page 286 describes an instance of female genital mutilation that took place in California.

 For information on female genital mutilation, see http://www.amnesty.org/ailib/intcam/femgen/fgm1.htm

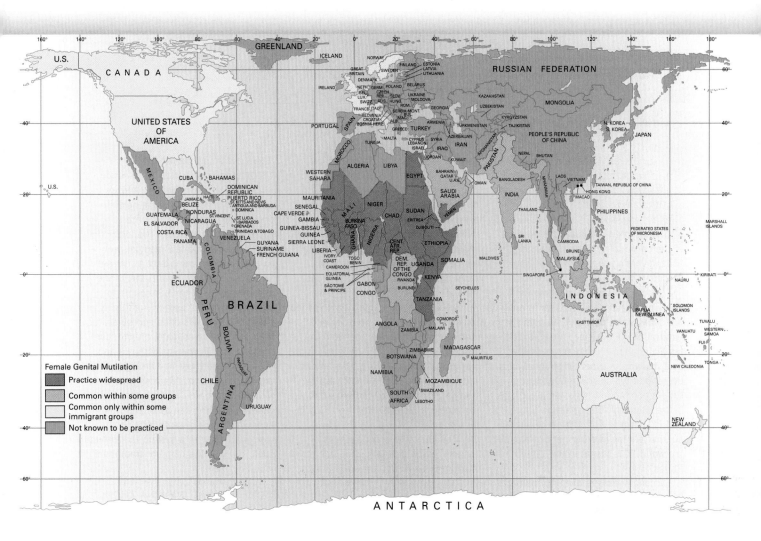

WINDOW ON THE WORLD

GLOBAL MAP 10-2 Female Genital Mutilation in Global Perspective

Female genital mutilation is known to be performed in more than forty countries around the world. Across Africa, the practice is common and affects a majority of girls in the eastern African nations of Sudan, Ethiopia, and Somalia. In several Asian nations, including India, the practice is limited to a few ethnic minorities. In the United States, Canada, several European nations, and Australia, there are reports of the practice among some immigrants.

Source: Data from Seager (2003).

VIOLENCE AGAINST MEN

If our way of life encourages violence against women, it may encourage even more violence against men. As noted in Chapter 7 ("Deviance"), in more than 80 percent of cases in which police make an arrest for a violent crime, including murder, robbery, and assault, the offender is a male. In addition, 59 percent of all victims of violent crime are also men (Federal Bureau of Investigation, 2005; U.S. Bureau of Justice Statistics, 2006).

Our culture tends to define masculinity in terms of aggression and violence. "Real men" work and play hard,

Female Genital Mutilation: Violence in the Name of Morality

Meserak Ramsey, a woman born in Ethiopia and now working as a nurse in California, paid a visit to an old friend's home. Soon after arriving, she noticed her friend's eighteen-month-old daughter huddled in the corner of a room in obvious pain. "What's wrong with her?" she asked.

Ramsey was shocked when the woman said her daughter had recently had a clitoridectomy, the surgical removal of the clitoris. This type of female genital mutilation—performed by a midwife, a tribal practitioner, or a doctor and typically without anesthesia—is common in Nigeria, Sierra Leone, Senegal, Somalia, and Egypt and is known to be practiced in certain cultural groups in other nations around the world. It is illegal in the United States.

Among members of highly patriarchal societies, husbands demand that their wives be virgins at marriage and remain sexually faithful thereafter. The point of female genital mutilation is to eliminate sexual feeling, which, people assume, makes the girl less likely to violate sexual norms and thus be more desirable to men. In about one-fifth of all cases, an even more severe procedure, called infibulation, is performed, in which the entire external genital area is removed and the surfaces are stitched together, leaving only a small hole for urination and menstruation. Before marriage, a husband

has the right to open the wound and ensure himself of his bride's virginity.

How many women have undergone female genital mutilation? Worldwide, estimates place the number at 135 million. In the United States, hundreds or even thousands of such procedures are performed every year. In most cases, immigrant mothers and grandmothers who have themselves been mutilated insist that young girls in their family follow their example. Indeed, many immigrant women demand the procedure *because* their daughters now live in the United States, where sexual mores are more lax. "I don't have to worry about her now," the girl's mother explained to Meserak Ramsey. "She'll be a good girl."

Medically, the consequences of female genital mutilation include more than loss of sexual pleasure. Pain is

intense and can persist for years. There is also the danger of infection, infertility, and even death. Ramsey knows this all too well: She herself underwent genital mutilation as a young girl. She is one of the lucky ones who has had few medical problems since. But the extent of her suffering is suggested by this story: She had invited a young U.S. couple to stay at her home. Late at night, she heard the woman's cries and burst into their room to investigate, only to learn that the couple was making love and the woman had just had an orgasm. "I didn't understand," Ramsey recalls. "I thought that there must be something wrong with American girls. But now I know that there is something wrong with me." Or with a system that inflicts such injury in the name of traditional morality.

These young women have just undergone female genital mutilation. What do you think should be done about this practice?

WHAT DO YOU THINK?

1. Is female genital mutilation a medical procedure or a means of social control? Explain your answer.

2. Can you think of other examples of physical mutilation imposed on women? What are they?

3. What do you think should be done about the practice of female genital mutilation in places where it is widespread? Do you think respect for human rights should override respect for cultural differences in this case?

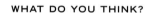

Sources: Crossette (1995) and Boyle, Songora, & Foss (2001).

speed on the highways, and let nothing stand in their way. A higher crime rate is one result. But even when no laws are broken, men's lives involve more stress and isolation than women's lives, which is one reason that the suicide rate for men is four times higher than for women. In addition, as noted earlier, men live, on average, about five fewer years than women.

Violence is not simply a matter of choices made by individuals. It is built into our way of life, with resulting harm to both men and women. In short, the way any culture constructs gender plays an important part in how violent or peaceful a society will be.

SEXUAL HARASSMENT

Sexual harassment refers to *comments, gestures, or physical contacts of a sexual nature that are deliberate, repeated, and unwelcome.* During the 1990s, sexual harassment became an issue of national importance that rewrote the rules for workplace interaction between women and men.

Most (but not all) victims of sexual harassment are women. The reason is that, first, our culture encourages men to be sexually assertive and to see women in sexual terms. As a result, social interaction in the workplace, on campus, and elsewhere can easily take on sexual overtones. Second, most people in positions of power—including business executives, doctors, bureau chiefs, assembly line supervisors, professors, and military officers—are men who oversee the work of women. Surveys carried out in widely different work settings show that half of women respondents receive unwanted sexual attention (NORC, 2005).

Sexual harassment is sometimes obvious and direct: A supervisor may ask for sexual favors from an employee and make threats if the advances are refused. Courts have declared that such *quid pro quo* sexual harassment (the Latin phrase means "one thing in return for another") is a violation of civil rights.

More often, however, the problem of unwelcome sexual attention is a matter of subtle behavior—sexual teasing, off-color jokes, comments about someone's looks—that may or may not be intended to harass anyone. But based on the *effect* standard, favored by many feminists, such actions add up to creating a *hostile environment.* Incidents of this kind are far more complex because they involve different perceptions of the same behavior. For example, a man may think that repeatedly complimenting a co-worker on her appearance is simply being friendly. The co-worker may believe the man is thinking of her in sexual terms and is not taking her work seriously, an attitude that could harm her job performance and prospects for advancement.

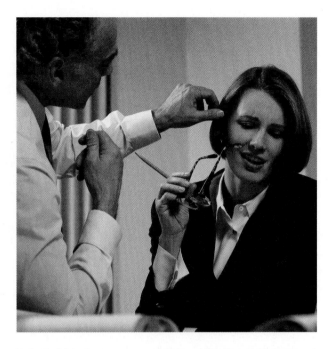

In the last twenty years, our society has defined sexual harassment as an important problem. As a result, at least officially, unwelcome sexual attention is no longer tolerated in the workplace. To what extent do you think sexual comments, off-color jokes, and unnecessary touching still take place on the job?

PORNOGRAPHY

Chapter 6 ("Sexuality and Society") defined *pornography* as sexually explicit material that causes sexual arousal. However, people take different views of exactly what is or is not pornographic; the law gives local communities the power to define whether sexually explicit material violates "community standards of decency" and lacks "any redeeming social value."

Traditionally, people have raised concerns about pornography as a *moral* issue. But pornography also plays a part in gender stratification. From this point of view, pornography is really a *power* issue because most pornography dehumanizes women, treating them as the playthings of men.

In addition, there is widespread concern that pornography encourages violence against women by portraying them as weak and undeserving of respect. Men show contempt for women defined in this way by striking out against them. National surveys show that about half of U.S. adults think that pornography encourages people to commit rape (NORC, 2005:293).

Like sexual harassment, pornography raises complex and sometimes conflicting concerns. Despite the fact that some material may offend just about everyone, many peo-

In the 1950s, Talcott Parsons proposed that sociologists interpret gender as a matter of *differences*. As he saw it, masculine men and feminine women formed strong families and made for an orderly society. In recent decades, however, social-conflict theory has reinterpreted gender as a matter of *inequality*. From this point of view, U.S. society places men in a position of dominance over women.

ple defend the rights of free speech and artistic expression. Nevertheless, pressure to restrict pornography has increased in recent decades, reflecting both the long-standing concern that pornography weakens morality and the more recent concern that it is demeaning and threatening to women.

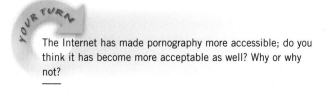

The Internet has made pornography more accessible; do you think it has become more acceptable as well? Why or why not?

Theoretical Analysis of Gender

Why is gender a part of all known societies? Sociology's macro-level approaches each address the central place of gender in social organization. The Applying Theory table summarizes the important insights offered by the structural-functional and social-conflict approaches.

STRUCTURAL-FUNCTIONAL ANALYSIS

The structural-functional approach views society as a complex system of many separate but integrated parts. From this point of view, gender serves as a means to organize social life.

As Chapter 2 ("Culture") explained, the earliest hunting and gathering societies had little power over the forces of biology. Lacking effective birth control, women could do

little to prevent pregnancy, and the responsibilities of child care kept them close to home. At the same time, men's greater strength made them better suited for warfare and hunting. Over the centuries, this sex-based division of labor became institutionalized and largely taken for granted (Lengermann & Wallace, 1985; Freedman, 2002).

Industrial technology opens up a much greater range of cultural possibilities. With human muscle power no longer the main energy source, the physical strength of men becomes less important. In addition, the ability to control reproduction gives women greater choices about how to live. Modern societies relax traditional gender roles as the societies become more meritocratic because rigid roles waste an enormous amount of human talent. Yet change comes slowly because gender is deeply rooted in culture.

Talcott Parsons: Gender and Complementarity

As Talcott Parsons (1942, 1951, 1954) observed, gender helps integrate society, at least in its traditional form. Gender forms a *complementary* set of roles that links women and men into family units and gives each sex responsibility for carrying out important tasks. Women take the lead in managing the household and raising children. Men connect the family to the larger world as they participate in the labor force.

Therefore, gender plays an important part in socialization. Society teaches boys—presumably destined for the labor force—to be rational, self-assured, and competitive. Parsons called this complex of traits *instrumental* qualities.

APPLYING THEORY

Gender

	Structural-Functional Approach	Social-Conflict Approach
What is the level of analysis?	Macro-level	Macro-level
What does gender mean?	Parsons described gender in terms of two complementary patterns of behavior: masculine and feminine.	Engels described gender in terms of the power of one sex over the other.
Is gender helpful or harmful?	Helpful. Gender gives men and women distinctive roles and responsibilities that help society operate smoothly. Gender builds social unity as men and women come together to form families.	Harmful. Gender limits people's personal development. Gender divides society by giving power to men to control the lives of women Capitalism makes patriarchy stronger.

To prepare girls for child rearing, socialization stresses *expressive* qualities, such as emotional responsiveness and sensitivity to others.

Society encourages gender conformity by instilling in men and women a fear that straying too far from accepted standards of masculinity or femininity will cause rejection by the opposite sex. In simple terms, women learn to reject nonmasculine men as sexually unattractive, and men learn to reject unfeminine women. In sum, gender integrates society both structurally (in terms of what we do) and morally (in terms of what we believe).

CRITICAL REVIEW Influential in the 1950s, this approach has lost much of its standing today. First, functionalism assumes a singular vision of society that is not shared by everyone. For example, historically, many women have worked outside the home because of economic need, a fact not reflected in Parsons's conventional, middle-class view of social life. Second, Parsons's analysis ignores the personal strains and social costs of rigid gender roles. Third, in the eyes of those seeking sexual equality, Parsons's gender "complementarity" amounts to little more than women submitting to male domination.

✓ **YOUR LEARNING** In Parsons's analysis, what functions does gender perform for society?

SOCIAL-CONFLICT ANALYSIS

From a social-conflict point of view, gender involves differences not just in behavior but in power as well. Consider the striking similarity between how traditional ideas about gender benefit men and the ways oppression of racial and eth-

nic minorities benefits white people. Conventional ideas about gender do not make society operate smoothly; they create division and tension, with men seeking to protect their privileges as women challenge the status quo.

As earlier chapters noted, the social-conflict approach draws heavily on the ideas of Karl Marx. Yet as far as gender is concerned, Marx was a product of his times, and his writings focused almost entirely on men. However, his friend and collaborator Friedrich Engels did develop a theory of gender stratification.

Friedrich Engels: Gender and Class

Looking back through history, Engels saw that in hunting and gathering societies, the activities of women and men, though different, had the same importance. A successful hunt brought men great prestige, but the vegetation gathered by women provided most of a group's food supply. As technological advances led to a productive surplus, social equality and communal sharing gave way to private property and ultimately a class hierarchy. At this point, men gained pronounced power over women. With surplus wealth to pass on to heirs, upper-class men needed to be sure who their sons were, which led them to control the sexuality of women. The desire to control property brought about monogamous marriage and the family. Women were taught to remain virgins until marriage, to remain faithful to their husbands thereafter, and to build their lives around bearing and raising one man's children.

According to Engels (1902, orig. 1884), capitalism intensifies this male domination. First, capitalism creates more wealth, which gives greater power to men as income earners and owners of property. Second, an expanding capitalist economy depends on turning people, especially

In the film *Iron Jawed Angels*, Hilary Swank portrays early women's rights activist Alice Paul, who worked tirelessly for passage of the Nineteenth Amendment to the Constitution giving women the right to vote. The United States was fighting World War I at the time, and there was little sympathy for what seemed to be radical ideas about gender. Alice Paul and others were taken to jail, where they began a hunger strike and refused to be force fed (which explains the name of the movie). With the ratification of the Nineteenth Amendment, women gained the right to vote in 1920.

women, into consumers who seek personal fulfillment by buying and using products. Third, society assigns women the task of maintaining the home to free men to work in factories. The double exploitation of capitalism, as Engels saw it, lies in paying low wages for male labor and paying women no wages at all.

CRITICAL REVIEW Social-conflict analysis is strongly critical of conventional ideas about gender, claiming that society would be better off if we minimized or even did away with this dimension of social structure. One problem with this approach is that it sees conventional families—supported by traditionalists as morally good—as a social evil. Second, social-conflict analysis minimizes the extent to which women and men live together cooperatively, and

often happily, in families. A third problem with this approach lies in its claim that capitalism is the root of gender stratification. Although agrarian societies typically are more patriarchal than industrial-capitalist societies, and socialist nations—including the People's Republic of China and the former Soviet Union—did move women into the labor force, by and large they provided women with very low pay in sex-segregated jobs (Rosendahl, 1997; Haney, 2002).

✓ **YOUR LEARNING** According to Engels, how does gender help support a capitalist class system?

Feminism

Feminism is *the advocacy of social equality for women and men, in opposition to patriarchy and sexism.* The "first wave" of the feminist movement in the United States began in the 1840s as women opposed to slavery, including Elizabeth Cady Stanton and Lucretia Mott, showed the similarities between the oppression of African Americans and the oppression of women. Their main objective was obtaining the right to vote, which was finally achieved in 1920. But other disadvantages persisted, causing a "second wave" of feminism to arise in the 1960s that continues today.

BASIC FEMINIST IDEAS

Feminism views the everyday lives of women and men through the lens of gender. How we think of ourselves (gender identity), how we act (gender roles), and our social standing as women or men (gender stratification) are all rooted in the operation of society.

Although people who consider themselves feminists disagree about many things, most support five general principles:

1. **Working to increase equality.** Feminist thinking is political; it relates ideas to action. Feminism is critical of the status quo, pushing for change toward social equality for women and men.

2. **Expanding human choice.** Feminists argue that cultural ideas about gender divide the full range of human qualities into two opposing and limiting spheres: the female world of emotion and cooperation and the male world of rationality and competition. As an alternative, feminists propose a "reintegration of humanity" by which all individuals develop all human traits (French, 1985).

3. **Eliminating gender stratification.** Feminism opposes laws and cultural norms that limit the education,

APPLYING THEORY

Feminism

	Liberal	Socialist	Radical
Does it accept the basic order of society?	Yes. Liberal feminism seeks change only to ensure equality of opportunity.	No. Socialist feminism supports an end to social classes and to family gender roles that encourage "domestic slavery."	No. Radical feminism supports an end to the family system.
How do women improve their social standing?	Individually, according to personal ability and effort.	Collectively, through socialist revolution.	Collectively, by working to eliminate gender itself.

income, and job opportunities of women. For this reason, feminists have long supported passage of the Equal Rights Amendment (ERA) to the U.S. Constitution, which states, "Equality of rights under the law shall not be denied or abridged by the United States or any State on account of sex." The ERA was first proposed in Congress in 1923. Although it has widespread support, it has yet to become law.

4. **Ending sexual violence.** Today's women's movement seeks to eliminate sexual violence. Feminists argue that patriarchy distorts relationships between women and men, encouraging violence against women in the form of rape, domestic abuse, sexual harassment, and pornography (A. Dworkin, 1987; Freedman, 2002).

5. **Promoting sexual freedom.** Finally, feminism advocates women's control over their sexuality and reproduction. Feminists support the free availability of birth control information. Most feminists also support a woman's right to choose whether to have children or to end a pregnancy, rather than allowing men—as fathers, husbands, doctors, and legislators—to control their reproduction. Many feminists also support gay people's efforts to overcome prejudice and discrimination in a predominantly heterosexual culture (Ferree & Hess, 1995; Armstrong, 2002).

YOUR TURN

On your campus, do men's organizations (such as athletic teams or fraternities) enjoy any special privileges? What about women's organizations (such as feminist groups or sororities)?

TYPES OF FEMINISM

Although feminists agree on the importance of gender equality, they disagree on how to achieve it: through liberal feminism, socialist feminism, or radical feminism (Stacey,

1983; L. Vogel, 1983; Ferree & Hess, 1995; Freedman, 2002). The Applying Theory table highlights key arguments made by each type of feminist thinking.

Liberal Feminism

Liberal feminism is rooted in classic liberal thinking that individuals should be free to develop their own talents and pursue their own interests. Liberal feminism accepts the basic organization of our society but seeks to expand the rights and opportunities of women, in part by passage of the Equal Rights Amendment. Liberal feminists also support reproductive freedom for all women. They respect the family as a social institution but seek changes in society, including more widely available maternity and paternity leave and child care for parents who work.

Given their beliefs in the rights of individuals, liberal feminists think that women should advance according to their individual efforts, rather than working collectively for change. Both women and men, through personal achievement, are capable of improving their lives, as long as society removes legal and cultural barriers.

Socialist Feminism

Socialist feminism evolved from the ideas of Karl Marx and Friedrich Engels, in part as a critical response to Marx's inattention to gender. From this point of view, capitalism increases patriarchy by concentrating wealth and power in the hands of a small number of men. Socialist feminists do not think the reforms supported by liberal feminists go far enough. The family form fostered by capitalism must change in order to replace "domestic slavery" with some collective means of carrying out housework and child care. Replacing the traditional family can come about only through a socialist revolution that creates a state-centered economy to meet the needs of all.

Radical Feminism

Like socialist feminism, *radical feminism* finds liberal feminism inadequate. Radical feminists believe that patriarchy is

January 28, 2005

Men Are Becoming the Ad Target of the Gender Sneer

By COURTNEY KANE

Are today's men incompetent, bumbling idiots? Judging by portrayals in some advertising, the answer seems to be yes—much to the dismay of some men.

The portrayals began as a clever reversal of traditional gender roles in campaigns, prompted by the ire of women and feminist organizations over decades of ads using stereotyped imagery of an incompetent, bumbling housewife who needed to be told which coffee or cleanser to buy.

As those images disappeared, the pendulum swung, producing campaigns portraying men in general, and husbands and fathers in particular, as objects of ridicule, pity or even scorn. Among them are ads for Bud Light, Domino's, Hummer, T-Mobile and Verizon.

The "man as a dope" imagery has gathered momentum over the last decade, and critics say that it has spiraled out of control. It is nearly impossible, they say, to watch commercials or read ads without seeing helpless, hapless men.

In the campaigns, which the critics consider misandry (the opposite of misogyny), men act like buffoons, ogling cars and women; are likened to dogs, especially in beer and pizza ads; and bungle every possible household task. It is common for the men in such ads to be set straight by wiser female counterparts, and even for women to smack, swat, punch or kick them in the groin, all in the name of humor.

Most marketers presenting incompetent, silly male characters say their campaigns provide a harmless comedic insight into the male mentality while also appealing to women. But men who describe themselves as rights activists are increasingly speaking out against the ads as a form of male-bashing, especially when the ads disparage the roles that fathers play in their children's lives. . . .

"Men are kind of the last target that's acceptable to make fun of, so they do it," said Glenn Sacks, a commentator who is the host of a national syndicated radio show that focuses on men's and fathers' rights.

Paul Nathanson, who wrote *Spreading Misandry: The Teaching of Contempt for Men in Popular Culture* with Katherine K. Young, said the issue was larger. . . .

"Negative imagery in advertising is part of negative imagery in popular culture in general," Dr. Nathanson said. . . .

Then there are the longer-term effects, Dr. Nathanson said, asking, "How do boys form a healthy identity?" if they are constantly exposed to anti-male stereotypes. . . .

---

so firmly entrenched that even a socialist revolution would not end it. Instead, reaching the goal of gender equality means that society must eliminate gender itself.

One possible way to achieve this goal is to use new reproductive technology (see Chapter 13, "Family and Religion") to separate women's bodies from the process of childbearing. With an end to motherhood, society could leave behind the entire family system, liberating women, men, and children from the oppression of family, gender, and sex itself (A. Dworkin, 1987). Radical feminism seeks an egalitarian and gender-free society, a revolution much more sweeping than that sought by Marx.

OPPOSITION TO FEMINISM

Because feminism calls for significant change, it has always been controversial. But today, just 20 percent of U.S. adults say they oppose feminism, a share that has declined over time (NORC, 2005). Figure 10–3 on page 294 shows a similar downward trend in opposition to feminism among college students after 1970. Note, however, that little change has occurred in recent years and that more men than women express antifeminist attitudes.

Feminism provokes criticism and resistance from both men and women who hold conventional ideas about gender. Some men oppose sexual equality for the same reasons that many white people have historically opposed social equality for people of color: They do not want to give up their privileges. Other men and women, including those who are neither rich nor powerful, distrust a social movement (especially its radical expressions) that attacks the traditional family and rejects patterns that have guided male-female relations for centuries.

Men who have been socialized to value strength and dominance may feel uneasy about feminist ideals of men as gentle and warm (Doyle, 1983). Similarly, women who have

Martyn Straw, chief strategy officer at BBDO Worldwide in New York, part of the Omnicom Group, offered an explanation.

"In advertising and in general communications," Mr. Straw said, "there is the notion that things that are 'negative' are always much funnier than 'positive,' which can get very schmaltzy.

"In order to not cross over the line into denigration," Mr. Straw said, the situation portrayed in an ad needs to be truthful and funny. If those elements are in place, he added, "it's not really bashing, it's just having a funny look at the way men work sometimes and the way they approach things."

Critics have compiled lists of ads they deem offensive. One Web site, Stand yourground.com, in cooperation with the Men's Activism News Network, lists 30 brands it asks men to avoid buying because of what they regard as male-bashing advertising; the list includes Budweiser, Hummer, J. C. Penney and Post-it notes.

One of the companies most cited is Verizon Communications, for a commercial for its Verizon DSL service created by McGarry Bowen in New York. The spot shows a computer-clueless father trying to help his Internet-savvy daughter with her homework online. Mom orders Dad to go wash the dog and leave their daughter alone; the girl flashes an exasperated look of contempt at him.

A Verizon spokesman in New York, John Bonomo, said, "It was not our intention certainly to portray fathers as inessential to families." The commercial has run its scheduled course, he added, and is no longer appearing.

In many ways, said Ann Simonton, coordinator of Media Watch in Santa Cruz, California, an organization that challenges what it considers to be racism, sexism and violence in the media, such commercials play on stereotypes of both sexes. For instance, speaking of the Verizon spot, Ms. Simonton said, "One might be able to interpret the women as being very nagging."

WHAT DO YOU THINK?

1. Do you see any connection between the rise of feminism and negative images of men in advertising? Explain your views.

2. Do you think the "man as dope" image appeals to women? Why or why not?

3. What effect does such advertising have on boys and young men?

Adapted from the original article by Courtney Kane published in *The New York Times* on January 28, 2005. Copyright © 2005 by The New York Times Company. Reprinted with permission.

built their lives around husbands and children think feminism does not value the social roles that give meaning to their lives. In general, opposition to feminism is greatest among women who have the least education and those who do not work outside the home (Marshall, 1985; Ferree & Hess, 1995).

Race and ethnicity play some part in shaping people's attitudes toward feminism. In general, African Americans (especially African American women) express the greatest support of feminist goals, followed by whites, with Hispanic Americans holding somewhat more traditional attitudes when it comes to gender (Kane, 2000).

Resistance to feminism is also found within academic circles. Some sociologists charge that feminism ignores a growing body of evidence that men and women do think and act in somewhat different ways, which may make complete gender equality impossible. Furthermore, say critics, with its drive to increase women's presence in the workplace, feminism undervalues the crucial and unique contribution women make to the development of children, especially in the first years of life (Baydar & Brooks-Gunn, 1991; Popenoe, 1993b; Gibbs, 2001).

As old questions about feminism continue to be debated, new issues are arising. "In the *Times*" draws attention to recent television advertising that has portrayed men in unfairly negative terms.

Finally, there is the question of *how* women should go about improving their social standing. A large majority of U.S. adults think that women should have equal rights, but 70 percent also say that women should advance individually, according to their training and abilities; only 10 percent favor women's rights groups or collective action (NORC, 2005:426).

For these reasons, most opposition to feminism is directed toward its socialist and radical forms, while support for liberal feminism is widespread. In addition, we are seeing an unmistakable trend toward gender equality. In 1977, 65

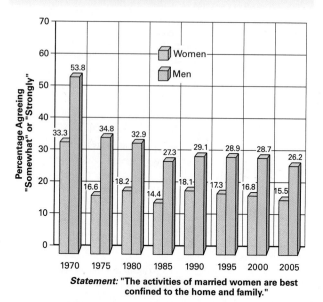

FIGURE 10-3 Opposition to Feminism among First-Year College Students, 1970–2005

The share of college students expressing antifeminist views declined after 1970. Men are still more likely than women to hold such attitudes.

Sources: Astin et al. (2002) and Pryor et al. (2005).

percent of all adults endorsed the statement "It is much better for everyone involved if the man is the achiever outside the home and the woman takes care of the home and family." By 2004, however, the share supporting this statement had dropped sharply, to 37 percent (NORC, 2005:314).

Gender: Looking Ahead

Predictions about the future are no more than educated guesses. Just as economists disagree about the likely inflation rate a year from now, sociologists can offer only general observations about the likely future of gender and society.

Change so far has been remarkable. A century ago, women were second-class citizens, without access to many jobs, barred from public office, and with no right to vote. Although women remain socially disadvantaged, the movement toward equality has surged ahead. Two-thirds of people entering the workforce in the 1990s were women, and in 2000, for the first time, a majority of families had both husband and wife in the paid labor force. Today's economy depends a great deal on the earnings of women.

Many factors have contributed to this transformation. Perhaps most important, industrialization and recent advances in computer technology have shifted the nature of work from physically demanding tasks that favored male strength to jobs that require thought and imagination. This change puts women and men on an even footing. Also, because birth control technology has given us greater control over reproduction, women's lives are less constrained by unwanted pregnancies.

Many women and men have deliberately pursued social equality. For example, sexual harassment complaints in the workplace are taken much more seriously today than they were a generation ago. As more women assume positions of power in the corporate and political worlds, social changes in the twenty-first century may be as great as those that have already taken place.

Despite real change, gender continues to involve controversy. But it seems likely that we are moving toward a society in which women and men will enjoy equal rights and opportunities.

APPLYING SOCIOLOGY IN EVERYDAY LIFE

1. Take a walk through a business area of your local community. Which businesses are frequented almost entirely by women? By men? By both men and women? Try to explain the patterns you find.

2. Watch several hours of children's television programming on a Saturday morning. Notice the advertising, which sells mostly toys and breakfast cereal. Keep track of what share of toys are "gendered," that is, aimed at one sex or the other. What traits do you associate with toys intended for boys and those intended for girls?

3. Do some research on the history of women's issues in your state. When was the first woman sent to Congress? What laws have existed restricting the work women could do? Do any such laws exist today? Did your state support the passage of the Equal Rights Amendment or not? What percentage of political officials in your state are women?

MAKING THE GRADE

CHAPTER 10 Gender Stratification

GENDER AND INEQUALITY

GENDER refers to the meaning a culture attaches to being female or male.
- Evidence that gender is rooted in culture includes global comparisons by Margaret Mead and others showing how societies define what is feminine and masculine in various ways.
- Gender is not only about difference: Because societies give more power and other resources to men than to women, gender is an important dimension of social stratification. *Sexism* is built into the operation of social institutions.
- Although some degree of *patriarchy* is found almost everywhere, it varies throughout history and from society to society.

pp 272–76

gender (p. 272) the personal traits and social positions that members of a society attach to being female or male

gender stratification (p. 272) the unequal distribution of wealth, power, and privilege between men and women

matriarchy (p. 274) a form of social organization in which females dominate males

patriarchy (p. 275) a form of social organization in which males dominate females

sexism (p. 275) the belief that one sex is innately superior to the other

GENDER AND SOCIALIZATION

Through the socialization process, gender becomes part of our personalities (*gender identity*) and our actions (*gender roles*). All the major agents of socialization—family, peer groups, schools, and the mass media—reinforce cultural definitions of what is feminine and masculine.

pp 276–78

gender roles (sex roles) (p. 276) attitudes and activities that a society links to each sex

GENDER AND SOCIAL STRATIFICATION

Gender stratification shapes **THE WORKPLACE:**
- A majority of women are now in the paid labor force, but 42% hold clerical or service jobs.
- Comparing full-time U.S. workers, women earn 77% as much as men.
- This gender difference in earnings results from differences in jobs, differences in family responsibilities, and discrimination.

pp 279–81

Gender stratification shapes **FAMILY LIFE:**
- Most unpaid housework is performed by women, whether or not they hold jobs outside the home.
- Pregnancy and raising small children keep many women out of the labor force at a time when their male peers are making important carreer gains.

pp 280–81

Gender stratification shapes **POLITICS:**
- Until a century ago, almost no women held any elected office in the United States.
- In recent decades, the number of women in politics has increased significantly.
- Even so, the vast majority of elected officials, especially at the national level, are men.
- Women make up only about 15% of U.S. military personnel.

pp 282–83

minority (p. 283) any category of people distinguished by physical or cultural difference that a society sets apart and subordinates

intersection theory (p. 283) the interplay of race, class, and gender, often resulting in multiple dimensions of disadvantage

sexual harassment (p. 287) comments, gestures, or physical contacts of a sexual nature that are deliberate, repeated, and unwelcome

INTERSECTION THEORY investigates the intersection of race, class, and gender, factors that combine to cause special disadvantages to some categories of people.
- Women of color encounter greater social disadvantages than white women and earn much less than white men.
- Because all women have a distinctive social identity and are disadvantaged, they are a minority, although most white women do not think of themselves this way.

pp 283–84

VIOLENCE AGAINST WOMEN AND MEN is a widespread problem that is linked to how a society defines gender. Related issues include
- *sexual harassment*, which mostly victimizes women because our culture encourages men to be assertive and to see women in sexual terms.
- *pornography*, which portrays women as sexual objects. Many see pornography as a moral issue; because pornography dehumanizes women, it is also a power issue.

pp 284–88

MAKING THE GRADE
CONTINUED...

THEORETICAL ANALYSIS OF GENDER

The **STRUCTURAL-FUNCTIONAL APPROACH**
suggests that

- in preindustrial societies, distinctive roles for males and females reflect biological differences between the sexes.
- in industrial societies, marked gender inequality becomes dysfunctional and gradually decreases.

Talcott Parsons described gender differences in terms of complementary roles that promote the social integration of families and society as a whole.

pp 288–89

The **SOCIAL-CONFLICT APPROACH**
suggests that

- gender is an important dimension of social inequality and social conflict.
- gender inequality benefits men and disadvantages women.
- Friedrich Engels tied gender stratification to the rise of private property and a class hierarchy. Marriage and the family are strategies by which men control their property through control of the sexuality of women. Capitalism exploits everyone by paying men low wages and assigning women the task of maintaining the home.

pp 289–90

See the Applying Theory table on page 289.

FEMINISM

FEMINISM

- endorses the social equality of women and men and opposes patriarchy and sexism.
- seeks to eliminate violence against women.
- advocates giving women control over their reproduction.

There are three types of feminism:

- Liberal feminism seeks equal opportunity for both sexes within the existing society.
- Socialist feminism claims that gender equality will come about by replacing capitalism with socialism.
- Radical feminism seeks to eliminate the concept of gender itself and to create an egalitarian and gender-free society.

pp 290–92

See the Applying Theory table on page 291.

feminism (p. 290) the advocacy of social equality for women and men, in opposition to patriarchy and sexism

These questions are similar to those found in the test bank that accompanies this textbook.

MULTIPLE-CHOICE QUESTIONS

1. Gender is not just a matter of difference but also a matter of
   a. power.
   b. wealth.
   c. prestige.
   d. All of the above are correct.

2. The anthropologist Margaret Mead studied gender in three societies in New Guinea and found that
   a. all societies define femininity in much the same way.
   b. all societies define masculinity in much the same way.
   c. what is feminine in one society may be masculine in another.
   d. the meaning of gender is changing everywhere toward greater equality.

3. For all of us raised in U.S. society, gender shapes our
   a. feelings.
   b. thoughts.
   c. actions.
   d. All of the above are correct.

4. There is a "beauty myth" in U.S. society that encourages
   a. women to believe that their personal importance depends on their looks.
   b. beautiful women to think they do not need men.
   c. men to strive to be attractive in order to attract women.
   d. women to think they are as physically attractive as today's men are.

5. In the United States, what share of women work for income?
   a. 79 percent
   b. 59 percent
   c. 39 percent
   d. 19 percent

6. In the U.S. labor force,
   a. men and women have the same kinds of jobs.
   b. men and women earn the same pay.
   c. women are still concentrated in several types of jobs.
   d. a majority of working women hold "pink-collar" jobs.

7. For which of the following categories of people in the United States is it true that women do more housework than men?
   a. people who work for income
   b. people who are married
   c. people who have children
   d. All of the above are correct.

8. In the United States, women in the labor force working full time earn how much for every dollar earned by men working full time?
   a. 77 cents
   b. 86 cents
   c. 97 cents
   d. 99 cents

9. In 2006, women held about what percentage of seats in Congress?
   a. 5 percent
   b. 15 percent
   c. 35 percent
   d. 55 percent

10. Which type of feminism accepts U.S. society as it is but wants to give women the same rights and opportunities as men?
    a. socialist feminism
    b. liberal feminism
    c. radical feminism
    d. All of the above are correct.

ANSWERS: 1 (d); 2 (c); 3 (d); 4 (a); 5 (b); 6 (c); 7 (d); 8 (a); 9 (b); 10 (b).

ESSAY QUESTIONS

1. How do the concepts "sex" and "gender" differ? In what ways are they related?

2. Why is gender considered a dimension of social stratification? How does gender intersect other dimensions of inequality, such as class, race, and ethnicity?

Ours is among the most racially and ethnically diverse of all societies. Racial and ethnic differences reflect heritage and traditions and they also are an important foundation of social stratification.

CHAPTER *11*

Race and Ethnicity

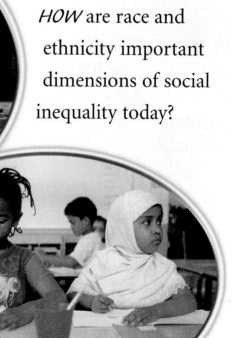

WHAT are race and ethnicity, and how are they created by society?

WHY does the United States have so much racial and ethnic diversity?

HOW are race and ethnicity important dimensions of social inequality today?

I n a sociology class at Bronx Community College in New York, the instructor is leading a small-group discussion of race and ethnicity. He explains that there has been a lot of change in how people think about these concepts. He suggests that the students find some examples in books published over the last few decades. Then he asks them "How do you describe yourself?"

Eva Rodriguez is quick to respond. "This is hard for me to answer. Most people think of race as black and white. But it's not. I have both black and white ancestry in me, but you know what? I don't think of myself in that way. I don't think of myself in terms of race at all. You can call me Puerto Rican or call me Hispanic. I prefer the term 'Latina.' Calling myself Latina says I have mixed racial heritage, and that's what I am. I wish more people understood that race is not clear-cut."

This chapter examines the meaning of race and ethnicity. We shall see that there are now millions of people in the United States who, like Eva Rodriguez, do not think of themselves in terms of a single category but as having a mix of ancestry.

The Social Meaning of Race and Ethnicity

As the opening to this chapter suggests, people often confuse "race" and "ethnicity." For this reason, we begin with some definitions.

RACE

A **race** is *a socially constructed category of people who share biologically transmitted traits that members of a society consider important*. People may classify one another racially based on physical characteristics such as skin color, facial features, hair texture, and body shape.

Racial diversity appeared among our human ancestors as the result of living in different regions of the world. In regions of intense heat, people developed darker skin (from the natural pigment melanin), which offers protection from the sun; in moderate climates, people developed lighter skin. Such traits are literally only skin deep because human beings the world over are members of a single biological species.

The striking variety of racial traits found today is also the product of migration; genetic characteristics once common to a single place are now found in many lands. Especially pronounced is the racial mix in the Middle East (that is, western Asia), historically a crossroads of migration. Greater racial uniformity characterizes more isolated peoples such as the island-dwelling Japanese. But every population has some genetic mixture, and increasing contact ensures even more racial blending of physical characteristics in the future.

Although we often think of race in terms of biological traits, race is a socially constructed concept. It is true that human beings differ in any number of ways involving physical traits, but a "race" comes into being only when the members of a society decide that some physical trait (such as skin color or eye shape) actually *matters*.

Because race is a matter of social definitions, it is a highly variable concept. For example, the members of our society consider racial differences more important than people of many other countries. We also tend to "see" three racial categories—typically, black, white, and Asian—while other societies identify many more categories. People in Brazil, for instance, distinguish between *branca* (white), *parda* (brown), *morena* (brunette), *mulata* (mulatto), *preta* (black), and *amarela* (yellow) (Inciardi, Surratt, & Telles, 2000). Of course, race may be defined differently by various categories of people within a society. In the United States, for example, research shows that white people "see" black people as having darker skin color than black people do (Hill, 2002).

The meaning and importance of race not only differ from place to place but also change over time. For example,

The range of biological variation in human beings is far greater than any system of racial classification allows. This fact is made obvious by trying to place all of the people pictured here into simple racial categories.

in 1900, it was common in the United States to consider people of Irish, Italian, or Jewish ancestry as "nonwhite." By 1950, however, this was no longer the case, and such people today are considered no different from other whites (Loveman, 1999; Brodkin, 2007).

Today, the Census Bureau allows people to describe themselves using more than one racial category (offering a total of sixty-three racial options). Our society officially recognizes a wide range of multiracial people (Porter, 2001).

YOUR TURN

Researchers have found that biracial and multiracial people choose different racial identities in different settings, depending on whom they are with (Harris & Sim, 2002). Have you ever experienced such a "racial shift"? Explain.

Racial Types

Scientists invented the concept of "race" more than a century ago as they tried to organize the world's physical diversity into three racial types. They called people with light skin and fine hair *Caucasoid,* people with dark skin and coarse hair *Negroid,* and people with yellow or brown skin and distinctive folds on the eyelids *Mongoloid.*

Sociologists consider such terms misleading at best and harmful at worst. For one thing, no society contains biologically "pure" people. The skin color of people we might call "Caucasoid" (or "Indo-European," "Caucasian," or more commonly, "white") ranges from very light (typical in Scandinavia) to very dark (in southern India). The same variation exists among so-called "Negroids" ("Africans" or, more commonly, "black" people) and "Mongoloids" ("Asians"). In fact, many "white" people (say, in southern India) actually have darker skin than many "black" people (such as the Negroid aborigines of Australia). Overall, the three racial categories differ in about 6 percent of their genes, and there is actually more genetic variation *within* each category than *between* categories. This means that two people in the European nation of Sweden, randomly selected, are likely to have at least as much genetic difference as a Swede and a person in the African nation of Senegal (Harris & Sim, 2002; American Sociological Association, 2003; California Newsreel, 2003).

So how important is race? From a biological point of view, knowing people's racial category allows us to predict nothing about them. Why, then, do societies make so much

More people in the United States consider themselves multiracial than ever before. A well-known example is actress Halle Berry, whose mother is white and whose father is African American.

of race? Such categories allow societies to rank people in a hierarchy, giving some people more money, power, and prestige than others and allowing some people to feel that they are naturally "better" than others. Because race may matter so much, societies sometimes construct racial categories in extreme ways. Throughout much of the twentieth century, for example, many southern states labeled as "colored" anyone with as little as one thirty-second African ancestry (that is, one African American great-great-great-grandparent). Today, the law allows parents to declare the race of a child (or not) as they wish. Even so, most members of our society are still very sensitive to people's racial backgrounds.

YOUR TURN

How much dating is there between people of different racial categories on your campus? Is the pattern changing over time?

A Trend toward Mixture

Over many generations and throughout the Americas, genetic traits from around the world have become mixed. Many "black" people have a significant Caucasoid ancestry, just as "white" people have some Negroid genes. Whatever people may think, race is not a black-and-white issue.

Today, people are more willing to define themselves as multiracial. When completing their 2000 census forms, almost 7 million people described themselves by checking two or more racial categories. The official number of interracial births tripled over the past twenty years to 172,000 annually, about 5 percent of all births.

ETHNICITY

Ethnicity is *a shared cultural heritage*. People define themselves—or others—as members of an *ethnic category* based on common ancestors, language, and religion that give them a distinctive social identity. The United States is a multiethnic society that favors the English language; even so, almost 52 million people (19 percent of the U.S. population over the age of five) speak Spanish, Italian, German, French, Chinese dialects, or some other language in their homes. In California, more than one-third of the population does so. With regard to religion, the United States is a predominantly Protestant nation, but most people of Spanish, Italian, and Polish ancestry are Roman Catholic, and many others of Greek, Ukrainian, and Russian descent belong to the Eastern Orthodox Church. More than 6 million Jewish Americans have ancestral ties to various nations around the world. The population of Muslim men and women is rapidly increasing and is variously estimated at between 2 and 8 million.

Like the reality of race, the reality of ethnicity is socially constructed. This means that it becomes important only when a society defines it that way. For example, U.S. society defines people of Spanish descent as "Latin," even though Italy probably has a more "Latin" culture than Spain. People of Italian descent are viewed not as Latin but as "European" and thus less "different" (Camara, 2000; Brodkin, 2007). Like racial differences, the importance of ethnic differences can change over time. A century ago, Catholics and Jews were considered "different" in the predominantly Protestant United States. This is much less true today.

Keep in mind that race is constructed from *biological* traits and ethnicity is constructed from *cultural* traits. Of course, the two may go hand in hand. For example, Japanese Americans have distinctive physical traits and, for those who maintain a traditional way of life, a distinctive culture as well. Table 11–1 shows the range of racial and ethnic diversity in the United States as recorded by the 2000 census.

On an individual level, people play up or play down their ethnicity, depending on whether they want to fit in or stand apart from the surrounding society: Immigrants may drop their cultural traditions over time or, like many people of Native American descent in recent years, try to revive their heritage. For most people, ethnicity is a more complex issue than race because they identify with several ethnic backgrounds. The golf star Tiger Woods describes himself as one-eighth American Indian, one-fourth Thai, one-fourth Chinese, one-eighth white, and one-fourth black (J. E. White, 1997).

MINORITIES

 March 3, Dallas, Texas. Sitting in the lobby of just about any hotel in a major U.S. city presents a lesson in contrasts: The majority of the guests checking in and out are white; the majority of the employees who carry the luggage, serve the food, and clean the rooms are minorities.

As defined in Chapter 10 ("Gender Stratification"), a **minority** is *any category of people distinguished by physical or cultural difference that a society sets apart and subordinates.* Minority standing can be based on race, ethnicity, or both. As shown in Table 11–1, white people of non-Hispanic background (71 percent of the total) are still a majority of the U.S. population. But the share of minorities is increasing. Today, minorities are a majority in four states (California, New Mexico, Texas, and Hawaii) and in half of the country's 100 largest cities. By about 2050, minorities are likely to form a majority of the entire U.S. population. National Map 11–1 on page 304 shows where a minority majority already exists.

Minorities have two important characteristics. First, they share a *distinct identity,* which may be based on physical or cultural traits. Second, minorities experience *subordination.* As the rest of this chapter shows, U.S. minorities typically have lower income, lower occupational prestige, and limited schooling. Class, race, and ethnicity, as well as gender, are overlapping and reinforcing dimensions of social stratification. The Thinking About Diversity box on page 305 describes the struggles of recent Latin American immigrants to the United States.

Of course, not all members of a minority category are disadvantaged. For example, some Latinos are quite wealthy, certain Chinese Americans are celebrated business leaders, and African Americans are among our nation's leading scholars. But even job success rarely allows individ-

TABLE 11-1
Racial and Ethnic Categories in the United States, 2000

Racial or Ethnic Classification*	Approximate U.S. Population	Percentage of Total Population
Hispanic descent	**35,305,818**	**12.5%**
Mexican	20,640,711	7.3
Puerto Rican	3,406,178	1.2
Cuban	1,241,685	0.4
Other Hispanic	10,017,244	3.6
African descent	**34,658,190**	**12.3**
Nigerian	165,481	0.1
Ethiopian	86,918	<
Cape Verdean	77,103	<
Ghanaian	49,944	<
South African	45,569	<
Native American descent	**2,475,956**	**0.9**
American Indian	1,815,653	0.6
Eskimo	45,919	<
Other Native American	614,384	0.2
Asian or Pacific Island descent	**10,641,833**	**3.8**
Chinese	2,432,585	0.9
Filipino	1,850,314	0.7
Asian Indian	1,678,765	0.6
Vietnamese	1,122,528	0.4
Korean	1,076,872	0.4
Japanese	796,700	0.3
Cambodian	171,937	<
Hmong	169,428	<
Laotian	168,707	<
Other Asian or Pacific Islander	1,173,997	0.4
West Indian descent	**1,869,504**	**0.7**
Arab descent	**1,202,871**	**0.4**
Non-Hispanic European descent	**194,552,774**	**70.9**
German	42,885,162	15.2
Irish	30,528,492	10.8
English	24,515,138	8.7
Italian	15,723,555	5.6
Polish	8,977,444	3.2
French	8,309,908	3.0
Scottish	4,890,581	1.7
Dutch	4,542,494	1.6
Norwegian	4,477,725	1.6
Two or more races	**6,826,228**	**2.4**

*People of Hispanic descent may be of any race. Many people also identify with more than one ethnic category. Therefore, figures total more than 100 percent.

< indicates less than 1/10 of 1 percent.

Sources: U.S. Census Bureau (2001, 2002, 2004).

By 2000, minorities had become a majority in four states—Hawaii, California, New Mexico and Texas—and the District of Columbia. At the other extreme, Vermont and Maine have the lowest share of racial and ethnic minorities (about 2 percent). Why are states with high minority populations located in the South and Southwest?

Source: "America 2000: A Map of the Mix," *Newsweek*, September 18, 2000, p. 48. Copyright © 2000 Newsweek, Inc. All rights reserved. Reprinted by permission.

Percentage of Total
Population Comprising
African Americans,
Hispanics, Asians,
Pacific Islanders, or
Native Americans

- 50% or higher
- 40% to 49%
- 30% to 39%
- 20% to 29%
- 10% to 19%
- 9% or lower

uals to escape their minority standing. As described in Chapter 4 ("Social Interaction in Everyday Life"), race or ethnicity often serves as a *master status* that overshadows personal accomplishments.

Minorities usually make up a small proportion of a society's population, but that is not always the case. Black South Africans are disadvantaged even though they are a numerical majority in their country. In the United States, women make up slightly more than half the population but are still struggling for the opportunities and privileges enjoyed by men.

Do you think all people of color, rich and poor alike, should be considered minorities? Why or why not?

Prejudice and Stereotypes

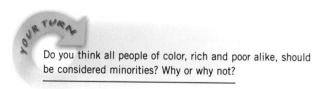

November 19, Jerusalem, Israel. We are driving along the edge of this historic city, a holy place to Jews, Christians, and Muslims, when Razi, our taxi driver, spots a small group of Falasha—Ethiopian Jews—on a street corner. "Those people over there," he begins, "they are different. They don't drive cars. They don't want to improve themselves. Even when our country offers them schooling, they don't take it." He shakes his head at the Ethiopians and drives on.

Prejudice is *a rigid and unfair generalization about an entire category of people.* Prejudice is unfair because such attitudes are supported by little or no direct evidence. Prejudice may target people of a particular social class, sex, sexual orientation, age, political affiliation, race, or ethnicity.

Prejudices are *prejudgments* that can be either positive or negative. Our positive prejudices exaggerate the virtues of people like ourselves, and our negative prejudices condemn those who are different from us.

Take a test for prejudice at http://www.tolerance.org/hidden_bias/index.html

Negative prejudice can be expressed as anything from mild dislike to outright hostility. Because such attitudes are rooted in culture, everyone has at least some measure of prejudice.

Prejudice often takes the form of a **stereotype** (*stereo* is derived from the Greek word for "hard" or "solid"), which is *an exaggerated description applied to every person in some category.* Many white people hold stereotypical views of minorities. Stereotyping is especially harmful to minorities in the workplace. If company officials see minority workers only in terms of a stereotype, they will make assumptions about their abilities, steer them toward certain jobs, and limit their access to better opportunities (R. L. Kaufman, 2002).

Minorities, too, stereotype whites and also other minorities (T. W. Smith, 1996; Cummings & Lambert, 1997). For example, recent surveys show that more African Americans than whites express the belief that Asians engage in unfair business practices and that more Asians than whites criticize Hispanics for having too many children (Perlmutter, 2002).

Hard Work: The Immigrant Life in the United States

Early in the morning, it is already hot in Houston as a line of pickup trucks snakes slowly into a dusty yard, where 200 laborers have been gathered since dawn, hoping for a day's work. The driver of the first truck opens his window and tells the foreman that he is looking for a crew to spread boiling tar on a roof. Abdonel Cespedes, the foreman, turns to the crowd, and after a few minutes, three workers step forward and climb into the back of the truck. The next driver is looking for two experienced housepainters. The scene is repeated over and over as men and a few women leave to dig ditches, spread cement, hang drywall, open clogged septic tanks, or crawl under houses to poison rats.

SOCIOLOGY 🔍 WORK

As each driver pulls into the yard, the foreman asks, "How much?" Most of the people in the trucks offer $5 an hour. Cespedes automatically responds, "$6.50; the going rate is $6.50 for an hour's hard work." Sometimes he convinces people to pay that much, but usually not. The workers, who come from Mexico, El Salvador, and Guatemala, know that dozens of them will end up with no work at all this day. Most jump at the offer of $5 an hour because they know that, when the day is over, $50 is better than nothing.

Labor markets like this one are common in large cities, especially across the southwestern United States.

The surge in immigration in recent years has brought millions of people to this country in search of work, and most have little schooling and speak little English.

Manuel Barrera has taken a day's work moving the entire contents of a store to a storage site as part of a repossession. He arrives at the boarded-up store and gazes at the mountains of heavy furniture that he must carry out to a moving van, drive across town, and then carry again. He sighs when he realizes how hot it is outside and that it is even hotter inside the building. He will have no break for

lunch. No one says anything about toilets. Barrera shakes his head. "I will do this kind of work because it puts food on the table. But I did not foresee it would turn out like this."

The hard truth is that immigrants to the United States do the jobs that no one else wants. Immigrants fill the bottom level of the national economy, working in restaurants and hotels, on construction crews, and in private homes cooking, cleaning, and caring for children. About half of all housekeepers, household cooks, tailors, and restaurant waiters in the United States were born abroad. Few immigrants make much more than the minimum wage ($5.15 per hour), and rarely do they receive any health or pension benefits. Many wealthy families take the labor of immigrants for granted as much as they do their sport utility vehicles and cell phones.

WHAT DO YOU THINK?

1. In what ways do you or members of your family depend on the low-paid labor of immigrants?

2. Do you favor allowing the 11 million immigrants who entered this country illegally to earn citizenship? What should be done?

3. Should the U.S. government act to reduce the number of immigrants entering the country in the future? Why or why not?

Sources: Based on Booth (1998) and Tumulty (2006).

Do you see stereotypes in common phrases such as "French kiss," "Dutch treat," "Indian giver," or being "gypped" (a reference to Gypsies)? Explain.

MEASURING PREJUDICE: THE SOCIAL DISTANCE SCALE

One measure of prejudice is *social distance*, which refers to how closely people are willing to interact with members of some category. Eighty years ago, the sociologist Emory Bog-

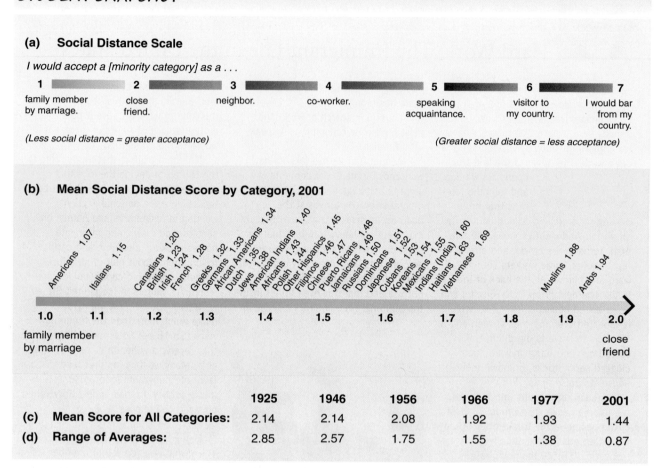

(a)   Social Distance Scale

I would accept a [minority category] as a . . .

1 — 2 — 3 — 4 — 5 — 6 — 7

| 1 family member by marriage. | 2 close friend. | 3 neighbor. | 4 co-worker. | 5 speaking acquaintance. | 6 visitor to my country. | 7 I would bar from my country. |

(Less social distance = greater acceptance)   *(Greater social distance = less acceptance)*

(b)   Mean Social Distance Score by Category, 2001

Americans 1.07, Italians 1.15, Canadians 1.20, British 1.23, Irish 1.24, French 1.28, Greeks 1.32, Germans 1.33, African Americans 1.34, Dutch 1.35, Jews 1.38, American Indians 1.40, Africans 1.43, Polish 1.44, Other Hispanics 1.45, Filipinos 1.46, Chinese 1.47, Puerto Ricans 1.48, Jamaicans 1.49, Russians 1.50, Dominicans 1.51, Japanese 1.52, Cubans 1.53, Koreans 1.54, Mexicans 1.55, Indians (India) 1.60, Haitians 1.63, Vietnamese 1.69, Muslims 1.88, Arabs 1.94

1.0   1.1   1.2   1.3   1.4   1.5   1.6   1.7   1.8   1.9   2.0

family member by marriage   close friend

	1925	1946	1956	1966	1977	2001
(c) Mean Score for All Categories:	2.14	2.14	2.08	1.92	1.93	1.44
(d) Range of Averages:	2.85	2.57	1.75	1.55	1.38	0.87

FIGURE 11-1   Bogardus Social Distance Research

The social distance scale is a good way to measure prejudice. Part (a) illustrates the complete social distance scale, from least social distance at the far left to greatest social distance at the far right. Part (b) shows the mean (average) social distance score received by each category of people in 2001. Part (c) presents the overall mean score (the average of the scores received by all racial and ethnic categories) in specific years. These scores have fallen from 2.14 in 1925 to 1.44 in 2001, showing that students express less social distance toward minorities today than they did in the past. Part (d) shows the range of averages, the difference between the highest and lowest scores in given years (in 2001, for instance, it was .87, the difference between the high score of 1.94 for Arabs and the low score of 1.07 for Americans). This figure has also become smaller since 1925, indicating that today's students tend to see fewer differences between various categories of people.

Source: Parrillo & Donoghue (2005).

ardus developed the *social distance scale* shown in Figure 11–1. Bogardus asked students at colleges and universities in the United States how closely they were willing to interact with people in thirty racial and ethnic categories. People express the greatest social distance (most negative prejudice) by declaring that some category of people should be barred from the country entirely (point 7 in the figure); at the other extreme, people express the least social distance (most social

acceptance) by saying they would accept a member of some category into their family through marriage.

Bogardus (1925, 1967; Owen, Elsner, & McFaul, 1977) found that people felt much more social distance from some categories than from others. In general, students in his surveys expressed the most social distance toward Hispanics, African Americans, Asians, and Turks by indicating that they would accept such people as co-workers but not as neighbors, close friends, or family members. People expressed the least social distance toward those from northern and western Europe, including English and Scottish people, and also Canadians, indicating that they were willing to include them in their families by marriage.

What patterns of social distance do we find among college students today? A recent study using the same social distance scale[1] reported three major findings (Parrillo & Donoghue, 2005):

1. **Student opinion shows a trend toward greater social acceptance.** Today's students express less social distance from all minorities than students did decades ago. Figure 11–1 shows that the mean (average) score on the social distance scale declined from 2.14 in 1925 to 1.93 in 1977 and to 1.44 in 2001. Respondents (81 percent of whom were white) showed notably greater acceptance of African Americans, a category of people that moved up from near the bottom in 1925 to the top one-third in 2001.

2. **People see less difference between various minorities.** The earliest studies found the difference between the highest- and lowest-ranked minorities (the range of averages) equal to almost three points on the scale. As the figure shows, the most recent research produced a range of averages less than one point, indicating that today's students tend to see fewer differences between various categories of people.

3. **The terrorist attacks of September 11, 2001, may have reduced social acceptance of Arabs and Muslims.** The most recent study was conducted just a few weeks after September 11, 2001. Perhaps the fact that the nineteen men who attacked the World Trade Center and the Pentagon were Arabs and Muslims is part of the reason that students ranked these categories last on the social distance scale. However, not a single student gave Arabs or Muslims a 7, indicating that they should be barred from the country. On the contrary, the 2001 mean scores (1.94 for Arabs and 1.88 for Muslims) show higher social acceptance than students in 1977 expressed toward eighteen of the thirty categories of people studied.

---

[1]Parrillo and Donoghue dropped seven of the categories used by Bogardus (Armenians, Czechs, Finns, Norwegians, Scots, Swedes, and Turks), claiming they were no longer visible minorities. He added nine new categories (Africans, Arabs, Cubans, Dominicans, Haitians, Jamaicans, Muslims, Puerto Ricans, and Vietnamese), claiming these are visible minorities today. This change probably encouraged higher social distance scores, making the trend toward decreasing social distance all the more significant.

Recent research measuring student attitudes shows declining prejudice towards all racial and ethnic categories of the U.S. population. Even so, attitudes towards Muslims and Arab Americans are the most negative, probably a result of publicity surrounding global terrorism. Here, Arab Americans speak out against what they feel is the negative depiction of Arabs in the film *True Lies.*

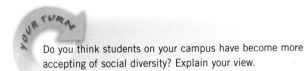

Do you think students on your campus have become more accepting of social diversity? Explain your view.

RACISM

A powerful and harmful form of prejudice, **racism** is *the belief that one racial category is innately superior or inferior to another.* Racism has existed throughout world history. Despite their many achievements, the ancient Greeks, the peoples of India, and the Chinese all considered people unlike themselves inferior.

Does Race Affect Intelligence?

Are Asian Americans smarter than white people? Is the typical white person more intelligent than the average African American? Throughout the history of the United States, we have painted one category of people as intellectually more gifted than another and used this thinking to justify the privileges of the allegedly superior category and even to bar supposedly inferior people from entering this country.

Scientists know that the distribution of the intelligence of individuals forms a bell-shaped curve, as shown in the figure. A person's *intelligence quotient* (IQ) is calculated as the person's mental age in years as measured by a test divided by the person's actual age in years, with the result multiplied by 100. An

eight-year-old who performs like a ten-year-old has an IQ of $10 \div 8 = 1.25 \times 100 = 125$. Average performance is defined as an IQ of 100.

Based on a controversial study of intelligence and social inequality, Richard Herrnstein and Charles Murray (1994) claim that overwhelming

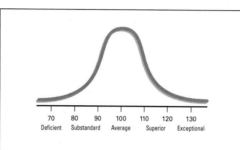

IQ: The Distribution of Intelligence

evidence shows that race is related to measures of intelligence. More specifically, they say that the average IQ for people of European ancestry is 100, for people of East Asian ancestry is 103, and for people of African ancestry is 90.

Statements like this go against our democratic and egalitarian beliefs that no racial type is naturally better than another. Some critics argue that intelligence tests are not valid and even that the concept of intelligence has little real meaning.

Most social scientists believe that IQ tests do measure something important that we think of as intelligence, and they agree that individuals vary in intellectual aptitude. But they reject the idea that any *category* of people, on average, is naturally smarter than any other. So how do we

---

Racism has also been widespread throughout the history of the United States, where ideas about racial inferiority supported slavery. Today, overt racism in this country

Racism can give rise to hate crimes. For more information, go to http://www.civilrights.org/issues/hate/

has decreased because more people believe in evaluating others, in Dr. Martin Luther King's words, "not by the color of their skin but by the content of their character."

Even so, racism remains a serious social problem, as some people still argue that certain racial and ethnic categories are smarter than others. As the Applying Sociology box explains, however, racial differences in mental abilities result from environment rather than biology.

THEORIES OF PREJUDICE

Where does prejudice come from? Social scientists provide several answers to this vexing question, focusing on frustration, personality, culture, and social conflict.

Scapegoat Theory

Scapegoat theory holds that prejudice springs from frustration among people who are themselves disadvantaged (Dollard et al., 1939). Take the case of a white woman who is frustrated by her low-paying job in a textile factory. Directing her hostility at the powerful factory owners carries the obvious risk of being fired; therefore, she may blame her low pay on the presence of minority co-workers. Her prejudice does not improve her situation, but it is a relatively safe way to express anger, and it may give her the comforting feeling that at least she is superior to someone.

A **scapegoat**, then, is *a person or category of people, typically with little power, whom other people unfairly blame for their own troubles.* Because they have little power and thus are usually "safe targets," minorities often are used as scapegoats.

Authoritarian Personality Theory

Theodor Adorno and his colleagues (1950) considered extreme prejudice a personality trait of certain individ-

explain the overall differences in IQ scores by race?

Thomas Sowell (1994, 1995) explains that most of the documented differences in intelligence result not from biology but from environment. In some skillful sociological detective work, Sowell traced IQ scores for various racial and ethnic categories throughout the twentieth century. He found that on average, early-twentieth-century immigrants from European nations such as Poland, Lithuania, Italy, and Greece, as well as Asian countries including China and Japan, scored 10 to 15 points below the U.S. average, but by the end of the twentieth century, people in these same categories had IQ scores that were average or above average. Among Italian Americans, for example, average IQ jumped almost 10 points; among Polish and Chinese Americans, the increase was almost 20 points.

Because genetic changes occur over thousands of years and most peo-ple in the various categories married others like themselves, biological factors cannot explain such a rapid rise in IQ scores. The only reasonable explanation is changing cultural patterns. The descendants of early immigrants improved their intellectual performance as their standard of living rose and their opportunity for schooling increased.

Sowell found that much the same was true of African Americans. Historically, the average IQ score of African Americans living in the North has been about 10 points higher than the average score of those living in the South. Among the descendants of African Americans who migrated from the South to the North after 1940, IQ scores went up just as they did for descendants of European and Asian immigrants. Thus environmental factors appear to go a long way toward explaining differences in IQ among various categories of people.

According to Sowell, these test score differences tell us that *cultural patterns matter.* Asians who score high on tests are no smarter than other people, but they have been raised to value learning and pursue excellence. For their part, African Americans are no less intelligent than anyone else, but they carry a legacy of disadvantage that can undermine self-confidence and discourage achievement.

WHAT DO YOU THINK?

1. If IQ scores reflect people's environment, are they valid measures of intelligence? Could they be harmful?

2. According to Thomas Sowell, why do some racial and ethnic categories show dramatic short-term gains in average IQ scores?

3. Do you think parents and schools influence a child's IQ score? If so, how?

uals. This conclusion is supported by research indicating that people who show strong prejudice toward one minority usually are intolerant of all minorities. These *authoritarian personalities* rigidly conform to conventional cultural values and see moral issues as clear-cut matters of right and wrong. According to Adorno, people who grow up developing authoritarian personalities also view society as naturally competitive, with "better" people (like themselves) dominating those who are weaker (all minorities).

Adorno and colleagues also found the opposite pattern to be true: People who express tolerance toward one minority are likely to be accepting of all. Such people tend to be more flexible in their moral judgments and treat all people as equals.

Adorno thought that people with little education and those raised by cold and demanding parents tend to develop authoritarian personalities. Filled with anger and anxiety as children, they grow into hostile and aggressive adults who seek out scapegoats.

Culture Theory

A third theory claims that although extreme prejudice is found in certain people, some prejudice is found in everyone. Why? Because prejudice is rooted in culture, as the Bogardus social distance studies illustrate. Bogardus found that students across the country had mostly the same attitudes toward specific racial and ethnic categories, feeling closer to some and more distant from others.

Finally, we know that prejudice is rooted in culture because minorities tend to express the same attitudes as white people toward categories other than their own. Such patterns suggest that individuals hold prejudices because we live in a "culture of prejudice" that has taught us to view certain categories of people as "better" or "worse" than others.

Conflict Theory

A fourth explanation proposes that prejudice is used as a tool by powerful people to oppress others. Anglos who look

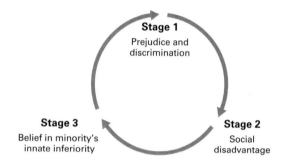

Stage 1
Prejudice and
discrimination

Stage 3
Belief in minority's
innate inferiority

Stage 2
Social
disadvantage

Stage 1: Prejudice and discrimination begin, often as an expression of ethnocentrism or an attempt to justify economic exploitation.

Stage 2: As a result of prejudice and discrimination, a minority is socially disadvantaged, occupying a low position in the system of social stratification.

Stage 3: This social disadvantage is then interpreted not as the result of earlier prejudice and discrimination but as evidence that the minority is innately inferior, unleashing renewed prejudice and discrimination by which the cycle repeats itself.

FIGURE 11–2 Prejudice and Discrimination: The Vicious Circle

Prejudice and discrimination can form a vicious circle, perpetuating themselves.

down on Latino immigrants in the Southwest, for example, can get away with paying the immigrants low wages for hard work. Similarly, all elites benefit when prejudice divides workers along racial and ethnic lines and discourages them from working together to advance their common interests (Geschwender, 1978; Olzak, 1989).

According to another conflict-based argument, made by Shelby Steele (1990), minorities themselves encourage *race consciousness* to win greater power and privileges. Because of their historical disadvantage, minorities claim that they are victims entitled to special consideration based on their race. Although this strategy may bring short-term gains, Steele cautions that such thinking often sparks a backlash from whites or others who oppose "special treatment" on the basis of race or ethnicity.

Discrimination

Closely related to prejudice is **discrimination,** *unequal treatment of various categories of people.* Prejudice refers to *attitudes;* discrimination is a matter of *action.* Like prejudice, discrimination can be either positive (providing spe-

cial advantages) or negative (creating obstacles) and ranges from subtle to blatant.

INSTITUTIONAL PREJUDICE AND DISCRIMINATION

We typically think of prejudice and discrimination as the hateful ideas or actions of specific people. But Stokely Carmichael and Charles Hamilton (1967) pointed out that far greater harm results from **institutional prejudice and discrimination,** *bias built into the operation of society's institutions,* including schools, hospitals, the police, and the

 Read the reports of the Housing Discrimination Study at http://www.huduser.org/publications/hsgfin/hds.html

workplace. For example, researchers have shown that banks reject home mortgage applications from minorities at a higher rate than those from white people, even when income and quality of neighborhood are held constant (Gotham, 1998).

According to Carmichael and Hamilton, people are slow to condemn or even recognize institutional prejudice and discrimination because it often involves respected public officials and long-established traditions. A case in point is *Brown v. Board of Education of Topeka,* the 1954 Supreme Court decision that ended legally segregated schools. The principle of "separate but equal" facilities had been the law of the land, supporting racial inequality by allowing school segregation. Despite the change in the law, fifty years later, most U.S. students still attend schools that are overwhelmingly one race or the other (Barnes, 2004). Indeed, in 1991, the courts declared that neighborhood schools will never provide equal education as long as our population is segregated, with most African Americans living in central cities and most white people (and Asian Americans) living in suburbs.

PREJUDICE AND DISCRIMINATION: THE VICIOUS CIRCLE

Prejudice and discrimination reinforce each other. The Thomas theorem, discussed in Chapter 4 ("Social Interaction in Everyday Life"), offers a simple explanation of this fact: *Situations that are defined as real become real in their consequences* (W. I. Thomas, 1966:301, orig. 1931).

As Thomas recognized, stereotypes become real to people who believe them and sometimes even to those victimized by them. For example, prejudice on the part of white people toward people of color can produce social inferiority, pushing minorities into low-paying jobs, inferior schools, and racially segregated housing. Then, as white people interpret that social disadvantage as evidence that minorities are *naturally* inferior, they unleash a new round of prejudice and discrimination, giving rise to a self-perpetuating vicious circle, as shown in Figure 11–2.

In May of 2006, immigrants and their supporters held rallies in cities across the United States demanding reform to immigration laws and reminding us that countless businesses across the country depend on immigrants' labor. Do you think that the millions of people who have entered this country illegally should be granted citizenship? Why or why not?

Majority and Minority: Patterns of Interaction

Social scientists describe interaction between majority and minority members of a society in terms of four models: pluralism, assimilation, segregation, and genocide.

PLURALISM

Pluralism is *a state in which people of all races and ethnicities are distinct but have equal social standing.* In other words, people who differ in appearance or social heritage all share resources roughly equally.

The United States is pluralistic to the extent that all people have equal standing under the law. In addition, large cities contain countless "ethnic villages" where people proudly display the traditions of their immigrant ancestors. These include New York's Spanish Harlem, Little Italy, and Chinatown; Philadelphia's Italian "South Philly"; Chicago's "Little Saigon"; and Latino East Los Angeles. New York City alone has 189 different ethnic newspapers (P. Paul, 2001; Logan, Alba, & Zhang, 2002). "In the *Times*" on pages 312–13 describes the remarkable and changing ethnic diversity of New York City's neighborhoods.

But the United States is not really pluralistic, for three reasons. First, although most of us value our cultural heritage, few want to live with only people exactly like ourselves (NORC, 2005). Second, our tolerance for social diversity goes only so far. One reaction to the growing proportion of minorities in the United States is a social movement to make English the nation's official language. Third, as we shall see later in this chapter, people of various colors and cultures do *not* have equal social standing.

ASSIMILATION

Many people think of the United States as a "melting pot" in which different nationalities blend together. But rather than everyone "melting" into some new cultural pattern, most minorities have adopted the dominant culture established by the earliest settlers. Why? Because doing so is both the avenue to upward social mobility and a way to escape the prejudice and discrimination directed against more visible foreigners. Sociologists use the term **assimilation** to describe *the process by which minorities gradually adopt patterns of the dominant culture.* Assimilation involves changing styles of dress, values, religion, language, and friends.

The amount of assimilation varies by category. For example, in the United States, Canadians have "melted" more than Cubans, the Dutch more than Dominicans, Germans more than the Japanese. Multiculturalists oppose making assimilation a goal because it suggests that minorities are "the problem" and the ones who need to do all the changing.

Note that assimilation involves changes in ethnicity but not in race. For example, many descendants of Japanese

January 30, 2005

Around the World in Five Boroughs

By JOSEPH BERGER

In a growing number of New York City neighborhoods, it is English that is the foreign language. "The Newest New Yorkers 2000," a 265-page report released last week on how immigration has transformed the city's landscape and life, counted 17 neighborhoods where a majority of the residents were born outside the United States.

In one, Elmhurst in Queens, seven out of 10 residents were born abroad. A stranger stepping out of the neighborhood's subway exit at 75th Street and Broadway would quickly see a large sign proclaiming "Learn English" at the entrance to the American Language Communication Center. There, 1,200 people a week take English classes, some to achieve something as modest as advancing to waiter from busboy.

On that block and the next, a beauty parlor is Indian, a money transmission shop is Ecuadorean, a bakery and Seventh-Day Adventist Church are Chinese, and a video store and dry cleaner are Korean. The owner of Bollywood Beauty Salon, Karim Budhwani, an Indian Muslim from Bombay, has learned a smattering of Spanish so he can intelligently give a *corte de pelo* (a haircut) to a Latino customer. He is also proud that for three years he has employed a Jew from the former Soviet Union, Alex Arkadiy, as a hair stylist. . . .

Elmhurst's polyglot character has become commonplace for much of the city, even in neighborhoods not previously known for their diversity. Several communities have been refashioned by the immigrant tide that gave New York City 2.9 million foreign-born residents in 2000 compared with 2.1 million in 1990.

Bensonhurst and Bay Ridge, once so inherently third- and fourth-generation Italian-American that the character of Tony Manero and his family were based there in the 1977 film classic *Saturday Night Fever*, now have a population that is 40 percent foreign born. One-fifth of that foreign-born population of 78,585 residents are from China, while Russians and Ukrainians also abound, and immigrants from Italy make up only 11 percent. Woodside and Sunnyside in Queens were once Irish bastions, but now, six out of 10 residents were born abroad in countries like Bangladesh, China, Colombia and Ecuador. . . .

The ethnic history of New York has been characterized by a checkerboard, with Italians tending to live in Italian neighborhoods, Jews in Jewish neighborhoods, and so on. But the report found neighborhoods where a stew would be a more apt metaphor.

Of the 74,639 foreign-born residents of Elmhurst, 19 percent came from China, 12 percent from Colombia, 11.7 percent from Ecuador, 8.4 percent from

immigrants have discarded their ethnic traditions but retain their racial identity. For racial traits to diminish over generations, **miscegenation,** or *biological reproduction by partners of different racial categories,* must occur. Although interracial marriage is becoming more common, it still amounts to only 3 percent of all marriages (U.S. Census Bureau, 2004).

SEGREGATION

Segregation is *the physical and social separation of categories of people.* Sometimes minorities, especially religious orders such as the Amish, voluntarily segregate themselves. However, majorities usually segregate minorities by excluding them. Neighborhoods, schools, occupations, hospitals, and even cemeteries can be segregated. Pluralism encourages cultural distinctiveness without disadvantage; segregation enforces separation that harms a minority.

Racial segregation has a long history in the United States, beginning with slavery and evolving into racially separate housing, schooling, buses, and trains. Decisions such as the 1954 *Brown* case have reduced *de jure* (Latin, "by law") discrimination in the United States. However, *de facto* ("in fact") segregation continues in the form of countless neighborhoods that are home to people of a single race.

Despite some recent decline, segregation continues in the United States. For example, Livonia, Michigan, is 96 percent white, while neighboring Detroit is 83 percent African American. Kurt Metzger (2001) explains, "Livonia was pretty much created by white flight [from Detroit]." Further, research shows that across the country, whites (especially those with young children) continue to avoid neighborhoods where African Americans live (Emerson, Yancey, & Chai, 2001; Krysan, 2002). At the extreme, Douglas Massey and Nancy Denton (1989) documented the *hypersegregation* of poor African Americans in some inner

Mexico, 7.1 percent from Korea, 5.6 percent from India and 5.2 percent from the Philippines. The exotic flavor would have been portrayed as even richer if the census had included children born here to immigrant parents among its count. . . .

Other neighborhoods are also becoming more cosmopolitan. Bedford-Stuyvesant, long identified as black American, had 16,200 residents who were born abroad, about 28 percent. Most were Caribbean blacks from Jamaica, Trinidad and Tobago, and Guyana. While Borough Park has long been depicted as Hasidic, the report found that it has 35,900 immigrants, one-fifth of whom are Chinese. Park Slope may be identified with brownstone-dwelling children of privilege, but it has 18,700 immigrants, 11 percent of whom are Mexicans. . . .

Despite the amalgamated example of Elmhurst, the report found that many newer immigrants still choose to live among compatriots, at least at first. Guyanese immigrants are settling in Richmond Hill, Queens, once a heavily German and Irish enclave that saw its immigrant population double during the 1990s. People from the Caribbean countries of Guyana (17,555) and Trinidad and Tobago (4,975) now predominate, and almost all are descendants of contract laborers who left India for the Caribbean in the 19th and early 20th centuries. . . .

The immigrant wave touched every corner of the city. The Bronx has not only had surges of Dominicans moving from apartments in Washington Heights to those in Highbridge, but Jamaicans now make up almost a quarter of the residents of Wakefield, a northeastern neighborhood of one- and two-family homes. Even Staten Island, the whitest of the city's boroughs, has changed. Neighborhoods like New Springville have large numbers of Koreans, Indians and Chinese, and New Brighton–Grymes Hill is home to 8,000 Mexicans.

None of these trends surprise Mr. Budhwani, the Elmhurst, hair salon owner.

"Every stranger can stay in New York City and feel more comfortable here than in any other state," he said.

WHAT DO YOU THINK?

1. In what specific ways does an increasing number of immigrants change city life?

2. Is the immigrant character of many New York neighborhoods anything new? Why or why not?

3. Why are more of today's neighborhoods ethnically mixed, in contrast to the one-ethnicity pattern of neighborhoods in the past?

---

cities. Hypersegregation means having little contact of any kind with people beyond the local community. Hypersegregation is the daily experience of about 20 percent of poor African Americans.

In your city or town, are there minority neighborhoods? Which category of people live there? To what extent is your city or town racially and ethnically segregated?

GENOCIDE

Genocide is *the systematic killing of one category of people by another.* This deadly form of racism and ethnocentrism violates nearly every recognized moral standard, yet it has occurred time and again in human history.

Genocide was common in the history of contact between Europeans and the original inhabitants of the Americas. From the sixteenth century on, the Spanish, Portuguese, English, French, and Dutch forcibly colonized vast empires. Although most native people died from diseases brought by Europeans, to which they had no natural defenses, many who opposed the colonizers were killed deliberately (Matthiessen, 1984; Sale, 1990).

Genocide also occurred in the twentieth century. Unimaginable horror befell European Jews during Adolf Hitler's reign of terror, known as the Holocaust. From about 1935 to 1945, the Nazis murdered more than 6 million Jewish men, women, and children, along with gay people, Gypsies, and people with handicaps. The Soviet dictator Josef Stalin murdered on an even greater scale, killing some 30 million real and imagined enemies during decades of violent rule. Between 1975 and 1980, Pol Pot's Communist regime in Cambodia butchered all "capitalists," which

In an effort to force assimilation, the U.S. Bureau of Indian Affairs took American Indian children from their families and placed them in boarding schools like this one—Oklahoma's Riverside Indian School. There, they were taught the English language by non-Indian teachers with the goal of making them into "Americans."

included anyone able to speak a Western language. In all, some 2 million people (one-fourth of the population) perished in the Cambodian "killing fields" (Shawcross, 1979).

Tragically, genocide continues even today. Recent examples include Hutus killing Tutsis in the African nation of Rwanda, Serbs killing Bosnians in the Balkans of Eastern Europe, and the killing of hundreds of thousands of people in the Darfur region of Sudan.

These four patterns of minority-majority contact have all been played out in the United States. Although many people proudly point to patterns of pluralism and assimilation, it is also important to recognize the degree to which U.S. society has been built on segregation (of African Americans) and genocide (of Native Americans). The remainder of this chapter examines how these four patterns have shaped the past and present social standing of major racial and ethnic categories in the United States.

Race and Ethnicity in the United States

Give me your tired, your poor,
Your huddled masses yearning to breathe free,
The wretched refuse of your teeming shore,
Send these, the homeless, tempest-tossed to me:
I lift my lamp beside the golden door.

These words by Emma Lazarus, inscribed on the base of the Statue of Liberty, express cultural ideals of human dignity, personal freedom, and economic opportunity. Indeed, the United States has provided more of the "good life" to more immigrants than any other nation. About 1 million immigrants come to this country every year, and their ways of life create a social mosaic that is especially evident in large cities.

However, as a survey of racial and ethnic minorities in the United States will show, our country's golden door has opened more widely for some than for others. We turn to the history and current social standing of the major categories of the U.S. population.

NATIVE AMERICANS

The term "Native Americans" refers to the hundreds of societies—including Aleuts, Cherokee, Zuni, Sioux, Mohawk, Aztec, and Inca—who first settled the Western Hemisphere. Some 30,000 years before Christopher Columbus (1446–1506) landed in the Americas, migrating peoples crossed a land bridge from Asia to North America where the Bering Strait (off the coast of Alaska) lies today. Gradually, they spread throughout North and South America.

When the first Europeans arrived late in the fifteenth century, Native Americans numbered in the millions. But by 1900, after centuries of conflict and acts of genocide, the

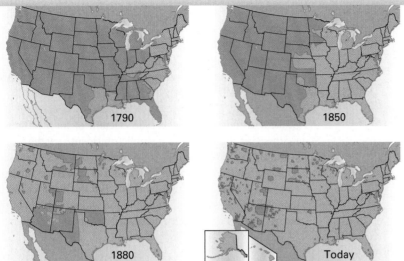

"vanishing Americans" numbered just 250,000 (Dobyns, 1966; Tyler, 1973). The land they controlled also shrank dramatically, as National Map 11–2 shows.

Columbus first referred to the Native Americans that he encountered as "Indians" because he mistakenly thought he had reached the coast of India. Columbus found the native people passive and peaceful, in stark contrast to the materialistic and competitive Europeans (Matthiessen, 1984; Sale, 1990). Yet Europeans justified the seizure of Native American lands by calling their victims thieves and murderers (Josephy, 1982; Matthiessen, 1984; Sale, 1990).

After the Revolutionary War, the new U.S. government adopted a pluralistic approach to Native American societies and tried to gain more land through treaties. Payment for land was far from fair, however, and when Native Americans resisted surrendering their homelands, the U.S. government simply used its superior military power to evict them. By the early 1800s, few Native Americans remained east of the Mississippi River.

In 1871, the United States declared Native Americans wards of the government and adopted a strategy of forced assimilation. Relocated to specific territories designated as "reservations," Native Americans continued to lose their land and were well on their way to losing their culture as well. Reservation life encouraged dependency on outsiders, replacing ancestral languages with English and traditional religion with Christianity. Officials took many children from their parents and handed them over to boarding schools, where they were resocialized as "Americans." Authorities gave local control of reservations to the few Native Americans who supported government policies, and they distributed reservation land, traditionally held collectively, as private property to individual families (Tyler, 1973).

Not until 1924 were Native Americans entitled to U.S. citizenship. After that, many migrated from the reservations, adopting mainstream cultural patterns and marrying non–Native Americans. Today, four out of ten Native Americans consider themselves biracial or multiracial (Raymond, 2001; Wellner, 2001), and many large cities now contain sizable Native American populations. However, as Table 11–2 shows, the income of Native Americans is far below the U.S. average, and relatively few Native Americans earn a college degree.[2]

From in-depth interviews with Native Americans in a western city, Joan Albon (1971) concluded that their low social standing was a result of cultural factors, including their noncompetitive view of life and reluctance to pursue higher education. In addition, she noted, many Native Americans have dark skin, which makes them targets of prejudice and discrimination.

 For more information on Native Americans, visit http://www.nativeweb.org

---

[2]In making comparisons of education and income, keep in mind that various categories of the U.S. population have different median ages. In 2000, the median age for all U.S. people was 35.4 years; for Native Americans, the figure was 28.5 years. Because people's schooling and income increase over time, this age difference accounts for some of the disparities shown in Table 11–2.

TABLE 11–2

The Social Standing of Native Americans, 2000

	Native Americans	Entire U.S. Population
Median family income	$33,144*	$50,891
Percentage in poverty	25.7%*	11.3%
Completion of four or more years of college (age 25 and over)	11.5%	24.4%

*Data are for 1999.

Sources: U.S. Census Bureau (2004, 2006).

Members of the more than 500 American Indian nations in the United States today are reclaiming pride in their cultural heritage. Traditional cultural organizations report a surge in new membership applications, and many children can now speak native languages better than their parents. The legal right of Native Americans to govern their reservations has enabled some tribes to build profitable gaming casinos. But the wealth produced from gambling has enriched relatively few Native peoples, and most profits go to non-Indian investors (Bartlett & Steele, 2002). While some prosper, most Native Americans remain severely disadvantaged, with a profound sense of the injustice they have suffered at the hands of white people.

WHITE ANGLO-SAXON PROTESTANTS

White Anglo-Saxon Protestants (WASPs) were not the first people to inhabit the United States, but they soon dominated the nation after European settlement began. Most WASPs are of English ancestry, but this category also includes people from Scotland and Wales. With some 31 million people claiming English, Scottish, or Welsh ancestry, 11 percent of our society has some WASP background, and WASPs are found at all class levels.

Historically, WASP immigrants were highly skilled and motivated to achieve by what we now call the Protestant work ethic. Because of their numbers and power, WASPs were not subject to the prejudice and discrimination experienced by other categories of immigrants. In fact, the historical dominance of WASPs has led others to want to become more like them (K. W. Jones, 2001).

WASPs were never one single group; especially during colonial times, hostility separated English Anglicans from Scottish Presbyterians (Parrillo, 1994). But in the nineteenth century, most WASPs joined together to oppose the arrival of "undesirables" such as the Germans in the 1840s

and Italians in the 1880s. Those who could afford it sheltered themselves in exclusive suburbs and restrictive clubs. Thus the 1880s—the decade when the Statue of Liberty first welcomed immigrants to the United States—also saw the founding of the first country club with exclusively WASP members (Baltzell, 1964).

By about 1950, however, WASP wealth and power had peaked, as indicated by the 1960 election of John Fitzgerald Kennedy as the first Irish Catholic president. Yet the WASP cultural legacy remains. English is this country's dominant language and Protestantism the majority religion. Our legal system also reflects its English origins. But the historical dominance of WASPs is most evident in the widespread use of the terms "race" and "ethnicity" to describe everyone but them.

AFRICAN AMERICANS

Africans accompanied Spanish explorers to the New World in the fifteenth century. But most accounts trace the beginning of black history in the United States to 1619, when a Dutch trading ship brought twenty Africans to Jamestown, Virginia. Whether these people arrived as slaves or as indentured servants who paid their passage by agreeing to work for a period of time, being of African descent on these shores soon became virtually synonymous with being a slave. In 1661, Virginia enacted the first law recognizing slavery (Sowell, 1981).

Slavery was the foundation of the southern colonies' plantation system. White people ran plantations using slave labor, and until 1808, some were also slave traders. Traders—including North Americans, Africans, and Europeans—forcibly transported some 10 million Africans to various countries in the Americas, including 400,000 to the United States. On small sailing ships, hundreds of slaves were chained for the several weeks it took to cross the Atlantic Ocean. Filth and disease killed many and drove others to suicide. Overall, perhaps half died en route (Franklin, 1967; Sowell, 1981).

Surviving the miserable journey was a mixed blessing, bringing with it a life of servitude. Although some slaves worked in cities at various trades, most labored in the fields, often from daybreak until sunset and even longer during the harvest. The law allowed owners to use whatever disci-

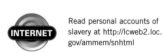 Read personal accounts of slavery at http://lcweb2.loc.gov/ammem/snhtml

plinary measures they deemed necessary to ensure that slaves were obedient and hardworking. Even killing a slave rarely prompted legal action. Owners also broke up slave families at public auctions, where human beings were bought and sold as pieces of property. Unschooled and dependent on their owners for all their

The efforts of these four women greatly advanced the social standing of African Americans in the United States. Pictured above, from left to right: Sojourner Truth (1797–1883), born a slave, became an influential preacher and outspoken abolitionist who was honored by President Lincoln at the White House. Harriet Tubman (1820–1913), after escaping from slavery herself, masterminded the flight from bondage of hundreds of African American men and women via the "Underground Railroad." Ida Wells-Barnett (1862–1931), born to slave parents, became a partner in a Memphis newspaper and served as a tireless crusader against the terror of lynching. Marian Anderson (1902–1993), an exceptional singer whose early career was restrained by racial prejudice, broke symbolic "color lines" by singing in the White House (1936) and on the steps of the Lincoln Memorial to a crowd of almost 100,000 people (1939).

basic needs, slaves had little control over their lives (Franklin, 1967; Sowell, 1981).

Some free people of color lived in both the North and the South, laboring as small-scale farmers, skilled workers, and small business owners. But the lives of most African Americans stood in glaring contradiction to the principles of freedom on which the United States was founded. The Declaration of Independence states,

> We hold these Truths to be self-evident, that all Men are created equal, that they are endowed by their Creator with certain unalienable Rights, that among these are Life, Liberty, and the Pursuit of Happiness.

However, most white people did not apply these ideals to African Americans. In the *Dred Scott* case in 1857, the U.S. Supreme Court addressed the question "Are blacks citizens?" by writing, "We think they are not, and that they are not included, and were not intended to be included, under the word 'citizens' in the Constitution, and can therefore claim none of the rights and privileges which that instrument provides for and secures for citizens of the United States" (quoted in Blaustein & Zangrando, 1968:160). Thus arose what the Swedish sociologist Gunnar Myrdal (1944) called the "American dilemma": a democratic society's denial of basic rights and freedoms to an entire category of people. To resolve this dilemma, many white people simply defined African Americans as naturally inferior and undeserving of equality (Leach, 2002).

In 1865, the Thirteenth Amendment to the Constitution outlawed slavery. Three years later, the Fourteenth Amendment reversed the *Dred Scott* ruling, granting citizenship to all people born in the United States. The Fifteenth Amendment, ratified in 1870, stated that neither race nor previous condition of servitude should deprive anyone of the right to vote. However, so-called *Jim Crow laws*—classic cases of institutionalized discrimination—segregated U.S. society into two racial castes. Especially in the South, white people beat and lynched black people (and some white people) who challenged the racial hierarchy.

The twentieth century brought dramatic changes for African Americans. After World War I, tens of thousands of women and men fled the rural South for jobs in northern factories. Although most did find economic opportunities, few escaped racial prejudice and discrimination, which placed them lower in the social hierarchy than white immigrants arriving from Europe.

In the 1950s and 1960s, a national civil rights movement grew out of landmark judicial decisions that outlawed segregated schools and overt discrimination in employment and public accommodations. The Black Power movement in the 1960s and 1970s gave African Americans a renewed sense of pride and purpose.

TABLE 11–3
The Social Standing of African Americans, 2005

	African Americans[*]	Entire U.S. Population
Median family income	$35,464	$56,194
Percentage in poverty	24.9%	12.6%
Completion of four or more years of college (age 25 and over)	17.6%	27.7%

[*]For comparison with other tables in this chapter, 2000 data are as follows: median family income, $34,204; percentage in poverty, 22.1%; completion of four or more years of college, 16.6%.

Sources: U.S. Census Bureau (2000, 2001, 2006).

Despite these gains, people of African descent continue to occupy a lower social position in the United States, as shown in Table 11–3. The median income of African American families in 2005 ($35,464) was only 56 percent of non-Hispanic white family income ($63,156), a ratio that has changed little in thirty years.[3] Black families remain three times as likely as white families to be poor.

The number of African American families securely in the middle class rose by more than half between 1980 and 2005; 36 percent earn $50,000 or more each year. But most African Americans are still working-class or poor, and in recent years, many have seen earnings slip as factory jobs, vital to residents of central cities, have been lost to other countries where labor costs are lower. This is one reason that black unemployment is more than twice as high as white unemployment; among African American teenagers in many cities, the figure exceeds 40 percent (R. A. Smith, 2002; U.S. Department of Labor, 2006).

Since 1980, African Americans have made remarkable educational progress. The share of adults completing high school rose from half to almost three-fourths, nearly closing the gap between whites and blacks. Between 1980 and 2005, the share of African American adults with at least a college degree rose from 8 percent to more than 17 percent. But as Table 11–3 shows, African Americans are still well below the national average when it comes to completing four years of college.

---

[3]Here again, a median age difference (non-Hispanic white people, 38.6; black people, 30.2) accounts for some of the income and educational disparities. More important is a higher proportion of one-parent families among blacks than whites. If we compare only married-couple families, African Americans (median income $56,054 in 2005) earned 80 percent as much as non-Hispanic whites ($70,307).

The political clout of African Americans has greatly increased. As a result of both black migration to the cities and white flight to the suburbs, half of this country's ten largest cities have elected African American mayors. Yet in 2006, African Americans accounted for just 39 members of the House of Representatives (8.9 percent of 435), no members (out of 100) in the Senate, and no state governors.

In sum, for nearly 400 years, people of African ancestry in the United States have struggled for social equality. As a nation, the United States has come far in this pursuit. Overt discrimination is now illegal, and research documents a long-term decline in prejudice against African Americans (Firebaugh & Davis, 1988; J. Q. Wilson, 1992; NORC, 2005).

In 1913, fifty years after the abolition of slavery, W. E. B. Du Bois proudly noted the extent of black achievement. But Du Bois also cautioned that racial caste remained strong in the United States. Almost a century later, the racial hierarchy persists.

In your opinion, how much change have you seen in racial prejudice and discrimination against African Americans during your lifetime? Explain your position.

ASIAN AMERICANS

Although Asian Americans share some racial traits, enormous cultural diversity marks this category of people. In 2000, the total number of Asian Americans exceeded 10 million, approaching 4 percent of the U.S. population. The largest category of Asian Americans is people of Chinese ancestry (2.4 million), followed by those of Filipino (1.8 million), Asian Indian (1.7 million), Vietnamese (1.1 million), Korean (1 million), and Japanese (800,000) descent. More than one-third of Asian Americans live in California.

Many young Asian Americans have commanded attention and respect as high achievers and are disproportionately represented at our country's best colleges and universities. Many of their elders also have made economic and social gains; most Asian Americans now live in middle-class suburbs. Yet despite (and sometimes because of) this achievement, Asian Americans are sometimes avoided or treated with outright hostility (O'Hare, Frey, & Fost, 1994; Chua-Eoan, 2000).

The achievement of some Asian Americans has given rise to a "model minority" stereotype that is misleading because it hides the differences in class standing and outright poverty that are found among their ranks. We will focus on the history and current standing of Chinese Americans and Japanese Americans—the longest-established Asian American minorities—and conclude with a brief look at the most recent arrivals.

Chinese Americans

Chinese immigration to the United States began in 1849 with the economic boom of California's Gold Rush. New towns and businesses sprang up overnight, and the demand for cheap labor attracted some 100,000 Chinese immigrants. Most Chinese workers were young, hardworking men willing to take low-status jobs that whites did not want. But the economy soured in the 1870s, and desperate whites began to compete with the Chinese for whatever work could be found. Suddenly, the hardworking Chinese were seen as a threat. In short, economic hard times led to prejudice and discrimination (Ling, 1971; Boswell, 1986). Soon laws were passed barring Chinese people from many occupations, and public opinion turned strongly against the "Yellow Peril."

In 1882, the U.S. government passed the first of several laws limiting Chinese immigration. This action caused domestic hardship because in the United States, Chinese men outnumbered Chinese women by twenty to one. This sex imbalance drove the Chinese population down to only 60,000 by 1920. Because Chinese women already in the United States were in high demand, they soon lost much of their traditional submissiveness to men (Hsu, 1971; Lai, 1980; Sowell, 1981).

Responding to racial hostility, some Chinese moved east; many more sought the relative safety of urban Chinatowns. There Chinese traditions flourished, and kinship networks, called *clans,* offered financial assistance to individuals and represented the interests of all. At the same time, however, living in an all-Chinese community discouraged people from learning English, which limited their job opportunities (Wong, 1971).

A renewed need for labor during World War II prompted President Franklin Roosevelt to end the ban on Chinese immigration in 1943 and to extend the rights of citizenship to Chinese Americans born abroad. Many responded by moving out of Chinatowns and seeking cultural assimilation. In turn-of-the-century Honolulu, for example, 70 percent of the Chinese people lived in Chinatown; today, the figure is below 20 percent.

By 1950, many Chinese Americans had experienced upward social mobility. Today, people of Chinese ancestry are no longer limited to self-employment in laundries and restaurants; many hold high-prestige positions, especially in fields related to science and new information technology.

Although sometimes portrayed as a successful "model minority," Asian Americans are highly diverse and, like other categories of people, include both rich and poor. These young people contend with many of the same patterns of prejudice and discrimination familiar to members of other minorities.

As shown in Table 11–4 on page 320, the median family income of Chinese Americans in 1999 ($60,058) stood above the national average of $50,046 for 1999. However, the higher income of all Asian Americans reflects a larger number of family members in the labor force.[4] Chinese Americans also have an enviable record of educational achievement, with almost twice the national average of college graduates.

Despite their success, many Chinese Americans still deal with subtle (and sometimes blatant) prejudice and discrimination. Such hostility is one reason that poverty among Chinese Americans stands near the national average. Poverty is higher still among those who remain in the socially isolated Chinatowns working in restaurants or other low-paying jobs. Sociologists debate whether racial and ethnic enclaves help their residents or exploit them (Portes & Jensen, 1989; Kinkead, 1992; Gilbertson & Gurak, 1993).

Visit the Organization of Chinese Americans at http://www.ocanatl.org/

---

[4]Median age for all Asian Americans in 2000 was 32.7 years, somewhat below the national median of 35.4 and the non-Hispanic white median of 38.6. But specific categories vary widely in median age: Japanese, 42; Chinese, 35; Filipino, 35; Korean, 32; Asian Indian, 30; Cambodian, 23; Hmong, 16 (U.S. Census Bureau, 2002, 2006).

TABLE 11-4

The Social Standing of Asian Americans, 2005

	All Asian Americans**	Chinese Americans*	Japanese Americans*	Korean Americans*	Filipino Americans*	Entire U.S. Population
Median family income	$68,957	$60,058	$70,849	$47,624	$65,189	$56,194
Percentage in poverty	11.1%	13.2%	9.5%	14.4%	6.2%	12.6%
Completion of four or more years of college (age 25 and over)	49.4%	48.1%	41.9%	43.8%	43.8%	27.7%

*Income data are for 1999; poverty and college completion data are for 2000.

**For comparison with other tables in this chapter, 2000 data for all Asians are as follows: median family income, $62,617; percentage in poverty, 10.8%, completion of four or more years of college, 43.9%.

Sources: U.S. Census Bureau (2000, 2001, 2006).

Japanese Americans

Japanese immigration to the United States began slowly in the 1860s, reaching only 3,000 by 1890. Most of these immigrants came to the Hawaiian Islands (annexed by the United States in 1898 and made a state in 1959) to take low-paying jobs. After 1900, as the number of Japanese immigrants to California increased (reaching 140,000 by 1915), white hostility increased (Takaki, 1998). In 1907, the United States signed an agreement with Japan limiting the entry of men—the chief economic threat—while allowing Japanese women to immigrate to ease the sex ratio imbalance. In the 1920s, state laws in California and dozens of other states mandated segregation and banned interracial marriage, virtually ending further Japanese immigration. Not until 1952 did the United States extend citizenship to foreign-born Japanese.

Japanese and Chinese immigrants differed in three important ways. First, there were fewer Japanese immigrants, so they escaped some of the hostility directed at the more numerous Chinese. Second, the Japanese knew much more about the United States than the Chinese did, which helped them assimilate (Sowell, 1981). Third, Japanese immigrants preferred rural farming to clustering in cities, which made them less visible. But many white people objected to Japanese ownership of farmland, so in 1913, California barred further purchases. Many foreign-born Japanese (called the *Issei*) responded by operating farms legally owned by their U.S.-born children (*Nisei*), who were constitutionally entitled to citizenship.

Japanese Americans faced their greatest crisis after Japan bombed the U.S. naval fleet at Pearl Harbor, Hawaii, on December 7, 1941. Rage was directed at the Japanese living in the United States. Some people feared that the Japa-

nese here would spy for Japan or commit acts of sabotage. President Franklin Roosevelt soon signed Executive Order 9066, an unprecedented action intended to protect national security by detaining people of Japanese descent in military camps. Authorities soon relocated 110,000 people (90 percent of all U.S. Japanese) to remote inland reservations (Sun, 1998).

Concern about national security always rises in times of war, but Japanese internment was sharply criticized. First, it targeted an entire category of people, not one of whom was ever known to have committed a disloyal act. Second, roughly two-thirds of those imprisoned were *Nisei*, U.S. citizens by birth. Third, the United States was also at war with Germany and Italy, but no comparable action of this kind was taken against people of German or Italian ancestry.

Relocation meant selling homes, furnishings, and businesses on short notice for pennies on the dollar. As a result, almost the entire Japanese American population was economically devastated. Herded into military prisons, surrounded by barbed wire and guarded by armed soldiers, families crowded into single rooms, often in buildings that had previously sheltered livestock. The internment ended in 1944 when the Supreme Court declared it unconstitutional. In 1988, Congress awarded $20,000 to each victim as token compensation for the hardships they endured.

After World War II, Japanese Americans staged a dramatic recovery. Having lost their traditional businesses, many entered new occupations, and driven by cultural values stressing the importance of education and hard work, Japanese Americans have enjoyed remarkable success. In 1999, the median income of Japanese American households was more than 40 percent above the national average. The rate of poverty among Japanese Americans was considerably less than the national figure.

Upward social mobility has encouraged cultural assimilation and interracial marriage. Younger generations of Japanese Americans rarely live in residential enclaves, as many Chinese Americans still do, and most marry non-Japanese partners. In the process, many have abandoned their traditions, including the Japanese language. Many Japanese Americans belong to ethnic associations as a way of maintaining their ethnic identity. Still, some appear to be caught between two worlds, no longer culturally Japanese yet, because of racial differences, not completely accepted in the larger society.

 To learn about Japanese culture and society, go to http://www.jinjapan.org

Recent research on social distance (see page 306) indicates that most of today's college students say they are more accepting of African Americans than Asian Americans. Does this square with your experiences? What about white people in the country as a whole—is there more social acceptance of Asian Americans or African Americans? Why?

Recent Asian Immigrants

More recent immigrants from Asia include Koreans, Filipinos, Indians, Vietnamese, Guamanians, and Samoans. Overall, the Asian American population increased by 48 percent between 1990 and 2000 and currently accounts for one-third of all immigration to the United States (U.S. Department of Homeland Security, 2006). A brief look at Koreans and Filipinos—both from countries that have had special ties to the United States—shows the social diversity of people arriving from Asia.

Korean immigration to the United States followed the U.S. involvement in the Korean War (1950–53). U.S. troops in South Korea experienced Korean culture firsthand, and some soldiers took Korean spouses. For South Koreans, contact with the troops increased interest in the United States.

The entrepreneurial spirit is strong among Asian immigrants. Asians are slightly more likely than Latinos, three times more likely than African Americans, and eight times more likely than Native Americans to own and operate small businesses (U.S. Small Business Administration, 2001a). Among all Asian Americans, Koreans are the most likely to own small businesses. For example, most small grocery stores in New York City are Korean-owned; in Los Angeles, Koreans operate a large share of liquor stores.

Although many Koreans work long hours in businesses such as these, Korean American families earn lower than average incomes, as shown in Table 11–4. To add to their

Of all categories of Asian Americans, immigrants from India have the greatest economic achievement due, in part, to overrepresentation in many high-paying professions. Parminda Nagra, who plays an Indian doctor, is featured on the popular television show *ER*.

burden, Korean Americans face limited social acceptance, even among other categories of Asian Americans.

The large number of immigrants from the Philippines is explained partly by the fact that the United States controlled the Philippine Islands between 1898, when Spain ceded it in partial settlement of the Spanish-American War, and 1946, when the Philippines became an independent republic.

The data in Table 11–4 show that Filipinos generally have fared well. But a closer look reveals a mixed pattern, with some Filipinos highly successful in the professions (especially in medicine) and others holding low-skill jobs (Parrillo, 1994).

For many Filipino families, the key to high income is working women. Almost three-fourths of Filipino American women are in the labor force, compared with just half of Korean American women. Moreover, many of these women

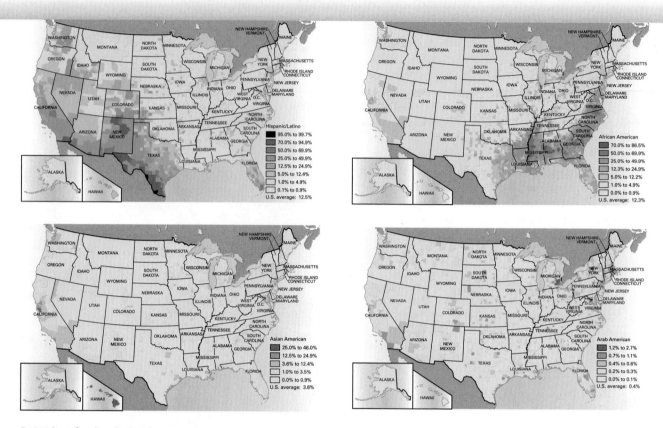

SEEING OURSELVES

NATIONAL MAP 11–3
The Concentration of Hispanics or Latinos, African Americans, Asian Americans, and Arab Americans, by County, 2000

In 2000, people of Hispanic or Latino descent represented 12.5 percent of the U.S. population, compared with 12.3 percent African Americans, 3.6 percent Asian Americans, and 0.4 percent Arab Americans. These maps show the geographic distribution of these categories of people in 2000. Comparing them, we see that the southern half of the United States is home to far more minorities than the northern half. But do they all concentrate in the same areas? What patterns do the maps reveal?

Sources: U.S. Census Bureau (2001, 2003).

are professionals, reflecting the fact that 42 percent of Filipino American women have a four-year college degree, compared with 26 percent of Korean American women.

In sum, a survey of Asian Americans presents a complex picture. The Japanese come closest to having achieved social acceptance, but some surveys reveal greater prejudice against Asian Americans than against African Americans (Parrillo, 2003a). Median income data suggest that many Asian Americans have prospered. But these numbers reflect the fact that many Asian Americans live in Hawaii, Califor-

nia, or New York, where incomes are high but so are living costs (Takaki, 1998). Then, too, many Asian Americans remain poor. One thing is clear—their high immigration rate means that people of Asian ancestry will play a central role in U.S. society in the decades to come.

HISPANIC AMERICANS/LATINOS

In 2000, the number of Hispanics in the United States topped 35 million (12.5 percent of the U.S. population), surpassing the number of African Americans (12.3 percent)

The strength of family bonds and neighborhood ties is evident in Carmen Lomas Garza's painting *Barbacoa para Cumpleanos* (Birthday Party Barbecue).

Carmen Lomas Garza, *Barbacoa para Cumpleanos* (Birthday Party Barbecue). Alkyds on canvas, 38 × 48 inches. (C) 1993 Carmen Lomas Garza (reg. 1994). Photo credit: M. Lee Fatherree. Collection of Federal Reserve Bank of Dallas.

and making Hispanics the largest racial or ethnic minority. Keep in mind that few who fall in this category describe themselves as "Hispanic" or "Latino." Like Asian Americans, Hispanics are really a cluster of distinct populations, each of which identifies with a particular ancestral nation (Marín & Marín, 1991). About two out of three Hispanics (some 20 million) are Mexican Americans. Puerto Ricans are next in number (3 million), followed by Cuban Americans (1.2 million). Many other nations of Latin America are represented by smaller numbers.

Although the Hispanic population is increasing all over the country, most Hispanic Americans live in the Southwest. One of four Californians is Latino (in greater Los Angeles, almost half the people are Latino). National Map 11–3 shows the distribution of the Hispanic, African American, Asian American, and Arab American populations across the United States.

For information about Hispanic/Latino culture, go to http://www1.lanic.utexas.edu/la/region/hispanic

Median family income for all Hispanics—$37,867 in 2005—stands well below the national average.[5] As the following sections explain, however, some categories of Hispanics have fared better than others.

---

[5]The 2000 median age of the U.S. Hispanic population was 25.8 years, well below the national median of 35.4 years. This difference accounts for some of the disparity in income and education.

Mexican Americans

Some Mexican Americans are descendants of people who lived in a part of Mexico annexed by the United States after the Mexican American War (1846–48). However, most Mexican Americans are recent immigrants. Today, more immigrants come to the United States from Mexico than from any other country.

Like many other immigrants, many Mexican Americans have worked as low-wage laborers, on farms or elsewhere. Table 11–5 on page 324 shows that the 2003 median family income for Mexican Americans was $32,263, about two-thirds the national average. Almost one-fourth of Chicano families are poor—nearly twice the national average. Finally, despite gains since 1980, Mexican Americans still have a high dropout rate and receive much less schooling, on average, than U.S. adults as a whole.

Puerto Ricans

The island of Puerto Rico, like the Philippines, became a U.S. possession when the Spanish-American War ended in 1898. In 1917, Puerto Ricans (but not Filipinos) became U.S. citizens.

New York City is home to nearly 1 million Puerto Ricans. However, about one-third of this community is severely disadvantaged. Adjusting to cultural patterns on the U.S. mainland—including, for many, learning English—is one major challenge; also, Puerto Ricans with

TABLE 11-5

The Social Standing of Hispanic Americans, 2005

	All Hispanics**	Mexican Americans*	Puerto Ricans*	Cuban Americans*	Entire U.S. Population
Median family income	$37,867	$32,263	$34,519	$44,847	$56,194
Percentage in poverty	21.8%	24.1%	23.7%	14.4%	12.6%
Completion of four or more years of college (age 25 and over)	12.1%	7.9%	14.1%	24.0%	27.7%

*Income and poverty data are for 2003; college completion data are for 2005.

**For comparison with other tables in this chapter, 2000 data for all Hispanics are as follows: median family income, $35,050; percentage in poverty, 21.2%; completion of four or more years of college, 10.6%.

Sources: U.S. Census Bureau (2000, 2001, 2005, 2006).

darker skin encounter much prejudice and discrimination. As a result, more people return to Puerto Rico each year than arrive: During the 1990s, the Puerto Rican population of New York actually fell by about 100,000 (Navarro, 2000).

This "revolving door" pattern limits assimilation. Three-fourths of Puerto Rican families in the United States speak Spanish at home, compared with about half of Mexican American families (Sowell, 1981; Stevens & Swicegood, 1987). Speaking only Spanish maintains a strong ethnic identity, but it also limits economic opportunity. Puerto Ricans also have a higher rate of women-headed households than other Hispanics, a pattern that puts families at greater risk of poverty.

Table 11–5 shows that the 2003 median family income for Puerto Ricans was $34,519, little more than 60 percent of the national average. Although long-term mainland residents have made economic gains, more recent immigrants from Puerto Rico struggle to find good work. Overall, Puerto Ricans remain the most socially disadvantaged Hispanic minority.

Cuban Americans

Within little more than a decade after the 1959 revolution led by Fidel Castro, 400,000 Cubans had fled to the United States. Most settled with other Cuban Americans in Miami. Many immigrants were highly educated business and professional people who wasted little time becoming as successful in the United States as they had been in their homeland.

Table 11–5 shows that the median family income for Cuban Americans in 2003 was $44,847, above that of other Hispanics but still well below the national average. The 1.2 million Cuban Americans living in the United States today

have managed a delicate balancing act, achieving in the larger society while holding on to much of their traditional culture. Of all Hispanics, Cubans are the most likely to speak Spanish in their homes: eight out of ten families do so. However, cultural distinctiveness and living in highly visible communities such as Miami's Little Havana provoke hostility from some people.

ARAB AMERICANS

Arab Americans are another U.S. minority that is increasing in size. Like Hispanic Americans, these are people whose ancestors lived in one or more different countries. What is sometimes called "the Arab world" includes twenty-two nations and stretches across northern Africa, from Mauritania and Morocco on Africa's west coast to Egypt and Sudan on Africa's east coast, and extends into the Middle East (western Asia), including Iraq and Saudi Arabia. Not all the people who live in these nations are Arabs, however; for example, the Berber people in Morocco and the Kurds of Iraq are not Arab.

Arab cultures differ from society to society, but they share widespread use of the Arabic alphabet and language and have Islam as their dominant religion. But keep in mind that "Arab" (an ethnic category) is not the same as "Muslim" (a follower of Islam). A majority of the people living in most Arab countries are Muslims, but some Arabs are Christians or followers of other religions. In addition, most of the world's Muslims are not Arabs and do not live in Africa or the Middle East.

Because Arabs have come to the United States from so many nations, they are a culturally diverse population. Some Arab Americans are Muslims and some are not; some speak Arabic and some do not; some maintain the traditions of their homeland and some do not. As is the case with Hispanic Americans and Asian Americans, some are recent immigrants and some have lived in this country for decades or even for generations.

As noted back in Table 11–1, the government gives the official number of Arab Americans as 1.2 million, but because people may not declare their ethnic background it is likely that the actual number is at least twice as high.[6] The largest populations of Arab Americans have ancestral ties to Lebanon (29 percent of all Arab Americans), Syria (15 percent), and Egypt (9 percent). Most Arab Americans (71 percent) report ancestral ties to one nation, but 28 percent report both Arab and non-Arab ancestry (U.S. Census Bureau, 2003). A look back at National Map 11–3 shows the distribution of the Arab American population throughout the United States.

Included in the Arab American population are people of all social classes. Some are highly educated professionals who work as physicians, engineers, and professors; others are working-class people who perform various skilled jobs in factories or on construction sites; still others do service work in restaurants, hospitals, or other settings or work in small family businesses. As shown in Table 11–6, median family income for Arab Americans is slightly above the national average ($52,318 compared to the national median of $50,046 in 1999), but Arab Americans have a higher than average poverty rate (16.7 percent versus 12.4 percent for the population as a whole in 1999). Arab Americans are highly educated; 41 percent have a college degree, compared to 12 percent of the population as a whole (U.S. Census Bureau, 2005).

Arab American communities can be found in many large cities on the east and west coasts of the United States, but the heaviest concentrations are found across the upper Midwest. This mosque rises above the cornfields in a rural area near Toledo, Ohio.

YOUR TURN

Do you know of any highly educated immigrants who worked as professionals in their birth nations and who are now performing working-class jobs here in the United States? Why might immigrants have to do this?

There are large, visible Arab American communities in a number of U.S. cities, including New York, Chicago, Los Angeles, Houston, and Dearborn (Michigan). Even so, Arab Americans may choose to downplay their ethnicity as a way to avoid prejudice and discrimination. The fact that many of the terrorist attacks against the United States and other nations were carried out by Arabs has fueled a stereotype

that links being Arab (or Muslim) with being a terrorist. This stereotype, like all stereotypes, is unfair because it blames an entire category of people for the actions of a few individuals. But it is probably the reason that the social distance research discussed earlier in this chapter shows students expressing more negative attitudes toward Arabs than toward any other racial or ethnic category. Its also helps explain why Arab Americans have been targets of an increasing number of hate crimes and why many Arab

---

[6]The 2000 median age for Arab Americans was 33.1 years, only slightly below the national median of 35.4 years.

TABLE 11–6

The Social Standing of Arab Americans, 1999

	Arab Americans	Entire U.S. Population
Median family income	$52,318	$50,046
Percentage in poverty	16.7%	12.4%
Completion of four or more years of college (age 25 and over)	41.2%*	24.4%*

*Data for for 2000.

Source: U.S. Census Bureau (2005).

THINKING CRITICALLY

Affirmative Action: Solution or Problem?

Barbara Gruttner, who is white, claimed that she was the victim of racial discrimination. She maintained that the University of Michigan Law School had unfairly denied her application for admission while admitting many less qualified African American applicants. The basis of her claim was the fact that Michigan, a state university, admitted just 9 percent of white students with her grade point average and law school aptitude test scores while admitting 100 percent of African American applicants with comparable scores.

In 2003, the Supreme Court heard Gruttner's complaint in a review of the admissions policies of both the law school and the undergraduate program at the University of Michigan. In a 6–3 decision, the court ruled against Gruttner, claiming that the University of Michigan Law School could use a policy of affirmative action that takes account of the race of applicants in the interest of creating a socially diverse student body. At the same time, however, the court struck down the university's undergraduate admissions policy, which awarded points not only for grades and college board scores but also for being a member of an underrepresented minority. A point system of this kind, the Court ruled, is too close

to the rigid quota systems rejected by the Court in the past.

With this ruling, the Supreme Court continued to oppose any quotalike systems while at the same time reaffirming the importance of racial diversity on campus. Thus colleges and universities can take account of race in order to increase the number of traditionally underrepresented students as long as race is treated as one variable in a process that evaluates each applicant as an individual (Stout, 2003).

How did the controversial policy of affirmative action begin? The answer takes us back to the end of World War II, when the U.S. government funded higher education for veterans of all races. The so-called G.I. Bill held special promise for African Americans, most of whom needed financial assistance to enroll in college. The program was so successful that by 1960, some 350,000 black men and women were on college campuses with government funding.

There was just one problem: These individuals were not finding the kinds of jobs for which they were qualified. In short, educational opportunity was not producing economic opportunity.

So in the early 1960s, the Kennedy administration devised a program of "affirmative action" to provide broader opportunities to qualified minorities. Employers and educators were instructed to carefully monitor hiring, promotion, and admissions policies to eliminate discrimination—even if unintended—against minorities.

Defenders of affirmative action see it, first, as a sensible response to our nation's racial and ethnic history, especially for African Americans, who suffered through two centuries of slavery and a century of segregation under Jim Crow laws. Throughout our history, they

Americans feel that they are subject to "ethnic profiling" that threatens their privacy and civil liberties (Ali & Juarez, 2003; Ali, Lipper, & Mack, 2004; Hagopian, 2004).

WHITE ETHNIC AMERICANS

The term "white ethnics" recognizes the ethnic heritage and social disadvantages of many white people. White ethnics

are non-WASPs whose ancestors lived in Ireland, Poland, Germany, Italy, or other European countries. More than half of the U.S. population falls into one or more white ethnic category.

High rates of emigration from Europe in the nineteenth century first brought Germans and Irish and then Italians and Jews to this country. Despite cultural differences, all shared the hope that the United States would offer

claim, being white gave people a big advantage. They see minority preference today as a step toward fair compensation for unfair majority preference in the past.

Second, given our racial history, many analysts doubt that the United States will ever become a color-blind society. They claim that because prejudice and discrimination are rooted deep in the fabric of U.S. society, simply claiming that we are color-blind does not mean that everyone will compete fairly.

Third, supporters maintain that affirmative action has worked. Where would minorities be if the government had not enacted this policy four decades ago? Major employers, such as fire and police departments in large cities, began hiring minorities and women for the first time only because of affirmative action. This program has played an important part in expanding the African American middle class. Affirmative action has also increased racial diversity on campus, which benefits everyone, and has advanced the careers of an entire generation of black students.

About 80 percent of African Americans claim that affirmative action is needed to secure equal opportunity. But affirmative action draws criticism from others. A 2003 poll shows that 73 percent of white people and 56 percent of Hispanics oppose preferences for African Americans (NORC, 2005). As this opposition to affirmative action

was building during the 1990s, courts began to trim back such policies. Critics argue, first, that affirmative action started out as a temporary remedy to ensure fair competition but became a system of "group preferences" and quotas. In other words, the policy did not remain true to the goal of promoting color blindness as set out in the 1964 Civil Rights Act. By the 1970s, it had become "reverse discrimination," favoring people not because of performance but because of their race, ethnicity, or sex.

Second, critics argue that affirmative action divides society. If racial preferences were wrong in the past, they are wrong now. Why should whites today, many of whom are far from privileged, be penalized for past discrimination that was in no way their fault? Our society has undone most of the institutional prejudice and discrimination of earlier times, opponents continue, so that minorities can and do enjoy success according to personal merit. Giving entire categories of people special treatment compromises standards of excellence, calls into question the real accomplishments of minorities, and offends public opinion.

A third argument against affirmative action is that it benefits those who need it least. Favoring minority-owned corporations or holding places in law school for minorities helps already privileged people. Affirmative action has done little for the African American underclass that needs the most help.

In sum, there are good arguments for and against affirmative action, and people who want our society to have more racial and ethnic equality fall on both sides of the debate. The disagreement is not whether people of all colors should have equal opportunity but whether the current policy of affirmative action is part of the solution or part of the problem.

WHAT DO YOU THINK?

1. In view of the fact that society historically has favored males over females and whites over people of color, would you agree that white males have received more "affirmative action" than anyone? Why or why not?

2. Should affirmative action include only disadvantaged categories of minorities (say, African Americans and Native Americans) and exclude more affluent categories (such as Japanese Americans)? Why or why not?

3. Should state universities admit applicants with an eye toward advancing minorities in order to lessen racial inequality? Do you think that goal is more or less important than the goal of admitting the most qualified individuals? Explain your answer.

Sources: Bowen & Bok (1999), Kantrowitz & Wingert (2003), and NORC (2005).

greater political freedom and economic opportunity than their homelands. Most did live better in this country, but the belief that "the streets of America were paved with gold" turned out to be a far cry from reality. Many immigrants found only hard labor for low wages.

White ethnics also endured their share of prejudice and discrimination. Many employers shut their doors to immigrants, posting signs such as "None need apply but Americans" (Handlin, 1941:67). By 1921, Congress had enacted a quota system greatly limiting immigration, especially by southern and eastern Europeans, who were likely to have darker skin and different cultural backgrounds than the dominant WASPs. This system continued until 1968.

In response to prejudice and discrimination, many white ethnics formed supportive residential enclaves. Some also gained footholds in certain businesses and trades: Italian Americans entered the construction industry, Irish Americans worked in construction and took civil service jobs, Jews predominated in the garment industry, and many Greeks (like the Chinese) worked in the retail food business (W. M. Newman, 1973).

Many white ethnics still live in traditional working-class neighborhoods, although those who prospered have gradually assimilated. Most descendants of immigrants who labored in sweatshops and lived in crowded tenements now make enough money to lead comfortable lives. As a result, their ethnic heritage has become a source of pride.

Race and Ethnicity: Looking Ahead

The United States has been, and will remain, a land of immigrants. Immigration has brought striking cultural diversity and tales of hope, struggle, and success told in hundreds of languages.

Most immigrants arrived in a great wave that peaked about 1910. The next two generations brought economic gains and at least some assimilation. The government also extended citizenship to Native Americans (1924), foreign-born Filipinos (1942), Chinese Americans (1943), and Japanese Americans (1952).

Another wave of immigration began after World War II and swelled as the government relaxed immigration laws in the 1960s. Today, about 1.5 million people come to the United States each year—about 1 million legally and another 500,000 illegally. This is twice the number that arrived dur-ing the "Great Immigration" a century ago (although newcomers now enter a country that has five times as many people). Most of today's immigrants come not from Europe but from Latin America and Asia, with Mexicans, Asian Indians, and Chinese arriving in the largest numbers.

Many new arrivals face much the same prejudice and discrimination experienced by those who came before them. In fact, recent years have witnessed rising hostility toward foreigners (an expression of *xenophobia*, from Greek roots meaning "fear of what is strange"). In 1994, California voters passed Proposition 187, cutting social services (including schooling) to illegal immigrants. More recently, voters there have mandated that all children learn English in school. Since 2000, there has been rising concern about the flow of illegal immigrants over the nation's southern border. Some landowners in the Southwest have taken up arms to defend themselves against large numbers of illegal immigrants crossing from Mexico, and the entire country is struggling to decide how to deal with the more than 11 million illegal immigrants already here.

Finally, as the Thinking Critically box on pages 326–27 explains, the debate over affirmative action rages as hotly as ever.

Like those of an earlier generation, today's immigrants try to blend into U.S. society without completely giving up their traditional culture. Some still build racial and ethnic enclaves, so that in many cities across the country, the Little Havanas and Koreatowns of today stand alongside the Little Italys and Chinatowns of the past. In addition, new arrivals still carry the traditional hope that their racial and ethnic diversity can be a source of pride rather than a badge of inferiority.

APPLYING SOCIOLOGY IN EVERYDAY LIFE

1. Does your college or university take account of race and ethnicity in its admissions policies? Ask to speak with an admissions officer to see what you can learn about your school's use of race and ethnicity in admissions. Ask whether there is a "legacy" policy that favors children of parents who attended the school.
2. Give several of your friends or family members a quick quiz, asking them what share of the U.S. pop-ulation is white, Hispanic, African American, and Asian (see Table 11–1 on page 303). Why do you think white people exaggerate the African American population? (C. A. Gallagher, 2003)
3. Interview immigrants on your campus or in your local community about their homelands and their experiences since arriving in the United States. Were they surprised by their experiences in this country? If so, why?

MAKING THE GRADE

CHAPTER 11 Race and Ethnicity

THE SOCIAL MEANING OF RACE AND ETHNICITY

RACE refers to socially constructed categories based on biological traits a society defines as important.

- The meaning and importance of race varies from place to place and over time.
- Societies use racial categories to rank people in a hierarchy, giving some people more money, power, and prestige than others.
- In the past, scientists created three broad categories—Caucasoids, Mongoloids, and Negroids—but there are no biologically pure races.

pp 300–302

ETHNICITY refers to socially constructed categories based on cultural traits a society defines as important.

- Ethnicity reflects common ancestors, language, and religion.
- The importance of ethnicity varies from place to place and over time.
- People choose to play up or play down their ethnicity.
- Societies may or may not set categories of people apart based on differences in ethnicity.

pp 302–303

race (p. 300) a socially constructed category of people who share biologically transmitted traits that members of a society consider important

ethnicity (p. 302) a shared cultural heritage

minority (p. 303) any category of people distinguished by physical or cultural difference that a society sets apart and subordinates

 Minorities are people of various racial and ethnic categories who are visually distinctive and disadvantaged by a society (p 303).

PREJUDICE AND STEREOTYPES

PREJUDICE is a rigid and unfair generalization about a category of people.

- The social distance scale is one measure of prejudice.
- One type of prejudice is the **STEREOTYPE**, an exaggerated description applied to every person in some category.
- **RACISM**, a very destructive type of prejudice, asserts that one race is innately superior or inferior to another.

pp 304–308

There are four **THEORIES OF PREJUDICE**:

- *Scapegoat theory* claims that prejudice results from frustration among people who are disadvantaged.
- *Authoritarian personality theory* (Adorno) claims prejudice is a personality trait of certain individuals, especially those with little education and those raised by cold and demanding parents.
- *Culture theory* (Bogardus) claims that prejudice is rooted in culture; we learn to feel greater social distance from some categories of people.
- *Conflict theory* claims that prejudice is a tool used by powerful people to divide and control the population.

pp 308–310

prejudice (p. 304) a rigid and unfair generalization about an entire category of people

stereotype (p. 304) an exaggerated description applied to every person in some category

racism (p. 307) the belief that one racial category is innately superior or inferior to another

scapegoat (p. 308) a person or category of people, typically with little power, whom other people unfairly blame for their own troubles

DISCRIMINATION

DISCRIMINATION refers to actions by which a person treats various categories of people unequally.

- Prejudice refers to *attitudes*; discrimination involves *actions*.
- Institutional prejudice and discrimination is bias built into the operation of society's institutions, including schools, hospitals, the police, and the workplace.
- Prejudice and discrimination perpetuate themselves in a vicious circle, resulting in social disadvantage that fuels additional prejudice and discrimination.

p 310

discrimination (p. 310) unequal treatment of various categories of people

institutional prejudice and discrimination (p. 310) bias built into the operation of society's institutions

MAKING THE GRADE

CONTINUED...

MAJORITY AND MINORITY: PATTERNS OF INTERACTION

PLURALISM means that racial and ethnic categories, although distinct, have roughly equal social standing.

- U.S. society is pluralistic in that all people in the United States, regardless of race or ethnicity, have equal standing under the law.
- U.S. society is not pluralistic in that all racial and ethnic categories do not have equal social standing.

p 311

ASSIMILATION is a process by which minorities gradually adopt the patterns of the dominant culture.

- Assimilation involves changes in dress, language, religion, values, and friends.
- Assimilation is a strategy to escape prejudice and discrimination and to achieve upward social mobility.
- Some categories of people have assimilated more than others.

pp 311–12

pluralism (p. 311) a state in which people of all races and ethnicities are distinct but have equal social standing

assimilation (p. 311) the process by which minorities gradually adopt patterns of the dominant culture

miscegenation (p. 312) biological reproduction by partners of different racial categories

segregation (p. 312) the physical and social separation of categories of people

genocide (p. 313) the systematic killing of one category of people by another

SEGREGATION is the physical and social separation of categories of people.

- Although some segregation is voluntary (for example, the Amish), majorities usually segregate minorities by excluding them from neighborhoods, schools, and occupations.
- *De jure* segregation is segregation by law; *de facto* segregation describes settings that contain only people of one category.
- Hypersegregation means having little social contact with people beyond the local community.

pp 312–13

GENOCIDE is the systematic killing of one category of people by another.

- Historical examples of genocide include the extermination of Jews by the Nazis and the killing of Western-leaning people in Cambodia by Pol Pot.
- Genocide continues in the modern world, with Hutus killing Tutsis in the African nation of Rwanda and Serbs killing Bosnians in the Balkans of Eastern Europe.

pp 313–14

RACE AND ETHNICITY IN THE UNITED STATES

NATIVE AMERICANS, the earliest human inhabitants of the Americas, have endured genocide, segregation, and forced assimilation. Today, the social standing of Native Americans is well below the national average.

pp 314–16

WHITE ANGLO-SAXON PROTESTANTS (WASPS) were most of the original European settlers of the United States, and many continue to enjoy high social position today.

p 316

AFRICAN AMERICANS experienced two centuries of slavery. Emancipation in 1865 gave way to segregation by law (the so-called Jim Crow laws). In the 1950s and 1960s, a national civil rights movement resulted in legislation that outlawed segregated schools and overt discrimination in employment and public accommodations. Today, despite legal equality, African Americans are still disadvantaged.

pp 316–18

ASIAN AMERICANS have suffered both racial and ethnic hostility. Although some prejudice and discrimination continue, both Chinese and Japanese Americans now have above-average income and schooling. Asian immigrants, especially Koreans and Filipinos, now account for one-third of all immigration to the United States.

pp 318–22

HISPANIC AMERICANS/LATINOS, the largest U.S. minority, include many ethnicities sharing a Spanish heritage. Mexican Americans, the largest Hispanic minority, are concentrated in the Southwest. Cubans, concentrated in Miami, are the most affluent Hispanic category; Puerto Ricans, 1 million of whom live in New York City, are the poorest.

pp 322–24

ARAB AMERICANS are a growing U.S. minority. Because they come to the United States from so many different nations, Arab Americans are a culturally diverse population, and they are represented in all social classes. They have been a target of prejudice and hate crimes in recent years as a result of a stereotype that links all Arab Americans with terrorism.

pp 324–26

WHITE ETHNIC AMERICANS are non-WASPs whose ancestors emigrated from Europe in the nineteenth and twentieth centuries. In response to prejudice and discrimination, many white ethnics formed supportive residential enclaves.

pp 326–28

These questions are similar to those found in the test bank that accompanies this textbook.

MULTIPLE-CHOICE QUESTIONS

1. *Race* refers to _____ considered important by a society, and *ethnicity* refers to _____.
   a. biological traits; cultural traits
   b. cultural traits; biological traits
   c. differences; what we have in common
   d. what we have in common; differences

2. People of Hispanic ancestry make up what share of the U.S. population?
   a. 42.5 percent
   b. 32.5 percent
   c. 22.5 percent
   d. 12.5 percent

3. A minority is defined as a category of people who
   a. have physical traits that make them different.
   b. are less than half the society's population.
   c. are defined as both different and disadvantaged.
   d. are below average in terms of income.

4. In this country, four states now have a "minority majority." Which of the following states is not one of them?
   a. California
   b. Florida
   c. Texas
   d. New Mexico

5. Research using the Bogardus social distance scale shows that U.S. college students
   a. are less prejudiced than students fifty years ago.
   b. believe that Arabs and Muslims should be kept out of the country.
   c. have the strongest prejudice against African Americans.
   d. All of the above are correct.

6. Prejudice is a matter of _____, and discrimination is a matter of _____.
   a. biology; culture
   b. attitudes; behavior
   c. choice; social structure
   d. what rich people think; what rich people do

7. The United States is not truly pluralistic because
   a. part of our population lives in "ethnic enclaves."
   b. this country has a history of slavery.
   c. different racial and ethnic categories are unequal in social standing.
   d. All of the above are correct.

8. Which term is illustrated by immigrants from Ecuador learning to speak the English language?
   a. genocide
   b. segregation
   c. assimilation
   d. pluralism

9. During the late 1400s, when the first Europeans came to the Americas, Native Americans
   a. followed shortly thereafter.
   b. had just migrated from Asia.
   c. came on ships with them from Europe.
   d. had inhabited this land for 30,000 years.

10. Which is the largest category of Asian Americans in the United States?
    a. Chinese American
    b. Japanese American
    c. Korean American
    d. Vietnamese American

ANSWERS: 1 (a); 2 (d); 3 (c); 4 (b); 5 (a); 6 (b); 7 (c); 8 (c); 9 (d); 10 (a).

ESSAY QUESTIONS

1. What is the difference between race and ethnicity? What does it mean to say that race and ethnicity are socially constructed?

2. What is a minority? Pointing to specific facts in this chapter, support the claim that African Americans and Asian Americans are both minorities in the United States.

SAMPLE TEST

331

Economics and politics are two social institutions that affect how wealth and power are distributed throughout a society's population. Although young people have a big stake in the way our society is organized, currently only a small share of them are registered to vote!

CHAPTER *12*

Economics
and Politics

WHAT is a social
institution?

HOW does change
in the economy
reshape society?

WHY do some critics say that
the United States is not
really a democracy?

Here's a quick quiz about the U.S. economy. (Hint: All five questions have the same right answer.)

- Which business do more than 130 million people in the United States visit each week?

- Which U.S. company, on average, opens a new store every day?

- Which U.S. company is the largest employer in the country after the federal government?

- Which U.S. company will create nearly 800,000 new jobs over the next five years?

- Which single company accounted for 25 percent of all the growth in U.S. economic output during the second half of the 1990s?

You have probably guessed that the correct answer is Wal-Mart, the global discount store chain founded by Sam Walton, who opened his first store in Arkansas in 1962. By mid-2006, Wal-Mart was making $312 billion in annual sales through 3,877 stores in the United States and 2,679 stores in other countries from Brazil to China.

But not everyone is happy with the expansion of Wal-Mart. Across the United States, people have formed a social movement to keep Wal-Mart out of their local communities, fearing the loss of local businesses and, in some cases, local culture. Critics claim that the merchandising giant pays low wages at home, keeps out unions, and sells many products made in sweatshops abroad.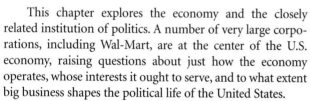

This chapter explores the economy and the closely related institution of politics. A number of very large corporations, including Wal-Mart, are at the center of the U.S. economy, raising questions about just how the economy operates, whose interests it ought to serve, and to what extent big business shapes the political life of the United States.

Economics and politics are each a **social institution,** *a major sphere of social life, or societal subsystem, organized to meet human needs.* The two chapters that follow consider other social institutions: Chapter 13 focuses on family and religion, and Chapter 14 highlights education and health. These discussions explain how social institutions have changed over the course of history, describe how they operate today, and point out controversies that are likely to shape them tomorrow.

The Economy: Historical Overview

The **economy** is *the social institution that organizes a society's production, distribution, and consumption of goods and*

services. The economy operates, for better or worse, in a generally predictable manner. *Goods* are commodities ranging from necessities (such as food, clothing, and shelter) to luxury items (such as automobiles, swimming pools, and yachts). *Services* are activities that benefit people (including the work of priests, doctors, teachers, and computer software specialists).

THE AGRICULTURAL REVOLUTION

As Chapter 2 ("Culture") explained, the earliest societies were made up of hunters and gatherers living off the land. In such societies, there was no distinct economy; producing and consuming were simply part of family life.

Harnessing animals to plows around 5,000 years ago permitted the development of agriculture, which was fifty times more productive than hunting and gathering. The resulting surpluses meant that not everyone had to produce food, so many people took on specialized work: making tools, raising animals, and building dwellings. Soon towns sprang up, linked by networks of traders dealing in food, animals, and other goods. These four factors—agricultural

As societies industrialize, a smaller share of the labor force works in agriculture. In the United States, much of the agricultural work that remains is performed by immigrants from lower-income nations. These farm workers, who came to this country from Mexico, travel throughout North Carolina during the tobacco harvest.

technology, specialized work, permanent settlements, and trade—made the economy a distinct social institution.

THE INDUSTRIAL REVOLUTION

By the mid-eighteenth century, a second technological revolution was under way, starting in England and spreading to the United States and elsewhere. Industrialization brought five changes to the economy:

1. **New sources of energy.** Throughout history, "energy" had meant the muscle power of people or animals. Then, in 1765, the English inventor James Watt introduced the steam engine. A hundred times more powerful than muscle power, early steam engines soon drove heavy machinery.

2. **Centralization of work in factories.** Steam-powered machinery moved work from homes to factories, centralized workplaces that housed the machines.

3. **Manufacturing and mass production.** Before the Industrial Revolution, most people grew or gathered raw materials such as grain, wood, or wool. In an industrial economy, the focus shifts so that most people turn raw materials into a wide range of finished products such as furniture and clothing.

4. **Specialization.** Centuries ago, people worked at home making products from start to finish. In the factory, a laborer repeats a single task over and over, making only a small contribution to the finished product.

5. **Wage labor.** Instead of working for themselves, factory workers became wage laborers who sold their labor to strangers, who often cared less for them than for the machines they operated.

YOUR TURN

Look back at the Chapter 9 opening story on page 244 about the fire in the Bangladesh sweatshop. What was the owner's biggest concern?

The Industrial Revolution raised the standard of living as countless new products fueled an expanding marketplace. However, the benefits of industrial technology were shared very unequally, especially at the beginning. Some factory owners made huge fortunes, but the majority of workers lived close to poverty. Children, too, worked in factories or in coal mines for pennies a day. With time, workers formed labor unions to collectively represent their interests to factory owners. Over the course of the twentieth century, new laws banned child labor, set minimum wage levels, improved workplace safety, and extended schooling and political rights to a larger segment of the population.

THE INFORMATION REVOLUTION AND POSTINDUSTRIAL SOCIETY

By about 1950, the nature of production was changing once again. The United States was creating a **postindustrial economy,** *a productive system based on service work and high technology.* Automated machinery (and more recently, robotics) reduced the role of human labor in production

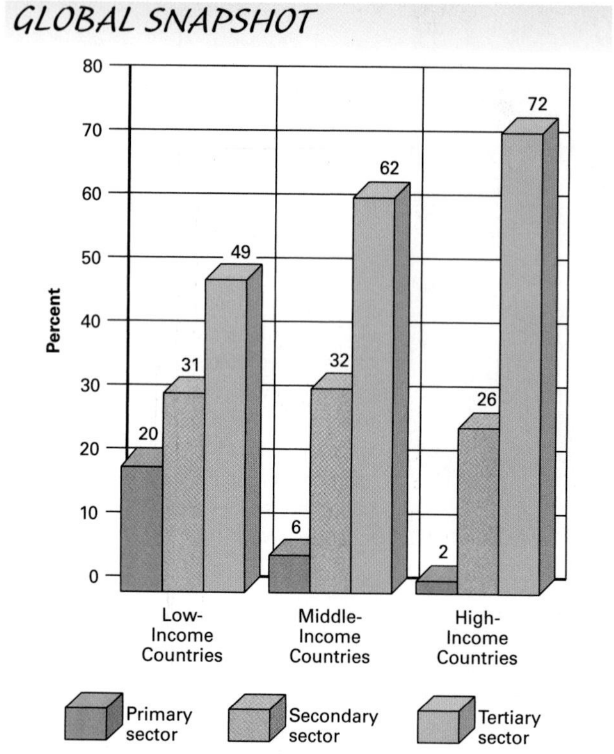

FIGURE 12–1 The Size of Economic Sectors by Income Level of Country

As countries become richer, the primary sector of the economy becomes smaller and the tertiary or service sector becomes larger.
Source: Author estimates based on World Bank (2006).

ing and writing well and, of course, using computers. People able to communicate effectively enjoy new opportunities; people without these skills face fewer opportunities.

3. **From factories to almost anywhere.** Industrial technology drew workers to factories located near power sources, but computer technology allows people to work almost anywhere. Laptop computers, cell phones, and portable fax machines can turn the home, car, or even an airplane into a "virtual office." What this means for everyday life is that new information technology blurs the line between work and home life.

YOUR TURN

Can you think of advantages and also disadvantages of being able to work almost anywhere? Do the benefits of the "anywhere office" outweigh the downsides?

SECTORS OF THE ECONOMY

The three revolutions just described reflect a shifting balance among the three sectors of a society's economy. The **primary sector** is *the part of the economy that draws raw materials from the natural environment.* The primary sector—agriculture, ranching, fishing, forestry, and mining—is largest in low-income nations. Figure 12–1 shows that 20 percent of the economic output of low-income countries is in the primary sector, compared with 6 percent of economic activity among middle-income nations and just 2 percent in high-income countries like the United States.

The **secondary sector** is *the part of the economy that transforms raw materials into manufactured goods.* This sector expands quickly as societies industrialize. It includes operations such as refining petroleum into gasoline and turning metals into tools and automobiles. The globalization of industry means that just about all the world's countries have a significant share of their workers in the secondary sector. Figure 12–1 shows that the secondary sector now accounts for a greater share of economic output in low-income nations than it does in high-income countries.

The **tertiary sector** is *the part of the economy that involves services rather than goods.* Accounting for 49 percent of economic output in low-income countries, the tertiary sector grows with industrialization and dominates the economies of middle-income countries (62 percent) and high-income, postindustrial nations (72 percent). About 76 percent of the U.S. labor force is in service work, including secretarial and clerical jobs and work in food service, sales, law, health care, advertising, and teaching.

while expanding the ranks of clerical workers and managers. The postindustrial era is marked by a shift from industrial work to service work.

Driving this economic change is a third technological breakthrough: the computer. Just as the Industrial Revolution did two centuries ago, the Information Revolution has introduced new kinds of products and new forms of communication and has changed the character of work. There have been three important changes:

1. **From tangible products to ideas.** The industrial era was defined by the production of goods; in the postindustrial era, people work with symbols. Computer programmers, writers, financial analysts, advertising executives, architects, editors, and various types of consultants make up the labor force of the information age.

2. **From mechanical skills to literacy skills.** The Industrial Revolution required mechanical skills, but the Information Revolution requires literacy skills: speak-

WINDOW ON THE WORLD

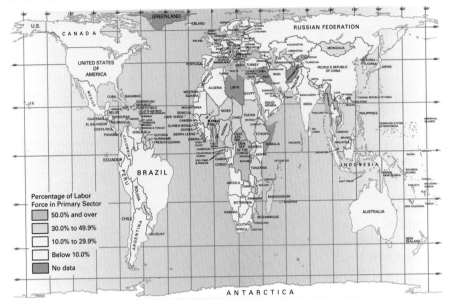

Percentage of Labor
Force in Primary Sector

- 50.0% and over
- 30.0% to 49.9%
- 10.0% to 29.9%
- Below 10.0%
- No data

GLOBAL MAP 12–1
Agricultural Employment in Global Perspective

The primary sector of the economy is largest in the nations that are least developed. Thus in the poor countries of Africa and Asia, up to half of all workers are farmers. This picture is altogether different in the world's most economically developed countries—including the United States, Canada, Great Britain, and Australia—in which only 2 percent of their labor force is engaged in agriculture.

Sources: Data from United Nations Development Programme (2000) and World Bank (2000, 2001); map projection from *Peters Atlas of the World* (1990).

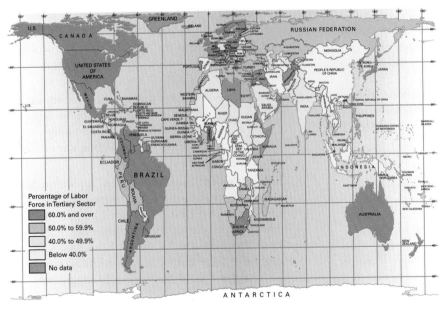

Percentage of Labor
Force in Tertiary Sector

- 60.0% and over
- 50.0% to 59.9%
- 40.0% to 49.9%
- Below 40.0%
- No data

GLOBAL MAP 12–2
Service-Sector Employment in Global Perspective

The tertiary sector of the economy becomes ever larger as a nation's income level rises. In the United States, Canada, the countries of Western Europe, much of South America, Australia, and Japan, about two-thirds of the labor force performs service work.

Sources: Data from United Nations Development Programme (2000) and World Bank (2000, 2001); map projection from *Peters Atlas of the World* (1990).

THE GLOBAL ECONOMY

If you look at many of the products we buy today in the United States, including cameras, televisions, furniture, kitchen appliances, computers, and cell phones, you will find that they are made in China, Mexico, and other countries. This is evidence of an expanding **global economy,**

economic activity that crosses national borders. The development of a global economy has five major consequences.

First, we see a global division of labor: Different regions of the world come to specialize in one sector of economic activity. As Global Map 12–1 shows, agriculture represents a large share—more than half—of the economy in the world's poorest countries. Global Map 12–2 shows that most workers living in high-income countries, including the United States, have jobs in the service sector.

Second, more and more products pass through more than one nation. Look no further than your morning coffee: It may have been grown in Colombia and transported to New Orleans on a freighter that was registered in Liberia, made in Japan using steel from Korea, and fueled by oil from Venezuela.

Third, national governments no longer control the economic activity that takes place within their borders. In fact, governments cannot even regulate the value of their national currencies because dollars, euros, pounds sterling, yen, and other currencies are traded around the clock in the financial markets of New York, London, and Tokyo.

A fourth consequence of the global economy is that a small number of businesses, operating internationally, now controls a vast share of the world's economic activity. A rough estimate is that the 600 largest multinational companies account for half the world's economic output (Kidron & Segal, 1991; Gergen, 2002).

Fifth and finally, the globalization of the economy affects the lives of workers in the United States. Critics of globalization claim that the United States is losing jobs—especially factory jobs—to China and other lower-income nations. This means that workers here face lower wages and higher unemployment; many workers abroad are paid wages that are far lower.

The world is organized into 192 politically distinct nations. But the rising level of international trade makes "nationhood" less significant than it was even a decade ago.

Economic Systems: Paths to Justice

 October 20, Saigon, Vietnam. Sailing up the narrow Saigon River is an unsettling experience for anyone who came of age in the 1960s. People like me need to remember that Vietnam is a country, not a war, and that forty years have passed since the last U.S. helicopter lifted off the rooftop of the U.S. embassy, ending our country's presence there.

Saigon is now a boomtown. Neon signs bathe the city's waterfront in color; hotels, bankrolled by Western corporations, push skyward from a dozen construction sites; taxi meters record fares in U.S. dollars, not Vietnamese dong; and Visa and American Express stickers decorate the doors of trendy restaurants and fashionable shops that cater to tourists from Japan, France, and the United States.

There is heavy irony here: After decades of fighting, millions of lives lost on both sides, and the victory of Communist forces, the Vietnamese are doing an about-face and turning toward capitalism. What we see today is what might well have happened had the U.S. forces won the war.

Every society's economy makes a statement about justice by determining who gets what. Two general economic models are capitalism and socialism. However, no nation anywhere in the world has an economy that is completely one or the other; rather, capitalism and socialism are two ends of a continuum along which all real-world economies can be located. We will look, in turn, at each of these two models.

CAPITALISM

Capitalism is *an economic system in which natural resources and the means of producing goods and services are privately owned.* An ideal capitalist economy has three distinctive features:

1. **Private ownership of property.** In a capitalist economy, individuals can own almost anything. The more capitalist an economy is, the more private ownership there is of wealth-producing property such as factories, real estate, and natural resources.

2. **Pursuit of personal profit.** A capitalist society seeks to create profit and wealth. The profit motive is the reason people try new jobs or open new businesses. Making money is considered the natural way of economic life.

3. **Competition and consumer choice.** A purely capitalist economy is a free-market system with no government interference (sometimes called a *laissez-faire* economy, from the French words meaning "leave it alone"). According to the Scottish economist Adam Smith (1723–1790), a freely competitive economy regulates itself by the "invisible hand" of supply and demand (1937, orig. 1776).

   Consumers guide a market economy, Smith explained, by choosing the goods and services that offer the greatest value. As producers compete for the customer's business, they provide the highest-quality goods at the lowest possible prices. In Smith's time-honored phrase, from narrow self-interest comes "the greatest good for the greatest number of people." Government control of an economy, on the other hand, distorts market forces and reduces the quantity and quality of goods, in the process shortchanging consumers.

Capitalism still thrives in Hong Kong (left), evident in streets choked with advertising and shoppers. Socialism is more the rule in China's capital of Beijing (right), a city dominated by government buildings rather than a downtown business district.

"Justice" in a capitalist system amounts to freedom of the marketplace, where anyone can produce, buy, and invest according to individual self-interest. The increasing popularity of Wal-Mart, described in the opening to this chapter, reflects the fact that the company's customers think they get a lot for their money.

The United States is considered a capitalist nation because most businesses are privately owned. However, it is not completely capitalist because the government plays a large role in the economy. The government owns and operates a number of businesses, including almost all of this country's schools, roads, parks, museums, the U.S. Postal Service, the Amtrak railroad system, and the entire U.S. military. The U.S. government also had a hand in building the Internet. In addition, governments use taxation and other forms of regulation to influence what companies produce, to control the quality and cost of merchandise, and to motivate consumers to conserve natural resources.

The U.S. government also sets minimum wage levels, enforces workplace safety standards, regulates corporate mergers, provides farm price supports, and gives income in the form of Social Security, public assistance, student loans, and veterans' benefits to a majority of its people. Local, state, and federal governments together are the nation's biggest employer, with 16 percent of the nonfarm labor force on their payrolls (U.S. Census Bureau, 2005).

SOCIALISM

Socialism is *an economic system in which natural resources and the means of producing goods and services are collectively owned*. In its ideal form, a socialist economy rejects each of the three characteristics of capitalism just described in favor of three opposite features:

1. **Collective ownership of property.** A socialist economy limits rights to private property, especially property used to generate income. Government controls such property and makes housing and other goods available to all, not just to the people with the most money.

2. **Pursuit of collective goals.** The individualistic pursuit of profit goes against the collective orientation of socialism. What capitalism celebrates as the "entrepreneurial spirit," socialism condemns as greed; individuals are urged to work for the common good of all.

3. **Government control of the economy.** Socialism rejects capitalism's laissez-faire approach in favor of a *centrally controlled* or *command economy* operated by the government. Commercial advertising thus plays a minimal role in socialist economies.

"Justice" in a socialist context means not competing to gain wealth but meeting everyone's basic needs in a roughly

Societies with mostly capitalist economies are very productive, providing a high overall standard of living. At the same time, however, these societies distribute income and wealth very unequally. In what social classes do you think people express the most, and the least, support for the mostly capitalist economy of the United States?

equal manner. From a socialist point of view, the common capitalist practice of giving workers as little in wages and benefits as possible to boost company earnings is putting profits before people and is unjust.

The People's Republic of China and more than two dozen other nations in Asia, Africa, and Latin America model their economies on socialism, placing much of their wealth-generating property under state control (Freedom House, 2006). The extent of world socialism declined during the 1990s as countries in Eastern Europe and the former Soviet Union have geared their economies toward a market system. In recent years, however, voters in Bolivia, Brazil, Venezuela, and other nations in South America have elected leaders who are moving the national economies in a socialist direction.

YOUR TURN

Do you think the United States could ever become a socialist nation? Explain.

WELFARE CAPITALISM AND STATE CAPITALISM

Most of the nations in Western Europe, especially Sweden and Italy, have market-based economies but also offer broad social welfare programs. Analysts call this third type of economic system **welfare capitalism,** *an economic and political system that combines a mostly market-based economy with extensive social welfare programs.*

Under welfare capitalism, the government owns some of the largest industries and services, such as transportation, the mass media, and health care. In Sweden and Italy,

about 12 percent of economic production is *nationalized,* or state-controlled. Most industry is left in private hands but is subject to extensive government regulation. High taxation (aimed especially at the rich) funds a wide range of social welfare programs, including universal health care and child care (Olsen, 1996).

Another alternative is **state capitalism,** *an economic and political system in which companies are privately owned but cooperate closely with the government.* State capitalism is the rule in the nations along the Pacific Rim. Japan, South Korea, and Singapore are all capitalist countries, but their governments work in partnership with large companies, supplying financial assistance and controlling foreign imports to help their businesses compete in world markets (Gerlach, 1992).

RELATIVE ADVANTAGES OF CAPITALISM AND SOCIALISM

Which economic system works best? Comparing economies is difficult because all countries mix capitalism and socialism to varying degrees. Nations also differ in cultural attitudes toward work, natural resources, technological development, and patterns of trade. Despite such complicating factors, some crude comparisons are revealing.

Economic Productivity

One key dimension of economic performance is productivity. A commonly used measure of economic output is *gross domestic product* (GDP), the total value of all goods and services produced annually. Per capita (per-person) GDP allows us to compare the economic performance of nations of different population sizes.

The output of mostly capitalist countries at the end of the 1980s—before the end of socialist economies in the Soviet Union and Eastern Europe—varied somewhat, but averaging the figures for the United States, Canada, and the nations of Western Europe yielded a per capita GDP of about $13,500. The comparable figure for the former Soviet Union and the nations of Eastern Europe was about $5,000. This means that the capitalist countries outproduced the socialist nations by a ratio of 2.7 to 1 (United Nations Development Programme, 1990). A recent comparison of socialist North Korea (per capita GDP of $1,000) and capitalist South Korea ($18,000) provides an even sharper contrast (Omestad, 2003).

Economic Equality

The distribution of resources within the population is another important measure of how well an economic system works. A comparative study of Europe back when that region was split between mostly capitalist and mostly socialist countries compared the earnings of the richest 5 percent of the population and the poorest 5 percent (Wiles, 1977). Societies with mostly capitalist economies had an income ratio of about 10 to 1; the figure for socialist countries was 5 to 1. In other words, capitalist economies support a higher overall standard of living but with greater income inequality. Said another way, socialist economies create more economic equality but provide a lower overall living standard.

Personal Freedom

One additional consideration in evaluating capitalism and socialism is the personal freedom each system gives its people. Capitalism emphasizes the *freedom to* pursue self-interest and depends on the freedom of producers and consumers to interact with little interference by the state. Socialism, by contrast, emphasizes *freedom from* basic want. The goal of equality requires the state to regulate the economy, which in turn limits personal choices and opportunities for citizens.

No system has yet been able to offer both political freedom and economic equality. In the capitalist United States, our political system offers many personal freedoms, but they are not worth as much to a poor person as to a rich one. By contrast, North Korea or Cuba has more economic equality, but people cannot speak out or travel freely within or outside of the country.

CHANGES IN SOCIALIST AND CAPITALIST COUNTRIES

In 1989 and 1990, the nations of Eastern Europe, which had been seized by the former Soviet Union at the end of World War II, overthrew their socialist regimes. These nations—including the former German Democratic Republic, the Czech Republic, Slovakia, Hungary, Romania, and Bulgaria—are all moving toward capitalist market systems after decades of state-controlled economies. At the end of 1991, the Soviet Union itself formally dissolved and has introduced some free-market principles. Ten years later, three-fourths of former Soviet government enterprises were partly or entirely in private hands (Montaigne, 2001).

There were many reasons for these sweeping changes. First, the capitalist economies far outproduced their socialist counterparts. The socialist economies were successful in achieving economic equality, but living standards were low compared with those of Western Europe. Second, Soviet socialism was heavy-handed, rigidly controlling the media and restricting individual freedoms. In other words, socialism did away with *economic* elites, as Karl Marx predicted, but as Max Weber foresaw, socialism increased the power of *political* elites.

So far, the market reforms in Eastern Europe are proceeding unevenly. Some nations (Czech Republic, Slovakia, Poland, and the Baltic states of Latvia, Estonia, and Lithuania) are doing relatively well. But other countries (Romania, Bulgaria, and the Russian Federation) have been buffeted by price increases and falling living standards. Officials hope that expanding production will gradually bring a turnaround. However, the introduction of a market economy has brought with it an increase in economic inequality (Buraway, 1997; World Bank, 2006).

A number of countries, primarily in South America, have recently begun moving in a more socialist direction. In 2005, the people of Bolivia elected Evo Morales, a former farmer, union leader, and activist, as their new president, over a wealthy business leader who was educated in the United States. This election placed Bolivia in a group of South American nations—including Ecuador, Venezuela, Brazil, Chile, and Uruguay—that are moving toward more socialist economies. The reasons for the shift toward socialism vary from country to country, but the common element is economic inequality. In Bolivia, for example, the economy has grown in recent decades, but most of the benefits have gone to a wealthy business elite. By contrast, more than half the country's people remain very poor (Howden, 2005).

YOUR TURN

Do you think the nations of the world are moving toward more capitalism or more socialism? What change would you support? Why?

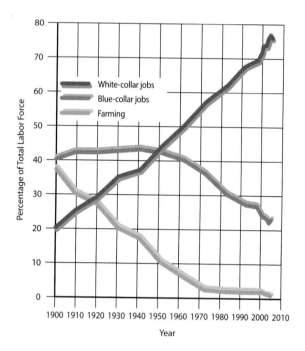

FIGURE 12-2 The Changing Pattern of Work in the United States, 1900–2005

Compared to a century ago, when the economy involved a larger share of factory and farm work, making a living in the United States now involves mostly white-collar service jobs.

Source: Estimates based on U.S. Department of Labor (2006).

Work in the Postindustrial U.S. Economy

Economic change is occurring not just around the world but also in the United States. In 2005, a total of 142 million people in this country—almost two-thirds of those aged sixteen and over—were working for income. A larger share of men (69.6 percent) than women (56.2 percent) had jobs, a gap that is holding steady over time. Among men, 60.2 percent of African Americans were employed, compared with 70.8 percent of whites, 71.8 percent of Asians, and 75.8 percent of Hispanics. Among women, 55.7 percent of African Americans were employed, compared with 56.3 percent of whites, 55.9 percent of Asians, and 51.5 percent of Hispanics (U.S. Department of Labor, 2006).

The Bureau of Labor Statistics Web site offers a wide range of data and reports at http://www.bls.gov

THE CHANGING WORKPLACE

In 1900, roughly 40 percent of U.S. workers were farmers. In 2005, just 1 percent were in agriculture. The family farm of

yesterday has been replaced by *corporate agribusinesses.* Land is now more productive, but this change has caused painful adjustments across the country as a way of life is lost (Dudley, 2000). Figure 12–2 illustrates the shrinking role of the primary sector in the U.S. economy.

A century ago, industrialization swelled the ranks of blue-collar workers. By 1950, however, a white-collar revolution had moved most workers from factories into service occupations. By 2005, some 76 percent of the labor force worked in the service sector, and 92 percent of new jobs were being created in this sector (U.S. Department of Labor, 2006).

As Chapter 8 ("Social Stratification") explained, much service work—including sales, clerical positions, and work in hospitals and restaurants—pays much less than older factory jobs paid. This means that many jobs in the postindustrial era provide only a modest standard of living. Women and other minorities are the most likely to have jobs doing low-paying service work (J. I. Nelson, 1994; Kalleberg, Reskin, & Hudson, 2000).

Do you think the jobs given to students as part of their financial aid provide a fair level of pay and benefits? Explain your view.

LABOR UNIONS

The changing U.S. economy has seen a decline in *labor unions,* organizations that seek to improve wages and working conditions. During the Great Depression of the 1930s, union membership increased rapidly until it reached more than one-third of nonfarm workers by 1950. By 1970, union rolls peaked at almost 25 million. Since then, membership has declined to about 13 percent of nonfarm workers, or some 15.7 million men and women. Looking more closely, 36 percent of government workers are members of unions, compared with just 8 percent of private (nongovernment) workers (Clawson & Clawson, 1999; Goldfield, 2000).

The pattern of union decline holds in most other high-income countries, yet most have a larger share of workers in labor unions than the United States. From about 20 percent in Japan, union membership climbs to 28 percent in Canada, to between 20 and 40 percent in much of Europe, and to a high of 78 percent in Sweden (Visser, 2006).

The widespread decline in union membership follows the shrinking industrial sector of the economy. Newer service jobs—such as sales jobs at retailers such as Wal-Mart, described in the opening to this chapter—are less likely to be unionized. Citing low wages and worker complaints, unions have been trying to organize Wal-Mart employees, so far without success. The weak economy of the past few years has given unions a short-term boost. But long-term gains probably depend on the ability of unions to adapt to the new global economy. Union members in the United States, used to seeing foreign workers as "the enemy," will have to build new international alliances (Greenhouse, 2000; Rousseau, 2002).

PROFESSIONS

All kinds of jobs today are called *professional;* there are professional tennis players, professional house cleaners, and even professional exterminators. As distinct from an *amateur* (from the Latin for "lover," meaning one who acts out of love for the activity itself), a professional performs some task to earn a living. But what exactly is a profession?

A **profession** is *a prestigious white-collar occupation that requires extensive formal education.* People performing this kind of work make a *profession,* or public declaration, of their willingness to work according to certain principles. Professions include the ministry, medicine, law, academia, and fields such as architecture, accountancy, and social work. Occupations are professional to the extent that they demonstrate the following four characteristics (W. J. Goode, 1960; Ritzer & Walczak, 1990):

1. **Theoretical knowledge.** Professionals have theoretical knowledge of their field rather than mere technical training. Anyone can master first-aid skills, for example, but doctors have a theoretical understanding of human health. This means that tennis players, house cleaners, and exterminators do not really qualify as "professionals."

2. **Self-regulating practice.** The typical professional is self-employed, "in private practice" rather than working for a company. Professionals oversee their own work and observe a code of ethics.

3. **Authority over clients.** Because of their expertise, professionals are sought out by clients, who value their advice and follow their directions.

4. **Community orientation rather than self-interest.** The traditional professing of duty states an intention to serve the community rather than merely to seek income.

In almost all cases, professional work requires a college degree and a graduate degree. Not surprisingly, professions are well represented among the jobs beginning college students say they hope to get after graduation, as shown in Figure 12–3.

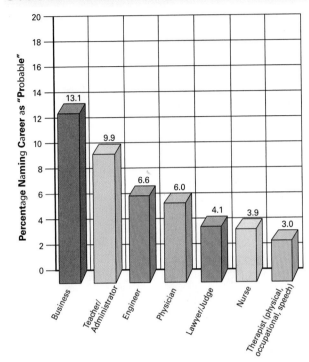

FIGURE 12-3 The Careers Most Commonly Named as Probable by First-Year College Students, 2005

Today's college students expect to enter careers that pay well and carry high prestige.

Source: Pryor et al. (2005).

Many occupations that do not qualify as true professions nonetheless seek to *professionalize* their services. Claiming professional standing usually begins by renaming the work to suggest special, theoretical knowledge, moving the field away from its original, lesser reputation. Stockroom workers become "inventory supply managers," and exterminators are reborn as "insect control specialists."

Interested parties may also form a professional association that certifies their skills. The organization then licenses its members, writes a code of ethics, and emphasizes the work's importance in the community. To win public acceptance, a professional association may also establish schools or other training facilities and perhaps start a professional journal. Not all occupations try to claim professional status. Some *paraprofessionals,* including paralegals and medical technicians, have specialized skills but lack the extensive theoretical education required of full professionals.

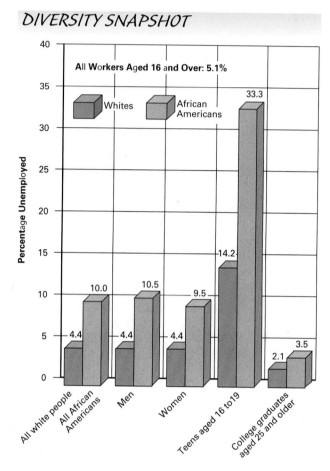

All Workers Aged 16 and Over: 5.1%

Whites

African Americans

FIGURE 12–4   Official U.S. Unemployment Rates for Various Categories of Adults, 2005

Although college graduates have low risk of unemployment, race is related to unemployment for all categories of people.

Source: U.S. Department of Labor (2006).

SELF-EMPLOYMENT

Self-employment—earning a living without being on the payroll of a large organization—was once common in the United States. About 80 percent of the labor force was self-employed in 1800, compared with just 7.4 percent of workers today (8.7 percent of men and 5.8 percent of women) (U.S. Department of Labor, 2006).

Lawyers, doctors, architects, and other highly paid professionals are well represented among the ranks of the self-employed in the United States. But most self-employed

Visit the Web site of the Small Business Administration at http://www.sba.gov

workers are small business owners, plumbers, farmers, carpenters, freelance writers and editors, artists, and long-distance truck drivers. In all, the self-

employed are more likely to have blue-collar than white-collar jobs.

Women own nearly 40 percent of this nation's small businesses, and the share is rising. The 9.1 million firms owned by U.S. women now employ almost 30 million people and generate close to $4 trillion in annual sales (U.S. Small Business Administration, 2001b).

UNEMPLOYMENT AND UNDEREMPLOYMENT

Every society has some level of unemployment. Few young people entering the labor force find a job right away. And workers may leave their jobs to seek new work or to stay at home raising children, some may be on strike, others suffer from long-term illnesses, and still others are without the skills to perform useful work.

But unemployment is not just an individual situation; it is also caused by the economy. Jobs disappear as occupations become obsolete, companies downsize to become

For an article on minority unemployment, go to http:// www.brookings.edu/es/urban/ publications/offnerexsum.htm

more profitable, or firms close in the face of foreign competition or economic recession. Since 1980, the

500 largest U.S. businesses have eliminated some 5 million jobs—one-fourth of the total—while creating even more new jobs. An economic slowdown between 2000 and 2003 resulted in millions of lost jobs, especially among white-collar workers who had typically weathered downturns in the past (Cullen, 2002).

By 2005, the economy had turned around, but there were still 7.6 million people over the age of sixteen who were unemployed—about 5.1 percent of the civilian labor force (U.S. Department of Labor, 2006). Some regions of the United States, especially rural areas, have unemployment rates double the national average.

Figure 12–4 shows that unemployment among African Americans (10.0 percent) is more than twice the rate among white people (4.4 percent). Among all categories of people, unemployment is lower among whites than among African Americans, although the gap between white and black teenagers is especially large and is actually growing.

The economic downturn after 2000 has also encouraged *underemployment*. Backruptcies of large corporations, including Enron and WorldCom, and efforts to cut costs at dozens of other companies have left millions of workers— the lucky ones who still have their jobs—with lower salaries, fewer benefits such as health insurance, and reduced pensions or no pensions at all. In an era of greater global competition and weaker worker organizations, many people have been able to keep their jobs only by agreeing to cutbacks in pay or to the loss of other benefits (Eisenberg, 2001; K. Clark, 2002).

WORKPLACE DIVERSITY: RACE AND GENDER

In the past, white men were the mainstay of the U.S. labor force. However, the nation's proportion of minorities has been rising rapidly. The African American population is increasing faster than the population of non-Hispanic white people. The rate of increase in the Asian American population is even greater. And the rate of increase in the Hispanic population is greatest of all.

Such dramatic changes are likely to affect U.S. society in countless ways. Not only will more and more workers be women and other minorities, but employers will have to develop programs and policies to meet the needs of a socially diverse workforce and also encourage everyone to work together effectively and respectfully. The Thinking About Diversity box on page 346 takes a closer look at some of the issues involved in our changing workplace.

NEW INFORMATION TECHNOLOGY AND WORK

July 2, Ticonderoga, New York. The manager of the local hardware store scans the bar codes of a bagful of items. "The computer doesn't just total the costs," she explains. "It also keeps track of inventory, places orders with the warehouse, and decides which products to continue to sell and which to drop." "Sounds like what you used to do, Maureen," I respond with a smile. "Yep," she nods, with no smile at all.

Another workplace issue is the increasing role of computers and other new information technology. The Information Revolution is changing what people do in a number of ways (Rule & Brantley, 1992; Vallas & Beck, 1996):

1. **Computers are deskilling labor.** Just as industrial machines replaced the master craftsworkers of an earlier era, computers now threaten the skills of managers. More business operations are based not on executive decisions but on computer modeling. A machine, not a person, decides whether to place an order, resupply a client, or approve a loan application.

2. **Computers are making work more abstract.** Most industrial workers have a hands-on relationship with their product. Postindustrial workers manipulate symbols to perform abstract tasks, such as making a company more profitable or making software more user-friendly.

3. **Computers limit workplace interaction.** Spending time at computer terminals, workers become isolated from one another.

Unemployment means not having a job and the income it provides. But it also means not having the respect that comes from being self-reliant in a society that expects people to take care of themselves. How does the sociological perspective help us to understand being out of work as more than a personal problem?

4. **Computers increase employers' control of workers.** Computers allow supervisors to check employees' output continuously, whether they work at keyboard terminals or on assembly lines.

5. **Computers allow companies to relocate work.** Because computer technology allows information to flow almost anywhere instantly, the symbolic work in today's economy may not take place where we might think. We have all had the experience of calling a business (say, a hotel or bookstore) located in our own town only to find out that we are talking to a person at a computer workstation thousands of miles away. Computer technology provides the means to

Twenty-First-Century Diversity:
Changes in the Workplace

An upward trend in the U.S. minority population is changing the workplace. As the figure shows, the number of non-Hispanic white men in the U.S. labor force will rise by a modest 3 percent between 2004 and 2014, but the number of African American men will increase by 17 percent, the number of Hispanic men will increase by 29 percent, and the number of Asian men will increase by 30 percent.

Among non-Hispanic white women, the projected rise is 4 percent; among African American women, 17 percent; and among Asian women, 35 percent. Hispanic women will show the greatest gains, estimated at 41 percent.

Within a decade, non-Hispanic white men will represent 35 percent of all workers, and that figure will continue to drop (Toossi, 2005). As a result, companies that welcome social diversity will tap the largest pool of talent and enjoy a competitive advantage.

Welcoming social diversity means, first, recruiting talented workers of both sexes and all racial and cultural backgrounds. But developing the potential of all employees requires meeting the needs of women and other minorities, which may not be the same as those of white men. For example, child care at the workplace is a big issue for working mothers with small children.

Second, businesses must develop effective ways to deal with tension that arises from social differences. They will have to work harder to ensure that workers are treated equally and respectfully, which means having zero tolerance for racial or sexual harassment.

Third, companies will have to rethink current promotion practices. At present, only 9 percent of *Fortune* 500 top executives are women, and just 4 percent are other minorities (Catalyst, 2006b). In a survey of U.S. companies, the U.S. Equal Employment Opportunity Commission (2005) confirmed that non-Hispanic white men, who make up 34 percent of adults aged twenty to sixty-four, hold 56 percent of management jobs; the comparable figures are 34 and 29 percent, respectively, for non-Hispanic white women, 13 and 6 percent for non-Hispanic African Americans, and 13 and 5 percent for Hispanics.

WHAT DO YOU THINK?

1. What underlying factors are increasing the social diversity of the U.S. workplace?

2. In what specific ways do you think businesses should support minority workers?

3. In what other settings (such as schools) is social diversity becoming more important?

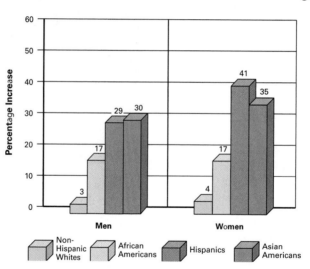

Projected Increase in the Numbers of People in the U.S. Labor Force, 2004–2014

Looking ahead, the share of minorities in the U.S. labor force will increase much faster than the share of white men and women.
Source: Toossi (2005).

outsource many jobs to other places where wages may be lower.

Such changes remind us that technology is not socially neutral. Rather, it changes the relationships between people in the workplace, shapes the way we work, and often alters the balance of power between employers and employees. Understandably, then, people welcome some aspects of the Information Revolution and oppose others.

Corporations

At the core of today's capitalist economy is the **corporation,** *an organization with a legal existence, including rights and liabilities, separate from that of its members.* Incorporating makes an organization a legal entity, able to enter into contracts and own property. Of more than 26 million businesses in the United States, 5 million are incorporated (U.S. Census Bureau, 2005). Incorporating protects the wealth of owners from lawsuits that result from business debts or harm to consumers; it can also mean a lower tax rate on the company's profits.

ECONOMIC CONCENTRATION

Most U.S. corporations are small, with assets of less than $500,000, so it is the largest corporations that dominate our nation's economy. In 2002, some 1,909 corporations had assets exceeding $2.5 billion, representing three-fourths of all corporate assets (Internal Revenue Service, 2005).

The largest U.S. corporation is ExxonMobil, with more than $208 billion in total assets. Its sales ($340 billion in 2005) equal the tax revenues of nearly two-thirds of the states.

In today's corporate world, computers are changing the nature of work just as factories did more than a century ago. In what ways is computer-based work different from factory work? In what ways is it the same?

> **YOUR TURN**
>
> Do you think that being very big benefits the public by making a corporation efficient? Or does being very big make a corporation so powerful that it doesn't need to be accountable to the public? Explain your position.

CONGLOMERATES AND CORPORATE LINKAGES

Economic concentration creates *conglomerates,* giant corporations composed of many smaller corporations. Conglomerates form as corporations enter new markets, spin off new companies, or merge with other companies. For example, PepsiCo is a conglomerate that includes Pepsi-Cola, Frito-Lay, Gatorade, Tropicana, and Quaker.

Many conglomerates are linked because they own each other's stock, the result being worldwide corporate alliances of staggering size. General Motors, for example, owns Opel (Germany), Vauxhall (Great Britain), and half of Saab (Sweden) and has partnerships with Suzuki, Isuzu, and Toyota (Japan). Similarly, Ford owns Jaguar and Aston Martin (Great Britain) and a share of Mazda (Japan), Kia (Korea), and Volvo (Sweden).

Corporations are also linked through *interlocking directorates,* networks of people who serve as directors of many corporations (Weidenbaum, 1995; Kono et al., 1998). These boardroom connections provide access to valuable information about other companies' products and marketing strategies. While perfectly legal, such linkages encourage illegal activity, such as price fixing, as companies share information about their pricing policies.

CORPORATIONS: ARE THEY COMPETITIVE?

According to the capitalist model, businesses operate independently in a competitive market. But in light of the extensive linkages that exist between them, it is obvious that large corporations do not operate independently. Also, a few large corporations dominate many markets, so they are not truly competitive.

Federal law forbids a large company from establishing a **monopoly,** *the domination of a market by a single producer,* because with no competition, such a company could simply dictate prices. But **oligopoly,** *the domination of a market by a few producers,* is both legal and common. This pattern results from the huge investment needed to enter a major market, such as the auto industry, which is beyond the reach of all but the biggest companies. In addition, true competition involves risk, which any company tries to avoid.

Big Corporations Getting Richer: The Case of Corporate Welfare

Would you like the government to slash your income taxes and cancel sales tax on your purchases? What about offering you money to buy a new house at a below-market interest rate? Would you like the government to hook up all your utilities for free and pay your water and electric bills?

For an ordinary person, such deals sound too good to be true. But our tax money is doing exactly that—not for families but for big corporations. All a large company has to do is declare a willingness to relocate and then wait for the offers from state and local governments to come pouring in.

Supporters call government aid to corporations "public-private partnerships." They point to the jobs corporations create, sometimes in areas hard hit by earlier business closings. For a city or county with a high unemployment rate, the promise of a new factory is simply too good to pass up. If incentives in the form of tax relief or free utilities are needed to seal the deal, the money is considered well spent.

Critics call such arrangements "corporate welfare." They agree that companies create new jobs, but they point out that the corporations get much more than they give. In 1991, for example, the state of Indiana offered $451 million in incentives to lure United Airlines to build an aircraft maintenance facility there. United built the facility and hired 6,300 people. But some simple math shows that the cost to Indiana was a whopping $72,000 per job. Much the same happened in 1993, when Alabama offered $253 million in incentives to Mercedes-Benz to build an automobile assembly plant in Tuscaloosa. The plant opened and 1,500 people were hired—at an average cost to Alabama of $169,000 for each worker. In 1997, Pennsylvania gave $307 million in incentives to a Norwegian company to reopen part of Philadelphia's naval shipyard. Once the deal was signed, 950 people were hired, at a cost of $323,000 per job. In 2002, Georgia spent $67,000 per job to bring in a new Daimler-Benz auto plant. Across the country, the pattern is much the same. Overall, government support to corporations exceeds $15 billion each year, far more than the total welfare dollars given to people who are poor.

Although new plants do create some jobs, most jobs are simply moved from one place to another. In addition, not all jobs pay well. Nor is there any guarantee that once settled, a corporation will stay, since businesses are free to make a better deal and move to another location.

WHAT DO YOU THINK?

1. Why are local government officials so eager to attract business?

2. Do ordinary people benefit from corporate tax relief policies? Explain your answer.

3. Overall, do you support tax breaks for corporations? Why or why not?

Sources: Based on Bartlett & Steele (1998) and various news reports.

The federal government seeks to regulate corporations in order to protect the public interest. Yet as recent corporate scandals have shown, regulation is often too little too late, resulting in harm to millions of people. The U.S. government is also the corporate world's single biggest customer, and sometimes it steps in to support struggling corporations with billion-dollar bailout programs. As the Applying Sociology box explains, state governments' aid to corporations has drawn fire from critics as "corporate welfare."

CORPORATIONS AND THE GLOBAL ECONOMY

Corporations have grown so large that they now account for most of the planet's economic output. The biggest corporations are based in the United States, Japan, and Western Europe, but their marketplace is the entire world. Many large companies such as McDonald's and the chipmaker Intel earn most of their money outside the United States.

Global corporations know that poor countries contain most of the world's people and resources. In addition, labor costs there are attractively low: A manufacturing worker in Mexico, who earns about $2.25 an hour, labors for more than a week to earn about what a worker in the United States (who averages about $17.85 an hour) or Japan ($18.20 an hour) earns in a single day.

As Chapter 9 ("Global Stratification") explained, the impact of multinational corporations on low-income countries is controversial. Modernization theorists claim that multinational corporations, by unleashing the great productivity of capitalism, raise living standards in poor

Where the Jobs Will Be:
Projections to 2010

The economic prospects of counties across the United States are not the same. Much of the midsection of the country is projected to lose jobs. By contrast, the coastal regions and most of the West are rapidly gaining jobs. What factors might account for this pattern?

Source: Woods & Poole Economics, Washington, D.C. Used with permission.

Employment
Growth or Decline,
Projections to 2010

Big gain:
17% to 58%

Moderate gain:
9% to 16%

Small gain:
1% to 8%

Job loss:
–10% to 0%

No data

nations, offering them tax revenues, capital investment, new jobs, and advanced technology that together accelerate economic growth (Berger, 1986; Firebaugh & Beck, 1994; Firebaugh & Sandu, 1998).

Dependency theorists respond that multinationals make global inequality worse, blocking the development of local industries and pushing poor countries to produce goods for export rather than food and other products for local people. From this standpoint, multinationals make poor nations increasingly dependent on rich nations (Wallerstein, 1979; Dixon & Boswell, 1996; Kentor, 1998).

The Economy: Looking Ahead

Social institutions are a society's ways of meeting people's needs. But as we have seen, the U.S. economy only partly succeeds in this mission. Although highly productive, our economy provides for some people much better than for others.

The Information Revolution has caused tremendous changes in the economy. First, the share of the U.S. labor force engaged in manufacturing is now half of what it was in 1960; service work, especially computer-related jobs, makes up the difference. For industrial workers, the postindustrial economy has brought unemployment and declining wages. "In the *Times*" on pages 350–51 takes a look at the everyday lives of low-paid workers in New York City's laundries.

Our society must face up to the challenge of providing millions of men and women with the language and computer skills needed in the new economy. Yet as the economic collapse of many dot-coms in 2001 shows, even this new type of work can experience a downturn. In addition, there are regional differences in the economic outlook: National Map

12–1 shows which regions are projected to gain jobs and which are expected to lose them by the end of the decade.

YOUR TURN

Make a list of the likely consequences for a community of the decline in industrial jobs.

A second transformation that will mark the new century is the expansion of the global economy. Two centuries ago, the ups and downs of a local economy reflected events and trends in a single town. One century ago, communities across the country became economically linked so that one town's prosperity depended on producing goods demanded by people elsewhere in the country. Today, it makes little sense to speak of a national economy because most markets have become global. For example, what we pay at the pump for gasoline here in the United States has as much to do with increasing demand for oil in China and India as it does with domestic demand, policies, and production. As both producers and consumers, we are now subject to factors and forces that are both distant and unseen.

Finally, analysts around the world are rethinking conventional economic models. The global economy shows that socialism is less productive than capitalism, one important reason for the collapse of socialist regimes in Eastern Europe and the former Soviet Union. But capitalism has its own problems, including corporate irresponsibility, social inequality, and government regulation.

What will be the long-term effects of these changes? Two conclusions seem certain. First, the economic future of

POLITICS: HISTORICAL OVERVIEW

POLITICS is the major social institution by which a society distributes power and organizes decision making. Max Weber claimed that raw power is transformed into *legitimate authority* in three ways:

- Preindustrial societies rely on tradition to transform power into authority. *Traditional authority* is closely linked to kinship.
- As societies industrialize, the expansion of rational bureaucracy is linked to the rise of *rational-legal authority*, which is closely linked to offices and law.
- At any time, however, some individuals transform power into authority through charisma. *Charismatic authority* is linked to extraordinary personal qualities (as found in Jesus of Nazareth, Adolf Hitler, Mahatma Gandhi).

pp 350–52

politics (p. 350) the social institution that distributes power, sets a society's goals, and makes decisions

power (p. 350) the ability to achieve desired ends despite resistance from others

government (p. 350) a formal organization that directs the political life of a society

authority (p. 350) power that people perceive as legitimate rather than coercive

routinization of charisma (p. 351) the transformation of charismatic authority into some combination of traditional and bureaucratic authority

POLITICS IN GLOBAL PERSPECTIVE

MONARCHY is common in agrarian societies; leadership is based on kinship.

p 352

DEMOCRACY is common in modern societies; leadership is linked to elective office.

p 352

AUTHORITARIANISM is any political system that denies the people participation in government.

pp 352–53

TOTALITARIANISM concentrates all political power in one centralized leadership.

pp 353–54

 The world is divided into 192 politically independent nation-states. A political trend, however, is the growing wealth and power of multinational corporations. In an age of computers and other new information technology, governments can no longer control the flow of information across their borders (p 354).

monarchy (p. 352) a political system in which a single family rules from generation to generation

democracy (p. 352) a political system that gives power to the people as a whole

authoritarianism (p. 352) a political system that denies the people participation in government

totalitarianism (p. 354) a highly centralized political system that extensively regulates people's lives

POLITICS IN THE UNITED STATES

U.S. government has expanded over the past two centuries, although the *welfare state* in the United States is smaller than in most other high-income nations.

p 355

The *political spectrum*, from the liberal left to the conservative right, involves attitudes on both economic issues and social issues.

pp 355–56

Special-interest groups advance the political aims of specific segments of the population.

p 357

Voter apathy runs high in the United States: Only 60% of eligible voters went to the polls in the 2004 presidential election.

pp 357–58

welfare state (p. 355) a system of government agencies and programs that provides benefits to the population

THEORETICAL ANALYSIS OF POWER

The **PLURALIST MODEL** claims that political power is spread widely in the United States.

p 358

The **POWER-ELITE MODEL** claims that power is concentrated in a small, wealthy segment of the population.

pp 358–59

The **MARXIST POLITICAL-ECONOMY MODEL** claims that our political agenda is determined by a capitalist economy, so true democracy is impossible.

pp 359–60

See the Applying Theory table on page 359.

pluralist model (p. 358) an analysis of politics that sees power as spread among many competing interest groups

power-elite model (p. 358) an analysis of politics that sees power as concentrated among the rich

Marxist political-economy model (p. 359) an analysis that explains politics in terms of the operation of a society's economic system

POWER BEYOND THE RULES

- **REVOLUTION** radically transforms a political system.
- **TERRORISM** employs violence in the pursuit of political goals and is used by a group against a much more powerful enemy.

pp 360–61

WAR AND PEACE

- The development and spread of nuclear weapons have increased the threat of global catastrophe
- World peace ultimately depends on resolving the tensions and conflicts that fuel militarism.

pp 362–66

political revolution (p. 360) the overthrow of one political system in order to establish another

terrorism (p. 361) acts of violence or the threat of violence used as a political strategy by an individual or a group

war (p. 362) organized, armed conflict among the people of two or more nations, directed by their governments

military-industrial complex (p. 363) the close association of the federal government, the military, and defense industries

In recent years, the world has become aware of the death and mutilation caused by millions of land mines placed in the ground during wartime and left there afterward. Civilians—many of them children—maimed by land mines receive treatment in this Kabul, Afghanistan, clinic.

contrast, there is no draft, and fighting is done by a volunteer military. But not every member of our society is equally likely to volunteer.

One recent study concluded that the military has few young people who are rich and few who are very poor. Rather, working-class people look to the military for a job, to get some money to go to college, or simply to get out of the small town where they grew up. In addition, the largest number of volunteers comes from the South, where regional culture is more supportive of the military and where most military bases are located. As two analysts put it, "America's military seems to resemble the makeup of a two-year commuter or trade school outside Birmingham or Biloxi far more than that of a ghetto or barrio or four-year university in Boston" (Halbfinger & Holmes, 2003:1).

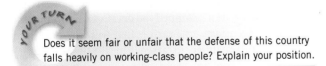

Does it seem fair or unfair that the defense of this country falls heavily on working-class people? Explain your position.

IS TERRORISM A NEW KIND OF WAR?

In recent years, we have heard government officials speak of terrorism as a new kind of war. War has historically followed certain patterns: It is played out according to at least some basic rules, the warring parties are known to each other, and the objectives of the warring parties—which generally involve control of territory—are clearly stated.

Terrorism breaks from these patterns. The identity of terrorist individuals and organizations may not be known, those involved may deny their responsibility, and their goals may be unclear. The 2001 terrorist attacks against the United States were not attempts to defeat the nation militarily or to secure territory. They were carried out by people representing not a country but a cause, one not well understood in the United States. In short, they were expressions of anger and hate intended to create widespread fear.

Conventional warfare is symmetrical, with two nations sending armies into battle. By contrast, terrorism is a new kind of war: an asymmetrical conflict in which a small number of attackers uses terror and their own willingness to die as a means to level the playing field against a much more powerful enemy. Although the terrorists may be ruthless, the nation under attack must use caution in its response to terrorism because little may be known about the identity and location of the parties responsible.

THE COSTS AND CAUSES OF MILITARISM

The cost of armed conflict extends far beyond battlefield casualties. Together, the world's nations spend almost $1 trillion annually for military purposes. Spending this much diverts resources from the desperate struggle for survival by hundreds of millions of poor people.

Defense is the U.S. government's second biggest expenditure (after Social Security), accounting for about 20 percent of all federal spending, which amounted to almost $500 billion in 2005. The United States has emerged as the world's single military superpower, with more military might than the next nine countries combined (Gergen, 2002).

For decades, military spending went up because of the *arms race* between the United States and the former Soviet Union, which dropped out of the race after its collapse in 1991. But some analysts (who support power-elite theory) link high military spending to the domination of U.S. society by a **military-industrial complex,** *the close association of the federal government, the military, and defense industries.* The roots of militarism, then, lie not just in external threats but also in institutional structures here at home (Marullo, 1987; Barnes, 2002b).

A final reason for continuing militarism is regional conflict. In the 1990s, localized wars broke out in Bosnia,

THINKING GLOBALLY

Islam and Freedom: A "Democracy Gap"?

I s freedom a goal that is celebrated everywhere? That depends—primarily because freedom means different things in different cultural settings.

Freedom House, an organization that monitors political freedom around the world, tracks people's right to vote, to freely express ideas, and to move about without undue interference from government. It reports that the region of the world with the least political freedom stretches from Africa through the Middle East to Asia (look back at Global Map 12–3 on page 353).

Many of the nations that Freedom House characterizes as "not free"

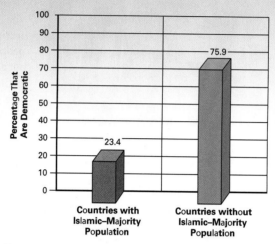

Democracy in Countries with and without Islamic-Majority Populations

Today, democratic government is much less common in countries with Islamic-majority populations. Fifty years ago, the same was true of countries with Catholic-majority populations.

Source: Karatnycky (2002).

have populations that are largely Muslim. This organization reports that in 2002, 47 of the world's 192 nations had an Islamic majority population. As the accompanying figure shows, just 11 (23.4 percent) of these 47 countries had democratic governments, and Freedom House rated only one—Mali—as "free." Of the 145 nations without a majority Islamic population, 110 (75.9 percent) had democratic governments, and 84 are described as "free." In other words, countries without Islamic majorities are three times more likely to have democratic governments than countries with Islamic majorities. Freedom House concludes that countries with Islamic majority populations display a disturbing "democracy gap."

This relative lack of democracy holds for all world regions that have

---

Chechnya, and Zambia, and today tensions run high between Israel and the Palestinians and between India and Pakistan. Even limited wars have the potential to grow and involve other countries, including the United States. India and Pakistan, both nuclear powers, moved to the brink of war in 2002. In 2003, the announcement by North Korea that it, too, had nuclear weapons raised tensions in Asia. In 2006, Iran continues to develop nuclear technology, raising fears that this nation may soon have an atomic bomb.

NUCLEAR WEAPONS

Despite the easing of superpower tensions, the world still contains 20,000 nuclear warheads, representing a destructive power equal to five tons of TNT for every person on the planet. If even a small fraction of this arsenal is used in war, life as we know it would end. Albert Einstein, whose genius contributed to the development of nuclear weapons, reflected, "The unleashed power of the atom has changed everything *save our modes of thinking,* and we thus drift

toward unparalleled catastrophe." In short, nuclear weapons make full-scale war unthinkable in a world not yet capable of peace.

The United States, the Russian Federation, Great Britain, France, the People's Republic of China, Israel, India, Pakistan, and North Korea all have nuclear weapons. Although a few nations stopped the development of nuclear weapons—Argentina and Brazil halted work in 1990, and South Africa dismantled its arsenal in 1991—by 2025, as many as fifty countries could have the ability to fight a nuclear war. Such a trend makes any regional conflict very dangerous to the entire planet.

MASS MEDIA AND WAR

The Iraq War was the first war in which television crews traveled with U.S. troops, reporting as the campaign unfolded. The mass media provided ongoing and detailed reports of events; cable television made available live coverage of the war twenty-four hours a day, seven days a week.

Islamic-majority nations—Africa, Central Europe, the Middle East, and Asia. The pattern is especially strong among the sixteen Islamic-majority states in the Middle East and North Africa that are ethnically Arabic—none is an electoral democracy.

What explains this "democracy gap"? Freedom House points to four factors. First, countries with Islamic-majority populations are typically less developed economically, with limited schooling for their people and widespread poverty. Second, these countries have cultural traditions that rigidly control the lives of women, providing them with few economic, educational, or political opportunities. Third, while most countries limit the power of religious elites in government, and some (including the United States) even require a "separation of church and state," Islamic-majority nations support giving Islamic leaders political power. In just two recent cases—Iran and Afghanistan under the Taliban—Islamic leaders have actually taken formal control of government; more commonly, religious leaders do not hold office but exert considerable influence on political outcomes.

Fourth and finally, the enormous wealth that comes from Middle Eastern oil plays a part in preventing democratic government. In Iraq, Saudi Arabia, Kuwait, Qatar, and other nations, this resource has provided astounding riches to a small number of families, money they can use to shore up their political control. In addition, oil wealth permits elites to build airports and other modern facilities without encouraging broader economic development that would raise the living standards of the majority.

For all these reasons, Freedom House concludes that the road to democracy for Islamic-majority nations is likely to be long. Yet there are also reasons to think that change will come. In 1950, very few Catholic-majority countries (mostly in Europe and Latin America) had democratic governments. Today, however, most of these nations are democratic. Note too that a majority of the world's Muslims—who live in Nigeria, Turkey, Bangladesh, India, Indonesia, and the United States—already live under democratic governments. But perhaps the best indicator that change is already under way: By the end of 2005, Freedom House had added two more countries with Islamic majorities to the list of "free" nations of the world.

WHAT DO YOU THINK?

1. Is the United States right or wrong in trying to bring about a democratic political system in Iraq? Explain your answer.

2. Do you expect to see greater democracy in Islamic-majority countries fifty years from now? Why or why not?

3. Can you point to several reasons that Muslims might object to the kind of political system we call "democracy"? Explain.

Those media outlets critical of the war—especially the Arab news channel Al-Jazeera—tended to report the slow pace of the conflict, the casualties to the U.S. and allied forces, and the deaths and injuries suffered by Iraqi civilians, information that increased pressure to end the war. Media outlets supportive of the war—including most news organizations in the United States—tended to report the rapid pace of the war and the casualties to Iraqi forces and to downplay harm to Iraqi civilians as minimal and unintended. In sum, the power of the mass media to provide selective information to a worldwide audience means that television and other media may be almost as important to the outcome of a conflict as the military who are doing the actual fighting.

PURSUING PEACE

How can the world reduce the dangers of war? Looking back over the last several decades, here are the most recent approaches to peace:

1. **Deterrence.** The logic of the arms race holds that security comes from a balance of terror between the superpowers. The principle of *mutual assured destruction* (MAD) means that a nation launching a first strike against another will face greater retaliation. This deterrence policy kept the peace for almost fifty years during the Cold War. Yet it encouraged an enormous arms race and cannot control nuclear proliferation, which poses a growing threat to peace. Deterrence also does little to stop terrorism or to prevent war started by a stronger nation (such as the United States) against a weaker foe (such as the Taliban government in Afghanistan or Saddam Hussein's Iraq).

2. **High-technology defense.** If technology created the weapons, perhaps it can also protect us from them; such is the claim of the *strategic defense initiative* (SDI). Under SDI, satellites and ground installations would destroy enemy missiles soon after they were launched. In a survey shortly after the September 11

attacks, two-thirds of U.S. adults supported SDI (Thompson & Waller, 2001; "Female Opinion," 2002). However, critics claim that the system, which they refer to as "Star Wars," would be, at best, a leaky umbrella. Others worry that building such a system will spark another massive arms race.

3. **Diplomacy and disarmament.** Some analysts believe that the best road to peace is diplomacy rather than technology (Dedrick & Yinger, 1990). Teams of diplomats working together can increase security by reducing, rather than building, weapons stockpiles.

   But disarmament has limitations. No nation wants to be weakened by eliminating its defenses. Successful diplomacy depends on everyone involved sharing responsibility for a common problem (Fisher & Ury, 1988). Although the United States and the Soviet Union succeeded in negotiating arms reduction agreements, the world now faces threats from other nations such as North Korea and Iran.

4. **Resolving underlying conflict.** In the end, reducing the dangers of war may depend on resolving underlying conflicts by promoting a more just world. Poverty, hunger, and illiteracy are all root causes of war. Perhaps the world needs to reconsider the wisdom of spending thousands of times as much money on militarism as we do on efforts to find peaceful solutions (Sivard, 1988; Kaplan & Schaffer, 2001).

Politics: Looking Ahead

Just as economies are changing, so are political systems. Several problems and trends are likely to be important as the century unfolds.

One troublesome problem in the United States is inconsistency between our democratic ideals and our low turnout at the polls. Perhaps, as conservative pluralist theorists say, many people do not bother to vote because they are content with their lives. On the other hand, the liberal power-elite theorists may be right when they say that people withdraw from a system that concentrates so much wealth and power in the hands of a few people. Or perhaps, as radical Marxist critics claim, people find that our political system offers little real choice, limiting options and policies to those that support our capitalist economy. In any case, the current high level of apathy indicates that significant political reform is needed.

A second major trend is the global rethinking of political models. The Cold War cast political debate in the form of two opposing models, capitalism and socialism. Today, however, discussion includes a broader range of political systems that links government to the economy in a variety of ways. Welfare capitalism, as found in Sweden, or state capitalism, as found in South Korea and Japan, are just two possibilities. The Thinking Globally box on pages 364–65 takes a look at the debate over the chances for the emergence of democratic governments in the world's Islamic countries.

Third, we still face the danger of war in many parts of the world. Even as the United States and the Russian Federation dismantle some warheads, vast stockpiles of nuclear weapons remain, and nuclear technology continues to spread around the world. In addition, new superpowers are likely to arise (the People's Republic of China and India are likely candidates), just as regional conflicts and terrorism are likely to continue. We can only hope (and vote!) for leaders who will find nonviolent solutions to the age-old problems that provoke war, putting us on the road to world peace.

APPLYING SOCIOLOGY IN EVERYDAY LIFE

1. Do some research to learn about the economy of your own state, including the type of work people do, the unemployment rate, and what trends are under way. A good place to start is the Web site for the U.S. Bureau of Labor Statistics at http://www.bls.org

2. Visit a discount store such as Wal-Mart or Kmart and do a little "fieldwork" in an area of the store that interests you. Pick ten products and see where they are made. Do the results support the existence of a global economy?

3. The following Web site provides data on how people voted in the 2004 presidential election by gender, age, race, and income: http://www.cnn.com/ELECTION/2004/pages/results/states/US/P/100/epolls.0.html Visit this site and develop a profile of the typical Democratic voter and the typical Republican voter. Which variables seem most closely linked to how people vote?

4. Freedom House, the organization that studies civil rights and political liberty around the world, publishes an annual report, *Freedom in the World*. Find a copy in the library or visit the Freedom House Web site, http://www.freedomhouse.org, and learn more about politics in countries of interest to you.

MAKING THE GRADE

CHAPTER 12   Economics and Politics

THE ECONOMY: HISTORICAL OVERVIEW

The **ECONOMY** is the major social institution through which a society produces, distributes, and consumes goods and services.

- In technologically simple societies, economic activity is simply part of family life.
- The Agricultural Revolution (5,000 years ago) made the economy a distinct social institution based on agricultural technology, specialized work, permanent settlements, and trade.
- The Industrial Revolution (beginning around 1750) expanded the economy based on new sources of energy and specialized work in factories that turned raw materials into finished products.
- The postindustrial economy is based on a shift to service work and computer technology.

pp 334–36

 Today's expanding global economy produces and consumes products and services with little regard for national borders. The world's 600 largest corporations account for half of the world's economic output (pp 337–38).

PRIMARY SECTOR
- draws raw materials from the natural environment
- is of greatest importance (20% of the economy) in low-income nations

p 336

SECONDARY SECTOR
- transforms raw materials into manufactured goods
- is a significant share (26-32%) of the economy in low-, middle-, and high-income nations

p 336

TERTIARY SECTOR
- produces services rather than goods
- is the largest sector (49-72%) in low-, middle-, and high-income countries

p 336

ECONOMIC SYSTEMS: PATHS TO JUSTICE

CAPITALISM is based on private ownership of property and the pursuit of profit in a competitive marketplace. Capitalism offers

- greater productivity ⟷
- higher overall standard of living ⟷
- greater income inequality ⟷
- freedom to act according to self-interest ⟷

SOCIALISM is grounded in collective ownership of productive property through government control of the economy. Socialism offers

- less productivity
- lower overall standard of living
- less income inequality
- freedom from basic want

pp 338–41

WORK IN THE POSTINDUSTRIAL U.S. ECONOMY

JOBS
- Agricultural work represents only 1% of jobs.
- Blue-collar, industrial work has declined to 23% of jobs.
- White-collar, service work has increased to 76% of jobs.

p 342

SELF-EMPLOYMENT
- 7.4% of U.S. workers are self-employed.
- Many professionals fall into this category, but most self-employed people have blue-collar jobs.

p 344

UNEMPLOYMENT
- Unemployment has many causes, including the operation of the economy itself.
- In 2005, 5.1% of the country's labor force was unemployed.
- At highest risk for unemployment are young people and African Americans.

p 344

CORPORATIONS

CORPORATIONS form the core of the U.S. economy.

- The largest corporations, which are conglomerates, account for most corporate assets and profits.
- Many large corporations operate as multinationals, producing and distributing products in nations around the world.

pp 347–49

social institution (p. 334) a major sphere of social life, or societal subsystem, organized to meet human needs

economy (p. 334) the social institution that organizes a society's production, distribution, and consumption of goods and services

postindustrial economy (p. 335) a productive system based on service work and high technology

primary sector (p. 336) the part of the economy that draws raw materials from the natural environment

secondary sector (p. 336) the part of the economy that transforms raw materials into manufactured goods

tertiary sector (p. 336) the part of the economy that involves services rather than goods

global economy (p. 337) economic activity that crosses national borders

capitalism (p. 338) an economic system in which natural resources and the means of producing goods and services are privately owned

socialism (p. 339) an economic system in which natural resources and the means of producing goods and services are collectively owned

welfare capitalism (p. 340) an economic and political system that combines a mostly market-based economy with extensive social welfare programs

state capitalism (p. 340) an economic and political system in which companies are privately owned but cooperate closely with the government

profession (p. 343) a prestigious white-collar occupation that requires extensive formal education

corporation (p. 347) an organization with a legal existence, including rights and liabilities, separate from that of its members

monopoly (p. 347) the domination of a market by a single producer

oligopoly (p. 347) the domination of a market by a few producers

MAKING THE GRADE
CONTINUED...

POLITICS: HISTORICAL OVERVIEW

POLITICS is the major social institution by which a society distributes power and organizes decision making. Max Weber claimed that raw power is transformed into *legitimate authority* in three ways:

- Preindustrial societies rely on tradition to transform power into authority. *Traditional authority* is closely linked to kinship.
- As societies industrialize, the expansion of rational bureaucracy is linked to the rise of *rational-legal authority*, which is closely linked to offices and law.
- At any time, however, some individuals transform power into authority through charisma. *Charismatic authority* is linked to extraordinary personal qualities (as found in Jesus of Nazareth, Adolf Hitler, Mahatma Gandhi).

pp 350–52

politics (p. 350) the social institution that distributes power, sets a society's goals, and makes decisions

power (p. 350) the ability to achieve desired ends despite resistance from others

government (p. 350) a formal organization that directs the political life of a society

authority (p. 350) power that people perceive as legitimate rather than coercive

routinization of charisma (p. 351) the transformation of charismatic authority into some combination of traditional and bureaucratic authority

POLITICS IN GLOBAL PERSPECTIVE

MONARCHY is common in agrarian societies; leadership is based on kinship.

p 352

DEMOCRACY is common in modern societies; leadership is linked to elective office.

p 352

AUTHORITARIANISM is any political system that denies the people participation in government.

pp 352–53

TOTALITARIANISM concentrates all political power in one centralized leadership.

pp 353–54

monarchy (p. 352) a political system in which a single family rules from generation to generation

democracy (p. 352) a political system that gives power to the people as a whole

authoritarianism (p. 352) a political system that denies the people participation in government

totalitarianism (p. 354) a highly centralized political system that extensively regulates people's lives

 The world is divided into 192 politically independent nation-states. A political trend, however, is the growing wealth and power of multinational corporations. In an age of computers and other new information technology, governments can no longer control the flow of information across their borders (p 354).

welfare state (p. 355) a system of government agencies and programs that provides benefits to the population

POLITICS IN THE UNITED STATES

U.S. government has expanded over the past two centuries, although the *welfare state* in the United States is smaller than in most other high-income nations.

p 355

The *political spectrum*, from the liberal left to the conservative right, involves attitudes on both economic issues and social issues.

pp 355–56

Special-interest groups advance the political aims of specific segments of the population.

p 357

Voter apathy runs high in the United States: Only 60% of eligible voters went to the polls in the 2004 presidential election.

pp 357–58

THEORETICAL ANALYSIS OF POWER

The **PLURALIST MODEL** claims that political power is spread widely in the United States.

p 358

The **POWER-ELITE MODEL** claims that power is concentrated in a small, wealthy segment of the population.

pp 358–59

The **MARXIST POLITICAL-ECONOMY MODEL** claims that our political agenda is determined by a capitalist economy, so true democracy is impossible.

pp 359–60

See the Applying Theory table on page 359.

pluralist model (p. 358) an analysis of politics that sees power as spread among many competing interest groups

power-elite model (p. 358) an analysis of politics that sees power as concentrated among the rich

Marxist political-economy model (p. 359) an analysis that explains politics in terms of the operation of a society's economic system

political revolution (p. 360) the overthrow of one political system in order to establish another

terrorism (p. 361) acts of violence or the threat of violence used as a political strategy by an individual or a group

war (p. 362) organized, armed conflict among the people of two or more nations, directed by their governments

military-industrial complex (p. 363) the close association of the federal government, the military, and defense industries

POWER BEYOND THE RULES

- **REVOLUTION** radically transforms a political system.
- **TERRORISM** employs violence in the pursuit of political goals and is used by a group against a much more powerful enemy.

pp 360–61

WAR AND PEACE

- The development and spread of nuclear weapons have increased the threat of global catastrophe
- World peace ultimately depends on resolving the tensions and conflicts that fuel militarism.

pp 362–66

MAKING THE GRADE
Sample Test Questions
CHAPTER 12

These questions are similar to those found in the test bank that accompanies this textbook.

MULTIPLE-CHOICE QUESTIONS

1. The economy is the social institution that guides
   a. the production of goods and services.
   b. the distribution of goods and services.
   c. the consumption of goods and services.
   d. All of the above are correct.

2. Building houses and making cars are examples of production in which economic sector?
   a. the primary sector
   b. the secondary sector
   c. the tertiary sector
   d. the service sector

3. The globalization of the economy is causing which of the following?
   a. Certain areas of the world specialize in one sector of economic activity.
   b. Industrial jobs in the United States are being lost.
   c. More and more products pass through several nations.
   d. All of the above are correct.

4. Socialist economies differ from capitalist economies by
   a. being more productive.
   b. creating less economic equality.
   c. creating more economic equality.
   d. making greater use of commercial advertising.

5. The largest 1,900 corporations, each with assets exceeding $2.5 billion, represent about what share of all corporate assets in the United States?
   a. 75 percent
   b. 50 percent
   c. 25 percent
   d. 5 percent

6. Modern societies, including the United States, rely mostly on which type of authority?
   a. charismatic authority
   b. traditional authority
   c. rational-legal authority
   d. Modern societies have no authority at all.

7. In which type of political system does power reside in the hands of the people as a whole?
   a. democracy
   b. aristocracy
   c. totalitarianism
   d. monarchy

8. In the 2004 U.S. presidential election, about what share of registered voters actually cast a vote?
   a. 100 percent
   b. 80 percent
   c. 60 percent
   d. 20 percent

9. The Marxist political-economy model suggests that
   a. power is concentrated in the hands of a small "power elite."
   b. an antidemocratic bias is built into the capitalist system.
   c. power is widely spread throughout society.
   d. many people do not vote because they are basically satisfied with their lives.

10. Which of the following wars resulted in the highest loss of life to people in the United States?
    a. Civil War
    b. World War II
    c. Korean War
    d. Vietnam War

ANSWERS: 1 (d); 2 (b); 3 (d); 4 (c); 5 (c); 6 (a); 7 (a); 8 (c); 9 (b); 10 (a).

ESSAY QUESTIONS

1. In what specific ways did the Industrial Revolution change the economy and the broader society of the United States? How is the Information Revolution changing our economy and broader society today?

2. Compare the pluralist, power-elite, and Marxist models of political power. What does each model lead you to conclude about politics in the United States?

Family and religion are two social institutions that shape people's behavior and beliefs. These two institutions often come together when people gather for ritual events, such as a wedding.

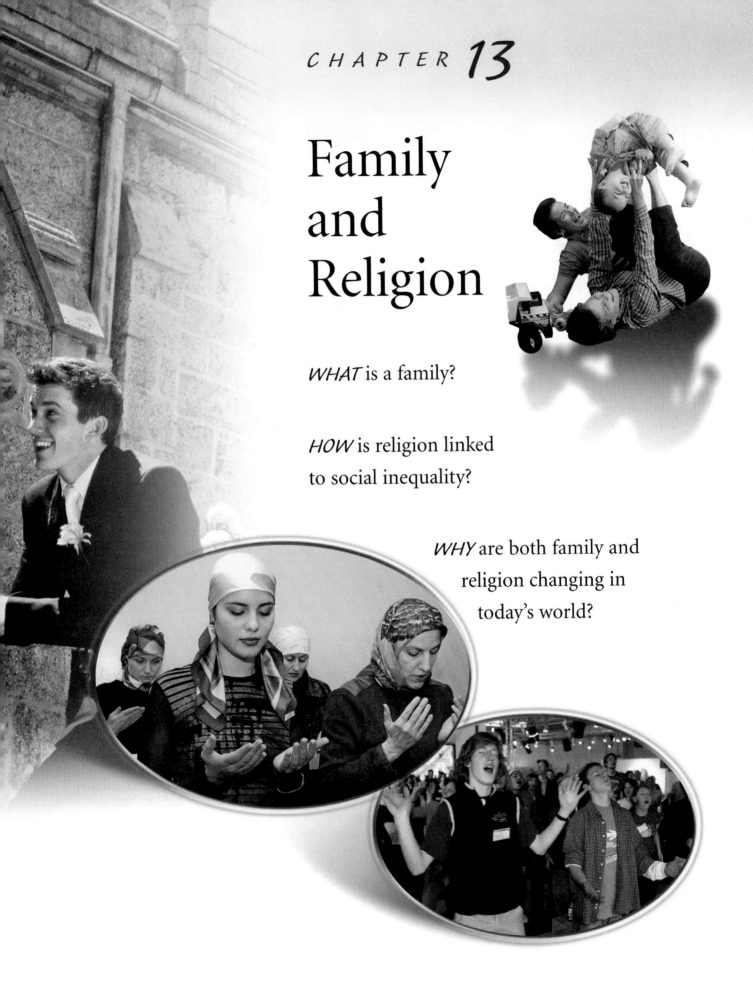

Family and Religion

WHAT is a family?

HOW is religion linked
to social inequality?

WHY are both family and
religion changing in
today's world?

Rosa Yniguez is one of seven children who grew up in Jalisco, Mexico, in a world in which families worked hard, went to church regularly, and were proud of having many children. Rosa remembers friends of her parents who had a clock in their living room with a picture of each of their twelve children where the numbers on the clock face would be.

Now thirty-five years old, Rosa is living in San Francisco, attends a local Catholic church, and works as a cashier in a department store. In some respects, she has carried on her parents' traditions—but not in every way. Recalling her childhood, she says, "In Mexico, many of the families I knew had six, eight, ten children. Sometimes more. But I came to this country to get ahead. That is simply impossible with too many kids." As a result of her desire to keep her job and make a better life for her family, Rosa has decided to have no more than the three children she has now.

A tradition of having large families has helped make Hispanics the largest racial or ethnic minority in the United States. But today, more and more Latinas are making the same decision as Rosa Yniguez and opting to have fewer children. Studies show that the birth rate for all immigrant women has dropped by 30 percent during the last decade (Navarro, 2004).

Families have been with us for a very long time. But as this story indicates, U.S. families are changing in response to a number of factors, including the desire of women to have more career options and to provide better lives for their children. In fact, the family is changing faster than any other social institution (Bianchi & Spain, 1996).

Religion is changing too as membership in long-established denominations is declining and new religious organizations are flourishing. This chapter examines family and religion, which are closely linked as society's *symbolic institutions.* Both help set standards of morality, maintain traditions, and join people together. Focusing on the United States and making comparisons to other countries, we will examine why many people consider family and religion the foundations of society while others predict—and may even encourage—the decline of both institutions.

Family: Basic Concepts

The **family** is *a social institution found in all societies that unites people in cooperative groups to care for one another, including any children.* Family ties are also called **kinship,** *a social bond based on common ancestry, marriage, or adop-* *tion.* All societies contain families, but exactly who people call their kin has varied through history and varies today from one culture to another. Here and in other countries, families form around **marriage,** *a legal relationship, usually involving economic cooperation as well as sexual activity and childbearing.*

Today, some people object to defining only married couples or parents and children as families because it endorses a narrow standard of behavior. Because some business and government programs still use this conventional definition, many unmarried but committed partners of the same or opposite sex are excluded from family health care and other benefits. However, organizations are gradually coming to recognize as families people with or without legal or blood ties who feel they belong together and define themselves as a family.

Because the U.S. Census Bureau uses the conventional definition of family,[1] sociologists who use Census Bureau

---

[1]According to the Census Bureau, there were 114 million U.S. households in 2005. Of these, 77.4 million (68 percent) meet the bureau's definition of "family." The remaining living units contained single people or unrelated people living together. In 1950, 90 percent of all households were families.

Families in the United States have many diverse forms, and celebrity couples represent them all. After living together, Ashton Kutcher, age 27, and Demi Moore, age 42, were recently married. They live with her three children from a previous marriage, who refer to Kutcher as "My Other Dad." Rosie O'Donnell and Kelli Carpenter married in San Francisco in 2004, but their marriage was later voided by the California Supreme Court. They live with Rosie's three adopted children.

data describing "families" must accept it. But as noted, the national trend is toward a broader definition.

Family: Global Variations

In preindustrial societies, people take a broad view of family ties, recognizing the **extended family,** *a family composed of parents and children as well as other kin.* This group is also called the *consanguine family* because it includes everyone with "shared blood." With industrialization, however, increasing social mobility and geographic migration give rise to the **nuclear family,** *a family composed of one or two parents and their children.* The nuclear family is also called the *conjugal family,* meaning "based on marriage." Although many people in our society live in extended families, far more live in nuclear families.

MARRIAGE PATTERNS

Cultural norms, and often laws, identify people as suitable or unsuitable marriage partners. Some norms promote **endogamy,** *marriage between people of the same social category.* Endogamy limits marriage prospects to others of the same age, village, race, religion, or social class. By contrast, **exogamy** is *marriage between people of different social categories.* In rural India, for example, a person is expected to marry someone from the same caste (endogamy) but from a different village (exogamy). The reason for endogamy is that people of similar position pass along their standing to

their children, maintaining the traditional social hierarchy. Exogamy, on the other hand, links communities and encourages the spread of culture.

In higher-income nations, laws permit only **monogamy** (from the Greek, meaning "one union"), *marriage that unites two partners.* Global Map 13–1 on page 374 shows that monogamy is the rule throughout the Americas and Europe. But many lower-income countries, especially in Africa and southern Asia, permit **polygamy** (Greek, "many unions"), *marriage that unites a person with two or more spouses.* Polygamy has two forms. By far the more common is *polygyny* (Greek, "many women"), a form of marriage that unites one man and two or more women. For example, Islamic nations in the Middle East and Africa permit men up to four wives. Even so, most Islamic families are monogamous because few men can afford to support several wives and even more children. *Polyandry* (Greek, "many men") unites one woman and two or more men. This extremely rare pattern exists in Tibet, a mountainous land where agriculture is difficult. There, polyandry discourages the division of land into parcels too small to support a family and divides the work of farming among many men.

Most of the world's societies at some time have permitted more than one marital pattern. Even so, most marriages have been monogamous (Murdock, 1965, orig. 1949). The historical preference for monogamy reflects two facts of life: Supporting several spouses is very expensive, and the number of men and women in most societies is roughly equal.

WINDOW ON THE WORLD

GLOBAL MAP 13-1 Marital Form in Global Perspective

Monogamy is the only legal form of marriage throughout the Western Hemisphere and in much of the rest of the world. In most African nations and in southern Asia, however, polygamy is permitted by law. In many cases, this practice reflects the historic influence of Islam, a religion that allows a man to have up to four wives. Even so, most marriages in these countries are monogamous, primarily for financial reasons.

Source: *Peters Atlas of the World* (1990).

Given the high level of divorce in the United States, do you think it would be more accurate to call our marriage system "serial monogamy" (one partner after another)? Explain.

RESIDENTIAL PATTERNS

Just as societies regulate mate selection, they also designate where a couple may live. In preindustrial societies, most newlyweds live with one set of parents who offer protection, support, and assistance. Most often, married couples live with or near the husband's family, an arrangement called *patrilocality* (Greek, "place of the father"). But some societies, including the North American Iroquois, favor *matrilocality* ("place of the mother"), in which couples live with or near the wife's family. Societies that engage in frequent local warfare tend toward patrilocality so that sons remain close to home to offer protection. Societies that engage in distant warfare may be patrilocal or matrilocal, depending on whether sons or daughters have greater economic value (Ember & Ember, 1971, 1991).

Industrial societies show yet another pattern. Finances permitting, they favor *neolocality* (Greek, "new place"), in which a married couple lives apart from both sets of parents.

PATTERNS OF DESCENT

Descent refers to *the system by which members of a society trace kinship over generations.* Most preindustrial societies trace kinship through just one side of the family. *Patrilineal descent,* the more common pattern, traces kinship through males, and property flows from fathers to sons. Patrilineal descent characterizes most pastoral and agrarian societies, in which men produce the most valued resources. *Matrilineal descent,* by which people define only the mother's side as kin and property passes from mothers to daughters, is found in horticultural societies where women are the main food producers.

Industrial societies with greater gender equality recognize *bilateral descent* ("two-sided descent"), in which children recognize people on both the father's side and the mother's side of the family as relatives. Property may also pass from parents to both sons and daughters.

> YOUR TURN
>
> In terms of patterns of descent, how would you describe the common practice of a woman's adopting her husband's last name after marriage?

PATTERNS OF AUTHORITY

Worldwide, polygyny, patrilocality, and patrilineal descent are dominant and reflect the global pattern of patriarchy. In industrial societies such as the United States, men are still typically heads of households, and most U.S. parents give children their father's last name. However, more egalitarian families are evolving, especially as the share of women in the labor force goes up.

Theoretical Analysis of Family

As in earlier chapters, the various theoretical approaches offer a range of insights about family.

FUNCTIONS OF FAMILY: STRUCTURAL-FUNCTIONAL ANALYSIS

According to the structural-functional approach, the family performs many vital tasks. For this reason, the family is sometimes called the "backbone of society."

1. **Socialization.** As noted in Chapter 3 ("Socialization: From Infancy to Old Age"), the family is the first and most important setting for child rearing. Ideally, parents help children develop into well-integrated and contributing members of society (Parsons & Bales, 1955). Of course, family socialization continues throughout the life cycle. Adults change within marriage, and as any parent knows, mothers and fathers learn as much from their children as their children learn from them.

2. **Regulation of sexual activity.** Every culture regulates sexual activity in the interest of maintaining kinship organization and property rights. As discussed in Chapter 6 ("Sexuality and Society"), the **incest taboo** is *a norm forbidding sexual relations or marriage between certain relatives.* Although the incest taboo exists in every society, exactly which relatives cannot marry varies from one culture to another (Murdock, 1965, orig. 1949).

   Reproduction between close relatives of any species can result in mental and physical damage to offspring. Yet only humans observe an incest taboo, suggesting that the key reason for controlling incest is social. Why? First, the incest taboo limits sexual competition in families by restricting sex to spouses. Second, because kinship defines people's rights and obligations toward one another, reproduction between close relatives would hopelessly confuse kinship ties and threaten the social order. Third, forcing people to marry beyond their immediate families ties together the larger society.

3. **Social placement.** Families are not needed for people to reproduce, but they do help maintain social organization. Parents pass on their own social identity—in terms of race, ethnicity, religion, and social class—to their children at birth.

4. **Material and emotional security.** Many people view the family as a "haven in a heartless world," offering physical protection, emotional support, and financial

Women have long been taught to see marriage as the key to a happy life. Social-conflict theory, however, points to the fact that marriage often means a lifetime sentence of unpaid domestic labor. Susan Pyzow's painting, *Bridal Bouquet,* makes the point.

© Susan Pyzow, *Bridal Bouquet,* watercolor on paper, 10 × 13.5 in. Studio SPM Inc.

assistance. Perhaps this is why people living in families tend to be happier, healthier, and wealthier than people living alone (Goldstein & Kinney, 2001; U.S. Census Bureau, 2006).

CRITICAL REVIEW Structural-functional analysis explains why society, at least as we know it, is built on families. But this approach glosses over the diversity of U.S. family life and ignores how other social institutions (such as government) could meet at least some of the same human needs. Finally, structural-functionalism overlooks

the negative aspects of family life, including patriarchy and family violence.

✔ **YOUR LEARNING** Identify four important functions of family for society.

INEQUALITY AND FAMILY: SOCIAL-CONFLICT AND FEMINIST ANALYSIS

Like the structural-functional approach, the social-conflict approach, including feminist analysis, considers the family as central to our way of life. But instead of focusing on ways that kinship benefits society, this approach points out how family perpetuates social inequality.

1. **Property and inheritance.** Friedrich Engels (1902, orig. 1884) traced the origin of the family to men's need (especially in the higher classes) to identify heirs so that they could hand down property to their sons. Families thus concentrate wealth and reproduce the class structure in each new generation.

2. **Patriarchy.** Feminists link the family to patriarchy. To know their heirs, men must control the sexuality of women. Families therefore transform women into the sexual and economic property of men. A century ago in the United States, most wives' earnings belonged to their husbands. Today, women still bear most of the responsibility for child rearing and housework (Benokraitis & Feagin, 1995; Stapinski, 1998; England, 2001).

3. **Race and ethnicity.** Racial and ethnic categories persist over generations only to the degree that people marry others like themselves. Endogamous marriage supports racial and ethnic hierarchies.

CRITICAL REVIEW Social-conflict and feminist analysis shows another side of family life: its role in social stratification. Friedrich Engels criticized the family as part and parcel of capitalism. But noncapitalist societies also have families (and family problems). The family may be linked to social inequality, as Engels argued, but it carries out societal functions not easily accomplished by other means.

✔ **YOUR LEARNING** Point to three ways in which families support social inequality.

CONSTRUCTING FAMILY LIFE: MICRO-LEVEL ANALYSIS

Both the structural-functional and social-conflict approaches view the family as a structural system. By contrast, micro-level analysis explores how individuals shape and experience family life.

APPLYING THEORY

Family

	Structural-Functional Approach	Social-Conflict and Feminist Approaches	Symbolic-Interaction and Social-Exchange Approaches
What is the level of analysis?	Macro-level	Macro-level	Micro-level
What is the importance of family for society?	The family performs vital tasks, including socializing the young and providing emotional and financial support for members. The family helps regulate sexual activity.	The family perpetuates social inequality by handing down wealth from one generation to the next. The family supports patriarchy as well as racial and ethnic inequality.	The symbolic-interaction approach explains that the reality of family life is constructed by members in their interaction. The social-exchange approach shows that courtship typically brings together people who offer the same level of advantages.

The Symbolic-Interaction Approach

Ideally, family living offers an opportunity for *intimacy*, a word with Latin roots that mean "sharing fear." As family members share many activities and establish trust, they build emotional bonds. Of course, the fact that parents act as authority figures often limits their closeness with younger children. Only as young people approach adulthood do kinship ties open up to include sharing confidences with greater intimacy (Macionis, 1978).

The Social-Exchange Approach

Social-exchange analysis, another micro-level approach, describes courtship and marriage as forms of negotiation (Blau, 1964). Dating allows each person to assess the advantages and disadvantages of a potential spouse. In essence, exchange analysts suggest, people "shop around" to make the best "deal" they can.

In patriarchal societies, gender roles dictate the elements of exchange: Men bring wealth and power to the marriage marketplace, and women bring beauty. The importance of beauty explains women's traditional concern with their appearance and sensitivity about revealing their age. But as women have joined the labor force and have become less dependent on men to support them, the terms of exchange are converging for men and women.

CRITICAL REVIEW Micro-level analysis balances structural-functional and social-conflict visions of the family as an institutional system. Both the symbolic-interaction and social-exchange approaches focus on the individual experience of family life. However, micro-level analysis misses the bigger picture: The experience of family life is similar for people in the same social and economic categories.

The Applying Theory table summarizes what we learn from the three theoretical approaches to family life.

✓ **YOUR LEARNING** How does a micro-level approach to understanding family differ from a macro-level approach?

Stages of Family Life

Members of our society recognize several distinct stages of family life across the life course.

COURTSHIP AND ROMANTIC LOVE

 November 2, Kandy, Sri Lanka. Winding through the rain forest of this beautiful island, our van driver, Harry, recounts how he met his wife. Actually, it was more of an arrangement: The two families were Buddhist and of the same caste. "We got along well, right from the start," recalls Harry. "We had the same background. I suppose either she or I could have said no. But 'love marriages' happen in the city, not in the village where I grew up."

In rural Sri Lanka, as in preindustrial societies throughout the world, most people consider courtship too important to be left to the young. *Arranged marriages* are alliances between two extended families of similar social standing and usually involve an exchange not just of chil-

Early to Wed: A Report from Rural India

Sumitra Jogi cries as her wedding is about to begin. Are they tears of joy? Not exactly. This "bride" is an eleven-month-old squirming in the arms of her mother. The groom? A boy of six.

In a remote village in India's western state of Rajasthan, the two families gather at midnight to celebrate a traditional wedding ritual. It is May 2, in Hindu tradition an especially good day to marry. Sumitra's father smiles as the ceremony begins; her mother cradles the infant, who has fallen asleep. The groom, wearing a special costume and a red and gold turban on his head, gently reaches up and grasps the baby's hand. Then, as the ceremony ends, the young boy leads the child and mother around the wedding fire three-and-one-half times while the audience beams at the couple's first steps together as husband and wife.

Child weddings are illegal in India, but traditions are strong in rural regions, and marriage laws are hard to enforce. As a result, thousands of children marry each year. "In rural Rajasthan," explains one social worker, "all the girls are married by age fourteen. These are poor, illiterate families, and they don't want to keep girls past their first menstrual cycle."

For now, Sumitra Jogi will remain with her parents. But in eight or ten years, a second ceremony will send her to live with her husband's family, and her married life will begin.

If the reality of marriage is years in the future, why do families push their children to marry at such an early age? Parents of girls know that the younger the bride, the smaller the dowry offered to the groom's family. Also, when girls marry this young, there is no question about their virginity, which raises their value on the marriage market. No one in these situations thinks about love or the fact that the children are too young to understand what is taking place (J. W. Anderson, 1995).

The two-year-old girl on the left is breastfeeding during her wedding ceremony in a small village in the state of Rajasthan, India; her new husband is eight years old. Although outlawed, such arranged marriages involving children are still known to take place in traditional, remote areas of India.

WHAT DO YOU THINK?

1. Why are arranged marriages common in very traditional communities?

2. List several advantages and disadvantages of arranged marriages from the point of view of the families involved.

3. Can you point to ways in which mate selection in the United States is "arranged" by society?

---

dren but also of wealth and favors. Romantic love has little to do with marriage, and parents may make such arrangements when their children are very young. A century ago in Sri Lanka and India, half of all girls married before age fifteen (Mayo, 1927; Mace & Mace, 1960). As the Thinking Globally box explains, in some parts of rural India, child marriage is still found today.

Industrialization both erodes the importance of extended families and weakens traditions. As young people begin the process of choosing their own mate, dating sharpens courtship skills and allows sexual experimentation. Mar-

riage is delayed until young people complete their education and gain the experience needed to select a suitable partner.

Our culture celebrates *romantic love*—affection and sexual passion toward another person—as the basis for marriage. We find it hard to imagine marriage without love, and popular culture—from fairy tales such as "Cinderella" to today's television sitcoms and dramas—portrays love as the key to a successful marriage.

Our society's emphasis on romantic love motivates young people to "leave the nest" to form families of their own; physical passion may also help a new couple through difficult adjustments in living together (W. J. Goode, 1959). On the other hand, because feelings change over time, romantic love is a less stable foundation for marriage than

 Check out how people use the internet to find partners at http://www.syl.com

social and economic considerations, one reason that the divorce rate is much higher in the United States than in nations where culture limits the choice of a partner.

But even in our country, sociologists point out, society aims Cupid's arrow more than we like to think. Most people fall in love with others of the same race, of comparable age, and of similar social class. Our society "arranges" marriages by encouraging **homogamy** (literally, "like marrying like"), *marriage between people with the same social characteristics.*

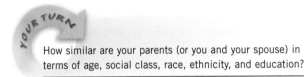

How similar are your parents (or you and your spouse) in terms of age, social class, race, ethnicity, and education?

SETTLING IN: IDEAL AND REAL MARRIAGE

Our culture gives young people an idealized, "happily ever after" picture of marriage. Such optimism can lead to disappointment, especially for women, who are taught that marriage is the key to happiness. Also, romantic love involves a lot of fantasy: We fall in love with others not always as they are but as we want them to be.

Sexuality, too, can be a source of disappointment. In the romantic haze of falling in love, people may see marriage as an endless sexual honeymoon, only to face the sobering realization that sex eventually becomes a less-than-all-consuming passion. Although the frequency of marital sex does decline over time, about two in three married people report that they are satisfied with the sexual dimension of their relationship. In general, couples with the best sexual relationships experience the most satisfaction in their marriages. Sex may not be the key to marital happiness, but more often than not, good sex and good relationships go together (Blumstein & Schwartz, 1983; Laumann et al., 1994).

Infidelity—sexual activity outside marriage—is another area where the reality of marriage does not match our cultural ideal. In a recent survey, 92 percent of U.S. adults said sex outside of marriage is "always wrong" or "almost always wrong." Even so, 21 percent of men and 13 percent of women indicated (in a private, written questionnaire) that they had been sexually unfaithful to their partners at least once (NORC, 2005:291, 1702).

Although the trend is toward less and less homogamy, it is still true that people who get married are likely to have many factors in common, including age, class, race and ethnicity, and level of education.

CHILD REARING

Despite the demands children make on us, U.S. adults overwhelmingly identify raising children as one of life's great joys (NORC, 2005:1480). Today, about half of U.S. adults say that two children is the ideal number, and few people want more than three (NORC, 2005:1478–79, 287). This is a change from two centuries ago, when *eight* children was the U.S. average.

Big families pay off in preindustrial societies because children supply needed labor. People therefore regard having children as a wife's duty, and in the absence of effective birth control, childbearing is a regular event. Of course, a high death rate in preindustrial societies prevents many children from reaching adulthood; as late as 1900, one-third of children in the United States died by age ten.

Economically speaking, industrialization transforms children from an asset to a liability. It now costs more than $200,000 to raise one child, including college tuition (Lino, 2006). No wonder the U.S. average steadily dropped during the twentieth century to one child per family![2]

---

[2]According to the U.S. Census Bureau, the mean number of children per family was 0.86 in 2005. Among all families, the medians were 0.83 for whites, 1.04 for African Americans, and 1.21 for Hispanics.

"Son, you're all grown up now. You owe me two hundred and fourteen thousand dollars."

The trend toward smaller families is most pronounced in high-income nations. The picture differs in low-income countries in Latin America, Asia, and especially Africa, where many women have few alternatives to bearing children. In such societies, as a glance back at Global Map 1–1 on page 3 shows, between four and six children is still the norm.

Parenting is a very expensive, lifelong commitment. As our society has given people greater choice about family life, more U.S. adults have decided to delay childbirth or to remain childless. In 1960, almost 90 percent of women between the ages of twenty-five and twenty-nine who had ever married had at least one child; today, this proportion is just 70 percent (U.S. Census Bureau, 2005).

About two-thirds of parents in the United States claim they would like to devote more of their time to child rearing (Snell, 1990; K. Clark, 2002). But unless we accept a lower standard of living, the need for income demands that most parents pursue careers outside the home, even if that means giving less attention to their families. For many families, including Rosa Yniguez's family described in the opening to this chapter, having fewer children is an important step toward raising their standard of living.

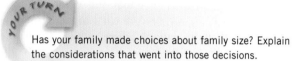

Has your family made choices about family size? Explain the considerations that went into those decisions.

Children of working parents spend most of the day at school. But after school, about 3.3 million youngsters (15 percent of six- to twelve-year-olds) are *latchkey kids* who must fend for themselves (Vandivere et al., 2003). Traditionalists in the "family values" debate charge that many mothers work at the expense of their children, who receive less parenting. Progressives reply that such criticism unfairly blames women for wanting the same opportunities men have long enjoyed.

Congress took a small step toward easing the conflict between family and job responsibilities by passing the Family and Medical Leave Act in 1993. This law allows up to ninety days' unpaid leave from work for either parent to care for a new child or deal with a serious family emergency. Still, most adults in this country have to juggle parental and job responsibilities. When mothers 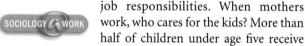 work, who cares for the kids? More than half of children under age five receive care from a parent (27 percent) or a relative (26 percent). The remaining 47 percent of young children are cared for by a nonrelative: 29 percent attend day care or preschool, 13 percent are cared for in a nonrelative's home, and 5 percent are cared for in their own home by a nanny or babysitter (Urban Institute, 2004).

THE FAMILY IN LATER LIFE

Increasing life expectancy in the United States means that couples who stay married do so for a longer time. By age sixty, most have completed the task of raising children. At this point, marriage brings a return to living with only a spouse.

Like the birth of children, their departure—creating an "empty nest"—requires adjustments, although a marriage often becomes closer and more satisfying. Years of living together may lessen a couple's sexual passion, but understanding and commitment often increase.

Personal contact with children usually continues because most older adults live near at least one of their grown children. One-third of all U.S. adults (60 million) are grandparents, many of whom help with child care and other responsibilities. Among African Americans (who have a high rate of single parenting), grandmothers have an especially important position in family life (Clemetson, 2000; U.S. Census Bureau, 2003).

The other side of the coin is that adults in midlife now provide more care for aging parents. The "empty nest" may not be filled by a parent coming to live in the home, but many adults find that caring for parents living to eighty and beyond can be as taxing as raising young children. The oldest of the "baby boomers"—now sixty—are called the "sandwich generation" because many, especially women, will spend as many years caring for their aging parents as they did caring for their children (Lund, 1993).

The final and surely the most difficult transition in married life comes with the death of a spouse. Wives typically outlive husbands because of their greater life expectancy and the fact that women usually marry men several years older than themselves. Wives can thus expect to spend some years as widows. The challenge of living alone after the death of a spouse is especially great for men, who usually have fewer friends than widows and may lack housekeeping skills.

U.S. Families: Class, Race, and Gender

Dimensions of inequality—social class, ethnicity, race, and gender—are powerful forces that shape marriage and family life. This discussion addresses each of these factors in turn, but bear in mind that they overlap in our lives.

SOCIAL CLASS

Social class determines both a family's financial security and its range of opportunities. Interviewing working-class women, Lillian Rubin (1976) found that wives thought a good husband was a man who held a steady job, did not drink too much, and was not violent. Rubin's middle-class respondents, by contrast, never mentioned such things; these women simply *assumed* that a husband would provide a safe and secure home. Their ideal husband was a man with whom they could talk easily, sharing feelings and experiences.

Clearly, what women (and men) hope for in marriage—and what they end up with—is linked to their social class. Much the same holds for children: Boys and girls lucky enough to be born into more affluent families enjoy better mental and physical health, develop more self-confidence, and go on to greater achievement than children born

to poor parents (McLeod & Shanahan, 1993; Duncan et al., 1998).

ETHNICITY AND RACE

Although ethnicity and race also shape families, American Indian, Latino, and African American families (like all families) do not fit any one stereotype (Allen, 1995).

American Indian Families

American Indians display a wide variety of family types. Some patterns emerge, however, among people who migrate from tribal reservations to cities. Women and men who arrive in cities often seek out others—especially kin and members of the same tribe—for help in getting settled. One recent study tells the story of two women migrants to the San Francisco area who met at a meeting of an Indian organization and realized they were of the same tribe. The women and their children decided to share an apartment, and soon after, the children began to refer to one another as brothers, sisters, and cousins. As the months passed, the two mothers came to think of themselves as sisters (Lobo, 2002).

Migration also creates "fluid households" with changing membership. In another case from this same study, a woman, her aunt, and their children rented a large apartment in San Francisco. Over the course of several months, they welcomed into their home more than thirty other urban migrants, each of whom stayed for a short time while looking for housing of their own. Such patterns of mutual assistance, involving real or fictional kinship, are common among low-income people.

American Indians who leave tribal reservations for the cities typically are better off than those who stay behind. Because people in reservations have a hard time finding work, they cannot easily form stable marriages, and problems such as alcoholism and drug abuse shatter the ties between parent and child. "In the *Times*" on pages 382–83 describes the crisis facing families on the Lummi Indian reservation in Washington, where half the children do not live with even one of their biological parents.

Latino Families

Many Latinos enjoy the loyalty and support of extended families. Traditionally, Hispanic parents exercise greater control over children's courtship, considering marriage an alliance of families and not just a union based on romantic love. Some Hispanic families also follow conventional gender roles, prizing *machismo*—strength, daring, and sexual conquest—among men and treating women with respect but also close supervision.

The New York Times

April 5, 2005

Crisis of Indian Children Intensifies as Families Fail

By SARAH KERSHAW

LUMMI INDIAN RESERVATION, Wash., March 29—The very full house on Gumel Place was steeped in the usual loud weekend chaos when 14-year-old Cecilia Morris burst through the door.

"Hey," she said. "Is Mom in jail?"

No, said her uncle, Jasper Cladoosby, but her mother had gone back into drug treatment. Her father is the one in prison.

Mr. Cladoosby, 27, who is raising four of his own children along with Cecilia and two of her sisters, is one of possibly hundreds of uncles, aunts, grandparents and others caring for children whose parents are unable to raise them because of dire poverty, alcoholism and epidemic drug abuse on this reservation on Bellingham Bay in Northwest Washington. . . .

Tribal officials here estimate that fewer than half of the 1,500 children on the reservation are living with a parent full time. A breakdown of the American Indian family, mirrored throughout reservations across the country, has been building for generations but is now growing worse, tribal and outside experts say.

The crisis gained new attention this month after a troubled youth went on a shooting rampage on the Red Lake reservation in northern Minnesota. The broken family of the teenager, Jeff Weise, 16, who the police say killed nine people and then himself, is typical among Indians. With his father dead and his mother disabled by a drunken-driving accident, he was staying with his grandmother on the reservation, after living with his mother, before her accident, in Minneapolis. . . .

Even though tribes have made great strides over the last two decades in keeping children from troubled homes, a cascade of statistics paints a bleak picture of the roughly 850,000 Indian and Alaska Native youths, about half of them living on Indian reservations, according to the Census Bureau. Compared with whites and with other minorities, Indians have extremely high teenage suicide rates, are more likely to get into fights at school and carry weapons to school, and have high rates of substance abuse, several recent reports show. . . .

According to the latest federal statistics, nearly 10,000 Indian and Alaska Native children, or about 1.2 percent, are in foster care, living with relatives or others. (Indians and Alaska Natives make up 1.5 percent of the nation's population.) The federal data, from the Department of Health and Human Services, show

However, assimilation into the larger society is changing these traditional patterns. In the opening story of this chapter, we explained that many women who come to California from Mexico favor smaller families. Similarly, many Puerto Ricans who migrate to New York do not maintain the strong extended families they knew in Puerto Rico. Traditional male authority over women has also lessened, especially among wealthy Latino families, whose number has tripled in the past twenty years (Lach, 1999; Navarro, 2004).

Overall, however, the typical Hispanic family had an income of just $37,867 in 2005, or 67 percent of the national average (U.S. Census Bureau, 2006). Many Hispanic families suffer the stress of unemployment and other poverty-related problems.

African American Families

The U.S. Census Bureau reports that the typical African American family earned $35,464 in 2005, which was 63 percent of the national average. People of African ancestry are three times as likely as non-Hispanic whites to be poor, and poverty means that parents and children are likely to experience unemployment, substandard housing, and poor health.

Under these circumstances, maintaining stable family ties is difficult. Consider that 28 percent of African American women in their forties have never married, compared with about 8 percent of non-Hispanic white women of the same age. This means that African American women—often with children—are more likely to be single heads of households. Figure 13–1 on page 384 shows that women headed 45 percent of African American families in 2005, compared with 23 percent of Hispanic families, 13 percent of non-Hispanic white families, and 7 percent of Asian and Pacific Islander families (U.S. Census Bureau, 2006).

Regardless of race, single-mother families are always at high risk of poverty. Twenty-two percent of U.S. families headed by non-Hispanic white women are poor. The higher poverty rate among families headed by African American women (36 percent) and Hispanic women (39 percent) is

that about 1.8 percent of black children and about 0.5 percent of white children are in foster care. . . .

Many experts say the crisis for Indian children stems not so much from living without their parents—the role of the extended family in child rearing is crucial in Indian culture—but from a lack of mental health services and recreation on reservations, some so destitute that there is no swimming pool or basketball court, let alone a counselor.

Money for health and mental health care on reservations, which comes mostly from the federal government but is increasingly supplemented by gambling revenues, falls far short of the demand, many experts say.

Here at Lummi Nation, the Silver Reef Casino opened in 2002 but has only recently begun to yield steady profits. The tribe has invested $2 million in a new home, scheduled to open April 13, that can hold 28 troubled children; a "safe home" for youths; and more counselors. Now, there are seven counselors available for the 1,500 children, well above the national average for Indians.

But tribal officials acknowledge that Lummi families still bear the brunt of caring for neglected children and emotionally supporting them. . . .

Justin Zollner, . . . 16, has an anger problem. The . . . father has "been out of the picture" for a long time. . . .

Justin has uncles who live nearby, and they attend his football games and take him canoe racing, a passionate pursuit for the tribe. . . .

Still, it is painful when Justin talks, fairly often, about missing his father. "Right now, I kind of wish my dad was still here because I've played football for like seven years now, and he never got to watch me." . . .

WHAT DO YOU THINK?

1. How does this article show the effect of societal structures such as poverty on families?

2. How do you think poverty and weak parent-child ties affect the children described in this article?

3. What should be done to address the problems discussed in this article?

Adapted from the original article by Sarah Kershaw published in *The New York Times* on April 5, 2005. Copyright © 2005 by The New York Times Company. Reprinted with permission.

strong evidence of how the intersection of class, race, and gender can put women at a disadvantage. African American families with both wife and husband in the home, which represent 46 percent of the total, are much stronger economically, earning 80 percent as much as comparable non-Hispanic white families. But 68 percent of African American children are born to single women, and 35 percent of African American boys and girls are growing up poor today, meaning that these families carry much of the burden of child poverty in the United States (Martin et al., 2005; U.S. Census Bureau, 2006).

Ethnically and Racially Mixed Marriages

Most spouses have similar social backgrounds with regard to class and race. But over the course of the twentieth century, ethnicity came to matter less and less. A woman of German and French ancestry might readily marry a man of Irish and English background without inviting disapproval from their families or from society in general.

Race has been a more powerful barrier. Before a 1967 Supreme Court decision (*Loving* v. *Virginia*), interracial marriage was illegal in sixteen states. Today, African, Asian, and Native Americans make up 17 percent of the U.S. population; if people ignored race in choosing spouses, we would expect about the same share of marriages to be mixed. The actual proportion of mixed marriages is 4 percent, showing that race still matters in social relations. But the number of racially mixed marriages is rising steadily.

The single most common type of interracial married couple is a white husband and an Asian wife, which accounts for about 14 percent of all interracial married couples. About one-fourth of all interracial married couples contain at least one partner who claimed a multiracial identity in the 2000 census. Interracial married couples are most likely to live in the West; in five states—Hawaii, Alaska, California, Nevada, and Oklahoma—more than 10 percent of all married couples are interracial (Lee & Edmonston, 2005).

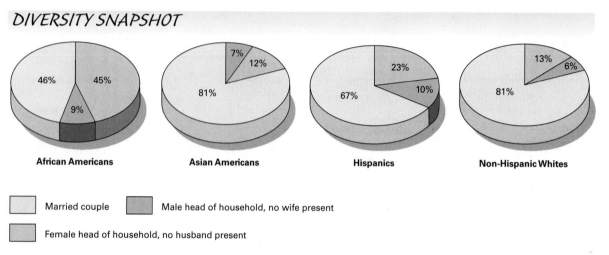

African Americans — 46%, 45%, 9%

Asian Americans — 81%, 7%, 12%

Hispanics — 67%, 23%, 10%

Non-Hispanic Whites — 81%, 13%, 6%

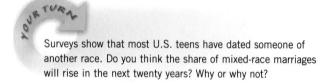

Married couple

Male head of household, no wife present

Female head of household, no husband present

FIGURE 13–1 Family Form in the United States, 2005

All racial and ethnic categories show variations in family form.

Source: U.S. Census Bureau (2006).

YOUR TURN

Surveys show that most U.S. teens have dated someone of another race. Do you think the share of mixed-race marriages will rise in the next twenty years? Why or why not?

GENDER

Jessie Bernard (1982, orig. 1973) says that every marriage is actually two different relationships: the woman's marriage and the man's marriage. The reason is that few marriages have two equal partners. Although patriarchy has diminished, many people still expect husbands to be older and taller than their wives and to have more important, better-paid jobs.

Why, then, do many people think that marriage benefits women more than men? The positive stereotype of the carefree bachelor contrasts sharply with the negative image of the lonely spinster, suggesting that women are fulfilled only through being wives and mothers.

However, Bernard concluded, married women actually have poorer mental health, less happiness, and more passive attitudes toward life than single women do. Married men, on the other hand, generally live longer, are mentally better off, and report being happier than single men. These differences suggest why, after divorce, men are more eager than women to find a new partner.

Bernard concludes that there is no better assurance of long life, health, and happiness for a man than having a woman well socialized to devote her life to taking care of

him and providing the security of a well-ordered home. She is quick to add that marriage *could* be healthful for women if husbands did not dominate wives and expect them to do almost all the housework.

Transitions and Problems in Family Life

The newspaper columnist Ann Landers once remarked that one marriage in twenty is wonderful, five in twenty are good, ten in twenty are tolerable, and the remaining four are "pure hell." Families can be a source of joy, but the reality of family life often falls short of the ideal.

DIVORCE

U.S. society strongly supports marriage, and about nine out of ten people at some point "tie the knot." But many of today's marriages unravel. Figure 13–2 shows the tenfold increase in the U.S. divorce rate over the past century. By 2005, almost four in ten marriages were ending in divorce (for African Americans, the rate was about six in ten). Ours is the highest divorce rate in the world, about one-and-one-half times as high as in Canada and Japan and nearly six times higher than in Italy (Japanese Ministry of Health, Labour, and Welfare, 2006).

Causes of Divorce

The high U.S. divorce rate has many causes (Furstenberg & Cherlin, 1991; Etzioni, 1993; Popenoe, 1999; Greenspan, 2001):

1. **Individualism is on the rise.** Today's family members spend less time together. We have become more individualistic, more concerned with our own personal happiness than with the well-being of our families and children.

2. **Romantic love fades.** Because our culture bases marriage on romantic love, relationships may fail as sexual passion fades. Many people end a marriage in favor of a new relationship that promises renewed excitement and romance.

3. **Women are less dependent on men.** Women's increasing participation in the labor force has reduced wives' financial dependency on their husbands. Thus women find it easier to leave unhappy marriages.

4. **Many of today's marriages are stressful.** With both partners working outside the home in most cases, jobs leave less time and energy for family life. This makes raising children harder than ever. Children do stabilize some marriages, but divorce is most common during the early years of marriage when many couples have young children.

5. **Divorce is socially acceptable.** Divorce no longer carries the powerful stigma it did several generations ago. Family and friends are now less likely to discourage couples in conflict from divorcing.

6. **A divorce is easier to get.** In the past, courts required divorcing couples to demonstrate that one or both were guilty of behavior such as adultery or physical abuse. Today, all states allow divorce if a couple simply states that the marriage has failed. Concern about easy divorce, shared by more than half of U.S. adults, has led some states to consider rewriting their marriage laws (Phillips, 2001; NORC, 2005).

Who Divorces?

At greatest risk of divorce are young couples—especially those who marry after a brief courtship—who lack money and emotional maturity. The chance of divorce also rises if a couple marries after an unexpected pregnancy or if one or both partners have substance abuse problems. People whose parents divorced also have a higher divorce rate themselves. Research suggests that a role-modeling effect is at work: Children who see parents go through divorce are more likely to consider divorce themselves (Amato, 2001). Finally, people who are not religious are more likely to divorce than those who have strong religious beliefs.

Divorce is also more common if both partners have successful careers, perhaps because of the strains of a two-career marriage but also because financially secure people may not

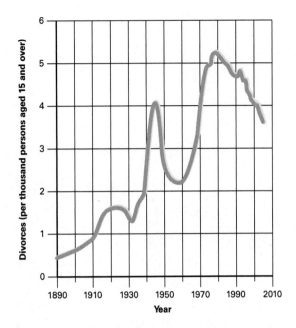

FIGURE 13-2 Divorce Rate for the United States, 1890–2005

Over the long term, the U.S. divorce rate has gone up. Since about 1980, however, the trend has been downward.

Source: Munson & Sutton (2006).

feel that they have to remain in an unhappy home. Finally, men and women who divorce once are more likely to divorce again, probably because high-risk factors follow them from one marriage to another (Glenn & Shelton, 1985).

Divorce and Children

Because mothers usually gain custody of children but fathers typically earn more income, the well-being of many children depends on fathers' making court-ordered child support payments. Courts award child support in 60 percent of all divorces involving children. Yet in any given year, half of children legally entitled to support receive partial payments or no payments at all. Some 3.5 million "deadbeat dads" fail to support their youngsters. In response, federal legislation now requires employers to withhold money from the earnings of fathers or mothers who fail to pay up; it is a serious crime to refuse to make child support payments or move to another state to avoid making such payments (U.S. Census Bureau, 2006).

REMARRIAGE AND BLENDED FAMILIES

Four out of five people who divorce remarry, most within five years. Nationwide, about half of all marriages are now

Divorce may be a solution for a couple in an unhappy marriage, but it can be a problem for children who experience the withdrawal of a parent from their social world. In what ways can divorce be harmful to children? Is there a positive side to divorce? How might separating parents better prepare their children for the transition of parental divorce?

remarriages for at least one partner. Men, who benefit more from wedlock, are more likely than women to remarry.

Remarriage often creates *blended families,* composed of children and some combination of biological parents and stepparents. Members of blended families must therefore

 Learn more about remarriage and other family issues at http://www.cdc.gov/nchs/data/series/sr_23/sr23_022.pdf

define precisely who is part of the nuclear family. Adjustments are necessary; for example, a former "only child" may suddenly find that she now has two older brothers. At the same time, blended families offer both young and old the chance to relax rigid family roles (Furstenberg & Cherlin, 2001; McLanahan, 2002).

A girl who has been an only child becomes a part of a blended family and suddenly has two older brothers. What adjustments might she have to make?

FAMILY VIOLENCE

The ideal family is a source of pleasure and support. However, the disturbing reality of many homes is **family violence,** *emotional, physical, or sexual abuse of one family member by another.* The sociologist Richard J. Gelles calls the family "the most violent group in society with the exception of the police and the military" (quoted in Roesch, 1984:75).

Violence against Women

Family brutality often goes unreported to police. Even so, the U.S. Bureau of Justice Statistics (2005) estimates that about 700,000 people are victims of domestic violence each year. Of this total, 73 percent of cases involve violence against women, and the remaining 27 percent involve violence against men. Fully 33 percent of women who are victims of homicide (but just 3 percent of men) are killed by spouses or, more often, ex-spouses. Nationwide, the death toll from family violence is about 1,250 women each year. Overall, women are more likely to be injured by a family member than to be mugged or raped by a stranger or hurt in an automobile accident (Shupe, Stacey, & Hazlewood, 1987; Blankenhorn, 1995; Federal Bureau of Investigation, 2005).

Historically, the law defined wives as the property of their husbands, so no man could be charged with raping his wife. Today, however, all fifty states have *marital rape laws.* The law no longer regards domestic violence as a private, family matter and thus gives victims more options. Now, even without separation or divorce, a woman can obtain court protection from an abusive spouse, and all states have stalking laws that prohibit a person from following or otherwise threatening an estranged partner. Finally, communities across North America have established shelters to provide counseling and temporary housing for women and children driven from their homes by domestic violence.

Violence against Children

Family violence also victimizes children. Each year, there are roughly 3 million reports of alleged child abuse or neglect, with about 1,500 of them involving a child's death. Child

 See the articles and resources on this Web site to learn more about child abuse: http://www.nncc.org

abuse involves more than physical injury; abusive adults can also misuse power and trust to damage a child's emotional well-being. Child abuse and neglect are most common among the youngest and most vulnerable children (Besharov & Laumann, 1996).

Although child abusers conform to no simple stereotype, they are more likely to be women (58 percent) than men (42 percent). But almost all abusers share one trait: having been abused themselves as children. Researchers have found that violent behavior in close relationships is learned; in families, violence begets violence (S. Levine, 2001; U.S. Department of Health and Human Services, 2006).

Alternative Family Forms

Most families in the United States are still composed of a married couple who, at some point in their lives, raise children. But in recent decades, our society has displayed increasing diversity in family life.

ONE-PARENT FAMILIES

Thirty-one percent of U.S. families with children under eighteen have only one parent in the household, a proportion that doubled during the past generation. Put another way, more than one-fourth of U.S. children now live with only one parent, and about half will do so before reaching eighteen. One-parent families, 73 percent of which are headed by a single mother, result from divorce, death, or an unmarried person's decision to have a child.

Single parenthood increases a woman's risk of poverty because it limits her ability to work and to further her education. The opposite is also true: Poverty raises the odds that a woman will become a single mother. But single parenthood goes well beyond the poor: One-third of women in the United States become pregnant as teenagers, and many decide to raise their children whether they marry or not. Looking back at Figure 13–1, note that 54 percent of African American families are headed by a single parent. Single parenthood is less common among Hispanics (33 percent), Asian Americans (19 percent), and non-Hispanic whites (19 percent). In many single-parent families, mothers turn to their own mothers for support. In the United States, then, the rise in single parenting is tied to a declining role for fathers and the growing importance of grandparenting.

Research shows that growing up in a one-parent family usually puts children at a disadvantage. Some studies claim that because a father and a mother each make a distinctive contribution to a child's social development, it is unrealistic to expect a single parent to do as good a job alone. But the most serious problem for one-parent families, especially if that parent is a woman, is poverty. On average, children growing up in a single-parent family start out poorer, get less schooling, and end up with lower incomes as adults. Such children are also more likely to become single parents themselves (Popenoe, 1993a; Blankenhorn, 1995; Wu, 1996;

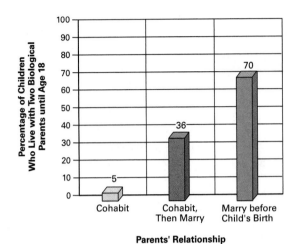

FIGURE 13-3 Parental Involvement in Children's Lives: Cohabiting and Married Parents

Marriage increases the odds that parents will share the same household with their child.

Source: Phillips (2001).

Duncan et al., 1998; Kantrowitz & Wingert, 2001; McLanahan, 2002).

COHABITATION

Cohabitation is *the sharing of a household by an unmarried couple.* In global perspective, cohabitation as a long-term form of family life, with or without children, is especially common in Sweden and other Scandinavian countries and is increasing in popularity in other European nations. In the United States, the number of cohabiting couples has increased from about 500,000 in 1970 to about 5.6 million today (4.9 million heterosexual couples and 700,000 homosexual couples), or about 9 percent of all couples. Almost half of people between twenty-five and forty-four years of age have cohabited at some point (U.S. Census Bureau, 2005).

Cohabiting tends to appeal more to independent-minded people and those who favor gender equality (Brines & Joyner, 1999). Most couples cohabit for no more than a few years; at that point, about half decide to marry and half split up. Mounting evidence suggests that living together may actually discourage marriage because partners (especially men) become used to low-commitment relationships. For this reason, cohabiting couples who have children—currently representing one-eighth of all births—are not always long-term parents. Figure 13–3 shows that just 5 percent of children born to cohabiting couples will live until age eighteen with both biological parents if the parents

APPLYING SOCIOLOGY

Should We Save the Traditional Family?

What are "traditional families"? Are they vital to our way of life or a barrier to progress? People use the term "traditional family" to mean a married couple who, at some point in their lives, raise children. Statistically speaking, traditional families are less common than they used to be. In 1950, as the figure shows, 90 percent of U.S. households were families: two or more people related by blood, marriage, or adoption. By 2005, owing to rising levels of divorce, cohabitation, and singlehood, just 68 percent of households were families.

"Traditional family" is more than just a term; it is also a moral statement. Support for the traditional family implies giving high value to becoming and staying married, putting children ahead of careers, and favoring two-parent families over various alternatives.

On one side of the debate, David Popenoe (1993a) warns of the decline of the traditional family since 1960. Back then, married couples with children living at home accounted for almost half of all households; today, the figure is 24 percent. Singlehood is

up, from 10 percent of households in 1960 to 26 percent today. And the divorce rate has risen by 60 percent since 1960, so that almost four in ten of today's marriages end in permanent separation. Because of both divorce

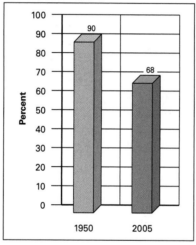

Share of U.S. Households That the Census Bureau Classifies as Families, 1950 and 2005

Families were a smaller share of all U.S. households in 2005 compared to 1950.

and the increasing number of children born to single women, the share of youngsters who will live with just one parent before age eighteen has quadrupled since 1960 to 50 percent. In other words, just one in four of today's children will grow up with two parents and go on to maintain a stable marriage as an adult.

In light of such data, Popenoe claims that it may not be an exaggeration to say that the family is falling apart. He sees a fundamental shift from a "culture of marriage" to a "culture of divorce," where traditional vows of marital commitment—"till death us do part"—now amount to little more than "as long as I am happy." Daniel Yankelovich (1994:20) summed it up this way:

> The quest for greater individual choice clashed directly with the obligations and social norms that held families and communities together in earlier years. People came to feel that questions of how to live and with whom to live were a matter of individual choice not to be governed by restrictive norms.

remain unmarried. The share rises to 36 percent among children whose parents marry at some point, but this is still half of the 70 percent figure for children whose parents married before they were born. When cohabiting couples with children separate, the involvement of both parents, especially with respect to financial support, is highly uncertain (Popenoe & Whitehead, 1999; Smock, 2000; Phillips, 2001; Scommegna, 2002).

GAY AND LESBIAN COUPLES

In 1989, Denmark became the first country to permit legal same-sex marriages. This change extended social legitimacy

to gay and lesbian couples and equalized advantages in inheritance, taxation, and joint property ownership. The Netherlands (2001), Belgium (2003), Canada (2003), and Spain (2005) have followed suit. Fifteen other European countries now recognize gay civil partnerships (Knox, 2004).

In the United States, the states of Vermont, Connecticut, and Hawaii, as well as a number of major cities including San Francisco and New York, have passed laws giving limited spousal benefits to gay and lesbian couples. Still, the U.S. Congress passed a law in 1996 defining marriage as joining one man and one woman, and until 2004, gay marriage remained illegal in all fifty states.

As a nation, we came to experience the bonds to marriage, family, children, job, community, and country as constraints that were no longer necessary. Commitments have loosened.

The negative consequences of the cultural trend toward weaker families, Popenoe continues, are obvious everywhere: As we pay less and less attention to children, the crime rate goes up, along with a host of other problem behaviors, including underage smoking and drinking, premarital sex, and teen suicide.

As Popenoe sees it, we must work hard and quickly to reverse current trends. Government cannot be the solution and may even be part of the problem: Since 1960, as families have weakened, government spending on social programs has soared fivefold. To save the traditional family, says Popenoe, we need a cultural turnaround, similar to what has happened with regard to cigarette smoking. In this case, we must replace our "me first" attitudes with commitment to spouses and children and publicly endorse the two-parent family as best for the well-being of children.

Judith Stacey (1993) provides a feminist viewpoint, saying "good riddance" to the traditional family. She claims that the traditional family is more problem than solution:

The family is not here to stay. Nor should we wish it were. On the contrary, I believe that all democratic people, whatever their kinship preferences, should work to hasten its demise (Stacey, 1990:269).

The main reason for rejecting the traditional family, Stacey explains, is that it perpetuates social inequality. Families play a key role in maintaining the class hierarchy by transferring wealth as well as "cultural capital" from one generation to the next. Feminists criticize the traditional family's patriarchal form, which subjects women to their husbands' authority and expects them to take most of the responsibility for housework and child care. Stacey adds that a society that values traditional families also denies homosexual men and women equal participation in social life.

Stacey thus applauds the breakdown of the traditional family as a measure of social progress. She does not consider the family a basic social institution but a political construction that elevates one category of people—affluent white men—above others, including women, homosexuals, and poor people.

Stacey also claims that the concept of the "traditional family" is increasingly irrelevant in a diverse society in which both men and women work for income. What our society needs, she concludes, is not a return to some golden age of the family but political and economic change, including income equality for women, universal health care, programs to reduce unemployment, and expanded sex education in the schools. Such measures not only help families but also ensure that people in diverse family forms receive the respect and dignity they deserve.

WHAT DO YOU THINK?

1. To strengthen families, David Popenoe suggests that parents put children ahead of their own careers by limiting their joint workweek to sixty hours. Do you agree? Why or why not?

2. Judith Stacey thinks that marriage is weaker today because women are rejecting patriarchal relationships. What do you think about this claim?

3. Do we need to change family patterns for the well-being of our children? As you see it, what specific changes are called for?

In 2004, however, the supreme court of Massachusetts ruled that gay couples had a right to marry, and legal marriages began in May of that year. The Massachusetts court decision prompted officials in San Francisco and a number of other U.S. cities to perform thousands of marriages for gay couples, despite state laws that banned such unions. Courts later declared those marriages to be illegal. In the November 2004 elections, voters in thirteen states passed ballot measures changing their state constitutions to recognize only marriages between one man and one woman.

The trend in public opinion is toward greater acceptance of homosexual relationships. About one-third of U.S. adults support gay marriage, and half support civil unions providing the rights enjoyed by married couples (Gallup, 2002; NORC, 2005:1477).

Most gay couples with children in the United States are raising the offspring of previous heterosexual unions; others have adopted children. But many gay parents are quiet about their sexual orientation, not wanting to draw unwelcome attention to their children or to themselves. In several widely publicized cases, courts have removed children from the custody of homosexual couples, citing the "best interests" of the children.

Gay parenting challenges many traditional ideas. But it also shows that many gay couples value family life as highly as heterosexuals do.

SINGLEHOOD

Because nine out of ten people in the United States marry, we tend to see singlehood as a temporary stage of life. However, increasing numbers of people are choosing to live alone. In 1950, only one household in ten contained a single person. By 2005, this share had risen to one in four, a total of 30 million single adults (U.S. Census Bureau, 2006).

Most striking is the rising number of single young women. In 1960, some 28 percent of women aged twenty to twenty-four were single; by 2003, the proportion had soared to 74 percent. Underlying this trend is women's greater participation in the labor force. Women who are economically secure view a husband as a matter of choice rather than a financial necessity and marry later or, in some cases, not at all (Edwards, 2000).

By midlife, many unmarried women sense a lack of available men. Because our society expects women to "marry up," the older a woman is, the more education she has, and the better her job, the more difficulty she has finding a suitable husband.

New Reproductive Technologies and Family

Recent medical advances involving new reproductive technologies are also changing families. In 1978, England's Louise Brown became the world's first "test-tube baby"; since then, tens of thousands of children have been conceived outside the womb.

Test-tube babies are the product of *in vitro fertilization,* in which doctors unite a woman's egg and a man's sperm "in glass" (usually not a test tube but a shallow dish) rather than in a woman's body. Doctors then either implant the resulting embryo in the womb of the woman who is to bear the child or freeze it for use at a later time.

At present, new reproductive technologies allow some couples who cannot conceive normally to have children. Looking ahead, these techniques may also help reduce the incidence of birth defects. Genetic screening of sperm and eggs would allow medical specialists to increase the odds for the birth of a healthy baby. But new reproductive technologies also raise difficult and troubling questions: When one woman carries an embryo developed from the egg of another, who is the mother? When a couple divorces, which spouse is entitled to use, or destroy, their frozen embryos? Should parents use genetic screening to select the traits of their child? Such questions remind us that technology changes faster than our ability to understand the consequences of its use (A. Cohen, 1998; Nock, Wright, & Sanchez, 1999).

Families: Looking Ahead

Family life in the United States will continue to change in years to come, and with change comes controversy. Advocates of "traditional family values" line up against those who support greater personal choice; the Applying Sociology box on pages 388–89 outlines some of the issues. Sociologists cannot predict the outcome of this debate, but we can suggest five likely future trends.

First, the divorce rate is likely to remain high, even in the face of evidence that marital breakups put children at higher risk of poverty. Today's marriages are about as durable as they were a century ago, when many were cut short by death. The difference is that now more couples *choose* to end marriages that fail to meet their expectations. Although the divorce rate has declined since 1980, it is unlikely that we will ever return to the low rates that marked the early decades of the twentieth century.

Second, family life in the future will be more diverse than ever. Cohabiting couples, one-parent families, gay and lesbian families, and blended families are all on the rise. Most families are still based on marriage, and most married couples still have children. But the diversity of family forms implies a trend toward more personal choice.

Third, men will play a limited role in child rearing. In the 1950s, a decade many people consider the "golden age" of families, men began to withdraw from active parenting (Snell, 1990; Stacey, 1990). In recent years, a countertrend

 Visit a Web site for stay-at-home fathers at http://www.slowlane.com

has become evident, with some older, highly educated fathers staying at home with young children, many using computer technology to continue their work. But the stay-at-home dad represents no more than 10 percent of fathers with young children (U.S. Census Bureau, 2004). The bigger picture is that the high divorce rate in the United States and the increase in single motherhood are weakening children's ties to fathers and increasing children's risk of poverty.

Fourth, families will continue to feel the effects of economic change. In many homes, both household partners work, reducing marriage and family to the interaction of weary men and women trying to fit a little "quality time" with their children into an already full schedule. The long-term effects of the two-career couple on families as we have known them are likely to be mixed.

Fifth and finally, the importance of new reproductive technologies will increase. Ethical concerns about whether what *can* be done *should* be done will surely slow these developments, but new reproductive technologies will continue to alter the traditional meaning of parenthood.

Despite the changes and controversies that have shaken the family in the United States, most people still report being happy as partners and parents. Marriage and family life will likely remain a foundation of our society for some time to come.

Religion: Basic Concepts

Like family, religion has played a central part in the drama of human history. Families have long used religious rituals to celebrate birth, recognize adulthood, and mourn the dead.

The French sociologist Emile Durkheim stated that religion involves "things that surpass the limits of our knowledge" (1965:62, orig. 1915). As human beings, we define most objects, events, and experiences as **profane** (from Latin, meaning "outside the temple"), *occurring as an ordinary element of everyday life.* But we also consider some things **sacred,** *set apart as extraordinary, inspiring awe and reverence.* Setting the sacred apart from the profane is the essence of all religious belief. **Religion,** then, is *a social institution involving beliefs and practices based on recognizing the sacred.*

There is great diversity in matters of faith, and nothing is sacred to everyone on Earth. Although people regard most books as profane, Jews believe that the Torah (the first five books of the Hebrew Bible or the Old Testament) is sacred, in the same way that Christians revere the Old and New Testaments of the Bible and Muslims exalt the Qur'an (Koran).

But no matter how a community of believers draws religious lines, Durkheim (1965:62, orig. 1915) explained, people understand profane things in terms of their everyday usefulness: We log on to the Internet with our computer or turn a key to start our car. What is sacred we reverently set apart from daily life, giving it a "forbidden" or "holy" aura. For example, Muslims remove their shoes before entering a mosque to avoid defiling a sacred place with soles that have touched the profane ground outside.

The sacred is embodied in *ritual,* or formal ceremonial behavior. Holy Communion is the central ritual of Christianity; to the Christian faithful, the wafer and wine consumed during Communion are treated not in a profane way as food but as the sacred symbols of the body and blood of Jesus Christ.

Because religion deals with ideas that transcend everyday experience, neither common sense nor sociology can prove or disprove religious doctrine. Religion is a matter of **faith,** *belief based on conviction rather than on scientific evidence.* The New Testament of the Bible defines faith as "the conviction of things not seen" (Hebrews 11:1) and urges Christians to "walk by faith, not by sight" (2 Corinthians 5:7).

Regularly taking part in religious rituals sharpens the distinction between the sacred and the profane. The wafer used in the Christian ritual of holy communion is never thought of in the everyday sense of food; it is a sacred symbol of the body of Christ.

Some people with strong religious beliefs may be disturbed by the thought of sociologists turning a scientific eye on what they hold sacred. However, sociological study is no threat to anyone's faith. Sociologists study religion just as they study family, to understand religious experiences around the world and how religion is tied to other social institutions. They make no judgments about whether a specific religion is "right" or "wrong." Sociological analysis takes a more worldly approach, seeking to understand why religion takes a particular form in one society or another and how religious activity affects society as a whole.

 Find online resources for the study of religion at http://www.princeton.edu/~csrelig/links/links.html

Theoretical Analysis of Religion

Sociologists apply the major theoretical approaches to the study of religion just as they do to any other topic. Each provides distinctive insights about the ways religion shapes social life.

FUNCTIONS OF RELIGION: STRUCTURAL-FUNCTIONAL ANALYSIS

According to Emile Durkheim (1965, orig. 1915), society has a life and power of its own beyond the life of any individual. In a sense, society itself is godlike, shaping the lives

Religion is founded on the concept of the sacred—that which is set apart as extraordinary and which demands our submission. Bowing, kneeling, or prostrating oneself are all ways of symbolically surrendering to a higher power. These Buddhist pilgrims are making their way to a holy place on Mount Kallas in western Tibet.

Durkheim identified three major functions of religion that contribute to the operation of society:

1. **Social cohesion.** Religion unites people through shared symbolism, values, and norms. Religious thought and ritual establish rules of fair play, organizing our social life.

2. **Social control.** Society uses religious ideas to promote conformity. In medieval Europe, for example, monarchs claimed to rule by "divine right." Even today, our leaders publicly ask for God's blessing, implying to audiences that their efforts are right and just.

3. **Providing meaning and purpose.** Religious belief offers the comforting sense that our brief lives serve some greater purpose. Strengthened by such beliefs, people are less likely to despair in the face of change or even tragedy. For this reason, we mark major life transitions—including birth, marriage, and death—with religious observances.

Sports culture has a semireligious character. What is the function for local communities of supporting teams, such as the Ohio State Buckeyes, the Iowa State Cyclones, or the San Francisco 49ers?

CRITICAL REVIEW In Durkheim's structural-functional analysis, religion represents the collective life of society. The major weakness of this approach is that it downplays religion's dysfunctions, especially the fact that strongly held beliefs can generate social conflict. Terrorists have claimed that God supports their actions, and nations march to war under the banner of their God. Especially in light of recent world events, few people would deny that religious beliefs have provoked more violence in the world than differences of social class.

YOUR LEARNING What are Durkheim's three functions of religion for society?

CONSTRUCTING THE SACRED: SYMBOLIC-INTERACTION ANALYSIS

From a symbolic-interaction point of view, religion (like all of society) is socially constructed (although perhaps with divine inspiration). Through various rituals—from daily prayer to annual events such as Easter, Passover, or Ramadan—people sharpen the distinction between the sacred and the profane. Furthermore, says Peter Berger

of its members and living on beyond them. Practicing religion, people celebrate the awesome power of their society.

No wonder people around the world transform everyday objects into sacred symbols of their collective life. Members of technologically simple societies do this with a **totem,** *an object in the natural world collectively defined as sacred.* The totem—perhaps an animal or an elaborate work of art—becomes the centerpiece of ritual and symbolizes the power of collective life over the individual. In our society, the flag is a quasi-religious totem that is not to be used in a profane way (say, as clothing) or allowed to touch the ground.

Patriarchy is found in all the world's major religions, including Christianity, Judaism, and Islam. Male dominance can be seen in restrictions that limit religious leadership to men and also in regulations that prohibit women from worshipping along with men.

(1967:35–36), placing our small, brief lives within some "cosmic frame of reference" gives us the appearance of "ultimate security and permanence."

Marriage is a good example. If two people look on marriage as a simple contract, they can walk away whenever they want. Their bond makes much stronger claims on them when it is defined as holy matrimony, which is surely one reason for the lower divorce rate among people with strong religious beliefs. More generally, whenever humans face uncertainty or life-threatening situations—such as illness, natural disaster, terrorist attack, or war—we turn to our sacred symbols.

CRITICAL REVIEW Using the symbolic-interaction approach, religion gives everyday life sacred meaning. Berger adds that the sacred's ability to give meaning and stability to society depends on ignoring the fact that it is socially constructed. After all, how much strength could we gain from sacred beliefs if we saw them merely as a means of coping with tragedy? Also, this micro-level view ignores religion's link to social inequality, to which we turn next.

✔ **YOUR LEARNING** Following Berger's thinking, why would religious people have a low divorce rate?

INEQUALITY AND RELIGION: SOCIAL-CONFLICT ANALYSIS

The social-conflict approach highlights religion's support of social inequality. Religion, proclaimed Karl Marx, serves elites by legitimizing the status quo and diverting people's attention from social inequities.

Today, the British monarch is the formal head of the Church of England, illustrating the close ties between religious and political elites. In practical terms, working for political change may mean opposing the church and, by implication, God. Religion also encourages people to accept the social problems of this world while they look hopefully to a "better world to come." In a well-known statement, Marx dismissed religion as "the sigh of the oppressed creature, the sentiment of a heartless world, and the soul of soulless conditions. It is the opium of the people" (1964:27, orig. 1848).

Religion and social inequality are also linked through gender because virtually all the world's major religions are patriarchal. For example, the Qur'an, the sacred text of Islam, gives men social dominance over women:

Men are in charge of women.... Hence good women are obedient.... As for those whose rebelliousness you fear, admonish them, banish them from your bed, and scourge them. (quoted in W. Kaufman, 1976:163).

Christianity, the major religion in the Western Hemisphere, has also supported patriarchy. Although Christians revere Mary, the mother of Jesus, the New Testament instructs us:

A man ... is the image and glory of God; but woman is the glory of man. For man was not made from woman, but woman from man. Neither was man created for woman, but woman for man. (1 Corinthians 11:7–9).

As in all the churches of the saints, the women should keep silence in the churches. For they are not permitted

APPLYING THEORY
Religion

	Structural-Functional Approach	Symbolic-Interaction Approach	Social-Conflict Approach
What is the level of analysis?	Macro-level	Micro-level	Macro-level
What is the importance of religion for society?	Religion performs vital tasks, including uniting people and controlling behavior. Religion gives life meaning and purpose.	Religion strengthens marriage by giving it (and family life) sacred meaning. People often turn to sacred symbols for comfort when facing danger or uncertainty.	Religion supports social inequality by claiming that the social order is just. Religion turns attention from problems in this world to a "better world to come."

to speak, but should be subordinate, as even the law says. If there is anything they desire to know, let them ask their husbands at home. For it is shameful for a woman to speak in church. (1 Corinthians 14:33–35)

Wives, be subject to your husbands, as to the Lord. For the husband is the head of the wife as Christ is the head of the church. . . . As the church is subject to Christ, so let wives also be subject in everything to their husbands. (Ephesians 5:22–24)

Judaism has also traditionally supported patriarchy. Male Orthodox Jews recite the following prayer each day:

> Blessed art thou, O Lord our God, King of the Universe, that I was not born a gentile.
> Blessed art thou, O Lord our God, King of the Universe, that I was not born a slave.
> Blessed art thou, O Lord our God, King of the Universe, that I was not born a woman.

Despite patriarchal traditions, most religions now have women in leadership roles, and many are introducing more gender-neutral language in hymnals and prayer books. Such changes involve not just organizational patterns but conceptions of God. The theologian Mary Daly puts the matter bluntly: "If God is male, then male is God" (cited in Woodward, 1989:58).

CRITICAL REVIEW Social-conflict analysis emphasizes the power of religion to support social inequality. Yet religion also promotes change toward equality. For example, nineteenth-century religious groups in the United States played an important role in the movement to abolish slavery. In the 1950s and 1960s, religious organizations and their leaders were at the core of the civil rights movement. In the 1960s and 1970s, many clergy actively opposed the Vietnam War, and today many support any number of progressive causes such as feminism and gay rights.

The Applying Theory table summarizes the three theoretical approaches to understanding religion.

✓ **YOUR LEARNING** How does religion help maintain class inequality and gender stratification?

Religion and Social Change

Religion is not just the conservative force portrayed by Karl Marx. In fact, at some points in history, as Max Weber (1958, orig. 1904–05) explained, religion has promoted dramatic social change.

MAX WEBER: PROTESTANTISM AND CAPITALISM

Weber believed that particular religious ideas set into motion a wave of change that brought about the industrialization of Western Europe. The rise of industrial capitalism was encouraged by Calvinism, a movement within the Protestant Reformation.

Central to the religious thought of John Calvin (1509–1564) is the doctrine of *predestination:* An all-knowing, all-powerful God has selected some people for salvation while condemning most to eternal damnation. Each person's fate, sealed before birth and known only to God, is either eternal glory or endless hellfire.

Driven by anxiety over their fate, Calvinists understandably looked for signs of God's favor in this world and came to see prosperity as a sign of divine blessing. Religious conviction and a rigid devotion to duty thus led Calvinists to work hard, and many amassed great wealth. But money was not for selfish spending or even for sharing with the poor, whose plight they saw as a mark of God's rejection. As agents for God's work on Earth, Calvinists believed that they could best fulfill their "calling" by reinvesting profits and achieving ever-greater success in the process.

All the while, the Calvinists lived thrifty lives and embraced technological advances, thereby laying the groundwork for the rise of industrial capitalism. In time, the religious fervor that motivated early Calvinists weakened, resulting in a profane "Protestant work ethic." To Max Weber, industrial capitalism itself was a "disenchanted" religion, further showing the power of religion to change the shape of society.

LIBERATION THEOLOGY

Historically, Christianity has reached out to suffering and oppressed people, urging all to strengthen their faith in a better life to come. In recent decades, however, some church leaders and theologians have taken a decidedly political approach and endorsed **liberation theology,** *the combining of Christian principles with political activism, often Marxist in character.*

This social movement started in the late 1960s in Latin America's Roman Catholic Church. Today, Christian activists continue to help people in poor nations liberate themselves from abysmal poverty. Their message is simple: Social oppression runs counter to Christian morality, so as a matter of faith and justice, Christians must promote greater social equality.

Despite its Roman Catholic beginnings, Pope John Paul II condemned liberation theology for distorting church doctrine with left-wing politics. Nevertheless, the liberation theology movement has grown in Latin America, where many people's Christian faith drives them to improve conditions for the world's poor (Neuhouser, 1989; J. E. Williams, 2002).

Types of Religious Organizations

Sociologists categorize the hundreds of different religious organizations in the United States along a continuum with *churches* at one end and *sects* at the other. We can describe any religious organization by placing it on the church-sect continuum.

CHURCH

Drawing on the ideas of his teacher Max Weber, Ernst Troeltsch (1931) defined a **church** as *a type of religious organization that is well integrated into the larger society.* Churchlike organizations typically persist for centuries and include generations of the same families. Churches have well-established rules and regulations and expect leaders to be formally trained and ordained.

Though concerned with the sacred, a church accepts the ways of the profane world. Church members conceive of God in intellectual terms (say, as a force for good) and favor abstract moral standards ("Do unto others as you would have them do unto you"). By teaching morality in safely abstract terms, church leaders avoid social controversy. For example, many churches celebrate the unity of all peoples but say little about their own lack of social diversity. By downplaying this type of conflict, a church makes peace with the status quo (Troeltsch, 1931).

A church may operate as an arm of the state. A **state church** is *a church formally allied with the state.* For centuries, Roman Catholicism was the official religion of the Roman Empire, and Confucianism was the official religion in China until the early twentieth century. Today, the Anglican church is the official church of England, and Islam is the official religion of Pakistan and Iran. State churches consider everyone in a society as a member, which often limits tolerance of religious differences.

A **denomination,** by contrast, is *a church, independent of the state, that recognizes religious pluralism.* Denominations exist in nations that formally separate church and state, such as the United States. This nation has dozens of Christian denominations, including Catholics, Baptists, Episcopalians, Methodists, and Lutherans—as well as various branches of Judaism, Islam, and other traditions. Although members of a denomination hold to their own beliefs, they recognize the right of others to have different beliefs.

SECT

Unlike a church, which tries to fit into the larger society, a **sect** is *a type of religious organization that stands apart from the larger society.* Sect members have rigid religious convictions and deny the beliefs of others. In extreme cases, members of a sect may withdraw completely from society to practice their faith without interference. The Amish community is one example of a North American sect that isolates itself. Because U.S. culture generally considers religious tolerance a virtue, members of sects sometimes are accused of being narrow-minded in insisting that they alone follow the true religion (Kraybill, 1994; P. W. Williams, 2002).

In organizational terms, sects are less formal than churches. Sect members may be highly spontaneous and emotional in worship, compared to members of churches, who tend to listen passively to their leaders. Sects also reject the intellectualized religion of churches, stressing instead the personal experience of divine power. Rodney Stark (1985:314) contrasts a church's vision of a distant God—"Our Father, who art in Heaven"—with a sect's more immediate God—"Lord, bless this poor sinner kneeling before you now."

Animism is widespread among Native Americans, who live respectfully within the natural world on which they depend for their survival. These Aleuts live in Eklutna, a village north of Anchorage, Alaska, which has been inhabited by people with much the same way of life for almost 500 years. Animists see a divine force present not only in themselves but in everything around them.

Churches and sects also have different patterns of leadership. The more churchlike an organization, the more likely that its leaders are formally trained and ordained. Sectlike organizations, which celebrate the personal presence of God, expect their leaders to show divine inspiration in the form of **charisma** (from Greek, meaning "divine favor"), *extraordinary personal qualities that can infuse people with emotion and turn them into followers.*

Sects generally form as breakaway groups from established religious organizations (Stark & Bainbridge, 1979). Their psychic intensity and informal structure make them less stable than churches, and many sects blossom only to disappear soon after. The sects that do endure typically become more like churches, losing fervor as they become more bureaucratic.

To sustain their membership, many sects actively recruit (*proselytize*) new members. Sects value highly the experience of *conversion*, or religious rebirth. For example, Jehovah's Witnesses go door to door to share their faith with others in the hope of attracting new members.

Finally, churches and sects differ in their social composition. Because they are more closely tied to the world, well-established churches tend to include people of high social standing. Sects attract more disadvantaged people. A sect's openness to new members and promise of salvation and personal fulfillment appeal to people who feel they are social outsiders.

Cult

A **cult** is *a type of religious organization that is largely outside a society's cultural traditions.* Most sects spin off from a con-ventional religious organization. However, a cult typically forms around a highly charismatic leader who offers a compelling message of a new and very different way of life. As many as 5,000 cults exist in the United States (Marquand & Wood, 1997).

Because some cult principles or practices are unconventional, many people view cults as deviant or even evil. The suicides of thirty-nine members of California's Heaven's Gate cult in 1997—people who claimed that dying was the doorway to a higher existence, perhaps in the company of aliens from outer space—confirmed the negative image the public holds of many cults. In short, say some scholars, calling a religious community a "cult" amounts to dismissing its members as crazy (Shupe, 1995; Gleick, 1997).

This charge is unfair because there is nothing basically wrong with this kind of religious organization. Many religions—Christianity, Islam, and Judaism included—began as cults. Of course, few cults exist for very long. One reason is that they are even more at odds with the larger society than sects. Many cults demand that members not only accept their teaching but also adopt a radically new lifestyle. This is why people sometimes accuse cults of brainwashing their members, although research suggests that most people who join cults experience no psychological harm (Kilbourne, 1983; P. W. Williams, 2002).

Can you think of ways in which a religious organization that began as a cult becomes a church?

Religion in History

Like family, religion is a part of every known society. Also like family, religion shows marked variation according to time and place.

Early hunters and gatherers embraced **animism** (from the Latin, meaning "breath of life"), *the belief that elements of the natural world are conscious life forms that affect humanity.* Animistic people view forests, oceans, mountains, and even the wind as spiritual forces. Many Native American societies are animistic, which accounts for their reverence for the natural environment.

Belief in a single divine power responsible for creating the world arose with pastoral and horticultural societies, which first appeared 10,000 to 12,000 years ago. The conception of God as a "shepherd" arose because Judaism, Christianity, and Islam all had their beginnings among pastoral peoples.

Religion becomes more important in agrarian societies. The central role of religion in social life is seen in the huge cathedrals that dominated the towns of medieval Europe.

The Industrial Revolution introduced the growing importance of science to everyday life. More and more, people looked to physicians and scientists for the knowledge and comfort they used to get from priests. However, religion persists in industrial societies because science is powerless to address issues of ultimate meaning in human life. In other words, *how* this world works is a matter for scientists, but *why* we and the rest of the universe exist is a question of faith.

Religion in the United States

Just as people debate the state of family life in the United States, analysts disagree about the strength of religion in our society. Research shows that changes are under way but also confirms that religion remains important in social life.

RELIGIOUS COMMITMENT

As Figure 13–4 shows, about eight in ten people in our society claim to gain "comfort and strength" from religion, a greater share than in other high-income countries. National surveys show that about 85 percent of adults in the United States claim a religious preference (NORC, 2005:169). More than half of U.S. adults consider themselves Protestants, one-fourth are Catholics, and 2 percent are Jews. Significant numbers of people also hold to dozens of other religions, from animism to Zen Buddhism, making our society as religiously diverse as any on Earth (Eck, 2001). The religious

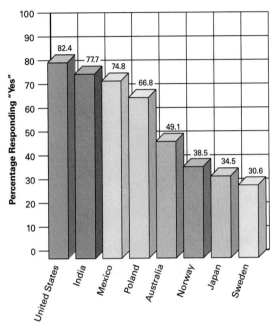

Survey Question: "Do you gain comfort and strength from religion?"

FIGURE 13-4   Religiosity in Global Perspective

Religion is stronger in the United States than in many other nations.

Source: Inglehart et al. (2000).

diversity of the United States stems from a constitutional ban on any government-sponsored religion and from our historically high numbers of immigrants from all over the world. National Map 13–1 on page 398 shows the share of people who claim to belong to a religious organization.

National Map 13–2 goes a step further, showing that the religion most people identify with varies by region. New England and the Southwest are predominantly Catholic, the South is overwhelmingly Baptist, and Lutherans predominate in the northern Plains states. In and around Utah, there is a heavy concentration of members of the Church of Jesus Christ of Latter-Day Saints (Mormons).

Religiosity is *the importance of religion in a person's life.* However, exactly how religious we are depends on precisely how we operationalize this concept. For example, 86 percent of adults in the United States claim to believe in a divine power, although just 60 percent claim that they "know that God exists and have no doubts about it" (NORC, 2005:442). Fifty-six percent of adults say they pray at least once a day, but just 30 percent report attending reli-

NATIONAL MAP 13-1
Religious Membership across the United States

In general, people in the United States are more religious than people in other high-income nations. Yet membership in a religious organization is more common in some parts of the country than in others. What pattern do you see in the map? Can you explain the pattern?

Source: From Rodger Doyle, *Atlas of Contemporary America.* Copyright © 1994 by Facts on File, Inc. Reprinted with the permission of Facts on File, Inc.

Percentage of Population Reporting Membership in Some Religious Organization
- 75% or more
- 50% to 74%
- 25% to 49%
- Less than 25%

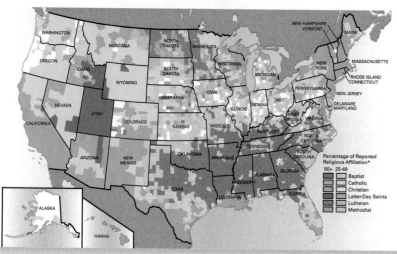

NATIONAL MAP 13-2
Religious Diversity across the United States

In most counties, at least 25 percent of people who report having an affiliation are members of the same religious organization. Thus although the United States is religiously diverse at the national level, most people live in communities where one denomination predominates. What historical facts might account for this pattern?

*When two or more churches have 25 to 49 percent of the membership in a county, the largest is shown. When no church has 25 percent of the membership, that county is left blank.

Source: Glenmary Research Center (2002).

Percentage of Reported Religious Affiliation*
50+ 25-49
- Baptist
- Catholic
- Christian
- Latter-Day Saints
- Lutheran
- Methodist

---

gious services on a weekly or almost weekly basis (NORC, 2005:171, 179).

Clearly, the question "How religious are we?" has no easy answer, and it is likely that many people claim to be more religious than they really are. Overall, although most people in the United States claim to be at least somewhat religious, probably no more than one-third actually are. Religiosity also varies among denominations. Members of sects are the most religious of all, followed by Catholics and then "mainstream" Protestant denominations such as Methodists, Presbyterians, and Episcopalians (Hadaway, Marler, & Chaves, 1993; Sherkat & Ellison, 1999; Miller & Stark, 2002).

INTERNET Answer 20 questions to find out what your spiritual type is at http://www.beliefnet.com/story/76/story_7665_1.html

What difference does being more religious make? Researchers have linked a number of social patterns to strong religious beliefs, including low rates of delinquency among young people and low rates of divorce among adults. According to one recent study, religiosity helps unite children, parents, and local communities in ways that benefit young people, enhancing their educational achievement (Muller & Ellison, 2001).

Do you think our society would be better off if more people were religious? Or would it be worse off? Explain your answer.

RELIGION: CLASS, ETHNICITY, AND RACE

Religious affiliation is related to a number of other factors, including social class, ethnicity, and race.

Social Class

A study of *Who's Who in America,* which profiles U.S. high achievers, showed that 33 percent of the people who gave a religious affiliation were Episcopalians, Presbyterians, and United Church of Christ members, denominations that together account for less than 10 percent of the population. Jews also enjoy high social position, with this 2 percent of the population accounting for 12 percent of listings in *Who's Who.*

Research shows that on average, members of other denominations, including Methodists and Catholics, have moderate social standing. Lower social standing is typical of Baptists, Lutherans, and members of sects. Of course, there is considerable variation within all denominations (Davidson, Pyle, & Reyes, 1995; Waters, Heath, & Watson, 1995; Keister, 2003).

Ethnicity

Throughout the world, religion is tied to ethnicity, largely because one religion stands out in a single nation or geographic region. Islam predominates in the Arab societies of the Middle East, Hinduism is fused with the culture of India, and Confucianism runs deep in Chinese society. Christianity and Judaism have cultural traditions as well, although significant numbers of Christians and Jews are found all over the world.

Religion and national identity are joined to a certain extent in the United States as well. For example, we have Anglo-Saxon Protestants, Irish Catholics, and Greek Orthodox. This linking of nation and religious belief results from the arrival of immigrants from nations with a distinctive major religion. Still, nearly every ethnic category displays some religious diversity. For example, people of English ancestry may be Protestants, Roman Catholics, Jews, Hindus, Muslims, or followers of other religions.

Race

Scholars claim that the church is both the oldest and the most important social institution in the African American community. Transported to the Western Hemisphere in slave ships, most Africans became Christians, the dominant religion in the Americas, but they blended Christian beliefs with elements of African religions they brought with them. As a result of this religious mix, Christian people of color in the United States have developed rituals that seem, by European standards, far more spontaneous and emotional (Frazier, 1965; Roberts, 1980; Paris, 2000).

When African Americans migrated from the rural South to the industrial cities of the North starting around 1940, the church played a major role in addressing problems of dislocation, poverty, and prejudice (Pattillo-McCoy, 1998). Black churches have also provided an important avenue of achievement for talented men and women. Ralph Abernathy, Martin Luther King Jr., and Jesse Jackson all achieved world recognition for their work as religious leaders.

Recent years have witnessed an increasing number of non-Christian African Americans, especially in large U.S. cities. Among them, the most common non-Christian religion is Islam, with an estimated 1 million African American followers (Paris, 2000).

Religion in a Changing Society

Like family life, religion is also changing in the United States. Sociologists focus on a major aspect of change: the process of secularization.

SECULARIZATION

Secularization is *the historical decline in the importance of the supernatural and the sacred.* Secularization (from a Latin word for "worldly," meaning literally "of the present age") is commonly associated with modern, technologically advanced societies in which science is the major way of understanding.

Today, we are more likely to experience the transitions of birth, illness, and death in the presence of physicians (with scientific knowledge) than church leaders (whose knowledge is based on faith). This shift alone suggests that religion's importance for our everyday lives has declined. Harvey Cox (1971:3) explains:

> The world looks less and less to religious rules and rituals for its morality or its meanings. For some [people] religion provides a hobby, for others a mark of national or ethnic identification, for still others an aesthetic delight. For fewer and fewer does it provide an inclusive and commanding system of personal and cosmic values and explanations.

If Cox is right, should we expect religion to disappear someday? Most sociologists say no. Although significant secularization does appear to have taken place in Europe, the vast majority of people in the United States still profess a belief in God, and more people claim to pray each day than vote in national elections. In addition, religious affiliation today in this country is higher than it was in 1850. And one of the most watched movies in recent years was Mel Gibson's *Passion of the Christ,* which portrayed the final days leading up to the crucifixion of Jesus.

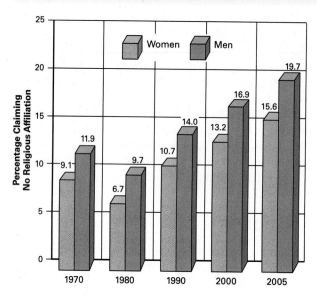

FIGURE 13-5 Religious Nonaffiliation among First-Year College Students, 1970–2005

The share of students claiming no religious affiliation has risen in recent decades.

Sources: Astin et al. (2002) and Pryor et al. (2005).

Our society does not seem to be on the road to secularization. Some dimensions of religiosity (such as belief in life after death) have declined, but others (such as religious affiliation) have increased. Similarly, some religious organizations have lost members, but others find their membership increasing. Among college students, as Figure 13–5 shows, the share of first-year students saying they have no religious preference has gone up, more than doubling between 1980 and 2005. But this share is still just a minority. Putting it all together, the claim that religion is declining in this country may be off the mark (Gorski, 2000; Stark & Finke, 2000; Hout & Fischer, 2002; Pryor et al., 2005).

As we look at religious change, people disagree whether it is good or bad. Conservatives see any weakening of religion as a mark of moral decline. Progressives view secularization as liberation from the dictatorial beliefs of the past, giving people greater choice about what to believe. Secularization has also brought many traditional religious practices (such as ordaining only men) into line with modern social attitudes that support greater gender equality.

An important event that helped spark the secularization debate occurred in 1963 when the U.S. Supreme Court banned organized prayer in school, ruling that is was a violation of the constitutional separation of church and state. In 1990, however, the Court stated that religious groups should be permitted to meet on school grounds as long as group membership is voluntary, groups meet outside of regular school hours, and students rather than teachers run the meetings.

CIVIL RELIGION

One dimension of secularization is what Robert Bellah (1975) calls **civil religion,** *a quasi-religious loyalty binding individuals in a basically secular society.* In other words, formal religion may lose power, but citizenship has its own religious qualities. Most people in the United States consider our way of life a force for moral good in the world. Many people also find religious qualities in political movements, whether liberal or conservative (Williams & Demerath, 1991).

Civil religion involves a range of rituals, from standing to sing the national anthem at sporting events to waving the flag at public parades. At all such events, the U.S. flag serves as a sacred symbol of our national identity, and we expect people to treat it with respect.

"NEW AGE" SEEKERS: SPIRITUALITY WITHOUT FORMAL RELIGION

 December 29, Machu Picchu, Peru. We are ending the first day exploring this magnificent city built by the Inca people at the top of the Andes Mountains. Lucas, a local shaman, or religious leader, is leading a group of twelve members of our tour group in a ceremony of thanks. He kneels on the dirt floor of the small stone building and places offerings—corn and beans, sugar, plants of all colors, and even bits of gold and silver—in front of him as gifts to Mother Earth as he prays for harmony, joy, and the will to do good for one another. His words and the magic of the setting make the ceremony very moving.

In recent decades, an increasing number of people have sought spiritual development outside of established religious organizations. This trend has led some analysts to conclude that the United States is becoming a *postdenominational society.* In simple terms, more people seem to be spiritual seekers, believing in a vital spiritual dimension to human existence that they pursue more or less separately from any formal denomination.

What exactly is the difference between this "New Age" focus on spirituality and a traditional concern with reli-

New Age "seekers" are people in pursuit of spiritual growth, often using the age-old technique of meditation. The goal of this activity is to quiet the mind so that, by moving away from everyday concerns, one can hear an inner, divine voice. Countless people attest to the spiritual value of meditation; it has also been linked to improved physical health.

gion? As one analysis (Cimino & Lattin, 1999:62) puts it, spirituality is

> the search for . . . a religion of the heart, not the head. It . . . downplays doctrine and dogma, and revels in direct experience of the divine—whether it's called the "holy spirit" or "divine consciousness" or "true self." It's practical and personal, more about stress reduction than salvation, more therapeutic than theological. It's about feeling good rather than being good. It's as much about the body as the soul.

Millions of people in the United States take part in New Age spirituality. Hank Wesselman (2001:39–42), an anthropologist and spiritual teacher, identifies five core values that define this approach:

1. **Seekers believe in a higher power.** There exists a higher power, a vital force that is within all things and all people. Humans, then, are partly divine.

2. **Seekers believe we're all connected.** Everything and everyone is interconnected as part of a universal divine pattern.

3. **Seekers believe in a spirit world.** The physical world is not all there is; a more important spiritual reality (or "spirit world") also exists.

4. **Seekers want to experience the spirit world.** Spiritual development means gaining the ability to experience the spirit world. Many seekers come to understand that helpers and teachers who dwell in the spirit world can and do touch their lives.

5. **Seekers pursue transcendence.** Various techniques (such as yoga, meditation, and prayer) give people an increasing ability to rise above the immediate physical world (the experience of "transcendence"), which is seen as the larger purpose of life.

From a traditional point of view, this New Age concern with spirituality may seem more like psychology than religion (Tucker, 2002). Yet it is an important new form of religious interest in the modern world.

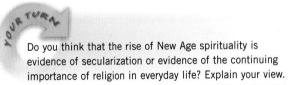

Do you think that the rise of New Age spirituality is evidence of secularization or evidence of the continuing importance of religion in everyday life? Explain your view.

RELIGIOUS REVIVAL: "GOOD OLD-TIME RELIGION"

At the same time as New Age spirituality is flourishing, a great deal of change has been going on in the world of organized religion. Membership in established, mainstream churches such as the Episcopalian and Presbyterian denominations has plummeted by almost 50 percent since 1960. During the same period, affiliation with other religious organizations (including the Mormons, Seventh-Day Adventists, and especially Christian sects) has risen just as fast.

In this outstanding example of U.S. folk art, Anna Bell Lee Washington's *Baptism 3* (1924) depicts the life-changing experience by which many people enter the Christian faith.

These opposing trends suggest that secularization itself may be self-limiting: As churchlike organizations become more worldly, many people leave them in favor of sectlike communities offering a more intense religious experience (Stark & Bainbridge, 1981; Roof & McKinney, 1987; Jacquet & Jones, 1991; Warner, 1993; Iannaccone, 1994; Hout, Greeley, & Wilde, 2001).

One striking religious trend today is the growth of **fundamentalism,** *a conservative religious doctrine that opposes intellectualism and worldly accommodation in favor of restoring traditional, otherworldly religion.* In the United States, fundamentalism has made the greatest gains among Protestants. Southern Baptists, for example, are the largest religious community in the United States. But fundamentalist groups have also grown among Roman Catholics, Jews, and Muslims.

In response to what they see as the growing influence of science and the weakening of the conventional family, religious fundamentalists defend what they call "traditional values." As they see it, liberal churches are simply too open to compromise and change. Religious fundamentalism is distinctive in five ways (Hunter, 1983, 1985, 1987):

1. **Fundamentalists take the words of sacred texts literally.** Fundamentalists insist on a literal reading of sacred texts such as the Bible to counter what they see as excessive intellectualism among more liberal religious organizations. For example, fundamentalist Christians believe God created the world in seven days precisely as described in the biblical book of Genesis.

2. **Fundamentalists reject religious pluralism.** Fundamentalists believe that tolerance and relativism water down personal faith. Therefore, they maintain that their religious beliefs are true and other beliefs are not.

3. **Fundamentalists pursue the personal experience of God's presence.** In contrast to the worldliness and intellectualism of other religious organizations, fundamentalists encourage a return to "good old-time religion" and spiritual revival. Among fundamentalist Christians, being "born again" and having a personal relationship with Jesus Christ should be evident in a person's everyday life.

4. **Fundamentalists oppose "secular humanism."** Fundamentalists think accommodation to the changing world undermines religious conviction. They reject "secular humanism," our society's tendency to look to scientific experts rather than God for guidance about how to live. There is nothing new in this tension between science and religion, as the Thinking Critically box explains.

5. **Many fundamentalists endorse conservative political goals.** Although fundamentalism tends to back away from worldly concerns, some fundamentalist leaders (including Christian fundamentalists Ralph Reed, Pat Robertson, and Gary Bauer) have entered politics to oppose the "liberal agenda," which includes feminism and gay rights. Fundamentalists oppose abortion, gay

Does Science Threaten Religion?

About 400 years ago, the Italian physicist and astronomer Galileo (1564–1642) helped start the Scientific Revolution with a series of startling discoveries. Dropping objects from the Leaning Tower of Pisa, he discovered some of the laws of gravity; making his own telescope, he observed the stars and found that Earth orbited the sun, not the other way around.

For his trouble, Galileo was challenged by the Roman Catholic Church, which had preached for centuries that Earth stood motionless at the center of the universe. Galileo only made matters worse by responding that religious leaders had no business talking about matters of science. Before long, he found his work banned and himself under house arrest.

As Galileo's treatment shows, right from the start, science has had an uneasy relationship with religion. In the twentieth century, the two clashed again over the issue of creation. Charles Darwin's masterwork, *On the Origin of Species,* states that humanity evolved from lower forms of life over a billion years. Yet this theory seems to fly in the face of the biblical account of creation found in Genesis, which states that "God created the heavens and the earth," introducing life on the third day and, on the fifth and sixth days, animal life, including human beings fashioned in God's own image.

Galileo would have been an eager observer of the famous "Scopes monkey trial." In 1925, the state of Tennessee put a small-town science teacher named John Thomas Scopes on trial for teaching evolution in the local high school. State law forbade teaching "any theory that denies the story of the Divine Creation of man as taught in the Bible" and especially the idea that "man descended from a lower order of animals." Scopes was found guilty and fined $100. His conviction was reversed on appeal, so the case never reached the U.S. Supreme Court, and the Tennessee law stayed on the books until 1967. A year after that, the Supreme Court (in *Epperson* v. *Arkansas*) struck down all such laws as unconstitutional government support of religion.

Today, almost four centuries after Galileo was silenced, many people still debate the apparently conflicting claims of science and religion. A third of U.S. adults believe that the Bible is the literal word of God, and many of them reject any scientific findings that run counter to it (NORC, 2005:198).

But a middle ground is emerging: Half of U.S. adults (including a number of church leaders) say the Bible is a book of truths inspired by God without being correct in a literal, scientific sense. That is, science and religion are two different types of understanding that answer different questions. Both Galileo and Darwin devoted their lives to investigating *how* the natural world works. Yet only religion can address *why* we and the natural world exist in the first place.

This basic difference between science and religion helps explain why our nation is both the most scientific and the most religious in the world. As one scientist recently noted, the mathematical odds that a cosmic Big Bang 12 billion years ago created the universe and led to the formation of life as we know it is even smaller than the chance of winning a state lottery twenty weeks in a row. To some people, such a scientific fact points to *intelligent design*—the idea that the universe is the creation of an intelligent and purposeful power. To others, the biological theory of evolution represents the best understanding of how we got here. Still others think that a person can be both religious and scientific at the same time.

In 1992, a Vatican commission concluded that the church's silencing of Galileo was wrong. Today, most scientific and religious leaders agree that science and religion represent important, but different, truths. Many also believe that in today's rush to scientific discovery, our world has never been more in need of the moral guidance provided by religion.

WHAT DO YOU THINK?

1. Why do some scientific people reject religious accounts of human creation? Why do some religious people reject scientific accounts?

2. Does the sociological study of religion challenge anyone's faith? Why or why not?

3. About half of U.S. adults think science is changing our way of life too fast. Do you agree? Why or why not?

Do you think religion threatens science? Does science threaten religion? Or do the two go together in your life?

Sources: Based on Gould (1981), Huchingson (1994), and Applebome (1996).

marriage, and liberal bias in the media; they support the traditional two-parent family, seek a return of prayer in schools, and criticize the mass media for approaching stories from a liberal viewpoint (Manza & Brooks, 1997; Thomma, 1997; Rozell, Wilcox, & Green, 1998).

Opponents regard fundamentalism as rigid and self-righteous. But many people find in fundamentalism, with its greater religious certainty and emphasis on experiencing God's presence, an appealing alternative to the more intellectual, tolerant, and worldly "mainstream" denominations (Marquand, 1997).

Which religious organizations are fundamentalist? In recent years, the world has become aware of an extreme form of fundamentalist Islam that supports violent attacks against Western culture. In the United States, the term is most commonly applied to conservative Christian organizations in the evangelical tradition, including Pentecostals, Southern Baptists, Seventh-Day Adventists, and the Assemblies of God. Several national religious movements, including Promise Keepers (a men's organization) and Chosen Women, have a fundamentalist orientation. In national surveys, 30 percent of U.S. adults describe their upbringing as "fundamentalist," 42 percent claim a "moderate" religious upbringing, and 25 percent cite a "liberal" background (NORC, 2005:190).

In contrast to local congregations of years past, some religious organizations, especially fundamentalist ones, have become *electronic churches* dominated by "prime-time preachers" (Hadden & Swain, 1981). Electronic religion is found only in the United States. It has made James Dobson, Franklin Graham, Robert Schuller, and others more famous than all but a few clergy in the past. Perhaps 5 percent of the national television audience (about 10 million people) are regular viewers of religious television, and 20 percent (about 40 million) watch some religious programming every week (NORC, 2005:441).

Religion: Looking Ahead

The popularity of media ministries, the growth of religious fundamentalism, new forms of spirituality, and the connection of millions of people to mainstream churches show that religion will remain a major part of modern society for decades to come. High levels of immigration from many religious countries in Latin America and elsewhere should intensify as well as diversify the religious character of U.S. society in the twenty-first century (Yang & Ebaugh, 2001).

The world is becoming more complex, and social change seems to move at a faster pace than our capacity to make sense of it all. But rather than weakening religion, this process fires the religious imagination. As new technology gives us the power to alter, sustain, and even create life, we are faced with increasingly difficult moral questions. Against this backdrop of uncertainty, it is little wonder that many people look to their faith for guidance and hope.

APPLYING SOCIOLOGY IN EVERYDAY LIFE

1. Parents and grandparents can be a wonderful source of information about changes in marriage and family. Ask them at what ages they married, what their married lives have been like, and what changes in family life today stand out to them. Compare the answers of people of different generations—how are they different?

2. Relationships with various family members differ. With which member of your family—mother, father, brother, sister—do you most easily, and least easily, share confidences? Why? Which family member would you turn to first in a crisis, and why?

3. Some colleges are decidedly religious; others are passionately secular. Investigate the place of religion on your campus. Is your school affiliated with a religious organization? Was it ever? Is there a chaplain or other religious official? See whether you can learn from sources on campus what percentage of students regularly attend any religious service.

4. Is religion getting weaker? To evaluate the theory that our society is undergoing secularization, go to the library or local newspaper office and find an issue of your local newspaper published fifty years ago and, if possible, another from 100 years ago. Page through the papers, comparing the amount of attention given to religious issues then and now. What pattern do you see?

MAKING THE GRADE

FAMILY: BASIC CONCEPTS

All societies are built on *kinship*. The **FAMILY** varies across cultures and over time:

- In industrialized societies such as the United States, *marriage* is monogamous.
- Many preindustrial societies permit *polygamy*, of which there are two types: *polygyny* and *polyandry*.
- In global perspective, *patrilocality* is most common, but industrial societies favor *neolocality* and a few societies have *matrilocal residence*.
- Industrial societies use bilateral *descent*; preindustrial societies are either patrilineal or matrilineal.

pp 372–75

THEORETICAL ANALYSIS OF FAMILY

The **STRUCTURAL-FUNCTIONAL APPROACH** identifies major family functions: socialization of the young, regulation of sexual activity, social placement, and providing material and emotional support.

pp 375–76

The **SOCIAL-CONFLICT APPROACH** and **FEMINIST APPROACH** explore how the family perpetuates social inequality by transmitting divisions based on class, ethnicity, race, and gender.

p 376

The **SYMBOLIC-INTERACTION APPROACH** and **SOCIAL-EXCHANGE APPROACH** highlight the variety of family life as experienced by various family members.

pp 376–77

See the Applying Theory table on page 377.

STAGES OF FAMILY LIFE

COURTSHIP AND ROMANTIC LOVE

- Courtship based on romantic love is central to mate selection in the United States.
- Arranged marriages are common in preindustrial societies.

pp 377–79

CHILD REARING

- Family size has decreased over time as industrialization increases the costs of raising children.
- Fewer children are born as more women go to school and join the labor force.

pp 379–80

THE FAMILY IN LATER LIFE

- Many middle-aged couples care for aging parents, and many older couples are active grandparents.
- The final transition in marriage begins with the death of a spouse.

pp 380–81

Most spouses have similar social background with regard to class and race, but over the last century, ethnicity has mattered less and less (p 383).

TRANSITIONS AND PROBLEMS IN FAMILY LIFE

- Four in ten of today's marriages will end in **DIVORCE**. Remarriage creates blended families that include children from previous marriages.
- **FAMILY VIOLENCE** is a widespread problem. Most adults who abuse family members were themselves abused as children.

pp 384–87

ALTERNATIVE FAMILY FORMS

Family life is becoming more varied:

- One-parent families, cohabitation, gay and lesbian couples, and singlehood have become more common in recent years.
- Although only Massachusetts has lawful same-sex marriage, many gay men and lesbians form long-lasting relationships and, increasingly, are becoming parents.

pp 387–90

NEW REPRODUCTIVE TECHNOLOGIES

- Although ethically controversial, new reproductive technologies are changing conventional ideas of parenthood.

p 390

VISUAL SUMMARY

family (p. 372) a social institution found in all societies that unites people in cooperative groups to care for one another, including any children

kinship (p. 372) a social bond based on common ancestry, marriage, or adoption

marriage (p. 372) a legal relationship, usually involving economic cooperation as well as sexual activity and childbearing

extended family (p. 373) a family composed of parents and children as well as other kin; also known as a *consanguine family*

nuclear family (p. 373) a family composed of one or two parents and their children; also known as a *conjugal family*

endogamy (p. 373) marriage between people of the same social category

exogamy (p. 373) marriage between people of different social categories

monogamy (p. 373) marriage that unites two partners

polygamy (p. 373) marriage that unites a person with two or more spouses

descent (p. 375) the system by which members of a society trace kinship over generations

incest taboo (p. 375) a norm forbidding sexual relations or marriage between certain relatives

homogamy (p. 379) marriage between people with the same social characteristics

family violence (p. 386) emotional, physical, or sexual abuse of one family member by another

cohabitation (p. 387) the sharing of a household by an unmarried couple

MAKING THE GRADE

CONTINUED...

RELIGION: BASIC CONCEPTS

- **RELIGION** is a major social institution based on setting the *sacred* apart from the *profane*.
- Religion is grounded in *faith* rather than scientific evidence, and people express their religious beliefs through various rituals.

p 391

profane (p. 391) occurring as an ordinary element of everyday life

sacred (p. 391) set apart as extraordinary, inspiring awe and reverence

religion (p. 391) a social institution involving beliefs and practices based on recognizing the sacred

faith (p. 391) belief based on conviction rather than on scientific evidence

THEORETICAL ANALYSIS OF RELIGION

The **STRUCTURAL-FUNCTIONAL APPROACH** suggests that religion unites people, promotes cohesion, and gives meaning and purpose to life; through religion, we celebrate the power of our society (Emile Durkheim).

pp 391–92

The **SYMBOLIC-INTERACTION APPROACH** explains that we socially construct religious beliefs; we are especially likely to seek religious meaning when faced with life's uncertainties and disruptions (Peter Berger).

pp 392–93

The **SOCIAL-CONFLICT APPROACH** claims that religion justifies the status quo. In this way, religion supports inequality and discourages change toward a more just and equal society (Karl Marx).

pp 393–94

See the Applying Theory table on page 394.

totem (p. 392) an object in the natural world collectively defined as sacred

liberation theology (p. 395) the combining of Christian principles with political activism, often Marxist in character

RELIGION AND SOCIAL CHANGE

- Max Weber argued, in opposition to Marx, that religion can encourage social change. He showed how Calvinist beliefs helped caused the rise of industrial capitalism.
- **LIBERATION THEOLOGY**, a fusion of Christian principles and political activism, tries to encourage social change.

pp 394–95

church (p. 395) a type of religious organization that is well integrated into the larger society

state church (p. 395) a church formally allied with the state

denomination (p. 395) a church, independent of the state, that recognizes religious pluralism

sect (p. 395) a type of religious organization that stands apart from the larger society

charisma (p. 396) extraordinary personal qualities that can infuse people with emotion and turn them into followers

cult (p. 396) a type of religious organization that is largely outside a society's cultural traditions

animism (p. 397) the belief that elements of the natural world are conscious life forms that affect humanity

TYPES OF RELIGIOUS ORGANIZATIONS

CHURCHES are religious organizations well integrated into their society. Churches fall into two categories: state churches and denominations.

p 395

SECTS are the result of religious division and are marked by charismatic leadership and members' suspicion of the larger society.

pp 395–96

CULTS are religious organizations based on new and unconventional beliefs and practices.

p 396

religiosity (p. 397) the importance of religion in a person's life

secularization (p. 399) the historical decline in the importance of the supernatural and the sacred

civil religion (p. 400) a quasi-religious loyalty binding individuals in a basically secular society

fundamentalism (p. 402) a conservative religious doctrine that opposes intellectualism and worldly accommodation in favor of restoring traditional, otherworldly religion

RELIGION IN THE UNITED STATES

The United States is one of the most religious and religiously diverse nations. How researchers operationalize "religiosity" affects how "religious" our people seem to be:

- 85% of adults identify with a religion
- 60% profess a firm belief in God
- just 30% say they attend religious services weekly

pp 397–98

Religious affiliation is tied to *social class*, *ethnicity*, and *race*.

- On average, Episcopalians, Presbyterians, and Jews enjoy high standing; lower social standing is typical of Baptists, Lutherans, and members of sects.
- Religion is often linked to ethnic background because people came to the United States from countries that have a major religion (e.g., most Irish-Americans are Catholics)
- Transported to this country in slave ships, most Africans became Christians, but they blended Christian beliefs with elements of African religions they brought with them

p 399

RELIGION IN A CHANGING SOCIETY

- **SECULARIZATION** is a decline in the importance of the supernatural and sacred.
- In the United States, while some indicators of religiosity (like membership in mainstream churches) have declined, others (such as membership in sects) have increased.
- Today, **CIVIL RELIGION** takes the form of a quasi-religious patriotism that ties people to their society

pp 399–400

- *Spiritual seekers* are part of the "New Age" movement, which pursues spiritual development outside conventional religious organizations.
- **FUNDAMENTALISM** opposes religious accommodation to the world, interprets religious texts literally, and rejects religious diversity.

pp 400–404

VISUAL SUMMARY

These questions are similar to those found in the test bank that accompanies this textbook.

MULTIPLE-CHOICE QUESTIONS

1. **The family is a social institution that is found in**
   a. every society.
   b. low-income nations but typically not in high-income nations.
   c. high-income nations but typically not in low-income nations.
   d. most but not all societies.

2. **What is the term sociologists use for a group containing parents, children, and other kin?**
   a. extended family
   b. nuclear family
   c. family of affinity
   d. conjugal family

3. **Sociologists claim that marriage in the United States follows the principle of homogamy, which means that partners are**
   a. people of the same sex.
   b. people who are socially alike in terms of class, age, and race.
   c. people who marry due to social pressure.
   d. selected based on love rather than by parents.

4. **Which theoretical approach states that people select partners who have about the same to offer as they do?**
   a. the structural-functional approach
   b. the social-conflict approach
   c. the social-exchange approach
   d. the feminist approach

5. **In the United States, many Latino families are characterized by**
   a. strong extended kinship.
   b. parents exerting a great deal of control over their children's courtship.
   c. traditional gender roles.
   d. All of the above are correct.

6. **What term did Emile Durkheim use to describe the everyday aspects of our lives?**
   a. religion
   b. sacred
   c. profane
   d. ritual

7. **Peter Berger claims that we are most likely to turn to religion when we experience**
   a. social conflict.
   b. the best of times.
   c. familiar, everyday routines.
   d. important events that are out of our control.

8. **Which type of religious organization is most integrated into the larger society?**
   a. cult
   b. church
   c. sect
   d. counterculture

9. **A sect is a type of religious organization that**
   a. stands apart from the larger society.
   b. is well integrated into the larger society.
   c. rejects the importance of charisma.
   d. has formally trained leaders.

10. **The term "secularization" refers to which of the following?**
    a. religion's becoming more important in people's lives
    b. the increasing popularity of fundamentalism
    c. a decline in the importance of religion and the sacred
    d. churches' resisting social change

ANSWERS: 1 (a); 2 (a); 3 (b); 4 (c); 5 (d); 6 (c); 7 (d); 8 (b); 9 (a); 10 (c).

ESSAY QUESTIONS

1. Point to a number of changes in the family since 1960. What factors are responsible for these changes?
2. Explain Karl Marx's claim that religion tends to support the status quo. Develop a counterclaim, based on Max Weber's analysis of Calvinism and the rise of capitalism.

In the modern world, education emerges as a new social institution as societies develop schooling to prepare people for future work. Modernity also sparks the development of medicine, and members of society gain an increasing concern for human health.

CHAPTER 14

Education, Health, and Medicine

HOW are schooling and health linked to social inequality in the United States?

WHAT changes in schooling and health have taken place in the United States in recent generations?

WHY do people in poor nations have little access to schooling and medical care?

dents can vary from one setting to another, a focus of the symbolic-interaction approach discussed next. In addition, structural-functional analysis says little about many problems of our educational system and how schooling helps reproduce the class structure in each generation, which is the focus of the social-conflict approach, covered in the final theoretical section on schooling.

✔ **YOUR LEARNING** Identify five functions of schooling for the operation of society.

Schooling and Social Interaction

The basic idea of the symbolic-interaction approach is that people create the reality they experience in their day-to-day interactions. We use this approach to explain how stereotypes can shape what goes on in the classroom.

THE SELF-FULFILLING PROPHECY

Chapter 4 ("Social Interaction in Everyday Life") presented the Thomas theorem, which states that situations people define as real become real in their consequences. Put another way, people who expect others to act in certain ways often encourage that very behavior. In doing so, people set up a *self-fulfilling prophecy.*

Jane Elliott, an elementary school teacher in the all-white community of Riceville, Iowa, carried out a simple experiment that showed how a self-fulfilling prophecy can take place in the classroom. In 1968, Elliot was teaching a fourth-grade class when Martin Luther King Jr. was murdered. Her students were puzzled and asked why a national hero had been brutally shot. Elliott responded by asking her white students what they thought about people of color and was stunned to learn that they held many powerful negative stereotypes.

To show the class the harmful effects of such stereotypes, Elliott performed a classroom experiment. She found that almost all of the children in her class had either blue eyes or brown eyes. She told the class that children with brown eyes were smarter and worked harder than children with blue eyes. To be sure everyone could easily tell which category a child fell into, a piece of brown or blue cloth was pinned to each student's collar.

Elliott recalls the effect of this "lesson" on the way students behaved: "It was just horrifying how quickly they became what I told them they were." Within half an hour, Elliot continued, a blue-eyed girl named Carol had changed from a "brilliant, carefree, excited little girl to a frightened, timid, uncertain, almost-person." Not surprisingly, in the hours that followed, the brown-eyed students came to life,

speaking up more and performing better than they had before. The prophecy had been fulfilled: Because the brown-eyed children thought they were superior, they became superior in their classroom performance; they also became "arrogant, ugly, and domineering" toward the blue-eyed children. For their part, the blue-eyed children began underperforming, becoming the inferior people they believed themselves to be.

At the end of the day, Elliott explained to the students what they had experienced. She applied the lesson to race, pointing out that if white children thought they were superior to black children, they would expect to do better in school, just as many children of color who live in the shadow of the same stereotypes would underperform in school. The children also realized that the society that teaches these stereotypes, as well as the hate that often accompanies them, encourages the kind of violence that ended the life of Martin Luther King Jr. (Kral, 2000).

CRITICAL REVIEW The symbolic-interaction approach explains how we all build reality in our everyday interactions with others. When school officials define some students as "gifted," for example, we can expect teachers to treat them differently and expect the students themselves to behave differently as a result of having been labeled in this way. If students and teachers come to believe that one race is academically superior to another, the behavior that follows may be a self-fulfilling prophecy.

One limitation of this approach is that people do not just make up such beliefs about superiority and inferiority. Rather, these beliefs are built into a society's system of social inequality, which brings us to the social-conflict approach.

✔ **YOUR LEARNING** How can the labels that schools place on some students affect the students' actual performance and the reactions of others?

Schooling and Social Inequality

Social-conflict analysis challenges the structural-functional idea that schooling develops everyone's talents and abilities. Instead, this approach emphasizes three ways in which schooling causes and perpetuates social inequality:

1. **Social control.** As Samuel Bowles and Herbert Gintis (1976) see it, the demand for public education in the late nineteenth century was based on capitalists' need for an obedient and disciplined workforce. Once in school, immigrants learned not only the English language but also the importance of following orders.

CHAPTER *14*

Education, Health, and Medicine

HOW are schooling and health linked to social inequality in the United States?

WHAT changes in schooling and health have taken place in the United States in recent generations?

WHY do people in poor nations have little access to schooling and medical care?

409

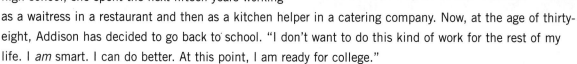

When Lisa Addison was growing up in Baltimore, her teachers always said she was smart and should go to college. "I liked hearing that," she recalls. "But I didn't know what to do about it. No one in my family had ever gone to college. I didn't know what courses to take in high school. I had no idea of how to apply to a college. How would I pay for it? What would it be like if I got there?"

Discouraged and uncertain, Addison found herself "kind of goofing off in school." After finishing high school, she spent the next fifteen years working as a waitress in a restaurant and then as a kitchen helper in a catering company. Now, at the age of thirty-eight, Addison has decided to go back to school. "I don't want to do this kind of work for the rest of my life. I *am* smart. I can do better. At this point, I am ready for college."

Addison took a giant step through the door of the Community College of Baltimore County, speaking to counselors and setting her sights on an associate's degree in business. When she finishes the two-year program, she plans to transfer to a four-year university to complete a bachelor's degree. Then she hopes to go back into the food service industry—but this time as a better-paid manager (Toppo & DeBarros, 2005).

This chapter begins by exploring *education,* a social institution that has particular importance to people looking to advance their own careers. You will learn *why* schooling is so important in the United States today and *who* benefits most from schooling. The second half of the chapter examines *health* and the social institution of *medicine.* Good health, like good schooling, is distributed unequally throughout our society's population. In addition, like education, the practice of medicine reveals striking differences from society to society.

Education: A Global Survey

Education is *the social institution through which society provides its members with important knowledge, including basic facts, job skills, and cultural norms and values.* Education takes place in many ways, from informal family discussions around the dinner table to lectures and labs at large universities. In high-income nations, education is largely a matter of **schooling,** *formal instruction under the direction of specially trained teachers.*

SCHOOLING AND ECONOMIC DEVELOPMENT

The extent of schooling in any society is tied to its level of economic development. In low- and middle-income coun- tries, which are home to most of the world's people, families and local communities teach young people important knowledge and skills. Formal schooling, and especially learning that is not directly connected to survival, is available mainly to wealthy people who can afford to pursue personal enrichment. The word *school* is from a Greek root that means "leisure." In ancient Greece, famous teachers such as Plato, Socrates, and Aristotle taught aristocratic, upper-class men who had plenty of spare time. The same was true in ancient China, where the famous philosopher K'ung Fu-tzu (Confucius) shared his wisdom with just a privileged few.

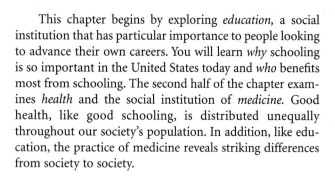 **December 30, the Quecha region, Peru.** High in the Andes Mountains of Peru, families send their children to the local school. But "local" can mean 3 miles away or more, and there are no buses, so these children, almost all from poor families, walk an hour or more each way. Schooling is required by law, but in the rural highlands, some parents prefer to keep their children at home where they can help with the farming and livestock.

Today, schooling in low-income countries reflects the national culture. In Iran, for example, schooling is closely

GLOBAL MAP 14-1 Illiteracy in Global Perspective

Reading and writing skills are widespread in high-income countries, where illiteracy rates generally are below 5 percent. In much of Latin America, however, illiteracy is more common, one consequence of limited economic development. In twenty-two nations—sixteen of them in Africa—illiteracy is the rule rather than the exception; there, people rely on the oral tradition of face-to-face communication rather than the written word.

Source: United Nations Development Programme (2005); map projection from *Peters Atlas of the World* (1990).

tied to Islam. Similarly, schooling in Bangladesh (Asia), Zimbabwe (Africa), and Nicaragua (Latin America) has been shaped by the distinctive cultural traditions of these nations.

All low-income countries have one trait in common when it comes to schooling: There is not very much of it. In the poorest nations (including several in Central Africa), only half of all children ever get to school; worldwide, only half of all children ever get to the secondary grades. As a result, about one-third of the world's people cannot read or write. Global Map 14–1 shows the extent of illiteracy around the world, and the following national comparisons

TABLE 14–1

Educational Achievement in the United States, 1910–2004[*]

Year	High School Graduates	College Graduates	Median Years of Schooling
1910	13.5%	2.7%	8.1
1920	16.4	3.3	8.2
1930	19.1	3.9	8.4
1940	24.1	4.6	8.6
1950	33.4	6.0	9.3
1960	41.1	7.7	10.5
1970	55.2	11.0	12.2
1980	68.7	17.0	12.5
1990	77.6	21.3	12.4
2000	84.1	25.6	12.7
2004	85.2	27.7	n/a

[*]For people twenty-five years of age and over. Percentage of high school graduates includes those who go on to college. Percentage of high school dropouts can be calculated by subtracting percentage of high school graduates from 100 percent.

Source: U.S. Census Bureau (2005).

illustrate the link between schooling and economic development.

SCHOOLING IN INDIA

India has recently become a middle-income country, but people there still earn only about 8 percent of the average U.S. income, and most poor families depend on the earnings of children. Even though India has outlawed child labor, many children continue to work in factories—weaving rugs or making handicrafts—up to sixty hours a week, which greatly limits their chances for schooling.

Today, 84 percent of children in India complete primary school, typically in crowded schoolrooms where one teacher may face as many as sixty children, twice as many as in the average U.S. public school classroom. Less than half go on to secondary education, and very few enter college. As a result, 39 percent of India's people are unable to read and write.

Patriarchy also shapes Indian education. Indian parents are joyful at the birth of a boy because he and his future wife will both contribute income to the family. But there are economic costs to raising a girl: Parents must provide a dowry (a gift of wealth to the groom's family), and after her marriage, a daughter's work benefits her husband's family. Therefore, many Indians see less reason to invest in the schooling of girls, which is why only 30 percent of girls

(compared with 45 percent of boys) reach the secondary grades. So what do the girls do while the boys are in school? Most of the children working in Indian factories are girls— a family's way of benefiting from their daughters while they can (United Nations Development Programme, 1995).

SCHOOLING IN JAPAN

Schooling has not always been part of the Japanese way of life. Before industrialization brought mandatory education in 1872, only a privileged few attended school. Today, Japan's educational system is widely praised for training some of the world's highest achievers.

The early grades concentrate on transmitting Japanese traditions, especially a sense of obligation to family. Starting in their early teens, students take a series of rigorous and highly competitive examinations. These written tests, which resemble the Scholastic Assessment Tests (SATs) used for college admissions in the United States, decide the future of all Japanese students.

More men and women graduate from high school in Japan (96 percent) than in the United States (85 percent). But competitive examinations allow for just half of high school graduates—compared to 67 percent in the United States—to enter college. Understandably, Japanese students take entrance examinations very seriously, and about half attend special "cram schools" to prepare for them.

Japanese schooling produces impressive results. In a number of fields, notably mathematics and science, young Japanese students outperform students in every other high-income nation, including the United States.

SCHOOLING IN THE UNITED STATES

The United States was among the first countries to set a goal of mass education. By 1850, about half the young people between the ages of five and nineteen were enrolled in school. By 1918, all states had passed *mandatory education laws* requiring children to attend school until the age of sixteen or completion of the eighth grade. Table 14–1 shows that this country reached a milestone in the mid-1960s, when for the first time a majority of U.S. adults had high school diplomas. Today, more than four out of five adults have high school educations, and more than one in four have a four-year college degree.

The U.S. educational system is shaped by both our high standard of living (which means that most young people do not have to work) and our democratic principles (the idea that schooling should be provided to everyone). Thomas Jefferson thought the new nation could become democratic only if people learned how to read. Today, the United States has an outstanding record of higher education for its people: No other country has as large a share of adults with university degrees (U.S. Census Bureau, 2005).

Schooling in the United States also tries to promote *equal opportunity*. National surveys show that most people think schooling is crucial to personal success, and a majority believe that everyone has the chance to get an education consistent with personal ability and talent (NORC, 2005). However, this opinion expresses cultural ideals rather than reality. A century ago, for example, women were all but excluded from higher education; even today, most people who attend college come from families with above-average incomes.

In the United States, the educational system stresses the value of *practical* learning, knowledge that prepares people for their future jobs. This is in line with what the education philosopher John Dewey (1859–1952) called

For the report, "Trends in Educational Equity of Girls and Women," go to http:// nces.ed.gov/pubs2005/equity/

progressive educa-tion, by which schools in the United States gener-ally try to make learning relevant to people's lives. In line with this philosophy, students seek out subjects of study that they believe will give them an advantage when they are ready to compete in the job market. For example, as concerns about international terrorism have risen in recent years, so have the numbers of students choosing to study geography, international conflict, and Middle Eastern history and culture (M. Lord, 2001).

The Functions of Schooling

Structural-functional analysis focuses on ways in which schooling supports the operation and stability of society:

1. **Socialization.** Technologically simple societies look to families to transmit a way of life from one genera-tion to the next. As societies gain complex technology, they turn to trained teachers to pass on specialized knowledge that adults will need for their jobs.

2. **Cultural innovation.** Faculty at colleges and universi-ties invent culture as well as pass it along to students. Especially at centers of higher education, scholars conduct research that leads to discoveries and changes our way of life.

3. **Social integration.** Schools mold a diverse popula-tion into one society sharing norms and values. This

Graduation from college is an important event in the lives of an ever-increasing number of people in the United States. Look over the discussion of the functions of schooling. How many of these functions do you think people in college are aware of? Can you think of other social consequences of going to college?

is one reason that states enacted mandatory education laws a century ago when immigration was very high. In light of the ethnic diversity of many urban areas today, schooling continues to serve this purpose.

4. **Social placement.** Schools identify talent and match instruction to ability. Schooling increases meritocracy by rewarding talent and hard work regardless of social background and provides a path to upward social mobility.

5. **Latent functions.** Schooling serves several less widely recognized functions. It provides child care for the growing number parents who work outside the home. In addition, it occupies thousands of young people in their twenties who would otherwise be competing for limited opportunities in the job market. High schools, colleges, and universities also bring together people of marriageable age. Finally, school networks can be a valuable career resource throughout life.

CRITICAL REVIEW Structural-functional analysis stresses ways in which formal education supports the operation of a modern society. However, this approach overlooks how the classroom behavior of teachers and students can vary from one setting to another, a focus of the symbolic-interaction approach discussed next. In addition, structural-functional analysis says little about many problems of our educational system and how schooling helps reproduce the class structure in each generation, which is the focus of the social-conflict approach, covered in the final theoretical section on schooling.

✓ YOUR LEARNING Identify five functions of schooling for the operation of society.

Schooling and Social Interaction

The basic idea of the symbolic-interaction approach is that people create the reality they experience in their day-to-day interactions. We use this approach to explain how stereotypes can shape what goes on in the classroom.

THE SELF-FULFILLING PROPHECY

Chapter 4 ("Social Interaction in Everyday Life") presented the Thomas theorem, which states that situations people define as real become real in their consequences. Put another way, people who expect others to act in certain ways often encourage that very behavior. In doing so, people set up a *self-fulfilling prophecy.*

Jane Elliott, an elementary school teacher in the all-white community of Riceville, Iowa, carried out a simple experiment that showed how a self-fulfilling prophecy can take place in the classroom. In 1968, Elliot was teaching a fourth-grade class when Martin Luther King Jr. was murdered. Her students were puzzled and asked why a national hero had been brutally shot. Elliott responded by asking her white students what they thought about people of color and was stunned to learn that they held many powerful negative stereotypes.

To show the class the harmful effects of such stereotypes, Elliott performed a classroom experiment. She found that almost all of the children in her class had either blue eyes or brown eyes. She told the class that children with brown eyes were smarter and worked harder than children with blue eyes. To be sure everyone could easily tell which category a child fell into, a piece of brown or blue cloth was pinned to each student's collar.

Elliott recalls the effect of this "lesson" on the way students behaved: "It was just horrifying how quickly they became what I told them they were." Within half an hour, Elliot continued, a blue-eyed girl named Carol had changed from a "brilliant, carefree, excited little girl to a frightened, timid, uncertain, almost-person." Not surprisingly, in the hours that followed, the brown-eyed students came to life,

speaking up more and performing better than they had before. The prophecy had been fulfilled: Because the brown-eyed children thought they were superior, they became superior in their classroom performance; they also became "arrogant, ugly, and domineering" toward the blue-eyed children. For their part, the blue-eyed children began underperforming, becoming the inferior people they believed themselves to be.

At the end of the day, Elliott explained to the students what they had experienced. She applied the lesson to race, pointing out that if white children thought they were superior to black children, they would expect to do better in school, just as many children of color who live in the shadow of the same stereotypes would underperform in school. The children also realized that the society that teaches these stereotypes, as well as the hate that often accompanies them, encourages the kind of violence that ended the life of Martin Luther King Jr. (Kral, 2000).

CRITICAL REVIEW The symbolic-interaction approach explains how we all build reality in our everyday interactions with others. When school officials define some students as "gifted," for example, we can expect teachers to treat them differently and expect the students themselves to behave differently as a result of having been labeled in this way. If students and teachers come to believe that one race is academically superior to another, the behavior that follows may be a self-fulfilling prophecy.

One limitation of this approach is that people do not just make up such beliefs about superiority and inferiority. Rather, these beliefs are built into a society's system of social inequality, which brings us to the social-conflict approach.

✓ YOUR LEARNING How can the labels that schools place on some students affect the students' actual performance and the reactions of others?

Schooling and Social Inequality

Social-conflict analysis challenges the structural-functional idea that schooling develops everyone's talents and abilities. Instead, this approach emphasizes three ways in which schooling causes and perpetuates social inequality:

1. **Social control.** As Samuel Bowles and Herbert Gintis (1976) see it, the demand for public education in the late nineteenth century was based on capitalists' need for an obedient and disciplined workforce. Once in school, immigrants learned not only the English language but also the importance of following orders.

Sociological research has documented the fact that young children living in low-income communities typically learn in classrooms like the one on the left, with large class sizes and low budgets that do not provide for high technology and other instructional materials. Children from high-income communities typically enjoy classroom experiences such as the one shown on the right, with small classes and the latest learning technology.

2. **Standardized testing.** Critics claim that the assessment tests widely used by schools reflect our society's dominant culture, placing minority students at a disadvantage. By defining majority students as smarter, standardized tests transform privilege into personal merit (Crouse & Trusheim, 1988; Putka, 1990).

3. **Tracking.** Despite controversy over standardized tests, most U.S. schools use them for **tracking,** *assigning students to different types of educational programs,* such as college preparatory classes, general education, and vocational and technical training. Tracking supposedly helps teachers meet each student's individual abilities and interests. However, the education critic Jonathan Kozol (1992) considers tracking one of the "savage inequalities" in our school system. Most students from privileged backgrounds get into higher tracks, where they receive the best the school can offer. Students from disadvantaged backgrounds end up in lower tracks, where teachers stress memorization and put little focus on creativity (Bowles & Gintis, 1976; Oakes, 1982, 1985; Kilgore, 1991; Gamoran, 1992).

PUBLIC AND PRIVATE EDUCATION

Across the United States, 90 percent of the 54 million primary and secondary school children attend state-funded public schools. The rest go to private schools.

Most private school students attend one of the more than 8,200 *parochial* schools (from Latin, meaning "of the parish") operated by the Roman Catholic Church. The Catholic school system grew rapidly a century ago as cities swelled with immigrants. Today, after decades of flight from the inner city by white people, many parochial schools enroll non-Catholics, including a growing number of African Americans whose families seek an alternative to the neighborhood public school.

Protestants also have private schools, often known as Christian academies. These schools are favored by parents who want religious instruction for their children, as well as parents of all backgrounds who seek higher academic and disciplinary standards.

Some 6,700 nonreligious private schools enroll young people, mostly from well-to-do families. These are typically prestigious and expensive preparatory ("prep") schools, modeled on British boarding schools, that not only provide strong academic programs but also teach the way of life of the upper class. Many "preppies" maintain lifelong school-based networks of personal contacts that provide numerous social advantages.

Are private schools better than public schools? Research shows that holding social background constant, students in private schools do outperform those in public schools. The advantages of private schools include smaller classes, more demanding coursework, and greater discipline (Coleman, Hoffer, & Kilgore, 1981; Coleman & Hoffer, 1987).

NATIONAL MAP 14-1

Teachers' Salaries across the United States

In 2004, the average public school teacher in the United States earned $46,752. The map shows the average teacher salary for all the states; they range from a low of $33,236 in South Dakota to a high of $57,337 in Connecticut. Looking at the map, what pattern do you see? What do high-salary (and low-salary) states have in common?

Source: National Education Association, *Rankings and Estimates: Rankings of the States, 2004, and Estimates of School Statistics, 2005.* Washington, D.C.: National Education Association, 2004, p. 19.

Average Annual Teacher Salaries
- $55,000 and above
- $50,000 to $54,999
- $45,000 to $49,999
- $40,000 to $44,999
- Below $40,000

U.S. average: $46,752

But even public schools are not all the same. Differences in funding between rich and poor communities result in unequal resources; this means that children in more affluent areas receive a better education than children in low-income communities. National Map 14–1 shows one key dimension of difference: Average teacher salaries vary by more than $20,000 in a state-by-state comparison.

At the local level, differences in school funding can be dramatic. Winnetka, Illinois, one of the richest suburbs in the United States, spends more than $13,000 each year on each of its students, compared to less than $8,000 in poor areas like Laredo, Texas, and in recent years, these differences have grown (Edwards, 1998; Winter, 2004). The Thinking About Diversity box shows the effects of funding differences in the everyday lives of students.

Because school funding often reflects local property values, schools in more affluent areas will offer better schooling than schools in poor communities. This difference also benefits whites over minorities, which is why some districts started a policy of *busing,* transporting students to achieve racial balance and equal opportunity in schools. Although only 5 percent of U.S. students are bused to schools outside their neighborhoods, the practice is controversial. Supporters claim that given the reality of racial segregation, the only way governments will adequately fund schools in poor, minority neighborhoods is if white children from richer areas attend. Critics respond that busing is expensive and undermines the concept of neighborhood schools. But almost everyone agrees on one thing: Given the racial imbalance of most urban areas, an effective busing policy would have to join inner cities and suburbs—a plan that has never been politically possible.

Another response to unequal school funding is to provide money equally across a state. This is the approach taken by Vermont, which passed a law that distributes tax money equally to all communities.

But not everyone thinks money is the key to good schooling. A classic report by a research team headed by James Coleman (1966) confirmed that schools in low-income communities and with mostly minority populations suffer problems ranging from large class size to insufficient libraries and too few science labs. But the Coleman report cautioned that more money by itself will not magically improve schooling. More important are the cooperative efforts of teachers, parents, and the students themselves. In other words, even if school funding were exactly the same everywhere, students who benefit from more *social capital*—that is, those whose families value schooling, read to their children, and encourage the development of imagination—would still perform better. In short, we should not expect schools alone to overcome marked social inequality in the United States (Schneider et al., 1998; Israel, Beaulieu, & Hartless, 2001).

Recent research confirms the important influence of home environment on school performance. A research team led by Douglas Downey (2004) studied the rate at which school-age children gain skills in reading and mathematics. Because U.S. children go to school six to seven hours a day, five days a week, and do not attend school during summer months, the researchers calculate that children spend only about 13 percent of their waking hours in school. During the school year, high-income children learn somewhat more quickly than low-income children, but the learning gap is far greater during the summer season when

Schooling in the United States: Savage Inequality

"Public School 261? Head down Jerome Avenue and look for the mortician's office." Off for a day studying the New York City schools, Jonathan Kozol parks his car and walks toward PS 261. Finding PS 261 is not easy because the school has no sign. In fact, the building is a former roller rink and doesn't look much like a school at all.

The principal explains that this is in a minority area of the North Bronx, so the population of PS 261 is 90 percent African American and Hispanic. Officially, the school should serve 900 students, but it actually enrolls 1,300. The rules say class size should not exceed 32, but Kozol observes that it sometimes approaches 40. Because the school has just one small cafeteria, the children must eat in three shifts. After lunch, with no place to play, students squirm in their seats until they are told to return to their classrooms. Only one classroom in the entire school has a window to the world outside.

Toward the end of the day, Kozol remarks to a teacher about the overcrowding and the poor condition of the building. She sums up her thoughts: "I had an awful room last year. In the winter, it was 56 degrees. In the summer, it was up to 90." "Do the children ever comment on the building?" Kozol asks. "They don't say," she responds, "but they know. All these kids see TV. They know what suburban schools are like. Then they look around them at their school. They don't comment on it, but you see it in their eyes. They understand."

Several months later, Kozol visits PS 24, in the affluent Riverdale section of New York City. This school is set back from the road, beyond a lawn planted with magnolia and dogwood trees, which are now in full bloom. On one side of the building is a playground for the youngest children; behind the school are playing fields for the older kids. Many people pay the high price of a house in Riverdale because the local schools have such an excellent reputation. There are 825 children here; most are white and a few are Asian, Hispanic, or African American. The building is in good repair. It has a large library and even a planetarium. All the classrooms have windows with bright curtains.

Entering one of the many classes for gifted students, Kozol asks the children what they are doing today. A young girl answers confidently, "My name is Laurie, and we're doing problem solving." A tall, good-natured boy continues, "I'm David. One thing that we do is logical thinking. Some problems, we find, have more than one good answer." Kozol asks if such reasoning is innate or if it is something a child learns. Susan, whose smile reveals her braces, responds, "You know some things to start with when you enter school. But we learn some things that other children don't. We learn certain things that other children don't know because we're *taught* them."

WHAT DO YOU THINK?

1. Are there differences between schools in your city or town? Explain.

2. Why is there so little public concern about schooling inequality?

3. What changes would our society have to make to eliminate schooling inequality? Would you support such changes? Why or why not?

Source: Adapted from Kozol (1992:85–88, 92–96).

children are not in school. This means that differences in the home and local neighborhood matter most in children's learning. As shown in Figure 14–1 on page 418, schools may not be equal for all children, but they do level the playing field somewhat by reducing the great differences in children's home environments.

YOUR TURN

Are there specific ways in which parents can improve children's learning? How did your parents affect your school performance?

ACCESS TO HIGHER EDUCATION

Schooling is the main path to good jobs. But only 67 percent of U.S. high school graduates enroll in college immediately after graduation. Among young people aged eighteen to twenty-four years, about 38 percent are enrolled in college (National Center for Education Statistics, 2006).

A crucial factor affecting access to higher education is income. College is expensive: Even at state-supported colleges and universities, annual tuition averages at least $3,000, and admission to the most expensive private colleges and universities exceeds $40,000 a year. As a result, two-thirds of the children in families with incomes above

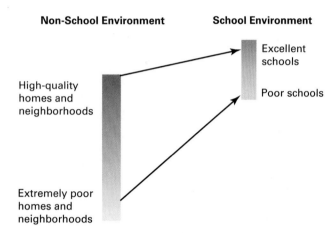

Non-School Environment | **School Environment**

High-quality homes and neighborhoods → Excellent schools

Poor schools

Extremely poor homes and neighborhoods →

FIGURE 14-1 Home and School Environments: Effects on Learning

Because U.S. children spend only 13 percent of their waking hours in school, the home environment has a greater effect on learning than the school environment. Schools—even poor ones—help narrow the learning gap between advantaged and disadvantaged children, but they are not able to close the gap completely.

Source: D. B. Downey, P. T. von Hippel, and B. A. Broh, "Are Schools the Great Equalizer?" *American Sociological Review*, vol. 69 no. 5 (October 2004), p. 614, Fig. 1. Reprinted by permission.

$75,000 per year (roughly the richest 30 percent, who fall within the upper-middle or upper class) attend college, but only 23 percent of children from families earning less than $20,000 a year go on to higher education (U.S. Census Bureau, 2006).

These economic differences are one reason that the educational gap between whites and minorities widens at the college level. As Figure 14–2 shows, African Americans are not quite as likely as non-Hispanic whites to graduate from high school and are much less likely to complete four or more years of college. Schooling is an important path to social mobility in our society, but the promise of schooling has not overcome the racial inequality that exists in the United States.

Completing college brings many rewards, including higher earnings. In the last forty years, as our economy has shifted to work that requires processing information, the gap in average income between people who complete only  high school and those who earn a four-year college degree has more than doubled. In fact, today, a college degree can add as much as $1 million to a person's lifetime income. Table 14–2 shows why. In 2005, men who were high school graduates averaged $36,302, and college graduates averaged

$60,020. The ratios in parentheses show that a man with a bachelor's degree earns 2.7 times in annual income as much as a man with eight or fewer years of schooling. Across the board, women earn less than men, although like men, added years of schooling boosts their income. Keep in mind that for both men and women, some of the greater earnings have to do with social background, because the people with the most schooling are likely to come from well-off families to begin with.

GREATER OPPORTUNITY: EXPANDING HIGHER EDUCATION

With some 17.3 million people enrolled in colleges and universities, the United States is the world leader in providing a college education to its people. This country also enrolls more students from abroad than any other.

One reason for this achievement is that there are more than 4,200 colleges and universities in the United States. This number includes 2,533 four-year institutions (which award bachelor's degrees) and 1,683 two-year colleges (which award associate's degrees). Some two-year colleges are private, but most are publicly funded community colleges that serve a local area (usually a county) and charge low tuition (National Center for Education Statistics, 2006).

 For general news and information about higher education, go to http://chronicle.com

Because higher education is a key path to better jobs and higher income, the government makes money available to help certain categories of people pay the costs of college. After World War II, the GI Bill provided college funds to veterans, with the result that tens of thousands of men and women were able to attend college. Some branches of the military continue to offer college money to enlistees; in addition, veterans continue to benefit from a number of government grants and scholarships.

COMMUNITY COLLEGES

Since the 1960s, the expansion of state-funded community colleges has further increased access to higher education. According to the National Center for Education Statistics (2006), the 1,683 two-year colleges across the United States now enroll 38 percent of all college undergraduates.

Community colleges provide a number of specific benefits. First, their low cost places college courses and degrees within reach of millions of families who could not otherwise afford them. Many students at community colleges today are the first in their families to pursue a college degree. The low cost of community colleges is especially important during periods of economic recession. When the economy slumps and people lose their jobs, college enrollments soar, especially at community colleges.

Second, community colleges have special importance to minorities. Currently, half of all African American and Hispanic undergraduates in the United States attend community colleges.

Third, although community colleges serve local populations, some attract students from around the world. Many community colleges recruit students from abroad, and more than one-third of all foreign students enrolled on a U.S. campus are studying at community colleges (Briggs, 2002; D. Golden, 2002).

Finally, the top priority of faculty who work at large universities is typically research, but the most important job for community college faculty is teaching. Thus although teaching loads are heavy (typically four or five classes each semester), community colleges appeal to faculty who find their greatest pleasure in the classroom. Community college students often get more attention from faculty than students at large universities (Jacobson, 2003).

PRIVILEGE AND PERSONAL MERIT

If attending college is a rite of passage for rich men and women, as social-conflict analysis suggests, then *schooling transforms social privilege into personal merit.* But given our cultural emphasis on individualism, we tend to see credentials as badges of ability rather than as symbols of family affluence (Sennett & Cobb, 1973).

When we congratulate the new graduate, we rarely recognize the financial and social resources that made this achievement possible. Yet young people from families with incomes exceeding $100,000 a year average more than 200 points higher on the SAT college entrance examination than young people from families with less than $10,000 in annual income. The richer students are thus more likely to get into college; once there, they are also more likely to complete their studies and get a degree. In a *credential society*—one that evaluates people based on their schooling—companies hire those with the best education. This process ends up helping people who are already advantaged and hurting those who are already disadvantaged (Collins, 1979).

CRITICAL REVIEW Social-conflict analysis links formal education to social inequality to show how schooling transforms privilege into personal worthiness and disadvantage into personal deficiency. However, the social-conflict approach overlooks the extent to which schooling provides upward mobility for talented women and men from all backgrounds. In addition, despite claims that schooling supports the status quo, today's college curricula challenge social inequality on many fronts.

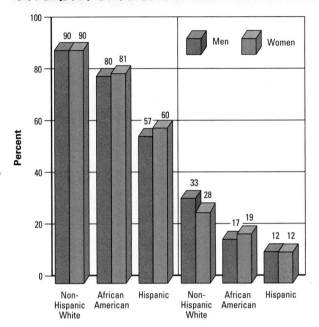

DIVERSITY SNAPSHOT

FIGURE 14-2 Educational Achievement for Various Categories of People, Aged 25 Years and Older, 2004

U.S. society still provides less education to minorities.

Source: U.S. Census Bureau (2005).

TABLE 14-2

Median Income by Sex and Educational Attainment*

Education	Men	Women
Professional degree	$100,000 (4.5)	$80,458 (5.0)
Doctorate	85,864 (3.8)	66,852 (4.1)
Master's	75,025 (3.4)	51,412 (3.2)
Bachelor's	60,020 (2.7)	42,172 (2.6)
1–3 years of college	42,418 (1.9)	31,399 (1.9)
4 years of high school	36,302 (1.6)	26,289 (1.6)
9–11 years of school	27,189 (1.2)	20,125 (1.2)
0–8 years of school	22,330 (1.0)	16,142 (1.0)

*Persons aged twenty-five years and over working full time, 2005. The earnings ratio, in parentheses, indicates how many times the lowest income level a person with additional schooling earns.

Source: U.S. Census Bureau (2006).

APPLYING THEORY

Education

	Structural-Functional Approach	Symbolic-Interaction Approach	Social-Conflict Approach
What is the level of analysis?	Macro-level	Micro-level	Macro-level
What is the importance of education for society?	Schooling performs many vital tasks for the operation of society, including socializing the young and encouraging discovery and invention to improve our lives. Schooling helps unite a diverse society by teaching shared norms and values.	How teachers and others define students can become real to everyone and affect students' educational performance.	Schooling maintains social inequality through unequal schooling for rich and poor. Within individual schools, tracking provides privileged children with a better education than poor children.

The Applying Theory table sums up what the theoretical approaches show us about education.

✓ **YOUR LEARNING** Explain several ways in which education is linked to social inequality.

Problems in the Schools

An intense debate revolves around schooling in the United States. Because we expect schools to do so much—equalize opportunity, instill discipline, and fire the imagination—people are divided on whether public schools are doing their job. Although almost half of adults give their local schools a grade of A or B, just as many give a grade of C or below (Rose & Gallup, 2006).

 For details on this national poll, go to http://www.pdkintl.org/kappan/k0609pol.htm

DISCIPLINE AND VIOLENCE

When many of today's older teachers think back to their own student days, school "problems" consisted of talking out of turn, chewing gum, breaking the dress code, or cutting class. Today, schools are grappling with serious issues such as drug and alcohol abuse, teenage pregnancy, and outright violence. Although almost everyone agrees that schools should teach personal discipline, many people think the job is no longer being done.

Schools do not create violence; in most cases, violence spills into schools from the surrounding society. In the wake of a number of school shootings in recent years, many school districts have adopted zero-tolerance policies that require suspension or expulsion for serious misbehavior or bringing weapons on campus.

STUDENT PASSIVITY

If some schools are plagued by violence, many more are filled with students who are bored. Some of the blame for their passivity can be placed on the fact that electronic devices, from television to iPods, now claim far more of young people's time than school, parents, and community activities. But schools must share the blame because the educational system itself encourages student passivity (Coleman, Hoffer, & Kilgore, 1981).

Bureaucracy

The small, personal schools that served local communities a century ago have evolved into huge education factories. In a study of high schools across the United States, Theodore Sizer (1984:207–9) identified five ways in which large, bureaucratic schools undermine education:

1. **Rigid uniformity.** Bureaucratic schools run by outside specialists (such as state education officials) generally ignore the cultural character of local communities and the personal needs of their children.

2. **Numerical ratings.** School officials define success in terms of numerical attendance rates and dropout rates, and "teach to the tests," hoping to raise test scores. In the process, they overlook dimensions of schooling that are difficult to quantify, such as creativity and enthusiasm.

3. **Rigid expectations.** Officials expect fifteen-year-olds to be in the tenth grade and eleventh graders to score at a certain level on a standardized verbal achievement test. Rarely are exceptionally bright and motivated students permitted to graduate early. Likewise, poor performers are pushed from grade to grade.

4. **Specialization.** High school students learn Spanish from one teacher, receive guidance from another, and are coached in sports by still others. Students shuffle between fifty-minute periods throughout the school day. As a result, no school official comes to know the child well.

5. **Little individual responsibility.** Highly bureaucratic schools do not empower students to learn on their own. Similarly, teachers have little say in how they teach their classes; any change in the pace of learning risks disrupting the system.

Of course, with 54 million schoolchildren in the United States, schools have to be bureaucratic to get the job done. But Sizer recommends that we "humanize" schools by eliminating rigid scheduling, reducing class size, and training teachers more broadly to make them more involved in the lives of their students. Overall, as James Coleman (1993) has suggested, schools should be less "administratively driven" and more "output-driven." Perhaps this transformation could begin by ensuring that graduation from high school depends on what students have learned rather than on how many years they have spent in the building.

College: The Silent Classroom

Passivity is also common among college and university students (Gimenez, 1989). Sociologists rarely study the college classroom—a curious fact considering how much time they spend there. One exception was a study of a coeducational university where David Karp and William Yoels (1976) found that even in small classes, only a few students speak up. Thus passivity is a classroom norm, and students even become irritated if one of their number is especially talkative.

According to Karp and Yoels, most students think classroom passivity is their own fault. But as anyone who watches young people outside of class knows, they are usually active and vocal. It is clearly the schools that teach students to be passive and to view instructors as experts who serve up "truth." Students see their proper role as quietly listening and taking notes. As a result, the researchers estimate, just 10 percent of college class time is used for discussion.

Faculty can bring students to life in their classrooms by making use of four teaching strategies: (1) calling on students by name when they volunteer, (2) positively reinforcing student participation, (3) asking analytical rather than factual questions and giving students time to answer, and (4) asking for student opinions even when no one volunteers a response (Auster & MacRone, 1994).

For all categories of people in the United States, dropping out of school greatly reduces the chances to get a good job and earn a secure income. Why is the dropout rate particularly high among Hispanic Americans?

How many of your classes encourage student discussion? Is participation more common in some disciplines than in others? Why?

DROPPING OUT

If many students are passive in class, others are not there at all. The problem of *dropping out*—quitting before earning even a high school diploma—leaves young people (many of whom are disadvantaged to begin with) unprepared for the world of work and at high risk for poverty.

The dropout rate has declined slightly in recent decades; currently, 10.3 percent of people between the ages of sixteen and twenty-four are high school dropouts, a total of 3.8 million young women and men. Dropping out is least common among non-Hispanic whites (6.8 percent), more likely among non-Hispanic African Americans (11.8 percent), and most common among Hispanics (23.8 percent) (National Center for Education Statistics, 2006).

Some students drop out because of problems with the English language, others because of pregnancy, and some because they must work to support their family. The dropout rate (17.7 percent) among children growing up in the poorest 25 percent of all households is five times as high

The New York Times

The College Dropout Boom

May 24, 2005

BY DAVID LEONHARDT

CHILHOWIE, Va.—One of the biggest decisions Andy Blevins has ever made . . . never seemed like much of a decision at all. . . .

In the summer of 1995, he was moving boxes of soup cans, paper towels and dog food across the floor of a supermarket warehouse. . . . The job had sounded impossible when he arrived fresh off his first year of college. . . .

But hard work done well was something he understood, even if he was the first college boy in his family. Soon he was making bonuses on top of his $6.75 an hour, more money than either of his parents made. His girlfriend was around, and so were his hometown buddies. . . .

It was just about the perfect summer. . . .

So he quit college . . . and . . . joined one of the largest and fastest-growing groups of young adults in America. He became a college dropout, though *non-graduate* may be the more precise term.

Many people like him plan to return to get their degrees, even if few actually do. Almost one in three Americans in their mid-20s now fall into this group, up from one in five in the late 1960s, when the Census Bureau began keeping such data. Most come from poor and working-class families.

The phenomenon has been largely overlooked in the glare of positive news about the country's gains in education. Going to college has become the norm throughout most of the United States. . . . At elite universities, classrooms are filled with women, blacks, Jews and Latinos, groups largely excluded two generations ago. The American system of higher learning seems to have become a great equalizer.

In fact, though, colleges have come to reinforce many of the advantages of birth. On campuses that enroll poorer students, graduation rates are often low. . . . Only 41 percent of low-income students entering a four-year college managed to graduate within five years, the Department of Education found in a study last year, but 66 percent of high-income students did. That gap had grown over recent years. . . .

That loss of ground is all the more significant because a college education matters much more now than it once did. . . . College graduates have received steady pay increases over the past two decades, while the pay of everyone else has risen little more than the rate of inflation.

As a result, despite one of the great education explosions in modern history, economic mobility . . . has stopped rising, researchers say. Some recent studies

---

as that (3.5 percent) for youngsters living in the richest 25 percent of households (National Center for Education Statistics, 2006). These data suggest that many dropouts are young people whose parents also have little schooling, revealing a multigenerational cycle of disadvantage. "In the *Times*" shows how class position plays into the decision by young people to leave college.

ACADEMIC STANDARDS

Perhaps the most serious educational issue confronting our society is the quality of schooling. *A Nation at Risk,* a 1983 study of the quality of U.S. schools by the National Commission on Excellence in Education, begins with this alarming statement:

> If an unfriendly foreign power had attempted to impose on America the mediocre educational performance that exists today, we might well have viewed it as an act of

war. As it stands, we have allowed this to happen to ourselves. (1983:5)

Supporting this claim, the report notes that "nearly 40 percent of seventeen-year-olds cannot draw inferences from written material; only one-fifth can write a persuasive essay; and only one-third can solve mathematical problems requiring several steps" (1983:9). Furthermore, scores on the Scholastic Assessment Test (SAT) show little improvement over time. In 1967, median scores were 516 on the mathematics test and 543 on the verbal test; by 2006, the average in mathematics had risen slightly to 518, and the verbal average had slipped to just 503. Nationwide, one-third of high school students—and more than half of those in urban schools—fail to master even the basics in reading, math, and science on the National Assessment of Education Progress examination (Marklein, 2000; Barnes, 2002a).

For many people, even basic literacy is at issue. **Functional illiteracy,** *a lack of the reading and writing skills*

suggest that it has declined over the last generation. . . . Ten years after trading college for the warehouse, Mr. Blevins . . . has worked his way up to produce buyer, earning $35,000 a year with health benefits and a 401(k) plan. He is on a path typical for someone who attended college without getting a four-year degree. Men in their early 40s in this category made an average of $42,000 in 2000. Those with a four-year degree made $65,000. . . .

Mr. Blevins says he has many reasons to be happy. He lives with his wife, Karla, and their year-old son, Lucas, in a small blue-and-yellow house at the end of a cul-de-sac in the middle of a stunningly picturesque Appalachian valley. . . .

But he does think about what might have been. . . .

College degree or not, Mr. Blevins has the kind of life that many Americans say they aspire to. He fills it with family, friends, church and a five-handicap golf game. . . .

Mr. Blevins also sings in a quartet called the Gospel Gentlemen. . . .

On a still-dark February morning, with the winter's heaviest snowfall on the ground, Andy Blevins scraped off his Jeep and began his daily drive to the supermarket warehouse. As he passed the home of Mike Nash, his neighbor and fellow gospel singer, he noticed that the car was still in the driveway. For Mr. Nash, a school counselor and the only college graduate in the singing group, this was a snow day.

Mr. Blevins later sat down with his calendar and counted to 280: the number of days he had worked last year. Two hundred and eighty days—six days a week most of the time—without ever really knowing what the future would hold. . . .

So the decision was made. On May 31, Andy Blevins says, he will return to Virginia Highlands, taking classes at night. . . .

He thinks he can get his bachelor's degree in three years. If he gets it at all, he will have defied the odds.

WHAT DO YOU THINK?

1. Is it correct to say that society is responsible for the high dropout rate among certain categories of people? Explain your answer.

2. Would more financial aid to needy students reduce the dropout rate? Why or why not?

3. Overall, does higher education makes U.S. society more equal or more unequal? Why?

needed for everyday living, is a problem for one in eight U.S. children who leave secondary school. For older people, the problem is even worse, with about 40 million U.S. adults (about 20 percent of the total) reading and writing at an eighth-grade level or below.

A Nation at Risk recommended drastic reform. First, it called for schools to require *all* students to complete several years of English, mathematics, social studies, general science, and computer science. Second, it warned schools not to promote students until they meet achievement standards. Third, it stated that teacher training must improve and teachers' salaries be raised to draw talent into the profession. The report concluded that schools must meet public expectations and that citizens must be prepared to pay for a job well done.

What has happened in the years since *A Nation at Risk* was issued? In some respects, schools have improved. A report by the Center on Education Policy (2000) noted a decline in the dropout rate, a trend toward schools' offering more challenging courses, and a larger share of high school graduates going to college. Despite several tragic cases of shootings, school violence overall was down during the 1990s. At the same time, the evidence suggests that a majority of elementary school students are falling below standards in reading; in many cases, they can't read at all. In short, although some improvement is evident, much remains to be done.

The United States spends more on schooling its children than almost any other country. Even so, a recent government report comparing the academic performance of twelfth graders in twenty-one countries found that the United States placed sixteenth in science and nineteenth in mathematics. Such statistics fuel fears that our country is losing its leadership in science to other nations, including China, India, and South Korea (Kingsbury, 2006; Lemonick, 2006).

Cultural values play a part in how hard students work at their schooling. For example, U.S. students generally are less motivated and do less homework than students in Japan. Japanese young people also spend sixty more days in school each year than U.S. students. Perhaps one approach to improving schools is simply to have students spend more time there.

YOUR TURN

Recall that U.S. students spend only about 13 percent of their waking hours in school. Do you think they should spend more time in school? Explain your answer.

GRADE INFLATION

Academic standards depend on the use of grades that have clear meaning and are awarded for work of appropriate quality. Yet in recent decades, there has been a substantial amount of *grade inflation,* the awarding of ever-higher grades for average work. While not necessarily found in every school, grade inflation is evident in both high schools and colleges.

One recent study of high school grades showed the dramatic change in the distribution of grades between 1968 and 2005. In 1968, the high school records of students who had just entered college included more grades of C+ and below than grades of A–, A, and A+. By 2005, however, these A grades outnumbered grades of C+ and below by almost nine to one (Pryor et al., 2005).

A few colleges and universities have enacted policies that limit the share of A's (generally to one-third of all grades). But there is little evidence that grade inflation will be reversed anytime soon. As a result, the C grade (which used to mean "average") may all but disappear, making just about every student "above average."

What accounts for grade inflation? In part, today's teachers are concerned about the morale and self-esteem of their students and perhaps their own popularity. In any case, teachers clearly are not as "tough" as they used to be. At the same time, the ever more competitive process of getting into college and graduate school puts pressure on high schools and colleges to award high grades (Astin et al., 2002).

Recent Issues in U.S. Education

Our society's schools continuously confront new challenges. Here we explore several recent and important educational issues.

SCHOOL CHOICE

Some analysts claim that our schools teach poorly because they have no competition. Giving parents options about schooling their children might force all schools to do a better job. This is the essence of a policy called *school choice.*

The goal of school choice is to create a market for education so that parents and students can shop for the best value. According to one proposal, the government would provide vouchers to families with school-aged children and allow them to spend the money at public, private, or parochial schools. In recent years, major cities, including Indianapolis, Minneapolis, Milwaukee, Cleveland, Chicago, and Washington, D.C., as well as the states of Florida and Illinois, have experimented with choice plans designed to make public schools perform better to win the confidence of families.

Supporters claim that giving parents a choice about where to enroll their children is the only sure way to improve all schools. But critics (including teachers' unions) charge that school choice amounts to giving up on our nation's commitment to public education and that it will do little to improve schools in the central cities, where the need is greatest (A. Cohen, 1999; Morse, 2002b).

In 2002, President George W. Bush signed a new education bill (popularly known as "No Child Left Behind") that downplayed vouchers in favor of another approach to greater choice. Starting in the 2005–06 school year, all public schools must test every child in reading, mathematics, and science in grades three through eight. Although the federal government may provide more aid to schools with students who do not perform well, if those schools do not show improvements in test scores over time, low-income students will have the choice of special tutoring or transportation to another school (Lindlaw, 2002).

A more modest form of school choice involves *magnet schools,* almost 2,000 of which now exist across the country. Magnet schools offer special facilities and programs to promote educational excellence in a particular field, such as computer science, foreign languages, science and mathematics, or the arts. In school districts with magnet schools, parents can choose the one best suited to their child's particular talents and interests.

Another school choice strategy involves *charter schools,* public schools that are given more freedom to try new policies and programs. There are about 3,500 such schools in forty states, Washington, D.C., and Puerto Rico; they enroll more than 1 million students, about half of whom are minorities. In many of these schools, students have demonstrated high academic achievement—a requirement for renewal of the charter (U.S. Charter Schools, 2006).

A final development in the school choice movement is *schooling for profit.* Supporters of this plan say school systems can be operated more efficiently by private profit-making companies than by local governments. Private schooling is nothing new, of course; more than 29,000 schools in the United States are currently run by private organizations and religious groups. What is new is that hundreds of public schools, enrolling hundreds of thousands of students, are now run by private businesses for profit.

Research confirms that many public school systems suffer from bureaucratic bloat, spending far too much and teaching far too little. And our society has long looked to competition to improve quality. Evidence suggests that for-profit schools have greatly reduced administrative costs, but the educational results appear mixed. Although companies claim to improve student learning, some cities have cut back on business-run schooling. In recent years, school boards in Baltimore, Miami, Hartford, and Boston have canceled the contracts of for-profit schooling corporations. But other cities are still willing to give for-profit schooling a try. For example, after Philadelphia's public school system failed to graduate one-third of its students, the state of Pennsylvania took over that city's schools and turned over most of them to for-profit companies. Emotions both for and against privately run public schools run high, and each side claims it speaks for the well-being of the schoolchildren caught in the middle (McGurn, 2002; Winters, 2002; Sizer, 2003).

HOME SCHOOLING

Home schooling is gaining popularity across the United States. About 1.1 million children (more than 2 percent of all school-aged children) have their formal schooling at home, and the number is increasing rapidly. This means that home schooling involves more school-age children than magnet schools, charter schools, and for-profit schools combined.

Why do parents undertake the enormous challenge of schooling their own children? Some twenty years ago, many of the parents who pioneered home schooling (which is now legal in every state) did not believe in public education, often because they wanted to give their children a strongly religious upbringing. Today, however, the majority are mothers and fathers who simply do not believe that public schools are doing a good job, and they think they can do better. To benefit their children, many parents are willing to change work schedules and to relearn algebra or other necessary subjects. Many belong to groups in which parents combine their efforts, specializing in what each knows best.

Advocates of home schooling point out that given the poor performance of many public schools, no one should be surprised that a growing number of parents are stepping up to teach their own children. In addition, this system works—on average, students who learn at home outper-

Educators have long debated the best way to teach children with disabilities. On one hand, such children may benefit from separate facilities staffed by specially trained teachers. On the other hand, children are less likely to be stigmatized as "different" if they are included in regular classrooms. One way to "mainstream" children with special needs is to provide them with teaching assistants who offer the help they need throughout the day.

form those who learn in school. Critics argue that home schooling reduces the amount of funding going to local public schools, which ends up hurting the majority of students. Moreover, as one critic points out, home schooling "takes some of the most affluent and articulate parents out of the system. These are the parents who know how to get things done with administrators" (Chris Lubienski, quoted in Cloud & Morse, 2001:48).

SCHOOLING PEOPLE WITH DISABILITIES

Many of the 6 million children with disabilities in the United States have difficulty getting to and from school; once there, many with crutches or wheelchairs cannot negotiate stairs and other obstacles in school buildings. Children with developmental disabilities such as mental retardation need extensive personal attention from specially trained teachers. As a result, many children with mental and physi-

The Twenty-First-Century Campus: Where Are the Men?

A century ago, the campuses of colleges and universities across the United States might as well have hung out a sign that read "Men Only." Almost all of the students and faculty were male. There were a small number of women's colleges, but many more schools—including some of the best-known U.S. universities, such as Yale, Harvard, and Princeton—barred women outright.

Since then, women have won greater social equality. By 1980, the number of women enrolled at U.S. colleges finally matched the number of men.

In a surprising trend, however, the share of women on campus has continued to increase. As a result, in 2004, men accounted for only 43 percent of all U.S. undergraduates. Meg DeLong noticed the gender imbalance right away when she moved into her dorm at the University of Georgia at Athens; she soon learned that just 39 percent of her first-year classmates were men. In some classes there were few men, and women usually dominated discussions. Out of class, DeLong and many other women soon complained that having so few men on campus hurt their social life. Not surprisingly, most of the men felt otherwise (Fonda, 2000).

What accounts for the shifting gender balance on U.S.

campuses? One theory is that young men are drawn away from college by the lure of jobs, especially in high technology. This pattern is sometimes termed the "Bill Gates syndrome," after the Microsoft founder, who dropped out of college and soon became the world's richest person. In addition, analysts point to an anti-intellectual male culture. Young women are drawn to learning and seek to do well in school, but young men attach less importance to studying. Rightly or wrongly, more men seem to think they can get a good job without investing years of their lives and a considerable amount of money in getting a college degree.

The gender gap is evident in all racial and ethnic categories and at all class levels. Among African Americans on campus, only 35 percent are men.

The lower the income level, the greater the gender gap in college attendance.

Many college officials are concerned about a lack of men on campus. In an effort to attract more balanced enrollments, some colleges are adopting what amounts to affirmative action programs that favor males. But courts in several states have already ruled such policies illegal. Many colleges, therefore, are turning to more active recruitment; admissions officers are paying special attention to male applicants and stressing a college's strength in mathematics and science—areas that traditionally have attracted men. In the same way that colleges across the country are striving to increase their share of minority students, the hope is that they can also succeed in attracting a larger share of men.

WHAT DO YOU THINK?

1. Among high school students, are men less concerned than women about academic achievement? Why or why not?

2. Is there a gender imbalance on your campus? Does it create problems? If so, what problems? For whom?

3. What programs or policies do you think might increase the number of men going to college?

---

cal disabilities have received a public education only after persistent efforts by parents and other concerned citizens (Horn & Tynan, 2001).

About half of all children with disabilities are schooled in special facilities; the rest attend public schools, many joining regular classes. Including students with disabilities

in the overall educational program is called *mainstreaming*. This form of *inclusive education* works best for physically impaired students who have no difficulty keeping up with the rest of the class. Another benefit is that mainstreaming allows all students to learn to interact with people who are different from themselves.

ADULT EDUCATION

In 2001, more than 92 million U.S. adults were enrolled in some type of schooling. These older students range in age from the mid-twenties to the seventies and beyond and make up 21 percent of students in degree-granting programs. Adults in school are more likely to be women than men, and most have above-average incomes.

Why do adults return to the classroom? The most common reasons given are to advance a career or train for a new job (30 percent), but many (21 percent) are in class simply for personal enrichment (U.S. Census Bureau, 2005).

THE TEACHER SHORTAGE

A final challenge for U.S. schools is hiring enough teachers to fill the classrooms. A number of factors—including low salaries, frustration, and retirement, as well as rising enrollment and increases in class size—have combined to create more than 200,000 teaching vacancies in the United States each year.

How will these slots be filled? About the same number of people graduate with education degrees annually. Most of them do not have a degree in a specific field, such as mathematics, biology, or English, and many have trouble passing state certification tests in the area they want to teach.

As a result, schools have adopted new recruitment strategies. Some analysts suggest that community colleges can play a larger role in teacher education. Others support using incentives such as higher salaries and signing bonuses to draw into teaching people who have already had successful careers. Another approach is for states to make teaching certification easier to get. Finally, many school districts are going global, actively recruiting in countries such as Spain, India, and the Philippines to bring talented women and men from around the world to U.S. classrooms (M. Lord, 2001; Philadelphia, 2001; Evelyn, 2002).

Debate about education in the United States extends beyond the issues noted here. The Seeing Sociology in Everyday Life box highlights the declining share of college students who are men.

Schooling: Looking Ahead

Although the United States still leads the world in sending people to college, the public school system continues to struggle with serious problems. In terms of quality of schooling, this country is falling behind many other nations, a fact that calls into question the future strength of the United States on the world stage.

Many of the problems of schooling discussed in this chapter have their roots in the larger society. We cannot expect schools *by themselves* to provide high-quality education. Schools will improve only to the extent that students, teachers, parents, and local communities commit themselves to educational excellence. In short, educational problems are *social* problems for which there is no quick fix.

For much of the twentieth century, there were just two models for education in the United States: public schools run by the government and private schools operated by nongovernmental organizations. In recent decades, however, many new ideas about schooling have emerged, including schooling for profit and a wide range of "school choice" programs. In the decades ahead, we will probably see some significant changes in mass education, guided in part by the results of social science research into the outcomes of different strategies.

Another factor that will continue to shape schools is information technology. Today, all but the poorest primary and secondary schools use computers for instruction. Computers prompt students to be more active and allow them to progress at their own pace. Even so, computers will never bring to the educational process the personal insights or imagination of a motivated human teacher. Nor will technology ever solve all the problems that plague our schools, including violence and rigid bureaucracy. What we need is a broad plan for social change that refires this country's ambition to provide universal schooling of the highest quality—a goal that we have yet to achieve.

Health and Medicine

Another institution that expands greatly in modern societies is **medicine,** *the social institution that focuses on* Learn more about the World Health Organization at http://www.who.int/en/ *fighting disease and improving health.* In ideal terms, according to the World Health Organization (1946:3), **health** is *a state of complete physical, mental, and social well-being.* This definition underscores the important fact that health is as much a social as a biological issue.

HEALTH AND SOCIETY

Society affects people's health in four major ways:

1. **Cultural patterns define health.** Standards of health vary from culture to culture. A century ago, yaws, a contagious skin disease, was so common in tropical Africa that people there considered it normal (Dubos, 1980, orig. 1965). "Health," therefore, is sometimes a matter of having the same diseases as one's neighbors (Pinhey, Rubinstein, & Colfax, 1997).

TABLE 14-3

Leading Causes of Death in the United States, 1900 and 2004

1900	2004
1. Influenza and pneumonia	1. Heart disease
2. Tuberculosis	2. Cancer
3. Stomach and intestinal disease	3. Stroke
4. Heart disease	4. Lung disease (noncancerous)
5. Cerebral hemorrhage	5. Accidents
6. Kidney disease	6. Diabetes
7. Accidents	7. Alzheimer's disease
8. Cancer	8. Influenza and pneumonia
9. Disease in early infancy	9. Kidney disease
10. Diphtheria	10. Blood disease

Sources: Information for 1900 is from William C. Cockerham, *Medical Sociology*, 2d ed. (Englewood Cliffs, N.J.: Prentice Hall, 1986), p. 24; information for 2004 is from Arialdi M. Miniño, Melonie P. Heron, & Betty L. Smith, *National Vital Statistics Reports*, vol. 54, no. 19 (Hyattsville, Md.: National Center for Health Statistics, 2006).

What people see as healthful also reflects what they think is morally good. Members of our society (especially men) think a competitive way of life is "healthy" because it fits our cultural mores, but stress contributes to heart disease and many other illnesses. On the other hand, people who object to homosexuality on moral grounds often call it "sick," even though it is natural from a biological point of view. Thus ideas about health act as a form of social control, encouraging conformity to cultural norms.

2. **Cultural standards of health change over time.** Early in the twentieth century, some doctors warned women not to go to college because higher education strained the female brain. Others claimed that masturbation was a threat to health. We now know that both of these ideas are false. Fifty years ago, on the other hand, few doctors understood the dangers of cigarette smoking or too much sun exposure, practices that we now recognize as serious health risks. Even patterns of basic hygiene change over time. Today, most people in the United States bathe every day; this is three times as many as fifty years ago (Gallup, 2000).

3. **A society's technology affects people's health.** In poor nations, infectious diseases are widespread because of malnutrition and poor sanitation. As industrialization raises living standards, people become healthier. But industrial technology also cre-

ates new threats to health. As Chapter 15 ("Population, Urbanization, and Environment") explains, rich societies endanger health by overtaxing the world's resources and creating pollution.

4. **Social inequality affects people's health.** All societies distribute resources unequally. Overall, the rich have far better physical, mental, and emotional health than the poor.

Health: A Global Survey

Because health is closely linked to social life, human well-being has improved over the long course of history as societies developed more advanced technology. Differences in societal development are also the cause of striking differences in health around the world today.

HEALTH IN LOW-INCOME COUNTRIES

With only simple technology, our ancestors could do little to improve health. Hunters and gatherers faced frequent food shortages, which sometimes forced mothers to abandon their children. Those lucky enough to survive infancy were still vulnerable to injury and illness, so half died by age twenty and few lived to forty (Scupin, 2000; Nolan & Lenski, 2004).

As societies developed agriculture, food became more plentiful. Yet social inequality also increased, so that elites enjoyed better health than peasants and slaves, who lived in crowded, unsanitary shelters and often went hungry. In the growing cities of medieval Europe, human waste and refuse piled up in the streets, spreading infectious diseases, and plagues periodically wiped out entire towns (Mumford, 1961).

In much of the world, poverty cuts decades off the life expectancy found in rich countries. A look back at Global Map 9–2 on page 252 shows that people in most parts of Africa have a life expectancy of barely fifty, and in the poorest countries, most people die before reaching their teens.

The World Health Organization reports that 1 billion people around the world—one person in six—suffer from serious illness due to poverty. Poor sanitation and malnutrition kill people of all ages. In a classic vicious circle, poverty breeds disease, which reduces people's ability to work, increasing poverty. When medical technology is used to control infectious disease, the populations of poor nations soar. But without enough resources to provide for the current population, poor societies can ill afford population increases. Therefore, programs that lower death rates in poor countries will succeed only if they are coupled with programs that reduce birth rates.

HEALTH IN HIGH-INCOME COUNTRIES

By 1800, as the Industrial Revolution took hold, factory jobs in cities attracted people from all over the countryside. Cities quickly became overcrowded, a condition creating serious sanitation problems. Factories fouled the air with smoke, and workplace accidents were common.

Gradually, industrialization raised living standards, providing better nutrition and safer housing for most people, so that by about 1850, health began to improve. About this time, medical advances began to control infectious diseases. For example, in 1854, a researcher named John Snow mapped the street addresses of London's cholera victims and found that they had all drunk water from the same well. Not long afterward, scientists linked cholera to a specific bacterium and developed a vaccine against the deadly disease. Armed with scientific knowledge, early environmentalists campaigned against common practices such as discharging raw sewage into rivers used for drinking water. By the early twentieth century, death rates from infectious diseases had fallen sharply.

A look at Table 14–3 shows that the leading killers in 1900—influenza and pneumonia—account for just a few percent of deaths in the United States today. It is now chronic illnesses, such as heart disease, cancer, and stroke, that cause most deaths, usually in old age.

Health in the United States

Because the United States is a rich nation, health is generally good by world standards. Still, some categories of people have much better health than others.

WHO IS HEALTHY? AGE, GENDER, CLASS, AND RACE

Social epidemiology is *the study of how health and disease are distributed throughout a society's population.* Social epidemiologists examine the origin and spread of epidemic

 For information on nutrition and health, go to http://www.nal.usda.gov/fnic/etext/000056.html

diseases and show how people's health is tied to their physical and social environments. In the United States, there is a twenty-year difference in average life expectancy between the richest and poorest communities. This difference can be viewed in terms of age, gender, social class, and race.

Age and Gender

Death is now rare among young people. Still, young people do fall victim to accidents and in recent decades, to acquired immune deficiency syndrome (AIDS).

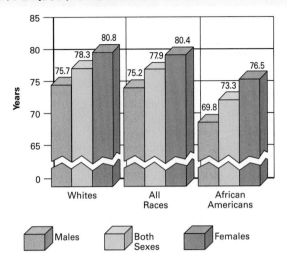

FIGURE 14-3 Life Expectancy of U.S. Children Born in 2004

Both gender and race have a powerful effect on life expectancy.
Source: Miniño, Heron, & Smith (2006).

Throughout the life course, women have better health than men. First, girls are less likely than boys to die before or immediately after birth. As socialization begins, males become more aggressive and individualistic, resulting in higher rates of accidents, violence, and suicide. As the Applying Sociology box on page 430 explains, the combination of chronic impatience, uncontrolled ambition, and outbursts of hostility that doctors call "coronary-prone behavior" is a fairly close match with our culture's definition of masculinity.

Social Class and Race

Government researchers tell us that 74 percent of people in families with incomes over $75,000 think their health is excellent or very good, but only 44 percent of people in families earning less than $20,000 say the same. Conversely, only about 6 percent of higher-income people describe their health as fair or poor, compared with 27 percent of low-income people (Lethbridge-Çejku, Rose, & Vickerie, 2006).

Poverty among African Americans—three times the rate for whites—helps explain why black people are more likely to die in infancy and, as adults, to suffer the effects of violence, drug abuse, and poor health (Hayward et al., 2000). Figure 14–3 shows that the life expectancy of white children born in 2004 is five years greater than for African American children (78.3 years versus 73.3). Gender is an even stronger predictor of health than race, since African

Masculinity: A Threat to Health?

Doctors call it "coronary-prone behavior." Psychologists call it "Type A personality." Sociologists recognize it as our culture's idea of masculinity. This combination of attitudes and behavior, common among men in our society, includes (1) chronic impatience ("C'mon! Get outta my way!"), (2) uncontrolled ambition ("I've gotta have it. I *need* that!"), and (3) free-floating hostility ("Why are so many people *such idiots?*").

This pattern, although normal from a cultural point of view, is one major reason that men who are driven to succeed are at high risk for heart disease. By acting out the Type A personality, we may get the job done, but we set in motion complex biochemical processes that are very hard on the human heart.

Here are a few questions to help you determine your own degree of risk (or that of someone important to you):

1. **Do you believe that you have to be aggressive to succeed? Do nice guys finish last?** For your heart's sake, try to remove hostility from your life. One starting point: Eliminate pro-

fanity from your speech. Try to replace aggression with compassion, which can be surprisingly effective in dealing with other people. Medically speaking, compassion and humor—rather than irritation and aggravation—will improve your health.

2. **How well do you handle uncertainty and opposition?** Do you have moments when you fume, "Why won't the waiter take my order?" or "This jerk just doesn't get it!"? We all like to know what's going on, and we want others to agree with us. But the world often doesn't work this way. Accepting uncertainty and opposition makes us

more mature and certainly healthier.

3. **Are you uncomfortable showing positive emotion?** Many men think that giving and accepting love—from women, from children, and from other men—is a sign of weakness. But the medical truth is that love supports health and anger damages it.

As human beings, we have a great deal of choice about how we live. Think about the choices you make, and reflect on how our society's idea of masculinity often makes us hard on others (including those we love) and, just as important, hard on ourselves.

WHAT DO YOU THINK?

1. What aspects of masculinity are harmful to health?

2. Why are so many people unaware of how masculinity can be harmful to health?

3. How can sociology play a part in changing men's health for the better?

Sources: Friedman & Rosenman (1974) and M. P. Levine (1990).

American women outlive men of either race. From another angle, 80 percent of white men but just 66 percent of African American men will live to age sixty-five. The comparable figures for women are 88 percent for whites and 79 percent for African Americans.

Infant mortality—the death rate among children under one year of age—is twice as high for disadvantaged children in the United States as for children born into privileged families. Although the health of the richest children in our country is the best in the world, our poorest children are as vulnerable to disease as those in low-income nations such as Nigeria and Vietnam.

CIGARETTE SMOKING

Cigarette smoking tops the list of preventable health hazards in the United States. Only after World War I did smoking become popular in this country. Despite growing evidence of its dangers, smoking remained fashionable until around a generation ago. Today, however, an increasing number of people consider smoking a mild form of social deviance.

The popularity of cigarettes peaked in 1960, when 45 percent of U.S. adults smoked. By 2004, only 21 percent were lighting up. Quitting is difficult because cigarette smoke contains nicotine, a physically addictive drug. Many people smoke to cope with stress: Divorced and separated people are likely to smoke, as are lower-income people, the unemployed, and people in the armed forces. A larger share of U.S. men (23 percent) than women (19 percent) smoke. But cigarettes, the only form of tobacco use popular among women, have taken a toll on women's health. By 1987, lung cancer surpassed breast cancer as a cause of death among U.S. women, who now account for 41 percent of all smoking-related deaths (Centers for Disease Control and Prevention, 2005b).

Some 440,000 men and women die prematurely each year as a direct result of cigarette smoking, a figure that exceeds the death toll from alcohol, cocaine, heroin, homicide, suicide, automobile accidents, and AIDS combined (Centers for Disease Control and Prevention, 2005a). Smokers also suffer more often from minor illnesses such as the flu, and pregnant women who smoke increase the likelihood of spontaneous abortion, prenatal death, and low-birthweight babies. Even nonsmokers exposed to cigarette smoke have a high risk of smoking-related diseases.

Tobacco is an $83 billion industry in the United States. In 1997, the tobacco industry admitted that cigarette smoking is harmful to health and agreed to stop marketing cigarettes to young people. Despite the antismoking trend in the United States, the percentage of college students who smoke has been creeping up, to 29 percent in 2001 (Centers for Disease Control and Prevention, 2002). In addition, the use of chewing tobacco, also a threat to health, is increasing among the young.

The tobacco industry has increased marketing abroad, where there is less regulation of tobacco products. In many countries, especially in Asia, a large majority of men smoke. Worldwide, more than 1 billion adults (about 30 percent of the total) smoke, consuming some 6 trillion cigarettes annually, and smoking is on the rise. The good news is that about ten years after quitting, an ex-smoker's health is about as good as that of someone who never smoked at all.

YOUR TURN

Researchers report that the less schooling people have, the more likely they are to smoke. Why do you think this is the case?

EATING DISORDERS

An **eating disorder** is *an intense type of dieting or other unhealthy method of weight control driven by the desire to be*

Mary-Kate Olsen, shown on the right with her twin sister Ashley Olsen, is among the many young women celebrities who have struggled with an eating disorder. To what extent do you think the mass media are responsible for encouraging young women to be so thin that some even put their lives at risk? Explain your view.

very thin. One eating disorder, *anorexia nervosa,* is characterized by dieting to the point of starvation; another is *bulimia,* which involves binge eating followed by induced vomiting to avoid weight gain.

About half of college women have engaged in such behavior, showing that eating disorders have a significant cultural component. Of people who suffer from anorexia nervosa or bulimia, 95 percent are women, mostly from white, affluent families. For women, U.S. culture equates slimness with being successful and attractive to men. Conversely, we tend to stereotype overweight women (and to a lesser extent men) as lazy, sloppy, and even stupid (M. P. Levine, 1987; A. E. Becker, 1999).

Research shows that most college-age women believe that "guys like thin girls," that being thin is crucial to physical attractiveness, and that they are not as thin as men would like. In fact, most college women actually want to be thinner than most college men want them to be. Men typi-

SEEING OURSELVES

NATIONAL MAP 14-2
Obesity across the United States

According to the government, two-thirds of U.S. adults are overweight, meaning that they are at least 10 pounds over a healthy weight. About half of all overweight people are clinically obese, which means they are at least 30 pounds overweight. This map shows the share of the population that is obese for counties across the nation. Looking at the map, what can you say about the regions that have the highest rates of obesity?

Source: *Time* (June 7, 2004). Copyright © 2004 Time, Inc. Reprinted by permission.

Percentage of Population with a Body Mass Index between 30 and 40
- 21.1% to 27.0%
- 19.1% to 21.0%
- 15.1% to 19.0%
- 11.4% to 15.0%

cally express more satisfaction with their own body shapes (Fallon & Rozin, 1985).

Because few women are able to meet our culture's unrealistic standards of beauty, many women develop a low self-image. Our idealized image of beauty leads many young women to diet to the point of risking their health and even their lives.

OBESITY

Eating disorders such as anorexia nervosa and bulimia are not the biggest eating-related problem in the United States. Obesity in the population as a whole is rapidly reaching crisis proportions. The government reports that two-thirds of U.S. adults are overweight, which is defined in terms of a *body mass index* (BMI) of 25.0–29.9, or roughly 10 to 30 pounds over a healthy weight for one's height. Half of all overweight people in the United States are clinically obese with a BMI over 30.0, which means that they are at least 30 pounds over their healthy weight. National Map 14–2 shows the percentage of people who are medically obese in the United States.

This government Web site provides health news and statistical data on a wide range of health topics: http://www.cdc.gov

Being overweight can limit physical activity and raises the risk of a number of serious diseases, including heart disease, stroke, and diabetes. According to the U.S. government, the cost of treating diseases caused by obesity plus the cost of lost days at work due to such illnesses equals about $117 billion every year. Most seriously, some 300,000 people die each year in the United States from diseases related to being overweight (Carmona, 2003; Ferraro & Kelley-Moore, 2003).

A cause for national concern is the fact that about one in four young people in this country is already overweight, and the proportion is increasing. This trend suggests that the members of this new generation will experience more medical problems as they reach middle age and may ultimately reverse the historical trend toward greater life expectancy.

What are the social causes of obesity? One factor is that we live in a society in which more and more people have jobs that keep them sitting in front of computer screens rather than engaging in the type of physical labor that was common a century ago. Even when we are not on the job, most of the work around the house is done by machines (or other people). Children spend more of their time sitting as well, watching television or playing video games.

Then, of course, there is diet. The typical person in the United States is eating more salty and fatty foods than ever before. And meals are also getting bigger: The Department of Agriculture recently reported that in 2000, the typical U.S. adult consumed 140 more pounds of food each year than was true a decade earlier. Comparing old and new editions of cookbooks, recipes that used to say they would feed six now say they will feed four. The odds of being overweight go up among people with lower incomes partly because they may lack the education to make healthy choices and partly because stores in low-income communities offer a greater selection of low-cost, high-fat snack foods and fewer healthful fruits and vegetables (Hellmich, 2002).

Calculate your *body mass index* (BMI): [weight in pounds ÷ (height in inches)^2] × 703. Or, go to http://www.cdc.gov/nccdphp/dnpa/bmi/adult_BMI/english_bmi_calculator/bmi_calculator.htm to do a quick calculation (Normal: 18.5–24.9; overweight: 25.0–29.9; obese: 30 and over). Where does your BMI fall? Were you surprised by the results?

SEXUALLY TRANSMITTED DISEASES

Sexual activity, though both pleasurable and vital to the continuation of our species, can transmit more than fifty kinds of infection, or *venereal disease* (named for Venus, the Roman goddess of love). Because U.S. culture associates sex with sin, some people regard sexually transmitted diseases (STDs) not only as illnesses but also as marks of immorality.

STDs grabbed national attention during the "sexual revolution" of the 1960s, when infection rates rose dramatically as people began sexual activity earlier and had a greater number of partners. This means that STDs are an exception to the general decline in infectious diseases over the course of the past century. By the late 1980s, the rising danger of STDs, especially AIDS, generated a sexual counterrevolution as people moved away from casual sex (Kain, 1987; Laumann et al., 1994). The following sections briefly describe several common STDs.

Gonorrhea and Syphilis

Gonorrhea and syphilis, among the oldest known diseases, are caused by microscopic organisms that are almost always transmitted by sexual contact. Untreated, gonorrhea causes sterility, and syphilis can damage major organs and result in blindness, mental disorders, and death.

In 2004, some 330,000 cases of gonorrhea and 33,000 instances of syphilis were recorded in the United States, although the actual numbers may be several times higher. Most cases are contracted by non-Hispanic African Americans (70 percent), with lower numbers among non-Hispanic whites (20 percent), Latinos (9 percent), and Asian and Native Americans (under 2 percent) (Centers for Disease Control and Prevention, 2005d).

Both gonorrhea and syphilis can be cured easily with antibiotics such as penicillin. Thus neither is a major health problem in the United States.

Genital Herpes

Genital herpes is a virus that infects at least 45 million adults in the United States (one in five). Though far less

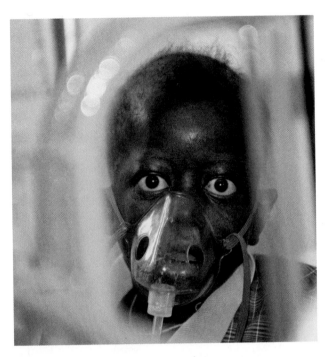

In the African nation of Kenya, there are about 500 deaths from AIDS every day. In parts of sub-Saharan Africa, the epidemic is so great that half of all children will become infected with HIV. This young Nairobi child, who already has AIDS, is fighting for his life.

serious than gonorrhea and syphilis, herpes is incurable. People with genital herpes may not have any symptoms, or they may experience periodic, painful blisters on the genitals accompanied by fever and headache. Although it is not fatal to adults, women with active genital herpes can transmit the disease during a vaginal delivery, and it can be deadly to newborns. Therefore, infected women often give birth by cesarean section (Sobel, 2001).

AIDS

The most serious of all sexually transmitted diseases is acquired immune deficiency syndrome (AIDS). Identified in 1981, it is incurable and almost always fatal. AIDS is caused by the human immunodeficiency virus (HIV), which attacks white blood cells, weakening the immune system. AIDS thus makes a person vulnerable to a wide range of other diseases that eventually cause death.

AIDS deaths in the United States numbered 15,798 in 2004. But officials recorded some 42,514 new cases in the United States that year, raising the total number of cases on record to 944,306. Of these, about 529,113 have died (Centers for Disease Control and Prevention, 2005c).

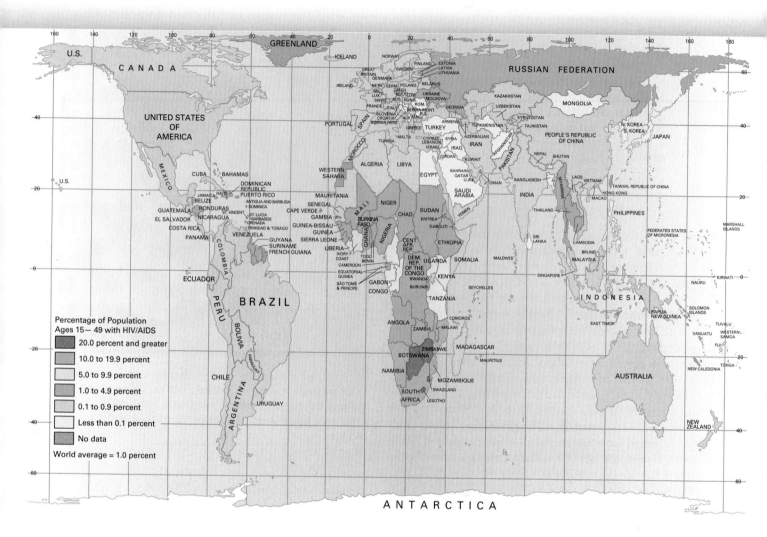

WINDOW ON THE WORLD

GLOBAL MAP 14–2   HIV/AIDS Infection of Adults in Global Perspective

Sixty-four percent of all global HIV infections are in sub-Saharan Africa. In Swaziland, one-third of people between the ages of fifteen and forty-nine are infected with HIV/AIDS. This very high infection rate reflects the prevalence of other sexually transmitted diseases and infrequent use of condoms, two factors that promote transmission of HIV. All of Southeast Asia accounts for about 17 percent of global HIV infections. In Cambodia, nearly 2 percent of people aged fifteen to forty-nine are now infected. All of North and South America taken together account for 8 percent of global HIV infections. In the United States, 0.6 percent of people aged fifteen to forty-nine are infected. The incidence of infection in Muslim nations is extremely low by world standards.

Sources: Population Reference Bureau (2003, 2006) and United Nations (2006); map projection from *Peters Atlas of the World* (1990).

Globally, HIV infects some 40 million people—half of them under age twenty-five—and the number is rising rapidly. The global death toll now exceeds 25 million, with about 2 percent of all deaths occurring in the United States. Global Map 14–2 shows that Africa (more specifically,

countries south of the Sahara) has the highest HIV infection rate and accounts for 64 percent of all world cases. A recent United Nations study found that across much of sub-Saharan Africa, fifteen-year-olds face a fifty-fifty chance of becoming infected with HIV. The risk is especially high for girls, not only because HIV is transmitted more easily from men to women but also because many African cultures encourage women to be submissive to men. According to For information on United Nations efforts to combat AIDS, go to http://www.unaids.org some analysts, the AIDS crisis now threatens the political and economic security of Africa, which affects the entire world (Ashford, 2002; United Nations, 2006).

Upon infection, people with HIV display no symptoms at all, so most are unaware of their condition. Symptoms of AIDS may not appear for a year or longer, during which time an infected person may infect others. Within five years, one-third of infected people develop full-blown AIDS; half develop AIDS within ten years, and almost all become sick within twenty years.

HIV is infectious but not contagious. That means that HIV is transmitted from person to person through blood, semen, or breast milk but not through casual contact such as shaking hands, hugging, sharing towels or dishes, swimming together, or even coughing and sneezing. The risk of transmitting AIDS through saliva (as in kissing) is extremely low. The risk of transmitting HIV through sexual activity is greatly reduced by the use of latex condoms. However, abstinence or an exclusive relationship with an uninfected person is the only sure way to avoid infection.

Specific behaviors place people at high risk for HIV infection. The first is *anal sex*, which can cause rectal bleeding, allowing easy transmission of HIV from one person to another. The fact that many homosexual and bisexual men engage in anal sex helps explain why these categories of people account for 48 percent of AIDS cases in the United States.

Sharing needles used to inject drugs is a second high-risk behavior. At present, intravenous drug users account for 27 percent of people with AIDS, so sex with an intravenous drug user is also very risky. Because intravenous drug use is more common among poor people in the United States, AIDS is becoming a disease of the socially disadvantaged. Minorities make up a majority of all people with AIDS: Non-Hispanic African Americans (12 percent of the population) account for 43 percent of people with AIDS, and Latinos (13 percent of the population) represent 20 percent of all AIDS cases. Almost 80 percent of all women and children with the disease are African American or Latino. By contrast, Asian Americans and Native Americans together account for only about 1 percent of people with AIDS (Centers for Disease Control and Prevention, 2005d).

Use of *any drug*, including alcohol, also increases the risk of being infected with HIV to the extent that it impairs judgment. In other words, even people who understand the risks may make bad choices regarding sexual activity or intravenous drug use once they are under the influence of alcohol, marijuana, or some other drug.

In the United States, 47 percent of people with AIDS became infected through homosexual contact. Only 17 percent of people with AIDS became infected through heterosexual contact, although heterosexuals, infected in various ways including intravenous drug use, account for more than 30 percent of AIDS cases. But heterosexual activity can transmit HIV, and the danger rises with the number of sexual partners one has, especially if they fall into high-risk categories. Worldwide, heterosexual relations are the primary means of HIV transmission, accounting for two-thirds of all infections.

Treating just one person with AIDS costs hundreds of thousands of dollars, and this figure may rise as new therapies appear. At present, government health programs, private insurance, and personal savings rarely cover more than a fraction of the cost of treatment. In addition, there is the mounting cost of caring for at least 75,000 U.S. children orphaned by AIDS. Overall, there is little doubt that AIDS is both a medical and a social problem of monumental proportions.

The U.S. government responded slowly to the AIDS crisis, largely because gays and intravenous drug users are widely viewed as deviant. But funding for AIDS research has increased (now totaling some $17 billion annually), and researchers have identified some drugs, including protease inhibitors, that suppress the symptoms of the disease. But educational programs remain the most effective weapon against AIDS because prevention is the only way to stop a disease that so far has no cure.

ETHICAL ISSUES SURROUNDING DEATH

Now that technological advances are giving human beings the power to draw the line separating life and death, people often must make the decision about how and when life ends. In other words, questions about the use of medical technology have added an ethical dimension to health and illness.

When Does Death Occur?

Common sense suggests that life ends when breathing and heartbeat stop. But the ability to revive or replace a heart and artificially sustain respiration makes this definition of death obsolete. Thus medical and legal experts in the United States define death as an *irreversible* state involving no response to stimulation, no movement or breathing, no reflexes, and no indication of brain activity (Ladd, 1979; Wall, 1980; D. G. Jones, 1998).

Do People Have a Right to Die?

Today, medical personnel, family members, and patients themselves face the burden of deciding when the life of a terminally ill person should end. Among the most difficult cases are the 10,000 people in the United States in a permanent vegetative state who cannot express their own desires about life and death.

Generally speaking, the first duty of doctors and hospitals is to protect a patient's life. Even so, a mentally competent person in the process of dying can refuse medical treatment or even nutrition either at the time or, in advance, through a document called a *living will* that states the extent of medical care a person would want or not want in the event of an illness or injury that leaves the person unable to make decisions.

"Mercy killing" is the common term for **euthanasia,** *assisting in the death of a person suffering from an incurable disease.* Euthanasia (from the Greek for "a good death") poses an ethical dilemma, being at once an act of kindness and a form of killing.

Whether there is a "right to die" is one of today's most difficult issues. All people with incurable diseases have a right to refuse treatment that might prolong their lives. But whether a doctor should be allowed to help bring about death is at the heart of today's debate. In 1994, three states—Washington, California, and Oregon—asked voters whether doctors should be able to help people who wanted to die. Only Oregon's proposition passed, and the law was quickly challenged and remained tied up in court until 1997, when voters again endorsed it. Since then, Oregon doctors have legally assisted in the death of a small number of terminally ill patients. In 1997, however, the U.S. Supreme Court decided that under the U.S. Constitution, there is no "right to die," a decision that has slowed the spread of such laws.

Supporters of *active* euthanasia—allowing a dying person to enlist the services of a doctor to bring on a quick death—argue that there are circumstances (such as when a dying person is suffering great pain) that make death preferable to life. Critics counter that permitting active euthanasia invites abuse. They fear that patients will feel pressure to end their lives to spare family members the burden of caring for them and the high costs of hospitalization. Research in the Netherlands, where physician-assisted suicide is legal, indicates that about one-fifth of all such deaths have occurred without a patient's explicitly requesting to die (Gillon, 1999).

In the United States, a majority of adults express support for giving dying people the right to choose to die with a doctor's help (NORC, 2005). Therefore, the right-to-die debate is sure to continue.

The Medical Establishment

Throughout most of human history, health care was the responsibility of individuals and their families. Medicine emerges as a social institution only as societies become more productive and people take on specialized work.

Members of agrarian societies today still turn to various traditional health practitioners, including acupuncturists and herbalists. In industrial societies, medical care falls to specially trained and licensed professionals, from anesthesiologists to X-ray technicians. The medical establishment of modern, industrial societies took form over the past 200 years.

THE RISE OF SCIENTIFIC MEDICINE

In colonial times, herbalists, druggists, barbers, midwives, and ministers practiced the healing arts. But not all were effective. Unsanitary instruments, lack of anesthesia, and simple ignorance made surgery a terrible ordeal, and doctors probably killed as many people as they saved.

Doctors made medicine into a science by following scientific procedures to study the human body and how it works, emphasizing surgery and the use of drugs to fight disease. Pointing to their specialized knowledge, doctors gradually established themselves as self-regulating professionals with medical degrees. The American Medical Association (AMA), founded in 1847, symbolized the growing acceptance of a scientific model of medicine.

Still, traditional practitioners of health care had their supporters. The AMA opposed them by seeking control of the certification process. In the early 1900s, state licensing boards agreed to certify only doctors trained in the scientific programs approved by the AMA. As a result, schools teaching other healing skills began to close, which soon limited the practice of medicine to individuals holding an M.D. degree. Accordingly, the prestige and income of doctors rose dramatically; today, men and women with M.D. degrees earn, on average, $250,000 annually.

Practitioners who did things differently, such as osteopathic physicians, concluded that they had no choice but to fall in line and follow AMA standards. Thus osteopaths (with D.O. degrees), originally concerned with treating illness by manipulating the skeleton and muscles, today treat illness with drugs in much the same way as medical doctors (with M.D. degrees). Chiropractors, herbal healers, and midwives still practice with their own special approaches but have lower standing within the medical profession.

Scientific medicine, taught in expensive, urban medical schools, also changed the social profile of doctors so that most physicians came from privileged backgrounds and practiced in cities. Women, who had played a large part in many fields of healing, were pushed aside by the AMA. Some early medical schools did train women and African Americans, but with few financial resources, most of these schools eventually closed. Only in recent decades has the social diversity of the medical profession increased, with women and African Americans representing 32 percent and 5 percent of physicians, respectively (U.S. Department of Labor, 2006).

HOLISTIC MEDICINE

The scientific model of medicine has been tempered by the introduction of **holistic medicine,** *an approach to health care that emphasizes prevention of illness and takes into account a person's entire physical and social environment.* Holistic practitioners agree on the need for drugs, surgery, artificial organs, and high technology, but they emphasize treating the whole person instead of just symptoms of disease. There are three foundations of holistic health care (Gordon, 1980; Patterson, 1998):

1. **Treat patients as people.** Holistic practitioners are concerned not only with symptoms but also with how people's environment and lifestyle affect health. Holistic practitioners extend the bounds of conventional medicine, taking an active role in fighting poverty, environmental pollution, and other dangers to public health.

2. **Encourage responsibility, not dependency.** A scientific approach to medicine puts doctors in charge of health, and patients are to follow doctors' orders. Holistic medicine tries to shift some responsibility for health from doctor to patient by emphasizing health-promoting behavior. Holistic medicine favors an *active* approach to *health* rather than a *reactive* approach to *illness.*

3. **Provide personal treatment.** Scientific medicine treats patients in impersonal offices and hospitals, both disease-centered settings. Holistic practitioners favor, as much as possible, a personal and relaxed environment such as the home.

In sum, holistic care does not oppose scientific medicine but shifts the emphasis from treating disease to achieving the greatest well-being for everyone. Considering that the AMA certifies more than fifty medical specialties, there is a need for practitioners concerned with the whole patient.

YOUR TURN

Point to specific ways in which you think people should take personal responsibility for their own health. In what ways should society change to promote public health?

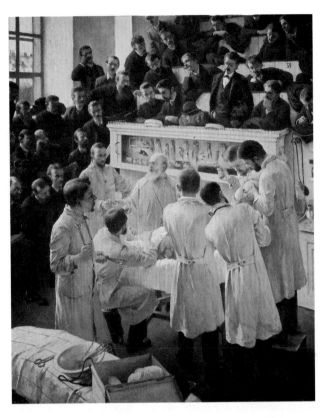

The rise of scientific medicine during the nineteenth century resulted in new skills and technology for treating many common ailments that had afflicted humanity for centuries. At the same time, however, scientific medicine pushed forms of health care involving women to the margins and placed medicine under the control of men living in cities. We see this pattern in the A. F. Seligmann painting *General Hospital*, showing an obviously all-male medical school class in Vienna in 1880.

PAYING FOR MEDICAL CARE: A GLOBAL SURVEY

As medicine has come to rely on high technology, the costs of medical care in industrial societies have skyrocketed. Countries throughout the world have adopted different strategies to meet these costs.

People's Republic of China

This economically growing but still mostly agrarian nation faces the immense task of providing for the health of more than 1.3 billion people. China has experimented with private medicine, but the government controls most health care.

China's "barefoot doctors," roughly comparable to U.S. paramedics, bring some modern methods of medical care to peasants in rural villages. Traditional healing arts, involving acupuncture and medicinal herbs, are still widely practiced. The Chinese approach to health is based on a holistic concern for the interplay of mind and body (Kaptchuk, 1985).

Russian Federation

The Russian Federation is transforming a state-dominated economy into more of a market system. For this reason, medical care is in transition. Nevertheless, the idea that everyone has a right to basic medical care remains widespread.

As in China, people in the Russian Federation do not choose a doctor but report to a local government health facility. Physicians have much lower incomes than medical doctors in the United States, earning about the same salary as skilled industrial workers (by contrast, U.S. doctors earn roughly five times as much as industrial workers in the United States). Also, about 70 percent of Russia's doctors are women, compared to 32 percent in the United States. As in our society, occupations dominated by women in the Russian Federation offer fewer financial rewards.

In recent years, the Russian Federation has suffered setbacks in health, partly due to a falling standard of living. A rising demand for medical care has strained a bureaucratic system that at best provides highly standardized and impersonal care. The optimistic view is that as market reforms proceed, both living standards and the quality of medical service will improve. In Russia's uncertain times, what does seem clear is that inequalities in medical care will increase (Specter, 1995; Landsberg, 1998).

Sweden

In 1891, Sweden began a mandatory, comprehensive system of government medical care. Citizens pay for this program with their taxes, which are among the highest in the world. Typically, doctors are government employees, and most hospitals are government-managed. Sweden's system is called **socialized medicine**, *a medical care system in which the government owns and operates most medical facilities and employs most physicians.*

Great Britain

In 1948, Great Britain also established socialized medicine by creating a dual system of medical services. All British citizens are entitled to medical care provided by the National Health Service, but those who can afford it can also go to doctors and hospitals that operate privately.

Canada

Since 1972, Canada has had a "single-payer" model of medical care that provides care to all Canadians. Like a vast

insurance company, the Canadian government pays doctors and hospitals according to a set schedule of fees. But Canada's system, like Great Britain's, has two tiers, with some doctors working outside the government-funded system and setting their own fees, although costs are regulated by the government.

Canada boasts of providing care for everyone at a lower cost than the (nonuniversal) medical system in the United States. However, the Canadian system uses less state-of-the-art technology and responds more slowly, meaning that people may wait months to receive major surgery. The Canadian system provides care for all its citizens, regardless of income, unlike the United States, in which lower-income people are often denied medical care (Rosenthal, 1991; Macionis & Gerber, 2005).

 July 31, Montreal, Canada. I am visiting the home of an oral surgeon who appears (judging by the large home) to be doing pretty well. Yet he complains that the Canadian government, in an effort to hold down medical costs, caps doctors' salaries at about $125,000 (U.S.). Therefore, he explains, many specialists have left for the United States, where they can earn much more; other doctors and dentists simply limit their practices.

Japan

Physicians in Japan operate privately, but a combination of government programs and private insurance pays medical costs. As shown in Figure 14–4, the Japanese approach medical care much like the Europeans, with most medical expenses paid through the government.

PAYING FOR MEDICAL CARE: THE UNITED STATES

The United States stands alone among high-income nations in having no universal, government-operated program of medical care. Ours is a **direct-fee system,** *a medical care system in which patients pay directly for the services of physicians and hospitals.* Europeans look to government to fund 70 to 80 percent of medical costs (paid for through taxation), but the U.S. government pays just 46 percent of this country's medical costs (U.S. Census Bureau, 2005).

 Read the government report *Healthy People 2010* at http://www.cdc.gov/nchs/hphome.htm

In the United States, rich people can buy the best medical care in the world, but poor people are worse off than their counterparts in Europe. This difference translates into relatively high death rates among both infants and adults in the United States compared with many European countries (United Nations Development Programme, 2005).

Why does the United States have no national medical care program? First, because our culture stresses self-reliance, our society has limited government. Second, political support for a national medical program has not been strong, even among labor unions, which have concentrated on winning medical care benefits from employers. Third, the AMA and the insurance industry have strongly and consistently opposed national medical care (Starr, 1982).

Medical expenditures in the United States have increased dramatically, from $12 billion in 1950 to more than $1.9 trillion in 2004 (National Coalition on Health Care, 2006). This amounts to more than $5,000 per person, more than any other nation spends for medical care. Who pays the medical bills?

YOUR TURN

The head of the Ford Motor Company said recently that in building a car, the cost of medical care for workers is now greater than the cost of steel. How do you think the rising cost of medical care affects an average family's budget?

Private Insurance Programs

In 2005, about 175 million people in the United States (59 percent) received medical care benefits from a family member's employer or labor union. Another 27 million people (9 percent) purchased some private coverage on their own. Combining these figures, 68 percent of the U.S. population has private insurance, although few such programs pay all medical costs (U.S. Census Bureau, 2006).

Public Insurance Programs

In 1965, Congress created Medicare and Medicaid. Medicare pays some of the medical costs for people over age sixty-five; in 2005, it covered 40 million men and women, 14 percent of the population. In the same year, Medicaid, a medical insurance program for the poor, provided benefits to 38 million people, about 13 percent of the population. An additional 11 million veterans (4 percent) can obtain free care in government-operated hospitals. In all, 27 percent of this country's people get medical benefits from the government, but most also have private insurance.

Health Maintenance Organizations

About 72 million people (25 percent) in the United States belong to a **health maintenance organization (HMO),** *an organization that provides comprehensive medical care to subscribers for a fixed fee.* HMOs vary in cost and benefits, and none provides full coverage. Fixed fees make these organi-

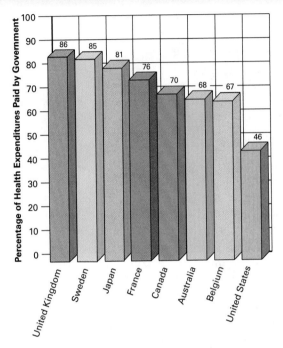

GLOBAL SNAPSHOT

FIGURE 14-4 Extent of Socialized Medicine in Selected Countries

Of all high-income countries, the United States has the smallest percentage of government-provided medical care.

Sources: U.S. Census Bureau (2005) and World Bank (2006).

zations profitable if subscribers stay healthy; therefore, many take a preventive approach to health. However, HMOs have been criticized for refusing to pay for medical procedures that they consider unnecessary. Congress is currently debating the extent to which patients can sue HMOs to obtain better care.

In all, 84 percent of the U.S. population has some medical care coverage, either private or public. Yet most plans do not provide full coverage, so serious illness threatens even middle-class people with financial hardship. Most programs also exclude many medical services, such as dental care and treatment for mental health and substance abuse problems. Worse, 47 million people (about 16 percent of the population) have no medical insurance at all, even though 78 percent of these people are working. Almost as many lose their coverage temporarily each year because of layoffs or job changes. Caught in the medical care bind are mostly low- to moderate-income people who cannot afford the cost of the preventive medical care they need to stay healthy (Brink, 2002; U.S. Census Bureau, 2006).

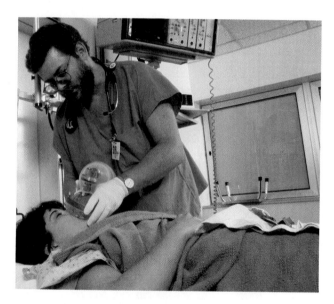

Throughout the United States, there is a serious shortage of nurses. One strategy for filling the need is for nursing programs to recruit more men into this profession; currently, men account for only 8 percent of nurses with R.N. degrees.

THE NURSING SHORTAGE

Another issue in medical care is the shortage of nurses across the United States. In 2005, there were some 2.4 million registered nurses (people with the degree of R.N.), but about 7 percent of the available jobs (roughly 140,000 positions) were unfilled.

The immediate cause of the shortage is that fewer people are entering the nursing profession. In the past decade, enrollments in nursing programs have dropped by one-third, even as the need for nurses, driven by the aging of the U.S. population, goes up. Why this decline? One factor is that today's young women have a wide range of job choices, and fewer are drawn to the traditionally female occupation of nursing. This fact is evident in the rising median age of working nurses, which is now forty-three. Another is that many of today's nurses are unhappy with their working conditions, citing heavy patient loads, too much required overtime, a stressful working environment, and a lack of recognition and respect from supervisors, physicians, and hospital managers. In fact, one recent survey found that a majority of working nurses say they would not recommend the field to others, and many R.N.s are leaving the field for other jobs.

A hopeful sign is that the nursing shortage is bringing change to this profession. Salaries, which range from about $45,000 for general-duty nurses to $100,000 for certified nurse anesthetists, are rising, although slowly. Some hospitals and doctors are also offering signing bonuses in efforts to attract new nurses. In addition, nursing programs are trying harder to recruit a more diverse population, seeking more minorities (which are currently underrepresented) and, especially, more men (who now make up only 8 percent of R.N.s) (DeFrancis, 2002a, 2002b; R. W. Dworkin, 2002; Yin, 2002).

Theoretical Analysis of Health and Medicine

Each of the theoretical approaches in sociology helps us organize and understand facts and issues concerning human health.

STRUCTURAL-FUNCTIONAL ANALYSIS: ROLE THEORY

Talcott Parsons (1951) viewed medicine as society's strategy to keep its members healthy. Parsons considered illness to be dysfunctional because it reduces people's abilities to perform their roles.

The Sick Role

Society responds to illness not only by providing medical care but also by allowing people a **sick role,** *patterns of behavior defined as appropriate for people who are ill.* According to Parsons, the sick role releases people from everyday obligations such as going to work or attending classes. However, people cannot simply claim to be ill; they must "look the part" and, in serious cases, get the help of a medical expert. After assuming the sick role, the patient must want to get better and must do whatever is needed to regain good health, including cooperating with health professionals.

The Physician's Role

Physicians evaluate people's claims of sickness and help restore the sick to normal routines. To do this, physicians use their specialized knowledge and expect patients to follow "doctor's orders" in order to complete treatment.

CRITICAL REVIEW Parsons's analysis links illness and medicine to the broader organization of society. Others have extended the concept of the sick role to some nonillness situations such as pregnancy (Myers & Grasmick, 1989).

One limitation of the sick-role concept is that it applies to acute conditions (like the flu or a broken leg) better than to chronic illnesses (like heart disease), which may not be reversible. In addition, a sick person's ability to assume the sick role (to take time off from work to regain

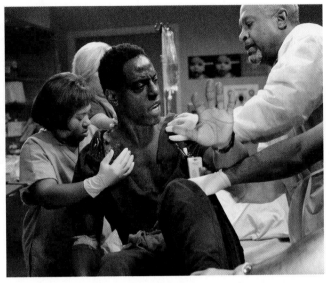

Our national view of medicine has changed during the last several decades. Television viewers in the 1970s watched doctors like Marcus Welby, M.D., confidently take charge of situations in a fatherly—and almost godlike—manner. By the 1990s, programs like *E.R.* gave a more realistic view of the limitations of medicine to address illness, as well as the violence that wracks our society. © American Broadcasting Companies, Inc.

health) depends on the person's resources. Finally, illness is not completely dysfunctional; it can have some positive consequences. Many people who experience a serious illness consider it an opportunity to reevaluate their lives and gain a better sense of what is truly important to them (D. G. Myers, 2000; Ehrenreich, 2001).

✓ **YOUR LEARNING** Define the sick role. How does turning illness into a role in this way help society operate?

SYMBOLIC-INTERACTION ANALYSIS: THE MEANING OF HEALTH

Using the symbolic-interaction approach, society is less a grand system than a complex and changing reality. In this view, health and medical care are socially constructed by people in everyday interaction.

The Social Construction of Illness

If both health and illness are socially constructed, people in a poor society may view malnutrition as normal. Similarly, many members of our own society give little thought to the harmful effects of a rich diet.

Our response to illness is based also on social definitions that may or may not square with medical facts. People with AIDS may be forced to deal with prejudice that has no medical basis. Likewise, students may pay no attention to symptoms of illness on the eve of vacation but head for the infirmary hours before a midterm examination with a case

of the sniffles. In short, health is less an objective fact than a negotiated outcome.

How people define a medical situation may actually affect how they feel. Medical experts marvel at *psychosomatic* disorders (a fusion of the Greek words for "mind" and "body"), when state of mind guides physical sensations (Hamrick, Anspaugh, & Ezell, 1986). Applying sociologist W. I. Thomas's theorem (presented in Chapter 4, "Social Interaction in Everyday Life"), we can say that once health or illness is defined as real, it can become real in its consequences.

The Social Construction of Treatment

Also in Chapter 4, we used Erving Goffman's dramaturgical approach to explain how doctors tailor their physical surroundings (their office) and their behavior (the "presentation of self") so that others see them as competent and in charge.

The sociologist Joan Emerson (1970) further illustrates this process of reality construction in her analysis of the gynecological examination carried out by a male doctor. The situation could be seriously misinterpreted because a man touching a woman's genitals is conventionally viewed as a sexual act and possibly an assault.

To ensure that the situation is defined as impersonal and professional, medical personnel wear uniforms, and the examination room is furnished with nothing but medical equipment. The doctor's manner is designed to make the patient feel that to him, examining the genital area is no different from treating any other part of the body. A female

APPLYING THEORY

Health

	Structural-Functional Approach	Symbolic-Interaction Approach	Social-Conflict and Feminist Approaches
What is the level of analysis?	Macro-level	Micro-level	Macro-level
How is health related to society?	Illness is dysfunctional for society because it prevents people from carrying out their daily roles. The sick role releases people who are ill from responsibilities while they try to get well.	Societies define "health" and "illness" differently according to their living standards. How people define their own health affects how they actually feel (psychosomatic conditions).	Health is linked to social inequality, with rich people having more access to care than poor people. Capitalist medical care places the drive for profits over the needs of people, treating symptoms rather than addressing poverty and sexism as causes of illness.

nurse usually is present during the examination, not only to assist the physician but also to avoid any impression that a man and woman are "alone together."

Managing situational definitions is rarely taught in medical schools. This oversight is unfortunate, because as Emerson's analysis shows, understanding how medical personnel construct reality in the examination room is as important as mastering the medical skills needed for treatment.

CRITICAL REVIEW The symbolic-interaction approach reveals that what people view as healthful or harmful depends on a host of factors that are not, strictly speaking, medical. This approach also shows that in any medical procedure, both patient and medical staff engage in a subtle process of reality construction.

Critics fault the symbolic-interaction approach for implying that there are no objective standards of well-being. Certain physical conditions do indeed cause specific changes in people, regardless of how we may view those conditions. For example, people who lack sufficient nutrition and safe water suffer from their unhealthy environment, whether they define their surroundings as normal or not.

A recent study shows that since 1985, the share of beginning college students in the United States who describe their physical health as "above average" has been dropping. Do you think this trend reflects changing perceptions or a real decline in health (due, say, to eating more unhealthy food)? Why do you think more men than women see their health as above average?

✔ **YOUR LEARNING** Explain what it means to say that both health and the treatment of illness are socially constructed.

SOCIAL-CONFLICT AND FEMINIST ANALYSIS

Social-conflict analysis points out the connection between health and social inequality. Some analysts, taking a cue from Karl Marx, tie medicine to the operation of capitalism. In addition, feminists link medicine to sexism and gender stratification. Most attention has gone to three main issues: access to medical care, the effects of the profit motive, and the politics of medicine.

Access to Care

Health is important to everyone. But by requiring individuals to pay for medical care, capitalist societies allow the richest people to have the best health. The access problem is more serious in the United States than in most other high-income nations because we do not have a universal medical care system.

Conflict theorists argue that capitalism provides excellent health care for the rich but at the expense of the rest of the population. Most of the 47 million people in the United States who lack any medical care coverage at present have moderate to low incomes.

The Profit Motive

Some social-conflict analysts go further, arguing that the real problem is not access to medical care but capitalist medicine itself. The profit motive turns doctors, hospitals, and the pharmaceutical industry into multibillion-dollar corporations. The drive for higher profits encourages unnecessary tests and surgery and a reliance on expensive drugs rather than focusing on improving people's lifestyles and living conditions.

Of about 25 million surgical operations performed in the United States each year, three-fourths are elective, meaning that they are intended to promote long-term health and are not prompted by a medical emergency. Of course, any medical procedure or use of drugs is risky and harms between 5 and 10 percent of patients. Therefore, social-conflict theorists argue that surgery reflects not just the medical needs of patients but also the financial interests of surgeons and hospitals (Cowley, 1995; Nuland, 1999).

Finally, say conflict theorists, our society is too tolerant of doctors' having a direct financial interest in the tests and procedures they order for their patients (Pear & Eckholm, 1991). Medical care should be motivated by a concern for people, not profits.

Medicine as Politics

Although science declares itself to be politically neutral, feminists claim that scientific medicine often takes sides on significant social issues. For example, the medical establishment has always strongly opposed government medical care programs and only recently allowed a significant number of women to join the ranks of physicians. The history of medicine shows that not only have racial and sexual discrimination kept women and people of color out of medicine, but discrimination has been supported by "scientific" opinions about, say, the inferiority of women and other minorities (Leavitt, 1984). Consider the diagnosis of "hysteria," a term that has its origins in the Greek word *hyster,* meaning "uterus." In choosing this word to describe a wild, emotional state, the medical profession suggested that being a woman is somehow the same as being irrational.

Even today, according to conflict theory, scientific medicine explains illness in terms of bacteria and viruses, ignoring the damaging effects of poverty, racism, and sexism. In effect, scientific medicine hides the bias in our medical system by transforming this social issue into simple biology.

CRITICAL REVIEW Social-conflict analysis provides still another view of the relationships among health, medicine, and society. According to this approach, social inequality is the reason some people have better health than others.

The most common objection to the conflict approach is that it minimizes the advances in U.S. health brought about by scientific medicine and higher living standards. Though there is plenty of room for improvement, health indicators for our population as a whole rose steadily over the course of the twentieth century, and they compare well with those in other high-income nations.

☑ YOUR LEARNING Explain how health and medical care are linked to social classes, to capitalism, and to gender stratification.

In sum, sociology's three major theoretical approaches explain why health and medicine are social issues. The Applying Theory table sums up what they teach us.

But advancing technology will not solve every health problem. On the contrary, as the Thinking Critically box on page 444 explains, today's advancing technology is raising new questions and concerns.

The famous French scientist Louis Pasteur (1822–1895), who spent much of his life studying how bacteria cause disease, said just before he died that health depends less on bacteria than on the social environment in which bacteria operate (Gordon, 1980:7). Explaining Pasteur's insight is sociology's contribution to human health.

Health and Medicine: Looking Ahead

In the early 1900s, deaths from infectious diseases such as diphtheria and measles were widespread. Because scientists had not yet developed penicillin and other antibiotics, even a simple infection from a minor wound was sometimes life-threatening. Today, a century later, most members of our society take good health and long life for granted. It seems reasonable to expect improvements in U.S. health to continue throughout the twenty-first century.

Another encouraging trend is that more people are taking responsibility for their own health (Caplow et al., 1991). Every one of us can live better and longer if we avoid tobacco, eat sensibly and in moderation, and exercise regularly.

Yet health problems will continue to plague U.S. society in the decades to come. The biggest problem, discussed throughout this chapter, is this nation's double standard in health: well-being for the rich but higher rates of disease for the poor. International comparisons reveal that the United States lags in some measures of human health because we neglect the people at the margins of our society. An important question, then, is how a rich society can afford to let millions of people live without the security of medical care.

Finally, we find that health problems are far greater in low-income nations than in the United States. The good news is that life expectancy for the world as a whole has been rising—from forty-eight years in 1950 to sixty-seven years today—and the biggest gains have been in poor countries (Population Reference Bureau, 2006). But in much of Latin America, Asia, and especially Africa, hundreds of millions of adults and children lack not only medical attention but adequate food and safe water as well. Improving the health of the world's poorest people is a critical challenge in the years to come.

The Genetic Crystal Ball: Do We Really Want to Look?

The liquid in the laboratory test tube seems ordinary enough, like syrupy water. But this liquid is one of the greatest medical breakthroughs of all time; it may even hold the key to life itself. The liquid is deoxyribonucleic acid, or DNA, the spiraling molecule found in every cell of the human body that contains the blueprint for making each one of us human as well as different from every other person.

The human body is composed of some 100 trillion cells, most of which contain a nucleus of twenty-three pairs of chromosomes (one of each pair comes from each parent). Each chromosome is packed with DNA in segments called genes. Genes guide the production of protein, the building block of the human body.

If genetics sounds complicated (and it is), the social implications of genetic knowledge are even more complex. Scientists discovered the structure of the DNA molecule in 1952, but it wasn't until 2000 that scientists neared the goal of mapping the human genome. Charting our genetic landscape may lead to understanding how each bit of DNA shapes our being. But do we really want to turn the key to understand life itself? And what do we do with this knowledge once we have it?

In the Human Genome Project, many scientists see the chance to stop certain illnesses before they even begin. Research has already identified genetic abnormalities that cause some forms of cancer, sickle-cell anemia, muscular dystrophy, Huntington's disease, cystic fibrosis, and other crippling and deadly afflictions. In the future, genetic screening—gazing into a scientific "crystal ball"—could tell people their medical destiny and allow doctors to manipulate segments of DNA to prevent diseases before they appear.

But many people urge caution in such research, warning that genetic information can easily be abused. At its worst, genetic mapping opens the door to Nazi-like efforts to breed a "super race." Indeed, in 1994, the People's Republic of China began to regulate marriage and childbirth with the purpose of avoiding "new births of inferior quality."

It seems inevitable that some parents will want to use genetic testing to predict the health (or even the eye color) of their future children. What if they want to abort a fetus because it falls short of their standards? When genetic manipulations become possible, should parents be able to create "designer children"?

Then there is the issue of "genetic privacy." Can a bride-to-be request a genetic evaluation of her fiancé before

agreeing to marry him? Can life insurance companies demand genetic testing before issuing policies? Should employers be allowed to screen job applicants to weed out those whose future illnesses might drain their company's health care funds? Clearly, what is scientifically possible is not always morally desirable. Society is already struggling with questions about the proper use of our expanding knowledge of human genetics. Such ethical dilemmas will multiply as genetic research moves forward in the years to come.

WHAT DO YOU THINK?

1. Traditional wedding vows join couples "in sickness and in health." Do people have a right to know the future health prospects of a partner before marriage? Why or why not?

2. Should parents be permitted to genetically "design" their children? Why or why not?

3. Should genetic research companies be allowed to patent their discoveries so that they can profit from the results, or should this information be made available to everyone? Explain your answer.

Sources: D. Thompson (1999) and Golden & Lemonick (2000).

APPLYING SOCIOLOGY IN EVERYDAY LIFE

1. Visit a secondary school near your college or home. Does it have a tracking policy? If so, find out how it works. How much importance does a student's family background have in making a tracking assignment?

2. Given the importance of sexuality in our thinking about women in the United States (and how they think about themselves), how do you think medical procedures such as mastectomy (surgical removal of

part or all of a breast) affect women's personal and social identity? (To learn more about these experiences, see Elson, 2004.)

3. Interview a midwife (many list their services in the Yellow Pages) about her work helping women deliver babies. How do midwives differ from medical obstetricians in their approach?

MAKING THE GRADE

CHAPTER 14   Education, Health, and Medicine

EDUCATION: A GLOBAL SURVEY

EDUCATION is the major social institution for transmitting knowledge and skills, as well as teaching cultural norms and values.

- In preindustrial societies, education occurs informally within the family.
- Industrial societies develop formal systems of schooling to educate their children.

pp 410–13

education (p. 410) the social institution through which society provides its members with important knowledge, including basic facts, job skills, and cultural norms and values

schooling (p. 410) formal instruction under the direction of specially trained teachers

THEORETICAL ANALYSIS OF SCHOOLING

The **STRUCTURAL-FUNCTIONAL APPROACH** highlights major functions of schooling, including, socialization, cultural innovation, social integration, and the placement of people in the social hierarchy.

- Latent functions of schooling include providing child care and building social networks.

pp 413–14

The **SYMBOLIC-INTERACTION APPROACH** helps us understand that stereotypes can have important consequences for how people act. If students think they are academically superior, they are likely to perform better; students who think they are inferior are likely to perform less well.

p 414

tracking (p. 415) assigning students to different types of educational programs

The **SOCIAL-CONFLICT APPROACH** links schooling to the hierarchy involving class, race, and gender.

- Formal education serves as a means of generating conformity to produce obedient adult workers.
- Standardized achievement tests have been criticized as culturally biased tools that may lead to labeling less privileged students as personally deficient.
- *Tracking* has been challenged by critics as a program that gives privileged youngsters a richer education.
- The great majority of young people in the United States attend state-funded public schools. A small proportion of students—usually the most well-to-do—attend elite private college preparatory schools.
- Largely due to the high cost of college, only 67% of U.S. students enroll in college directly after high school graduation.

pp 414–20

⊞   See the Applying Theory table on page 420.

PROBLEMS IN THE SCHOOLS

- *Violence* permeates many schools, especially in poor neighborhoods.
- The bureaucratic character of schools fosters *high dropout rates* and *student passivity*.
- *Declining academic standards* are reflected in today's lower average scores on achievement tests, the functional illiteracy of a significant proportion of high school graduates, and grade inflation.

pp 420–24

functional illiteracy (p. 422) a lack of the reading and writing skills needed for everyday living

RECENT ISSUES IN U.S. EDUCATION

The **SCHOOL CHOICE MOVEMENT** seeks to make schools more accountable to the public. Innovative options include

- magnet schools
- schooling for profit
- charter schools

pp 424–25

HOME SCHOOLING

- The original pioneers of home schooling did not believe in public education because they wanted to give their chidren a strongly religious upbringing.
- Home schooling advocates today point to the poor performance of public schools.

p 425

SCHOOLING PEOPLE WITH DISABILITITES

- Children with mental or physical disabilities historically have been schooled in special classes.
- *Mainstreaming* affords them broader opportunities and exposes all children to a more diverse student population.

pp 425–26

ADULT EDUCATION

- Adults represent a growing proportion of students in the United States.
- Most older learners are women who are engaged in job-related study.

p 427

THE TEACHER SHORTAGE

- More than 200,000 teaching vacancies exist in the United States each year due to low salaries, frustration, retirements, and rising enrollment and class size.
- To address this shortage, many school districts are recruiting teachers from abroad.

p 427

MAKING THE GRADE

CONTINUED...

HEALTH AND MEDICINE

HEALTH is a social issue because personal well-being depends on a society's level of technology and its distribution of resources. A society's culture shapes definitions of health.

pp 427–28

medicine (p. 427) the social institution that focuses on fighting disease and improving health

health (p. 427) a state of complete physical, mental, and social well-being

HEALTH: A GLOBAL SURVEY

HEALTH VARIES OVER TIME:
- With industrialization, health improved dramatically in Western Europe and North America in the nineteenth century.
- A century ago, infectious diseases were leading killers; today, most people in the United States die in old age of chronic illnesses such as heart disease, cancer, or stroke.

p 428

HEALTH VARIES AROUND THE WORLD:
- Poor nations suffer from inadequate sanitation, hunger, and other problems linked to poverty.
- Life expectancy in low-income nations is about twenty years less than in the United States; in the poorest nations, half the children do not survive to adulthood.

pp 428–29

HEALTH IN THE UNITED STATES

HEALTH FACTS
- More than three-fourths of U.S. children born today will live to at least age sixty-five.
- Throughout the life course, women have better health than men, and people of high social position enjoy better health than the poor.

pp 429–30

CURRENT ISSUES in U.S. health care include
- cigarette smoking, which is the greatest preventable cause of death
- eating disorders and obesity
- the increase in sexually transmitted diseases
- ethical dilemmas associated with advancing medical technology and the right to die

pp 430–36

social epidemiology (p. 429) the study of how health and disease are distributed throughout a society's population

eating disorder (p. 431) an intense type of dieting or other unhealthy method of weight control driven by the desire to be very thin

euthanasia (p. 436) assisting in the death of a person suffering from an incurable disease; also known as *mercy killing*

THE MEDICAL ESTABLISHMENT

THE RISE OF SCIENTIFIC MEDICINE
- Health care was historically a family concern but with industrialization became the responsibility of trained specialists.
- The model of scientific medicine is the foundation of the U.S. medical establishment.

pp 436–37

PAYING FOR MEDICAL CARE: A GLOBAL SURVEY
- Socialist societies define medical care as a right; governments offer basic care equally to everyone.
- Capitalist societies view medical care as a commodity to be purchased, although most capitalist governments help pay for medical care through socialized medicine or national health insurance.

pp 437–38

PAYING FOR MEDICAL CARE: THE UNITED STATES
- The United States, with a direct-fee system, is the only high-income nation with no comprehensive medical care program.
- Most people have private or government health insurance, but about 47 million people in the United States do not have medical insurance.

pp 438–40

holistic medicine (p. 437) an approach to health care that emphasizes prevention of illness and takes into account a person's entire physical and social environment

socialized medicine (p. 438) a medical care system in which the government owns and operates most medical facilities and employs most physicians

direct-fee system (p. 438) a medical care system in which patients pay directly for the services of physicians and hospitals

health maintenance organization (HMO) (p. 439) an organization that provides comprehensive medical care to subscribers for a fixed fee

sick role (p. 440) patterns of behavior defined as appropriate for people who are ill

THEORETICAL ANALYSIS OF HEALTH AND MEDICINE

The **STRUCTURAL-FUNCTIONAL APPROACH** considers illness to be dysfunctional because it reduces people's abilities to perform their roles (Talcott Parsons). Society responds to illness by defining roles:
- The *sick role* excuses the ill person from routine social responsibilities.
- The *physician's role* is to use specialized knowledge to take charge of the patient's recovery.

pp 440–41

The **SYMBOLIC-INTERACTION APPROACH** investigates how health and medical care are socially constructed by people in everyday interaction:
- Our response to illness is not always based on medical facts.
- How people define a medical situation may affect how they feel.

pp 441–42

The **SOCIAL-CONFLICT** and **FEMINIST APPROACHES** focus on the unequal distribution of health and medical care. They criticize the U.S. medical establishment for
- its overreliance on drugs and surgery
- the dominance of the profit motive
- overemphasis on the biological rather than the social causes of illness.

pp 442–43

See the Applying Theory table on page 442.

MAKING THE GRADE
Sample Test Questions
CHAPTER 14

These questions are similar to those found in the test bank that accompanies this textbook.

MULTIPLE-CHOICE QUESTIONS

1. In the United States and in other countries, laws requiring all children to attend school were enacted following
   a. national independence.
   b. the Industrial Revolution.
   c. World War II.
   d. the invention of computers.

2. Japan differs from the United States in that getting into college depends more on
   a. athletic ability.
   b. race and ethnicity.
   c. scores on achievement tests.
   d. family money.

3. Using a structural-functional approach, schooling carries out the task of
   a. tying together a diverse population.
   b. creating new culture.
   c. socializing young people.
   d. All of the above are correct.

4. A social-conflict approach highlights how education
   a. reflects and reinforces social inequality.
   b. helps prepare students for their future careers.
   c. has both latent and manifest functions.
   d. All of the above are correct.

5. The importance of community colleges to U.S. higher education is reflected in the fact that they
   a. greatly expand the opportunity to attend college.
   b. enroll almost 40 percent of all U.S. college students.
   c. enroll half of all African American and Hispanic college students.
   d. All of the above are correct.

6. Health is a social issue because
   a. cultural patterns define what people view as healthy.
   b. social inequality affects people's health.
   c. a society's technology affects people's health.
   d. All of the above are correct.

7. In the very poorest nations of the world today, a majority of people die before reaching
   a. their teens.
   b. the age of fifty.
   c. the age of sixty-five.
   d. the age of seventy-five.

8. Which is the greatest cause of death among young people in the United States?
   a. cancer
   b. AIDS
   c. accidents
   d. influenza

9. In the United States, the greatest preventable cause of death is
   a. sexually transmitted diseases.
   b. automobile accidents.
   c. cigarette smoking.
   d. AIDS.

10. About what share of U.S. adults are overweight?
    a. two-thirds
    b. half
    c. one-third
    d. one-fifth

ANSWERS: 1 (b); 2 (c); 3 (d); 4 (a); 5 (d); 6 (d); 7 (a); 8 (c); 9 (c); 10 (a).

ESSAY QUESTIONS

1. Why does industrialization lead societies to expand their systems of schooling? In what ways has schooling in the United States been shaped by our economic, political, and cultural systems?
2. Using the structural-functional approach, why is schooling important to the operation of society? From a social-conflict point of view, how does schooling reproduce social inequality in each generation?
3. Why is health a social issue as much as a biological issue? What are several ways in which health and medicine are linked to social inequality?

S A M P L E   T E S T

447

Most people in the United States live in face-paced cities and suburbs. Sociologists study the differences between rural and urban life, and they also track global population increase and how human societies are altering the natural environment.

CHAPTER 15

Population, Urbanization, and Environment

WHY should we worry about the rapid rate of global population increase?

WHAT makes city and rural living different?

HOW is the state of the natural environment a social issue?

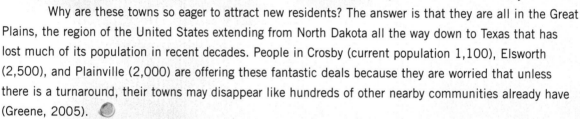

L ooking for a new place to live after you finish college? Crosby, North Dakota, would really like you to call it home. The town's officials will do more than welcome you—they will give you a free piece of land on which to build a house. As a bonus, they will throw in a free membership in the local country club.

Ellsworth, Kansas, also wants you. The town leaders will match Crosby's offer of free land and go one better, paying you $1,000 cash toward your down payment on a new home.

Perhaps the best deal of all is found in Plainville, Kansas. In addition to free land, you can forget about property taxes for the next ten years!

Why are these towns so eager to attract new residents? The answer is that they are all in the Great Plains, the region of the United States extending from North Dakota all the way down to Texas that has lost much of its population in recent decades. People in Crosby (current population 1,100), Elsworth (2,500), and Plainville (2,000) are offering these fantastic deals because they are worried that unless there is a turnaround, their towns may disappear like hundreds of other nearby communities already have (Greene, 2005).

All across the Great Plains, towns are hanging on by a thread. This chapter investigates population patterns, explaining why people move from place to place, why some cities get so large, and why small towns sometimes die. It will also look at the effects on the physical environment of population change and our way of life.

Demography: The Study of Population

When humans first began to cultivate plants some 12,000 years ago, Earth's entire *Homo sapiens* population was about 5 million, or about the number of people living in Minnesota today. Very slow growth pushed the total in 1 C.E. to perhaps 300 million, or about the population of the United States today.

Starting around 1750, world population began to spike upward. We now add more than 74 million people to the planet each year; the world now holds 6.5 billion people.

The causes and consequences of this drama are the focus of **demography,** *the study of human population.* Demography (from Greek, meaning "description of people") is a cousin of sociology that analyzes the size and composition of a population and studies how and why people move from place to place. Demographers not only collect statistics but also pose important questions about the effects of population growth and suggest how it might be controlled. The following sections present basic demographic concepts.

FERTILITY

The study of human population begins with how many people are born. **Fertility** is *the incidence of childbearing in a country's population.* During her childbearing years, from the onset of menstruation (typically in the early teens) to menopause (usually in the late forties), a woman is capable of bearing more than twenty children. But *fecundity,* or maximum possible childbearing, is sharply reduced by cultural norms, finances, and personal choice.

Demographers describe fertility using the **crude birth rate,** *the number of live births in a given year for every 1,000 people in a population.* To calculate a crude birth rate, divide the number of live births in a year by the society's total population and multiply the result by 1,000. In the United States in 2005, there were 4.1 million live births in a population of 297 million, yielding a crude birth rate of 13.8 (Munson & Sutton, 2006).

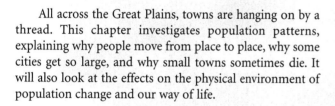

January 18, Coshocton County, Ohio.
Having just finished off the mountains of meat and potatoes that make up a typical

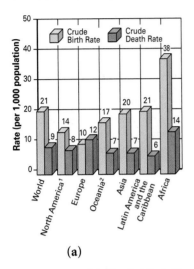
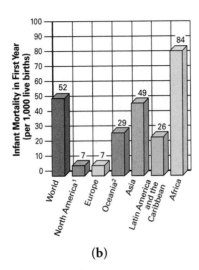
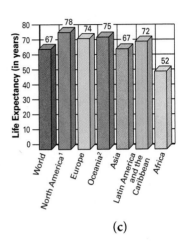

(a)   (b)   (c)

FIGURE 15-1   (a) Crude Birth Rates and Crude Death Rates,

(b) Infant Mortality Rates, and

(c) Life Expectancy around the World, 2005

By world standards, North America has low birth and death rates, very low infant mortality rates, and high life expectancy.

[1] United States and Canada.
[2] Australia, New Zealand, and South Pacific Islands.
Source: Population Reference Bureau (2006).

Amish meal, our group of college students has gathered in the living room of Jacob Raber, a member of this rural Amish community. Mrs. Raber, a mother of four, is telling us about Amish life. "Most of the women I know have five or six children," she says with a smile, "but certainly not everybody—some have eleven or twelve!"

A country's birth rate is described as "crude" because it is based on the entire population, not just women in their childbearing years. In addition, this measure ignores differences among various categories of the population: Fertility among the Amish, for example, is quite high, and fertility among Asian Americans is low. But this measure is easy to calculate and allows rough comparisons of the fertility of one country or region in relation to others. Part (a) of Figure 15–1 shows that compared to the rest of the world, the crude birth rate of North Americans is low.

How do you think low-fertility societies differ from high-fertility societies with respect to (1) age at first marriage, (2) opportunities available to women, and (3) attitudes toward homosexuality? Explain your responses.

MORTALITY

Population size also reflects **mortality,** *the incidence of death in a country's population.* To measure mortality, demographers use the **crude death rate,** *the number of deaths in a given year for every 1,000 people in a population.* This time, we take the number of deaths in a year, divide by the total population, and multiply the result by 1,000. In 2005, there were 2.4 million deaths in the U.S. population of 297 million, yielding a crude death rate of 8.1 (Munson & Sutton, 2006). Part (a) of Figure 15–1 shows that in global context, this rate is about average.

A third useful demographic measure is the **infant mortality rate,** *the number of deaths among infants under one year of age for each 1,000 live births in a given year.* To compute infant mortality, divide the number of deaths of children under one year of age by the number of live births during the same year and multiply the result by 1,000. In 2005, there were 28,000 infant deaths and 4.1 million live births in the United States. Dividing the first number by the second and multiplying the result by 1,000 yields an infant mortality rate of 6.8. Part (b) of Figure 15–1 indicates that by world standards, North American infant mortality is low.

NATIONAL MAP 15–1
Population Change
across the United States

This map, based on results of the 2000 census, shows that population is moving from the heartland of the United States toward the coasts. What do you think is causing this internal migration? What types of people do you think remain in counties that are losing population?

Source: U.S. Census Bureau (2001).

Change in Population, 1990 to 2000

- Gain 50.0% to 191.0%
- 25.0% to 49.9%
- 13.2% to 24.9%
- Gain up to 13.1%
- Loss up to 10.0%
- Loss 10.1% to 42.3%

But remember the differences among various categories of people. For example, African Americans, with nearly three times the burden of poverty as whites, have an infant mortality rate of 14.4—more than twice the white rate of 5.8.

Low infant mortality greatly raises **life expectancy,** *the average life span of a country's population.* U.S. males born in 2004 can expect to live 75.2 years, and females can look forward to 80.4 years. As part (c) of Figure 15–1 shows, life expectancy for North Americans is twenty-six years greater than that typical of low-income countries of Africa.

MIGRATION

Population size is also affected by **migration,** *the movement of people into and out of a specified territory.* Movement into a territory, or *immigration,* is measured as an *in-migration rate,* calculated as the number of people entering an area for every 1,000 people in the population. Movement out of a territory, or *emigration,* is measured in terms of an *out-migration rate,* the number leaving for every 1,000 people. Both types of migration usually happen at once; the difference is the *net migration rate.*

All nations experience some degree of internal migration, that is, movement within their borders, from one region to another. National Map 15–1 shows where the U.S. population is moving and the places being left behind (as suggested by the chapter opening, notice the heavy losses in the Plain States in the middle of the country).

Migration is sometimes voluntary, as when people leave a small town to move to a larger city. In such cases, "push-pull" factors are usually at work; a lack of jobs

"pushes" people to move, and more opportunity elsewhere "pulls" people to someplace new. Migration can also be involuntary, such as the forced transport of 10 million Africans to the Western Hemisphere as slaves.

POPULATION GROWTH

Fertility, mortality, and migration all affect the size of a society's population. In general, rich nations (such as the United States) grow almost as much from immigration as natural increase; poorer nations (such as Pakistan) grow almost entirely from natural increase.

To calculate a population's *natural growth rate,* demographers subtract the crude death rate from the crude birth rate. The natural growth rate of the U.S. population in 2005 was 5.7 per 1,000 (the crude birth rate of 13.8 minus the crude death rate of 8.1), or about 0.6 percent annual growth.

Global Map 15–1 shows that population growth in the United States and other high-income nations is well below the world average of 1.2 percent. Earth's low-growth continents are Europe (currently posting a slight decline, expressed as a *negative* 0.1 percent annual rate), North America (0.6 percent), and Oceania (1.0 percent). Near the global average are Asia (1.2 percent) and Latin America (1.5 percent). The highest-growth region of the world is Africa (2.3 percent).

A handy rule for estimating population growth is to divide a society's population growth into the number 70; this yields the *doubling time* in years. Thus an annual growth rate of 2 percent (found in parts of Latin America) doubles a population in thirty-five years, and a 3 percent

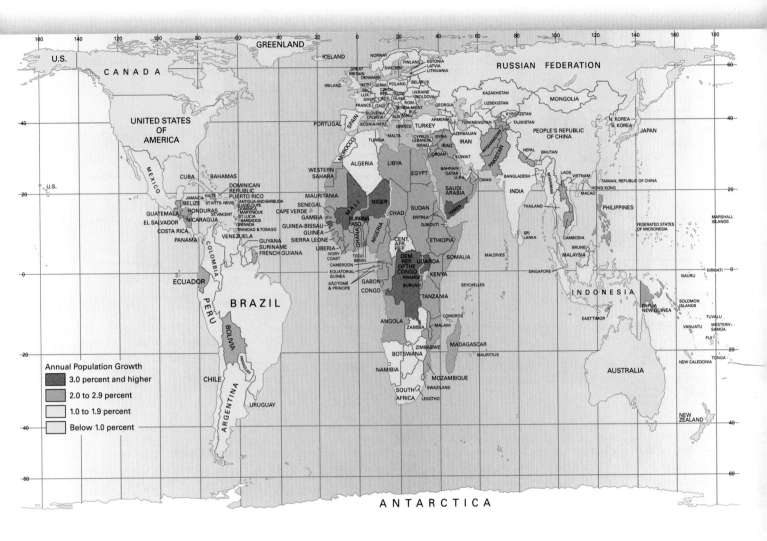

GLOBAL MAP 15-1 Population Growth in Global Perspective

The richest countries of the world—including the United States, Canada, and the nations of Europe—have growth rates below 1 percent. The nations of Latin America and Asia typically have growth rates around 1.5 percent, which double a population in forty-seven years. Africa has an overall growth rate of 2.3 percent (despite only small increases in countries with a high rate of AIDS), which cuts the doubling time to thirty years. In global perspective, we see that a society's standard of living is closely related to its rate of population growth: Population is rising fastest in the world regions that can least afford to support more people.

Source: Population Reference Bureau (2006); map projection from *Peters Atlas of the World* (1990).

growth rate (found in some countries in Africa) drops the doubling time to just twenty-three years. The rapid population growth of the poorest countries is deeply troubling because these countries can barely support the populations they have now.

POPULATION COMPOSITION

Demographers also study the makeup of a society's population at a given point in time. One variable is the **sex ratio,** *the number of males for every 100 females in a nation's popu-*

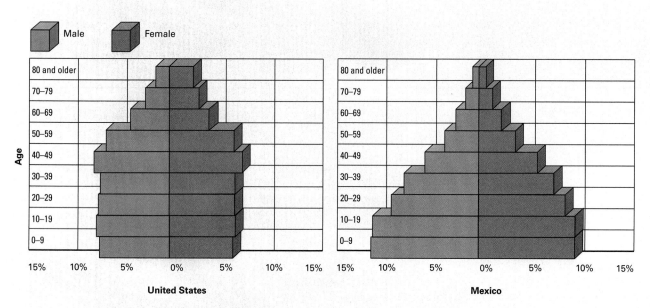

FIGURE 15-2   Age-Sex Population Pyramids for the United States and Mexico, 2005

By looking at the shape of a country's population pyramid, you can tell its level of economic development and predict future levels of population increase.

Source: U.S. Census Bureau (2005).

lation. In 2005, the sex ratio in the United States was 96, or 96 males for every 100 females. Sex ratios are ordinarily below 100 because, on average, women outlive men. In India, however, the sex ratio is 106 because parents value sons more than daughters and may either abort a female fetus or, after birth, give more care to a male infant, raising the odds that a female child will die.

A more complex measure is the **age-sex pyramid,** *a graphic representation of the age and sex of a population.* Figure 15–2 presents the age-sex pyramids for the United States and Mexico. Higher death rates as people age give these figures a rough pyramid shape. In the U.S. pyramid, the bulge in the middle reflects the high birth rates during the "baby boom" from the mid-1940s to the mid-1960s. The contraction for people in their twenties and thirties reflects the subsequent "baby bust." The birth rate has continued to decline from its high of 25.3 in 1957 to 13.8 in 2005.

The U.S. and Mexican age-sex pyramids show different demographic trends. The pyramid for Mexico, like that of other lower-income nations, is wide at the bottom (reflecting higher birth rates) and narrows quickly by what we would call middle age (due to higher mortality). In short, Mexico is a much younger society, with a median age of twenty-five, compared to thirty-five in the United States. With a larger share of women still in their childbearing

years, therefore, Mexico's crude birth rate (22) is nearly twice our own (13.8), and its annual rate of population growth (1.7 percent) is almost three times the U.S. rate (0.6 percent).

Using the age-sex pyramid for the United States shown in Figure 15–2, explain why many people are concerned that there will not be enough workers to pay for the retirement of the baby boom generation.

History and Theory of Population Growth

In the past, people wanted large families because human labor was the key to productivity. In addition, until rubber condoms were invented 150 years ago, preventing pregnancy was uncertain at best. But high death rates from infectious diseases put a constant brake on population growth.

A major demographic shift began about 1750 as the world's population turned upward, reaching the 1 billion mark by 1800. This milestone (which took all of human history to reach) was matched barely a century later in 1930, when a second billion people were added to the planet. In other words, not only was population increasing,

 To find out more about U.S. demography, go to http://www.census.gov

but the *rate* of growth was accelerating. Global population reached 3 billion by 1962 (just thirty-two years later) and 4 billion by 1974 (only twelve years later). The rate of world population increase has slowed recently, but the planet passed the 5 billion mark in 1987 and the 6 billion mark in 1999 (the 6.5 billion mark was passed early in 2006). In no previous century did the world's population even double. In the twentieth century, it quadrupled.

Currently, the world is gaining 74 million people each year, with 96 percent of this increase in poor countries. Experts predict that Earth's population will be between 8 and 9 billion in 2050 (O'Neill & Balk, 2001). Given the world's troubles feeding its present population, such an increase is a matter of urgent concern.

MALTHUSIAN THEORY

The sudden population growth 250 years ago sparked the development of demography. Thomas Robert Malthus (1766–1834), an English economist and clergyman, warned that rapid population increase would lead to social chaos. Malthus (1926, orig. 1798) calculated that population would increase in what mathematicians call a *geometric progression*, illustrated by the series of numbers 2, 4, 8, 16, 32, and so on. At such a rate, Malthus concluded, world population would soon soar out of control.

Food production would also increase, Malthus explained, but only in an *arithmetic progression* (as in the series 2, 3, 4, 5, 6, etc.) because even with new agricultural technology, farmland is limited. Thus Malthus presented a troubling vision of the future: people reproducing beyond what the planet could feed, leading ultimately to widespread starvation and war over what resources were left.

Malthus recognized that artificial birth control or abstaining from sex might change his prediction. But he considered one as morally wrong and the other as impractical. Famine and war therefore stalked humanity in Malthus's mind, and he was justly known as "the dismal parson."

CRITICAL REVIEW Fortunately, Malthus's prediction was flawed. First, by 1850, the European birth rate began to drop, partly because with industrialization, children were becoming an economic liability rather than an asset

and partly because people began using artificial birth control. Second, Malthus underestimated human ingenuity: Modern irrigation techniques, fertilizers, and pesticides have increased farm production far more than he could have imagined.

Some criticized Malthus for ignoring the role of social inequality in world abundance and famine. For example, Karl Marx (1967, orig. 1867) objected to his view of suffering as a "law of nature" rather than the curse of capitalism. More recently, "critical demographers" have claimed that saying poverty is caused by a high birth rate in low-income countries amounts to blaming the victims. On the contrary, they see global inequality as the real issue (Horton, 1999; Kuumba, 1999).

Still, Malthus offers an important lesson. Habitable land, clean water, and fresh air are limited resources, and increased economic productivity has taken a heavy toll on the natural environment. In addition, medical advances have lowered death rates, pushing up world population. In principle, of course, no level of population growth can go on forever. People everywhere must become aware of the dangers of population increase.

YOUR LEARNING What did Malthus predict about human population increase? About food production? What was his overall conclusion?

DEMOGRAPHIC TRANSITION THEORY

A more complex analysis of population change is **demographic transition theory,** *a thesis that links population patterns to a society's level of technological development.* Figure 15–3 on page 456 shows the demographic consequences at four levels of technological development. Preindustrial, agrarian societies (Stage 1) have high birth rates because of the economic value of children and the absence of birth control. Death rates are also high due to low living standards and limited medical technology. Outbreaks of disease cancel out births, so population rises and falls with only a modest overall increase. This was the case for thousands of years in Europe before the Industrial Revolution.

Stage 2, the onset of industrialization, brings a demographic transition as death rates fall due to greater food supplies and scientific medicine. But birth rates remain high, resulting in rapid population growth. It was during Europe's Stage 2 that Malthus formulated his ideas, which accounts for his pessimistic view of the future. The world's poorest countries today are in this high-growth stage.

In Stage 3, a mature industrial economy, the birth rate drops, curbing population growth once again. Fertility falls because most children survive to adulthood, so fewer are

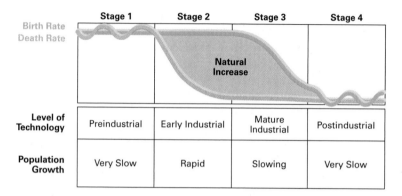

	Stage 1	Stage 2	Stage 3	Stage 4
Birth Rate Death Rate		Natural Increase		
Level of Technology	Preindustrial	Early Industrial	Mature Industrial	Postindustrial
Population Growth	Very Slow	Rapid	Slowing	Very Slow

FIGURE 15-3 Demographic Transition Theory

Demographic transition theory links population change to a society's level of technological development.

needed, and because high living standards make raising children expensive. In short, affluence transforms children from economic assets into economic liabilities. Smaller families, made possible by effective birth control, are also favored by women working outside the home. As birth rates follow death rates downward, population growth slows further.

Stage 4 corresponds to a postindustrial economy in which the demographic transition is complete. The birth rate remains low for a number of reasons: Two-income couples gradually become the norm, birth control use becomes the norm, and the cost of raising and schooling children continues to increase. This trend, coupled with steady death rates, means that population grows only very slowly or even decreases. This is the case today in Japan, Europe, and the United States.

CRITICAL REVIEW Demographic transition theory suggests that the key to population control lies in technology. Instead of the runaway population increase feared by Malthus, this theory sees technology slowing growth and spreading material plenty.

Demographic transition theory is linked to modernization theory, one approach to global development discussed in Chapter 9 ("Global Stratification"). Modernization theorists are optimistic that poor countries will solve their population problems as they industrialize. But critics, notably dependency theorists, strongly disagree. Unless there is a redistribution of global resources, they maintain, our planet will become increasingly divided into affluent "haves," enjoying low population growth, and poor "have-nots," struggling in vain to feed more and more people.

YOUR LEARNING Explain the four stages of demographic transition theory.

GLOBAL POPULATION TODAY: A BRIEF SURVEY

What can we say about population in today's world? Drawing on the discussion so far, we can identify important patterns and reach several conclusions.

The Low-Growth North

When the Industrial Revolution began in the Northern Hemisphere, population growth in Western Europe and North America was a high 3 percent annually. But in the centuries since, the growth rate has steadily declined, and in 1970, it fell below 1 percent. As our postindustrial society settles into Stage 4, the U.S. birth rate is less than the replacement level of 2.1 children per woman, a point demographers call **zero population growth,** *the level of reproduction that maintains population at a steady level.* More than sixty nations, almost all of them rich, are at or below the point of zero population growth.

 To find out more about population growth, go to http://www.populationconnection.org

Among the factors that serve to hold down population in these postindustrial societies are the high proportion of men and women in the labor force, the rising costs of raising children, trends toward later marriage and singlehood, and the widespread use of contraceptives and abortion.

In high-income nations, then, population increase is not the pressing problem that it is in poor countries. On the contrary, many governments in high-income countries are concerned about a future problem of *underpopulation,* because declining population size may be difficult to reverse and because the swelling ranks of the elderly have fewer and fewer young people to look to for support in old age (P. McDonald, 2001; Kent & Mather, 2002).

Fertility in the United States has fallen during the past century and is now quite low. But some categories of the U.S. population have much higher fertility rates. One example is the Amish, a religious society living in rural areas of Ohio, Pennsylvania, and other states. It is common for Amish couples to have five, six, or more children. Why do you think the Amish favor large families?

YOUR TURN

Typically, immigrants are younger than most people in their new country. What is the likely effect of high immigration on a country's ability to support more and more older people?

The High-Growth South

Population is a critical problem in poor nations of the Southern Hemisphere. No nation in the world lacks industrial technology entirely; demographic transition theory's Stage 1 applies only to remote rural areas of low-income nations. But much of Latin America, Africa, and Asia is at Stage 2, with a mix of agrarian and industrial economies. Advanced medical technology, supplied by rich societies, has sharply reduced death rates, but birth rates remain high. This is why poor societies now account for two-thirds of Earth's people and 96 percent of global population increase.

In poor countries throughout the world, birth rates have fallen from an average of about six children per woman

INTERNET — Read about population control in South Asia at http://www.asia-initiative.org/index.html

in 1950 to about three today. But fertility this high will only intensify global poverty. At a 1994 global population conference in Cairo, delegates from 180 nations agreed that a key element in controlling world population growth is to raise the status of women. The Thinking Globally box on page 458 takes a closer look.

In much of the world today, mortality is falling. To limit population increase, the world—especially poor nations—must control births as successfully as it is fending off deaths.

Urbanization: The Growth of Cities

October 8, Hong Kong. The cable train grinds to the top of Victoria Peak, where we behold one of the world's most spectacular vistas: the city of Hong Kong at night. A million bright, colorful lights ring the harbor as ships, ferries, and traditional Chinese junks churn by. Few cities match Hong Kong for sheer energy: This small city is as economically productive as the state of Wisconsin or the nation of Finland. We could sit here for hours entranced by the spectacle of Hong Kong.

Throughout most of human history, the sights and sounds of great cities such as Hong Kong, New York, and Paris were simply unimaginable. Our distant ancestors lived in small, nomadic groups, moving from place to place as they depleted vegetation or hunted migratory game. The small settlements that marked the emergence of civilization in the Middle East some 12,000 years ago held only a small fraction of Earth's people. Today, the largest three or four cities of the world hold as many people as the entire planet did back then.

Urbanization is *the concentration of population into cities.* Urbanization both redistributes population within a society and transforms many patterns of social life. We will trace these changes in terms of three urban revolutions: the emergence of cities beginning 10,000 years ago, the development of industrial cities after 1750, and the explosive growth of cities in poor countries today.

Empowering Women: The Key to Controlling Global Population Growth

Sohad Ahmad lives with her husband in a farming village 50 miles south of Cairo, Egypt's capital city. Ahmad lives a poor life, like hundreds of millions of other women in the world. Yet her situation differs in an important respect: She has had only two children and will have no more.

Why do Ahmad and her husband reject the conventional wisdom that children are an economic asset? One part of the answer is that Egypt's growing population has already created such a demand for land that Ahmad's family could not afford more even if they had the children to farm it. But the main reason is that she does not want her life defined only by childbearing.

Like Ahmad, more women in Egypt are taking control of their fertility and seeking educational and economic opportunities. Indeed, this country has made great progress in reducing its annual population growth from 3.0 percent in the 1990s to 2.1 percent today.

With its focus on raising the standing of women, the 1994 Cairo conference on global population broke new ground. Past population control programs simply tried to make birth control technology available to women, a vital effort because only half of the world's married women use effective birth control. But even with available birth control, population continues to increase in societies that define women's primary responsibility as raising children.

Nafis Sadik, the female Egyptian physician who leads the United Nations' efforts at population control, sums up the new approach to lowering birth rates this way: *Give women more life choices, and they will have fewer children.* In other words, women with access to schooling and jobs, who can decide when and whether to marry, and who bear children as a matter of choice will limit their own fertility. Schooling must be available to older women, too, Sadik adds, because elders exercise great influence in local communities.

Evidence from countries around the world supports the idea that controlling population and raising the social standing of women go hand in hand.

WHAT DO YOU THINK?

1. Why do many analysts claim that controlling global population depends on expanding women's choices?

2. What specific laws or programs can you think of that might reduce women's childbearing?

3. Is population control an issue for people in rich countries as well as poor countries? Why or why not?

A simple truth: Women who have more opportunity for schooling and paid work have fewer children. As more women attend school in traditional societies, the fertility rate in these countries is falling.

Sources: Ashford (1995), Axinn & Barber (2001), and Population Reference Bureau (2006).

THE EVOLUTION OF CITIES

Cities are a relatively new development in human history. Only about 12,000 years ago did our ancestors begin founding permanent settlements, which paved the way for the *first urban revolution.*

The First Cities

Hunting and gathering forced people to move all the time; however, once our ancestors discovered how to domesticate animals and cultivate crops, they were able to stay in one place. Raising their own food also created a material surplus, which freed some people from food production and allowed them to build shelters, make tools, weave cloth, and take part in religious rituals. The emergence of cities led to both specialization and higher living standards.

The first city that we know of was Jericho, which lies to the north of the Dead Sea in what is now the West Bank. Dating back 10,000 years, it was home to only 600 people. But as the centuries passed, cities grew to tens of thousands of people and became the centers of vast empires. By 3000 B.C.E., Egyptian cities flourished, as did cities in China about

2000 B.C.E. and in Central and South America about 1500 B.C.E. In North America, however, only a few Native American societies formed settlements; widespread urbanization did not take place until the arrival of European settlers in the seventeenth century.

Preindustrial European Cities

European cities date back some 5,000 years to the Greeks and, later, the Romans, both of whom formed great empires and founded cities across Europe, including Vienna, Paris, and London. With the fall of the Roman Empire, the so-called Dark Ages began as people withdrew within defensive walled settlements and warlords battled for territory. Only in the eleventh century did Europe become more peaceful; trade flourished once again, allowing cities to grow.

Medieval cities were quite different from those familiar to us today. Beneath towering cathedrals, the narrow, winding streets of London, Brussels, and Florence teemed with merchants, artisans, priests, peddlers, jugglers, nobles, and servants. Occupational groups such as bakers, carpenters, and metalworkers clustered in distinct sections or "quarters." Ethnicity also defined communities as people sought to keep out those who differed from themselves. The term "ghetto" (from the Italian word *borghetto,* meaning "outside the city walls") was first used to describe the neighborhood into which the Jews of Venice were segregated.

Industrial European Cities

As the Middle Ages came to a close, steadily increasing commerce enriched a new urban middle class called the *bourgeoisie* (French for "townspeople"). Earning more and more money, the bourgeoisie soon rivaled the hereditary nobility.

By about 1750, the Industrial Revolution triggered a *second urban revolution,* first in Europe and then in North America. The tremendous productive power of factories caused cities to grow bigger than ever before. London, the largest European city, reached 550,000 people by 1700 and exploded to 6.5 million by 1900 (A. F. Weber, 1963, orig. 1899; Chandler & Fox, 1974).

Cities not only grew but changed shape as well. Older winding streets gave way to broad, straight boulevards to handle the increasing flow of commercial traffic. Steam and electric trolleys soon crisscrossed the expanding cities. Because land was now a commodity to be bought and sold, developers divided cities into regular-sized lots (Mumford, 1961). The center of the city was no longer the cathedral but a bustling central business district filled with banks, retail stores, and tall office buildings.

With a new focus on business, cities became ever more crowded and impersonal. Crime rates rose. Especially at the outset, a few industrialists lived in grand style, but most

TABLE 15-1

Urban Population of the United States, 1790–2000

Year	Population (in millions)	Percentage Urban
1790	3.9	5.1%
1800	5.3	6.1
1820	9.6	7.3
1840	17.1	10.5
1860	31.4	19.7
1880	50.2	28.1
1900	76.0	39.7
1920	105.7	51.3
1940	131.7	56.5
1960	179.3	69.9
1980	226.5	73.7
2000	281.4	79.0

Source: U.S. Census Bureau (2005).

men, women, and children barely survived by working in factories.

Organized efforts by workers eventually brought improvements to the workplace, better housing, and the right to vote. Public services such as water, sewer systems, and electricity further improved urban living. Today, some urbanites still live in poverty, but a rising standard of living has partly fulfilled the city's historical promise of a better life.

THE GROWTH OF U.S. CITIES

As noted, most of the Native Americans who inhabited North America for thousands of years before the arrival of Europeans were migratory people who formed few permanent settlements. The spread of villages and towns came after European colonization.

Colonial Settlement, 1565–1800

In 1565, the Spanish built a settlement at Saint Augustine, Florida, and in 1607, the English founded Jamestown, Virginia. However, the first lasting settlement came in 1624 when the Dutch established New Amsterdam, later renamed New York.

New York and Boston (founded by the English in 1630) started out as tiny villages in a vast wilderness. They resembled medieval towns in Europe, with narrow, winding streets that still curve through lower Manhattan and downtown Boston. When the first census was completed in 1790, as Table 15–1 shows, just 5 percent of the nation's people lived in cities.

A century ago, as this scene from the film *Gangs of New York* suggests, people living in cities used the streets for most of their daily activities. Today, by contrast, the idea of "living on the streets" is associated with the poor and homeless. Why do you think street life is less valued today than it was in the past?

Urban Expansion, 1800–1860

Early in the nineteenth century, towns sprang up along the transportation routes that opened the American West. By 1860, Buffalo, Cleveland, Detroit, and Chicago were all changing the face of the Midwest, and about one-fifth of the U.S. population lived in cities.

Urban expansion was greatest in the northern states; New York City, for example, had ten times the population of Charleston, South Carolina. The evolution of the United States into the industrial-urban North and the agrarian-rural South was one major cause of the Civil War (A. M. Schlesinger, 1969).

The Metropolitan Era, 1860–1950

The Civil War (1861–1865) gave an enormous boost to urbanization as factories strained to produce weapons. Waves of people deserted the countryside for cities in hopes of finding better jobs. Joining them were tens of millions of immigrants, most from Europe, forming a culturally diverse urban mix.

In 1900, New York's population soared past the 4 million mark, and Chicago, a city that had scarcely 100,000 people in 1860, was closing in on 2 million. Such growth marked the era of the **metropolis** (from Greek words meaning "mother city"), *a large city that socially and economically dominates an urban area.* Metropolises became the economic centers of the United States. By 1920, urban areas were home to a majority of the U.S. population.

Industrial technology pushed city populations higher and higher. In the 1880s, the tallest buildings, supported by steel girders and equipped with mechanical elevators, were ten stories high. In 1930, New York's Empire State Building was hailed as an urban wonder; this early skyscraper was the highest point in the New York skyline, soaring 102 stories into the clouds.

Urban Decentralization, 1950–Present

The industrial metropolis reached its peak about 1950. Since then, something of a turnaround, called *urban decentralization,* has occurred as people have left downtown areas for outlying **suburbs,** *urban areas beyond the political boundaries of a city.* The old industrial cities of the Northeast and Midwest stopped growing, and some lost considerable population in the decades after 1950. The urban landscape of densely packed central cities evolved into sprawling suburban regions.

SUBURBS AND URBAN DECLINE

Imitating European nobility, some of the rich in the United States had town houses in the city as well as country homes beyond the city limits. But not until after World War II did ordinary people find a suburban home within their reach. With more and more cars, new four-lane highways, government-backed mortgages, and inexpensive tract homes, suburbs grew as never before. By 1999, most of the U.S. population lived in suburbs, where they frequented nearby shopping malls rather than the older downtown shopping districts (Pederson, Smith, & Adler, 1999; Macionis & Parrillo, 2007).

As many older cities of the Snowbelt—the Northeast and Midwest—lost higher-income taxpayers to the suburbs, they struggled to pay for expensive social programs for the poor who remained. Many cities fell into financial crisis, and inner-city decay became severe. Especially to white suburbanites, the inner cities became synonymous with slum housing, crime, drugs, unemployment, the poor, and minorities (Stahura, 1986; Galster, 1991).

The urban critic Paul Goldberger (2002) points out that the decline of central cities also has led to a decline in the importance of public space. Historically, city life was played out on the streets. The French word for a sophisticated person is *boulevardier,* which literally means "street person." However, this term has a negative meaning in the United States today. The activity that once took place on public streets and in public squares now takes place in shopping malls, cineplex lobbies, and gated communities—all private spaces. Further reducing the vitality of today's urban places is the spread of television, the Internet, and other media that people use without leaving home.

YOUR TURN

Is there a class difference in people's use of the streets as a place to meet and greet others? For example, do you think working-class people are more likely to use the streets in this way than middle-class suburbanites?

POSTINDUSTRIAL SUNBELT CITIES AND SPRAWL

As the older Snowbelt cities fell into decline, Sunbelt cities in the South and West grew rapidly. The soaring populations of cities such as Los Angeles and Houston reflect a population shift to the Sunbelt, where 60 percent of U.S. people now live. In addition, most of today's immigrants enter the country in the Sunbelt region. In 1950, nine of the ten largest U.S. cities were in the Snowbelt; in 2004, six of the top ten were in the Sunbelt (U.S. Census Bureau, 2005).

Unlike their colder counterparts, these cities came of age *after* urban decentralization began. So while Snowbelt cities have long been enclosed by a ring of politically independent suburbs, Sunbelt cities have pushed their boundaries outward along with the population flow. Chicago covers 227 square miles; Houston is more than twice that size, and the greater Houston metropolitan region covers almost 9,000 square miles—an area the size of the state of New Jersey.

The great sprawl of Sunbelt cities has its drawbacks. Many people in cities such as Atlanta, Dallas, Phoenix, and Los Angeles argue that the growth follows no plan and results in traffic-clogged roads leading to poorly planned housing developments and schools that cannot keep up with the inflow of children. Not surprisingly, voters in many communities across the United States have passed ballot initiatives seeking to limit urban sprawl (Lacayo, 1999; Romero & Liserio, 2002).

MEGALOPOLIS: THE REGIONAL CITY

Another result of urban decentralization is urban regions, or regional cities. The U.S. Census Bureau (2005) recognizes 362 *metropolitan statistical areas* (MSAs). These areas include at least one city with 50,000 or more people. The bureau also recognizes 560 *micropolitan statistical areas,* urban areas with at least one city of 10,000 to 50,000 people. *Core-based statistical areas* (CBSAs) include both metropolitan and micropolitan statistical areas.

The biggest CBSAs contain millions of people and cover areas that extend into several states. In 2000, the biggest CBSA was New York and its adjacent urban areas in Long Island, western Connecticut, and northern New Jersey and Pennsylvania, with a total population of more than 21 million. Next in size is the CBSA in southern California that includes Los Angeles, Riverside, and Long Beach, with a population of more than 16 million.

As regional cities grow, they begin to overlap. In the early 1960s, the French geographer Jean Gottmann (1961) coined the term **megalopolis** to designate *a vast urban region containing a number of cities and their surrounding suburbs.* Along the East Coast, a 400-mile megalopolis stretches all the way from New England to Virginia. Other supercities cover the eastern coast of Florida and stretch from Cleveland west to Chicago.

EDGE CITIES

Urban decentralization has also created *edge cities,* business centers some distance from the old downtowns. Edge cities—a mix of corporate office buildings, shopping malls, hotels, and entertainment complexes—differ from suburbs, which contain mostly homes. The population of suburbs peaks at night, but the population of edge cities peaks during the workday.

As part of expanding urban regions, most edge cities have no clear physical boundaries. Some do have names, including Las Colinas (near the Dallas–Fort Worth airport), Tyson's Corner (in Virginia, near Washington, D.C.), and King of Prussia (northwest of Philadelphia). Other edge cities are known only by the major highways that flow

The rural rebound has been most pronounced in towns that offer spectacular natural beauty. There are times when people living in the scenic town of Park City, Utah, cannot even find a parking space.

through them, including Route 1 in Princeton, New Jersey, and Route 128 near Boston (Garreau, 1991; Macionis & Parrillo, 2007).

THE RURAL REBOUND

Over the course of U.S. history, as shown by the data in Table 15–1, the urban population of the nation has increased steadily. Immigration has played a part in this increase because most newcomers settle in cities. There has also been considerable migration from rural areas to urban places, typically by people seeking greater economic opportunity.

However, in the 1990s, three-fourths of the rural counties across the United States gained population, a trend analysts have called the "rural rebound." Most of this gain resulted from migration of people from urban areas. This trend has not affected all rural places: As the opening to this chapter explains, many small towns in rural areas (especially in the Plain States) are struggling to stay alive. But even in these areas, the losses slowed during the 1990s (K. M. Johnson, 1999; D. Johnson, 2001).

The greatest gains have come to rural communities that offer scenic and recreational attractions, such as lakes, mountains, and ski areas. People are drawn not only to the natural beauty of rural communities but also to their slower pace: less traffic, a lower crime rate, and cleaner air. A number of companies have relocated to rural counties as well, which has increased economic opportunity for the rural population (K. M. Johnson, 1999; Johnson & Fuguitt, 2000).

Urbanism as a Way of Life

Early sociologists in Europe and the United States focused their attention on the rise of cities. We briefly present their accounts of urbanism as a way of life.

FERDINAND TÖNNIES: GEMEINSCHAFT AND GESELLSCHAFT

In the nineteenth century, the German sociologist Ferdinand Tönnies (1855–1937) studied how life in the new industrial metropolis differed from life in rural villages. From this contrast, he developed two concepts that have become a lasting part of sociology's terminology.

Tönnies (1963, orig. 1887) used the German word *Gemeinschaft* ("community") to refer to *a type of social organization in which people are closely tied by kinship and tradition.* The *Gemeinschaft* of the rural village, Tönnies explained, joins people in what amounts to a single primary group.

By and large, argued Tönnies, *Gemeinschaft* is absent in the modern city. On the contrary, urbanization creates *Gesellschaft* ("association"), *a type of social organization in which people come together only on the basis of individual self-interest.* In the *Gesellschaft* way of life, individuals are motivated by their own needs rather than by a desire to help improve the well-being of everyone. By and large, city dwellers have little sense of community or common identity and look to other people mainly when they need something. Tönnies saw in urbanization the weakening of

Peasant Dance (above, c. 1565), by Pieter Breughel the Elder, conveys the essential unity of rural life forged by generations of kinship and neighborhood. By contrast, Ernest Fiene's *Nocturne* (left) communicates the impersonality common to urban areas. Taken together, these paintings capture Tönnies's distinction between *Gemeinschaft* and *Gesellschaft*.

Pieter Breughel the Elder (c. 1525/30–1569), *Peasant Dance*, c. 1565, Kunsthistorisches Museum, Vienna/Superstock. Ernest Fiene (1894–1965), *Nocturne*. Photograph © Christie's Images.

close, long-lasting social relations in favor of the brief and impersonal ties or secondary relationships typical of business.

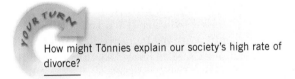

How might Tönnies explain our society's high rate of divorce?

EMILE DURKHEIM: MECHANICAL AND ORGANIC SOLIDARITY

The French sociologist Emile Durkheim agreed with much of Tönnies's thinking about cities. However, Durkheim countered that urbanites do not lack social bonds; they simply organize social life differently than rural people.

Durkheim described traditional, rural life as *mechanical solidarity*, social bonds based on common sentiments and shared moral values. With its emphasis on tradition, Durkheim's concept of mechanical solidarity bears a striking similarity to Tönnies's *Gemeinschaft*. Urbanization erodes mechanical solidarity, Durkheim explained, but it also generates a new type of bonding, which he called *organic solidarity*, social bonds based on specialization and

interdependence. This concept, which parallels Tönnies's *Gesellschaft*, reveals an important difference between the two thinkers. Both felt that the growth of industrial cities weakened tradition, but Durkheim optimistically pointed to a new kind of solidarity. Where societies had been built on *likeness*, Durkheim now saw social life based on *difference*.

For Durkheim, urban society offers more individual choice, moral tolerance, and personal privacy than people find in rural villages. In sum, Durkheim thought that something is lost in the process of urbanization, but much is gained.

GEORG SIMMEL: THE BLASÉ URBANITE

The German sociologist Georg Simmel (1858–1918) offered a microanalysis of cities, studying how urban life shapes individual experience. According to Simmel, individuals see the city as a crush of people, objects, and events. To prevent being overwhelmed by all this stimulation, urbanites develop a *blasé attitude*, tuning out much of what goes on around them. Such detachment does not mean that city dwellers lack compassion for others; they simply keep their distance as a survival strategy so that they can focus their time and energy on the people and things that really matter to them.

How would Simmel explain cases of people turning away from others in need on the grounds that they simply "don't want to get involved"?

THE CHICAGO SCHOOL: ROBERT PARK AND LOUIS WIRTH

Sociologists in the United States soon joined the study of rapidly growing cities. Robert Park (1864–1944), a leader of the first U.S. sociology program at the University of Chicago, sought to add a street-level perspective by getting out and studying real cities. As he said of himself, "I suspect that I have actually covered more ground, tramping about in cities in different parts of the world, than any other living man" (1950:viii). Walking the streets, Park found the city to be an organized mosaic of distinctive ethnic communities, commercial centers, and industrial districts. Over time, he observed, these "natural areas" develop and change in relation to one another. To Park, the city was a living organism—a human kaleidoscope.

Another major figure in the Chicago School of urban sociology was Louis Wirth (1897–1952). Wirth (1938) is best known for blending the ideas of Tönnies, Durkheim, Simmel, and Park into a comprehensive theory of urban life.

Wirth began by defining the city as a setting with a large, dense, and socially diverse population. These traits result in an impersonal, superficial, and transitory way of life. Living among millions of others, urbanites come into contact with many more people than residents of rural areas. Thus when city people notice others at all, they usually know them not in terms of *who they are* but *what they do*—as, for instance, the bus driver, the florist, or the grocery store clerk. Specialized urban relationships are sometimes pleasant for all concerned, but we should remember that self-interest rather than friendship is the main reason for the interaction.

The impersonal nature of urban relationships, together with the great social diversity found in cities today, makes city dwellers more tolerant than rural villagers. Rural communities often jealously enforce their narrow traditions, but the heterogeneous population of a city rarely shares any single code of moral conduct (T. C. Wilson, 1985, 1995).

CRITICAL REVIEW In both Europe and the United States, early sociologists presented a mixed view of urban living. Rapid urbanization troubled Tönnies and Wirth, who saw personal ties and traditional morality lost in the anonymous rush of the city. Durkheim and Park emphasized urbanism's positive face, pointing to more personal freedom and choice.

One problem with all of these views is that they paint urbanism in broad strokes that overlook the effects of class, race, and gender. There are many kinds of urbanites—rich and poor, black and white, Anglo and Latino, women and men—all leading distinctive lives (Gans, 1968). As the Thinking About Diversity box explains, the share of racial and ethnic minorities in the largest U.S. cities increased sharply during the 1990s. We see social diversity most clearly in cities, where various categories of people are large enough to form visible communities (Macionis & Parrillo, 2007).

YOUR LEARNING Of these urban sociologists—Tönnies, Durkheim, Park, and Wirth—which were more positive about urban life? Which were more negative? In each case, explain why.

URBAN ECOLOGY

Sociologists (especially members of the Chicago School) developed **urban ecology,** *the study of the link between the physical and social dimensions of cities.* For example, why are cities located where they are? The first cities emerged in fertile regions where the ecology favored raising crops. Preindustrial people, concerned with defense, built their cities on mountains (ancient Athens was perched on an outcropping of rock) or surrounded by water (Paris and Mexico City were built on islands). With the Industrial Revolution, economic considerations placed all major U.S. cities near rivers and natural harbors that facilitated trade.

Urban ecologists also study the physical design of cities. In 1925, Ernest W. Burgess, a student and colleague of Robert Park's, described land use in Chicago in terms of *concentric zones.* City centers, Burgess observed, are business districts bordered by a ring of factories, followed by residential rings with housing that becomes more expensive the farther it is from the noise and pollution of the city's center.

Homer Hoyt (1939) refined Burgess's observations, noting that distinctive districts sometimes form *wedge-shaped sectors.* For example, one fashionable area may develop next to another, or an industrial district may extend outward from a city's center along a train or trolley line.

Chauncy Harris and Edward Ullman (1945) added yet another insight: As cities decentralize, they lose their single-center form in favor of a *multicentered model.* As cities grow, residential areas, industrial parks, and shopping districts

THINKING ABOUT DIVERSITY: RACE, CLASS, AND GENDER

Census 2000: Minorities Now a Majority in the Largest U.S. Cities

The 2000 U.S. census reported that minorities—Hispanics, African Americans, and Asians—are now a majority of the population in 48 of the 100 largest U.S. cities, up from 30 in 1990.

What accounts for the change? One reason is that large cities have been losing their non-Hispanic white populations. For example, by 2000, Santa Ana, California, had lost 38 percent of the white population it had in 1990; the drop was 40 percent in Birmingham, Alabama, and a whopping 53 percent in Detroit, Michigan. The white share of the population of all 100 of the largest cities fell from 52.1 percent in 1990 to 43.8 percent in 2000.

But perhaps the biggest reason for the minority-majority trend is the increase in immigration. Immigration, coupled with higher birth rates among new immigrants, resulted in a 43 percent gain in the Hispanic population (almost 4 million people) of the largest

100 cities between 1990 and 2000. The Asian population also surged by 40 percent (more than 1.1 million people).

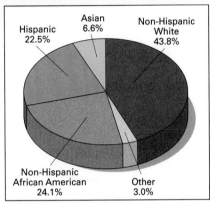

Population Profile for the 100 Largest U.S. Cities, 2000

Racial and ethnic minorities make up a majority of the population of this country's 100 largest cities.

Source: U.S. Census Bureau (2001).

The African American population was steady over the course of the 1990s.

Political officials and other policy-makers are examining these figures closely. Clearly, the future vitality of the largest U.S. cities depends on meeting the needs and taking advantage of the contributions of their swelling minority populations.

WHAT DO YOU THINK?

1. Why are the minority populations of large U.S. cities increasing?

2. What positive changes and what challenges does a minority-majority bring to a city?

3. Before Hurricane Katrina, African Americans represented 60 percent of the population of New Orleans; afterward, the share was about 40 percent. What difference might this change make in the city's immediate future?

Sources: Schmitt (2001) and U.S. Census Bureau (2005).

---

typically push away from one another. Few people want to live close to industrial areas, for example, so the city becomes a mosaic of distinct districts.

Social area analysis investigates what people in particular neighborhoods have in common. Three factors seem to explain most of the variation in neighborhood types: family patterns, social class, and race and ethnicity (Shevky & Bell, 1955; R. J. Johnston, 1976). Families with children look for areas with large apartments or single-family homes and good schools. The rich seek high-prestige neighborhoods, often in the central city near cultural attractions. People with a common race or ethnic heritage cluster in distinctive communities.

Finally, Brian Berry and Philip Rees (1969) tied together many of these insights. They explained that dis-

tinct family types tend to settle in the concentric zones described by Burgess. Specifically, households with few children tend to cluster toward the city's center, and those with more children live farther away. Social class differences are primarily responsible for the sector-shaped districts described by Hoyt; the rich occupy one "side of the tracks" and the poor the other. And racial and ethnic neighborhoods are found at various places throughout the city, consistent with Harris and Ullman's multicentered model.

URBAN POLITICAL ECONOMY

In the late 1960s, many large U.S. cities were rocked by major riots. As public awareness of racial and economic inequality increased, some analysts turned away from the ecological approach to a social-conflict understanding of

April 3, 2006

Dump Trash, Add Scavengers, Mix and Get a Big Mess

By HOWARD W. FRENCH

SHANGHAI—Song Tiping, a peasant from rural Jiangsu Province, and Bernie Kearsley-Pratt, an Australian executive, would not at first glance seem to have much in common, and they do not, except for one thing: both were drawn here by the unlikely financial promise of garbage, towering mountains of refuse that attest to this city's status as a raging boomtown. . . .

The Australian, who works for a French company that is helping manage this city's garbage, says his difficult job is made all the harder—indeed, on some days he himself would say impossible—by the cruel fact that even in the heartland of a booming China, peasants can make far more money collecting plastic trash bags, tin cans and the rubber soles

of shoes than they can as farmers or ordinary day laborers.

Most days Mr. Song . . . spends several hours dodging monstrous earthmoving equipment in the landfill, one of the largest in Asia, to pick trash.

Were it not for dangers of the job, like being crushed by a bulldozer, inhaling noxious gases while wading knee-deep in fetid refuse or being beaten by warring gangs of scrap pickers for the mere prize of an unbroken bottle, it might even be considered a good job.

"We worked really hard as laborers before, doing 12- to- 15-hour days for a mere few hundred yuan," about $35, Mr. Song said. "You have to work even if you are sick or tired. Here we are working for ourselves, and there is a lot more freedom—four to five hours a day, plus we can earn a lot more." . . .

"Everyone has a big challenge when they come to China," Mr. Kearsley-Pratt said. . . . "As soon as you tip the truck there will be 40 or 50 people running all about the machines—quite big machines," he said. "I don't have the statistics, but quite a few people have been crushed like this." . . .

All about, as Mr. Kearsley-Pratt looked on helplessly, scavengers were loading their day's haul onto pushcarts, onto rickety wagons hitched to the back of motorcycles to be sorted out offsite and sold to buyers who specialize in different kinds of refuse, whether rubber, plastic, aluminum or tin.

"Last year my daughter was admitted to high school and we have to pay 10,000 yuan for her registration," Mr. Song said. In addition to that, the equivalent of $1,250, he said, he also has to pay $125

---

city life. The *urban political-economy model* applies Karl Marx's analysis of conflict in the workplace to conflict in the city (Lindstrom, 1995).

Political economists reject the ecological approach's view of the city as a natural organism with particular districts and neighborhoods developing according to an internal logic. Instead, they see city life as defined by people with power: corporate leaders and political officials. Capitalism, which transforms the city into real estate traded for profit and concentrates wealth in the hands of the few, is the key to understanding city life. From this point of view, the decline in industrial Snowbelt cities after 1950 was the result of deliberate decisions by the corporate elite to move their production facilities to the Sunbelt (where labor is cheaper and less likely to be unionized) or move them out of the country entirely to low-income nations (Molotch, 1976; Castells, 1977, 1983; Lefebvre, 1991; Jones & Wilson, 1999).

CRITICAL REVIEW The fact that many U.S. cities are in crisis, with widespread poverty, high crime, and barely functioning schools, seems to favor the political-economy

view over the urban ecology approach. But one criticism applies to both: They focus on U.S. cities during a limited period of history. Much of what we know about industrial cities does not apply to preindustrial towns in our own past or the rapidly growing cities in many poor nations today. It is unlikely that any single model of cities can account for the full range of urban diversity.

✔ **YOUR LEARNING** In your own words, explain what the urban ecology theories and the urban political-economy theory teach us about cities.

Urbanization in Poor Nations

November 16, Cairo, Egypt. People call the vast Muslim cemetery in Old Cairo the "City of the Dead." In truth, it is very much alive: Tens of thousands of squatters have moved into the mausoleums, making this place an eerie mix of life and death. Children run across the stone floors, clotheslines stretch between the monu-

for his second daughter's school. . . . Zuo Xilian, another garbage picker, said he was working his way through college while supporting a 60-year-old father in fragile health. . . .

The landfill's management has thought about sitting down with the scavengers to cut a deal that would allow them to keep picking without endangering themselves or the dump's operations. But the potential bonanza of the trash has proved, like a gold rush, impossible to manage. The dimensions of the problem are on clear display most days, when 120 huge trucks per hour, freshly loaded with garbage from the barges, rumble down the plant's access road with squadrons of trash pickers on motorbikes following in their wake.

The city is vague about its plans for dealing with the trash pickers, saying only that they will be "phased out" eventually. "Right now, we don't have a city regulation on scavenging," said Wu Xiwei, an official of the city sanitation bureau.

Zhu Feixiang, 46, a scavenger who lives on the edge of the dump on a trash-strewn plot with sheep and dogs and more old plastic bags than you've ever seen, doubts the city will stop him or any others. "They can call the police, but it's not against law or regulation to pick garbage," he said. "We don't steal. We don't rob. We only make a living. Besides, recycling garbage benefits the nation."

Mr. Zhu . . . stopped raking the garbage blowing around in his yard to contemplate that for a moment. "Plus, we're dirty and we stink, so the police would never take us in," he said.

Adapted from the original article by Howard W. French published in *The New York Times* on April 3, 2006. Copyright © 2006 by The New York Times Company. Reprinted with permission.

WHAT DO YOU THINK?

1. Most people in the United States have trouble imagining why people would flock to a city dump looking for work. Based on this article, explain the pattern.

2. Can you think of ways that city officials might be able to protect the safety of trash-pickers in Shanghai?

3. Chapter 9 ("Global Stratification") provides several ways of understanding the poverty that draws people to work in urban dumps. If you have read that chapter, apply modernization theory and dependency theory to better understand this article.

ments, and an occasional television antenna protrudes from a tomb roof. With Cairo gaining 1,000 people a day, families live where they can.

Twice in its history, the world has experienced a revolutionary expansion of cities. The first urban revolution began about 8000 B.C.E. with the first urban settlements and continued until permanent settlements were in place on several continents. About 1750, the second urban revolution took off; it lasted for two centuries as the Industrial Revolution spurred rapid growth of cities in Europe and North America.

A third urban revolution is now under way. Today, 75 percent of people in high-income countries are already city dwellers. But extraordinary urban growth is occurring in poor nations. In 1950, about 25 percent of the people in low-income countries lived in cities; in 2005, the figure was close to 50 percent. In addition, in 1950, only seven cities in the world had populations over 5 million, and only two of these were in low-income countries. By 2005, forty-nine cities had passed this mark, and thirty-two of them were in less developed nations (Brockerhoff, 2000; GeoHive, 2005).

This third urban revolution is the result of many poor nations entering the high-growth Stage 2 of demographic transition theory. Falling death rates have fueled population increase in Latin America, Asia, and especially Africa. For urban areas, the rate of increase is *twice* as high because, in addition to natural increase, millions of people leave the countryside each year in search of jobs, health care, education, and conveniences such as running water and electricity.

Cities do offer more opportunities than rural areas, but they provide no quick fix for the problems of escalating population and grinding poverty. Many cities in less developed nations—including Mexico City, Egypt's Cairo, India's Calcutta, and Manila in the Philippines—are simply unable to meet the basic needs of much of their population. All these cities are surrounded by wretched shantytowns, settlements of makeshift homes built from discarded materials. As noted in Chapter 9 ("Global Stratification"), even city dumps are home to thousands of poor people, who pick through the waste hoping to find enough to make it through another day. "In the *Times*" explains why the city dump in Shanghai, China, attracts so many people.

Environment and Society

The human species has prospered, rapidly expanding over the entire planet. An increasing share of the global population now lives in large, complex settlements that offer the promise of a better life than that found in rural villages.

But these advances have come at a high price. Never before in history have human beings placed such demands on Earth. This disturbing development brings us to focus on the interplay of the natural environment and society. Like demography, **ecology** is another cousin of sociology, formally defined as *the study of the interaction of living organisms and the natural environment*. Ecology rests on the research of natural scientists as well as social scientists. We shall focus on the aspects of ecology that involve familiar sociological concepts and issues.

The **natural environment** is *Earth's surface and atmosphere, including living organisms, air, water, soil, and other resources necessary to sustain life*. Like every other species, humans depend on the natural environment to survive. Yet with our capacity for culture, humans stand apart from other species; we alone take deliberate action to remake the world according to our own interests and desires, for better and for worse.

Why is the environment of interest to sociologists? Environmental problems, from pollution to global warming, do not arise from the natural world operating on its own. Such problems result from the specific actions of human beings, making them *social* problems (L. Marx, 1994).

THE GLOBAL DIMENSION

The study of the natural environment must be approached from a global perspective. The reason is simple: Regardless of political divisions between nations, the planet is a single **ecosystem,** *a system composed of the interaction of all living organisms and their natural environment.*

The Greek meaning of *eco* is "house," reminding us that this planet is our home and that all living things and their natural environment are interrelated. A change in any part of the natural environment sends ripples through the entire global ecosystem.

Consider, from an ecological point of view, our national love of eating hamburgers. People in North America (and, increasingly, around the world) have created a huge demand for beef, which has greatly expanded ranching in Brazil, Costa Rica, and other Latin American nations. To produce the lean meat sought by fast-food corporations, cattle in Latin America feed on grass, which uses a great deal of land. Latin American ranchers clear the land for grazing

by cutting down thousands of square miles of forests each year. These tropical forests are vital to maintaining Earth's atmosphere. Deforestation ends up threatening everyone, including the people back in the United States enjoying their hamburgers (N. Myers, 1984b).

TECHNOLOGY AND THE ENVIRONMENTAL DEFICIT

Sociologists point to a simple formula: $I = PAT$, where environmental impact (I) reflects a society's population (P), its level of affluence (A), and its level of technology (T). Members of societies with simple technology—the hunters and gatherers described in Chapter 2 ("Culture")—hardly affect the environment because they are small in number, are poor, and have only simple technology. On the contrary, nature affects their lives as they follow the migration of game, watch the rhythm of the seasons, and suffer from natural catastrophes, such as fires, floods, droughts, and storms.

Societies at intermediate stages of sociocultural evolution have a somewhat greater capacity to affect the environment. But the environmental impact of horticulture (small-scale farming), pastoralism (the herding of animals), and even agriculture (the use of animal-drawn plows) is limited because people still rely on muscle power for producing food and other goods.

Human control of the natural environment increased dramatically with the Industrial Revolution. Muscle power gave way to engines that burn fossil fuels: coal at first and then oil. Such machinery affects the environment in two ways: by consuming natural resources and by releasing pollutants into the atmosphere. Even more important, humans armed with industrial technology are able to bend nature to their will, tunneling through mountains, damming rivers, irrigating deserts, and drilling for oil in the arctic wilderness and on the ocean floor. This explains why people in rich nations, who represent just 18 percent of humanity, use 80 percent of the world's energy (G. T. Miller, 1992; York, Rosa, & Deitz, 2002).

The environmental impact of industrial technology goes beyond energy consumption. Just as important is the fact that members of industrial societies produce 100 times more goods than people in agrarian societies. Higher living standards, in turn, increase the problems of solid waste (because people ultimately throw away most of what they produce) and pollution (industrial production generates smoke and other toxic substances).

From the start, people recognized the material benefits of industrial technology. But only a century later did they begin to see its long-term effects on the natural environment. Today, we realize that the technological power to make our lives better can also put the lives of future generations at risk, and there is a national debate about how to address this issue.

Evidence is mounting that we are running up an **environmental deficit,** *profound long-term harm to the natural environment caused by humanity's focus on short-term material affluence* (Bormann, 1990). The concept of environmental deficit is important for three reasons. First, it reminds us that environmental concerns are *sociological,* reflecting societies' priorities about how people should live. Second, it suggests that much environmental damage—to the air, land, or water—is *unintended.* By focusing on the short-term benefits of, say, cutting down forests, strip mining, or using throwaway packaging, we fail to see their long-term environmental effects. Third, in some respects, the environmental deficit is *reversible.* Inasmuch as societies have created environmental problems, societies can undo many of them.

CULTURE: GROWTH AND LIMITS

Whether we recognize environmental dangers and decide to do something about them is a cultural matter. Thus along with technology, culture has powerful environmental consequences.

The Logic of Growth

One of the core values that underlie social life in the United States is *material comfort,* the belief that money and the things it buys enrich our lives. We also believe in the idea of *progress,* thinking that the future will be better than the present. In addition, we look to *science* to make our lives easier and more rewarding. In simpler terms, "having things is good," "life gets better," and "people are clever." Taken together, such cultural values form the *logic of growth.*

YOUR TURN

Identify ways in which the mass media and our popular culture (music, films, and television) encourage people to accept the logic of growth.

An optimistic view of the world, the logic of growth holds that more powerful technology has improved our lives and that new discoveries will continue to do so into the future. Throughout the history of the United States and other high-income nations, the logic of growth has been the driving force behind settling the wilderness, building towns and roads, and pursuing material affluence.

The most important insight sociology offers about our physical world is that environmental problems do not simply "happen." Rather, the state of the natural environment reflects the ways in which social life is organized—how people live and what they think is important. The greater the technological power of a society, the greater that society's ability to threaten the natural environment.

However, "progress" can lead to unexpected problems, including strain on the environment. The logic of growth responds by arguing that people (especially scientists and other technology experts) will find a way out of any problem placed in our path. If, for example, the world runs short of oil, scientists will come up with hydrogen, solar, or nuclear engines or some as yet unknown technology to meet the world's energy needs.

Environmentalists counter that the logic of growth is flawed because it assumes that natural resources such as clean air, fresh water, and topsoil will always be plentiful. We can and will exhaust these *finite* resources if we continue to pursue growth at any cost. Echoing Malthus, environmentalists warn that if we call on the planet to support increasing numbers of people, we will surely destroy the environment—and ourselves—in the process.

The Limits to Growth

If we cannot invent our way out of the problems created by the logic of growth, perhaps we need another way of think-

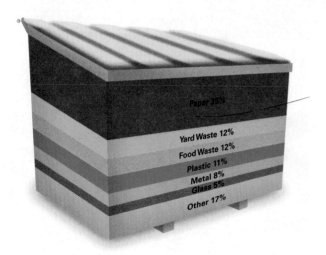

FIGURE 15-4 Composition of Community Trash

We throw away a wide range of material, with paper the single largest part of our trash.

Source: U.S. Environmental Protection Agency (2006).

ing about the world. Environmentalists claim that growth must have limits. Stated simply, the *limits-to-growth* thesis is that humanity must put in place policies to control population increase, pollution, and the use of resources in order to avoid environmental collapse.

In *The Limits to Growth,* a controversial book that had a large hand in launching the environmental movement, Donella Meadows and her colleagues (1972) used a computer model to calculate the planet's available resources, rates of population growth, amount of land available for cultivation, levels of industrial and food production, and amount of pollutants released into the atmosphere. The model reflects changes that have occurred since 1900 and projects forward to the end of the twenty-first century. The authors concede that such long-range predictions are speculative, and some critics think they are plain wrong (Simon, 1981). But given the high stakes, the general conclusions of the study call for serious consideration. The authors claim that we are quickly consuming Earth's finite resources. Supplies of oil, natural gas, and other energy sources are already falling sharply with prices on the rise, and the shortage will only get worse as large nations such as India and China industrialize. By the end of this century, these resources will almost certainly be gone, crippling industrial output and causing a decline in food production.

This limits-to-growth theory shares Malthus's pessimism about the future. People who accept it doubt that current patterns of life are sustainable for even another cen-

tury. If this is true, we face a fundamental choice: Either we make deliberate changes in how we live, or widespread calamity will force change on us.

Are you willing to pay more for products (such as hybrid cars or things made from recycled materials) that are better for the environment? Explain your view.

SOLID WASTE: THE DISPOSABLE SOCIETY

Across the United States, people generate a massive amount of solid waste—about 1.4 billion pounds *each and every day*. Figure 15–4 shows the composition of a typical community's trash.

As a rich nation of people who value convenience, the United States has become a *disposable society*. We consume more products than virtually any other nation on Earth, many of which have throwaway packaging. For example, fast food is served in cardboard, plastic, and Styrofoam containers that we throw away within minutes. But countless other products, from film to fishhooks, are elaborately packaged to make them more attractive to the customer and to discourage tampering and theft.

Manufacturers market soft drinks, beer, and fruit juices in aluminum cans, glass jars, and plastic containers, which not only use up finite resources but also create mountains of solid waste. Countless items are intentionally designed to be disposable: pens, razors, flashlights, batteries, even cameras. Other goods, from light bulbs to automobiles, are designed to have a limited useful life after which they become unwanted junk. As Paul Connett (1991) points out, even the words we use to describe what we throw away—"waste," "trash," "refuse," "garbage," "rubbish"—show how little we value what we cannot immediately use. But this was not always the case, as the Applying Sociology box explains.

Living in a rich society, the average person in the United States consumes hundreds of times more energy, plastics, lumber, and other resources than someone living in a low-income nation such as Bangladesh or Tanzania (and nearly twice as much as someone living in many other high-income countries such as Japan or Sweden). This high level of consumption means that we in the United States not only use a disproportionate share of the planet's natural resources but also generate most of the world's refuse.

We like to say that we throw things "away." But 80 percent of our solid waste never goes away. It ends up in landfills, which are, literally, filling up. Material in landfills also can pollute groundwater stored under Earth's surface. Although in most places laws now regulate what can be dis-

APPLYING SOCIOLOGY

Why Grandma Macionis Had No Trash

Grandma Macionis, we always used to say, never threw away anything. She was born and raised in Lithuania—the "old country"—where growing up in a poor village shaped her in ways that never changed, even after she came to the United States as a young woman and settled in Philadelphia.

After opening a birthday present, she would carefully save the box, wrapping paper, and ribbon, which meant as much to her as the gift they contained. Buying a present for her was difficult because Grandma never wore new clothes or wanted anything that she did not already have. Her kitchen knives were worn thin from decades of sharpening, and all her garbage was recycled as compost for her vegetable garden.

As strange as Grandma sometimes seemed to her grandchildren, she was a product of her culture. A century ago, there was little "trash." If a pair of

socks wore thin, Grandma mended them, probably more than once. When they were beyond repair, they were used as rags for cleaning or sewn, along with other old clothing, into a quilt. For her, everything had value, if not in one way, then in another.

During the twentieth century, as women joined men working outside of

the home, income went up and families began buying more and more "time-saving" products. Before long, few people cared about the home recycling that Grandma practiced. Soon cities sent crews from block to block to pick up truckloads of discarded material. The era of "trash" had begun.

WHAT DO YOU THINK?

1. Just as Grandma Macionis was a product of her culture, so are we. What cultural values make people today "consumers" who demand so many products and time-saving devices?

2. Will the recycling of household waste in the United States expand in the decades to come? Why or why not?

3. How does this box demonstrate that the state of the natural environment is a social issue?

---

carded in a landfill, the Environmental Protection Agency has identified 30,000 dump sites across the United States containing hazardous materials that are polluting water both above and below the ground. In addition, what goes into landfills all too often stays there, sometimes for centuries. Tens of millions of tires, diapers, and other items that we bury in landfills each year do not decompose and will be an unwelcome legacy for future generations.

Environmentalists argue that we should address the problem of solid waste by doing what many of our grandparents did: turn "waste" into a resource. One way to do this is through *recycling,* reusing resources we would otherwise throw away. Recycling is an accepted practice in Japan and many other nations, and it is becoming more common in the United States, where we now reuse about 30 percent of waste materials. The share is increasing as laws mandate reuse of certain materials such as glass bottles and aluminum cans and as the business of recycling becomes more profitable.

WATER AND AIR

Oceans, lakes, and streams are the lifeblood of the global ecosystem. Humans depend on water for drinking, bathing, cooling, cooking, recreation, and a host of other activities.

According to what scientists call the *hydrologic cycle,* the planet naturally recycles water and refreshes the land. The process begins as heat from the sun causes Earth's water, 97 percent of which is in the oceans, to evaporate and form clouds. Because water evaporates at lower temperatures than most pollutants, the water vapor that rises from the seas is relatively pure, leaving various contaminants behind. Water then falls to the Earth as rain, which drains into streams and rivers and finally returns to the sea. Two major concerns about water, then, are supply and pollution.

Water Supply

Only about 1 percent of Earth's water is suitable for drinking. It is not surprising, then, that for thousands of years, water rights have figured prominently in laws around the world. Today, some regions of the world, especially the tropics, enjoy plentiful fresh water, using only a small share of the available supply. High demand, coupled with modest reserves, makes water supply a matter of concern in much of North America and Asia, where people look to rivers rather than rainfall for their water. In China, deep aquifers are dropping rapidly. In the Middle East, water supply is reaching a critical level. Iran is rationing water in its capital city. In Egypt, people can consume just one-sixth as much water from the Nile River today as in 1900. All the nations of northern Africa and the Middle East will probably face a water crisis by about 2035 ("China Faces Water Shortage," 2001; International Development Research Center, 2006).

Rising population and the development of more complex technology have greatly increased the world's appetite for water. The global consumption of water (now estimated at 4 billion cubic feet per year) has doubled since 1950 and is rising steadily. As a result, even in parts of the world that receive plenty of rainfall, people are using groundwater faster than it can be replenished naturally. In the Tamil Nadu region of southern India, for example, people are drawing so much groundwater that the local water table has fallen 100 feet over the last several decades. Mexico City—which has sprawled to some 1,400 square miles—has pumped so much water from its underground aquifer that the city has sunk 30 feet in the past century and continues to drop about 2 inches per year. Farther north in the United States, the Ogallala aquifer, which lies below seven states from South Dakota to Texas, is now being pumped so rapidly that some experts fear it could run dry within several decades.

In light of such developments, we must face the reality that water is a valuable and finite resource. Greater conservation of water by individuals (the average person on our planet consumes 10 million gallons in a lifetime) is part of the answer. However, households around the world account for just 10 percent of water use. We need to curb water consumption by industry, which uses 20 percent of the global total, and farming, which consumes 70 percent of the total for irrigation.

Perhaps new irrigation technology will reduce demand for water in the future. But here again, we see how population increase, as well as economic growth, strains our ecosystem (Postel, 1993; Population Action International, 2000).

Water is vital to life, and it is also in short supply. The state of Gujarat, in western India, has experienced a decade-long drought. In the village of Natwarghad, people crowd together, lowering pots into the local well, taking what little water is left.

Las Vegas is one of the fastest-growing U.S. cities—and it is built in a desert. Do you think the future water needs of this city's people (and those of the entire Southwest) are ensured?

Water Pollution

In large cities—from Mexico City to Cairo to Shanghai—many people have no choice but to drink contaminated water. Infectious diseases such as typhoid, cholera, and dysentery, all caused by waterborne microorganisms, spread rapidly through these populations. In addition to ensuring ample *supplies* of water, we must protect the *quality* of water.

Water quality in the United States is generally good by global standards. However, even here the problem of water pollution is steadily growing. According to the Sierra Club, an environmental activist organization, rivers and streams across the United States absorb some 500 million pounds of toxic waste each year. This pollution results not just from intentional dumping but also from the runoff of agricultural fertilizers and lawn chemicals.

A special problem is *acid rain*—rain made acidic by air pollution—which destroys plant and animal life. Acid rain (or snow) begins with power plants burning fossil fuels (oil and coal) to generate electricity; this burning process releases sulfuric and nitrous oxides into the air. As the wind sweeps these gases into the atmosphere, they react with the air to form sulfuric and nitric acids, which turn atmospheric moisture acidic.

This is a clear case of one type of pollution causing another: Air pollution (from smokestacks) ends up contaminating water (in lakes and streams that collect acid rain). Acid rain is truly a global phenomenon because the regions that suffer the harmful effects may be thousands of miles from the source of the pollution. For instance, British power plants have caused acid rain that has devastated forests and fish in Norway and Sweden, 1,000 miles to the northeast. In the United States, we see a similar pattern as midwestern smokestacks have harmed the natural environment of upstate New York and New England.

Air Pollution

Because we are surrounded by air, most people in the United States are more aware of air pollution than contaminated water. One of the unexpected consequences of industrial technology—especially the factory and the motor vehicle—has been a decline in air quality. In London, fifty years ago, factory smokestacks, automobiles, and coal fires used to heat households all added up to what was probably the worst urban air quality in the world. The fog that some British jokingly called "pea soup" was in reality a deadly mix of pollution: During five days in 1952, an especially thick haze that hung over London killed 4,000 people.

Air quality improved in the final decades of the twentieth century. Rich nations passed laws that banned high-pollution heating, including the coal fires that choked London fifty years ago. In addition, scientists devised ways to make factories as well as motor vehicles operate much more cleanly.

If high-income countries can breathe a bit more easily than they once did, the problem of air pollution in poor societies is becoming more serious. One reason is that people in low-income countries still rely on wood, coal, peat, or other "dirty" fuels to cook their food and heat their homes. In addition, nations eager to encourage short-term industrial development may pay little attention to the longer-term dangers of air pollution. As a result, many cities in Latin America, Eastern Europe, and Asia are plagued by air pollution as bad as London's pea soup fifty years ago.

THE RAIN FORESTS

Rain forests are *regions of dense forestation, most of which circle the globe close to the equator.* The largest tropical rain forests are in South America (notably Brazil), west-central Africa, and Southeast Asia. In all, the world's rain forests cover some 2 billion acres, or 7 percent of Earth's total land surface.

Like other global resources, rain forests are falling victim to the needs and appetites of the surging world population. As noted earlier, to meet the demand for beef, ranchers in Latin America clear forested areas to increase their supply of grazing land. We are also losing rain forests to the hardwood trade. People in rich nations pay high prices for mahogany and other woods because, as environmentalist Norman Myers (1984c:88) puts it, they have "a penchant for parquet floors, fine furniture, fancy paneling, weekend yachts, and high-grade coffins." Under such economic pressure, the world's rain forests are now just half their original size, and they continue to shrink by about 1 percent (65,000 square miles) annually. Unless we stop this loss, the rain forests will vanish before the end of this century, and with them will go protection for Earth's biodiversity and climate.

For more information about rain forests, visit http://www.rainforestweb.org

Global Warming

Why are rain forests so important to our natural environment? One reason is that they cleanse the atmosphere of carbon dioxide (CO_2). Since the beginning of the Industrial Revolution, the amount of carbon dioxide produced by humans (mostly from factories and automobiles) has risen sharply. Much of this CO_2 is absorbed by the oceans. But plants take in carbon dioxide and expel oxygen. This is why the rain forests are vital to maintaining the chemical balance of the atmosphere.

The problem is that production of carbon dioxide is rising while the amount of plant life on Earth is shrinking. To make matters worse, rain forests are being destroyed mostly by burning, which releases even more CO_2 into the atmosphere. Experts estimate that the atmospheric concentration of carbon dioxide is now 20 to 30 percent higher than it was 150 years ago (Revkin, 2002).

High above Earth, carbon dioxide acts like the glass roof of a greenhouse, letting heat from the sun pass through to the surface while preventing much of it from radiating away from the planet. The result of this *greenhouse effect,* say ecologists, is **global warming,** *a rise in Earth's average temperature due to an increasing concentration of carbon dioxide in the atmosphere.* Over the past century, the global temperature has risen about 1° Fahrenheit (to an average of 58° F). Scientists warn that it could rise by 5° to 10° F during this century, which would melt vast areas of the polar ice caps and raise the sea level to cover low-lying land around the world. Were this to happen, water would cover all of Bangladesh, for example, and much of the coastal United States, including Washington, D.C., right up to the steps of the White House. On the other hand, the U.S. Midwest, cur-

Members of small, simple societies, such as the Tan't Batu in the Philippines, live in harmony with nature; they do not have the technological means to greatly affect the natural world. Although we in complex societies like to think of ourselves as superior to such people, the truth is that there is much we can—and must—learn from them.

rently one of the most productive agricultural regions in the world, probably would become arid.

Not all scientists share this vision of future global warming. Some point out that global temperature changes have been taking place throughout history, apparently having little or nothing to do with rain forests. Higher concentrations of carbon dioxide in the atmosphere might speed up plant growth (because plants thrive on this gas), which would correct the imbalance and nudge Earth's temperature downward once again. But a consensus is building that global warming is a problem that threatens the future for all of us (K. A. McDonald, 1999; Kerr, 2005).

 The Heinz Center publishes analyses of society's effect on the natural environment at http://www.heinzctr.org/publications.htm

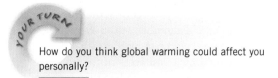

How do you think global warming could affect you personally?

Declining Biodiversity

Clearing rain forests also reduces Earth's *biodiversity* because rain forests are home to almost half of the planet's living species. On Earth, there are as many as 30 million species of animals, plants, and microorganisms. Several dozen unique species of plants and animals cease to exist each day. But given the vast number of living species, why should we be concerned about the loss of a few? Environmentalists give four reasons. First, our planet's biodiversity provides a varied source of human food. Using agricultural high technology, scientists can "splice" familiar crops with more exotic plant life, making food more bountiful and more resistant to insects and disease. Thus biodiversity helps feed our planet's rapidly increasing population.

Second, Earth's biodiversity is a vital genetic resource used by medical and pharmaceutical researchers to provide hundreds of new compounds each year that cure disease and improve our lives. For example, children in the United States now have a good chance of surviving leukemia, a disease that was almost a sure killer two generations ago, because of a compound derived from a pretty tropical flower called the rosy periwinkle. The oral birth control pill, used by tens of millions of women in this country, is another product of plant research, this one involving the Mexican forest yam.

Third, with the loss of any species of life—whether it is the magnificent California condor, the famed Chinese panda, the spotted owl, or even a single species of ant—the beauty and complexity of our natural environment are diminished. And there are clear warning signs: Three-fourths of the world's 9,000 bird species are declining in number.

Finally, unlike pollution, the extinction of any species is irreversible and final. An important ethical question is whether people living today have the right to impoverish the world for those who will live tomorrow (N. Myers, 1991; E. O. Wilson, 1991; Brown et al., 1993).

ENVIRONMENTAL RACISM

Conflict theory has given birth to the concept of **environmental racism**, *patterns that make environmental hazards greatest for poor people, especially minorities.* Historically, factories that spew pollution have stood near neighborhoods housing the poor and people of color. Why? In part, the poor themselves were drawn to factories in search of work, and their low incomes often meant they could afford housing only in undesirable neighborhoods. Sometimes the only housing that fit their budgets stood in the very shadow of the plants and mills where they worked.

Nobody wants a factory or dump nearby, but the poor have little power to resist. Through the years, the most serious environmental hazards have been placed near Newark, New Jersey (not in upscale Bergen County), in southside Chicago (not in wealthy Lake Forest), or on Native Ameri-

THINKING CRITICALLY

Apocalypse: Will People Overwhelm the Planet?

Are you worried about the world's increasing population? Think about this: By the time you finish reading this box, more than 1,000 people will have been added to our planet. By this time tomorrow, global population will have risen by more than 200,000. Currently, as the table shows, there are about four births for every two deaths on the planet, pushing the world's population upward by more than 74 million annually. Put another way, global population growth amounts to adding another Ethiopia to the world every year.

It is no wonder that many demographers and environmentalists are deeply concerned about the future. Earth has an unprecedented population: The 2 billion people we have added since 1974 alone exceeds the planet's total in 1900. Might Thomas Malthus—who

predicted that overpopulation would use up Earth's resources and plunge humanity into war and suffering—be right after all? Lester Brown and other *neo-Malthusians* predict a coming apocalypse if we do not change our ways. Brown admits that Malthus failed to imagine how much technology (especially fertilizers and altering plant genetics) could boost the planet's agricultural output. But he maintains that Earth's rising population is nevertheless rapidly outstripping its finite resources. Families in many poor countries can find little firewood, members of rich societies are depleting worldwide oil reserves, and everyone is draining our supply of clean water and poisoning the planet with waste. Some analysts argue that we have already passed Earth's "carrying capacity" for population and we need to hold the line or even reduce

population to ensure our long-term survival.

But other analysts, the *anti-Malthusians,* sharply disagree. Julian Simon points out that centuries after Malthus predicted catastrophe, Earth supports almost six times as many people, who live longer, healthier lives than ever before. With more advanced technology, people have devised ways to increase productivity and limit population increase. As Simon sees it, this is cause for celebration. Human ingenuity has consistently proven the doomsayers wrong, and Simon is betting it will continue to do so.

WHAT DO YOU THINK?

1. Where do you place your bet? Do you think Earth can support 8 or 10 billion people? Explain your position.

2. Ninety-six percent of current population growth is in poor countries. What does this mean for the future of rich nations? For the future of poor ones?

3. What should people in rich countries do to ensure the future of children everywhere?

Global Population Increase

	Births	Deaths	Net Increase
Per year	130,860,569	56,579,396	74,281,173
Per month	10,905,047	4,714,950	6,190,098
Per day	358,522	155,012	203,510
Per hour	14,938	6,459	8,480
Per minute	249	108	141
Per second	4.1	1.8	2.4

Sources: Brown (1995), Simon (1995), Scanlon (2001), and Smail (2007).

can reservations in the West (not in affluent suburbs of Denver or Phoenix) (Commission for Racial Justice, 1994; Bohon & Humphrey, 2000).

Looking Ahead: Toward a Sustainable Society and World

The demographic analysis presented in this chapter points to some disturbing trends. First, Earth's population has reached record levels because birth rates remain high in

poor nations and death rates have fallen just about everywhere. Reducing fertility will remain a pressing issue throughout this century. Even with some recent decline in the rate of population increase, the nightmare of Thomas Malthus is still a real possibility, as the Thinking Critically box explains.

Further, population growth remains greatest in the poorest countries of the world, those without the means to support their present populations, much less their future ones. Supporting 74 million additional people on our planet each year, 70 million of whom are in poor societies, will take a global commitment to provide not only food but also housing, schools, and employment. The security of the entire world may ultimately depend on resolving the economic and social problems of poor, overly populated countries and bridging the widening gulf between "have" and "have-not" nations.

Urbanization is continuing, especially in poor countries. People have always sought out cities in the hope of finding a better life. But the sheer numbers of people who live in the emerging global supercities, including Mexico City, São Paulo (Brazil), Kinshasa (Democratic Republic of the Congo), Bombay (India), and Manila (Philippines), have created urban problems on a massive scale.

Throughout the world, humanity is facing a serious environmental challenge. Part of this problem is population increase, which is greatest in poor societies. But part of the problem is the high levels of consumption in rich nations such as our own. By increasing the planet's environmental deficit, our present way of life is borrowing against the well-being of our children and their children. Globally, members of rich societies, who currently consume so much of Earth's resources, are mortgaging the future security of the poor countries of the world.

The answer, in principle, is to create an **ecologically sustainable culture**, *a way of life that meets the needs of the present generation without threatening the environmental legacy of future generations.* Sustainable living depends on three strategies.

First, the world needs to *bring population growth under control.* The current population of 6.5 billion is already straining the natural environment. Clearly, the higher world population climbs, the more difficult environmental problems will become. Even if the recent slowing of population growth continues, the world will have 8 billion people by 2050. Few analysts think that Earth can

To read more about population increase, the environment, and global inequality, go to http:// www.peopleandplanet.net

support this many people; most argue that we must hold the line at about 7 billion, and some argue that we must *decrease* population in the coming decades (Smail, 2007).

A second strategy is to *conserve finite resources.* This means meeting our needs with a responsible eye toward the future by using resources efficiently, seeking alternative sources of energy, and in some cases, learning to live with less.

A third strategy is to *reduce waste.* Whenever possible, simply using less is the best way to do this. But recycling programs are also part of the answer.

In the end, making all three of these strategies work depends on a more basic change in the way we think about ourselves and our world. Our *egocentric* outlook sets our own interests as standards for how to live; a sustainable environment demands an *ecocentric* outlook that helps us see that the present is tied to the future and that everyone must work together. Most nations in the southern half of the world are *underdeveloped,* unable to meet the basic needs of their people. At the same time, most countries in the northern half of the world are *overdeveloped,* using more resources than Earth can sustain over time. Changes needed to create a sustainable ecosystem will not come easily. But the price of not responding to the growing environmental deficit will certainly be greater (Kellert & Bormann, 1991; Brown et al., 1993; Population Action International, 2000).

Finally, consider that the great dinosaurs dominated this planet for some 160 million years and then perished forever. Humanity is far younger, having existed for a mere 250,000 years. Compared to the rather dimwitted dinosaurs, our species has the gift of great intelligence. But how will we use this ability? What are the chances that humans will continue to flourish 160 million years—or even 1,000 years—from now? The answer depends on the choices made by one of the 30 million species living on Earth: human beings.

⬤ APPLYING SOCIOLOGY IN EVERYDAY LIFE

1. Here is an illustration of the problem of runaway growth (Milbrath, 1989:10): *A pond has a single water lily growing on it. The lily doubles in size each day. In thirty days, it covers the entire pond. On which day does it cover half the pond?* Discuss the implications of your answer for population increase.

2. Draw a "mental map" of a city familiar to you with as much detail of specific places, districts, roads, and transportation facilities as you can. Compare your

map with a published one or, better yet, a map drawn by someone you know. Try to account for the differences in how people visualize their city.

3. As an interesting exercise, carry a trash bag around with you for a single day, and collect everything you throw away. Most people are surprised to find that the average person in the United States discards close to 5 pounds of paper, metal, plastic, and other materials daily (over a lifetime, that's about 50 tons).

MAKING THE GRADE

DEMOGRAPHY: THE STUDY OF POPULATION

 Demography analyzes the size and composition of a population and how and why people move from place to place. Demographers collect data and study several factors that affect population (p 450).

FERTILITY

- Fertility is the incidence of childbearing in a country's population.
- Demographers describe fertility using the *crude birth rate*.

pp 450–51

MORTALITY

- Mortality is the incidence of death in a country's population.
- Demographers measure mortality using both the *crude death rate* and the *infant mortality rate*.

pp 451–52

MIGRATION

The *net migration rate* is the difference between the in-migration rate and the out-migration rate.

p 452

POPULATION GROWTH

In general, rich nations grow almost as much from immigration as from natural increase; poorer nations grow almost entirely from natural increase.

pp 452–53

POPULATION COMPOSITION

Demographers use *age-sex pyramids* to show graphically the composition of a population and to project population trends.

pp 453–54

demography (p. 450) the study of human population

fertility (p. 450) the incidence of childbearing in a country's population

crude birth rate (p. 450) the number of live births in a given year for every 1,000 people in a population

mortality (p. 451) the incidence of death in a country's population

crude death rate (p. 451) the number of deaths in a given year for every 1,000 people in a population

infant mortality rate (p. 451) the number of deaths among infants under one year of age for each 1,000 live births in a given year

life expectancy (p. 452) the average life span of a country's population

migration (p. 452) the movement of people into and out of a specified territory

sex ratio (p. 453) the number of males for every 100 females in a nation's population

age-sex pyramid (p. 454) a graphic representation of the age and sex of a population

HISTORY AND THEORY OF POPULATION GROWTH

- Historically, world population grew slowly because high birth rates were offset by high death rates.
- About 1750, a demographic transition began as world population rose sharply, mostly due to falling death rates.
- In the late 1700s, *Thomas Robert Malthus* warned that population growth would outpace food production, resulting in social calamity.
- *Demographic transition theory* contends that technological advances gradually slow population increase.
- World population is expected to reach between 8 billion and 9 billion by 2050.

pp 454–57

demographic transition theory (p. 455) a thesis that links population patterns to a society's level of technological development

zero population growth (p. 456) the level of reproduction that maintains population at a steady level

 Currently, the world is gaining 74 million people each year, with 96% of this increase taking place in poor countries (p 455).

URBANIZATION: THE GROWTH OF CITIES

The **FIRST URBAN REVOLUTION** began with the appearance of cities about 10,000 years ago.

- By about 2,000 years ago, cities had emerged in most regions of the world except North America and Antarctica.
- Preindustrial cities have low-rise buildings; narrow, winding streets; and personal social ties.

pp 457–59

A **SECOND URBAN REVOLUTION** began about 1750 as the Industrial Revolution propelled rapid urban growth in Europe.

- The physical form of cities changed as planners created wide, regular streets to allow for more trade.
- The emphasis on commerce, as well as the increasing size of cities, made urban life more impersonal.

p 459

urbanization (p. 457) the concentration of population into cities

metropolis (p. 460) a large city that socially and economically dominates an urban area

suburbs (p. 460) urban areas beyond the political boundaries of a city

megalopolis (p. 461) a vast urban region containing a number of cities and their surrounding suburbs

IN THE UNITED STATES, urbanization has been going on for more than 400 years and continues today.

- Urbanization came to North America with European colonists.
- By 1850, hundreds of new cities had been founded from coast to coast.
- By 1920, a majority of the U.S. population lived in urban areas.
- Since 1950, the decentralization of cities has resulted in the growth of suburbs and edge cities and a "rebound" in rural population.
- Nationally, Sunbelt cities—but not the older Snowbelt cities—are increasing in size and population.

pp 459–62

VISUAL SUMMARY

MAKING THE GRADE

URBANISM AS A WAY OF LIFE

☑ *Rapid urbanization during the nineteenth century led early sociologists to study the differences between rural and urban life. These early sociologists included, in Europe, Tönnies, Durkheim, and Simmel, and in the United States, Park and Wirth.*

FERDINAND TÖNNIES built his analysis on the concepts of *Gemeinschaft*, and *Gesellschaft*.

- *Gemeinschaft*, typical of the rural village, joins people in what amounts to a single primary group.
- *Gesellschaft*, typical of the modern citiy, describes individuals motivated by their own needs rather than by a desire to help improve the well-being of the community.

pp 462–63

EMILE DURKHEIM agreed with much of Tönnies's thinking but claimed that urbanites do not lack social bonds; the basis of social soldarity simply differs in the two settings. He described

- *mechanical solidarity*—social bonds based on common sentiments and shared moral values. This type of social solidarity is typical of traditional, rural life.
- *organic solidarity*—social bonds based on specialization and interdependence. This type of social solidarity is typical of modern, urban life.

p 463

Gemeinschaft (p. 462) a type of social organization in which people are closely tied by kinship and tradition

Gesellschaft (p. 462) a type of social organization in which people come together only on the basis of individual self-interest

urban ecology (p. 464) the study of the link between the physical and social dimensions of cities

GEORG SIMMEL claimed that the over-stimulation of city life produced a blasé attitude in urbanites.

p 463

ROBERT PARK, at the University of Chicago, claimed that cities permit greater social freedom.

p 464

LOUIS WIRTH saw large, dense, heterogeneous populations creating an impersonal and self-interested, though tolerant, way of life.

p 464

URBANIZATION IN POOR NATIONS

- The world's first urban revolution took place about 8,000 B.C.E. with the first urban settlements.
- The second urban revolution took place after 1750 in Europe and North America with the Industrial Revolution.
- A third urban revolution is now occurring in poor countries. Today, most of the world's largest cities are found in less developed nations.

pp 466–67

ENVIRONMENT AND SOCIETY

The state of the **ENVIRONMENT** is a social issue because it reflects how human beings organize social life.

- Societies increase the *environmental deficit* by focusing on short-term benefits and ignoring the long-term consequences brought on by their way of life.
- The more complex a society's technology, the greater its capacity to alter the natural environment.

pp 468–69

- The *logic-of-growth* thesis supports economic development, claiming that people can solve environmental problems as they arise.
- The *limits-to-growth* thesis states that societies must curb development to prevent eventual environmental collapse.

pp 469–70

ecology (p. 468) the study of the interaction of living organisms and the natural environment

natural environment (p. 468) Earth's surface and atmosphere, including living organisms, air, water, soil, and other resources necessary to sustain life

ecosystem (p. 468) a system composed of the interaction of all living organisms and their natural environment

environmental deficit (p. 469) profound long-term harm to the natural environment caused by humanity's focus on short-term material affluence

rain forests (p. 473) regions of dense forestation, most of which circle the globe close to the equator

global warming (p. 473) a rise in Earth's average temperature due to an increasing concentration of carbon dioxide in the atmosphere

environmental racism (p. 474) patterns that make environmental hazards greatest for poor people, especially minorities

ecologically sustainable culture (p.476) a way of life that meets the needs of the present generation without threatening the environmental legacy of future generations

ENVIRONMENTAL ISSUES include

- DISPOSING OF SOLID WASTE—80% of what we throw away ends up in landfills, which are filling up and which can pollute groundwater under Earth's surface.
- PROTECTING THE QUALITY OF WATER AND AIR—The supply of clean water is already low in some parts of the world. Industrial technology has caused a decline in air quality.
- PROTECTING THE RAIN FORESTS—Rain forests help remove carbon dioxide from the atmosphere and are home to a large share of this planet's living species. Under pressure from development, the world's rain forests are now half their original size and are shrinking by about 1% annually.
- ENVIRONMENTAL RACISM—Conflict theory has drawn attention to the pattern by which the poor, especially minorities, suffer most from environmental hazards.

pp 470–75

VISUAL SUMMARY

MAKING THE GRADE
Sample Test Questions
CHAPTER 15

These questions are similar to those found in the test bank that accompanies this textbook.

MULTIPLE-CHOICE QUESTIONS

1. *Demography* is defined as the study of
   a. democratic political systems.
   b. human culture.
   c. human population.
   d. the natural environment.

2. Which region of the world has *both* the lowest birth rate and the lowest infant mortality rate?
   a. Latin America
   b. Europe
   c. Africa
   d. Asia

3. Typically, high-income nations grow mostly from _____, while low-income nations grow from _____.
   a. immigration; natural increase
   b. emigration; natural increase
   c. natural increase; immigration
   d. internal migration; natural increase

4. In general, the higher the average income of a country,
   a. the faster the population increase.
   b. the slower the population increase.
   c. the lower the level of immigration.
   d. the lower the level of urbanization.

5. In the United States, urban decentralization has caused
   a. the expansion of suburbs.
   b. the development of vast urban regions.
   c. the growth of edge cities.
   d. All of the above are correct.

6. Which term was used by Ferdinand Tönnies to refer to social organization in which people come together on the basis of individual self-interest?
   a. mechanical solidarity
   b. organic solidarity
   c. *Gesellschaft*
   d. *Gemeinschaft*

7. The world's third urban revolution is now taking place in
   a. the United States.
   b. Europe and Japan.
   c. middle-income nations.
   d. low-income nations.

8. When environmentalists speak of an environmental deficit, they are referring to
   a. long-term harm to the environment caused by a short-sighted focus on material affluence.
   b. the public's lack of interest in the natural environment.
   c. the fact that natural scientists ignore the social dimensions of environmental problems.
   d. the lack of funding for important environmental programs.

9. Which of the following statements reflects the limits-to-growth thesis?
   a. People are rapidly consuming Earth's finite resources.
   b. Whatever problems technology creates, technology can solve.
   c. Quality of life on Earth is getting better.
   d. Higher living standards today will benefit future generations.

10. *Environmental racism* refers to
    a. the presence of few minorities within the environmental movement.
    b. the claim that prejudice is the major cause of pollution and other environmental problems.
    c. the fact that environmental dangers are greatest for the poor and minorities.
    d. All of the above are correct.

ANSWERS: 1 (c); 2 (b); 3 (a); 4 (b); 5 (d); 6 (c); 7 (d); 8 (a); 9 (a); 10 (c).

ESSAY QUESTIONS

1. According to demographic transition theory, how does economic development affect population patterns?

2. According to Ferdinand Tönnies, Emile Durkheim, Georg Simmel, and Louis Wirth, what characterizes urbanism as a way of life? Note several differences in the ideas of these thinkers.

Social change often brings together traditional and modern ways of life. For centuries, members of Eskimo communities have relied on dogs to pull sleds; today, dogs can hitch a ride on gasoline-powered snowmobiles.

CHAPTER *16*

Social Change: Modern and Postmodern Societies

WHY do societies change?

HOW do social movements both encourage and resist social change?

WHAT do sociologists say is good and bad about today's society?

481

The five-story red brick apartment building at 253 East Tenth Street in New York has been standing for more than a century. In 1900, one of the twenty small apartments in the building was occupied by thirty-nine-year-old Julius Streicher; Christine Streicher, age thirty-three; and their four young children. The Streichers were immigrants, both having come in 1885 from their native Germany to New York, where they met and married.

The Streichers probably considered themselves successful. Julius operated a small clothing shop a few blocks from his apartment; Christine stayed at home, raised the children, and did housework. Like most people in the country at that time, neither Julius nor Christine had graduated from high school, and they worked for ten to twelve hours a day, six days a week. Their income—average for that time—was about $35 a month, or about $425 per year. (In today's dollars, that would be slightly more than $8,000, which would put the family well below the poverty line.) They spent almost half of their income on food; most of the rest went for rent.

Today, Dorothy Sabo resides at 253 East Tenth Street, living alone in the same apartment where the Streichers spent much of their lives. Now eighty-seven, she is retired from a career teaching art at a nearby museum. In many respects, Sabo's life has been far easier than the life the Streichers knew. For one thing, when the Streichers lived there, the building had no electricity (people used kerosene lamps and candles) and no running water (Christine Streicher spent most of every Monday doing laundry using water she carried from a public fountain at the end of the block). There were no telephones, no television, and of course no computers. Today, Dorothy Sabo takes such conveniences for granted. Although she is hardly rich, her pension and Social Security amount to several times as much (in constant dollars) as the Streichers earned.

Sabo has her own worries. She is concerned about the environment and often speaks out about global warming. But a century ago, if the Streichers and their neighbors were concerned about "the environment," they probably would have meant the smell coming up from the street. At a time when motor vehicles were just beginning to appear in New York City, carriages, trucks, and trolleys were all pulled by horses—thousands of them. These animals dumped 60,000 gallons of urine and 2.5 million pounds of manure on the streets every day (Simon & Cannon, 2001).

It is difficult for most people today to imagine how different life was a century ago. Not only was life much harder

Learn about the lives of men and women, black and white, living in New York City a century ago at http://www.albany.edu/mumford/1920/groups.html

back then, but it was also much shorter. Statistical records show that life expectancy was just forty-six years for men and forty-eight years for women (compared to seventy-five and eighty years today).

Over the course of the past century, much has changed for the better. Yet as this chapter explains, social change is not all positive. Change has negative consequences too, causing unexpected new problems. As we shall see, early sociologists were mixed in their assessment of *modernity,* changes brought about by the Industrial Revolution. Likewise, today's sociologists point to both good and bad aspects of *postmodernity,* the recent transformations caused by the Information Revolution and the postindustrial economy. One thing is clear: For better or worse, the rate of change has never been faster than it is now.

What Is Social Change?

In earlier chapters, we examined relatively fixed or *static* social patterns, including status and role, social stratification, and social institutions. We also looked at the *dynamic* forces that have shaped our way of life, ranging from innovations in technology to the growth of bureaucracy and the expansion of cities. These are all dimensions of **social change,** *the transformation of culture and social institutions over time.* This complex process has four major characteristics:

1. **Social change happens all the time.** "Nothing is constant except death and taxes," goes the old saying. Yet our thoughts about death have changed dramatically as life expectancy in the United States has nearly doubled in the past 100 or so years. And back in 1900, the Streichers, like nearly everyone else in the United States, paid little or no taxes on their earnings; taxation increased dramatically over the course of the twentieth century, along with the size and scope of government. In short, just about everything is subject to the twists and turns of change.

   Still, some societies change faster than others. As Chapter 2 ("Culture") explained, hunting and gathering societies change quite slowly; members of technologically complex societies, by contrast, can witness significant change within a single lifetime.

   YOUR TURN

   What would you say have been the two most important changes that have occurred during your lifetime? Explain your answer.

   It is also true that in any society, some cultural elements change faster than others. William Ogburn's theory of *cultural lag* (see Chapter 2) asserts that material culture (that is, things) changes faster than nonmaterial culture (ideas and attitudes). For example, genetic technology that allows scientists to alter and perhaps even create life has developed more rapidly than our ethical standards for deciding when and how to use it.

2. **Social change is sometimes intentional but often unplanned.** Industrial societies actively promote many kinds of change. Scientists seek more efficient forms of energy, and advertisers try to convince us that we cannot live without an iPod or some other gadget. Yet rarely can anyone envision all the consequences of changes as they are set in motion.

   Back in 1900, when the country still relied on horses for transportation, people looked ahead to motor vehicles that would take a single day to carry them distances that used to take weeks or months. But no one could see how much the mobility provided by automobiles would alter life in the United States, scattering family members, threatening the environment, and reshaping cities and suburbs. Nor could automotive pioneers have predicted the more than 42,000 deaths that occur in car accidents each year in the United States alone.

   YOUR TURN

   Try to imagine some of the unexpected consequences of the popularity of iPods, especially among young people. What changes are likely?

3. **Social change is controversial.** The history of the automobile shows that social change brings both good and bad consequences. Capitalists welcomed the Industrial Revolution because advancing technology increased productivity and swelled profits. However, workers feared that machines would make their skills obsolete and resisted the push toward "progress."

   Today, as in the past, people disagree about how we ought to live. As a result, the changing patterns of social interaction between black people and white people, women and men, and gays and straights are welcomed by some people but opposed by others.

4. **Some changes matter more than others.** Some changes (such as clothing fads) have only passing significance; other changes (like computers) last a long time and may change the entire world. Will the Information Revolution turn out to be as important as the Industrial Revolution? Like the automobile and television, computers have both positive and negative effects, providing new kinds of jobs while eliminating old ones, isolating people in offices while linking people in global electronic networks, offering vast amounts of information while threatening personal privacy.

These young boys are performing in a hip-hop dance competition in Chengdu, China, in 2005. Hip-hop music, dress style, and dancing have become popular in China, a clear case of cultural diffusion. Cultural patterns move from place to place, but not always with the same understandings of what they mean. How might Chinese youth understand hip hop differently from the young African Americans in the United States who originated it?

Causes of Social Change

Social change has many causes. In a world linked by sophisticated communication and transportation technology, change in one place often sets off change elsewhere.

CULTURE AND CHANGE

Chapter 2 ("Culture") identified three important sources of cultural change. First, *invention* produces new objects, ideas, and social patterns. Rocket propulsion research, which began in the 1940s, has produced sophisticated spacecraft that can reach toward the stars. Today we take such technology for granted; during the twenty-first century, a significant number of people may well travel in space.

Second, *discovery* occurs when people take notice of existing elements of the world. For example, medical advances offer a growing understanding of the human body. Beyond their direct effects on human health, medical discoveries have extended life expectancy, setting in motion the "graying" of U.S. society (see Chapter 3, "Socialization: From Infancy to Old Age").

Third, *diffusion* creates change as products, people, and information spread from one society to another. Ralph Linton (1937a) recognized that many familiar aspects of our culture came from other lands. For example, the cloth used to make our clothing was developed in Asia, the clocks we see all around us were invented in Europe, and the coins we carry in our pockets were devised in what is now Turkey.

In general, material things change more quickly than cultural ideas. For example, new breakthroughs such as the science of cloning occur faster than our understanding of when—and even whether—they are morally desirable.

CONFLICT AND CHANGE

Inequality and conflict within a society also produce change. Karl Marx saw class conflict as the engine that drives societies from one historical era to another. In industrial-capitalist societies, he maintained, the struggle between capitalists and workers pushes society toward a socialist system of production.

In the century and a quarter since Marx's death, this model has proved simplistic. Yet Marx correctly foresaw that social conflict arising from inequality (involving not just class but also race and gender) would force changes in every society, including our own, to improve the lives of working people.

IDEAS AND CHANGE

Max Weber also contributed to our understanding of social change. Although Weber acknowledged that conflict could bring about change, he traced the roots of most social changes to ideas. For example, people with charisma (Martin Luther King Jr. was one example) can carry a message that changes the world.

Weber highlighted the importance of ideas by revealing how the religious beliefs of early Protestants set the stage for the spread of industrial capitalism (see Chapter 13, "Family and Religion"). The fact that industrial capitalism developed primarily in areas of Western Europe where the Protestant work ethic was strong proved to Weber (1958, orig. 1904–05) the power of ideas to bring about change.

DEMOGRAPHIC CHANGE

Population patterns also play a part in social change. The typical U.S. household (4.8 people) was almost twice as large in 1900 as it is today (2.6 people). Women are having fewer children, and more people are living alone. Change is also taking place as our population grows older. As Chapter 3 ("Socialization: From Infancy to Old Age") explained, 12 percent of the U.S. population was over age sixty-five in

2000, three times the proportion back in 1900. By the year 2030, seniors will account for 20 percent of the total (U.S. Census Bureau, 2004). Medical research and health care services already focus extensively on the elderly, and life will change in countless other ways as homes and household products are redesigned to meet the needs of growing numbers of older consumers.

Migration within and between societies is another demographic factor that promotes change. Between 1870 and 1930, tens of millions of immigrants entered the industrial cities in the United States. Millions more from rural areas joined the rush. As a result, farm communities declined, cities expanded, and by 1920 the United States had for the first time become a mostly urban nation. Similar changes are taking place today as people moving from the Snowbelt to the Sunbelt mix with new immigrants from Latin America and Asia.

Where in the United States have demographic changes been greatest and which areas have been least affected? National Map 16–1 provides one answer, showing counties where the largest share of people have lived in their present homes for thirty years or more.

SOCIAL MOVEMENTS AND CHANGE

A final cause of social change lies in the efforts of people like us. People commonly band together to form a **social movement,** *an organized activity that encourages or discourages social change.* Our nation's history includes all kinds of social movements, from the colonial drive for independence to today's organizations supporting or opposing abortion, gay rights, and the death penalty.

Types of Social Movements

Researchers classify social movements according to the type of change they seek (Aberle, 1966; Cameron, 1966; Blumer, 1969). One variable asks, Who is changed? Some movements target selected people, and others try to change everyone. A second variable asks, How much change? Some movements seek only limited change in our lives; others pursue a radical transformation of society. Combining these variables results in four types of social movements, shown in Figure 16–1 on page 486.

Alterative social movements are the least threatening to the status quo because they seek limited change in only part of the population. Their aim is to help certain people *alter* their lives. Promise Keepers is one example of an alterative social movement; it encourages men to live more spiritual lives and be more supportive of their families.

Visit the Promise Keepers Web site at http://www.promisekeepers.org

Redemptive social movements also target specific individuals, but they seek more radical change. Their aim is to help certain people *redeem* their lives. For example, Alcoholics Anonymous is an organization that helps people with an alcohol addiction achieve a sober life.

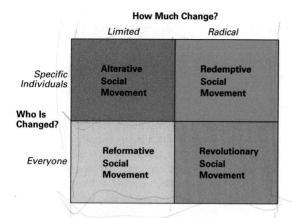

How Much Change?

	Limited	Radical
Specific Individuals	Alterative Social Movement	Redemptive Social Movement
Everyone	Reformative Social Movement	Revolutionary Social Movement

Who Is Changed?

FIGURE 16–1 Four Types of Social Movements

There are four types of social movements, reflecting who is changed and how great the change is.

Source: Based on Aberle (1966).

Reformative social movements aim for only limited change but target everyone. The environmental movement seeks to interest everyone in protecting the natural environment.

Revolutionary social movements are the most extreme of all, working for major transformation of an entire society. Sometimes pursuing specific goals, sometimes spinning utopian dreams, these social movements, including both the left-wing Communist party (pushing for government control of the entire economy) and right-wing militia groups (seeking the destruction of "big government") seek to radically change our way of life.

Have you ever taken part in a social movement or witnessed one in action on your campus? If so, which one of the four types best describes the movement?

Claims Making

In 1981, the Centers for Disease Control and Prevention began to track a strange disease that was killing people, most of them homosexual men. The disease came to be known as AIDS (acquired immune deficiency syndrome). Although this is a deadly disease, there was little public attention and few stories in the mass media. It was only about five years later that the public became aware of the rising number of deaths and began to think of AIDS as a serious social threat.

The change in public thinking was the result of **claims making,** *the process of trying to convince the public and public officials of the importance of joining a social movement to address a particular issue.* In other words, for a social movement to form, some issue has to be defined as a problem that demands public attention. Usually, claims making begins with a small number of people. In the case of AIDS, the gay community in large cities (notably San Francisco and New York) mobilized to convince people of the dangers posed by this deadly disease. Over time, if the mass media give the issue attention and public officials speak out on behalf of the problem, it is likely that the social movement will gain strength.

Considerable public attention has now been given to AIDS, and there is ongoing research aimed at finding a cure for this deadly disease. The process of claims making goes on all the time for dozens of issues. Today, for example, a movement to ban the use of cellular telephones in automobiles has pointed to the thousands of automobile accidents each year related to the use of phones while driving; some states have now passed laws banning this practice, and debate continues in others (McVeigh, Welch, & Bjarnason, 2003; Macionis, 2005).

Explaining Social Movements

Sociologists have developed several explanations of social movements. *Deprivation theory* holds that social movements arise among people who feel deprived of something, such as income, safe working conditions, or political rights. Whether you feel deprived or not, of course, depends on what you expect in life. Thus people band together in response to **relative deprivation,** *a perceived disadvantage arising from some specific comparison.* This concept helps explain why movements for change surface in both good and bad times: It is not people's absolute standing that counts but how they perceive their situation in relation to the situations of others (J. C. Davies, 1962; Merton, 1968).

Mass-society theory, a second explanation, argues that social movements attract socially isolated people who join a movement in order to gain a sense of identity and purpose. From this point of view, social movements have a personal as well as a political agenda (Melucci, 1989).

Resource mobilization theory, a third theoretical scheme, links the success of any social movement to available resources, including money, human labor, and the mass media. Because most social movements begin small, they must look beyond themselves to mobilize the resources required for success (Meyer & Whittier, 1994; Valocchi, 1996; Zhao, 1998).

Fourth, *culture theory* points out that social movements depend not only on money and other material resources but

Social movements are often given great energy by powerful visual images, which is one key idea of culture theory. During World War II, this photo of six soldiers raising the U.S. flag on the tiny Pacific island of Iwo Jima increased morale at home and, later, was the inspiration for a memorial sculpture. Some twenty-five years later, the news included the photo on the right, showing children running from a napalm strike by U.S. planes in South Vietnam. The girl in the middle of the picture had ripped the flaming clothes from her body. This photo increased the strength of the social movement against the war in Vietnam.

also on cultural symbols. People must have a shared understanding of injustice in the world before they will mobilize to bring about change. In addition, specific symbols (such as photographs of the burning World Trade Center after the September 11 attacks) helped mobilize people to support the military campaigns in Afghanistan and Iraq (McAdam, McCarthy, & Zald, 1996:6; J. E. Williams, 2002).

Fifth, *new social movements theory* points out the distinctive character of recent social movements in postindustrial societies. Rather than being local matters, these movements are typically national or international in scope, and most focus on quality-of-life issues—including the natural environment, world peace, or animal rights—rather

 For information on laws involving animal rights, see http://www.animal-law.org

than more traditional economic issues. This broader scope of contemporary social movements

results from closer ties between governments and between ordinary people around the world, who are now linked by the mass media and new information technology (Kriesi, 1989; Pakulski, 1993; Jenkins & Wallace, 1996).

Sixth and finally, *political economy theory* is a Marxist approach that claims that social movements arise in capitalist societies because the capitalist economic system fails to meet the needs of the majority of people. Despite great economic productivity, U.S. society is in crisis, with millions of people unable to find good jobs, living below the

poverty line, and surviving without health insurance. Social movements arise as workers organize to demand higher wages, citizens rally for a health policy that protects everyone, and people march in opposition to spending billions to fund wars while ignoring basic needs at home (Buechler, 2000).

Stages in Social Movements

Social movements typically unfold in four stages: emergence, coalescence, bureaucratization, and decline. The *emergence* of social movements occurs as people think that all is not well. Some, such as the civil rights and women's movements, are born of widespread dissatisfaction. Others emerge as a small group tries to mobilize the population, as when gay activists raised public concern about AIDS.

Coalescence takes place when a social movement defines itself and develops a strategy for attracting new members and "going public." Leaders determine policies and decide on tactics, which may include demonstrations or rallies to attract media attention.

As it gains members and resources, a social movement may undergo *bureaucratization*. As a movement becomes established, it depends less on the charisma and talents of a few leaders and more on a professional staff, which increases the chances for the movement's long-term survival.

Sociologists classify disasters into three types. Hurricane Katrina, which brought massive flooding to New Orleans, is an example of a natural disaster. The 1989 grounding of the tanker ship *Exxon Valdez*, which spilled 11 million gallons of crude oil off the coast of Alaska, was a technological disaster. The slaughter of hundreds of thousands of people and the displacement of millions more from their homes in the Darfur region of Sudan since 2003 is an example of intentional disaster.

Finally, social movements *decline* as resources dry up, the group faces overwhelming opposition, or members achieve their goals and lose interest. Some well-established organizations outlive their original causes and move on to new crusades; others lose touch with the idea of changing society and choose instead to become part of the "system" (Piven & Cloward, 1977; F. D. Miller, 1983).

DISASTERS: UNEXPECTED CHANGE

Sometimes change results from events that are both unexpected and unwelcome. A **disaster** is *an event that is generally unexpected and that causes extensive harm to people and damage to property.* Disasters are of three types[1]. Floods, earthquakes, forest fires, and hurricanes (such as Katrina, which devastated the Gulf Coast in 2005) are examples of *natural disasters.* A second type is the *technological disaster,* which is widely regarded as an *accident* but is more accurately the result of our inability to control technology. The

nuclear accident at the Chernobyl power plant in Ukraine in 1986 and the 11 millions of gallons of oil spilled when the *Exxon Valdez* tanker ran aground off the coast of Alaska in 1989 were both technological disasters. A third type of disaster is the *intentional disaster,* in which one or more organized groups deliberately harm others. War, terrorist attacks, and the genocide that took place in Yugoslavia (1992–1995), Rwanda (2000), and Darfur (2006) are examples of intentional disasters.

The full scope of the harm caused by disasters may become evident only many years after the event takes place. The Applying Sociology box provides an example of a technological disaster that is still affecting people and their descendants more than fifty years after it took place.

Kai Erikson (1976; 1994; 2005a) has investigated disasters of all types. From his investigations of floods, nuclear contamination, oil spills, and genocide, Erikson reached three major conclusions about the social consequences of disasters. First, we all know that disasters harm people and destroy property, but what most people don't realize is that disasters also cause serious damage to human community. When a dam burst and sent a mountain of water down West Virginia's Buffalo Creek in 1972, it killed 125 people,

---

[1]The first two types are based on Erikson (2005). The third type is added by the author.

A Never-Ending Atomic Disaster

It was just after dawn on March 1, 1954, and the air was already warm on Utrik Island, a small bit of coral and volcanic rock in the South Pacific that is one of the Marshall Islands. The island was home to 159 people, who lived by fishing much as their ancestors have done for centuries. The population knew only a little about the outside world—a missionary from the United States taught the local children, and two dozen military personnel lived at a small U.S. weather station with an airstrip that received one plane each week.

At 6:45 A.M., the western sky suddenly lit up brighter than anyone had ever seen, and seconds later, a rumble like a massive earthquake rolled across the island. Some of the Utrik people thought the world was coming to an end. Their world, at least as they had known it, had changed forever.

About 160 miles to the west, on Bikini Island, the United States military had just detonated an atomic bomb, a huge device with 1,000 times the power of the bomb used at the end of World War II to destroy the Japanese city of Hiroshima. The enormous blast vaporized the island and sent a massive cloud of dust and radiation into the atmosphere. The military expected the winds to take the cloud north into an open area of the ocean, but the cloud blew east instead. By noon, the radiation cloud had engulfed a Japanese fishing boat ironically called the *Lucky Dragon,* exposing the twenty-three people on board to a dose of radiation that

would eventually sicken or kill them all. By the end of the afternoon, the deadly cloud had reached Utrik Island.

The cloud was made up of coral and rock dust, all that was left of Bikini Island. The dust fell softly on Utrik Island, and the children, who remembered pictures of snow shown to them by their missionary teacher, ran out to play in the white powder that was piling up everywhere. No one realized that it was contaminated with deadly radiation.

Three-and-one-half days later, the U.S. military landed planes on Utrik Island and informed all the people that they would have to leave immediately,

bringing nothing with them. For three months, the island people were held on another military base, and then they were taken home.

Many of the people who were on the island that fateful morning died young, typically from cancer or other diseases associated with radiation exposure. But even today, those who survived consider themselves and their island poisoned by the radiation, and they believe that the poison will never go away. The radiation may or may not still be in their bodies, but it has worked its way deep into their culture. More than fifty years after the bomb exploded, people still talk about the morning that "everything changed." The damage from this disaster turns out to be much more than medical—it was a social transformation that left the people with a deep belief that they are all sick, that life will never be the same, and that the people who could have prevented the disaster failed to do so.

WHAT DO YOU THINK?

1. In what sense is a disaster like this one never really over?

2. In what ways did the atomic bomb test change the culture of the Utrik people?

3. What does this account lead us to expect about the long-term consequences of other disasters such as Hurricane Katrina, which destroyed much of the Gulf Coast in 2005?

Source: Based on K. T. Erikson (2005a).

destroyed 1,000 homes, and left 4,000 people homeless. After the waters had gone and help was streaming into the area, the people were paralyzed not only by the loss of family members and friends but also by the loss of their way of life. Even more than thirty years later, they have been unable to rebuild the community life that they once knew. We can know when disasters start, Erikson points out, but we cannot know when they will end.

Second, Erikson explains that the social damage is more serious when an event involves some toxic substance, as is

TABLE 16-1

The United States: A Century of Change

	1900	2000
National population	76 million	281 million
Percentage urban	40%	80%
Life expectancy	46 years (men), 48 years (women)	74 years (men), 79 years (women)
Median age	22.9 years	35.3 years
Average household income	$8,000 (in 2000 dollars)	$40,000 (in 2000 dollars)
Share of income spent on food	43%	15%
Share of homes with flush toilets	10%	98%
Average number of cars	1 car for every 2,000 households	1.3 cars for every household
Divorce rate	about 1 in 20 marriages	about 8 in 20 marriages
Average gallons of petroleum products consumed per person per year	34	1,100

common with technological disasters. As the case of radiation falling on Utrik Island shows us, people feel "poisoned" when they have been exposed to a dangerous substance that they fear and over which they have no control. People in the Ukraine felt much the same way after the 1986 explosion and radiation leak at the Chernobyl nuclear plant.

Third, the social damage is most serious when the disaster is caused by the actions of other people. This can happen through negligence or carelessness (in the case of technological disasters) or through willful action (as in the case of intentional disasters). Our belief that "other people will do us no harm" is a basic foundation of social life, Erikson claims. But when others act carelessly (as in the case of the *Exxon Valdez* oil spill in Alaska) or intentionally in ways that harm us (as in the case of genocide in Yugoslavia), survivors typically lose their trust in others to a degree that may never go away.

Many people who were forced from New Orleans when Hurricane Katrina hit believed that government officials had not done all they could to help them. How does such a belief intensify the effects of a disaster?

Modernity

A central concept in the study of social change is **modernity,** *social patterns resulting from industrialization.* In everyday terms, modernity (its Latin root means "lately") refers to the present in relation to the past. Sociologists use this catchall concept to describe the many social patterns set in

motion by the Industrial Revolution beginning in Western Europe in the mid-eighteenth century. **Modernization,** then, is *the process of social change begun by industrialization.* The timeline inside the front cover of this book highlights important events that mark the emergence of modernity. Table 16–1 provides a summary of change in the United States over the course of the twentieth century.

Peter Berger (1977) identified four major characteristics of modernization:

1. **The decline of small, traditional communities.** Modernity involves "the progressive weakening, if not destruction, of the . . . relatively cohesive communities in which human beings have found solidarity and meaning throughout most of history" (1977:72). For thousands of years, in the camps of hunters and gatherers and in the rural villages of Europe and North America, people lived in small communities where life revolved around family and neighborhood. Such traditional worlds give each person a well-defined place that, while limiting choice, offers a strong sense of identity, belonging, and purpose.

   Small, isolated communities still exist in the United States, of course, but they are home to only a tiny percentage of our nation's people. These days, their isolation is only geographic: Cars, telephones, television, and computers give most rural families the pulse of the larger society and connect them to the entire world.

2. **The expansion of personal choice.** People in traditional, preindustrial societies view their lives as shaped by forces beyond human control—gods, spirits, or simply fate. As the power of tradition weakens, people

George Tooker's 1950 painting *The Subway* depicts a common problem of modern life: Weakening social ties and eroding traditions create a generic humanity in which everyone is alike yet each person is an anxious stranger in the midst of others.

George Tooker, *The Subway*, 1950, egg tempera on gesso panel, 18$\frac{1}{8}$ × 36$\frac{1}{8}$", Whitney Museum of American Art, New York. Purchased with funds from the Juliana Force Purchase Award, 50.23. Photograph © Whitney Museum of American Art.

come to see their lives as an unending series of options, a process Berger calls *individualization*. For instance, many people in the United States choose a particular "lifestyle" (sometimes adopting one after another), showing an openness to change. Indeed, it is a common belief that people *should* take control of their lives.

3. **Increasing social diversity.** In preindustrial societies, strong family ties and powerful religious beliefs enforce conformity and discourage diversity and change. Modernization promotes a more rational, scientific worldview as tradition loses its hold and people gain more and more individual choice. The growth of cities, the expansion of impersonal bureaucracy, and the social mix of people from various backgrounds combine to encourage diverse beliefs and behavior.

4. **Orientation toward the future and a growing awareness of time.** Premodern people focus on the past; people in modern societies think more about the future. Modern people are not only forward-looking but also optimist that new inventions and discoveries will improve their lives.

   Modern people organize daily routines down to the very minute. With the introduction of clocks in the late Middle Ages, Europeans began to think not in terms of sunlight and seasons but in terms of hours and minutes. Focused on personal gain, modern people demand precise measurement of time and are likely to agree that "time is money." Berger points out that one good indicator of a society's degree of modernization is the share of people wearing wristwatches.

Finally, recall that modernization touched off the development of sociology itself. As Chapter 1 ("Sociology:

Perspective, Theory, and Method") explained, the discipline originated in the wake of the Industrial Revolution in Western Europe, at a point when social change was proceeding rapidly. Early European and U.S. sociologists tried to analyze the rise of modern society and its consequences, both good and bad, for human beings.

FERDINAND TÖNNIES: THE LOSS OF COMMUNITY

The German sociologist Ferdinand Tönnies produced a lasting account of modernization in his theory of *Gemeinschaft* and *Gesellschaft* (see Chapter 15, "Population, Urbanization, and Environment"). Like Peter Berger, whose work he influenced, Tönnies (1963, orig. 1887) viewed modernization as the progressive loss of *Gemeinschaft*, or human community. As Tönnies saw it, the Industrial Revolution weakened the social fabric of family and tradition by introducing a businesslike emphasis on facts, efficiency, and money. European and North American societies gradually became rootless and impersonal as people came to associate with one another mostly on the basis of self-interest—the state Tönnies termed *Gesellschaft*.

 For a short biography of Tönnies, visit the Gallery of Sociologists at http://www.TheSociologyPage.com

Early in the twentieth century, at least some parts of the United States could be described using Tönnies's concept of *Gemeinschaft*. Families that had lived for many generations in small villages and towns were bound together into a hardworking and slowly changing way of life. Telephones (invented in 1876) were rare; not until 1915 could one place a coast-to-coast call (see the timeline inside the front cover of this book). Living without television (introduced commercially in 1933 and not widespread until after 1950), families entertained themselves, often gathering with friends in the evening to share stories, sorrows, or song.

In traditional societies, such as Amish communities in the United States, everyone does much the same work. These societies are held together by strong moral beliefs. Modern societies, illustrated by urban areas in this country, are held together by a system of production in which people perform specialized work and rely on one another.

Lacking rapid transportation (Henry Ford's assembly line began in 1908, but cars became common only after World War II), many people knew little of the world beyond their hometown.

Inevitable tensions and conflicts divided these communities of the past. But according to Tönnies, the traditional spirit of *Gemeinschaft* meant that people were "essentially united in spite of all separating factors" (1963:65, orig. 1887).

Modernity turns society inside out so that, as Tönnies put it, people are "essentially separated in spite of uniting factors" (1963:65, orig. 1887). This is the world of *Gesellschaft*, where, especially in large cities, most people live among strangers and ignore the people they pass on the street. Trust is hard to come by in a mobile and anonymous society in which, according to researchers, people tend to put their personal needs ahead of group loyalty and an increasing majority of adults believe "you can't be too careful" in dealing with people (NORC, 2005:226). No wonder researchers conclude that even as we have become more affluent, the social health of modern societies has declined (D. G. Myers, 2000).

CRITICAL REVIEW Tönnies's theory of *Gemeinschaft* and *Gesellschaft* is the most widely cited model of modernization. The theory's strength lies in its synthesis of various dimensions of change: growing population, the rise of cities, and increasingly impersonal interaction. But modern life, though often impersonal, still has some degree of *Gemeinschaft*. Even in a world of strangers, modern friendships can be strong and lasting. In addition, some analysts think that Tönnies favored—perhaps even romanticized—traditional societies while overlooking bonds of family and friendship that continue to flourish in modern societies.

 **YOUR LEARNING** As forms of social organization, how do *Gemeinschaft* and *Gesellschaft* differ?

EMILE DURKHEIM: THE DIVISION OF LABOR

The French sociologist Emile Durkheim shared Tönnies's interest in the important social changes that resulted from the Industrial Revolution. For Durkheim (1964a, orig. 1893), modernization was marked by an increasing **division of labor,** or *specialized economic activity*. Every member of a traditional society performs more or less the same activities; modern societies function by having people perform highly specialized roles.

Durkheim explained that preindustrial societies are held together by *mechanical solidarity,* or *shared moral sentiments* (see Chapter 15). Members of such societies view everyone as basically alike, doing the same work and belonging together. Durkheim's concept of mechanical solidarity is virtually the same as Tönnies's *Gemeinschaft*.

With modernization, the division of labor becomes more and more pronounced. To Durkheim, this change means less mechanical solidarity but more of another kind of tie: *organic solidarity,* or the mutual dependency between people engaged in specialized work. Put simply, modern societies are held together not by likeness but by difference: All of us must depend on others to meet most of our needs. Organic solidarity corresponds to Tönnies's concept of *Gesellschaft.*

Despite obvious similarities in their thinking, Durkheim and Tönnies viewed modernity somewhat differently. To Tönnies, modern *Gesellschaft* amounted to the loss of social solidarity because people lose the "natural" and "organic" bonds of the rural village, leaving only the "artificial" and "mechanical" ties of the big city. Durkheim had a different view of modernity, even reversing Tönnies's language to bring home the point. Durkheim labeled modern society "organic," arguing that modern society is no less natural than any other, and he described traditional societies as "mechanical" because they are so regimented. Durkheim viewed modernization not so much as a loss of community as a change from community based on bonds of likeness (kinship and neighborhood) to community based on economic interdependence (the division of labor). Durkheim's view of modernity is thus both more complex and more positive than Tönnies's view.

CRITICAL REVIEW Durkheim's work, which resembles that of Tönnies, is a highly influential analysis of modernity. Of the two, Durkheim was the more optimistic; still, he feared that modern societies might become so diverse that they would collapse into **anomie,** *a condition in which society provides little moral guidance to individuals.* Living with weak moral norms, modern people can become egocentric, placing their own needs above those of others and finding little purpose in life.

The suicide rate, which Durkheim considered a good index of anomie, did in fact increase in the United States over the course of the twentieth century, and the vast majority of adults report that they see moral questions not in clear terms of right and wrong but as confusing "shades of gray" (NORC, 2005:445). Yet shared norms and values seem strong enough to give most people a sense of meaning and purpose. Whatever the hazards of anomie, most people value the personal freedom modern society gives us.

✔ **YOUR LEARNING** In his view of the modern world, what makes Durkheim more optimistic than Tönnies?

To Max Weber, modernity meant the rise of a rational worldview, which is illustrated in the spread of bureaucracy. The efforts of large, formal organizations to deal with vast numbers of people efficiently is evident in the endless collection of files that accumulate in storerooms (and, increasingly, on computer drives). Why did Weber worry that modern rationality threatened our basic humanity?

MAX WEBER: RATIONALIZATION

For Max Weber, modernity meant replacing a traditional worldview with a rational way of thinking. In preindustrial societies, tradition acts as a constant brake on social change. To traditional people, "truth" is roughly the same as "what has always been" (1978:36, orig. 1921). To modern people, however, "truth" is the result of rational calculation. Because they value efficiency and have little reverence for the past, modern people adopt whatever social patterns allow them to achieve their goals.

Echoing Tönnies's and Durkheim's claim that industrialization weakens tradition, Weber declared modern society to be "disenchanted." The unquestioned truths of an earlier time had been challenged by rational thinking. In short, said Weber, modern society turns away from the gods. Throughout his life, Weber studied various modern "types"—the scientist, the capitalist, the bureaucrat—all of whom share the detached worldview that he believed was coming to dominate humanity.

CRITICAL REVIEW Compared with Tönnies and especially Durkheim, Weber was very critical of modern society. He knew that science could produce technological and organizational wonders, yet he worried that science was carrying us away from more basic questions about the meaning and purpose of human existence. Weber feared that rationalization, especially in bureaucracies, would erode the human spirit with endless rules and regulations.

 YOUR LEARNING What did Weber mean by describing the modern world as "disenchanted"? In what ways are scientists, capitalists, and bureaucrats all "disenchanted"?

Some of Weber's critics think that the alienation Weber attributed to bureaucracy actually stemmed from social inequality. This issue leads us to the ideas of Karl Marx.

KARL MARX: CAPITALISM

For Karl Marx, modern society was synonymous with capitalism; he saw the Industrial Revolution primarily as a *capitalist revolution.* Marx traced the emergence of the bourgeoisie in medieval Europe to the expansion of commerce. The bourgeoisie gradually displaced a feudal aristocracy as the Industrial Revolution gave it control of a powerful new productive system.

Marx agreed that modernity weakened small communities (as described by Tönnies), increased the division of labor (as noted by Durkheim), and encouraged a rational worldview (as Weber claimed). But he saw these simply as conditions necessary for capitalism to flourish. According to Marx, capitalism draws population

 For more on Durkheim, Weber, and Marx, visit the Gallery of Sociologists at http://www. TheSociologyPage.com

from farms and small towns into an ever-expanding market system centered in the cities; specialization is needed for efficient factories; and rationality is illustrated by the capitalists' endless pursuit of profit.

Earlier chapters have painted Marx as a spirited critic of capitalist society, but his vision of modernity also incorporates a considerable measure of optimism. Unlike Weber, who viewed modern society as an "iron cage" of bureaucracy, Marx believed that social conflict in capitalist societies would sow the seeds of revolutionary change, leading to an egalitarian socialism. Such a society, as he saw it, would harness the wonders of industrial technology to enrich people's lives and rid the world of social classes, the source of conflict and so much suffering. Although Marx's evaluation of modern capitalist society was highly negative, he imagined a future of human freedom, creativity, and community.

CRITICAL REVIEW Marx's theory of modernization is a complex theory of capitalism. But he underestimated the dominance of bureaucracy in shaping modern societies. In socialist societies, in particular, the stifling effects of bureaucracy have turned out to be as bad as, or even worse than, the dehumanizing aspects of capitalism. The upheavals in Eastern Europe and the former Soviet Union in the 1990s reveal the depth of popular opposition to oppressive state bureaucracies.

 YOUR LEARNING Of the four theorists just discussed—Tönnies, Durkheim, Weber, and Marx—who comes across as the most optimistic about modern society? Who was the most pessimistic? Explain your responses.

Structural-Functional Analysis: Modernity as Mass Society

November 11, on Interstate 275. From the car window, we see BP and Sunoco gas stations, a Kmart and a Wal-Mart, an AmeriSuites hotel, a Bob Evans, a Chi-Chi's Mexican restaurant, and a McDonald's. This road happens to circle Cincinnati, Ohio. But it could be just about anywhere in the United States.

The rise of modernity is a complex process involving many dimensions of change, described in previous chapters and reviewed in the Summing Up table. How can we make sense of so many changes going on at once? Sociologists have two broad explanations of modern society, one guided by the structural-functional approach and the other based on social-conflict theory.

The first explanation—guided by the structural-functional approach and drawing on the ideas of Tönnies, Durkheim, and Weber—understands modernity as the emergence of a *mass society* (Kornhauser, 1959; Nisbet, 1969; Berger, Berger, & Kellner, 1974; Pearson, 1993). A **mass society** is *a society in which prosperity and bureaucracy have weakened traditional social ties.* A mass society is productive; on average, people have more income than ever. At the same time, it is marked by weak kinship and impersonal neighborhoods, leaving individuals to feel socially isolated. Although many people have material plenty, they are spiritually weak and often experience moral uncertainty about how to live.

THE MASS SCALE OF MODERN LIFE

Mass-society theory argues, first, that the scale of modern life has greatly increased. Before the Industrial Revolution, Europe and North America formed a mosaic of countless rural villages and small towns. In these local communities, which inspired Tönnies's concept of *Gemeinschaft,* people lived out their lives surrounded by kin and guided by a shared heritage. Gossip was an informal yet highly effective

SUMMING UP

Traditional and Modern Societies: The Big Picture

Elements of Society	Traditional Societies	Modern Societies
Cultural Patterns		
Values	Homogeneous; sacred character; few subcultures and countercultures	Heterogeneous; secular character; many subcultures and countercultures
Norms	Great moral significance; little tolerance of diversity	Variable moral significance; high tolerance of diversity
Time orientation	Present linked to past	Present linked to future
Technology	Preindustrial; human and animal energy	Industrial; advanced energy sources
Social Structure		
Status and role	Few statuses, most ascribed; few specialized roles	Many statuses, some ascribed and some achieved; many specialized roles
Relationships	Typically primary; little anonymity or privacy	Typically secondary; much anonymity and privacy
Communication	Face to face	Face-to-face communication supplemented by mass media
Social control	Informal gossip	Formal police and legal system
Social stratification	Rigid patterns of social inequality; little mobility	Fluid patterns of social inequality; high mobility
Gender patterns	Pronounced patriarchy; women's lives centered on the home	Declining patriarchy; increasing number of women in the paid labor force
Settlement patterns	Small-scale; population typically small and widely dispersed in rural villages and small towns	Large-scale; population typically large and concentrated in cities
Social Institutions		
Economy	Based on agriculture; much manufacturing in the home; little white-collar work	Based on industrial mass production; factories become centers of production; increasing white-collar work
State	Small-scale government; little state intervention in society	Large-scale government; much state intervention in society
Family	Extended family as the primary means of socialization and economic production	Nuclear family retains some socialization functions but is more a unit of consumption than of production
Religion	Religion guides worldview; little religious pluralism	Religion weakens with the rise of science; extensive religious pluralism
Education	Formal schooling limited to elites	Basic schooling becomes universal, with growing proportion receiving advanced education
Health	High birth and death rates; short life expectancy because of low standard of living and simple medical technology	Low birth and death rates; longer life expectancy because of higher standard of living and sophisticated medical technology
Social Change	Slow; change evident over many generations	Rapid; change evident within a single generation

way of ensuring conformity to community standards. Such small communities tolerated little social diversity—the state of mechanical solidarity described by Durkheim.

For example, before 1690, English law demanded that everyone participate regularly in the Christian ritual of Holy Communion (P. Laslett, 1984). On the North American continent, only Rhode Island among the New England colonies tolerated any religious dissent. Because social differences were repressed in favor of conformity to established norms, subcultures and countercultures were few, and change proceeded slowly.

Increasing population, the growth of cities, and specialized economic activity driven by the Industrial Revolution gradually altered this pattern. People came to know one another by their jobs (for example, as "the doctor" or "the bank clerk") rather than by their kinship group or hometown. People looked on most others simply as strangers. The face-to-face communication of the village was eventually replaced by the impersonal mass media: newspapers, radio, television, and more recently, computer networks. Large organizations steadily assumed more and more responsibility for the daily needs that had once been fulfilled by family, friends, and neighbors; public education drew more and more people to schools; police, lawyers, and courts supervised a formal criminal justice system. Even charity became the work of faceless bureaucrats working for various social welfare agencies.

Geographic mobility, mass communication, and exposure to diverse ways of life all weaken traditional values. People become more tolerant of social diversity, defending individual rights and freedom of choice. Treating people differently because of their race, sex, or religion comes to be defined as backward and unjust. In the process, minorities at the margins of society gain greater power and broader participation in public life.

The mass media give rise to a national culture that washes over the traditional differences that used to set off one region from another. As one analyst put it, "Even in Baton Rouge, La., the local kids don't say 'y'all' anymore; they say 'you guys' just like on TV" (Gibbs, 2000:42). Mass-society theorists fear that the transformation of people of various backgrounds into a generic mass may end up dehumanizing everyone.

YOUR TURN

Identify five elements of "mass culture" that are the same throughout the United States. Name five more that differ from region to region.

THE EVER-EXPANDING STATE

In the small-scale preindustrial societies of Europe, government amounted to little more than a local noble. A royal family formally reigned over an entire nation, but in the absence of swift transportation and efficient communication, even absolute monarchs had far less power than today's political leaders.

As technological innovation allowed government to expand, the centralized state grew in size and importance. At the time the United States gained independence from Great Britain, the federal government was a tiny organization with the primary function of providing national defense. Since then, government has assumed responsibility for more and more areas of social life: schooling, regulating wages and working conditions, establishing standards for products of all sorts, and providing financial assistance to the elderly, the ill, and the unemployed. To pay for such programs, taxes have soared: Today's average worker in the United States labors more than four months each year just to pay for the broad array of services the government provides.

In a mass society, power resides in large bureaucracies, leaving people in local communities with little control over their lives. For example, state officials mandate that local schools must meet educational standards, local products must be government-certified, and every citizen must maintain extensive tax records. Although such regulations may protect people and enhance social equality, they also force us to deal more and more with nameless officials in distant and often unresponsive bureaucracies, and they undermine the autonomy of families and local communities.

CRITICAL REVIEW The growing scale of modern life certainly has positive aspects, but only at the cost of our cultural heritage. Modern societies increase individual rights, have greater tolerance of social differences, and raise living standards (Inglehart & Baker, 2000). But they are prone to what Weber feared most—excessive bureaucracy—as well as to Tönnies's self-centeredness and Durkheim's anomie. The size, complexity, and tolerance of diversity of modern societies all but doom traditional values and families, leaving individuals isolated, powerless, and materialistic. As Chapter 12 ("Economics and Politics") noted, voter apathy is a serious problem in the United States. But should we be surprised that individuals in vast, impersonal societies such as ours end up thinking that no one person can make much of a difference?

Critics sometimes say that mass-society theory romanticizes the past. They remind us that many people in the small towns of our past were eager to set out for a better standard of living in cities. This approach also ignores problems of social inequality. Critics say mass-society theory attracts social and economic conservatives who defend conventional morality and are indifferent to the historical inequality of women and other minorities.

✔ YOUR LEARNING In your own words, state the mass-society analysis of modernity.

Social-Conflict Analysis: Modernity as Class Society

The second explanation of modernity derives mostly from the ideas of Karl Marx. From a social-conflict perspective, modernity takes the form of a **class society,** *a capitalist society with pronounced social stratification.* While agreeing that modern societies have expanded to a mass scale, this approach views the heart of modernization as an expanding capitalist economy, marked with inequality (Habermas, 1970; Harrington, 1984; Buechler, 2000).

Social-conflict theory sees modernity not as a mass society but as a class society in which some categories of people are second-class citizens. This six-year-old boy waits for his mother to finish cooking a simple dinner outside their trailer on the Navajo Reservation near Window Rock, Arizona. The family lives without electricity or running water—a situation shared by thousands of other Navajo families.

CAPITALISM

Class-society theory follows Marx in claiming that the increasing scale of social life in modern times has resulted from the growth and greed unleashed by capitalism. Because a capitalist economy pursues ever-greater profits, both production and consumption steadily increase.

According to Marx, capitalism rests on "naked self-interest" (Marx & Engels, 1972:337, orig. 1848). This self-centeredness weakens the social ties that once united small communities. Capitalism also treats people as commodities: a source of labor and a market for capitalist products.

Capitalism supports science not just as the key to greater productivity but also as an ideology that justifies the status quo. Modern societies encourage people to view human well-being as a technical puzzle that can be solved by engineers and other experts rather than through the pursuit of social justice. For example, a capitalist culture seeks to improve health through advances in scientific medicine rather than by eliminating poverty, which is a core cause of poor health.

Businesses also raise the banner of scientific logic, trying to increase profits through greater efficiency. As Chapter 12 ("Economics and Politics") explained, capitalist corporations have reached enormous size and control unimaginable wealth by "going global" as multinationals. From the class-society point of view, the expanding scale of life is less a function of *Gesellschaft* than the inevitable and destructive consequence of capitalism.

PERSISTENT INEQUALITY

Modernity has gradually worn away some of the rigid categories that divided preindustrial societies. But class-society theory maintains that elites persist as capitalist millionaires rather than nobles born to wealth and power. In the United States, we may have no hereditary monarchy, but the richest 5 percent of the population controls about 60 percent of all privately held property.

What of the state? Mass-society theorists argue that the state works to increase equality and fight social problems. Marx disagreed; he doubted that the state could accomplish more than minor reforms because, as he saw it, real power lies in the hands of the capitalists who control the economy. Other class-society theorists add that to the extent that working people and minorities do enjoy greater political rights and a higher standard of living today, these changes were the result of political struggle, not government goodwill. Despite our pretensions of democracy, they conclude, most people are powerless in the face of wealthy elites.

CRITICAL REVIEW Class-society theory dismisses Durkheim's argument that people in modern societies suffer from anomie, claiming instead that most people deal with alienation and powerlessness. Not surprisingly, the class-society interpretation of modernity enjoys widespread support among liberals and radicals who favor greater equality and seek extensive regulation (or abolition) of the capitalist marketplace.

A basic criticism of class-society theory is that it overlooks the increasing prosperity of modern societies and the fact that discrimination based on race, ethnicity, religion, and gender is now illegal and is widely regarded as a social problem. In addition, most people in the United States do not want an egalitarian society; they prefer a system of unequal rewards that reflects personal differences in talent and effort.

SUMMING UP

Two Interpretations of Modernity

	Mass Society	Class Society
Process of modernization	Industrialization; growth of bureaucracy	Rise of capitalism
Effects of modernization	Increasing scale of life; rise of the state and other formal organizations	Expansion of the capitalist economy; persistence of social inequality

Based on socialism's failure to generate a high overall standard of living, few observers think that a centralized economy would cure the ills of modernity. Many other problems in the United States—including unemployment, industrial pollution, and unresponsive government—are also found in socialist nations such as China, North Korea, and the former Soviet Union.

✓ YOUR LEARNING In your own words, state the class-society analysis of modernity.

The Summing Up table compares views of modern society offered by mass-society theory and class-society theory. Mass-society theory focuses on the increasing impersonality of social life and the growth of government; class-society theory stresses the expansion of capitalism and the persistence of inequality.

Modernity and the Individual

Both mass- and class-society theories look at the broad patterns of change since the Industrial Revolution. From these macro-level approaches, we can also draw micro-level insights into how modernity shapes individual lives.

MASS SOCIETY: PROBLEMS OF IDENTITY

Modernity freed individuals from the small, tightly knit communities of the past. Most members of modern societies have the privacy and freedom to express their individuality. However, mass-society theory suggests that so much social diversity, widespread isolation, and rapid social change make it difficult for many people to establish any coherent identity at all (Wheelis, 1958; Berger, Berger, & Kellner, 1974).

Chapter 3 ("Socialization: From Infancy to Old Age") explained that people's personalities are mostly a product of their social experiences. The small, homogeneous, and slowly changing societies of the past provided a firm, if nar-

row, foundation for building a personal identity. Even today, Amish communities that flourish in the United States teach young men and women "correct" ways to think and behave. Not everyone born into an Amish community can tolerate such rigid demands for conformity, but most members establish a well-integrated and satisfying personal identity (Hostetler, 1980; Kraybill & Olshan, 1994).

Mass societies are quite another story. Socially diverse and rapidly changing, they offer only shifting sands on which to build a personal identity. Left to make many life decisions on their own, people—especially those with greater wealth—face a confusing range of options. The freedom to choose has little value without standards to guide the selection process; in a tolerant mass society, people may find little reason to choose one path over another. As a result, many people shuttle from one identity to another, changing their lifestyles, relationships, and even religions in search of an elusive "true self." Given the widespread relativism of modern societies, people without a moral compass lack the security and certainty once provided by tradition.

To David Riesman (1970, orig. 1950), modernization brings changes in **social character,** *personality patterns common to members of a particular society.* Preindustrial societies promote what Riesman calls **tradition-directedness,** *rigid conformity to time-honored ways of living.* Members of such societies model their lives on those of their ancestors, so that "living the good life" amounts to "doing what people have always done."

Tradition-directedness corresponds to Tönnies's *Gemeinschaft* and Durkheim's mechanical solidarity. Culturally conservative, tradition-directed people think and act alike. Unlike the conformity often found in modern societies, the uniformity of tradition-directedness is not an effort to imitate a popular celebrity or follow the latest trend. Instead, people are alike because they all draw on the same solid cultural foundation. Amish women and men exemplify tradition-directedness; in the Amish culture, tra-

Mass-society theory relates feelings of anxiety and lack of meaning in the modern world to rapid social change that washes away tradition. This notion of modern emptiness is captured in the photo at the left. Class-society theory, by contrast, ties such feelings to social inequality, by which some categories of people are made into second-class citizens (or not made citizens at all), an idea expressed in the photo at the right.

dition ties everyone to ancestors and descendants in an unbroken chain of righteous living.

Members of diverse and rapidly changing societies define a tradition-directed personality as deviant because it seems so rigid. Modern people prize personal flexibility, the capacity to adapt, and sensitivity to others. Riesman calls this type of social character **other-directedness,** *openness to the latest trends and fashions, often expressed by imitating others.* Because their socialization occurs in societies that are continuously in flux, other-directed people develop fluid identities marked by superficiality, inconsistency, and change. They try on different "selves" almost like new clothing, seek out role models, and engage in varied performances as they move from setting to setting (Goffman, 1959). In a traditional society, such "shiftiness" marks a person as untrustworthy, but in a changing, modern society, the chameleonlike ability to fit in virtually anywhere is very useful.

In societies that value the up-to-date rather than the traditional, people look to others for approval, using members of their own generation rather than elders as role models. Peer pressure can be irresistible to people without strong standards to guide them. Our society urges people to be true to themselves, but when social surroundings change so rapidly, how can people develop the self to which they

should be true? This problem lies at the root of the identity crisis so widespread in industrial societies today. "Who am I?" is a nagging question that many of us struggle to answer. In truth, this problem is not so much us as the inherently unstable mass society in which we live.

Have you felt difficulty deciding "who you are"? Do you try to be a different person in different settings?

CLASS SOCIETY: PROBLEMS OF POWERLESSNESS

Class-society theory paints a different picture of modernity's effects on individuals. This approach maintains that persistent inequality undermines modern society's promise of individual freedom. For some people, modernity serves up great privilege, but for many others, everyday life means coping with economic uncertainty and a gnawing sense of powerlessness (K. S. Newman, 1993; Ehrenreich, 2001).

For racial and ethnic minorities, the problem of relative disadvantage looms even larger. Similarly, although women participate more broadly in modern societies, they continue

Does "Modernity" Equal "Progress"?
Brazil's Kaiapo and Georgia's Gullah Community

The firelight flickers in the gathering darkness. Chief Kanhonk sits, as he has done at the end of the day for many years, ready to begin an evening of animated talk and storytelling (Simons, 2007). This is the hour when the Kaiapo, a small society in Brazil's lush Amazon region, celebrate their heritage. Because the Kaiapo are a traditional people with no written language, the elders rely on evenings by the fire to pass along their culture to their children and grandchildren. In the past, evenings like this have been filled with tales of brave Kaiapo warriors fighting off Portuguese traders in pursuit of slaves and gold.

But as the minutes pass, just a few older villagers assemble for the evening ritual. "It is the Big Ghost," one man grumbles, explaining the poor turnout. The "Big Ghost" has indeed descended on them; its bluish glow spills from windows throughout the village. The Kaiapo children—and many adults as well—are watching sitcoms on television. Buying a television and a satellite dish several years ago has had consequences far greater than anyone imagined. In the end, what their enemies failed to do with guns, the Kaiapo may well do to themselves with prime-time programming.

The Kaiapo are among the 230,000 native peoples who inhabit Brazil. They

To see pictures of Brazil's Kaipo, go to http://www. ddbstock.com/largeimage/ amindns.html

stand out because of their striking body paint and ornate ceremonial dress. During the 1980s, they became rich from gold mining and harvesting mahogany trees. Now they must decide if their newfound fortune is a blessing or a curse.

To some, affluence means the opportunity to learn about the outside world through travel and television. Others, like Chief Kanhonk, are not so sure. Sitting by the fire, he thinks aloud, "I have been saying that people must buy useful things like knives and fishing hooks. Television does not fill the stomach. It only shows our children and grandchildren white people's things." Bebtopup, the oldest priest, nods in agreement: "The night is the time the old people teach the young people. Television has stolen the night" (Simons, 2007:522).

to run up against traditional barriers of sexism. This approach rejects mass-society theory's claim that people suffer from too much freedom; according to class-society theory, our society still denies a majority of people full participation in social life.

As Chapter 9 ("Global Stratification") explained, the expanding scope of world capitalism has placed more of Earth's population under the influence of multinational corporations. As a result, more than three-fourths of the world's income is concentrated in high-income nations, where just 18 percent of its people live. Is it any wonder, class-society theorists ask, that people in poor nations seek greater power to shape their own lives?

The problem of widespread powerlessness led Herbert Marcuse (1964) to challenge Max Weber's claim that modern society is rational. Marcuse condemned modern society as irrational for failing to meet the needs of so many people. Although modern capitalist societies produce unparalleled wealth, poverty remains the daily plight of more than 1 billion people. Marcuse added that technological advances further reduce people's control over their own lives. The advent of high technology has generally conferred a great deal of power on a core of specialists—not the majority of people—who now dominate discussion of when to go to war, what our energy policy should be, and how people should pay for health care. Countering the popular view

Far to the north, half an hour by ferry from the coast of Georgia, lies the swampy island community of Hog Hammock. The seventy African American residents of the island today trace their ancestry back to the first slaves who settled here in 1802.

Walking past the brightly painted houses that stand among yellow pine trees draped with Spanish moss, a visitor can easily feel transported back in time. The local people, known as Gullahs (or, in some places, Geechees), speak a *creole* or mixture of English and West African languages. They fish, living much the same as they have for hundreds of years.

But the future of this way of life is now in doubt. Few young people who are raised in Hog Hammock can find work; beyond fishing and making traditional crafts, there are simply no jobs to do. "We have been here nine generations and we are still here," says one local. Then, referring to the nineteen children who now live on the island, she adds, "It's not that they don't want to be here; it's that there's nothing here for them—they need to have jobs" (Curry, 2001:41).

INTERNET Learn more about Gullah culture at http://www.knowitall.org/gullahnet

Just as important, with people on the mainland looking for waterside homes for vacations or year-round living, the island is now becoming prime real estate. Not long ago, one larger house went up for sale and the community was shocked to learn of an asking price over $1 million. The locals know only too well that higher property values will mean high taxes that few can afford to pay. In short, Hog Hammock is likely to become another Hilton Head, once a Gullah community on the South Carolina coast that is now home to well-to-do people from the mainland.

The odds are that before long, the people of Hog Hammock will be selling their homes and moving inland. But few people are happy at the thought of selling out, even for a good price. On the contrary, moving away will mean the end of their cultural heritage.

The stories of both the Kaiapo and the people of Hog Hammock show us that change is not a simple path toward "progress." These people may be moving toward modernity, but this process will have both positive and negative consequences. In the end, both groups of people may enjoy a higher standard of living with better shelter, more clothing, and new technology. But their new affluence will come at the price of their traditions. The drama of these people is now being played out around the world as more and more traditional cultures are being lured away from their heritage by the affluence and materialism of rich societies.

WHAT DO YOU THINK?

1. Why is social change both a winning and a losing proposition for traditional people?

2. Do the changes described here improve the lives of the Kaiapo? What about the Gullah community?

3. Do traditional people have the power to choose to become more modern? Explain your view.

that technology *solves* the world's problems, Marcuse suggested that it is more accurate to say that science *causes* them. In sum, class-society theory asserts that people suffer because modern societies have concentrated both wealth and power in the hands of a privileged few.

Modernity and Progress

In modern societies, most people expect and applaud social change. We link modernity to the idea of *progress* (from Latin, meaning "moving forward"), a state of continual improvement. By contrast, we see stability as stagnation.

Given our cultural bias in favor of change, members of our society tend to regard traditional cultures as backward. But change, particularly toward material affluence, turns our to be a mixed blessing. As the Thinking Globally box shows, social change is too complex to equate simply with progress.

Even getting rich has both advantages and disadvantages, as the cases of the Kaiapo and Gullah show. Historically, among people in the United States, a rising standard of living has made lives longer and materially more comfortable. At the same time, many people wonder whether today's routines are too stressful, with families often having little time to relax or to spend time together. Indeed, in most

November 25, 2004

Modernity Tips Balance in a Remote Corner of Kashmir

By AMY WALDMAN

LEH, Kashmir—The young man wore Western clothes, but he paused as he passed the prayer wheel. Then, without self-consciousness, he mounted the steps and spun, circumambulating the wheel in search of good fortune.

"I feel great because I'm doing something for my God," he said afterward.

The young man, Tsewang Tamchos, 16, is a product of Ladakh, a remote repository of Tibetan Buddhism on a high-altitude Himalayan plateau in the northern areas of Kashmir, a disputed state. But he is a product of a wider world, too: his school in Delhi, the music of Eminem, the ambitions of an upwardly mobile family whose material fortunes improve with each generation.

As in many cultures, the people of Ladakh, a sparsely populated region, live in the fold between tradition and modernity. But few places have provided as concentrated a laboratory for how modernization is tipping that balance.

In less than four decades, Ladakh has gone from being closed to the outside world to reflecting it. With each generation, the ties to the land, to the past, weaken as options and opportunities widen. The culture and economy have moved from community-oriented to competitive, from living off the land to working for cash and spending it.

For generations, Ladakh, a barren, moonlike landscape punctuated by monasteries, was almost cut off from the outside world. . . . It took 16 days to get to Srinagar, the state's summer capital, across passes that soar above 13,000 feet. Its people developed a way of life attuned to the land, and in tune with one another. Nothing was wasted. . . . Human waste fertilized fields; worn-out clothes patched irrigation channels. . . .

In 1974, Ladakh opened to foreign tourists for the first time, and they quickly became a pillar of the economy. . . .

The influence of outsiders has gradually leached into Ladakh's way of life. Before [as one long-time resident noted], the economy was not based on money. Rich and poor alike needed each other for the harvest. Now rich men can hire laborers from Nepal or poorer Indian states, and many do. "There is a lot of competition now," he said. "Everyone is trying to have a car."

The notion, and the novelty, of competition surfaces in conversations in the car-choked streets of Leh or nearby villages.

At 35, Tashi Palzes is old enough to remember a time with no competition in her village, Phyang Puluhu, which sits on several steep terraces in the valley behind the Phyang monastery.

Today, she, like everyone, is racing against her neighbors, and sees herself

high-income countries, measures of happiness show a decline over the course of recent decades (D. G. Myers, 2000).

Science, too, has its pluses and minuses. We in the United States are more confident than people living in most other industrial societies that science improves our everyday lives (Inglehart et al., 2000). But surveys also show that many of us are concerned that science "makes our way of life change too fast" (NORC, 2005:427). Could it be that science and even increasing affluence are not the keys to happiness?

New technology has always been a mixed blessing. A century ago, the introduction of automobiles and telephones allowed more rapid transportation and more efficient communication, improving people's lives. At the same time, such technology also weakened traditional attachments to hometowns and even to families. Today, people might wonder whether computer technology will do the same thing: giving us access to people around the world but shielding us from the community right outside our doors; providing more information than ever before but in the process threatening personal privacy. In short, we all realize that social change comes faster all the time, but we may disagree about whether a particular change is good or bad for society.

In 1970, Alvin Toffler coined the expression "future shock" to describe the effect of social change that was becoming so rapid that it overwhelms individuals. Do you think our world needs more change, or are we suffering from future shock? Explain your position.

as winning. She has not one, but two televisions—the second one in color—and a satellite dish on her roof. She wears not the handspun traditional dress of a Ladakhi woman but a second-hand Gap sweatshirt, bought at the Leh bazaar.

Earlier, she said, villagers did not have much and did not need much. Now they have more needs—better clothes, better education, more televisions—and thus more work. Life is simultaneously more comfortable and more difficult.

. . .

In the Leh home of Tsewang Tamchos, too, each generation brings substantial change. His grandparents live in the Nubra Valley, about 75 miles away.

They do not read or write; they farm. They grew up drinking unlimited quantities of butter tea, the salty staple of Ladakhi life.

His father, Tsering Tundup, 44, is a government forester. He says butter tea is bad for his blood pressure, and limits his intake to two cups a day. The house he has built his family in Leh has elements of tradition—the Buddhist prayer room, the wooden ceiling in the kitchen—but in most respects is modern.

His children study out of the state, Tsewang in Delhi and his 19-year-old sister, Tsering, in Chandigarh.

Tsewang's parents want him to be an engineer, and he does as well, but Ladakh has few opportunities for engineers. He would like to live here, but does not know if he will.

He does plan to marry a Ladakhi woman. "I don't want to change my culture," he said. "That's the only thing I have."

WHAT DO YOU THINK?

1. List five examples of cultural diffusion in the article, and explain how they are causing changes to this traditional society.

2. Do you think the only way societies can save their traditions is to remain isolated from the rest of the world? What advantages and disadvantages do you see in doing so?

3. In what specific ways does modern life differ from traditional life in Ladakh?

Modernity: Global Variation

 October 1, Kobe, Japan. Riding the computer-controlled monorail high above the streets of Kobe or the 200-mile-per-hour bullet train to Tokyo, we see Japan as the society of the future, in love with high technology. Yet the Japanese remain strikingly traditional in other respects: Few corporate executives and almost no politicians are women, young people still show seniors great respect, and public orderliness contrasts with the chaos of cities in the United States.

Japan is a nation at once traditional and modern. This contradiction reminds us that although it is useful to contrast traditional and modern social patterns, the old and the new often coexist in unexpected ways. In the People's Republic of China, ancient Confucian principles are mixed with contemporary socialist thinking. In Saudi Arabia and Qatar, a love of the latest modern technology is mixed with respect for the ancient principles of Islam. Likewise, in Mexico and much of Latin America, people observe centuries-old Christian rituals even as they struggle to move ahead economically. In short, combinations of traditional and modern are far from unusual—rather, they are found throughout the world. "In the *Times*" describes the patterns of change coming to a traditional village in Tibet.

Postmodernity

If modernity was the product of the Industrial Revolution, could the Information Revolution be creating a postmodern era? A number of scholars think so, and they use the

THINKING CRITICALLY

Tracking Change: Is Life in the United States Getting Better or Worse?

We began this chapter with a look at what life was like in 1900, more than a century ago. It is easy to see that in many ways, life is far better today than it was for our grandparents and great-grandparents. In recent decades, however, not all indicators have been good. Here is a look at some trends that have shaped the United States since 1970 (Miringoff & Miringoff, 1999; D. G. Myers, 2000).

First, the good news: By some measures, shown in the first set of figures, life in this country is clearly improving. Infant mortality has fallen steadily, meaning that fewer and fewer children die soon after birth. In addition, an increasing share of people are reaching old age, and after reaching sixty-five, they are living longer than ever. More good news: The poverty rate among the elderly is well below what it was in 1970. Schooling is another area of improvement: The share of people dropping out of high school is down, and the share completing college is up.

Second, some "no news" results: A number of indicators show that life is about the same as it was in the 1970s.

The good news

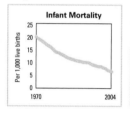

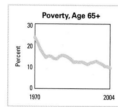

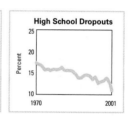

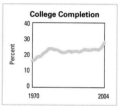

No news

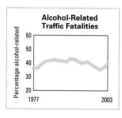

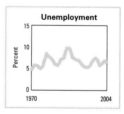

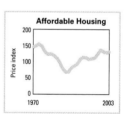

term **postmodernity** to refer to *social patterns characteristic of postindustrial societies.*

Precisely what postmodernism is remains a matter of debate. The term has been used for decades in literary, philosophical, and even architectural circles. It has moved into sociology on a wave of social criticism that has been building since the spread of left-leaning politics in the 1960s. Although there are many variations of postmodern thinking, all share the following five themes (Hall & Neitz, 1993; Inglehart, 1997; Rudel & Gerson, 1999):

1. **In important respects, modernity has failed.** The promise of modernity was a life free from want. As postmodernist critics see it, however, the twentieth century was unsuccessful in solving social problems such as poverty because many people still lack financial security.

2. **The bright light of "progress" is fading.** Modern people look to the future expecting that their lives will improve in significant ways. Members (and even leaders) of a postmodern society are less confident about

504   CHAPTER 16   SOCIAL CHANGE: MODERN AND POSTMODERN SOCIETIES

The bad news

Child Abuse

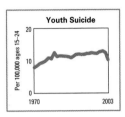

Child Poverty

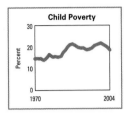

Youth Suicide

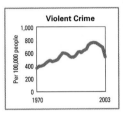

Violent Crime

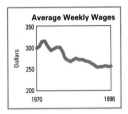

Average Weekly Wages

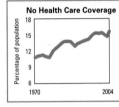

No Health Care Coverage

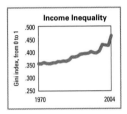

Income Inequality

For example, teenage drug use was about the same in 2004 as a generation before. Likewise, alcohol-related traffic deaths number about the same. Unemployment has had its ups and downs, but the overall level has stayed about the same. Finally, there was about the same amount of affordable housing in the United States in 2003 as in 1970.

Then there's the bad news, shown in the third set of figures: By some measures, several having to do with children, the quality of life in the United States has actually fallen. The official rate of child abuse is up, as is the level of child poverty and the rate of suicide among young people.

Although the level of violent crime fell through most of the 1990s, it still remains above the 1970 level. Average weekly wages, one measure of basic economic security, show a downward trend, meaning that more families have had to rely on two or more wage earners to maintain family income. The number of people without health insurance is also on the rise. Finally, economic inequality in this country has been increasing.

Overall, the evidence does not support any simple ideas about "progress over time." Social change has been, and probably will continue to be, a complex and uneven process that reflects the priorities we set for this

nation as well as our will to achieve them.

WHAT DO YOU THINK?

1. Some analysts claim that U.S. society is experiencing rising economic health but falling social health. Based on the data presented here, do you agree? Why or why not?

2. Which of the trends do you find most important? Why?

3. Overall, is the quality of life in the United States improving or not? Why?

what the future holds. The strong optimism that carried society into the modern era more than a century ago has given way to widespread pessimism: Most U.S. adults believe that life is getting worse (NORC, 2005:259). The Thinking Critically box offers evidence suggesting that life in the United States is and is not getting better.

3. **Science no longer holds the answers.** The defining trait of the modern era was a scientific outlook and a confident belief that technology would make life bet-

ter. But postmodern critics argue that science has failed to solve many old problems (such as poor health) and has even created new problems (such as air and water pollution and declining natural resources).

Postmodernist thinkers discredit science, claiming that it implies a singular truth. On the contrary, they maintain, there is no one truth. This means that objective reality does not exist; rather, many realities result from social construction.

Do Personal Freedom and Social Responsibility Go Together?

One issue we all have to work out is making personal decisions that take proper account of other people. But what, exactly, do we owe others? To see the problem, consider an event that took place in New York in 1964. Shortly after midnight on a crisp March evening, Kitty Genovese drove into the parking lot of her apartment complex. She turned off the engine, locked the car doors, and headed across the blacktop toward the entrance to her building. Out of nowhere, a man holding a knife lunged at her, and as she screamed in terror and pain, he stabbed her repeatedly. Windows opened above as curious neighbors looked down to see what was going on. The attack continued for more than thirty minutes until Genovese lay dead in her doorway. The police never identified her killer, and the follow-up investigation revealed the stunning fact that *not one of the dozens of neighbors who witnessed the attack on Kitty Genovese went to her aid or even called the police.*

Decades after this tragic event, we still confront the question of what we owe others. As members of a modern society, we prize our individual rights and personal privacy, but we sometimes withdraw from public responsibility and turn a cold shoulder to people in need. When a cry for help is met by indifference, have we pushed our modern idea of personal freedom too far? In a society of expanding individual rights, can we keep a sense of human community?

These questions highlight the tension between traditional and modern social systems, which is evident in the writings of all the sociologists discussed in this chapter. Tönnies, Durkheim, and others concluded that in some respects, traditional community and modern individualism don't mix. That is, society can unite its members as a moral community only by limiting their range of personal choices about how to live. In short, although we value both community and freedom, we can't have it both ways.

The sociologist Amitai Etzioni (1993, 1996, 2003) has tried to strike a middle ground. The *communitarian movement* rests on the simple idea that with rights must come responsibilities. Put another way, our pursuit of self-interest must be balanced by a commitment to the larger community.

Etzioni claims that modern people have become too concerned about individual rights. We expect the system to work for us, but we are reluctant to support the system. For example, we believe that people accused of a crime deserve their day in court, but fewer and fewer of us are willing to perform jury duty; similarly, we are quick to accept government services but reluctant to support these services with our taxes.

The communitarians advance four proposals toward balancing individual rights with public responsibilities. First, our society should stop the expanding "culture of rights" by which we put our own interests ahead of social responsibility. The Constitution, which is

4. **Cultural debates are intensifying.** Many people have all the material things they really need, which allows ideas to take on more importance. In this sense, postmodernity is also a postmaterialist era in which issues such as social justice, the environment, and animal rights command more and more public attention.

5. **Social institutions are changing.** Just as industrialization brought sweeping transformation to social institutions, the rise of postindustrial society is remaking society all over again. For example, the Industrial Revolution placed *material things* at the center of productive life; the Information Revolution emphasizes *ideas*. Similarly, the postmodern family no longer conforms to any one pattern; on the con-

trary, individuals are choosing among many family forms.

CRITICAL REVIEW Analysts who claim that the United States and other high-income nations are entering a postmodern era criticize modernity for failing to meet human needs. In defense of modernity, there have been marked increases in longevity and living standards over the past century. Even if we were to accept postmodernist views that science is bankrupt and progress is a sham, what are the alternatives?

✔ **YOUR LEARNING** In your own words, state the defining characteristics of a postmodern society.

quoted so often when discussing individual rights, does not guarantee us the right to do whatever we want. Second, we must remember that we cannot take from society without giving something back. Third, the well-being of everyone may require limiting our individual rights; for example, pilots and bus drivers who are responsible for public safety may be asked to take drug tests. Fourth, no one can ignore key responsibilities such as obeying the law and responding to a cry for help from someone like Kitty Genovese.

The communitarian movement appeals to many people who believe in both personal freedom and social responsibility. But Etzioni's proposals have drawn criticism from both sides of the political spectrum. To those on the left, problems ranging from voter apathy to street crime cannot be solved by some vague idea of "social responsibility." As they see it, what is needed is expanded government programs to protect people and lessen inequality.

Conservatives, on the political right, see different problems in Etzioni's proposals (Pearson, 1995). As they see it, the communitarian movement favors liberal goals, such as confronting prejudice and protecting the environment, but says little about conservative goals, such as strengthening religious belief and supporting traditional families.

Etzioni responds that the criticism coming from both sides suggests he has found a moderate, sensible answer to a serious problem. But the debate may also indicate that in a society as diverse as the United States, people who are so quick to assert their rights are not so ready to agree on their responsibilities.

WHAT DO YOU THINK?

1. Have you ever failed to come to the aid of someone in need or danger? Why?

2. Nearly half a century ago, President Kennedy stated, "Ask not what your country can do for you; ask what you can do for your country." Do you think people today support this idea? Why or why not?

3. Are you willing to serve on a jury? Do you mind paying your fair share of taxes? Would you be willing to perform a year of national service? Explain your answers.

In today's world, people can find new ways to express age-old virtues such as concern for their neighbors and extending a hand to those in need. Habitat for Humanity, an organization with chapters in cities and towns across the United States, is made up of people who want to help local families realize their dream of owning a home.

Looking Ahead: Modernization and Our Global Future

Imagine the entire world's population reduced to a single village of 1,000 people. About 180 residents of this "global village" come from high-income countries. Another 180 people are so poor that their lives are at risk.

The tragic plight of the world's poor shows that some desperately needed change has not yet occurred. Chapter 9 ("Global Stratification") presented two competing views of why 1 billion people the world over are poor. *Modernization theory* claims that in the past, the entire world was poor and that technological change, especially the Industrial Revolu-

tion, enhanced human productivity and raised living standards in many nations. From this point of view, the solution to global poverty is to promote technological development around the world.

For reasons suggested earlier, however, global modernization may be difficult. Recall that David Riesman portrayed preindustrial people as *tradition-directed* and likely to resist change. So modernization theorists claim that rich nations should help poor countries grow economically. Industrial nations can speed development by exporting technology to poor regions, welcoming students from these countries, and providing foreign aid to stimulate economic growth.

The review of modernization theory in Chapter 9 points to some success for these policies in Latin America and more dramatic results in the small Asian countries of Taiwan, South Korea, Singapore, and Hong Kong (now part of the People's Republic of China). But jump-starting development in the poorest countries of the world poses greater challenges. Even where dramatic change has occurred, modernization involves a trade-off. Traditional people, such as Brazil's Kaiapo, may gain wealth through economic development, but only at the cost of losing their traditional identity and values as they are drawn into a global "McCulture" based on Western materialism, pop music, trendy clothes, and fast food. One Brazilian anthropologist expressed optimism about the future of the Kaiapo: "At least they quickly understood the consequences of watching television. . . . Now [they] can make a choice" (Simons, 2007, 523).

But not everyone thinks that modernization is really an option. According to a second approach to global stratification, *dependency theory,* today's poor societies have little ability to modernize, even if they want to. From this point of view, the major barrier to economic development is not traditionalism but global domination by rich capitalist societies.

Dependency theory asserts that rich nations achieved their modernization at the expense of poor ones, by taking their valuable natural resources and exploiting their human labor. Even today, the world's poorest countries remain locked in a disadvantageous economic relationship with rich nations, dependent on wealthy countries to buy their raw materials and in return provide them with whatever manufactured products they can afford. According to this view, continuing ties with rich societies will only perpetuate current patterns of global inequality.

Whichever approach one finds more convincing, we can no longer isolate the study of the United States from the rest of the world. At the beginning of the twentieth century, a majority of people in even the richest nations lived in relatively small settlements with limited awareness of the larger world. Today, a century later, the entire world has become one huge village because the lives of all people are increasingly linked.

The last century witnessed unprecedented human achievement. Yet solutions to many problems of human existence—including finding meaning in life, resolving conflicts between societies, and eliminating poverty—have eluded us. The Seeing Sociology in Everyday Life box on pages 506–7 examines one dilemma: balancing individual freedom and personal responsibility. To this list of pressing matters new concerns have been added, such as controlling population growth and establishing an environmentally sustainable society. In the next 100 years, we must be prepared to tackle such problems with imagination, compassion, and determination. Our growing understanding of human society gives us reason to be hopeful that we can get the job done.

◄ APPLYING SOCIOLOGY IN EVERYDAY LIFE

1. Ask an elderly relative or friend to name the most important social changes during his or her lifetime. Do you think your world will change as much during your lifetime?

2. Ask people in your class or friendship group to make five predictions about U.S. society in the year 2050, when today's twenty-year-olds will be senior citizens. On what issues do they agree?

3. Do you think the rate of social change has been increasing? Do some research about modes of travel, including walking, riding animals, trains, cars, airplanes, and rockets. At what point in history did each of these ways of moving come into being? What pattern do you see?

MAKING THE GRADE

CHAPTER 16   Social Change:
Modern and Postmodern Societies

WHAT IS SOCIAL CHANGE?

SOCIAL CHANGE is the transformation of culture and social institutions over time. Every society changes all the time, sometimes faster, sometimes more slowly. Social change often generates controversy.

p 483

social change (p. 483) the transformation of culture and social institutions over time

CAUSES OF SOCIAL CHANGE

CULTURE

- *Invention* produces new objects, ideas, and social patterns.
- *Discovery* occurs when people take notice of existing elements of the world.
- *Diffusion* creates change as products, people, and information spread from one society to another.

p 484

SOCIAL CONFLICT

- Karl Marx claimed that class conflict between capitalists and workers pushes society toward a socialist system of production.
- Social conflict arising from class, race, and gender inequality has resulted in social changes that have improved the lives of working people.

p 484

social movement (p. 485) an organized activity that encourages or discourages social change

claims making (p. 486) the process of trying to convince the public and public officials of the importance of joining a social movement to address a particular issue

relative deprivation (p. 486) a perceived disadvantage arising from some specific comparison

disaster (p. 488) an event that is generally unexpected and that causes extensive harm to people and damage to property

IDEAS

Max Weber traced the roots of most social changes to ideas:

- The fact that industrial capitalism developed first in areas of Western Europe where the Protestant work ethic was strong demonstrates the power of ideas to bring about change.

p 484

DEMOGRAPHIC FACTORS

Population patterns play a part in social change:

- The aging of U.S. society has resulted in changes to family life and the development of consumer products to meet the needs of the elderly.
- Migration within and between societies promotes change.

pp 484–85

DISASTERS

Disasters cause unexpected social change:

- *natural disasters* (Example: Hurricane Katrina)
- *technological disasters* (Example: nuclear accident at the Chernobyl power plant)
- *intentional disasters* (Example: Rwanda genocide)

pp 488–90

Social Movements

TYPES OF SOCIAL MOVEMENTS

- *Alterative social movements* seek limited change in specific individuals. (Example: Promise Keepers)
- *Redemptive social movements* seek radical change in specific individuals. (Example: Alcoholics Anonymous)
- *Reformative social movements* seek limited change in the whole society. (Example: the environmental movement)
- *Revolutionary social movements* seek radical change in the whole society. (Example: the Communist party)

pp 485–86

EXPLANATIONS OF SOCIAL MOVEMENTS

- *Deprivation theory*: Social movements arise among people who feel deprived of something, such as income, safe working conditions, or political rights.
- *Mass-society theory*: Social movements attract socially isolated people who join a movement in order to gain a sense of identity and purpose.
- *Resource mobilization theory*: Success of a social movement is linked to available resources, including money, labor, and the mass media.
- *Culture theory*: Social movements depend not only on money and resources but also on cultural symbols that motivate people.
- *New social movements theory*: Social movements in postindustrial societies are typically international in scope and focus on quality-of-life issues.

pp 486–87

WHAT IS MODERNITY?

MODERNITY refers to the social consequences of industrialization, which include the decline of traditional communities, the expansion of personal choice, increasing social diversity, and a focus on the future.

- Ferdinand Tönnies described modernization as the transition from *Gemeinschaft* to *Gesellschaft*, characterized by the loss of traditional community and the rise of individualism.
- Emile Durkheim saw modernization as a society's expanding division of labor. *Mechanical solidarity*, based on shared activities and beliefs, is gradually replaced by *organic solidarity*, in which specialization makes people interdependent.
- Max Weber saw modernity as the decline of a traditional worldview and the rise of rationality. Weber feared the dehumanizing effects of rational organization.
- Karl Marx saw modernity as the triumph of capitalism over feudalism. Capitalism creates social conflict, which Marx claimed would bring about revolutionary change leading to an egalitarian socialist society.

pp 490–94

modernity (p. 490) social patterns resulting from industrialization

modernization (p. 490) the process of social change begun by industrialization

division of labor (p. 492) specialized economic activity

anomie (p. 493) Durkheim's term for a condition in which society provides little moral guidance to individuals

MAKING THE GRADE
CONTINUED...

THEORETICAL ANALYSIS OF MODERNITY

STRUCTURAL-FUNCTIONAL THEORY: MODERNITY AS MASS SOCIETY

- According to mass-society theory, modernity increases the scale of life, enlarging the role of government and other formal organizations in carrying out tasks previously performed by families in local communities.
- Cultural diversity and rapid social change make it difficult for people in modern societies to develop stable identities and to find meaning in their lives.

pp 494–96

SOCIAL-CONFLICT THEORY: MODERNITY AS CLASS SOCIETY

- According to class-society theory, modernity involves the rise of capitalism into a global economic system resulting in persistent social inequality.
- By concentrating wealth in the hands of a few, modern capitalist societies generate widespread feelings of alienation and powerlessness.

pp 496–98

mass society (p. 494) a society in which prosperity and bureaucracy have weakened traditional social ties

class society (p. 496) a capitalist society with pronounced social stratification

See the Summing Up tables on pp 495 and 498.

MODERNITY AND THE INDIVIDUAL

Both mass-society theory and class-society theory are macro-level approaches; from them, however, we can also draw micro-level insights into how modernity shapes individual lives.

p 498

social character (p. 498) personality patterns common to members of a particular society

tradition-directedness (p. 498) rigid conformity to time-honored ways of living

other-directedness (p. 499) openness to the latest trends and fashions, often expressed by imitating others

MASS SOCIETY: PROBLEMS OF IDENTITY

- Mass-society theory suggests that the great social diversity, widespread isolation, and rapid social change of modern societies make it difficult for individuals to establish a stable social identity.
- David Riesman described the changes in social character that modernity causes:
- Preindustrial societies exhibit *tradition-directedness*: Everyone in society draws on the same solid cultural foundation, and people model their lives on those of their ancestors.
- Modern societies exhibit *other-directedness*: Because their socialization occurs in societies that are continuously in flux, other-directed people develop fluid identities marked by superficiality, inconsistency, and change.

pp 498–99

CLASS SOCIETY: PROBLEMS OF POWERLESSNESS

- Class-society theory claims that the problem facing most people today is economic uncertainty and powerlessness.
- Herbert Marcuse claimed that modern society is irrational because it fails to meet the needs of so many people.
- Marcuse also believed that technological advances further reduce people's control over their own lives.
- People suffer because modern societies have concentrated both wealth and power in the hands of a privileged few.

pp 499–501

MODERNITY AND PROGRESS

Social change is too complex and controversial simply to be equated with progress:

- A rising standard of living has mades lives longer and materially more comfortable; at the same time, many people are stressed and have little time to relax with their families; measures of happiness have declined over recent decades.
- Science and technology have brought many conveniences to our everyday lives, yet many people are concerned that life is changing too fast; the introduction of automobiles and advanced communications technology have weakened traditional attachments to hometowns and even to families.

pp 501–2

MODERNITY: GLOBAL VARIATION

Although we often think of tradition and modernity as opposites, traditional and modern elements coexist in most societies.

p 503

POSTMODERNITY

POSTMODERNITY refers to the cultural traits of postindustrial societies. Postmodern criticism of society centers on the failure of modernity, and specifically science, to fulfill its promise of prosperity and well-being.

pp 503–6

postmodernity (p. 504) social patterns characteristic of postindustrial societies

MAKING THE GRADE
Sample Test Questions

CHAPTER 16

These questions are similar to those found in the test bank that accompanies this textbook.

MULTIPLE-CHOICE QUESTIONS

1. Sociologists use the term "modernity" to refer to social patterns that emerged
   a. with the first human civilizations.
   b. with the founding of cities.
   c. after the Industrial Revolution.
   d. along with the Information Revolution.

2. Which of the following are common causes of social change?
   a. invention of new ideas and things
   b. diffusion from one cultural system to another
   c. discovery of existing things
   d. All of the above are correct.

3. Karl Marx highlighted the importance of which of the following in the process of social change?
   a. immigration and demographic factors
   b. ideas
   c. social conflict
   d. cultural diffusion

4. Max Weber's analysis of how Calvinism helped create the spirit of capitalism highlighted the importance of which of the following in the process of social change?
   a. invention
   b. ideas
   c. social conflict
   d. cultural diffusion

5. Which term was used by Ferdinand Tönnies to describe a modern society?
   a. *Gesellschaft*
   b. *Gemeinschaft*
   c. mechanical solidarity
   d. organic solidarity

6. According to Emile Durkheim, modern societies have
   a. respect for established tradition.
   b. widespread alienation.
   c. common values and beliefs.
   d. an increasing division of labor.

7. Hurricane Katrina is one recent case of
   a. a technological disaster.
   b. a natural disaster.
   c. an intentional disaster.
   d. an everyday disaster.

8. Which of the following statements about modernity as a mass society is *not* correct?
   a. There is more poverty than in past centuries.
   b. Kinship ties have become weaker.
   c. Bureaucracy, including government, has increased in size.
   d. People experience moral uncertainty about how to live.

9. Sociologists who describe modernity in terms of class-society theory focus on which of the following?
   a. rationality as a way of thinking about the world
   b. mutual interdependency
   c. the rise of capitalism
   d. the high risk of anomie

10. David Riesman described the other-directed social character typical of modern people as
    a. rigid conformity to tradition.
    b. eagerness to follow the latest fashions and fads.
    c. highly individualistic.
    d. All of the above are correct.

ANSWERS: 1 (c); 2 (d); 3 (c); 4 (b); 5 (a); 6 (d); 7 (b); 8 (a); 9 (c); 10 (b).

ESSAY QUESTIONS

1. Discuss how Tönnies, Durkheim, Weber, and Marx described modern society. Point out the similarities and differences in their understandings of modernity.
2. What traits lead some people to call the United States a "mass society"? Why do other analysts describe the United States as a "class society"?

S A M P L E   T E S T

511

GLOSSARY

abortion   the deliberate termination of a pregnancy

absolute poverty   a deprivation of resources that is life-threatening

achieved status   a social position a person takes on voluntarily that reflects personal ability and effort

Afrocentrism   emphasizing and promoting African cultural patterns

age-sex pyramid   a graphic representation of the age and sex of a population

ageism   prejudice and discrimination against older people

agriculture   large-scale cultivation using plows harnessed to animals or machines

alienation   the experience of isolation and misery resulting from powerlessness

animism   the belief that elements of the natural world are conscious life forms that affect humanity

anomie   Durkheim's term for a condition in which society provides little moral guidance to individuals

anticipatory socialization   learning that helps a person achieve a desired position

ascribed status   a social position a person receives at birth or takes on involuntarily later in life

asexuality   no sexual attraction to people of either sex

assimilation   the process by which minorities gradually adopt patterns of the dominant culture

authoritarianism   a political system that denies the people participation in government

authority   power that people perceive as legitimate rather than coercive

beliefs   specific statements that people hold to be true

bisexuality   sexual attraction to people of both sexes

blue-collar occupations   lower-prestige jobs that involve mostly manual labor

bureaucracy   an organizational model rationally designed to perform tasks efficiently

bureaucratic inertia   the tendency of bureaucratic organizations to perpetuate themselves

bureaucratic ritualism   a focus on rules and regulations to the point of interfering with an organization's goals

capitalism   an economic system in which natural resources and the means of producing goods and services are privately owned

capitalists   people who own and operate factories and other businesses in pursuit of profits

caste system   social stratification based on ascription, or birth

cause and effect   a relationship in which change in one variable (the independent variable) causes change in another (the dependent variable)

charisma   extraordinary personal qualities that can infuse people with emotion and turn them into followers

church   a type of religious organization that is well integrated into the larger society

civil religion   a quasi-religious loyalty binding individuals in a basically secular society

claims making   the process of trying to convince the public and public officials of the importance of joining a social movement to address a particular issue

class society   a capitalist society with pronounced social stratification

class system   social stratification based on both birth and individual achievement

cohabitation   the sharing of a household by an unmarried couple

cohort   a category of people with something in common, usually their age

colonialism   the process by which some nations enrich themselves through political and economic control of other nations

community-based corrections   correctional programs operating within society at large rather than behind prison walls

concept   a mental construct that represents some part of the world in a simplified form

concrete operational stage   Piaget's term for the level of human development at which individuals first see causal connections in their surroundings

conspicuous consumption   buying and using products with an eye to the "statement" they make about social position

corporate crime   the illegal actions of a corporation or people acting on its behalf

corporation   an organization with a legal existence, including rights and liabilities, separate from that of its members

correlation   a relationship in which two (or more) variables change together

counterculture   cultural patterns that strongly oppose those widely accepted within a society

crime   the violation of a society's formally enacted criminal law

crimes against property (property crimes)   crimes that involve theft of property belonging to others

crimes against the person (violent crimes)   crimes that direct violence or the threat of violence against others

criminal justice system   a formal response by police, courts, and prison officials to alleged violations of the law

criminal recidivism   later offenses by people previously convicted of crimes

critical sociology   the study of society that focuses on the need for social change

crude birth rate   the number of live births in a given year for every 1,000 people in a population

crude death rate   the number of deaths in a given year for every 1,000 people in a population

cult   a type of religious organization that is largely outside a society's cultural traditions

cultural integration   the close relationships among various elements of a cultural system

cultural lag   the fact that some cultural elements change more quickly than others, disrupting a cultural system

cultural relativism   the practice of judging a culture by its own standards

cultural transmission   the process by which one generation passes culture to the next

cultural universals   traits that are part of every known culture

culture   the ways of thinking, the ways of acting, and the material objects that together form a people's way of life

culture shock   personal disorientation when experiencing an unfamiliar way of life

Davis-Moore thesis   the assertion that social stratification exists in every society because it has beneficial consequences for the operation of society

democracy   a political system that gives power to the people as a whole

demographic transition theory   a thesis that links population patterns to a society's level of technological development

demography   the study of human population

denomination   a church, independent of the state, that recognizes religious pluralism

dependency theory   a model of economic and social development that explains global inequality in terms of the historical exploitation of poor nations by rich ones

descent   the system by which members of a society trace kinship over generations

deterrence   the attempt to discourage criminality through the use of punishment

deviance   the recognized violation of cultural norms

direct-fee system   a medical care system in which patients pay directly for the services of physicians and hospitals

disaster   an event that is generally unexpected and that causes extensive harm to people and damage to property

discrimination   unequal treatment of various categories of people

division of labor   specialized economic activity

dramaturgical analysis   Erving Goffman's term for the study of social interaction in terms of theatrical performance

dyad   a social group with two members

eating disorder   an intense type of dieting or other unhealthy method of weight control driven by the desire to be very thin

ecologically sustainable culture   a way of life that meets the needs of the present generation without threatening the environmental legacy of future generations

ecology   the study of the interaction of living organisms and the natural environment

economy   the social institution that organizes a society's production, distribution, and consumption of goods and services

ecosystem   a system composed of the interaction of all living organisms and their natural environment

education   the social institution through which society provides its members with important knowledge, including basic facts, job skills, and cultural norms and values

ego   Freud's term for a person's conscious efforts to balance innate pleasure-seeking drives with the demands of society

empirical evidence   information we can verify with our senses

endogamy   marriage between people of the same social category

environmental deficit   profound long-term harm to the natural environment caused by humanity's focus on short-term material affluence

environmental racism   patterns that make environmental hazards greatest for poor people, especially minorities

ethnicity   a shared cultural heritage

ethnocentrism   the practice of judging another culture by the standards of one's own culture

ethnomethodology   Harold Garfinkel's term for the study of the way people make sense of their everyday surroundings

Eurocentrism   the dominance of European (especially English) cultural patterns

euthanasia   assisting in the death of a person suffering from an incurable disease; also known as *mercy killing*

exogamy   marriage between people of different social categories

experiment   a research method for investigating cause and effect under highly controlled conditions

expressive leadership   group leadership that focuses on the group's well-being

extended family   a family composed of parents and children as well as other kin; also known as a *consanguine family*

faith   belief based on conviction rather than on scientific evidence

family   a social institution found in all societies that unites people in cooperative groups to care for one another, including any children

family violence   emotional, physical, or sexual abuse of one family member by another

feminism   the advocacy of social equality for women and men, in opposition to patriarchy and sexism

feminization of poverty   the trend of women making up an increasing proportion of the poor

fertility   the incidence of childbearing in a country's population

folkways   norms for routine or casual interaction

formal operational stage   Piaget's term for the level of human development at which individuals think abstractly and critically

formal organization   a large secondary group organized to achieve its goals efficiently

functional illiteracy   a lack of the reading and writing skills needed for everyday living

fundamentalism   a conservative religious doctrine that opposes intellectualism and worldly accommodation in favor of restoring traditional, otherworldly religion

Gemeinschaft   a type of social organization in which people are closely tied by kinship and tradition

gender   the personal traits and social positions that members of a society attach to being female or male

gender roles (sex roles)   attitudes and activities that a society links to each sex

gender stratification   the unequal distribution of wealth, power, and privilege between men and women

gender-conflict approach   a point of view that focuses on inequality and conflict between women and men

generalized other   George Herbert Mead's term for widespread cultural norms and values we use as a reference in evaluating ourselves

genocide   the systematic killing of one category of people by another

gerontocracy   a form of social organization in which the elderly have the most wealth, power, and prestige

gerontology   the study of aging and the elderly

Gesellschaft   a type of social organization in which people come together only on the basis of individual self-interest

global economy   economic activity that crosses national borders

global perspective   the study of the larger world and our society's place in it

global stratification   patterns of social inequality in the world as a whole

global warming   a rise in Earth's average temperature due to an increasing concentration of carbon dioxide in the atmosphere

government   a formal organization that directs the political life of a society

groupthink   the tendency of group members to conform, resulting in a narrow view of some issue

hate crime   a criminal act against a person or a person's property by an offender motivated by racial or other bias

health   a state of complete physical, mental, and social well-being

health maintenance organization (HMO)   an organization that provides comprehensive medical care to subscribers for a fixed fee

heterosexism   a view that labels anyone who is not heterosexual as "queer"

heterosexuality sexual attraction to someone of the other sex

high culture cultural patterns that distinguish a society's elite

high-income countries the nations with the highest overall standards of living

holistic medicine an approach to health care that emphasizes prevention of illness and takes into account a person's entire physical and social environment

homogamy marriage between people with the same social characteristics

homophobia discomfort over close personal interaction with people thought to be gay, lesbian, or bisexual

homosexuality sexual attraction to someone of the same sex

horticulture the use of hand tools to raise crops

hunting and gathering the use of simple tools to hunt animals and gather vegetation for food

id Freud's term for the human being's basic drives

ideology cultural beliefs that justify particular social arrangements, including patterns of inequality

in-group a social group toward which a member feels respect and loyalty

incest taboo a norm forbidding sexual relations or marriage between certain relatives

income earnings from work or investments

industry the production of goods using advanced sources of energy to drive large machinery

infant mortality rate the number of deaths among infants under one year of age for each 1,000 live births in a given year

institutional prejudice and discrimination bias built into the operation of society's institutions

instrumental leadership group leadership that focuses on the completion of tasks

intergenerational social mobility upward or downward social mobility of children in relation to their parents

interpretive sociology the study of society that focuses on the meanings people attach to their social world

intersection theory the interplay of race, class, and gender, often resulting in multiple dimensions of disadvantage

intersexual people people whose bodies (including genitals) have both female and male characteristics

intragenerational social mobility a change in social position occurring during a person's lifetime

kinship a social bond based on common ancestry, marriage, or adoption

labeling theory the idea that deviance and conformity result not so much from what people do as from how others respond to those actions

language a system of symbols that allows people to communicate with one another

latent functions the unrecognized and unintended consequences of any social pattern

liberation theology the combining of Christian principles with political activism, often Marxist in character

life expectancy the average life span of a country's population

looking-glass self Charles Horton Cooley's term for a self-image based on how we think others see us

low-income countries nations with a low standard of living in which most people are poor

macro-level orientation a broad focus on social structures that shape society as a whole

manifest functions the recognized and intended consequences of any social pattern

marriage a legal relationship, usually involving economic cooperation as well as sexual activity and childbearing

Marxist political-economy model an analysis that explains politics in terms of the operation of a society's economic system

mass media the means for delivering impersonal communications to a vast audience

mass society a society in which prosperity and bureaucracy have weakened traditional social ties

master status a status that has special importance for social identity, often shaping a person's entire life

matriarchy a form of social organization in which females dominate males

measurement a procedure for determining the value of a variable in a specific case

medicalization of deviance the transformation of moral and legal deviance into a medical condition

medicine the social institution that focuses on fighting disease and improving health

megalopolis a vast urban region containing a number of cities and their surrounding suburbs

meritocracy social stratification based on personal merit

metropolis a large city that socially and economically dominates an urban area

micro-level orientation a close-up focus on social interaction in specific situations

middle-income countries nations with a standard of living about average for the world as a whole

migration the movement of people into and out of a specified territory

military-industrial complex the close association of the federal government, the military, and defense industries

minority any category of people distinguished by physical or cultural difference that a society sets apart and subordinates

miscegenation biological reproduction by partners of different racial categories

modernity social patterns resulting from industrialization

modernization the process of social change begun by industrialization

modernization theory a model of economic and social development that explains global inequality in terms of technological and cultural differences between nations

monarchy a political system in which a single family rules from generation to generation

monogamy marriage that unites two partners

monopoly the domination of a market by a single producer

mores norms that are widely observed and have great moral significance

mortality the incidence of death in a country's population

multiculturalism a perspective recognizing the cultural diversity of the United States and promoting respect and equal standing for all cultural traditions

multinational corporation a large business that operates in many countries

natural environment Earth's surface and atmosphere, including living organisms, air, water, soil, and other resources necessary to sustain life

neocolonialism a new form of global power relationships that involves not direct political control but economic exploitation by multinational corporations

network a web of weak social ties

nonverbal communication communication using body movements, gestures, and facial expressions rather than speech

norms rules and expectations by which a society guides the behavior of its members

nuclear family a family composed of one or two parents and their children; also known as a *conjugal family*

oligarchy the rule of the many by the few

oligopoly the domination of a market by a few producers

organizational environment factors outside an organization that affect its operation

organized crime a business supplying illegal goods or services

other-directedness openness to the latest trends and fashions, often expressed by imitating others

out-group a social group toward which a person feels a sense of competition or opposition

participant observation a research method in which investigators systematically observe people while joining them in their routine activities

pastoralism the domestication of animals

patriarchy a form of social organization in which males dominate females

peer group a social group whose members have interests, social position, and age in common

personal space the surrounding area over which a person makes some claim to privacy

personality a person's fairly consistent patterns of acting, thinking, and feeling

plea bargaining a legal negotiation in which a prosecutor reduces a charge in exchange for a defendant's guilty plea

pluralism a state in which people of all races and ethnicities are distinct but have equal social standing

pluralist model an analysis of politics that sees power as spread among many competing interest groups

political revolution the overthrow of one political system in order to establish another

politics the social institution that distributes power, sets a society's goals, and makes decisions

polygamy marriage that unites a person with two or more spouses

popular culture cultural patterns that are widespread among a society's population

pornography sexually explicit material intended to cause sexual arousal

positivism a way of understanding based on science

postindustrial economy a productive system based on service work and high technology

postmodernity social patterns characteristic of postindustrial societies

power the ability to achieve desired ends despite resistance from others

power-elite model an analysis of politics that sees power as concentrated among the rich

prejudice a rigid and unfair generalization about an entire category of people

preoperational stage Piaget's term for the level of human development at which individuals first use language and other symbols

presentation of self Erving Goffman's term for a person's efforts to create specific impressions in the minds of others

primary group a small social group whose members share personal and lasting relationships

primary sector the part of the economy that draws raw materials from the natural environment

primary sex characteristics the genitals, organs used for reproduction

profane occurring as an ordinary element of everyday life

profession a prestigious white-collar occupation that requires extensive formal education

proletarians working people who sell their labor for wages

prostitution the selling of sexual services

queer theory a body of research findings that challenges the heterosexual bias in U.S. society

race a socially constructed category of people who share biologically transmitted traits that members of a society consider important

race-conflict approach a point of view that focuses on inequality and conflict between people of different racial and ethnic categories

racism the belief that one racial category is innately superior or inferior to another

rain forests regions of dense forestation, most of which circle the globe close to the equator

rationality a way of thinking that emphasizes deliberate, matter-of-fact calculation of the most efficient way to accomplish a particular task

rationalization of society Weber's term for the historical change from tradition to rationality as the main mode of human thought

reference group a social group that serves as a point of reference in making evaluations and decisions

rehabilitation a program for reforming the offender to prevent later offenses

relative deprivation a perceived disadvantage arising from some specific comparison

relative poverty the deprivation of some people in relation to those who have more

reliability consistency in measurement

religion a social institution involving beliefs and practices based on recognizing the sacred

religiosity the importance of religion in a person's life

research method a systematic plan for doing research

resocialization radically changing an inmate's personality by carefully controlling the environment

retribution an act of moral vengeance by which society makes the offender suffer as much as the suffering caused by the crime

role behavior expected of someone who holds a particular status

role conflict conflict among the roles connected to two or more statuses

role set a number of roles attached to a single status

role strain tension among the roles connected to a single status

routinization of charisma the transformation of charismatic authority into some combination of traditional and bureaucratic authority

sacred set apart as extraordinary, inspiring awe and reverence

Sapir-Whorf thesis the idea that people see and understand the world through the cultural lens of language

scapegoat a person or category of people, typically with little power, whom other people unfairly blame for their own troubles

schooling formal instruction under the direction of specially trained teachers

science a logical system that bases knowledge on direct, systematic observation

scientific management Frederick Taylor's term for the application of scientific principles to the operation of a business or other large organization

scientific sociology the study of society based on systematic observation of social behavior

secondary group a large and impersonal social group whose members pursue a specific goal or activity

secondary sector the part of the economy that transforms raw materials into manufactured goods

secondary sex characteristics bodily development, apart from the genitals, that distinguishes biologically mature females and males

sect a type of religious organization that stands apart from the larger society

secularization the historical decline in the importance of the supernatural and the sacred

segregation the physical and social separation of categories of people

self George Herbert Mead's term for the part of an individual's personality composed of self-awareness and self-image

sensorimotor stage Piaget's term for the level of human development at which individuals experience the world only through their senses

sex the biological distinction between females and males

sex ratio the number of males for every 100 females in a nation's population

sexism the belief that one sex is innately superior to the other

sexual harassment comments, gestures, or physical contacts of a sexual nature that are deliberate, repeated, and unwelcome

sexual orientation a person's romantic and emotional attraction to another person

sick role patterns of behavior defined as appropriate for people who are ill

significant others people, such as parents, who have special importance for socialization

social change the transformation of culture and social institutions over time

social character personality patterns common to members of a particular society

social-conflict approach a framework for building theory that sees society as an arena of inequality that generates conflict and change

social construction of reality the process by which people creatively shape reality through social interaction

social control attempts by society to regulate people's thoughts and behavior

social dysfunction any social pattern that may disrupt the operation of society

social epidemiology the study of how health and disease are distributed throughout a society's population

social functions the consequences of a social pattern for the operation of society as a whole

social group two or more people who identify and interact with one another

social institution a major sphere of social life, or societal subsystem, organized to meet human needs

social interaction the process by which people act and react in relation to others

socialism an economic system in which natural resources and the means of producing goods and services are collectively owned

socialization the lifelong social experience by which people develop their human potential and learn culture

socialized medicine a medical care system in which the government owns and operates most medical facilities and employs most physicians

social mobility a change in position within the social hierarchy

social movement an organized activity that encourages or discourages social change

social stratification a system by which a society ranks categories of people in a hierarchy

social structure any relatively stable pattern of social behavior

societal protection rendering an offender incapable of further offenses temporarily through imprisonment or permanently by execution

society people who interact in a defined territory and share a culture

sociobiology a theoretical approach that explores ways in which human biology affects how we create culture

socioeconomic status (SES) a composite ranking based on various dimensions of social inequality

sociological perspective the special point of view of sociology that sees general patterns of society in the lives of particular people

sociology the systematic study of human society

state capitalism an economic and political system in which companies are privately owned but cooperate closely with the government

state church a church formally allied with the state

status a social position that a person holds

status consistency the degree of consistency in a person's social standing across various dimensions of social inequality

status set all the statuses a person holds at a given time

stereotype an exaggerated description applied to every person in some category

stigma a powerfully negative label that greatly changes a person's self-concept and social identity

structural-functional approach a framework for building theory that sees society as a complex system whose parts work together to promote solidarity and stability

structural social mobility a shift in the social position of large numbers of people due more to changes in society than to individual efforts

subculture cultural patterns that set apart some segment of a society's population

suburbs urban areas beyond the political boundaries of a city

superego Freud's term for the cultural values and norms internalized by an individual

survey a research method in which subjects respond to a series of statements or questions in a questionnaire or an interview

symbol anything that carries a particular meaning recognized by people who share a culture

symbolic-interaction approach a framework for building theory that sees society as the product of the everyday interactions of individuals

technology knowledge that people use to make a way of life in their surroundings

terrorism acts of violence or the threat of violence used as a political strategy by an individual or a group

tertiary sector the part of the economy that involves services rather than goods

theoretical approach   a basic image of society that guides thinking and research

theory   a statement of how and why specific facts are related

Thomas theorem   W. I. Thomas's statement that situations defined as real are real in their consequences

total institution   a setting in which people are isolated from the rest of society and manipulated by an administrative staff

totalitarianism   a highly centralized political system that extensively regulates people's lives

totem   an object in the natural world collectively defined as sacred

tracking   assigning students to different types of educational programs

tradition   values and beliefs passed from generation to generation

tradition-directedness   rigid conformity to time-honored ways of living

transsexuals   people who feel they are one sex even though biologically they are the other

triad   a social group with three members

urban ecology   the study of the link between the physical and social dimensions of cities

urbanization   the concentration of population into cities

validity   actually measuring exactly what you intend to measure

values   culturally defined standards that people use to decide what is desirable, good, and beautiful and that serve as broad guidelines for social living

variable   a concept whose value changes from case to case

victimless crimes   violations of law in which there are no obvious victims

war   organized, armed conflict among the people of two or more nations, directed by their governments

wealth   the total value of money and other assets, minus outstanding debts

welfare capitalism   an economic and political system that combines a mostly market-based economy with extensive social welfare programs

welfare state   a system of government agencies and programs that provides benefits to the population

white-collar crime   crime committed by people of high social position in the course of their occupations

white-collar occupations   higher-prestige jobs that involve mostly mental activity

zero population growth   the level of reproduction that maintains population at a steady level

REFERENCES

ABERLE, DAVID F. *The Peyote Religion among the Navaho.* Chicago: Aldine, 1966.

"Abramoff Effect: Leaping out of Bed with the Lobbyists." *New York Times* (January 16, 2006). [Online] Available June 3, 2006, at http://www. researchnavigator.com

ADLER, JERRY. "When Harry Called Sally . . ." *Newsweek* (October 1, 1990):74.

ADORNO, THEODOR W., ET AL. *The Authoritarian Personality.* New York: Harper, 1950.

AKERS, RONALD L., MARVIN D. KROHN, LONN LANZA-KADUCE, and MARCIA RADOSEVICH. "Social Learning and Deviant Behavior." *American Sociological Review.* Vol. 44, No. 4 (August 1979):636–55.

ALAN GUTTMACHER INSTITUTE. "Teen Pregnancy: Trends and Lessons Learned." Issues in Brief. 2002 Series, No. 1. 2002. [Online] Available May 2, 2006 at http://www.guttmacher.org/pubs/ib_1_02.pdf

———. "U.S. Teenage Pregnancy Statistics: Overall Trends, Trends by Race and Ethnicity and State-by-State Information." Updated February 19, 2004. [Online] Available May 2, 2006 at http://www.guttmacher.org/pubs/ state_pregnancy_trends.pdf

ALBON, JOAN. "Retention of Cultural Values and Differential Urban Adaptation: Samoans and American Indians in a West Coast City." *Social Forces.* Vol. 49, No. 3 (March 1971):385–93.

ALFORD, RICHARD. "The Structure of Human Experience: Expectancy and Affect: The Case of Humor." Unpublished paper, Department of Sociology, University of Wyoming, 1979.

ALLAN, EMILIE ANDERSEN, and DARRELL J. STEFFENSMEIER. "Youth, Underemployment, and Property Crime: Differential Effects of Job Availability and Job Quality on Juvenile and Young Adult Arrest Rates." *American Sociological Review.* Vol. 54, No. 1 (February 1989):107–23.

ALLEN, THOMAS B., and CHARLES O. HYMAN. *We Americans: Celebrating a Nation, Its People, and Its Past.* Washington, D.C.: National Geographic, 1999.

ALLEN, WALTER R. "African American Family Life in Social Context: Crisis and Hope." *Sociological Forum.* Vol. 10, No. 4 (December 1995):569–92.

ALTONJI, JOSEPH G., ULRICH DORASZELSKI, and LEWIS SEGAL. "Black/White Differences in Wealth." *Economic Perspectives.* Vol. 24, No. 1 (First Quarter 2000):38–50.

AMATO, PAUL R. "What Children Learn from Divorce." *Population Today.* Vol. 29, No. 1 (January 2001):1, 4.

AMERICAN BAR ASSOCIATION. "First-Year and Total J.D. Enrollment by Gender, 1947–2005." 2006. [Online] Available May 24, 2006, at http://www. abanet.org/legaled/statistics/charts/enrollmentbygender.pdf

American Demographics. Zandi Group survey. Vol. 20 (March 3, 1998):38.

AMERICAN PSYCHOLOGICAL ASSOCIATION. *Violence and Youth: Psychology's Response.* Washington, D.C.: American Psychological Association, 1993.

AMERICAN SOCIOLOGICAL ASSOCIATION. "Code of Ethics." Washington, D.C.: American Sociological Association, 1997.

———. *Careers in Sociology.* 6th ed. Washington, D.C.: American Sociological Association, 2002.

———. *The Importance of Collecting Data and Doing Social Scientific Research on Race.* Washington, D.C.: American Sociological Association, 2003.

AMNESTY INTERNATIONAL. "Abolitionist and Retentionist Countries." [Online] Available May 9, 2006a, at http://web.amnesty.org/pages/deathpenalty -countries-eng

———. "Facts and Figures on the Death Penalty." [Online] Available May 9, 2006b, at http://web.amnesty.org/pages/deathpenalty-facts-eng

ANDERSON, ELIJAH. "The Code of the Streets." *Atlantic Monthly.* Vol. 273 (May 1994):81–94.

———. "The Ideologically Driven Critique." *American Journal of Sociology.* Vol. 197, No. 6 (May 2002):1533–50.

ANDERSON, JOHN WARD. "Early to Wed: The Child Brides of India." *Washington Post* (May 24, 1995):A27, A30.

ANNAN, KOFI. "Astonishing Facts." *New York Times* (September 27, 1998):16.

APPLEBOME, PETER. "70 Years after Scopes Trial, Creation Debate Lives." *New York Times* (March 10, 1996):1, 10.

ARIÈS, PHILIPPE. *Centuries of Childhood: A Social History of Family Life.* New York: Vintage Books, 1965.

ARMSTRONG, ELISABETH. *The Retreat from Organization: U.S. Feminism Reconceptualized.* Albany: State University of New York Press, 2002.

ARONOWITZ, STANLEY. *The Politics of Identity: Class, Culture, and Social Movements.* New York: Routledge, 1992.

ASANTE, MOLEFI KETE. *Afrocentricity.* Trenton, N.J.: Africa World Press, 1988.

ASCH, SOLOMON. *Social Psychology.* Englewood Cliffs, N.J.: Prentice Hall, 1952.

ASHFORD, LORI S. "New Perspectives on Population: Lessons from Cairo." *Population Bulletin.* Vol. 50, No. 1 (March 1995).

———. "Young Women in Sub-Saharan Africa Face a High Risk of HIV Infection." *Population Today.* Vol. 30, No. 2 (February/March 2002):3, 6.

ASTIN, ALEXANDER W., LETICIA OSEGUERA, LINDA J. SAX, and WILLIAM S. KORN. *The American Freshman: Thirty-Five-Year Trends.* Los Angeles: University of California Higher Education Research Institute, 2002.

AUSTER, CAROL J., and MINDY MACRONE. "The Classroom as a Negotiated Social Setting: An Empirical Study of the Effects of Faculty Members' Behavior on Students' Participation." *Teaching Sociology.* Vol. 22, No. 4 (October 1994):289–300.

AXINN, WILLIAM G., and JENNIFER S. BARBER. "Mass Education and Fertility Transition." *American Sociological Review.* Vol. 66, No. 4 (August 2001):481–505.

BAINBRIDGE, JAY, MARCIA K. MEYERS, and JANE WALDFOGEL. "Childcare Reform and the Employment of Single Mothers." *Social Science Quarterly.* Vol. 84, No. 4 (December 2003):771–91.

BAKALAR, NICHOLAS. "Reactions: Go On, Laugh Your Heart Out." *New York Times* (March 8, 2005). [Online] Available March 11, 2005, at http://www. nytimes.com/2005/03/08/health/08reac.html

BAKER, PATRICIA S., WILLIAM C. YOELS, JEFFREY M. CLAIR, and RICHARD M. ALLMAN. "Laughter in the Triadic Geriatric Encounters: A Transcript-Based Analysis." In REBECCA J. ERIKSON and BEVERLY CUTHBERTSON-JOHNSON, eds., *Social Perspectives on Emotion.* Vol. 4. Greenwich, Conn.: JAI Press, 1997:179–207.

BAKER, ROSS. "Business as Usual." *American Demographics.* Vol. 19, No. 4 (April 1997):28.

BALTZELL, E. DIGBY. *The Protestant Establishment: Aristocracy and Caste in America.* New York: Vintage Books, 1964.

———. "Introduction to the 1967 Edition." In W.E.B. DU BOIS, *The Philadelphia Negro: A Social Study.* New York: Schocken Books, 1967; orig. 1899.

———. *Puritan Boston and Quaker Philadelphia.* New York: Free Press, 1979b.

———. *Sporting Gentlemen: From the Age of Honor to the Cult of the Superstar.* New York: Free Press, 1995.

BANFIELD, EDWARD C. *The Unheavenly City Revisited.* Boston: Little, Brown, 1974.

BARASH, DAVID P. *The Whisperings Within.* New York: Penguin Books, 1981.

BARNES, JULIAN E. "Wanted: Readers." *U.S. News & World Report* (September 9, 2002a):44–45.

———. "War Profiteering." *U.S. News & World Report* (May 13, 2002b):20–24.

———. "Unequal Education." *U.S. News & World Report* (March 22, 2004):66–75.

BARON, JAMES N., MICHAEL T. HANNAN, and M. DIANE BURTON. "Building the Iron Cage: Determinants of Managerial Intensity in the Early Years of Organizations." *American Sociological Review.* Vol. 64, No. 4 (August 1999):527–47.

BARONE, MICHAEL. "Lessons of History." *U.S. News & World Report* (May 20, 2002):24.

———. "Cultures Aren't Equal." *U.S. News & World Report.* Vol. 139, No. 6 (August 22, 2005):26.

BAROVICK, HARRIET. "Tongues That Go Out of Style." *Time* (June 10, 2002):22.

BARR, ROBERT. "Archbishop of Canterbury Is Enthroned." [Online] Available February 27, 2003, at http://news.yahoo.com

BARTLETT, DONALD L., and JAMES B. STEELE. "Corporate Welfare." *Time* (November 9, 1998):36–54.

———. "How the Little Guy Gets Crunched." *Time* (February 7, 2000):38–41.

———. "Wheel of Misfortune." *Time* (December 16, 2002):44–58.

BASSUK, ELLEN J. "The Homelessness Problem." *Scientific American.* Vol. 251, No. 1 (July 1984):40–45.

BAUER, P. T. *Equality, the Third World, and Economic Delusion.* Cambridge, Mass.: Harvard University Press, 1981.

BAYDAR, NAZLI, and JEANNE BROOKS-GUNN. "Effect of Maternal Employment and Child-Care Arrangements on Preschoolers' Cognitive and Behavioral Outcomes: Evidence from Children from the National Longitudinal Survey of Youth." *Developmental Psychology.* Vol. 27 (1991):932–35.

BEARAK, BARRY. "Lives Held Cheap in Bangladesh Sweatshops." *New York Times* (April 15, 2001):A1, A12.

BECKER, ANNE E. "The Association of Television Exposure with Disordered Eating Among Ethnic Fijian Adolescent Girls." Paper presented at the annual meeting of the American Psychiatric Association, Washington, D.C., May 19, 1999.

BECKER, HOWARD S. *Outside: Studies in the Sociology of Deviance.* New York: Free Press, 1966.

BEDARD, PAUL. "Washington Whispers." *U.S. News & World Report* (March 25, 2002):2.

BEEGHLEY, LEONARD. *The Structure of Social Stratification in the United States.* Needham Heights, Mass.: Allyn & Bacon, 1989.

BEGLEY, SHARON. "Gray Matters." *Newsweek* (March 7, 1995):48–54.

———. "How to Beat the Heat." *Newsweek* (December 8, 1997):34–38.

BELLAH, ROBERT N. *The Broken Covenant.* New York: Seabury Press, 1975.

BELLAH, ROBERT N., et al. *Habits of the Heart: Individualism and Commitment in American Life.* New York: Harper & Row, 1985.

BELLUCK, PAM. "Black Youths' Rate of Suicide Rising Sharply." *New York Times* (March 20, 1998):A1, A18.

BEM, SANDRA LIPSITZ. *The Lenses of Gender: Transforming the Debate on Sexual Inequality.* New Haven, Conn.: Yale University Press, 1993.

BENEDICT, RUTH. "Continuities and Discontinuities in Cultural Conditioning." *Psychiatry.* Vol. 1 (May 1938):161–67.

BENJAMIN, LOIS. *The Black Elite: Facing the Color Line in the Twilight of the Twentieth Century.* Chicago: Nelson-Hall, 1991.

BENJAMIN, MATTHEW. "Suite Deals." *U.S. News & World Report* (April 29, 2002):32–34.

BENOKRAITIS, NIJOLE V., and JOE R. FEAGIN. *Modern Sexism: Blatant, Subtle, and Overt Discrimination.* 2d ed. Upper Saddle River, N.J.: Prentice Hall, 1995.

BERGAMO, MONICA, and GERSON CAMAROTTI. "Brazil's Landless Millions." *World Press Review.* Vol. 43, No. 7 (July 1996):46–47.

BERGER, PETER L. *Invitation to Sociology.* New York: Anchor Books, 1963.

———. *The Sacred Canopy: Elements of a Sociological Theory of Religion.* Garden City, N.Y.: Doubleday, 1967.

———. *Facing Up to Modernity: Excursions in Society, Politics, and Religion.* New York: Basic Books, 1977.

———. *The Capitalist Revolution: Fifty Propositions about Prosperity, Equality, and Liberty.* New York: Basic Books, 1986.

———. "Sociology: A Disinvitation?" *Society.* Vol. 30, No. 1 (November/December 1992):12–18.

BERGER, PETER L., BRIGITTE BERGER, and HANSFRIED KELLNER. *The Homeless Mind: Modernization and Consciousness.* New York: Vintage Books, 1974.

BERGESEN, ALBERT, ed. *Crises in the World-System.* Beverly Hills, Calif.: Sage, 1983.

BERNARD, JESSIE. *The Female World.* New York: Free Press, 1981.

———. *The Future of Marriage.* New Haven, Conn.: Yale University Press, 1982; orig. 1973.

BERRILL, KEVIN T. "Anti-Gay Violence and Victimization in the United States: An Overview." In GREGORY M. HEREK and KEVIN T. BERRILL, eds., *Hate Crimes: Confronting Violence against Lesbians and Gay Men.* Newbury Park, Calif.: Sage, 1992:19–45.

BERRY, BRIAN L., and PHILIP H. REES. "The Factorial Ecology of Calcutta." *American Journal of Sociology.* Vol. 74, No. 5 (March 1969):445–91.

BERTEAU, CELESTE. "Disconnected Intimacy: AOL Instant Messenger Use among Kenyon College Students." Senior thesis. Kenyon College, 2005.

BESHAROV, DOUGLAS J., and PETER GERMANIS. "Welfare Reform: Four Years Later." *Public Interest.* No. 140 (Summer 2000):17–35.

BESHAROV, DOUGLAS J., and LISA A. LAUMANN. "Child Abuse Reporting." *Society.* Vol. 34, No. 4 (May/June 1996):40–46.

BEST, RAPHAELA. *We've All Got Scars: What Boys and Girls Learn in Elementary School.* Bloomington: Indiana University Press, 1983.

BIANCHI, SUZANNE M., and LYNNE M. CASPER. "American Families." *Population Bulletin.* Vol. 55, No. 4 (December 2000):3–43.

BIANCHI, SUZANNE M., and DAPHNE SPAIN. "Women, Work, and Family in America." *Population Bulletin.* Vol. 51, No. 3 (December 1996).

BLACKWOOD, EVELYN, and SASKIA WIERINGA, eds. *Female Desires: Same-Sex Relations and Transgender Practices across Cultures.* New York: Columbia University Press, 1999.

BLANKENHORN, DAVID. *Fatherless America: Confronting Our Most Urgent Social Problem.* New York: HarperCollins, 1995.

BLAU, JUDITH R., and PETER M. BLAU. "The Cost of Inequality: Metropolitan Structure and Violent Crime." *American Sociological Review.* Vol. 47, No. 1 (February 1982):114–29.

BLAU, PETER M. *Exchange and Power in Social Life.* New York: Wiley, 1964.

———. *Inequality and Heterogeneity: A Primitive Theory of Social Structure.* New York: Free Press, 1977.

BLAU, PETER M., TERRY C. BLUM, and JOSEPH E. SCHWARTZ. "Heterogeneity and Intermarriage." *American Sociological Review.* Vol. 47, No. 1 (February 1982):45–62.

BLAU, PETER M., and OTIS DUDLEY DUNCAN. *The American Occupational Structure.* New York: Wiley, 1967.

BLAUSTEIN, ALBERT P., and ROBERT L. ZANGRANDO. *Civil Rights and the Black American.* New York: Washington Square Press, 1968.

BLUMER, HERBERT G. "Collective Behavior." In ALFRED MCCLUNG LEE, ed., *Principles of Sociology.* 3d ed. New York: Barnes & Noble Books, 1969:65–121.

BLUMSTEIN, PHILIP, and PEPPER SCHWARTZ. *American Couples.* New York: Morrow, 1983.

BOBO, LAWRENCE D., and VINCENT L. HUTCHINGS. "Perceptions of Racial Group Competition: Extending Blumer's Theory of Group Position to a Multiracial Social Context." *American Sociological Review.* Vol. 61, No. 6 (December 1996):951–72.

BOERNER, CHRISTOPHER, and THOMAS LAMBERT. "Environmental Injustice." *Public Interest* (Winter 1995):61–82.

BOGARDUS, EMORY S. "Social Distance and Its Origins." *Sociology and Social Research.* Vol. 9 (July/August 1925):216–25.

———. *A Forty-Year Racial Distance Study.* Los Angeles: University of Southern California Press, 1967.

BOHANNAN, CECIL. "The Economic Correlates of Homelessness in Sixty Cities." *Social Science Quarterly.* Vol. 72, No. 4 (December 1991):817–25.

BOHLEN, CELESTINE. "Facing Oblivion, Rust-Belt Giants Top Russian List of Vexing Crises." *New York Times* (November 8, 1998):1, 6.

BOHON, STEPHANIE A., and CRAIG R. HUMPHREY. "Courting LULUs: Characteristic of Suitor and Objector Communities." *Rural Sociology.* Vol. 65, No. 3 (September 2000):376–95.

BONANNO, ALESSANDRO, DOUGLAS H. CONSTANCE, and HEATHER LORENZ. "Powers and Limits of Transnational Corporations: The Case of ADM." *Rural Sociology.* Vol. 65, No. 3 (September 2000):440–60.

BONNER, JANE. Research presented in *The Two Brains.* Public Broadcasting System telecast, 1984.

BONO, AGOSTINO. "John Jay Study Reveals the Extent of Abuse Problem." [Online] Available September 13, 2006, at http://www.americancatholic.org/news/clergysexabuse/johnjaycns.asp

BOOTH, ALAN, and JAMES DABBS. "Male Hormone Is Linked to Marital Problems." *Wall Street Journal* (August 19, 1992):B1.

BOOTH, WILLIAM. "By the Sweat of Their Brows: A New Economy." *Washington Post* (July 13, 1998):A1, A10–A11.

BORMANN, F. HERBERT. "The Global Environmental Deficit." *BioScience.* Vol. 40 (1990):74.

BOSWELL, TERRY E. "A Split Labor Market Analysis of Discrimination against Chinese Immigrants, 1850–1882." *American Sociological Review.* Vol. 51, No. 3 (June 1986):352–71.

BOSWELL, TERRY E., and WILLIAM J. DIXON. "Marx's Theory of Rebellion: A Cross-National Analysis of Class Exploitation, Economic Development, and Violent Revolt." *American Sociological Review.* Vol. 58, No. 5 (October 1993):681–702.

BOTT, ELIZABETH. *Family and Social Network.* New York: Free Press, 1971; orig. 1957.

BOWEN, WILLIAM G., and DEREK K. BOK. *The Shape of the River: Long-Term Consequences of Considering Race in College and University Admissions.* Princeton, N.J.: Princeton University Press, 1999.

BOWLES, SAMUEL, and HERBERT GINTIS. *Schooling in Capitalist America: Educational Reform and the Contradictions of Economic Life.* New York: Basic Books, 1976.

BOYER, DEBRA. "Male Prostitution and Homosexual Identity." *Journal of Homosexuality.* Vol. 17, Nos. 1–2 (Fall/Winter 1989):151–84.

BOYLE, ELIZABETH HEGER, FORTUNATA SONGORA, and GAIL FOSS. "International Discourse and Local Politics: Anti-Female-Genital-Cutting Laws in Egypt, Tanzania, and the United States." *Social Problems.* Vol. 48, No. 4 (November 2001):524–44.

BRECHIN, STEVEN R., and WILLETT KEMPTON. "Global Environmentalism: A Challenge to the Postmaterialism Thesis." *Social Science Quarterly.* Vol. 75, No. 2 (June 1994):245–69.

BRIANS, CRAIG LEONARD, and BERNARD GROFMAN. "Election Day Registration's Effect on U.S. Voter Turnout." *Social Science Quarterly.* Vol. 82, No. 1 (March 2001):170–83.

BRIGGS, TRACEY WONG. "Two Years, Changed Lives." *USA Today* (April 22, 2002):D1–D2.

BRINES, JULIE, and KARA JOYNER. "The Ties That Bind: Principles of Cohesion in Cohabitation and Marriage." *American Sociological Review.* Vol. 64, No. 3 (June 1999):333–55.

BRINK, SUSAN. "Living on the Edge." *U.S. News & World Report* (October 14, 2002):58–64.

BROCKERHOFF, MARTIN P. "An Urbanizing World." *Population Bulletin*. Vol. 55, No. 3 (September 2000).

BRODER, DAVID S. "Stock Options Belong in the Line of Fire." *Columbus Dispatch* (April 21, 2002):G3.

BRODKIN, KAREN B. "How Did Jews Become White Folks?" In JOHN J. MACIONIS and NIJOLE V. BENOKRAITIS, eds. *Seeing Ourselves: Classic, Contemporary, and Cross-Cultural Readings in Sociology*. 7th ed. Upper Saddle River, N.J.: Prentice Hall, 2007.

BROOKS, DAVID. *Bobos in Paradise: The New Upper Class and How They Got There*. New York: Simon & Schuster, 2000.

BROWN, LESTER R. "Reassessing the Earth's Population." *Society*. Vol. 32, No. 4 (May/June 1995):7–10.

BROWN, LESTER R., ET AL., eds. *State of the World, 1993: A Worldwatch Institute Report on Progress toward a Sustainable Society*. New York: Norton, 1993.

BUCKS, BRIAN K., ARTHUR B. KENNICKEL, and KEVIN B. MOORE. "Recent Change in U.S. Family Finances: Evidence from the 2001 and 2004 Survey of Consumer Finances." *Federal Reserve Bulletin*. 2006. [Online] Available May 11, 2006, at http://www.federalreserve.gov/pubs/bulletin/2006/financesurvey.pdf

BUECHLER, STEVEN M. *Social Movements in Advanced Capitalism: The Political Economy and Cultural Construction of Social Activism*. New York: Oxford University Press, 2000.

BURAWAY, MICHAEL. "Review Essay: The Soviet Descent into Capitalism." *American Journal of Sociology*. Vol. 102, No. 5 (March 1997):1430–44.

BURKETT, ELINOR. "God Created Me to Be a Slave." *New York Times Sunday Magazine* (October 12, 1997):56–60.

CALIFORNIA NEWSREEL. "Race: The Power of an Illusion: Genetic Diversity Quiz." 2003. [Online] Available February 9, 2006, at http://www.pbs.org/race/000_About/002_04_a-godeeper.htm

CAMARA, EVANDRO. Personal communication, 2000.

CAMERON, WILLIAM BRUCE. *Modern Social Movements: A Sociological Outline*. New York: Random House, 1966.

CAPEK, STELLA A. "The 'Environmental Justice' Frame: A Conceptual Discussion and an Application." *Social Problems*. Vol. 40, No. 1 (February 1993):5–24.

CAPLOW, THEODORE, HOWARD M. BAHR, JOHN MODELL, and BRUCE A. CHADWICK. *Recent Social Trends in the United States, 1960–1990*. Montreal: McGill-Queen's University Press, 1991.

CARLSON, NORMAN A. "Corrections in the United States Today: A Balance Has Been Struck." *American Criminal Law Review*. Vol. 13, No. 4 (Spring 1976):615–47.

CARMICHAEL, STOKELY, and CHARLES V. HAMILTON. *Black Power: The Politics of Liberation in America*. New York: Vintage Books, 1967.

CARMONA, RICHARD H. "The Obesity Crisis in America." Testimony before the Subcommittee on Education Reform, Committee on Education and the Workforce, United States House of Representatives. July 16, 2003. [Online] Available September 25, 2005, at http://www.surgeongeneral.gov/news/testimony/obesity07162003.htm

CARROLL, JAMES R. "Congress Is Told of Coal-Dust Fraud; Senator from Minnesota Rebukes Industry." *Louisville Courier Journal* (May 27, 1999):1A.

CARSON, RACHEL. *Silent Spring*. Boston: Houghton Mifflin, 1962.

CARYL, CHRISTIAN. "Iraqi Vice." *Newsweek* (December 22, 2003):38–39.

CASTELLS, MANUEL. *The Urban Question*. Cambridge, Mass.: MIT Press, 1977.

———. *The City and the Grass Roots*. Berkeley: University of California Press, 1983.

CATALYST. "2005 Catalyst Census of Women Board Directors of the *Fortune* 500 Shows 10-Year Trend of Slow Progress and Persistent Challenges." Press release. March 29, 2006. [Online] Available August 10, 2006, at http://www.catalyst.org/pressroom/press_releases/3_29_06%20-20WBD%20release.pdf

———. *2005 Catalyst Census of Women Corporate Officers and Top Earners of the* Fortune *500*. 2006. [Online] Available August 10, 2006, at http://www.catalystwomen.org/files/full/2005%20COTE.pdf

CENTER FOR AMERICAN WOMEN AND POLITICS. "Women in State Legislatures, 2005." Eagleton Institute of Politics, Rutgers University. June 2005. [Online] Available June 23, 2005, at http://www.cawp.rutgers.edu/Facts/Officeholders/stleg.pdf

———. "Women in Elected Office: Fact Sheets and Summaries." Eagleton Institute of Politics, Rutgers University. May 2006. [Online] Available May 24, 2006, at http://www.cawp.rutgers.edu/Facts.html

CENTER FOR RESPONSIVE POLITICS. "The Big Picture, 2004 Cycle: Where the Money Came From." May 16, 2005a. [Online] Available September 24, 2006, at http://www.opensecrets.org/bigpicture/wherefrom.asp?cycle=2004

———. "The Big Picture, 2004 Cycle: Totals by Sector." May 16, 2005b. [Online] Available September 24, 2006, at http://www.opensecrets.org/bigpicture/sectors.asp?cycle=2004

CENTER ON EDUCATION POLICY AND AMERICAN YOUTH POLICY FORUM. *Do You Know . . . the Good News about American Education?* Washington, D.C.: Center on Education Policy and American Youth Policy Forum, 2000. [Online] Available on October 1, 2006, at http://www.aypf.org/publications/good_news.pdf

CENTERS FOR DISEASE CONTROL AND PREVENTION. "Trends in Cigarette Smoking among High School Students—United States, 1991–2001." *Morbidity and Mortality Weekly Report*. Vol. 51, No. 19 (May 17, 2002):409–12.

———. "Annual Smoking-Attributable Mortality, Years." *Morbidity and Mortality Weekly Report*. Vol. 54, No. 25 (July 1, 2005a):625–28.

———. "Cigarette Smoking among Adults—United States, 2004." *Morbidity and Mortality Weekly Report*. Vol. 54, No. 44 (November 11, 2005b): 1121–24.

———. *HIV/AIDS Surveillance Report, 2004*. Vol. 16. 2005c. [Online] Available September 27, 2006, at http://www.cdc.gov/hiv/topics/surveillance/resources/reports/2004report/default.htm

———. *Sexually Transmitted Disease Surveillance, 2004*. September 2005d. [Online] Available September 27, 2006, at http://www.cdc.gov/std/stats/toc2004.htm

———. "Youth Risk Behavior Surveillance—United States, 2005." *Morbidity and Mortality Weekly Report*. Vol. 55, No. 5 (June 9, 2006).

CERE, DANIEL. "Courtship Today: The View from Academia." *Public Interest*. No. 143 (Spring 2001):53–71.

CHAGNON, NAPOLEON A. *Yąnomamö: The Fierce People*. 4th ed. Austin, Tex.: Holt, Rinehart and Winston, 1992.

CHANDLER, TERTIUS, and GERALD FOX. *3000 Years of Urban History*. New York: Academic Press, 1974.

CHAVEZ, LINDA. "Promoting Racial Harmony." In GEORGE E. CURRY, ed., *The Affirmative Action Debate*. Reading, Mass.: Addison-Wesley, 1996.

CHEN, SHAOHUA, and MARTIN RAVALLION. "How Have the World's Poorest Fared since the Early 1980s?" World Bank Policy Research Working Paper 3341, June 2004. [Online] Available May 22, 2006, at http://www.worldbank.org

"China Faces Water Shortage." *Popline*. Vol. 23 (December 2001):1–4.

CHIRICOS, TED, RANEE MCENTIRE, and MARC GERTZ. "Perceived Racial and Ethnic Composition of Neighborhood and Perceived Risk of Crime." *Social Problems*. Vol. 48, No. 3 (August 2001):322–40.

CHODOROW, NANCY. *Femininities, Masculinities, Sexualities: Freud and Beyond*. Lexington: University of Kentucky Press, 1994.

CHOLDIN, HARVEY M. "How Sampling Will Help Defeat the Undercount." *Society*. Vol. 34, No. 3 (March/April 1997):27–30.

CHRONICLE OF HIGHER EDUCATION. *Almanac 2006–07*. 2006. [Online] Available September 20, 2006, at http://chronicle.com/free/almanac/2006/index.htm

CHUA-EOAN, HOWARD. "Profiles in Outrage." *Time* (September 25, 2000):38–39.

CIMINO, RICHARD, and DON LATTIN. "Choosing My Religion." *American Demographics*. Vol. 21, No. 4 (April 1999):60–65.

CLARK, KIM. "Bankrupt Lives." *U.S. News & World Report* (September 16, 2002):52–54.

CLARK, MARGARET S., ed. *Prosocial Behavior*. Newbury Park, Calif.: Sage, 1991.

CLAWSON, DAN, and MARY ANN CLAWSON. "What Has Happened to the U.S. Labor Movement? Union Decline and Renewal." *Annual Review of Sociology*. Vol. 25 (1999):95–119.

CLEMETSON, LYNETTE. "Grandma Knows Best." *Newsweek* (June 12, 2000):60–61.

CLOUD, JOHN. "What Can the Schools Do?" *Time* (May 3, 1999):38–40.

CLOUD, JOHN, and JODIE MORSE. "Home Sweet School." *Time* (August 27, 2001):46–54.

CLOWARD, RICHARD A., and LLOYD E. OHLIN. *Delinquency and Opportunity: A Theory of Delinquent Gangs*. New York: Free Press, 1966.

COAKLEY, JAY J. *Sport in Society: Issues and Controversies*. 4th ed. St. Louis, Mo.: Mosby, 1990.

COHEN, ADAM. "Test-Tube Tug-of-War." *Time* (April 6, 1998):65.

———. "A First Report Card on Vouchers." *Time* (April 26, 1999):36–38.

COHEN, ALBERT K. *Delinquent Boys: The Culture of the Gang*. New York: Free Press, 1971; orig. 1955.

COHEN, PHILIP N., and MATT L. HUFFMAN. "Individuals, Jobs, and Labor Markets: The Devaluation of Women's Work." *American Sociological Review*. Vol. 68, No. 3 (June 2003):443–63.

COLE, GEORGE F., and CHRISTOPHER E. SMITH. *Criminal Justice in America*. 3d ed. Belmont, Calif.: Wadsworth, 2002.

COLEMAN, JAMES S. "The Design of Organizations and the Right to Act." *Sociological Forum.* Vol. 8, No. 4 (December 1993):527–46.

COLEMAN, JAMES S., and THOMAS HOFFER. *Public and Private High Schools: The Impact of Communities.* New York: Basic Books, 1987.

COLEMAN, JAMES S., THOMAS HOFFER, and SALLY KILGORE. *Public and Private Schools: An Analysis of Public Schools and Beyond.* Washington, D.C.: National Center for Education Statistics, 1981.

COLEMAN, JAMES S., ET AL. *Equality of Educational Opportunity.* Washington, D.C.: U.S. Government Printing Office, 1966.

COLEMAN, RICHARD P., and LEE RAINWATER. *Social Standing in America.* New York: Basic Books, 1978.

COLLEGE BOARD. "2006 College-Bound Seniors Tables and Related Items." [Online] Available September 24, 2006, at http://www.collegeboard.com/about/news_info/cbsenior/yr2006/links.html

COLLINS, RANDALL. *The Credential Society: A Historical Sociology of Education and Stratification.* New York: Academic Press, 1979.

COLLYMORE, YVETTE. "Migrant Street Children on the Rise in Central America." *Population Today.* Vol. 30, No. 2 (February/March 2002):1, 4.

COLTON, HELEN. *The Gift of Touch: How Physical Contact Improves Communication, Pleasure, and Health.* New York: Seaview/Putnam, 1983.

COMMISSION FOR RACIAL JUSTICE AND UNITED CHURCH OF CHRIST. *CRJ Reporter.* New York: Commission for Racial Justice and United Church of Christ, 1994.

COMTE, AUGUSTE. *Auguste Comte and Positivism: The Essential Writings.* GERTRUD LENZER, ed. New York: Harper Torchbooks, 1975; orig. 1851–54.

CONNETT, PAUL H. "The Disposable Society." In F. HERBERT BORMANN and STEPHEN R. KELLERT, eds., *Ecology, Economics, and Ethics: The Broken Circle.* New Haven, Conn.: Yale University Press, 1991:99–122.

COOLEY, CHARLES HORTON. *Social Organization.* New York: Schocken Books, 1962; orig. 1909.

———. *Human Nature and the Social Order.* New York: Schocken Books, 1964; orig. 1902.

CORCORAN, MARY, SANDRA K. DANZIGER, ARIEL KALIL, and KRISTIN S. SEEFELDT. "How Welfare Reform Is Affecting Women's Work." *Annual Review of Sociology.* Vol. 26 (2000):241–69.

CORNELL, BARBARA. "Pulling the Plug on TV." *Time* (October 16, 2000):F16.

CORRELL, SHELLEY J. "Gender and the Career Choice Process: The Role of Biased Self-Assessment." *American Journal of Sociology.* Vol. 106, No. 6 (May 2001):1691–1730.

CORTESE, ANTHONY J. *Provocateur: Images of Women and Minorities in Advertising.* Lanham, Md.: Rowman & Littlefield, 1999.

COSE, ELLIS. "The Good News about Black America." *Newsweek* (June 7, 1999):28–40.

COSER, LEWIS. *The Functions of Social Conflict.* New York: Free Press, 1956.

———. *Masters of Sociological Thought: Ideas in Historical and Social Context.* 2d ed. New York: Harcourt Brace Jovanovich, 1977.

COURTWRIGHT, DAVID T. *Violent Land: Single Men and Social Disorder from the Frontier to the Inner City.* Cambridge, Mass.: Harvard University Press, 1996.

COWLEY, GEOFFREY. "The Prescription That Kills." *Newsweek* (July 17, 1995):54.

COX, HARVEY. *The Secular City.* Rev. ed. New York: Macmillan, 1971.

COYOTE (CALL OFF YOUR OLD TIRED ETHICS). "What Is COYOTE?" 2004. [Online] Available October 11, 2005, at http://www.coyotela/what-is.html

CROSSETTE, BARBARA. "Female Genital Mutilation by Immigrants Is Becoming Cause for Concern in the U.S." *New York Times International* (December 10, 1995):11.

CROUSE, JAMES, and DALE TRUSHEIM. *The Case against the SAT.* Chicago: University of Chicago Press, 1988.

CRUTSINGER, MARTIN. "Trade Deficit Hits $665.9 Billion in 2004." [Online] Available March 16, 2005, at http://news.yahoo.com

CULLEN, LISA TAKEUCHI. "Will Manage for Food." *Time* (October 14, 2002):52–56.

CUMMINGS, SCOTT, and THOMAS LAMBERT. "Anti-Hispanic and Anti-Asian Sentiments among African Americans." *Social Science Quarterly.* Vol. 78, No. 2 (June 1997):338–53.

CURRIE, ELLIOTT. *Confronting Crime: An American Challenge.* New York: Pantheon Books, 1985.

CURRY, ANDREW. "The Gullahs' Last Stand?" *U.S. News & World Report* (June 18, 2001):40–41.

CURTIS, JAMES E., DOUGLAS E. BAER, and EDWARD G. GRABB. "Nations of Joiners: Explaining Voluntary Association Membership in Democratic Societies." *American Sociological Review.* Vol. 66, No. 6 (December 2001):783–805.

CURTISS, SUSAN. *Genie: A Psycholinguistic Study of a Modern-Day "Wild Child."* New York: Academic Press, 1977.

DAHL, ROBERT A. *Who Governs?* New Haven, Conn.: Yale University Press, 1961.

———. *Dilemmas of Pluralist Democracy: Autonomy vs. Control.* New Haven, Conn.: Yale University Press, 1982.

DAHRENDORF, RALF. *Class and Class Conflict in Industrial Society.* Stanford, Calif.: Stanford University Press, 1959.

DARROCH, JACQUELINE E., JENNIFER J. FROST, SUSHEELA SINGH, and the Study Team. "Teenage Sexual and Reproductive Behavior in Developed Countries: Can More Progress Be Made?" Alan Guttmacher Institute (November 2001). [Online] Available August 14, 2002, at http://www.agi-usa

DAVIDSON, JAMES D., RALPH E. PYLE, and DAVID V. REYES. "Persistence and Change in the Protestant Establishment, 1930–1992." *Social Forces.* Vol. 74, No. 1 (September 1995):157–75.

DAVIDSON, JULIA O'CONNELL. *Prostitution, Power, and Freedom.* Ann Arbor: University of Michigan Press, 1998.

DAVIES, CHRISTIE. *Ethnic Humor around the World: A Comparative Analysis.* Bloomington: Indiana University Press, 1990.

DAVIES, JAMES C. "Toward a Theory of Revolution." *American Sociological Review.* Vol. 27, No. 1 (February 1962):5–19.

DAVIES, MARK, and DENISE B. KANDEL. "Parental and Peer Influences on Adolescents' Educational Plans: Some Further Evidence." *American Journal of Sociology.* Vol. 87, No. 2 (September 1981):363–87.

DAVIS, BYRON BRADLEY. "Sports World." *Christian Science Monitor* (September 9, 1997):11.

DAVIS, DONALD M., cited in "TV Is a Blonde, Blonde World." *American Demographics* (special issue): "Women Change Places" (1993).

DAVIS, KINGSLEY. "Extreme Social Isolation of a Child." *American Journal of Sociology.* Vol. 45, No. 4 (January 1940):554–65.

———. "Final Note on a Case of Extreme Isolation." *American Journal of Sociology.* Vol. 52, No. 5 (March 1947):432–37.

———. "The Myth of Functional Analysis as a Special Method in Sociology and Anthropology." *American Sociological Review.* Vol. 24, No. 1 (February 1959):75ff.

———. "Sexual Behavior." In ROBERT K. MERTON and ROBERT NISBET, eds., *Contemporary Social Problems.* 3d ed. New York: Harcourt Brace Jovanovich, 1971:313–60.

DAVIS, KINGSLEY, and WILBERT MOORE. "Some Principles of Stratification." *American Sociological Review.* Vol. 10, No. 2 (April 1945):242–49.

DEDRICK, DENNIS K., and RICHARD E. YINGER. "MAD, SDI, and the Nuclear Arms Race." Unpublished manuscript. Georgetown College, Georgetown, Ky., 1990.

DEFINA, ROBERT H., and THOMAS M. ARVANITES. "The Weak Effect of Imprisonment on Crime, 1971–1998." *Social Science Quarterly.* Vol. 83, No. 3 (September 2002):635–53.

DEFRANCIS, MARC. "U.S. Elder Care Is in a Fragile State." *Population Today.* Vol. 30, No. 1 (January 2002a):1–3.

———. "A Spiraling Shortage of Nurses." *Population Today.* Vol. 30, No. 2 (February) March 2002b):8–9.

DELACROIX, JACQUES, and CHARLES C. RAGIN. "Structural Blockage: A Cross-National Study of Economic Dependency, State Efficacy, and Underdevelopment." *American Journal of Sociology.* Vol. 86, No. 6 (May 1981):1311–47.

DEMERATH, N. J., III. "Who Now Debates Functionalism? From *System, Change, and Conflict* to 'Culture, Choice, and Praxis.'" *Sociological Forum.* Vol. 11, No. 2 (June 1996):333–45.

DEMUTH, STEPHEN, and DARRELL STEFFENSMEIER. "The Impact of Gender and Race-Ethnicity in the Pretrial Release Process." *Social Problems.* Vol. 51, No. 2 (May 2004):222–42.

DERBER, CHARLES. *The Wilding of America: Money, Mayhem, and the New American Dream.* 3d ed. New York: Worth, 2004.

DICKINSON, AMY. "When Dating Is Dangerous." *Time* (August 27, 2001):76.

DIXON, WILLIAM J., and TERRY BOSWELL. "Dependency, Disarticulation, and Denominator Effects: Another Look at Foreign Capital Penetration." *American Journal of Sociology.* Vol. 102, No. 2 (September 1996):543–62.

DOBYNS, HENRY F. "An Appraisal of Techniques with a New Hemispheric Estimate." *Current Anthropology.* Vol. 7, No. 4 (October 1966):395–446.

DOLLARD, JOHN, ET AL. *Frustration and Aggression.* New Haven, Conn.: Yale University Press, 1939.

DOMHOFF, G. WILLIAM. *Who Rules America Now? A View of the '80s.* Englewood Cliffs, N.J.: Prentice Hall, 1983.

DONAHUE, JOHN J., III, and STEVEN D. LEAVITT. Research cited in "New Study Claims Abortion Is Behind Decrease in Crime." *Population Today*. Vol. 28, No. 1 (January 2000):1, 4.

DONOVAN, VIRGINIA K., and RONNIE LITTENBERG. "Psychology of Women: Feminist Therapy." In BARBARA HABER, ed., *The Women's Annual, 1981: The Year in Review*. Boston: Hall, 1982:211–35.

DOWNEY, DOUGLAS B., PAUL T. VON HIPPEL, and BECKETT A. BROH. "Are Schools the Great Equalizer? Cognitive Inequality during the Summer Months and School Year." *American Sociological Review*. Vol. 69, No. 5 (October 2004):613–35.

DOYLE, JAMES A. *The Male Experience*. Dubuque, Iowa: Brown, 1983.

DU BOIS, W. E. B. *The Philadelphia Negro: A Social Study*. New York: Schocken Books, 1967; orig. 1899.

DUBOS, RENÉ. *Man Adapting*. New Haven, Conn.: Yale University Press, 1980; orig. 1965.

DUDLEY, KATHRYN MARIE. *Debt and Dispossession: Farm Loss in America's Heartland*. Chicago: University of Chicago Press, 2000.

DUNBAR, LESLIE. *The Common Interest: How Our Social Welfare Policies Don't Work and What We Can Do about Them*. New York: Pantheon, 1988.

DUNCAN, CYNTHIA M. *Worlds Apart: Why Poverty Persists in Rural America*. New Haven, Conn.: Yale University Press, 1999.

DUNCAN, GREG J., W. JEAN YEUNG, JEANNE BROOKS-GUNN, and JUDITH R. SMITH. "How Much Does Childhood Poverty Affect the Life Chances of Children?" *American Sociological Review*. Vol. 63, No. 3 (June 1998):406–23.

DUNN, LUCIA F. "Is Combat Pay Effective? Evidence from Operation Desert Storm." *Social Science Quarterly*. Vol. 84, No. 2 (June 2003):344–58.

DUNPHY, HARRY. "World Bank: Sub-Saharan Africa Sees Growth." 2006. [Online] Available April 24, 2006, at http://news.yahoo.com

DUREX GLOBAL SEX SURVEY. Reported in *Time* (October 30, 2000):31.

DURKHEIM, EMILE. *The Division of Labor in Society*. New York: Free Press, 1964a; orig. 1893.

———. *The Rules of Sociological Method*. New York: Free Press, 1964b; orig. 1895.

———. *The Elementary Forms of Religious Life*. New York: Free Press, 1965; orig. 1915.

———. *Suicide*. New York: Free Press, 1966; orig. 1897.

DWORKIN, ANDREA. *Intercourse*. New York: Free Press, 1987.

DWORKIN, RONALD W. "Where Have All the Nurses Gone?" *Public Interest*. Vol. 148 (Summer 2002):23–36.

EBAUGH, HELEN ROSE FUCHS. *Becoming an Ex: The Process of Role Exit*. Chicago: University of Chicago Press, 1988.

EBOH, CAMILLUS. "Nigerian Woman Loses Appeal against Stoning Death." [Online] Available August 19, 2002, at http://news.yahoo.com

ECK, DIANA L. *A New Religious America: How a "Christian Country" Has Become the World's Most Religiously Diverse Nation*. San Francisco: HarperSanFrancisco, 2001.

EDWARDS, TAMALA M. "Revolt of the Gentry." *Time* (June 15, 1998):34–35.

———. "Flying Solo." *Time* (August 28, 2000):47–55.

EHRENREICH, BARBARA. *The Hearts of Men: American Dreams and the Flight from Commitment*. Garden City, N.Y.: Anchor Books, 1983.

———. "The Real Truth about the Female Body." *Time* (March 15, 1999):56–65.

———. *Nickel and Dimed: On (Not) Getting By in America*. New York: Holt, 2001.

EICHLER, MARGRIT. *Nonsexist Research Methods: A Practical Guide*. Winchester, Mass.: Unwin Hyman, 1988.

EISENBERG, DANIEL. "Paying to Keep Your Job." *Time* (October 15, 2001):80–83.

EKMAN, PAUL. "Biological and Cultural Contributions to Body and Facial Movements in the Expression of Emotions." In AMELIE OKSENBURG RORTY, ed., *Explaining Emotions*. Berkeley: University of California Press, 1980a:73–101.

———. *Face of Man: Universal Expression in a New Guinea Village*. New York: Garland Press, 1980b.

———. *Telling Lies: Clues to Deceit in the Marketplace, Politics, and Marriage*. New York: Norton, 1985.

ELIAS, ROBERT. *The Politics of Victimization: Victims, Victimology and Human Rights*. New York: Oxford University Press, 1986.

ELLIOT, DELBERT S., and SUZANNE S. AGETON. "Reconciling Race and Class Differences in Self-Reported and Official Estimates of Delinquency." *American Sociological Review*. Vol. 45, No. 1 (February 1980):95–110.

ELLISON, CHRISTOPHER G., JOHN P. BARTKOWSKI, and MICHELLE L. SEGAL. "Do Conservative Protestant Parents Spank More Often? Further Evidence from the National Survey of Families and Households." *Social Science Quarterly*. Vol. 77, No. 3 (September 1996):663–73.

ELMER-DEWITT, PHILIP. "Now for the Truth about Americans and Sex." *Time* (October 17, 1994):62–70.

EMBER, MELVIN, and CAROL R. EMBER. "The Conditions Favoring Matrilocal versus Patrilocal Residence." *American Anthropologist*. Vol. 73, No. 3 (June 1971):571–94.

———. *Anthropology*. 6th ed. Englewood Cliffs, N.J.: Prentice Hall, 1991.

EMERSON, JOAN P. "Behavior in Private Places: Sustaining Definitions of Reality in Gynecological Examinations." In HANS PETER DREITZEL, ed., *Recent Sociology*. Vol. 2. New York: Collier, 1970:74–97.

EMERSON, MICHAEL O., GEORGE YANCEY, and KAREN J. CHAI. "Does Race Matter in Residential Segregation? Exploring the Preferences of White Americans." *American Sociological Review*. Vol. 66, No. 6 (December 2001):922–35.

ENGELS, FRIEDRICH. *The Origin of the Family*. Chicago: Kerr, 1902; orig. 1884.

ENGLAND, PAULA. "Three Reviews on Marriage." *Contemporary Sociology*. Vol. 30, No. 6 (November 2001):564–65.

ENGLAND, PAULA, JOAN M. HERMSEN, and DAVID A. COTTER. "The Devaluation of Women's Work: A Comment on Tam." *American Journal of Sociology*. Vol. 105, No. 6 (May 2000):1741–60.

ERIKSON, ERIK H. *Childhood and Society*. New York: Norton, 1963; orig. 1950.

ERIKSON, KAI T. *Everything in Its Path: Destruction of Community in the Buffalo Creek Flood*. New York: Simon & Schuster, 1976.

———. *A New Species of Trouble: Explorations in Disaster, Trauma, and Community*. New York: Norton, 1994.

———. Lecture delivered at Kenyon College, Gambier, Ohio, February 7, 2005a.

———. *Wayward Puritans: A Study in the Sociology of Deviance*. New York: Wiley, 2005b; orig. 1966.

ERIKSON, ROBERT S., NORMAN R. LUTTBEG, and KENT L. TEDIN. *American Public Opinion: Its Origins, Content, and Impact*. 2d ed. New York: Wiley, 1980.

ESTES, RICHARD J. "The Commercial Sexual Exploitation of Children in the U.S., Canada, and Mexico." Reported in "Study Explores Sexual Exploitation." [Online] Available September 10, 2001, at http://news.yahoo.com

ETZIONI, AMITAI. *A Comparative Analysis of Complex Organization: On Power, Involvement, and Their Correlates*. Rev. and enlarged ed. New York: Free Press, 1975.

———. "How to Make Marriage Matter." *Time* (September 6, 1993):76.

———. "The Responsive Community: A Communitarian Perspective." *American Sociological Review*. Vol. 61, No. 1 (February 1996):1–11.

———. *My Brother's Keeper: A Memoir and a Message*. Lanham, Md.: Rowman & Littlefield, 2003.

EVELYN, JAMILAH. "Community Colleges Play Too Small a Role in Teacher Education, Report Concludes." *Chronicle of Higher Education Online*. [Online] Available October 24, 2002, at http://chronicle.com/daily/2002/10/2002102403n.htm

FAGAN, JEFFREY, FRANKLIN E. ZIMRING, and JUNE KIM. "Declining Homicide in New York City: A Tale of Two Trends." *National Institute of Justice Journal*. Vol. 237 (October 1998):12–13.

FALLON, A. E., and P. ROZIN. "Sex Differences in Perception of Desirable Body Shape." *Journal of Abnormal Psychology*. Vol. 94, No. 1 (1985):100–05.

FARLEY, CHRISTOPHER JOHN. "Winning the Right to Fly." *Time* (August 28, 1995):62–64.

FATTAH, HASSAN. "A More Diverse Community." *American Demographics*. Vol. 24, No. 7 (July/August 2002):39–43.

FEAGIN, JOE R., and VERA HERNÁN. *Liberation Sociology*. Boulder, Colo.: Westview Press, 2001.

FEATHERMAN, DAVID L., and ROBERT M. HAUSER. *Opportunity and Change*. New York: Academic Press, 1978.

FEDARKO, KEVIN. "Land Mines: Cheap, Deadly, and Cruel." *Time* (May 13, 1996):54–55.

FEDERAL BUREAU OF INVESTIGATION. *Crime in the United States, 2004*. 2005. [Online] Available May 3, 2006, at http://www.fbi.gov/publications.htm

FEDERAL ELECTION COMMISSION. "PAC Financial Activity Increases." August 30, 2006. [Online] Available September 24, 2006, at http://www.fec.gov/press/press2006/20060828pac/20060830pac.html

FELLMAN, BRUCE. "Taking the Measure of Children's TV." *Yale Alumni Magazine* (April 1995):46–51.

"Female Opinion and Defense since September 11th." *Society*. Vol. 39, No. 3 (March/April 2002):2.

FERNANDEZ, ROBERTO M., and NANCY WEINBERG. "Sifting and Sorting: Personal Contacts and Hiring in a Retail Bank." *American Sociological Review*. Vol. 62, No. 6 (December 1997):883–902.

FERRARO, KENNETH F., and JESSICA A. KELLEY-MOORE. "Cumulative Disadvantage and Health: Long-Term Consequences of Obesity?" *American Sociological Review.* Vol. 68, No. 5 (October 2003):707–29.

FERREE, MYRA MARX, and BETH B. HESS. *Controversy and Coalition: The New Feminist Movement across Four Decades of Change.* 3d ed. New York: Routledge, 1995.

FETTO, JOHN. "Lean on Me." *American Demographics.* Vol. 22, No. 12 (December 2000):16–17.

———. "Gay Friendly?" *American Demographics.* Vol. 24, No. 5 (May 2002a):16.

———. "Roomier Rentals." *American Demographics.* Vol. 24, No. 5 (May 2002b):17.

———. "Me Gusta TV." *American Demographics.* Vol. 24, No. 11 (January 2003):14–15.

FIREBAUGH, GLENN. "Growth Effects of Foreign and Domestic Investment." *American Journal of Sociology.* Vol. 98, No. 1 (July 1992):105–30.

———. "Does Foreign Capital Harm Poor Nations? New Estimates Based on Dixon and Boswell's Measures of Capital Penetration." *American Journal of Sociology.* Vol. 102, No. 2 (September 1996):563–75.

———. "Empirics of World Income Inequality." *American Journal of Sociology.* Vol. 104, No. 6 (May 1999):1597–1630.

———. "The Trend in Between-Nation Income Inequality." *Annual Review of Sociology.* Vol. 26 (2000):323–39.

FIREBAUGH, GLENN, and FRANK D. BECK. "Does Economic Growth Benefit the Masses? Growth, Dependence, and Welfare in the Third World." *American Sociological Review.* Vol. 59, No. 5 (October 1994):631–53.

FIREBAUGH, GLENN, and KENNETH E. DAVIS. "Trends in Antiblack Prejudice, 1972–1984: Region and Cohort Effects." *American Journal of Sociology.* Vol. 94, No. 2 (September 1988):251–72.

FIREBAUGH, GLENN, and DUMITRU SANDU. "Who Supports Marketization and Democratization in Post-Communist Romania?" *Sociological Forum.* Vol. 13, No. 3 (September 1998):521–41.

FISHER, ELIZABETH. *Woman's Creation: Sexual Evolution and the Shaping of Society.* Garden City, N.Y.: Anchor/Doubleday, 1979.

FISHER, ROGER, and WILLIAM URY. "Getting to Yes." In WILLIAM M. EVAN and STEPHEN HILGARTNER, eds., *The Arms Race and Nuclear War.* Englewood Cliffs, N.J.: Prentice Hall, 1988:261–68.

FISKE, ALAN PAIGE. "The Cultural Relativity of Selfish Individualism: Anthropological Evidence That Humans Are Inherently Sociable." In MARGARET S. CLARK, ed., *Prosocial Behavior.* Newbury Park, Calif.: Sage, 1991:176–214.

FITZGERALD, JIM. "Martha Stewart Enjoys Comforts of Home." [Online] Available March 6, 2005, at http://news.yahoo.com.

FITZGERALD, JOAN, and LOUISE SIMMONS. "From Consumption to Production: Labor Participation in Grass-Roots Movements in Pittsburgh and Hartford." *Urban Affairs Quarterly.* Vol. 26, No. 4 (June 1991):512–31.

FLAHERTY, MICHAEL G. "A Formal Approach to the Study of Amusement in Social Interaction." *Studies in Symbolic Interaction.* Vol. 5. New York: JAI Press, 1984:71–82.

———. "Two Conceptions of the Social Situation: Some Implications of Humor." *Sociological Quarterly.* Vol. 31, No. 1 (Spring 1990).

FOBES, RICHARD. "Creative Problem Solving." *Futurist.* Vol. 30, No. 1 (January/February 1996):19–22.

FONDA, DAREN. "The Male Minority." *Time* (December 11, 2000):58–60.

———. "Selling in Tongues." *Time* (Global Business edition, November 2001):B12–B16.

FORD, CLELLAN S., and FRANK A. BEACH. *Patterns of Sexual Behavior.* New York: Harper Bros., 1951.

FOUCAULT, MICHEL. *The History of Sexuality: An Introduction.* Vol. 1. ROBERT HURLEY, trans. New York: Vintage Books, 1990; orig. 1978.

FRANK, ANDRÉ GUNDER. *On Capitalist Underdevelopment.* Bombay: Oxford University Press, 1975.

———. *Crisis in the World Economy.* New York: Holmes & Meier, 1980.

———. *Reflections on the World Economic Crisis.* New York: Monthly Review Press, 1981.

FRANKLIN, JOHN HOPE. *From Slavery to Freedom: A History of Negro Americans.* 3d ed. New York: Vintage Books, 1967.

FRAZIER, E. FRANKLIN. *Black Bourgeoisie: The Rise of a New Middle Class.* New York: Free Press, 1965.

FREDRICKSON, GEORGE M. *White Supremacy: A Comparative Study in American and South African History.* New York: Oxford University Press, 1981.

FREEDMAN, ESTELLE B. *No Turning Back: The History of Feminism and the Future of Women.* New York: Ballantine Books, 2002.

FREEDOM HOUSE. *Freedom in the World, 2006.* [Online] Available June 2, 2006, at http://www.freedomhouse.org

FRENCH, MARILYN. *Beyond Power: On Women, Men, and Morals.* New York: Summit Books, 1985.

FRIEDMAN, MEYER, and RAY H. ROSENMAN. *Type A Behavior and Your Heart.* New York: Fawcett Crest, 1974.

FUGITA, STEPHEN S., and DAVID J. O'BRIEN. "Structural Assimilation, Ethnic Group Membership, and Political Participation among Japanese Americans: A Research Note." *Social Forces.* Vol. 63, No. 4 (June 1985):986–95.

FULLER, REX, and RICHARD SCHOENBERGER. "The Gender Salary Gap: Do Academic Achievement, Intern Experience, and College Major Make a Difference?" *Social Science Quarterly.* Vol. 72, No. 4 (December 1991):715–26.

FURSTENBERG, FRANK F., JR., and ANDREW CHERLIN. *Divided Families: What Happens to Children When Parents Part.* Cambridge, Mass.: Harvard University Press, 1991.

GAGNÉ, PATRICIA, and RICHARD TEWKSBURY. "Conformity Pressures and Gender Resistance among Transgendered Individuals." *Social Problems.* Vol. 45, No. 1 (February 1998):81–101.

GAGNÉ, PATRICIA, RICHARD TEWKSBURY, and DEANNA McGAUGHEY. "Coming Out and Crossing Over: Identity Formation and Proclamation in a Transgender Community." *Gender and Society.* Vol. 11, No. 4 (August 1997):478–508.

GALLAGHER, CHARLES A. "Miscounting Race: Explaining Whites' Misperceptions of Racial Group Size." *Sociological Perspectives.* Vol. 46, No. 3 (2003):381–96.

GALLAGHER, MAGGIE. "Does Bradley Know What Poverty Is?" *New York Post* (October 28, 1999):37.

GALLUP ORGANIZATION. Data reported in "Americans and Homosexual Civil Unions." *Society.* Vol. 40, No. 1 (December 2002):2.

GALSTER, GEORGE. "Black Suburbanization: Has It Changed the Relative Location of Races?" *Urban Affairs Quarterly.* Vol. 26, No. 4 (June 1991):621–28.

GAMORAN, ADAM. "The Variable Effects of High-School Tracking." *American Sociological Review.* Vol. 57, No. 6 (December 1992):812–28.

GANS, HERBERT J. *People and Plans: Essays on Urban Problems and Solutions.* New York: Basic Books, 1968.

GARDYN, REBECCA. "The Mating Game." *American Demographics.* Vol. 24, No. 7 (July/August 2002):33–37.

GARFINKEL, HAROLD. "Conditions of Successful Degradation Ceremonies." *American Journal of Sociology.* Vol. 61, No. 2 (March 1956):420–24.

———. *Studies in Ethnomethodology.* Cambridge, Mass.: Polity Press, 1967.

GARREAU, JOEL. *Edge City.* New York: Doubleday, 1991.

GEERTZ, CLIFFORD. "Common Sense as a Cultural System." *Antioch Review.* Vol. 33, No. 1 (Spring 1975):5–26.

GELLES, RICHARD J., and CLAIRE PEDRICK CORNELL. *Intimate Violence in Families.* 2d ed. Newbury Park, Calif.: Sage, 1990.

GEOHIVE. "Agglomerations." [Online] Available October 3, 2005, at http://www.geohive.com/charts/city_million.php

GERBER, THEODORE P., and MICHAEL HOUT. "More Shock Than Therapy: Market Transition, Employment, and Income in Russia, 1991–1995." *American Journal of Sociology.* Vol. 104, No. 1 (July 1998):1–50.

GERGEN, DAVID. "King of the World." *U.S. News & World Report* (February 25, 2002):84.

GERLACH, MICHAEL L. *The Social Organization of Japanese Business.* Berkeley: University of California Press, 1992.

GESCHWENDER, JAMES A. *Racial Stratification in America.* Dubuque, Iowa: Brown, 1978.

GEWERTZ, DEBORAH. "A Historical Reconsideration of Female Dominance among the Chambri of Papua New Guinea." *American Ethnologist.* Vol. 8, No. 1 (1981):94–106.

GIBBS, NANCY. "The Pulse of America along the River." *Time* (July 10, 2000):42–46.

———. "What Kids (Really) Need." *Time* (April 30, 2001):48–49.

GIDDENS, ANTHONY. *The Transformation of Intimacy.* Cambridge: Polity Press, 1992.

GILBERTSON, GRETA A., and DOUGLAS T. GURAK. "Broadening the Enclave Debate: The Dual Labor Market Experiences of Dominican and Colombian Men in New York City." *Sociological Forum.* Vol. 8, No. 2 (June 1993):205–20.

GILLIGAN, CAROL. *In a Different Voice: Psychological Theory and Women's Development.* Cambridge, Mass.: Harvard University Press, 1982.

GILLON, RAANAN. "Euthanasia in the Netherlands: Down the Slippery Slope?" *Journal of Medical Ethics.* Vol. 25, No. 1 (February 1999):3–4.

GIMENEZ, MARTHA E. "Silence in the Classroom: Some Thoughts about Teaching in the 1980s." *Teaching Sociology.* Vol. 17, No. 2 (April 1989):184–91.

GIOVANNINI, MAUREEN. "Female Anthropologist and Male Informant: Gender Conflict in a Sicilian Town." In JOHN J. MACIONIS and NIJOLE V. BENOKRAITIS, eds., *Seeing Ourselves: Classic, Contemporary, and Cross-Cultural Readings in Sociology.* 2d ed. Englewood Cliffs, N.J.: Prentice Hall, 1992:27–32.

GLEICK, ELIZABETH. "The Marker We've Been Waiting For." *Time* (April 7, 1997):28–42.

GLENMARY RESEARCH CENTER. *Major Religious Families by Counties of the United States: 2000* (map). Nashville, Tenn.: Glenmary Research Center, 2002.

GLENN, NORVAL D., and BETH ANN SHELTON. "Regional Differences in Divorce in the United States." *Journal of Marriage and the Family.* Vol. 47, No. 3 (August 1985):641–52.

GLUECK, SHELDON, and ELEANOR GLUECK. *Unraveling Juvenile Delinquency.* New York: Commonwealth Fund, 1950.

GOESLING, BRIAN. "Changing Income Inequalities within and between Nations: New Evidence." *American Sociological Review.* Vol. 66, No. 5 (October 2001):745–61.

GOFFMAN, ERVING. *The Presentation of Self in Everyday Life.* Garden City, N.Y.: Anchor Books, 1959.

———. *Asylums: Essays on the Social Situation of Mental Patients and Other Inmates.* Garden City, N.Y.: Anchor Books, 1961.

———. *Stigma: Notes on the Management of Spoiled Identity.* Englewood Cliffs, N.J.: Prentice Hall, 1963.

———. *Interactional Ritual: Essays on Face-to-Face Behavior.* Garden City, N.Y.: Anchor Books, 1967.

———. *Gender Advertisements.* New York: Harper Colophon, 1979.

GOLDBERG, BERNARD. *Bias: A CBS Insider Exposes How the Media Distort the News.* Washington, D.C.: Regnery, 2002.

GOLDBERG, STEVEN. *The Inevitability of Patriarchy.* New York: Morrow, 1974.

GOLDBERGER, PAUL. Lecture delivered at Kenyon College, Gambier, Ohio, September 22, 2002.

GOLDEN, DANIEL. "Some Community Colleges Fudge the Facts to Attract Foreign Students." *Wall Street Journal* (April 2, 2002):B1, B4.

GOLDEN, FREDERIC. "Lying Faces Unmasked." *Time* (April 5, 1999):52.

GOLDEN, FREDERIC, and MICHAEL D. LEMONICK. "The Race Is Over." *Time* (July 3, 2000):18–23.

GOLDFIELD, MICHAEL. "Rebounding Unions Target Service Sector." *Population Today.* Vol. 28, No. 7 (October 2000):3, 10.

GOLDSMITH, H. H. "Genetic Influences on Personality from Infancy." *Child Development.* Vol. 54, No. 2 (April 1983):331–35.

GOLDSTEIN, JOSHUA R., and CATHERINE T. KENNEY. "Marriage Delayed or Marriage Forgone? New Cohort Forecasts of First Marriage for U.S. Women." *American Sociological Review.* Vol. 66, No. 4 (August 2001):506–19.

GOODE, WILLIAM J. "The Theoretical Importance of Love." *American Sociological Review.* Vol. 24, No. 1 (February 1959):38–47.

———. "Encroachment, Charlatanism, and the Emerging Profession: Psychology, Sociology and Medicine." *American Sociological Review.* Vol. 25, No. 6 (December 1960):902–14.

GORDON, JAMES S. "The Paradigm of Holistic Medicine." In ARTHUR C. HASTINGS ET AL., eds., *Health for the Whole Person: The Complete Guide to Holistic Medicine.* Boulder, Colo.: Westview Press, 1980:3–27.

GORSKI, PHILIP S. "Historicizing the Secularization Debate: Church, State, and Society in Late Medieval and Early Modern Europe, ca. 1300 to 1700." *American Sociological Review.* Vol. 65, No. 1 (February 2000):138–67.

GOTHAM, KEVIN FOX. "Race, Mortgage Lending, and Loan Rejections in a U.S. City." *Sociological Focus.* Vol. 31, No. 4 (October 1998):391–405.

GOTTFREDSON, MICHAEL R., and TRAVIS HIRSCHI. "National Crime Control Policies." *Society.* Vol. 32, No. 2 (January/February 1995):30–36.

GOTTMANN, JEAN. *Megalopolis.* New York: Twentieth Century Fund, 1961.

GOUGH, KATHLEEN. "The Origin of the Family." In JOHN J. MACIONIS and NIJOLE V. BENOKRAITIS, eds., *Seeing Ourselves: Classic, Contemporary, and Cross-Cultural Readings in Sociology.* Englewood Cliffs, N.J.: Prentice Hall, 1989.

GOULD, STEPHEN J. "Evolution as Fact and Theory." *Discover* (May 1981):35–37.

GRATTET, RYKEN. "Hate Crimes: Better Data or Increasing Frequency?" *Population Today.* Vol. 28, No. 5 (July 2000):1, 4.

GREELEY, ANDREW M. "Religious Revival in Eastern Europe." *Society.* Vol. 39, No. 2 (January/February 2002):76–77.

GREEN, GARY PAUL, LEANN M. TIGGES, and DANIEL DIAZ. "Racial and Ethnic Differences in Job-Search Strategies in Atlanta, Boston, and Los Angeles." *Social Science Quarterly.* Vol. 80, No. 2 (June 1999):263–90.

GREENBERG, DAVID F. *The Construction of Homosexuality.* Chicago: University of Chicago Press, 1988.

GREENE, BOB. "Empty House on the Prairie." *New York Times* (March 2, 2005). [Online] Available May 24, 2005, at http://www.researchnavigator.com

GREENFIELD, LAWRENCE A. *Child Victimizers: Violent Offenders and Their Victims.* Washington, D.C.: U.S. Bureau of Justice Statistics, 1996.

GREENSPAN, STANLEY I. *The Four-Thirds Solution: Solving the Child-Care Crisis in America.* Cambridge, Mass.: Perseus, 2001.

GURAK, DOUGLAS T., and JOSEPH P. FITZPATRICK. "Intermarriage among Hispanic Ethnic Groups in New York City." *American Journal of Sociology.* Vol. 87, No. 4 (January 1982):921–34.

GURNETT, KATE. "On the Forefront of Feminism." *Albany Times Union* (July 5, 1998):G1, G6.

GWYNNE, S. C., and JOHN F. DICKERSON. "Lost in the E-Mail." *Time* (April 21, 1997):88–90.

HABERMAS, JÜRGEN. *Toward a Rational Society: Student Protest, Science, and Politics.* JEREMY J. SHAPIRO, trans. Boston: Beacon Press, 1970.

HACKER, HELEN MAYER. "Women as a Minority Group." *Social Forces.* Vol. 30 (October 1951):60–69.

HADAWAY, C. KIRK, PENNY LONG MARLER, and MARK CHAVES. "What the Polls Don't Show: A Closer Look at U.S. Church Attendance." *American Sociological Review.* Vol. 58, No. 6 (December 1993):741–52.

HADDEN, JEFFREY K., and CHARLES E. SWAIN. *Prime Time Preachers: The Rising Power of Televangelism.* Reading, Mass.: Addison-Wesley, 1981.

HAGAN, JACQUELINE MARIA. "Social Networks, Gender, and Immigrant Incorporation: Resources and Restraints." *American Sociological Review.* Vol. 63, No. 1 (February 1998):55–67.

HAIG, ROBIN ANDREW. *The Anatomy of Humor: Biopsychosocial and Therapeutic Perspectives.* Springfield, Ill.: Thomas, 1988.

HALBERSTAM, DAVID. *The Reckoning.* New York: Avon Books, 1986.

HALBFINGER, DAVID M., and STEVEN A. HOLMES. "Military Mirrors Working-Class America." *New York Times* (March 20, 2003). [Online] Available April 28, 2005, at http://www.researchnavigator.com

HALEDJIAN, DEAN. *How to Tell a Businessman from a Businesswoman.* Annandale: Northern Virginia Community College, 1997.

HALL, JOHN R., and MARY JO NEITZ. *Culture: Sociological Perspectives.* Englewood Cliffs, N.J.: Prentice Hall, 1993.

HALL, KELLEY J., and BETSY LUCAL. "Tapping in Parallel Universes: Using Superhero Comic Books in Sociology Courses." *Teaching Sociology.* Vol. 27, No. 1 (January 1999):60–66.

HALLINAN, MAUREEN T. "The Sociological Study of Social Change." *American Sociological Review.* Vol. 62, No. 1 (February 1997):1–11.

HAMER, DEAN, and PETER COPELAND. *The Science of Desire: The Search for the Gay Gene and the Biology of Behavior.* New York: Simon & Schuster, 1994.

HAMILTON, ANITA. "Speeders, Say Cheese." *Time* (September 17, 2001):32.

HAMILTON, BRADY E., ET AL. "Births: Preliminary Data for 2004." *National Vital Statistics Reports.* Vol. 54, No. 8 (December 29, 2005).

HAMRICK, MICHAEL H., DAVID J. ANSPAUGH, and GENE EZELL. *Health.* Columbus, Ohio: Merrill, 1986.

HAN, WENJUI, and JANE WALDFOGEL. "Child Care Costs and Women's Employment: A Comparison of Single and Married Mothers with Preschool-Aged Children." *Social Science Quarterly.* Vol. 83, No. 5 (September 2001):552–68.

HANDLIN, OSCAR. *Boston's Immigrants, 1790–1865: A Study in Acculturation.* Cambridge, Mass.: Harvard University Press, 1941.

HANEY, CRAIG, CURTIS BANKS, and PHILIP G. ZIMBARDO. "Interpersonal Dynamics in a Simulated Prison." *International Journal of Criminology and Penology.* Vol. 1 (1973):69–97.

HANEY, LYNNE. "After the Fall: East European Women since the Collapse of State Socialism." *Contexts.* Vol. 1, No. 3 (Fall 2002):27–36.

HARLOW, HARRY F., and MARGARET KUENNE HARLOW. "Social Deprivation in Monkeys." *Scientific American* (November 1962):137–46.

HARPSTER, PAULA, and ELIZABETH MONK-TURNER. "Why Men Do Housework: A Test of Gender Production and the Relative Resources Model." *Sociological Focus.* Vol. 31, No. 1 (February 1998):45–59.

HARRIES, KEITH D. *Serious Violence: Patterns of Homicide and Assault in America.* Springfield, Ill.: Thomas, 1990.

HARRINGTON, MICHAEL. *The New American Poverty.* New York: Penguin, 1984.

HARRIS, CHAUNCY D., and EDWARD L. ULLMAN. "The Nature of Cities." *Annals.* Vol. 242 (November 1945):7–17.

HARRIS, DAVID R., and JEREMIAH JOSEPH SIM. "Who Is Multiracial? Assessing the Complexity of Lived Race." *American Sociological Review.* Vol. 67, No. 4 (August 2002):614–27.

HARRIS, MARVIN. *Cultural Anthropology.* 2d ed. New York: Harper & Row, 1987.

HARRISON, C. KEITH. "Black Athletes at the Millennium." *Society.* Vol. 37, No. 3 (March/April 2000):35–39.

HAUB, CARL. "How Many People Have Ever Lived on Earth?" *Population Today.* Vol. 30, No. 8 (November/December 2002):3–4.

HAWTHORNE, PETER. "South Africa's Makeover." *Time* (July 12, 1999). [Online] Available September 29, 2006, at http://jcgi.pathfinder.com/time/magazine/article/0,9171,991487,00.html

HAYDEN, THOMAS. "Losing Our Voices." *U.S. News & World Report* (May 26, 2003):42.

HAYWARD, MARK D., EILEEN M. CRIMMINS, TONI P. MILES, and YU YANG. "The Significance of Socioeconomic Status in Explaining the Racial Gap in Chronic Health Conditions." *American Sociological Review.* Vol. 65, No. 6 (December 2000):910–30.

HEATH, JULIA A., and W. DAVID BOURNE. "Husbands and Housework: Parity or Parody?" *Social Science Quarterly.* Vol. 76, No. 1 (March 1995):195–202.

HELGESEN, SALLY. *The Female Advantage: Women's Ways of Leadership.* New York: Doubleday, 1990.

HELIN, DAVID W. "When Slogans Go Wrong." *American Demographics.* Vol. 14, No. 2 (February 1992):14.

HELLMICH, NANCI. "Environment, Economics Partly to Blame." *USA Today* (October 9, 2002):9

HENLEY, D., NANCY, MYKOL HAMILTON, and BARRIE THORNE. "Womanspeak and Manspeak: Sex Differences in Communication, Verbal and Nonverbal." In JOHN J. MACIONIS and NIJOLE V. BENOKRAITIS, eds., *Seeing Ourselves: Classic, Contemporary, and Cross-Cultural Readings in Sociology.* 2d ed. Englewood Cliffs, N.J.: Prentice Hall, 1992:10–15.

HEREK, GREGORY M. "Myths about Sexual Orientation: A Lawyer's Guide to Social Science Research." *Law and Sexuality.* Vol. 1 (1991):133–72.

HERMAN, DIANNE. "The Rape Culture." In JOHN J. MACIONIS and NIJOLE V. BENOKRAITIS, eds., *Seeing Ourselves: Classic, Contemporary, and Cross-Cultural Readings in Sociology.* 5th ed. Upper Saddle River, N.J.: Prentice Hall, 2001.

HERPERTZ, SABINE C., and HENNING SASS. "Emotional Deficiency and Psychopathy." *Behavioral Sciences and the Law.* Vol. 18, No. 5 (September/October 2000):567–80.

HERRING, HUBERT B. "An Aging Nation Is Choosing Younger Bosses." *New York Times* (February 20, 2005). [Online] Available April 12, 2005, at http://www.researchnavigator.com

HERRNSTEIN, RICHARD J., and CHARLES MURRAY. *The Bell Curve: Intelligence and Class Structure in American Life.* New York: Free Press, 1994.

HERZOG, BRAD. "A Man of His Words." *Cornell Alumni Magazine.* Vol. 106, No. 4 (January/February 2004):58–63.

HESS, BETH B. "Breaking and Entering the Establishment: Committing Social Change and Confronting the Backlash." *Social Problems.* Vol. 46, No. 1 (February 1999):1–12.

HEYMANN, PHILIP B. "Civil Liberties and Human Rights in the Aftermath of September 11." *Harvard Journal of Law and Public Policy.* Vol. 25, No. 2 (Spring 2002):441–57.

HILL, MARK E. "Race of the Interviewer and Perception of Skin Color: Evidence from the Multi-City Study of Urban Inequality." *American Sociological Review.* Vol. 67, No. 1 (February 2002):99–108.

HIRSCHI, TRAVIS. *Causes of Delinquency.* Berkeley: University of California Press, 1969.

HOBSON, KATHERINE. "Kissing Cousins." *U.S. News & World Report* (April 15, 2002):77.

HOCHSCHILD, ARLIE RUSSELL. "Emotion Work, Feeling Rules, and Social Structure." *American Journal of Sociology.* Vol. 85, No. 3 (November 1979):551–75.

———. *The Managed Heart.* Berkeley: University of California Press, 1983.

HOGAN, RICHARD, and CAROLYN C. PERRUCCI. "Producing and Reproducing the Class and Status Differences: Racial and Gender Gaps in U.S. Employment and Retirement Income." *Social Problems.* Vol. 45, No. 4 (November 1998):528–49.

HOLMES, THOMAS H., and RICHARD H. RAHE. "The Social Readjustment Rating Scale." *Journal of Psychosomatic Research.* Vol. 11 (1967):213–18.

HOPE, TRINA L., HAROLD G. GRASMICK, and LAURA J. POINTON. "The Family in Gottfredson and Hirschi's General Theory of Crime: Structure, Parenting, and Self-Control." *Sociological Focus.* Vol. 36, No. 4 (November 2003): 291–311.

HORN, WADE F., and DOUGLAS TYNAN. "Revamping Special Education." *Public Interest* (Summer 2001):36–53.

HORTON, HAYWARD DERRICK. "Critical Demography: The Paradigm of the Future?" *Sociological Forum.* Vol. 14, No. 3 (September 1999):363–67.

HOSTETLER, JOHN A. *Amish Society.* 3d ed. Baltimore: Johns Hopkins University Press, 1980.

HOUT, MICHAEL. "More Universalism, Less Structural Mobility: The American Occupational Structure in the 1980s." *American Journal of Sociology.* Vol. 95, No. 6 (May 1998):1358–400.

HOUT, MICHAEL, CLEM BROOKS, and JEFF MANZA. "The Persistence of Classes in Post-Industrial Societies." *International Sociology.* Vol. 8, No. 3 (September 1993):259–77.

HOUT, MICHAEL, and CLAUDE W. FISCHER. "Why More Americans Have No Religious Preference: Politics and Generations." *American Sociological Review.* Vol. 67, No. 2 (April 2002):165–90.

HOUT, MICHAEL, ANDREW M. GREELEY, and MELISSA J. WILDE. "The Demographic Imperative in Religious Change in the United States." *American Journal of Sociology.* Vol. 107, No. 2 (September 2001):468–500.

HOWDEN, DANIEL. "Latin America's New Socialist Revolution." *New Zealand Herald* (December 20, 2005). [Online] Available February 13, 2006, at http://www.nzherald.co.nz

HOYERT, DONNA L., MELONIE P. HERON, SHERRY L. MURPHY, and HSIANG-CHING KUNG. "Deaths: Final Data for 2003." *National Vital Statistics Reports.* Vol. 54, No. 13 (April 19, 2006).

HOYERT, DONNA L., HSIANG-CHING KUNG, and BETTY L. SMITH. "Deaths: Preliminary Data for 2003." *National Vital Statistics Report.* Vol. 53, No. 15 (February 28, 2005).

HOYT, HOMER. *The Structure and Growth of Residential Neighborhoods in American Cities.* Washington, D.C.: Federal Housing Administration, 1939.

HSU, FRANCIS L. K. *The Challenge of the American Dream: The Chinese in the United States.* Belmont, Calif.: Wadsworth, 1971.

HUCHINGSON, JAMES E. "Science and Religion." *Miami* (Fla.) *Herald* (December 25, 1994):1M, 6M.

HUFFMAN, KAREN. *Psychology in Action.* New York: Wiley, 2000.

HUGHES, MICHAEL, and MELVIN E. THOMAS. "The Continuing Significance of Race Revisited: A Study of Race, Class, and Quality of Life in America, 1972 to 1996." *American Sociological Review.* Vol. 63, No. 6 (December 1998):785–95.

HUMAN RIGHTS WATCH. "Children's Rights: Child Labor." 2006. [Online] Available April 9, 2006, at http://www.hrw.org/children/labor.htm

HUMMER, ROBERT A., RICHARD G. ROGERS, CHARLES B. NAM, and FELICIA B. LE CLERE. "Race/Ethnicity, Nativity, and U.S. Adult Mortality." *Social Science Quarterly.* Vol. 80, No. 1 (March 1999):136–53.

HUNTER, JAMES DAVISON. *American Evangelicalism: Conservative Religion and the Quandary of Modernity.* New Brunswick, N.J.: Rutgers University Press, 1983.

———. "Conservative Protestantism." In PHILIP E. HAMMOND, ed., *The Sacred in a Secular Age.* Berkeley: University of California Press, 1985:50–66.

———. *Evangelicalism: The Coming Generation.* Chicago: University of Chicago Press, 1987.

HYMOWITZ, CAROL. "World's Poorest Women Advance by Entrepreneurship." *Wall Street Journal* (September 9, 1995):B1.

IANNACCONE, LAURENCE R. "Why Strict Churches Are Strong." *American Journal of Sociology.* Vol. 99, No. 5 (March 1994):1180–211.

IDE, THOMAS R., and ARTHUR J. CORDELL. "Automating Work." *Society.* Vol. 31, No. 6 (September/October 1994):65–71.

INCIARDI, JAMES A. *Elements of Criminal Justice.* 2d ed. New York: Oxford University Press, 2000.

INCIARDI, JAMES A., HILARY L. SURRATT, and PAULO R. TELLES. *Sex, Drugs, and HIV/AIDS in Brazil.* Boulder, Colo.: Westview Press, 2000.

INGLEHART, RONALD. *Modernization and Postmodernization: Cultural, Economic, and Political Change in 43 Societies.* Princeton, N.J.: Princeton University Press, 1997.

INGLEHART, RONALD, and WAYNE E. BAKER. "Modernization, Cultural Change, and the Persistence of Traditional Values." *American Sociological Review.* Vol. 65, No. 1 (February 2000):19–51.

INGLEHART, RONALD, ET AL. *World Values Surveys and European Values Surveys, 1981–1984, 1990–1993, and 1995–1997.* [Computer file] ICPSR version. Ann Arbor, Mich. Interuniversity Consortium for Political and Social Research, 2000.

INTERNAL REVENUE SERVICE. "Corporation Income Tax Returns, 2001." *Statistics of Income Bulletin.* Summer 2004. [Online] Available November 3, 2004, at http://www.irs.gov/pub/irs-soi/01corart.pdf

———. "Corporation Income Tax Returns, 2002." *Statistics of Income Bulletin.* Summer 2005. [Online] Available June 2, 2006, at http://www.irs.gov/pub/irs-soi/02corart.pdf

INTERNATIONAL MONETARY FUND. *World Economic Outlook: Asset Prices and the Business Cycle.* May 2000. [Online] Available October 9, 2004, at http://www.imf.org/external/pubs/ft/weo/2000/01/index.htm

INTERNATIONAL TELECOMMUNICATION UNION. *World Telecommunication Development Report.* Data cited in WORLD BANK, *2006 World Development Indicators.* Washington, D.C.: World Bank, 2006.

INTER-PARLIAMENTARY UNION. "Women in National Parliaments." 2006. [Online] Available May 24, 2006, at http://www.ipu.org/wmn-e/classif.htm and http://www.ipu.org/wmn-e/world.htm

ISRAEL, GLENN D., LIONEL J. BEAULIEU, and GLEN HARTLESS. "The Influence of Family and Community Social Capital on Educational Achievement." *Rural Sociology.* Vol. 66, No. 1 (March 2001):43–68.

JACOBS, DAVID, and JASON T. CARMICHAEL. "The Political Sociology of the Death Penalty: A Pooled Time-Series Analysis." *American Sociological Review.* Vol. 67, No. 1 (February 2002):109–31.

JACOBS, DAVID, and RONALD E. HELMS. "Toward a Political Model of Incarceration: A Time-Series Examination of Multiple Explanations for Prison Admission Rates." *American Journal of Sociology.* Vol. 102, No. 2 (September 1996):323–57.

JACOBSON, JENNIFER. "Professors Are Finding Better Pay and More Freedom at Community Colleges." *Chronicle of Higher Education Online* (March 7, 2003). [Online] Available March 7, 2003, at http://www.chronicle.com

JACQUET, CONSTANT H., and ALICE M. JONES. *Yearbook of American and Canadian Churches, 1991.* Nashville, Tenn.: Abingdon Press, 1991.

JANIS, IRVING L. *Victims of Groupthink.* Boston: Houghton Mifflin, 1972.

———. *Crucial Decisions: Leadership in Policymaking and Crisis Management.* New York: Free Press, 1989.

JAPANESE MINISTRY OF HEALTH, LABOUR, AND WELFARE. *International Comparisons of Divorce Rates.* June 1, 2005. [Online] Available June 13, 2006, at http://web-jpn.org/stat/stats/02VIT33.html

JENKINS, J. CRAIG. *Images of Terror: What We Can and Can't Know about Terrorism.* Hawthorne, N.Y.: Aldine de Gruyter, 2003.

JENKINS, J. CRAIG, and MICHAEL WALLACE. "The Generalized Action Potential of Protest Movements: The New Class, Social Trends, and Political Exclusion Explanations." *Sociological Forum.* Vol. 11, No. 2 (June 1996):183–207.

JENNESS, VALERIE, and RYKEN GRATTET. *Making a Hate Crime: From Movement to Law Enforcement.* New York: Russell Sage Foundation, 2001.

JOHNSON, BARRY W., and BRIAN G. RAUB. "Personal Wealth, 2001." *Statistics of Income Bulletin* (Winter 2005–06). 2006. [Online] Available September 20, 2006, at http://www.irs.gov/pub/irs-soi/01pwart.pdf

JOHNSON, CATHRYN. "Gender, Legitimate Authority, and Leader–Subordinate Conversations." *American Sociological Review.* Vol. 59, No. 1 (February 1994):122–35.

JOHNSON, DIRK. "Death of a Small Town." *Newsweek* (September 10, 2001):30–31.

JOHNSON, KENNETH M. "The Rural Rebound." *Population Reference Bureau Reports on America.* Vol. 1, No. 3 (September 1999). [Online] Available October 9, 2004, at http://www.prb.org/Content/NavigationMenu/PRB/AboutPRB/Reports_on_America/ReportonAmericaRuralRebound.pdf

JOHNSON, KENNETH M., and GLENN V. FUGUITT. "Continuity and Change in Rural Migration Patterns, 1950–1995." *Rural Sociology.* Vol. 65, No. 1 (March 2000):27–49.

JOHNSON, PAUL. "The Seven Deadly Sins of Terrorism." In BENJAMIN NETANYAHU, ed., *International Terrorism.* New Brunswick, N.J.: Transaction Books, 1981:12–22.

JOHNSTON, DAVID CAY. "Voting, America's Not Keen On. Coffee Is Another Matter." *New York Times* (November 10, 1996):sec.4, p. 2.

JOHNSTON, R. J. "Residential Area Characteristics." In DAVID T. HERBERT and R. J. JOHNSTON, eds., *Social Areas in Cities.* Vol. 1: *Spatial Processes and Form.* New York: Wiley, 1976:193–235.

JONES, ANDREW E. G., and DAVID WILSON. *The Urban Growth Machine: Critical Perspectives.* Albany: State University of New York Press, 1999.

JONES, D. GARETH. "Brain Death." *Journal of Medical Ethics.* Vol. 24, No. 4 (August 1998):237–43.

JONES, JUDY. "More Miners Will Be Offered Free X-Rays; Federal Agency Wants to Monitor Black-Lung Cases." *Louisville Courier Journal* (May 13, 1999):1A.

JONES, KATHARINE W. *Accent on Privilege: English Identities and Anglophilia in the U.S.* Philadelphia: Temple University Press, 2001.

JORDAN, ELLEN, and ANGELA COWAN. "Warrior Narratives in the Kindergarten Classroom: Renegotiating the Social Contract?" *Gender and Society.* Vol. 9, No. 6 (December 1995):727–43.

JOSEPHY, ALVIN M., JR. *Now That the Buffalo's Gone: A Study of Today's American Indians.* New York: Knopf, 1982.

JOYNSON, ROBERT B. "Fallible Judgments." *Society.* Vol. 31, No. 3 (March/April 1994):45–52.

KAIN, EDWARD L. "A Note on the Integration of AIDS into the Sociology of Human Sexuality." *Teaching Sociology.* Vol. 15, No. 4 (July 1987):320–23.

———. *The Myth of Family Decline: Understanding Families in a World of Rapid Social Change.* Lexington, Mass.: Lexington Books, 1990.

KALLEBERG, ARNE L., BARBARA F. RESKIN, and KEN HUDSON. "Bad Jobs in America: Standard and Nonstandard Employment Relations and Job Quality in the United States." *American Sociological Review.* Vol. 65, No 2 (April 2000):256–78.

KALLEBERG, ARNE L., and MARK E. VAN BUREN. "Is Bigger Better? Explaining the Relationship between Organization Size and Job Rewards." *American Sociological Review.* Vol. 61, No. 1 (February 1996):47–66.

KAMINER, WENDY. "Volunteers: Who Knows What's in It for Them?" *Ms.* (December 1984):93–96, 126–28.

———. "Demasculinizing the Army." *New York Times Review of Books* (June 15, 1997):7.

KANE, EMILY W. "Racial and Ethnic Variations in Gender-Related Attitudes." *Annual Review of Sociology.* Vol. 26 (2000):419–39.

KANTER, ROSABETH MOSS. *Men and Women of the Corporation.* New York: Basic Books, 1977.

KANTER, ROSABETH MOSS, and BARRY A. STEIN. "The Gender Pioneers: Women in an Industrial Sales Force." In ROSABETH MOSS KANTER and BARRY A. STEIN, eds., *Life in Organizations.* New York: Basic Books, 1979:134–60.

KANTROWITZ, BARBARA, and PAT WINGERT. "Unmarried with Children." *Newsweek* (May 28, 2001):46–52.

———. "What's at Stake." *Newsweek* (January 27, 2003):30–37.

KAO, GRACE. "Group Images and Possible Selves among Adolescents: Linking Stereotypes to Expectations by Race and Ethnicity." *Sociological Forum.* Vol. 15, No. 3 (September 2000):407–30.

KAPLAN, DAVID E., and MICHAEL SCHAFFER. "Losing the Psywar." *U.S. News & World Report* (October 8, 2001):46.

KAPTCHUK, TED. "The Holistic Logic of Chinese Medicine." In SHEPARD BLISS ET AL., eds., *The New Holistic Health Handbook.* Lexington, Mass.: Steven Greene Press/Penguin, 1985:41.

KARATNYCKY, ADRIAN. "The 2001–2002 Freedom House Survey of Freedom: The Democracy Gap." In *Freedom in the World, 2001–2002.* New York: Freedom House, 2002:7–18.

KARP, DAVID A., and WILLIAM C. YOELS. "The College Classroom: Some Observations on the Meaning of Student Participation." *Sociology and Social Research.* Vol. 60, No. 4 (July 1976):421–39.

KARRFALT, WAYNE. "A Multicultural Mecca." "*American Demographics.* Vol. 25, No. 4 (May 2003):54–55.

KATES, ROBERT W. "Ending Hunger: Current Status and Future Prospects." *Consequences.* Vol. 2, No. 2 (Summer 1996):3–11.

KAUFMAN, ROBERT L. "Assessing Alternative Perspectives on Race and Sex Employment Segregation." *American Sociological Review.* Vol. 67, No. 4 (August 2002):547–72.

KAUFMAN, WALTER. *Religions in Four Dimensions: Existential, Aesthetic, Historical, and Comparative.* New York: Reader's Digest Press, 1976.

KAY, PAUL, and WILLETT KEMPTON. "What Is the Sapir-Whorf Hypothesis?" *American Anthropologist.* Vol. 86, No. 1 (March 1984):65–79.

KEISTER, LISA A. *Wealth in America: Trends in Wealth Inequality.* New York: Cambridge University Press, 2000.

———. "Religion and Wealth: The Role of Religious Affiliation and Participation in Early Adult Asset Accumulation." *Social Forces,* Vol. 82, No. 1 (September 2003):173–205.

KEISTER, LISA A., and STEPHANIE MOLLER. "Wealth Inequality in the United States." *Annual Review of Sociology.* Vol. 26 (2000):63–81.

KELLER, HELEN. *The Story of My Life.* New York: Doubleday, 1903.

KELLERT, STEPHEN R., and F. HERBERT BORMANN. "Closing the Circle: Weaving Strands among Ecology, Economics, and Ethics." In F. HERBERT BORMANN and STEPHEN R. KELLERT, eds., *Ecology, Economics, and Ethics: The Broken Circle.* New Haven, Conn.: Yale University Press, 1991:205–10.

KENT, MARY M., and MARK MATHER. "What Drives U.S. Population Growth?" *Population Bulletin.* Vol. 57, No. 4 (December 2002):3–40.

KENTOR, JEFFREY. "The Long-Term Effects of Foreign Investment Dependence on Economic Growth, 1940–1990." *American Journal of Sociology.* Vol. 103, No. 4 (January 1998):1024–46.

———. "The Long-Term Effects of Globalization on Income Inequality, Population Growth, and Economic Development." *Social Problems*. Vol. 48, No. 4 (November 2001):435–55.

KERCKHOFF, ALAN C., RICHARD T. CAMPBELL, and IDEE WINFIELD-LAIRD. "Social Mobility in Great Britain and the United States." *American Journal of Sociology*. Vol. 91, No. 2 (September 1985):281–308.

KERR, RICHARD A. "Climate Models Heat Up." *Science Now* (January 26, 2005):1–3.

KEYS, JENNIFER. "Feeling Rules That Script the Abortion Experience." Paper presented at the annual meeting of the American Sociological Association, Chicago, August 2002.

KIDRON, MICHAEL, and RONALD SEGAL. *The New State of the World Atlas*. New York: Simon & Schuster, 1991.

KILBOURNE, BROCK K. "The Conway and Siegelman Claims against Religious Cults: An Assessment of Their Data." *Journal for the Scientific Study of Religion*. Vol. 22, No. 4 (December 1983):380–85.

KILGORE, SALLY B. "The Organizational Context of Tracking in Schools." *American Sociological Review*. Vol. 56, No. 2 (April 1991):189–203.

KING, KATHLEEN PIKER, and DENNIS E. CLAYSON. "The Differential Perceptions of Male and Female Deviants." *Sociological Focus*. Vol. 21, No. 2 (April 1988):153–64.

KINGSBURY, ALEX. "Did Bush Do the Math?" *U.S. News & World Report*. Vol. 140, No. 5 (February 13, 2006):28.

KINKEAD, GWEN. *Chinatown: A Portrait of a Closed Society*. New York: Harper-Collins, 1992.

KINSEY, ALFRED C., WARDELL B. POMEROY, and CLYDE E. MARTIN. *Sexual Behavior in the Human Male*. Philadelphia: Saunders, 1948.

KINSEY, ALFRED C., WARDELL B. POMEROY, CLYDE E. MARTIN, and PAUL H. GEBHARD. *Sexual Behavior in the Human Female*. Philadelphia: Saunders, 1953.

KITTRIE, NICHOLAS N. *The Right to Be Different: Deviance and Enforced Therapy*. Baltimore: Johns Hopkins University Press, 1971.

KITZINGER, CELIA. "Heteronormativity in Action: Reproducing the Heterosexual Nuclear Family in After-Hours Medical Calls." *Social Problems*. Vol. 52, No. 4 (November 2005):477–98.

KLEINFELD, JUDITH. "Student Performance: Males versus Females." *Public Interest* (Winter 1999):3–20.

KLUCKHOHN, CLYDE. "As an Anthropologist Views It." In ALBERT DEUTH, ed., *Sex Habits of American Men*. New York: Prentice Hall, 1948.

KNOX, NOELLE. "European Gay Union Trends Influence U.S. Debate." *USA Today* (July 14, 2004):5A.

KOHLBERG, LAWRENCE. *The Psychology of Moral Development: The Nature and Validity of Moral Stages*. New York: Harper & Row, 1981.

KOHLBERG, LAWRENCE, and CAROL GILLIGAN. "The Adolescent as Philosopher: The Discovery of Self in a Postconventional World." *Daedalus*. Vol. 100 (Fall 1971):1051–86.

KOHN, MELVIN L. *Class and Conformity: A Study in Values*. 2d ed. Homewood, Ill.: Dorsey Press, 1977.

KONO, CLIFFORD, DONALD PALMER, ROGER FRIEDLAND, and MATTHEW ZAFONTE. "Lost in Space: The Geography of Corporate Interlocking Directorates." *American Journal of Sociology*. Vol. 103, No. 4 (January 1998):863–911.

KOONTZ, STEPHANIE. *The Way We Never Were: American Families and the Nostalgia Trap*. New York: Basic Books, 1992.

KORNHAUSER, WILLIAM. *The Politics of Mass Society*. New York: Free Press, 1959.

KORZENIEWICZ, ROBERTO P., and KIMBERLY AWBREY. "Democratic Transitions and the Semiperiphery of the World Economy." *Sociological Forum*. Vol. 7, No. 4 (December 1992):609–40.

KOZOL, JONATHAN. *Rachel and Her Children: Homeless Families in America*. New York: Crown, 1988.

———. *Savage Inequalities: Children in America's Schools*. New York: Harper Perennial, 1992.

KRAL, BRIGITTA. "The Eyes of Jane Elliott." *Horizon*. 2000. [On-line] Available June 8, 2005, at http://www.horizonmag.com/4/jane-elliott.asp

KRAYBILL, DONALD B. *The Riddle of Amish Culture*. Baltimore: Johns Hopkins University Press, 1989.

———. "The Amish Encounter with Modernity." In DONALD B. KRAYBILL and MARC A. OLSHAN, eds., *The Amish Struggle with Modernity*. Hanover, N.H.: University Press of New England, 1994:21–33.

KRAYBILL, DONALD B., and MARC A. OLSHAN, eds. *The Amish Struggle with Modernity*. Hanover, N.H.: University Press of New England, 1994.

KRIESI, HANSPETER. "New Social Movements and the New Class in the Netherlands." *American Journal of Sociology*. Vol. 94, No. 5 (March 1989):1078–116.

KRUGMAN, PAUL. "For Richer: How the Permissive Capitalism of the Boom Destroyed American Equality." *New York Times Magazine* (September 20, 2002):62 ff.

KRUKS, GABRIEL N. "Gay and Lesbian Homeless/Street Youth: Special Issues and Concerns." *Journal of Adolescent Health*. Special Issue No. 12 (1991):515–18.

KRYSAN, MARIA. "Community Undesirability in Black and White: Examining Racial Residential Preferences through Community Perceptions." *Social Problems*. Vol. 49, No. 4 (November 2002):521–43.

KÜBLER-ROSS, ELISABETH. *On Death and Dying*. New York: Macmillan, 1969.

KUBURSI, ATIF. "Water Crisis, the Environment, and Arab Sustainable Development." 2004. [Online] Available September 15, 2006, at http://www.idrc.ca/en/ev-96888-201-1-DO_TOPIC.html

KUNKEL, DALE, ET AL. *Sex on TV, 2005*. Menlo Park, Calif.: Henry J. Kaiser Family Foundation, 2005. [Online] Available September 13, 2006, at http://www.kff.org/entmedia/upload/Sex-on-TV-4-Full-Report.pdf

KUUMBA, M. BAHATI. "A Cross-Cultural Race/Class/Gender Critique of Contemporary Population Policy: The Impact of Globalization." *Sociological Forum*. Vol. 14, No. 3 (March 1999):447–63.

KUZNETS, SIMON. "Economic Growth and Income Inequality." *American Economic Review*. Vol. 14, No. 1 (March 1955):1–28.

———. *Modern Economic Growth: Rate, Structure, and Spread*. New Haven, Conn.: Yale University Press, 1966.

LACAYO, RICHARD. "The Brawl over Sprawl." *Time* (March 22, 1999):44–48.

LACH, JENNIFER. "The Color of Money." *American Demographics*. Vol. 21, No. 2 (February 1999):59–60.

LADD, JOHN. "The Definition of Death and the Right to Die." In JOHN LADD, ed., *Ethical Issues Relating to Life and Death*. New York: Oxford University Press, 1979:118–45.

LAI, H. M. "Chinese." In *Harvard Encyclopedia of American Ethnic Groups*. Cambridge, Mass.: Harvard University Press, 1980:217–33.

LANDSBERG, MITCHELL. "Health Disaster Brings Early Death in Russia." *Washington Times* (March 15, 1998):A8.

LANGBEIN, LAURA I., and ROSEANA BESS. "Sports in School: Source of Amity or Antipathy?" *Social Science Quarterly*. Vol. 83, No. 2 (June 2002):436–54.

LAPCHICK, RICHARD. "The 2005 Racial and Gender Report Cards." Institute for Diversity and Ethics in Sport, University of Central Florida. 2006. [Online] Available October 1, 2006, at http://www.bus.ucf.edu/sport/cgi-bin/site/sitew.cgi?page=/ides/index.htm

LAPPÉ, FRANCES MOORE, and JOSEPH COLLINS. *World Hunger: Twelve Myths*. New York: Grove Press/Food First Books, 1986.

LAREAU, ANNETTE. "Invisible Inequality: Social Class and Childrearing in Black Families and White Familes." *American Sociological Review*. Vol. 67, No. 5 (October 2002):747–76.

LAROSSA, RALPH, and DONALD C. REITZES. "Two? Two and One-Half? Thirty Months? Chronometrical Childhood in Early Twentieth-Century America." *Sociological Forum*. Vol. 166, No. 3 (September 2001):385–407.

LASLETT, BARBARA. "Family Membership, Past and Present." *Social Problems*. Vol. 25, No. 5 (June 1978):476–90.

LASLETT, PETER. *The World We Have Lost: England before the Industrial Age*. 3d ed. New York: Scribner, 1984.

LASSWELL, MARK. "A Tribe at War: Not the Yanomami, the Anthropologists." *Wall Street Journal* (November 17, 2000):A17.

LAUMANN, EDWARD O., JOHN H. GAGNON, ROBERT T. MICHAEL, and STUART MICHAELS. *The Social Organization of Sexuality: Sexual Practices in the United States*. Chicago: University of Chicago Press, 1994.

LEACH, COLIN WAYNE. "Democracy's Dilemma: Explaining Racial Inequality in Egalitarian Societies." *Sociological Forum*. Vol. 17, No. 4 (December 2002):681–96.

LEACOCK, ELEANOR. "Women's Status in Egalitarian Societies: Implications for Social Evolution." *Current Anthropology*. Vol. 19, No. 2 (June 1978):247–75.

LEAVITT, JUDITH WALZER. "Women and Health in America: An Overview." In JUDITH WALZER LEAVITT, ed., *Women and Health in America*. Madison: University of Wisconsin Press, 1984:3–7.

LEBON, GUSTAVE. *The Crowd: A Study of the Popular Mind*. New York: Viking Press, 1960; orig. 1895.

LEE, SHARON M., and BARRY EDMONSTON. "New Marriages, New Families: U.S. Racial and Hispanic Intermarriage." *Population Bulletin*. Vol. 60, No. 2 (June 2005):3–36.

LEFEBVRE, HENRI. *The Production of Space*. Oxford: Blackwell, 1991.

LELAND, JOHN. "Bisexuality." *Newsweek* (July 17, 1995):44–49.

LEMERT, EDWIN M. *Social Pathology.* New York: McGraw-Hill, 1951.

———. *Human Deviance, Social Problems, and Social Control.* 2d ed. Englewood Cliffs, N.J.: Prentice Hall, 1972.

LEMONICK, MICHAEL D. "The Search for a Murder Gene." *Time.* Vol. 164, No. 3 (January 20, 2003):100.

———. "Are We Losing Our Edge?" *Time.* Vol. 167, No. 7 (February 13, 2006):22–33.

LENGERMANN, PATRICIA MADOO, and JILL NIEBRUGGE-BRANTLEY. *The Women Founders: Sociology and Social Theory, 1830–1930.* New York: McGraw-Hill, 1998.

LENGERMANN, PATRICIA MADOO, and RUTH A. WALLACE. *Gender in America: Social Control and Social Change.* Englewood Cliffs, N.J.: Prentice Hall, 1985.

LENSKI, GERHARD E. *Power and Privilege: A Theory of Social Stratification.* New York: McGraw-Hill, 1966.

LEONARD, EILEEN B. *Women, Crime, and Society: A Critique of Theoretical Criminology.* White Plains, N.Y.: Longman, 1982.

LETHBRIDGE-ÇEJKU, MARGARET, DEBORAH ROSE, and JACKLINE VICKERIE. *Summary Health Statistics for U.S. Adults: National Health Interview Survey, 2004.* Vital and Health Statistics, Series 10, No. 228. Hyattsville, Md.: National Center for Health Statistics, 2006.

LETHBRIDGE-ÇEJKU, MARGARET, and JACKLINE VICKERIE. *Summary Health Statistics for U.S. Adults: National Health Interview Survey, 2003.* Vital and Health Statistics, Series 10, No. 225. Hyattsville, Md.: National Center for Health Statistics, 2005.

LETSCHER, MARTIN. "Tell Fads from Trends." *American Demographics.* Vol. 16, No. 12 (December 1994):38–45.

LEVAY, SIMON. *The Sexual Brain.* Cambridge, Mass.: MIT Press, 1993.

LEVER, JANET. "Sex Differences in the Complexity of Children's Play and Games." *American Sociological Review.* Vol. 43, No. 4 (August 1978):471–83.

LEVIN, JACK, and ARNOLD ARLUKE. *Gossip: The Inside Scoop.* New York: Plenum, 1987.

LEVINE, MICHAEL P. *Student Eating Disorders: Anorexia Nervosa and Bulimia.* Washington, D.C.: National Educational Association, 1987.

———. "Reducing Hostility Can Prevent Heart Disease." *Mount Vernon News* (August 7, 1990):4A.

LEVINE, SAMANTHA. "The Price of Child Abuse." *U.S. News & World Report* (April 9, 2001):58.

———. "Playing God in Illinois." *U.S. News & World Report* (January 13, 2003):13.

LEWIS, FLORA. "The Roots of Revolution." *New York Times Magazine* (November 11, 1984):70–86.

LEWIS, OSCAR. *The Children of Sanchez.* New York: Random House, 1961.

LIAZOS, ALEXANDER. "The Poverty of the Sociology of Deviance: Nuts, Sluts, and Preverts." *Social Problems.* Vol. 20, No. 1 (Summer 1972):103–20.

———. *People First: An Introduction to Social Problems.* Needham Heights, Mass.: Allyn & Bacon, 1982.

LICHTER, DANIEL T., and MARTHA L. CROWLEY. "Poverty in America: Beyond Welfare Reform." *Population Bulletin.* Vol. 57, No. 2 (June 2002):3–34.

LICHTER, DANIEL T., and RUKMALIE JAYAKODY. "Welfare Reform: How Do We Measure Success?" *Annual Review of Sociology.* Vol. 28 (2002):117–41.

LICHTER, S. ROBERT, and DANIEL R. AMUNDSON. "Distorted Reality: Hispanic Characters in TV Entertainment." In CLARA E. RODRIGUEZ, ed., *Latin Looks: Images of Latinas and Latinos in the U.S. Media.* Boulder, Colo.: Westview Press, 1997:57–79.

LIN, NAN, KAREN COOK, and RONALD S. BURT, eds. *Social Capital: Theory and Research.* Hawthorne, N.Y.: Aldine de Gruyter, 2001.

LIN, NAN, and WEN XIE. "Occupational Prestige in Urban China." *American Journal of Sociology.* Vol. 93, No. 4 (January 1988):793–832.

LINDAUER, DAVID L., and AKILA WEERAPANA. "Relief for Poor Nations." *Society.* Vol. 39, No. 3 (March/April 2002):54–58.

LINDLAW, SCOTT. "President Signs Education Bill." [Online] Available January 8, 2002, at http://news.yahoo.com

LINDSTROM, BONNIE. "Chicago's Post-Industrial Suburbs." *Sociological Focus.* Vol. 28, No. 4 (October 1995):399–412.

LING, PYAU. "Causes of Chinese Emigration." In AMY TACHIKI, ed., *Roots: An Asian American Reader.* Los Angeles: UCLA Asian American Studies Center, 1971:134–38.

LINN, MICHAEL. "Class Notes 1970." *Cornell Alumni News.* Vol. 99, No. 2 (September 1996):25.

LINO, MARK. *Expenditures on Children by Families, 2005.* U.S. Department of Agriculture, Center for Nutrition Policy and Promotion. Miscellaneous Publication No. 1528-2005. Washington, D.C.: U.S. Government Printing Office, 2006.

LINTON, RALPH. "One Hundred Percent American." *American Mercury.* Vol. 40, No. 160 (April 1937a):427–29.

———. *The Study of Man.* New York: Appleton-Century, 1937b.

LIPSET, SEYMOUR MARTIN. *Canada and the United States.* CHARLES F. DONAN and JOHN H. SIGLER, eds. Englewood Cliffs, N.J.: Prentice Hall, 1985.

LISKA, ALLEN E., and BARBARA D. WARNER. "Functions of Crime: A Paradoxical Process." *American Journal of Sociology.* Vol. 96, No. 6 (May 1991):1441–63.

LITTLE, CRAIG, and ANDREA RANKIN. "Why Do They Start It? Explaining Reported Early Teen Sexual Activity." *Sociological Forum.* Vol. 16, No. 4 (December 2001):703–29.

LIVINGSTON, KEN. "Politics and Mental Illness." *Public Interest.* No. 143 (Winter, 1999):105–9.

LOBO, SUSAN. "Census-Taking and the Invisibility of Urban American Indians." *Population Today.* Vol. 30, No. 4 (May/June 2002):3–4.

LOGAN, JOHN R., RICHARD D. ALBA, and WENQUAN ZHANG. "Immigrant Enclaves and Ethnic Communities in New York and Los Angeles." *American Sociological Review.* Vol. 67, No. 2 (April 2002):299–322.

LORD, MARY. "Good Teachers, the Newest Imports." *U.S. News & World Report* (April 9, 2001):54.

LORD, WALTER. *A Night to Remember.* Rev. ed. New York: Holt, Rinehart and Winston, 1976.

LOVEMAN, MARA. "Is 'Race' Essential?" *American Sociological Review.* Vol. 64, No. 6 (December 1999):890–98.

LUND, DALE A. "Caregiving." In *Encyclopedia of Adult Development.* Phoenix, Ariz.: Oryx Press, 1993:57–63.

LUNDMAN, RICHARD L. Correspondence with author, 1999.

LYNCH, MICHAEL, and DAVID BOGEN. "Sociology's Asociological 'Core': An Examination of Textbook Sociology in Light of the Sociology of Scientific Knowledge." *American Sociological Review.* Vol. 62, No. 3 (June 1997):481–93.

LYND, ROBERT S., and HELEN MERRELL LYND. *Middletown in Transition.* New York: Harcourt, Brace & World, 1937.

LYNOTT, PATRICIA PASSUTH, and BARBARA J. LOGUE. "The 'Hurried Child': The Myth of Lost Childhood in Contemporary American Society." *Sociological Forum.* Vol. 8, No. 3 (September 1993):471–91.

MABRY, MARCUS, and TOM MASLAND. "The Man after Mandela." *Newsweek* (June 7, 1999):54–55.

MACE, DAVID, and VERA MACE. *Marriage East and West.* Garden City, N.Y.: Doubleday/Dolphin, 1960.

MACIONIS, JOHN J. "Intimacy: Structure and Process in Interpersonal Relationships." *Alternative Lifestyles.* Vol. 1, No. 1 (February 1978):113–30.

———. "A Sociological Analysis of Humor." Presentation to the Texas Junior College Teachers Association, Houston, 1987.

MACIONIS, JOHN J., and LINDA M. GERBER. *Sociology.* 5th Canadian ed. Toronto: Pearson Prentice Hall, 2005.

MACIONIS, JOHN J., and VINCENT R. PARRILLO. *Cities and Urban Life.* 4th ed. Upper Saddle River, N.J.: Prentice Hall, 2007.

MACKAY, JUDITH. *The Penguin Atlas of Human Sexual Behavior.* New York: Penguin, 2000.

MACPHERSON, KAREN. "Children Have a Full-Time Media Habit, Study Says." *Toledo Blade* (November 18, 1999):3.

MADDOX, SETMA. "Organizational Culture and Leadership Style: Factors Affecting Self-Managed Work Team Performance." Paper presented at the annual meeting of the Southwest Social Science Association, Dallas, February 1994.

MALTHUS, THOMAS ROBERT. *First Essay on Population, 1798.* London: Macmillan, 1926; orig. 1798.

MANZA, JEFF, and CLEM BROOKS. "The Religious Factor in U.S. Presidential Elections, 1960–1992." *American Journal of Sociology.* Vol. 103, No. 1 (July 1997):38–81.

MARATHONGUIDE.COM. "Marathon Records." 2006. [Online] Available May 24, 2006, at http://www.marathonguide.com/#Records

MARCUSE, HERBERT. *One-Dimensional Man.* Boston: Beacon Press, 1964.

MARÍN, GERARDO, and BARBARA VAN OSS MARÍN. *Research with Hispanic Populations.* Newbury Park, Calif.: Sage, 1991.

MARKLEIN, MARY BETH. "Optimism Rises as SAT Math Scores Hit 30-Year High." *USA Today* (August 30, 2000):1A.

MARKOFF, JOHN. "Remember Big Brother? Now He's a Company Man." *New York Times* (March 31, 1991):7.

MARKS, ALEXANDRA. "U.S. Shelters Swell—with Families." *Christian Science Monitor.* [Online] Available December 4, 2001, at http://www.csmonitor.com

MARQUAND, ROBERT. "Worship Shift: Americans Seek Feeling of 'Awe.'" *Christian Science Monitor* (May 28, 1997):1, 8.

MARQUAND, ROBERT, and DANIEL B. WOOD. "Rise in Cults as Millennium Approaches." *Christian Science Monitor* (March 28, 1997):1, 18.

MARQUARDT, ELIZABETH, and NORVAL GLENN. *Hooking Up, Hanging Out, and Hoping for Mr. Right.* New York: Institute for American Values, 2001.

MARSHALL, SUSAN E. "Ladies against Women: Mobilization Dilemmas of Antifeminist Movements." *Social Problems.* Vol. 32, No. 4 (April 1985):348–62.

MARTIN, CAROL LYNN, and RICHARD A. FABES. "The Stability and Consequences of Young Children's Same-Sex Peer Interactions. "*Developmental Psychology.* Vol. 37, No. 3 (May 2001):431–46.

MARTIN, JOHN M., and ANNE T. ROMANO. *Multinational Crime: Terrorism, Espionage, Drug and Arms Trafficking.* Newbury Park, Calif.: Sage, 1992.

MARTIN, JOYCE A., ET AL. "Births: Final Data for 2003." *National Vital Statistics Report.* Vol. 54, No. 2 (September 8, 2005).

MARTINEZ, RAMIRO, JR. "Latinos and Lethal Violence: The Impact of Poverty and Inequality." *Social Problems.* Vol. 43, No. 2 (May 1996):131–46.

MARULLO, SAM. "The Functions and Dysfunctions of Preparations for Fighting Nuclear War." *Sociological Focus.* Vol. 20, No. 2 (April 1987):135–53.

MARX, KARL. *Karl Marx: Selected Writings in Sociology and Social Philosophy.* T. B. Bottomore, trans. New York:McGraw-Hill, 1964.

———. *Capital.* FRIEDRICH ENGELS, ed. New York: International Publishers, 1967; orig. 1867.

MARX, KARL, and FRIEDRICH ENGELS. "Manifesto of the Communist Party." In ROBERT C. TUCKER, ed., *The Marx-Engels Reader.* New York: Norton, 1972:331–62; orig. 1848.

MARX, LEO. "The Environment and the 'Two Cultures' Divide." In JAMES RODGER FLEMING and HENRY A. GEMERY, eds., *Science, Technology, and the Environment: Multidisciplinary Perspectives.* Akron, Ohio: University of Akron Press, 1994:3–21.

MASSEY, DOUGLAS S. "Housing Discrimination 101." *Population Today.* Vol. 28, No. 6 (August/September 2000):1, 4.

MASSEY, DOUGLAS S., and NANCY A. DENTON. "Hypersegregation in U.S. Metropolitan Areas: Black and Hispanic Segregation along Five Dimensions." *Demography.* Vol. 26, No. 3 (August 1989):373–91.

MATHEWS, T. J., and BRADY E. HAMILTON. "Trend Analysis of the Sex Ratio at Birth in the United States." *National Vital Statistics Reports.* Vol. 53, No. 20 (June 14, 2005).

MATTHIESSEN, PETER. *Indian Country.* New York: Viking Press, 1984.

MAUER, MARC. *The Crisis of the Young African American Male and the Criminal Justice System.* Report prepared for U.S. Commission on Civil Rights. Washington, D.C., April 15–16, 1999. [Online] Available October 1, 2004, at http://www.sentencingproject.org/pdfs/5022.pdf

MAYO, KATHERINE. *Mother India.* New York: Harcourt, Brace, 1927.

MCADAM, DOUG, JOHN D. MCCARTHY, and MAYER N. ZALD, eds. *Comparative Perspectives on Social Movements: Political Opportunities, Mobilizing Structures, and Cultural Framings.* New York: Cambridge University Press, 1996.

MCALLISTER, J. F. O. "Cinderella, Career Gal." *Time* (April 23, 2001):8.

MCBROOM, WILLIAM H., and FRED W. REED. "Recent Trends in Conservatism: Evidence of Non-Unitary Patterns." *Sociological Focus.* Vol. 23, No. 4 (October 1990):355–65.

MCDONALD, KIM A. "Debate over How to Gauge Global Warming Heats Up Meeting of Climatologists." *Chronicle of Higher Education.* Vol. 45, No. 22 (February 5, 1999):A17.

MCDONALD, PETER. "Low Fertility Not Politically Sustainable." *Population Today.* Vol. 29, No. 6 (August/September 2001):3, 8.

MCGURN, WILLIAM. "Philadelphia Dims Edison's Light." *Wall Street Journal* (March 20, 2002):A22.

MCKEE, VICTORIA. "Blue Blood and the Color of Money." *New York Times* (June 9, 1996):49–50.

MCLANAHAN, SARA. "Life without Father: What Happens to the Children?" *Contexts.* Vol. 1, No. 1 (Spring 2002):35–44.

MCLEOD, JANE D., and MICHAEL J. SHANAHAN. "Poverty, Parenting, and Children's Mental Health." *American Sociological Review.* Vol. 58, No. 3 (June 1993):351–66.

MCLEOD, JAY. *Ain't No Makin' It: Aspirations and Attainment in a Low-Income Neighborhood.* Boulder, Colo.: Westview Press, 1995.

MEAD, GEORGE HERBERT. *Mind, Self, and Society.* CHARLES W. MORRIS, ed. Chicago: University of Chicago Press, 1962; orig. 1934.

MEAD, MARGARET. *Sex and Temperament in Three Primitive Societies.* New York: Morrow, 1963; orig. 1935.

MEADOWS, DONELLA H., DENNIS L. MEADOWS, JORGAN RANDERS, and WILLIAM W. BEHRENS III. *The Limits to Growth: A Report on the Club of Rome's Project on the Predicament of Mankind.* New York: Universe, 1972.

MELTZER, BERNARD N. "Mead's Social Psychology." In JEROME G. MANIS and BERNARD N. MELTZER, eds., *Symbolic Interaction: A Reader in Social Psychology.* 3d ed. Needham Heights, Mass.: Allyn & Bacon, 1978.

MELUCCI, ALBERTO. *Nomads of the Present: Social Movements and Individual Needs in Contemporary Society.* Philadelphia: Temple University Press, 1989.

MENJIVAR, CECILIA. "Immigrant Kinship Networks and the Impact of the Receiving Context: Salvadorans in San Francisco in the Early 1990s." *Social Problems.* Vol. 44, No. 1 (February 1997):104–23.

MERTON, ROBERT K. "Social Structure and Anomie." *American Sociological Review.* Vol. 3, No. 6 (October 1938):672–82.

———. *Social Theory and Social Structure.* New York: Free Press, 1968.

METZ, MICHAEL E., and MICHAEL H. MINER. "Psychosexual and Psychosocial Aspects of Male Aging and Sexual Health." *Canadian Journal of Human Sexuality.* Vol. 7, No. 3 (Summer 1998):245–60.

METZGER, KURT. "Cities and Race." *Society.* Vol. 39, No. 1 (December 2001):2.

MEYER, DAVIS S., and NANCY WHITTIER. "Social Movement Spillover." *Social Problems.* Vol. 41, No. 2 (May 1994):277–98.

MICHELS, ROBERT. *Political Parties.* Glencoe, Ill.: Free Press, 1949; orig. 1911.

MILBRATH, LESTER W. *Envisioning a Sustainable Society: Learning Our Way Out.* Albany: State University of New York Press, 1989.

MILGRAM, STANLEY. "Behavioral Study of Obedience." *Journal of Abnormal and Social Psychology.* Vol. 67, No. 4 (1963):371–78.

———. "Group Pressure and Action against a Person." *Journal of Abnormal and Social Psychology.* Vol. 69, No. 2 (August 1964):137–43.

———. "Some Conditions of Obedience and Disobedience to Authority." *Human Relations.* Vol. 18 (February 1965):57–76.

———. "The Small World Problem." *Psychology Today* (May 1967):60–67.

MILLER, ALAN S., and RODNEY STARK. "Gender and Religiousness: Can Socialization Explanations Be Saved?" *American Journal of Sociology.* Vol. 107, No. 6 (May 2002):1399–423.

MILLER, ARTHUR G. *The Obedience Experiments: A Case of Controversy in Social Science.* New York: Praeger, 1986.

MILLER, FREDERICK D. "The End of SDS and the Emergence of Weatherman: Demise through Success." In JO FREEMAN, ed., *Social Movements of the Sixties and Seventies.* White Plains, N.Y.: Longman, 1983:279–97.

MILLER, G. TYLER, JR. *Living in the Environment: An Introduction to Environmental Science.* Belmont, Calif.: Wadsworth, 1992.

MILLER, MATTHEW, and PETER NEWCOMB, eds. "The Forbes 400." *Forbes* (Special issue, October 10, 2005).

MILLER, WALTER B. "Lower-Class Culture as a Generating Milieu of Gang Delinquency." In MARVIN E. WOLFGANG, LEONARD SAVITZ, and NORMAN JOHNSTON, eds., *The Sociology of Crime and Delinquency.* 2d ed. New York: Wiley, 1970:351–63; orig. 1958.

MILLER, WILLIAM J., and RICK A. MATTHEWS. "Youth Employment, Differential Association, and Juvenile Delinquency." *Sociological Focus.* Vol. 34, No. 3 (August 2001):251–68.

MILLS, C. WRIGHT. *The Power Elite.* New York: Oxford University Press, 1956.

———. *The Sociological Imagination.* New York: Oxford University Press, 1959.

MINIÑO, ARIALDI M., MELONIE P. HERON, and BETTY L. SMITH. "Deaths: Preliminary Data for 2004." *National Vital Statistics Reports.* Vol. 54, No. 19 (June 28, 2006).

MIRACLE, TINA S., ANDREW W. MIRACLE, and ROY F. BAUMEISTER. *Human Sexuality: Meeting Your Basic Needs.* Upper Saddle River, N.J.: Prentice Hall, 2003.

MIRINGOFF, MARC, and MARQUE-LUISA MIRINGOFF. "The Social Health of the Nation." *Economist.* Vol. 352, No. 8128 (July 17, 1999):suppl. 6–7.

MIROWSKY, JOHN. "The Psycho-Economics of Feeling Underpaid: Distributive Justice and the Earnings of Husbands and Wives." *American Journal of Sociology.* Vol. 92, No. 6 (May 1987):1404–34.

MITCHELL, ALISON. "Give Me a Home Where the Buffalo Roam Less." *New York Times* (January 20, 2002):sec. 4, p. 5.

MOGELONSKY, MARCIA. "Reconfiguring the American Dream (House)." *American Demographics.* Vol. 19, No. 1 (January 1997):31–35.

MOLOTCH, HARVEY. "The City as a Growth Machine." *American Journal of Sociology.* Vol. 82, No. 2 (September 1976):309–33.

MONTAIGNE, FEN. "Russia Rising." *National Geographic* (September 2001):2–31.

MOORE, GWEN, ET AL. "Elite Interlocks in Three U.S. Sectors: Nonprofit, Corporate, and Government." *Social Science Quarterly.* Vol. 83, No. 3 (September 2002):726–44.

MOORE, WILBERT E. "Modernization as Rationalization: Processes and Restraints." In MANNING NASH, ed., *Essays on Economic Development and Cultural Change in Honor of Bert F. Hoselitz.* Chicago: University of Chicago Press, 1977:29–42.

———. *World Modernization: The Limits of Convergence.* New York: Elsevier, 1979.

MORSE, JODIE. "A Victory for Vouchers." *Time* (July 8, 2002b):32–34.

MOUW, TED. "Job Relocation and the Racial Gap in Unemployment in Detroit and Chicago, 1980 to 1990." *American Sociological Review.* Vol. 65, No. 5 (October 2000):730–53.

MULLER, CHANDRA, and CHRISTOPHER G. ELLISON. "Religious Involvement, Social Capital, and Adolescents' Academic Progress: Evidence from the National Education Longitudinal Study of 1988." *Sociological Focus.* Vol. 34, No. 2 (May 2001):155–83.

MUMFORD, LEWIS. *The City in History: Its Origins, Its Transformations, and Its Prospects.* New York: Harcourt, Brace & World, 1961.

MUNSON, MARTHA L., and PAUL D. SUTTON. "Births, Marriages, Divorces, and Deaths: Provisional Data for 2003." *National Vital Statistics Report.* Vol. 52, No. 22 (June 10, 2004).

———. "Births, Marriages, Divorces, and Deaths: Provisional Data for 2005." *National Vital Statistics Reports.* Vol. 54, No. 20 (July 21, 2006).

MURDOCK, GEORGE PETER. "Comparative Data on the Division of Labor by Sex." *Social Forces.* Vol. 15, No. 4 (May 1937):551–53.

———. "The Common Denominator of Cultures." In RALPH LINTON, ed., *The Science of Man in World Crisis.* New York: Columbia University Press, 1945:123–42.

———. *Social Structure.* New York: Free Press, 1965; orig. 1949.

MURRAY, STEPHEN O., and WILL ROSCOE, eds. *Studies of African Homosexualities.* New York: St. Martin's Press, 1998.

MYERS, DAVID G. *The American Paradox: Spiritual Hunger in an Age of Plenty.* New Haven, Conn.: Yale University Press, 2000.

MYERS, NORMAN. "Humanity's Growth." In SIR EDMUND HILLARY, ed., *Ecology 2000: The Changing Face of the Earth.* New York: Beaufort Books, 1984a:16–35.

———. "The Mega-Extinction of Animals and Plants." In SIR EDMUND HILLARY, ed., *Ecology 2000: The Changing Face of the Earth.* New York: Beaufort Books, 1984b:82–107.

———. "Biological Diversity and Global Security." In F. HERBERT BORMANN and STEPHEN R. KELLERT, eds., *Ecology, Economics, and Ethics: The Broken Circle.* New Haven, Conn.: Yale University Press, 1991:11–25.

MYERS, SHEILA, and HAROLD G. GRASMICK. "The Social Rights and Responsibilities of Pregnant Women: An Application of Parsons's Sick Role Model." Paper presented to the Southwestern Sociological Association, Little Rock, Arkansas, March 1989.

MYRDAL, GUNNAR. *An American Dilemma: The Negro Problem and Modern Democracy.* New York: Harper Bros., 1944.

NATIONAL CENTER FOR EDUCATION STATISTICS. *Dropout Rates in the United States, 2001.* Washington, D.C.: U.S. Government Printing Office, 2004. [Online] Available November 6, 2004, at http://www.nces.ed.gov/pubs2005/2005046.pdf

———. *Digest of Education Statistics.* 2005 Tables. [Online] Available May 24, 2006, at http://nces.ed.gov/programs/digest/d05_tf.asp

NATIONAL COALITION ON HEALTH CARE. "Health Insurance Cost." 2006. [Online] Available September 15, 2006, at http://www.nchc.org/facts/cost.shtml

NATIONAL COMMISSION ON EXCELLENCE IN EDUCATION. *A Nation at Risk.* Washington, D.C.: U.S. Government Printing Office, 1983.

NAVARRO, MIREYA. "Puerto Rican Presence Wanes in New York." *New York Times* (February 28, 2000):A1, A20.

———. "For Younger Latinas, a Shift to Smaller Families." *New York Times* (December 5, 2004). [Online] Available April 30, 2005, at http://www.researchnavigator.com

NELSON, AMY L. "The Effect of Economic Restructuring on Family Poverty in the Industrial Heartland, 1970–1990." *Sociological Focus.* Vol. 31, No. 2 (May 1998):201–16.

NELSON, JOEL I. "Work and Benefits: The Multiple Problems of Service Sector Employment." *Social Problems.* Vol. 42, No. 2 (May 1994):240–55.

NEUHOUSER, KEVIN. "The Radicalization of the Brazilian Catholic Church in Comparative Perspective." *American Sociological Review.* Vol. 54, No. 2 (April 1989):233–44.

NEWMAN, KATHERINE S. *Declining Fortunes: The Withering of the American Dream.* New York: Basic Books, 1993.

NEWMAN, WILLIAM M. *American Pluralism: A Study of Minority Groups and Social Theory.* New York: Harper & Row, 1973.

NIELSEN MEDIA RESEARCH. "Nielsen Reports Americans Watch TV at Record Levels." News release. September 29, 2005. [Online] Available August 27, 2006, at http://www.nielsenmedia.com/newsreleases/2005/AvgHoursMinutes92905.pdf

NISBET, ROBERT A. *The Quest for Community.* New York: Oxford University Press, 1969.

NOCK, STEVEN L., JAMES D. WRIGHT, and LAURA SANCHEZ. "America's Divorce Problem." *Society.* Vol. 36, No. 4 (May/June 1999):43–52.

NOLAN, PATRICK, and GERHARD LENSKI. *Human Societies.* 9th ed. Boulder, Colo.: Paradigm, 2004.

NORC. *General Social Surveys, 1972–2004: Cumulative Codebook.* Chicago: National Opinion Research Center, 2005.

NORD, MARK. "Does It Cost Less to Live in Rural Areas? Evidence from New Data on Food Scarcity and Hunger." *Rural Sociology.* Vol. 65, No. 1 (March 2000):104–25.

NOVAK, VIVECA. "The Cost of Poor Advice." *Time* (July 5, 1999):38.

NULAND, SHERWIN B. "The Hazards of Hospitalization." *Wall Street Journal* (December 2, 1999):A22.

OAKES, JEANNIE. "Classroom Social Relationships: Exploring the Bowles and Gintis Hypothesis." *Sociology of Education.* Vol. 55, No. 4 (October 1982):197–212.

———. *Keeping Track: How High Schools Structure Inequality.* New Haven, Conn.: Yale University Press, 1985.

OGBURN, WILLIAM F. *On Culture and Social Change.* Chicago: University of Chicago Press, 1964.

O'HARE, WILLIAM P., WILLIAM H. FREY, and DAN FOST. "Asians in the Suburbs." *American Demographics.* Vol. 16, No. 9 (May 1994):32–38.

O'HARROW, ROBERT, JR. "ID Theft Scam Hits D.C. Area Residents." [Online] Available February 21, 2005, at http://news.yahoo.com

OLSEN, GREGG M. "Re-Modeling Sweden: The Rise and Demise of the Compromise in a Global Economy." *Social Problems.* Vol. 43, No. 1 (February 1996):1–20.

OLZAK, SUSAN. "Labor Unrest, Immigration, and Ethnic Conflict in Urban America, 1880–1914." *American Journal of Sociology.* Vol. 94, No. 6 (May 1989):1303–33.

OMESTAD, THOMAS. "A Balance of Terror." *U.S. News & World Report* (February 3, 2003):33–35.

O'NEILL, BRIAN, and DEBORAH BALK. "World Population Futures." *Population Bulletin.* Vol. 56, No. 3 (September 2001):3–40.

"Online Privacy: It's Time for Rules in Wonderland." *Business Week* (March 20, 2000):82–96.

ORECKLIN, MICHELLE. "Earnings Report: J.K. and Judy." *Time* (January 13, 2003):72.

ORHANT, MELANIE. "Human Trafficking Exposed." *Population Today.* Vol. 30, No. 1 (January 2002):1, 4.

ORLANSKY, MICHAEL D., and WILLIAM L. HEWARD. *Voices: Interviews with Handicapped People.* Columbus, Ohio: Merrill, 1981.

ORWIN, CLIFFORD. "All Quiet on the Western Front?" *Public Interest* (Spring 1996): 3–9.

OSTRANDER, SUSAN A. "Upper-Class Women: The Feminine Side of Privilege." *Qualitative Sociology.* Vol. 3, No. 1 (Spring 1980):23–44.

———. *Women of the Upper Class.* Philadelphia: Temple University Press, 1984.

OUCHI, WILLIAM. *Theory Z: How American Business Can Meet the Japanese Challenge.* Reading, Mass.: Addison-Wesley, 1981.

"Our Cheating Hearts." Editorial. *U.S. News & World Report* (May 6, 2002):4.

OVADIA, SETH. "Race, Class, and Gender Differences in High School Seniors' Values: Applying Intersection Theory in Empirical Analysis." *Social Science Quarterly.* Vol. 82, No. 2 (June 2001):341–56.

OWEN, CAROLYN A., HOWARD C. ELSNER, and THOMAS R. MCFAUL. "A Half-Century of Social Distance Research: National Replication of the Bogardus Studies." *Sociology and Social Research.* Vol. 66 (1977):80–98.

PACKARD, MARK. Personal communication, 2002.

PAKULSKI, JAN. "Mass Social Movements and Social Class." *International Sociology.* Vol. 8, No. 2 (June 1993):131–58.

PARIS, PETER J. "The Religious World of African Americans." In Jacob Neusner, ed. *World Religions in America: An Introduction.* Rev. and exp. ed. Louisville, Ky.: Westminster/John Knox Press, 2000:48–65.

PARK, ROBERT E. *Race and Culture.* Glencoe, Ill.: Free Press, 1950.

PARRILLO, VINCENT N. "Diversity in America: A Sociohistorical Analysis." *Sociological Forum.* Vol. 9, No. 4 (December 1994):42–45.

———. *Strangers to These Shores.* 7th ed. Boston: Allyn & Bacon, 2003.

PARRILLO, VINCENT, and CHRISTOPHER DONOGHUE. "Updating the Bogardus Social Distance Studies: A New National Survey." *Social Science Journal.* Vol. 42, No. 2 (April 2005):257–71.

PARSONS, TALCOTT. "Age and Sex in the Social Structure of the United States." *American Sociological Review.* Vol. 7, No. 4 (August 1942):604–16.

———. *The Social System.* Glencoe, Ill.: Free Press, 1951.

———. *Essays in Sociological Theory.* Glencoe, Ill.: Free Press, 1954.

———. *Societies: Evolutionary and Comparative Perspectives.* Englewood Cliffs, N.J.: Prentice Hall, 1966.

PARSONS, TALCOTT, and ROBERT F. BALES, eds. *Family, Socialization and Interaction Process.* Glencoe, Ill.: Free Press, 1955.

PATTERSON, ELISSA F. "The Philosophy and Physical of Holistic Health Care: Spiritual Healing as a Workable Interpretation." *Journal of Advanced Nursing.* Vol. 27, No. 2 (February 1998):287–94.

PATTILLO-MCCOY, MARY. "Church Culture as a Strategy of Action in the Black Community." *American Sociological Review.* Vol. 63, No. 6 (December 1998):767–84.

PAUL, PAMELA. "News, Noticias, Nouvelles." *American Demographics.* Vol. 23, No. 11 (November 2001):26–31.

PEAR, ROBERT, and ERIK ECKHOLM. "When Healers Are Entrepreneurs: A Debate over Costs and Ethics." *New York Times* (June 2, 1991):1, 17.

PEARSON, DAVID E. "Post-Mass Culture." *Society.* Vol. 30, No. 5 (July/August 1993):17–22.

———. "Community and Sociology." *Society.* Vol. 32, No. 5 (July/August 1995):44–50.

PEASE, JOHN, and LEE MARTIN. "Want Ads and Jobs for the Poor: A Glaring Mismatch." *Sociological Forum.* Vol. 12, No. 4 (December 1997):545–64.

PEDERSON, DANIEL, VERN E. SMITH, and JERRY ADLER. "Sprawling, Sprawling. . . ." *Newsweek* (July 19, 1999):23–27.

PERLMUTTER, PHILIP. "Minority Group Prejudice." *Society.* Vol. 39, No. 3 (March/April 2002):59–65.

PERRUCCI, ROBERT. "Inventing Social Justice: SSSP and the Twenty-First Century." *Social Problems.* Vol. 48, No. 2 (May 2001):159–67.

PESSEN, EDWARD. *Riches, Class, and Power: America before the Civil War.* New Brunswick, N.J.: Transaction, 1990.

Peters Atlas of the World. New York: HarperCollins, 1990.

PETERSEN, TROND, ISHAK SAPORTA, and MARC-DAVID L. SEIDEL. "Offering a Job: Meritocracy and Social Networks." *American Journal of Sociology.* Vol. 106, No. 3 (November 2000):763–816.

PETERSILIA, JOAN. "Probation in the United States: Practices and Challenges." *National Institute of Justice Journal.* No. 233 (September 1997):4.

PHILADELPHIA, DESA. "Rookie Teacher, Age 50." *Time* (April 9, 2001):66–68.

———. "Tastier, Plusher—and Fast." *Time* (September 30, 2002):57.

PHILLIPS, MELANIE. "What about the Overclass?" *Public Interest* (Fall 2001):38–43.

PINCHOT, GIFFORD, and ELIZABETH PINCHOT. *The End of Bureaucracy and the Rise of the Intelligent Organization.* San Francisco: Berrett-Koehler, 1993.

PINHEY, THOMAS K., DONALD H. RUBINSTEIN, and RICHARD S. COLFAX. "Overweight and Happiness: The Reflected Self-Appraisal Hypothesis Reconsidered." *Social Science Quarterly.* Vol. 78, No. 3 (September 1997):747–55.

PINKER, STEVEN. "Are Your Genes to Blame?" *Time* (January 20, 2003):98–100.

PIRANDELLO, LUIGI. "The Pleasure of Honesty." In *To Clothe the Naked and Two Other Plays.* New York: Dutton, 1962:143–98.

PITNEY, JOHN J., JR. "What Scholars Don't Know about Term Limits." *Chronicle of Higher Education.* Vol. 41, No. 33 (April 28, 1995):A76.

PIVEN, FRANCES FOX, and RICHARD A. CLOWARD. *Poor People's Movements: Why They Succeed, How They Fail.* New York: Pantheon Books, 1977.

"Places Where the System Broke Down." *Time.* Vol. 166, No. 12 (September 19, 2005):34–41.

PODOLNY, JOEL M., and JAMES N. BARON. "Resources and Relationships: Social Networks and Mobility in the Workplace." *American Sociological Review.* Vol. 62, No. 5 (October 1997):673–93.

POLLARD, KELVIN. "Play Ball! Demographics and Major League Baseball." *Population Today.* Vol. 24, No. 4 (April 1996):3.

POLSBY, NELSON W. "Three Problems in the Analysis of Community Power." *American Sociological Review.* Vol. 24, No. 6 (December 1959):796–803.

POMER, MARSHALL I. "Labor Market Structure, Intragenerational Mobility, and Discrimination: Black Male Advancement out of Low-Paying Occupations, 1962–1973." *American Sociological Review.* Vol. 51, No. 5 (October 1986):650–59.

POPENOE, DAVID. "American Family Decline, 1960–1990: A Review and Appraisal." *Journal of Marriage and the Family.* Vol. 55, No. 3 (August 1993a):527–55.

———. "Parental Androgyny." *Society.* Vol. 30, No. 6 (September/October 1993b):5–11.

———. "Can the Nuclear Family Be Revived?" *Society.* Vol. 36, No. 5 (July/August 1999):28–30.

POPENOE, DAVID, and BARBARA DAFOE WHITEHEAD. *Should We Live Together? What Young Adults Need to Know about Cohabitation before Marriage.* New Brunswick, N.J.: National Marriage Project, 1999.

POPULATION ACTION INTERNATIONAL. *People in the Balance: Population and Resources at the Turn of the Millennium.* Washington, D.C.: Population Action International, 2000.

POPULATION REFERENCE BUREAU. *2003 World Population Data Sheet.* Washington, D.C.: Population Reference Bureau, 2003.

———. *2004 World Population Data Sheet.* Washington, D.C.: Population Reference Bureau, 2004.

———. *2006 World Population Data Sheet.* Washington, D.C.: Population Reference Bureau, 2006.

PORTER, EDUARDO. "Even 126 Sizes Do Not Fit All." *Wall Street Journal* (March 2, 2001):B1.

PORTES, ALEJANDRO, and LEIF JENSEN. "The Enclave and the Entrants: Patterns of Ethnic Enterprise in Miami before and after Mariel." *American Sociological Review.* Vol. 54, No. 6 (December 1989):929–49.

POSTEL, SANDRA. "Facing Water Scarcity." In LESTER R. BROWN ET AL., eds., *State of the World 1993: A Worldwatch Institute Report on Progress toward a Sustainable Society.* New York: Norton, 1993:22–41.

POWELL, CHRIS, and GEORGE E. C. PATON, eds. *Humor in Society: Resistance and Control.* New York: St. Martin's Press, 1988.

PRIMEGGIA, SALVATORE, and JOSEPH A. VARACALLI. "Southern Italian Comedy: Old to New World." In JOSEPH V. SCELSA, SALVATORE J. LA GUMINA, and LYDIO TOMASI, eds., *Italian Americans in Transition.* New York: American Italian Historical Association, 1990:241–52.

PRYOR, JOHN H., ET AL. *The American Freshman: National Norms for Fall 2005.* Los Angeles: UCLA Higher Education Research Institute, 2005.

PUTKA, GARY. "SAT to Become a Better Gauge." *Wall Street Journal* (November 1, 1990):B1.

PYLE, RALPH E., and JEROME R. KOCH. "The Religious Affiliation of American Elites, 1930s to 1990s: A Note on the Pace of Disestablishment." *Sociological Focus.* Vol. 34, No. 2 (May 2001):125–37.

QUILLIAN, LINCOLN, and DEVAH PAGER. "Black Neighbors, Higher Crime? The Role of Racial Stereotypes in Evaluations of Neighborhood Crime." *American Journal of Sociology.* Vol. 107, No. 3 (November 2001):717–67.

QUINNEY, RICHARD. *Class, State and Crime: On the Theory and Practice of Criminal Justice.* New York: McKay, 1977.

RABKIN, JEREMY. "The Supreme Court in the Culture Wars." *Public Interest* (Fall 1996):3–26.

RANK, MARK R., and THOMAS A. HIRSCHL. "Rags or Riches? Estimating the Probabilities of Poverty and Affluence across the Adult American Life Span." *Social Science Quarterly.* Vol. 82, No. 4 (December 2001):651–69.

RAPHAEL, RAY. *The Men from the Boys: Rites of Passage in Male America.* Lincoln: University of Nebraska Press, 1988.

RATNESAR, ROMESH. "Lost in the Middle." *Time* (September 14, 1998):60–62.

RAYMOND, JOAN. "The Multicultural Report." *American Demographics.* Vol. 23, No. 11 (November 2001):S1–S6.

RECKLESS, WALTER C., and SIMON DINITZ. "Pioneering with Self-Concept as a Vulnerability Factor in Delinquency." *Journal of Criminal Law, Criminology, and Police Science.* Vol. 58, No. 4 (December 1967):515–23.

RECTOR, ROBERT. "America Has the World's Richest Poor People." *Wall Street Journal* (September 24, 1998):A18.

REMOFF, HEATHER TREXLER. *Sexual Choice: A Woman's Decision.* New York: Dutton/Lewis, 1984.

RESKIN, BARBARA F., and DEBRA BRANCH MCBRIER. "Why Not Ascription? Organizations' Employment of Male and Female Managers." *American Sociological Review.* Vol. 65, No. 2 (April 2000):210–33.

REVKIN, ANDREW C. "Can Global Warming Be Studied Too Much?" *New York Times* (December 3, 2002):D1, D4.

RHODES, STEVE. "The Luck of the Draw." *Newsweek* (April 26, 1999):41.

RIDDLE, JOHN M., J. WORTH ESTES, and JOSIAH C. RUSSELL. "Ever since Eve: Birth Control in the Ancient World." *Archaeology.* Vol. 47, No. 2 (March/April 1994):29–35.

RIDGEWAY, CECILIA L. *The Dynamics of Small Groups.* New York: St. Martin's Press, 1983.

RIESMAN, DAVID. *The Lonely Crowd: A Study of the Changing American Character.* New Haven, Conn.: Yale University Press, 1970; orig. 1950.

RITZER, GEORGE. *The McDonaldization of Society: An Investigation into the Changing Character of Contemporary Social Life.* Thousand Oaks, Calif.: Pine Forge Press, 1993.

———. *The McDonaldization Thesis: Explorations and Extensions.* Thousand Oaks, Calif.: Sage, 1998.

———. "The Globalization of McDonaldization." *Spark* (February 2000):8–9.

RITZER, GEORGE, and DAVID WALCZAK. *Working: Conflict and Change.* 4th ed. Englewood Cliffs, N.J.: Prentice Hall, 1990.

ROBERTS, J. DEOTIS. *Roots of a Black Future: Family and Church.* Philadelphia: Westminster Press, 1980.

ROBINSON, LINDA. "A Timeworn Terrorism List." *U.S. News & World Report* (May 20, 2002):18, 21.

ROBINSON, THOMAS N., ET AL. "Effects of Reducing Children's Television and Video Game Use on Aggressive Behavior." *Archives of Pediatrics and Adolescent Medicine.* Vol. 155, No. 1 (January 2001):17–23.

RODGERS, JOAN R. "An Empirical Study of Intergenerational Transmission of Poverty in the United States." *Social Science Quarterly.* Vol. 76, No. 1 (March 1995):178–94.

ROESCH, ROBERTA. "Violent Families." *Parents* (September 1984):74–76, 150–52.

ROGERS, RICHARD G., REBECCA ROSENBLATT, ROBERT A. HUMMER, and PATRICK M. KRUEGER. "Black-White Differentials in Adult Homicide Mortality in the United States." *Social Science Quarterly.* Vol. 82, No. 3 (September 2001):435–52.

ROGERS-DILLON, ROBIN H. "What Do We Really Know about Welfare Reform?" *Society.* Vol. 38, No. 2 (January/February 2001):7–15.

ROMERO, FRANCINE SANDERS, and ADRIAN LISERIO. "Saving Open Spaces: Determinants of 1998 and 1999 'Antisprawl' Ballot Measures." *Social Science Quarterly.* Vol. 83, No. 1 (March 2002):341–52.

ROOF, WADE CLARK, and WILLIAM MCKINNEY. *American Mainline Religion: Its Changing Shape and Future.* New Brunswick, N.J.: Rutgers University Press, 1987.

ROSE, LOWELL C., and ALEC M. GALLUP. *The 38th Annual Phi Delta Kappa/Gallup Poll of the Public's Attitudes toward the Public Schools.* 2006. [Online] Available September 26, 2006, at http://www.pdkintl.org/kappan/k0609pol.pdf

ROSEN, ELLEN ISRAEL. *Bitter Choices: Blue-Collar Women in and out of Work.* Chicago: University of Chicago Press, 1987.

ROSEN, JEFFREY. *The Unwanted Gaze.* New York: Random House, 2000.

ROSENDAHL, MONA. *Inside the Revolution: Everyday Life in Socialist Cuba.* Ithaca, N.Y.: Cornell University Press, 1997.

ROSENFELD, RICHARD. "Crime Decline in Context." *Contexts.* Vol. 1, No. 1 (Spring 2002):20–34.

ROSENTHAL, ELIZABETH. "Canada's National Health Plan Gives Care to All, with Limits." *New York Times* (April 30, 1991):A1, A16.

ROSSI, ALICE S. "Gender and Parenthood." In ALICE S. ROSSI, ed., *Gender and the Life Course.* New York: Aldine, 1985:161–91.

ROSTOW, WALT W. *The Stages of Economic Growth: A Non-Communist Manifesto.* Cambridge: Cambridge University Press, 1960.

———. *The World Economy: History and Prospect.* Austin: University of Texas Press, 1978.

ROTHMAN, STANLEY, and AMY E. BLACK. "Who Rules Now? American Elites in the 1990s." *Society.* Vol. 35, No. 6 (September/October 1998):17–20.

ROTHMAN, STANLEY, STEPHEN POWERS, and DAVID ROTHMAN. "Feminism in Films." *Society.* Vol. 30, No. 3 (March/April 1993):66–72.

ROZELL, MARK J., CLYDE WILCOX, and JOHN C. GREEN. "Religious Constituencies and Support for the Christian Right in the 1990s." *Social Science Quarterly.* Vol. 79, No. 4 (December 1998):815–27.

RUBIN, JOEL. "E-Mail Too Formal? Try a Text Message." Columbia News Service. March 7, 2003. [Online] Available April 25, 2005, at http://www.jrn.columbia.edu/studentwork/cns/2003-03-07/85.asp

RUBIN, LILLIAN BRESLOW. *Worlds of Pain: Life in the Working-Class Family.* New York: Basic Books, 1976.

RUDEL, THOMAS K., and JUDITH M. GERSON. "Postmodernism, Institutional Change, and Academic Workers: A Sociology of Knowledge." *Social Science Quarterly.* Vol. 80, No. 2 (June 1999):213–28.

RUDOLPH, ELLEN. "Women's Talk: Japanese Women." *New York Times Magazine* (September 1, 1991).

RULE, JAMES, and PETER BRANTLEY. "Computerized Surveillance in the Workplace: Forms and Delusions." *Sociological Forum.* Vol. 7, No. 3 (September 1992):405–23.

RUSSELL, CHERYL. "Are We in the Dumps?" *American Demographics.* Vol. 17, No. 1 (January 1995a):6.

———. "True Crime." *American Demographics.* Vol. 17, No. 8 (August 1995b):22–31.

RUTHERFORD, MEGAN. "Women Run the World." *Time* (June 28, 1999):72.

RYAN, WILLIAM. *Blaming the Victim.* Rev. ed. New York: Vintage Books, 1976.

RYMER, RUSS. *Genie.* New York: Harper Perennial, 1994.

SACHS, JEFFREY. "The Real Causes of Famine." *Time* (October 26, 1998):69.

SAINT JEAN, YANICK, and JOE R. FEAGIN. *Double Burden: Black Women and Everyday Racism.* Armonk, N.Y.: Sharpe, 1998.

SALA-I-MARTIN, XAVIER. "The World Distribution of Income." Working Paper No. 8933. Cambridge, Mass.: National Bureau of Economic Research, 2002.

SALE, KIRKPATRICK. *The Conquest of Paradise: Christopher Columbus and the Columbian Legacy.* New York: Knopf, 1990.

SAMUELSON, ROBERT J. "The Rich and Everyone Else." *Newsweek* (January 27, 2003):57.

SANSOM, WILLIAM. *A Contest of Ladies.* London: Hogarth, 1956.

SAPIR, EDWARD. "The Status of Linguistics as a Science." *Language.* Vol. 5 (1929):207–14.

———. *Selected Writings of Edward Sapir in Language, Culture, and Personality.* David G. MANDELBAUM, ed. Berkeley: University of California Press, 1949.

SAX, LINDA J., ET AL. *The American Freshman: National Norms for Fall 2003.* Los Angeles: UCLA Higher Education Research Institute, 2003.

SCANLON, STEPHAN J. "Food Availability and Access in Less-Industrialized Societies: A Test and Interpretation of Neo-Malthusian and Technoecological Theories." *Sociological Forum.* Vol. 16, No. 2 (June 2001):231–62.

SCHAFFER, MICHAEL. "American Dreamers." *U.S. News & World Report* (August 26, 2002):12–16.

SCHAUB, DIANA. "From Boys to Men." *Public Interest.* No. 127 (Spring 1997): 108–14.

SCHEFF, THOMAS J. *Being Mentally Ill: A Sociological Theory.* 2d ed. New York: Aldine, 1984.

SCHLESINGER, ARTHUR M., JR. "The City in American Civilization." In ALEXANDER B. CALLOW JR., ed., *American Urban History.* New York: Oxford University Press, 1969:25–41.

SCHLESINGER, JACOB M. "Finally, U.S. Median Income Approaches Old Heights." *Wall Street Journal* (September 25, 1998):B1.

SCHLOSSER, ERIC. *Fast Food Nation: The Dark Side of the All-American Meal.* New York: Perennial, 2002.

SCHMITT, ERIC. "Whites in Minority in Largest Cities, the Census Shows." *New York Times* (April 30, 2001):A1, A12.

SCHNAIBERG, ALLAN, and KENNETH ALAN GOULD. *Environment and Society: The Enduring Conflict.* New York: St. Martin's Press, 1994.

SCHNEIDER, MARK, MELISSA MARSCHALL, PAUL TESKE, and CHRISTINE ROCH. "School Choice and Culture Wars in the Classroom: What Different Parents Seek from Education." *Social Science Quarterly.* Vol. 79, No. 3 (September 1998):489–501.

SCHOFER, EVAN, and MARION FOURCADE-GOURINCHAS. "The Structural Contexts of Civil Engagement: Voluntary Association Membership in Comparative Perspective." *American Sociological Review.* Vol. 66, No. 6 (December 2001):806–28.

SCHULTZ, T. PAUL. "Inequality in the Distribution of Personal Income in the World: How It Is Changing and Why." *Journal of Population Economics.* Vol. 11, No. 2 (1998):307–44.

SCHUMAN, HOWARD, and MARIA KRYSAN. "A Historical Note on Whites' Beliefs about Racial Inequality." *American Sociological Review.* Vol. 64, No. 6 (December 1999):847–55.

SCHUR, LISA A., and DOUGLAS L. KRUSE. "What Determines Voter Turnout? Lessons from Citizens with Disabilities." *Social Science Quarterly.* Vol. 81, No. 2 (June 2000): 571–87.

SCHUTT, RUSSELL K. "Objectivity versus Outrage." *Society.* Vol. 26, No. 4 (May/June 1989):14–16.

SCHWARTZ, FELICE N. "Management, Women, and the New Facts of Life." *Harvard Business Review.* Vol. 89, No. 1 (January/February 1989):65–76.

SCOMMEGNA, PAOLA. "Increased Cohabitation Changing Children's Family Settings." *Population Today.* Vol. 30, No. 7 (July 2002):3, 6.

SEAGER, JONI. *The Penguin Atlas of Women in the World.* 3d ed. New York: Penguin Putnam, 2003.

SEGAL, MADY WECHSLER, and AMANDA FAITH HANSEN. "Value Rationales in Policy Debates on Women in the Military: A Content Analysis of Congressional Testimony, 1941–1985." *Social Science Quarterly.* Vol. 73, No. 2 (June 1992):296–309.

SEIDMAN, STEVEN, ed. *Queer Theory/Sociology.* Cambridge, Mass.: Blackwell, 1996.

SENNETT, RICHARD. *The Corrosion of Character: The Personal Consequences of Work in the New Capitalism.* New York: Norton, 1998.

SENNETT, RICHARD, and JONATHAN COBB. *The Hidden Injuries of Class.* New York: Vintage Books, 1973.

SENTENCING PROJECT. "Facts about Prisons and Prisoners." October 2005. [Online] Available September 13, 2006, at http://www.sentencingproject.org/pdfs/1035.pdf

SHARPE, ANITA. "The Rich Aren't So Different After All." *Wall Street Journal* (November 12, 1996):B1, B10.

SHAWCROSS, WILLIAM. *Sideshow: Kissinger, Nixon and the Destruction of Cambodia.* New York: Pocket Books, 1979.

SHEA, RACHEL HARTIGAN. "The New Insecurity." *U.S. News & World Report* (March 25, 2002):40.

SHELDON, WILLIAM H., EMIL M. HARTL, and EUGENE MCDERMOTT. *Varieties of Delinquent Youth.* New York: Harper Bros., 1949.

SHERKAT, DARREN E., and CHRISTOPHER G. ELLISON. "Recent Developments and Current Controversies in the Sociology of Religion." *Annual Review of Sociology.* Vol. 25 (1999):363–94.

SHERMAN, LAWRENCE W., and DOUGLAS A. SMITH. "Crime, Punishment, and Stake in Conformity: Legal and Informal Control of Domestic Violence." *American Sociological Review.* Vol. 57, No. 5 (October 1992):680–90.

SHEVKY, ESHREF, and WENDELL BELL. *Social Area Analysis.* Palo Alto, Calif.: Stanford University Press, 1955.

SHIPLEY, JOSEPH T. *Dictionary of Word Origins.* Totowa, N.J.: Roman & Allanheld, 1985.

SHIVELY, JOELLEN. "Cowboys and Indians: Perceptions of Western Films among American Indians and Anglos." *American Sociological Review.* Vol. 57, No. 6 (December 1992):725–34.

SHUPE, ANSON. *In the Name of All That's Holy: A Theory of Clergy Malfeasance.* Westport, Conn.: Praeger, 1995.

SHUPE, ANSON, WILLIAM A. STACEY, and LONNIE R. HAZLEWOOD. *Violent Men, Violent Couples: The Dynamics of Domestic Violence.* Lexington, Mass.: Lexington Books, 1987.

SIMMEL, GEORG. *The Sociology of Georg Simmel.* KURT WOLFF, ed. New York: Free Press, 1950:118–69; orig. 1902.

SIMON, JULIAN. *The Ultimate Resource.* Princeton, N.J.: Princeton University Press, 1981.

———. "More People, Greater Wealth, More Resources, Healthier Environment." In THEODORE D. GOLDFARB, ed., *Taking Sides: Clashing Views on Controversial Environmental Issues.* 6th ed. Guilford, Conn.: Dushkin, 1995.

SIMON, ROGER, and ANGIE CANNON. "An Amazing Journey." *U.S. News & World Report* (August 6, 2001):10–19.

SIMONS, MARLISE. "The Price of Modernization: The Case of Brazil's Kaiapo Indians." In JOHN J. MACIONIS and NIJOLE V. BENOKRAITIS, eds., *Seeing Ourselves: Classic, Contemporary, and Cross-Cultural Readings in Sociology.* 7th ed. Upper Saddle River, N.J.: Prentice Hall, 2007.

SIMPSON, GEORGE EATON, and J. MILTON YINGER. *Racial and Cultural Minorities: An Analysis of Prejudice and Discrimination.* 4th ed. New York: Harper & Row, 1972.

SIPES, RICHARD G. "War, Sports, and Aggression: An Empirical Test of Two Rival Theories." *American Anthropologist.* Vol. 75, No. 1 (January 1973):64–86.

SIVARD, RUTH LEGER. *World Military and Social Expenditures, 1987–88.* 12th ed. Washington, D.C.: World Priorities, 1988.

———. *World Military and Social Expenditures, 1992–93.* 17th ed. Washington, D.C.: World Priorities, 1993.

SIZER, THEODORE R. *Horace's Compromise: The Dilemma of the American High School.* Boston: Houghton Mifflin, 1984.

———. "Private Profit, Public Good?" *Frontline* interview. July 3, 2003. [Online] Available May 20, 2006, at http://www.pbs.org/wgbh/pages/frontline/shows/edison/etc/private.html

SKOCPOL, THEDA. *States and Social Revolutions: A Comparative Analysis of France, Russia, and China.* Cambridge: Cambridge University Press, 1979.

SMAIL, J. KENNETH. "Let's Reduce Global Population!" In JOHN J. MACIONIS and NIJOLE V. BENOKRAITIS, eds., *Seeing Ourselves: Classic, Contemporary, and Cross-Cultural Readings in Sociology.* 7th ed. Upper Saddle River, N.J.: Prentice Hall, 2007.

SMITH, ADAM. *An Inquiry into the Nature and Causes of the Wealth of Nations.* New York: Modern Library, 1937; orig. 1776.

SMITH, CRAIG S. "Authorities Took Victim's Organs, His Brother Says." *Columbus Dispatch* (March 11, 2001):A3.

SMITH, DOUGLAS A. "Police Response to Interpersonal Violence: Defining the Parameters of Legal Control." *Social Forces.* Vol. 65, No. 3 (March 1987):767–82.

SMITH, DOUGLAS A., and PATRICK R. GARTIN. "Specifying Specific Deterrence: The Influence of Arrest on Future Criminal Activity." *American Sociological Review.* Vol. 54, No. 1 (February 1989):94–105.

SMITH, DOUGLAS A., and CHRISTY A. VISHER. "Street-Level Justice: Situational Determinants of Police Arrest Decisions." *Social Problems.* Vol. 29, No. 2 (December 1981):167–77.

SMITH, RYAN A. "Race, Gender, and Authority in the Workplace: Theory and Research." *Annual Review of Sociology.* Vol. 28 (2002):509–42.

SMITH, TOM W. "Anti-Semitism Decreases but Persists." *Society.* Vol. 33, No. 3 (March/April 1996):2.

———. "Are We Grown Up Yet? U.S. Study Says Not 'til 26." [Online] Available May 23, 2003, at http://news.yahoo.com

SMITH-LOVIN, LYNN, and CHARLES BRODY. "Interruptions in Group Discussions: The Effects of Gender and Group Composition." *American Journal of Sociology.* Vol. 54, No. 3 (June 1989):424–35.

SMOCK, PAMELA J. "Cohabitation in the United States: An Appraisal of Research Themes, Findings, and Implications." *Annual Review of Sociology.* Vol. 26 (2000):1–20.

SMOLOWE, JILL. "When Violence Hits Home." *Time* (July 4, 1994):18–25.

SNELL, MARILYN BERLIN. "The Purge of Nurture." *New Perspectives Quarterly.* Vol. 7, No. 1 (Winter 1990):1–2.

SOBEL, RACHEL K. "Herpes Tests Give Answers You Might Need to Know." *U.S. News & World Report* (June 18, 2001):53.

SOUTH, SCOTT J., and KIM L. LLOYD. "Spousal Alternatives and Marital Dissolution." *American Sociological Review.* Vol. 60, No. 1 (February 1995):21–35.

SOUTH, SCOTT J., and STEVEN F. MESSNER. "Structural Determinants of Intergroup Association: Interracial Marriage and Crime." *American Journal of Sociology.* Vol. 91, No. 6 (May 1986):1409–30.

SOWELL, THOMAS. *Ethnic America.* New York: Basic Books, 1981.

———. *Compassion versus Guilt and Other Essays.* New York: Morrow, 1987.

———. *Race and Culture.* New York: Basic Books, 1994.

———. "Ethnicity and IQ." In STEVEN FRASER, ed., *The Bell Curve Wars: Race, Intelligence, and the Future of America.* New York: Basic Books, 1995:70–79.

SPECTER, MICHAEL. "Plunging Life Expectancy Puzzles Russia." *New York Times* (August 2, 1995):A1, A2.

SPEIER, HANS. "Wit and Politics: An Essay on Laughter and Power." ROBERT JACKALL, ed. and trans. *American Journal of Sociology.* Vol. 103, No. 5 (March 1998):1352–401.

SPITZER, STEVEN. "Toward a Marxian Theory of Deviance." In DELOS H. KELLY, ed., *Criminal Behavior: Readings in Criminology.* New York: St. Martin's Press, 1980:175–91.

STACEY, JUDITH. *Patriarchy and Socialist Revolution in China.* Berkeley: University of California Press, 1983.

———. *Brave New Families: Stories of Domestic Upheaval in Late-Twentieth-Century America.* New York: Basic Books, 1990.

———. "Good Riddance to 'The Family': A Response to David Popenoe." *Journal of Marriage and the Family.* Vol. 55, No. 3 (August 1993):545–47.

STACK, CAROL B. *All Our Kin: Strategies for Survival in a Black Community.* New York: Harper & Row, 1975.

STACK, STEVEN. "Occupation and Suicide." *Social Science Quarterly.* Vol. 82, No. 2 (June 2001):384–96.

STACK, STEVEN, IRA WASSERMAN, and ROGER KERN. "Adult Social Bonds and the Use of Internet Pornography." *Social Science Quarterly.* Vol. 85, No. 1 (March 2004):75–88.

STAHURA, JOHN M. "Suburban Development, Black Suburbanization, and the Black Civil Rights Movement since World War II." *American Sociological Review.* Vol. 51, No. 1 (February 1986):131–44.

STAPINSKI, HELENE. "Let's Talk Dirty." *American Demographics.* Vol. 20, No. 11 (November 1998):50–56.

STARK, RODNEY. *Sociology.* Belmont, Calif.: Wadsworth, 1985.

STARK, RODNEY, and WILLIAM SIMS BAINBRIDGE. "Of Churches, Sects, and Cults: Preliminary Concepts for a Theory of Religious Movements." *Journal for the Scientific Study of Religion.* Vol. 18, No. 2 (June 1979):117–31.

———. "Secularization and Cult Formation in the Jazz Age." *Journal for the Scientific Study of Religion.* Vol. 20, No. 4 (December 1981):360–73.

STARK, RODNEY, and ROGER FINKE. *Acts of Faith: Explaining the Human Side of Religion.* Berkeley: University of California Press, 2000.

STARR, PAUL. *The Social Transformation of American Medicine.* New York: Basic Books, 1982.

"State Laws regarding Marriages between First Cousins." National Conference on State Legislatures. 2006. [Online] Available September 13, 2006, at http://www.ncsl.org/programs/cyf/cousins.htm

STEELE, RANDY. "Awful but Lawful." *Boating* (June 2000):36.

STEELE, SHELBY. *The Content of Our Character: A New Vision of Race in America.* New York: St. Martin's Press, 1990.

STEINBERG, LAURENCE. "Failure outside the Classroom." *Wall Street Journal* (July 11, 1996):A14.

STEPHENS, JOHN D. *The Transition from Capitalism to Socialism.* Urbana: University of Illinois Press, 1986.

STERKE, CLAIRE E. *Tricking and Tripping: Prostitution in the Era of AIDS.* Putnam Valley, N.Y.: Social Change Press, 2000.

STEVENS, GILLIAN, and GRAY SWICEGOOD. "The Linguistic Context of Ethnic Endogamy." *American Sociological Review.* Vol. 52, No. 1 (February 1987):73–82.

STIER, HAYA. "Continuity and Change in Women's Occupations following First Childbirth." *Social Science Quarterly.* Vol. 77, No. 1 (March 1996):60–75.

STONE, PAMELA. "Ghettoized and Marginalized: The Coverage of Racial and Ethnic Groups in Introductory Sociology Texts." *Teaching Sociology.* Vol. 24, No. 4 (October 1996):356–63.

STORMS, MICHAEL D. "Theories of Sexual Orientation." *Journal of Personality and Social Psychology.* Vol. 38, No. 5 (May 1980):783–92.

STOUFFER, SAMUEL A., ET AL. *The American Soldier: Adjustment during Army Life.* Vol. 1. Princeton, N.J.: Princeton University Press, 1949.

STOUT, DAVID. "Supreme Court Splits on Diversity Efforts at University of Michigan." [Online] Available June 23, 2003, at http://news.yahoo.com

STRATTON, LESLIE S. "Why Does More Housework Lower Women's Wages? Testing Hypotheses Involving Job Effort and Hours Flexibility." *Social Sciences Quarterly.* Vol. 82, No. 1 (March 2001):67–76.

STROSS, RANDALL E. "The McPeace Dividend." *U.S. News & World Report* (April 1, 2002):36.

SULLIVAN, ANDREW. Lecture delivered at Kenyon College, Gambier, Ohio, April 4, 2002.

SULLIVAN, BARBARA. "McDonald's Sees India as Golden Opportunity." *Chicago Tribune* (April 5, 1995):B1.

SUMNER, WILLIAM GRAHAM. *Folkways.* New York: Dover, 1959; orig. 1906.

SUN, LENA H. "WWII's Forgotten Internees Await Apology." *Washington Post* (March 9, 1998):A1, A5, A6.

SUTHERLAND, EDWIN H. "White-Collar Criminality." *American Sociological Review.* Vol. 5, No. 1 (February 1940):1–12.

SWARTZ, STEVE. "Why Michael Milken Stands to Qualify for Guinness Book." *Wall Street Journal.* Vol. 70, No. 117 (March 31, 1989):1, 4.

SZASZ, THOMAS S. *The Myth of Mental Illness: Foundations of a Theory of Personal Conduct.* New York: Dell, 1961.

———. *The Manufacturer of Madness: A Comparative Study of the Inquisition and the Mental Health Movement.* New York: Harper & Row, 1970.

———. "Idleness and Lawlessness in the Therapeutic State." *Society.* Vol. 32, No. 4 (May/June 1995):30–35.

———. "Cleansing the Modern Heart." *Society.* Vol. 40, No. 4 (May/June 2003):52–59.

———. "Protecting Patients against Psychiatric Intervention." *Society.* Vol. 41, No. 3 (March/April 2004):7–10.

TAJFEL, HENRI. "Social Psychology of Intergroup Relations." *Annual Review of Psychology.* Palo Alto, Calif.: Annual Reviews, 1982:1–39.

TAKAKI, RONALD. *Strangers from a Different Shore.* Boston: Back Bay Books, 1998.

TALLICHET, SUZANNE E. "Barriers to Women's Advancement in Underground Coal Mining." *Rural Sociology.* Vol. 65, No. 2 (June 2000):234–52.

TANNEN, DEBORAH. *You Just Don't Understand: Women and Men in Conversation.* New York: Morrow, 1990.

———. *Talking from 9 to 5: How Women's and Men's Conversational Styles Affect Who Gets Heard, Who Gets Credit, and What Gets Done at Work.* New York: Morrow, 1994.

TAVRIS, CAROL, and CAROL WADE. *Psychology in Perspective.* 3d ed. Upper Saddle River, N.J.: Prentice Hall, 2001.

TAX FOUNDATION. [Online] Available June 15, 2000, at http://www.taxfoundation.org

———. "America Celebrates Tax Freedom Day." Report No. 134 (April 2005). [Online] Available October 19, 2005, at http://www.taxfoundation.org/publications/showtype/27.html

TAYLOR, FREDERICK WINSLOW. *The Principles of Scientific Management.* New York. Harper Bros., 1911.

"Terrorist Attacks Spur Unseen Human Toll." *Popline* (December 2001):1–2.

TERRY, DON. "In Crackdown on Bias, A New Tool." *New York Times* (June 12, 1993):8.

THOMAS, PAULETTE. "Success at a Huge Personal Cost." *Wall Street Journal* (July 26, 1995):B1, B6.

THOMAS, PIRI. *Down These Mean Streets.* New York: Signet, 1967.

THOMAS, W. I. "The Relation of Research to the Social Process." In MORRIS JANOWITZ, ed., *W. I. Thomas on Social Organization and Social Personality.* Chicago: University of Chicago Press, 1966:289–305; orig. 1931.

THOMMA, STEVEN. "Christian Coalition Demands Action from GOP." *Philadelphia Inquirer* (September 14, 1997):A2.

THOMPSON, DICK. "Gene Maverick." *Time* (January 11, 1999):54–55.

THOMPSON, MARK, and DOUGLAS WALLER. "Shield of Dreams." *Time* (May 8, 2001):45–47.

THORNBERRY, TERRANCE P., and MARGARET FARNSWORTH. "Social Correlates of Criminal Involvement: Further Evidence on the Relationship between Social Status and Criminal Behavior." *American Sociological Review.* Vol. 47, No. 4 (August 1982):505–18.

THORNE, BARRIE, CHERIS KRAMARAE, and NANCY HENLEY, eds. *Language, Gender, and Society.* Rowley, Mass.: Newbury House, 1983.

TILLY, CHARLES. "Does Modernization Breed Revolution?" In JACK A. GOLDSTONE, ed., *Revolutions: Theoretical, Comparative, and Historical Studies.* New York: Harcourt Brace Jovanovich, 1986:47–57.

TITTLE, CHARLES R., WAYNE J. VILLEMEZ, and DOUGLAS A. SMITH. "The Myth of Social Class and Criminality: An Empirical Assessment of the Empirical Evidence." *American Sociological Review.* Vol. 43, No. 5 (October 1978):643–56.

TOCQUEVILLE, ALEXIS DE. *The Old Regime and the French Revolution.* STUART GILBERT, trans. Garden City, N.Y.: Anchor/Doubleday, 1955; orig. 1856.

TOFFLER, ALVIN. *Future Shock.* New York: Random House, 1970.

TOLSON, JAY. "The Trouble with Elites." *Wilson Quarterly.* Vol. 19, No. 1 (Winter 1995):6–8.

TÖNNIES, FERDINAND. *Community and Society (Gemeinschaft und Gesellschaft).* New York: Harper & Row, 1963; orig. 1887.

TOOSSI, MITRA. "Labor Force Projections to 2014: Retiring Boomers." *Monthly Labor Review* (November 2005):25–44. [Online] Available June 2, 2006, at http://www.bls.gov/opub/mlr/2005/11/art3full.pdf

TOPPO, GREG, and ANTHONY DEBARROS. "Reality Weighs Down Dreams of College." *USA Today* (February 2, 2005):A1.

TORRES, LISA, and MATT L. HUFFMAN. "Social Networks and Job Search Outcomes among Male and Female Professional, Technical, and Managerial Workers." *Sociological Focus.* Vol. 35, No. 1 (February 2002):25–42.

TREAS, JUDITH. "Older Americans in the 1990s and Beyond." *Population Bulletin.* Vol. 50, No. 2 (May 1995).

TROELTSCH, ERNST. *The Social Teaching of the Christian Churches.* New York: Macmillan, 1931.

TUCKER, JAMES. "New Age Religion and the Cult of the Self." *Society.* Vol. 39, No. 2 (February 2002):46–51.

TUMIN, MELVIN M. "Some Principles of Stratification: A Critical Analysis." *American Sociological Review.* Vol. 18, No. 4 (August 1953):387–94.

TURNER, JONATHAN. *On the Origins of Human Emotions: A Sociological Inquiry into the Evolution of Human Emotions.* Stanford, Calif.: Stanford University Press, 2000.

TURNER, RALPH H., and LEWIS M. KILLIAN. *Collective Behavior.* 3rd ed. Englewood Cliffs, N.J.: Prentice Hall, 1987. TYLER, S. LYMAN. *A History of Indian Policy.* Washington, D.C.: U.S. Department of the Interior, Bureau of Indian Affairs, 1973.

UDRY, J. RICHARD. "Biological Limitations of Gender Construction." *American Sociological Review.* Vol. 65, No. 3 (June 2000):443–57.

UGGEN, CHRISTOPHER. "Ex-Offenders and the Conformist Alternative: A Job-Quality Model of Work and Crime." *Social Problems.* Vol. 46, No. 1 (February 1999):127–51.

UGGEN, CHRISTOPHER, and JEFF MANZA. "Democratic Contraction? Political Consequences of Felon Disenfranchisement in the United States." *American Sociological Review.* Vol. 67, No. 6 (December 2002):777–803.

UNESCO. Data reported in "Tower of Babel Is Tumbling Down—Slowly." *U.S. News & World Report* (July 2, 2001):9.

UNITED NATIONS. *2006 Report on the Global AIDS Epidemic.* 2006a. [Online] Available September 27, 2006, at http://www.unaids.org/en/HIV_data/2006GlobalReport/default.asp

———. *The World's Women, 2005: Progress in Statistics.* New York: United Nations, 2006b.

UNITED NATIONS DEVELOPMENT PROGRAMME. *Human Development Report, 1990.* New York: Oxford University Press, 1990.

———. *Human Development Report, 1995.* New York: Oxford University Press, 1995.

———. *Human Development Report, 1996.* New York: Oxford University Press, 1996.

———. *Human Development Report, 2000.* New York: Oxford University Press, 2000.

———. *Human Development Report, 2001.* New York: Oxford University Press, 2001.

———. *Human Development Report, 2004.* New York: Oxford University Press, 2004.

———. *Human Development Report, 2005.* New York: Oxford University Press, 2005.

UPTHEGROVE, TAYNA R., VINCENT J. ROSCIGNO, and CAMILLE ZUBRINSKY CHARLES. "Big Money Collegiate Sports: Racial Concentration, Contradictory Pressures, and Academic Performance." *Social Science Quarterly.* Vol. 80, No. 4 (December 1999):718–37.

URBAN INSTITUTE. "Nearly 3 Out of 4 Young Children with Employed Mothers Are Regularly in Child Care." April 28, 2004. [Online] Available September 25, 2006, at http://www.urban.org/UploadedPDF/900706.pdf

U.S. BUREAU OF JUSTICE STATISTICS. *Criminal Victimization, 2004.* Washington, D.C.: U.S. Government Printing Office, 2005. [Online] Available October 13, 2005, at http://www.ojp.usdoj.gov/bjs/pub/pdf/cv04.pdf

———. *Family Violence Statistics: Including Statistics on Strangers and Acquaintances.* Washington, D.C.: U.S. Government Printing Office, 2005.

———. *Criminal Victimization, 2005.* Washington, D.C.: U.S. Government Printing Office, 2006. [Online] Available September 13, 2006, at http://www.ojp.usdoj.gov/bjs/pub/pdf/cv05.pdf

———"Defendants Sentenced in U.S. District Courts." *Sourcebook of Criminal Justice Statistics Online.* [Online] Available May 8, 2006, at http://www.albany.edu/sourcebook

———. *Prison and Jail Inmates at Midyear 2005.* Washington, D.C.: U.S. Government Printing Office, 2006. [Online] Available July 8, 2006, at http://www.ojp.usdoj.gov/bjs/pub/pdf/pjim05.pdf

U.S. CENSUS BUREAU. *65+ in the United States.* Washington, D.C.: U.S. Government Printing Office, 1996.

———. "Census Bureau Counts 170,000 at Homeless Shelters." News release, October 31, 2000.

———. *Educational Attainment in the United States, March 2000* (Update). Current Population Reports, P20-536. Washington, D.C.: U.S. Government Printing Office, 2000.

———. *Age: 2000.* Census 2000 Brief, C2KBR/01-12. Washington, D.C.: U.S. Government Printing Office, 2001.

———. *The Black Population, 2000.* Census 2000 Brief, C2KBR/01-5. Washington, D.C.: U.S. Government Printing Office, 2001. [Online] Available October 24, 2002, at http://www.census.gov/population/www/cen2000/briefs.html

———. *The Hispanic Population, 2000.* Census 2000 Brief, C2KBR/01-3. Washington, D.C.: U.S. Government Printing Office, 2001. [Online] Available October 24, 2002, at http://www.census.gov/population/www/cen2000/ briefs.html

———. *Mapping Census 2000: The Geography of U.S. Diversity.* Census Special Reports, Series CENSR/01-1. Washington, D.C.: U.S. Government Printing Office, 2001.

———. *Money Income in the United States, 2000.* Current Population Reports, P60-213. Washington, D.C.: U.S. Government Printing Office, 2001.

———. *The Native Hawaiian and Other Pacific Islander Population, 2000.* Census 2000 Brief, C2KBR/01-14. Washington, D.C.: U.S. Government Printing Office, 2001. [Online] Available October 24, 2002, at http://www.census.gov/population/www/cen2000/briefs.html

———. *Population Change and Distribution, 1990 to 2000.* Census 2000 Brief, C2KBR/01-2. Washington, D.C.: U.S. Government Printing Office, 2001.

———. *Poverty in the United States, 2000.* Current Population Reports, P60-214. Washington, D.C.: U.S. Government Printing Office, 2001.

———. *The Two or More Races Population, 2000.* Census 2000 Brief, C2KBR/01-6. Washington, D.C.: U.S. Government Printing Office, 2001. [Online]

Available October 24, 2002, at http://www.census.gov/population/www/cen2000/briefs.html

———. *The White Population, 2000.* Census 2000 Brief, C2KBR/01-4. Washington, D.C.: U.S. Government Printing Office, 2001. [Online] Available October 24, 2002, at http://www.census.gov/population/www/cen2000/briefs.html

———. *The American Indian and Alaska Native Population, 2000.* Census 2000 Brief, C2KBR/01-15. Washington, D.C.: U.S. Government Printing Office, 2002. [Online] Available October 24, 2002, at http://www.census.gov/population/www/cen2000/briefs.html

———. *The Asian Population, 2000.* Census 2000 Brief, C2KBR/01-16. Washington, D.C.: U.S. Government Printing Office, 2002. [Online] Available October 24, 2002, at http://www.census.gov/population/www/cen2000/briefs.html

———. *The Arab Population, 2000.* Census 2000 Brief, C2KBR-23. Washington, D.C.: U.S. Government Printing Office, 2003.

———. *Grandparents Living with Grandchildren, 2000.* Census 2000 Brief, C2KBR-31. Washington, D.C.:U.S. Government Printing Office, 2003.

———. *Language Use and English-Speaking Ability, 2000.* Census 2000 Brief, C2KBR-29. Washington, D.C.: U.S. Government Printing Office, 2003.

———. *Ancestry, 2000.* Census 2000 Brief, C2KBR-35. Washington, D.C.: U.S. Government Printing Office, 2004.

———. *Statistical Abstract of the United States, 2004–2005.* Washington, D.C.: U.S. Government Printing Office, 2004.

———. "(Table) MS-3. Interracial Married Couples, 1980 to 2002." Rev. September 15, 2004. [Online] Available September 22, 2006, at http://www.census.gov/population/socdemo/hh-fam/tabMS-3.pdf

———. "(Table) 2a. Projected Population of the United States, by Age and Sex: 2000 to 2050." Rev. March 18, 2004. [Online] Available July 24, 2005, at http://www.census.gov/ipc/www/usinterimproj/natprojtab02a.pdf

———. "About Metropolitan and Micropolitan Statistical Areas." Rev. June 7, 2005. [Online] Available September 28, 2006, at http://www.census.gov/population/www/estimates/aboutmetro.html

———. *Educational Attainment in the United States, 2004.* Detailed tables. Rev. March 27, 2005. [Online] Available October 21, 2005, at http://www.census.gov/population/www/socdemo/education/cps2004.html

———. *Fertility of American Women, June 2004.* Current Population Reports (P20-555). Washington, D.C.: U.S. Government Printing Office, 2005.

———. *The Hispanic Population of the United States, 2004.* Detailed tables. Rev. December 14, 2005. [Online] Available September 22, 2006, at http://www.census.gov/population/www/socdemo/hispanic/cps2004.html

———. Historical Income Tables—Families. "(Tables) F-2, F-7." Rev. December 20, 2005. [Online] Available September 15, 2006, at http://www.census.gov/hhes/www/income/histinc/incfamdet.html

———. "International Database: IDB Population Pyramids." Rev. April 26, 2005. [Online] Available July 24, 2006, at http://www.census.gov/ipc/www/idbpyr.html

———. *Number, Timing, and Duration of Marriages and Divorces, 2001.* Current Population Reports (P70-97). Washington, D.C.: U.S. Government Printing Office, 2005.

———. "Percent Total Population in Poverty, 2003" (map). Small Area Income and Poverty Estimates. Rev. November 29, 2005. [Online] Available September 17, 2006, at http://www.census.gov/hhes/www/saipe/maps/maps2003.html

———. Voting and Registration in the Election of November 2004. "(Tables) 1, 2, 8." Rev. May 25, 2005. [Online] Available September 24, 2006, at http://www.census.gov/population/www/socdemo/voting/cps2004.html

———. "Annual Estimates of the Population by Selected Age Groups and Sex for the United States, April 1, 2000 to July 1, 2005 (NC-EST2005-02)." Rev. May 9, 2006. [Online] Available September 13, 2006, at http://www.census.gov/popest/national/asrh/NC-EST2005/NC-EST2005-02.xls

———. "Annual Estimates of the Population by Sex and Five-Year Age Groups for the United States, April 1, 2000 to July 1, 2005 (NC-EST2005-01)." Rev. May 9, 2006. [Online] Available September 13, 2006, at http://www.census.gov/popest/national/asrh/NC-EST2005/NC-EST2005-01.xls

———. "Census 2000 Demographic Profile Highlights." [Online] Available September 22, 2006, at http://factfinder.census.gov

———. Current Population Survey, 2006 Annual Social and Economic Supplement. "(Tables) FINC-01, FINC-02, FINC-07." Rev. August 29, 2006.

[Online] Available September 16, 2006, at http://pubdb3.census.gov/macro/032006/faminc/toc.htm

———. Current Population Survey, 2006 Annual Social and Economic Supplement. "(Tables) POV01, POV04, POV14, POV41." Rev. August 29, 2006. [Online] Available September 17, 2006, at http://pubdb3.census.gov/macro/032006/pov/toc.htm

———. Custodial Mothers and Fathers and Their Child Support, 2003. Current Population Reports (P60-230). Washington, D.C.: U.S. Government Printing Office, 2006.

———. Historical Income Tables—Families. "(Tables) F-1, F-2, F-3." Rev. September 15, 2006. [Online] Available September 16, 2006, at http://www.census.gov/hhes/www/income/histinc/incfamdet.html

———. Historical Income Tables—Households. "(Table) H-9." Rev. August 29, 2006. [Online] Available September 16, 2006, at http://www.census.gov/hhes/www/income/histinc/inchhtoc.html

———. Historical Income Tables—People. "(Tables) P-32, P-33, P-34, P-35." Rev. January 13, 2006. [Online] Available September 17, 2006, at http://www.census.gov/hhes/www/income/histinc/incpertoc.html

———. Housing Vacancies and Homeownership. (CPS/HVS). Annual Statistics, 2005. Table 20. Rev. March 1, 2006. [Online] Available September 16, 2006, at http://www.census.gov/hhes/www/housing/hvs/annual05/ann05ind.html

———. Income, Poverty, and Health Insurance Coverage in the United States, 2005. Current Population Reports (P60-231). Washington, D.C.: U.S. Government Printing Office, 2006.

———. "(Table) S1601. Language Spoken at Home." 2005 American Community Survey. Rev. August 15, 2006. [Online] Available September 22, 2006, at http://factfinder.census.gov

———. We the People: American Indians and Alaska Natives in the United States. Census 2000 Special Reports, CENSR-28. Washington, D.C.: U.S. Government Printing Office, 2006.

U.S. CHARTER SCHOOLS. "About the Charter School Movement." [Online] Available September 26, 2006, at http://www.uscharterschools.org/pub/uscs_docs/o/movement.htm

U.S. CITIZENSHIP AND IMMIGRATION SERVICES. "U.S. Legal Permanent Residents, 2005." Annual Flow Report. April 2006. [Online] Available September 22, 2006, at http://www.uscis.gov/graphics/shared/statistics/publications/USLegalPermEst_5.pdf

U.S. DEPARTMENT OF HEALTH AND HUMAN SERVICES, ADMINISTRATION ON CHILDREN, YOUTH, AND FAMILIES. Child Maltreatment, 2004. Washington, D.C.: U.S. Government Printing Office, 2006.

U.S. DEPARTMENT OF HOMELAND SECURITY. 2004 Yearbook of Immigration Statistics. Rev. June 24, 2005. [Online] Available July 23, 2005, at http://uscis.gov/graphics/shared/statistics/yearbook/YrBk04Im.htm

U.S. DEPARTMENT OF HOUSING AND URBAN DEVELOPMENT. "The Forgotten Americans: Homelessness—Programs and the People They Serve." December 1999. [Online] Available October 4, 2004, at http://www.huduser.org/publications/homeless/homelessness/contents.html

U.S. DEPARTMENT OF JUSTICE. The Sexual Victimization of College Women. December 2000. [Online] Available September 20, 2006, at http://www.ncjrs.gov/pdffiles1/nij/182369.pdf

U.S. DEPARTMENT OF LABOR, BUREAU OF LABOR STATISTICS. Women in the Labor Force: A Databook. Report 985. Washington, D.C.: U.S. Government Printing Office, 2005.

———. Employment and Earnings. Vol. 53, No. 1 (January 2006). [Online] Available July 8, 2006, at http://www.bls.gov/cps/#annual

U.S. DEPARTMENT OF STATE. Country Reports on Terrorism, 2005. April 2006. [Online] Available June 3, 2006, at http://www.state.gov/s/ct/rls

U.S. ENVIRONMENTAL PROTECTION AGENCY. "Municipal Solid Waste." February 22, 2006. [Online] Available June 16, 2006, at http://www.epa.gov/msw/facts.htm

U.S. EQUAL EMPLOYMENT OPPORTUNITY COMMISSION. "Occupational Employment in Private Industry by Race/Ethnic Group/Sex, and by Industry, United States, 2003." Rev. June 8, 2005. [Online] Available September 24, 2006, at http://www.eeoc.gov/stats/jobpat/2003/national.html

U.S. HOUSE OF REPRESENTATIVES. 1991 Green Book. Washington, D.C.: U.S. Government Printing Office, 1991.

U.S. SMALL BUSINESS ADMINISTRATION. Minorities in Business, 2001. November 2001a. [Online] Available September 22, 2006, at http://www.sba.gov/advo/stats/min01.pdf

———. Women in Business, 2001. October 2001b. [Online] Available September 22, 2006, at http://www.sba.gov/advo/stats/wib01.pdf

VALDEZ, A. "In the Hood: Street Gangs Discover White-Collar Crime." Police. Vol. 21, No. 5 (May 1997):49–50, 56.

VALLAS, STEPHEN P., and JOHN P. BECK. "The Transformation of Work Revisited: The Limits of Flexibility in American Manufacturing." Social Problems. Vol. 43, No. 3 (August 1996):339–61.

VALOCCHI, STEVE. "The Emergence of the Integrationist Ideology in the Civil Rights Movement." Social Problems. Vol. 43, No. 1 (February 1996):116–30.

VANDIVERE, SHARON, KATHRYN TOUT, MARTHA ZASLOW, JULIA CALKINS, and JEFFREY CAPIZZANO. Unsupervised Time:Factors Associated with Self-Care. Washington, D.C.: The Urban Institute, 2003. [Online] Available November 4, 2004, at http://www.urban.org/UploadedPDF/310894_OP71.pdf

VEDDER, RICHARD, and LOWELL GALLAWAY. "Declining Black Employment." Society. Vol. 30, No. 5 (July/August 1993):56–63.

VINOVSKIS, MARIS A. "Have Social Historians Lost the Civil War? Some Preliminary Demographic Speculations." Journal of American History. Vol. 76, No. 1 (June 1989):34–58.

VIOLENCE POLICY CENTER. "An Analysis of the Decline in Gun Dealers, 1994 to 2005." 2006. [Online] Available September 13, 2006, at http://www.vpc.org/studies/dealers.pdf

VISSER, JELLE. "Union Membership Statistics in 24 Countries." Monthly Labor Review (January 2006):38–49. [Online] Available June 2, 2006, at http://www.bls.gov/opub/mlr/2006/01/art3full.pdf

VOGEL, EZRA F. The Four Little Dragons: The Spread of Industrialization in East Asia. Cambridge, Mass.: Harvard University Press, 1991.

VOGEL, LISE. Marxism and the Oppression of Women: Toward a Unitary Theory. New Brunswick, N.J.: Rutgers University Press, 1983.

VOLD, GEORGE B., and THOMAS J. BERNARD. Theoretical Criminology. 3d ed. New York: Oxford University Press, 1986.

WALDER, ANDREW G. "Career Mobility and the Communist Political Order." American Sociological Review. Vol. 60, No. 3 (June 1995):309–28.

WALDFOGEL, JANE. "The Effect of Children on Women's Wages." American Sociological Review. Vol. 62, No. 2 (April 1997):209–17.

WALKER, KAREN. "'Always There for Me': Friendship Patterns and Expectations among Middle- and Working-Class Men and Women." Sociological Forum. Vol. 10, No. 2 (June 1995):273–96.

WALL, THOMAS F. Medical Ethics: Basic Moral Issues. Washington, D.C.: University Press of America, 1980.

WALLERSTEIN, IMMANUEL. The Modern World-System: Capitalist Agriculture and the Origins of the European World-Economy in the Sixteenth Century. New York: Academic Press, 1974.

———. The Capitalist World Economy. New York: Cambridge University Press, 1979.

———. "Crises: The World Economy, the Movements, and the Ideologies." In ALBERT BERGESEN, ed., Crises in the World System. Beverly Hills, Calif.: Sage, 1983:21–36.

———. The Politics of the World Economy: The States, the Movements, and the Civilizations. Cambridge: Cambridge University Press, 1984.

WARNER, R. STEPHEN. "Work in Progress toward a New Paradigm for the Sociological Study of Religion in the United States." American Journal of Sociology. Vol. 98, No. 5 (March 1993):1044–93.

WARNER, W. LLOYD, and PAUL S. LUNT. The Social Life of a Modern Community. New Haven, Conn.: Yale University Press, 1941.

WARR, MARK, and CHRISTOPHER G. ELLISON. "Rethinking Social Reactions to Crime: Personal and Altruistic Fear in Family Households." American Journal of Sociology. Vol. 106, No. 3 (November 2000):551–78.

WATERS, MELISSA S., WILL CARRINGTON HEATH, and JOHN KEITH WATSON. "A Positive Model of the Determination of Religious Affiliation." Social Science Quarterly. Vol. 76, No. 1 (March 1995):105–23.

WATTS, DUNCAN J. "Networks, Dynamics, and the Small-World Phenomenon." American Journal of Sociology. Vol. 105, No. 2 (September 1999):493–527.

WEBER, ADNA FERRIN. The Growth of Cities. New York: Columbia University Press, 1963; orig. 1899.

WEBER, MAX. The Protestant Ethic and the Spirit of Capitalism. New York: Scribner, 1958; orig. 1904–05.

———. Economy and Society. GNNTER ROTH and CLAUS WITTICH, eds. Berkeley: University of California Press, 1978; orig. 1921.

WEBSTER, ANDREW. Introduction to the Sociology of Development. London: Macmillan, 1984.

WEIDENBAUM, MURRAY. "The Evolving Corporate Board." Society. Vol. 32, No. 3 (March/April 1995):9–20.

WEINBERG, GEORGE. *Society and the Healthy Homosexual.* Garden City, N.Y.: Anchor Books, 1973.

WEISBERG, D. KELLY. *Children of the Night: A Study of Adolescent Prostitution.* Lexington, Mass.: Heath, 1985.

WEITZMAN, LENORE J. *The Divorce Revolution: The Unexpected Social and Economic Consequences for Women and Children in America.* New York: Free Press, 1985.

———. "The Economic Consequences of Divorce Are Still Unequal: Comment on Peterson." *American Sociological Review.* Vol. 61, No. 3 (June 1996):537–38.

WELLNER, ALISON STEIN. "Discovering Native America." *American Demographics.* Vol. 23, No. 8 (August 2001):21.

———. "The Power of the Purse." *American Demographics.* Vol. 24, No. 7 (January/February 2002):S3–S10.

WESSELMAN, HANK. *Visionseeker: Shared Wisdom from the Place of Refuge.* Carlsbad, Calif.: Hay House, 2001.

WESTERN, BRUCE. "The Impact of Incarceration on Wage Mobility and Inequality." *American Sociological Review.* Vol. 67, No. 4 (August 2002):526–46.

WHEELIS, ALLEN. *The Quest for Identity.* New York: Norton, 1958.

WHITAKER, MARK. "Ten Ways to Fight Terrorism." *Newsweek* (July 1, 1985):26–29.

WHITE, JACK E. "I'm Just Who I Am." *Time.* Vol. 149, No. 18 (May 5, 1997):32–36.

WHITE, RALPH, and RONALD LIPPITT. "Leader Behavior and Member Reaction in Three 'Social Climates.'" In DORWIN CARTWRIGHT and ALVIN ZANDER, eds., *Group Dynamics.* Evanston, Ill.: Row & Peterson, 1953:586–611.

WHITMAN, DAVID. "Shattering Myths about the Homeless." *U.S. News & World Report* (March 20, 1989):26, 28.

WHORF, BENJAMIN LEE. "The Relation of Habitual Thought and Behavior to Language." In *Language, Thought, and Reality: Selected Writings of Benjamin Lee Whorf.* JOHN B. CARROLL, ed. Cambridge, Mass.: MIT Press, 1956:134–59; orig. 1941.

WHYTE, WILLIAM FOOTE. *Street Corner Society.* Chicago: University of Chicago Press, 1981; orig. 1943.

WICKHAM, DE WAYNE. "Homeless Receive Little Attention from Candidates." *USA Today Online.* [Online] Available October 24, 2000, at http://www.usatoday.com/usatonline

WILCOX, CLYDE. "Race, Gender, and Support for Women in the Military." *Social Science Quarterly.* Vol. 73, No. 2 (June 1992):310–23.

WILDAVSKY, BEN. "Small World, Isn't It?" *U.S. News & World Report* (April 1, 2002):68.

WILES, P. J. D. *Economic Institutions Compared.* New York: Halsted Press, 1977.

WILKINSON, DORIS. "Transforming the Social Order: The Role of the University in Social Change." *Sociological Forum.* Vol. 9, No. 3 (September 1994):325–41.

WILLIAMS, JOHNNY E. "Linking Beliefs to Collective Action: Politicized Religious Beliefs and the Civil Rights Movement." *Sociological Forum.* Vol. 17, No. 2 (June 2002):203–22.

WILLIAMS, PETER W. *America's Religions: From Their Origins to the Twenty-First Century.* Urbana: University of Illinois Press, 2002.

WILLIAMS, RHYS H., and N. J. DEMERATH III. "Religion and Political Process in an American City." *American Sociological Review.* Vol. 56, No. 4 (August 1991):417–31.

WILLIAMS, ROBIN M., JR. *American Society: A Sociological Interpretation.* 3d ed. New York: Knopf, 1970.

WILLIAMSON, JEFFREY G., and PETER H. LINDERT. *American Inequality: A Macroeconomic History.* New York: Academic Press, 1980.

WILSON, BARBARA J. "National Television Violence Study." Reported by JULIA DUIN, "Study Finds Cartoon Heroes Initiate Too Much Violence." *Washington Times* (April 17, 1998):A4.

WILSON, EDWARD O. "Biodiversity, Prosperity, and Value." In F. HERBERT BORMANN and STEPHEN R. KELLERT, eds., *Ecology, Economics, and Ethics: The Broken Circle.* New Haven, Conn.: Yale University Press, 1991:3–10.

WILSON, JAMES Q. "Crime, Race, and Values." *Society.* Vol. 30, No. 1 (November/December 1992):90–93.

WILSON, THOMAS C. "Urbanism and Tolerance: A Test of Some Hypotheses Drawn from Wirth and Stouffer." *American Sociological Review.* Vol. 50, No. 1 (February 1985):117–23.

———. "Urbanism and Unconventionality: The Case of Sexual Behavior." *Social Science Quarterly.* Vol. 76, No. 2 (June 1995):346–63.

WILSON, WILLIAM JULIUS. *When Work Disappears: The World of the New Urban Poor.* New York: Knopf, 1996a.

———. "Work." *New York Times Magazine* (August 18, 1996b):26 ff.

WINNICK, LOUIS. "America's 'Model Minority.'" *Commentary.* Vol. 90, No. 2 (August 1990):22–29.

WINSHIP, CHRISTOPHER, and JENNY BERRIEN. "Boston Cops and Black Churches." *Public Interest* (Summer 1999):52–68.

WINTER, GREG. "Wider Gap Found between Wealthy and Poor Schools." *New York Times* (October 6, 2004). [Online] Available June 8, 2005, at http://www.researchnavigator.com

WINTERS, REBECCA. "Trouble for School Inc." *Time* (May 27, 2002):53.

WIRTH, LOUIS. "Urbanism as a Way of Life." *American Journal of Sociology.* Vol. 44, No. 1 (July 1938):1–24.

WITKIN, GORDON. "The Crime Bust." *U.S. News & World Report* (May 25, 1998):28–40.

WITKIN-LANOIL, GEORGIA. *The Female Stress Syndrome: How to Recognize and Live with It.* New York: Newmarket Press, 1984.

WOLF, NAOMI. *The Beauty Myth: How Images of Beauty Are Used against Women.* New York: Morrow, 1990.

WOLFF, EDWARD N. "Changes in Household Wealth in the 1980s and 1990s in the U.S." Working Paper No. 407. Levy Economics Institute. May 2004. [Online] Available May 11, 2006, at http://www.levy.org/default.asp?view=research_distro

WOLFGANG, MARVIN E., ROBERT M. FIGLIO, and THORSTEN SELLIN. *Delinquency in a Birth Cohort.* Chicago: University of Chicago Press, 1972.

WOLFGANG, MARVIN E., TERRENCE P. THORNBERRY, and ROBERT M. FIGLIO. *From Boy to Man, from Delinquency to Crime.* Chicago: University of Chicago Press, 1987.

WONDERS, NANCY A., and RAYMOND MICHALOWSKI. "Bodies, Borders, and Sex Tourism in a Globalized World: A Tale of Two Cities—Amsterdam and Havana." *Social Problems.* Vol. 48, No. 4 (November 2001):545–71.

WONG, BUCK. "Need for Awareness: An Essay on Chinatown, San Francisco." In AMY TACHIKI ET AL., eds., *Roots: An Asian American Reader.* Los Angeles: UCLA Asian American Studies Center, 1971:265–73.

WOODWARD, KENNETH L. "Feminism and the Churches." *Newsweek* (February 13, 1989):58–61.

———. "Talking to God." *Newsweek* (January 6, 1992):38–44.

WORLD BANK. *1999 World Development Indicators.* Washington, D.C.: World Bank, 1999.

———. *Entering the 21st Century: World Development Report, 1999/2000.* Washington, D.C.: World Bank, 2000.

———. *World Development Report, 2000/2001.* Washington, D.C.: World Bank, 2001.

———. *2005 World Development Indicators.* Washington, D.C.: World Bank, 2005.

———. *2006 World Development Indicators.* Washington, D.C.: World Bank, 2006.

"World Divorce Rates." [Online] Available October 21, 2005, at http://www.divorcereform.org/gul.html

WORLD HEALTH ORGANIZATION. *Constitution of the World Health Organization.* New York: World Health Organization Interim Commission, 1946.

WORLD VALUES SURVEY. "Latest Publications: Predict 2005—FIGURE." 2004. [Online] Available April 25, 2005, at http://www.worldvaluessurvey.com/library/index.html

WORSLEY, PETER. "Models of the World System." In MIKE FEATHERSTONE, ed., *Global Culture: Nationalism, Globalization, and Modernity.* Newbury Park, Calif.: Sage, 1990:83–95.

WREN, CHRISTOPHER S. "In Soweto-by-the-Sea, Misery Lives on as Apartheid Fades." *New York Times* (June 9, 1991):1, 7.

WRIGHT, JAMES D. "Ten Essential Observations on Guns in America." *Society.* Vol. 32, No. 3 (March/April 1995):63–68.

WRIGHT, QUINCY. "Causes of War in the Atomic Age." In WILLIAM M. EVAN and STEPHEN HILGARTNER, eds., *The Arms Race and Nuclear War.* Englewood Cliffs, N.J.: Prentice Hall, 1987:7–10.

WRIGHT, RICHARD A. *In Defense of Prisons.* Westport, Conn.: Greenwood Press, 1994.

WRIGHT, ROBERT. "Sin in the Global Village." *Time* (October 19, 1998):130.

WU, LAWRENCE L. "Effects of Family Instability, Income, and Income Instability on the Risk of a Premarital Birth." *American Sociological Review.* Vol. 61, No. 3 (June 1996):386–406.

YANG, FENGGANG, and HELEN ROSE EBAUGH. "Transformations in New Immigrant Religions and Their Global Implications." *American Sociological Review.* Vol. 66, No. 2 (April 2001):269–88.

YANKELOVICH, DANIEL. "How Changes in the Economy Are Reshaping American Values." In HENRY J. AARON, THOMAS E. MANN, and TIMOTHY TAYLOR, eds., *Values and Public Policy.* Washington, D.C.: Brookings Institution, 1994.

YEATTS, DALE E. "Creating the High-Performance Self-Managed Work Team: A Review of Theoretical Perspectives." Paper presented at the annual meeting of the Southwest Social Science Association, Dallas, Tex., February 1994.

YIN, SANDRA. "Wanted: One Million Nurses." *American Demographics.* Vol. 24, No. 8 (September 2002):63–65.

YOELS, WILLIAM C., and JEFFREY MICHAEL CLAIR. "Laughter in the Clinic: Humor in Social Organization." *Symbolic Interaction.* Vol. 18, No. 1 (1995):39–58.

YORK, RICHARD, EUGENE A. ROSA, and THOMAS DEITZ. "Bridging Environmental Science with Environmental Policy: Plasticity of Population, Affluence, and Technology." *Social Science Quarterly.* Vol. 83, No. 1 (March 2002):18–34.

ZAKARIA, FAREED. "How to Wage the Peace." *Newsweek* (April 21, 2003):38–48.

ZALMAN, MARVIN, and STEVEN STACK. "The Relationship between Euthanasia and Suicide in the Netherlands: A Time-Series Analysis, 1950–1990." *Social Science Quarterly.* Vol. 77, No. 3 (September 1996):576–93.

ZHAO, DINGXIN. "Ecologies of Social Movements: Student Mobilization during the 1989 Prodemocracy Movement in Beijing." *American Journal of Sociology.* Vol. 103, No. 6 (May 1998):1493–529.

ZICKLIN, G. "Re-Biologizing Sexual Orientation: A Critique." Paper presented at the annual meeting of the Society for the Study of Social Problems, Pittsburgh, 1992.

ZIMBARDO, PHILIP G. "Pathology of Imprisonment." *Society.* Vol. 9 (April 1972):4–8.

ZIPP, JOHN F. "The Impact of Social Structure on Mate Selection: An Empirical Evaluation of an Active-Learning Exercise." *Teaching Sociology.* Vol. 30, No. 2 (April 2002):174–84.

ZOGBY INTERNATIONAL. Poll, reported in SANDRA YIN, "Race and Politics." *American Demographics.* Vol. 23, No. 8 (August 2001):11–13.

PHOTO CREDITS

Bettmann, 301 (*top right*); Charles O'Rear/Corbis/Bettmann, 301 (*bottom left*); Paul W. Liebhardt, 301 (*bottom center*); Lisi Dennis/Lisl Dennis, 301 (*bottom right*); AP Wide World Photos, 302; Bob Daemmrich Photography, Inc., 305; Paul Conklin/PhotoEdit Inc., 307; Marcio Jose Sanchez/AP Wide World Photos, 311; Western History Collections, University of Oklahoma Libraries, 314; Corbis/Bettmann, 317 (*left*); Culver Pictures, Inc., 317 (*left center*); Photographs and Prints Division, Schomburg Center for Research in Black Culture/The New York Public Library/Astor, Lenox and Tilden Foundations, 317 (*right center*); UPI/Corbis/Bettmann, 317 (*right*); A. Ramey/Woodfin Camp & Associates, 319; Warner Bros./Amblin TV/Picture Desk, Inc./Kobal Collection, 321; Carmen Lomas Garza, *Barbacoa para Cumpleanos (Birthday Party Barbecue)*. Alkyds on canvas, 36 × 48 inches. © 1993 Carmen Lomas Garza (reg. 1994). Photo credit: M. Lee Fatherree. Collection of Federal Reserve Bank of Dallas, 323; Peter Yates/Corbis/Bettmann, 325; Carl D. Walsh/Aurora & Quanta Productions Inc., 326.

CHAPTER 12: Spencer Platt/Getty Images, 332; Amy Etra/PhotoEdit Inc., 333 (*top*); Beawiharta/Reuters/Corbis/Bettmann, 333 (*left*); Jim Pickerell/The Stock Connection, 333 (*right*); AP Wide World Photos, 334; AP Wide World Photos, 335; Bellavia/REA/Rea Agency, 339 (*left*); John Bryson/Corbis/Sygma, 339 (*right*); Alamy Images, 340; Najlah Feanny/Corbis/Bettmann, 345; Matthew Borkoski/Index Stock Imagery, Inc., 347; Durand/SIPA Press, 352; Ramin Talaie/Corbis/Bettmann, 355 (*left*); Joel Gordon Photography, 355 (*right*); Karen Ballard/Dreamworks SKG/Universal/Picture Desk, Inc./Kobal Collection, 361; Joe McNally, Life Magazine © TimePix, 363.

CHAPTER 13: Corbis Royalty Free, 370; Bob Daemmrich/The Image Works, 371 (*top*); Mashkov Yuri/ITAR-TASS/Corbis/Bettmann, 371 (*left*); Friedrich Stark/Das Fotoarchiv/Peter Arnold, Inc., 371 (*right*); Michael Newman/PhotoEdit Inc., 372; Getty Images, 373 (*left*); Tina Fineberg/AP Wide World Photos, 373 (*right*); © Susan Pyzow, *Bridal Bouquet*, watercolor on paper, 10 × 13.5 in. Studio SPM Inc., 376; AP Wide World Photos, 378; LWA-Dann Tardif/Corbis/Bettmann, 379; © The New Yorker Collection 1983 Robert Weber from cartoonbank.com, All Rights Reserved, 380; Mark J. Barrett/Creative Eye/MIRA.com, 386; Michael Newman/PhotoEdit Inc., 391; Shaul Schwarz/Getty Images, Inc., 392; David H. Wells/Corbis Digital Stock, 393; Ian Berry/Magnum Photos, Inc., 396; Philip North-Coombes/Getty Images Inc.—Stone Allstock, 401; Anna Belle Lee Washington/SuperStock, Inc., 402; © Gary Braasch/Bettmann/CORBIS All Rights Reserved, 403.

CHAPTER 14: Jon Feingersh/Masterfile Corporation, 408; Corbis Royalty Free, 409 (*top*); Gideon Mendel/CORBIS—NY, 409 (*left*); Michael Rosenfeld/Getty Images, Inc.—Stone Allstock, 409 (*right*); © Andrew Holbrooke/Bettmann/CORBIS All Rights Reserved, 410; Bob Daemmrich Photography, Inc., 413; Michael Newman/PhotoEdit Inc., 415 (*left*); Jim Cummins/Getty Images, Inc., 415 (*right*); Lawrence Migdale/Pix, 421; Bob Daemmrich Photography, Inc., 425; Kevin Virobik-Adams, Progressive Photo, 426; Steve Prezant/Corbis/Stock Market, 430; © Lucy Nicholson/Bettmann/CORBIS All Rights Reserved, 431; George Mulala/Peter Arnold, Inc., 433; Adalbert Franz Seligmann, *Allgemeines Krankenhaus (General Hospital)*, 19th Century Painting, canvas, *Professor Theodor Billroth Lectures at the General Hospital, Vienna*, 1880, Erich Lessing/Art Resource, N.Y., 437; Billy E. Barnes/PhotoEdit Inc., 440; ABC Television/Globe Photos, Inc., 441 (*left*); Copyright 2006 ABC News/ABC Photography Archives, 441 (*right*).

CHAPTER 15: Brad Rickerby/Getty Images, Inc.—Stone Allstock, 448; Clark J. Mishler/Creative Eye/MIRA.com, 449 (*top*); Dinodia/The Image Works, 449 (*left*); Lester Lefkowitz/Corbis/Bettmann, 449 (*right*); © Annie Griffiths/Bettmann/CORBIS All Rights Reserved, 450; David and Peter Turnley/Corbis/Bettmann, 457; Lauren Goodsmith/The Image Works, 458; Mario Tursi/Miramax/Dimension Films/The Kobal Collection, 460; Steve C. Wilson/Online USA, Inc., 462; Christie's Images Inc./Ernest Fiene (1894–1965) "Nocturne." Photograph © Christie's Images, 463 (*left*); Pieter Breughel the Elder (c. 1525/30–1569), *Peasant Dance*, c. 1565, Kunsthistorisches Museum, Vienna/Superstock, Inc., 463 (*right*); Wilfried Krecichwost/Zefa/Corbis Zefa Collection, 469; Culver Pictures, Inc., 471; Dave Amit/Reuters/Landov LLC, 472; TCS—Jean Erick Pasquier, 474.

CHAPTER 16: Tiziana and Gianni Baldizzone/Corbis/Bettmann, 480; Pam Francis/Getty Images, 481 (*top*); Ed Kashi/Corbis/Bettmann, 481 (*left*); B.S.P.I./Corbis/Bettmann, 481 (*right*); Culver Pictures, Inc., 482; China Images/Getty Images, Inc., 484; © CORBIS, 487 (*left*); Huynh Cong "Nick" Ut/AP Wide World Photos, 487 (*right*); Rick Wilking/Reuters/Corbis/Bettmann, 488 (*left*); Al Grillo/Peter Arnold, Inc., 488 (*center*); Salah Omar/AFP/Getty Images, Inc.—Agence France Presse, 488 (*right*); CORBIS—NY, 489; George Tooker, *The Subway*, 1950, egg tempera on gesso panel, 18 1/8 × 36 1/8″, Whitney Museum of American Art, New York, purchased with funds from the Juliana Force Purchase Award, 50.23. Photograph © 2000 Whitney Museum of American Art, 491; Peter Finger/Corbis/Bettmann, 492 (*left*); Mikael Karlsson/Arresting Images, 492 (*right*); Peter Frischmuth/argus/Peter Arnold, Inc., 493; Eric Draper/AP Wide World Photos, 497; Ed Pritchard/Getty Images, Inc.—Stone Allstock, 499 (*left*); Mark Richards/PhotoEdit Inc., 499 (*right*); Mauri Rautkari/WWF UK (World Wide Fund For Nature), 500; Kelly-Mooney Photography/Corbis/Bettmann, 501; Paul Howell/Getty Images, Inc.—Liaison, 507.

TIMELINE: 1807: Getty Images, Inc.—Hulton Archive Photos; 1829: Association of American Railroads; 1848: North Carolina Museum of History; 1876: Property of AT&T Archives, Courtesy of AT&T Archives and History Center, Warren, NJ; 1886 (*top*): Irene Springer/Pearson Education/PH College; 1886 (*bottom*): "Coca-Cola" is a registered trademark of The Coca-Cola Company and is reproduced with kind permission from The Coca-Cola Company; 1893: Library of Congress; 1910: Tim Ridley © Dorling Kindersley; 1912: Wilton, Chris Alan/Getty Images, Inc.—Image Bank; 1913: Library of Congress; 1921: Getty Images, Inc.—Hulton Archive Photos; 1927: Corbis/Bettmann; 1931: Texas State Library and Archives Commission; 1945: U.S. Air Force; 1946: Photo courtesy of Unisys Corporation; 1947: © CORBIS/Bettmann; 1950: Corbis/Bettmann; 1952: © Dorling Kindersley; 1955: AP Wide World Photos; 1964: Getty Images, Inc.—Hulton Archive Photos; 1969 (*top*): AP Wide World Photos; 1969 (*bottom*): NASA/Johnson Space Center; 1970: Jason Laure/Woodfin Camp & Associates; 1980: Laima Druskis/Pearson Education/PH College; 1981: Jan Butchofsky-Houser/AP Wide World Photos; 1987: John Serafin; 1990s: Gerald Lopez © Dorling Kindersley; 2000: Brady/Pearson Education/PH College.

INSIDE BACK COVER: George Breithaup.

NAME INDEX

SUBJECT INDEX

Chukchee Eskimo, 156
Church(es)
  black, 399
  defined, 395
  electronic, 404
  state, 395
Church of England, 393, 395
Church of Jesus Christ of Latter-Day
  Saints (see Mormons)
Cigarette smoking (see Smoking)
Circumcision
  female, 165
  male, 165
Cities (see also Urbanization/urban-
  ism)
  decentralization, 460
  decline of, 460–61
  edge, 461–62
  ethnic villages/enclaves, 310,
    312–13, 327–28
  evolution of, 458–59
  ghettos, 459
  growth of, 12, 457–60
  growth of U.S., 459–60
  homelessness, 236–38
  megalopolis, 461
  metropolises, 460
  minorities in, 465
  political economy, 465–66
  presidential election of 2004 and,
    357
  rural rebound, 462
  shantytowns, 250, 256, 261,
    264–65
  Snowbelt, 461
  Sunbelt, 461
  urban ecology, 464–65
  white flight from, 461
Civil law, focus of, 184
Civil religion, 400
Civil Rights Act (1964), 327
Civil rights movement, 317
Civil War, urbanization during, 460
Claims making, 486
Class conflict, Marxist views on,
  215–17
Class society, modernity and, 496–98
  mass society versus, 498
Class struggle (see Class conflict)
Class system, 255, 258
  in Britain, 210–11
  in China, 212–13
  defined, 208
  estate system, 210–11
  industrialization and, 210
  meritocracy, 208, 210
  in the Soviet Union, 211–12
  status consistency and, 210
Closed systems, 207
Coalescence, social movements and,
  487
Coercive organizations, 127–28
Cognitive theory, Piaget's, 73–74
Cohabitation, 387–88
Cohort, 88
Colleges
  access to, 417–18
  affirmative action, 326–27
  African Americans in, 318
  Asian Americans in, 318, 319
  community, 418–19
  family income and, 417–18
  gender differences in 277, 281–82,
    426
  GI Bill, 418
  illegal immigrants and, 8, 10–11
  latent and manifest functions, 14

privilege and personal merit, 419
  research at, 25
  violence at, 284
College students
  capital punishment and, 198
  career aspirations, 343
  date rape, 162–63, 284
  dropping out, 422–423
  feminism, opposition to, 293, 294
  homosexuality, attitudes toward,
    157–58
  hooking up, 162
  life objectives of, 57
  passive, 420–21
  political party identification, 356
  religion and, 400
  social distance and, 307
Colombia
  drug trade in, 193
  income inequality, 221
Colonial America, cities in, 459
Colonialism
  defined, 256
  dependency theory, 260–63
  neo-, 257
  poverty and, 256
Command economy, 339
Common sense
  debunking, 8, 9
  versus scientific evidence, 19
Communication (see also E-mail;
  Languages)
  cultural differences, 44
  global, 59
  grapevines, 130
  nonverbal, 103–6
Communism
  in China, 212
  collapse of, in the Soviet Union,
    211
Communitarian movement, 506–7
Community
  Gemeinschaft and Gesellschaft,
    462–63, 491–92
  Gullah, 500–501
  las colonias, 250
  modernization and loss of, 490
Community-based corrections,
  199–200
Community colleges, 418–19
Comparable worth, 280
Competition
  capitalism and, 338
  corporations and, 347–48
  workplace, 136
Complementary, gender, 288–89
Computers (see also Information
  technology)
  impact of, 336, 345–46
  privacy issues, 138–39
  work and, 345–46
Concentric zones, 464
Concept
  defined, 19
  scientific sociology and, 19
Concrete operational stage, 73–74
Conflict
  class, 215–17
  cultural, 54
  gender-conflict approach, 15–17
  humor and, 114
  race-conflict approach, 17
  resolving underlying, 366
  role, 99
  social-conflict analysis, 15–17, 18
  social stratification and, 215–17
  sports and, 20–21

subcultures, 178
  theory and racism, 309–10
  values and, 48–49
Conformity
  deviance versus, 174
  differential association theory, 182
  group, 122–24
  groupthink, 124
  social control and, 182
  tradition-directedness, 498
Conglomerates, 347
Conjugal family, 373
Consanguine family, 373
Conscience, superego, 175
Conservatives, social issues, 356
Conspicuous consumption, 218
Constitution, U.S.
  African American rights, 317
  Bill of Rights, 193, 355
Constitutional monarchs, 352
Consumerism, capitalism and, 338
Containment theory, 176
Contraception (see Birth control)
Control
  McDonaldization and, 139–40
  social, 174
  theory, Hirschi's, 182–83
Conventional level, Kohlberg's moral
  development theory, 74
Conversion, religious, 396
Core-based statistical areas (CBSAs),
  461
Cornerville study, 30–31
Corporate agribusiness, 342
Corporate crime, 185
Corporate welfare, 348
Corporations (see also Multinational
  corporations)
  competitiveness and, 347–48
  conglomerates, 347
  crime, 185
  defined, 347
  economic concentration, 347
  global, 348–49
Correction systems
  community-based, 199–200
  death penalty, global map, 192
  deterrence, 195–96
  rehabilitation, 196
  retribution, 195
  societal protections, 196–99
Correlation
  defined, 22
  spurious, 22
  variables, relationships among, 22
Counterculture, 56–57
Courts, role in criminal justice system, 194–95
Courtship, 377–79
  social-exchange analysis, 377
Cousin marriage laws in U.S., first-,
  149
Creative freedom, in the workplace,
  136
Credential society, 419
Creoles, 54–55
Crime (see also Deviance; Violence)
  against people, 187–88
  against property, 188
  age and, 189
  community-based corrections,
    199–200
  corporate, 185
  cultural differences, 191–93
  defined, 174, 186
  deterrence, 195–45, 198
  economy and effects on, 199

gender differences, 189–90
  genetics and, 175
  global perspective, 191–93
  hate, 186, 187
  organized, 185
  prostitution as a victimless, 161
  race and ethnicity, 190–91
  rape, 161–63
  social class and, 190
  statistics on, 188, 189
  subcultures, 178–79
  types of, 187–88
  victimless, 161, 188
  violent, rates down, 198–99
  white-collar, 184
Crime in the United States (FBI), 187
Criminal intent, 186
Criminal justice system
  courts, 194
  defined, 174
  due process, 193–94
  plea bargaining, 194–95
  police role of, 194
  punishment, reasons for, 195–99
Criminal law, focus of, 184
Criminal recidivism, 197
Criminals
  profile of, 188–91
  voting and, 358
Crisis, social, 4–5
Critical sociology, 23–24
Crowds, defined, 120
Crude birth rate, 450–51
Crude death rte, 451
Cuba
  Bay of Pigs and groupthink, 124
  meeting with foreigners, banned,
    176
Cuban Americans
  education and, 324
  ethnic communities, 324
  income of, 324
  poverty and, 324
  social standing of, 324
Cults, 396
Cultural capital
  defined, 78
  family and, 78
Cultural change
  causes of, 57
  cultural lag, 57
Cultural differences
  affection, showing, 149
  beauty and, 147
  child labor and, 58
  communication and, 44
  crime and, 192–93
  deviance and, 176
  education, 410–12
  emotions, showing, 108
  homosexuality and, 156
  humor and, 112–13
  intelligence and, 308–9
  languages and, 46
  male circumcision, 165
  modesty and, 149
  nonverbal communication and,
    104, 106, 107
  personal space and, 104
  sexual expression and, 149–50
  sexuality and, 165
  sexual practices and, 149–50, 165
  symbols and, 44–45
  U.S. and Canada compared, 63
Cultural diversity
  cultural change, 57–58
  counterculture, 56–57

ethnocentrism, 58–59
high versus popular, 52–53
multiculturalism, 55–56
subculture, 53–54
virtual, 53
Cultural integration, 57
Cultural lag, 57, 483
Cultural relativism, 58–59
Cultural shock, 41–42, 43, 45
Cultural transmission, 46
Cultural universals, 60–61
Culture
aging and, 85–86
change, 57
counter-, 56–57
defined, 40–42, 44
diversity in, 52–58
elements of, 44–50
emotions and influence of, 108
evolution and, 62, 64
freedom and, 64
functions of, 60–61
gender and, 273–74
global, 59–60
high versus popular, 52–53
ideal versus real, 50
inequality and, 61
information technology and, 52
intelligence and, 42–44
language and, 44, 46, 47
material, 50
modernization theory, 258
multi-, 55–56
norms, 50
poverty and, 234, 255
reality building and, 102
shock, 41–42, 43, 45
social change and, 484
social-conflict analysis, 61
sociobiology approach, 62, 65
structural-functional analysis, 60–61
sub-, 53–54
symbols, 44–46
technology and, 50–52
theoretical analysis of, 60–64
theory, 486–87
theory and racism, 309
transmission of, 46
values and beliefs, 46, 48–49
Curriculum, hidden, 79
Czechoslovakia, socialism, decline of, 341
Czech Republic, market reforms, 341

Darfur, genocide, 488
Data
qualitative versus quantitative, 23
using existing research, 31–34
Date rape, 162–63
Dating, 377–78
Davis-Moore thesis, 214–15
Death and dying (see also Mortality rates)
defining, 435
ethical issues, 435–36
euthanasia, 436
leading causes of, in U.S., 428
penalty, 192
right-to-die debate, 436
of a spouse, 381
as a stage of life, 87
stages of, 87
Death instinct, 72
Death rates, crude, 451
Debt bondage, 254

Debunking common sense, 8, 9
Deception, spotting, 104
Declaration of Independence, 12, 317
Decline, social movements and, 488
De facto segregation, 312
Degradation ceremony, 181
De jure segregation, 312
Demeanor, social interaction and, 104
Democracy
bureaucracy and, 352
defined, 352
economic inequality and, 352
freedom and, 352, 364–65
gap, 364–65
political freedom, map of, 353
U.S. value, 48
Democratic leadership, 122
Democratic party, 356
Democratic Republic of the Congo
gross domestic product, 251
as a low-income country, 247, 248, 251
quality of life, 251
Demographic transition theory, 455–56
Demography (see also Population/population growth)
defined, 450
fertility, 450–51
migration, 452
mortality, 451–52
social change and, 484–85
Denial of death, 87
Denmark
homosexual marriages, 388
women in government positions, 282
Denominations, 395
Dependency theory
capitalist world economy, 261–62
colonialism and, 260–61
compared to modernization theory, 263
defined, 260
evaluation of, 262–63
high-income countries and, 262
historical, 260
modernity and, 508
Dependent variables, 22, 25–26
Deprivation theory, 486
Descent patterns, 375
Descriptive statistics, 19
Desegreation, 310
Deterrence
of criminals, 195–96, 198
of war, 365
Development, human (see Human development)
Deviance (see also Crime)
biological context, 175
capitalism and, 183–84
control theory, 182–83
cultural differences, 176
defined, 174
differential association theory, 182
Durkheim's work, 176–77
functions of, 176
gender differences and, 186
Hirschi's control theory, 182–83
labeling theory, 179–83
medicalization of, 181
Merton's strain theory, 177–78
personality factors, 175–76
power and, 183
primary, 179–80

Puritans, example of, 177
secondary, 179–80
social-conflict analysis, 183–85
social control, 174
social foundations of, 176
stigma, 180–81
strain theory, 177–78
structural-functional analysis, 176–79, 185
subcultures, 178–79, 180
Sutherland's differential association theory, 182
symbolic-interaction analysis, 179–83, 185
Deviant career, 180
Dharma, 256
Differential association theory, 182
Diffusion
culture, 57
social change and, 484
Diplomacy, peace and, 366
Direct-fee system, 438
Disabled
education for, 425–26
master status, 98
Disarmament, peace and, 366
Disasters
defined, 488
impact of, 488–90
intentional, 488
natural, 488
technological, 488
Discipline problems, school, 420
Discoveries
cultural change and, 57
social change and, 484
Discrimination (see also Racial discrimination)
defined, 310
institutional, 310
prejudice and, 310
women and, 280
workplace, 134–35
Disposable society, 470
Diversity (see also Cultural diversity; Social diversity)
biodiversity, declining, 474
language, in the U.S., 56
racial, in the U.S., 79
religious, across U.S., 398
workplace, 345, 346
Divine right, 352
Division of labor, 492–93
Divorce
causes of, 384–85
children and, 385
child support, 385
rates for U.S., 385
reproductive technology and effects on, 390
Doe v. Bolton, 166
Domestication of animals, 51
Domestic violence, 386–87
Double standards, 25
sexual behavior and, 62, 64, 152, 153
Down These Mean Streets (Thomas), 100–101
Downward social mobility, 228
Dramaturgical analysis
defined, 102
elements of, 18
embarrassment, 106–7
idealization, 106
nonverbal communication, 103–6
performances, 103

Dred Scott case, 317
Dropout, school, 421–23
Drug abuse
AIDS/HIV and, 435
deviance and medicalization of, 181
Drug trade
crime and, 193, 199
decline in, 199
Due process, 193–194
Durkheim, work of
on deviance, 176–77
division of labor, 492–93
on mechanical and organic solidarity, 463
on religion, 391–92
Dyad, 125

Earnings (see Economy; Global economy; Income)
Eastern Europe (see Europe, eastern)
Eating disorders, 431–32
Ecologically sustainable culture, 476
Ecology
defined, 468
urban, 464–65
Economic elites, 341
Economic equality, capitalism versus socialism and, 341
Economic inequality (see also Income inequality)
in China, 212–13
in selected countries, 213
in the Soviet Union, 211
Economic productivity, capitalism versus socialism and, 340–41
Economic systems
capitalism, 338–39
socialism, 339–41
state capitalism, 340
welfare capitalism, 340
Economy (see also Global economy; Income)
agricultural revolution, 334–35
capitalism, 338–39
capitalism, state, 340
capitalism, welfare, 340
in China, 212
command, 339
corporations, 347–49
crime rates and, 199
defined, 334
education and role of, 410–12
future issues, 349–50
historical overview, 334–38
Industrial Revolution, 335
information revolution, 335–36, 345–46
laissez-faire, 338
map, agricultural employment 337
map, service sector work, 337
perestroika, in Soviet Union, 211
political-economy model/theory, 359, 487
politics and, 355–56
postindustrial, 335–36
postindustrial society and, 336–36, 342–49
sectors of, 336
socialism, 339–40, 341
urban political, 465–66
Wallerstein's capitalist world, 261–62
Ecosystem, 468
Ecuador
beauty in, 147

in high-income countries, 429
insurance, 438–39
in low-income countries, 428
marriage and, 385
obesity, 432
poverty and effects on, 252–53
racial differences, 429–30
sexually transmitted diseases,
433–35
smoking, 430–31
social class and, 227, 429–30
social-conflict analysis, 442–43
social inequality and, 428
society and, 428
structural-functional analysis,
440–41, 442
symbolic-interaction analysis,
441–42
in the U.S., 429–43
Health insurance, U.S., 438–39
Health maintenance organizations
(HMOs), 439
Heaven's Gate cult, 396
Hermaphrodites, 148
Herpes, genital, 433
Heterosexism, 167
Heterosexuality, defined, 155
Hidden curriculum, 79
High culture, 52–53
Higher education (see Colleges; Education)
High-income countries (see also
name of country)
age at death, global median, 252,
253
childbearing, map on, 3
countries considered, 245–246,
247
defined, 5, 245
dependency theory, 262–63
economic sectors, 336
family size, 379
gross domestic product (GDP),
247n, 251
health in, 429
income inequality, 220, 221
map of, 247
modernization theory, 259–60
per capita income, 246
population growth, 456
productivity of, 245–46, 247
prostitution in, 160
quality of life index, 251
television ownership, 80
values in, 49
Hispanic Americans/Latinos (see also
Race; Racial discrimination;
Racial segregation; Racism)
AIDS/HIV and, 435
conducting research with, 26
Cuban Americans, 324
demographics map, 322
education and, 323
ethnic villages, 311
family life, 381–82
family size, 379n
feminism and, 293
income inequality, 224, 231, 284,
323, 324, 382
income of, 323, 324, 382
las colonias, 250
machismo, 381
Mexican Americans, 323
parenting, single (one), 384, 387,
390
personal space and, 26

political party identification and,
356
poverty and, 233, 324
Puerto Ricans, 323–24
sexually transmitted diseases and,
433
social standing, 324
statistics on, 322–23
stereotypes, 304
voting participation and, 358
work and, 342, 346
Hispanic American women (see
Women, Hispanic American)
HMOs (health maintenance organizations), 439
Holistic medicine, 437
Holocaust, 313
Homelessness
description of, 236–38
deviance and, 181
Home schooling, 425
Homogamy, 379
Homophobia, 158
Homosexuality (homosexuals)
AIDS/HIV and, 435
attitudes toward, 156–58
cultural differences, 156
defined, 155
families, 388–89
gay rights movements, 157–58
genetics and, 156–57
hate crimes, 186
marriages, 388–89
parenting, 389
prostitution and, 161
queer theory, 167–68
statistics on, 157
Hong Kong
description of, 457
as a high-income country, 246, 247
modernization theory, 259
Hooking up, 162
Horizontal social mobility, 229
Horticulture societies
description of, 51
social stratification and, 219
Houses of correction, 196
Housework, 98, 100, 281
Hull House, 16
Human development
cognitive development, 73–74
moral development, 74
nature versus nurture, 71–72
personality development, 72–73
self, development of, 75–76
social isolation and, 71–72
socialization and, 72–88
stages of, 76–77
Human Genome Project, 444
Human immunodeficiency virus
(HIV) (see AIDS/HIV)
Human trafficking, 254
Humor
conflict and, 114
cultural differences, 112–13
dynamics of, 111–12
foundation of, 111
function of, 114
social interaction and, 111–14
topics of, 112–14
Hungary, socialism, decline of, 341
Hunting and gathering societies
description of, 50–51
gender differences/roles, 274
religion and, 51, 397
social stratification and, 219

Hurricane Katrina, 54–55, 131
Hutus, 314
Hydrologic cycle, 471
Hypersegregation, 312–13
Hypothesis
defined, 25
testing, 25–26

"I," Mead's self, 76
Iceland, social status of women, 275
Id, 72–73
Ideal culture, 50
Idealism, 60
Idealization, 106
Identity
Erikson's developmental stages,
76–77
modernity/mass society and,
498–99
Ideology
defined, 213
historical patterns, 213
Marx, views of, 213
Plato's views, 213
social stratification and, 213
Illiteracy
functional, 422–23
global, 411
Imagination, sociological, 6
Imitation, 76
Immigrants
college attendance and illegal, 8,
10–11
social change and, 485
work for, 305
Immigration
defined, 452
growth of, 12, 457–61
Hull House/settlement houses, 16
multiculturalism, 311–12
statistics on, 328
Impression management, 103
Incarceration (see Correction systems; Prisons)
Incest taboo, 149–50, 375
Inclusive education, 426
Income
African Americans and, 223–24,
229, 231, 283–84, 318, 382
Arab Americans and, 325
Asian Americans and, 318, 319, 320
defined, 220–21
distribution of, in the U.S., 221, 222
distribution of world, 273
elderly and, 86–87
Hispanic Americans, 224, 231, 284,
323, 324, 382
mean annual, U.S., 229
median annual, U.S., 232
Native Americans and, 315
social mobility and, 229
Income inequality
African Americans, 223–24, 229,
231, 283–84, 318, 382–83
democracy and, 352
gender differences, 231, 279–81,
419
global, 211, 212, 213, 220, 221
Hispanic Americans, 224, 231, 284,
323, 324, 382
Kuznets curve, 220
race and, 223–25, 229, 231
in the U.S., 220–23
Independent variables, 22, 25
India
caste system, 208

child labor in, 412
child weddings in, 378
crime in, 191
education in, 412
family size, 3
female genital mutilation, 285
marriage in, 373, 378
as a middle-income country, 247,
248
poverty, 256
servile forms of marriage, 254
water supply problems, 472
Indians (see also Native Americans)
use of term, 315
Individualism
divorce and, 385
modernization theory, 258, 491,
498–99
U.S., 355
Individualization, modernity and,
491
Individual liberty, 12
Individual rights, 12
(see also Bill of Rights, U.S.; Rights)
Indonesia, child labor in, 82–83
Industrial Revolution
cities, 459
effects on the economy, 335
modernization theory and, 257
population growth, 456
social change and, 11–12, 490
social stratification and, 210
Industrial societies
cities in, 459
description of, 52
inequality in, 217
population growth, 455
religion in, 397
social stratification and, 219–20
Inefficiency, bureaucratic, 131–32
Inequality (see Gender inequality;
Income inequality; Racial
inequality; Social inequality)
Inertia, bureaucratic, 132–33
Infants
mortality rates, 430, 451–52
self development, 76–77
sensorimotor stage, 73
Infidelity, 379
Information technology
computers, impact of, 345–46
culture and, 52
Internet users map, 128
modernization theory, 259
networks and, 127, 128
postindustrial, 52
postindustrial society and, 335–36
privacy issues, 138–39
work and, 345–46
Informed consent, 25
In-groups, 124–25
Inheritance rules, 376
Innovation, deviance, 178
Instant messaging, symbols of, 45
Institutional prejudice and discrimination, 310
Institutional review boards (IRBs), 25
Institutional sexism, 275–76
Institutions
social, 334
total, 89
Instrumental leadership, 122
Insurance, health, 438–39
Intelligence
bell curve, 308
culture and, 42–44

Modernization theory
  compared to dependency theory, 263
  culture and, 258
  defined, 257
  evaluation of, 259–60
  high-income countries and, 259–60
  historical, 257–58
  stages of, 258–59
Modesty, cultural differences, 149
Monarchy (monarchies)
  absolute, 352
  constitutional, 352
  countries that have, 352
  defined, 352
Money (see Economy; Income)
Mongoloid, racial type, 301
Monoculture, 52
Monogamy, 373
Monopolies, 347
Moral development
  gender differences, 74–75
  Gilligan's theory, 74–75
  Kohlberg's theory, 74
Moral reasoning, 74
Mores, 50
Mormons, 397, 401
Mortality rates
  children and, 379, 429, 451
  gender differences, 452
  infant, 429, 451–52
  measuring, 451–52
  racial differences, 452
Morocco
  beauty in, 147
  child labor in, 58
  as a middle-income country, 247, 248
MSAs (metropolitan statistical areas), 461
Multicentered model, 464–65
Multiculturalism, 40
  assimilation, 311–12
  controversies over, 55–56
  defined, 55–56
Multinational corporations (see also Corporations)
  defined, 257
  growth and control by, 338
  neocolonialism and, 257
Mundugumor, New Guinea, Mead's gender studies, 273–74
Muslims (see also Arab Americans; Arabs; Islam; Islamic societies)
  difference between the terms Arab and, 324
  social distance and, 307
Muslim women (see Women, Islamic)
Musuo, 274
Mutual assured destruction (MAD), 365
Myanmar (Burma), beauty in, 147

NAACP (National Association for the Advancement of Colored People), 16, 17
Namibia, as a middle-income country, 247, 248
National Rifle Association, 357
Nation at Risk, A (NCEE), 422–23
Native Americans
  AIDS/HIV and, 435
  animism and, 396, 397
  assimilation of, 314
  citizenship for, 315
  cultural revival, 316

descent patterns, 375
education of, 314, 315
family life, 381, 382–83
gambling, 316
genocide, 314–15
incest taboo, 149
income of, 315
Indians, use of term, 315
intersexual people and, 148
land controlled by, map of, 315
migration to North America, 314
norms and, 50
on reservations, 315, 382–83
sexually transmitted diseases and, 433
social standing, 316
use of term, 314
Natural disasters, 488
Natural environment (see also Environment)
  defined, 468
Natural selection, 62
Nature versus nurture, 70–71
Navajo
  incest taboo, 149
  intersexual people and, 148
  Nazis, Holocaust, 313
Needs, basic human, 72
Negroid, racial type, 301
Neocolonialism
  defined, 257
  poverty and, 257
Neolocality, 375
Netherlands, homosexual marriages, 388
Networks
  defined, 126
  gender differences, 127
  grapevines, 130
  Internet, 127, 128
  social groups and, 126–27
New Age religion, 400–401
New Guinea, Mead's gender studies, 273–74
New social movements theory, 487
New York City, changing neighborhoods, 312–13
New York Times, 10–11, 54–55, 84–85, 112–13, 132–33, 150–51, 196–97, 236–37, 264–65, 292–93, 312–13, 350–51, 382–83, 422–23, 466–67, 502–3
New Zealand, as a high-income country, 246, 247
Nicaragua
  education in, 411
  modernization theory, 259
  quality of life, 259
Niger
  modernization theory, 259
  quality of life, 323
  women, social status of, 275
Nigeria
  affection, display of, 149
  beauty in, 147
  constraints put on women, 186
  female genital mutilation, 286
Nike Corp., 82–83
Nineteenth Amendment, 290
No Child Left Behind, 424
Nongovernmental organizations (NGOs), 354
Nonmaterial culture, 40
Nonverbal communication
  body language, 104, 105
  deception, spotting, 104
  defined, 104

demeanor, 104
eye contact, 104, 105
facial expressions, 104, 105
gender differences, 104–5
hand gestures, 105, 106
personal space, 104
social interaction and, 103–6
Normative organizations, 127
Norms
  defined, 50
  folkways and mores, 50
  superego, 73
  totalitarianism, 354
North American Free Trade Agreement (NAFTA), 264
North Korea
  nuclear weapons in, 364
  totalitarianism in, 354
Norway
  gross domestic product, 251
  as a high-income country, 251
  quality of life index, 251
  women, social status of, 275
  women in government positions, 282
Nuclear family, 373
Nuclear weapons, 364
Nursing shortage, in U.S., 440
Nurture
  in early childhood, 78
  nature versus, 70–71

Obesity
  causes of, 432
  health effects, 432
  in the U.S., map of, 432
Objectivity
  defined, 22
  scientific, 22–23
Observation, participant, 28, 30–31
Occupations (see also Work/workplace)
  prestige, 223, 224
  versus professions, 343
Old age (see Elderly)
Oligarchy, 133
Oligopoly, 347
One-parent families, 381, 382, 384, 387, 390
On the Origin of Species (Darwin), 62
Open systems, 207
Operationalize variables, 19
Opportunity
  relative, 178
  U.S. value, 48
Oral contraceptives, 152
Organic solidarity, 463, 493
Organizational environment, 129–30
Organizations (see also Bureaucracy; Formal organizations)
  coercive, 127–28
  environment, 129–30
  flexible, 136
  models, 137
  normative, 127
  utilitarian, 127
Organized crime
  defined, 185
  human trafficking, 254
Other-directedness, 499
Out-groups, 124–25
Overgeneralizing, 24

PACs (political action committees), 357

Pakistan
  gross domestic product, 251
  as a low-income country, 247, 248, 251
  quality of life, 251
  state religion, 395
Paraprofessions, 343
Parenting
  cohabiting couples, 387
  cost of, 379
  homosexuals, 389
  number of children in families, 379–80
  single (one)-parent, 381, 382, 387, 390
  traditional, 388–89
  who is taking care of children, 381
Parochial schools, 415
Parole, 200
Participant observation, 28, 30–31
Passive students, 420–21
Pastoralism, defined, 51
Pastoral societies
  development of, 51
  social stratification and, 219
Patriarchy
  authority and, 350
  defined, 275
  family and, 376
  in India, 412
  inevitableness of, 276
  sexism and, 275–76
Patrilineal descent, 375
Patrilocality, 375
Peace, approaches to, 365–66
Pearl Harbor, 320
Peer group
  defined, 79
  gender socialization and, 277
  socialization and, 79–80
Pentagon attack (see September 11, 2001 attacks)
Pentecostals, 404
People's Republic of China (see China)
People with disabilities (see Disabled)
Perestroika, 211
Performances, social interaction and, 103
Personal choice, 4
Personal freedom
  capitalism versus socialism and, 341
  social responsibility versus, 506–7
Personal growth, sociology and, 8–9
Personality
  authoritarian personality theory, 308–9
  charisma, 396
  defined, 70
  development, 73
  deviance and, 175–76
  Erikson's developmental stages, 76–77
  Freud's model of, 72–73
  Type A, 276, 430
Personal space
  Hispanics and, 26
  social interaction and, 104
Peru
  crime in, 192
  sibling marriages, 149
Philadelphia Negro: A Social Study, The (Du Bois), 16
Philippines
  crime in, 193
  wealth and poverty, 249

Physical appearance/attractiveness
  beauty myth and advertising, 278
  cultural differences, 147
  eating disorders, 431–32
  obesity, 432
  racial differences, 300–301
Physical disabilities, 98
Physically disabled (*see* Disabled)
Physicians
  licensing of, 436, 437
  role of, 440–41
Piaget's cognitive theory, 73–74
Pink-collar jobs, 279
Play
  gender socialization and, 277
  self development, 76
Plea bargaining, 194–95
Pluralism, 311
Pluralist model, 358, 359
Pokot, 148
Poland
  market reforms, 341
  as a middle-income country, 247,
    248
Police
  community-based, 199
  role of, 194
Political action committees (PACs),
    357
Political change, sociology and, 12
Political-economy model/theory, 359,
    487
Political elites, 341
Political parties
  college students and, 356
  Democratic party, 356
  gender differences and, 356
  identification, 356–57
  liberals, 356
  racial differences and, 356
  Republican party, 356
  rural-urban divide, 357
  social class and, 356
  social issues and, 356
Political revolution
  common traits, 360
  defined, 360
Political spectrum, U.S., 355–56
Political systems
  in agrarian societies, 52
  authoritarianism, 352–53
  democracy, 352
  global, 354
  monarchy, 352
  totalitarianism, 353–54
Politics
  authority and, 350–51
  critical sociology and, 23–24
  defined, 350
  future for, 366
  gender differences, 282–83
  global perspective, 352–54
  pornography and, 159
  power and, 350
  social class and, 227–28
  television and, 80–81
  women in, 282–83
Politics, U.S.
  class, race, and gender issues, 356
  culture and the welfare state, 355
  economic issues, 355–56
  Marxist political-economy model,
    359
  medicine and, 443
  party identification, 356–57
  pluralist model, 358, 359
  political spectrum, 355–56

power-elite model, 358–59
  social issues, 356
  special-interest groups, 357
  voter apathy, 357–58
Pollution
  air, 473
  solid waste, 470–71
  water, 472–73
Polyandry, 373
Polygamy, 373
Polygyny, 373
Popular culture, 52–53
Population/population growth (*see
  also* Demography)
  age-sex pyramid, 454
  composition, 453–54
  control and role of women, 458
  demographic transition theory,
    455–56
  future for, 475–76
  growth, estimating, 452–53
  growth, global, 453, 456–57
  growth, zero, 456
  historical, 454–55
  Malthusian theory, 455
  modernization theory and control
    of, 259
  poverty and increase in, 255
  sex ratio, 453–54
  social change and, 484–85
  surveys, 27
  urban, in U.S., 459
  U.S., map, 452, 485
  zero population growth, 456
Pornography
  defined, 159, 287
  as a power issue, 159
  violence and, 159, 287–88
Positivism, defined, 13
Postconventional level, Kohlberg's
  moral development theory, 74
Postdenomination society, 400–401
Postindustrial economy
  computers, impact of, 345–36
  defined, 335–361
  Kuznets curve, 220
  professions, 343
  self-employment, 344
  work and, 342–49
Postindustrial societies
  information revolution and, 335
  information technology, 52
  population growth, 456
  work in, 335, 342–49
Postmodernity, 503–6
Poverty (*see also* Global poverty)
  absolute, 232, 251
  age and, 233
  causes of, 234
  children and, 232–33, 253, 382–83
  culture of, 234, 236
  elderly and, 233
  extents of, 232–33, 252–53
  family, 233–34, 382–83
  feminization of, 233–34, 253–54
  health and, 428
  homelessness, 237–38
  race and, 233
  rates, 234
  relative, 232, 251
  serverity of, 249–51
  shantytowns, 250
  single (one)-parent and, 382–83, 387
  urban versus rural, 234
  in the U.S., 232–38
  welfare dilemma, 235
  working poor, 236–37

Power
  authority and, 350
  defined, 350
  deviance and, 183
  -elite model, 358–59
  global relationships and, 256
  in-groups and, 125
  language and, 108
  Marxist political-economy model,
    359
  pluralist model, 358, 359
  poverty and, 256
  wealth and, 223
Powerlessness, modernity and,
    499–501
Practicality, U.S. value, 48
Prayer, in schools, 400
Preconventional level, Kohlberg's
  moral development theory, 74
Predestination, 394
Pregnancy
  abortion, 109
  adolescents and, 158–59
Preindustrial societies (*see* Agricul-
    tural societies; Hunting and gath-
    ering societies; Pastoral societies)
Prejudice
  authoritarian personality theory,
    308–9
  conflict theory, 309–10
  culture theory, 309
  defined, 304
  discrimination and, 310
  ethnocentrism, 58–59
  measuring, 305–7
  racism and, 307–8
  scapegoat theory, 308
  stereotypes, 304
  theories of, 308–10
Premarital sex, 153–54
Preoperational stage, 73
Presbyterians
  Scottish, 316
  social class and, 399
Presentation of self, 103
Presidential election of 2004
  popular vote by county, map, 357
  rural-urban division, 357
Prestige, occupational, 223, 224
Primary deviance, 179
Primary economic sectors, 336
Primary groups, 121–22
Primary sex characteristics, 147–48
Primates
  importance of, 42
  Rhesus monkeys social isolation
    experiment, 71
Primogeniture, 210
Prisons
  community-based corrections ver-
    sus, 199
  increase in inmates, 196–97
  justification for, 195–98
  resocialization, 89–90
  setting, 27
  Stanford County prison experi-
    ment, 27
  statistics on number of inmates,
    196–97
  voting and criminals, 358
Privacy
  laws related to, 139
  surveillance methods, 138
  technology and erosion of,
    138–39
Private schools, in the U.S., 415
Probation, 199–200

Productivity, economic, 340–41
Profane, defined, 391
Professions
  characteristics of, 343
  defined, 343
  para-, 343
Profit
  capitalism and personal, 338
  medicine and, 442–43
  schooling for, 424–25
Progress
  modernity/social change and,
    501–2
  U.S. value, 48
Progressive education, 413
Prohibition, 185
Projective labeling, 181
Proletarians, 215
Promise Keepers, 404
Property crimes, 188
Property ownership
  capitalism and, 338
  collective, 339
  estate system, 210–11
  inheritance rules, 376
  socialism and, 339
Proselytize, religious, 396
Prostitution
  defined, 159
  global, 159–160
  human trafficking, 254
  latent functions, 164
  legalized, 159
  types of, 160–61
  as a victimless crime, 161
Protestantism
  capitalism and, 394–95
  denominations, 395
  fundamentalism, 402, 404
  social class and, 399
  suicide rates, 4
  white Anglo-Saxon, 316
  work ethic, 316
Psychoanalysis, 72
Public policy, sociology and, 8
Public schools, in the U.S., 415
Puerto Ricans, 323
  income of, 324
  poverty and, 324
  revolving door policy, 324
  social standing of, 324
  Spanish language, use of, 324
Puerto Rico, modernization theory,
    259
Punishment, for criminals, 195–99
*Puritan Boston and Quaker Philadel-
    phia* (Baltzell), 31–34
Puritans, 150, 177
Pygmies, 50

Qualitative data, 23
Quality circles, work in Japan, 135
Quality of life, globally, 251
Quantitative data, 23
Queer theory, 167–68
Questionnaires, research, 27
Quid pro quo, sexual harassment and,
    287
Qur'an (Koran), 391, 393

Race (*see also* Ethnicity)
  assimilation, 311–12
  categories/types, 301–2, 303
  -conflict approach, 17
  consciousness, 310
  crime and, 190–91
  defined, 300–301

diversity map for the U.S., 79
future issues, 328
group dynamics and, 126
hate crimes, 187
income inequality and, 223–25
intelligence and, 308–9
majority/minority patterns of interaction, 311–14
pluralism, 311
poverty and, 233
prejudice, 304–10
religion and, 399
socialization and, 78
socially constructed, 300
stereotypes, 304
Racial blends, 302
Racial differences
feminism and, 293
health and, 429–30
infant mortality rates, 452
physical traits and, 300–301
political party identification and, 356
suicide rates, 4
television and, 277
unemployment and, 344
work and, 342, 344, 346
Racial discrimination
affirmative action, 326–27
African Americans and, 316–18
apartheid, 209, 213
Arab Americans and, 324–26
arrests and, 190
Asian Americans and, 318–22
civil rights movement, 317–18
Dred Scott case, 317
Du Bois, work of, 16, 17, 318
Hispanic Americans and, 322–24
institutional, 310
Japanese Americans and, 320–21
Jim Crow laws, 317
lynching, 317
Native Americans and, 314–16
prejudice, 304–10
sports and, 20–21
successful African Americans and, 28
in the U.S., 48, 134, 316–18
voting rights, 318
in the workplace, 134
Racial segregation
apartheid, 209
Brown v. *Board of Education of Topeka,* 310
civil rights movement, 317–18
de jure and *de facto,* 312
history of, in the U.S., 312–13
hyper-, 312–13
Japanese American internment, 320
in schools, 310, 416, 417
in U.S. cities, 312
Racism
defined, 307–8
environmental, 474–75
future issues, 328
hate crimes, 187
intelligence and, 308–9
lynching, 317
Radical feminism, 291–92
Rain forests, 473
Rape
date, 162–63
defined, 162
marital, 386
of men, 162
pornography and, 159
statistics on, 161–62, 284

Rationality
alienation and, 131
defined, 129
McDonaldization concept, 140
modernization and, 493–94
Weber and, 493–94
Rationalization of society, 129
Rational-legal authority, 351
Raves, 30
Real culture, 50
Reality
building, 102
language and, 46
social construction of, 99–102
Rebellion, 178
Recidivism, criminal, 197
Recycling, 471
Redemptive social movements, 485, 486
Red tape, bureaucratic, 132–33
Reference groups, 124
Reformative social movements, 486
Reformatories, 196
Rehabilitation, of criminals, 196, 198
Relative deprivation, 486
Relative opportunity, 178
Relative poverty, 232, 251
Reliability, 19, 22
Religion (*see also* name of)
in agrarian societies, 52, 397
basic concepts, 391
capitalism and, 394–95
civil, 400
in colonial America, 316
defined, 391
diversity across U.S., map, 398
electronic, 404
ethnicity and, 399
functions of, 391–92
fundamentalism, 402, 404
future for, 404
in history, 397
in horticultural societies, 51
in hunting and gathering societies, 51, 397
in industrial societies, 397
membership across U.S., map, 398
New Age, 400–401
in pastoral societies, 51
postdenomination society, 400–401
in preindustrial societies, 397
race and, 399
revival, 401–4
science and, 403
secularization, 399–400
social change and, 394–95
social class and, 399
social-conflict analysis, 393–94
sociology and, 391
structural-functional analysis, 391–92, 394
symbolic-interaction analysis, 392–93, 394
in the U.S., 397–99
Religiosity
defined, 397
globally, 397
importance of, 397–98
Religious affiliation
college students and, 400
diversity across U.S., map, 398
membership across U.S., map, 398
racial/ethnic, 399
social class and, 399
Religious organization, types of churches, 395

cults, 396
denominations, 395
sects, 395–96
state church, 395
Remarriage, 385–86
Renaissance, 13
Repression, 73
Reproduction
family and new technology, 390
in vitro fertilization, 390
sex determination, 146–47
test tube babies, 390
Republican party, 356
Research (*see* Sociological investigation)
Research methods
data, using existing, 31–34
defined, 25
experiments, 25–27
participant observation, 28, 30–31
surveys, 27–28
Reservations
Japanese Americans on, 320
Native Americans on, 315
Residential patterns
industrial societies and, 375
preindustrial societies and, 374–75
Resocialization, 89–90
Resource-mobilization theory, 486
Retreatist subcultures, 178
Retribution, 195
Retrospective labeling, 181
Revivalism, 401–4
Revolution, capitalist, 494
Revolution, political
common traits, 360
defined, 360
Revolutionary social movements, 486
Revolutionary War, 360
Rhesus monkeys, social isolation experiment, 71
Right(s)
individual, 12
informed consent, 25
-to-die debate, 436
Ritual, defined, 391
Ritualism
bureaucratic, 132
deviance, 1786
Roe v. *Wade,* 166
Roles
conflict, 99
defined, 98–99
exit, 99
gender, 98, 99
set, 98
strain, 99
Roman Catholic Church (*see also* Catholicism)
liberation theology, 395
parochial schools, 415
Roman Empire, early cities in, 459
Romania
gross domestic product, 251
market reforms, 341
as a middle-income country, 251
quality of life, 251
socialism, decline of, 341
Romantic love, 377–79, 385
Routinization of charisma, 351–52
Rural areas
political party identification and, 357
population growth in, 462
poverty, 234
presidential election of 2004 and, 357

Rural life (*Gemeinschaft*), 462–63, 491–92
Russia (*see also* Soviet Union)
economic inequality, 211
gross domestic product, 251
market reforms, 341
medicine in, 438, 439
as a middle-income country, 246, 247, 248, 251
quality of life, 251
social stratification in, 211–12
Russian Revolution, 211, 360
Rwanda
genocide, 314, 488
quality of life, 259

Sacred, defined, 391
Sambia, homosexuality and, 156
Same-sex marriage, 158
Sampling, 27
snowball, 28
Sandwich generation, 381
Sapir-Whorf thesis, 46
SAT (Scholastic Assessment Test) scores, 422
Saudi Arabia
ban on red flowers, 176
constraints put on women, 186
as a high-income country, 5, 246, 247
modernity, 503
monarchy in, 352
Scapegoat theory, 308
Scholastic Assessment Test (SAT) scores, 422
Schooling (*see also* Education)
defined, 41
for profit, 424–25
School problems (*see* Education)
Schools (*see also* Education)
charter, 424
choice of, 424–25
Christian academies, 415
home, 425
inequality in, 414–20
magnet, 424
parochial, 415
prayer in, 400
private boarding, 415
public, 412–13
public versus private, in the U.S., 415–17
socialization and, 79
tracking, 15, 415
Science
defined, 19
medicine and, 436–37
religion and, 403
sociology and, 12–13
U.S. value, 48
Scientific management, 134
Scientific medicine, 436–37
Scientific sociology
cause and effect, 22
concepts, 19
correlation, 22
defined, 19
measurement, 19
objectivity and, 22–23
reliability and validity, 19, 22
statistics, 19
summary of, 24
variables, 19, 22
Scientific stage, 13
SDI (strategic defense initiative), 365–66
Secondary deviance, 179–80

Values
  beliefs and, 46, 48
  clusters, 48
  conflict and, 48–49
  defined, 46
  emerging, 49
  global, 49
  language and, 108–10
  social class, 227
  in the U.S., 48
Variables
  defined, 19
  dependent, 22, 25–26
  independent, 22, 25
  operationalize, 19
  relationships among, 22
  scientific sociology and, 19, 22
Venereal disease (see Sexually trans-
    mitted diseases)
Venezuela
  gross domestic product, 251
  as a middle-income country, 251
  quality of life, 251
Verstehen (understanding), 23
Veto groups, 358
Victimization surveys, 188
Victimless crimes, 161, 188
Video games, violence and, 81
Vietnam
  capitalism in, 338
  description of street traffic, 96
  meeting with foreigners, banned,
    176
  totalitarianism in, 354
Virginity, 165
Virtual culture, 53
Violence (see also Terrorism; Women,
    violence against)
  against men, 285, 287
  assault, 284
  child abuse, 386–87
  at colleges, 284
  crime rates down, 198–99
  date rape, 162–63
  family, 386–87
  female genital mutilation, 165, 284,
    285, 286
  pornography and, 159, 287–88
  prostitution and, 161
  rape, 161–63
  school, 420
  sexual harassment, 287
  television and, 81
  video games and, 81
  Yąnomamö views on, 41, 43
Voluntary associations, 127
Voting
  apathy, 357–58
  criminals and, 358
  presidential election of 2004, 357
Voting rights
  African Americans and, 317
  criminals and, 358
  Fifteenth Amendment, 317
  Nineteenth Amendment, 290
  for women, 290

Wage gap, 231
Wage labor, 335
Wal-Mart, 334, 339, 342–43
War
  causes of, 362
  children, effects on, 72
  costs of, 363–64
  defined, 362
  media, role of, 364–65

military social class, 362–63
  nuclear weapons, 364
  peace, approaches to, 365–66
  statistics on, 362
  terrorism as, 363
WASPs (see White Anglo-Saxon
    Protestants)
Water
  pollution, 472–73
  quality, 472
  supply problems, 471–72
Wealth (see also Income)
  of chief executive officers (CEOs),
    230
  defined, 221
  distribution of, in the U.S., 222
  power and, 223
  super rich, 358–59
Weber, work of
  authority and, 350
  concept of Verstehen (understand-
    ing), 23
  modernization and, 493–94
  power and, 350
  rationalization and, 493–94
  religion and, 394–95
  social change and, 484
  social stratification and, 217
Wedge-shaped sectors, 464
Welfare
  capitalism, 340
  corporate, 348
  state, 355
  in the U.S., 234, 235, 355
White Anglo-Saxon Protestants
    (WASPs), 316
White-collar crime, defined, 184
White-collar occupations
  defined, 216
  social class and, 224
White ethnic Americans, use of term,
    326–28
Whites
  crime rates, 190
  family size, 379n
  income inequality and, 223–24
  poverty and, 233
  suicide rates, 4
  unemployment and, 344
  voting participation and, 358
  white Anglo-Saxon, 316
  women, working, 342, 346
  work and, 342, 346
Wodaabe, 274
Women (see also Gender differences;
    Gender inequality)
  abortion issue, 166–67
  in agrarian societies, 51–52
  care and responsibility perspective,
    74
  childbearing, map, 3
  discrimination, 280
  eating disorders, 431–32
  education and, 273, 277, 281–82
  extramarital sex, 155
  feminism, 16, 290–94
  feminization of poverty, 233–34,
    253–54
  gender roles, 99
  in government positions, 282, 283
  homosexual, 156, 157
  housework and, 98, 100, 281
  in hunting and gathering societies,
    50–51
  matrilineal descent, 375
  in the military, 283

as minorities, 283–84
  political party identification and,
    356
  politics and, 282–83
  population growth and role of, 458
  poverty and, 233–34, 253–54
  premarital sex, 153
  prostitution, 159–61
  sexual revolution, 151–52
  single (one)-parenthood, 381, 382,
    384, 387, 390
  as slaves, 254, 255
  social mobility and, 231
  in sports, 20, 272–73, 277
  status of, globally, 275
  upper-upper class, 226
Women, African American
  as head of household, 384
  as leaders, 317
  life expectancy and, 430
  parenting and role of grandmoth-
    ers, 381
  work and, 283–84, 342, 346
Women, Asian American
  as head of household, 384
  work and, 321–22, 342, 346
Women, Hispanic American/Latinos
  as head of household, 382, 384
  work and, 284, 342, 346
Women, Islamic
  constraints put on, 186
  female genital mutilation, 165
  modesty, 149
  wearing of makeup banned, 176
Women, violence against
  assaults, 284
  date rape, 162–63
  domestic, 386
  female genital mutilation, 165, 284,
    285, 286
  pornography as a cause, 159,
    287–88
  prostitution and, 161
  rape, 161–63
  rape, marital, 386
  sexual harassment, 287
Women, in the workplace
  African American, 283–84, 342,
    346
  Asian American, 342, 346
  comparable worth, 280
  discrimination, 134–35
  earnings gap, 231
  as entrepreneurs, 280
  female advantage, 135
  Filipino Americans, 321–22
  gender inequality, 279–81
  glass ceiling, 280
  Hispanic American, 284, 342, 346
  income inequality, 231, 280–81
  laundry, 350–51
  in managerial positions, 135
  occupations, 279–80
  pink-collar jobs, 279
  racial differences, 342
  self-employed, 344
  statistics on, 279
  whites, 342, 346
Women's movement, feminism, 16,
    290–94
Work/workplace (see also Women, in
    the workplace)
  blue-collar, 216
  changing nature of, 135–37, 342
  child labor, 58, 82–83, 257, 412
  computers, effects of, 345–46

debt bondage, 254
  discrimination, 134–35
  diversity, 345, 346
  division of labor, 492–93
  ethic, Protestant, 316
  expressing emotions at, 108
  factories, 335, 336
  garment industry, in Bangladesh,
    244
  gender differences, 279–81, 342,
    346
  global economy and effects on U.S.,
    231–32
  housework and, 98, 100, 281
  immigrants and, 305
  income inequality, 231, 280–81
  Industrial Revolution, 335
  in industrial societies, 52
  information revolution and, 335,
    345–46
  Japanese, 135
  job projections to 2010, 349
  jobs with the highest concentra-
    tions of women, 279
  lack of, and poverty, 234, 236
  laundry, 350–51
  legal protections, 217
  managerial positions in the U.S.,
    135
  pink-collar jobs, 279
  in postindustrial economy, 335–36,
    342–49
  prestige, 223, 224
  professions, 343
  projections of, to 2010, map of, 349
  Protestant work ethic, 316
  prostitution as, 160–61
  racial differences, 342, 346
  scientific management, 134
  self-employment, 344
  social class and, 223, 224
  teams, 136
  technology and, 345–46
  unemployment, 344
  unions, 217, 342–43
  U.S. value, 48
  white-collar, 216
Workforce diversity, 345, 346
Working class
  blue-collar, 216
  defined, 226–27
  marriages, 228
Working poor, 227, 236–37
WorldCom, 344
World economy, Wallerstein's capital-
    ist, 261–62
World Trade Center (see September
    11, 2001 attacks)
World War II
  Japanese American internment, 320
  reference group study, 124

Xenophobia, 328

Yąnomamö, 41, 43, 50, 52, 362
Yemen, family size, 3
Yugoslavia
  cultural conflict in, 54
  genocide, 488

Zambia, economic inequality, 213
Zero population growth, 456
Zimbabwe, education in, 411